Historic Documents on Presidential Elections 1787-1988

Historic Documents on Presidential Elections 1787-1988

Michael Nelson
Editor

Washington, D.C.

Congressional Quarterly Inc.

Congressional Quarterly Inc., an editorial research service and publishing company, serves clients in the fields of news, education, business, and government. It combines Congressional Quarterly's specific coverage of Congress, government, and politics with the more general subject range of an affiliated service, *The CQ Researcher*.

Congressional Quarterly publishes the *Congressional Quarterly Weekly Report* and a variety of books, including college political science textbooks under the CQ Press imprint and public affairs paperbacks on developing issues and events. CQ also publishes information directories and reference books on the federal government, national elections, and politics, including the *Guide to the Presidency*, the *Guide to Congress*, the *Guide to the U.S. Supreme Court*, the *Guide to U.S. Elections, Politics in America*, and *Congress A to Z: CQ's Ready Reference Encyclopedia*. The *CQ Almanac*, a compendium of legislation for one session of Congress, is published each year. *Congress and the Nation*, a record of government for a presidential term, is published every four years.

CQ publishes *The Congressional Monitor*, a daily report on current and future activities of congressional committees, and several newsletters including *Congressional Insight*, a weekly analysis of congressional action, and *Campaign Practices Reports*, a semimonthly update on campaign laws.

An electronic online information system, Washington Alert, provides immediate access to CQ's databases of legislative action, votes, schedules, profiles, and analyses.

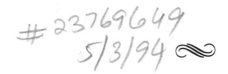
Library of Congress Cataloging-in-Publication Data
Historic documents on presidential elections/Michael Nelson, Editor.
    p.   cm.
    Includes index.
    ISBN 0-87187-607-8
    1. Elections--United States--History--Sources.   I. Nelson, Michael, 1949-
    JK1965.H56 1991   91-18729
    324.973--dc20   CIP

To four outstanding institutions of higher learning, with gratitude

The College of William and Mary
The Johns Hopkins University
Vanderbilt University
Rhodes College

Table of Contents

Preface

Readers may fairly ask: How does the editor of a one-volume collection of documents on the history of U.S. presidential elections choose the seventy most important, interesting, and illustrative of the many thousands of campaign speeches, party platforms, newspaper articles, congressional debates, and other written and spoken artifacts of two centuries of national politics?

My answer resembles—but with a twist—my answer to a similar question posed in the preface to the companion volume to this collection, *Historic Documents on the Presidency, 1776-1989* (Congressional Quarterly, 1989). In that book, documents were included because they embodied either the most significant activities of particular presidents or the major landmarks in the development of the presidency as an institution. The emphasis, however, was clearly on the institution.

In this book, too, documents were chosen to highlight either particular presidential elections or the institutional development of the presidential election process. Here, however, the emphasis is on the particular. After all, elections are episodic—quadrennial, not ongoing—occurrences.

The vast majority of the individual presidential elections that took place from 1789 to 1988 are represented in this book, including every election after 1912. Modern and other especially important elections, such as the elections of 1860, 1896, 1912, and 1932, and every election since 1960 receive more than one entry. The documents include:

~ *important political party platforms*, such as the Democratic platforms of 1840 (the first party platform in U.S. history), 1860, and 1932, and the Republican platforms of 1856, 1896, and 1980.

~ *landmark speeches*, including the acceptance speeches of Franklin D. Roosevelt (the first ever by a presidential candidate), Harry S Truman, Barry M. Goldwater, Richard Nixon, and George Bush; other historical convention speeches by political leaders such as William Jennings Bryan, Hubert H. Humphrey, Edward M. Kennedy, and Jesse Jackson; and a number of memorable speeches and addresses by George Washington, Woodrow Wilson, Dwight D. Eisenhower, Adlai Stevenson, John F. Kennedy, and others.

~ *candidate debates*, beginning with the first Kennedy-Nixon debate in 1960 and continuing through the debates of 1976, 1980, 1984, and 1988.

~ *news articles and campaign broadsides*, such as "the Lincoln Catechism," the *New York World*'s account of the "Rum, Romanism, and Rebellion" affair, H. L. Mencken's attack on anti-Catholic prejudice in the 1928 election, and Jimmy Carter's interview with *Playboy* magazine.

~ *significant third parties,* including Theodore Roosevelt's "Bull Moose" platform and speeches by Henry A. Wallace, George C. Wallace, and John B. Anderson.

The documents concerning the historical development of the presidential election process fall mostly into these categories:

~ *constitutional origins and development,* including the debates on presidential selection at the Constitutional Convention, excerpts from *The Federalist Papers,* congressional debates on various constitutional amendments, and the Supreme Court's ruling in *Buckley v. Valeo.*

~ *landmark events in the history of the presidential election process,* such as the official call for the first presidential election, the proceedings of the 1824 congressional caucus, the vote to abolish the two-thirds rule for nominations at the 1936 Democratic national convention, and the report of the McGovern-Fraser Commission.

~ *the vice presidency,* including Richard Nixon's "Checkers" speech, statements concerning the "Eagleton affair," Geraldine A. Ferraro's acceptance speech, and the Bentsen-Quayle debate.

Finally, several documents deal with the processes of what might be called unusual presidential selection—that is, the selection of the president when the normal electoral process is not adequate. These include the elections by the House of Representatives of Thomas Jefferson in 1800 and John Quincy Adams in 1824, the disputed election of 1876, and the Presidential Succession Act of 1947.

Some of the documents have been edited for clarity, but not at the expense of completeness or historical accuracy. (For example, we have included all footnotes from those documents that had them and retained the original spelling even in the few instances in which conventions have changed.) In addition, each document is introduced by a headnote that places it into its contemporary setting, into broad historical context, and, through numerous cross-references to other documents, into the structure of the volume. Taken together, the headnotes constitute a virtual history of presidential elections.

The book also includes helpful appendices—a complete chart of U.S. presidents and vice presidents and a summary of presidential elections, 1789-1988.

I would like to thank: David R. Tarr, director of CQ's Book Department; Margaret Seawell Benjaminson, project editor for this book; and Jamie R. Holland, the book's production editor, for all their hard and good work. I rejoice, as always, in the love and support of my wife, Linda E. Nelson, and my boys, Michael and Sam.

Michael Nelson

The Constitutional Convention: Debates on Presidential Selection (1787)

Few issues vexed the delegates to the Constitutional Convention of 1787 more than how to elect the president. A number of far-fetched ideas were proposed, including one to entrust presidential selection to the state governors and another to have a randomly picked group of national legislators make the choice. Alexander Hamilton, a New York delegate who admired the British monarchy, even suggested that the president be elected for a lifetime term. Popular election was dismissed out of hand. "It would be as unnatural to refer the choice of a proper character for chief Magistrate to the people," said George Mason of Virginia, "as it would, to refer a trial of colours to a blind man." (Mason's fellow Virginian, James Madison, kept the notes on the convention's debates from which all quotations are drawn.)

Most of the delegates seem to have preferred, at least initially, that Congress elect the president: its members presumably would know and could judge the candidates best. The delegates also wanted the president to be eligible for reelection, both to allow the nation a way to keep a good leader in office and to give the president what Gouverneur Morris of Pennsylvania described as "the great motive to good behavior, the hope of being rewarded with a re-appointment." Morris also warned, "Shut the Civil road to Glory,

& he may be compelled to seek it by the sword."

The problem, as many delegates saw it, was that their two desiderata were in conflict. Mason stated the concern of the convention best: if Congress could reelect the president, there would be a constant "temptation on the side of the Executive to intrigue with the Legislature for a re-appointment." As a strategy to win another term, Mason and some other delegates argued, the president would have every incentive to use political patronage and illegitimate favors in effect to buy the votes of legislators.

In mid- and late July, beginning on the seventeenth, the convention struggled to find some way around its dilemma. On July 26, frustrated by their inability to develop an acceptable method to elect the president that did not involve Congress, the delegates reluctantly voted for legislative selection of the president to a single, seven-year term.

The search for an alternative mechanism was renewed with fresh urgency after August 24, however. Until that day, no consideration had been given to how Congress would choose the president. Now the convention voted that the election would be by "joint ballot" of the House of Representatives, which was apportioned according to population, and the much smaller Senate, in

1

which the states were represented equally. The decision alienated the small-state delegates, who realized that this method would vastly diminish their states' influence on the choice of the president. Small-staters quickly joined forces with proexecutive delegates like Morris and James Wilson of Pennsylvania, who wanted the president to have an electoral base independent of Congress. On August 31, the new coalition pressed successfully to have the entire issue of presidential selection reexamined by a specially appointed committee.

On September 4, the Committee on Postponed Matters (also known as the Committee of Eleven) recommended that the president be chosen for a four-year term by an electoral college, with no restriction on the right to seek reelection. The committee also proposed that a vice president be elected, with responsibility to preside over the Senate (voting only to break ties) and to step in as president if the president died, resigned, or was impeached and convicted. On September 7, eager for compromise, the delegates readily adopted a slightly modified version of the committee's recommendation. (See "United States Constitution," p. 35.)   ~

Tuesday, July 17.
In Convention.

...9th Resol: "that Natl. Executive consist of a single person." Agd. to nem. con.

"To be chosen by the National Legisl:"

Mr. Governr. Morris was pointedly agst. his being so chosen. He will be the mere creature of the Legisl: if appointed & impeachable by that body. He ought to be elected by the people at large, by the freeholders of the Country. That difficulties attend this mode, he

admits. But they have been found superable in N.Y. & in Ct. and would he believed be found so, in the case of an Executive for the U. States. If the people should elect, they will never fail to prefer some man of distinguished character, or services; some man, if he might so speak, of continental reputation. If the Legislature elect, it will be the work of intrigue, of cabal, and of faction; it will be like the election of a pope by a conclave of cardinals; real merit will rarely be the title to the appointment. He moved to strike out "National Legislature" & insert "citizens of U.S."

Mr. Sherman thought that the sense of the Nation would be better expressed by the Legislature, than by the people at large. The latter will never be sufficiently informed of characters, and besides will never give a majority of votes to any one man. They will generally vote for some man in their own State, and the largest State will have the best chance for the appointment. If the choice be made by the Legislre. A majority of voices may be made necessary to constitute an election.

Mr. Wilson. Two arguments have been urged agst. an election of the Executive Magistrate by the people. I the example of Poland where an Election of the supreme Magistrate is attended with the most dangerous commotions. The cases he observed were totally dissimilar. The Polish nobles have resources & dependents which enable them to appear in force, and to threaten the Republic as well as each other. In the next place the electors all assemble in one place: which would not be the case with us. The 2d. argt. is that a *majority* of the people would never concur. It might be answered that the concurrence of a majority of people is not a necessary principle of election, nor required as such in any of the States. But allowing the objection all its force, it may be obviated by the expedient used in Masts. where the Legislature by majority of voices, decide in case a majority of people do not concur in favor of one of the candidates. This would restrain the choice to a good nomination at least, and prevent in a great degree intrigue & cabal. A particular objection with him agst. an absolute election by the Legislre. was that the Exec: in that case would be too dependent to stand the mediator between the intrigues & sinister views of the Representatives and the general liberties & interests of the people.

Mr. Pinkney did not expect this question would again have been brought forward; An Election by the people being liable to the most obvious & striking objections. They will be led by a few active & designing men. The most populous States by combining in favor of the same individual will be able to carry their points. The Natl. Legislature being most immediately interested in the laws made by themselves, will be most attentive to the choice of a fit man to carry them properly into execution.

Mr. Govr. Morris. It is said that in case of an election by the people the populous States will combine & elect whom they please. Just the reverse. The people of such States cannot combine. If their be any combination it must be among their representatives in the Legislature. It is said the people will be led by a few designing men. This might happen in a small district. It can never happen throughout the continent. In the election of a Govr. of N. York, it sometimes is the case in particular spots, that the activity & intrigues of little partizans are successful, but the general voice of the State is never influenced by such artifices. It is said the multitude will be uninformed. It is true they would be uninformed of what passed in the Legislative Conclave, if the election were to be made there; but they will not be uninformed of those great & illustrious characters which have merited their esteem & confidence. If the Executive be chosen by the Natl. Legislature, he will not be inde-

pendent on it; and if not independent, usurpation & tyranny on the part of the Legislature will be the consequence. This was the case in England in the last Century. It has been the case in Holland, where their Senates have engrossed all power. It has been the case every where. He was surprised that an election by the people at large should ever have been likened to the polish election of the first Magistrate. An election by the Legislature will bear a real likeness to the election by the Diet of Poland. The great must be the electors in both cases, and the corruption & cabal weh. are known to characterise the one would soon find their way into the other. Appointments made by numerous bodies, are always worse than those made by single responsible individuals, or by the people at large.

Col. Mason. It is curious to remark the different language held at different times. At one moment we are told that the Legislature is entitled to thorough confidence, and to indifinite power. At another, that it will be governed by intrigue & corruption, and cannot be trusted at all. But not to dwell on this inconsistency he would observe that a Government which is to last ought at least to be practicable. Would this be the case if the proposed election should be left to the people at large. He conceived it would be as unnatural to refer the choice of a proper character for chief Magistrate to the people, as it would, to refer a trial of colours to a blind man. The extent of the Country renders it impossible that the people can have the requisite capacity to judge of the respective pretensions of the Candidates.

Mr. Wilson could not see the contrariety stated [by Col. Mason] The Legislre. might deserve confidence in some respects, and distrust in others. In acts which were to affect them & yr. Constituents precisely alike confidence was due. In others jealousy was warranted. The appointment to great offices, where the Legislre. might feel many motives, not common to the public confidence was surely misplased. This branch of business it was notorious was most corruptly managed of any that had been committed to legislative bodies.

Mr. Williamson conceived that there was the same difference between an election in this case, by the people and by the legislature, as between an appt. by lot, and by choice. There are at present distinguished characters, who are known perhaps to almost every man. This will not always be the case. The people will be sure to vote for some man in their own State, and the largest State will be sure to succeed. This will not be Virga. however. Her slaves will have no suffrage. As the Salary of the Executive will be fixed, and he will not be eligible a 2d. time, there will not be such a dependence on the Legislature as has been imagined.

Question on an election by the people instead of the legislature; which passed in the negative.

Mas. no. Ct. no. N.J. no. Pa. ay. Del. no. Md. no. Va. no. N.C. no. S.C. no. Geo. no.

Mr. L. Martin moved that the Executive be chosen by Electors appointed by the several Legislatures of the individual States.

Mr. Broome 2ds. On the Question, it passed in the negative.

Mas. no. Ct. no. N.J. no. Pa. no. Del. ay. Md. ay. Va. no. N.C. no. S.C. no. Geo. no.

On the question on the words "to be chosen by the Nationl. Legislature" it passed unanimously in the affirmative.

"For the term of seven years"—postponed nem. con. on motion of Mr. Houston & Gov. Morris.

"to carry into execution the nationl. laws"—agreed to nem. con.

"to appoint to offices in cases not otherwise provided for."—agreed to nem. con.

"to be inteligible a second time"—

Mr. Houston moved to strike out this clause.

Mr. Sherman 2ds. the motion.

Mr. Govr. Morris espoused the motion. The ineligibility proposed by the clause as it stood tended to destroy the great motive to good behavior, the hope of being rewarded by a re-appointment. It was saying to him, make hay while the sun shines.

On the question for striking out as moved by Mr. Houston, it passed in the affirmative

Mas. ay. Ct. ay. N.J. ay. Pa. ay. Del. no. Md. ay. Va. no. N.C. no. S.C. no. Geo. ay.

"For the term of 7 years" resumed

Mr. Broom was for a shorter term since the Executive Magistrate was now to be re-eligible. Had he remained ineligible a 2d. time, he should have preferred a longer term.

Docr. McClurg moved[1] to strike out 7 years, and insert "during good behavior." By striking out the words declaring him not re-eligible, he was put into a situation that would keep him dependent for ever on the Legislature; and he conceived the independence of the Executive to be equally essential with that of the Judiciary department.

Mr. Govr. Morris 2ded. the motion. He expressed great pleasure in hearing it. This was the way to get a good Government. His fear that so valuable an ingredient would not be attained had led him to take the part he had done. He was indifferent how the Executive should be chosen, provided he held his place by this tenure.

Mr. Broome highly approved the motion. It obviated all his difficulties.

Mr. Sherman considered such a tenure as by no means safe or admissible. As the Executive Magistrate is now re-eligible, he will be on good behavior as far as will be necessary. If he behaves well he will be continued; if otherwise, displaced, on a succeeding election.

Mr. Madison[2] If it be essential to the preservation of liberty that the Legisl:

Execut: & Judiciary powers be separate, it is essential to a maintenance of the separation, that they should be independent of each other. The Executive could not be independent of the Legislure, if dependent on the pleasure of that branch for a reappointment. Why was it determined that the Judges should not hold their places by such a tenure? Because they might be tempted to cultivate the Legislature, by an undue complaisance, and thus render the Legislature the virtual expositor, as well the maker of the laws. In like manner a dependence of the Executive on the Legislature, would render it the Executor as well as the maker of laws; & then according to the observation of Montesquieu, tyrannical laws may be made that they may be executed in a tyrannical manner. There was an analogy between the Executive & Judiciary departments in several respects. The latter executed the laws in certain cases as the former did in others. The former expounded & applied them for certain purposes, as the latter did for others. The difference between them seemed to consist chiefly in two circumstances—

(I.) the collective interest & security were much more in the power belonging to the Executive than to the Judiciary department.

2. in the administration of the former much greater latitude is left to opinion and discretion than in the administration of the latter. But if the 2d. consideration proves that it will be more difficult to establish a rule sufficiently precise for trying the Execut: than the Judges, & forms an objection to the same tenure of office, both considerations prove that it might be more dangerous to suffer a union between the Executive & Legisl: powers, than between the Judiciary & Legislative powers. He conceived it to be absolutely necessary to a well constituted Republic that the two first shd. be kept distinct & independent of each other. On the other hand, respect for the mover entitled his proposition to a fair hearing & discussion, until a less objectionable expedient should be applied for guarding against a dangerous union of the Legislative & Executive departments.

Col. Mason. This motion was made some time ago, & negatived by a very large majority. He trusted that it would be again negatived. It would be impossible to define the misbehaviour in such a manner as to subject it to a proper trial; and perhaps still more impossible to compel so high an offender holding his office by such a tenure to submit to a trial. He considered an Executive during good behavior as a softer name only for an Executive for life. And that the next would be an easy step to hereditary Monarchy. If the motion should finally succeed, he might himself live to see such a Revolution. If he did not it was probable his children or grand children would. He trusted there were few men in that House who wished for it. No state he was sure had so far revolted from Republican principles as to have the least bias in its favor.

Mr. Madison, was not apprehensive of being thought to favor any step towards monarchy. The real object with him was to prevent its introduction. Experience had proved a tendency in our governments to throw all power into the Legislative vortex. The Executives of the States are in general little more than Cyphers; the legislatures omnipotent. If no effectual check be devised for restraining the instability & encroachments of the latter, a revolution of some kind or other would be inevitable. The preservation of Republican Government therefore required some expedient for the purpose, but required evidently at the same time that in devising it, the genuine principles of that form should be kept in view.

Mr. Govr. Morris was as little a friend to monarchy as any gentleman. He concurred in the opinion that the way to keep out monarchical Government was to establish such a Republican Government as would make the people happy and prevent a desire of change.

Docr. McClurg was not so much afraid of the shadow of monarchy as to be unwilling to approach it; nor so wedded to Republican Government as not to be sensible of the tyrannies that had been & may be exercised under that form. It was an essential object with him to make the Executive independent of the Legislature; and the only mode left for effecting it, after the vote destroying his ineligibility a second time, was to appoint him during good behavior.

On the question for inserting "during good behavior" in place of 7 years [with a re-eligibility] it passed in the negative.

Mas. no. Ct. no. N.J. ay. Pa. ay. Del. ay. Md. no. Va. ay. N.C. no. S.C. no. Geo. no.[3]

On the motion "to strike out seven years" it passed in the negative.

Mas. ay. Ct. no. N.J. no. Pa. ay. Del. ay. Md. no. Va. no. N.C. ay. S.C. no. Geo. no.[4]

It was now unanimously agreed that the vote which had struck out the words "to be ineligible a second time" should be reconsidered to-morrow.

Adjd.

Thursday, July 19.
In Convention

On reconsideration of the vote rendering the Executive re-eligible a 2d. time, Mr. Martin moved to reinstate the words, "to be ineligible a 2d. time."

Mr. Governeur Morris. It is necessary to take into one view all that relates to the establishment of the Executive; on the due formation of which must depend the efficacy & utility of the Union among the present and future States. It has been a maxim in Political Science that Republican Government is not adapted to a large extent of Country, because the energy of the Executive Magistracy can not reach the extreme parts of it. Our Country is an extensive one. We must either then renounce the blessings of the Union, or provide an Executive with sufficient vigor to pervade every part of it. This subject was of so much importance that he hoped to be indulged in an extensive view of it. One great object of the Executive is to control the Legislature. The Legislature will continually seek to aggrandize & perpetuate themselves; and will sieze those critical moments produced by war, invasion or convulsion for that purpose. It is necessary then that the Executive Magistrate should be the guardian of the people, even of the lower classes, against Legislative tyranny, against the Great & the wealthy who in the course of things will necessarily compose the Legislative body. Wealth tends to corrupt the mind & to nourish its love and power, and to stimulate it to oppression. History proves this to be the spirit of the opulent. The check provided in the 2d. branch was not meant as a check on Legislative usurpations of power, but on the abuse of lawful powers, on the propensity in the 1st. branch to legislate too much to run into projects of paper money & similar expedients. It is no check on Legislative tyranny. On the contrary it may favor it, and if the 1st branch can be seduced may find the means of success. The Executive therefore ought to be so constituted as to be the great protector of the Mass of the people.—It is the duty of the Executive to appoint the officers & to command the forces of the Republic: to appoint 1. ministerial officers for the administration of public affairs. 2. officers for the dispensation of Justice. Who will be the best Judges whether these appointments be well made? The people at large, who will know, will see, will feel the effects of them. Again who can judge so well of the discharge of military duties for the protection & security of the people, as the people themselves who are to be protected & secured?—He finds too that the Executive is not to be re-eligible. What effect will this have? 1. it will destroy the great incitement to merit public esteem by taking away the hope of being rewarded with a reappointment. It may give a dangerous turn to one of the strongest passions in the human breast. The love of fame is the great spring to noble & illustrious actions. Shut the Civil road to Glory & he may be compelled to seek it by the sword. 2. It will tempt him to make the most of the short space of time allotted him, to accumulate wealth and provide for his friends. 3. It will produce violations of the very constitution it is meant to secure. In moments of pressing danger the tried abilities and established character of a favorite Magistrate will prevail over respect for the forms of the Constitution. The Executive is also to be impeachable. This is a dangerous part of the plan. It will hold him in such dependence that he will be no check on the Legislature, will not be a firm guardian of the people and of the public interest. He will be the tool of a faction, of some leading demagogue in the Legislature. These then are the faults of the Executive establishment as now proposed. Can no better establishment be devised? If he is to be the Guardian of the people let him be appointed by the people? If he is to be a check on the Legislature let him not be impeachable. Let him be of short duration, that he may with propriety be re-eligible. It has been said that the candidates for this office will not be known to the people. If they be known to the Legislature, they must have such a notoriety and eminence of Character, that they can not possibly be unknown to the people at large. It cannot be possible that a man shall have sufficiently distinguished himself to merit this high trust without having his character proclaimed by fame throughout the Empire. As to the

danger from an unimpeachable magistrate he could not regard it as formidable. There must be certain great officers of State; a minister of finance, of war, of foreign affairs &c. These he presumes will exercise their functions in subordination to the Executive, and will be amenable by impeachment to the public Justice. Without these ministers the Executive can do nothing of consequence. He suggested a biennial election of the Executive at the time of electing the 1st. branch, and the Executive to hold over, so as to prevent any interregnum in the administration. An election by the people at large throughout so great an extent of country could not be influenced, by those little combinations and those momentary lies which often decide popular elections within a narrow sphere. It will probably, be objected that the election will be influenced by the members of the Legislature; particularly of the 1st. branch, and that it will be nearly the same thing with an election by the Legislature itself. It could not be denied that such an influence would exist. But it might be answered that as the Legislature or the candidates for it would be divided, the enmity of one part would counteract the friendship of another: that if the administration of the Executive were good, it would be unpopular to oppose his re-election, if bad it ought to be opposed & a reappointment prevented; and lastly that in every view this indirect dependence on the favor of the Legislature could not be so mischievous as a direct dependence for his appointment. He saw no alternative for making the Executive independent of the Legislature but either to give him his office for life, or make him eligible by the people— Again, it might be objected that two years would be too short a duration. But he believes that as long as he should behave himself well, he would be continued in his place. The extent of the Country would secure his re-election against the factions & discontents of particular States. It deserved consideration also that such an ingredient in the plan would render it extremely palatable to the people. These were the general ideas which occurred to him on the subject, and which led him to wish & move that the whole constitution of the Executive might undergo reconsideration.

Mr. Randolph urged the motion of Mr. L. Martin for restoring the words making the Executive ineligible a 2nd. time. If he ought to be independent, he should not be left under a temptation to court a re-appointment. If he should be re-appointable by the Legislature, he will be no check on it. His revisionary power will be of no avail. He had always thought & contended as he still did that the danger apprehended by the little States was chimerical; but those who thought otherwise ought to be peculiarly anxious for the motion. If the Executive be appointed, as has been determined, by the Legislature, he will probably be appointed either by joint ballot of both houses, or be nominated by the 1st. and appointed by the 2d. branch. In either case the large States will preponderate. If he is to court the same influence for his re-appointment, will he not make his revisionary power, and all the other functions of his administration subservient to the views of the large States. Besides, is there not great reason to apprehend that in case he should be re-eligible, a false complaisance in the Legislature might lead them to continue an unfit man in office in preference to a fit one. It has been said that a constitutional bar to reappointment will inspire unconstitutional endeavours to perpetuate himself. It may be answered that his endeavours can have no effect unless the people be corrupt to such a degree as to render all precautions hopeless: to which may be added that this argument supposes him to be more powerful & dangerous, than other arguments which have been used, admit, and consequently calls for stron-

ger fetters on his authority. He thought an election by the legislature with an incapacity to be elected a second time would be more acceptable to the people than the plan suggested by Mr. Govr. Morris.

Mr. King did not like the ineligibility. He thought there was great force in the remark of Mr. Sherman, that he who has proved himself to be most fit for an Office, ought not to be excluded by the constitution from holding it. He would therefore prefer any other reasonable plan that could be substituted. He was much disposed to think that in such cases the people at large would chuse wisely. There was indeed some difficulty arising from the improbability of a general concurrence of the people in favor of any one man. On the whole he was of opinion that an appointment by electors chosen by the people for the purpose, would be liable to fewest objections.

Mr. Patterson's ideas nearly coincided he said with those of Mr King. He proposed that the Executive should be appointed by Electors to be chosen by the States in a ratio that would allow one elector to the smallest and three to the largest States.

Mr. Wilson. It seems to be the unanimous sence that the Executive should not be appointed by the Legislature, unless he be rendered in-eligible a 2d. time: he perceived with pleasure that the idea was gaining ground, of an election mediately or immediately by the people.

Mr. Madison. If it be a fundamental principle of free Government that the Legislative, Executive & Judiciary powers should be *separately* exercised, it is equally so that they be *independently* exercised. There is the same & perhaps greater reason why the Executive should be independent of the Legislature, than why the Judiciary should: A coalition of the two former powers would be more immediately & certainly dangerous to public liberty. It is essential then that the appointment of the Executive should either be drawn from some source, or held by some tenure, that will give him a free agency with regard to the Legislature. This could not be if he was to be appointable from time to time by the Legislature. It was not clear that an appointment in the 1st instance even with an eligibility afterwards would not establish an improper connection between the two departments. Certain it was that the appointment would be attended with intrigues and contentions that ought not to be unnecessarily admitted. He was disposed for these reasons to refer the appointment to some other source. The people at large was in his opinion the fittest in itself. It would be as likely as any that could be devised to produce an Executive Magistrate of distinguished Character. The people generally could only know & vote for some Citizen whose merits had rendered him an object of general attention & esteem. There was one difficulty however of a serious nature attending an immediate choice by the people. The right of suffrage was much more diffusive in the Northern than the Southern States; and the latter could have no influence in the election on the score of the Negroes. The substitution of electors obviated this difficulty and seemed on the whole to be liable to fewest objections.

Mr. Gerry. If the Executive is to be elected by the Legislature he certainly ought not to be re-eligible. This would make him absolutely dependent. He was against a popular election. The people are uninformed, and would be misled by a few designing men. He urged the expediency of an appointment of the Executive by Electors to be chosen by the State Executives. The people of the States will then choose the 1st. branch: The legislatures of the States the 2d. branch of the National Legislature, and the Executives of the States, the National Executive. This he thought would form a strong attach-

ment in the States to the National System. The popular mode of electing the chief Magistrate would certainly be the worst of all. If he should be so elected & should do his duty, he will be turned out for it like Govr. Bowdoin in Massts. & President Sullivan in N. Hamshire.

On the question on Mr. Govr. Morris motion to reconsider generally the constitution of the Executive.

Mas. ay. Ct. ay. N.J. ay & all others ay.

Mr. Elseworth moved to strike out the appointment by the National Legislature, and insert "to be chosen by electors appointed, by the Legislatures of the States in the following ratio; towit—one for each State not exceeding 200,000 inhab. two for each above yt. number & not exceeding 300,000 and three for each State exceeding 300,000.—Mr. Broome 2ded. the motion.

Mr. Rutlidge was opposed to all the modes except the appointment by the National Legislature. He will be sufficiently independent, if he be not re-eligible.

Mr. Gerry preferred the motion of Mr. Elseworth to an appointment by the National Legislature, or by the people; tho' not to an appointment by the State Executives. He moved that the electors proposed by Mr. E. should be 25 in number, and allotted in the following proportion. to N.H. 1. to Mas. 3. to R.I. 1. to Ct. 2. to N.Y. 2. N.J. 2. Pa. 3. Del. 1 Md. 2. Va. 3. N.C. 2. S.C. 2. Geo. 1.

The question as moved by Mr. Elseworth being divided, on the 1st. part shall ye Nat. Executive be appointed by Electors?

Mas. divd Ct. ay. N.J. ay. Pa. ay. Del. ay. Md. ay. Va. ay. N.C. no. S.C. no. Geo. no.

On 2d. part shall the Electors be chosen by State Legislatures?

Mas. ay. Ct. ay. N.J. ay. Pa. ay. Del. ay. Md. ay. Va. no. N.C. ay. S.C. no.

Geo. ay.

The part relating to the ratio in which the States sd. chuse electors was postponed nem. con.

Mr. L. Martin moved that the Executive be ineligible a 2d. time.

Mr. Williamson 2ds. the motion. He had no great confidence in the Electors to be chosen for the special purpose. They would not be the most respectable citizens; but persons not occupied in the high offices of Government. They would be liable to undue influence, which might the more readily be practised as some of them will probably be in appointment 6 or 8 months before the object of it comes on.

Mr. Elseworth supposed any persons might be appointed Electors, excepting solely, members of the National Legislature.

On the question shall he be ineligible a 2d. time?

Mas. no. Ct. no. N.J. no. Pa. no. Del. no. Md. no. Va. no. N.C. ay. S.C. ay. Geo. ay.

On the question Shall the Executive continue for 7 years? It was passed in the negative

Mas. divd. Ct. ay. N.J. no. Pa. no. Del. no. Md. no. Va. no. N.C. divd. S.C. ay. Geo. ay.

Mr. King was afraid we should shorten the term too much.

Mr. Govr. Morris was for a short term, in order to avoid impeachments which would be otherwise necessary.

Mr. Butler was against a frequency of the elections. Geo. & S.C. were too distant to send electors often.

Mr. Elseworth was for 6 years. If the elections be too frequent, the Executive will not be firm eno'. There must be duties which will make him unpopular for the moment. There will be *outs* as well as *ins*. His administration therefore will be attacked and misrepresented.

Mr. Williamson was for 6 years. The expence will be considerable & ought not to be unnecessarily repeated.

If the Elections are too frequent, the best men will not undertake the service and those of an inferior character will be liable to be corrupted.

On question for 6 years?

Mas. ay. Ct. ay. N.J. ay. Pa. ay. Del. no. Md. ay. Va. ay. N.C. ay. S.C. ay. Geo. ay.

Adjourned

The postponed Ratio of Electors for appointing the Executive; to wit 1 for each State whose inhabitants do not exceed 100,000, &c. being taken up.

Mr. Madison observed that this would make in time all or nearly all the States equal. Since there were few that would not in time contain the number of inhabitants intitling them to 3 Electors: that this ratio ought either to be made temporary, or so varied as that it would adjust itself to the growing population of the States.

Mr. Gerry moved that in the 1st *instance* the Electors should be allotted to the States in the following ratio: to N.H. 1. to Mas. 3. to R.I. 1. to Ct. 2. to N.Y. 2. N.J. 2. Pa. 3. Del. 1 Md. 2. Va. 3. N.C. 2. S.C. 2. Geo. 1.

On the question to postpone in order to take up this motion of Mr. Gerry. It passed in the affirmative.

Mas. ay. Ct. no. N.J. no. Pa. ay. Del. no. Md. no. Va. ay. N.C. ay. S.C. ay. Geo. ay.

Mr. Elseworth moved that 2 Electors be allotted to N.H. Some rule ought to be pursued; and N.H. has more than 100,000 inhabitants. He thought it would be proper also to allot 2. to Georgia.

Mr. Broom & Mr. Martin moved to postpone Mr. Gerry's allotment of Electors, leaving a fit ratio to be reported by the Committee to be appointed for detailing the Resolutions.

On this motion.

Mas. no. Ct. no. N.J. ay. Pa. no. Del. ay. Md. ay. Va. no. N.C. no. S.C. no. Geo. no.

Mr. Houston 2ded. the motion of Mr. Elseworth to add another Elector to

N.H. & Georgia. On the Question:

Mas. no. Ct. ay. N.J. no. Pa. no. Del. no. Md. no. Va. no. N.C. no. S.C. ay. Geo. ay.

Mr. Williamson moved as an amendment to Mr. Gerry's allotment of Electors in the 1st. instance that in future elections of the National Executive, the number of Electors to be appointed by the several States shall be regulated by their respective numbers of Representatives in the 1st. branch pursuing as nearly as may be the present proportions....

Tuesday, July 24.
In Convention

The appointment of the Executive by Electors reconsidered.

Mr. Houston moved that he be appointed by the "National Legislature," instead of "Electors appointed by the State Legislatures" according to the last decision of the mode. He dwelt chiefly on the improbability, that capable men would undertake the service of Electors from the more distant States.

Mr. Spaight seconded the motion.

Mr. Gerry opposed it. He thought there was no ground to apprehend the danger urged by Mr. Houston. The election of the Executive Magistrate will be considered as of vast importance and will excite great earnestness. The best men, the Governours of the States will not hold it derogatory from their character to be the electors. If the motion should be agreed to, it will be necessary to make the Executive ineligible a 2d. time, in order to render him independent of the Legislature; which was an idea extremely repugnant to his way of thinking.

Mr. Strong supposed that there would be no necessity, if the Executive should be appointed by the Legislature, to make him ineligible a 2d. time; as new elections of the Legislature will

have intervened; and he will not depend for his 2d. appointment on the same set of men as his first was recorded from. It had been suggested that *gratitude* for his past appointment would produce the same effect as dependence for his future appointment. He thought very differently. Besides this objection would lie against the Electors who would be objects of gratitude as well as the Legislature. It was of great importance not to make the Government too complex which would be the case if a new set of men like the Electors should be introduced into it. He thought also that the first characters in the States would not feel sufficient motives to undertake the office of Electors.

Mr. Williamson was for going back to the original ground; to elect the Executive for 7 years and render him ineligible a 2d. time. The proposed Electors would certainly not be men of the 1st. nor even the 2d. grade in the States. These would all prefer a seat either in the Senate or the other branch of the Legislature. He did not like the Unity in the Executive. He had wished the Executive power to be lodged in three men taken from three districts into which the States should be divided. As the Executive is to have a kind of veto on the laws, and there is an essential difference of interests between the N. & S. States, particularly in the carrying trade, the power will be dangerous, if the Executive is to be taken from part of the Union, to the part from which he is not taken. The case is different here from what it is in England; where there is a sameness of interests throughout the Kingdom. Another objection against a single Magistrate is that he will be an elective King, and will feel the spirit of one. He will spare no pains to keep himself in for life, and will then lay a train for the succession of his children. It was pretty certain he thought that we should at some time or other have a King; but he wished no precaution to be omitted that might postpone the event as long as possible.—Ineligibility a 2d. time appeared to him to be the best precaution. With this precaution he had no objection to a longer term than 7 years. He would go as far as 10 or 12 years.

Mr. Gerry moved that the Legislatures of the States should vote by ballot for the Executive in the same proportions as it had been proposed they should chuse electors; and that in case a majority of the votes should not center on the same person, the 1st branch of the National Legislature should chuse two out of the 4 candidates having most votes, and out of these two, the 2nd branch should chuse the Executive.

Mr. King seconded the motion—and on the Question to postpone in order to take it into consideration. The *noes* were so predominant, that the States were not counted.

Question on Mr. Houston's motion that the Executive be appointed by National Legislature

N.H. ay. Mas. ay. Ct. no. N.J. ay. Pa. no. Del. ay. Md. no. Va. no. N.C. ay. S.C. ay. Geo. ay.

Mr. L. Martin & Mr. Gerry moved to re-instate the ineligibility of the Executive a 2d. time.

Mr. Elseworth. With many this appears a natural consequence of his being elected by the Legislature. It was not the case with him. The Executive he thought should be reelected if his conduct proved him worthy of it. And he will be more likely to render himself, worthy of it if he be rewardable with it. The most eminent characters also will be more willing to accept the trust under this condition, than if they foresee a necessary degradation at a fixt period.

Mr. Gerry. That the Executive should be independent of the Legislature is a clear point. The longer the duration of his appointment the more will his dependence be diminished. It will be better than for him to continue 10, 15, or even 20, years and be ineligible afterwards.

Mr. King was for making him re-eligible. This is too great an advantage to be given up for the small effect it will have on his dependence, if impeachments are to lie. He considered these as rendering the tenure during pleasure.

Mr. L. Martin, suspending his motion as to the ineligibility, moved "that the appointment of the Executive shall continue for Eleven years.

Mr. Gerry suggested fifteen years.

Mr. King twenty years. This is the medium life of princes.[5]

Mr. Davie Eight years.

Mr. Wilson. The difficulties & perplexities into which the House is thrown proceed from the election by the Legislature which he was sorry had been reinstated. The inconveniency of this mode was such that he would agree to almost any length of time in order to get rid of the dependence which must result from it. He was persuaded that the longest term would not be equivalent to a proper mode of election; unless indeed it should be during good behavior. It seemed to be supposed that at a certain advance in life, a continuance in office would cease to be agreeable to the officer, as well as desirable to the public. Experience had shewn in a variety of instances that both a capacity & inclination for public service existed—in very advanced stages. He mentioned the instance of a Doge of Venice who was elected after he was 80 years of age. The popes have generally been elected at very advanced periods, and yet in no case had a more steady or a better concerted policy been pursued than in the Court of Rome. If the Executive should come into office at 35 years of age, which he presumes may happen & his continuance should be fixt at 15 years at the age of 50 in the very prime of life, and with all the aid of experience, he must be cast aside like a useless hulk. What an irreparable loss would the British Jurisprudence have sustained, had the age of 50 been fixt there as the ultimate limit of capacity or readiness to serve the public. The great luminary [Lord Mansfield] held his seat for thirty years after his arrival at that age. Notwithstanding what had been done he could not but hope that a better mode of election would yet be adopted; and one that would be more agreeable to the general sense of the House. That time might be given for further deliberation he would move that the present question be postponed till tomorrow.

Mr. Broom seconded the motion to postpone.

Mr. Gerry. We seem to be entirely at a loss on this head. He would suggest whether it would not be advisable to refer the clause relating to the Executive to the Committee of detail to be appointed. Perhaps they will be able to hit on something that may unite the various opinions which have been thrown out.

Mr. Wilson. As the great difficulty seems to spring from the mode of election, he would suggest a mode which had not been mentioned. It was that the Executive be elected for 6 years by a small number, not more than 15 of the National Legislature, to be drawn from it, not by ballot, but by lot and who should retire immediately and make the election without separating.

By this mode intrigue would be avoided in the first instance, and the dependence would be diminished. This was not he said a digested idea and might be liable to strong objections.

Mr. Govr. Morris. Of all possible modes of appointment that by the Legislature is the worst. If the Legislature is to appoint, and to impeach or to influence the impeachment, the Executive will be the mere creature of it. He had been opposed to the impeachment but was now convinced that impeachments must be provided for, if the appointment was to be of any duration. No man wd. say, that an Executive known to be in the pay of an Enemy, should not be removable in some way or other. He had been charged heretofore [by Col. Mason] with inconsistency in pleading for confidence in the legislature on some occasions, & urging a distrust on others. The charge was not well founded. The Legislature is worthy of unbounded confidence in some respects, and liable to equal distrust in others. When their interest coincides precisely with that of their Constituents, as happens in many of their Acts, no abuse of trust is to be apprehended. When a strong personal interest happens to be opposed to the general interest, the Legislature can not be too much distrusted. In all public bodies there are two parties. The Executive will necessarily be more connected with one than with the other. There will be a personal interest therefore in one of the parties to oppose as well as in the other to support him. Much had been said of the intrigues that will be practised by the Executive to get into office. Nothing had been said on the other side of the intrigues to get him out of office. Some leader of party will always covet his seat, will perplex his administration, will cabal with the Legislature, till he succeeds in supplanting him. This was the way in which the King of England was got out, he meant the real King, the Minister. This was the way in which Pitt [Lord Chatham] forced himself into place. Fox was for pushing the matter still farther. If he carried his India bill, which he was very near doing, he would have made the Minister, the King in form almost as well as in substance. Our President will be the British Minister, yet we are about to make him appointable by the Legislature. Something had been said of the danger of Monarchy. If a good government should not now be formed, if a good organization of the Executive should not be provided, he doubted whether we should not have something worse than a limited Monarchy. In order to get rid of the dependence of the Executive on the Legislature, the expedient of making him ineligible a 2d. time had been devised. This was as much as to say we should give him the benefit of experience, and then deprive ourselves of the use of it. But make him ineligible a 2d. time—and prolong his duration even to 15-years, will he by any wonderful interposition of providence at that period cease to be a man? No he will be unwilling to quit his exaltation, the road to his object thro' the Constitution will be shut; he will be in possession of the sword, a civil war will ensue, and the Commander of the victorious army on which ever side, will be the despot of America. This consideration renders him particularly anxious that the Executive should be properly constituted. The vice here would not, as in some other parts of the system be curable. It is the most difficult of all rightly to balance the Executive. Make him too weak: The Legislature will usurp his powers: Make him too strong. He will usurp on the Legislature. He preferred a short period, a re-eligibility, but a different mode of election. A long period would prevent an adoption of the plan: it ought to do so. He should himself be afraid to trust it. He was not prepared to decide on Mr. Wilson's mode of election just hinted by him. He thought it deserved consideration. It would be better that chance should decide than intrigue.

On a question to postpone the consideration of the Resolution on the subject of the Executive.

N.H. no. Mas. no. Ct. ay. N.J. no. Pa. ay. Del. divd. Md. ay. Va. ay. N.C. no. S.C. no. Geo. no.

Mr. Wilson then moved that the Executive be chosen every ——— years by ——— Electors to be taken by lot from the Natl Legislature who shall proceed immediately to the choice of the Executive and not separate until it be made.

Mr. Carrol 2ds. the motion

Mr. Gerry. This is committing too much to chance. If the lot should fall on a set of unworthy men, an unworthy Executive must be saddled on the Country. He thought it had been demonstrated that no possible mode of electing by the Legislature could be a good one.

Mr. King. The lot might fall on a majority from the same State which would ensure the election of a man from that State. We ought to be governed by reason, not by chance. As nobody seemed to be satisfied, he wished the matter to be postponed.

Mr. Wilson did not move this as the best mode. His opinion remained unshaken that we ought to resort to the people for the election. He seconded the postponement.

Mr. Govr. Morris observed that the chances were almost infinite against a majority of electors from the same State.

On a question whether the last motion was in order, it was determined in the affirmative; 7 ays. 4 noes.

On the question of postponement it was agreed to nem. con.

Mr. Carrol took occasion to observe that he considered the clause declaring that direct taxation on the States should be in proportion to representation, previous to the obtaining an actual census, as very objectionable, and that he reserved to himself the right of opposing it, if the Report of the Committee of detail should leave it in the plan.

Mr. Govr. Morris hoped the Committee would strike out the whole of the clause proportioning direct taxation to representation. He had only meant it as a bridge[6] to assist us over a certain gulph; having passed the gulph the bridge may be removed. He thought the principle laid down with so much strictness, liable to strong objections.

On a ballot for a Committee to report a Constitution conformable to the Resolutions passed by the Convention, the members chosen were

Mr. Rutlidge, Mr. Randolph, Mr. Ghorum, Mr. Elseworth, Mr Wilson—

On motion to discharge the Committee of the whole from the propositions submitted to the Convention by Mr. C. Pinkney as the basis of a constitution, and to refer them to the Committee of detail just appointed, it was agd. to nem: con.

A like motion was then made & agreed to nem: con: with respect to the propositions of Mr. Patterson

Adjourned.

Wednesday, July 25.
In Convention

Clause relating to the Executive again under consideration.

Mr. Elseworth moved "that the Executive be appointed by the Legislature," except when the magistrate last chosen shall have continued in office the whole term for which he was chosen, & be reliable, in which case the choice shall be by Electors appointed by the legislatures of the States for that purpose. By this means a deserving magistrate may be reelected without making him dependent on the Legislature.

Mr. Gerry repeated his remark that an election at all by the Natl. Legislature was radically and incurably wrong; and moved that the Executive be appointed by the Governors & Presidents of the States, with advice of their Councils, and where there are no Councils by Electors chosen by the Legislatures. The executives to vote in the following proportions: viz—

Mr. Madison. There are objections agst. every mode that has been, or perhaps can be proposed. The election must be made either by some existing authority under the Natl. or State Constitutions—or by some special authority derived from the people—or by the people themselves.—The two Existing authorities under the Natl. constitutional wd. be the Legislative & Judiciary. The latter he presumed was out of the ques-

tion. The former was in his Judgment liable to insuperable objections. Besides the general influence of that mode on the independence of the Executive, 1. the election of the Chief Magistrate would agitate & divide the legislature so much that the public interest would materially suffer by it. Public bodies are always apt to be thrown into contentions, but into more violent ones by such occasions than by any others. 2. the candidate would intrigue with the Legislature, would derive his appointment from the predominant faction, and be apt to render his administration subservient to its views. 3. The Ministers of foreign powers would have and make use of, the opportunity to mix their intrigues & influence with the Election. Limited as the powers of the Executive are, it will be an object of great moment with the great rival powers of Europe who have American possessions, to have at the head of our Government a man attached to their respective politics & interests. No pains, nor perhaps expence, will be spared, to gain from the Legislature an appointment favorable to their wishes. Germany & Poland are witnesses of this danger. In the former, the election for the Head of the Empire, till it became in a manner hereditary, interested all Europe, and was much influenced by foreign interference. In the latter, although the elective Magistrate has very little real power, his election has at all times produced the most eager interference of forign princes, and has in fact at length slid entirely into foreign hands. The existing authorities in the States are the Legislative, Executive & Judiciary. The appointment of the Natl. Executive by the first, was objectionable in many points of view, some of which had been already mentioned. He would mention one which of itself would decide his opinion. The Legislatures of the States had betrayed a strong propensity to a variety of pernicious measures. One object of the National Legislre. was to control this propensity. One object of the Natl. Executive, so far as it would have a negative on the laws, was to control the Natl. Legislature, so far as it might be infected with similar propensity. Refer the appointmt. of the Natl. Executive to the State Legislatures, and this controuling purpose may be defeated. The Legislatures can & will act with some kind of regular plan, and will promote the appointmt. of a man who will not oppose himself to a favorite object. Should a majority of the Legislatures at the time of election have the same object, or different objects of the same kind, The Natl. Executive would be rendered subservient to them.—An appointment by the State Executives, was liable among other objections to this insuperable one, that being standing bodies, they could & would be courted, and intrigued with by the Candidates, by their partizans, and by the Ministers of foreign powers. The State Judiciarys had not & he presumed would not be proposed as a proper source of appointment. The option before us then lay between an appointment by Electors chosen by the people—and an immediate appointment by the people. He thought the former mode free from many of the objections which had been urged against it, and greatly preferable to an appointment by the Natl. Legislature. As the electors would be chosen for the occasion, would meet at once, & proceed immediately to an appointment, there would be very little opportunity for cabal, or corruption. As a farther precaution, it might be required that they should meet at some place distinct from the seat of Government and even that no person within a certain distance of the place at the time should be eligible. This Mode however had been rejected so recently & by so great a majority that it probably would not be proposed anew. The remaining mode was an election by the people or rather by the qualified part of

them, at large: With all its imperfections he liked this best. He would not repeat either the general arguments for or the objections against this mode. He would only take notice of two difficulties which he admitted to have weight. The first arose from the disposition in the people to prefer a Citizen of their own State, and the disadvantage this would throw on the smaller States. Great as this objection might be he did not think it equal to such as lay against every other mode which had been proposed. He thought too that some expedient might be hit upon that would obviate it. The second difficulty arose from the disproportion of qualified voters in the N. & S. States, and the disadvantages which this mode would throw on the latter. The answer to this objection was 1. that this disproportion would be continually decreasing under the influence of the Republican laws introduced in the S. States, and the more rapid increase of their population. 2. That local considerations must give way to the general interest. As an individual from the S. States he was willing to make the sacrifice.

Mr. Elseworth. The objection drawn from the different sizes of the States, is unanswerable. The Citizens of the largest States would invariably prefer the Candidate within the State; and the largest States would invariably have the man.

Question on Mr. Elseworth's motion as above.

N.H. ay. Mas. no. Ct. ay. N.J. no. Pa. ay. Del. no. Md. ay. Va. no. N.C. no. S.C. no. Geo. no.

Mr. Pinkney moved that the election by the Legislature be qualified with a proviso that no person be eligible for more than 6 years in any twelve years. He thought this would have all the advantage & at the same time avoid in some degree the inconveniency, of an absolute ineligibility a 2d. time.

Col. Mason approved the idea. It had the sanction of experience in the instance of Congs. and some of the Executives of the States. It rendered the Executive as effectually independent, as an ineligibility after his first election, and opened the way at the same time for the advantage of his future services. He preferred on the whole the election by the Natl. Legislature: Tho' Candor obliged him to admit, that there was great danger of foreign influence, as had been suggested. This was the most serious objection with him that had been urged.

Mr. Butler. The two great evils to be avoided are cabal at home, and influence from abroad. It will be difficult to avoid either if the Election be made by the Natl. Legislature. On the other hand: The Government should not be made so complex and unwieldy as to disgust the States. This would be the case, if the election shd. be referred to the people. He liked best an election by Electors chosen by the Legislatures of the States. He was against a re-eligibility at all events. He was also agst. a ratio of votes in the States. An equality should prevail in this case. The reasons for departing from it do not hold in the case of the Executive as in that of the Legislature.

Mr. Gerry approved of Mr. Pinkney's motion as lessening the evil.

Mr. Govr. Morris was against a rotation in every case. It formed a political School, in wch we were always governed by the scholars, and not by the Masters. The evils to be guarded agst. in this case are 1. the undue influence of the Legislature. 2. instability of Councils. 3. misconduct in office. To guard agst. the first, we run into the second evil. We adopt a rotation which produces instability of Councils. To avoid Sylla we fall into Charibdis. A change of men is ever followed by a change of measures. We see this fully exemplified in the vicissitudes among ourselves, particularly in the State of Pena. The self-sufficiency of a victorious party scorns to tread in the paths of their predecessors. Rehoboam will not imitate Soloman. 2. the Rotation in office will not prevent intrigue and dependence on the Legislature. The man in office will look forward to the period at which he will become re-eligible. The distance of the period, the improbability of such a protraction of his life will be no obstacle. Such is the nature of man, formed by his benevolent author no doubt for wise ends, that altho' he knows his existence to be limited to a span, he takes his measures as if he were to live for ever. But taking another supposition, the inefficacy of the expedient will be manifest. If the magistrate does not look forward to his re-election to the Executive, he will be pretty sure to keep in view the opportunity of his going into the Legislature itself. He will have little objection then to an extension of power on a theatre where he expects to act a distinguished part; and will be very unwilling to take any step that may endanger his popularity with the Legislature, on his influence over which the figure he is to make will depend. 3. To avoid the third evil, impeachments will be essential, and hence an additional reason against an election by the Legislature. He considered an election by the people as the best, by the Legislature as the worst, mode. Putting both these aside, he could not but favor the idea of Mr. Wilson, of introducing a mixture of lot. It will diminish, if not destroy both cabal and dependence.

Mr. Williamson was sensible that strong objections lay agst. an election of the Executive by the Legislature, and that it opened a door for foreign influence. The principal objection agst. an election by the people seemed to be, the disadvantage under which it would place the smaller States. He suggested as a cure for this difficulty, that each man should vote for 3 candidates, One of these he observed would be probably of his own State, the other 2. of some other States; and as probably of a small as a large one.

Mr. Govr. Morris liked the idea, suggesting as an amendment that each man should vote for two persons one of whom at least should not be of his own State.

Mr. Madison also thought something valuable might be made of the suggestion with the proposed amendment of it. The second best man in this case would probably be the first, in fact. The only objection which occurred was that each Citizen after having given his vote for his favorite fellow Citizen, wd. throw away his second on some obscure Citizen of another State, in order to ensure the object of his first choice. But it could hardly be supposed that the Citizens of many States would be so sanguine of having their favorite elected, as not to give their second vote with sincerity to the next object of their choice. It might moreover be provided in favor of the smaller States that the Executive should not be eligible more than ―――― times in ―――― years from the same State.

Mr. Gerry. A popular election in this case is radically vicious. The ignorance of the people would put it in the power of some one set of men dispersed through the Union & acting in Concert to delude them into any appointment. He observed that such a Society of men existed in the Order of the Cincinnati. They are respectable, United, and influencial. They will in fact elect the chief Magistrate in every instance, if the election be referred to the people. His respect for the characters composing this Society could not blind him to the danger & impropriety of throwing such a power into their hands.

Mr. Dickenson. As far as he could judge from the discussions which had taken place during his attendance, insuperable objections lay agst. an election of the Executive by the Natl. Legislature; as also by the Legislatures or Executives of the States. He had long leaned towards an election by the people which he regarded as the best & purest source. Objections he was aware lay agst. this mode, but not so great he thought as agst. the other modes. The greatest difficulty in the opinion of the House seemed to arise from the partiality of the States to their respective Citizens. But, might not this very partiality be turned to a useful purpose. Let the people of each State chuse its best Citizen. The people will know the most eminent characters of their own States, and the people of different States will feel an emulation in selecting those of which they will have the greatest reason to be proud. Out of the thirteen names thus selected, an Executive Magistrate may be chosen either by the Natl. Legislature, or by Electors appointed by it.

On a Question which was moved for postponing Mr. Pinkney's motion; in order to make way for some such proposition as had been hinted by Mr. Williamson and others: it passed in the negative.

N.H. no. Mas. no. Ct. no. N.J. ay. Pa. ay. Del. no. Md. ay. Va. ay. N.C. no. S.C. no. Geo. no.

On Mr. Pinkney's motion that no person shall serve in the Executive more than 6 years in 12 years, it passed in the negative.

N.H. ay. Mas. ay. Ct. no. N.J. no. Pa. no. Del. no. Md. no. Va. no. N.C. ay. S.C. ay. Geo. ay.

On a motion that the members of the Committee be furnished with copies of the proceedings it was so determined; S. Carolina alone being in the negative.

It was then moved that the members of the House might take copies of the Resolutions which had been agreed to; which passed in the negative. N.H. no. Mas. no. Ct. ay. N.J. ay. Pa. no. Del. ay. Md. no. Va. ay. N.C. ay. S.C. no. Geo. no.

Mr. Gerry & Mr. Butler moved to refer the resolution relating to the Executive (except the clause making it consist of a single person) to the Committee of detail.

Mr. Wilson hoped that so important a branch of the System would not be committed until a general principle shd. be fixed by a vote of the House.

Mr. Langdon, was for the Commitment—Adjd.

Thursday, July 26.
In Convention

Col. Mason. In every Stage of the Question relative to the Executive, the difficulty of the subject and the diversity of the opinions concerning it have appeared. Nor have any of the modes of constituting that department been satisfactory. 1. It has been proposed that the election should be made by the people at large; that is that an act which ought to be performed by those who know most of Eminent characters & qualifications, should be performed by those who know least. 2. that the election should be made by the Legislatures of the States. 3. by the Executives of the States. Agst. these modes also strong objections have been urged. 4. It has been proposed that the election should be made by Electors chosen by the people for that purpose. This was at first agreed to: But on further consideration has been rejected. 5. Since which, the mode of Mr. Williamson, requiring each freeholder to vote for several candidates has been proposed. This seemed like many other propositions, to carry a plausible face, but on closer inspection is liable to fatal objections. A popular election in any form, as Mr. Gerry has observed, would throw the appointment into the hands of the Cincinnati, a Society for the members of which he had a great respect; but which he never wished to have a preponderating influence in the Govt. 6. Another expedient was proposed by Mr. Dickenson, which is liable to so palpable & material an inconvenience that he had little doubt of its being by this time rejected by himself. It would exclude every man who happened not to be popular within his own State; tho' the causes of his local unpopularity might be of such a nature as to recommend him to the States at large. 7. Among other expedients, a lottery has been introduced. But as the tickets do not appear to be in much demand, it will probably, not be carried on, and nothing therefore need be said on that subject. After reviewing all these various modes, he was led to conclude, that an election by the Natl. Legislature as originally proposed, was the best. If it was liable to objections, it was liable to fewer than any other. He conceived at the same time that a second election ought to be absolutely prohibited. Having for his primary object, for the pole-star of his political conduct, the preservation of the rights of the people, he held it as an essential point, as the very palladium of Civil liberty, that the great officers of the State, and particularly the Executive should at fixed periods return to that mass from which they were at first taken, in order that they may feel & respect those rights and interests which are again to be personally valuable to them. He concluded with moving that the constitution of the Executive as reported by the Come. of the whole be re-instated, viz. "that the Executive be appointed for seven years, & be ineligible a 2d time."

Mr. Davie seconded the motion

Docr. Franklin. It seems to have been imagined by some that the returning to the mass of the people was degrading the magistrate. This he thought was contrary to republican principles. In free Governments the rulers are the servants, and the people their superiors & sovereigns. For the former therefore to return among the latter was not to *degrade* but to promote them. And it would be imposing an unreasonable burden on them, to keep them always in a State of servitude, and not allow them to become again one of the Masters.

Questions on Col. Masons motion as above; which passed in the affirmative

N.H. ay. Mas. not on floor. Ct. no. N.J. ay. Pa. no. Del. no. Md. ay. Va. ay. N.C. ay. S.C. ay. Geo. ay.

Mr. Govr. Morris was now agst. the whole paragraph. In answer to Col. Mason's position that a periodical return of the great officers of the State into the mass of the people, was the palladium of Civil liberty he wd. observe that on the same principle the Judiciary ought to be periodically degraded; certain it was that the Legislature ought on very principle, yet no one had proposed, or conceived that the members of it should not be re-eligible. In answer to Docr. Franklin, that a return into the mass of the people would be a promotion, instead of a degradation, he had no doubt that our Executive like most others would have too much modesty not to be willing to decline the promotion.

On the question on the whole resolution as amended in the words following— "that a National Executive be instituted—to consist of a single person—to be chosen by the Natl. legislature—for the term of seven years—to be ineligible a 2d. time—with power to carry into execution the natl. laws—to appoint to offices in cases not otherwise provided for—to be removable on impeachment & conviction of malpractice or neglect of duty—to receive a fixt compensation for the devotion of his time to the public service, to be paid out of the Natl. treasury"—it passed in the affirmative.

N.H. ay. Mas. not on floor. Ct. ay. N.J. ay. Pa. no. Del. no. Md. no. Va. divd. Mr. Blair & Col. Mason ay. Gen. Washington & Mr. Madison no. Mr. Randolph happened to be out of the House. N.C. ay. S.C. ay. Geo. ay....

... Art. X. sect. 1. "The executive power" of the U.S. shall be vested in a single person. His stile shall be "The President of the U.S. of America" and his title shall be "His Excellency." He shall be elected by ballot by the Legislature. He shall hold his office during the term of seven years; but shall not be elected a second time.

On the question for vesting the power in a *single person*. It was agreed to nem: con: So also on the *Stile* and *title*.

Mr. Rutledge moved to insert "joint" before the word "ballot," as the most convenient mode of electing.

Mr. Sherman objected to it as depriving the *States* represented in the *Senate* of the negative intended them in that house.

Mr. Ghorum said it was wrong to be considering at every turn whom the Senate would represent. The public good was the true object to be kept in view. Great delay and confusion would ensue if the two Houses shd. vote separately, each having a negative on the choice of the other.

Mr. Dayton. It might be well for those not to consider how the Senate was constituted, whose interest it was to keep it out of sight.—If the amendment should be agreed to, a *joint* ballot would in fact give the appointment to one House. He could never agree to the clause with such an amendment. There could be no doubt of the two Houses separately concurring in the same person for President. The importance & necessity of the case would ensure a concurrence.

Mr. Carrol moved to strike out "by the Legislature" and insert "by the people." Mr. Wilson 2ded him and on the question

N.H. no. Mas. no. Ct. no. N.J. no. Pa. ay. Del. ay. Md. no. Va. no. N.C. no. S.C. no. Geo. no.

Mr. Brearly was opposed to the motion for inserting the word "joint." The argument that the small States should not put their hands into the pockets of the large ones did not apply in this case.

Mr. Wilson urged the reasonableness of giving the larger States a larger share of the appointment, and the danger of delay from a disagreement of the two Houses. He remarked also that the Senate had peculiar powers balancing the advantage given by a joint ballot in this case to the other branch of the Legislature.

Mr. Langdon. This general officer ought to be elected by the joint & general voice. In N. Hampshire the mode of separate votes by the two Houses was productive of great difficulties. The negative of the Senate would hurt the feelings of the man elected by the votes of the other branch. He was for inserting "joint" tho' unfavorable to N. Hampshire as a small State.

Mr. Wilson remarked that as the President of the Senate was to be President of the U.S. that Body in cases of vacancy might have an interest in throwing dilatory obstacles in the way, if its separate concurrence should be required.

Mr. Madison. If the amendment be agreed to the rule of voting will give to the largest State, compared with the smallest, an influence as 4 to 1 only, although the population is as 10 to 1. This surely can not be unreasonable as the President is to act for the *people* not for the *States*. The President of the *Senate* also is to be occasionally President of the U.S. and by his negative alone can make ¾ of the other branch necessary to the passage of the law. This is another advantage enjoyed by the Senate.

On the question for inserting "joint," it passed in the affirmative.

N.H. ay. Mas. ay. Ct. no. N.J. no. Pa. ay. Del. ay. Md. no. Va. ay. N.C. ay. S.C. ay. Geo. no.

Mr. Dayton then moved to insert, after the word "Legislatures" the words "each State having one vote" Mr. Brearley 2ded him, and on the question it passed in the negative.

N.H. no. Mas. no. Ct. ay. N.J. ay. Pa. no. Del. ay. Md. ay. Va. no. N.C. no. S.C. no. Geo. ay.

Mr. Pinkney moved to insert after the word "Legislature" the words "to

which election a majority of the votes of the members present shall be required" & on this question, it passed in the affirmative.

N.H. ay. Mas. ay. Ct. ay. N.J. no. Pa. ay. Del. ay. Md. ay. Va. ay. N.C. ay. S.C. ay. Geo. ay.

Mr. Read moved "that in case the numbers for the two highest in votes should be equal, then the President of the Senate shall have an additional casting vote," which was disagreed to by a general negative.

Mr. Govr. Morris opposed the election of the President by the Legislature. He dwelt on the danger of rendering the Executive uninterested in maintaining the rights of his Station, as leading to Legislative tyranny. If the Legislature have the Executive dependent on them, they can perpetuate & support their usurpations by the influence of tax-gatherers & other officers, by fleets armies &c. Cabal and corruption are attached to that mode of election: so also is ineligibility a second time. Hence the Executive is interested in Courting popularity in the Legislature by sacrificing his Executive Rights; & then he can go into that Body, after the expiration of his Executive office, and enjoy there the fruits of his policy. To these considerations he added that rivals would be continually intrigueing to oust the President from his place. To guard against all these evils he moved that the President "shall be chosen by Electors to be chosen by the People of the several States" Mr. Carrol 2ded him & on the question it passed in the negative.

N.H. no. Mas. no. Ct. ay. N.J. ay. Pa. ay. Del. ay. Md. no. Va. ay. N.C. no. S.C. no. Geo. no.

Mr. Dayton moved to postpone the consideration of the two last clauses of Section I. art. X. which was disagreed to without a count of the States.

Mr. Broome moved to refer the two clauses to a Committee of a member from each State, & on the question, it failed the States being equally divided

N.H. no. Mas. no. Ct. divd. N.J. ay. Pa. ay. Del. ay. Md. ay. Va. ay. N.C. no. S.C. no. Geo. no.

On the question taken on the first part of Mr. Govr. Morris's Motion towit "shall be chosen by electors" as an abstract question, it failed the States being equally divided.

N.H. no. Mas. abst. Ct. divided. N.J. ay. Pa. ay. Del. ay. Md. divided. Va. ay. N.C. no. S.C. no. Geo. no. . . .

Adjourned

Tuesday, September 4. In Convention

Mr. Brearly from the Committee of eleven made a further partial Report as follows

"The Committee of Eleven to whom sundry resolutions &c were referred on the 31st of August, report that in their opinion the following additions and alterations should be made to the Report before the Convention, viz

1. The first clause of section 1. art 7. to read as follows— 'The Legislature shall have power to lay and collect taxes duties imposts & excises, to pay the debts and provide for the common defence and general welfare, of the U.S.'

2. At the end of the 2d clause of section 1. art 7. add 'and with the Indian Tribes.'

3. In the place of the 9th art. section 1. to be inserted 'The Senate of the U.S. shall have power to try all impeachments; but no person shall be convicted without the concurrence of two thirds of the members present.'

4. After the word 'Excellency' in sect. 1. art. 10. to be inserted. 'He shall hold his office during the term of four years, and together with the vice-President, chosen for the same term, be elected in the following manner viz. Each State shall appoint in such manner as its Legislature may direct, a number of electors equal to the whole number of Senators and members of the House of Representatives to which the State may be entitled in the Legislature. The Electors shall meet in their respective States, and vote by ballot for two persons, of whom one at least shall not be an inhabitant of the same State with themselves; and they shall make a list of all the persons voted for, and of the number of votes for each, which list they shall sign and certify and transmit sealed to the Seat of the General Government, directed to the President of the Senate—The President of the Senate shall in that House open all the certificates; and the votes shall be then and there counted. The Person having the greatest number of votes shall be the President, if such number be a majority of that of the electors; and if there be more than one who have such majority, and have an equal number of votes, then the Senate shall immediately choose by ballot the President. And in every case after the choice of the President, the person having the greatest number of votes shall be vice-president: but if there should remain two or more who have equal votes, the Senate shall choose from them the vice-President. The Legislature may determine the time of choosing and assembling the Electors, and the manner of certifying and transmitting their votes.'

5. 'Sect. 2. No person except a natural born citizen or a Citizen of the U.S. at the time of the adoption of this Constitution shall be eligible to the office of President; nor shall any person be elected to that office, who shall be under the age of thirty five years, and who has not been in the whole, at least fourteen years a resident within the U.S.'

6. 'Sect. 3. The vice-president shall be ex officio President of the Senate, except when they sit to try the impeachment of the President, in which case the Chief Justice shall preside, and excepting also when he shall exercise the powers and duties of President, in

which case and in case of his absence, the Senate shall chuse a President pro tempore—'The vice-President when acting as President of the Senate shall not have a vote unless the House be equally divided.'

7. 'Sect. 4. The President by and with the advice and Consent of the Senate, shall have power to make Treaties; and he shall nominate and by and with the advice and consent of the Senate shall appoint ambassadors, and other public Ministers, Judges of the Supreme Court, and all other Officers of the U.S., whose appointments are not otherwise herein provided for. But no Treaty shall be made without the consent of two thirds of the members present.'

8. After the words— "into the service of the U.S." in sect. 2. art: 10. add 'and may require the opinion in writing of the principal officer in each of the Executive Departments, upon any subject relating to the duties of their respective offices."

The latter part of Sect. 2. Art: 10. to read as follows.

9. 'He shall be removed from his office on impeachment by the House of Representatives, and conviction by the Senate, for Treason, or bribery, and in case of his removal as aforesaid, death, absence, resignation or inability to discharge the powers or duties of his office, the vice-president shall exercise those powers and duties until another President be chosen, or until the inability of the President be removed.'

The (1st.) clause of the Report was agreed to, nem. con.

The (2) clause was also agreed to nem: con:

The (3) clause was postponed in order to decide previously on the mode of electing the President.

The (4th) clause was accordingly taken up.

Mr. Gorham disapproved of making the next highest after the President, the vice-President, without referring the decision to the Senate in case the next highest should have less than a majority of votes. As the regulation stands a very obscure man with very few votes may arrive at that appointment.

Mr. Sherman said the object of this clause of the report of the Committee was to get rid of the ineligibility, which was attached to the mode of election by the Legislature, and to render the Executive independent of the Legislature. As the choice of the President was to be made out of the five highest, obscure characters were sufficiently guarded against in that case; and he had no objection to requiring the vice-President to be chosen in like manner, where the choice was not decided by a majority in the first instance.

Mr. Madison was apprehensive that by requiring both the President & vice President to be chosen out of the five highest candidates, the attention of the electors would be turned too much to making candidates instead of giving their votes in order to a definitive choice. Should this turn be given to the business, the election would, in fact be consigned to the Senate altogether. It would have the effect at the same time, he observed, of giving the nomination of the candidates to the largest States.

Mr. Govr. Morris concurred in, & enforced the remarks of Mr. Madison.

Mr. Randolph & Mr. Pinkney wished for a particular explanation & discussion of the reasons for changing the mode of electing the Executive.

Mr. Govr. Morris said he would give the reasons of the Committee and his own. The 1st. was the danger of intrigue and faction if the appointment should be made by the Legislature. 2. the inconveniency of an ineligibility required by that mode in order to lessen its evils. 3. The difficulty of establishing a Court of Impeachments, other than the Senate which would not be so proper for the trial nor the other branch for the impeachment of the President, if appointed by the Legislature, 4. No body had appeared to be satisfied with an appointment by the Legislature. 5. Many were anxious even for an immediate choice by the people. 6. the indispensible necessity of making the Executive independent of the Legislature.—As the Electors would vote at the same time throughout the U.S. and at so great a distance from each other, the great evil of cabal was avoided. It would be impossible also to corrupt them. A conclusive reason for making the Senate instead of the Supreme Court the Judge of impeachments, was that the latter was to try the President after the trial of the impeachment.

Col. Mason confessed that the plan of the Committee had removed some capital objections, particularly the danger of cabal and corruption. It was liable however to this strong objection, that nineteen times in twenty the President would be chosen by the Senate, an improper body for the purpose.

Mr. Butler thought the mode not free from objections, but much more so than an election by the Legislature, where as in elective monarchies, cabal faction and violence would be sure to prevail.

Mr. Pinkney stated as objections to the mode 1. that it threw the whole appointment in fact into the hands of the Senate. 2. The Electors will be strangers to the several candidates and of course unable to decide on their comparative merits. 3. It makes the Executive reeligible which will endanger the public liberty. 4. It makes the same body of men which will in fact elect the President his Judges in case of an impeachment.

Mr. Williamson had great doubts whether the advantage of re-eligibility would balance the objection to such a dependence of the President on the Senate for his reappointment. He thought at least the Senate ought to be restrained to the *two* highest on the list.

Mr. Govr. Morris said the principal advantage aimed at was that of taking away the opportunity for cabal. The President may be made if thought necessary ineligible on this as well as on any other mode of election. Other inconveniences may be no less redressed on this plan than any other.

Mr. Baldwin thought the plan not so objectionable when well considered, as at first view. The increasing intercourse among the people of the States, would render important characters less and less unknown; and the Senate would consequently be less & less likely to have the eventual appointment thrown into their hands.

Mr. Wilson. This subject has greatly divided the House, and will also divide people out of doors. It is in truth the most difficult of all on which we have had to decide. He had never made up an opinion on it entirely to his own satisfaction. He thought the plan on the whole a valuable improvement on the former. It gets rid of one great evil, that of cabal & corruption; & Continental Characters will multiply as we more & more coalesce, so as to enable the electors in every part of the Union to know and judge of them. It clears the way also for a discussion of the question of re-eligibility on its own merits, which the former mode of election seems to forbid. He thought it might be better however to refer the eventual appointment to the Legislature than to the Senate, and to confine it to a smaller number than five of the Candidates. The eventual election by the Legislature wd. not open cabal anew, as it would be restrained to certain designated objects of choice, and as these must have had the previous sanction of a number of the States: and if the election be made as it ought as soon as the votes of the electors are opened and it is known that no one has a majority of the whole, there can be little danger of corruption. Another reason for preferring the Legislature to the Senate in this business, was that the House of Reps. will be so often changed as to be free from the influence and faction to which the permanence of the Senate may subject that branch.

Mr. Randolph preferred the former mode of constituting the Executive, but if the change was to be made, he wished to know why the eventual election was referred to the *Senate* and not to the *Legislature?* He saw no necessity for this and many objections to it. He was apprehensive also that the advantage of the eventual appointment would fall into the hands of the States near the Seat of Government.

Mr. Govr. Morris said the *Senate* was preferred because fewer could then, say to the President, you owe your appointment to us. He thought the President would not depend so much on the Senate for his re-appointment as on his general good conduct.

The further consideration of the Report was postponed that each member might take a copy of the remainder of it.

The following motion was referred to the Committee of Eleven—to wit,— "To prepare & report a plan for defraying the expences of the Convention"

Mr. Pinkney moved a clause declaring "that each House should be judge of the privilege of its own members. Mr. Govr. Morris 2ded. the motion.

Mr. Randolph & Mr. Madison expressed doubts as to the propriety of giving such a power, & wished for a postponement.

Mr. Govr. Morris thought it so plain a case that no postponement could be necessary.

Mr. Wilson thought the power involved, and the express insertion of it needless. It might beget doubts as to the power of other public bodies, as Courts &c. Every Court is the judge of its own privileges.

Mr. Madison distinguished between the power of Judging of privileges previously & duly established, and the effect of the motion which would give a discretion to each House as to the extent of its

own privileges. He suggested that it would be better to make provision for ascertaining by *law*, the privileges of each House, than to allow each House to decide for itself. He suggested also the necessity of considering what privileges ought to be allowed to the Executive.

Adjourned

Wednesday, September 5.
In Convention

Mr. Brearley from the Committee of Eleven made a farther report as follows,

1. To add to the clause "to declare war" the words "and grant letters of marque and reprisal"

"Ordered that the Secretary make out and transmit to the Treasury office of the U.S. an accord for the said Services, & for the incidental expenses of this Convention"

The resolution & order were separately agreed to nem: con:

Mr. Gerry gave notice that he should move to reconsider articles XIX. XX. XXI. XXII.

Mr. Williamson gave like notice as to the Article fixing the number of Representatives, which he thought too small. He wished also to allow Rho. Island more than one, as due to her probable number of people, and as proper to stifle any pretext arising from her absence on the occasion.

The Report made yesterday as to the appointment of the Executive being taken up. Mr. Pinkney renewed his opposition to the mode, arguing 1. that the electors will not have sufficient knowledge of the fittest men, & will be swayed by an attachment to the eminent men of their respective States. Hence 2dly the dispersion of the votes would leave the appointment with the Senate, and as the President's reappointment will thus depend on the Senate he will be the mere creature of that body. 3. He will combine with the Senate agst. the House of Representatives. 4. This change in the mode of election was meant to get rid of the ineligibility of the President a second time, whereby he will become fixed for life under the auspices of the Senate.

Mr. Gerry did not object to this plan of constituting the Executive in itself, but should be governed in his final vote by the powers that may be given to the President.

Mr. Rutlidge was much opposed to the plan reported by the Committee. It would throw the whole power into the Senate. He was also against a re-eligibility. He moved to postpone the Report under consideration & take up the original plan of appointment by the Legislature, to wit. "He shall be elected by joint ballot by the Legislature to which election a majority of the votes of the members present shall be required: He shall hold his office during the term of seven years; but shall not be elected a second time."

On this motion to postpone

N.H. divd. Mas. no. Ct. no. N.J. no. Pa. no. Del. no. Md. no. Va. no. N.C. ay. S.C. ay. Geo. no.

Col. Mason admitted that there were objections to an appointment by the Legislature as originally planned. He had not yet made up his mind, but would state his objections to the mode proposed by the Committee. 1. It puts the appointment in fact into the hands of the Senate, as it will rarely happen that a majority of the whole votes will fall on any one candidate: and as the Existing President will always be one of the 5 highest, his reappointment will of course depend on the Senate. 2. Considering the powers of the President and those of the Senate, if a coalition should be established between these two branches, they will be able to subvert the Constitution—The great objection with him would be removed by depriving the Senate of the eventual election.

He accordingly moved to strike out the words "if such number be a majority of that of the electors."

Mr. Williamson 2ded. the motion. He could not agree to the clause without some such modification. He preferred making the highest tho' not having a majority of the votes, President, to a reference of the matter to the Senate. Referring the appointment to the Senate lays a certain foundation for corruption and aristocracy.

Mr. Govr. Morris thought the point of less consequence than it was supposed on both sides. It is probable that a majority of votes will fall on the same man. As each elector is to give two votes, more than ¼ will give a majority. Besides as one vote is to be given to a man out of the State, and as this vote will not be thrown away, ½ the votes will fall on characters eminent and generally known. Again if the President shall have given satisfaction, the votes will turn on him of course, and a majority of them will reappoint him, without resort to the Senate: If he should be disliked, all disliking him, would take care to unite their votes so as to ensure his being supplanted.

Col. Mason those who think there is no danger of there not being a majority for the same person in the first instance, ought to give up the point to those who think otherwise.

Mr. Sherman reminded the opponents of the new mode proposed that if the small states had the advantage in the Senate's deciding among the five highest candidates, the large States would have in fact the nomination of these candidates.

On the motion of Col. Mason

N.H. no. Mas. no. Ct. no. N.J. no. Pa. no. Del. no. Md. ay. Va. no. N.C. ay. S.C. no. Geo. no.

Mr. Wilson moved to strike out "Senate" and insert the word "Legislature"

Mr. Madison considered it as a primary object to render an eventual resort to any part of the Legislature improbable. He was apprehensive that the proposed alteration would turn the attention of the large States too much to the appointment of candidates, instead of aiming at an effectual appointment of the officer, as the large States would predominate in the Legislature which would have the final choice out of the Candidates. Whereas if the Senate in which the small States predominate should have this final choice, the concerted effort of the large States would be to make the appointment in the first instance conclusive.

Mr. Randolph. We have in some revolutions of this plan made a bold stroke for Monarchy. We are now doing the same for an aristocracy. He dwelt on the tendency of such an influence in the Senate over the election of the President in addition to its other powers, to convert that body into a real and dangerous Aristocracy.

Mr. Dickinson was in favor of giving the eventual election to the Legislature, instead of the Senate. It was too much influence to be superadded to that body.

On the question moved by Mr. Wilson

N.H. divd. Mas. no. Ct. no. N.J. no. Pa. ay. Del. no. Md. no. Va. ay. N.C. no. S.C. ay. Geo. no.

Mr. Madison & Mr. Williamson moved to strike out the word "majority" and insert "one third" so that the eventual power might not be exercised if less than a majority, but not less than 1/3 of the Electors should vote for the same person.

Mr. Gerry objected that this would put it in the power of three or four States to put in whom they pleased.

Mr. Williamson. There are seven States which do not contain one third of the people. If the Senate are too appoint, less than one sixth of the people will have the power.

On the question

N.H. no. Mas. no. Ct. no. N.J. no. Pa. no. Del. no. Md. no. Va. ay. N.C. ay. S.C. no. Geo. no.

Mr. Gerry suggested that the eventual election should be made by six Senators and seven Representatives chosen by joint ballot of both Houses.

Mr. King observed that the influence for the Small States in the Senate was somewhat balanced by the influence of the large States in bringing forward the candidates;[7] and also by the Concurrence of the small States in the Committee in the clause vesting the exclusive origination of Money bills in the House of Representatives.

Col. Mason moved to strike out the word "five" and insert the word "three" as the highest candidates for the Senate to choose out of.

Mr. Gerry 2ded. the motion

Mr. Sherman would sooner give up the plan. He would prefer seven or thirteen.

On the question moved by Col. Mason & Mr. Gerry

N.H. no. Mas. no. Ct. no. N.J. no. Pa. no. Del. no. Md. no. Va. ay. N.C. ay. S.C. no. Geo. no.

Mr. Spaight and Mr. Rutledge moved to strike out "five" and insert "thirteen"—to which all the States disagreed—except N.C. & S.C.

Mr. Madison & Mr. Williamson moved to insert after "Electors" the words "who shall have balloted" so that the non voting electors not being counted might not increase the number necessary as a majority of the whole, to decide the choice without the agency of the Senate.

On this question

N.H. no. Mas. no. Ct. no. N.J. no. Pa. ay. Del. no. Md. ay. Va. ay. N.C. ay. S.C. no. Geo. no.

Mr. Dickinson moved, in order to remove ambiguity from the intention of the clause as explained by the vote, to add, after the words "if such number be majority of the whole number of the Electors" the word "appointed"

On this motion

N.H. ay. Mas. ay. Ct. ay. N.J. ay. Pa. ay. Del. ay. Md. ay. Va. no. N.C. no. S.C. ay. Geo. ay.

Col. Mason. As the mode of appointment is now regulated, he could not forbear expressing his opinion that it is utterly inadmissible. He would prefer the Government of Prussia to one which will put all power into the hands of seven or eight men, and fix an Aristocracy worse than absolute monarchy.

The words "and of their giving their votes" being inserted on motion for that purpose, after the words "The Legislature may determine the time of chusing and assembling the Electors."

The House adjourned

Thursday, September 6.
In Convention

Mr. King and Mr. Gerry moved to insert in the clause of the Report (see Sept. 4) after the words "may be entitled in the Legislature" the words following—"But no person shall be appointed an elector who is a member of the Legislature of the U.S. or who holds any office of profit or trust under the U.S." which passed nem: con:

Mr. Gerry proposed, as the President was to be elected by the Senate out of the five highest candidates, that if he should not at the end of his term be re-elected by a majority of the Electors, and no other candidate should have a majority, the eventual election should be made by the Legislature. This he said would relieve the President from his particular dependence on the Senate for his continuance in office.

Mr. King liked the idea, as calculated to satisfy particular members & promote unanimity, as likely to operate but seldom.

Mr. Read opposed it, remarking that if individual members were to be indulged, alterations would be necessary to satisfy most of them.

Mr. Williamson espoused it as a reasonable precaution against the undue influence of the Senate.

Mr. Sherman liked the arrangement as it stood, though he should not be averse to some amendments. He thought he said that if the Legislature were to have the eventual appointment instead of the Senate, it ought to vote in the case by States, in favor of the small States, as the large States would have so great an advantage in nominating the candidates.

Mr. Govr. Morris thought favorably of Mr. Gerry's proposition. It would free the President from being tempted in naming to Offices, to Conform to the will of the Senate, and thereby virtually give the appointments to office, to the Senate.

Mr. Wilson said that he had weighed carefully the report of the Committee for remodelling the constitution of the Executive; and on combining it with other parts of the plan, he was obliged to consider the whole as having a dangerous tendency to aristocracy; as throwing a dangerous power into the hands of the Senate. They will have in fact, the appointment of the President, and through his dependence on them, the virtual appointment to offices; among others the offices of the Judiciary Department. They are to make Treaties; and they are to try all impeachments. In allowing them thus to make the Executive and Judiciary appointments, to be the Court of impeachments, and to make Treaties which are to be laws of the land, the Legislative, Executive & Judiciary powers are all blended in one branch of the Government. The power of making Treaties involves the case of subsidies, and here as an additional evil, foreign influence is to be dreaded. According to the plan as it now stands, the President will not be the man of the people as he ought to be, but the Minion of the

Senate. He cannot even appoint a tide-waiter without the Senate. He had always thought the Senate too numerous a body for making appointments to office. The Senate, will moreover in all probability be in constant Session. They will have high salaries. And with all those powers, and the President in their interest, they will depress the other branch of the Legislature, and aggrandize themselves in proportion. Add to all this, that the Senate sitting in conclave, can by holding up to their respective States various and improbable candidates, contrive so to scatter their votes, as to bring the appointment of the President ultimately before themselves. Upon the whole he thought the new mode of appointing the President, with some amendments, a valuable improvement; but he could never agree to purchase it at the price of the ensuing parts of the Report, nor befriend a system of which they make a part.

Mr. Govr. Morris expressed his wonder at the observations of Mr. Wilson so far as they preferred the plan in the printed Report to the new modification of it before the House, and entered into a comparative view of the two, with an eye to the nature of Mr. Wilsons objections to the last. By the first the Senate he observed had a voice in appointing the President out of all the Citizens of the U.S.: by this they were limited to five candidates previously nominated to them, with a probability of being barred altogether by the successful ballot of the Electors. Here surely was no increase of power. They are now to appoint Judges nominated to them by the President. Before they had the appointment without any agency whatever of the President. Here again was surely no additional power. If they are to make Treaties as the plan now stands, the power was the same in the printed plan. If they are to try impeachments, the Judges must have been triable by them before. Wherein then lay

the dangerous tendency of the innovations to establish an aristocracy in the Senate? As to the appointment of officers, the weight of sentiment in the House, was opposed to the exercise of it by the President alone; though it was not the case with himself. If the Senate would act as was suspected, in misleading the States into a fallacious disposition of their votes for a President, they would, if the appointment were withdrawn wholly from them, make such representations in their several States where they have influence, as would favor the object of their partiality.

Mr. Williamson replying to Mr. Morris: observed that the aristocratic complexion proceeds from the change in the mode of appointing the President which makes him dependent on the Senate.

Mr. Clymer said that the aristocratic part to which he could never accede was that in the printed plan, which gave the Senate the power of appointing to offices.

Mr. Hamilton said that he had been restrained from entering into the discussions by his dislike of the Scheme of Gov. in General; but as he meant to support the plan to be recommended, as better than nothing, he wished in this place to offer a few remarks. He liked the new modification, on the whole, better than that in the printed Report. In this the President was a Monster elected for seven years, and ineligible afterwards; having great powers in appointments to office, & continually tempted by this constitutional disqualification to abuse them in order to subvert the Government. Although he should be made re-eligible, still if appointed by the Legislature, he would be tempted to make use of corrupt influence to be continued in office. It seemed peculiarly desireable therefore that some other mode of election should be devised. Considering the different views of different States, & the different districts Northern Middle & Southern, he concurred with those who thought that the votes would not be concentered, and that the appointment would consequently in the present mode devolve on the Senate. The nomination to offices will give great weight to the President. Here then is a mutual connection & influence, that will perpetuate the President, and aggrandize both him & the Senate. What is to be the remedy? He saw none better than to let the highest number of ballots, whether a majority or not, appoint the President. What was the objection to this? Merely that too small a number might appoint. But as the plan stands, the Senate may take the candidate having the smallest number of votes, and make him President.

Mr. Spaight & Mr. Williamson moved to insert "seven" instead of "four" years for the term of the President—

On this motion

N.H. ay. Mas. no. Ct. no. N.J. no. Pa. no. Del. no. Md. no. Va. ay. N.C. ay. S.C. no. Geo. no.

Mr. Spaight & Mr. Williamson, then moved to insert "six" instead of "four."

On which motion

N.H. no. Mas. no. Ct. no. N.J. no. Pa. no. Del. no. Md. no. Va. no. N.C. ay. S.C. ay. Geo. no.

On the term "four" all the States were ay, except N. Carolina, no.

On the question (Clause 4. in the Report) for Appointing President by electors—down to the words,—"entitled in the Legislature" inclusive.

N.H. ay. Mas. ay. Ct. ay. N.J. ay. Pa. ay. Del. ay. Md. ay. Va. ay. N.C. no. S.C. no. Geo. ay.

It was moved that the Electors meet at the seat of the General Government which passed in the Negative. N.C. only being ay.

It was moved to insert the words "under the seal of the State" after the word "transmit" in 4th clause of the Report which was disagreed to; as was

another motion to insert the words "and who shall have given their votes" after the word "appointed" in the 4th Clause of the Report as added yesterday on motion of Mr. Dickinson.

On several motions, the words "in presence of the Senate and House of Representatives" were inserted after the word "counted" and the word "immediately" before the word "choose"; and the words "of the Electors" after the word "votes."

Mr. Spaight said if the election by Electors is to be crammed down, he would prefer their meeting altogether and deciding finally without any reference to the Senate and moved "That the Electors meet at the seat of the General Government."

Mr. Williamson 2ded. the motion, on which all the States were in the negative except N. Carolina.

On the motion the words "But the election shall be on the same day throughout the U.S." were added after the words "transmitting their votes"

N.H. ay. Mas. no. Ct. ay. N.J. no. Pa. ay. Del. no. Md. ay. Va. ay. N.C. ay. S.C. ay. Geo.—ay.

On a question on the sentence in clause (4). "if such number be a majority of that of the Electors appointed."

N.H. ay. Mas. ay. Ct. ay. N.J. ay. Pa. no. Del. ay. Md. ay. Va. no. N.C. no. S.C. ay. Geo. ay.

On a question on the clause referring to the eventual appointment of the President to the Senate

N.H. ay. Mas. ay. Ct. ay. N.J. ay. Pa. ay. Del. ay. Md. ay. Va. ay. N.C. no. Here the call ceased.

Mr. Madison made a motion requiring 2/3 at least of the Senate to be present at the choice of a President. Mr. Pinkney 2ded. the motion.

Mr. Gorham thought it a wrong principle to require more than a majority in any case. In the present case it might prevent for a long time any choice of a President. On the question moved by Mr. M. & Mr. P.

N.H. ay. Mas. abst. Ct. no. N.J. no. Pa. no. Del. no. Md. ay. Va. ay. N.C. ay. S.C. ay. Geo. ay.

Mr. Williamson suggested as better than an eventual choice by the Senate, that this choice should be made by the Legislature, voting *by States* and not *per capita.*

Mr. Sherman suggested the House of Reps. as preferable to the Legislature, and moved, accordingly,

To strike out the words "The Senate shall immediately choose &c" and insert "The House of Representatives shall immediately choose by ballot one of them for President, the members from each State having one vote."

Col. Mason liked the latter mode best as lessening the aristocratic influence of the Senate.

On the Motion of Mr. Sherman

N.H. ay. Mas. ay. Ct. ay. N.J. ay. Pa. ay. Del. no. Md. ay. Va. ay. N.C. ay. S.C. ay. Geo. ay.

Mr. Govr. Morris suggested the idea of providing that in all cases, the President in office, should not be one of the five Candidates; but be only re-eligible in case a majority of the electors should vote for him [This was another expedient for rendering the President independent of the Legislative body for his continuance in office.]

Mr. Madison remarked that as a majority of members wd. make a quorum in the H. of Reps. it would follow from the amendment of Mr. Sherman giving the election to a majority of States, that the President might be elected by two States only, Virga. and Pen. which have 18 members, if these States alone should be present.

On a motion that the eventual election of President in case of *an equality* of the votes of the electors be referred to the House of Reps.

N.H. ay. Mas. ay. N.J. no. Pa. ay. Del. no. Md. no. Va. ay. N.C. ay. S.C. ay. Geo. ay.

Mr. King moved to add to the amendment of Mr. Sherman "But a quorum for this purpose shall consist of a member or members from two thirds of the States," and also of a majority of the whole number of the House of Representatives."

Col. Mason liked it as obviating the remark of Mr. Madison—The motion as far as "States" inclusive was agd. to. On the residue to wit, "and also of a majority of the whole number of the House of Reps. it passed in the Negative.

N.H. no. Mas. ay. Ct. ay. N.J. no. Pa. ay. Del. no. Md. no. Va. ay. N.C. ay. S.C. no. Geo. no.

The Report relating to the appointment of the Executive stands as amended, as follows,

"He shall hold his office during the term of four years, and together with the vice-President, chosen for the same term, be elected in the following manner.

Each State shall appoint in such manner as its Legislature may direct, a number of electors equal to the whole number of Senators and members of the House of Representatives, to which the State may be entitled in the Legislature.

But no person shall be appointed an Elector who is a member of the Legislature of the U.S. or who holds any office of profit or trust under the U.S.

The Electors shall meet in their respective States and vote by ballot for two persons, of whom one at least shall not be an inhabitant of the same States with themselves; and they shall make a list of the persons voted for, and of the number of votes for each, which list they shall sign and certify, and transmit sealed to the Seat of the General Government, directed to the President of the Senate.

The President of the Senate shall in the presence of the Senate and House of Representatives open all the certificates & the votes shall then be counted.

The person having the greatest number of votes shall be the President (if such number be a majority of the whole number of electors appointed) and if there be more than one who have such majority, and have an equal number of votes, then the House of Representatives shall immediately choose by ballot one of them for President, the Representation from each State having one vote. But if no person have a majority, then from the five highest on the list, the House of Representatives shall in like manner choose by ballot the President. In the choice of a President by the House of Representatives, a Quorum shall consist of a member or members from two thirds of the States and the [concurrence of a majority of all the States shall be necessary to such choice.]—And in every case after the choice of the President, the person having the greatest number of votes of the Electors shall be the vice-president: But, if there should remain two or more who have equal votes, the Senate shall choose from them the vice-President.

The Legislature may determine the time of choosing the Electors, and of their giving their votes; and the manner of certifying and transmitting their votes—But the election shall be on the same day throughout the U. States."

Adjourned

Friday, September 7.
In Convention.

The mode of constituting the Executive being resumed, Mr. Randolph moved, to insert in the first Section of the report made yesterday.

"The Legislature may declare by law what officer of the U.S. shall act as President in case of the death, resignation, or disability of the President and Vice-President; and such officer shall act accordingly until the time of electing a President shall arrive."

Mr. Madison observed that this, as worded, would prevent a supply of the vacancy by an intermediate election of the President, and moved to substitute—"until such disability be removed, or a President shall be elected. Mr. Governr. Morris 2ded. the motion, which was agreed to.

It seemed to be an objection to the provision with some, that according to the process established for chusing the Executive there would be difficulty in effecting it at other than the fixed periods; with others, that the Legislature was restrained in the temporary appointment to "*officers*" of the *U.S.* They wished it to be at liberty to appoint others than such.

On the Motion of Mr. Randolph as amended, it passed in the affirmative.

N.H. divided. Mas. no. Ct. no. N.J. ay. Pa. ay. Del. no. Md. ay. Va. ay. N.C. no. S.C. ay. Geo. ay.

Mr. Gerry moved "that in the election of President by the House of Representatives, no State shall vote by less than three members, and where that number may not be allotted to a State, it shall be made up by its Senators; and a concurrence of a majority of all the States shall be necessary to make such choice." Without some such provision five individuals might possibly be competent to an election; these being a majority of two thirds of the existing number of States; and two thirds being a quorum for this business.

Mr. Madison 2ded. the motion.

Mr. Read observed the the States having but one member only in the House of Representatives would be in danger of having no vote at all in the election: the sickness or absence either of the Representative or one of the Senators would have that effect.

Mr. Madison replied that, if one member of the House of Representatives, should be left capable of voting for the State, the states having one Representative only would still be subject to that danger. He thought it an evil that so small a number at any rate should be authorized, to elect. Corruption would be greatly faciliated by it.

The mode itself was liable to this further weighty objection that the representatives of a *majority* of the *States* and of the *people*. He wished some cure for this inconveniency might yet be provided.

Mr. Gerry withdrew the first part of his motion; and on the,—Question on the 2d. part viz. "and a concurrence of a majority of all the States shall be necessary to make such choice" to follow the words "a member or members from two thirds of the States"—It was agreed to nem: con:

The section 2. (see Sept. 4) requiring that the President should be a natural-born Citizen, &c. and should have been resident for fourteen years, & be thirty five years of age, was agreed to nem: con:

Section 3. (see Sept. 4). "The vice President shall be ex-officio President of the Senate"

Mr. Gerry opposed this regulation. We might as well put the President himself at the head of the Legislature. The close intimacy that must subsist between the President & vice-president makes it absolutely improper. He was agst. having any vice President.

Mr. Gov. Morris. The vice president then will be the first heir apparent that ever loved his father. If there should be no vice president, the President of the Senate would be temporary successor, which would amount to the same thing.

Mr. Sherman saw no danger in the case. If the vice-President were not to be President of the Senate, he would be without employment, and some member by being made President must be deprived of his vote, unless when an equal division of votes might happen in the Senate, which would be but seldom.

Mr. Randolph concurred in the opposition to the clause.

Mr. Williamson, observed that such an officer as vice-President was not wanted. He was introduced only for the sake of a valuable mode of election which required two to be chosen at the same time.

Col. Mason, thought the office of vice-President an encroachment on the rights of the Senate; and that it mixed too much the Legislative & Executive, which as well as the Judiciary departments, ought to be kept as separate as possible. He took occasion to express his dislike of any reference whatever of the power to make appointments to either branch of the Legislature. On the other hand he was averse to vest so dangerous a power in the President alone. As a method for avoiding both, he suggested that a privy Council of six members to the president should be established; to be chosen for six years by the Senate, two out of the Eastern two out of the middle, and two out of the Southern quarters of the Union, & to go out in rotation two every second year; the concurrence of the Senate to be required only in the appointment of Ambassadors, and in making treaties, which are more of a legislative nature. This would prevent the constant sitting of the Senate which he thought dangerous, as well as keep the departments separate & distinct. It would also save the expence of constant sessions of the Senate. He had he said always considered the Senate as too unwieldy & expensive for appointing officers, especially the smallest, such as tide waiters &c. He had not reduced his idea to writing, but it could be easily done if it should be found acceptable.

On the question shall the vice President be ex officio President of the Senate?

N.H. ay. Mas. ay. Ct. ay. N.J. no. Pa. ay. Del. ay. Md. no. Va. ay. N.C. abst. S.C. ay. Geo. ay.

The other parts of the same Section (3) were then agreed to.

The Section 4.—to wit, "The President by & with the advice and consent of the Senate shall have power to make Treaties &c."

Mr. Wilson moved to add, after the word "Senate" the words, "and House of Representatives." As treaties he said are to have the operation of laws, they ought to have the sanction of laws also. The circumstance of secrecy in the business of treaties formed the only objection; but this he thought, so far as it was inconsistent with obtaining the Legislative sanction, was outweighed by the necessity of the latter.

Mr. Sherman thought the only question that could be made was whether the power could be safely trusted to the Senate. He thought it could; and that the necessity of secresy in the case of treaties forbade a reference of them to the whole Legislature.

Mr. Fitzimmons 2ded. the motion of Mr. Wilson, & on the question

N.H. no. Mas. no. Ct. no. N.J. no. Pa. ay. Del. no. Md. no. Va. no. N.C. no. S.C. no. Geo. no.

Notes

1. The probable object of this motion was merely to enforce the argument against the re-eligibility of the Executive Magistrate, by holding out a tenure during good behaviour as the alternative for keeping him independent of the Legislature.
2. The view here taken of the subject was meant to aid in parrying the animadversions likely to fall on the motion of Dr. McClurg, for whom J. M. had a particular regard. The Doctor, though possessing talents of the highest order, was modest & unaccustomed to exert them in public debate.
3. This vote is not to be considered as any certain index of opinion, as a number in the affirmative probably had it chiefly in view to alarm those attached to a dependence of the Executive on the Legislature, & thereby facilitate some final arrangement of a contrary tendency. The avowed friends of an Executive, "during good behaviour" were not more than three or four, nor is it certain they would finally have adhered to such a tenure. An independence of the three great departments of each other, as far as possible, and the responsibility of all to the will of the community seemed to be generally admitted as the true basis of a well constructed government.
4. There was no debate on this motion, the apparent object of many in the affirmative was to secure the re-eligibility by shortening the term, and of many in the negative to embarrass the plan of referring the appointment & dependence of the Executive to the Legislature.
5. This might possibly be meant as a carricature of the previous motions in order to defeat the object of them.
6. The object was to lessen the eagerness on one side, & the opposition on the other, to the share of representation claimed by the S. Sothern States on account of the Negroes.
7. This explains the compromise mentioned above by Mr. Govr. Morris. Col. Mason, Mr. Gerry & other members from large States set great value on this privilege of originating money bills. Of this the members from the small states, with some from the large States who wished a high mounted Govt endeavored to avail themselves, by making that privilege, the price of arrangements in the constitution favorable to the small States, and to the elevation of the Government.

United States Constitution (1789)

Few features of the Constitution are as complicated as the electoral college, the mechanism for choosing the president that was created by Article I, Section 1, and was modified substantially in 1804 by the Twelfth Amendment.

Here is how the electoral college works, both constitutionally and in practice:

~ The president is elected by a majority vote of the electors, who are chosen every four years by the states using whatever methods each state individually adopts. Since 1860, every elector has been chosen by popular vote.

~ Each state has a number of electoral votes equal to the size of its delegation in Congress. In the 1990s, the apportionment of electors ranges from California's 52 to the minimum of three (corresponding to two senators and one representative) that are allotted to each of the 6 smallest states and, because of the Twenty-third Amendment (1961), to the District of Columbia.

~ Electors may not be federal officeholders, nor do they ever assemble as a national body. Instead, each state's electors meet in their own state capital, then send their ballots to Washington to be counted. By federal law, electors are chosen on election day—the first Tuesday after the first Monday in November—and vote on the first Monday after the second Wednesday in December.

ber. All electoral votes are opened and tallied publicly at a joint session of Congress in early January.

~ If no one receives a majority of electoral votes, the House of Representatives must choose the president from among the top three candidates. In making this decision, each state delegation in the House has one vote, with a majority of states needed for election. Two presidents have been elected by the House: Thomas Jefferson in 1800 (see "The House of Representatives Elects Thomas Jefferson: Rules and Ballots," p. 73), and John Quincy Adams in 1824 ("The House of Representatives Elects John Quincy Adams: Debate and Balloting," p. 127).

Under the original Constitution, each elector was required to vote for two presidential candidates, with the runner-up in the presidential election becoming the vice president. The Twelfth Amendment separated the balloting for president and vice president. (See "The Twelfth Amendment: Senate Debate," p. 89.) It also stated that if no one received a majority of electoral votes for vice president, the Senate would choose the vice president from among the top two candidates. Only one vice president—Richard M. Johnson in 1837—has been elected by the Senate.

With rare exception, electors have voted as instructed by the people of their states. (The most recent of history's nine *"faithless electors" reversed the order of the Democratic party's ticket and voted for Lloyd Bentsen for president and Michael S. Dukakis for vice president in 1988.) Even so, the outcome of the state-by-state contest for electoral votes has not always mirrored the national popular vote. In 1824, 1876, and 1888, the presidential and vice presidential candidates who received the most votes from the people were not elected. In twentieth-century elections, however, the electoral vote invariably has magnified the popular vote: in percentage terms, the winning candidate's majority in the former always has exceeded his plurality in the latter.*

In addition to the Twelfth and Twenty-third amendments, the presidential election process has been modified by the Twentieth Amendment and, especially, by the Twenty-second Amendment. (See "The Twentieth Amendment: Senate Debate," p. 301, and "The Twenty-second Amendment: House Debate," p. 370.) *The Twenty-fifth Amendment altered vice-presidential selection in certain unusual circumstances.* (See "The Twenty-fifth Amendment: Senate Debate," p. 522.) *Hundreds of amendments have been proposed in Congress to abolish the electoral college (more than on any other subject), but none has been approved and sent to the states for ratification.* ~

We the People of the United States, in Order to form a more perfect Union, establish Justice, insure domestic Tranquility, provide for the common defence, promote the general Welfare, and secure the Blessings of Liberty to ourselves and our Posterity, do ordain and establish this Constitution for the United States of America.

Article I

Section 1. All legislative Powers herein granted shall be vested in a Congress of the United States, which shall consist of a Senate and House of Representatives.

Section 2. The House of Representatives shall be composed of Members chosen every second Year by the People of the several States, and the Electors in each State shall have the Qualifications requisite for Electors of the most numerous Branch of the State Legislature.

No Person shall be a Representative who shall not have attained to the age of twenty five Years, and been seven Years a Citizen of the United States, and who shall not, when elected, be an Inhabitant of that State in which he shall be chosen.

[Representatives and direct Taxes shall be apportioned among the several States which may be included within this Union, according to their respective Numbers, which shall be determined by adding to the whole Number of free Persons, including those bound to Service for a Term of Years, and excluding Indians not taxed, three fifths of all other Persons.][1] The actual Enumeration shall be made within three Years after the first Meeting of the Congress of the United States, and within every subsequent Term of ten Years, in such Manner as they shall by Law direct. The Number of Representatives shall not exceed one for every thirty Thousand, but each State shall have at Least one Representative; and until such enumeration shall be made, the State of New Hampshire shall be entitled to chuse three, Massachusetts eight, Rhode-Island and Providence Plantations one, Connecticut five, New-York six, New Jersey four, Pennsylvania eight, Delaware one, Maryland six, Virginia ten, North Carolina five, South Carolina five, and Georgia three.

When vacancies happen in the Representation from any State, the Executive Authority thereof shall issue Writs of Election to fill such Vacancies.

The House of Representatives shall

and shall have the sole Power of Impeachment.

Section 3. The Senate of the United States shall be composed of two Senators from each State, [chosen by the Legislature thereof,][2] for six Years; and each Senator shall have one Vote.

Immediately after they shall be assembled in Consequence of the first Election, they shall be divided as equally as may be into three Classes. The Seats of the Senators of the first Class shall be vacated at the Expiration of the second Year, of the second Class at the Expiration of the fourth Year, and of the third Class at the Expiration of the sixth Year, so that one third may be chosen every second Year; [and if Vacancies happen by Resignation, or otherwise, during the Recess of the Legislature of any State, the Executive thereof may make temporary Appointments until the next Meeting of the Legislature, which shall then fill such Vacancies.][3]

No Person shall be a Senator who shall not have attained to the Age of thirty Years, and been nine Years a Citizen of the United States, and who shall not, when elected, be an Inhabitant of that State for which he shall be chosen.

The Vice President of the United States shall be President of the Senate, but shall have no Vote, unless they be equally divided.

The Senate shall chuse their other Officers, and also a President pro tempore, in the Absence of the Vice President, or when he shall exercise the Office of President of the United States.

The Senate shall have the sole Power to try all Impeachments. When sitting for that Purpose, they shall be on Oath or Affirmation. When the President of the United States is tried the Chief Justice shall preside: And no Person shall be convicted without the Concurrence of two thirds of the Members present.

Judgment in Cases of Impeachment shall not extend further than to removal from Office, and disqualification to hold and enjoy any Office of honor, Trust or Profit under the United States: but the Party convicted shall nevertheless be liable and subject to Indictment, Trial, Judgment and Punishment, according to Law.

Section 4. The Times, Places and Manner of holding Elections for Senators and Representatives, shall be prescribed in each State by the Legislature thereof; but the Congress may at any time by Law make or alter such Regulations, except as to the Places of chusing Senators.

The Congress shall assemble at least once in every Year, and such Meeting shall [be on the first Monday in December],[4] unless they shall by Law appoint a different Day.

Section 5. Each House shall be the Judge of the Elections, Returns and Qualifications of its own Members, and a Majority of each shall constitute a Quorum to do Business; but a smaller Number may adjourn from day to day, and may be authorized to compel the Attendance of absent Members, in such Manner, and under such Penalties as each House may provide.

Each House may determine the Rules of its Proceedings, punish its Members for disorderly Behaviour, and, with the Concurrence of two thirds, expel a Member.

Each House shall keep a Journal of its Proceedings, and from time to time publish the same, excepting such Parts as may in their Judgment require Secrecy; and the Yeas and Nays of the Members of either House on any question shall, at the Desire of one fifth of those Present, be entered on the Journal.

Neither House, during the Session of Congress, shall, without the Consent of the other, adjourn for more than three days, nor to any other Place than that in which the two Houses shall be sitting.

Section 6. The Senators and Representatives shall receive a Compensation for their Services, to be ascertained by Law, and paid out of the Treasury of the United States. They shall in all Cases, except Treason, Felony and Breach of the Peace, be privileged from Arrest during their Attendance at the Session of their respective Houses, and in going to and returning from the same; and for any Speech or Debate in either House, they shall not be questioned in any other Place.

No Senator or Representative shall, during the Time for which he was elected, be appointed to any civil Office under the Authority of the United States, which shall have been created, or the Emoluments whereof shall have been encreased during such time; and no Person holding any Office under the United States, shall be a Member of either House during his Continuance in Office.

Section 7. All Bills for raising Revenue shall originate in the House of Representatives; but the Senate may propose or concur with amendments as on other Bills.

Every Bill which shall have passed the House of Representatives and the Senate, shall, before it become a Law, be presented to the President of the United States; If he approve he shall sign it, but if not he shall return it, with his Objections to that House in which it shall have originated, who shall enter the Objections at large on their Journal, and proceed to reconsider it. If after such Reconsideration two thirds of that House shall agree to pass the Bill, it shall be sent, together with the Objections, to the other House, by which it shall likewise be reconsidered, and if approved by two thirds of that House, it shall become a Law. But in all such Cases the Votes of both Houses shall be determined by yeas and Nays, and the Names of the Persons voting for and against the Bill shall be entered on the Journal of each House respectively. If any Bill shall not be returned by the President within ten Days (Sundays excepted) after it shall have been presented to him, the Same shall be a Law, in like Manner as if he had signed it, unless the Congress by their Adjournment prevent its Return, in which Case it shall not be a Law.

Every Order, Resolution, or Vote to which the Concurrence of the Senate and House of Representatives may be necessary (except on a question of Adjournment) shall be presented to the President of the United States; and before the Same shall take Effect, shall be approved by him, or being disapproved by him, shall be repassed by two thirds of the Senate and House of Representatives, according to the Rules and Limitations prescribed in the Case of a Bill.

Section 8. The Congress shall have Power To lay and collect Taxes, Duties, Imposts and Excises, to pay the Debts and provide for the common Defence and general Welfare of the United States; but all Duties, Imposts and Excises shall be uniform throughout the United States;

To borrow Money on the credit of the United States;

To regulate Commerce with foreign Nations, and among the several States, and with the Indian Tribes;

To establish an uniform Rule of Naturalization, and uniform Laws on the subject of Bankruptcies throughout the United States;

To coin Money, regulate the Value thereof, and of foreign Coin, and fix the Standard of Weights and Measures;

To provide for the Punishment of counterfeiting the Securities and current Coin of the United States;

To establish Post Offices and post Roads;

To promote the Progress of Science and useful Arts, by securing for limited Times to Authors and Inventors the exclusive Right to their respective Writings and Discoveries;

To constitute Tribunals inferior to the supreme Court;

To define and punish Piracies and Felonies commited on the high Seas, and Offences against the Law of Nations;

To declare War, grant Letters of Marque and Reprisal, and make Rules concerning Captures on Land and Water;

To raise and support Armies, but no Appropriation of Money to that Use shall be for a longer Term than two Years;

To provide and maintain a Navy;

To make Rules for the Government and Regulation of the land and naval Forces;

To provide for calling forth the Militia to execute the Laws of the Union, suppress Insurrections and repel Invasions;

To provide for organizing, arming, and disciplining, the Militia, and for governing such Part of them as may be employed in the Service of the United States, reserving to the States respectively, the Appointment of the Officers, and the Authority of training the Militia according to the discipline prescribed by Congress;

To exercise exclusive Legislation in all Cases whatsoever, over such District (not exceeding ten Miles square) as may, by Cession of Particular States, and the Acceptance of Congress, become the Seat of the Government of the United States, and to exercise like Authority over all Places purchased by the Consent of the Legislature of the State in which the Same shall be, for the Erection of Forts, Magazines, Arsenals, dock-Yards, and other needful Buildings;— And

To make all Laws which shall be necessary and proper for carrying into Execution the foregoing Powers, and all other Powers vested by this Constitution in the Government of the United States, or in any Department or Officer thereof.

Section 9. The Migration or Importation of such Persons as any of the States now existing shall think proper to admit, shall not be prohibited by the Congress prior to the Year one thousand eight hundred and eight, but a Tax or duty may be imposed on such Importation, not exceeding ten dollars for each Person.

The Privilege of the Writ of Habeas Corpus shall not be suspended, unless when in Cases of Rebellion or Invasion the public Safety may require it.

No Bill of Attainder or ex post facto Law shall be passed.

No capitation, or other direct, Tax shall be laid, unless in Proportion to the Census of Enumeration herein before directed to be taken.[5]

No Tax or Duty shall be laid on Articles exported from any State.

No Preference shall be given by any Regulation of Commerce or Revenue to the Ports of one State over those of another; nor shall Vessels bound to, or from, one State, be obliged to enter, clear or pay Duties in another.

No Money shall be drawn from the Treasury, but in Consequence of Appropriations made by Law; and a regular Statement and Account of the Receipts and Expenditures of all public Money shall be published from time to time.

No Title of Nobility shall be granted by the United States: And no Person holding any Office of Profit or Trust under them, shall, without the Consent of the Congress, accept of any present, Emolument, Office, or Title, of any kind whatever, from any King, Prince or foreign State.

Section 10. No State shall enter into any Treaty, Alliance, or Confederation; grant Letters of Marque and Reprisal; coin Money; emit Bills of Credit; make any Thing but gold and silver Coin a Tender in Payment of Debts; pass any Bill of Attainder, ex post facto Law, or Law impairing the Obligation of Contracts, or grant any Title of Nobility.

No State shall, without the Consent of the Congress, lay any Imposts or Duties on Imports or Exports, except what may be absolutely necessary for executing it's inspection Laws: and the net Produce of all Duties and Imposts, laid by any State on Imports or Exports, shall be for the Use of the Treasury of the United States; and all such Laws shall be subject to the Revision and Controul of the Congress.

No State shall, without the Consent of Congress, lay any Duty of Tonnage, keep Troops, or Ships of War in time of Peace, enter into any Agreement or Compact with another State, or with a foreign Power, or engage in War, unless actually invaded, or in such imminent Danger as will not admit of delay.

Article II

Section 1. The executive Power shall be vested in a President of the United States of America. He shall hold his Office during the Term of four Years, and, together with the Vice President, chosen for the same Term, be elected, as follows.

Each State shall appoint, in such Manner as the Legislature thereof may direct, a Number of Electors, equal to the whole Number of Senators and Representatives to which the State may be entitled in the Congress: but no Senator or Representative, or Person holding an Office of Trust or Profit under the United States, shall be appointed an Elector.

[The Electors shall meet in their respective States, and vote by Ballot for two Persons, of whom one at least shall not be an Inhabitant of the same State with themselves. And they shall make a List of all the Persons voted for, and of the Number of Votes for each; which List they shall sign and certify, and transmit sealed to the Seat of the Government of the United States, directed to the President of the Senate. The President of the Senate shall, in the Presence of the Senate and House of Representatives, open all the Certificates, and the Votes shall then be counted. The Person having the greatest Number of Votes shall be the President, if such Number be a Majority of the whole Number of Electors appointed; and if there be more than one who have such Majority, and have an equal Number of Votes, then the House of Representatives shall immediately chuse by Ballot one of them for President; and if no Person have a Majority, then from the five highest on the list the said House shall in like Manner chuse the President. But in chusing the President, the Votes shall be taken by States, the Representation from each State having one Vote; a quorum for this Purpose shall consist of a Member or Members from two thirds of the States, and a Majority of all the States shall be necessary to a Choice. In every Case, after the Choice of the President, the Person having the greatest Number of Votes of the Electors shall be the Vice President. But if there should remain two or more who have equal Votes, the Senate shall chuse from them by Ballot the Vice President.][6]

The Congress may determine the Time of chusing the Electors, and the Day on which they shall give their Votes; which Day shall be the same throughout the United States.

No Person except a natural born Citizen, or a Citizen of the United States, at the time of the Adoption of this Constitution, shall be eligible to the Office of President; neither shall any Person be eligible to that Office who shall not have attained to the Age of thirty five Years, and been fourteen Years a Resident within the United States.

In Case of the Removal of the President from Office, or of his Death, Resignation, or Inability to discharge the Powers and Duties of the said Office,[7] the Same shall devolve on the Vice President, and the Congress may by Law provide for the Case of Removal, Death, Resignation or Inability, both of the President and Vice President, declaring what Officer shall then act as

President, and such Officer shall act accordingly, until the Disability be removed, or a President shall be elected.

The President shall, at stated Times, receive for his Services, a Compensation, which shall neither be encreased nor diminished during the Period for which he shall have been elected, and he shall not receive within that Period any other Emolument from the United States, or any of them.

Before he enter on the Execution of his Office, he shall take the following Oath or Affirmation:—"I do solemnly swear (or affirm) that I will faithfully execute the Office of President of the United States, and will to the best of my Ability, preserve, protect and defend the Constitution of the United States."

Section 2. The President shall be Commander in Chief of the Army and Navy of the United States, and of the Militia of the several States, when called into the actual Service of the United States; he may require the Opinion, in writing, of the principal Officer in each of the executive Departments, upon any Subject relating to the Duties of their respective Offices, and he shall have Power to grant Reprieves and Pardons for Offenses against the United States, except in Cases of Impeachment.

He shall have Power, by and with the Advice and Consent of the Senate, to make Treaties, provided two thirds of the Senators present concur; and he shall nominate, and by and with the Advice and Consent of the Senate, shall appoint Ambassadors, other public Ministers and Consuls, Judges of the supreme Court, and all other Officers of the United States, whose Appointments are not herein otherwise provided for, and which shall be established by Law: but the Congress may by Law vest the Appointment of such inferior Officers, as they think proper, in the President alone, in the Courts of Law, or in the Heads of Departments.

The President shall have Power to fill up all Vacancies that may happen dur-ing the Recess of the Senate, by granting Commissions which shall expire at the End of their next Session.

Section 3. He shall from time to time give to the Congress Information of the State of the Union, and recommend to their Consideration such Measures as he shall judge necessary and expedient; he may, on extraordinary Occasions, convene both Houses, or either of them, and in Case of Disagreement between them, with Respect to the Time of Adjournment, he may adjourn them to such Time as he shall think proper; he shall receive Ambassadors and other public Ministers; he shall take Care that the Laws be faithfully executed, and shall Commission all the Officers of the United States.

Section 4. The President, Vice President and all Civil Officers of the United States, shall be removed from office on Impeachment for, and Conviction of, Treason, Bribery, or other high Crimes and Misdemeanors.

Article III

Section 1. The judicial Power of the United States, shall be vested in one supreme Court, and in such inferior Courts as the Congress may from time to time ordain and establish. The Judges, both of the supreme and inferior Courts, shall hold their Offices during good Behaviour, and shall, at stated Times, receive for their Services, a Compensation, which shall not be diminished during their Continuance in Office.

Section 2. The judicial Power shall extend to all Cases, in Law and Equity, arising under this Constitution, the Laws of the United States, and Treaties made, or which shall be made, under their Authority;—to all Cases affecting Ambassadors, other public Ministers and Consuls;—to all Cases of admiralty and maritime Jurisdiction;—to Controversies to which the United States shall be a Party;—to Controversies between two or more States;—between a State and Citizens of another State;[8]— between Citizens of different States;— between Citizens of the same State claiming Lands under Grants of different States, and between a State, or the Citizens thereof, and foreign States, Citizens or Subjects.[9]

In all Cases affecting Ambassadors, other public Ministers and Consuls, and those in which a State shall be Party, the supreme Court shall have original Jurisdiction. In all the other Cases before mentioned, the supreme Court shall have appellate Jurisdiction, both as to Law and Fact, with such Exceptions, and under such Regulations as the Congress shall make.

The Trial of all Crimes, except in cases of Impeachment, shall be by Jury; and such Trial shall be held in the State where the said Crimes shall have been committed; but when not committed within any State, the Trial shall be at such Place or Places as the Congress may by Law have directed.

Section 3. Treason against the United States, shall consist only in levying War against them, or in adhering to their Enemies, giving them Aid and Comfort. No Person shall be convicted of Treason unless on the Testimony of two Witnesses to the same overt Act, or on Confession in open Court.

The Congress shall have Power to declare the Punishment of Treason, but no Attainder of Treason shall work Corruption of Blood, or Forfeiture except during the Life of the Person attainted.

Article IV

Section 1. Full Faith and Credit shall be given in each State to the public Acts, Records, and judicial Proceedings of every other State. And the Congress may by general Laws prescribe the Manner in which such Acts, Records and Proceedings shall be proved, and the Effect thereof.

Section 2. The Citizens of each State shall be entitled to all Privileges and Immunities of Citizens in the several States.

A Person charged in any State with Treason, Felony, or other Crime, who shall flee from Justice, and be found in another State, shall on Demand of the executive Authority of the State from which he fled, be delivered up, to be removed to the State having Jurisdiction of the Crime.

[No Person held to Service or Labour in one State, under the Laws thereof, escaping into another, shall, in Consequence of any Law or Regulation therein, be discharged from such Service or Labour, but shall be delivered up on Claim of the Party to whom such Service or Labour may be due.][10]

Section 3. New States may be admitted by the Congress into this Union; but no new State shall be formed or erected within the Jurisdiction of any other State; nor any State be formed by the Junction of two or more States, or Parts of States, without the Consent of the Legislatures of the States concerned as well as of the Congress.

The Congress shall have Power to dispose of and make all needful Rules and Regulations respecting the Territory or other Property belonging to the United States; and nothing in this Constitution shall be so construed as to Prejudice any Claims of the United States, or of any particular State.

Section 4. The United States shall guarantee to every State in this Union a Republican Form of Government, and shall protect each of them against Invasion; and on Application of the Legislature, or of the Executive (when the Legislature cannot be convened) against domestic Violence.

Article V

The Congress, whenever two thirds of both Houses shall deem it necessary, shall propose Amendments to this Constitution, or, on the Application of the Legislatures of two thirds of the several States, shall call a Convention for proposing Amendments, which, in either Case, shall be valid to all Intents and Purposes, as Part of this Constitution, when ratified by the Legislatures of three fourths of the several States, or by Conventions in three fourths thereof, as the one or the other Mode of Ratification may be proposed by the Congress; Provided [that no Amendment which may be made prior to the Year One thousand eight hundred and eight shall in any Manner affect the first and fourth Clauses in the Ninth Section of the first Article; and][11] that no State, without its Consent, shall be deprived of its equal Suffrage in the Senate.

Article VI

All Debts contracted and Engagements entered into, before the Adoption of this Constitution, shall be as valid against the United States under this Constitution, as under the Confederation.

This Constitution, and the Laws of the United States which shall be made in Pursuance thereof; and all Treaties made, or which shall be made, under the Authority of the United States, shall be the supreme Law of the Land; and the Judges in every State shall be bound thereby, any Thing in the Constitution or Laws of any State to the Contrary notwithstanding.

The Senators and Representatives before mentioned, and the Members of the several State Legislatures, and all executive and judicial Officers, both of the United States and of the several States, shall be bound by Oath or Affirmation, to support this Constitution; but no religious Test shall ever be required as a Qualification to any Office or public Trust under the United States.

Article VII

The Ratification of the Conventions of nine States, shall be sufficient for the Establishment of this Constitution between the States so ratifying the Same. Done in Convention by the Unanimous Consent of the States present the Seventeenth Day of September in the Year of our Lord one thousand seven hundred and Eighty seven and of the Independence of the United States of America the Twelfth. In witness whereof We have hereunto subscribed our Names, George Washington, President and deputy from Virginia.

New Hampshire:	John Langdon, Nicholas Gilman.
Massachusetts:	Nathaniel Gorham, Rufus King.
Connecticut:	William Samuel Johnson, Roger Sherman.
New York:	Alexander Hamilton.
New Jersey:	William Livingston, David Brearley, William Paterson, Jonathan Dayton.
Pennsylvania:	Benjamin Franklin, Thomas Mifflin, Robert Morris, George Clymer, Thomas FitzSimons, Jared Ingersoll, James Wilson, Gouverneur Morris.
Delaware:	George Read, Gunning Bedford Jr., John Dickinson, Richard Bassett, Jacob Broom.
Maryland:	James McHenry, Daniel of St. Thomas Jenifer, Daniel Carroll.
Virginia:	John Blair, James Madison Jr.
North Carolina:	William Blount, Richard Dobbs Spaight, Hugh Williamson.

South Carolina: John Rutledge,
                  Charles Cotesworth
                    Pinckney,
                  Charles Pinckney,
                  Pierce Butler.

Georgia: William Few,
                  Abraham Baldwin.

[The language of the original Constitution, not including the Amendments, was adopted by a convention of the states on Sept. 17, 1787, and was subsequently ratified by the states on the following dates: Delaware, Dec. 7, 1787; Pennsylvania, Dec. 12, 1787; New Jersey, Dec. 18, 1787; Georgia, Jan. 2, 1788; Connecticut, Jan. 9, 1788; Massachusetts, Feb. 6, 1788; Maryland, April 28, 1788; South Carolina, May 23, 1788; New Hampshire, June 21, 1788.
Ratification was completed on June 21, 1788.
The Constitution subsequently was ratified by Virginia, June 25, 1788; New York, July 26, 1788; North Carolina, Nov. 21, 1789; Rhode Island, May 29, 1790; and Vermont, Jan. 10, 1791.]

Amendments

Amendment I
(First ten amendments ratified December 15, 1791.)

Congress shall make no law respecting an establishment of religion, or prohibiting the free exercise thereof; or abridging the freedom of speech, or of the press; or the right of the people peaceably to assemble, and to petition the Government for a redress of grievances.

Amendment II

A well regulated Militia, being necessary to the security of a free State, the right of the people to keep and bear Arms, shall not be infringed.

Amendment III

No Soldier shall, in time of peace be quartered in any house, without the consent of the Owner, nor in time of war, but in a manner to be prescribed by law.

Amendment IV

The right of the people to be secure in their persons, houses, papers, and effects, against unreasonable searches and seizures, shall not be violated, and no Warrants shall issue, but upon probable cause, supported by Oath or affirmation, and particularly describing the place to be searched, and the persons or things to be seized.

Amendment V

No person shall be held to answer for a capital, or otherwise infamous crime, unless on a presentment or indictment of a Grand Jury, except in cases arising in the land or naval forces, or in the Militia, when in actual service in time of War or public danger; nor shall any person be subject for the same offence to be twice put in jeopardy of life or limb; nor shall be compelled in any criminal case to be a witness against himself, nor be deprived of life, liberty, or property, without due process of law; nor shall private property be taken for public use, without just compensation.

Amendment VI

In all criminal prosecutions, the accused shall enjoy the right to a speedy and public trial, by an impartial jury of the State and district wherein the crime shall have been committed, which district shall have been previously ascertained by law, and to be informed of the nature and cause of the accusation; to be confronted with the witnesses against him; to have compulsory process for obtaining witnesses in his favor, and to have the Assistance of Counsel for his defence.

Amendment VII

In Suits at common law, where the value in controversy shall exceed twenty dollars, the right of trial by jury shall be preserved, and no fact tried by a jury, shall be otherwise re-examined in any Court of the United States, than according to the rules of the common law.

Amendment VIII

Excessive bail shall not be required, nor excessive fines imposed, nor cruel and unusual punishments inflicted.

Amendment IX

The enumeration in the Constitution, of certain rights, shall not be construed to deny or disparage others retained by the people.

Amendment X

The powers not delegated to the United States by the Constitution, nor prohibited by it to the States, are reserved to the States respectively, or to the people.

Amendment XI
(Ratified February 7, 1795)

The Judicial power of the United States shall not be construed to extend to any suit in law or equity, commenced or prosecuted against one of the United States by Citizens of another State, or by Citizens or Subjects of any Foreign State.

Amendment XII
(Ratified June 15, 1804)

The Electors shall meet in their respective states and vote by ballot for President and Vice-President, one of whom, at least, shall not be an inhabitant of the same state with themselves; they shall name in their ballots the person voted for as President, and in distinct ballots the person voted for as Vice-President, and they shall make distinct lists of all persons voted for as President, and of all persons voted for as Vice-President, and of the number of votes for each, which lists they shall sign and certify, and transmit sealed to the seat of the government of the United States, directed to the President of the Senate; —The President of the Senate shall, in the presence of the Senate and House of Representatives, open all the certificates and the votes shall then be counted; —The person having the greatest number of votes for President, shall be the President, if such number be a majority of the whole number of Electors appointed; and if no person have such majority, then from the persons having the highest numbers not exceeding three on the list of those voted for as President, the House of Representatives shall choose immediately, by ballot, the President. But in choosing the President, the votes shall be taken by states, the representation from each state having one vote; a quorum for this purpose shall consist of a member or members from two-thirds of the states, and a majority of all the states shall be necessary to a choice. [And if the House of Representatives shall not choose a President whenever the right of choice shall devolve upon them, before the fourth day of March next following, then the Vice-President shall act as President, as in the case of the death or other constitutional disability of the President—][12] The person having the greatest number of votes as Vice-President, shall be the Vice-President, if such number be a majority of the whole number of Electors appointed, and if no person have a majority, then from the two highest numbers on the list, the Senate shall choose the Vice-President; a quorum for the purpose shall consist of two-thirds of the whole number of Senators, and a majority of the whole number shall be necessary to a choice. But no person constitutionally ineligible to the office of President shall be eligible to that of Vice-President of the United States.

Amendment XIII
(Ratified December 6, 1865)

Section 1. Neither slavery nor involuntary servitude, except as a punishment for crime whereof the party shall have been duly convicted, shall exist within the United States, or any place subject to their jurisdiction.

Section 2. Congress shall have power to enforce this article by appropriate legislation.

Amendment XIV
(Ratified July 9, 1868)

Section 1. All persons born or naturalized in the United States and subject to the jurisdiction thereof, are citizens of the United States and of the State wherein they reside. No State shall make or enforce any law which shall abridge the privileges or immunities of citizens of the United States; nor shall any State deprive any person of life, liberty, or property, without due process of law; nor deny to any person within its jurisdiction the equal protection of the laws.

Section 2. Representatives shall be apportioned among the several States according to their respective numbers, counting the whole number of persons in each State, excluding Indians not taxed. But when the right to vote at any election for the choice of electors for President and Vice President of the United States, Representatives in Congress, the Executive and Judicial officers of a State, or the members of the Legislature thereof, is denied to any of the male inhabitants of such State, being twenty-one years of age,[13] and citizens of the United States, or in any way abridged, except for participation in rebellion, or other crime, the basis of representation therein shall be reduced in the proportion which the number of such male citizens shall bear to the whole number of male citizens twenty-one years of age in such State.

Section 3. No person shall be a Senator or Representative in Congress, or elector of President and Vice President, or hold any office, civil or military, under the United States, or under any State, who, having previously taken an oath, as a member of Congress, or as an officer of the United States, or as a member of any State legislature, or as an executive or judicial officer of any State, to support the Constitution of the United States, shall have engaged in insurrection or rebellion against the same, or given aid or comfort to the enemies thereof. But Congress may by a vote of two-thirds of each House, remove such disability.

Section 4. The validity of the public debt of the United States, authorized by law, including debts incurred for payment of pensions and bounties for services in suppressing insurrection or rebellion, shall not be questioned. But neither the United States nor any State shall assume or pay any debt or obligation incurred in aid of insurrection or rebellion against the United States, or any claim for the loss or emancipation of any slave; but all such debts, obligations and claims shall be held illegal and void.

Section 5. The Congress shall have power to enforce, by appropriate legislation, the provisions of this article.

Amendment XV
(Ratified February 3, 1870)

Section 1. The right of citizens of the United States to vote shall not be denied or abridged by the United States or by any State on account of race, color, or previous condition of servitude.

Section 2. The Congress shall have power to enforce this article by appropriate legislation.

Amendment XVI
(Ratified February 3, 1913)

The Congress shall have power to lay and collect taxes on incomes, from whatever source derived, without apportionment among the several States, and without regard to any census or enumeration.

Amendment XVII
(Ratified April 8, 1913)

The Senate of the United States shall be composed of two Senators from each State, elected by the people thereof, for six years; and each Senator shall have one vote. The electors in each State shall have the qualifications requisite for electors of the most numerous branch of the State legislatures.

When vacancies happen in the representation of any State in the Senate, the executive authority of such State shall issue writs of election to fill such vacancies: *Provided,* That the legislature of any State may empower the executive thereof to make temporary appointments until the people fill the vacancies by election as the legislature may direct.

This amendment shall not be so construed as to affect the election or term of any Senator chosen before it becomes valid as part of the Constitution.

[Amendment XVIII
(Ratified January 16, 1919)

Section 1. After one year from the ratification of this article the manufacture, sale, or transportation of intoxicating liquors within, the importation thereof into, or the exportation thereof from the United States and all territory subject to the jurisdiction thereof for beverage purposes is hereby prohibited.

Section 2. The Congress and the several States shall have concurrent power to enforce this article by appropriate legislation.

Section 3. This article shall be inoperative unless it shall have been ratified as an amendment to the Constitution by the legislatures of the several States, as provided in the Constitution, within seven years from the date of the submission hereof to the States by the Congress.]14

Amendment XIX
(Ratified August 18, 1920)

The right of citizens of the United States to vote shall not be denied or abridged by the United States or by any State on account of sex.

Congress shall have power to enforce this article by appropriate legislation.

Amendment XX
(Ratified January 23, 1933)

Section 1. The terms of the President and Vice President shall end at noon on the 20th day of January, and the terms of Senators and Representatives at noon on the 3d day of January, of the years in which such terms would have ended if this article had not been ratified; and the terms of their successors shall then begin.

Section 2. The Congress shall assemble at least once in every year, and such meeting shall begin at noon on the 3d day of January, unless they shall by law appoint a different day.

Section 3.15 If, at the time fixed for the beginning of the term of the President, the President elect shall have died, the Vice President elect shall become President. If a President shall not have been chosen before the time fixed for the beginning of his term, or if the President elect shall have failed to qualify, then the Vice President elect shall act as President until a President shall have qualified; and the Congress may by law provide for the case wherein neither a President elect nor a Vice President elect shall have qualified, declaring who shall then act as President, or the manner in which one who is to act shall be selected, and such person shall act accordingly until a President or Vice President shall have qualified.

Section 4. The Congress may by law provide for the case of the death of any of the persons from whom the House of Representatives may choose a President whenever the right of choice shall have devolved upon them, and for the case of the death of any of the persons from whom the Senate may choose a Vice President whenever the right of choice shall have devolved upon them.

Section 5. Sections 1 and 2 shall take effect on the 15th day of October following the ratification of this article.

Section 6. This article shall be inoperative unless it shall have been ratified as an amendment to the Constitution by the legislatures of three-fourths of the several States within seven years from the date of its submission.

Amendment XXI
(Ratified December 5, 1933)

Section 1. The eighteenth article of amendment to the Constitution of the United States is hereby repealed.

Section 2. The transportation or importation into any State, Territory or possession of the United States for delivery or use therein of intoxicating liquors, in violation of the laws thereof, is hereby prohibited.

Section 3. This article shall be inoperative unless it shall have been ratified as an amendment to the Constitution by conventions in the several States, as provided in the Constitution, within seven years from the date of the submission hereof to the States by the Congress.

Amendment XXII
(Ratified February 27, 1951)

Section 1. No person shall be elected to the office of the President more than twice, and no person who has held the office of President, or acted as President, for more than two years of a term to which some other person was elected President shall be elected to the office of the President more than once. But this Article shall not apply to any person holding the office of President when this Article was proposed by the Congress, and shall not prevent any person who may be holding the office of President, or acting as President, during the term within which this Article becomes operative from holding the office of President or acting as President during the remainder of such term.

Section 2. This Article shall be inoperative unless it shall have been ratified as an amendment to the Constitution by the legislatures of three-fourths of the several States within seven years

from the date of its submission to the States by the Congress.

Amendment XXIII
(Ratified March 29, 1961)

Section 1. The District constituting the seat of Government of the United States shall appoint in such manner as the Congress may direct:

A number of electors of President and Vice President equal to the whole number of Senators and Representatives in Congress to which the District would be entitled if it were a State, but in no event more than the least populous State; they shall be in addition to those appointed by the States, but they shall be considered, for the purposes of the election of President and Vice President, to be electors appointed by a State; and they shall meet in the District and perform such duties as provided by the twelfth article of amendment.

Section 2. The Congress shall have power to enforce this article by appropriate legislation.

Amendment XXIV
(Ratified January 23, 1964)

Section 1. The right of citizens of the United States to vote in any primary or other election for President or Vice President, for electors for President or Vice President, or for Senator or Representative in Congress, shall not be denied or abridged by the United States or any State by reason of failure to pay any poll tax or other tax.

Section 2. The Congress shall have power to enforce this article by appropriate legislation.

Amendment XXV
(Ratified February 10, 1967)

Section 1. In case of the removal of the President from office or of his death or resignation, the Vice President shall become President.

Section 2. Whenever there is a vacancy in the office of the Vice President, the President shall nominate a Vice President who shall take office upon confirmation by a majority vote of both Houses of Congress.

Section 3. Whenever the President transmits to the President pro tempore of the Senate and the Speaker of the House of Representatives his written declaration that he is unable to discharge the powers and duties of his office, and until he transmits to them a written declaration to the contrary, such powers and duties shall be discharged by the Vice President as Acting President.

Section 4. Whenever the Vice President and a majority of either the principal officers of the executive departments or of such other body as Congress may by law provide, transmit to the President pro tempore of the Senate and the Speaker of the House of Representatives their written declaration that the President is unable to discharge the powers and duties of his office, the Vice President shall immediately assume the powers and duties of the office as Acting President.

Thereafter, when the President transmits to the President pro tempore of the Senate and the Speaker of the House of Representatives his written declaration that no inability exists, he shall resume the powers and duties of his office unless the Vice President and a majority of either the principal officers of the executive department or of such other body as Congress may by law provide, transmit within four days to the President pro tempore of the Senate and the Speaker of the House of Representatives their written declaration that the President is unable to discharge the powers and duties of his office. Thereupon Congress shall decide the issue, assembling within forty-eight hours for that purpose if not in session. If the Congress, within twenty-one days after receipt of the latter written declaration, or, if Congress is not in session, within twenty-one days after Congress is required to assemble, determines by two-thirds vote of both houses that the President is unable to discharge the powers and duties of his office, the Vice President shall continue to discharge the same as Acting President; otherwise, the President shall resume the powers and duties of his office.

Amendment XXVI
(Ratified July 1, 1971)

Section 1. The right of citizens of the United States, who are eighteen years of age or older, to vote shall not be denied or abridged by the United States or by any State on account of age.

Section 2. The Congress shall have power to enforce this article by appropriate legislation.

Notes

1. The part in brackets was changed by section 2 of the Fourteenth Amendment.
2. The part in brackets was changed by section 1 of the Seventeenth Amendment.
3. The part in brackets was changed by the second paragraph of the Seventeenth Amendment.
4. The part in brackets was changed by section 2 of the Twentieth Amendment.
5. The Sixteenth Amendment gave Congress the power to tax incomes.
6. The material in brackets has been superseded by the Twelfth Amendment.
7. This provision has been affected by the Twenty-fifth Amendment.
8. This clause was affected by the Eleventh Amendment.
9. This clause was affected by the Eleventh Amendment.
10. This paragraph has been superseded by the Thirteenth Amendment.
11. Obsolete.
12. The part in brackets has been superseded by section 3 of the Twentieth Amendment.
13. See the Twenty-sixth Amendment.
14. This Amendment was repealed by section 1 of the Twenty-first Amendment.
15. See the Twenty-fifth Amendment.

The Federalist Papers, *Nos. 68, 71, 72 (1788)*

During the final week of the Constitutional Convention, Alexander Hamilton told his fellow delegates that he would reluctantly sign the proposed constitution, even though no one's ideas were "more remote" from the document than his own. (See "The Constitutional Convention: Debates on Presidential Selection," p. 1.) Nonetheless, swallowing his reservations, Hamilton returned to New York after the convention and fought to ratify the Constitution as ardently as if he had written every jot and tittle of the plan of government himself.

Hamilton's main contribution to the state-by-state battle for ratification was to organize the writing of The Federalist Papers, *a series of newspaper articles that explained and defended the Constitution. Hamilton recruited* The Federalist's *other authors, Secretary of Foreign Affairs John Jay of New York and James Madison of Virginia, who was serving in the then-capital city of New York as a member of Congress. The articles appeared pseudonymously above the pen name "Publius," which Hamilton probably borrowed from the celebrated defender of the ancient Roman Republic, Publius Valerius Publicola.*

Hamilton's role in the history of The Federalist *went beyond creating the series. He also helped to distribute the articles to newspapers in New York and around the country, arming the* Constitution's defenders in almost every state with arguments that they could use against the document's "Anti-Federalist" critics. Finally, Hamilton wrote around fifty of the eighty-five papers, including Federalist Nos. 68-77, which dealt with the presidency.

Hamilton began his essays on the executive by noting that the presidential selection process had turned out to be one of the least controversial parts of the Constitution. In Federalist No. 68, *he avowed that the electoral college offered "a constant probability of seeing the [presidency] filled by characters pre-eminent for ability and virtue." Interestingly, however, some aspects of the electoral college that Hamilton singled out for special praise have turned out in practice to be of little consequence. He proudly asserted, for example, that the absence of a single meeting place for the electors would make foreign "cabal, intrigue, and corruption" of presidential elections less likely. Similarly, he claimed, the Constitution's prohibition on federal officeholders serving as electors would make the presidential election "free from any sinister byass."*

In Federalist No. 71, *after arguing in No. 70 that unity was the first requisite for "energy in the executive," Hamilton defended the president's four-year term as being conducive to "duration," the second such requisite. (The third and fourth requisites for executive energy—"an adequate provision for its support; and competent powers," respectively—were dealt with in Nos. 73-77.) According to Hamilton, who had urged lifetime presidential tenure at the Constitutional Convention, the president's term was just long enough: "a duration of four years will contribute to the firmness of the executive in a sufficient degree to render it a very valuable ingredient in the composition; so on the other, it is not long enough to justify any alarm for the public liberty." In* Federalist *No. 72, Hamilton addressed the aspect of presidential selection that was of greatest importance to the convention, namely, the president's eligibility for reelection. Echoing an argument by Gouverneur Morris of Pennsylvania, Hamilton wrote that the Constitution, by allowing the president to stand for more than one term, shrewdly "admitted that the desire of reward is one of the strongest incentives of human conduct." Even a president whose behavior was motivated by personal goals such as "avarice" or "ambition" would do a good job in order to hold onto the office that promised to fulfill those desires.*   ~

Federalist No. 68
March 12, 1788

To the People of the State of New York.

The mode of appointment of the chief magistrate of the United States is almost the only part of the system, of any consequence, which has escaped without severe censure, or which has received the slightest mark of approbation from its opponents. The most plausible of these, who has appeared in print, has even deigned to admit, that the election of the president is pretty well guarded. I venture somewhat further; and hesitate not to affirm, that if the manner of it be not perfect, it is at least excellent. It unites in an eminent degree all the advantages; the union of which was to be desired.

It was desirable, that the sense of the people should operate in the choice of the person to whom so important a trust was to be confided. This end will be answered by committing the right of making it, not to any pre-established body, but to men, chosen by the people for the special purpose, and at the particular conjuncture.

It was equally desirable, that the immediate election should be made by men most capable of analyzing the qualities adapted to the station, and acting under circumstances favorable to deliberation and to a judicious combination of all the reasons and inducements, which were proper to govern their choice. A small number of persons, selected by their fellow citizens from the general mass, will be most likely to possess the information and discernment requisite to so complicated an investigation.

It was also peculiarly desirable, to afford as little opportunity as possible to tumult and disorder. This evil was not least to be dreaded in the election of a magistrate, who was to have so important an agency in the administration of the government, as the president of the United States. But the precautions which have been so happily concerted in the system under consideration, promise an effectual security against this mischief. The choice of *several* to form an intermediate body of electors, will be much less apt to convulse the community, with any extraordinary or violent movements, than the choice of *one* who was himself to be the final object of the public wishes. And as the electors, chosen in each state, are to assemble and vote in the state, in which they are chosen, this detached and divided situation will expose them much less to heats and ferments, which might be communicated from them to the people, than if they were all to be convened at one time, in one place.

Nothing was more to be desired, than that every practicable obstacle should be opposed to cabal, intrigue and corruption. These most deadly adversaries of republican government might naturally have been expected to make their approaches from more than one quarter, but chiefly from the desire in foreign powers to gain an improper ascendant in our councils. How could they better gratify this, than by raising a creature of their own to the chief magistracy of the union? But the convention have guarded against all danger of this sort with the most provident and judicious attention. They have not made the appointment of the president to depend on any pre-existing bodies of men who might be tampered with before hand to prostitute their votes; but they have referred it in the first instance to an immediate act of the people of America, to be exerted in the choice of persons for the temporary and sole purpose of making the appointment. And they have excluded from eligibility to this trust, all those who from situation might be suspected of too great devotion to the president in office. No senator, representative, or other person holding a place of trust or profit under the United States, can be of the number of the electors. Thus, without corrupting the body of the people, the immediate agents in the election will at least enter upon the task, free from any sinister byass. Their transient existence, and their detached situation, already taken notice of, afford a satisfactory prospect of their continuing so, to the conclusion of it. The business of corruption, when it is to embrace so considerable a number of men, requires time, as well as means. Nor would it be found easy suddenly to embark them, dispersed as they would be over thirteen states, in any combinations,

founded upon motives, which though they could not properly be denominated corrupt, might yet be of a nature to mislead them from their duty.

Another and no less important desideratum was, that the executive should be independent for his continuance in office on all, but the people themselves. He might otherwise be tempted to sacrifice his duty to his complaisance for those whose favor was necessary to the duration of his official consequence. This advantage will also be secured, by making his re-election to depend on a special body of representatives, deputed by the society for the single purpose of making the important choice.

All these advantages will be happily combined in the plan devised by the convention; which is, that the people of each state shall choose a number of persons as electors, equal to the number of senators and representatives of such state in the national government, who shall assemble within the state and vote for some fit person as president. Their votes, thus given, are to be transmitted to the seat of the national government, and the person who may happen to have a majority of the whole number of votes will be the president. But as a majority of the votes might not always happen to centre on one man and as it might be unsafe to permit less than a majority to be conclusive, it is provided, that in such a contingency, the house of representatives shall select out of the candidates, who shall have the five highest numbers of votes, the man who in their opinion may be best qualified for the office.

This process of election affords a moral certainty, that the office of president, will seldom fall to the lot of any man, who is not in an eminent degree endowed with the requisite qualifications. Talents for low intrigue and the little arts of popularity may alone suffice to elevate a man to the first honors in a single state; but it will require other talents and a different kind of merit to establish him in the esteem and confidence of the whole union, or of so considerable a portion of it as would be necessary to make him a successful candidate for the distinguished office of president of the United States. It will not be too strong to say, that there will be a constant probability of seeing the station filled by characters pre-eminent for ability and virtue. And this will be thought no inconsiderable recommendation of the constitution, by those, who are able to estimate the share, which the executive in every government must necessarily have in its good or ill administration. Though we cannot acquiesce in the political heresy of the poet who says—

"For forms of government let fools contest—

That which is best administered is best."

—yet we may safely pronounce, that the true test of a good government is its aptitude and tendency to produce a good administration.

The vice-president is to be chosen in the same manner with the president; with this difference, that the senate is to do, in respect to the former, what is to be done by the house of representatives, in respect to the latter.

The appointment of an extraordinary person, as vice president, has been objected to as superfluous, if not mischievous. It has been alledged, that it would have been preferable to have authorised the senate to elect out of their own body an officer, answering that description. But two considerations seem to justify the ideas of the convention in this respect. One is, that to secure at all times the possibility of a definitive resolution of the body, it is necessary that the president should have only a casting vote. And to take the senator of any state from his seat as senator, to place him in that of president of the senate, would be to exchange, in regard to the state from which he came, a constant for a contingent vote. The other consideration is, that as the vice-president may occasionally become a substitute for the president, in the supreme executive magistracy, all the reasons, which recommend the mode of election prescribed for the one, apply with great, if not with equal, force to the manner of appointing the other. It is remarkable, that in this as in most other instances, the objection, which is made, would be against the constitution of this state. We have a Lieutenant Governor chosen by the people at large, who presides in the senate, and is the constitutional substitute for the Governor in casualties similar to those, which would authorise the vice-president to exercise the authorities and discharge the duties of the president.

PUBLIUS.

Federalist No. 71
March 18, 1788

To the People of the State of New York. Duration in office has been mentioned as the second requisite to the energy of the executive authority. This has relation to two objects: To the personal firmness of the Executive Magistrate in the employment of his constitutional powers; and to the stability of the system of administration which may have been adopted under his auspices. With regard to the first, it must be evident, that the longer the duration in office, the greater will be the probability of obtaining so important an advantage. It is a general principle of human nature, that a man will be interested in whatever he possesses, in proportion to the firmness of precariousness of the tenure, by which he holds it; will be less attached to what he holds by a momentary or uncertain title, than to what he enjoys by a durable or certain title; and of course will be willing to risk more for the sake of the one, than for the sake of the other. This remark is not less applicable to a political privilege, or honor, or trust, than to any article of ordinary property. The inference from it is, that a man acting in the capacity of Chief Magistrate, under a consciousness, that in a very short time he *must* lay down his office, will be apt to feel himself too little interested in it, to hazard any material censure or perplexity, from the independent exertion of his powers, or from encountering the ill-humors, however transient, which may happen to prevail either in a considerable part of the society itself, or even in a predominant faction in the legislative body. If the case should only be, that he *might* lay it down, unless continued by a new choice; and if he should be desirous of being continued, his wishes conspiring with his fears would tend still more powerfully to corrupt his integrity, or debase his fortitude. In either case feebleness and irresolution must be the characteristics of the station.

There are some, who would be inclined to regard the servile pliancy of the executive to a prevailing current, either in the community, or in the Legislature, as its best recommendation. But such men entertain very crude notions, as well of the purposes for which government was instituted, as of the true means by which the public happiness may be promoted. The republican principle demands, that the deliberate sense of the community should govern the conduct of those to whom they entrust the management of their affairs; but it does not require an unqualified complaisance to every sudden breeze of passion, or to every transient impulse which the people may receive from the arts of men, who flatter their prejudices to betray their interests. It is a just observation, that the people commonly *intend* the Public Good. This often applies to their very errors. But their good sense would despise the adulator, who should pretend that they always *reason right* about the *means* of promoting it. They know from experience, that they

sometimes err; and the wonder is, that they so seldom err as they do; beset as they continually are by the wiles of parasites and sycophants, by the snares of the ambitious, and avaricious, the desperate; by the artifices of men, who possess their confidence more than they deserve it, and of those who seek to possess, rather than to deserve it. When occasions present themselves in which the interests of the people are at variance with their inclinations, it is the duty of the persons whom they have appointed to be the guardians of those interests, to withstand the temporary delusions, in order to give them time and opportunity for more cool and sedate reflection. Instances might be cited, in which a conduct of this kind has saved the people from very fatal consequences of their own mistakes, and has procured lasting monuments of their gratitude to the men, who had courage and magnanimity enough to serve them at the peril of their displeasure.

But however inclined we might be to insist upon an unbounded complaisance in the executive to the inclinations of the people, we can with no propriety contend for a like complaisance to the humors of the Legislature. The latter may sometimes stand in opposition to the former; and at other times the people may be entirely neutral. In either supposition, it is certainly desirable that the executive should be in a situation to dare to act his own opinion with vigor and decision.

The same rule, which teaches the propriety of a partition between the various branches of power, teaches us likewise that this partition ought to be so contrived as to render the one independent of the other. To what purpose separate the executive, or the judiciary, from the legislative, if both the executive and the judiciary are so constituted as to be at the absolute devotion of the legislative? Such a separation must be merely nominal and incapable of producing the ends for which it was established. It is one thing to be subordinate to the laws, and another to be dependent on the legislative body. The first comports with, the last violates, the fundamental principles of good government; and whatever may be the forms of the Constitution, unites all power in the same hands. The tendency of the legislative authority to absorb every other, has been fully displayed and illustrated by examples, in some preceding numbers. In governments purely republican, this tendency is almost irresistible. The representatives of the people, in a popular assembly, seem sometimes to fancy that they are the people themselves; and betray strong symptoms of impatience and disgust at the least sign of opposition from any other quarter; as if the exercise of its rights by either the executive or judiciary, were a breach of their privilege and an outrage to their dignity. They often appear disposed to exert an imperious control over the other departments; and as they commonly have the people on their side, they always act with such momentum as to make it very difficult for the other members of the government to maintain the balance of the Constitution.

It may perhaps be asked how the shortness of the duration in office can affect the independence of the executive on the legislature, unless the one were possessed of the power of appointing or displacing the other? One answer to this enquiry may be drawn from the principle already remarked, that is from the slender interest a man is apt to take in a short lived advantage, and the little inducement it affords him to expose himself on account of it to any considerable inconvenience or hazard. Another answer, perhaps more obvious, though not more conclusive, will result from the consideration of the influence of the legislative body over the people, which might be employed to prevent the reelection of a man, who by an upright

resistance to any sinister project of that body, should have made himself obnoxious to its resentment.

It may be asked also whether a duration of four years would answer the end proposed, and if it would not, whether less period which would at least be recommended by greater security against ambitious designs, would not for that reason be preferable to a longer period, which was at the same time too short for the purpose of inspiring the desired firmness and independence of the magistrate?

It cannot be affirmed, that a duration of four years or any other limited duration would completely answer the end proposed; but it would contribute towards it in a degree which would have a material influence upon the spirit and character of the government. Between the commencement and termination of such a period there would always be a considerable interval, in which the prospect of annihilation would be sufficiently remote not to have an improper effect upon the conduct of a man endued with a tolerable portion of fortitude; and in which he might reasonably promise himself, that there would be time enough, before it arrived, to make the community sensible of the propriety of the measures he might incline to pursue. Though it be probable, that as he approached the moment when the public were by a new election to signify their sense of his conduct, his confidence and with it, his firmness would decline; yet both the one and the other would derive support from the opportunities, which his previous continuance in the station had afforded him of establishing himself in the esteem and good will of his constituents. He might then hazard with safety, in proportion to the proofs he had given of his wisdom and integrity, and to the title he had acquired to the respect and attachment of his fellow citizens. As on the one hand, a duration of four years will contribute to the firmness of the executive in a sufficient degree to render it a very valuable ingredient in the composition; so on the other, it is not long enough to justify any alarm for the public liberty. If a British House of Commons, from the most feeble beginnings, *from the mere power of assenting or disagreeing to the imposition of a new tax,* have by rapid strides, reduced the prerogatives of the crown and the privileges of the nobility within the limits they conceived to be compatible with the principles of a free government; while they raised themselves to the rank and consequence of a coequal branch of Legislature; if they have been able in one instance to abolish both the royalty and the aristocracy, and to overturn all the ancient establishments as well in the church as State; if they have been able on a recent occasion to make the monarch tremble at the prospect of an innovation[1] attempted by them; what would be to be feared from an elective magistrate of four years duration, with the confined authorities of a President of the United States? What but that he might be unequal to the task which the Constitution assigns him? I shall only add that if his duration be such as to leave a doubt of his firmness, that doubt is inconsistent with a jealousy of his encroachments.

PUBLIUS.

Federalist No. 72
March 19, 1788

To the People of the State of New York. The Administration of government, in its largest sense, comprehends all the operations of the body politic, whether legislative, executive or judiciary, but in its most usual and perhaps in its most precise signification, it is limited to executive details, and falls peculiarly within the province of the executive department. The actual conduct of foreign negotiations, the preparatory plans of finance, the application and disbursement of the public monies, in conformity to the general appropriations of the legislature, the arrangement of the army and navy, the direction of the operations of war; these and other matters of a like nature constitute what seems to be most properly understood by the administration of government. The persons therefore, to whose immediate management these different matters are committed, ought to be considered as the assistants or deputies of the chief magistrate; and, on this account, they ought to derive their offices from his appointment, at least from his nomination, and ought to be subject to his superintendence. This view of the subject will at once suggest to us the intimate connection between the duration of the executive magistrate in office, and the stability of the system of administration. To reverse and undo what has been done by a predecessor is very often considered by a successor, as the best proof he can give of his own capacity and desert; and, in addition to this propensity, where the alteration has been the result of public choice, and person substituted is warranted in supposing, that the dismission of his predecessor has proceeded from a dislike to his measures, and that the less he resembles him the more he will recommend himself to the favor of his constituents. These considerations, and the influence of personal confidences and attachments, would be likely to induce every new president to promote a change of men to fill the subordinate stations; and these causes together could not fail to occasion a disgraceful and ruinous mutability in the administration of the government.

With a positive duration of considerable extent, I connect the circumstance of re-eligibility. The first is necessary to give to the officer himself the inclination and the resolution to act his part well, and to the community time and leisure to observe the tendency of his measures, and thence to form an experimental estimate of their merits. The last is necessary to enable the people, when they see reason to approve of his conduct, to continue him in the station, in order to prolong the utility of his talents and virtues, and to secure to the government, the advantage of permanency in a wise system of administration.

Nothing appears more plausible at first sight, nor more ill founded upon close inspection, than a scheme, which in relation to the present point has had some respectable advocates—I mean that of continuing the chief magistrate in office for a certain time, and then excluding him from it, either for a limited period, or for ever after. This exclusion whether temporary or perpetual would have nearly the same effects; and these effects would be for the most part rather pernicious than salutary.

One ill effect of the exclusion would be a diminution of the inducements to good behaviour. There are few men who would not feel much less zeal in the discharge of a duty, when they were conscious that the advantages of the station, with which it was connected, must be relinquished at a determinate period, then when they were permitted to entertain a hope of *obtaining* by *meriting* a continuance of them. This position will not be disputed, so long as it is admitted that the desire of reward is one of the strongest incentives of human conduct, or that the best security for the fidelity of mankind is to make their interest coincide with their duty. Even the love of fame, the ruling passion of the noblest minds, which would prompt a man to plan and undertake extensive and arduous enterprises for the public benefit, requiring considerable time to mature and perfect them, if he could flatter himself with the prospect of being allowed to finish what he had begun, would on the contrary deter him from the undertaking, when he foresaw that he must quit the scene, before he could accomplish the work, and must commit that, together with his own reputation, to hands which be unequal or unfriendly to the task. The most to be expected from the generality of men, in such a situation, is the negative merit of not doing harm instead of the positive merit of doing good.

Another ill effect of the exclusion would be the temptation to sordid views, to peculation, and in some instances, to usurpation. An avaricious man, who might happen to fill the offices, looking forward to a time when he must at all events yield up the emoluments he enjoyed, would feel a propensity, not easy to be resisted by such a man, to make the best use of the opportunity he enjoyed, while it lasted; and might not scruple to have recourse to the most corrupt expedients to make the harvest as abundant as it was transitory; though the same man probably, with a different prospect before him, might content himself with the regular perquisites of his station, and might even be unwilling to risk the consequences of an abuse of his opportunities. His avarice might be a guard upon his avarice. Add to this, that the same man might be vain or ambitious as well as avaricious. And if he could expect to prolong his honors, by his good conduct, he might hesitate to sacrifice his appetite for them to his appetite for gain. But with the prospect before him of approaching and inevitable annihilation, his avarice would be likely to get the victory over his caution, his vanity or his ambition.

An ambitious man too, when he found himself seated on the summit of his country's honors, when he looked forward to the time at which he must descend from the exalted eminence forever; and reflected that no exertion of merit on his part could save him from the unwelcome reverse: Such a man, in such a situation, would be much more violently tempted to embrace a favorable conjuncture for attempting the prolongation of his power, at every personal hazard, than if he had the probability of answering the same end by doing his duty.

Would it promote the peace of the community, or the stability of the government, to have half a dozen men who had had credit enough to be raised to the seat of the supreme magistracy, wandering among the people like discontented ghosts, and sighing for a place which they were destined never more to possess?

A third ill effect of the exclusion would be the depriving the community of the advantage of the experience gained by the chief magistrate in the exercise of his office. That experience is the parent of wisdom is an adage, the truth of which is recognized by the wisest as well as the simplest of mankind. What more desirable or more essential than this quality in the governors of nations? Where more desirable or more essential than in the first magistrate of a nation? Can it be wise to put this desirable and essential quality under the ban of the constitution; and to declare that the moment it is acquired, its possessor shall be compelled to abandon the station in which it was acquired, and to which it is adapted? This nevertheless is the precise import of all those regulations, which exclude men from serving their country, by the choice of their fellow citizens, after they have, by a course of service fitted themselves for doing it with a greater degree of utility.

A fourth ill effect of the exclusion would be the banishing men from stations, in which in certain emergencies of the state their presence might be of the greatest moment to the public interest or safety. There is no nation which has not at one period or another experienced an absolute necessity of the services of particular men, in particular situations, perhaps it would not be too strong to say, to the preservation of its political existence. How unwise therefore must be every such self-denying ordinance, as serves to prohibit a nation from making use of its own citizens, in the manner best suited to its exigences and circumstances! Without supposing the personal essentiality of the man, it is evident that a change of the chief magistrate, at the breaking out of a war, or at any similar crisis, for another even of equal merit, would at all times be detrimental to the community; inasmuch as it would substitute inexperience to experience and would tend to unhinge and set afloat the already settled train of the administration.

A fifth ill effect of the exclusion would be, that it would operate as a constitutional interdiction of stability in the administration. *By necessitating* a change of men, in the first office in the nation, it would necessitate a mutability of measures. It is not generally to be expected, the men will vary; and measures remain uniform. The contrary is the usual course of things. And we need not be apprehensive there will be too much stability, while there is even the option of changing; nor need we desire to prohibit the people from continuing their confidence, where they think it may be safely placed, and where by constancy on their part they may obviate the fatal inconveniences of fluctuating councils and a variable policy.

These are some of the disadvantages, which would flow from the principle of exclusion. They apply most forcibly to the scheme of a perpetual exclusion; but when we consider that even a partial exclusion would always render the re-admission of the person a remote and precarious object, the observations which have been made will apply nearly as fully to one case as to the other.

What are the advantages promised to counterbalance these disadvantages? They are represented to be 1st. Greater independence in the magistrate: 2dly. Greater security to the people. Unless the exclusion be perpetual there will be no pretence to infer the first advantage. But even in that case, may he have no object beyond his present station to which he may sacrifice his independence? May he have no connections, no friends, for whom he may sacrifice it? May he not be less willing, by a firm conduct, to make personal enemies, when he acts under the impression, that a time is fast approaching, on the arrival of which he not only may, but must be exposed to their resentments, upon an equal, perhaps upon an inferior footing? It is not an easy point to determine whether his independence would be most promoted or impaired by such an arrangement.

As to the second supposed advantage, there is still greater reason to entertain doubts concerning it. If the exclusion were to be perpetual, a man of irregular ambition, of whom alone there could be reason in any case to entertain apprehensions, would with infinite reluctance yield to the necessity of taking his leave forever of a post, in which his passion for power and pre-eminence had acquired the force of habit. And if he had been fortunate or adroit enough to conciliate the good will of people he might induce them to consider as a very odious and unjustifiable restraint upon themselves, a provision which was calculated to debar them of the right of giving a fresh proof of their attachment to a favorite. There may be conceived circumstances, in which this disgust of the people, seconding the thwarted ambition of such a favourite, might occasion greater danger to liberty, than could ever reasonably be dreaded from the possibility of a perpetuation in office, by the voluntary suffrages of the community, exercising a constitutional privilege.

There is an excess of refinement in the idea of disabling the people to continue in office men, who had entitled themselves, in their opinion, to approbation and confidence; the advantages of which are at best speculative and equivocal; and are overbalanced by disadvantages far more certain and decisive.

PUBLIUS.

Note

1. This was the case with respect to Mr. Fox's India bill which was carried in the House of Commons, and rejected in the House of Lords, to the entire satisfaction, as it is said, of the people.

Official Call for the
First Presidential Election (1788)

On September 13, 1788, after eleven states (two more than were required) had ratified the Constitution, the outgoing Congress of the Articles of Confederation passed an election ordinance to get the new government under way. The ordinance called upon the states to choose their presidential electors on January 7, the first Wednesday in January 1789. The electors were to meet to vote in their state capitals on February 4, 1789, the first Wednesday of that month. The first Wednesday in March —March 4, 1789—was established as the day for "commencing Proceedings under the said Constitution."

With less than four months to invent suitable methods to choose electors, the states improvised. Some states allowed the voters to make the decision, others the legislature. One state, Massachusetts, used a hybrid system in which the voters nominated electors and the legislature chose from among the nominees. No two states adopted exactly the same procedure. New York, its legislature bitterly divided between a Federalist senate and an Anti-Federalist assembly, chose no electors at all.

The outcome of the first presidential election was virtually foreordained. To some extent, at least, the Constitutional Convention had created the presidency in the image of Gen. George Washington, the hero of the Revolutionary War. "[M]any of the delegates," wrote South Carolina delegate Pierce Butler to a British kinsman, "cast their eyes toward General Washington as President; and shaped their Ideas of the Powers to be given to a President, by their opinions of his Virtue."

Yet Washington was a reluctant presidential candidate, despite the importuning of supporters such as Alexander Hamilton, who told him (quite accurately) in a September 1788 letter that "the point of light in which you stand at home and abroad will make an infinite difference in the respectability with which the government will begin its operations in the alternative of your being or not being at the head of it." Weary in his country's service, longing to remain at his Mount Vernon, Virginia, home, Washington replied to Hamilton on October 3 by begging "to pass an unclouded evening, after the stormy day of life, in the bosom of domestic tranquility." (The general was never more eloquent than in contemplation of retirement.)

Washington's letter to Hamilton also contained an additional, more important concern: he did not want to suffer the indignity of having to face an Anti-Federalist (or any other) opponent in the election. When none emerged, Washington allowed his name to go forward. He was elected to the presidency unanimously after the electors assembled in their state capitals, as scheduled, on

February 4, 1789. To provide the new government with a regional balance, Hamilton and other Federalists engineered the election of John Adams of Massachusetts to be the vice president.

Much to Washington's chagrin, the new Congress was slow to gather in the temporary capital city of New York. March 4 came and went; not until April 6 did a quorum assemble in Congress to count the electoral votes and declare Washington the president. He, in turn, waited at Mount Vernon until April 14 for official notification of his election, then proceeded slowly northward, accepting the adulation of ecstatic crowds along the way. On April 30, nearly two months past the scheduled inauguration date, Washington took the oath of office as president.

Although the new government was late in getting started, a law passed by Congress in 1792 retained March 4 as the date on which the president's term begins. This date prevailed until 1933, when the adoption of the Twentieth Amendment advanced the inauguration to January 20. (See "The Twentieth Amendment: Senate Debate," p. 301.) In 1845, a law was enacted to schedule election day—that is, the day on which the electors are chosen—on the first Tuesday after the first Monday in November.   ~

Whereas the Convention assembled in Philadelphia, pursuant to the Resolution of Congress of the 21st February, 1787, did, on the 17th of September in the same year, report to the United States in Congress assembled, a Constitution for the People of the United States; whereupon Congress, on the 28th of the same September, did resolve unanimously, "That the said report, with the Resolutions and Letter accompanying the same, be transmitted to the several Legislatures, in order to be submitted to a Convention of Delegates chosen in each State by the people thereof, in conformity to the Resolves of the Convention made and provided in that case:" And whereas the Constitution so reported by the Convention, and by Congress transmitted to the several Legislatures, has been ratified in the manner therein declared to be sufficient for the establishment of the same, and such Ratifications duly authenticated have been received by Congress, and are filed in the Office of the Secretary—therefore,

Resolved, That the first Wednesday in January next, be the day for appointing Electors in the several States, which before the said day shall have ratified the said Constitution; that the first Wednesday in February next, be the day for the Electors to assemble in their respective States, and vote for a President; and that the first Wednesday in March next, be the time, and the present Seat of Congress the place for commencing Proceedings under the said Constitution.

George Washington's Farewell Address (1796)

George Washington did not want to serve a second term as president—he even asked Rep. James Madison of Virginia to draft a farewell address for him in 1792—but he was prevailed upon to stand for reelection by almost every political leader in the country. One of the reasons that Washington wanted to retire—the angry divisions that had developed during his first term between the Federalist party, led by Alexander Hamilton, and the Democratic-Republican party, led by Thomas Jefferson—was also the reason that he reluctantly agreed to remain in office for another four years. As Attorney General Edmund Randolph, with some hyperbole, had warned the president, "Should a civil war arise, you cannot stay at home. And how much easier it will be, to disperse the factions which are rushing to this catastrophe, than to subdue them, after they shall appear in arms?"

Washington's election in 1792—by a unanimous electoral vote, as in 1789—did not arrest the development of political parties, but it did provide the country with a much-needed four more years of unifying leadership. By 1796, however, Washington had had all that he could stand of politics and government. (He longed, he said, for "the shade of retirement.") On September 19, 1796, Washington published his Farewell Address, which included ele-

ments from Madison's 1792 draft, a new draft by former secretary of the treasury Hamilton, and the president's own notes. The address, which Washington himself never delivered to an audience, is read aloud every year on February 22, his birthday, in the House of Representatives.

The Farewell Address is best remembered for its warnings about the threats to national unity that Washington foresaw, especially the "common and continued mischiefs of the Spirit of Party" and the inclination among Americans to choose sides in foreign conflicts.

Equally important, however, were the immediate political consequences of the address. Washington's withdrawal meant that, for the first time, the presidential election would be contested by opposing candidates. The late date of his announcement left the parties only a few weeks to select their 1796 nominees before the states would have to begin choosing electors. A 1792 law required each state to act within the thirty-four days prior to the first Wednesday in December.

Jefferson, the only Democratic-Republican of national stature, was the clear choice of his party's leaders, even though he showed no interest in running for president and made no efforts in his own behalf. Vice President John Adams was the obvious Federalist can-

didate. Hamilton's dislike of Adams, however, led him to entertain the hope that the party's vice-presidential nominee, the diplomat Thomas Pinckney of South Carolina, would receive more electoral votes than Adams. Because the Constitution originally did not distinguish between votes for president and votes for vice president, a vice presidential candidate with broader national support than either party's presidential candidate could actually win the presidency. (See "United States Constitution," p. 35, and "The House of Representatives Elects Thomas Jefferson: Rules and Ballots," p. 73.)

The election of 1796 was close. Jefferson swept the South, but Adams's unanimous support in the more populous North earned him a narrow majority. Some Federalist electors in New England subverted Hamilton's anti-Adams scheme by withholding one of their two votes for president from Pinckney. The final electoral vote tally was Adams 71, Jefferson 68, and Pinckney 59. (The Democratic-Republicans had not agreed upon a vice-presidential nominee.) On March 4, 1797, Adams was inaugurated as president and his rival, Jefferson, as vice president. ~

Friends and Fellow-Citizens:

The period for a new election of a citizen, to administer the Executive Government of the United States being not far distant, and the time actually arrived when your thoughts must be employed in designating the person who is to be clothed with that important trust, it appears to me proper, especially as it may conduce to a more distinct expression of the public voice, that I should now apprise you of the resolution I have formed to decline being considered among the number of those out of whom a choice is to be made.

I beg you at the same time to do me the justice to be assured that this reso-lution has not been taken without a strict regard to all the considerations appertaining to the relation which binds a dutiful citizen to his country; and that in withdrawing the tender of service, which silence in my situation might imply, I am influenced by no diminution of zeal for your future interest, no deficiency of grateful respect for your past kindness, but am supported by a full conviction that the step is compatible with both.

The acceptance of and continuance hitherto in the office to which your suffrages have twice called me, have been a uniform sacrifice of inclination to the opinion of duty and to a deference for what appeared to be your desire. I constantly hoped that it would have been much earlier in my power, consistently with motives which I was not at liberty to disregard, to return to that retirement from which I had been reluctantly drawn. The strength of my inclination to do this previous to the last election had even led to the preparation of an address to declare it to you; but mature reflection on the then perplexed and critical nature of our affairs with foreign nations and the unanimous advice of persons entitled to my confidence impelled me to abandon the idea. I rejoice that the state of your concerns, external as well as internal, no longer renders the pursuit of inclination incompatible with the sentiment of duty or propriety, and am persuaded, whatever partiality may be retained for my services, that in the present circumstances of our country you will not disapprove my determination to retire.

The impressions with which I first undertook the arduous trust were explained on the proper occasion. In the discharge of this trust I will only say that I have, with good intentions, contributed towards the organization and administration of the Government the best exertions of which a very fallible judgment was capable. Not unconscious in the outset of the inferiority of my qualifications, experience in my own eyes, perhaps still more in the eyes of others, has strengthened the motives to diffidence of myself; and every day the increasing weight of years admonishes me more and more that the shade of retirement is as necessary to me as it will be welcome. Satisfied that if any circumstances have given peculiar value to my services they were temporary, I have the consolation to believe that, while choice and prudence invite me to quit the political scene, patriotism does not forbid it.

In looking forward to the moment which is intended to terminate the career of my political life my feelings do not permit me to suspend the deep acknowledgment of that debt of gratitude which I owe to my beloved country for the many honors it has conferred upon me; still more for the steadfast confidence with which it has supported me, and for the opportunities I have thence enjoyed of manifesting my inviolable attachment by services faithful and persevering, though in usefulness unequal to my zeal. If benefits have resulted to our country from these services, let it always be remembered to your praise and as an instructive example in our annals that under circumstances in which the passions, agitated in every direction, were liable to mislead; amidst appearances sometimes dubious; vicissitudes of fortune often discouraging; in situations in which not unfrequently want of success has countenanced the spirit of criticism, the constancy of your support was the essential prop of the efforts and the guaranty of the plans by which they were effected. Profoundly penetrated with this idea, I shall carry it with me to my grave as a strong incitement to unceasing vows that Heaven may continue to you the choicest tokens of its beneficence; that your union and brotherly affection may be perpetual; that the free Constitution which is the work of your hands may be sacredly maintained; that its adminis-

tration in every department may be stamped with wisdom and virtue; that, in fine, the happiness of the people of these States, under the auspices of liberty, may be made complete by so careful preservation and so prudent a use of this blessing as will acquire to them the glory of recommending it to the applause, the affection, and adoption of every nation which is yet a stranger to it.

Here, perhaps, I ought to stop. But a solicitude for your welfare which can not end but with my life, and the apprehension of danger natural to that solicitude, urge me on an occasion like the present to offer to your solemn contemplation and to recommend to your frequent review some sentiments which are the results of much reflection, of no inconsiderable observation, and which appear to me all important to the permanency of your felicity as a people. These will be offered to you with the more freedom as you can only see in them the disinterested warnings of a parting friend, who can possibly have no personal motive to bias his counsel. Nor can I forget as an encouragement to it your indulgent reception of my sentiments on a former and not dissimilar occasion.

Interwoven as is the love of liberty with every ligament of your hearts, no recommendation of mine is necessary to fortify or confirm the attachment.

The unity of government which constitutes you one people is also now dear to you. It is justly so, for it is a main pillar in the edifice of your real independence, the support of your tranquillity at home, your peace abroad, of your safety, of your prosperity, of that very liberty which you so highly prize. But as it is easy to foresee that from different causes and from different quarters much pains will be taken, many artifices employed, to weaken in your minds the conviction of this truth, as this is the point in your political fortress against which the batteries of internal and external enemies will be most constantly and actively (though often covertly and insidiously) directed, it is of definite moment that you should properly estimate the immense value of your national union to your collective and individual happiness; that you should cherish a cordial, habitual, and immovable attachment to it; accustoming yourselves to think and speak of it as of the palladium of your political safety and prosperity; watching for its preservation with jealous anxiety; discountenancing whatever may suggest even a suspicion that it can in any event be abandoned, and indignantly frowning upon the first dawning of every attempt to alienate any portion of our country from the rest or to enfeeble the sacred ties which now link together the various parts.

For this you have every inducement of sympathy and interest. Citizens by birth or choice of a common country, that country has a right to concentrate your affections. The name of American, which belongs to you in your national capacity, must always exalt the just pride of patriotism more than any appellation derived from local discriminations. With slight shades of difference, you have the same religion, manners, habits, and political principles. You have in a common cause fought and triumphed together. The independence and liberty you possess are the work of joint councils and joint efforts, of common dangers, sufferings, and successes.

But these considerations, however powerfully they address themselves to your sensibility, are greatly outweighed by those which apply more immediately to your interest. Here every portion of our country finds the most commanding motives for carefully guarding and preserving the union of the whole.

The *North*, in an unrestrained intercourse with the *South*, protected by the equal laws of a common government, finds in the productions of the latter great additional resources of maritime and commercial enterprise and precious materials of manufacturing industry. The *South*, in the same intercourse, benefiting by the same agency of the *North*, sees its agriculture grow and its commerce expand. Turning partly into its own channels the seamen of the *North*, it finds its particular navigation invigorated; and while it contributes in different ways to nourish and increase the general mass of the national navigation, it looks forward to the protection of a maritime strength to which itself is unequally adapted. The *East*, in a like intercourse with the *West*, already finds, and in the progressive improvement of interior communications by land and water will more and more find, a valuable vent for the commodities which it brings from abroad or manufactures at home. The *West* derives from the *East* supplies requisite to its growth and comfort, and what is perhaps of still greater consequence, it must of necessity owe the *secure* enjoyment of indispensable *outlets* for its own productions to the weight, influence, and the future maritime strength of the Atlantic side of the Union, directed by an indissoluble community of interest as *one nation*. Any other tenure by which the *West* can hold this essential advantage, whether derived from its own separate strength or from an apostate and unnatural connection with any foreign power, must be intrinsically precarious.

While, then, every part of our country thus feels an immediate and particular interest in union, all the parts combined can not fail to find in the united mass of means and efforts greater strength, greater resource, proportionably greater security from external danger, a less frequent, interruption of their peace by foreign nations, and what is of inestimable value, they must derive from union an exemption from those broils and wars between themselves which so frequently afflict neighboring countries not tied together by the same governments, which their own rivalships alone would be sufficient to produce, but which opposite foreign alliances, attachments, and intrigues would stimulate and imbitter. Hence, likewise, they will avoid the necessity of those overgrown military establishments which, under any form of government, are inauspicious to liberty, and which are to be regarded as particularly hostile to republican liberty. In this sense it is that your union ought to be considered as a main prop of your liberty, and that the love of the one ought to endear to you the preservation of the other.

These considerations speak a persuasive language to every reflecting and virtuous mind, and exhibit the continuance of the union as a primary object of patriotic desire. Is there a doubt whether a common government can embrace so large a sphere? Let experience solve it. To listen to mere speculation in such a case were criminal. We are authorized to hope that a proper organization of the whole, with the auxiliary agency of governments for the respective subdivisions, will afford a happy issue to the experiment. It is well worth a fair and full experiment. With such powerful and obvious motives to union affecting all parts of our country, while experience shall not have demonstrated its impracticability, there will always be reason to distrust the patriotism of those who in any quarter may endeavor to weaken its bands.

In contemplating the causes which may disturb our union it occurs as matter of serious concern that any ground should have been furnished for characterizing parties by *geographical* discriminations—*Northern* and *Southern, Atlantic* and *Western*—whence designing men may endeavor to excite a belief that there is a real difference of local interests and views. One of the expedients of party to acquire influence within particular districts is to misrepresent the opinions and aims of other districts. You can not shield yourselves

too much against the jealousies and heart-burnings which spring from these misrepresentations; they tend to render alien to each other those who ought to be bound together by fraternal affection. The inhabitants of our Western country have lately had a useful lesson on this head. They have seen in the negotiation by the Executive and in the unanimous ratification by the Senate of the treaty with Spain, and in the universal satisfaction at that event throughout the United States, a decisive proof how unfounded were the suspicions propagated among them of a policy in the General Government and in the Atlantic States unfriendly to their interests in regard to the Mississippi. They have been witnesses to the formation of two treaties—that with Great Britain and that with Spain—which secure to them everything they could desire in respect to our foreign relations toward confirming their prosperity. Will it not be their wisdom to rely for the preservation of these advantages on the union by which they were procured? Will they not henceforth be deaf to those advisors, if such there are, who would sever them from their brethren and connect them with aliens?

To the efficacy and permanency of your union a government for the whole is indispensable. No alliances, however strict, between the parts can be an adequate substitute. They must inevitably experience the infractions and interruptions which all alliances in all times have experienced. Sensible of this momentous truth, you have improved upon your first essay by the adoption of a Constitution of Government better calculated then your former for an intimate union and for the efficacious management of your common concerns. This Government, the offspring of your own choice, uninfluenced and unawed, adopted upon full investigation and mature deliberation, completely free in its principles, in the distribution of its powers, uniting security with energy, and containing within itself a provision for its own amendment, has a just claim to your confidence and your support. Respect for its authority, compliance with its laws, acquiescence in its measures, are duties enjoined by the fundamental maxims of true liberty. The basis of our political systems is the right of the people to make and to alter their constitutions of government. But the constitution which at any time exists till changed by an explicit and authentic act of the whole people is sacredly obligatory upon all. The very idea of the power and the right of the people to establish government presupposes the duty of every individual to obey the established government.

All obstructions to the execution of the laws, all combinations and associations, under whatever plausible character, with the real design to direct, control, counteract, or awe the regular deliberation and action of the constituted authorities, are destructive of this fundamental principle and of fatal tendency. They serve to organize faction; to give it an artificial and extraordinary force; to put in the place of the delegated will of the nation the will of a party, often a small but artful and enterprising minority of the community, and, according to the alternate triumphs of different parties, to make the public administration the mirror of the ill-concerted and incongruous projects of faction rather than the organ of consistent and wholesome plans, digested by common counsels and modified by mutual interests.

However combinations or associations of the above description may now and then answer popular ends, they are likely in the course of time and things to become potent engines by which cunning, ambitious, and unprincipled men will be enabled to subvert the power of the people, and to usurp for themselves the reins of government, destroying afterwards the very engines which have lifted them to unjust dominion.

Toward the preservation of your Government and the permanency of your present happy state, it is requisite not only that you steadily discountenance irregular oppositions to its acknowledged authority, but also that you resist with care the spirit of innovation upon its principles, however specious the pretexts. One method of assault may be to effect in the forms of the Constitution alterations which will impair the energy of the system, and thus to undermine what can not be directly overthrown. In all the changes to which you may be invited remember that time and habit are at least as necessary to fix the true character of governments as of other human institutions; that experience is the surest standard by which to test the real tendency of the existing constitution of a country that facility in changes upon the credit of mere hypothesis and opinion exposes to perpetual change, from the endless variety of hypothesis and opinion; and remember especially that for the efficient management of your common interests in a country so extensive as ours a government of as much vigor as is consistent with the perfect security of liberty is indispensable. Liberty itself will find in such a government, with powers properly distributed and adjusted, its surest guardian. It is, indeed, little else than a name where the government is too feeble to withstand the enterprises of faction, to confine each member of the society within the limits prescribed by the laws, and to maintain all in the secure and tranquil enjoyment of the rights of person and property.

I have already intimated to you the danger of parties in the State, with particular reference to the founding of them on geographical discriminations. Let me now take a more comprehensive view, and warn you in the most solemn manner against the baneful effects of the spirit of party generally.

This spirit, unfortunately, is inseparable from our nature, having its root in the strongest passions of the human mind. It exists under different shapes in all governments, more or less stifled, controlled, or repressed; but, in those of the popular form, it is seen in its greatest rankness and is truly their worst enemy.

The alternate domination of one faction over another, sharpened by the spirit of revenge natural to party dissension, which in different ages and countries has perpetrated the most horrid enormities, is itself a frightful despotism. But this leads at length to a more formal and permanent despotism. The disorders and miseries which result gradually incline the minds of men to seek security and repose in the absolute power of an individual, and sooner or later the chief of some prevailing faction, more able or more fortunate than his competitors, turns this disposition to the purposes of his own elevation on the ruins of public liberty.

Without looking forward to an extremity of this kind (which nevertheless ought not to be entirely out of sight), the common and continual mischiefs of the spirit of party are sufficient to make it the interest and duty of a wise people to discourage and restrain it.

It serves always to distract the public councils and enfeeble the public administration. It agitates the community with ill-founded jealousies and false alarms; kindles the animosity of one part against another; foments occasionally riot and insurrection. It opens the door to foreign influence and corruption, which find a facilitated access to the government itself through the channels of party passion. Thus the policy and the will of one country are subjected to the policy and will of another.

There is an opinion that parties in free countries are useful checks upon the administration of the government, and serve to keep alive the spirit of liberty. This within certain limits is probably true; and in governments of a monarchical cast patriotism may look with indulgence, if not with favor, upon the spirit of party. But in those of the popular character, in governments purely elective, it is a spirit not to be encouraged. From their natural tendency it is certain there will always be enough of that spirit for every salutary purpose; and there being constant danger of excess, the effort ought to be by force of public opinion to mitigate and assuage it. A fire not to be quenched, it demands a uniform vigilance to prevent its bursting into a flame, lest, instead of warming, it should consume.

It is important, likewise, that the habits of thinking in a free country should inspire caution in those intrusted with its administration to confine themselves within their respective constitutional spheres, avoiding in the exercise of the powers of one department to encroach upon another. The spirit of encroachment tends to consolidate the powers of all the departments in one, and thus to create, whatever the form of government, a real despotism. A just estimate of that love of power and proneness to abuse it which predominates in the human heart is sufficient to satisfy us of the truth of this position. The necessity of reciprocal checks in the exercise of political power, by dividing and distributing it into different depositories, and constituting each the guardian of the public weal against invasions by the others, has been evinced by experiments ancient and modern, some of them in our country and under our own eyes. To preserve them must be as necessary as to institute them. If in the opinion of the people the distribution or modification of the constitutional powers be in any particular wrong, let it be corrected by an amendment in the way which the Constitution designates. But let there be no change by usurpation; for though this in one instance may be the instrument of good, it is the customary weapon by which free governments are destroyed. The precedent must always greatly overbalance in permanent evil any partial or transient benefit which the use can at any time yield.

Of all the dispositions and habits which lead to political prosperity, religion and morality are indispensable supports. In vain would that man claim the tribute of patriotism who should labor to subvert these great pillars of human happiness—these firmest props of the duties of men and citizens. The mere politician, equally with the pious man, ought to respect and to cherish them. A volume could not trace all their connections with private and public felicity. Let it simply be asked, Where is the security for property, for reputation, for life, if the sense of religious obligation *desert* the oaths which are the instruments of investigation in courts of justice? And let us with caution indulge the supposition that morality can be maintained without religion. Whatever may be conceded to the influence of refined education on minds of peculiar structure, reason and experience both forbid us to expect that national morality can prevail in exclusion of religious principle.

It is substantially true that virtue or morality is a necessary spring of popular government. The rule indeed extends with more or less force to every species of free government. Who that is a sincere friend to it can look with indifference upon attempts to shake the foundation of the fabric? Promote, then, as an object of primary importance, institutions for the general diffusion of knowledge. In proportion as the structure of a government gives force to public opinion, it is essential that public opinion should be enlightened.

As a very important source of strength and security, cherish public credit. One method of preserving it is to use it as sparingly as possible, avoiding occasions of expense by cultivating peace, but remembering also that timely disbursement to prepare for danger frequently prevent much greater disbursements to repel it; avoiding occasions of expense by cultivating peace, but remembering also that timely disbursements to prepare for danger frequently prevent much greater disbursements to repel it; avoiding likewise the accumulation of debt, not only by shunning occasions of expense, but by vigorous exertions in time of peace to discharge the debts which unavoidable wars have occasioned, not ungenerously throwing upon posterity the burthen which we ourselves ought to bear. The execution of these maxims belongs to your representatives; but it is necessary that public opinion should cooperate. To facilitate to them the performance of their duty it is essential that you should practically bear in mind that toward the payment of debts there must be revenue; that to have revenue there must be taxes; that no taxes can be devised which are not more or less inconvenient and unpleasant; that the intrinsic embarrassment inseparable from the selection of the proper objects (which is always a choice of difficulties), ought to be a decisive motive for a candid constriction of the conduct of the Government in making it, and for a spirit of acquiescence in the measures for obtaining revenue which the public exigencies may at any time dictate.

Observe good faith and justice towards all nations. Cultivate peace and harmony with all. Religion and morality enjoin this conduct. And can it be that good policy does not equally enjoin it? It will be worthy of a free, enlightened, and at no distant period a great nation to give to mankind the magnanimous and too novel example of a people always guided by an exalted justice and benevolence. Who can doubt that in the course of time and things the fruits of such a plan would richly repay any temporary advantages which might be lost by a steady adherence to it? Can it be that Providence has not connected the permanent felicity of a nation with its virtue? The experiment, at least, is recommended by every sentiment which ennobles human nature. Alas! is it rendered impossible by its vices?

In the execution of such a plan nothing is more essential than that permanent, inveterate antipathies against particular nations and passionate attachments for others should be excluded and that in place of them just and amicable feelings towards all should be cultivated. The nation which indulges towards another an habitual hatred or an habitual fondness is in some degree a slave. It is a slave to its animosity or to its affection, either of which is sufficient to lead it astray from its duty and its interest. Antipathy in one nation against another disposes each more readily to offer insult and injury, to lay hold of slight causes of umbrage, and to be haughty and intractable when accidental or trifling occasions of dispute occur.

Hence frequent collisions, obstinate, envenomed and bloody contests. The nation promoted by ill will and resentment sometimes impels to war the government, contrary to the best calculations of policy. The government sometimes participates in the national propensity, and adopts through passion what reason would reject. At other times it makes the animosity of the nation subservient to projects of hostility, instigated by pride, ambition, and other sinister and pernicious motives. The peace often, sometimes perhaps the liberty, of nations has been the victim.

So, likewise, a passionate attachment of one nation for another produces a variety of evils. Sympathy for the favorite nation, facilitating the illusion of an imaginary common interest in cases where no real common interest exists, and infusing into one the enmities of the other, betrays the former into a participation in the quarrels and wars of the latter without adequate inducement or justification. It leads also to concessions to the favorite nation of privileges denied to others, which is apt doubly to injure the nation making the concessions by unnecessarily parting with what ought to have been retained, and by exciting jealousy, ill-will, and a disposition to retaliate in the parties from whom equal privileges are withheld; and it gives to ambitious, corrupted, or deluded citizens (who devote themselves to the favorite nation) facility to betray or sacrifice the interests of their own country without odium, sometimes even with popularity, gliding with the appearances of a virtuous sense of obligation, a commendable deference for public opinion, or a laudable zeal for public good the base or foolish compliances of ambition, corruption, or infatuation.

As avenues to foreign influence in innumerable ways, such attachments are particularly alarming to the truly enlightened and independent patriot. How many opportunities do they afford to tamper with domestic factions, to practice the arts of seduction, to mislead public opinion, to influence or awe the public councils! Such an attachment of a small or weak toward a great and powerful nation dooms the former to be the satellite of the latter. Against the insidious wiles of foreign influence (I conjure you to believe me, fellow-citizens) the jealousy of a free people ought to be *constantly* awake, since history and experience prove that foreign influence is one of the most baneful foes of republican government. But that jealousy, to be useful, must be impartial, else it becomes the instrument of the very influence to be avoided, instead of a defense against it. Excessive partiality for one foreign nation and excessive dislike of another cause those whom they actuate to see danger only on one side, and serve to veil and even second the arts of influence on the other. Real patriots who may resist the intrigues of the favorite are liable to become suspected and odious, while its tools and dupes usurp the applause and confidence of the people to surrender their interests.

The great rule of conduct for us in regard to foreign nations is, in extending our commercial relations to have with them as little *political* connection as possible. So far as we have already formed engagements let them be fulfilled with perfect good faith. Here let us stop.

Europe has a set of primary interests which to us have none or a very remote relation. Hence she must be engaged in frequent controversies, the causes of which are essentially foreign to our concerns. Hence, therefore, it must be unwise in us to implicate ourselves by artificial ties in the ordinary vicissitudes of her politics or the ordinary combinations and collisions of her friendships or enmities.

Our detached and distant situation invites and enables us to pursue a different course. If we remain one people, under an efficient government, the period is not far off when we may defy material injury from external annoyance; when we may take such an attitude as will cause the neutrality we may at any time resolve upon to be scrupulously respected; when belligerent nations, under the impossibility of making acquisitions upon us, will not lightly hazard the giving us provocation; when we may choose peace or war, as our interest, guided by justice, shall counsel.

Why forego the advantages of so peculiar a situation? Why quit our own to stand upon foreign ground? Why, by interweaving our destiny with that of any part of Europe, entangle our peace and prosperity in the toils of European ambition, rivalship, interest, humor, or caprice?

It is our true policy to steer clear of permanent alliances with any portion of the foreign world, so far, I mean, as we are now at liberty to do it; for let me not be understood as capable of patronizing infidelity to existing engagements. I

hold the maxim no less applicable to public than to private affairs that honesty is always the best policy. I repeat, therefore, let those engagements be observed in their genuine sense. But in my opinion it is unnecessary and would be unwise to extend them.

Taking care always to keep ourselves by suitable establishments on a respectable defensive posture, we may safely trust to temporary alliances for extraordinary emergencies.

Harmony, liberal intercourse with all nations are recommended by policy, humanity, and interest. But even our commercial policy should hold an equal and impartial hand, neither seeking nor granting exclusive favors or preferences; consulting the natural course of things; diffusing and diversifying by gentle means the streams of commerce, but forcing nothing; establishing with powers so disposed, in order to give trade a stable course, to define the rights of our merchants, and to enable the Government to support them, conventional rules of intercourse, the best that present circumstances and mutual opinion will permit, but temporary and liable to be from time to time abandoned or varied as experience and circumstance shall dictate; constantly keeping in view that it is folly in one nation to look for disinterested favors from another; that it must pay with a portion of its independence for whatever it may accept under that character; that by such acceptance it may place itself in the condition of having given equivalents for nominal favors, and yet of being reproached with ingratitude for not giving more. There can be no greater error than to expect or calculate upon real favors from nation to nation. It is an illusion which experience must cure, which a just pride ought to discard.

In offering to you, my countrymen, these counsels of an old and affectionate friend I dare not hope they will make the strong and lasting impression

I could wish—that they will control the usual current of the passions or prevent our nation from running the course which has hitherto marked the destiny of nations. But if I may even flatter myself that they may be productive of some partial benefit, some occasional good—that they may now and then recur to moderate the fury of party spirit, to warn against the mischiefs of foreign intrigue, to guard against the impostures of pretended patriotism—this hope will be a full recompense for the solicitude for your welfare by which they have been dictated.

How far in the discharge of my official duties I have been guided by the principles which have been delineated in the public records and other evidences of my conduct must witness to you and to the world. To myself, the assurance of my own conscience is that I have at least believed myself to be guided by them.

In relation to the still subsisting war in Europe my proclamation of the 22nd of April, 1793, is the index to my plan. Sanctioned by your approving voice and by that of your representatives in both Houses of Congress, the spirit of that measure has continually governed me, uninfluenced by any attempts to deter or divert me from it.

After deliberate examination, with the aid of the best lights I could obtain, I was well satisfied that our country, under all the circumstances of the case, had a right to take, and was bound in duty and interest to take, a neutral position. Having taken it, I determined as far as should depend upon me to maintain it with moderation, perseverance, and firmness.

The considerations which respect the right to hold this conduct it is not necessary on this occasion to detail. I will only observe that, according to my understanding of the matter, that right, so far from being denied by any of the belligerent powers, has been virtually admitted by all.

The duty of holding a neutral conduct may be inferred, without anything more, from the obligation which justice and humanity impose on every nation, in cases in which it is free to act, to maintain inviolate the relations of peace and amity toward other nations.

The inducements of interest for observing that conduct will best be referred to your own reflections and experience. With me, a predominant motive has been to endeavor to gain time to our country to settle and mature its yet recent institutions, and to progress without interruption to that degree of strength and consistency, which is necessary to give it, humanly speaking, the command of its own fortunes.

Though in reviewing the incidents of my Administration I am unconscious of intentional error, I am nevertheless too sensible of my defects not to think it probable that I may have committed many errors. Whatever they may be I fervently beseech the Almighty to avert or mitigate the evils to which they may tend. I shall also carry with me the hope that my country will never cease to view them with indulgence, and that after forty-five years of my life dedicated to its service with an upright zeal, the faults of incompetent abilities will be consigned to oblivion, as myself must soon be to the mansions of rest.

Relying on its kindness in this as in other things, and actuated by that fervent love towards it which is so natural to a man who views in it the native soil of himself and his progenitors for several generations, I anticipate with pleasing expectation that retreat in which I promise myself to realize without alloy the sweet enjoyment of partaking in the midst of my fellow-citizens the benign influence of good laws under a free government—the ever-favorite object of my heart, and the happy reward, as I trust, of our mutual cares, labors, and dangers.

The House of Representatives Elects Thomas Jefferson: Rules and Ballots (1801)

The election of 1800 was the first in which both political parties organized to nominate candidates for president and vice president. On May 3, 1800, Federalist members of Congress "caucused" in the temporary capital city of Philadelphia to nominate John Adams for a second term as president and Gen. Charles Cotesworth Pinckney of South Carolina (the elder brother of Thomas Pinckney—the party's 1796 vice-presidential nominee) for vice president. Eight days later, the Democratic-Republican congressional caucus chose Vice President Thomas Jefferson to run for president and Aaron Burr, a party leader in New York, for vice president.

As in 1796, the election of 1800 was closely divided along regional lines, but this time Democratic-Republican inroads in the North gave the party a 73-65 electoral vote majority. Despite the clear verdict, however, a constitutional catastrophe occurred when the electors met to vote in the various state capitals on December 3, 1800. Democratic-Republican electors, fully aware that Jefferson was their party's presidential candidate and Burr the candidate for vice president, cast their two votes in the only faithfully partisan way the Constitution then allowed: one for Jefferson and one for Burr. (See "United States Constitution," p. 35.) When the votes were tallied from around the country, Jefferson and Burr each had seventy-three electoral votes—for president.

Instantly, the third paragraph of Article II, Section 1, of the Constitution came into play. It stated plainly that "if there be more than one [presidential candidate] who have such Majority [of electoral votes], and have an equal Number of Votes, then the House of Representatives shall immediately chuse by ballot one of them for President." The Constitution further provided that each of the by-now sixteen state delegations in the House would be granted a single vote in the presidential election, with a majority vote of nine states required for victory. Although Democratic-Republican candidates had swept the House elections in 1800, the "lame-duck" Federalist majority was still in office when the House assembled in 1801 to choose the president. (See "The Twentieth Amendment: Senate Debate," p. 301.)

Tacitly encouraged by Burr, who in any case impressed Federalists as more politically pliable than Jefferson, many Federalist representatives voted for the Democratic-Republicans' vice presidential nominee when the House began balloting on February 11, 1801. Through six days and thirty-five ballots, Jefferson consistently received the support of eight states to

Burr's six. Two state delegations were evenly divided. According to the Constitution, their votes did not count.

Alexander Hamilton, still a Federalist leader, was furious at the conduct of his fellow partisans in the House. Aware that to defeat Jefferson through political chicanery would jeopardize the new and still-fragile Constitution, Hamilton fumed in a letter to Sen. Gouverneur Morris of Pennsylvania that Burr's "elevation can only promote the purposes of the desperate and profligate. If there be a man in the world I ought to hate, it is Jefferson. With Burr I have always been personally well. But the public good must be paramount to every private consideration."

On February 16, Federalist representative James Bayard of Delaware warned his party's caucus that to prolong the election any further would jeopardize the entire constitutional system of government. Having received word through Samuel Smith, a Democratic-Republican leader in Maryland, that Jefferson would not indiscriminately overturn the policies or personnel of the Washington and Adams administrations, Bayard encouraged his colleagues to abstain in the next day's voting. On February 17, enough Federalists took his advice to elect Jefferson by ten states to four states on the thirty-sixth ballot.

Jefferson was inaugurated as president (and Burr as vice president) on March 4, 1801. Not only was Jefferson the first president to be inaugurated in the new permanent capital city of Washington, but his ascendancy marked the new nation's first peaceful transfer of power from one political party to another.

Fittingly, the president struck a conciliatory note in his inaugural address. "We have called by different names brethren of the same princi-

ple," Jefferson said. "We are all Republicans, we are all Federalists." ~

Friday, February 6.

A new member, to wit: Levi Lincoln, returned to serve in this House as a member from Massachusetts, in the room of Dwight Foster, elected a Senator of the United States, appeared, produced his credentials, and took his seat in the House.

Mr. Bird, from the committee appointed, presented a bill for the purpose of ascertaining the northwardly boundary line of a tract of land between the Little Miami and the Scioto rivers, reserved by the State of Virginia to satisfy the troops of the line of the said State, who in the Revolutionary war served on the Continental establishment; which was read twice, and committed a Committee of the whole House on Tuesday next.

The House proceeded to consider the amendments reported yesterday from the Committee of the whole House to whom was committed the bill for the government of the District of Columbia: Whereupon,

Ordered, That the said bill and amendments be recommitted to the Committee of the whole House to whom is committed the bill sent from the Senate, entitled "An Act concerning the District of Columbia."

Mr. Platt, from the Committee of Revisal and Unfinished Business, to whom it was referred to examine what laws have expired, or are near expiring, and require to be revived or further continued, made a further report, in part; which was read, and ordered to lie on the table.

On motion, it was

Resolved, That the Committee of Commerce and Manufacturers be instructed to inquire into the expediency of making provision to secure the property of prints to inventors and engravers.

Rules for Election of President

Mr. Rutledge, from the committee appointed, on the second instant, to prepare and report such rules as, in their opinion, are proper to be adopted by this House to be observed in the choice of a President of the United States, made a report; which was read, as follows.

The committee appointed the second instant, report, in part, the following resolution:

Resolved, That the following rules be observed in the choice by the House of Representatives of the President of the United States, whose term is to commence on the fourth day of March next.

1st. In the event of its appearing, upon the counting and ascertaining of the votes given for President and Vice President, according to the mode prescribed by the Constitution, that no person has a Constitutional majority, and the same shall have been duly declared and entered on the journals of this House, the Speaker accompanied by the members of this House, shall return to their Chamber.

2nd. Seats shall be provided in this House for the President and members of the Senate; and notification of the same shall be made to the Senate.

3rd. The House, on their return from the Senate Chamber, it being ascertained that the Constitutional number of States are present, shall immediately proceed to choose one of the persons from whom the choice is to be made for President; and in case upon the first ballot there shall not appear to be a majority of the States in favor of one of them, in such case the House shall continue to ballot for a President, without interruption by other business, until it shall appear that a President is duly chosen.

4th. After commencing the balloting for President, the house shall not adjourn until a choice be made.

5th. The doors of the House shall be closed during the balloting, except against the officers of the House.

6th. In balloting, the following mode shall be observed, to wit: The representatives of the respective States shall be so seated that the delegation of each State shall be together. The representatives of each State shall, in the first instance, ballot among themselves, in order to ascertain the vote of that State; and it shall be allowed, where deemed necessary by the delegation, to name one or more persons of the representation, to be tellers of the ballots. After the vote of each State is ascertained, duplicates thereof shall be made; and in case the vote of the State be for one person, then the name of that person shall be written on each of the duplicates; and in case the ballots of the State be equally divided, then the word "divided" shall be written on each duplicate, and the said duplicates shall be deposited in manner hereafter prescribed, in boxes to be provided. That, for the conveniently taking the ballots of the several representatives of the respective States, there be sixteen ballot boxes provided for the purpose of receiving the votes of the State; that after the delegation of each State shall have ascertained the vote of the States the Sergeant-at-Arms shall carry to the respective delegations the two ballot boxes, and the delegation of each State, in the presence and subject to the examination of the members of the delegation, shall deposit a duplicate of the vote of the State in each ballot box; and where there is more than one representative of a State the duplicates shall not both be deposited by the same person. When the votes of the States are all thus taken in, the Sergeant-at-Arms shall carry one of the general ballot boxes to one table, and the other to a second and separate table. Sixteen members shall then be appointed as tellers of the ballots; one of whom shall be taken from each State and be nominated by the delegation of the State from which he was taken. The said tellers shall be divided into two equal sets, according to such agreement as shall be made among themselves; and one of the said sets of tellers shall proceed to count the votes in one of the said boxes, and the other set the votes in the other box; and in the event of no appointment of teller by any delegation, the speaker shall in such case appoint. When the votes of the States are counted by the respective sets of tellers, the result shall be reported to the House; and if the reports agree, the same shall be accepted as the true votes of the States; but if the reports disagree, the States shall immediately proceed to a new ballot, in manner aforesaid.

7th. If either of the persons voted for shall have a majority of the votes of all the States, the Speaker shall declare the same; and official notice thereof shall be immediately given to the President of the United States and to the Senate.

8th. All questions which shall arise after the balloting commences, and which shall require the decision of the House, shall be decided without debate.

Resolved, That this House will consider the said report on Monday next.

Mr. Harper, from the committee appointed, presented a bill to continue in force the act entitled "An act to augment the salaries of the officers therein mentioned;" which was read twice and committed to a Committee of the whole House on Monday next.

Mr. Otis from the committee appointed, presented a bill supplementary to an act, entitled, "An act to divide the Territory of the United States northwest of the Ohio, into two separate governments," which was read twice and committed to a Committee of the whole House on Monday next.

Mr. Harper, from the committee appointed, presented a bill to extend to aliens who arrived and became residents in the United States, before a certain period, the benefits of the act of one thousand seven hundred and ninety-five, on the subject of naturalization; which was read twice and committed to a Committee of the Whole on Monday next.

The House went into a Committee of the Whole on the bill to amend the act, entitled "An act to provide for the valuation of lands and dwelling-houses, and the enumeration of slaves, within the United States, and to repeal the act, entitled "An act to enlarge the powers of the Surveyors of the Revenue;" and, after some time spent therein, the Committee rose, reported progress and had leave to sit again.

Monday, February 9.

Ordered, That the Committee of Claims, to whom was referred on the thirtieth ultimo, the memorial of sundry clerks employed in the different departments, be discharged from the further consideration thereof, and that the same be referred to the Committee of Revisal and Unfinished Business.

Mr. Rutledge, from the Committee appointed on the part of this House, jointly, with the Committee on the part of the Senate, to ascertain and report a mode of examining the votes given for President and Vice President of the United States; of notifying the persons elected of their election, and the time, place, and manner of administering the oath of office to the President, reported that the Committee had taken the subject referred to them under consideration, but had come to no agreement thereupon.

A message from the Senate, informed the House that the Senate would be ready to receive the House in the Senate chamber on Wednesday next, at twelve o'clock, for the purpose of being present at the opening and counting of the votes for President of the United States; and that the Senate have appointed a teller on their part, to make a list of the votes for President of the United States as they shall be declared.

Rules for Election of President

The House proceeded to consider the report made on Friday last, from the committee appointed to prepare and report rules proper to be observed in the choice of a President of the United States: Whereupon,

Ordered, That the said report be committed to a Committee of the whole House immediately.

The House, accordingly, resolved itself into a Committee of the Whole on the said report; and, after some time spent therein, the Chairman reported that the committee had had the said report under consideration, and directed him to report to the House their agreement to the same, with an amendment; which he delivered in at the Clerk's table, where the same was read. The House then proceeded to consider the report: whereupon, the amendment reported from the Committee of the whole House to the said report was, on the question put thereupon, agreed to by the House.

A motion was then made and seconded that the House do disagree with the Committee of the whole House in their agreement to the fourth rule contained in the said report, in the words following, to wit:

"4th. After commencing the balloting for president, the House shall not adjourn until a choice is made:"

And, the question being taken thereupon, it passed in the negative—yeas 47, nays 53, as follows:

Yeas—Willis Alston, George Baer, Theodorus Bailey, Phanuel Bishop, Robert Brown, Samuel J. Cabell, Gabriel Christie, Matthew Clay, William Charles Cole Claiborne, John Condit, John Dawson, Joseph Eggleston, Lucas Elmendorf, John Fowler, Albert Gallatin, Samuel Goode, Edwin Gray, John A. Hanna, Joseph Heister, David Holmes, George Jackson, Aaron Kitchell, Michael Leib, Levi Lincoln, Matthew Lyon, James Lynn, Edward Livingston, Nathaniel Macon, Peter Muhlenberg, Anthony New, John Nicholas, Robert Page, John Randolph, John Smilie, John Smith, Samuel Smith, Richard Dobbs Spaight, Richard Stanford, David Stone, John Stewart, Benjamin Taliaferro, John Thompson, Abram Trigg, John Trigg, Littleton W. Tazewell, Philip Van Cortlandt, and Joseph B. Varnum.

Nays—Bailey Bartlett, James A. Bayard, John Bird, John Brown, Christopher G. Champlin, William Cooper, William Craik, John Davenport, Franklin Davenport, Thomas T. Davis, John Dennis, George Dent, Joseph Dickson, William Edmond, Thomas Evans, Abiel Foster, Jonathan Freeman, Henry Glen, Chauncey Goodrich, Elizur Goodrich, Andrew Gregg, Roger Griswold, William Barry Grove, Robert Goodloe Harper, Archibald Henderson, William H. Hill, Benjamin Huger, James H. Imlay, Henry Lee, Silas Lee, Ebenezer Mattoon, Lewis R. Morris, Abraham Nott, Harrison G. Otis, Josiah Parker, Thomas Pinckney, Jonas Platt, Leven Powell, John Reed, Nathan Read, John Rutledge, William Shepard, John C. Smith, James Sheafe, Samuel Tenney, George Thatcher, John Chew Thomas, Richard Thomas, Peleg Wadsworth, Robert Waln, Robert Williams, Lemuel Williams, and Henry Woods.

A motion was then made and seconded that the House do disagree with the Committee of the whole House in their agreement to the fifth rule contained in the said report, in the words following, to wit:

"5th. The doors of the House shall be closed during the balloting, except against the officers of the House:"

And, the question being taken thereupon, it passed in the negative—yeas 45, nays 54, as follows:

Yeas—Willis Alston, Theodorus Bailey, Phanuel Bishop, Robert Brown, Samuel J. Cabell, Gabriel Christie,

Matthew Clay, William Charles Cole Claiborne, John Condit, Thomas T. Davis, John Dawson, George Dent, Joseph Eggleston, Lucas Elmendorf, John Fowler, Albert Gallatin, Edwin Gray, Andrew Gregg, John A. Hanna, Joseph Heister, David Holmes, George Jackson, Michael Leib, Matthew Lyon, Edward Livingston, Nathaniel Macon, Peter Muhlenberg, Anthony New, John Nicholas, John Randolph, John Smilie, John Smith, Samuel Smith, Richard Dobbs Spaight, Richard Stanford, David Stone, John Stewart, Benjamin Taliaferro, John Thompson, Abram Trigg, John Trigg, Littleton W. Tazewell, Philip Van Cortlandt, Joseph B. Varnum, and Robert Williams.

Nays—George Baer, Bailey Bartlett, James A. Bayard, John Bird, John Brown, Christopher G. Champlin, William Cooper, William Craik, John Davenport, Franklin Davenport, John Dennis, Joseph Dickson, William Edmond, Thomas Evans, Abiel Foster, Jonathan Freeman, Henry Glen, Samuel Goode, Chauncey Goodrich, Elizur Goodrich, Roger Griswold, William Barry Grove, Robert Goodloe Harper, Archibald Henderson, William H. Hill, Benjamin Huger, James H. Imlay, Henry Lee, Silas Lee, Levi Lincoln, James Lynn, Ebenezer Mattoon, Lewis R. Morris, Abraham Nott, Harrison G. Otis, Robert Page, Josiah Parker, Thomas Pinckney, Jonas Platt, Levin Powell, John Reed, Nathan Read, John Rutledge, William Shepard, John C. Smith, James Sheafe, Samuel Tenney, George Thatcher, John Chew Thomas, Richard Thomas, Peleg Wadsworth, Robert Waln, Lemuel Williams, and Henry Woods.

Resolved, That this House doth agree with the Committee of the whole House in their agreement to the said report, as amended, in the words following, to wit:

"That the following rules be observed in the choice by the House of Representatives of a President of the United States, whose term is to commence on the fourth day of March next.

"1st. In the event of its appearing, upon the counting and Ascertaining of the votes given for President and Vice President, according to the mode prescribed by the Constitution, that no person has a Constitutional majority, and the same shall have been duly declared and entered on the Journals of this House, the Speaker accompanied by the members of the House, shall return to their Chamber.

"2d. Seats shall be provided in this House for the President and members of the Senate; and notification of the same shall be made to the Senate.

"3d. The House, on their return from the Senate Chamber, it being ascertained that the Constitutional number of States were present, shall immediately proceed to choose one of the persons from whom the choice is to be made for President; and in case upon the first ballot there shall not appear to be a majority of the States in favor of one of them, in such case the House shall continue to ballot for a President, without interruption by other business, until it shall appear that a President is duly chosen.

"4th. After commencing the balloting for President, the House shall not adjourn until a choice be made.

"5th. The doors of the House shall be closed during the balloting, except against the officers of the House.

"6th. In balloting, the following mode shall be observed, to wit: The representatives of the respective States shall be so seated that the delegation of each State shall be together. The representatives of each State, shall, in the first instance, ballot among themselves, in order to ascertain the votes of the State; and it shall be allowed, where deemed necessary by the delegation, to name one or more persons of the representation, to be tellers of the ballots. After the vote of each State is ascertained, duplicates thereof shall be made; and in case the vote of the State be for one person, then the name of that person shall be written on each of the duplicates; and in case the ballots of the State be equally divided, then the word *"divided"* shall be written on each duplicate, and the said duplicates shall be deposited in manner hereafter prescribed, in boxes to be provided. That, for the conveniently making the ballots of the several representatives of the respective States, there be sixteen ballot boxes provided: and that there be, additionally, two boxes provided for the purpose of receiving the votes of the States; that after the delegation of each State shall have ascertained the vote of the State, the Sergeant-at-Arms shall carry to the respective delegations the two ballot boxes, and the delegation of each State, in the presence and subject to the examination of all the members of the delegation, shall deposit a duplicate of the vote of the State in each ballot box; and where there is more than one representative of a State, the duplicates shall not both be deposited by the same person. When the votes of the States are all thus taken in, the Sergeant-at-Arms shall carry one of the general ballot boxes to one table, and the other to a second and separate table. Sixteen members shall then be appointed as tellers of the ballots; one of whom shall be taken from each State, and be nominated by the delegation of the State from which he was taken. The said tellers shall be divided into two equal sets, according to such agreement as shall be made among themselves; and one of the said sets of tellers shall proceed to count the votes on one of the said boxes, and the other set the votes in the other box; and in the event of no appointment of teller by any delegation, the Speaker shall in such case appoint. When the votes of the States are counted by the respective sets of tellers, the result shall be reported to the House; and if the reports agree, the same shall be accepted as the true votes of the States; but if the reports disagree, the States shall immediately proceed to a new ballot, in manner aforesaid.

"7th. If either of the persons voted for, shall have a majority of the votes of all the States, the Speaker shall declare the same; and official notice thereof shall be immediately given to the president of the United States, and to the Senate.

"8th. All questions which shall arise after the balloting commences, and which shall be decided by the House voting *per capita* to be incidental to the power of choosing the President, and which shall require the decision of the House, shall be decided by States, and without debate; and in case of an equal division of the votes of States, the question shall be lost."

Election of President

Mr. Bayard moved an additional rule in relation to the Presidential election, viz: that five hundred tickets should be printed, on which should be the name of Thomas Jefferson, and five hundred on which should be the name of Aaron Burr, and the members in balloting should be confined exclusively to these.

The Speaker requested Mr. Bayard to modify his motion, so that six hundred tickets should be printed, and that after Thomas Jefferson, should be printed "of Virginia," and after Aaron Burr, "of New York," as he (the Speaker) had given directions to this effect; to which Mr. Bayard agreed.

The question was taken that the House do agree to the same, and it passed in the negative—yeas 36, nays 59, as follows:

Yeas—Bailey, Bartlett, James A. Bayard, John Bird, John Brown, William Cooper, John Davenport, Franklin Davenport, John Dennis, Joseph Dickson, William Edmond, Abiel Foster, Henry Glen, Chauncey Goodrich, Elizur Goodrich, Roger Griswold, Wm. B. Grove, Robert B. Harper, Archibald Henderson, Benjamin Huger, Henry

Lee, Lewis R. Morris, Abraham Nott, Harrison G. Otis, Thomas Pinckney, Jonas Platt, Leven Powell, Nathan Reed, John Rutledge, Jr., William Shepard, John C. Smith, James Sheafe, Samuel Tenney, George Thatcher, John Chew Thomas, Richard Thomas, and Lemuel Williams.

Nays—Willis Alston, George Baer, Theodorus Bailey, Phanuel Bishop, Robert Brown, Samuel J. Cabell, Christopher G. Champlin, Gabriel Christie, Matthew Clay, William Charles Cole Claiborne, John Condit, William Craik, Thomas T. Davis, John Dawson, George Dent, Joseph Eggleston, Lucas Elmendorf, Thomas Evans, John Fowler, Albert Gallatin, Samuel Goode, Edwin Gray, Andrew Gregg, John A. Hanna, Joseph Heister, William H. Hill, David Holmes, George Jackson, Aaron Kitchell, Michael Leib, Levi Lincoln, Matthew Lyon, James Linn, Edward Livingston, Nathaniel Macon, Ebenezer Mattoon, Peter Muhlenberg, Anthony New, John Nicholas, Robert Page, Josiah Parker, John Randolph, John Smilie, John Smith, Samuel Smith, Richard Dobbs Spaight, Richard Stanford, David Stone, John Steward, Benjamin Taliaferro, John Thompson, Abram Trigg, John Trigg, Littleton W. Tazewell, Philip Van Cortlandt, Joseph B. Varnum, Peleg Wadsworth, Robert Williams, and Henry Woods.

Resolved, That this House will attend in the Chamber of the Senate on Wednesday next, at twelve o'clock, for the purpose of being present at the opening and counting of the votes for President and Vice President of the United States; that Mr. Rutledge and Mr. Nicholas be appointed tellers, to act jointly with the teller appointed on the part of the Senate, to make a list of the votes for President and Vice President of the United States, as they shall be declared; that the result shall be delivered to the President of the Senate, who shall announce the state of the vote, which shall be entered on the

Journals; and if it shall appear that a choice hath been made agreeably to the Constitution, such entry on the Journals shall be deemed a sufficient declaration thereof.

Ordered, That the Clerk of this House do acquaint the Senate therewith.

Wednesday, February 11.

On motion, it was
Resolved, That all letters and packets to John Adams, now President of the United States, after the expiration of his term of office, and during his life, may be transmitted by post, free of postage.

Ordered, That a bill, or bills, be brought in pursuant to the said resolution; and that Mr. Otis, Mr. Thatcher, and Mr. Shepard, be appointed a committee to prepare and bring in the same.

Election of the President

On this day, being the day by law appointed for counting the votes of the Electors of President and Vice President, there were present the following Representatives, respectively, that is to say:

*From New Hampshire—*Abiel Foster, Jonathan Freeman, James Sheafe, and Samuel Tenney.

*From Massachusetts—*Theodore Sedgwick, Speaker, John Reed, Joseph B. Varnum, William Shepard, Peleg Wadsworth, Silas Lee, Lemuel Williams, George Thatcher, Bailey Bartlett, Phanuel Bishop, Harrison G. Otis, Nathan Reed, Levi Lincoln, and Ebenezer Mattoon.

*From Connecticut—*John Davenport, Roger Griswold, Samuel W. Dana, Chauncey Goodrich, Elizur Goodrich, William Edmond, and John C. Smith.

*From Vermont—*Matthew Lyon, and Lewis R. Morris.

*From Rhode Island—*Christopher G.

Champlin, and John Brown.

From New York—John Smith, Philip Van Cortlandt, Jonas Platt, Henry Glen, John Thompson, Theodorus Bailey, John Bird, William Cooper, Lucias Elmendorf, and Edward Livingston.

From New Jersey—James Linn, Aaron Kitchell, John Condit, James H. Imlay, and Franklin Davenport.

From Pennsylvania—Robert Brown, Albert Gallatin, Andrew Gregg, John A. Hanna, Joseph Heister, John Wilkes Kittera, Michael Leib, Peter Muhlenberg, John Smilie, John Steward, Richard Thomas, Robert Wain, and Henry Woods.

From Delaware—James A. Bayard.

From Maryland—John Chew Thomas, Samuel Smith, Gabriel Christie, William Craik, Joseph H. Nicholson, George Dent, George Baer, and John Dennis.

From Virginia—Samuel J. Cabell, Matthew Clay, John Dawson, Joseph Eggleston, Thomas Evans, Samuel Goode, Edwin Gray, David Holmes, George Jackson, Henry Lee, Anthony New, John Nicholas, Robert Page, Josiah Parker, Leven Powell, John Randolph, Abram Trigg, John Trigg and Littleton W. Tazewell.

From North Carolina—Willis Alston, Joseph Dickson, William Barry Grove, Archibald Henderson, William H. Hill, Nathaniel Macon, Richard Dobbs Spaight, Richard Stanford, David Stone, and Robert Williams.

From South Carolina—Robert Goodloe Harper, Benjamin Huger, Abraham Nott, Thomas Pinckney, and John Rutledge.

From Georgia—Benjamin Taliaferro.

From Kentucky—John Fowler, and Thomas T. Davis.

From Tennessee—William Charles Cole Claiborne.

Mr. Speaker, attended by the House, then went into the Senate Chamber, and took seats therein, when both Houses being assembled, Mr. Rutledge and Mr. Nicholas, the tellers on the part of this House, together with Mr. Wells, the teller on the part of the Senate, took seats at a table provided for them, in the front of the President of the Senate.

The President of the Senate, in the presence of both Houses, proceeded to open the certificates of the Electors of the several States, beginning with the State of New Hampshire; and as the votes were read, the tellers on the part of each House, counted and took lists of the same, which, being compared, were delivered to the President of the Senate, and are as follows:

	Thomas Jefferson	Aaron Burr	John Adams	Charles C. Pinckney	John Jay
New Hampshire	—	—	6	6	—
Massachusetts	—	—	16	16	—
Rhode Island	—	—	4	3	1
Connecticut	—	—	9	9	—
Vermont	—	—	4	4	—
New York	12	12	—	—	—
New Jersey	—	—	7	7	—
Pennsylvania	8	8	7	7	—
Delaware	—	—	3	3	—
Maryland	5	5	5	5	—
Virginia	21	21	—	—	—
Kentucky	4	4	—	—	—
North Carolina	8	8	4	4	—
Tennessee	3	3	—	—	—
South Carolina	8	8	—	—	—
Georgia	4	4	—	—	—
Total	73	73	65	64	1

Recapitulation of the votes of the Electors.

Thomas Jefferson	73
Aaron Burr	73
John Adams	65
Charles Cotesworth Pinckney	64
John Jay	1

The President of the Senate, in pursuance of the duty enjoined upon him, announced the state of the votes to both Houses, and declared that Thomas Jefferson, of Virginia, and Aaron Burr, of New York, having the greatest number, and a majority of the votes of all the Electors appointed, and, being equal, it remained for the House of Representatives to determine the choice.

The two Houses then separated; and the House of Representatives, being returned to their Chamber, proceeded, in the manner prescribed by the Constitution, to the choice of a President of the United States, and the following members were appointed tellers of the respective States, to examine ballots of each State, pursuant to the sixth rule adopted by the House on the ninth instant, to wit:

For the State of New Hampshire, Abiel Foster; Massachusetts, Harrison G. Otis; Rhode Island, Christopher G. Champlin; Connecticut, Roger Griswold; Vermont, Lewis R. Morris; New York, Theodorus Bailey; New Jersey, James Linn; Pennsylvania, Albert Gallatin; Delaware, James A. Bayard; Maryland, George Dent; Virginia, Littleton W. Tazewell; North Carolina, Nathaniel Macon; South Carolina, Thomas Pinckney; Georgia, Benjamin Taliaferro; Kentucky, John Fowler; Tennessee, William Charles Cole Claiborne.

The members of the respective States then proceeded to ballot, in the manner prescribed by the rule aforesaid, and the tellers appointed by the States, respectively, having put duplicates of their votes into the general ballot boxes prepared for the purpose, the votes contained therein were taken out and counted, and the result being reported to the Speaker, he declared to the House that the votes of eight States had been given for Thomas Jefferson, of Virginia; the votes of six States for Aaron Burr, of New York; and that the votes of two States were divided.[1]

The Constitution of the United States requiring that the votes of nine States should be necessary to constitute a choice of president of the United States, a motion was made and seconded, that the ballot for the President be repeated in one hour; and, the question being taken by States, it passed in the negative.

The States then proceeded in the manner aforesaid, to a second ballot; and, upon examination of the ballot boxes, it appeared that that votes of eight States had been given for Thomas Jefferson, of Virginia; and the votes of six States for Aaron Burr, of New York; and that the votes of two States were divided.

The States then proceeded in like manner to a third ballot; and, upon examination thereof, the result was declared to be the same.

The States then proceeded in like manner to a fourth ballot; and, upon examination thereof, the result was declared to be the same.

The States then proceeded in like manner to a fifth ballot; and, upon examination thereof, the result was declared to be the same.

The States then proceeded in like manner to a sixth ballot; and, upon examination thereof, the result was declared to be the same.

The States then proceeded in like manner to a seventh ballot; and, upon examination thereof, the result was declared to be the same.

A motion was then made and seconded, that the States proceed again to ballot in one hour; and, the question being taken thereupon, it was resolved in the affirmative—the votes of the States being ayes 12, noes 4.

The time agreed upon by the last-mentioned vote being expired, the States proceeded, in manner aforesaid, to the eighth ballot; and, upon examination thereof, the result was declared to be the same, to wit:

The votes of eight States for Thomas Jefferson, of Virginia; the votes of six States for Aaron Burr, of New York; and the votes of two States were divided.

The States then proceeded to a ninth, tenth, eleventh, twelfth, thirteenth, fourteenth, and fifteenth ballots; and, upon examination of the ballots, respectively, the result was declared to be the same.

A motion was then made and seconded, that the States proceed again to ballot at ten o'clock; and the question being taken thereupon, it passed in the negative—the votes of the States being ayes 7, noes 9.

Ordered, That the next ballot be repeated at nine o'clock, and not before.

The time agreed upon by the last-mentioned vote being expired, the States proceeded in manner aforesaid to the sixteenth ballot; and upon examination thereof, the result was declared to be the same.

Ordered, That the ballot be repeated in one hour.

The time agreed upon by the last-mentioned vote being expired, the States proceeded in manner aforesaid to the seventeenth ballot; and, upon examination thereof, the result was declared to be the same.

Ordered, That the ballot be repeated at eleven o'clock.

The time agreed upon by the last-mentioned vote being expired, the States proceeded in manner aforesaid to the eighteenth ballot; and, upon examination thereof, the result was declared to be the same.

A motion was then made and seconded, that the ballot be repeated to-morrow at eleven o'clock, and not before.

The question being taken thereupon, it passed in the negative.

Ordered, That the ballot be repeated at twelve o'clock.

The time agreed upon by the last-mentioned vote being expired, the States proceeded in manner aforesaid to the nineteenth ballot; and, upon examination thereof, the result was declared to be the same.

Ordered, That the ballot be repeated in one hour.

February 12 – 1 o'clock, a.m.

The time agreed upon by the last-mentioned vote being expired, the States proceeded in manner aforesaid to the twentieth ballot; and, upon examination thereof, the result was declared to be the same.

Ordered, That the ballot be repeated at two o'clock.

The time agreed upon by the last-mentioned vote being expired, the States proceeded in manner aforesaid to the twenty-first ballot; and, upon examination thereof, the result was declared to be the same.

Ordered, That the ballot be repeated at half after two o'clock.

The time agreed upon by the last-mentioned vote being expired, the States proceeded in manner aforesaid to the twenty-second ballot; and, upon examination thereof, the result was declared to be the same.

Ordered, That the ballot be repeated at four o'clock.

The time agreed upon by the last-mentioned vote being expired, the States proceeded in manner aforesaid to the twenty-third ballot; and, upon examination thereof, the result was declared to be the same.

Ordered, That the ballot be repeated at five o'clock.

The time agreed upon by the last-mentioned vote being expired, the States proceeded in manner aforesaid to the twenty-fourth ballot; and, upon examination thereof, the result was declared to be the same.

Ordered, That the ballot be repeated at six o'clock.

The time agreed upon by the last-mentioned vote being expired, the States proceeded in manner aforesaid to the twenty-fifth ballot; and, upon examination thereof, the result was declared to be the same.

Ordered, That the ballot be repeated at seven o'clock.

The time agreed upon by the last-mentioned vote being expired, the States proceeded in manner aforesaid to the twenty-sixth ballot; and, upon examination thereof, the result was declared to be the same.

Ordered, That the ballot be repeated at eight o'clock.

The time agreed upon by the last-mentioned vote being expired, the States proceeded in manner aforesaid to the twenty-seventh ballot; and, upon examination thereof, the result was declared to be the same.

Ordered, That the ballot be repeated to-morrow at eleven o'clock, and not before.

February 13

The time agreed upon by the last-mentioned vote being expired, the States proceeded in manner aforesaid to the twenty-ninth ballot; and, upon examination thereof, the result was declared to be the same.

Ordered, That the ballot be repeated to-morrow at twelve o'clock and not before.

February 14

The time agreed upon by the last-mentioned vote being expired, the States proceeded in manner aforesaid to the thirtieth ballot; and, upon examination thereof, the result was declared to be the same.

Ordered, That the ballot be repeated at one o'clock.

The time agreed upon by the last-mentioned vote being expired, the States proceeded in manner aforesaid to the thirty-first ballot; and, upon examination thereof, the result was declared to be the same.

Ordered, That the ballot be repeated at two o'clock.

The time agreed upon by the last-

mentioned vote being expired, the States proceeded in manner aforesaid to the thirty-second ballot; and, upon examination thereof, the result was declared to be the same.

Ordered, That the ballot be repeated at three o'clock.

The time agreed upon by the last-mentioned vote being expired, the States proceeded in manner aforesaid to the thirty-third ballot; and, upon examination thereof, the result was declared to be the same.

Ordered, That the ballot be repeated on Monday next at twelve o'clock, and not before.

February 16

The time agreed upon by the last-mentioned vote being expired, the States proceeded in manner aforesaid to the thirty-fourth ballot; and, upon examination thereof, the result was declared to be the same.

Ordered, That the ballot be repeated to-morrow at twelve o'clock, and not before.

February 17

The time agreed upon by the last-mentioned vote being expired, the States proceeded in manner aforesaid to the thirty-fifth ballot; and, upon examination thereof, the result was declared to be the same.

Ordered, That the ballot be repeated at one o'clock, and not before.

The time agreed upon by the last-mentioned vote being expired, the States proceeded in manner aforesaid to the thirty-fifth ballot; and, upon examination thereof, the result being reported by the tellers to the speaker, the speaker declared to the House that the votes of ten States had been given for Thomas Jefferson, of Virginia; the votes of four States for Aaron Burr, of New York; and that the votes of two States had been given in blank; and that, consequently, Thomas Jefferson, of Virginia, has been, agreeably to the

Constitution, elected President of the United States, for the term of four years, commencing on the fourth day of March next.[2]

Ordered, That Mr. Pinckney, Mr. Tazewell, and Mr. Bayard, be appointed a committee to wait on the President of the United States, and notify him that Thomas Jefferson is elected President of the United States, for the term commencing on the fourth day of March next.

Ordered, That a message be sent to the Senate to inform them that Thomas Jefferson has been duly elected President of the United States, for the term of four years, commencing on the fourth day of March next; and that the Clerk of this House do go with the said message.

Notes

1. During the time the States were employed in balloting, sundry messages from the President of the United States, from the Senate, and communications from Departments were received, and reports from committees made; but, it being contrary to the rules established on the 9th instant for the House to take them into consideration at that time, they were taken up and acted upon after the balloting had been completed, and the final result declared. Among which documents was a Message from the President of the United States, concerning the disposition of the property of the United States now in his possession.
2. The following account of the ballotings and incidents connected therewith in the House, is taken from the national Intelligencer, of February 13, 16, and 18, 1801.

[From the National Intelligencer, Feb. 13.]

"The votes having been entered on the Journals of the House of Representatives, the House returned to its own Chamber, and with closed doors proceeded to the ballot, as follows:

Whereupon the votes of the first ballot being counted, the following was the result:

Jefferson, 8 States; Burr, 6; divided, 2 viz: Maryland and Vermont. No election.

	Jefferson	Burr
New Hampshire	—	4
Massachusetts	3	11
Vermont	1	1
Rhode Island	—	2
Connecticut	—	7
New York	6	4
New Jersey	3	2
Pennsylvania	9	4
Delaware	—	1
Maryland	4	4
Virginia	16	3
Kentucky	2	—
North Carolina	9	1
South Carolina	—	5
Georgia	1	—
Tennessee	1	—
Total	55	49

The individual votes on the succeeding ballots occasionally fluctuated without changing the general result.

The House proceeded immediately to the second ballot, the result of which was the same, as well as that of the succeeding ballots, including the 8th, which being declared about 4 P.M., the House determined to suspend taking the next ballot for ne hour; on which the members separated.

The reader will observe that this postponement of the ballot was a virtual adjournment of the House, and that it was pursued in preference to adjournment, to avoid violating the rule previously adopted not to adjourn until a President should be elected.

About 5 P.M. the 9th ballot was entered upon, and the same result with the former produced.

After going through a number of other ballots, terminating in the same issue, it was agreed to take each ballot at the interval of an hour. In this manner the ballots were repeated until about 9 o'clock A.M., on Thursday—no separation of the members having taken place during the whole night.

The same invariable result followed each ballot, including the 27th, when, at 9 o'clock A.M., it was agreed to postpone the next ballot till 12 o'clock at noon; when the members separated.

At 12 o'clock the 28th ballot was taken—the result of which corresponded with the preceeding ballots. After which further balloting was postponed until Friday at 11 o'clock.

On Thursday morning the Speaker stated that persons were in waiting to deliver messages from the President and the Senate, and he wished a decision of the House whether they could be received. On the suggestion of a member it was agreed, without formally putting the question, to receive the messages.

On Wednesday, Mr. Nicholson, who had been for several days very ill, appeared on the floor, and had a place assigned him in an anti-chamber adjacent to the room in which the House assembled, to which room, to enable him to vote, the ballot box was carried by the tellers of Maryland. He rapidly progresses in recovery. His vote for Mr. Jefferson was important as it divided Maryland, and would, with the accession to Mr. Jefferson of one Federal vote from that State, have made him President.

At 12 o'clock on Friday (this day) the 29th ballot was taken, which produced the same result.

At 1 o'clock the 30th ballot was taken, the result the same.

It was then determined that the next ballot would be taken to-morrow at 12 o'clock. ·

[From the National Intelligencer, of Feb. 16.]

On Saturday, the 14th instant, at 12 o'clock at noon, the House of Representatives went into the thirty-first balloting, the result of which was the same with the preceding ballots.

It was then determined that the next ballot should be at one o'clock.

On going into the thirty-second ballot, General Dickson, from North Carolina, declared, that it was high time to come to a final vote, and that he would henceforward vote for Mr. Jefferson.

The result of this ballot presented the same issue.

At two o'clock, the thirty-third ballot was taken; the result still the same.

It was then determined that the next ballot should be taken on Monday at 12 o'clock.

On Friday, during one of the intervals of balloting, the Speaker informed the House that he had received a letter from the Secretary of the Treasury, which he would, with the permission of the House, read.

A member expressed his opinion that to read the letter would be an infraction of the rule established by the House.

The Speaker declared that, in his opinion, the rule would not be violated, a reading of the letter would be gone through before the hour assigned for the next ballot arrived.

It was replied that, though it had been agreed to postpone taking the next ballot for an hour, yet it was clearly understood that, in the interval, the Representatives of the Several States were consulting on the votes to be given.

The reading of the letter was overruled.

After the thirtieth ballot, on Friday, a motion was made and seconded by individual members, to postpone the next ballot to the 3d of March; the motion was rejected by the unanimous votes of all the States.

The Speaker then informed the House that, unless otherwise instructed, he should in future not consider a question before the House, unless moved by one State, and seconded by another.

The decision of the Chair was, on all hands, acquiesced in.

On Monday, the 16th instant, the thirty-fourth ballot was taken, the result was the same as before.

The next ballot was postponed till to-morrow at 12 o'clock.

All the accounts received from individuals at a distance, as well as the feelings of citizens on the spot, concur in establishing the conviction that the present is among the most solemn eras which have existed in the annals of our country.

That confidence, which has hitherto reposed in tranquil security, on the wisdom and patriotism of Congress, stands appalled at dangers which threaten the peace of society, and the existence of the constitution.

Placed in the midst of such circumstances, with the solicitudes of millions centering on the deliberations of their Representatives, it becomes the sacred duty of the press to make that people, whose rights are involved, the depositary of the earliest and most correct information.

For four days, the Republican and Federal parties have remained immoveable in their original vote for President.

The Republicans possess eight States, with half the delegation of two other States.

The Federalists possess six States with half the delegation of two States.

The Federal party apparently, for some time, entertained hopes of gaining over some Republican votes. But they are now convinced that the hope is abortive. What will be the result?

The answer to this interesting question will be made with the utmost coolness and integrity. Though it will in a degree involve opinions as to future measures, yet it is confidently believed that these opinions are entitled to the most unlimited confidence.

1. The Representatives of the eight States that vote for Mr. Jefferson will remain immutable in their adherence to the public will.

2. It is said that the six States that vote for Mr. Burr will not yield.

But it is believed that they will yield. The unanimous and firm decision of the people throughout the United States in favor of Mr. Jefferson will be irresistible. In Maryland, there is scarcely a dissenting voice, and among the first who have avowed a preference for Mr. Jefferson, are Federalists of the largest wealth and most respectable talents.

3. Some of the Representatives of those States that vote for Mr. Burr have declared a determination, in case neither he nor Mr. Jefferson shall be elected, to make by law a President *pro tempore*.

The determination was avowed; but it is believed that it is not now seriously entertained. So hostile would the voice of America appear to be to this measure, that it is doubtful whether any man would propose it, and more doubtful whether any man would accept the station, if offered to him.

During that period of deep suspense which may be yet to come, it behooves the people of the United States to manifest that spirit of dignified and commanding fortitude, that, while it stands prepared for any crisis, is resolved not to commit the cause in which it is embarked, by any act of indiscretion. It is right that public opinion should express itself. Let the Representatives of the people know the will of the people, and they will obey it.

That the people may know how the votes of their Representatives have been given, we present a statement:

New Hampshire—4 for Burr, viz.: Mr. Foster, Mr. Sheafe, Mr. Tenney, and Mr. Freeman.

Massachusetts—11 for Burr, viz: Mr. S. Lee, Mr. Otis, Mr. N. Read, Mr. Shepard, Mr. Thatcher, Mr. Wadsworth, Mr. L. Williams, Mr. Bartlett, Mr. Mattoon, Mr. J. Reed, Mr. Sedgwick.

Three for Jefferson, viz: Mr. Bishop, Mr. Varnum, Mr. Lincoln.

Rhode Island—2 for Burr, viz: Mr. Champlin, and Mr. J. Brown.

Connecticut—7 for Burr, viz: Mr. C. Goodrich, Mr. E. Goodrich, Mr. Griswold, Mr. Dana, Mr. J. Davenport, Mr. Edmond, Mr. J. C. Smith.

Vermont—1 for Jefferson, viz: Mr. Lyon.

One for Burr, viz: Mr. Morris.

New York—6 for Mr. Jefferson, viz: Mr. Bailey, Mr. Thompson, Mr. Livingston, Mr. Elmendorf, Mr. Van Cortlandt, Mr. J. Smith.

Four for Mr. Burr, viz: Mr. Bird, Mr. Glen, Mr. Cooper, Mr. Platt.

New Jersey—3 for Jefferson, viz: Mr. Kitchell, Mr. Condit, Mr. Lynn.

Two for Burr, viz: Mr. F. Davenport, Mr. Imlay.

Pennsylvania—9 for Mr. Jefferson, viz: Mr. Gallatin, Mr. Gregg, Mr. Hanna, Mr. Leib, Mr. Smilie, Mr. Muhlenberg, Mr. Heister, Mr. Stewart, Mr. R. Brown.

Four for Burr, viz: Mr. Waln, Mr. Kittera, Mr. Thomas, Mr. Woods.

Delaware—1 for Mr. Burr, viz: Mr. Bayard.

Maryland—4 for Mr. Jefferson, viz: Mr. S. Smith, Mr. Dent, Mr. Nicholson, Mr. Christie.

Four for Mr. Burr, viz: Mr. J. C. Thomas, Mr. Craik, Mr. Dennis, and Mr. Baer.

Virginia—14 invariably for Mr. Jefferson, viz: Mr. Nicholas, Mr. Clay, Mr. Cabell, Mr. Dawson, Mr. Eggleston, Mr. Goode, Mr. Gray, Mr. Holmes, Mr. Jackson, Mr. New, Mr. Randolph, Mr. A. Trigg, Mr. J. Trigg, Mr. Tazewell.

Five for Mr. Burr on same ballots, (two of whom on the first ballot voted for Mr. Jefferson,) viz: Mr. Evans, Mr. H. Lee, Mr. Page, Mr. Parker, Mr. Powell.

North Carolina—6 invariably for Mr. Jefferson, viz: Mr. Alston, Mr. Macon, Mr. Stanford, Mr. Stone, Mr. R. Williams, Mr. Spaight.

Four for Burr on some ballots, (3 of whom on the first ballot voted for Mr. Jefferson,) viz: Mr. Henderson, Mr. Hill, Mr. Dickson, Mr. Grove.

South Carolina—Mr. Sumter being sick has not attended, but will attend, at every hazard, the moment his vote can be of any avail. The individual votes of the Representatives of this State are not accurately known, but it is generally believed that Mr. Huger votes for Mr. Jefferson; and Mr. Rutledge, Mr. Pinckney, and Mr. Harper, vote for Mr. Burr. Mr. Nott's vote is doubtful. He has gone home.

Georgia—1 for Jefferson, viz: Mr. Taliaferro—Mr. Jones, who is dead, would have voted the same way.

Kentucky—2 for Mr. Jefferson, viz: Mr. Davis and Mr. Fowler.

Tennessee—1 for Mr. Jefferson, viz: Mr. Claiborne.

On Saturday last a memorial was presented to John Chew Thomas, representative in Congress for this District, from a respectable number of his constituents, recommending him to vote for Thomas Jefferson, and declaring that at least two-thirds of his constituents were in favor of the election of Mr. Jefferson.

The memorial was signed by the most respectable Federal gentlemen of the City of Washington.

[From the National Intelligencer, of Feb. 18].

On Tuesday at 12 o'clock the 35th ballot was taken; the result the same with that of the preceeding ballots.

At 1 o'clock the 36th ballot was taken which issued in the election of Thomas Jefferson.

On this ballot there were,

Ten States for Mr. Jefferson, viz: Vermont, New York, New Jersey, Pennsylvania, Maryland, Virginia, North Carolina, Georgia, Kentucky, and Tennessee.

Four States for Mr. Burr, viz: Rhode Island, New Hampshire, Connecticut, and Massachusetts.

Two States voted by blank ballots, viz: Delaware and South Carolina.

In the instance of Vermont, Mr. Morris withdrew.

In that of South Carolina, Mr. Huger, who is understood previously uniformly to have voted for Mr. Jefferson, also withdrew, from a spirit of accommodation, which enabled South Carolina to give a blank vote.

And in the instance of Maryland, four votes were for Jefferson and four blank.

The Twelfth Amendment: Senate Debate (1803)

The electoral college method of electing the president and the vice president was one of the least controversial provisions of the Constitution, both in the late stages of the Constitutional Convention and in the ratification debates that followed. (See "The Constitutional Convention: Debates on Presidential Selection," p. 1, and "The Federalist Papers: Nos. 68, 71, 72," p. 50.) It is all the more ironic, then, that the electoral college was the first institution created by the new Constitution to undergo a major overhaul.

The flaw in the original electoral college was the assumption that underlay its formulation, namely, that political parties would not arise to dominate presidential elections. Instead, the framers believed, states and ad hoc groups would nominate candidates for president. Individual electors would then vote for two of these candidates, one of them perhaps a local favorite but the other a leader of national stature. The most popular (and, presumably, the best qualified) candidate would be elected as president and the second most qualified candidate as vice president.

The framers' expectations were soon disappointed. By 1796, two political parties—the Federalists and the Democratic-Republicans—had taken charge of the presidential nominating process. In 1800, every Democratic-Republican elector cast one vote each for Thomas Jefferson and Aaron Burr, the party's nominees for president and vice president, respectively. Constitutionally incapable of distinguishing presidential from vice presidential votes, Congress declared the election a tie, ana the House of Representatives, which was controlled by a "lame duck" Federalist majority, nearly elected Burr as president. (See "The House of Representatives Elects Thomas Jefferson," p. 73.) When Jefferson won, some disgruntled Federalists actually began plotting to subvert his bid for reelection: if the Democratic-Republican ticket won a majority of electoral votes in 1804, they decided, Federalist electors would cast one of their votes for the victorious vice presidential nominee, thus electing him, not Jefferson, as president.

In December 1803, a Democratic-Republican-controlled Congress voted to amend the Constitution to accommodate the new partisan political realities. In order to separate the balloting for president and vice president, the amendment stated: "The Electors ... shall name in their ballots the person voted for as President, and in distinct ballots the person voted for as Vice President." In further recognition that a two-party system had emerged, the amendment reduced from five to three the number of candidates from whom the House could choose the president *in the absence of an electoral-vote majority. Finally, the amendment provided that if no one received a majority of electoral votes for vice president, the Senate would choose, by a majority vote of all senators, the vice president "from the two highest numbers on the list."*

Despite some Federalist grumbling, the Twelfth Amendment passed easily through Congress in December 1803 and was ratified quickly by the states. It became part of the Constitution on June 15, 1804, in time for the presidential election of 1804.

The Twelfth Amendment completely solved the problem that occasioned its enactment: not since 1800 has there been any confusion about which candidates are running for president and which for vice president.

Less benign, however, were the amendment's effects on the vice presidency. The position, always constitutionally weak, now was stripped of its status as the office awarded to the second most successful presidential candidate. Under the original Constitution, the nation's first and second vice presidents, John Adams and Thomas Jefferson, had risen to become its second and third presidents. Under the Twelfth Amendment, talented political leaders shunned the vice presidency, sinking the office into a century-long torpor, during which it frequently was occupied by aged or incompetent politicians.   ~

[December 1, 1803]

Mr. Hillhouse: ... The Complex mode provided by the Constitution was conceived in great wisdom. It was necessary, when the country was agitated, to operate as a check upon party and irregular passions. Parties will always have their champions, and they will be always well known; to attack another champion is to restrain the passions by some degree of uncertainty during the contest. But, by the new amendment, it would be every man to his own book, and every demagogue would be a leader and a champion, and, in the contest, parties would be divided between the two principal champions, and a third would come in and win the race.

If every man were to act correctly, no party passions would prevail on an occasion so important; but carry the champions of two opposite parties to the House of Representatives, and instead of voting thirty-seven times before they decide, as on the last occasion, they will vote thirty hundred times. You are told that, at the last election, one was intended by the people for President, and the other for Vice President; but the Constitution knows no vote for Vice President. Alter it as you now propose, and let two candidates be equal, and then you will be told that they were both intended for President. What will be the consequences? On the third day of March neither party will give out, and it will end in the choice of a third man, who will not be the choice of the people, but one who will, by artful contrivances, bring himself to that place with the sole intention of getting in between them. Choice by lot would certainly be better than this. Would not any man prefer a choice by lot rather than such a course, as it would break up the Constitution, and leave the people without a President in whom they would confide?

The principle of the Constitution, of electing by electors, is certainly preferable to all others. One of the greatest evils that can happen is the throwing of the election into the House of Representatives. There, Pennsylvania, Virginia, Massachusetts, and New York, may combine; they may say to the other States, we will not vote for your man; for either of those States giving their whole votes to a third character may bring him in. We see the practice daily in Congressional elections, when both parties obstinately adhere to their candidate; a third is set up and carried in to the rejection of both. By the new mode proposed every man will have an interest to intrigue for himself to obtain the eminent station. Gentlemen may suppose that such is the predominancy of their party, they may carry in any President. But no party can long hold an ascendancy in power; they will ill treat each other—or some of them will disagree, and from the fragments new parties will arise, who will gain power and forget themselves, and again disagree, to make way for new parties. The Constitution was predicated upon the existence of parties; they will always exist, and names will not be wanting to rally under, and difference of interests will not be wanting for pretexts: the agricultural will be arrayed against the mercantile; the South against the East; the seaboard against the inland. As to what he had heard about cutting off heads, he supposed that could not have been meant as a threat; in his part of the country such a crime could not take place. The gentleman, however, must be supposed to know his neighbors better than he did, but he could not suspect such danger from a valiant people.

Mr. Pickering said the amendment he had offered was suggested to him by the alarming picture of danger drawn by the gentleman from Maryland. He thought the dangers indeed exaggerated, though possibly they might not be; but he thought it proper to provide how elections should be conducted, and to determine between tumult or civil war and law.

Mr. Smith did say that, at the last Presidential election, the party opposed to the present Chief Magistrate did contemplate laying aside the popular choice and electing a President by a law to be passed for the occasion, at the time: he had also said, that had the measure been carried into effect, the person, whoever he might have been, would have met the fate of an usurper, and his head would not have remained on his shoulders twenty-four hours.

Mr. Wright: It had been said, that we meant to precipitate this amendment of the Constitution—to make the minority swallow it; he hoped the gentlemen, in their eagerness to render it insipid, would not make it totally unpalatable to us: as they had proceeded, the modes they had proposed struck him at least by their novelty. Since what was offered was not satisfactory, and they were willing to commit it to chance, why did they not take up the ancient mode of *grande bataille?* We should have no objection to have it decided by the champions of both parties armed with tomahawks! Gentlemen talk of the danger and of the rights of the small States, do they expect that any man can think their professions serious, when they are, at the same time, willing to commit their rights to the chance of a lottery? The rights of freemen are not to be gambled away, or committed to chance, or sorcery, or witchcraft; we look to reason and experience for our guides; we seek for the means most conducive to the general happiness; to this, reason conducts us. By experience, we correct what may have escaped our sagacity at first, or may have been defective or erroneous in practice. It is upon these principles our Constitution is founded; it is for these words that the provision is made in the Constitution itself for its own amendment; and it is not compatible with reason, or with the principles of the Constitution, to commit anything to capricious fortune, in which reason and human rights are concerned. Gentlemen charge us now with a wish to press this amendment forward with precipitation; what do gentlemen mean by this? A few days only have passed, when the same gentlemen were eager for an immediate decision; they declared their readiness to decide immediately; that the subject was as well understood then as ever it would be; and that we delayed the decision to the exhaustion of their patience. The subject has, nevertheless, undergone a long discussion, and the time has only served to prove that the gentlemen were at first mistaken, or that the numerous amendments which they have brought forward have their origin in other considerations.

Mr. Adams had declared that he was ready to give his vote upon the amendment in the first stage; but it did not therefore follow, that when his opinion on the whole was not likely to prevail, that he should endeavor to render it as palatable as possible. He was totally adverse to any decision by lot, and agreed perfectly with the gentleman from Maryland, that it was not a mode suited to the principles of our Government. But gentlemen say there is a defect, and wish to provide a remedy. He had drawn up an amendment which he should offer to the House, if that of his colleague should not be approved. He confessed he did approve of the designating principle, and for one among other reasons, that the present mode is too much like choice by lot. For instance, A may be intended by a large majority of the people for President, and B as Vice President; yet the votes might be so disposed, or chance might operate so contrary to intention, that the votes for B should exceed by a vote those for A. This was a defect in the Constitution; and there was a further reason why he was in favor of the designating principle, and that was, that it appeared to be called for from all parts of the United States. It was very true, as had been observed, that some time ago the opposers of the amendment did press for a decision; but he had seen those dispositions prevail alternately; but the minority had not so much pressed for a decision as for the discussion of the question.

Mr. Pickering suggested his wish to substitute forty-eight hours for twenty-four, in his amendment; and if the election should not then take place, a choice to be made in such manner as the House should direct.

The question, on Mr. Pickering's motion, was then put and negatived, without a division.

Mr. Adams then moved the following amendment: In the 37th line, after the word "choice," insert—

> And in case the House of Representatives shall not, within ____ days, effect the choice in manner aforesaid, and there be a Vice President duly elected, the said Vice President shall discharge the powers and duties of the President of the United States. But if the office of Vice President be also vacant, then the said powers and duties of President of the United States shall be discharged by such person as Congress may by law direct, until a new election shall be had, in manner already prescribed by law.

Mr. Hillhouse thought that there should be provision made for the choice so made, to remain only until such period as the Electors could be called again.

Mr. Dayton hoped the gentleman did not mean to lay a larger patch upon the Constitution than the hole they make in it required. Had gentlemen considered, that when there is a Vice President, that in case of death or inability, he alone can exercise the powers of the Executive, and that you cannot place any person over his head?

Mr. Adams: The gentleman is certainly right; he had offered his proposition hastily. The observations which arise in this discussion evidently prove that we have not as full a consideration of the subject as it is susceptible of.

Mr. Wright: Gentlemen did not perceive that the House of Representatives are Constitutionally bound and impelled to choose when it devolves upon them: they are sworn to do their duty. The amendments offered are wholly founded on the presumed corruption of the House of Representatives. You may as well make provisions against the corruption of a jury.

Mr. Hillhouse: There is another point which gentlemen appear not to have taken into view: how the objections of their oaths are to operate or be enforced, when the functions themselves expire on the third of March. There is another view of the subject, which ought not to be passed over: The members are sworn, to be sure, but one half of the House may sincerely believe that A is the popular choice; while the other half may as sincerely believe that the wishes of the majority are with B; and how are we to compel them by moral obligations, when the obligation rests wholly on the consciences of the individuals? The true principle, then, would be to make provision for the appointment of a person who should carry on the functions of Government till the Electors may again meet and choose a President. A provision vesting in the Senate the right of choice, even for one year, may be a motive for the other house to perform their duty promptly. It was not pleasant to discuss some topics, but we must discuss them, if we mean to avoid evil. We must suppose the existence of faction, of party, and even corruption, for we know that evil passions do and will exist, and that, by discussing, we guard against them. A House of Representatives elected two years before your Presidential election, may hold sentiments very different from him; the public mind may change in the time; and a party losing power may be led away by passion to conspire and throw every difficulty in the way.

Mr. Bradley thought the sentiments of the gentleman last up perfectly correct. He was satisfied that, if the House made no choice, the Vice President would administer the Government.

Mr. Wright said that although the functions of the House of Representatives would expire with the third of March, yet there was, assuredly, time enough between the second Wednesday in February, and the third of March, to make a proper choice; nothing but obstinacy, or worse, would prevent an election; he would shut them up, like a jury, until they had made a choice: he could not conceive a case wherein any number of men in Congress would dare to set themselves up against the country, and put its happiness and their own lives at hazard, in such a way as the gentleman supposed.

Mr. S. Smith: The gentleman from Massachusetts (Mr. Adams) appears not to be perfectly satisfied with his own amendment; and certainly the gentleman from Connecticut had shown that the amendment was effective; the candor of that gentleman he must acknowledge, he had taken the strongest hold possible of the subject; he had laid the fruits of experience before you, and pointed out the weakness which you had to protect. He would recommend it to the gentleman from Massachusetts to alter his amendment, so as to make it, that, in case the House should fail to choose, then, in four days after, the Vice President shall be President.

Mr. Adams saw a new difficulty there also, for there may not be a majority for both, and provision will be necessary for the vacancy of the Vice Presidency.

Mr. Hillhouse thought there would be no danger of the Senate omitting to elect their President, who is, on a vacancy, the Vice President in fact. As to shutting the House up like a jury in a dark room, depriving them of fire, light, and food, he thought the measure too strong; he did not wish to see them at the mercy of the sheriff, who upon their laches might call in the *posse comitatus*, and trundle them out of the District, or send them to Coventry. If the House of Representatives should not make a choice, he saw no reason why the Government should not go on until an election should take place.

Mr. Cocke was astonished to see gentlemen going over so much unnecessary ground. Could they suppose the people so indifferent to their own rights as not to make an election? Or, do gentlemen mean all these cavillings as amusement—to display their ingenuity at finding fault? If there should be any failure of choice, why could not the Secretary of State arrange and carry on the Executive business until an election should again take place?

Mr. Tracy rose.

Mr. Cocke called for the question—the question!

Mr. Tracy: Does the gentleman mean to call for the question while I am on the floor? I will not sit down upon such a call. What is the question, sir?

Mr. Dayton hoped the gentleman from Massachusetts (Mr. Adams) would withdraw his amendment.

Mr. Adams thought the deliberation of one or two hours could not be thrown away.

Mr. Wright hoped the decision on the amendment would not be pressed upon the House. What! is it proposed to take the choice of President out of the hands of the Electors and place it wholly in the House of Representatives, and tell them, hold out only four days, and you will then have the whole power in your hands; you may set aside all consideration for the wishes of your constituents—set popular opinion at defiance, and please yourselves by choosing a President of whom the people never thought? Gentlemen should avoid this dangerous path which they wish to prepare; the people will not bear to be frowned upon by those whom their breath has made, and can unmake.

Sir, it is our wish to prevent all these dangerous or fatal courses and consequences; and we should keep in mind, that whatever we may conclude upon here, is completely guarded, not alone by the necessary consent of the other House, but that of three-fourths of the States. The Constitution, sir, would be preferable as it is, without the odious and anti-republican forms which gentlemen propose to engross upon it. What, sir, determine a most important principle of effective government by a non-

effective act—determine an election by holding out a temptation to non-election! He should prefer having the choice open to the Representatives bound by oath, by duty, and by the Constitution, to such an alternative....

An observation of the gentleman from Massachusetts (Mr. Adams) produced a sensation which at once showed that something besides the care of the people's rights had an influence here. He proposes that the proper officer, the Vice President, should succeed to the Presidential chair upon a failure of election or vacancy after a few short months. Whence arose the agitation and interest excited by his proposition? Is it because we wish not to see a man seated in the Executive chair whom the people never contemplated to place there, and who never had a vote?

Mr. Dayton: You are about to designate who shall be President and who Vice President; and some gentlemen have gone so far as to favor the choice of one who had not a vote for either office. The gentleman from Massachusetts, (Mr. Adams) indeed, professes to have in view the succession of the Vice President to the Executive Chair when vacant. But gentlemen should perceive, that if you designate, the principle will be totally changed. He could not assent to the conclusion of some gentlemen on another point. If anything could be understood from the Constitution more clearly than another, it was that the votes are given to two persons for President, and that, as has been observed before, the Constitution never notices a vote for the office of Vice President. Now, then, can it be said which was the person intended? The gentleman from Maryland (Mr. Wright) had said that one of the candidates at the late election had not a single vote for President, while the official returns show that each and every vote was the same for both candidates as President.

Mr. Taylor: That matter appears susceptible of a very simple explanation. There can be no question that in form, the votes for each candidate were equal; but that is not the question; the *quo animo* must be taken into view. Would any gentleman say no preference was intended? It is very true that such was the form, but looking to the well known intention, have you not in the very fact stated an evidence that the principle of designation is essential, were it only to prevent the consummation of an act never contemplated or expected?

[December 2, 1803]

Mr. Taylor, of Virginia, desired to withdraw his motion of the preceding day in order to accommodate the terms of his proposition to the wishes of gentlemen. His only object was to obtain the principle, and provided that was obtained in such a manner as to promise an accomplishment of the good intended thereby, he should consider the words in which the provision was to be couched of inferior moment. In lieu of the addition which he offered before, he now proposed to insert after the word *choice,* in the 37th line, the following words:

> And if the House of Representatives shall not choose a President whenever the right of choice shall devolve upon them, before the 4th day of March next following, then the Vice President shall act as President, as in case of the death or other Constitutional disability of the President.

Mr. Adams had no sort of objection to this addition to the paragraph; it reached his ideas as far as it went; but he conceived that though this made a very necessary provision for the case of the President, it did not go far enough, inasmuch as no provision was made in case there should be no Vice President. He would submit this case to gentlemen, that if there was no Vice President existing nor any more than a President chosen, in the event of a high state of party spirit, would it be difficult to foresee that there would be much room left for contention and evil? Unless provision should be made against the contingency, therefore, the amendment would be imperfect, in his mind. Like the gentleman from Virginia, he was not tied to words, but he thought it worth while to employ two liens to provide against the danger.

Mr. Pickering objected to the length of time allowed for the House of Representatives to decide. We have been told that the small States, from the smaller number of votes, are exposed to corruption; he wished not time to be left for corruption to operate, and he therefore desired that the period for the House of Representatives to decide should be limited to forty-eight hours or three days. . . .

The amendment was agreed to—. . . .

Mr. Adams offered another amendment, of the following effect, to be added to the provisions concerning the election of Vice President:

> if there shall be no Vice President duly elected within ten days after the fourth of March, then the power and duties of the President of the United States shall be discharged by such person as shall be by law invested with that power, until such time as a new election by Electors shall take place." . . .

Mr. Hillhouse was not disposed to concur with the proposed amendment; he did not think a period of agitation a proper one to make choice of an officer of so much power; he would prefer making provision by law before the happening of the event; for, in a high state of party he could see no likelihood of an agreement, and out of disagreement confusion might arise. His wish was to have some person designated who should discharge the Executive duties until an election should take place, and that this officer should be previously fixed upon, so that party spirit should have no room for agitation.

Mr. Jackson could not discern the necessity of the proposition now offered; the case proposed to be provided against, he thought so extreme as likely never to happen. Besides, the mover appeared not to have taken it into consideration that one-third of the Senate go out at the close of the second session of every Congress by rotation, and would he have only two-thirds to make the law which was to provide for this choice? upon the principle of the general amendment, he had not at first made up his convictions, but the amendment adopted had removed his doubts, and he thought this addition to this amendment unnecessary. He hoped the Senate would abide by that they had already agreed to, and preserve the right of choice to the people.

Mr. Wright: There was another difficulty which the gentleman from Massachusetts appears not to have foreseen. To make a law it is not enough that the Senate are present even if complete; the House of Representatives is necessary to an act of legislation, and that body can have no existence after the fourth day of March, nor within the ten days suggested, for they could not, if all elected, be called even by proclamation within that time; and further, if there should be no election of President, there would be no power to convene Congress; so that the proposed addition is improper altogether.

Mr. Adams did not feel extremely solicitous for the proposition; when the Constitution is proposed to be amended, however, he was disposed to offer every suggestion which might appear to him calculated to render it more perfect. The objections offered by the gentleman form Georgia, highly as he respected his opinion, did not appear to him conclusive; for his calculations of time and circumstances do not entirely correspond with experience past. The President has at all times heretofore been inaugurated after the House of Representatives had closed its session by limitation, and the Senate had been uniformly assembled for the purpose of the inauguration. Here then is a body in session, and if there shall not be a Vice President chosen, they can and must proceed to choose one, and that choice would of course fall, as proposed, upon one of the candidates. The gentleman from Connecticut (Mr. Hillhouse) had mistaken his view, concerning the choice of a person by law; his intention certainly was to provide for the future contingency by a previous law.

Mr. Jackson still conceived the gentleman's proposition founded in mistake; for it would be impracticable for the Senate to act, since, according to the rules of the Senate, two-thirds of the whole are necessary to form a quorum; one third must Constitutionally go out of that body at the time, and the absence of a single member would disable the Senate from business.

Mr. Adams: There would remain still two-thirds of the Senate, and it would be the duty of the Executive to call them together, as had been done in some cases; and as to the deduction of the third by rotation, there are several of the small States that elected their Senators several months before the period. To argue that they would neglect it, would be to argue that the States are indifferent to their representation on this floor.

Mr. Jackson: We know that vacancies do occur from other causes than indifference or neglect of States; we know that at this moment New York has but one Representative on this floor, and that New Jersey had but very lately been so much embarrassed by a faction as to leave her for sometime without more than one Senator. . . .

Mr. Taylor: The opposition to this discriminating amendment to the Constitution is condensed into a single stratagem, namely: an effort to excite the passion of jealousy in various forms. Endeavors have been made to excite geographical jealousies—a jealousy of the smaller against the larger States—a jealousy in the people against the idea of amending the Constitution; and even a jealousy against individual members of this House. Sir, is this passion a good medium through which to discern truth, or is it a mirror calculated to reflect error? Will it enlighten or deceive? Is it planted in good or in evil—in moral or in vicious principles? Wherefore, then, do gentlemen endeavor to blow it up? Is it because they distrust the strength of their arguments, that they resort to this furious and erring passion? Is it because they know that

    ——"Trifles light as air,
Are, to the jealous, confirmation strong
As proofs of holy writ?"

So far as these efforts have been directed towards a geographical demarcation of the interests of the Union into North and South, in order to excite a jealousy of one division against another; and, so far as they have been used to create suspicions of individuals, they have been either so feeble, inapplicable, or frivolous, as to bear but lightly upon the question, and to merit but little attention. But the attempts to array States against States because they differ in size, and to prejudice the people against the idea of amending their Constitution, bear a more formidable aspect, and ought to be repelled, because they are founded on principles the most mischievous and inimical to the Constitution, and could they be successful, are replete with great mischiefs.

Towards exciting this jealousy of smaller States against larger States, the gentleman from Connecticut (Mr. Tracy) had labored to prove that the federal principle of the Constitution of the United States was founded in the idea of minority invested with operative power. That, in pursuance of this principle, it was contemplated and intended that the election of a President should frequently come into the House of Representatives, and to divert it from thence by this amendment would trench upon the federal principle of our Constitution, and diminish the rights of the smaller States, bestowed by this principle upon them. This was the scope of his argument to excite their jealousy, and is the amount also of several other arguments delivered by gentlemen on the same side of the question. He did not question the words, but the ideas of gentlemen. Words, selected from their comrades, are easily asserted to misrepresent opinions, as he had himself experienced during the discussion on the subject.

This idea of federalism ought to be well discussed by the smaller States, before they will suffer it to produce the intended effect—that of exciting their jealousy against the larger. To him it appeared to be evidently incorrect. Two principles sustain our Constitution: one a majority of the people, the other a majority of the States; the first was necessary to preserve the liberty or sovereignty of the people; the last, to preserve the liberty or sovereignty of the States. But both are founded in the principle of majority; and the effort of the Constitution is to preserve this principle in relation both to the people and the States, so that neither species of sovereignty or independence should be able to destroy the other. Many illustrations might be adduced. That of amending the Constitution will suffice. Three-fourths of the States must concur in this object, because a less number or a majority of States might not contain a majority of people; therefore, the Constitution is not amendable by a majority of States, lest a species of State sovereignty might, under color of amending the Constitution, infringe the right of the people. On the other hand, a majority of the people residing in the large States cannot amend the Constitution, lest they should diminish or destroy the sovereignty of the small States, the federal Union, or federalism itself. Hence a concurrence of the States to amend the Constitution became necessary, not because federalism was founded in the idea of minority, but for a reason the very reverse of that idea— that is, to cover the will both of a majority of the people and a majority of States, so as to preserve the great element of self-government, as it regarded State sovereignty, and also as it regarded the sovereignty of the people.

For this great purpose certain political functions are assigned to be performed, under the auspices of the States or federal principle, and certain others under the popular principle. It was the intention of the Constitution that these functions should be performed in conformity to its principle. If that principle is in fact a government of a minority, then these functions ought to be performed by a minority. When the federal principle is performing a function, according to this idea, a majority of the States ought to decide. And, by the same mode of reasoning, when the popular principle is performing a function, then a minority of the people ought to decide. This brings us precisely to the question of the amendment. It is the intention of the Constitution that the popular principle shall operate in the election of a President and Vice President. It is also the intention of the Constitution that the popular principle, in discharging the functions committed to it by the Constitution, should operate by a majority and not by a minority. That the majority of the people should be driven, by an unforeseen state of parties, to the necessity of relinquishing their will in the election of one or the other of these officers, or that the principle of majority, in a function confided to the popular will, should be deprived of half its rights, and be laid under a necessity of violating its duty to preserve the other half, is not the intention of the Constitution.

But the gentleman from Connecticut had leaped over all this ground, and gotten into the House of Representatives, without considering the principles of the Constitution, as applicable to the election of President and Vice President by Electors, and distinguishing them from an election by the House of Representatives. And by mingling and interweaving the two modes of electing together, a considerable degree of complexity has been produced. If, however, it is admitted that in an election of a President and Vice President by Electors, that the will of the electing majority ought fairly to operate, and that an election by the will of a minority would be an abuse or corruption of the principles of the Constitution, then it follows that an amendment, to avoid this abuse, accords with, and is necessary to save these principles. In like manner, had an abuse crept into the same election, whenever it was to be made under the federal principle by the House of Representatives, enabling a minority of States to carry the election, it would not have violated the intention of the Constitution to have corrected this abuse, also, by an amendment. For, sir, I must suppose it to have been the intention of the Constitution that both the federal principle and the popular principle should operate in those functions respectively assigned to them, perfectly and not imperfectly—that is, the former by a majority of States, and the latter by a majority of the people.

Under this view of the subject, the amendment ought to be considered. Then the question will be, whether it is calculated or not to cause the popular principle, applied by the Constitution in the first instance, to operate perfectly, and to prevent the abuse of an election by a minority? If it is, it corresponds with the intention, diminishes nothing of the rights of the smaller States, and, of course, affords them no cause of jealousy.

Sir, it could never have been the intention of the Constitution to produce a state of things by which a majority of the popular principle should be under the necessity of voting against its judgment to secure a President, and by which a minor faction should acquire a power capable of defeating the majority in the election of President, or of electing a Vice President contrary to the will of the electing principle. To permit this abuse would be a fraudulent mode of defeating the operation of the popular principle in this election, in order to transfer it to the federal principle—to disinherit the people for the sake of endowing the House of Representatives; whereas it was an accidental and not an artificial disappointment in the election of a President, against which the Constitution intended to provide. A fair and not an unfair attempt to elect was previously to be made by the popular principle, before the election was to go into the House of Representatives. And if the people of all the States, both large and small, should by an abuse of the real design of the Constitution, be bubbled out of the election of Executive power, by leaving to them the nominal right of an abortive effort, and transferring to the House of Representatives the substantial right of a real election, nothing will remain but to corrupt the election in that House by some of those abuses of which elections by diets are susceptible, to bestow upon Executive power an aspect both formidable and inconsistent with the principles by which the Constitution intended to mold it.

The great check imposed upon Executive power was a popular mode of election; and the true object of jealousy, which ought to attract the attention of the people of every State, is any circumstance tending to diminish or destroy that check. It was also a primary intention of the Constitution to keep Executive power independent of Legislative; and although a provision was made for its election by the House of Representatives in the possible case, that possible case never was intended to be converted into the active rule, so as to destroy in a degree the line of separation and independency between the Executive and Legislative power. The controversy is not therefore between larger and smaller States, but between the people of every State and the House of Representatives. Is it better that the people—a fair majority of the popular principle—should elect Executive power; or, that a minor faction should be enabled to embarrass and defeat the judgment and will of this majority, and throw the election into the House of Representatives? This is the question. If this amendment should enable the popular principle to elect Executive power, and thus keep it separate and distinct from legislation, the intention of the Constitution, the interest of the people, and the principles of our policy, will be preserved; and if so, it is as I have often endeavored to prove in this debate, the interest of the smaller States themselves, that the amendment should prevail. For, sir, is an exposure of their Representatives to bribery and corruption (a thing which may possibly happen at some future day, when men lose that public virtue which now governs them) an acquisition more desirable than all those great objects best (if not exclusively) attainable by the election of Executive power by the popular principle of the Federal Government, as the Constitution itself meditates and prefers?

So far, then, the amendment strictly coincides with the Constitution and with the interests of the people of every State in the Union. But suppose by some rare accident the election should still be sent into the House of Representatives, does not the amendment then afford cause of jealousy to the smaller States? Sir, each State has but one vote, whether it is large or small; and the President and Vice President are still to be chosen out of five persons. Such is the Constitution in both respects now. To have enlarged the number of nominees, would have increased the occurrence of an election by the House of Representatives; and if, as I endeavored to prove, it is for the interest of every State, that the election should be made by the popular principle of Government and not by that House, then it follows, that whatever would have a tendency to draw the election to that House, is against the interest of every State in the Union; and that every State in the Union is interested to avoid an enlargement of the nominees, if it would have such a tendency.

Sir, the endeavor to excite a national jealousy against the idea of amending the Constitution, is in my view infinitely more dangerous and alarming than even the attempt to marshal States against States. The gentleman from Connecticut (Mr. Tracy) has twice pronounced with great emphasis, "man is man," and attempted to make inferences against all attempts to amend our Constitution from the evil moral qualities with which human nature is afflicted! Sir, he has forgotten that Governments as well as nations are constituted of men, and that if the vices of governed man ought to alarm us for the safety of liberty, the vices of governing man are not calculated to assuage our apprehensions. Sir, it is this latter species of depravity which has suggested to the people of America a new idea, enforced by constitutions. Permit me to illustrate this new idea by the terms political law and municipal law. The former is that law, called Constitutional, contrived and enacted in the United States, to control those evil moral qualities to which the creature "man" is liable when invested with power. The latter is that law enacted to control the vices of man in his private capacity. If the former species of law should be suffered to remain unchanged, the effects would be the same as if the latter should remain unchanged. But, unaltered, would be evaded by the ingenuity, avarice, and ambition of public man, as well as private man. And, therefore, it is as necessary for the preservation of liberty, that constitutions or political law should be amended from time to time, in order to preserve liberty against the avarice and ambition of men in power, by meeting and controlling their artifices, as it is occasionally to amend municipal law, for the preservation of property against the vicious practices of men not in power.

Thomas Jefferson's "No Third Term" Letter (1807)

Thomas Jefferson did not attend the Constitutional Convention of 1787. Like John Adams, who was the U.S. minister to Great Britain, Jefferson was representing his country abroad at the time, as the minister to France.

Although Jefferson admired both the delegates to the convention (an "assembly of demigods," he observed from Paris) and the plan of government that they produced, he objected strongly to the absence of a term limit on the president. "Their President seems like a bad edition of a Polish king," Jefferson lamented in a letter to Adams on November 13, 1787. "He may be reelected from 4. years to 4. years for life. . . . Once in office, and possessing the military force of the union, without either the aid or check of a council, he would not be easily dethroned, even if the people could be induced to withdraw their votes from him. I wish that at the end of the 4. years they had made him for ever ineligible a second time."

Jefferson, who was elected as president in 1800, managed to temper his objections to presidential reeligibility long enough to run for a second term in 1804. He was reelected easily, by a margin of 162 electoral votes to 14 electoral votes for the Federalist candidate, Charles Cotesworth Pinckney of South Carolina.

Still, Jefferson was not guided entirely, or even mainly, by expediency on the term issue. In 1807, six state legislatures petitioned him to run for a third term. Undoubtedly, Jefferson would have been reelected if he had allowed his name to go forward: the Federalists were growing steadily weaker, the president's hold on the Democratic-Republican party was strong, and his popularity, although not as great as in 1804, was more than sufficient to win a third term.

But two terms was Jefferson's limit. On December 10, 1807, in a letter to the legislature of Vermont, he stated his belief that no president should serve in office any longer than eight years. Echoing his two-decades-old letter to Adams, Jefferson wrote, "If some termination to the services of the Chief Magistrate be not fixed by the Constitution, or supplied by practice, his office, nominally four years, will in fact become for life, and history shows how easily that degenerates into an inheritance." To strengthen his argument for a two-term tradition, Jefferson even invoked "the sound precedent set by an illustrious predecessor," George Washington. In truth, Washington had retired more for personal reasons than reasons of state. (See "George Washington's Farewell Address," p. 62.)

Jefferson's withdrawal from the presidency was not a withdrawal from presidential politics. He prevailed upon the Democratic-Republican cau-

cus in Congress to nominate his long-time political ally and current secretary of state, James Madison, for president in 1808. Madison easily defeated Pinckney, by 122 electoral votes to 47 electoral votes. His election signified both that the Democratic-Republicans were the nation's majority party and that a new steppingstone to the presidency had replaced the vice presidency. (See "The Twelfth Amendment: Senate Debate," p. 89.) *From 1800 to 1824, every person who was elected president was a current or former secretary of state.*

Jefferson's longstanding desire to impose a limit on presidential reeligibility opposed the intention of the Constitution's framers. (See "The Constitutional Convention: Debates on Presidential Selection," p. 1, and *"The Federalist Papers:* Nos. 68, 71, 72," p. 50.) *Yet he won his argument in the court of history. For a time, a one-term tradition actually prevailed in the presidency.* (See "Campaign Speech by William Henry Harrison," p. 167.) *As for a third term, no president even was nominated for one until 1940, when Franklin D. Roosevelt ran and was elected.* (See "Alben W. Barkley's 'Third Term' Speech to the Democratic National Convention," p. 358.) *Far from shattering the Jeffersonian tradition, Roosevelt's successful reelections in 1940 and 1944 triggered such a political backlash that a two-term limit was added to the Constitution in 1951.* (See "The Twenty-second Amendment: House Debate," p. 370.)   ~

To the Legislature of Vermont. [1]

Washington, December 10, 1807

I received in due season the *address* of the legislature of Vermont, bearing date the 5th of November, 1806, in which, with their approbation of the general course of my administration, they were so good as to express their desire that I would consent to be proposed again, to the public voice, on the expiration of my present term of office. Entertaining, as I do, for the legislature of Vermont those sentiments of high respect which would have prompted an immediate answer, I was certain, nevertheless, they would approve a delay which had for its object to avoid a premature agitation of the public mind, on a subject so interesting as the election of a chief magistrate.

That I should lay down my charge at a proper period, is as much a duty as to have borne it faithfully. If some termination to the services of the chief magistrate be not fixed by the Constitution, or supplied by practice, his office, nominally for years, will, in fact, become for life; and history shows how easily that degenerates into an inheritance. Believing that a representative government, responsible at short periods of election, is that which produces the greatest sum of happiness to mankind, I feel it a duty to do no act which shall essentially impair that principle; and I should unwillingly be the person who, disregarding the sound precedent set by an illustrious predecessor, should furnish the first example of prolongation beyond the second term of office.

Truth, also, requires me to add, that I am sensible of that decline which advancing years bring on; and feeling their physical, I ought not to doubt their mental effect. Happy if I am the first to perceive and to obey this admonition of nature, and to solicit a retreat from cares too great for the wearied faculties of age.

For the approbation which the legislature of Vermont has been pleased to express of the principles and measures pursued in the management of their affairs, I am sincerely thankful; and should I be so fortunate as to carry into retirement the equal approbation and good will of my fellow citizens generally, it will be the comfort of my future days, and will close a service of forty years with the only reward it ever wished.

Report of the Hartford Convention (1815)

Competition between the political parties was fierce during the early years of the Republic. As the historian Lynn W. Turner has written, "Parties in power, in those days, assumed that they alone had the right to rule and equated opposition almost with treason, while parties out of power did not scruple to demand fundamental changes in the form of government or even a dissolution of the Union in order to recover their position."

From 1789 to 1801, the party in power was the Federalist party. Part of Alexander Hamilton's political genius was that he was able to transfer the Federalist label—that is, the label worn by those who had fought to ratify the Constitution—to the Federalist party, which supported a strong national government, executive power, and an alliance with Great Britain. In contrast, James Madison, whose interpretation of the Constitution inclined toward states' rights and legislative supremacy and who favored France in international affairs, joined the Democratic-Republican party, which Thomas Jefferson led.

The fortunes of the Federalist party began to decline at the beginning of the nineteenth century. Jefferson was elected as president in 1800 and 1804. Madison succeeded him in 1808. The election of 1812 was fairly close—Madison was reelected by a margin of 128

electoral votes to 89 electoral votes—but only because the Federalists decided not to nominate a candidate of their own and instead endorsed the independent Democratic-Republican candidacy of Lt. Gov. DeWitt Clinton of New York, the nephew of Vice President George Clinton.

What explains the Federalists' decline? More than anything else, the Federalist party failed because the Democratic-Republican party succeeded. Starting with the Jefferson administration, the Democratic-Republicans increasingly became the party of nationalism and executive leadership, stealing the Federalist party's thunder. The Federalists, in contrast, glumly retreated to their New England base and issued sullen complaints about national and presidential power. "Our two great parties have crossed over the valley and taken possession of each other's mountain," former president John Adams, a Federalist, observed ruefully in 1813.

Although the sources of the Federalist party's decline were external, its outright demise was self-inflicted. The Federalists bitterly opposed the entry of the United States into the War of 1812 against Great Britain. Federalist governors in New England contested federal calls on their state militia, resisted federal tax measures, boycotted federal loans, and tacitly encouraged *illegal trading with British Canada. Matters came to a head in October 1814, when the Massachusetts state legislature summoned a convention of the New England states to discuss their common grievances against the national government.*

The Hartford Convention convened in the capital city of Connecticut on December 15, 1815, and deliberated secretly for three weeks. The convention stopped short of calling upon the New England states to secede from the Union, but not by much. It passed a series of resolutions for constitutional amendments, including a two-thirds requirement for Congress to declare war or to admit new states, a bar on trade embargoes of more than sixty days, and a prohibition on the election of two consecutive presidents from the same state (read: Virginia). If these resolutions were ignored, the Hartford Convention concluded, another convention should be called and given "such powers and instructions as the exigency of the crisis may require."

Representatives from the Hartford Convention carried its resolutions to Washington. Their arrival could not have been more poorly timed. The capital was rejoicing over Gen. Andrew Jackson's victory in the Battle of New Orleans and the signing of the Treaty of Ghent, which ended the war with Great Britain. In this mood of nationalist triumph, the Federalist party and the resolutions that its supporters had adopted in Hartford were dismissed as disloyal, selfish, and provincial.

The death of the Federalist party, although certain, was slow. Against Secretary of State James Monroe, the Democratic-Republican nominee for president in 1816, the Federalists won 34 electoral votes, which they gave to Sen. Rufus King of New York. (Monroe won 183 electoral votes.) In 1820, Monroe ran unopposed and was reelected by a 231-1 margin in the electoral college. ～

The delegates from the legislatures of the states of Massachusetts, Connecticut, and Rhode-Island, and from the counties of Grafton and Cheshire in the state of New-Hampshire and the county of Windham in the state of Vermont, assembled in convention, beg leave to report the following result of their conference.

The convention is deeply impressed with a sense of the arduous nature of the commission which they were appointed to execute, of devising the means of defence against dangers, and of relief from oppressions proceeding from the acts of their own government, without violating constitutional principles, or disappointing the hopes of a suffering and injured people. To prescribe patience and firmness to those who are already exhausted by distress, is sometimes to drive them to despair, and the progress towards reform by the regular road, is irksome to those whose imaginations discern, and whose feelings prompt, to a shorter course. But when abuses, reduced to a system, and accumulated through a course of years, have pervaded every department of government, and spread corruption through every region of the state; when these are clothed with the forms of law, and enforced by an executive whose will is their source, no summary means of relief can be applied without recourse to direct and open resistance. This experiment, even when justifiable, cannot fail to be painful to the good citizen; and the success of the effort will be no security against the danger of the example. Precedents of resistance to the worst administration, are eagerly seized by those who are naturally hostile to the best. Necessity alone can sanction a resort to this measure; and it should never be extended in duration or degree beyond the exigency, until the people, not merely in the fervour of sudden excitement, but after full deliberation, are determined to change the constitution.

It is a truth, not to be concealed, that a sentiment prevails to no inconsiderable extent, that administration have given such constructions to that instrument, and practised so many abuses under colour of its authority, that the time for a change is at hand. Those who so believe, regard the evils which surround them as intrinsic and incurable defects in the constitution. They yield to a persuasion, that no change, at any time, or on any occasion, can aggravate the misery of their country. This opinion may ultimately prove to be correct. But as the evidence on which it rests is not yet conclusive, and as measures adopted upon the assumption of its certainty might be irrevocable, some general considerations are submitted, in the hope of reconciling all the course of moderation and firmness, which may save them from the regret incident to sudden decisions, probably avert the evil, or at least insure consolation and success in the last resort.

The constitution of the United States, under the auspices of a wise and virtuous administration, proved itself competent to all the objects of national prosperity comprehended in the views of its framers. No parallel can be found in history, of a transition so rapid as that of the United States from the lowest depression to the highest felicity— from the condition of weak and disjointed republics, to that of a great, united, and prosperous nation.

Although this high state of public happiness has undergone a miserable and afflicting reverse, through the prevalence of a weak and profligate policy, yet the evils and afflictions which have thus been induced upon the country, are not peculiar to any form of government. The lust and caprice of power, the corruption of patronage, the oppression of the weaker interests of the community by the stronger, heavy taxes, wasteful expenditures, and unjust and ruinous wars, are the natural offspring of bad administrations, in all ages and countries. It was indeed to be hoped, that the rulers of these states would not make such disastrous haste to involve their infancy in the embarrassments of old and rotten institutions. Yet all this have they done; and their conduct calls loudly for their dismission and disgrace. But to attempt upon every abuse of power to change the constitution, would be to perpetuate the evils of revolution.

Again, the experiment of the powers of the constitution to regain its vigour, and of the people to recover from their delusions, has been hitherto made under the greatest possible disadvantages arising from the state of the world. The fierce passions which have convulsed the nations of Europe, have passed the ocean, and finding their way to the bosoms of our citizens, have afforded to administration the means of perverting public opinion, in respect to our foreign relations, so as to acquire its aid in the indulgence of their animosities, and the increase of their adherents. Further, a reformation of public opinion, resulting from dear-bought experience, in the southern Atlantic states, at least, is not to be despaired of. They will have felt, that the eastern states cannot be made exclusively the victims of a capricious and impassioned policy. They will have seen that the great and essential interests of the people are common to the south and to the east. They will realize the fatal errors of a system which seeks revenge for commercial injuries in the sacrifice of commerce, and aggravates by needless wars, to an immeasurable extent, the injuries it professes to redress. They may discard the influence of visionary theorists, and recognize the benefits of a practical policy. Indications of this desirable revolution of opinion, among our brethren in those states are already manifested. While a hope remains of its ultimate completion, its progress should not be retarded or stopped, by exciting fears which must check these favourable tendencies, and frustrate the efforts of the wisest and best men in those states, to accelerate this propitious change.

Finally, if the Union be destined to dissolution, by reason of the multiplied abuses of bad administrations, it should, if possible, be the work of peaceable times, and deliberate consent. Some new forms of confederacy should be substituted among those states which shall intend to maintain a federal relation to each other. Events may prove that the causes of our calamities are deep and permanent. They may be found to proceed, not merely from the blindness of prejudice, pride of opinion, violence of party spirit, or the confusion of the times; but they may be traced to implacable combinations of individuals, or of states, to monopolize power and office, and to trample without remorse upon the rights and interests of commercial sections of the Union. Whenever it shall appear that these causes are radical and permanent, a separation, by equitable arrangement, will be preferable to an alliance by constraint, among nominal friends, but real enemies, inflamed by mutual hatred and jealousy, and inviting, by intestine divisions, contempt and aggression from abroad. But a severance of the Union by one or more states, against the will of the rest, and especially in a time of war, can be justified only by absolute necessity. These are among the principal objections against precipitate measures tending to disunite the states, and when examined in connection with the farewell address of the Father of his country, they must, it is believed, be deemed conclusive.

Under these impressions, the convention have proceeded to confer and deliberate upon the alarming state of public affairs, especially as affecting the interests of the people who have appointed them for this purpose, and they are naturally led to a consideration, in the first place, of the dangers and grievances which menace an immediate or speedy pressure, with a view of suggesting means of present relief; in the next place, of such as are of a more remote and general description, in the hope of attaining future security.

Among the subjects of complaint and apprehension, which might be comprised under the former of these propositions, the attention of the convention has been occupied with the claims and pretensions advanced, and the authority exercised over the militia, by the executive and legislative departments of the national government. Also, upon the destitution of the means of defense in which the eastern states are left; while at the same time they are doomed to heavy requisitions of men and money for national objects.

The authority of the national government over the militia is derived from those clauses in the constitution which give power to Congress "to provide for calling forth the militia to execute the laws of the Union, suppress insurrections and repel invasions;"—Also "to provide for organizing, arming, and disciplining the militia, and for governing such parts of them as may be employed in the service of the United States, reserving to the states respectively the appointment of the officers, and the authority of training the militia according to the discipline prescribed by Congress." Again, "the President shall be commander in chief of the army and navy of the United States, and of the militia of the several states, *when called into the actual service of the United States.*" In these specified cases only, has the national government any power over the militia; and it follows conclusively, that for all general and ordinary purposes, this power belongs to the states respectively, and to them alone. It is not only with regret, but with astonishment, the convention perceive that under colour of an authority conferred with such plain and precise limitations, a power is arrogated by the executive government, and in some instances sanctioned by the two houses of congress, of control over the militia, which if conceded will render nugatory the rightful authority of the individual states over that class of men, and by placing at the disposal of the national government the lives and services of the great body of the people, enable it at pleasure to destroy their liberties, and erect a military despotism on the ruins.

An elaborate examination of the principles assumed for the basis of these extravagant pretensions, of the consequences to which they lead, and of the insurmountable objections to their admission, would transcend the limits of this report. A few general observations, with an exhibition of the character of these pretensions, and a recommendation of a strenuous opposition to them, must not, however, be omitted.

It will not be contended that by the terms used in the constitutional compact, the power of the national government to call out the militia is other than a power expressly limited to three cases. One of these must exist, as a condition precedent to the exercise of that power—Unless the laws shall be opposed, or an insurrection shall exist, or an invasion shall be made, congress, and of consequence the President as their organ, has no more power over the militia than over the armies of a foreign nation.

But if the declaration of the President should be admitted to be an unerring test of the existence of these cases, this important power would depend, not upon the truth of the fact, but upon executive infallibility. And the limitation of the power would consequently be nothing more than merely nominal, as it might always be eluded. It follows therefore that the decision of the President in this particular cannot be conclusive. It is as much the duty of the state authorities to watch over the rights *reserved*, as of the United States to exercise the powers which are *delegated*.

The arrangement of the United States into military districts, with a small portion of the regular force, under an officer of high rank of the standing army, with power to call for the militia, as circumstances in his judgment may require; and to assume the command of them, is not warranted by the constitution or any law of the United States. It is not denied that Congress may delegate to the President of the United States the power to call forth the militia in the cases which are within their jurisdiction—But he has no authority to substitute military prefects throughout the Union, to use their own discretion in such instances. To station an officer of the army in a military district without troops corresponding to his rank, for the purpose of taking command of the militia that may be called into service, is a manifest evasion of that provision of the constitution which expressly reserves to the states the appointment of the officers of the militia; and the object of detaching such officer cannot be well concluded to be any other than that of superseding the governor or other officers of the militia in their right to command.

The power of dividing the militia of the states into classes, and obliging such classes to furnish by contract or draft, able-bodied men, to serve for one or more years for the defence of the frontier, is not delegated to Congress. If a claim to draft the militia for one year for such general object be admissible, no limitation can be assigned to it, but the discretion of those who make the law. Thus, with a power in Congress to authorize such a draft of conscription, and in the Executive to decide conclusively upon the existence and continuance of the emergency, the whole militia may be converted into a standing army disposable at the will of the President of the United States.

The power of compelling the militia, and other citizens of the United States, by a forcible draft or conscription, to serve in the regular armies as proposed in a late official letter of the Secretary of War, is not delegated to Congress by the constitution, and the exercise of it would be not less dangerous to their liberties, than hostile to the sovereignty of the states. The effort to deduce this power from the right of raising armies, is a flagrant attempt to pervert the sense of the clause in the constitution which confers that right, and is incompatible with other provisions in that instrument. The armies of the United States have always been raised by contract, never by conscription, and nothing more can be wanting to a government possessing the power thus claimed to enable it to usurp the entire control of the militia, in derogation of the authority of the state, and to convert it by impressment into a standing army.

It may be here remarked, as a circumstance illustrative of the determination of the Executive to establish an absolute control over all descriptions of citizens, that the rights of impressing seamen into the naval service is expressly asserted by the Secretary of the Navy in a late report. Thus a practice, which in a foreign government has been regarded with great abhorrence by the people, finds advocates among those who have been the loudest to condemn it.

The law authorising the enlistment of minors and apprentices into the armies of the United States, without the consent of parents and guardians, is also repugnant to the spirit of the constitution. By a construction of the power to raise armies, as applied by our present rulers, not only persons capable of contracting are liable to be impressed into the army, but those who are under legal disabilities to make contracts, are to be invested with the capacity, in order to enable them to annul at pleasure contracts made in their behalf by legal guardians. Such an interference with the municipal laws and rights of the several states, could never have been contemplated by the framers of the constitution. It impairs the salutary control and influence of the parent over his child—the master over his servant— the guardian over his ward—and thus destroys the most important relations in society, so that by the conscription of the father, and the seduction of the son, the power of the Executive over all the effective male population of the United States is made complete.

Such are some of the odious features of the novel system proposed by the rulers of a free country, under the limited powers derived from the constitution. What portion of them will be embraced in acts finally to be passed, it is yet impossible to determine. It is, however, sufficiently alarming to perceive, that these projects emanate from the highest authority nor should it be forgotten, that by the plan of the Secretary of War, the classification of the militia embraced the principle of direct taxation upon the white population only; and that, in the house of representatives, a motion to apportion the militia among the white population exclusively, which would have been in its operation a direct tax, was strenuously urged and supported.

In this whole series of devices and measures for raising men, this convention discern a total disregard for the constitution, and a disposition to violate its provisions, demanding from the individual states a firm and decided opposition. An iron despotism can impose no harder servitude upon the citizen, than to force him from his home and his occupation, to wage offensive wars, undertaken to gratify the pride or passions of his master. The example of France has recently shown that a cabal of individuals assuming to act in the name of the people, may transform the great body of citizens into soldiers, and deliver them over into the hands of a single tyrant. No war, not held in just abhorrence by the people, can require the aid of such stratagems to recruit an army. Had the troops already raised, and in great numbers sacrificed upon the frontier of Canada, been employed for the defence of the country, and had the millions which have been squandered with shameless profusion, been appropriated to their payment, to the protection of the coast, and to the naval service, there would have been no occasion for unconstitutional expedients. Even at this late hour, let government leave to New-England the remnant of her resources, and she is ready and able to defend her territory, and to resign the glories and advantages of the border war to those who are determined to persist in its prosecution.

That acts of Congress in violation of the constitution are absolutely void, is an undeniable position. It does not, however, consist with the respect and forbearance due from a confederate state towards the general government, to fly to open resistance upon every infraction of the constitution. The mode and the energy of the opposition, should always conform to the nature of the violation, the intention of its authors, the extent of the injury inflicted, the determination manifested to persist in it, and the danger of delay. But in cases of deliberate, dangerous, and palpable infractions of the constitution, affecting the sovereignty of a state, and liberties of the people; it is not only the right but the duty of such a state to interpose its authority for their protection, in the manner best calculated to secure that end. When emergencies occur which are either beyond the reach of the judicial tribunals, or too pressing to admit of the delay incident to their forms, states which have no common umpire, must be their own judges, and execute their own decisions. It will thus be proper for the several states to await the ultimate disposal of the obnoxious measures recommended by the Secretary of War, or pending before Congress, and so to use their power according to the character these measures shall finally assume, as effectually to protect their own sovereignty, and the rights and liberties of their citizens.

The next subject which has occupied the attention of the convention, is the means of defence against the common enemy. This naturally leads to the inquiries, whether any expectation can be reasonably entertained, that adequate provision for the defence of the eastern states will be made by the national government? Whether the several states can, from their own resources, provide for self-defence and fulfill the requisitions which are to be expected for the national treasury? And, generally, what course of conduct ought to be adopted by those states, in relation to the great object of defence.

Without pausing at present to comment upon the causes of the war, it may be assumed as a truth, officially announced, that to achieve the conquest of Canadian territory, and to hold it as a pledge for peace, is the deliberate purpose of administration. This enterprize, commenced at a period when government possessed the advantage of selecting the time and occasion for making a sudden descent upon an unprepared enemy, now languishes in the third year of the war. It has been prosecuted with various fortune, and occasional brilliancy of exploit, but without any solid acquisition. The British armies have been recruited by veteran regiments. Their navy commands Ontario. The American ranks are thinned by the casualties of war. Recruits are discouraged by the unpopular character of the contest, and by the uncertainty of receiving their pay.

In the prosecution of this favourite warfare, administration have left the exposed and vulnerable parts of the country destitute of all the efficient means of defence. The main body of the regular army has been marched to the frontier. The navy had been stripped of a great part of its sailors for the service of the lakes. Meanwhile the enemy scours the sea-coast, blockades our ports, ascends our bays and rivers, makes actual descents in various and distant places, holds some by force, and threatens all that are assailable with fire and sword. The sea-board of four of the New-England states, following its curvatures, presents an extent of more than seven hundred miles, generally occupied by a compact population, and accessible by a naval force, exposing a mass of people and property to the devastation of the enemy, which bears a great proportion to the residue of the maritime frontier of the United States. This extensive shore has been exposed to frequent attacks, repeated contributions, and constant alarms. The regular forces detached by the national government for its defence are mere pretexts for placing officers of high rank in command. They are besides confined to a few places, and are too insignificant in number to be included in any computation.

These states have thus been left to adopt measures for their own defence. The militia have been constantly kept on the alert, and harassed by garrison duties, and other hardships, while the expenses, of which the national government decline the reimbursement, threaten to absorb all the resources of the states. The President of the United States has refused to consider the expanse of the militia detached by state authority, for the indispensable defence of the state, as chargeable to the Union, on the ground of a refusal by the Executive of the state to place them under the command of officers of the regular army. Detachments of militia placed at the disposal of the general government, have been dismissed either without pay, or with depreciated paper. The prospect of the ensuing campaign is not enlivened by the promise of any alleviation of these grievances. From authentic documents, extorted by necessity from those whose inclination might lead them to conceal the embarrassments of the government, it is apparent that the treasury is bankrupt, and its credit prostrate. So deplorable is the state of the finances, that those who feel for the honour and safety of the country, would be willing to conceal the melancholy spectacle, if those whose infatuation has produced this state of fiscal concerns had not found themselves compelled to unveil it to public view.

If the war be continued, there appears no room for reliance upon the national government for the supply of those means of defence which must become indispensable to secure these states from desolation and ruin. Nor is it possible that the states can discharge this sacred duty from their own resources, and continue to sustain the burden of the national taxes. The administration, after a long perseverance in plans to baffle every effort of commercial enterprize, had fatally succeeded in their attempts at the epoch of the war. Commerce, the vital spring of New-England's prosperity, was annihilated. Embargoes, restrictions, and the rapacity of revenue officers, had completed its destruction. The various objects for the employment of productive labour, in the branches of business dependent on commerce, have disappeared. The fisheries have shared its fate. Manufactures, which government has professed an intention to favour and to cherish, as an indemnity for the failure of these branches of business, are doomed to struggle in their infancy with taxes and obstructions, which cannot fail most seriously to affect their growth. The specie is withdrawn from circulation. The landed interest, the last to feel these burdens, must prepare to become their principal support, as all other sources of revenue must be exhausted. Under these circumstances, taxes, of a description and amount unprecedented in this country, are in a train of imposition, the burden of which must fall with the heaviest pressure upon the states east of the Potomac. *The amount of these taxes for the ensuing year cannot be estimated at less than five millions of dollars upon*

*the New-England states, and the ex-
penses of the last year for defence, in
Massachusetts alone, approaches to
one million of dollars.*

From these facts, it is almost superfluous to state the irresistible inference
that these states have no capacity of
defraying the expense requisite for their
own protection, and, at the same time,
of discharging the demands of the national treasury.

The last inquiry, what course of conduct ought to be adopted by the aggrieved states, is in a high degree momentous. When a great and brave
people shall feel themselves deserted by
their government, and reduced to the
necessity either of submission to a foreign enemy, or of appropriating to their
own use those means of defence which
are indispensable to self-preservation,
they cannot consent to wait passive
spectators of approaching ruin, which it
is in their power to avert, and to resign
the last remnant of their industrious
earnings to be dissipated in support of
measures destructive of the best interests of the nation.

This convention will not trust themselves to express their conviction of the
catastrophe to which such a state of
things inevitably tends. Conscious of
their high responsibility to God and
their country, solicitous for the continuance of the Union, as well as the sovereignty of the states, unwilling to furnish
obstacles to peace—resolute never to
submit to a foreign enemy, and confid-
ing in the Divine care and protection,
they will, until the last hope shall be
extinguished, endeavor to avert such
consequences.

With this view they suggest an arrangement, which may at once be consistent with the honour and interest of
the national government, and the security of these states. This it will not be
difficult to conclude, if that government
should be so disposed. By the terms of
it these states might be allowed to assume their own defence, by the militia

or other troops. A reasonable portion,
also, of the taxes raised in each state
might be paid into its treasury, and
credited to the United States, but to be
appropriated to the defence of such
state, to be accounted for with the
United States. No doubt is entertained
that by such an arrangement, this portion of the country could be defended
with greater effect, and in a mode more
consistent with economy, and the public
convenience, than any which has been
practised.

Should an application for these purposes, made to Congress by the state
legislatures, be attended with success,
and should peace upon just terms appear to be unattainable, the people
would stand together for the common
defence, until a change of administration, or of disposition in the enemy,
should facilitate the occurrence of that
auspicious event. It would be inexpedient for this Convention to diminish the
hope of a successful issue to such an
application, by recommending, upon
supposition of a contrary event, ulterior
proceedings. Nor is it indeed within
their province. In a state of things so
solemn and trying as may then arise,
the legislatures of the states, or conventions of the whole people, or delegates
appointed by them for the express purpose in another Convention, must act as
such urgent circumstances may then
require.

But the duty incumbent on this Convention will not have been performed,
without exhibiting some general view of
such measures as they deem essential to
secure the nation against a relapse into
difficulties and dangers, should they, by
the blessing of Providence, escape from
their present condition, without absolute ruin. To this end a concise retrospect of the state of this nation under
the advantages of a wise administration,
contrasted with the miserable abyss
into which it is plunged by the profli-
gacy and folly of political theorists, will
lead to some practical conclusions. On

this subject, it will be recollected, that the immediate influence of the Federal Constitution upon its first adoption, and for twelve succeeding years, upon the prosperity and happiness of the nation, seemed to countenance a belief in the transcendency of its perfection over all human institutions. In the catalogue of blessings which have fallen to the lot of the most favoured nations, none could be enumerated from which our country was excluded—a free Constitution, administered by great and incorruptible statesmen, realized the fondest hopes of liberty and independence—The progress of agriculture was stimulated by the certainty of value in the harvest—and commerce, after traversing every sea, returned with the riches of every clime. A revenue, secured by a sense of honour, collected without oppression, and paid without murmurs, melted away the national debt; and the chief concern of the public creditor arose from its too rapid diminution. The wars and commotions of the European nations, and their interruptions of the commercial intercourse afforded to those who had not promoted, but who would have rejoiced to alleviate their calamities, a fair and golden opportunity, by combining themselves to lay a broad foundation for national wealth. Although occasional vexations to commerce arose from the furious collisions of the powers at war, yet the great and good men of that time conformed to the force of circumstances which they could not control, and preserved their country in security from the tempests which overwhelmed the old world, and threw the wreck of their fortunes on these shores. Respect abroad, prosperity at home, wise laws made by honored legislators, and prompt obedience yielded by a contented people, had silenced the enemies of republican institutions. The arts flourished—the sciences were cultivated—the comforts and conveniences of life were universally dif-

fused—and nothing remained for succeeding administrations but to reap the advantages and cherish the resources flowing from the policy of their predecessors.

But no sooner was a new administration established in the hands of the party opposed to the Washington policy, than a fixed determination was perceived and avowed of changing a system which had already produced these substantial fruits. The consequences of this change, for a few years after its commencement, were not sufficient to counteract the prodigious impulse towards prosperity, which had been given to the nation. But a steady perseverance in the new plans of administration, at length developed their weakness and deformity, but not until a majority of the people had been deceived by flattery, and inflamed by passion, into blindness to their defects. Under the withering influence of this new system, the declension of the nation has been uniform and rapid. The richest advantages for securing the great objects of the constitution have been wantonly rejected. While Europe reposes from the convulsions that had shaken down her ancient institutions, she beholds with amazement this remote country, once so happy and so envied, involved in a ruinous war, and excluded from intercourse with the rest of the world.

To investigate and explain the means whereby this fatal reverse has been effected, would require a voluminous discussion. Nothing more can be attempted in this report than a general allusion to the principal outlines of the policy which has produced this vicissitude. Among these may be enumerated—

First.—A deliberate and extensive system for effecting a combination among certain states, by exciting local jealousies and ambition, so as to secure to popular leaders in one section of the Union, the control of public affairs in perpetual succession. To which primary object most other characteristics of the system may be reconciled.

Secondly.—The political intolerance displayed and avowed in excluding from office men of unexceptionable merit, for want of adherence to the executive creed.

Thirdly.—The infraction of the judiciary authority and rights, by depriving judges of their offices in violation of the constitution.

Fourthly.—The abolition of existing taxes, requisite to prepare the country for those changes to which nations are always exposed, with a view to the acquisition of popular favour.

Fifthly.—The influence of patronage in the distribution of offices, which in these states has been almost invariably made among men the least entitled to such distinction, and who have sold themselves as ready instruments for distracting public opinion, and encouraging administration to hold in contempt the wishes and remonstrances of a people thus apparently divided.

Sixthly.—The admission of new states into the Union formed at pleasure in the western region, has destroyed the balance of power which existed among the original States, and deeply affected their interest.

Seventhly.—The easy admission of naturalized foreigners, to places of trust, honour or profit, operating as an inducement to the malcontent subjects of the old world to come to these States, in quest of executive patronage, and to replay it by an abject devotion to executive means.

Eighthly.—Hostility to Great Britain, and partiality to the late government of France, adopted as coincident with popular prejudice, and subservient to the main object, party power. Connected with these must be ranked erroneous and distorted estimates of the power and resources of those nations, of the probable results of their controversies, and of our political relations to them respectively.

Lastly and principally.—A visionary and superficial theory in regard to commerce, accompanied by a real hatred but a feigned regard to its interests, and a ruinous perseverance in efforts to render it an instrument of coercion and war.

But it is not conceivable that the obliquity of any administration could, in so short a period, have so nearly consummated the work of national ruin, unless favoured by defects in the constitution.

To enumerate all the improvements of which that instrument is susceptible, and to propose such amendments as might render it in all respects perfect, would be a task which this convention has not thought proper to assume. They have confined their attention to such as experience has demonstrated to be essential, and even among these, some are considered entitled to a more serious attention than others. They are suggested without any intentional disrespect to other states, and are meant to be such as all shall find an interest in promoting. Their object is to strengthen, and if possible to perpetuate, the union of the states, by removing the grounds of existing jealousies, and providing for a fair and equal representation, and a limitation of powers, which have been misused.

The first amendment proposed, relates to the apportionment of representatives among the slave holding states. This cannot be claimed as a right. Those states are entitled to the slave representation, by a constitutional compact. It is therefore merely a subject of agreement, which should be conducted upon principles of mutual interest and accommodation, and upon which no sensibility on either side should be permitted to exist. It has proved unjust and unequal in its operation. Had this effect been foreseen, the privilege would probably not have been demanded; certainly not conceded. Its tendency in future will be adverse to that harmony and mutual confidence which are more conducive to the happiness and prosperity of every confederated state, than a mere preponderance of power, the prolific source of jealousies and controversy, can be to any one of them. The time may therefore arrive, when a sense of magnanimity and justice will reconcile those states to acquiesce in a revision of this article, especially as a fair equivalent would result to them in the apportionment of taxes.

The next amendment relates to the admission of new states into the Union.

This amendment is deemed to be highly important, and in fact indispensable. In proposing it, it is not intended to recognize the right of Congress to admit new states without the original limits of the United States, nor is any idea entertained of disturbing the tranquillity of any state already admitted into the Union. The object is merely to restrain the constitutional power of Congress in admitting new states. At the adoption of the constitution, a certain balance of power among the original parties was considered to exist, and there was at that time, and yet is among those parties, a strong affinity between their great and general interests.—By the admission of these states that balance has been materially affected, and unless the practice be modified, must ultimately be destroyed. The southern states will first avail themselves of their new confederates to govern the east, and finally the western states, multiplied in number, and augmented in population, will control the interests of the whole. Thus for the sake of present power, the southern states will be common sufferers with the east, in the loss of permanent advantages. None of the old states can find an interest in creating prematurely an overwhelming western influence, which may hereafter discern (as it has heretofore) benefits to be derived to them by wars and commercial restrictions.

The next amendments proposed by the convention, relate to the powers of Congress, in relation to embargo and the interdiction of commerce.

Whatever theories upon the subject of commerce have hitherto divided the opinions of statesmen, experience has at last shown that it is a vital interest in the United States, and that its success is essential to the encouragement of agriculture and manufactures, and to the wealth, finances, defence, and liberty of the nation. Its welfare can never interfere with the other great interests of the state, but must promote and uphold them. Still those who are immediately concerned in the prosecution of commerce, will of necessity be always a minority of the nation. They are, however, best qualified to manage and direct its course by the advantages of experience, and the sense of interest. But they are entirely unable to protect themselves against the sudden and injudicious decisions of bare majorities, and the mistaken or oppressive projects of those who are not actively concerned in its pursuits. Of consequence, this interest is always exposed to be harassed, interrupted, and entirely destroyed, upon pretence of securing other interests. Had the merchants of this nation been permitted by their own government to pursue an innocent and lawful commerce, how different would have been the state of the treasury and of public credit! How short-sighted and miserable is the policy which has annihilated this order of men, and doomed their ships to rot in the docks, their capital to waste unemployed, and their affections to be alienated from the government which was formed to protect them! What security for an ample and unfailing revenue can ever be had, comparable to that which once was realized in the good faith, punctuality, and sense of honour, which attached the mercantile class to the interests of government! Without commerce, where can be found the aliment for a navy; and without a navy, what is to constitute the defence, and ornament, and glory of this nation!

No union can be durably cemented, in which every great interest does not find itself reasonably secured against the encroachment and combinations of other interests. When, therefore, the past system of embargoes and commercial restrictions shall have been reviewed— when the fluctuation and inconsistency of public measures, betraying a want of information as well as feeling in the majority, shall have been considered, the reasonableness of some restrictions upon the power of a bare majority to repeat these oppressions, will appear to be obvious.

The next amendment proposes to restrict the power of making offensive war. In the consideration of this amendment, it is not necessary to inquire into the justice of the present war. But one sentiment now exists in relation to its expediency, and regret for its declaration is nearly universal. No indemnity can ever be attained for this terrible calamity, and its only palliation must be found in obstacles to its future recurrence. Rarely can the state of this country call for or justify offensive war. The genius of our institutions is unfavourable to its successful prosecution; the felicity of our situation exempts us from its necessity. In this case, as in the former, those more immediately exposed to its fatal effects are a minority of the nation. The commercial towns, the shores of our seas and rivers, contain the population whose vital interests are most vulnerable by a foreign enemy. Agriculture, indeed, must feel at last, but this appeal to its sensibility comes too late. Again, the immense population which has swarmed into the west, remote from immediate danger, and which is constantly augmenting, will not be averse from the occasional disturbances of Altantic states. Thus interest may not unfrequently combine with passion and intrigue, to plunge the nation into needless wars, and compel it to become a military, rather than a happy and flourishing people. These

considerations, which it would be easy to augment, call loudly for the limitation proposed in the amendment.

Another amendment, subordinate in importance, but still in a high degree expedient, relates to the exclusion of foreigners hereafter arriving in the United States from the capacity of holding offices of trust, honour, or profit.

That the stock of population already in these states is amply sufficient to render this nation in due time sufficiently great and powerful, is not a controvertible question. Nor will it be seriously pretended, that the national deficiency in wisdom, arts, science, arms, or virtue, needs to be replenished from foreign countries. Still, it is agreed, that a liberal policy should offer the rights of hospitality, and the choice of settlement, to those who are disposed to visit the country. But why admit to a participation in the government aliens who were no parties to the compact— who are ignorant of the nature of our institutions, and have no stake in the welfare of the country but what is recent and transitory? It is surely a privilege sufficient, to admit them after due probation to become citizens, for all but political purposes. To extend it beyond these limits, is to encourage foreigners to come to these states as candidates for preferment. The Convention forbear to express their opinion upon the inauspicious effects which have already resulted to the honour and peace of this nation, from this misplaced and indiscriminate liberality.

The last amendment respects the limitation of the office of President in a single constitutional term, and his eligibility from the same state two terms in succession.

Upon this topic it is superfluous to dilate. The love of power is a principle in the human heart which too often impels to the use of all practicable means to prolong its incentives to this passion. The first and most natural exertion of a vast patronage is directed towards the security of a new election. The interest of the country, the welfare of the people, even honest fame and respect for the opinion of posterity, are secondary considerations. All the engines of intrigue, all the means of corruption are likely to be employed for this object. A President whose political career is limited to a single election, may find no other interest than will be promoted by making it glorious to himself, and beneficial to his country. But the hope of re-election is prolific of temptations, under which these magnanimous motives are deprived of their principal force. The repeated election of the President of the United States from any one state, affords inducements and means for intrigues, which tend to create an undue local influence, and to establish the domination of particular states. The justice, therefore, of securing to every state a fair and equal chance for the election of this officer from its own citizens is apparent, and this object will be essentially promoted by preventing an election from the same state twice in succession.

Such is the general view which this Convention has thought proper to submit, of the situation of these states, of their dangers and their duties. Most of the subjects which it embraces have separately received an ample and luminous investigation, by the great and able assertors of the rights of their country, in the national legislature; and nothing more could be attempted on this occasion than a digest of general principles, and of recommendations suited to the present state of public affairs. The peculiar difficulty and delicacy of performing even this undertaking, will be appreciated by all who think seriously upon the crisis. Negotiations for peace are at this hour supposed to be pending, the issue of which must be deeply interesting to all. No measures should be adopted which might unfavourably affect that issue; none

which should embarrass the administration, if their professed desire for peace is sincere; and none which on supposition of their insincerity, should afford them pretexts for prolonging the war, or relieving themselves from the responsibility of a dishonourable peace. It is also devoutly to be wished, that an occasion may be afforded to all friends of the country, of all parties, and in all places, to pause and consider the awful state to which pernicious counsels and blind passions have brought this people. The number of those who perceive, and who are ready to retrace errors, must, it is believed, be yet sufficient to redeem the nation. It is necessary to rally and unite them by the assurance that no hostility to the constitution is meditated, and to obtain their aid in placing it under guardians who alone can save it from destruction. Should this fortunate change be effected, the hope of happiness and honour may once more dispel the surrounding gloom. Our nation may yet be great, our union durable. But should this prospect be utterly hopeless, the time will not have been lost which shall have ripened a general sentiment of the necessity of more mighty efforts to rescue from ruin, at least some portion of our beloved country.

Therefore Resolved,

That it be and hereby is recommended to the legislatures of the several states represented in this Convention, to adopt all such measures as may be necessary effectually to protect the citizens of said states from the operation and effects of all acts which have been or may be passed by the Congress of the United States, which shall contain provisions, subjecting the militia or other citizens to forcible drafts, conscriptions, or impressments, not authorised by the constitution of the United States.

Resolved, That it be and hereby is recommended to the said Legislatures, to authorize an immediate and earnest application to be made to the government of the United States, requesting their consent to some arrangement, whereby the said states may, separately or in concert, be empowered to assume upon themselves the defence of their territory against the enemy; and a reasonable portion of the taxes, collected within said States, may be paid into the respective treasuries thereof, and appropriated to the payment of the balance due said states, and to the future defence of the same. The amount so paid into the said treasuries to be credited, and the disbursements made as aforesaid to be charged to the United States.

Resolved, That it be, and hereby is, recommended to the legislatures of the aforesaid states, to pass laws (where it has not already been done) authorizing the governors or commanders-in-chief of their militia to make detachments from the same, or to form voluntary corps, as shall be most convenient and conformable to their constitutions, and to cause the same to be well armed, equipped, and disciplined, and held in readiness for service; and upon the request of the governor of either of the other states to employ the whole of such detachment or corps, as well as the regular forces of the state, or such part thereof as may be required and can be spared consistently with the safety of the state, in assisting the state, making such request to repel any invasion thereof which shall be made or attempted by the public enemy.

Resolved, That the following amendments of the constitution of the United States be recommended to the states represented as aforesaid, to be proposed by them for adoption by the state legislatures, and in such cases as may be deemed expedient by a convention chosen by the people of each state.

And it is further recommended, that the said states shall persevere in their efforts to obtain such amendments, until the same shall be effected.

First. Representatives and direct taxes shall be apportioned among the several states which may be included within this Union, according to their respective numbers of free persons, including those bound to serve for a term of years, and excluding Indians not taxed, and all other persons.

Second. No new state shall be admitted into the Union by Congress, in virtue of the power granted by the constitution, without the concurrence of two thirds of both houses.

Third. Congress shall not have power to lay any embargo on the ships or vessels of the citizens of the United States, in the ports or harbours thereof, for more than sixty days.

Fourth. Congress shall not have power, without the concurrence of two thirds of both houses, to interdict the commercial intercourse between the United States and any foreign nation, or the dependencies thereof.

Fifth. Congress shall not make or declare war, or authorize acts of hostility against any foreign nation, without the concurrence of two thirds of both houses, except such acts of hostility be in defence of the territories of the United States when actually invaded.

Sixth. No person who shall hereafter be naturalized, shall be eligible as a member of the senate or house of representatives of the United States, nor capable of holding any civil office under the authority of the United States.

Seventh. The same person shall not be elected president of the United States for a second time; nor shall the president be elected from the same state two terms in succession.

Resolved, That if the application of these states to the government of the United States, recommended in a foregoing resolution, should be unsuccessful, and peace should not be concluded, and the defence of these states should be neglected, as it has been since the commencement of the war, it will, in the opinion of this convention, be expedient for the legislatures of the several states to appoint delegates to another convention, to meet at Boston in the state of Massachusetts, on the third Thursday of June next, with such powers and instructions as the exigency of a crisis so momentous may require.

Resolved, That the Hon. George Cabot, the Hon. Chauncey Goodrich, and the Hon. Daniel Lyman, or any two of them, be authorized to call another meeting of this convention, to be holden in Boston, at any time before new delegates shall be chosen, as recommended in the above resolution, if, in their judgment the situation of the country shall urgently require it.

George Cabot,
Nathan Dane,
William Prescott,
Harrison Gray Otis, Massachusetts
Timothy Bigelow,
Joshua Thomas,

Samuel Summer Wilde,
Joseph Lyman,
Stephen Longfellow, Jun.
Daniel Waldo,
Hodijah Baylies,
George Bliss

Chauncey Goodrich,
John Treadwell,
James Hillhouse
Zephaniah Swift Connecticut
Nathaniel Smith,
Calvin Goddard
Roger Minot Sherman.

Daniel Lyman,
Samuel Ward,
Edward Manton, Rhode-Island
Benjamin Hazard.

Benjamin West,
Mills Olcott. N. Hampshire

William Hall, Jun. Vermont

Proceedings of the Congressional Caucus (1824)

In creating the electoral college, the Constitutional Convention explicitly rejected a proposal to have Congress elect the president. (See "The Constitutional Convention: Debates on Presidential Selection," p. 1.) *But when political parties formed during the 1790s, they faced the logistical problem of how to nominate candidates for president and vice president. In an era of difficult and time-consuming travel, the practical solution was to have each party's members in Congress, who already were in the capital, choose the nominees.*

The Federalist party was the first to hold a congressional caucus (it nominated John Adams for president and Thomas Pinckney for vice president in May 1796), but the Democratic-Republicans made better use of the innovation. Indeed, the Federalist party held its last caucus in 1800, the same year that the Democratic-Republican party held its first. Federalist leaders chose their candidates informally in 1804 and 1808, the last presidential elections that the party contested seriously.

*The highwater mark for the congressional caucus was 1804. Not only did all but a handful of the Democratic-Republican representatives and senators attend the February caucus, but, after nominating Thomas Jefferson for reelection as president and Gov. George Clinton of New York for vice president, the caucus appointed a thir-*teen-member committee to organize the party's national campaign.

Subsequent caucuses were less well-attended. Around 60 percent of the Democratic-Republican members of Congress participated in the 1808 caucus, less than 50 percent in 1812, 40 percent in 1816, and 30 percent in 1820. Members typically would boycott a caucus if they expected it to nominate a candidate whom they disliked.

Among the voters, the congressional caucus became increasingly unpopular as an institution. In 1820, meetings were held around the country to protest what came to be known as "King Caucus." The caucus was attacked for being undemocratic and for violating the intentions of the framers, who had wanted to discourage the very courting of favors in Congress by presidential candidates that, because of the caucus, was actually occurring.

King Caucus was dethroned in 1824. The Democratic-Republican party, by now the only national political party, was divided among the supporters of five presidential candidates: Secretary of State John Quincy Adams of Massachusetts, Secretary of the Treasury William H. Crawford of Georgia, Sen. Andrew Jackson of Tennessee, Secretary of War John C. Calhoun of South Carolina, and Speaker of the House Henry Clay of Kentucky. Crawford appeared to be the leading (but by no means the consensus) candidate among his party's membership in Congress.

In early February 1824, two statements were issued by groups within Congress, one a formal call to caucus, the other a refusal to attend. The latter was signed by 24 members, who claimed to speak for 181 of their colleagues. When the caucus met on February 14, only 66 of the 231 Democratic-Republican representatives and senators were present. They voted overwhelmingly to nominate Crawford.

The 1824 congressional caucus resolved nothing, except the fate of the caucus itself. Supporters of Adams, Jackson, Calhoun, and Clay attacked the caucus as an illegitimate institution and derided Crawford's nomination as politically meaningless. In response to the growing propensity of the states to select their presidential electors by popular vote (in only six of the twenty-four states did the legislature still choose electors), all five of the remaining candidates took their campaigns directly to the people. Never again did a congressional caucus meet for the purpose of nominating a presidential candidate. ～

Anti-Caucus Resolution

In consequence of the statements which have gone abroad, in relation to a Congressional nomination of Candidates for President and Vice President of the United States, the undersigned have been requested, by many of their Republican colleagues and associates, to ascertain the number of the Members of Congress who deem it inexpedient, at this time, to make such a nomination; and to publish the same, for the information of the People of the United States.

In compliance with this request, they have obtained from gentlemen, representing the several states, satisfactory information, that, of two hundred and sixty-one, the whole number of Members composing the present Congress, there are ONE HUNDRED AND EIGHTY-ONE who deem it inexpedient, under existing circumstances, to meet in Caucus for the purpose of nominating Candidates for President and Vice President of the United States; and they have good reason to believe, that a portion of the remainder will be found unwilling to attend such a meeting.

Richard M. Johnson, of	Kentucky.
Jno. H. Eaton,	Tennessee.
David Barton,	Missouri.
Wm. Kelly,	Alabama.
Robert Y. Hayne,	South Carolina.
Charles Rich,	Vermont.
T. Fuller,	Massachusetts.
J. Sloane,	Ohio.
Geo. Holcombe,	New Jersey.
S. D. Ingham,	Pennsylvania.
R. Harris,	Pennsylvania.
Joseph Kent,	Maryland.
D. H. Miller,	Pennsylvania.
Thomas Metcalfe,	Kentucky.
Robert S. Garnett,	Virginia.
James Hamilton, Jr.,	South Carolina.
J. C. Isacks,	Tennessee.
Geo. Kremer,	Pennsylvania.
B. W. Crowninshield,	Massachusetts.
Wm. Burleigh,	Maine.
L. Whitman,	Connecticut.
Jonathan Jennings,	Indiana.
Sam. Houston,	Tennessee.
J. R. Poinsett,	South Carolina.

Caucus Call

The DEMOCRATIC MEMBERS OF CONGRESS are invited to meet in the Representatives' Chamber, at the Capitol, on the evening of the 14th of February, at 7 o'clock, to recommend candidates to the People of the United States for the offices of President and Vice President of the United States.

John Chandler,	Burwell Basset,
Noyes Barber,	H. G. Burton,
Elisha Litchfield,	John Forsyth
M. Dickerson,	J. B. Thomas,

Walter Lowrie,   Benjamin Ruggles.
Edward Lloyd,
                Washington, February 6, 1824

Proceedings of the Caucus

Chamber of the House of
Representatives of the United States
February 14, 1824

At a meeting of Republican Members
of Congress, assembled this evening,
pursuant to public notice, for the purpose of recommending to the People of
the United States suitable persons to be
supported at the approaching election,
for the offices of President and Vice
President of the United States:

On motion of Mr. James Barbour, of
Virginia—

Mr. Benjamin Ruggles, a Senator
from the State of Ohio, was called to the
chair, and Mr. Ela Collins, a Representative from the State of New York, was
appointed secretary.

The Meeting being thus organized—

Mr. Markley, of Pennsylvania submitted the following Preamble and
Resolution:

Whereas, it is highly important to
the preservation, the maintenance, and
the ascendancy of the democracy of the
country, that a concentration should be
effected, in the selection of Candidates
for the Presidency and Vice Presidency
of the United States—and a deviation
from the old and approved mode of
nomination by the Republican members of Congress, which has heretofore
secured and elevated to the Chief
Magistracy of the nation, a Jefferson, a
Madison, and a Monroe, may be dangerous to the democracy and best interest of the American people: And
the interest and prosperity of the country, in order to avoid sectional feelings
and jealousies, require every republican to make a sacrifice of personal

predilections, which alone can preserve
the permanency & stability of the
principles of democracy, & secure the
election in the hands of the people.
And whereas, a number of our republican brethren in Congress believe at
this time it is inexpedient to unite with
a large portion of their democratic
brethren, to make a nomination; and
this meeting, feeling a deep interest in
the union and triumph of republican
principles, which alone can be obtained
by a spirit of harmony and co-operation, and by a regard to those ancient
land marks which have heretofore
guided the operations and movements
of the democratic party of the Union.
But, in order to afford further time to
those who doubt, at this time, the expediency of co-operating with their republican brethren who approve of a
Congressional Convention, to reflect on
the subject, and advise with their republican brethren throughout the
Union.

Be it resolved, That this meeting
adjourn, to meet again in the Chamber
of the House of Representatives, on
Saturday, the 20th day of March next,
at 7 o'clock in the evening, for the
purpose of putting in nomination and
recommending candidates to the People of the United States, for the offices
of President and Vice President, and
that the Democratic Republican members of the 18th Congress be, and they
are hereby, invited to attend said
meeting.

And the question being taken
thereon, it was determined in the negative.

Mr. Dickerson, of New Jersey, then
submitted the following resolution, to
wit:

Resolved, That this Meeting do now
proceed to designate, by ballot, a Candidate for President of the United
States. And the question being taken
thereon, it was determined in the affirmative.

On motion of Mr. Van Buren, of New York, it was

Resolved, That the Chairman call up the Republican Members of Congress by States, in order to receive their respective ballots.

*   *   *

Mr. Bassett, of Virginia, and Mr. Cambreling, of New York, were appointed Tellers, and on counting the ballots, it appeared that

William H. Crawford had sixty-four votes.

John Quincy Adams two votes.

Andrew Jackson one vote, and

Nathaniel Macon one vote.

Mr. Dickerson, of New Jersey, then submitted the following resolution, which was agreed to:

Resolved, That this meeting do now proceed to designate, by ballot, a candidate for the office of Vice President of the United States.

Mr. Van Buren, of New York, then stated that he was authorized to say that the Vice President having, some time since, determined to retire from public life, did not wish to be regarded by his friends as a candidate for re-election to that office.

On counting the ballots, it appeared that *Albert Gallatin,* of Pennsylvania, had fifty-seven votes; *John Q. Adams,* of Massachusetts, one vote; *Samuel Smith,* of Maryland, one vote; *William King,* of Maine, one vote; *Richard Bush,* of Pennsylvania, one vote; *Brastus Root,* of New York, two votes; *John Tod,* of Pennsylvania, one vote; and *Walter Lowrie,* of Pennsylvania, one vote.

And, thereupon, Mr. Clark, of New York, submitted the following resolutions, to wit:

Resolved, As the sense of this Meeting, that *William H. Crawford* of Geor-gia, be recommended to the People of the United States as a proper Candidate for the Office of President, and *Albert Gallatin,* of Pennsylvania, for the Office of Vice President, of the United States, for four years from the 4th of March, 1825.

Resolved, That, in making the foregoing recommendation, the Members of this Meeting have acted in their individual characters, as citizens; that they have been induced to this measure from a deep and settled conviction of the importance of Union among Republicans, throughout the United States, and, as the best means of collecting and concentrating the feelings and wishes of the People of the Union, upon this important subject.

The question being put on these resolutions, they were unanimously agreed to.

Mr. Holmes, of Maine, then moved that the proceedings of the meeting be signed by the Chairman and Secretary, and published, together with an Address to the People of the United States, to be prepared by a Committee to be appointed for that purpose.

On motion, it was ordered that this Committee consist of the Chairman and Secretary of the Convention, together with the gentlemen whose names were signed to the notice calling the Meeting.

On motion, it was further

Resolved, That the Chairman and Secretary inform the gentlemen nominated for the offices of President and Vice President, of their nomination, and learn from them whether they are willing to serve in the said offices, respectively.

Benjamin Ruggles,
Chairman.
E. Collins,
Secretary.

Address of the Caucus

To the Republicans of the United States:

Fellow Citizens: Pursuant to notice, and conformable to usage, the Republican Members of both Houses of Congress, whose names are stated to you, have proceeded to recommend suitable persons to fill the offices of President and Vice President of the United States, for the term ensuing the expiration of the present. Existing circumstances will justify, if they do not require, a brief exposition of the grounds of this proceeding. In its adoption, and submission to your consideration, we have acted as members of the republican party, pursuing the footsteps of those who have gone before us, from the important revolution in the politics of the country, resulting in the choice of Mr. Jefferson, to the period of the first election of the present Chief Magistrate. That this course has not been sanctioned by all our republican colleagues, is a subject for regret. Others, with whom we wished to associate and unite in measures of conciliation and concord, have, though respectfully invited, declined to co-operate with us. We have been ready and anxious, in a general meeting of all the Republican Members, to submit their preferences to the will of the majority. Those who differ with us in opinion have refused their concurrence. It is your right, and becomes your duty, to decide between us. We intend no impeachment of the conduct or motives of others. We speak for ourselves only, without affecting to conceal our expectation of obtaining your approval of the course of proceeding we have adopted. It is now twenty-four years since the great political revolution to which we have alluded was effected, and the power which was then acquired by republicans in the government of the Union is still retained. Their enjoyment of this ascendancy has not, however, been undisturbed; on the contrary, they have had an unwearied struggle to maintain with the same adversary over whom their triumph was achieved. It is not to be doubted that it was by union and concert of action that the strength of the republican party was consolidated, and its success in the decisive controversy *effected*. It is as little to be doubted, that it is by adherence to the same principle and policy of action that its unbroken force and continued ascendancy can be preserved. The reasons for adhering to this policy of efficiency and safety derive, in our judgment, peculiar force from the circumstances which characterize the existing period. The correctness of this opinion is demonstrated by a revision of the grounds which have been assigned for a deviation from that policy. Those grounds we understand to be, the supposed obliteration of party distinctions, the change of opinion on the subject, which is apprehended to have taken place in the Republican body, and the improbability that a general attendance of the Republican members could be obtained. In relation to the correctness of the first of these grounds, the supposed obliteration of party distinctions, your ability to decide can derive little aid from any observations of ours. That, in some parts of the Union, where the Federal party have always been weaker and less violent, the fact is, in some degree, as stated, and that, since the late war, their exertions have no where been as efficient as formerly, we admit. But that danger is not to be apprehended from this source, in connection with the pending divisions in the Republican party, and the angry dissentions they are likely to engender, we deny. That our adversaries have not lost their disposition to avail themselves of those divisions, to regain their ascendancy, is confirmed by a reference to the past, and ought not to be doubted. There is not an instance to be found in the history of the politics of the different states, for the last twenty years, in which serious and continued divisions among republicans have not led to a temporary success of their opponents. The same cause will produce a more extended effect on a larger scale of operations, and, we are persuaded, that all calculations, of a different result, will, in the end, deceive and disappoint those who shall be so indiscreet as to indulge them. As it respects the supposed change of sentiment among the Republicans of the Union, on the question of the fitness of conventions of this character, the proceedings of the last twelve months have strongly impressed our minds with a different conclusion. Heretofore conventions of the Republican Members of the Congress, for the nomination of candidates for President and Vice President, have been held upon the *presumed* approbation of their constituents *only*. The question now, however, stands upon a very different footing. Resolutions expressive of their dissent to meetings of this character have, during their last session, been passed by the Legislature of the state of Tennessee, and transmitted to the Executives of the other states, for the purpose of being laid before their Legislatures for concurrence. No mode could have been adopted better devised to ascertain the state of public sentiment. It is known that those resolutions have been acted upon by the Legislatures of Maine, New York, Virginia, Georgia, North Carolina, Rhode Island, Ohio, Pennsylvania and Indiana; which states are entitled to one hundred and forty-six out of the *two hundred and sixty-one votes* to be given in the United States. By the republican members of the Legislatures of the four states first named, and entitled to seventy-eight votes, resolutions have been passed, with great unanimity, approving, in the warmest terms, such a meeting as has been held. In the remaining states mentioned, the resolutions of Tennessee have been postponed, in some instances, indefinitely, and in others disposed of in a manner evincive of a determination not to act upon them. In no state, except Maryland, entitled to eleven votes, has there been an expression of concurrence, by the Legislature, in the views of the Legislature of Tennessee. In South Carolina, entitled to the same number of votes, one branch of the Legislature, in opposition to the opinion of the other, has expressed such concurrence. Nor have the members of the Legislature of any state, in their individual capacity, expressed similar views. From reference to these facts, we feel authorized in the belief that a large majority of the Republicans of the Union have desired and expected the adoption of the course which, under the influence of those impressions, we have felt it our duty to pursue. On the remaining subject of review, we have a word only to offer. The circumstance of the absence of so many Republicans from our meeting has already been stated as a subject for regret. It is neither our privilege nor disposition to exercise any right of judgment on their conduct. We have been uniform in the expression of our readiness to abide by the sentiment of a general convention of our Republican brethren, and to renounce our predilections in obedience to its reward. Various causes have combined to reduce the number of those who have attended. Several who were friendly to the candidates nominated, had objections, which they conceived to be founded in principle; other circumstances have co-operated. Without detaining you by an enumeration, we content ourselves with a reference to the striking fact, that although the states of New York, Virginia, and Maine have, with unusual unanimity, recommended to their Members, in express terms, to attend this meeting, only thirty-four persons have represented the sixty-nine votes to which they will be entitled in the election.

We will not attempt to conceal the anxiety with which we are impressed by the present conjuncture. To our minds, the course of recent events points to the entire dismemberment of the party to which it is our pride to be attached. The admission, unreservedly made, that, on the question of the expediency of a convention, the entire amalgamation of parties has been assumed in, of itself, sufficient ground of solicitude. Other considerations justify apprehensions of the same character. The injurious consequences likely to be produced by a departure, at this time, from the ancient usages of the party, will not be confined to the election of President and Vice President. Exertions are everywhere making to break up the entire system of conventions for the nomination of candidates, in reference to state as well as federal elections. It is submitted, then, whether an abandonment of the practice here will not involve the ultimate prostration of the system wherever it prevails, and with it the securities of the republican ascendancy. It is from an apprehension of such results, in the event of the abandonment of established principles, and of the usage of the party, that we have adopted the proceedings now submitted to your consideration. *The question is, in our best judgment, one touching the dismemberment or preservation of the party.* This question it is your province to decide. The office we have sought to discharge has been to place the subject before you for this decision. The limits allotted to this address will not permit us to dwell on the many and pressing considerations of a more general nature, urging to union among republicans, with a view to the decision of the approaching election of the first officers of the governments by the people, and the avoidance of the unalleviated mischiefs of an election by the House of Representatives. Among the most striking of these considerations is to be ranked the inevitable inefficiency, as it respects the measures, both of domestic and foreign character, of an Executive administration having to rely for its support on the co-operation of a Legislature distracted by angry and implacable divisions. Of the persons recommended to you as candidates it has not been usual to speak. No motive exists to depart from the established usage in this respect. Known to you by a long course of public life, by their uniform devotion to the best interests of the nation, in stations of the highest responsibility, in which their zeal, integrity, and capacity have been amply proved, we are satisfied that we have only anticipated your wishes by giving them our recommendation. Without intending to derogate from the merits of others, for whom your confidence may be solicited, it is just to remind you that the candidate we recommend for the first office in your government, has established a peculiar claim to the esteem of the republican party, by his manly and disinterested conduct upon a former occasion, under the strongest temptation to become the instrument of compromising its integrity.

Benjamin Ruggles,
Chairman.
E. Collins,
Secretary.

The House of Representatives Elects John Quincy Adams: Debate and Balloting (1825)

The outcome of the election of 1824 was in some ways utterly predictable: the president, having served two terms, did not run for reelection and was succeeded by the secretary of state, who was a leader of the Democratic-Republican party. The events that brought about this outcome, however, were as unusual as any in the history of presidential elections.

Five candidates, all of them Democratic-Republicans, decided to seek the presidency in 1824: Secretary of State John Quincy Adams of Massachusetts, Secretary of the Treasury William H. Crawford of Georgia, Sen. Andrew Jackson of Tennessee, Secretary of War John C. Calhoun of South Carolina, and House Speaker Henry Clay of Kentucky. Even though the much-maligned congressional caucus nominated Crawford for president in February 1824, all five candidates remained in the race. (See "Proceedings of the Congressional Caucus," p. 120.)

During the summer and fall, Secretary of State Adams, the son of the former president, and General Jackson (as he preferred to be known), the hero of the War of 1812's Battle of New Orleans, emerged from the pack as the leading candidates. Crawford and Clay were beset by rumors of bad health, which in Crawford's case were true. When Calhoun found himself to be the first choice of few but the second choice

of many, he withdrew from the race and made himself available as a vice presidential candidate.

The results of the presidential election were inconclusive. Jackson led with ninety-nine electoral votes, mostly from the South; Adams swept New England and New York to finish second with eighty-four electoral votes; and Crawford and Clay trailed with forty-one electoral votes and thirty-seven electoral votes, respectively. In contrast, Calhoun received an overwhelming majority of electoral votes for vice president and was elected to that office.

Since no candidate for president won a majority of electoral votes, Article II, Section 1, of the Constitution and the Twelfth Amendment required the House of Representatives to choose from among the three highest electoral vote recipients, with each state delegation casting one vote and a majority (thirteen) of the twenty-four state delegations needed for election.

Although Clay, who had finished fourth, was eliminated as a candidate, he could not help but figure heavily in the outcome of the election in his capacity as the speaker of the House. (See "United States Constitution," p. 35, and "The Twelfth Amendment: Senate Debate," p. 89.)

In January 1825, Clay endorsed Adams, whom he disliked personally but whose experience in government he ad-

mired and whose views he shared on issues such as the federal government's responsibility for canals, highways, and other internal improvements. Shortly thereafter, a letter appeared in a Philadelphia newspaper charging that Adams had offered to appoint Clay as secretary of state in exchange for his support. On February 9, 1825, when the House met to vote, Clay helped to deliver to Adams the support not just of the three states that he had carried—Kentucky, Missouri, and Ohio—but also three of Jackson's states, Maryland, Illinois, and Louisiana. These six state delegations, joined to the seven that had supported Adams in the election, gave him the bare majority of thirteen states that he needed to be elected. Jackson won the votes of seven state delegations, Crawford of four.

Soon after the House election, President Adams appointed Clay as secretary of state, which provoked Jackson's already furious supporters to charge that the election had been stolen in a "corrupt bargain." ~

On motion of Mr. Cocke, the Committee of the Whole on the state of the Union were discharged from the further consideration of the rules referred to it; and they were laid on the table. They were then taken up and read in order. The first rule is in the following words:

"1st. In the event of its appearing, on opening all the certificates, and counting the votes given by the electors of the several States for President, that no person has a majority of the votes of the whole number of the electors appointed, and the result shall have been declared, the same shall be entered on the journals of this House."

This rule, having been read, was agreed to.

The second rule, on motion of Mr. Bassett, was amended by inserting, after the word "called," the words "by States;" and, thus amended, it reads as follows:

"2d. The roll of the House shall then be called, by States; and, on its appearing that a member or members from two thirds of the States are present, the House shall immediately proceed, by ballot, to choose a President from the persons having the highest numbers, not exceeding three, on the list of those voted for as President; and in case neither of those persons shall receive the votes of a majority of all the States on the first ballot, the House shall continue to ballot for a President, without interruption by other business, until a President be chosen."

And, thus amended, it was agreed to.

The third rule having been read, a motion was made to strike out the last clause, which orders the galleries to be cleared at the request of the delegation of any one State.

On this question, Mr. McDuffie rose and observed that he left it to the House to determine on whom the responsibility rested of giving to the present discussion the extensive range which it had taken. For himself, he had adopted as a constant rule not to consume the time of the House by any remarks which had not a direct reference to the subject before it, or which were not drawn out by other topics brought into the discussion by other gentlemen. As to the present discussion, he had considered the gentleman from Delaware as assuming, at the commencement of it, as the ground on which he thought it wise policy to clear the galleries, that members of this House, when engaged in electing a President, did not act as the delegates of the people, and were not responsible to them. The reply which he himself had made was directed only to this principle. It went no further. In replying to his remark, the gentleman from North Carolina and the gentleman from Delaware had extended the discussion still further, and had made a theoretical discussion of the powers of the House to bear on the question immediately before it. And now, at the close of one of the most eloquent and imposing arguments ever delivered in the House, a member rises in his place and suggests the impolicy of continuing this argument. He felt very great respect for that member, but he considered the matter to be discussed as of the greatest importance. The principle laid down had a very wide and extensive bearing, and he felt it his duty to submit to the dictates of his own judgment, and give the principle that discussion which he considered it entitled to receive. The responsibility rested upon him, and he well knew the impatience of the House, and was aware of the lateness of the hour: but he was compelled, notwithstanding these disadvantages, to go into the argument, and to reply both to the gentleman from North Carolina and the gentleman from Delaware.

Both of those gentlemen had put cases, urged with a great deal of ingenuity, to show that the doctrine for which he contended, viz: that, in electing a President, the people have a right to instruct their delegates, would operate, in practice, to defeat the election. Sir, said Mr. McD., if that consequence can be shown to be fairly deducible from the principle I advocate, I will abandon it. But I think that, so far from this being the case, the danger exists only in the imaginations of the gentlemen who urge it. What is the case supposed by the gentleman from North Carolina? That there are three candidates, and that eight States vote for each of them. Well, take that case. The gentlemen say, if the people have a right to instruct their delegates, then instructions once given cannot be resisted, and so the delegate must go on voting to the end, for the candidate designated by his own State, and thus the election will be prevented altogether. But this statement rises from an entire misapprehen-

sion of the ground I take. I did not contend that the delegate must go on voting to the end as he began, and so defeat the election. I only contended that the popular will of the State is as binding on me, as they say the dictate of conscience is binding on them.

I will therefore turn the gentlemen's case upon themselves. Suppose there are three candidates, and the members from eight States hold themselves bound in conscience to vote each of them, can there be an election in this case? No, sir. They say that if the popular will is to bind me, I must continue to submit to it. Well, sir, if conscience is to bind them, they must continue to submit to it. I do not say that the people have a legal right to instruct their delegates, but—

Here Mr. Webster observed that he rose with great pain. He hoped the gentleman from South Carolina would do him the justice to believe that nothing but an imperious conviction of duty induced him to interrupt an argument which he knew it would give him pleasure to hear, but he submitted whether it was in order to go into an argument in the House, in reply to an argument urged in Committee of the Whole, any more than if it had been urged in a select committee.

The Speaker decided that the observations of Mr. McDuffie were not in order, on the ground stated, and that they were not in order for another reason, viz: that the whole scope of the debate was irrelevant to the question actually before the House.

Mr. McDuffie, upon the latter ground, submitted to the decision of the Chair.

The question was then put on the amendment, and carried.

Mr. Wright moved further to amend the rule, by inserting, after the word "Senators," the word "stenographers;" which was carried.

And the rule, as amended, was adopted, and read, as follows:

"3. The doors of the hall shall be closed during the balloting, except against members of the Senate, stenographers, and the officers of the House."

The fourth rule was then read, and adopted, as follows:

"4th. From the commencement of the balloting until an election is made, no proposition to adjourn shall be received, unless on the motion of one State, seconded by another State; and the question shall be decided by States. The same rule shall be observed in regard to any motion to change the usual hour for the meeting of the House."

The fifth rule was then read, in the words following:

"5th. In balloting, the following mode shall be observed, to wit:

"The representatives of each State shall be arranged and seated together, beginning with the seat at the right hand of the Speaker's chair, with the members from the State of Maine; thence, proceeding with the members from the States in the order the States are usually named for receiving petitions, around the hall of the House, until all are seated:

"A ballot-box shall be provided for each State;

"The representatives of each State shall, in the first instance, ballot among themselves, in order to ascertain the vote of their State; and they may, if necessary, appoint tellers of their ballots;

After the vote of each State is ascertained, duplicates thereof shall be made out; and in case any one of the persons from whom the choice is to be made shall receive a majority of the votes given, on any one balloting, but the representatives of a State, the name of that person shall be written on each of the duplicates; and in case the votes so given shall be divided, so that neither of said persons shall have a majority of the whole number of votes given by such State on any one balloting, then the

word "divided" shall be written on each duplicate;

"After the delegation from each State shall have ascertained the vote of their State, the Clerk shall name the States in the order they are usually named for receiving petitions; and, as the name of each is called, the Sergeant-at-arms shall present to the delegation of each two ballot-boxes, in each of which shall be deposited, by some representative of the State, one of the duplicates, made as aforesaid, of the vote of said State, in the presence and subject to the examination of all the members from said State then present; and, where there is more than one representative from a State, the duplicates shall not both be deposited by the same person;

"When the votes of the States are thus all taken in, the Sergeant-at-arms shall carry one of the said ballot-boxes to one table, and the other to a separate and distinct table;

"One person from each State represented in the balloting shall be appointed by its representatives to tell off said ballots; but, in case the representatives fail to appoint a teller, the Speaker shall appoint;

"The said tellers shall divide themselves into two sets, as nearly equal in number as can be, and one of the said sets of tellers shall proceed to count the votes in one of said boxes, and the other set the votes in the other box;

"When the votes are counted by the different sets of tellers, the result shall be reported to the House; and if the reports agree, the same shall be accepted as the true votes of the States; but if the reports disagree, the States shall proceed, in the same manner as before, to a new ballot."

Mr. Hamilton, of S.C., then moved to amend this rule by striking out what follows the words "a ballot-box shall be provided for each State," and inserting the following:

"Labelled with the name of the State, placed in front of the Speaker's chair, on the Clerk's table, placed in the order of the States. The Clerk shall then proceed to call each delegation, in the order in which petitions are called, and the member of each delegation shall place his ballot in the box labelled with the name of the State. After all the States have thus voted, then the members of each delegation shall nominate a member of their delegation to act as teller, who shall proceed, with the rest of the tellers appointed by the several delegations, to count the votes of each State, commencing in the order in which they are called; at the close of which count, the separate vote of each State shall be declared by the senior member of the committee of tellers, as well as the result of the aggregate ballot. Should the delegation of any State fail to appoint a teller, then the Speaker shall nominate one; and where there is but one member of a State, he shall act as teller. These rules shall be observed in each successive ballot, until a choice is produced, in conformity with the provisions of the constitution of the United States."

Mr. Hamilton rose and observed that, in offering this amendment, he disclaimed any intention to provoke a debate on a subject which might be susceptible of extended and various considerations. My object (said Mr. H.) is to endeavor to adopt, within the provisions of the constitution, some mode by which the vote of each State (not the members of the several States) may be ascertained. To the members composing the delegations I know that the privilege of a secret ballot is secured. This I do not propose to violate; but I do propose that some mode should be adopted, by which the vote of the State, when given, should be put on record on the journals of this House, and the people be enabled, in an authentic form, to know how their representatives have given the vote of the States which they represent.

Now, by the mode reported by the committee, there are to be twenty-four distinct and secret colleges, each State acting under its own discretion; and the strange result might occur, that, in one delegation blank votes would be counted, and in another rejected, and by this clashing it might in effect arise that an election should be produced, which was not the result of a majority of the States.

The amendment he had submitted provided that the vote of each State should be in a separate ballot-box, and be thus told and declared. He felt satisfied that, although it seemed in its operation to disclose the vote of a member, when that person represented alone a whole state, yet this was an accident either of good fortune or bad, according to the pride and regret with which such gentlemen might view the situation. Besides, he did not suppose that any gentleman on that floor would desire to have any result produced by his acts attributed to another, which, in the portentous darkness which was about to veil their proceedings in relation to the mode of balloting, might occur.

In conclusion, he would say that we were bound, as far as it was admissible within the secret ballot accorded to each member, to allow the people to understand, at least in our condescension, how the vote of their different States have been given, in a shape more authentic than rumor, or even a newspaper report. He defied any man, in the odious contest of 1801, to determine how the States had voted, from the journals of this House; and he thought such a mysterious mode of choice suited rather the muffled secrecy of a Venetian Senate than an assembly representing a free people. Let us have no approach, even in appearance, in our transactions on this eventful occasion, to that terrible image of jealousy, secrecy, and prostration of public freedom, exhibited by the brazen lion of Venice, which, with his gaping mouth, receives a vote which comes whence nobody knows, and for which nobody is responsible.

Mr. Webster requested leave to make a single remark, which might save further discussion. The rule, as proposed by the gentleman from South Carolina, would be in direct violation of the constitution. The constitution says that the States shall vote by ballot. But the proposed amendment would defeat that intention. Some of the States are represented only by a single delegate; and, if the proposed amendment prevailed, each of those gentlemen is compelled to declare in what way he has voted.

Mr. Hamilton observed, in reply to the gentleman from Massachusetts, that, on a question involving a construction of the constitution, he would advance his own opinions with some deference, in opposition to the opinions of that gentleman. But he contended that, substantially, by his mode, the vote was given by States, which was all the constitution renders necessary; that, so long as the mode by which the sense and vote of each State were ascertained was by ballot, all the requisitions of the constitution were complied with. His amendment, in fact, merely provided for a separate ballot-box for each State, rather than a general one, by which the vote of the several States would be wholly unknown. Mr. H. then dwelt very briefly on several public considerations, which rendered such knowledge important, and concluded by saying that, from the lateness of the hour, and the short time which was allowed them now for the passage of the rules, he would not press the discussion further.

Mr. Wright, of Ohio, observed that if gentlemen would examine the rule reported by the committee, and the amendment proposed by the gentleman from South Carolina, [Mr. Hamilton,] with the constitution, they would find the rule was, and the amendment was not, consistent with it. The constitution requires the choice to be made by ballot; the votes to be taken by States, each

State having one vote. The amendment goes upon the principle that you must present to the House one vote for each member from a State, instead of one vote for each State, without regard to the number of members. The difference must be obvious. The rule prescribes the manner in which each State shall ascertain its vote, and, when ascertained, how that vote shall be presented to the House, and be told off; the amendment seeks to deprive the States of a vote by ballot, and to confer power on the tellers, who shall ascertain, by counting the ballots of the members, how the State would vote, to give that vote *viva voce,* not by ballot. The House, constitutionally, has little to do in determining the vote of the States. Its main power on the subject commences when that vote has been determined.

The amendment is objectionable in another point of view. It leaves to the tellers to settle the disputed question, (without the control of the delegation or the House,) whether the vote or ballot of a State shall result from a bare plurality, or depend on a majority, of the ballots in each delegation. This is a question, sir, of too much importance to leave for adjustment in such a way. It should be settled by the House, voting *per capita,* and before any result is known, calculated to influence the decision; it should be settled now. For himself, Mr. W. said, having carefully examined the provisions of the constitution relating to the election of President, with a view to understand their literal meaning, as well as to discover their spirit, he entertained no doubt but a majority of the delegation of any one State was necessary to determine its vote, and that nothing short of it would do. He felt confident the House would so determine.

Mr. Hamilton spoke in reply, and made some observations to show that his proposal was in conformity with the constitution. He hoped that at least so much of it as provides twenty-four separate ballot-boxes would be adopted. He insisted that it ought to be known, publicly and officially, how each State had voted, and regretted the want of this knowledge touching the election of 1801.

Mr. McDuffie advocated the amendment of the gentleman from South Carolina. The question now was, whether the constitution was to be so interpreted as to throw an impenetrable veil over the proceedings of this House, in so important an act as the choice of a Chief Magistrate. He felt bound to protect the honor of his State, and his own honor; but the rule, as it at present stood, rendered it impossible for him to show that he had been faithful to his constituents. Mr. McD. quoted the constitution, and insisted that the amendment was not inconsistent with it; that the constitution did not require that the vote of the States should be concealed; nor did it ever mean to screen the votes of the delegates themselves from the public scrutiny. In declaring that the votes should be by States, it meant no more than that all the States should have an equal voice. It directed not that they should vote by States, but that they should be counted by States. If it happened that some of the States had only one delegate, that did not alter the requirements of the constitution, nor the propriety of the plan proposed by his colleague. The constitution would still be obeyed. He had no suspicion that the gentleman from Delaware, or any other of those gentlemen who stood alone in representing States, had any wish to conceal the vote that they should give, and he expressed a hope that they would support the amendment.

Mr. Cook, of Illinois, disclaiming all wish to have his vote concealed, was yet opposed to the adoption of the amendment now proposed, which he considered as striking a deadly blow at the constitution. A fundamental principle

of that instrument was, that the legislative and executive departments should be kept entirely separate. While, on the one hand, the President was protected from having an improper influence exerted over him by members of this body, it was proper, on the other hand, that the members of this House should be protected from his resentment, arising from a knowledge that any particular portion of them were opposed to his elections. It was not proper that the President should know officially from whence his power was derived. He should receive it from the whole people, and exercise it alike for the good of every portion of them. When the constitution was revised, in 1801, this great fundamental principle was preserved untouched. The rule proposed by the gentleman from South Carolina was calculated to render the Chief Magistrate the President of a party, not the President of the nation. The practical tendency was to array some of the States against the President, and the President against them; to cherish the seeds of faction, and to give to party spirit still greater bitterness. It was the duty of the House to be umpires, not agitators; to pacify the nation, not to irritate it.

Mr. Wright again spoke in opposition to the amendment. He had supposed, he said, that no one could have doubted that the constitution required only one vote for each State, instead of one for each member of the House; in the present case, twenty-four ballots instead of two hundred and thirteen. And he had supposed it equally clear the framers of the constitution never contemplated that the proceeding should stop the moment you had ascertained whether the State intended to vote, before the ballot or vote was prepared and deposited; but in this he found himself mistaken. He should despair of removing those doubts, and would forbear further argument as to it. It is urged that the plan proposed by the rule makes the proceedings among the members of the States secret, and that you have no way to find out how each man voted. Why should that be known? What good could result from it? Does the constitution authorize you to require publicity in this proceeding? I think not. Individually, I have no desire to keep my vote secret; I am willing to proclaim it to the world. The gentleman from Illinois [Mr.Cook] has presented to you, much better than I could do, some of the principles which govern elections by ballot, and urged some forcible reasons why the votes should be secret. I agree with the gentleman in the views he has submitted. The requisition upon a voter by ballot, to endorse his name on the ballot, or to rise when about to vote, and proclaim for whom he voted, would entirely defeat the object of voting by ballot, and break down all the guards the constitution has established to protect the elector in the free enjoyment of this right.

Mr. Stewart, of Pennsylvania, regretted that time was not allowed more maturely to examine so important a proposition as that now before the House, before it was voted on. From the short consideration he had been able to give it, he could not perceive that it was inconsistent with the constitution; and he should vote for it, because he perceived that its object was to remove every thing like secrecy from the transaction which was approaching. It was well known that the proceedings of this House on that occasion would be regarded by the people with suspicion. Was it a likely way of removing this to throw a mantle of secrecy over its proceedings? Was not this the way to set the tongue of slander in motion? When an allegation was made, affecting the purity of any individual, would they be removed by his skulking and shrinking from observation? Would not this rather rivet the suspicion? If a man was charged with

theft, was it a way to remove the charge, if he shut his door, and refused all admittance and observation? But if he threw open the suspected place, invited observation, and displayed a frank, open, and candid deportment, the report would be disbelieved. So long as shadows, clouds, and darkness, were suffered to rest on any of the doings of this House, the suspicions of the people would only be fixed and confirmed. With a view, however, to the further examination of the amendment, he moved that the House adjourn.

This motion was negatived, by a large majority.

Mr. Stewart then demanded that, when the question was taken on the amendment, it should be taken by yeas and nays. The House refused to order them.

The question was then put on Mr. Hamilton's amendment, and decided in the negative: Yeas 52, nays 115.

And the rule, as above stated, was agreed to.

The remaining rules were then successively read, and adopted, as follows:

"6th. All questions arising after the balloting commences, requiring the decision of the House, which shall be decided by the House, voting *per capita,* to be incidental to the power of choosing a President, shall be decided by States, without debate; and in case of an equal division of the votes of States, the question shall be lost.

"7th. When either of the persons from whom the choice is to be made shall have received a majority of all the States, the Speaker shall declare the same, and that that person is elected President of the United States.

"8th. The result shall be immediately communicated to the Senate by message; and a committee of three persons shall be appointed to inform the President of the United States and the President elect of said election."

And then the House adjourned.

In Senate, Tuesday, February 8, 1825 Election of President

The committee on the part of the Senate, appointed to join such committee as might be appointed on the part of the House of Representatives, to ascertain and report a mode of examining the votes for President and Vice President of the United States, and of notifying the persons elected of their election, report, in part, the agreement of the joint committee to the following resolution:

Resolved, That the two Houses shall assemble in the chamber of the House of Representatives on Wednesday, the 9th day of February, 1825, at 12 o'clock; that one person be appointed teller on the part of the Senate, and two persons be appointed tellers on the part of the House, to make a list of the votes as they shall be declared; that the result shall be delivered to the President of the Senate, who shall announce to the two Houses, assembled as aforesaid, the state of the vote, and the person or persons elected, if it shall appear that a choice hath been made agreeably to the constitution of the United States; which annunciation shall be deemed a sufficient declaration of the person or persons elected, and, together with a list of the votes, shall be entered on the journals of the two Houses.

[The committee which made this report consisted, on the part of the Senate, of Mr. Tazewell, Mr. Van DYKE, Mr. King of Ala.

On the part of the House of Representatives, Mr. Taylor, Mr. Archer, Mr. Thompson of Pa.,]

Mr. Talbot suggested some difficulty in the order of proceeding recommended by the committee, and Mr. Holmes, of Maine, proposed some amendment, but which he subsequently withdrew. These suggestions gave rise to some discussion of the subject, in which Messrs. Holmes of Maine, Talbot, Tazewell, Lowrie, Barbour, Johnson of Ky., King of Ala., and Van Dyke, participated.

Mr. Tazewell went, at some length, into an explanation and justification of the course adopted by the committee. In some points, in which the committee on the part of the Senate would have preferred a different arrangement, they were overruled by the committee on the part of the other House, which had its rights as well as the Senate. The mode reported by the committee was precisely, however, the same as that adopted by the Senate, and agreed on by the two Houses, on similar occasions, from the year 1805 to 1817, inclusive.

Mr. Eaton then moved to add the following, as an amendment:

"If any objection shall arise to the vote or votes of any State, it shall be filed in writing and entered on the journals of the Senate and House of Representatives; but the two Houses shall not separate until the entire votes are counted and reported, which report shall be liable to be controlled and altered by the decision to be made by the two Houses, after their separation, relative to any objections that may be made and entered on the journals; provided no objection taken shall be considered valid unless concurred in by the two Houses."

This amendment was opposed by Mr. Hayne and Mr. Van Buren, on the ground that it was now too late to attempt to provide in anticipation for such an occurrence; that the Senate had, at the last session, passed a bill providing for every possible contingency for which the constitution prescribed no rule, which bill the House of Representatives had not acted on; that, therefore, if any difficulty should arise on the present occasion, the Senate could not be reproached for it; that as it was now too late to expect the two Houses to concur in any regulations of the kind, in time for the government of the proceedings to take place to-morrow, it was better to leave the remedy to be provided for in any case of difficulty that might unexpectedly arise, &c.

Mr. Eaton replied, and urged the necessity of making an effort to provide for possible difficulty beforehand, &c.

The question was then taken on his amendment, and negatived, without a division; and

The report of the committee was concurred in.

Mr. Tazewell was appointed teller on the part of the Senate.

House of Representatives, Same Day

Mr. Taylor, from the joint committee appointed to consider the mode of counting the votes for President and Vice President of the United States, made a report, in part; which was read.

[The report is the same as that before stated in the Senate proceedings.]

The House agreed to the resolution reported, and Mr. P. P. Barbour and Mr. Taylor were appointed tellers according thereto.

Election of President

At twelve o'clock, precisely, the members of the Senate entered the hall, preceded by their Sergeant-at-arms, and having the President of the Senate at their head, who was invited to a seat on the right hand of the Speaker of the House.

Seats were then assigned the Senators, who took their seats together, in front of the Speaker's chair, and toward the right hand of the entrance.

The President of the Senate [Mr. Gaillard] then rose and stated that the certificates forwarded by the electors from each State would be delivered to the tellers.

Mr. Tazewell, of the Senate, and Messrs. John W. Taylor and Philip P. Barbour, on the part of the House, took their places as tellers at the Clerk's table. The President of the Senate then opened two packets, one received by messenger and the other by mail, containing the certificates of the votes of the State of New Hampshire. One of these was then read by Mr. Tazewell, while the other was compared with it by Messrs. Taylor and Barbour. The whole having been read, and the votes of New Hampshire declared, they were set down by the Clerks of the Senate and of the House of Representatives, seated at different tables. Thus the certificates from all the States were gone through with.

The tellers then left the Clerk's table, and presenting themselves in front of the Speaker, Mr. Tazewell delivered their report of the votes given; which was then handed to the President of the Senate, who again read it to the two Houses, as follows:

The President of the Senate then rose and declared that no person had received a majority of the votes given for President of the United States; that Andrew Jackson John Quincy Adams, and William H. Crawford, were the three persons who had received the highest number of votes, and that the remaining duties in the choice of a President now devolved on the House of Representatives. He further declared that John C. Calhoon, of South Carolina, having received 182 votes, was duly elected Vice President of the United States, to serve for four years from the 4th day of March next.

The members of the Senate then retired.

The Speaker directed the roll of the House to be called by States, and the members of the respective delegations to take their seats in the order in which the States should be called, be-

	For President				For Vice President					
States	John Quincy Adams	William H. Crawford	Andrew Jackson	Henry Clay	John C. Calhoun	Nathaniel Macon	Andrew Jackson	Nathan Sanford	Henry Clay	Martin Van Buren
Maine	9	—	—	—	9	—	—	—	—	—
New Hampshire	8	—	—	—	7	—	1	—	—	—
Massachusetts	15	—	—	—	15	—	—	—	—	—
Rhode Island	4	—	—	—	3	—	—	—	—	—
Connecticut	8	—	—	—	—	—	8	—	—	—
Vermont	7	—	—	—	7	—	—	—	—	—
New York	26	5	1	4	29	—	—	7	—	—
New Jersey	—	—	8	—	8	—	—	—	—	—
Pennsylvania	—	—	28	—	28	—	—	—	—	—
Delaware	1	2	—	—	1	—	—	—	2	—
Maryland	3	1	7	—	10	—	1	—	—	—
Virginia	—	24	—	—	—	24	—	—	—	—
North Carolina	—	—	15	—	15	—	—	—	—	—
South Carolina	—	—	11	—	11	—	—	—	—	—
Georgia	—	9	—	—	—	—	—	—	—	9
Kentucky	—	—	—	14	7	—	—	7	—	—
Tennessee	—	—	11	—	11	—	—	—	—	—
Ohio	—	—	—	16	—	—	—	16	—	—
Louisiana	2	—	3	—	5	—	—	—	—	—
Mississippi	—	—	3	—	3	—	—	—	—	—
Indiana	—	—	5	—	5	—	—	—	—	—
Illinois	1	—	2	—	3	—	—	—	—	—
Alabama	—	—	5	—	5	—	—	—	—	—
Missouri	—	—	—	3	—	—	3	—	—	—
Total	84	41	99	37	182	24	13	30	2	9

ginning at the right hand of the Speaker.

The roll was called accordingly, when it appeared that every member of the House was present, with the exception of Mr. Garnett, of Va., who was known to be indisposed at his lodgings, in this city.

The delegations took their places accordingly, ballot-boxes were distributed to each delegation by the Sergeant-at-arms, and the Speaker directed that the balloting should proceed.

The ballots having all been deposited in the boxes, the following tellers were named by the respective delegations, being one from each State in the Union:

Mr. Cushman,
Livermore,
Mr. Hooks,
Campbell,

Webster,
Eddy,
Tomlinson,
Buck,
Taylor,
Condict,
Ingham,
McLane,
Kent,
Randolph,

Forsyth,
Trimble,
Allen of Tenn.,
Sloane,
Livingston,
Rankin,
Jennings,
Cook,
Owen,
Scott.

Mr. Webster, of Massachusetts, was appointed by those tellers who sat at one table, and Mr. Randolph, of Virginia, by those at the other, to announce the result of the balloting. After the ballots were counted out, Mr. Webster rose and said:

"Mr. Speaker: the tellers of the votes at this table have proceeded to count the ballots contained in the box set before them. The result they find to be, that there are—

For John Quincy Adams, of Massachusetts, 13 votes,

For Andrew Jackson, of Tennessee, 7 votes,

For William H. Crawford, of Georgia, 4 votes."

Mr. Randolph, from the other table, made a statement corresponding with that of Mr. Webster in the facts, but varying in the phraseology, so as to say that Mr. ADAMS, Mr. Jackson, and Mr. Crawford, had received the votes of so many States, instead of so many votes.

The Speaker then stated this result to the House, and announced that John Quincy Adams, having a majority of the votes of these United States, was duly elected President of the same for four years, commencing with the 4th day of March next.

On motion of Mr. Taylor, of New York, a committee was ordered to be appointed, to notify the President of the United States and the President elect of the result of the ballot.

And then the House adjourned.

[When the fact of Mr. Adams having 13 votes was announced by the tellers, some clapping and exultation took place in the galleries, and some slight hissing followed. The House suspended its proceedings until the galleries were cleared.]. . .

Anti-Adams Editorial (1828)

John Quincy Adams reigned as president under two dark political clouds: the bizarre and, many believed, corrupt circumstances of his election in 1824-1825 (see "The House of Representatives Elects John Quincy Adams," p. 127) and the breakup of the Democratic-Republican party. In a country as socially and economically dynamic as the United States was in the early nineteenth century, no single political party could hope to accommodate the varied interests of the city and the farm, the slaveholding South and the free North, the commercial East and the frontier West, laborers and owners, small businesses and large factories, importers and exporters, rich and poor.

Andrew Jackson of Tennessee was the thunder head that rumbled ominously in both of Adams's dark clouds. Having won the most popular and electoral votes in 1824, Jackson and his supporters were deeply aggrieved by Adams's election. Even more important, as a westerner, a self-made man, a political outsider, and a firm believer in equality of opportunity, which was the rising idea of the age, Jackson embodied the fastest growing sectors of American society.

The contrast between Jackson and Adams—a Massachusetts aristocrat who, like every previous president, had risen to power through the established ranks of the national government—could not have been sharper. An editorial in the leading anti-administration newspaper, the United States Telegraph, plainly stated both the case for Jackson (he represented "the great cause of the many against the few, of equal rights against privileged orders, of democracy against aristocracy") and the case against Adams ("indebted to Federalists ... devoid of sincerity ... an aristocrat").

The Telegraph, which was published in Washington, was typical of the early- and mid-nineteenth century press in its unabashed partisanship. Although the newspaper professed to speak for traditional Democratic-Republicanism, the old party no longer existed in any politically meaningful sense. Instead, it was in the process of splitting into two new parties, the National Republican party (later called the Whigs), led by Adams and Clay, and the Democratic party, led by Jackson and Adams's vice president, John C. Calhoun of South Carolina.

The major issues that divided the Democrats from the National Republicans concerned the proper role of the national government in American society and of the presidency within the national government. Whigs wanted a congressionally dominated, strong central government that would promote economic development through internal improvements and high tariffs.

Democrats, who were committed to equality of opportunity and were convinced that Washington and, especially, Congress were dominated by an eastern commercial elite, preferred to decentralize political power among the states. Within the national government, however, Jackson's Democratic supporters wanted a strong president, who would serve as the "tribune of the people."

With the demise of the congressional caucus in 1824, state legislatures informally assumed the responsibility to nominate candidates for president and vice president. (See "Proceedings of the Congressional Caucus," p. 120.) Jackson accepted Vice President Calhoun as his running mate, Adams ran with Secretary of the Treasury Richard Rush. Voter turnout in the 1828 election was triple that in 1824: the population was growing, states were abandoning property-owning qualifications for suffrage, and all but two states now chose their presidential electors by popular vote. Jackson won 642,553 popular votes (41.3 percent) to Adams's 500,897 (30.9 percent). In the electoral college, Jackson swept the West and South to win by a margin of 178-83.   ~

Among a people like that of the United States, who recognize no difference between political and social morals, and who believe that, he who would be false to one engagement would not be true to any, no quality is more highly estimated than party fidelity. They consider parties, and very justly, essential to the political health of a republic; for, viewing these parties as spies on each other, they consider their mutual distrust the best restraint against any improper courses. But besides the utility of parties in a republic, every member of the Democratic Republican party must feel that, to him in common with his associates, is confided the great cause of the many against the few, of

equal rights against privileged orders, of democracy against aristocracy. Therefore every member of this party must feel that, John Quincy Adams must be an object of particular distrust to Democratic Republicans.

Mr. Adams was educated among the Federal party, and indebted to Federalists for his first appearance in public employment. He afterwards abandoned this party, and joined that of the Democratic Republicans. Federalists have believed that he deserted and calumniated them. If this be true, he deserves no confidence from Democratic Republicans for having violated the principle of party fidelity, which, in this country, all parties do or ought to respect, he can justly claim the confidence of no party. Other Federalists maintain that, he joined the Democratic Republican party for the purpose of destroying it. If *this* be true, I need not say what he deserves from this party. In a former number, I endeavored to show, by the testimony of a witness who could not be impeached, who, as a Federalist viewed with just indignation the desertion of his own party, and as an honorable man, with equal indignation the attempt to destroy its opponent party by dishonorable means, that, Mr. Adams had associated himself with the Democratic Republican party, for the purpose of compassing its ruin.

1st. He is devoid of sincerity. To some politicians, who separate public from private morals, and believe that to obtain votes, any course or expedient is justifiable that may influence public opinion, want of sincerity in a candidate for public employment may seem a venial infirmity. But this class, it may be hoped, is not numerous in this land. The great majority of the American people, honest themselves, selecting agents to transact their most important business, the management of their institutions, will certainly—deem the honesty of such agents as important consideration. And how can they deem that agent honest, who holds one language to the world and another to the few; one to those whom he professes to have abandoned, and another to those whom he pretends to have joined? All mankind join in expressing veneration for truth and detestation of falsehood. This sentiment is not more general than necessary, for how can society be held together in peace, unless its members can confide in the statements and declarations of each other? Then as sincerity consists in strictly adhering to truth, and detesting the odious vice of falsehood, and as, in republic, honesty and fidelity in public agents are vitally important, with what propriety can we say that, want of sincerity affords no objection against a candidate for public office? — Admitting this, what citizen of honest feelings can approve the character of Mr. Adams, so far as it has been evinced by insincere professions to the Democratic party?

2d. He is regardless of means in seeking his object. Fraud, deceit, artifice, circumvention, seem, to him, excusable if not justifiable means of compassing a political design. What could be more deceptive, more fraudulent, than to join a party for the purpose of destroying it? Such conduct involves both espionage and treachery, and must meet the unqualified condemnation of all honorable minds. To compass this design, he must seem a traitor to his early friends and associates; for he could not, with any hope of success, confide his scheme to the whole Federal party. Such disclosure would publish it to the whole community, and put his opponents on their guard. He must, therefore, in pursuit of his design, necessarily deceive the majority of his Federal friends, and subject himself, in their estimation, to the charges of perfidy and ingratitude. In seeking admittance at the door of the Democratic party, he must assign some satisfactory or plausible reason for denouncing his old friends, or incur the imputation of

changing to gratify personal ambition. Accordingly, he accused the Federal party of plotting against the Union and institutions of their country.

This charge was true or false. If true, Mr. Adams sought the destruction of the Democratic party, for the purpose of restoring to power those whom he knew to be a band of traitors. If false, Mr. Adams stands before the world as a calumniator of his old friends, as a pretender to principles he condemns, and a promoter of policy he disapproves, and for the purpose of subverting the liberties of his country. In either case, his course is marked by double fraud, and should prepare for him a niche in the Temple of Fame, as a character which none can mistake.

3d. He is an aristocrat. Why should he be so solicitous about expelling the Democratic party from public trust, and restoring Federalism to power? He has assigned the reason; and to every Democrat, that reason *ought* to be *satisfactory*. His object was to change the democratic institutions of his country, and replace them by some more resembling the aristocratic institutions of England. On this point, comment is needless, for every Democratic Republican will know what sentence to pronounce.

4th. He is a moral traitor. To seek the destruction of the government, has, in all countries, been denommated *treason*, though in all cases, the epithet is not applied correctly. Our revolutionary fathers sought the destruction of a colonial tyranny, for the purpose of restoring to a people their plundered rights. They were not *traitors*, but *patriots*. But to seek the destruction of the liberty which they established, and for the purpose of restoring the tyranny which they overthrew, would be *treason*, and of the darkest hue, in one who had been nurtured and educated amid that liberty, and who saw and felt that, to its salutary influence must be ascribed the happiness, the prosperity, the security of his country. General Henry Lee, who aided Washington and LaFayette in fighting the battles of liberty, was no *traitor,* though an Englishman by birth, and for years an officer in the British military service. Yet Arnold was a traitor, though in drawing his sword against his native country, he followed the example of General Lee. What constitutes the difference? One abandoned an unjust and the other betrayed a righteous cause. In the estimation of every Democratic Republican, Mr. Adams has followed the example of Arnold, and not of General Lee; for he did not abandon an unjust in order to aid a righteous cause, but falsely pretended to abandon an unjust, for the purpose of betraying a righteous cause. A pretended disciple of liberty, he sought its ruin for the sake of arbitrary power; and therefore, in the estimation of all who deem liberty valuable, he must be pronounced a *traitor.*

Proceedings of the Anti-Masonic Convention (1831)

The political crusade that animated the Anti-Masonic party in 1831-1832— namely, to oppose the Freemasons and other "secret societies" in an election in which both major party candidates, President Andrew Jackson and Sen. Henry Clay of Kentucky, were members of the Masonic order—has faded into political obscurity. But the Anti-Masons are well remembered for two enduring institutional legacies that they left to the presidential election process: the "third party" and the national party convention.

The Anti-Masonic party was the first third party to have a serious influence on national politics. The Constitution, by requiring an electoral vote majority for the president and winner-take-all elections for Congress, inadvertently fostered the development of a two-party system. Yet, historically, the occasional failure of both major parties to speak to an important national or regional concern has prompted the formation of third parties. Eleven of these parties, beginning in 1832 with the Anti-Masons and their nominee for president, William Wirt, have won 5 percent or more of the popular vote in a presidential election: the Free Soil party (Martin Van Buren, 1848), the Whig-American party (Millard Fillmore, 1860), the Southern Democratic party (John C. Breckinridge, 1860), the Constitutional Union party (John Bell,

1860), the People's party (James B. Weaver, 1896), the Progressive or "Bull Moose" party (Theodore Roosevelt, 1912), the Socialist party (Eugene V. Debs, 1912), the Progressive party (Robert M. La Follette, 1924), the American Independent party (George C. Wallace, 1968), and the National Unity Campaign (John B. Anderson, 1980).

The other enduring legacy of the Anti-Masonic party is the national convention. Adapting a widely used state institution to the national political arena, Anti-Masonic leaders called for a convention to meet in Baltimore, Maryland, on September 26, 1831. The delegates, who were chosen by state conventions and caucuses, included Thurlow Weed and William H. Seward of New York, Thaddeus Stevens of Pennsylvania, and other nationally prominent political leaders. Chief Justice John Marshall, although not a delegate, attended the convention as a sympathetic observer. The 1831 Anti-Masonic convention did most of the things that national party conventions have done ever since: it elected officers, adopted rules, nominated candidates for president (former attorney general Wirt, a Marylander) and vice president (former Pennsylvania attorney general Amos Ellmaker), and approved a platform-like "Address to the People" that stated and defended the *party's principles. The proceedings of the Anti-Masonic convention were reported in the* Niles Register *in October 1831.*

On December 12, 1831, the National Republican party also convened in Baltimore, as did the Democrats on May 21, 1832. (Baltimore was the favored mid-nineteenth century convention city because of its central location.) Both parties followed approximately the same format as the Anti-Masons. The National Republicans chose Clay for president and former representative John Sergeant of Pennsylvania for vice president. The Democratic convention, which was summoned mainly to name a substitute for Vice President John C. Calhoun, nominated Jackson and his preferred running mate, former secretary of state Martin Van Buren of New York. (Calhoun had fallen out of favor with the president.)

Jackson swept the election of 1832 with a 54 percent to 37 percent majority over Clay in the popular vote and a 219-49 margin in the electoral college. (Wirt won 8 percent of the popular vote and 7 electoral votes.) The results confirmed that a political realignment had taken place in national politics. Under Jackson's leadership, the Democrats had become the nation's new majority party. They would remain so until the Civil War. ~

Sept. 26, 1831.

At 12 o'clock, M. the delegates to the national antimasonic convention assembled in the saloon of the Athenaeum, and were called to order by the hon. judge Burt, of New York, when the hon. John Ratherford was called to the chair, and the following officers being nominated were unanimously chosen:—

John C. Spencer, of	N.Y.,	President
John Rutherford,	N.J.	1st V.P.
Jonathan Sloan,	Ohio	2nd V.P.
Thomas Elder,	Penn.	3rd V.P.
John Bailey,	Mass.	4th V.P.
Benjamin F. Hallet,		

Edward D. Barber,	secretaries
S. C. Leavitt,	
Caleb Emery,	

On taking the chair, Mr. Spenser addressed the convention as follows:

Gentlemen—I return you my thanks for the distinguished honor you have conferred in calling upon me to preside over your deliberations. While I distrust my ability to discharge the duties of the chair, I have yet learnt in the school of anti-masonary to decline no duty to which I may be called in the promotion of our great and growing cause. But my reliance, gentlemen, will be on your patriotism and urbanity, to render the duties of the station light and easy. I ask your indulgence for any errors that may be committed, assuring you that nothing offensive to any member shall proceed from the chair, or be permitted in the deliberations of the convention.

On motion of *Mr. Phelps,* of Mass. voted, that the credentials of the delegates be now received and examined; upon so doing it appeared that there were present, from

New Hampshire	1
Maine	2
Massachusetts	13
Rhode Island	4
Connecticut	6
Vermont	5
New York	31
New Jersey	4
Pennsylvania	19
Ohio	5
Maryland	1
Delaware	1

On motion of *Mr. Walker,* of Mass. voted, that a regular roll of the members of this convention be now made, and the state, county and town, in which they reside, be fully designated.

On motion of *Mr. Morris,* of N.Y. voted, that a committee of three be appointed to invite the hon. Charles Carrol, of Carrollton, to take a seat in this convention. Messrs. Rutherford, of

N.J. Burt, of N.Y. and Elder, of Pa. were appointed said committee.

Voted, on motion of *Mr. Phelps,* that a committee of one from each state be appointed to report upon the business of this convention, viz:

Phelps, of	Massachusetts
Ward,	New York
Jones,	Pennsylvania
Hallett,	Rhode Island
Cram,	Maine
Emery,	New Hampshire
Terry, of	Connecticut
Barber,	Vermont
Vanderpool	New Jersey
Sloan,	Ohio
Gibbons,	Delaware
Shriver,	Maryland

Voted to adjourn to meet again at 4 P.M. Met agreeably to adjournment. *Mr. Phelps* from the committee reported on the business to be adopted by the convention, which was unanimously accepted.

On motion of *judge Hopkins,* of New York, voted, that Messrs. Hopkins, of N. York, Jones, of Pa. and Walker, of Mass. be a committee to wait on his hon. chief justice Marshall, now in this city, and request his attendance on the sitting of this body.

Mr. Ward, from the committee, at the call of the convention, submitted a report which was read and laid upon the table.

The president of the convention announced the appointment of the following committees:

On masonic penalties—Hallet, of R. I. Larned, of Maine, Morris, of N.Y. Grimshaw, of Pa. and Warner, of Ohio.

On judicial proceedings in the case of Morgan—J. C. Spencer, of N.Y. Ogle, of Pa. Walker, of Mass. Gibbons, of Del. Russell of N. York.

On the address to the people—Holly, of N.Y. Denny, of Pa. Leavitt of Connecticut.

On finance—Irwin, of Pa. Boynton,

of Conn. Beckman, of N.Y. Jenkins, of Ohio, Shriver, of Md.

The committee appointed to wait on *judge Marshall,* reported by their chairman that they had seen that gentleman, and that, in reply to their invitation, his honor politely stated that he should leave the city at 6 o'clock, tomorrow morning, and therefore be unable to attend, although it would afford him great pleasure to do so.

On motion of *Mr. St. John,* of N.Y. voted to adjourn till 10 o'clock, tomorrow morning.

Tuesday, Sept. 27, 10 o'clock, A.M.

Met pursuant to adjournment.

The proceedings of yesterday were read by the secretary.

Messrs. Oliver, of Mass. *Harvey, Heister, Rugle, Burrowes, Waters* and *Stevens,* of Pa. *Baker,* of Ohio, and *Strong* of N.Y. appeared and took their seats.

A letter direct to the president of the convention from *Samuel Stevens,* a delegate from N. York, was presented and read to the convention, and on motion of *Mr. Seward* of N.Y. was ordered to be entered at large on the journal of the convention.

Mr. Hopkins, of N.Y. announced that chief justice Marshall having been unexpectedly prevented from leaving the city, would soon be in the hall, to attend the deliberations of the convention.

Mr. Rutherford, of N.J. from the Committee appointed to wait on the venerable Charles Carroll, of Carrollton, and invited him to be present at the deliberations of the convention, reported,

"That the committee have seen the secretary of Mr. Carroll, and are informed that Mr. Carroll left this city in the month of June last, for his country residence on the manor of Carrollton, sixteen miles from Baltimore, and that he is not expected to return until the month of October next; that he is in good health, but is desirous to avoid the fatigue of journies to and from the city. The committee, therefore, did not proceed to Carrollton yesterday, more especially as the weather was inclement, and the visit and journey would occupy part of two days.

On motion of *Mr. Phelps,* of Mass.

Voted, That the time appointed to make nominations of president and vice president of the United States, be postponed till to-morrow at 10 o'clock, A.M.

Mr. David, of Vermont, submitted the following resolution:

Resolved, That this convention will adjourn without delay on Wednesday next, the 28th inst.

Ordered to lie on the table.

On motion of *Mr. Hallet,* of R.I.

Resolved, That the resolution of this convention inviting the venerable Charles Carroll, of Carrollton, to be present at the proceedings of this convention, together with the report of the committee appointed on that resolution, be transcribed and certified by the officers of this convention, and communicated to Mr. Carroll.

Mr. Burt, of N.Y. called for the reading of the rules and orders of this convention, which were accordingly read.

Chief justice Marshall, introduced by Mr. Hopkins, of N.Y. appeared in the hall, in pursuance of the invitation given him, and took a seat to attend the deliberations of the convention.

Mr. Hallett, from the committee appointed to report on the construction of masonic penalties, &c. made a report, which was read and laid on the table.

The president from the committee appointed to prepare a brief history of judicial proceedings, &c. made a report, which was read and laid on the table.

Convention adjourned to four o'clock, P.M.

Four o'clock, P.M. Convention met pursuant to adjournment.

Messrs. Pile and *Fowler,* from Ohio, appeared and took their seats.

The reports of the committees on the construction of masonic penalties, and on the history of judicial proceedings, being under consideration, a debate ensued in which *Messrs. Foote,* of N.Y. *Hallett,* of R.I. *Ward,* of N.Y. *Morris,* of N.Y. *Seward,* of N.Y. *Walker,* of Mass. and *Harvey,* of Pa. took part.

Mr. Northrup, of N.J. appeared and took his seat.

The reports on the construction of masonic penalties and on the history of judicial proceedings, were ordered to be printed.

On motion of *Mr. Jones,*

Resolved, That a committee of five be appointed to report on the extent to which the principles of free masonry are political, and opposition to them by an organised political party.

Messrs. Jones, of Pa. *Seward,* of N.Y. *Sloane,* of Ohio, *Bailey,* of Mass. *Emery,* of N.H. were appointed said committee.

The convention adjourned to nine o'clock to-morrow morning.

Wednesday, Sept. 28

Met pursuant to adjournment.

Mr. Wm. Vanderpool, of N.J. appeared and took his seat.

Mr. Seward, of N.Y. submitted the following preamble and resolution, which were read and passed.

Whereas, Wm. G. Verplanck, of Ballston, Saratoga County, N.Y. a delegate originally appointed by the state convention of the state of New York, has since the last adjournment, arrived in this city, having been detained by accident on his journey. And

Whereas, The place of said delegate has been supplied as a vacancy.

Resolved, That said Wm. G. Verplanck be admitted to a seat as an honorary member with the privilege of participating in the debates, but not in the votes of this convention.

Mr. Samuel J. Packer, of Pa. was also admitted to a seat in the convention in accordance with the aforegoing resolution.

On motion of *Mr. Phelps,* of Mass.

The resolution relative to the nomination of president, &c. was re-considered and amended, so as to strike out that part requiring the convention to go into committee of the whole for that purpose.

On motion of *Mr. Walker,* of Mass.

Voted, To proceed to ballot for candidates for the offices of president and vice president of the United States.

Messrs. Phelps, of Mass. and *Stevens,* of Pa. were appointed by the president tellers to receive and count the votes.

The convention then proceeded to ballot for president.

Mr. Hambly, of Pa. being absent, on motion of Mr. Irwin of Pa. Mr. Packer was admitted to vote in his stead.

Mr. Phelps, one of the tellers, reported as follows:—

Whole number of votes	111
Necessary to a choice	84
William Wirt, of Maryland	108
Richard Rush, of Pennsylvania	1
Blank	2

The president announced the result, and declared William Wirt, of Md. duly nominated as the anti-masonic candidate for the presidency of the United States.

On motion of *Mr. Stevens,* of Pa.

Resolved unanimously, That William Wirt, of Md. be nominated as the anti-masonic candidate for the office of president of the United States at the ensuing election.

Resolved, That a committee of three members be appointed to communicate the preceding resolution to Mr. Wirt, and to request his acceptance of the above nomination. Messrs. Rutherford, of N.J. Sloane, of Ohio, and Elder, of Pa. were appointed said committee.

The convention then proceeded to ballot for vice president.

Mr. Stevens, one of the tellers, reported as follows:

Whole number of votes given	110
Necessary to a choice	83

Amos Ellmaker, of Penn.	108
John C. Spencer, of New York	1
Blank	1

The president announced the result and declared Amos Ellmaker, of Pa. duly nominated as the anti-masonic candidate for vice president of the United States.

On motion of *Mr. Phelps,* of Mass.

Resolved, unanimously, That Amos Ellmaker, of Pa. be nominated by the convention, as the anti-masonic candidate for vice president of the United States, at the ensuing election.

Resolved, That a committee of three members be appointed to communicate the resolution above to Mr. Ellmaker, and request his acceptance of the above nomination. Messrs. Baily, of Mass. Lyman, of N.Y. and Shriver, of Maryland, were appointed said committee.

On motion of *Mr. Morris,* of N.Y.

Resolved, unanimously, That a committee of three members be appointed to express, by written communication, to the hon. Richard Rush, of Pa. the profound sense of this convention, of the patriotism, principle and firmness which dictated his eloquent exposition of the evils of free masonry, and their high appreciation of the beneficial results which it cannot fail to produce. Messrs. Morris, of N.Y. Denny, of Pa. and Gibbons, of Delaware, were appointed said committee.

Mr. Rutherford, from the committee appointed to wait on Mr. Wirt, &c. reported that the committee had performed that duty, and that he would send a written communication to the convention at 8 o'clock, P.M.

On motion of *Mr. Hopkins* of N.Y.

Resolved, unanimously, That the thanks of this convention, be presented to these citizens of Baltimore at whose expense the convention has been accommodated with the use of the splendid hall of the Athanaeum, and that this convention have felt peculiar pleasure in receiving such a proof of hospitality from the inhabitants of this elegant and polished city, and that the president of this convention be requested to transmit a copy of this resolution to the mayor of this city.

On motion of *Mr. Turner,* of R.I.

Resolved, That the president of this convention be requested to present a copy of the printed proceedings of this, and of the anti-masonic convention held at Philadelphia last year, to the president and vice president of the United States, to the ex-presidents of the United States, to the heads of the several departments, to the hon. John Marshall, chief justice, and to each of the justices of the supreme court of the United States, to the governors of the several states of the union, to gen. Lafayette, to the venerable Charles Carroll, of Carrollton, to the mayor of the city of Baltimore, to the trustees of the Athenaeum of Baltimore, and to such other distinguished individuals of this country, as he may deem expedient.

On the consideration of this resolution a debate ensued, in which *Messrs. Turner,* of R.I. *Vanderpool,* of N.J. *Hallett,* of R.I. *Phelps,* of Mass. *Denny,* of Pa. and *Miller,* of Pa. took part.

Mr. Bailey from the committee to wait on Mr. Ellmaker reported that the committee had performed the duty assigned them, and that Mr. Ellmaker would shortly make a communication to the convention.

Adjourned to 5 o'clock, P.M.

September 28, 5 o'clock, P.M.

Met pursuant to adjournment.

Mr. Ward, from the committee on resolutions, made a report which was trice read and unanimously adopted.

Messrs. Foote, Fuller and *Hopkins,* of *N.Y. Hallet,* of R.I. and *Stevens,* of Pa. severally addressed the convention in support of the resolutions.

Mr. Seward, of N.Y. submitted the following resolutions, which were read and passed unanimously.

Resolved, That the committee of finance be authorised to pay over any surplus funds which may remain in their hands, towards the expenses of the national corresponding committee to be distributed by the publishing committee.

Resolved, That the thanks of this convention be returned to the national corresponding committee for the faithful discharge of their duties during the past year, and that this convention entertain a profound conviction that the results of their labors must be eminently beneficial to the cause of anti-masonry.

The report of the national corresponding committee was called up and ordered to be printed.

Adjourned to 8 o'clock this evening.

Address of the Anti-Masonic Convention

To the American People

A large and growing political party, through us, respectfully addresses you. Numerous bodies of enlightened and honest freemen, in states containing more than half the electors of our union, have openly and fairly delegated us to represent them, in the performance of duties, which cannot fail to affect your essential rights. And believing that your rights are inseparably blended with theirs, we seek, most earnestly, so to perform these duties, as to produce effects equally and extensively beneficial upon the rights of all. These duties consist in nominating citizens to be supported, as candidates for the offices of president, and vice president, of the United States, at the next election, and in setting forth the grounds, on which you are invited to sustain the nomination.

The concurrence of millions of men, in any act of deliberation or decision, for objects, in which they have a common interest, presents to the mind a magnificent and exciting spectacle. If the men be intelligent, patriotic, and free, and the object be that of appointing the most suitable of their number, to guard the rights, and advance the prosperity, of the nation, which they constitute, human life can rarely exhibit a spectacle of equal interest and sublimity. Scarcely any approach towards such an exhibition has ever been witnessed, in any country, but ours. Let it be our ambition, so to continue and improve the exhibition, in all its stated recurrences, and shall more and more commend it to be approbation and esteem of the great brotherhood of communities, to which we belong, and most effectually tend to the establishment and support of free principles, in every community of our fellow men.

In selecting candidates for the highest offices, in the gift of the people, it is essential to consider—the peculiar frame and objects of our government—the personal qualifications of the candidates—the principles, which should govern their administration—the sources at danger to these principles—and the means of removing that danger. On each of these considerations, we wish to offer our opinions with that ingeniousness, fullness, and earnestness, which become freemen, in addressing their equals and brethren, upon subjects involving their dearest hopes, and most imperative duties.

Government has always been a business of the highest importance. In every form, it has exercised a mighty influence upon the individual and collective condition of its subjects. In most countries, it has generally been the prey of crafty and fortunate violence; and wielded for partial and selfish objects. With such an origin and such an object, it was impossible that it should not be the parent of innumerable mischiefs. But bad as it has been, it has not been without its advantages; and these have greatly outweighed its evils. Without government, there could have been no extensive associations among men. Their conflicting interests and passions, would have produced universal collisions, so fierce and frequent, as to have prevented much increase; and the human face would have existed, at this day, only in the condition of a few scattered, ignorant, indigent, feeble, ferocious, and insecure families. To raise them above this condition, government was absolutely, indispensable.

The great use of government is to secure rights—all the rights of those, who unite in its formation. These are comprehended in the liberty, and the pursuit of happiness. To the security of these, order is essential. Order cannot be maintained without a common and definite arbiter of the differences, that may arise between the individuals composing a nation, and a power to protect the whole against external aggression. Such an arbiter and power is government; which, to be perfect, should be just, intelligent, free from the bias of self interest, and effective, as to all the objects for which it is constituted. But such a government never existed. And so long as men are ignorant, selfish, and passionate, never will exist among them. The nearest possible approximation to such a government is a republic.

A republic acknowledges the rights of all, and seeks to avail itself of the wisdom and power of all, to promote their common welfare. Its theory is perfect. It is bounded upon the proper basis, pursues the proper end, and employs the proper means. And by the principles of elective representation and accountability, it may be so extended as ultimately to combine all nations—if not into one family—into a friendly association of several peaceful, prosperous, and numerous families. If right, duty, wisdom, and power, can contribute to the real exaltation and happiness of man; and if government can combine and apply them most comprehensively and beneficially to the regulation of human conduct, then republicanism offers a more majestic and reverend image of substantial glory, than can otherwise result, from the labors, and sufferings, and virtues of our race. It is a practical scheme of universal benevolence, sure to be approved, embraced, and sustained, by all men, in proportion to the just prevalence, in their minds, of intelligence, truth, and philanthropy. Such a government is the one, under which, it is our privilege to live.

Where it is the distinctive object of government to bring the public wisdom to the direction of the public will, for the public good; and the people understand their rights, their duties, and their interests, a designation to fill the high places of its administration, by a majority of their free voices, is the most precious reward, of earthly origin, which can be bestowed upon intellectual and moral merit; and imposes an accountability exactly proportioned to its value. No step should be taken towards its bestowment, without a lively and generous solitude.

The qualities, which should be possessed by every president of the U. States, are the most estimable, that can adorn a man. He should be industrious. No great end of human life can be obtained without great effort. Everything, which is good in the character and condition of man, is progressive, and cannot be otherwise. Knowledge, virtue, safety, happiness, are attainments, not gifts, nor inheritances. They are the slowly maturing, but precious fruits of exertion; not the capricious or unsought bounties of earth, or heaven. Free government, the most complicated and expansive good, that can spring from human effort, has not been acquired, and cannot be preserved, without perpetual and strenuous exertion. The chief magistrate of this government must therefore, be willing and accustomed to labor. Honest labor is always honorable. In the president of the U.

States, it is most honorable, because his labor is consecrated to the noblest purposes that can be advanced by human means, and requires the employment of the highest qualities, that can animate the soul.

He should be intelligent. The objects and provisions of our government, in all its relations both foreign and domestic—the sources of its power, and the means of its support—the history of its origin, its establishment, and its fruits, are topics of inquiry and mediation more pregnant with valuable instruction to the genuine friends of man, than all others supplied by civil records. They are themes of enlightened examination, discussion, and admiration, every where. And the most respectable nations of the old world are now agonising to disabuse themselves of their ancient, burdensome, and unequal institutions, for the sake of following our example. To understand these topics, will well repay the efforts it may cost, to every mind. It is an essential part of the education of every freeman. In him, who is entrusted with the most responsible application of all the knowledge they infold, to the holy purposes of rightful order and social advancement, it is equally the dictate of duty, self-respect, and honorable ambition, to understand them familiarly, and in all their details. Such understanding can be obtained, only by diligent study, deep reflection, candid observation, wise intercourse, and practical experience.

He should be honest. His conduct should be a perfect exemplification of the solemn claims of truth and right, in all his communications and influences, and of the strictest fidelity to the prescribed duties of his office. His manners should be plain, direct, and cordial, both in his official and private relations—the transcript of an upright, pure and benevolent mind, and suitable to aid in the accomplishment of all his grave and exalted functions. The greatest crime, which can be committed against freemen is the usurpation of power. It should be deemed the unpardonable sin of republics. It has been the unfathomable deep in which all the footsteps of liberty, in other countries, have been swallowed up, in all ancient and modern times. To it, the highest place of delegated powers affords both the most temptation, and the most probable means of success. Whoever fills that place should, therefore, be strong in honesty. If he yields to the temptations, and seeks to employ the means, entrusted to him only for the benefit of his fellow citizens, in endeavors, to raise himself upon their ruin, he should be branded like another Cain. His memory should be held in the most intense and immortal detestation.

He should be independent, following his own convictions of right, and not shrinking from any of his appropriate responsibilities. He should be swayed by no private and illegitimate influences, and never seek to cast his burthens upon others. In every act of the power lawfully assigned him, he should stand forth, as the personal agent of the public will, and answerable to all its just demands.

He should be vigilant. Our freedom, though well secured, may be invaded. In all other countries, freedom has been successfully invaded. Ours is too valuable, and has been too dearly purchased, to omit any means of its preservation. Without eternal vigilance, in all its sentinels, no means will be sufficient. With an awakened eye to every part of his charge, he who occupies the highest watch-tower of the nation, should carefully mark all the indications of good or evil, which may affect it, and weigh them well, the better to secure the objects of his care.

He should be wise in judgment. To this end, patient examination, cool deliberation, and impartial affections are requisite. Accordingly, he should be in the customary use of them. His judg-

ment is the great hinge of good or evil to millions. It should not therefore be hasty, wavering, or weak; but well informed, faithful and firm.

He should be prudent. This quality refers more to action than to speculation, but includes both: and consists in a sagacious foresight of evils, and an effective application of means to avoid them, as well as in an enlightened anticipation of benefits, and adequate efforts to secure them. It is an exalted merit; not often brilliant in its means, because they are such as common sense enjoins, and therefore excite no wonder; but blessed in its effects, because under all circumstances it leads to the utmost attainable good. Prudence obtains less praise than it deserves, because it is often confounded with the partial and sordid purpose, to which it may be made subservient.

He should be disinterested and patriotic. Yielding himself to the wishes of his fellow citizens for the momentous tasks of their leading civil service, he should in all its specifications and labors, lose himself in them. Their rights, their safety, their happiness, should be his undeviating aim. Regarding them as his political brethren and principals, he will be intent upon promoting their interests. In this way, he will secure his own. And grateful to them for his elevation to the noblest and widest sphere of beneficent exertion, to which wisdom and virtue can aspire, in this world, he will labor, unceasingly, for the good of his country. With a country distinguished above all others—for its exemption from time-honored abuses either civil, ecclesiastical or military—for the self-directing, and self-relying habits of its people—for its ingenuity and enterprise, in all the walks of productive industry—for its force and steadiness of resolve, in pursuit of practical utility— for its just distribution of social respect and honor—for its high and equal valuation of individual rights—for its anxiety and ability to disseminate useful knowledge, among all its children—for the spirit of improvement incorporated in its frame of government, exciting to the discovery, and inviting to the adoption, of every new and useful principle, and method of operation—for its unparalleled advancement in wealth, numbers, and strength—for its facilities of enlargement over half a continent, and of influence over all the world—for the adaptation of its employments, purposes and institutions, to the rights of man—for its large and increasing enjoyment of the esteem and favor of nations—and for its glorious hopes of perpetuity, it would be as natural as it would be necessary, that he should be a patriot. It would seem impossible for him to be otherwise. Penetrated with a just sense of the dignity and importance of his great trust, he should endeavor to discharge it, with parental and equal regard to every section and member of the national family.

What should be the principles of his administration? Such certainly as are found in the fundamental doctrines of the republic, and are best calculated to harmonise order and right. As drawn from our constitutions and illustrated by the writings and examples of our sages, they are chiefly the following—equal and exact justice to all men of whatever state, condition, or persuasion, religious or political—peace, commerce and honest friendship with all nations, entangling alliances with none—the support of the state governments, in all their rights, as the most competent administrations for our domestic concerns, and the surest bulwark against anti-republican tendencies—the preservation of the general government in its whole constitutional vigor, as the sheet anchor of our peace at home and safety abroad—a sacred regard to the principles and spirit of our union, which make us one people, and have been the essential means of our national power, honor, prosperity and freedom, as much as they were of the successful assertion

of our national independence—acquiescence in the decisions of the majority, even if deemed wrongful, till they can be lawfully changed, by the influence of intelligence and patriotism; such acquiescence being the vital principle of republics, from which there is no appeal but to force, the vital principle and immediate parent of despotism—a well organized militia, our best reliance in peace, and for the first moments of war, till regulars may relieve them—the supremacy of the civil over the military authority—economy in the public expense, that labor may be lightly burthened—the honest payment of our debts and careful preservation of the public faith—encouragement of the great interests of agriculture, commerce and manufactures, that every branch of productive industry may be profitable, protected and respected—the diffusion of information, by the reasonable patronage of elementary schools, and scientific establishments, as well as by the publicity of all governmental transactions, with those temporary exceptions only, which are dictated by prudence, in relation to foreign intercourse, and the initiatory steps in prosecuting crime—the arraignment of all abuses at the bar of the public reason—the strict accountability of placement and frequent rotation in office—the unbroken dominion of the laws over all men, whether private citizens, public officers, or associations of both—the prompt and lawful application of all the necessary powers of government to secure the liberty and life of any citizen from criminal invasion, when it is known to be threatened, and the most strenuous and perservering exertion, on all occasions, to disclose and bring to legal punishment, the perpetrators of crime; government is unwilling, or unable, to withstand the enterprises of faction and crime, whether proceeding in secret or in public; confine each member of the society, and association of members, within the limits prescribed by the laws, and to maintain all, in the secure and tranquil enjoyment of the rights of person and property. There are yet other rights of the people of which his administration should manifest a zealous care—that of political equality, implying general suffrage, and eligibility to office—of the independent and safe application of the right of voting to all cases, which the people shall think proper, as in this way it may become the mild and safe corrective of abuses, which must be lopped by the sword of revolution where peaceable remedies are unprovided—of freedom of religion; freedom of the press, and freedom of person, under the protection of the habeas corpus; of trial by juries and judges impartial in their obligations and impartially selected; and of security in person, house, papers, and effects, against unreasonable searches and seizures. These seem to us the essential principles of our freedom. They have been raised out of the precious mine of human rights, by the labors of ages; and having disengaged them from the rubbish and dross, under which all the workings of ignorance, faction and tyranny, would keep them eternally buried, by the post pure-hearted, arduous, and sagacious exertions, our political fathers have combined and set them up, for our shelter and guidance. Let us never be unmindful of them. We can have nothing of so much worth. They are the most brilliant jewels of our nation already rich and renowned. We cannot overvalue them. But, unlike the shining baubles of ostentatious and unrighteous power, they are valuable in their use. In that alone are they good; and their most important use is, to be made the touchstone of the merits of those we trust.

Are these principles in danger? Every candid man, who will enquire, must think so. They were never in danger so imminent. Their foe is rich, disciplined, and wily. He obeys no rules of civilized warfare, no restraint of truth, no injustice, no pleadings of humanity. He already occupies the principal posts heretofore relied on, as the chief defence of our liberty; every where lies in wait to deceive; endeavors to poison the springs of resistance to him; seduces the unwary, disloyal, and sordid, by flattery, lucrative employment, and offers of preferment; intimidates the irresolute and weak, by haughty exhibitions of his power, and assails by a thousand ambuscades, and by all sorts of weapons the most envenomed and condemned, the watchful, thoughtful, steadfast, and unconquerable friends of free principles. Such a foe is freemasonry.

This appears incredible to honest unreflecting men, till they fairly understand the character of freemasonry, and ascertain its conduct. Whenever they do this, the incredibility vanishes; they join the great rally of antimasons, and work with one mind and untiring zeal, in all the way of law and honor, for its abolition. The disinclination to take up impressions of evil against it arises, almost wholly, from the fair characters of some men, who have been connected with it, and from the support of it, by interested politicians, and the presses under its control.

Honorable men have joined it, in early life. Incited by unsuspected representations of its purity and value, and by curiosity to explore a mystery, they surrendered themselves to the wish of its members, and offered to be conducted into its dark chambers. Of these we know some stopped at the threshold; some, in the first degree; some in the second; and more, in the third. None of them knew any thing of its peculiar ceremonies, oaths, or objects, till they had sworn to conceal them. They have often praised the virtues it claimed, for they loved virtue, and hoped the claim was just. But they never imbibed its spirit, or knowingly approved its principles. From the first step of their initiation, they always suspected both. If they did not, we should have heard from some of the ten thousand conscientious and patriotic seceders, who have opened the door upon all its proceedings, of fathers leading their sons to the masonic altar. Among them all, the seceders have probably witnessed admissions to nearly every lodge in the union. No one has told you, that he ever assisted at the initiation of his own son, or knew any other father do so, in relation to his son. Is not this a most honest, legible, and fatal condemnation of the order, derived from witnesses the most competent and credible though unwilling—even from the very hearts of its adhering members? What! would not a father initiate his son, the pride of his life, the hope of his age, the object of his prayers, into an association of honorable men most exclusively designed, and most wisely adapted, to the inculcation of science, charity, religion? How have good fathers done, who have become freemasons? Let each one look around among his acquaintances, and recall his past observation, for the answer. They have discontinued attendance upon the lodges. They have preferred other schools of science, for their children. They have resorted to better means of impressing the love and practice of charity upon their hearts. They have looked higher for their religion. Either the best of fathers, who had joined the lodge, were anti-masons in the bottom of their hearts, knowing the institution to be a base imposture; or they hated their children.

But how have members, who were most distinguished for public honor and private virtue out of the lodge, conducted, in relation to it? Franklin is said to have replied to his brother, who asked his advice about joining the society, "one fool is enough in a family." When the reputable and benevolent Jeremy Gridley, was grand master of the Massachusetts masons, before the most criminal degrees of the order where known in our country, he was enquired of, by a young friend, whether it was worth his while to become a mason? and he answered NO—with this pregnant addition, "by aggregation to the society a young man might acquire a little *artificial* support, but that *he* did not need it; and there was *nothing* in the masonic institution *worthy of his seeking to be associated with it.*" The enquirer, afterwards, by his bold and freedom-freighted thoughts, and the high bearing of his devoted expression of them, was the most prominent agent in carrying the declaration of independence, in the illustrious congress of '76.

But, Washington, and his brother officers of glorious memory, were masons. True. They were admitted to three degrees. None of them went higher, in the early days of our independence. Washington never visited a lodge but once or twice after 1768; and never presided in one. He afterwards in effect, renounced it; and so did a large majority of the officers before alluded to, in their voluntary determination to extinguish the Cincinnati society. To this society they were bound by stronger ties than masonry can offer to uncorrupted minds—by those of a natural and general and generous sympathy, of which the golden links were struck out and forged, in the welding fires of our revolutionary war.

The origin of this society was innocent; its objects were laudable; its laws were published; its meetings were not secret; it administered no oaths, imposed no bloody penalties, had no division into degrees, and its members were respected and honored as the benefactors of their country; but it introduced distinctions between its members and other citizens; its associates wore badges, a ribbon and eagle; it was hereditary; admitted honorary members; and had funds for charity. Thus constituted all the whigs of the country, in civil life, as soon as it was known to them, opposed it, as eminently dangerous to liberty. It had no political objects. The conduct of its members, and the true purpose of the association were excellent. But it was liable to abuse. Political means were resorted to, for its abolition. Governors of states denounced it; legislative bodies expressed their opposition to it, by resolutions; assemblies of private citizens reprobated it; the press sternly and universally rebuked it; the whole country was excited to a flame against it.

Washington soon became sensible that it might produce political evils, which the pure and strong motives, in which it originated, had hidden from their observation of its members. And he attended its first annual meeting determined to exert all his influence for its suppression. He did so exert it. And the order was on the point of being annihilated by the vote of *the great majority* of its members. Its complete annihilation was prevented, only by a sense of courtesy and consistency towards their foreign brother officers, whom the members had officially and formally invited to join it, before they had well considered the abuses of which it was susceptible, and the political tendencies, which it might foster. They did destroy its essential features, by resolving that the order should be no longer hereditary, and that no new members should be admitted. They discontinued wearing its badges, in this country; and left nothing of its existence, but its name, its meetings, which were changed from being annual to triennial, and its charitable funds, which were ordered to be deposited with the state legislatures. This fundamental modification, with the well known cause of its continuance, in the shape it was made to assume by its own members, appeased the public; though Jefferson, and many others, expressed a decided disapprobation of its continuance at all.

Compare this society with freemasonry, in its motives, its origin, its degrading ceremonies, its accumulation of titles, its numerous expressive through fantastic badges; its exacting obedience in the lower degrees, and irresponsible authority in the higher; its secrecy; its oaths; its penalties; its claims of exclusive allegiance; its long list of degrees; its means of private recognition, command and universal concert; its affiliation with members in all foreign countries; its numbers; its boasted power; its crimes, and the pertinacity with which it is sustained, by its adhering members; and it is impossible not to be convinced, that it is exceedingly dangerous; and that those, who were willing to renounce the Cincinnati society, would be compelled, by the same patriotic motives, which controlled them, in that act, if they had lived till now, to renounce freemasonry. They would have insisted upon its total abrogation. It must be abrogated.

The unavoidable inference drawn by every prudent man, from observing the conduct of its best members, in all past time, is, that its character is bad. This inference is greatly strengthened, by the intelligible hints and friendly advice of the most trust worthy among them. It should be ripened into unhesitating conviction by a consideration of the secrecy which it enjoins. *Standing secrecy always implies shame and guilt.* It is utterly inconsistent with social improvement, confidence and happiness. All the descendants of Adam inherit his nature. While he was innocent, he was ingenuous, communicative, without the need, or the desire, of concealment. For the first crime he committed, even before the sentence of banishment from Paradise, was pronounced upon him, he sought concealment.

But we are not left to our own reasonable inferences, or to hints, and a few honest but guarded expressions, from its members, to decide upon the character of freemasonry. That character has been revealed, under oath, by its adhering members, and by a great band of seceders. And how does it stand? Infamous beyond all parallel in human annals. Its principles are vicious, murderous, treasonable; and so far as they prevail fatally hostile to those of our government.

In the first degree, the candidate pledges himself under oath, and upon forfeiture of his life if he does not redeem the pledge, to ever conceal and never reveal the secrets of freemasonry, which he had then received, is about to receive, or may thereafter be instructed in. Among the secrets, which the candidate may, and must be instructed in, if he takes the second degree, is that of his pledge of passive obedience to the laws of the lodge, and and all regular summonses sent him by a brother of that degree. If he takes the third degree, among those secrets are pledges to fly to the relief of a brother of that degree, when masonically required so to do, at the risk of life, should there be a great probability of saving the life of the brother requiring, than of losing his own to apprise a brother of all approaching danger if possible—and to conceal the secrets of a brother master mason when communicated to him as such, murder and treason only excepted, and they left at his discretion. And if he takes the royal arch degree, among those secrets are pledges—to extricate a brother of that degree from danger, if he can, whether that brother be right or wrong—to promote his political preferment before that of all others of equal qualifications—and to conceal his secrets, murder and treason not excepted. Thus is the concealment of crimes made a masonic duty; and the candidates expressly disclaim all equivocation, mental reservation or evasion of mind, both in the first degree and in the last.

How do these parts of masonry affect the moral character of its members? In the first degree, and every other, no man knows any of its obligations, till after he has sworn to conceal them. It is a first principle in morals, that there is no accountability without knowledge and free will. Such oaths, therefore, are not binding, and no forms, or objects, or

solemnities, can make them so. But what is the purpose of the order, in the ceremony of imposing them? Can it be good? It is certainly such as can be accomplished only by men divested of all sense of accountability. The less of this sense the better, for all the purposes of fraud and crime—and the more of it the better, for all the purposes of integrity and virtue. These are truths, which nobody can gainsay. All the history of piety, on the one hand, and of sin on the other, asserts them. They are obvious to the common sense of all men. This proceeding of freemasonry, is, therefore obviously in hostility to good morals. It is more than that. To take such an oath deliberately and with an intent to perform it, is an attempt at the voluntary extinguishment of the highest rights of the soul, and a complete foreclosure of the source of every duty. It is not possible to imagine a more aggravated crime. Rape, murder, treason, may be repented of, and their perpetrators reclaimed. But to forego the rights of knowledge and volition, in regard to every proposition, which can be offered to a moral agent, amounts to a desperate erasure of the image of God from the breast. It would necessarily preclude repentance, reformation, pardon, hope; and be death, in its most unutterable horrors. It would be as much worse than common suicide, as the value of the immortal spirit is greater than that of the corruptible body.

In the degrees, higher than the royal arch, the members swear to oppose the interest, derange the business, and destroy the reputation, of unfaithful brethren, through life,—to prefer the interests of a companion of the order; and of a companion's friend, for whom he pleads, to those of any mere man of the world, in matters of difference submitted to them—never to engage in mean party strife, nor conspiracies against the government or religion of their country, *whereby their reputation may suffer,* nor ever to associate with dishonorable men, for a moment, except *it be to secure* the interest of such person, his family, or friends, to a companion, whose necessities require this *degradation* at their hands—to follow strictly every command of the illustrious knights, and grand commander, and especially to *sacrifice the traitors of masonry.*

Have these points of masonic obligation any political bearing? All the rights of man are founded in his moral nature. It is the intention of free government to secure him in the possession of these rights. Whatever is hostile to good morals is therefore opposed to the civil policy of freemen. We have seen large numbers of the most intelligent, wealthy, and respectable freemasons in New York, debating in their lodges and elsewhere, on the means of suppressing a written disclosure of their secrets, by one of their number—we have seen notices of a slanderous character, simultaneously printed, a few days before the seizure and murder of Morgan, in newspapers a hundred miles apart, warning the public against the designs of the author of this disclosure and especially directed to the masonic brotherhood—about the same time we have seen masons set fire to a building prepared by them with peculiar care for sudden combustion, because it was supposed to contain this disclosure in manuscript—we have seen them employ a masonic printer, who was a stranger and an alien, to go into the office where it was printing, with the offer to aid in that work by labor and money, for the sole purpose of stealing the manuscript—we have afterwards seen them kidnap the writer of it, carry him hoodwinked and bound, with the greatest secrecy and caution, through a great extent of populous country, to a fort of the United States—unlawfully and forcibly imprison him there—collect together in frequent deliberation, upon the means of his final disposition—communicate,

while in this situation, with several members of a chapter of their body, then numerously attended in the neighborhood—and resolve unanimously, though with painful reluctance, on the part of some, that their masonic obligations required them to murder him; not for any offence against the state, but for the sole cause of his attempting to publish the secrets of the order, which he had a lawful right to do, and which, considering their character, he was bound to do, by every consideration of private morality and fidelity to his country. On the night of the 18th of September, 1826, they accordingly murdered him. To this tearful consummation none were privy, but those who had as masons, sworn to assist each other right or wrong, and to conceal each other's murder and treason. After the murder, all the precaution possible was taken for concealing it; but this not being wholly successful, and legal prosecutions being threatened, the criminals frequently met and consulted together, for their mutual safety. The most influential among them insisted, that if called by the legal authorities of our country to testify, they one and all must swear they knew nothing of the matter; otherwise they would be forsworn to masonry and might lose the life they would thus forfeit. As witnesses, as magistrates, as sheriffs, as grand jurors, as petit jurors, as legislators, these masons and others with whom they were intimate, *would* know nothing of it. In all their civil relations they violated their oaths and the most sacred duties. They flew to each others' assistance knowing their criminality. They gave each other notice of the approaching danger of legal prosecution. They spirited away witnesses who, they feared, would disclose too much. They perjured themselves in court. They contumaciously refused to answer questions decided to be legal. They declined to answer, on the ground, that if they should, they would criminate themselves in relation to the murder. They prevented the judicial ascertainment, and punishment of the foulest criminals. They made common cause in behalf of these criminals, against the rights of the citizen, and the laws of the land. Thousands of them were acquainted with some of the steps of these crimes against the state. Hundreds of them know the leading malefactors.

A good citizen cannot look on with indifference and see a fellow freeman kidnapped and murdered. He cannot know that such crimes are successfully protected, by an extensive, artful, and powerful conspiracy, without being excited against it. The sympathies of a patriot embrace his whole country. The poorest man, the most defenceless woman, the weakest child in it, cannot be assailed with unlawful violence, without quickening his pulse, and stiffening his sinews, with indignation. His blood is up in every case of high crime; and it keeps up against the aggressor, till the law performs its office upon him. To the law he is willing to submit, because he knows it is the deliberate expression of the public will for the public good; the great shield spread by the hands of all, over the rights of all.

Individual rights are, separately considered, of immeasurable and indefinable worth. They partake of the infinitude of moral existence and responsibility. As contemplated by our government, a single individual, and one as much as another, is an august being, entitled to inviolable reverence, and bearing upon him the badges of a most majestic origin, and the stamp of most transcendent destinations. His safety, his liberty, his life, his improvement, his happiness, it designs, at all times and places, faithfully to protect, by the application of all its delegated means. The law is the beneficial instrument of this protection, and should be appreciated by every reflecting man as the sacred, living, and most venerable expression of the national mind and

will. Break this, and the nation has but one right left, which it can peaceably enforce, the right of suffrage.

The masonic institution is answerable for the crimes to which we have referred. They were committed in obedience to its prescribed and specific oaths, and in fear of its penalties. The man-stealing and murder, were for no other than a masonic offence. The whole array of its frightful crimes, out of court, and in court, were no other than necessary means of carrying into effect the obligations it has deliberately and universally exacted of its members. All who uphold the obligations, uphold the crimes. No adhering mason has afforded the least willing assistance to the exposure and punishment of them. No lodge or chapter has called the criminals to account. Many of them are known to the public. Cheseboro, and Sawyer, and Lawson, and Bruce, and Whitney, have been convicted of the conspiracy to kidnap, and have been condemned and suffered infamous punishments, and the very murderers are known with moral, though not with strict judicial certainty. Not one of these men have been expelled. The grand lodge or grand chapter of which they were members, has the power of expulsion, but has declined to exercise it in relation to them; and such of them as are still living, are, in masonic estimation, worthy members of the order.

But the fraternity have gone much farther to make that crime their own. In 1837 the grand lodge gave 100 dollars to one of its members then under public accusation for kidnapping Morgan, and afterwards convicted of that offence; and the grand chapter, by its vote, placed 1,000 dollars at the control of another of its members, ostensibly for charitable uses, of which a part has been proved, in a court of justice, to have been applied for the benefit of other kidnappers; and the trustee of the charity has never been called to an account by the grand chapter, for any part of the sum, though in all other cases such accountability is enforced by the chapter. The records of this last body, apparently relating to this transaction, have been produced in court, and were seen to be mutilated.

The fraternity have also employed and paid able counsel to defend the criminals.

In this way, while the chief magistrate of the state of New York was, by proclamation, offering money, for the conviction of the offenders, the highest masonic bodies, in that state, were offering, and in their associate capacity actually paying money to protect and support them. Can it be justly thought surprising, then, that so few convictions have followed upon such enormous offences, and that no more of the facts have been ascertained in legal form?

The criminals, in all these atrocities, testified their devotion to the institution, and by its own laws are only the more entitled to its guardian care, by all the hazards they involved. That care has been extended to them in every term of expression tending to their relief and comfort. Besides the exertions of their brethren already alluded to, adhering masons have, at great expense, established and circulated newspapers to vilify all who were engaged in exposing the crimes, and to call into action the entire resources of the fraternity, in behalf of those who committed them. These newspapers have, with the most unblushing hardihood, asserted the innocence and praised the virtues of the convicts, several of whom they knew to have confessed their offences. They have commended the most stubborn refusal in court to reveal the truth by masonic witnesses, *as manly firmness.* They have in every form of misrepresentation, which they could devise, labored to darken all knowledge of the facts relating to the outrages; and to blot out the moral sense of the community.

Hundreds of the brethren in different counties in the state of New York, have published addresses, under their names, in which they have deliberately contradicted facts established judicially, by many of their adhering brethren and by many seceding masons; and which, under the sanction of a lawful oath, and subject to cross examination before the public, they would be compelled to admit. Similar falsehoods have been published in an address of a committee of the grand lodge of Rhode Island—and the grand secretary of the grand lodge of New York has recently issued an official letter, in which he represents that body as extending its dependants, confident in its strength, and determined to outbrave all the consequences of their detected guilt, and the public indignation. Nothing could account for this universal course of falsehood, but the unhappy truth, that the men who are engaged in it, have sworn, under the penalty of death, to conceal the secrets of freemasonry, a most essential branch of which consists in the crimes of its members. This course is countenanced by the president of the U. States, who is a mason, and who has recently appointed as heads of the departments in the national government, a majority of distinguished masons. One of these heads of departments—the post master general, the only one retained of the late cabinet, has removed a large number of his most competent and faithful deputies, in New York, for the sole cause of the zeal and patriotism with which they sought to bring into just disrepute the crimes and institution of freemasonry.

The course of these transactions is rapidly corroding and wearing away the very basis of all public and private virtue in our country; and eradicating that mutual confidence, upon which the business of life, its peace, and its enjoyments essentially depend. When men refuse to bear testimony in court, to public offences, of which they know the perpetrators, and are praised for it— when they perjure themselves, and are not disgraced—when they are convicted of a conspiracy to kidnap a free citizen, and are applauded as victims to the prejudices of their countrymen—when the distinctions between right and wrong are practically superseded, by the systematic and solemn injunctions of a wealthy, intelligent, numerous and powerful society, diffused and sustaining itself in all the places of social influence and honor—when in pursuance of this injunction, the laws of the land, in the solemn places of their judicial application for the admonition and punishment of the most flagrant offences, are foully baffled, set aside and scorned—then, the social fabric is trembling—then there can be but one alternative, that of reform or ruin—then, looking beyond, but not forgetting, all the considerations of attachment to the policy of encouraging this or that branch of national industry—this or that scheme of financial management,—this or that exposition of the principles of our political organization—this or that object of all our foreign and domestic policy, the considerate friend of his country will govern himself primarily, by the obvious necessity to which he is reduced of preserving for his country the power of determining for itself upon any course of policy, and of disengaging the heart of the body politic from the fangs of a monster more blood thirsty, remorseless and insatiable, than any, which has ever come to prey upon the hopes of man.

There is a bearing of freemasonry, not yet embraced in this address, which is replete with the most distressing apprehensions. There is located, in Boston, a masonic body denominated the African grand lodge, which dates its origin before the American revolution, and derived its existence from a Scottish duke. This body acknowledges no allegiance to any of the associations of American masonry. Its authority is co-extensive with our union. It has already granted many charters to African

lodges. We are afraid to intimate their location, to look in upon their proceedings, to count their inmates, or to specify their resources.

What are the means of removing these dangers? The dangers are confined to no one place, in our country, and to no one department of our social interests; but extend to all places, and infect every department. Common prudence demands, that the means should be capable of reaching them, wherever they exist, and susceptible of a safe application, in their utmost extent. Such means we have; and we are familiar with their use. They consist in the honest exercise of the right of suffrage, and the most patriotic employment of official patronage. The evils of freemasonry operate upon the moral and political condition of the nation, and can be removed only by moral and political means. It is the exalted excellence of our political institutions, that they are especially designed and adapted to secure our rights, all of which pertain to us as moral beings. In voting, every elector should always be governed by a knowledge of his rights, and the desire of preserving them. There can be no higher political duty than this.

But the use of our right of suffrage against freemasonry is termed proscription. Proscription cannot be imputed to a party, because it justly opposes what is wrong. It is not proscription to be resolute and active in detecting and denouncing opinions of which the obvious tendency is to unhinge society; or to resist, by every lawful means, the influence of men, who commit crimes, and confederate to support each other in their commission. To call such detection, denunciation and resistance, proscription, could never satisfy an honest mind. It would be like stigmatising, with an opprobrious epithet, those public benefactors, who teach men, that all violations of duty are criminal and disreputable, and make their best exertions to discourage them. Proscription can apply only to those, who oppose and lessen the influence of their fellow citizens, because they innocently and with good motives, think and act differently from themselves. Such proscription deserves reprehension, because it invades the equal rights of others, and is averse to the improvement and happiness of all.

The offences of freemasonry upon our individual and national rights, if they had been committed by a foreign nation would, by the law of nations, have justified a public war to avenge them. Shall we fall in love with crime because those who commit it are near us? Shall we spare the destroyed because we can subdue him peaceably? Freemasonry can be destroyed by the votes of freeman, and by nothing else. All who are truly opposed to it, will always vote against it. And they deceive nobody but themselves, who profess opposition to it, and yet dare to express that opposition by their vote.

No good reason has been rendered, or can be rendered, who a freeman, who is opposed to freemasonry, should not vote against it. The application of the right of suffrage against it is just, peaceable, effective and may be as comprehensive as the evils which alarm us. And no other means can be described, or imagined which unite these characteristics. Voting is the only decisive means by which public opinion can be distinctly ascertained upon the subject. And since many persons not initiated into the society, openly connect themselves with its fortunes, and make every exertion in their power to sustain it, by their votes, we cannot safely, if we would, betake ourselves to any other resort but the ballot boxes for its destruction. These persons affect to consider themselves as entitled to the praise of all candid and unexcited minds, by the course which they adopt; and profess to be neither masons nor anti-masons; claiming the respect of the community for their indifference to its

rights and welfare. If it has not been for the support of the order, by interested and profligate politicians, who were not members, the forfeiture of public confidence justly incurred, by its crimes, would have been so carried home to the minds of its most worthy members, as long ago to have induced its entire dissolution. It is an undoubted fact, that the men, who are neither masons nor anti-masons, are answerable for the continuance of the order. They have kept it from sinking into annihilation by its sins, and are thus equally censurable with its members. No association of men, however impudent and hardened can withstand, for years, the indignant, well founded, universal rebuke of their fellow citizens. So treated, the worst members would be driven from the face of the sun, and from public observation, into the fastnesses and caves of the earth, to take upon themselves the skulking habits, along with the flagitious purposes, of felons; and the best would be compelled to abandon it.

It is attempted to make anti-masonry odious, because it is political. But these attempts must recoil upon those with whom they originate. None but tyrants can think the use of political means degrading. And there seems to be peculiar effrontry required to impeach it, in a country where every thing most memorable, in its history has been inseparably connected with political movement, and every thing most animating in its prospects, is dependent upon political action and supervision. The exertions of our fathers to establish our independence, were political exertions. Even the revolutionary war and the war of 1812, were waged for political objects. The constitutions, by which our civil and religious rights are secured, are political constitutions. And this independence, these constitutions, and rights, can be preserved and perpetuated only by political means.

Voting for our public servants is the highest exercise of sovereign power known in our land. It is the paramount distinctive privilege of freemen. In countries where only a small minority of the people are authorised to vote, if oppressive measures are adopted, by their rules, they must either submit, or fight. In countries where all the citizens are authorised to vote, if they are oppressed, they can throw off the oppression, by their votes. And if the frowns of power, or the calumnies of malefactors have force to dissuade them from using their votes to throw it off, they are fit for slaves, and can be only slaves. The highest functionaries of the general and state governments are amenable to the people, for the proper discharge of their duties. But a freeman, when he votes for a candidate, exercises the right of selecting, among those who are eligible, subject to no authority under heaven. For his choice, he is accountable only to his conscience and his God. And who should he not, in the most sovereign act he can perform, do himself the great justice of giving expression to the honest conviction of his soul? If having the will, he cannot do it, he is a slave. If having the power, he will not do it, he is corrupt.

An enlightened exercise of the right of suffrage is the constitutional and equitable mode adopted by the antimasons to remove the evils they suffer, and produce the reforms they seek. But this mode, to be availing, must include a judicious selection of candidates. After diligent inquiry and mature deliberation we have selected, and now nominate, for your support, as a candidate for the office of president of the United States, at the next election,

WILLIAM WIRT, of Maryland

And for vice president,

AMOS ELLMAKER, of Pennsylvania.

These citizens we deem eminently possessed of the qualifications before set forth, as most essential for the offices, which they have associated their names—and confident of their devoted attachment to the principles

of administration contained in this address, and their concurrence in our views of the crimes of freemasonry, and the necessity of their removal, by directing against them the sovereign and the free remedy of public suffrage, and the bestowment of official favors, we earnestly recommend them to your support. Their election would be a great step towards the rescue of our republic from the odious and formidable power which endangers it; and we will labor to accomplish it, in the spirit of freemen. In this labor we invite you to participate.

Our free principles cannot be preserved without constant vigilance, and a continuance of the same disinterested and determined action, by which they were established. They are the best possession of the rich, and the only wealth of the poor. They are the common and peculiar property of the nation, embracing all its rights, its virtues and its fortunes.

Neither the price of our liberties nor their fruits will permit them to be regarded without emotion, by any intelligent mind. They have been purchased by ages of just, and earnest thought, of brave and generous effort, of vicissitude, and suffering, and blood. Nor have they been purchased in vain. They have taught man to form a just estimate of his own worth, and that of his fellow beings, to estimate the value of a reasonable and responsible creature, not by the place which he may hold in an artificial and unnatural state of society, but solely by the faculties conferred upon him, by his Maker, and the intelligence and virtues of his character. And while they have abased the proud from his stilted and haughty elevation, they have brought up the poor to the exalted standard of human rights and human hopes; and thus opened the way for the whole family of man, "to run the great career of justice." We have set out first in this career. Let us remove every impediment, which would obstruct our progress in it, and by the attractions of our success invite all nations to embrace it. If we are true to ourselves, our institutions, our fathers and our posterity, this is to be our glorious destiny.—The influence of our example is already great. In our foreign conflicts and negotiations, our vigor, prudence, and wisdom, have made us respected and illustrious. Let not these qualities be wanting in their proper domestic applications, that the values of our example may be enhanced, and its influence increased. Providence has manifestly cast upon us the high responsibility of determining the most interesting problem of social life, that of man's capacity for self-government. If we suppress all unsocial conspiracy and selfish faction, from within, as we hitherto have done all dictation and tyranny from without, we shall determine it in favor of liberty. Such a determination the great and good of every nation expect from us; and they are beginning, in the face of all their foes, to hazard upon it, their possessions, their honor and their lives. Let us neither disappoint them, nor betray ourselves. A disinterested and faithful adherence to the principles which we inculcate, and to the modes of sustaining them, which we recommend, becomes both our cause and our responsibility; and irresistably commending itself to the honest and free, it will give that cause success. If it fails, then right, duty, improvement, self-government, happiness, are phantoms. We shall be compelled to repudiate the memory of our immortal sires, and forego the great inheritance they have bequeathed us. But it will not fail. Freedom is not more the friend of man, than the favorite of heaven. It is equally our highest glory, our most sacred duty, our most assured hope and our promised possession.

Democratic Party Platform (1840)

Andrew Jackson's two terms as president forged a national majority for the Democratic party that included farmers, mechanics, and laborers from all regions of the country, especially the South and West. Reaping the political harvest of "Jacksonian Democracy," the president's handpicked successor, Vice President Martin Van Buren of New York, was elected to succeed him in 1836.

Van Buren and the Democrats were opposed by the two-year-old Whig party, which included virtually everyone who disliked Jackson: National Republicans, Anti-Masons, and disgruntled Democratic supporters of former vice president John C. Calhoun. (See "Proceedings of the Anti-Masonic Convention," p. 143.) So strange an assortment of political bedfellows were the Whigs that, instead of agreeing upon a single nominee for president in 1836, they ran three regional candidates against Van Buren: Sen. Daniel Webster of Massachusetts, Sen. Hugh L. White of Tennessee, and Gen. William Henry Harrison of Ohio, who had been a military hero during the War of 1812.

The Whigs' hope—to deny Van Buren enough electoral votes to throw the election into the House of Representatives— was foiled when the vice president won 764,176 popular votes (50.8 percent) and 170 electoral votes, more than his three opponents combined. Van Buren's vice presidential running mate, Rep. Richard M. Johnson of Kentucky, had to be elected by the Senate after Virginia's twenty-three Democratic electors, offended by Johnson's relationship with a series of slave mistresses, withheld their votes. (See "The Twelfth Amendment: Senate Debate," p. 89.)

Throughout his political career, Van Buren was a painstaking and skillful builder of grassroots political party organizations. By encouraging the practice of rewarding local party workers with government jobs and other forms of patronage—the so-called "spoils system"—Van Buren helped to transform the Democrats into the modern world's first mass-based political party. Whigs and, in later years, Republicans copied his techniques in their parties. Van Buren's posthumously published book, An Inquiry Into the Origin and Course of Political Parties in the United States (1867), revealed him to be as brilliant a theorist of political parties as he was a practitioner of party politics.

In 1840, Van Buren encouraged the Democratic national convention, which was meeting in Baltimore, Maryland, on May 5-6, to adopt the first national party platform in history. A model of brevity, the Democratic platform consisted of nine statements of orthodox Jacksonian principles. The convention enacted the platform after unani-

mously renominating Van Buren to run for a second term as president.

In future years, party platforms would become considerably longer than the 1840 Democratic platform, packed with programmatic promises and with rhetoric that was alternately boastful and alarmist. (See, for example, "Republican Party Platform [1980]," p. 677.) Widespread doubts would arise about both the sincerity and the actual influence of platforms, as evidenced by the familiar political saying, "A platform is what you start by running on and end by running from." Research by political scientists such as Gerald Pomper and Benjamin Ginsberg, however, indicates that, at various times, platforms have reflected both real differences between the political parties and a genuine commitment to governmental change. ～

1. *Resolved,* That the federal government is one of limited powers, derived solely from the constitution, and the grants of power shown therein, ought to be strictly construed by all the departments and agents of the government, and that it is inexpedient and dangerous to exercise doubtful constitutional powers.

2. *Resolved,* That the constitution does not confer upon the general government the power to commence and carry on, a general system of internal improvements.

3. *Resolved,* That the constitution does not confer authority upon the federal government, directly or indirectly, to assume the debts of the several states, contracted for local internal improvements, or other state purposes; nor would such assumption be just or expedient.

4. *Resolved,* That justice and sound policy forbid the federal government to foster one branch of industry to the detriment of another or to cherish the interests of one portion to the injury of another portion of our common country—that every citizen and every section of the country, has a right to demand and insist upon an equality of rights and privileges, and to complete and ample protection of person and property from domestic violence, or foreign aggression.

5. *Resolved,* That it is the duty of every branch of the government, to enforce and practice the most rigid economy, in conducting our public affairs, and that no more revenue ought to be raised, than is required to defray the necessary expenses of the government.

6. *Resolved,* That congress has no power to charter a national bank; that we believe such an institution one of deadly hostility to the best interests of the country, dangerous to our republican institutions and the liberties of the people, and calculated to place the business of the country within the control of a concentrated money power, and above the laws and the will of the people.

7. *Resolved,* That congress has no power, under the constitution, to interfere with or control the domestic institutions of the several states, and that such states are the sole and proper judges of everything appertaining to their own affairs, not prohibited by the constitution; that all efforts by abolitionists or others, made to induce congress to interfere with questions of slavery, or to take incipient steps in relation thereto, are calculated to lead to the most alarming and dangerous consequences, and that all such efforts have an inevitable tendency to diminish the happiness of the people, and endanger the stability and permanency of the union, and ought not to be countenanced by any friend to our political institutions.

8. *Resolved,* That the separation of the moneys of the government from banking institutions, is indispensable for the safety of the funds of the government, and the rights of the people.

9. *Resolved,* That the liberal principles embodied by Jefferson in the Declaration of Independence, and sanctioned in the constitution which makes ours the land of liberty, and the asylum of the oppressed of every nation, have ever been cardinal principles in the democratic faith; and every attempt to abridge the present privilege of becoming citizens, and the owners of soil among us, ought to be resisted with the same spirit which swept the alien and sedition laws from our statute-book.

Campaign Speech by William Henry Harrison (1840)

Somewhat to the surprise of party leaders, Gen. William Henry Harrison of Ohio turned out to be by far the strongest of the three Whig nominees for president in 1836: his seventy-three electoral votes and 550,816 popular votes far exceeded the combined totals of the party's other two candidates. (See "Democratic Party Platform [1840]," p. 164.) With the gaze of its delegates firmly fixed on victory in 1840, the Whig national convention, meeting in Baltimore, Maryland, in December 1839, rejected the candidacy of the party's preeminent leader, Sen. Henry Clay of Kentucky, and nominated Harrison for president.

The Harrison campaign was an early precursor of modern "image campaigning." President Andrew Jackson's appeal, Whig strategists believed, had been based on his reputation as a self-made man of the people ("Old Hickory") and a brilliant general (the "Hero of New Orleans"). Reaching out to the same socially and geographically broad electorate that had supported Jackson in 1824, 1828, and 1832, Whigs contrived to portray the well-born, college-educated Harrison as "Old Buckeye," the "hard-cider, log-cabin" candidate. Although Harrison's own military victory over the Shawnee chief, Tecumseh, in 1811 had been sloppily fought, Whigs also billed him as "the Hero of Tippecanoe." Indeed,

when Gov. John Tyler of Virginia was added to the ticket as Harrison's vice presidential running mate, the Whig party slogan became "Tippecanoe and Tyler Too."

The Democratic nominee in 1840, President Martin Van Buren, faced serious political problems because of the Panic of 1837. After years of feverish business growth, overspeculation in land and securities, and unregulated financial and commercial practices, the national economy had crashed just after Van Buren became president in March 1837. During the 1840 campaign, the Whigs added to Van Buren's woes with a series of personal attacks that portrayed him, somewhat unfairly, as a high-living, effete snob. Image campaigning and negative campaigning came together in a favorite Whig song:

> Let Van from his coolers of silver drink
> wine,
> And lounge on his cushioned settee;
> Our man on his buckeye bench can
> recline
> Content with hard cider is he.

Harrison's personal contribution to the history of presidential elections was to make the first campaign speech ever delivered to the voters by a major-party nominee. The prevailing custom, which was restored in future nineteenth-century elections, was for presidential candidates to remain silent

*while others campaigned in their be-
half. Harrison, sixty-eight years old
and riled by Democratic charges that
he was senile, insisted on speaking personally to twenty-three public audiences. Avoiding the issues (a wise decision in view of his party's divisions
among nationalists and states'-
rightsers, protectionists and free trad-
ers, and slaveholders and abolitionists), Harrison told a wildly cheering
crowd in Dayton, Ohio, on September
10, 1840, that "I cannot consent to
make mere* promises *the condition of
obtaining the office, which you kindly
wish to bestow upon me." Instead, he
spoke first of himself, then of the importance that the Whigs attached to
restoring to Congress the powers that
recent Democratic presidents had
seized for the executive.*

*Harrison's declamations against
presidential power notwithstanding—
he even promised "before Heaven and
earth, if elected President of these
United States, to lay down at the end
of the term faithfully that high trust at
the feet of the people!"—the election of
1840 illustrated the growing importance of the presidency as an institution. The campaign centered on the
personalities of the candidates. As to
substance, in contrast to the Panic of
1819, which was followed by President
James Monroe's near-unanimous reelection in 1820, the voters now attached much of the blame for the economic hard times to the president. In
one of the highest turnout elections in
history—80.2 percent of the eligible
voters in the country, a percentage
exceeded only in 1860 and 1876—Harrison defeated President Van Buren by
234 to 60 in the electoral college and by
1,275,390 (52.9 percent) to 1,128,854
(46.8 percent) in the popular vote.* ~

I rise, fellow citizens, (the multitude
was here agitated as the sea, when the
wild wind blows upon it, and it was a
full five minutes before the tumult of
joy, at seeing and hearing the next President of the United States, could be
calmed)—I rise, fellow citizens, to express to you from the bottom of a
grateful heart, my warmest thanks for
the kind and flattering manner in which
I have been received by the representatives of the valley of the Miami. I rise
to say to you, that however magnificent
my reception has been on this occasion,
I am not so vain as to presume that it
was intended for me; that this glorious
triumphal entry was designed for one
individual. No. I know too well that
person's imperfections to believe that
this vast assemblage has come up here
to do him honor. It is the glorious cause
of democratic rights that brought them
here. [Immense cheering.] It is the
proud anniversary of one of the
brightest victories that glows on the
pages of our country's history, which
hath summoned this multitude together. [Tremendous cheering.]

Fellow citizens, it was about this time
of the day, twenty-seven years ago, this
very hour, this very minute, that your
speaker, as commander-in-chief of the
North-Western army, was plunged into
an agony of feeling when the cannonad-
ing from our fleet announced an action
with the enemy. His hopes, his fears,
were destined to be soon quieted, for
the tidings of victory were brought to
him on the wings of the wind. With the
eagle of triumph perching upon our
banners on the lake, I moved on to
complete the overthrow of the foreign
foe. The anniversary of that day can
never be forgotten, for every American
has cause to rejoice at the triumph of
our arms on that momentous occasion;
but the brave and gallant hero of that
victory is gone, gone to that home
whither we are all hurrying, and to his
memory let us do that reverence due to
the deeds of so illustrious a patriot.
From Heaven does his soul look down
upon us, and gladden at the virtues
which still animate his generous coun-

trymen in recurring to his noble and glorious career while on earth. [Great sensation for several seconds.]

I am fully aware, my fellow citizens, that you expect from me some opinion upon the various questions which now agitate our country, from centre to circumference, with such fierce contention. Calumny, ever seeking to destroy all that is good in this world, hath proclaimed that I am averse from declaring my opinions on matters so interesting to you; but nothing can be more false. [Cheers.]

Have I not, time out of mind, proclaimed my opposition to a citizen's going forward among the people and soliciting votes for the Presidency? Have I not, many a time and often, said, that in my opinion, no man ought to aspire to the Presidency of these United States, unless he is designated as a candidate for that high office by the unbought wishes of the people? [Cheering.] If the candidate for so high an office be designated by a portion or a majority of the people, they will have come to the determination of sustaining such a man from a review of his past actions and life, and they will not exact pledges from him of what he will do and what he will not do, for their selection of him is proof enough that he will carry out the doctrines of his party. This plan of choosing a candidate for the Presidency is a much surer bar against corruption than the system of requiring promises. If the pledging plan is pursued, the effect will be, to offer the Presidential chair to the man who will make the *most* promises. [Laughter.] He who would pledge most, he who would promise most, would be the man to be voted for, and I have no hesitation in declaring my belief, that he would subject his course to be thus tied up by promises and pledges, would not stop to break them when once in office. [Cheering.] Are my views on this topic correct, or are they not? [With one voice the multitude indicated they were.]

If, fellow citizens, we examine the history of all Republics, we shall find as they receded from the purity of Representative Government, the condition of obtaining office was the making of promises. He who bid the highest in promises, was the favored candidate, and the higher the bids, the more marked and certain the corruption. Look at the progress of this thing in our own Republic. Were any pledges required of your Washington or your Adams? Adams was the candidate of the federal party, and as a statesman was bound to carry out the principles of his party. Was his successor, Thomas Jefferson, the high priest of constitutional democracy, called on for pledges? No. His whole like was a pledge of what he would do. And if we go back to this old system of selecting men for the Presidency, whose past career shall be a guarantee of their conduct when elected to the Chief Magistracy of the Republic, the nation would advance safely, rapidly, and surely in the path of prosperity. But of late years the other corrupting system of requiring pledges hath been adopted. The Presidency has been put up to the highest bidder in promises, and we see the result. It remains for you, my fellow citizens, to arrest this course of things.

While then, fellow citizens, I have never hesitated to declare my opinions on proper occasions upon the great questions before the nation, I cannot consent to make mere *promises* the condition of obtaining the office which you kindly wish to bestow upon me. My opinions I am free to express, but you already have them, sustained and supported by the acts of a long and arduous life. That life is a pledge of my future course, if I am elevated by your suffrages to the highest office in your gift. [Immense cheering for several seconds.]

It has been charged against me, fellow citizens, that I am a Federalist. While I acknowledge that the original Federal party of this country was actuated in its course by no improper motives, *I deny that I ever belonged to that class of politicians.* [Tremendous cheering.] How could I belong to that party? I was educated in the school of anti-federalism, and though too young to take an active part in the politics of the country, when at the reaction of the Constitution, the nation was divided into two great parties, my honored father had inducted me into the principles of Constitutional Democracy, and my teachers were the Henrys and the Masons of that period. He who declared that the seeds of monarchy were sown in the soil of the Constitution, was a leader in my school of politics. He, who said that "if this government be not a monarchy, it has an awful squinting towards a monarchy," was my Mentor. [Immense applause. Some time elapsed before order could be restored, at hearing these emphatic declarations of the General.] If I know my own feelings, if I know my own judgment, I believe now, as I did then, with the patriachs of the Jeffersonian school, that the seeds of monarchy were indeed sown in the fertile soil of our Federal Constitution; and that though for nearly fifty years they lay dormant, they at last sprouted and shot forth into strong and thriving plants, bearing blossoms and producing ripe fruit. *The Government is now a practical monarchy!* [Loud and long cheering indicating that the people felt full force of his declaration] Power is power, it matters not by what name it is called. The head of the Government exercising monarchical power, may be named King, Emperor, or Imaum, [great laughter] still he is a monarch. But this is not all. The President of these United States exercises a power superior to that vested in the hands of nearly all the European Kings. It is a power far greater than that ever dreamed of by the old Federal party.

It is an ultra federal power, it is despotism! [Cheering.] And I may here advert to an objection that has been made against me. It has been said, that if I ever should arrive at the dignified station occupied by my opponent, I would be glad and eager to retain the power enjoyed by the President of the United States. *Never, never.* [Tremendous cheering.] Though averse from pledges of every sort, I here openly and before the world declare that I will use all the power and influence vested in the office of President of the Union to abridge the power and influence of the National Executive! [It is impossible to describe the sensation produced by this declaration.] Is this federalism? [Cries of no, no, for several seconds.] In the Constitution, that glorious charter of our liberties, there is a defect, and that defect is, the term of service of the President,—not limited. This omission is the source of all the evil under which the country is laboring. If the privilege of being President of the United States had been limited to one term, the incumbent would devote all his time to the public interest, and there would be no cause to misrule the country. I shall not animadvert on the conduct of the present administration, lest you may in that case, conceive that I am aiming for the Presidency, to use it for selfish purposes. I should be an interested witness, if I entered into the subject. *But I pledge myself before Heaven and earth, if elected President of these United States, to lay down at the end of the term faithfully that high trust at the feet of the people!* [Here the multitude was so excited as to defy description.]

I go farther. I here declare before this vast assembly of the Miami Tribe (great laughter) that if I am elected, no human being shall ever know upon whom I would prefer to see the people's mantle fall; but I shall surrender this glorious badge of their authority into their own hands to bestow it as they please!— (nine cheers.) Is this federalism? (no, no, no.) Again in relation to the charge of being a federalist, I can refer to the doings previous to, and during, the late war. The federal party took ground against that war, and as a party, there never existed a purer band of patriots, for when the note of strife was sounded, they rallied under the banner of their country. But patriotic as they were, I do know *that I was not one of them!* [cheering.] I was denounced in unmeasured terms as one of the authors of that war, and was held up by the federal papers of the day as the marked object of the party. I could here name the man who came to me, and a more worthy man never lived, to say that he was mistaken in his views of my policy, as Governor of Indiana, when I was charged by the federalists as uselessly involving the country in an indian war. He told me that I acted rightly in that matter, and that the war was brought on by me as a matter of necessity. [Cries of name him, name him.] It was Mr. Gaston of North Carolina.—[Three cheers.] Is this a proof that I was a federalist?—[No, no, no.]

I have now got rid, my fellow citizens, of this baseless charge—no, I have not. There are a few more allegations to notice. I am not a professional speaker, nor a studied orator, but I am an old soldier and a farmer, and as my sole object is to speak what I think, you will excuse me if I do it in my own way. [Shouts of applause, and cries of—the old soldier and farmer for us.]

I have said that there were other allegations to notice.—To prove that I was a federalist, they assert that I supported the alien and sedition laws, and in doing so, violated the principles and express words of the Constitution. I did not, fellow citizens, ever participate in this measure—When these laws passed I was a soldier in the army of the United States! [Applause.]

Again, they censure me for my course in Congress, when I served you in that body as a representative of the North West Territory. And here I will advert to the fact that I represented, at the

time, a territory comprising now the States of Indiana, Illinois and Michigan. I was the sole representative of that immense extent of country. [A voice here cried—"And you are going to be again!" Tremendous cheering.] I understood federalism to be in its origin, so I understand it to be now. It was and is the accumulation of power in the Executive to be used and exercised for its own benefit. Was my conduct in Congress then such as to entitle me to the appellation of federalist?—[Cries of no, no, and cheering.]

I had the honor, as Chairman of a Committee in the year 1800, to devise a bill which had for its object to snatch from the grasp of speculators all this glorious country which now seems with rich harvests under the hands of the honest, industrious and virtuous husbandman. [Immense cheering.] Was I a federalist then? [Cries of no, no.] When I was Governor of Indiana, ask how unlimited power bestowed upon me was exercised—a power as high as that exercised by the present President of the United States! I was then sole monarch of the North West Territory! [Laughter.] Did I discharge my duties as Governor of that vast Territory in such a way as to show that I was in love with the tremendous powers invested in me? [Here some 4000 persons in one quarter of the crowd raised their hats in the air and rent it with shouts of—no, no, no. They were the delegation from Indiana. This prompt response from so many persons produced great sensation.] There is an essential difference between the President of the United States and me. When he was in the Convention which remodelled the Constitution of New York, he was for investing the Governor with the appointment of the Sheriffs.—When I was Governor of Indiana, and possessed the power of appointing all officers. I gave it up to the people! [Intense excitement and great cheering.] I never appointed any officer whatever, while Governor of Indiana, whether sheriff, coroner, judge, justice of the peace or aught else, without first consulting and obtaining the wishes of the people. [Shouts of applause.] Was this an evidence that I was a federalist? [No, no, no.]

I think I have now shown you, fellow citizens, conclusively, that my actions do not constitute me a federalist, and it is to them I proudly point as the shield against which the arrows of my calumniators will fall in vain. [Immense cheering.]

Methinks I hear a soft voice asking: Are you in favor of paper money? I AM. [Shouts of applause.] If you would know why I am in favor of the credit system, I can only say it is because I am a democrat. [Immense cheering.] The two systems are the only means, under Heaven, by which a poor industrious man may become a rich man without bowing to colossal wealth. [Cheers.] But with all this, I am not a Bank man. Once in my life I was, and then they cheated me out of every dollar I placed in their hands. [Shouts of laughter.] And I shall never indulge in this way again; for it is more than probable that I shall never again have money beyond the day's wants. But I am in favor of a correct banking system, for the simple reason, that the share of the precious metals, which, in the course of trade, falls to our lot, is much less than the circulating medium which our internal and external commerce demands, to raise our prices to a level with the prices of Europe, where the credit system does prevail. There must be some plan to multiply the gold and silver which our industry commands; and there is no other way to do this but by a safe banking system. [Great applause.] I do not pretend to say that a perfect system of banking can be devised. There is nothing in the offspring of the human mind that does not savor of imperfection. No plan of government or finance can be devised free from defect. After long deliberation, I have no hopes that this country

can ever go on to prosper under a pure specie currency. Such a currency but makes the poor poorer, and the rich richer. A properly devised banking system alone, possesses the capability of bringing the poor to a level with the rich.—[Tremendous cheering.]

I have peculiar notions of government. Perhaps I may err. I am no statesman by profession, but as I have already said, I am a half soldier and a half farmer, and it may be, that, if I am elected to the first office in your gift, my fellow citizens will be deceived in me, but I can assure them, that if, in carrying out their wishes, the head shall err, the heart is true. [Great huzzaing.]

My opinion of the power of Congress to charter a national bank remains unchanged. There is not in the Constitution any express grant of power for such purpose, and it could never be constitutional to exercise, save in the event, the powers granted to congress could not be carried into effect, without resorting to such an institution. [Applause] Mr. Madison signed the law creating a national bank, because he thought that the revenue of the country could not be collected or disbursed to the best advantage without the interposition of such an establishment. I said in my letter to Sherrod Williams, that, if it was plain that the revenues of the Union could only be collected and disbursed in the most effectual way by means of a bank, and if I was clearly of opinion that the majority of the people of the United States desired such an institution, then, and then only would I sign a bill going to charter a bank. [Shouts of applause.] I have never regarded the office of Chief Magistrate as conferring upon the incumbent the power of mastery over the popular will, but as granting him the power to execute the properly expressed will of the people and not to resist it. With my mother's milk did I suck in the principles on which the Declaration of Independence was founded. [Cheering.]

That declaration complained, that the King would not let the people make such laws as they wished. Shall a President or an executive officer undertake, at this late time of day, to control the people in the exercise of their supreme will? No. The people are the best guardians of their own rights, [applause,] and it is the duty of their Executive to abstain from interfering in or thwarting the sacred exercise of the law-making functions of their government.

In this view of the matter, I defend my having signed a well known bill which passed the legislature while I was Governor of Indiana. It is true, my opponents have attempted to cast odium upon me for having done so, but while they are engaged in such an effort, they impugn the honor and honesty of the inmates of the log cabins, who demanded the passage and signature of that bill. The men who now dare to arraign the people of Indiana for having exercised their rights as they pleased, were in their nurse's arms when that bill passed the legislature. What do they know of the pioneers of that vast wilderness? I tell them, that in the legislature which passed the bill exciting so much their horror, there were men as pure in heart, and as distinguished for their common sense and high integrity, as any who set themselves up for models in these days. [Immense cheering.] I glory in carrying out their views, for in doing so I submitted to the law-making power, in accordance with the declaration of independence, I did not prevent the people from making what laws they pleased. [Cheering.]

If the Augean stable is to be cleansed, it will be necessary to go back to the principles of Jefferson. [Cheers.] It has been said by the Henrys, the Madisons, the Graysons and others, that one of the great dangers in our government is, the powers vested in the general government would overshadow the government of the States. There is truth in this, and long since and often have I expressed the opinion that the interference of the general government with the elective franchise in the States would be the signal for the downfall of liberty. That interference has taken place, and while the mouths of professed democrats appeal to Jefferson, and declare they are governed by his principles, they are urging at the same time 100,000 office holders to meddle in the State elections! And if the rude hand of power be not removed from the elective franchise, there will soon be an end to the government of the Union. [Cries of assent.] It is a truth in government ethics, that when a larger power comes in contact with a smaller power, the latter is speedily destroyed or swallowed up by the former. So in regard to the general government and the State governments. Should I ever be placed in the Chief Magistrate's seat, I will carry out the principles of Jackson, and never permit the interference of office-holders in the elections. [Immense applause.] I will do more. While I will forbid their interference in elections, I will never do aught to prevent their going quietly to the polls and voting, even against me or my measures. No American citizen should be deprived of his power of voting as he pleases.

I have detained you, fellow-citizens, longer than I intended, but you now see that I am not the old man on crutches nor the imbecile they say I am—[cheering] not the prey to disease—a voice cried here; nor the bear in a cage, nor the caged animal they wittily described me to be. [Great laughter and cheering.]

But before I conclude, there are two or three other topics I must touch upon.

The violence of party spirit, as of late exhibited, is a serious mischief to the political welfare of the country. Party feeling is necessary in a certain degree to the health and stability of a Republic, but when pushed to too great an extent, it is detrimental to the body politic, it is the rock upon which many a Republic has been dashed to pieces. An old farmer told me the other day that he did not believe one of the stories circulated against me, and he would support me if I were only a Democrat. [Laughter.] But if I support and sustain democratic principles, what matters it how I am called? It matters a good deal, said he; you don't belong to the Democratic party! [Laughter] Can any thing be more ruinous in its tendency to our institutions, than this high party spirit, which looks to the shadow, and not to be the substance of things? Nothing, nothing. This running after names, after imaginings, is ominous of dangerous results. In the blessed Book we are told that the pretensions of false Christs shall be in future times so specious that even the elect will be deceived. And is it not so now with Democracy? The name does not constitute the Democrat.—It is the vilest imposture ever attempted upon the credulity of the public mind to array the poor of the country under the name of Democrats against the rich, and style them aristocrats. This is dealing in fables. The natural antagonist of Democracy is not aristocracy. It is monarchy.—There is no instance on record of a Republic like ours running into an aristocracy. It can hurry into a pure Democracy, and the confidence of that Democracy being once obtained by a Marius or Caesar, by a Bolivar or a Bonaparte, he strides rapidly from professions of love for the people to usurpation of their rights, and steps from that high eminence to a throne! [Cheering.] And thus, in the name of Democracy, the boldest crimes are committed. Who forgets the square in Paris, where ran rivers of the people's blood, shed in the name of Democracy at the foot of the statue of liberty! Cherish not the man, then, who under the guise and name of Democracy, tries to overthrow the principles of Republicanism, as professed and acted upon by Jefferson and Madison. [Immense cheering.]

Gen. Harrison here adverted to the calumnies put forth against his military fame by that noble pair of brothers, Allen and Duncan, and in severe but just terms exposed the falsehoods of these vilifiers. He proved that they were guilty of falsifying the records of the country, and in a brief and lucid manner vindicated himself and the honor of the nation from the aspersions of these and other reckless politicians. He showed that the received history of his brilliant career in the North West had been stamped by the impress of trust, and he will soon find that a generous and grateful people will testify their administration of his glorious services in their causes by raising the brave old soldier to the highest office in their gift.

A precious inheritance, continued the General, has been handed down to you by your forefathers. In Rome, the sacred fire of fabled gods was kept alive by vestal virgins, and they watched over the gift with eager eyes. In America, a glorious fire has been lighted upon the altar of liberty, and to you, my fellow citizens, has been entrusted its safe-keeping, to be nourished with care and fostered forever. Keep it burning, and let the sparks that continually go up from it fall on other altars, and light up in distant lands the fire of freedom. The Turk busies himself no longer with his harem or his bow string. To licentiousness have succeeded the rights of man, and constitutions are given to the people by once despotic rulers. Whence came the light that now shines in the land of darkness? It was a brand snatched from your own proud altar, and thrust into the pyre of Turkish oppression.

Shall then the far seen light upon the shrine of American liberty ever be extinguished? [No, no, no.] It would not be your loss only—it would be the loss of the whole world. The enemies of freedom in Europe are watching you with intense anxiety, and your friends, like a few planets of heaven, are praying for your success. Deceive them not, but keep the sacred fire burning steadily upon your altars, and the Ohio farmer whom you design to make your Chief Magistrate will, at the end of four years, cheerfully lay down the authority which you may entrust him with, free from all ambition. It will have been glorious enough for me to be honored as those pure and honest republicans. Washington, Jefferson and Madison were honored—with the high confidence of a great, noble, just and generous people! [The excitement and cheering continued for several minutes, and the multitude were swayed to and from, as the leaves of the forest in a storm of wind.]

Martin Van Buren's Letter on Texas Annexation (1844)

On April 6, 1841, just five weeks after his inauguration as president, William Henry Harrison succumbed to pneumonia, the first president ever to die in office. Taking advantage of the Constitution's ambiguity—its language was unclear as to whether the vice president was to become the president until the scheduled end of the departed president's term or merely the acting president until a special election could be called—Vice President John Tyler quickly took the presidential oath of office and declared his intention to serve out the remaining three years and forty-seven weeks of Harrison's term.

Tyler's presidency coincided with the rise of a strong national sense of "manifest destiny," the belief that the United States was ordained by Providence to expand ever westward. The leading object of expansion in the early 1840s was Texas, which had declared its independence from Mexico in 1836 and now sought admission to the Union. Southerners were all for annexation and statehood, but northerners resisted: they did not want to risk war with Mexico for the sake of adding another slave state.

President Tyler, in an effort to revive his desperately unpopular administration, endorsed annexation: In April 1844 he submitted to the Senate a treaty to grant statehood to Texas. Within days, former president Martin Van Buren declared his opposition to the treaty in a public letter to Rep. William H. Hammett of Mississippi.

Van Buren's politically courageous stand cost him the certain presidential nomination of his party in 1844. Although he won a majority of votes on the first ballot when the Democratic national convention met in Baltimore, Maryland, on May 27, 1844, unrelenting southern opposition prevented him from obtaining the two-thirds majority that party rules required for nomination. (See "Abolition of the Two-Thirds Rule: Proceedings of the Democratic National Convention," p. 344.) Former secretary of war Lewis Cass of Michigan—Van Buren's main rival—took the lead on the convention's fifth ballot, but he, too, came nowhere near the necessary two-thirds.

On the ninth ballot, the Democrats nominated history's first "dark-horse," or long-shot, candidate for president, James K. Polk. The former speaker of the House of Representatives and governor of Tennessee had two political virtues that made him an ideal compromise nominee: he favored admitting Texas to the Union but had maintained good personal relations with Van Buren and his supporters. The convention helped Polk's cause by endorsing the annexation not just of Texas but of the antislavery territory of Oregon, which Great Britain also claimed as its own.

The Whig party nominated Sen. Henry Clay of Kentucky for president. Clay waffled on the issue of Texas annexation after initially declaring against it. His intent seems to have been to add southern voters to his northern base; if so, the effect was the opposite—distrustful southerners and alienated northerners. Polk undermined Clay's candidacy by endorsing the orthodox Whig view that no president should serve more than one term. (See "Campaign Speech by William Henry Harrison," p. 167.)

Polk defeated Clay, winning 1,339,494 popular votes (49.5 percent) and 170 electoral votes to Clay's 1,300,004 popular votes (48.1 percent) and 105 electoral votes. The new president fulfilled his party's pledges to admit Texas to the Union, although at the expense of a war with Mexico in 1846, and to negotiate a settlement with the British over Oregon. Polk also kept his personal promise to retire at the end of one term.

Polk was not the last dark-horse candidate to emerge from a deadlocked convention. His successors in that role included Franklin Pierce in 1852, Rutherford B. Hayes in 1876, Warren G. Harding in 1920, and Wendell L. Willkie in 1940.   ~

My Dear Sir: Your letter of the 28th of March last, was duly received.

Acting as an unpledged delegate to the Baltimore convention you ask my opinion in regard to the constitutionality and expediency of an immediate annexation of Texas to the United States, or as soon as the assent of Texas may be had to such annexation.—Upon the receipt of your letter, I caused you to be forthwith informed that your request should be complied with in full season for the convention. This promise I shall now perform. But, lest my motives in making a public avowal of my opinions, whilst a negotiation is sup-

posed to be pending, should be misconstrued, I shall send this to a friend who will delay its delivery as long as that can be done consistently with a faithful compliance with the requirements of your letter, and the general objects for which it was written.

You by no means overrate the importance of the subject upon which you have been pleased to address me. It is not only a question of intense interest to every part of the country, but is unhappily also one in regard to which we may not promise ourselves that unanimity in opinions which is so important when great national questions like this are to be decided. That those which I am about to express will, in at least one important particular, differ from that of many friends, political and personal, whose judgments and purity of views I hold in high and habitual respect, I can well imagine; and it is quite evident, from the tenor of your letter, that they will not in all respects correspond with your own. If, however, such of my fellow citizens as are neither influenced by prejudices, nor warped by self-interest, concede to my opinions the merit of having been formed under views directed to the preservation and advancement of the honor and best interests of our common country, as a whole, and expressed with a sincerity which has overlooked, as far as our feeble natures will permit us to do, all personal considerations, my most favorable anticipations will be realized.

It has already been made my duty to act officially on at least several occasions, but in different forms, upon the subject matter to which your questions have reference.

Having charge of the department of state in 1829, I prepared, by direction of the president, instructions to our minister at Mexico, by which he was directed to open without delay, a negotiation with the Mexican government for the purchase of a greater part of the then province of Texas, and by which he was likewise authorized to insert in the treaty a provision similar to that in the Louisiana and Florida treaties, for the incorporation of the inhabitants of Texas into the Union as soon as it could be done consistently with the principles of the federal constitution. The reasons in favor of this measure I stated at large in that document.

In taking this step, the administration of president Jackson renewed (but, as was supposed, under more favorable circumstances) an attempt to accomplish the same object which had been made by its immediate predecessor. Instructions, similar in their general object, had, in the second year of the latter administration, been sent from the department of state to the same American minister at Mexico. I am not aware that there were any material differences between them, other than those of 1827 proposed an acquisition of territory as far west as the Rio del Norte—being, I believe, the extreme western boundary of Texas—whilst the cession asked for by president Jackson extended only as far west as the centre of the Desert or Grand Prairie, which lies east of the river Nueces; and that for the frontier the payment of one million of dollars was authorized whilst, by the administration of president Jackson, the American minister was permitted to go as high as four, and, if indispensable, five millions. Both authorized agreements for smaller portions of territory, and the payments were modified accordingly. In respect for the proposed stipulations for the ultimate incorporation of the inhabitants into the Union, both instructions were identical.

In August, 1837, a proposition was received at the department of state, from the Texan minister at Washington, proposing a negotiation for the annexation of Texas to the United States. This was the first time the question of a foreign independent state has ever been presented to this government. In deciding upon the disposition that ought to be made of it, I did not find it necessary to consider the question of constitutional power, nor the manner in which the object should be accomplished, if deemed expedient and proper. Both these points were therefore, in terms, passed over in the reply of the secretary of state to the Texan minister, as subjects the consideration of which had not been entered upon by the executive.

The first of these, viz: constitutional power—is now presented by your inquiries, not, however, in precisely the same form. Then the application was for the immediate admission of Texas into the Union as an independent state; your question looks only to its annexation as part of the territory of the United States. There is no express power giving to any department of the government to purchase territory except for the objects specified in the constitution, viz: for arsenals, etc.; but the power has, on several very important occasions, been regarded as embraced in the treaty-making power; and territories have been so annexed with a view and under engagements for their ultimate admission into the Union as states.

If there be nothing in the situation or condition of the territory of Texas, which would render its admission hereafter into the Union as a new state improper, I cannot perceive any objection, on constitutional grounds, to its annexation as a territory. In speaking of the right to admit new states, I must, of course, be understood as referring to the power of congress. The executive and senate may, as I have already observed, by the exercise of the treaty-making power, acquire territory; but new states can only be admitted by congress; and the sole authority over the subject, which is given to it by the constitution, is contained in the following provision, viz: "new states may be admitted by the congress into this Union." The only restrictions imposed upon this general power are, 1st, That no new states shall be formed or erected within the jurisdiction of any other state; nor 2dly, "Any state formed by the junction of two or more states, or parts of states, without the consent of the legislatures concerned, as well as of congress"—restrictions which have no bearing upon the present question. The matter, therefore, stands as it would do if the constitution said "new states may be admitted by the congress into this Union," without addition or restriction. That these words, taken by themselves, are broad enough to authorize the admission of the territory of Texas, cannot, I think, be well doubted; nor do I perceive upon what principle we can set up limitations to a power so unqualifiedly recognized by the constitution in the plain simple words I have quoted, and with which no other provision of that instrument conflicts in the slightest degree. But if, with no other guides than our own discretion, we assume limitations upon a power so general, we are at least bound to give to them some intelligible and definite character. The most natural, and indeed the only one of that nature which has been suggested, and which was presented by Mr. Jefferson whilst he entertained doubts in respect to the constitutional power to admit Louisiana, is, that the new states to be admitted must be formed out of territory, not foreign, but which constituted a part of the United States, at the declaration of independence, or the adoption of the constitution. So far from there being any thing in the language of the constitution, or to be found in the extraneous and contemporaneous circumstances which preceded and attended its adoption, to show that such was the intentions of its framers, they are, in my judgment, all strongly the other way. In the first place, the articles of confederation, under which the Union was originally formed, and which gave place to the present constitution, looked directly to a broader extension of the confederacy. It contained a provi-

sion that "Canada, acceding to the constitution, and joining in the measures of the United States, shall be admitted into, and entitled to all the advantages of the Union; but no other colony shall be admitted into the same, *unless* such admission be agreed to by nine states." The practicability, as well as expediency, of making Canada a member of the Union, did certainly, to some extent at least, occupy the minds of our public men, as well before the close of the revolution, as between that event and the formation of the new constitution. This is, however, only a link in the chain of evidence, to make probable what subsequent events make certain, that the framers of the constitution had their eyes upon this very question, when this section was finally settled. That part of the constitution, as appears by the journal of the proceedings of the convention, was presented in a variety of forms before it assumed the shape in which it was finally adopted.

In the resolutions offered by Mr. Edward Randolph, as a basis for the new constitution, and which contained the first propositions of the character which were submitted to it, the power in question was described as follows, viz: "that provisions ought to be made for the admission of states *lawfully arising within the limits of the United States,* whether arising from a voluntary junction of government or otherwise, with the consent of a number of voices in the legislature, less than the whole." In Mr. Charles Pinckney's draft, it was proposed that "the legislature shall have power to admit new states into the Union, on the same terms with the original states, provided two-thirds of the members present in both houses agree—leaving out the clause in respect to the character of the territory. Mr. Randolph's proposition, containing the restriction confining the power to states lawfully arising within the limits of the United States, was at one time adopted in committee of the whole; and in the state, referred with others to the committee of detail. In a draft of a constitution, reported by that committee, the article upon this subject contained the following propositions: 1st. That new states, lawfully constituted or established within the limits of the United States might be admitted by the legislature in this government. 2d. That to such admission, the consent of two-thirds of the members present in each house should be necessary. 3d. That if a new state should arise within the limits of any of the present states, the consent of the legislature of such states should also be necessary to its admission. 4th. That if the admission was consented to, the new states should be admitted on the same terms with the original states; and 5th. That the legislature might make conditions with new states concerning that public debt then subsisting. The 2d, 4th, and 5th clauses were stricken out by the votes of the convention; and after that had been done, the following was adopted as a substitute for the whole, viz: "New states may be admitted by the legislature into the union; but no new state shall be erected within the limits of any of the present states, without the consent of the legislature of such state, as well as of the general legislature"— leaving out that part of the first clause which related to the domestic character of the territory; and this substitute was consequently revised and amended, so as to make it conform in its phraseology to the section as it now stands in the constitution. These proceedings show that the proposition to restrict the power to admit new states to the territory without the original limits of the United States, was distinctly before the convention, once adopted by it, and finally rejected in favor of a clause making the power in this respect general. Whatever differences of opinion may exist as to the propriety of referring to extraneous matter to influence the construction of the constitution where its language is explicit, there can certainly be no objections to a resort to such aids to test the correctness of interferences, having no other basis than supposed improbabilities. I have not, therefore, been able to bring my mind to another satisfactory conclusion than that it was the intention of the convention to give the power of admitting new states to congress, with no other limitation than those which are specified in that instrument. The language employed, the specifications of certain restriction, the adoption and subsequent exclusion of that which is now referred to, together with the subsequent and continued action of the new government, all seem to combine to render this interpretation of the constitution the true one. Propositions for annexation can certainly be imagined, of a character so unwise and improvident as to strike the minds of all with repugnance. But if we look over the conceded powers of congress, we shall also find many others, the abuse of which might involve, to an equally great extent, the well being of the republic, and against which abuse the constitution has provided no other safeguards than the responsibilities to their constituents and to the laws of the land, of those whose sanction is necessary to the validity of an act of congress. Nor is it very unreasonable to suppose that those who based their government upon the great principle that it is the right of the people to alter or abolish it, and to institute new ones, in such form as they may think most likely to effect their safety and happiness, should feel themselves secure in trusting to their representatives in the house, in the senate, and in the executive chair, the right to admit new members into the confederacy, with no other restrictions than those which they have thought proper to specify.

It was under this view of the constitution that the purchase of Louisiana in 1803, only fifteen years after the adoption of the constitution, promising the incorporation of the ceded territory into the Union, and the admission, as soon as possible, of the inhabitants to the enjoyment of all the rights, advantages, and immunities of citizens of the United States, was ratified, confirmed, and finally executed by every branch of the federal government whose co-operation is required by the constitution. It is true that Mr. Jefferson, in the interval between the negotiation and submission of the treaty to the senate, thought that the opinion that the constitution had made no provision for our holding foreign territory, nor for incorporating foreign states into the Union. The fact of his approving the treaty, and the laws necessary to its execution, must, however, be regarded as conclusive proof that, upon looking further into the matter, his opinion was changed. The attempt to convince him of his error was made by his friend, governor Nicholas, as appears by Mr. Jeffersons' letter to him; and I have little doubt that, if his letters to Breckenridge and Nicholas had been published in his life-time, or his attention been in any other way directed to their contents, he would, from his habitual care in such matters, have avowed the change, and explained the grounds on which it was based. It is equally true that the acceptance of the cession, as well as the admission of the state, became party questions, and were contested with partisan warmth. Of the vital importance of that great acquisition to the safety, prosperity, and honor of the whole Union, there can however, now be no diversity of opinion. But the councils of the nation, in the course of time, cease to be at all divided upon the question of constitutional power to accept a cession of foreign territory, with the view of its ultimate admission into the Union. In 1819 the Spanish treaty for the cession of east and west Florida contain the usual stipulation for ultimate incorporation into the Union was ratified and upon the call of the names of the senators

present, it appeared that every one voted for the ratification. Upon the question of constitutional power, so far [as] that case went, the senate of the United States has therefore, become unanimous.

Certainly no remarks are necessary to show that there can be no possible difference produced in the constitutional question by the relative positions of the territory comprising Louisiana, the Floridas, and Texas, in respect to the old United States.

I have gone thus fully and minutely into this matter, as well from a deep sense of the vast importance of the question, as from a sincere desire to satisfy those of my friends who may differ from me on this point, and whose opinions I hold in the highest respect, that I have not yielded my assent hastily or unadvisedly to the views I have here taken of the subject.

Having thus given you my views upon the constitutional question, I will, with the same frankness answer the remaining portion of your inquiries, viz. The expediency of immediately annexing Texas to the United States, or so soon as her consent to such annexation may be obtained.

I have already referred to an application for the accomplishment of the same object that was made to this government by Texas, whilst I was president.

The history of the Texan revolution, and the condition of that republic, as well as the probable advantages to result to both from proposed annexation, were placed before us in an elaborate communication. It can scarcely be necessary to say that the application was considered with that attention and care which were due to so grave a proposition, and under the full influence of feeling of sincere solitude for the prosperity and permanent welfare of a young and neighboring state, whose dependence we had been the first to acknowledge feelings which constitute, and I sincerely hope, will constitute, the prevailing sentiment of the people of the United States. In coming to the decision which it became my duty to make, I was aided in addition to the other members of my cabinet, by the counsel and constitutional advice of two distinguished citizens of your own section of the Union, of the first order of intellect, great experience in public affairs, and whose devotion to their own, as well as every other section of the Union, was above all question.—The result of our united opinions was announced to the Texan minister, (Gen. Hunt,) in a communication from the late Mr. Forsyth, the substance of which I cannot better express than by incorporating one or two brief extracts from it in this letter. Upon the general subjects, my own views, as well as those of the cabinet, were thus stated:

So long as Texas shall remain at war, while the United States are at peace with her adversary, the proposition of the Texan minister plenipotentiary necessarily involves the question of war with that adversary. The United States are bound to Mexico by a treaty of amity and commerce, which will be scrupulously observed on their part so long as it can be reasonably hoped that Mexico will perform her duties, and respect our rights under it. The United States might justly be suspected of a disregard of the friendly purposes of the compact, if the overture of General Hunt were to be even reserved for future consideration, as this would imply a disposition on our part to espouse the quarrel of Texas with Mexico—a disposition wholly at variance with the spirit of the treaty with the uniform policy and all the obvious welfare of the United States.

The inducements mentioned, by general Hunt for the United States to annex Texas to their territory, are duly appreciated; but, powerful and weighty as certainly they are, they are light when opposed in the scale of reason to treaty obligations, and respect for that integrity of character by which the United States have sought to distinguish themselves since the establishment of their right to claim a place in the great family of nations.

The intimation in general Hunt's letter that Texas might be induced to extend commercial advantages to other nations to the prejudice of the United States, was thus noticed:

"It is presumed, however, that the motives by which Texas has been governed in making this overture, have equal force in impelling her to preserve, as an independent power, the most liberal commercial relations with the United States. Such a disposition will be cheerfully met, in a corresponding spirit, by this government. If the answer which the undersigned has been directed to give to the proposition of general Hunt should unfortunately work such a change in the sentiments of that government as to induce an attempt to extend commercial relations elsewhere, upon terms prejudicial to the United States, this government will be consoled by the rectitude of its intentions, and a certainty that, although the hazard of transient losses may be incurred by a rigid adherence to just principles, no lasting prosperity can be secured when they are disregarded." That these views were not altogether satisfactory to General Hunt, nor probably to his government, has been seen. But I think I may safely say that seldom, if ever, has the decision, by this government, of a question of equal magnitude, been more decidedly or more unanimously approved by the people of the U. States. The correspondence was, very soon after it took place, communicated to congress, and although the public mind was at the time in a state of the highest excitement, and the administration daily assailed through every avenue by which it was deemed approachable, I am yet to see the first sentence of complaint upon that point, in any quarter of the Union. Even a resolution offered in the senate, declaring annexation, "whenever it could be effected *consistently with the public faith and treaty stipulations of the United States,* desirable," was ordered to be laid upon the table; and a similar disposition was made in the house of the papers upon the subject, which had been referred to the committee on foreign relations, and that committee discharged from the further consideration of the matter, upon its own application:—Nor were the friendly relations then existing between that republic and the United States—to its honor be it said—in any perceptible degree impaired by this decision.

Standing in this position before the country, it becomes my duty to consider whether either the nature of the question, or the circumstances of the case, have so far changed as to justify me in now advising a policy from which I then, in the most solemn form, dissented.

In giving to you, and, through you to the public, the result of a very careful and dispassionate examination of this grave question, I should neither do justice to yourself, to the patriotic state which you, in conjunction with others, are to represent in the convention, to the people of the United States, nor to my own position, if I failed to accompany it with a brief exposition of the grounds upon which I have proceeded. It is in that way only that justice can be done to my intentions; and that is all I desire. The annexation of the territory, and the consequent assumption by us of a responsibility to protect and defend its inhabitants, would, in respect to the consideration to which I am about to refer, stand upon the same footing with that of its admission as a state. The recognition of Texas as an independent state, was a measure which received, in various and appropriate forms, the sanction of every department of the government, whose cooperation was

necessary to its validity, and had my hearty concurrence. From this act of our government just and proper in all respects as it was; an inference has, however, been drawn and brought to bear upon the present question, not only very far beyond its real bearing, but by which its true character is entirely reversed. Many persons who enter upon the consideration of the subject with the purest intention and are incapable of knowingly giving a false interpretation to anything connected with it, take it for granted that the United States, in recognizing the independence of Texas, declared to the world, not only that she was independent *in fact,* but also that she was such *of right.* Acting upon this erroneous construction, they very naturally conclude, that having gone thus far, having examined into and passed not only upon the existence of her independence, but also upon her right to its enjoyment, it is now (and more especially after the lapse of several years) too late to hesitate upon the question of annexation on the ground of any existing controversy upon those points. The fallacy of this reasoning will be apparent when it is considered that the usage of nations to acknowledge the government, *de facto,* of every country, was established for the express purpose of avoiding all inquiry into, or the expression of any opinion upon, the question of *right* between the contending parties. They acknowledge no other power in any country than that which is in fact supreme. They cannot inquire beyond that point without interfering with the internal concerns of other nations—a practice which all disclaim, and a disclaimer which it has been our invariable usage not only to make, but to enforce with scrupulous fidelity. To recognize the independence of the government *de facto,* is also a matter of state necessity; for without it, neither commercial nor diplomatic intercourse between any such power and the nations of the world could be carried on with success, and the social interests of mankind require that these should not be arrested by quarrels between contesting parties, in regard to their respective right to the supreme power. In respect to all beyond this, the laws and usages of nations require the observance of a strict neutrality between the contending parties, as long as the war lasts. It is due, also, from every government to its own citizens, to declare when a revolted colony shall be regarded as an independent nation. Because "it belongs to the government alone to make the declaration," and because "until it is made, or the parent state relinquishes her claims, courts of justice must consider the ancient state of things as remaining unaltered, and the sovereign power of the parent state over the colony as still subsisting." But nothing can be farther from giving to the act of recognition its true character, than to suppose that it has the slightest bearing upon the rights of the parties; it being, as I have already said resorted to for the express purpose of avoiding any such construction. Such is not only the law and usage of nations, but such also have been the reiterated avowals of our own government. I do not remember that the recognition of Texan independence gave rise to any correspondence between Mexico and our government; and if it did, I have not the means of stating its character. But the principles upon which all such acts are based, were fully set forth by this government upon the occasion of the recognition of the independence of the Spanish American States.—In the message of president Monroe, to the house of representatives, suggesting the propriety of that recognition, it was expressly declared that, in proposing this measure, it was "not contemplated to change thereby, in the slightest manner, our friendly relations with either of the parties; but to observe in all respects, as heretofore, should the war be continued, the most perfect neutrality between them." The committee

on foreign affairs in their elaborate report upon the subject says: "Our recognition must necessarily be co-existent only with the fact on which it is founded, and cannot survive it. While the nations of South America are actually independent, it is simply to speak the truth to acknowledge them to be so. *Should Spain, contrary to her avowed principle and acknowledged interest, renew the war for the conquest of South America, we shall, indeed, regret it; but we shall observe, as we have done between the independent parties an honest and impartial neutrality.*" The secretary of state, in defence of the act of recognition said to the Spanish minister: "This recognition is neither intended to invalidate any right of Spain, *nor to affect the employment of any means which she may yet be disposed or enabled to use, with the view of re-uniting those provinces to the rest of her dominions.*" That these avowals were in strict conformity to the true principles of the law of nations, there can be no doubt.—They were, at all events, those which this government has solemnly announced as its rule of action in regard to contests between rival parties for the supreme power in foreign states. That the admission of Texas as a member of this confederacy, whilst the contest for the maintenance of the independence she has acquired was still pending, and a consequent assumption of the responsibility of protecting her against invasion, would have been a plain departure from the laws and usages of nations, and a violation of the principles to which we had avowed our adherence in the face of the world, was too clear to be doubted. Thus believing. I had on the occasion to which I have referred, in the faithful discharge of the trust which the people had reposed in me, but one course to pursue; and that was promptly, but respectfully adopted.

I return now to the question. Has the condition of the contest between Texas and Mexico, for the sovereignty of the former, so far changed as to render these principles now inapplicable? What is the attitude which these two states at this moment occupy towards each other? Are they at war, or are they not? We cannot evade this question if we would [want to].—To enumerate all the circumstances bearing upon it, in a communication like this, would be impracticable, nor is it necessary. In respect to the parties themselves, there would seem to be no misunderstanding upon the subject. Mexico has been incessant in her avowal, as well to our government as to others, of the continuance of the war, and of her determination to prosecute it. How does Texas regard her position in respect to the war with Mexico? Three years subsequent to our recognition of her independence, we find her entering into a stipulation with a foreign power to accept of her mediation to bring about a cession of hostilities between her and Mexico, engaging to assume a million sterling of the debt due from Mexico to the subjects of that power, if she, through her influence, obtained from Mexico an unlimited truce in respect to the war then raging between her and Texas within one month and a treaty of peace in six. As late as last June, we see a proclamation of the president of Texas, declaring a suspension of hostilities between the two powers during the pendency of negotiations to be entered upon between them, issued on the supposition that a similar proclamation would be issued by Mexico; and actual hostilities are now only suspended by an armistice to be continued for a specified and short period, for the sake of negotiation. Nor are our own views upon the point less explicit. In the published letter of the late secretary of state, to the Mexican minister at Washington, written in December last, he says: "Nearly eight years have elapsed since Texas declared her independence. During *all that time* Mexico has asserted her right of jurisdiction and dominion over that country, and has endeavored to enforce it by arms." In the president's message to congress, it is stated "that the war which has existed for so long a time between Mexico and Texas, has, since the battle of San Jacinto, consisted for the most part of predatory incursions, which, while they have been attended with much of suffering to individuals, and kept the borders of the two countries in a state of constant alarm *have failed to approach to any definite result*." And after commenting with much truth upon the insufficiency of the armaments which Mexico has fitted out for the subjection of Texas—on the length of time which has elapsed since the latter declared her independence—on the perseverance, notwithstanding, in plans of reconquest by Mexico—on her refusal to acknowledge the independence of Texas, and on the evils of border warfare, the message adds: "The United States have an immediate interest in seeing an end put to the state of hostilities between Mexico and Texas;" following up the remark with a forcible remonstrance against the continuance of the war, and a very just and impressive statement of the reasons why it should cease. This remonstrance is, in my opinion, entirely just and perfectly proper. The government of the United States should be at all times ready to interpose its good offices to bring about a speedy, and, as far as practicable a satisfactory adjustment of this long pending controversy. Its whole influence should be exerted constantly zealously and in good faith, to advance so desirable an object, and in the process of time it can, without doubt, be accomplished. But what, my dear sir, is the true and undisguised character of the remedy for those evils, which would be applied by the "immediate annexation of Texas to the United States?" Is it more or less than saying to Mexico, We feel ourselves aggrieved by the continuance of this war between you and Texas; we have an interest in seeing it terminated; we will accomplish that object by taking the disputed territory to ourselves, we will make Texas a part of the United States, so that those plans of reconquest which we know you are maturing, to be successful, must be made so against the power that we can bring into the contest; if the war is to be continued as we understand to be your design, the United States are henceforth to be regarded as one of the belligerents?

We must look at this matter as it really stands—We shall act under the eye of an intelligent, observing world; and the affair cannot be made to wear a different aspect from what it deserves if even we had the disposition (which we have not) to throw over it disguises of any kind. We should consider whether there is any way in which the peace of the country can be preserved, should an immediate annexation take place, save one—and that is, according to present appearances, the improbable event that Mexico will be deterred from the farther prosecution of the war by the apprehension of our power. How does that matter stand? She has caused us to be informed, both at Mexico and here, in a manner the most formal and solemn, that she will feel herself constrained, by every consideration that can influence the conduct of a nation, to regard the fact of annexation as an act of war on the part of the United States and that she will, notwithstanding, prosecute her attempts to regain Texas, regardless of consequences. Exceptions are, however, taken by the president, and I think very justly taken, to the manner in which this determination has been announced. The Mexican government should certainly have applied in a becoming spirit to ours for explanation of its intention. If it found this government under the impression that Mexico, although it might not be willing to acknowledge its independence, has abandoned all serious hope of re-conquering Texas, Mexico should have as-

sured us of our error, and remonstrate against any action on our part based on that erroneous assumption and declared firmly, if it pleased, but in that courteous and respectful manner which is alone suited to the intercourse between nations who profess to be friends, its determination to oppose us. Instead of taking a course, the propriety of which was so obvious, she first assumes, upon grounds which were neither proper nor safe for her to act upon, that this government had designs upon Texas; then denounces the annexation as a great national crime, and forthwith proclaims instant war as the penalty of our persisting in such an attempt; and all this in language bearing certainly (although subsequently disavowed) every appearance of menace.

But this is a besetting and very ancient foible of the mother country, as well as of her descendants, in their diplomatic intercourse. Every one conversant with the subject of Spanish relations, knows that, at least from the time of Don Louis d'Onis to the present day, this government has been frequently—not to say continually—subjected to this species of diplomatic dogmatism. Partly in consequence of the genius of their language; partly from their peculiar temperament; much from habit, but more from a radical defeat of judgment,—they continue the use of language in their state papers, which better tempered, if not wiser diplomatists have almost every where laid aside as worse than useless. But at no time has our government suffered it actions upon great national questions to be influenced by such petulance. From the time of the modest, yet firm Madison, to the late Mr. Upshur, (whose melancholy fate is so justly and generally lamented,) has every secretary of state, acting under the direction of the executive, deemed it sufficient to place the government and minister employing it in the wrong, by showing its injustice as well as its futility. We have then heretofore, as I hope we shall now, decided to act in the matter under consideration in a manner which was deemed due to justice and to our own character, without being in any degree influenced by such unavailing menaces. It is foreign to my habit, and repugnant to my feelings, to say any thing that should offend the pride of any nation, if the declarations of individuals could possibly have that effect, being sincerely desirous that the United States should cultivate friendly relations with all. But with a population not equal to half that of the United States, and laboring under many and serious disadvantages, from which we are comparatively free, Mexico could not with propriety, be offended by the assumption that this government may act as it would have done had no such menaces been made, without the slightest danger of being regarded by the rest of the world—as having been intimidated by threats of war from that republic. So at least I should act, if the direction of public affairs were in my hands. The question then recurs, if, as sensible men, we cannot avoid the conclusion that the immediate annexation of Texas would, in all human probability, draw after it a war with Mexico, can it be expedient to attempt it? Of the consequences of such a war, the character it might be made to assume, the entanglements with other nations which the position of a belligerent almost unavoidably draws after it, and the undoubted injuries which might be inflicted upon each,—notwithstanding the great desparity of their respective forces, I will not say a word. God forbid that an American citizen should ever count the cost of any appeal to what is appropriately denominated the last resort of nations, whenever that resort becomes necessary either for the safety or to vindicate the honor of this country. There is, I trust, not one so base as not to regard himself and all he has to be forever and at all times subject to such a requisition. But would a war

with Mexico, brought on under such circumstances, be a contest of that character? Could we hope to stand justified in the eyes of mankind for entering into it; more especially if its commencement is to be preceded by the appropriation to our own uses of the territory, the sovereignty of which is in dispute between two nations one of which we are to join in the struggle? This sir, is a matter of the very gravest import, one in respect to which no American statesman or citizen can possibly be indifferent. We have a character among the nations of the earth to maintain.—All our public functionaries, as well those who advocate this measure as those who oppose it, however much they may differ as to its effects, will I am sure, be equally solicitous for the performance of this first of duties. It has hitherto been our pride and our boast, that whilst the lust of power, with fraud and violence in its train, has led other and differently constituted governments to aggression and conquest, our movements in these respects have always been regulated by reason and justice. A disposition to detract from our pretensions in this respect, will in the nature of things be always prevalent elsewhere; and has, at this very moment,—and from special causes assumed, in some quarters, the most rabid character. Should not every one, then who sincerely loves his country—who venerates its time-honored and glorious institutions—who dwells with pride and delight on associations connected with our rise, progress and present condition—on the steady step with which we have advanced to our present eminence, in despite of the hostility, and in contempt of the bitter revilings of the enemies of freedom in all parts of the globe,—consider and think deeply whether we would not by the immediate annexation of Texas, place a weapon in the hands of those who now look upon us and our institutions with distrustful and envious eyes, that would do us more real, lasting injury as a nation, than the acquisition of such a territory, valuable as it undoubtedly is, could possibly repair? It is said, and truly said, that this war between Texas and Mexico has already been of too long duration. We are and must continue to be more or less annoyed by its prosecution, and have undoubtedly, as has been remarked, an interest in seeing it terminated. But can we appeal to any principle in the law of nations, to which we practice a scrupulous adherence, that would, under present circumstances, justify us in interfering for its suppression in a manner that would unavoidably make us a party to its prosecution? Can this position be made sufficiently clear to justify us in committing the peace and honor of the country to its support.

In regard to the performance by us of that duty, so difficult for any government to perform,—the observance of an honest neutrality between nations at war—we can now look through our whole career, since our first admission into the family of nations, not only without a blush, but with feelings of honest pride and satisfaction. The way was opened by President Washington himself, under circumstances of the most difficult character, and at no less a hazard than that of exposing ourselves to plausible, yet unjust, imputations of infidelity to treaty stipulations. The path he trod with such unfaltering steps—and which led to such beneficial results, has hitherto been pursued with unvarying fidelity by every one of his successors of whom it becomes me to speak.

If our sympathies could induce a departure from a policy which has so much in its commencement to consecrate it, and such advantages to recommend its continuance, they would doubtless draw us to the side of Texas. That the happiness of her people would be promoted by the maintenance of her independence, I have no doubt. Few, if any, efforts for the extension of the blessings of free government in any part of the world have been made since the establishment of our own independence, that have failed to excite our earnest and sincere wishes for their success. But they have never been permitted to withdraw us from the faithful performance of our duty as a neutral nation. They were excited, and deeply too, at the commencement of the French revolution; they were revived in the struggle of the South American states for the establishment of their independence; they have been put to their severest trial in this very contest between Texas and Mexico. Yet, in that whole period of time, amidst the convulsions of empires and the lawlessness of power by which many of its possessors have been distinguished, it has been a cardinal point in the administration of affairs of this republic to adhere with the strictest fidelity to the rule which was laid down by Washington, enforced by Jefferson and respected with unabated sincerity by his successors.

There is another circumstance which is well calculated to mislead us upon this subject. Many, if not most, of the persons to be affected by the decision of this question, were once citizens of the U. States, and have still their relatives and friends amongst us. I am not unaware of the hazard to which I expose my standing with the latter, in speaking thus unreservedly upon a point so well calculated to excite deep feelings. This is perhaps more particularly applicable to the portion of my fellow citizens, of whom it was aptly and appropriately said by one of their own number, that "they are the children of the sun, and partake of its warm fire."—Yet, whether we stand or fall in the estimation of our countrymen, it is always true wisdom, as well as true morality, to hold fast to the truth. It is, moreover, a consolation to know, that if to nourish enthusiasm is one of the effects of a genial climate, it at the same time seldom fails to give birth to a chivalrous spirit, which will not permit itself to be outdone in the extent or sincerity of its sacrifices at the shrine of patriotism. To preserve our national escutcheon untarnished, has, consequently, if reliance can be placed upon our public archives, been an object of unceasing solicitude with southern statesmen.

Nothing is either more true or more extensively known than that Texas was wrested from Mexico, and her independence established through the instrumentality of citizens of the United States. Equally true is it that this was done not only against the wishes, but in direct contravention of the best efforts of our government to prevent our citizens from engaging in the enterprise. Efforts have nevertheless, not been wanting on the part of those who are not over-anxious for the credit of republican governments, to misrepresent our views in this respect—to cause it to be believed that our efforts to prevent unlawful participation by our citizens in that struggle were insincere; that we coveted this portion of the territory of Mexico; and having failed to obtain it by fair purchase, or by negotiation, we saw in this movement a preliminary step, which would, in the end, be equally subservient to our views upon Texas. No one can have had better opportunities of knowing how unfounded these injurious imputations were than myself. As early as when president Houston first went to Texas, I believe in 1829, I was consulted by general Jackson upon the subject of a private letter addressed by him to the honorable Mr. Fulton, now senator of the United States, then secretary of the territory of Arkansas, requesting him to cause the movements of general Houston to be watched, and to apprize the president of the first indication on his part of any intention to violate the laws of the United States by an armed incursion into Mexico. From that period to the end of general Jackson's term of

office, I am as well satisfied as I can be of any fact, that he was sincerely desirous to perform his whole duty as chief magistrate of the country, and to prevent in this respect, the slightest violation of the laws, with the execution of which he was charged. He no doubt sincerely believed that the incorporation of Texas into the Federal Union would be alike advantageous to her, to Mexico, and to the United States and was ever ready to adopt all proper measures for the accomplishment of that object. But they know very little of general Jackson's true character, who can for a moment permit themselves to believe him capable of doing, countenancing, or advising, a single act which he believed, or had even reason to apprehend, would violate the plighted faith of his country, or infringe upon the duty which it owes to the great family of nations. To prevent our people from going to Texas, and embarking in the war, was an impossibility which neither he nor any other chief magistrate could have accomplished. If they went there without military organization, or armaments, and chose to place themselves beyond the protection of this government, we had no right to control their action; nor do other governments exercise any such right in similar cases. For the suppression of military enterprises, organized and armed here against a nation with which we are at peace, the provisions of our laws are ample. But of the difficulties of enforcing them with a frontier and seaboard like those which open our communication with Texas, no sensible and well informed mind can be ignorant.

For the voluntary action of our government in regard to the subject of annexation, we can have no such explanation to give. The acquisition of so valuable a territory by means which are of questionable propriety, would be a departure from those just principles upon which this government has ever added and which have excited the admiration and secured the respect of the dispassionate and enlightened friends of freedom throughout the world. But I am very sure that we shall all, in the end, so act upon this subject as to put it out of the power of the national enemies of republican institutions to make a plausible charge of infidelity to our avowed principles in respect to it. No one was more deeply sensible of the necessity of the greatest prudence in this particular, or more anxious to secure its observance, than general Jackson. As late as December, 1836—only a few months before the recognition—he thus expresses himself, in a special message to the senate: "But there are circumstances in the relations of the two countries which require us to act, on this occasion, with ever more than our wonted caution. Texas was once claimed as a part of our property; and there are those among our citizens who, always reluctant to abandon that claim, cannot but regard with solicitude the prospect of the union of the territory of this country; a large proportion of its civilized inhabitants are emigrants from the United States, speak the same language with ourselves, cherish the same principles, political and religious, and are bound to many of our citizens by ties of friendship and kindred blood; and, more than all, it is known that the people of that country have instituted the same form of government with our own, and have, since the close of your session, openly resolved on the acknowledgment of their independence, to seek admission into the Union as one of the federal States. This last circumstance is a matter of peculiar delicacy, and forces upon us considerations of the gravest character. The title of Texas to the territory she claims, is identified with her independence. She asks us to acknowledge that title to the territory, with an avowed design to treat immediately of its transfer to the United States. It becomes us to beware of a early movement, as it might subject us,

however unjustly to the imputation of seeking to establish the claims of our neighbors to a territory, with a view to its subsequent acquisition by ourselves."

It has been urged, from a quarter entitled to great respect, and reasoned, too, with no inconsiderable degree of cogency, that the acquisition of Texas now, in the mode proposed, would be liable to no greater objection than the accomplishment of the same object would have been either in 1827 or 1829, when it was attempted by two successive administrations to purchase it from Mexico. If I were to go into a discussion of this question, and the facts necessarily connected with it, I should be writing a book instead of a letter; nor is it necessary that I should. I will therefore content myself with saying, that with every disposition to look at the subject in all its bearings with an impartial eye, I have not been able to see the analogy which is claimed to exist between the two cases. But if it were even admitted that the able men who were, at those respective periods, at the end of the government, under strong convictions of the importance of the acquisition of Texas to the U. States, so far precipitated their measures for the accomplishment of that object, as to have endangered the good faith and pacific relations of the United States (which I do not admit), we could still only convince ourselves on their failure, but could not thereby justify the present movement, if it is not right in itself, and capable of justification on other grounds. I by no means contend that a formal recognition of the independence of Texas by Mexico is necessary to justify us in assenting to her annexation to the United States. Time and circumstances may work such a change in the relations between those two countries, as to render an act of that character, on the part of Mexico, unnecessary and unimportant. What I mean to say, is, that from all the information I have been able to acquire upon the subject, no change has yet taken place in those regions that would make the objections, which I have here detailed, inapplicable.

It is said, also, that if Texas is not acquired now, the opportunity will be forever lost—that some other power will acquire it; and, indeed, some of the rumors of the day have gone so far as to say that the Texan minister is already instructed, in case of failure here, to proceed forthwith to Europe, with all authority for the accomplishment of that object. We must not forget, that besides great public considerations, there are extensive private interests involved in this matter; and we may therefore well be distrustful of the thousand rumors which are from day to day put afloat upon this subject. What a comparatively few individuals, acting under the influence of personal interest, may not desire to have done, I will not undertake to say, or to conjecture. But that the people of Texas—so many of whom carry in their veins the blood of our revolutionary ancestors—thousands of whom are thoroughly imbued with democratic principles—who achieved by their own gallantry that independence which we were the first to acknowledge—who have established and subsequently maintain institutions similar to our own; that such a people and such a government will ever be found capable of sending a minister to the crowned heads of Europe, to barter away their young and enterprising republic, and all that they have purchased with their blood, to the highest bidder, is what I cannot believe; in the possibility of "so apostate and unnatural a connexion?" I can have no faith.

It is also apprehended by many, that the British authorities, will attempt to make Texas a British colony or dependency. I find it difficult to credit the existence of such infatuation on the part of any European power. I cannot bring myself to believe that any European government which has not already made up its mind to provoke a war with this country, will ever attempt to colonize Texas, either in form or in substance. If there is any such power, the considerations to which I have adverted, would soon lose most of their importance; for opportunities would not then be slow in presenting themselves for the conquest of whatever territory might, in that event, be deemed necessary to our security, in legitimate self defence. Commercial favors Texas has, to the same extent as other independent powers, the right to dispose of as she thinks proper; subject only to the penalties which are certain, sooner or later, to follow in the wake of national injustice. But European colonization of Texas is another and a very different matter—a matter in respect to the ultimate consequence of which no European nation can possibly deceive either herself or us. I have no access to the sources of true information in respect to the degree of credit which may be due to these rumors; but our government ought, without doubt, to exercise a most jealous vigilance against the extension of British influence, and indeed foreign influence, or dominion of any kind, or from any quarter, either in Texas, or in any portions of the continent bordering on the Gulf of Mexico. If the time ever comes when the question resolves itself into whether Texas shall become a British dependency or colony, or a constitutional portion of this union, the great principle of self-defence, applicable as well to nations as to individuals, would, without doubt, produce as great a unanimity amongst us in favor of the latter alternative, as can ever be expected on any great question of foreign or domestic policy.

Having now replied, in the fullest and frankest manner, to both the questions which you have propounded to me, I might here close this letter; but being sincerely anxious to put you, and others occupying the same position, in possession of my views and opinions upon the whole subject, as far as they can with propriety be now formed and expressed, I will go a few steps farther.

Occasions do sometimes present themselves, in the administration of public affairs, when the decisions of great questions can be safely anticipated by those whose subsequent duty it may become to pass upon them; but to justify such a course, those questions must be such as are unavoidably dependent upon circumstances and considerations of a fixed and settled character. I have not been able to regard this as being, in all its respects, a case of that description. It is a matter affecting our foreign relations, in respect to which every enlightened nation makes it a rule to avoid, as far as practicable, public annunciation of its proceedings and intentions beyond what is deemed necessary either to justify its past course, or to make others sensible of its determination to resist aggression, whether present or prospective. As the action of the executive upon all questions that affect our relations with other countries, must be more or less influenced by their conduct towards us, it is, in general, desirable that his future course should not be embarrassed by assurances given at a period when no safe opinion could be formed of what that conduct would be. In respect even to motives of a domestic character, it could scarcely be deemed consistent with that prudence and calm discretion which, in public as well as private affairs, is of such inestimable value, to bind ourselves in advance in respect to the particular line of conduct we will hereafter adopt in a case of such magnitude as the present. When the period for definitive action shall have arrived, the considerations now taken into view may have lost its weight they at present possess in the estimation of the public; and others, not now regarded as of any value, may, in the mean time, arise to affect materially, if not to change, the

whole aspect of the subject. The present condition of the relations between Mexico and Texas may soon be so far changed as to weaken, and perhaps to obviate entirely, the objections against the immediate annexation of the latter to the United States, which I have here set forth, and to place the question on different grounds. Should such a state of things arise, and I be found in charge of the responsible duties of president, you may be assured that I would meet the question, if then presented to me, with a sincere desire to promote the result which I believed best calculated to advance the permanent welfare of the whole country. In the discharge of this, the common duty of all our public functionaries, I would not allow myself to be influenced by local or sectional feelings. I am not, I need hardly say to you, an untried man in respect to my disposition or ability to disregard any feelings of that character in the discharge of official duties. You, as well as all others, have therefore at least some grounds on which to form an opinion as to the probable fidelity with which these assurances would be observed.

I shall add a few words on another aspect of the question, and then dismiss the subject. Mexico may carry her persistance in refusing to acknowledge the independence of Texas, and in destructive but fruitless efforts to reconquer that state, so far as to produce, in connexion with other circumstances, a decided conviction on the part of a majority of the people of the United States, that the permanent welfare, if not absolute safety to all, make it necessary that the proposed annexation should be affected, be the consequences what they may. The question may be asked, what, under such circumstances, would be the use you would make of the executive power, if intrusted to your hands? Would it be wielded to defeat, or to carry into effect the ascertained wishes of our people? My reply to such a supposition is, that I can conceive of no public questions, in respect to which it is more eminently proper that the opinions and wishes of the people of the different states, should be consulted, and being ascertained, treated with greater respect than those which relate either to the admission of a new member into the confederacy, or the acquisition of additional territory, with a view to such a result; and that, if any application for annexation, under such circumstances, were made to me, I would feel it to be my duty to submit the same to congress for a public expression of their opinion, as well upon the propriety of annexation, as to regard to the terms upon which it should take place. If, after the whole subject had been brought before the country, and fully discussed, as it now will be, the senate and house of representatives, a large portion of the former, and the whole of the latter having been chosen by the people, after the question of annexation had been brought before the country for its mature consideration, should express an opinion in favor of annexation, I would hold it to be my farther duty to employ the executive power to carry into full and fair effect the wishes of a majority of the people of the existing states, thus constitutionally and solemnly expressed.

There may, notwithstanding, be those, on both sides of this great question, who are unwilling to confer their suffrages on one who is not prepared to give them specific pledges in regard to the course he would, if elected, pursue in respect to the various aspects in which this matter may hereafter be presented. To all such I have only to say—and I do so with the greatest sincerity—that I have not the slightest disposition to question their right so to regulate their conduct, and will be the last to complain of its exercise. If there be any one who they believe can be more safely intrusted with their interest in this or any other of the great questions of public policy which are likely to arise in the administration of the government, or whose assurances as to his future course are more satisfactory to the, they will, without doubt, be well warranted in giving him the preference, and they may be assured that no one will more cheerfully acquiesce in a decision made from such motives, than myself. I have expressed a willingness to discharge, to the best of my abilities, the responsible duties of the highest office in question, should the democracy of the U. States be able and willing to re-elect me to the same. But I can take no steps to obtain it by which my ability to discharge its duties impartially and usefully to every portion of our common country would be impaired; nor can I in any extremity, be induced to cast a shade over the motives of my past life, by changes or concealments of opinions maturely formed upon a great national question, for the unworthy purpose of increasing my chances for political promotion.

I am, sir, very respectfully, your friend and obedient servant,

M. Van Buren

Republican Party Platform (1856)

The intensifying controversy over slavery during the late 1840s and the 1850s strained the fabric of national unity at every seam, including the party system. The Democrats, with their Deep South and lower-class base, were able to survive as a political party, although in a much weakened condition. (See "Democratic Party Platform [1860]," p. 164.) The Whig party, which included both large slaveowners and passionate abolitionists and which lacked a solid regional base, was less successful.

The unusual circumstances of the Whigs' victory in the election of 1848 bore unwitting testimony to the party's fragility. As in 1840, the 1848 Whig national convention bypassed its most respected leaders, Sen. Henry Clay of Kentucky and Sen. Daniel Webster of Massachusetts, to nominate a popular but aging Mexican War general, Zachary Taylor. Not only were Taylor's views on the issues unknown (he was almost wholly apolitical), so were the party's. The Whig convention decided that the best way to deal with its wrenching differences over slavery was not to enact any platform at all.

Taylor narrowly defeated the Democratic nominee, Sen. Lewis Cass of Michigan, in the election of 1848, but, like General Harrison, he died less than halfway into his term, on July 9, 1850. Taylor's successor as president,

Millard Fillmore of New York, was replaced on the ticket in 1852 by yet another Mexican War general, Winfield Scott. By now the Whigs were reaching deep into the political barrel—"Old Fuss and Feathers" was hardly the candidate that his predecessor, "Old Rough and Ready," had been four years earlier.

The Whigs' efforts to paper over the slavery controversy in presidential elections were undone by developments in Congress. The legislative branch had no choice but to address issues such as the admission of new states with slave or free constitutions, the conflicting legal rights of fugitive slaves and their owners, and the slave trade in the nation's capitol. Battles between "Conscience" Whigs and "Cotton" Whigs tore the party asunder.

Internally weakened and weakly led, the Whigs were trounced in the election of 1852. The Democratic national convention's forty-ninth ballot, "darkhorse" nominee for president, Gov. Franklin Pierce of New Hampshire, was himself a pallid choice. But Pierce easily defeated Scott by 254-42 in the electoral college and by a margin of 220,568 popular votes. (See "Martin Van Buren's Letter on Texas Annexation," p. 176.)

Two years later, in a desperate effort to defuse the controversy over slavery, Democratic senator Stephen Douglas of Illinois proposed to Congress that the settlers of territories seeking statehood, such as Kansas and Nebraska, be allowed to decide whether or not to allow slavery within their borders. Hopelessly divided over the Kansas-Nebraska Act of 1854, which embodied Douglas's plan for "popular sovereignty," the Whig party simply collapsed.

The Whigs' demise forced the party's northern antislavery adherents to seek a new political home. Antislavery Democrats, many of whom had followed former president Martin Van Buren into the Free Soil party in 1848, joined the quest. (Van Buren won 10.1 percent of the popular vote but carried no states.) Gathering at Ripon, Wisconsin, on February 28, 1854, a group of activists with varied political backgrounds resolved to form a new party that would make no effort to accommodate slavery's southern supporters. The new party, which adopted the name "Republican," spread quickly through the West, then the Northeast, winning several state elections in November 1854.

On July 17, 1856, delegates from all of the free states and four border states gathered in Philadelphia at the first Republican national convention. The convention adopted a platform that was antislavery but not abolitionist. (It opposed only the expansion of slavery into the territories.) The platform also included some traditional Whig planks endorsing internal improvements.

As their presidential candidate, the Republicans nominated the celebrated western explorer, Col. John C. Fremont of California. Fremont lost to the Democratic nominee, the wholly uncontroversial former secretary of state James Buchanan of Pennsylvania, by 174-114 in the electoral college. This remarkable showing for the new party—Fremont carried all of the eleven northernmost states—emboldened Republicans as they looked ahead to 1860. ~

This Convention of Delegates, assembled in pursuance of a call addressed to the people of the United States, without regard to past political differences or divisions, who are opposed to the repeal of the Missouri Compromise; to the policy of the present Administration; to the extension of Slavery into Free Territory; in favor of the admission of Kansas as a free State; of restoring the action of the Federal Government to the principles of Washington and Jefferson; and for the purpose of presenting candidates for the offices of President and Vice-President, do

Resolved: That the maintenance of the principles promulgated in the Declaration of Independence, and embodied in the Federal Constitution are essential to the preservation of our Republican institutions, and that the Federal Constitution, the rights of the States, and the union of the States, must and shall be preserved.

Resolved: That, with our Republican fathers, we hold it to be a self-evident truth, that all men are endowed with the inalienable right to life, liberty, and the pursuit of happiness, and that the primary object and ulterior design of our Federal Government were to secure these rights to all persons under its exclusive jurisdiction; that, as our Republican fathers, when they had abolished Slavery in all our National Territory, ordained that no person shall be deprived of life, liberty, or property, without due process of law, it becomes our duty to maintain this provision of the Constitution against all attempts to violate it for the purpose of establishing Slavery in the Territories of the United States by positive legislation, prohibiting its existence or extension therein. That we deny the authority of Congress, of a Territorial Legislation, of any individual, or association of individuals, to give legal existance to Slavery in any Territory of the United States, while the present Constitution shall be maintained.

Resolved: That the Constitution confers upon Congress sovereign powers over the Territories of the United States for their government; and that in the exercise of this power, it is both the right and the imperative duty of Congress to prohibit in the Territories those twin relics of barbarism—Polygamy, and Slavery.

Resolved: That while the Constitution of the United States was ordained and established by the people, in order to "form a more perfect union, establish justice, insure domestic tranquility, provide for the common defense, promote the general welfare, and secure the blessings of liberty," and contain ample provision for the protection of the life, liberty, and property of every citizen, the dearest Constitutional rights of the people of Kansas have been fraudulently and violently taken from them.

Their Territory has been invaded by an armed force;

Spurious and pretended legislative, judicial, and executive officers have been set over them, by whose usurped authority, sustained by the military power of the government, tyrannical and unconstitutional laws have been enacted and enforced;

The right of the people to keep and bear arms has been infringed.

Test oaths of an extraordinary and entangling nature have been imposed as a condition of exercising the right of suffrage and holding office.

The right of an accused person to a speedy and public trial by an impartial jury has been denied;

The right of the people to be secure in their persons, houses, papers, and effects, against unreasonable searches and seizures, has been violated;

They have been deprived of life, liberty, and property without due process of law;

That the freedom of speech and of the press has been abridged;

The right to choose their representatives has been made of no effect;

Murders, robberies, and arsons have been instigated and encouraged, and the offenders have been allowed to go unpunished;

That all these things have been done with the knowledge, sanction, and procurement of the present National Administration; and that for this high crime against the Constitution, the Union, and humanity, we arraign that Administration, the President, his advisers, agents, supporters, apologists, and accessories, either *before* or *after* the fact, before the country and before the world; and that it is our fixed purpose to bring the actual perpetrators of these atrocious outrages and their accomplices to a sure and condign punishment thereafter.

Resolved, That Kansas should be immediately admitted as a state of this Union, with her present Free Constitution, as at once the most effectual way of securing to her citizens the enjoyment of the rights and privileges to which they are entitled, and of ending the civil strife now raging in her territory.

Resolved, That the highwayman's plea, that "might makes right," embodied in the Ostend Circular, was in every respect unworthy of American diplomacy, and would bring shame and dishonor upon any Government or people that gave it their sanction.

Resolved, That a railroad to the Pacific Ocean by the most central and practicable route is imperatively demanded by the interests of the whole country, and that the Federal Government ought to render immediate and efficient aid in its construction, and as an auxiliary thereto, to the immediate construction of an emigrant road on the line of the railroad.

Resolved, That appropriations by Congress for the improvement of rivers and harbors, of a national character, required for the accommodation and security of our existing commerce, are authorized by the Constitution, and justified by the obligation of the Government to protect the lives and property of its citizens.

Resolved, That we invite the affiliation and cooperation of the men of all parties, however differing from us in other respects, in support of the principles herein declared; and believing that the spirit of our institutions as well as the Constitution of our country, guarantees liberty of conscience and equality of rights among citizens, we oppose all legislation impairing their security.

Abraham Lincoln's Cooper Institute Speech (1860)

Abraham Lincoln was raised in humble circumstances in Kentucky and Indiana and settled as a young man in Illinois, where he studied law. In 1834, Lincoln was elected to the first of several terms as a Whig member of the state legislature; twelve years later, he was chosen to serve a term in the House of Representatives, where his principled opposition to the popular Mexican War did his political career little good. Neither, in the short term, did Lincoln benefit politically from his strong belief that slavery was evil and should not be allowed to spread beyond its southern boundaries. In 1854, Lincoln found a home in the fledgling Republican party.

Ironically, Lincoln's greatest prepresidential political triumph came in defeat. In 1858, he challenged Stephen Douglas's effort to be reelected as senator from Illinois. Although, under the provisions of the original Constitution, senators were chosen by the state legislatures (and continued to be, until the adoption of the Seventeenth Amendment in 1913), Lincoln and Douglas managed to transform the Illinois legislative elections of 1858 into a referendum on the two candidates.

Touring the state together, Lincoln and Douglas waged a series of seven brilliant debates about the future of slavery. In the end, the Democrats narrowly won the legislative elections and returned Douglas to the Senate. But reports of the debates were published throughout the country and made Lincoln an instantly credible candidate for the Republican presidential nomination in 1860.

Beginning in 1859, Lincoln made several widely reported speaking tours, including one to the East in early 1860. His most successful eastern speech was delivered on February 27 to a large and enthusiastic audience at the Cooper Institute in New York City. "Let us have faith that right makes might," Lincoln said of the need to oppose the spread of slavery, "and in that faith, let us, to the end, dare to do our duty as we understand it."

The Cooper Institute speech not only made a strong impression in New York (the home state of the leading candidate for the 1860 Republican presidential nomination, former governor William H. Seward) but raised Lincoln's stature back home as well. Impressed with his reviews in the eastern press, Illinois Republicans decided to support Lincoln for president at the Republican national convention in May 1860.

Lincoln benefited from the party's decision to hold its convention in Chicago. Just as Baltimore became the leading convention city when the United States was mainly an eastern country (See "Proceedings of the Anti-

Masonic Convention," p. 143), *so did Chicago's location draw conventions when the country spread westward: since 1856, twenty-four national party conventions have been held in Chicago. Not surprisingly, Lincoln's home-state supporters packed the galleries during the balloting for president.*

Seward, the most famous Republican in the country, led the other candidates on the first two ballots. But the delegates turned to Lincoln the third time the roll was called, persuaded that his humble birth, homely wit, skill in debate, and geographical and political centrism would attract votes in states like Illinois and Indiana, where the Democrats were strong.

To balance the ticket, the convention chose Gov. Hannibal Hamlin of Maine for vice president. Hamlin was an easterner and a leader of the Seward wing of the Republican party. The party's platform, although mainly an antislavery document, reached out to northern business and western agricultural interests with promises to seek a protective tariff, a transcontinental railroad, and a homestead act to provide land for frontier settlers.   ~

Mr. President and Fellow-Citizens of New-York:—The facts with which I shall deal this evening are mainly old and familiar, nor is there anything new in the general use I shall make of them. If there shall be any novelty, it will be in the mode of presenting the facts, and the inferences and observations following that presentation.

In his speech last autumn, at Columbus, Ohio, as reported in "The New-York Times," Senator Douglas said:

> "Our fathers, when they framed the government under which we live, understood this question just as well, and even better, than we do now."

I fully indorse this, and I adopt it as a text for this discourse. I so adopt it because it furnishes a precise and an agreed starting point for a discussion between Republicans and that wing of the Democracy headed by Senator Douglas. It simply leaves the inquiry: *"What was the understanding those fathers had of the question mentioned?"*

What is the frame of Government under which we live:

The answer must be: "The Constitution of the United States." That Constitution consists of the original, framed in 1787, (and under which the present government first went into operation,) and twelve subsequently framed amendments, the first ten of which were framed in 1789.

Who were our fathers that framed the Constitution? I suppose the "thirty-nine" who signed the original instrument may be fairly called our fathers who framed that part of the present Government. It is almost exactly true to say they framed it, and it is altogether true to say they fairly represented the opinion and sentiment of the whole nation at that time. Their names, being familiar to nearly all, and accessible to quite all, need not now be repeated.

I take these "thirty-nine" for the present, as being "our fathers who framed the Government under which we live."

What is the question which, according to the text, those fathers understood "just as well, and even better than we do now?"

It is this: Does the proper division of local from federal authority, or anything in the Constitution, forbid *our Federal Government* to control as to slavery in *our Federal Territories?*

Upon this, Senator Douglas holds the affirmative, and Republicans the negative. This affirmation and denial form an issue; and this issue—this question—is precisely what the text declares our fathers understood "better than we."

Let us now inquire whether the "thirty-nine," or any of them, ever acted upon this question; and if they did, how they acted upon it—how they expressed that better understanding?

In 1784, three years before the Constitution—the United States then owning the Northwestern Territory, and no other, the Congress of the Confederation had before them the question of prohibiting slavery in that Territory; and four of the "thirty-nine," who afterward framed the Constitution, were in that Congress, and voted on that question. Of these, Roger Sherman, Thomas Mifflin, and Hugh Williamson voted for the prohibition, thus showing that, in their understanding, no life dividing local from federal authority, nor anything else, properly forbade the Federal Government to control as to slavery in federal territory. The other of the four—James M'Henry—voted against the prohibition, showing that, for some cause, he thought it improper to vote for it.

In 1788, still before the Constitution, but while the Convention was in session framing it, and while the Northwestern Territory still was the only territory owned by the United States, the same question of prohibiting slavery in the territory again came before the Congress of the Confederation; and two more of the "thirty-nine" who afterward signed the Constitution, were in that Congress, and voted on the question. They were William Blount and William Few; and they both voted for the prohibition—thus showing that, in their understanding, no line dividing local from federal authority, nor anything else, properly forbade the Federal Government to control as to slavery in federal territory. This time the prohibition became a law, being part of what is now well known as the Ordinance of '87.

The question of federal control of slavery in the territories, seems not to have been directly before the Convention which framed the original Constitution; and hence it is not recorded that the "thirty-nine," or any of them, while engaged on that instrument, expressed any opinion of that precise question.

In 1789, by the first Congress which sat under the Constitution, an act was passed to enforce the Ordinance of '87, including the prohibition of slavery in the Northwestern Territory. The bill for this act was reported by one of the "thirty-nine," Thomas Fitzsimmons, then a member of the House of Representatives from Pennsylvania. It went through all its states without a word of opposition, and finally passed both branches without yeas and nays, which is equivalent to an unanimous passage. In this Congress there were sixteen of the thirty-nine fathers who framed the original Constitution. They were John Langdon, Nicholas Gilman, Wm. S. Johnson, Roger Sherman, Robert Morris, Thos. Fitzsimmons, William Few, Abraham Baldwin, Rufus King, William Paterson, George Clymer, Richard Bassett, George Read, Pierce Butler, Daniel Carroll, James Madison.

This shows that, in their understanding, no line dividing local from federal authority, nor anything else in the Constitution, properly forbade Congress to prohibit slavery in the federal territory; else both their fidelity to correct principle, and their oath to support the Constitution, would have constrained them to oppose the prohibition.

Again, George Washington, another of the "thirty-nine," was then President of the United States, and, as such, approved and signed the bill; thus completing its validity as a law, and thus showing that, in his understanding, no line dividing local from federal authority, nor anything in the Constitution, forbade the Federal Government, to control as to slavery in federal territory.

No great while after the adoption of the original Constitution, North Carolina ceded to the Federal Government the country now constituting the State of Tennessee; and a few years later

Georgia ceded that which now constitutes the States of Mississippi and Alabama. In both deeds of cession it was made a condition by the ceding States that the Federal Government should not prohibit slavery in the ceded country. Besides this, slavery was then actually in the ceded country. Under these circumstances, Congress, on taking charge of these countries, did not absolutely prohibit slavery within them. But they did interfere with it—take control of it—even there, to a certain extent. In 1798, Congress organized the Territory of Mississippi. In the act of organization, they prohibited the bringing of slaves into the Territory, from any place without the United States, by fine, and giving freedom to slaves so brought. This act passed both branches of Congress without yeas and nays. In that Congress were three of the "thirty-nine" who framed the original Constitution. They were John Langdon, George Read and Abraham Baldwin. They all, probably, voted for it. Certainly they would have placed their opposition to it upon record, if, in their understanding, any line dividing local from federal authority, or anything in the Constitution, properly forbade the Federal Government to control as to slavery in federal territory.

In 1803, the Federal Government purchased the Louisiana country. Our former territorial acquisitions came from certain of our own States; but this Louisiana country was acquired from a foreign nation. In 1804, Congress gave a territorial organization to that part of it which now constitutes the State of Louisiana. New Orleans, lying within that part, was an old and comparatively large city. There were other considerable towns and settlements, and slavery was extensively and thoroughly intermingled with the people. Congress did not, in the Territorial Act, prohibit slavery; but they did interfere with it— take control of it—in a more marked and extensive way than they did in the

case of Mississippi. The substance of the provision therein made, in relation to slaves, was:

First. That no slave should be imported into the territory from foreign parts.

Second. That no slave should be carried into it who had been imported into the United States since the first day of May, 1798.

Third. That no slave should be carried into it, except by the owner, and for his own use as a settler; the penalty in all the cases being a fine upon the violator of the law, and freedom to the slave.

This act also was passed without yeas and nays. In the Congress which passed it, there were two of the "thirty-nine." They were Abraham Baldwin and Jonathan Dayton. As stated in the case of Mississippi, it is probable they both voted for it. They would not have allowed it to pass without recording their opposition to it, if, in their understanding, it violated either the line properly dividing local from federal authority, or any provision of the Constitution.

In 1819-20, came and passed the Missouri question. Many votes were taken, by yeas and nays, in both branches of Congress, upon the various phases of the general question. Two of the "thirty-nine"—Rufus King and Charles Pinckney—were members of that Congress. Mr. King steadily voted for slavery prohibition and against all compromises, while Mr. Pinckney as steadily voted against slavery prohibition and against all compromises. By this, Mr. King showed that, in his understanding, no line dividing local from federal authority, nor anything in the Constitution, was violated by Congress prohibiting slavery in federal territory; while Mr. Pinckney, by his votes, showed that, in his understanding, there was some sufficient reason for opposing such prohibition in that case.

The cases I have mentioned are the only acts of the "thirty-nine," or of any of them, upon the direct issue, which I have been able to discover.

To enumerate the persons who thus acted, as being four in 1784, two in 1787, seventeen in 1789, three in 1798, two in 1804, and two in 1819-20—there would be thirty of them. But this would be counting John Langdon, Roger Sherman, William Few, Rufus King, and George Read, each twice; and Abraham Baldwin, three times. The true number of those of the "thirty-nine" whom I have shown to have acted upon the question, which, by the text, they understood better than we, is twenty-three, leaving sixteen not shown to have acted upon it in any way.

Here, then, we have twenty-three out of our thirty-nine fathers "who framed the Government under which we live," who have, upon their official responsibility and their corporal oaths, acted upon the very question which the text affirms they "understood just as well, and even better than we do now;" and twenty-one of them—a clear majority of the whole "thirty-nine"—so acting upon it as to make them guilty of gross political impropriety and willful perjury, if, in their understanding, any proper division between local and federal authority, or anything in the Constitution they had made themselves, and sworn to support, forbade the Federal Government to control as to slavery in the federal territories. Thus the twenty-one acted; and as actions speak louder than words, so actions, under such responsibility, speak still louder.

Two of the twenty-three voted against Congressional prohibition of slavery in the federal territories, in the instances in which they acted upon the question. But for what reasons they so voted is not known. They may have done so because they thought a proper division of local from federal authority, or some provision or principle of the Constitution, stood in the way; or they may, without any such question, have voted against the prohibition, on what

appeared to them to be sufficient grounds of expediency. No one who has sworn to support the Constitution, can conscientiously vote for what he understands to be an unconstitutional measure, however expedient he may think it; but one may and ought to vote against a measure which he deems constitutional, if, at the same time, he deems it inexpedient. It, therefore, would be unsafe to set down even the two who voted against the prohibition, as having done so because, in their understanding, any proper division of local from federal authority, or anything in the Constitution forbade the Federal Government to control as to slavery in federal territory.

The remaining sixteen of the "thirty-nine," so far as I have discovered, have left no record of their understanding upon the direct question of federal control of slavery in the federal territories. But there is much reason to believe that their understanding upon that question would not have appeared different from that of their twenty-three compeers, had it been manifested at all.

For the purpose of adhering rigidly to the text, I have purposely omitted whatever understanding may have been manifested by any person, however distinguished, other than the thirty-nine fathers who framed the original Constitution; and, for the same reason, I have also omitted whatever understanding may have been manifested by any of the "thirty-nine" even, on any other phase of the general question of slavery. If we should look into their acts and declarations on those other phases, as the foreign slave trade, and the morality and policy of slavery generally, it would appear to us that on the direct question of federal control of slavery in federal territories, the sixteen, if they had acted at all, would probably have acted just as the twenty-three did. Among that sixteen were several of the most noted anti-slavery men of those times—as Dr. Franklin, Alexander

Hamilton and Gouverneur Morris—while there was not one known to have been otherwise, unless it may be John Rutledge, of South Carolina.

The sum of the whole is, that of our thirty-nine fathers who framed the original Constitution, twenty-one—a clear majority of the whole—certainly understood that no proper division of local from federal authority, nor any part of the Constitution, forbade the Federal Government to control slavery in the federal territories; while all the rest probably had the same understanding. Such, unquestionably, was the understanding of our fathers who framed the original Constitution; and the text affirms that they understood the question "better than we."

But, so far, I have been considering the understanding of the question manifested by the framers of the original Constitution. In and by the original instrument, a mode was provided for amending it; and, as I have already stated, the present frame of "the Government under which we live" consists of that original, and twelve amendatory articles framed and adopted since. Those who now insist that federal control of slavery in federal territories violates the Constitution, point us to the provisions which they suppose it thus violates; and, as I understand, they all fix upon provisions in these amendatory articles, and not in the original instrument. The Supreme Court, in the Dred Scott case, plant themselves upon the fifth amendment, which provides that no person shall be deprived of "life, liberty or property without due process of law;" while Senator Douglas and his peculiar adherents plant themselves upon the tenth amendment, providing that "the powers not delegated to the United States by the Constitution," "are reserved to the States respectively, or to the people."

Now, it so happens that these amendments were framed by the first Congress which sat under the Constitution—the identical Congress which passed the act already mentioned, enforcing the prohibition of slavery in the Northwestern Territory. Not only was it the same Congress, but they were the identical, same individual men who, at the same session, and at the same time within the session, had under consideration, and in progress toward maturity, these Constitutional amendments, and this act prohibiting slavery in all the territory the nation then owned. The Constitutional amendments were introduced before, and passed after the act enforcing the Ordinance of '87; so that, during the whole pendency of the act to enforce the Ordinance, the Constitutional amendments were also pending.

The seventy-six members of that Congress, including sixteen of the framers of the original Constitution, as before stated, were pre-eminently our fathers who framed that part of "the Government under which we live," which is now claimed as forbidding the Federal Government to control slavery in the federal territories.

It is not a little presumptuous in any one at this day to affirm that the two things with the Congress deliberately framed, and carried to maturity at the same time, are absolutely inconsistent with each other? And does not such affirmation become impudently absurd when coupled with the other affirmation from the same mouth, that those who did the two things, alleged to be inconsistent, understood whether they really were inconsistent better than we—better than he who affirms that they are inconsistent?

It is surely safe to assume that the thirty-nine framers of the original Constitution, and the seventy-six members of the Congress which framed the amendments thereto, taken together, do certainly include those who may be fairly called "our fathers who framed the Government under which we live." And so assuming, I defy any man to show that any one of them ever, in his whole life, declared that, in his understanding, any proper division of local from federal authority, or any part of the Constitution, forbade the Federal Government to control as to slavery in the federal territories. I go a step further. I defy any one to show that any living man in the whole world ever did, prior to the beginning of the present century, (and I might almost say prior to the beginning of the last half of the present century,) declare that, in his understanding, any proper division of local from federal authority, or any part of the Constitution, forbade the Federal Government to control as to slavery in the federal territories. To those who now so declare, I give, not only "our fathers who framed the Government under which we live," but with them all other living men within the century in which it was framed, among whom to search, and they shall not be able to find the evidence of a single man agreeing with them.

Now, and here, let me guard a little against being misunderstood. I do not mean to say we are bound to follow implicitly in whatever our fathers did. To do so, would be to discard all the lights of current experience—to reject all progress—all improvement. What I do say is, that if we would supplant the opinions and policy of our fathers in any case, we should do so upon evidence so conclusive, and argument so clear, that even their great authority, fairly considered and weighted, cannot stand; and most surely not in a case whereof we ourselves declare they understood the question better than we.

If any man at this day sincerely believes that a proper division of local from federal authority, or any part of the Constitution, forbids the Federal Government to control as to slavery in the federal territories, he is right to say so, and to enforce his position by all truthful evidence and fair argument which he can. But he has no right to mislead others, who have less access to

history, and less leisure to study it, into the false belief that "our fathers, who framed the Government under which we live," were of the same opinion—thus substituting falsehood and deception for truthful evidence and fair argument. If any man at this day sincerely believes "our fathers who framed the Government under which we live," used and applied principles, in other cases, which ought to have led them to understand that a proper division of local from federal authority or some part of the Constitution, forbids the Federal Government to control as to slavery in the federal territories, he is right to say so. But he should, at the same time, brave the responsibility of declaring that, in his opinion, he understands their principles better than they did themselves; and especially should he not shirk that responsibility by asserting that they "understood the question just as well, and even better, than we do now."

But enough! *Let all who believe that "our fathers, who framed the Government under which we live, understood this question just as well, and even better, than we do now," speak as they spoke, and act as they acted upon it. This is all Republicans ask—all Republicans desire—in relation to slavery. As those fathers marked it, so let it be again marked, as an evil not to be extended, but to be tolerated and protected only because of and so far as its actual presence among us makes that toleration and protection a necessity. Let all the guaranties those fathers gave it, be, not grudgingly, but fully and fairly maintained.* For this Republicans contend, and with this, so far as I know or believe, they will be content.

And now, if they would listen—as I suppose they will not—I would address a few words to the Southern people.

I would say to them:—You consider yourselves a reasonable and a just people; and I consider that in the general qualities of reason and justice you are not inferior to any other people. Still, when you speak of us Republicans, you do so only to denounce us as reptiles, or, at the best, as no better than outlaws. You will grant a hearing to pirates or murderers, but nothing like it to "Black Republicans." In all your contentions with one another, each of you deems an unconditional condemnation of "Black Republicanism" as the first thing to be attended to. Indeed, such condemnation of us seems to be an indispensable prerequisite—license, so to speak—among you to be admitted or permitted to speak at all. Now, can you, or not, be prevailed upon to pause and to consider whether this is quite just to us, or even to yourselves? Bring forward your charges and specifications, and then be patient long enough to hear us deny or justify.

You say we are sectional. We deny it. That makes an issue; and the burden of proof is upon you. You produce your proof; and what is it? Why, that our party has no existence in your section—gets no votes in your section. The fact is substantially true; but does it prove the issue? If it does, then in case we should, without change of principle, begin to get votes in your section, we should thereby cease to be sectional. You cannot escape this conclusion; and yet, are you willing to abide by it? If you are, you will probably soon find that we have ceased to be sectional, for we shall get votes in your section this very year. You will then begin to discover, as the truth plainly is, that your proof does not touch the issue. The fact that we get no votes in your section, is a fact of your making, and not of ours. And if there be fault in that fact, that fault is primarily yours, and remains so until you show that we repel you by some wrong principle or practice. If we do repel you by any wrong principle or practice, the fault is ours; but this brings you to where you ought to have started—to a discussion of the right or wrong of our principle. If our principle, put in prac-

tice, would wrong your section for the benefit of ours, or for any other object, then our principle, and we with it, are sectional, and are justly opposed and denounced as such. Meet us, then, on the question of whether our principle, put in practice, would wrong your section; and so meet us as if it were possible that something may be said on our side. Do you accept the challenge? No! Then you really believe that the principle which "our fathers who framed the Government under which we live" thought so clearly right as to adopt it, and indorse it again and again, upon their official oaths, is in fact so clearly wrong as to demand your condemnation without a moment's consideration.

Some of you delight to flaunt in our faces the warning against sectional parties given by Washington in his Farewell Address. Less than eight years before Washington gave that warning, he had, as President of the United States, approved and signed an act of Congress, enforcing the prohibition of slavery in the Northwestern Territory, which act embodied the policy of the Government upon that subject up to and at the very moment he penned that warning; and about one year after he penned it, he wrote La Fayette that he considered that prohibition a wise measure, expressing in the same connection his hope that we should at some time have a confederacy of free States.

Bearing this in mind, and seeing that sectionalism has since arisen upon this same subject, is that warning a weapon in your hands against us, or in our hands against you? Could Washington himself speak, would he cast the blame of that sectionalism upon us, who sustain his policy, or upon you who repudiate it? We respect that warning of Washington, and we commend it to you, together with his example pointing to the right application of it.

But you say you are conservative—eminently conservative—while we are revolutionary, destructive, or something of the sort. What is conservatism? Is it not adherence to the old and tried, against the new and untried? We stick to, contend for, the identical old policy on the point in controversy which was adopted by "our fathers who framed the Government under which we live," while you with one accord reject, and scout, and spit upon that old policy, and insist upon substituting something new. True, you disagree among yourselves as to what that substitute shall be. You are divided on new propositions and plans, but you are unanimous in rejecting and denouncing the old policy of the fathers. Some of you are for reviving the foreign slave trade; some for a Congressional Slave-Code for the Territories; some for maintaining Slavery in the Territories through the judiciary; some for the "gur-reat pur-rinciple" that "if one man would enslave another, no third man should object," fantastically called "Popular Sovereignty;" but never a man among you in favor of federal prohibition of slavery in federal territories, according to the practice of "our fathers who framed the Government under which we live." Not one of all your various plans can show a precedent or an advocate in the century within which our Government originated. Consider, then, whether your claim of conservatism for yourselves, and your charge of destructiveness against us, are based on the most clear and stable foundations.

Again, you say we have made the slavery question more prominent than it formerly was. We deny it. We admit that it is more prominent, but we deny that we made it so. It was not we, but you, who discarded the old policy of the fathers. We resisted, and still resist, your innovation; and thence comes the greater prominence of the question. Would you have that question reduced to its former proportions? Go back to that old policy. What has been will be again, under the same conditions. If you would have the peace of the old times,

readopt the precepts and policy of the old times.

You charge that we stir up insurrections among your slaves. We deny it; and what is your proof? Harper's Ferry! John Brown!! John Brown was no Republican; and you have failed to implicate a single Republican in his Harper's Ferry enterprise. If any member of our party is guilty in that matter, you know it or you do not know it. If you do know it, you are inexcusable for not designating the man and proving the fact. If you do not know it, you are inexcusable for asserting it, and especially for persisting in the assertation after you have tried and failed to make the proof. You need not be told that persisting in a charge which one does not know to be true, is simply malicious slander.

Some of you admit that no Republican designedly aided or encouraged the Harper's Ferry affair; but still insist that our doctrines and declarations necessarily lead to such results. We do not believe it. We know we hold to no doctrine, and make no declaration, which were not held to and made by "our fathers who framed the government under which we live." You never dealt fairly by us in relation to this affair. When it occurred, some important State elections were near at hand, and you were in evident glee with the belief that, by charging the blame upon us, you could get an advantage of us in those elections. The elections came, and your expectations were not quite fulfilled. Every Republican man knew that, as to himself at least, your charge was a slander, and he was not much inclined by it to cast his vote in your favor. Republican doctrines and declarations are accompanied with a continual protest against any interference whatever with your slaves, or with you about your slaves. Surely, this does not encourage them to revolt. True, we do, in common with "our fathers, who framed the Government under which we live," declare our belief that slavery is wrong; but the slaves do not hear us declare even this. For anything we say or do, the slaves would scarcely know there is a Republican party. I believe they would not, in fact, generally know it but for your misrepresentations of us, in their hearing. In your political contests among yourselves, each faction charges the other with sympathy with Black Republicanism; and then, to give point to the charge, defines Black Republicanism to simply be insurrection, blood and thunder among the slaves.

Slave insurrections are no more common now than they were before the Republican party was organized. What induced the Southampton insurrection, twenty-eight years ago, in which, at least, three times as many lives were lost as at Harper's Ferry? You can scarcely stretch your very elastic fancy to the conclusion that Southampton was "got up by Black Republicanism." In the present state of things in the United States, I do not think a general, or even a very extensive slave insurrection, is possible. The indispensable concert of action cannot be attained. The slaves have no means of rapid communication; nor can incendiary freemen, black or white, supply it. The explosive materials are everywhere in parcels; but there neither are, nor can be supplied, the indispensable connecting trains.

Much is said by Southern people about the affection of slaves for their masters and mistresses; and a part of it, at least, is true. A plot for an uprising could scarcely be devised and communicated to twenty individuals before some one of them, to save the life of a favorite master or mistress, would divulge it. This is the rule; and the slave revolution in Hayti was not an exception to it, but a case occurring under peculiar circumstances. The gunpowder plot of British history, though not connected with slaves, was more in point. In that case, only about twenty were admitted to the secret; and yet one of them, in his anxiety to save a friend, betrayed the

plot to that friend, and, by consequence, averted the calamity. Occasional poisonings from the kitchen, and open or stealthy assassinations in the field, and local revolts extending to a score or so, will continue to occur as the natural results of slavery; but no general insurrection of slaves, as I think, can happen in this country for a long time. Whoever much fears, or much hopes for such an event, will be alike disappointed.

In the language of Mr. Jefferson, uttered many years ago, "It is still in our power to direct the process of emancipation, and deportation, peaceably, and in such slow degrees, as that the evil will wear off insensibly; and their places be, *pari passu,* filled up by free white laborers. If, on the contrary, it is left to force itself on, human nature must shudder at the prospect held up."

Mr. Jefferson did not mean to say, nor do I, that the power of emancipation is in the Federal Government. He spoke of Virginia; and, as to the power of emancipation, I speak of the slaveholding States only. The Federal Government, however, as we insist, has the power of restraining the extension of the institution—the power to insure that a slave insurrection shall never occur on any American soil which is now free from slavery.

John Brown's effort was peculiar. It was not a slave insurrection. It was an attempt by white men to get up a revolt among slaves, in which the slaves refused to participate. In fact, it was so absurd that the slaves, with all their ignorance, saw plainly enough it could not succeed. That affair, in its philosophy, corresponds with the many attempts, related in history, at the assassination of kings and emperors. An enthusiast broods over the oppression of a people till he fancies himself commissioned by Heaven to liberate them. He ventures the attempt, which ends in little else than his own execution. Orsini's attempt on Louis Napoleon, and John Brown's attempt at Harper's Ferry were, in their philosophy, precisely the same. The eagerness to cast blame on old England in the one case, and on New England in the other, does not disprove the sameness of the two things.

And how much would it avail you, if you could, by the use of John Brown, Helper's Book, and the like, break up the Republican organization? Human action can be modified to some extent, but human nature cannot be changed. There is a judgment and a feeling against slavery in this nation, which cast at least a million and a half of votes. You cannot destroy that judgment and feeling—that sentiment—by breaking up the political organization which rallies around it. You can scarcely scatter and disperse an army which has been formed into order in the face of your heaviest fire; but if you could, how much would you gain by forcing the sentiment which created it out of the peaceful channel of the ballot-box, into some other channel? What would that other channel probably be? Would the number of John Browns be lessened or enlarged by the operation?

But you will break up the Union rather than submit to a denial of your Constitutional rights.

That has a somewhat reckless sound, but it would be palliated, if not fully justified, were we proposing, by the mere force of numbers, to deprive you of some right, plainly written down in the Constitution. But we are proposing no such thing.

When you make these declarations, you have a specific and well-understood allusion to an assumed constitutional right of yours, to take slaves into the federal territories, and to hold them there as property. But no such right is specifically written in the Constitution. That instrument is literally silent about any such right. We, on the contrary, deny that such a right has any existence in the Constitution, even by implication.

Your purpose, then, plainly stated, is, that you will destroy the Government, unless you be allowed to construe and enforce the Constitution as you please, on all points in dispute between you and us. You will rule or ruin in all events.

This, plainly stated, is your language. Perhaps you will say the Supreme Court has decided the disputed Constitutional question in your favor. Not quite so. But waiving the lawyer's distinction between dictum and decision, the Court have decided the question for you in a sort of way. The Court have substantially said, it is your Constitutional right to take slaves into the federal territories, and to hold them there as property. When I say the decision was made in a sort of way, I mean it was made in a divided Court, by a bare majority of the Judges, and they not quite agreeing with one another in the reasons for making it; that it is so made as that its avowed supporters disagree with one another about its meaning, and that it was mainly based upon a mistaken statement of fact—the statement in the opinion that "the right of property in a slave is distinctly and expressly affirmed in the Constitution."

An inspection of the Constitution will show that the right of property in a slave is not "distinctly and expressly affirmed" in it. Bear in mind, the judges do not pledge their judicial opinion that such right is impliedly affirmed in the Constitution; but they pledge their veracity that it is "distinctly and expressly" affirmed there—"distinctly," that is, not mingled with anything else—"expressly," that is, in words meaning just that, without the aid of any inference, and susceptible of no other meaning.

If they had only pledged their judicial opinion that such right is affirmed in the instrument by implication, it would be open to others to show that neither the word "slave" nor "slavery" is to be found in the Constitution, nor the word "property" even, in any connection with language alluding to the things slave, or slavery, and that wherever in that instrument the slave is alluded to, he is called a "person;"—and wherever his master's legal right in relation to him is alluded to, it is spoken of as "service or labor which may be due,"—as a debt payable in service or labor. Also, it would be open to show, by contemporaneous history, that this mode of alluding to slaves and slavery, instead of speaking of them, was employed on purpose to exclude from the Constitution the idea that there could be property in man.

To show all this, is easy and certain.

When this obvious mistake of the Judges shall be brought to their notice, is it not reasonable to expect that they will withdraw the mistaken statement, and reconsider the conclusion based upon it?

And then it is to be remembered that "our fathers, who framed the Government under which we live"—the men who made the Constitution—decided this same Constitutional question in our favor, long ago—decided it without division among themselves, when making the decision; without division among themselves about the meaning of it after it was made, and, so far as any evidence is left, without basing it upon any mistaken statement of facts.

Under all these circumstances, do you really feel yourselves justified to break up the Government, unless such a court decision as yours is, shall be at once submitted to as a conclusive and final rule of political action? But you will not abide the election of a Republican President! In that supposed event, you say, you will destroy the Union; and then, you say, the great crime of having destroyed it will be upon us! That is cool. A highwayman holds a pistol to my ear, and mutters through his teeth, "Stand and deliver, or I shall kill you, and then you will be a murderer!"

To be sure, what the robber demanded of me—my money—was my own; and I had a clear right to keep it; but it was no more my own than my vote is my own; and the threat of death to me, to extort my money, and the threat of destruction to the Union, to extort my vote, can scarcely be distinguished in principle.

A few words now to Republicans. *It is exceedingly desirable that all parts of this great Confederacy shall be at peace, and in harmony, one with another. Let us Republicans do our part to have it so. Even though much provoked, let us do nothing through passion and ill temper. Even though the southern people will not so much as listen to us, let us calmly consider their demands, and yield to them if, in our deliberate view of our duty, we possibly can.* Judging by all they say and do, and by the subject and nature of their controversy with us, let us determine, if we can, what will satisfy them.

Will they be satisfied if the Territories be unconditionally surrendered to them? We know they will not. In all their present complaints against us, the Territories are scarcely mentioned. Invasions and insurrections are the rage now. Will it satisfy them, if, in the future, we have nothing to do with invasions and insurrections? We know it will not. We so know, because we know we never had anything to do with invasions and insurrections; and yet this total abstaining does not exempt us from the charge and the denunciation.

The question recurs, what will satisfy them? Simply this: We must not only let them alone, but we must, somehow, convince them that we do let them alone. This, we know by experience, is no easy task. We have been so trying to convince them from the very beginning of our organization, but with no success. In all our platforms and speeches we have constantly protested our purpose to let them alone; but this has had no tendency to convince them. Alike unavailing to convince them, is the fact that they have never detected a man of us in any attempt to disturb them.

These natural, and apparently adequate means all failing, what will convince them? This, and this only: cease to call slavery *wrong,* and join them in calling it *right,* and this must be done thoroughly—done in *acts* as well as in *words.* Silence will not be tolerated— we must place ourselves avowedly with them. Senator Douglas's new sedition law must be enacted and enforced, suppressing all declarations that slavery is wrong, whether made in politics, in presses, in pulpits, or in private. We must arrest and return their fugitive slaves with greedy pleasure. We must pull down our Free State constitutions. The whole atmosphere must be disinfected from all taint of opposition to slavery, before they will cease to believe that all their troubles proceed from us.

I am quite aware they do not state their case precisely in this way. Most of them would probably say to us, "Let us alone, *do* nothing to us, and *say* what you please about slavery." But we do let them alone—have never disturbed them—so that, after all, it is what we say, which dissatisfies them. They will continue to accuse us of doing, until we cease saying.

I am also aware they have not, as yet, in terms, demanded the overthrow of our Free-State Constitutions. Yet those Constitutions declare the wrong of slavery, with more solemn emphasis, than do all other sayings against it; and when all these other sayings shall have been silenced, the overthrow of these Constitutions will be demanded, and nothing be left to resist the demand. It is nothing to the contrary, that they do not demand the whole of this just now. Demanding what they do, and for the reason they do, they can voluntarily stop nowhere short of this consummation. Holding, as they do, that slavery is morally right, and socially elevating, they cannot cease to demand a full

national recognition of it, as a legal right, and a social blessing.

Nor can we justifiably withhold this, on any ground save our conviction that slavery is wrong. If slavery is right, all words, acts, laws, and constitutions against it, are themselves wrong, and should be silenced, and swept away. If it is right, we cannot justly object to its nationality—its universality; if it is wrong, they cannot justly insist upon its extension—its enlargement. All they ask, we could readily grant, if we thought slavery right; all we ask, they could as readily grant, if they thought it wrong. Their thinking it right, and our thinking it wrong, is the precise fact upon which depends the whole controversy. Thinking it right, as they do, they are not to blame for desiring its full recognition, as being right; but, thinking it wrong, as we do, can we yield to them? Can we cast our votes with their view, and against our own? In view of our moral, social, and political responsibilities, can we do this?

Wrong as we think slavery is, we can yet afford to let it alone where it is, because that much is due to the necessity arising from its actual presence in the nation; but can we, while our votes will prevent it, allow it to spread into the National Territories, and to overrun us here in these Free States? If our sense of duty forbids this, then let us stand by our duty, fearless and effectively. Let us be diverted by none of those sophistical contrivances wherewith we are so industriously plied and belabored—contrivances such as groping for some middle ground between the right and the wrong, vain as the search for a man who should be neither a living man nor a dead man—such as a policy of "don't care" on a question about which all true men do care—such as Union appeals beseeching true Union men to yield to Disunionists, reversing the divine rule, and calling, not the sinners, but the righteous to repentence—such as invocations to Washington, imploring men to unsay what Washington said, and undo what Washington did.

Neither let us be slandered from our duty by false accusations against us, nor frightened from it by menaces of destruction to the Government nor of dungeons to ourselves. *Let us have faith that right makes might, and in that faith, let us, to the end, dare to do our duty as we understand it.*

Democratic Party Platform: Proposals on Slavery (1860)

Sen. Stephen Douglas of Illinois labored mightily to stake out a middle ground in the raging controversy of the 1840s and 1850s, the extension of slavery into the western territories. In 1857, when the Supreme Court issued a politically inflammatory ruling in the case of Dred Scott v. Sanford, *Douglas's efforts collapsed. So did the national Democratic party and, in short order, the Union.*

Douglas had fought for the notion of popular sovereignty, in which the people of each territory would decide whether to allow slavery within their borders. In 1854 Congress accepted his position by passing the Kansas-Nebraska Act. (See "Republican Party Platform [1860]," p. 194.) Popular sovereignty was, at best, a plan of both dubious morality (it treated slavery as a matter of majority preference) and uncertain practicality, as the settlers in "Bleeding Kansas" learned when their territory became, literally, a battleground between abolitionists and the champions of slavery. But the Supreme Court eliminated popular sovereignty even as an expedient when, on March 6, 1857, it ruled in the Dred Scott *case that slavery was legal in the territories and that neither Congress nor a territorial legislature could do anything about it.*

When the 1860 Democratic national convention convened in Charleston, South Carolina, on April 23, delegates from the northern and southern wings of the party discovered that they no longer had any basis for compromise, much less agreement, on slavery. Southerners controlled the platform committee, northerners the convention. After several days of debate, the delegates voted narrowly to reject the platform committee's pro-Dred Scott proposal in favor of a minority plank that explicitly avoided the slavery issue by laying it on the doorstep of future courts. Southern delegates

walked out of the convention in protest. Unable to rouse the required two-thirds majority for any presidential candidate, the remaining Democrats voted to reassemble in Baltimore, Maryland.

On June 18, 1860, two Democratic conventions met in Baltimore. The northern-dominated convention chose Douglas to run for president; southern Democrats nominated Vice President John C. Breckinridge of Kentucky. The Republicans already had selected Abraham Lincoln as their presidential candidate in May. (See "Abraham Lincoln's Cooper Institute Speech," p. 198.) A convention of mainly southern former Whigs—the Constitutional Union party, which pledged only to preserve the Union—nominated a fourth candidate, former senator John Bell of Tennessee.

The election of 1860 devolved into two virtually separate contests—Lincoln versus Douglas in the North, Bell versus Breckinridge in the South. Courageously, however, Douglas conducted a speaking tour through the South to plead against secession in the event that Lincoln won. "The election of a man to the Presidency by the American people in conformity with the Constitution of the United States would not justify any attempt at dissolving this glorious confederacy," Douglas told skeptical southern audiences.

On election day, Lincoln received only 39.9 percent of the popular vote. (Douglas won 29.4 percent, Breckinridge 18.1 percent, and Bell 12.6 percent.) But the Republican nominee's solid northern and western support was enough to earn him 180 electoral votes, 28 more than were required for election.

On December 20, 1860, the South Carolina legislature voted to secede from the Union. Other southern states followed in short order. The Confederate States of America declared itself a nation on February 7, 1861. Lincoln was inaugurated on March 4. Less than six weeks later, on April 12, Confederates fired on the federal outpost at Fort Sumter, South Carolina. The Civil War had begun.   ~

Majority Platform

Resolved, That the platform adopted by the Democratic party at Cincinnati be affirmed, with the following explanatory resolutions:

1. That the Government of a Territory organized by an act of Congress is provisional and temporary, and during its existence all citizens of the United States have an equal right to settle with their property in the Territory, without their rights, either of person or property, being destroyed or impaired by Congressional or Territorial legislation.

2. That it is the duty of the Federal Government, in all its departments, to protect, when necessary, the rights of persons and property in the Territories, and wherever else its constitutional authority extends.

3. That when the settlers in a Territory, having an adequate population, form a State Constitution, the right of sovereignty commences, and being consummated by admission into the Union, they stand on an equal footing with the people of other States, and the State thus organized ought to be admitted into the Federal Union, whether its Constitution prohibits or recognizes the institution of slavery.

Resolved, That the Democratic party are in favor of the acquisition of the Island of Cuba, on such terms as shall be honorable to ourselves and just to Spain, at the earliest practicable moment.

Resolved, That the enactments of State Legislatures to defeat the faithful execution of the Fugitive Slave Law are hostile in character, subversive of the Constitution, and revolutionary in their effect.

Resolved, That the Democracy of the United States recognize it as the imperative duty of this Government to protect the naturalized citizen in all his rights, whether at home or in foreign lands, to the same extent as its native-born citizens.

Whereas, One of the greatest necessities of the age, in a political, commercial, postal and military point of view, is a speedy communication between the Pacific and Atlantic coasts. Therefore be it

Resolved, That the National Democratic party do hereby pledge themselves to use every means in their power to secure the passage of some bill, to the extent of the constitutional authority of

Congress, for the construction of a Pacific Railroad from the Mississippi River to the Pacific Ocean, at the earliest practicable moment.

Minority Platform

1. *Resolved,* That we, the Democracy of the Union in Convention assembled, hereby declare our affirmance of the resolutions unanimously adopted and declared as a platform of principles by the Democratic Convention at Cincinnati, in the year 1856, believing that Democratic principles are unchangeable in their nature, when applied to the same subject matters; and we recommend, as the only further resolutions, the following:

2. Inasmuch as difference of opinion exist in the Democratic party as to the nature and extent of the powers of a Territorial Legislature, and as to the powers and duties of Congress, under the Constitution of the United States, over the institution of slavery within the Territories.

Resolved, That the Democratic party will abide by the decision of the Supreme Court of the United States upon these questions of Constitutional law.

3. *Resolved,* That it is the duty of the United States to afford ample and complete protection to all its citizens, whether at home or abroad, and whether native or foreign born.

4. *Resolved,* That one of the necessities of the age, in a military, commercial, and postal point of view, is speedy communication between the Atlantic and Pacific States; and the Democratic party pledge such Constitutional Government aid as will insure the construction of a Railroad to the Pacific coast, at the earliest practicable period.

5. *Resolved,* That the Democratic party are in favor of the acquisition of the Island of Cuba on such terms as shall be honorable to ourselves and just to Spain.

6. *Resolved,* That the enactments of the State Legislatures to defeat the faithful execution of the Fugitive Slave Law, are hostile in character, subversive of the Constitution, and revolutionary in their effect.

7. *Resolved,* That it is in accordance with the interpretation of the Cincinnati platform, that during the existence of the Territorial Governments the measure of restriction, whatever it may be, imposed by the Federal Constitution on the power of the Territorial Legislature over the subject of the domestic relations, as the same has been, or shall hereafter be finally determined by the Supreme Court of the United States, should be respected by all good citizens, and enforced with promptness and fidelity by every branch of the general government.

"The Lincoln Catechism" (1864)

In March 1863, halfway through President Abraham Lincoln's first term, reelection in 1864 seemed unlikely. Tradition belied a second term: no president had even been renominated by his party since Martin Van Buren in 1840. So did recent circumstances. In 1861 and 1862, the Union army had been poorly led and militarily unsuccessful. The initial public response to the Emancipation Proclamation, Lincoln's September 22, 1862, pledge to abolish slavery in the still-rebellious states on January 1, 1863, had been mixed. In the midterm elections of 1862, the Democrats had made gains in the House of Representatives and in several state governments.

Victories in battles at Gettysburg, Pennsylvania, and Vicksburg, Mississippi, improved the Union's military (and Lincoln's political) fortunes in July 1863, but these successes made the army's slow progress in early and mid-1864 seem all the more frustrating. In anticipation of the election of 1864, rival candidates emerged within the Republican party, including Secretary of the Treasury Salmon P. Chase and Gen. John C. Fremont, the party's nominee for president in 1856. Democrats cohered around Gen. George B. McClellan, the first commander of the Army of the Potomac. Although Lincoln had relieved McClellan of his post for want of a fighting spirit, the general had been highly popular with his troops.

Some advisers urged the president to postpone or suspend the 1864 elections, but Lincoln demurred. "We cannot have free government without elections," he said, "and if the rebellion could force us to forgo, or postpone a national election, it might fairly claim to have already conquered and ruined us."

As the election year wore on, Lincoln's political fortunes continued to wax and wane with the progress of the fighting. The national party convention in Baltimore, Maryland—dubbed the National Union convention in an effort to attract the support of prowar Democrats—came at a high point, in June. Not only was Lincoln renominated without opposition, but he maneuvered successfully to secure the second slot on the ticket for Andrew Johnson of Tennessee. Johnson, a Democrat and the only southern senator not to support secession in 1861, lent a bipartisan luster to the Republican campaign. The convention also called for a constitutional amendment to bring about the "utter and complete extirpation of slavery."

Just two months later, however, in

August 1864, misfortunes on the battle-field made Lincoln so despondent about his political prospects that he obliged the members of his cabinet to sign a statement pledging that if, as "seems exceedingly probable ... this Administration will not be reelected," an orderly transition of power to the Democratic president would occur. The general election campaign was vindictive and abusive. Republicans ridiculed McClellan's generalship and questioned the Democrats' patriotism. Democrats vilified Lincoln in cruel personal terms; the so-called "Lincoln Catechism" was a typical campaign broadside.

Lincoln's campaign for reelection caught fire in the fall. October brought a politically timely series of Union triumphs in Georgia, Alabama, Virginia, and elsewhere. McClellan proved to be a weak candidate--he was alternately conciliatory toward the South and unwilling to abandon the cause for which his Union soldiers had fought. On election day, Lincoln triumphed easily in the purely northern and western balloting: he won 2,218,388 popular votes (55.0 percent) and 212 electoral votes to McClellan's 1,812,807 popular votes (45.0 percent) and 21 electoral votes. Of the twenty-five states that participated in the election, the president carried all but Delaware, Kentucky, and New Jersey.   ~

I.

What is the Constitution?
A compact with hell—now obsolete.

II.

By whom hath the Constitution been made obsolete?
By Abraham Africanus the First.

III.

To what end?
That his days may be long in office—and that he may make himself and his people the equal of the negroes.

IV.

What is a President?
A general agent for negroes.

V.

What is Congress?
A body organized for the purpose of taxing the people to buy negroes, and to make laws to protect the President from being punished for his crimes.

VI.

What is an army?
A provost guard, to arrest white men, and set negroes free.

VII.

Who are members of Congress supposed to represent?
The President and his Cabinet.

VIII.

What is the meaning of *coining money?*
Printing green paper.

IX.

What did the Constitution mean by freedom of the Press?
Throwing Democratic newspapers out of the mails.

X.

What is the meaning of the word Liberty?
Incarceration in a vermin-infested bastile.

XI.

What is the duty of a Secretary of War?
To arrest freemen by telegraph.

XII.

What are the duties of a Secretary of the Navy?
To build and sink gunboats.

XIII.

What is the business of a Secretary of the Treasury?

To destroy State Banks and fill the pockets of the people full of worthless, irredeemable U.S. shinplasters.

XIV.

What is the chief business of a Secretary of State?

To print five volumes a year of Foreign Correspondence with himself, to drink whisky, and prophesy about war.

XV.

What is the meaning of the word "patriot?"

A man who loves his country less, and the negro more.

XVI.

What is the meaning of the word "traitor?"

One who is a stickler for the Constitution and the laws.

XVII.

What is the meaning of the word "Copperhead?"

A man who believes in the Union as it was, the Constitution as it is, and who cannot be bribed with greenbacks, nor frightened by a bastile.

XVIII.

What is a "loyal league?"

A body of men banded together, with secret signs and pass words, for the purpose of making a negro of a white man, and of controlling elections by force or fraud.

XIX.

What is the meaning of the word "law?"

The will of the President.

XX.

How were the States formed?

By the United States.

XXI.

Is the United States Government older that the States which made it?

It is.

XXII.

Have the States any rights?

None whatever, except when the President allows.

XXIII.

Have the people any rights?

None but such as the President gives.

XXIV.

Who is the greatest martyr of history?

John Brown.

XXV.

Who is the wisest man?

Abraham Lincoln.

XXVI.

Who is Jeff. Davis?

The devil.

Lesson the Second

I.

What is the *"habeas corpus?"*

The power of the President to imprison whom he pleases, as long as he pleases.

II.

What is Trial by Jury?

Trial by military commission.

III.

What is "security from unreasonable searches and seizures?"

The liability of a man's house to be entered by any Provost Marshal who pleases.

IV.

What is the meaning of the promise that, "no person shall be held to answer for any crime unless on a presentment or indictment of a Grand Jury?"

That any person may be arrested whenever the President or any of his officers please.

V.

What is the meaning of the promise that, "no person shall be deprived of life, liberty or property, without due process of law?"

That any person may be deprived of life, liberty and property, whom the President orders to be so stripped.

VI.

What is the meaning of "the right to a speedy and public trial by an impartial jury?"

A remote secret inquisition conducted by a man's enemies.

VII.

What is the meaning of the promise that the accused shall be tried "in the State and district wherein the crime shall have been committed?"

That he shall be sent away from the State and beyond the jurisdiction of the district where the offence is said to be committed.

VIII.

What is the meaning of the declaration that the accused shall "have the assistance of counsel for his defense?"

That, in the language of Seward to the prisoners in Fort Warren, "the employment of counsel will be deemed new cause for imprisonment."

IX.

What is the meaning of the declaration that, "the right of the people to keep and bear arms shall not be infringed?"

That a man's house may be searched, and he be stripped of his arms, whenever and wherever a provost marshall

dare attempt it.

X.

What is the meaning of the declaration that "the accused shall be informed of the nature and cause of the accusation," against him?

That he shall not be informed of the nature of his offence.

XI.

What is the meaning of the promise that an accused man may "be confronted with the witnesses against him?"

That he shall not be allowed to confront them.

XII.

What is the meaning of the declaration that the accused "shall have compulsory process for obtaining witnesses in his favor?"

That he shall not be allowed any witnesses.

XIII.

What is the meaning of the declaration that "the judicial Power of the United States shall be vested in the Supreme Court," etc.?

That it shall be vested in the President and his provost marshals.

XIV.

What is the meaning of the declaration that "No bill of Attainder, or *ex post facto* law shall be passed?"

That such a law may be passed whenever Congress pleases.

XV.

What is the meaning of the President's oath that he, "will to the best of his ability, Preserve, protect and defend the Constitution of the United States?"

That he will do all in his power to subvert and destroy it.

XVI.

What is the meaning of that part of his oath in which he swears to "take care that the laws be faithfully executed?"

That he will appoint provost marshals to override and disobey the laws.

XVII.

What is the meaning of the declaration that "The United States shall guarantee to every state a Republican form of government?"

That Congress shall assist the President in destroying the Republican form of government in the States, and substituting a military government whenever he pleases—witness Missouri, Kentucky, Maryland, and Delaware.

XVIII.

What is the meaning of the declaration that "No attainder of Treason shall work corruption of blood, or forfeiture, except during the life of the person attained?"

That a person accused of Treason may have his property confiscated not only during his life, but for all time, so that his children and heirs shall be punished for the crimes alleged against him.

XIX.

What is the meaning of the declaration, that "No person shall be convicted of treason unless on the testimony of two witnesses to some overt act, or on confession in open court?"

That a man may be convicted of treason without any witness, and without judge or jury, and without having committed any overt act.

XX.

What is the meaning of the declaration that "No money shall be drawn from the Treasury but in consequence of appropriations made by law?"

That the President may draw money from the Treasury whenever he pleases, for such things as sending missionaries and teachers to teach contrabands to read and write, or to build sheds and houses for stolen or runaway negroes.

XXI.

What is the meaning of the government?

The President.

XXII.

What is the meaning of an oath?

To swear not to do the thing you promise.

XXIII.

What is truth?

A lie.

Lesson the Third

I.

Do loyal leaguers believe in the Ten Commandments?

They do.

II.

What are the Ten Commandments?

Thou shalt have no other God but the negro.

Thou shalt make an image of a negro, and place it on the Capitol as the type of the new American man.

Thou shalt swear that the negro shall be the equal of the white man.

Thou shalt fight thy battles on the Sabbath day, and thy generals, and thy captains, and thy privates, and thy servants, shall do all manner of murders, and thefts as on the other six days.

Thou shalt not honor nor obey thy father nor thy mother if they are Copperheads; but thou shalt serve, honor and obey Abraham Lincoln.

Thou shalt commit murder—of slaveholders.

Thou mayest commit adultery—with the contrabands.

Thou shalt steal—everything that belongeth to a slaveholder.

Thou shalt bear false witness—against all slaveholders.

Thou shalt covet the slaveholder's

man-servant and his maid-servant, and shalt steal his ox and his ass, and everything that belongeth to him.

For on these commandments hang all the law and the honor of loyal leaguers.

III.

Do loyal leaguers believe the teachings of the gospel?

They do.

IV.

What does the gospel teach?

That we shall hate those who believe not with us, and persecute those who never wronged us.

V.

What else does the gospel teach?

That we shall resist evil, and that we shall overcome evil with evil.

VI.

What does the gospel say of peacemakers?

That they shall be accursed.

VII.

Whose children are the peacemakers?

The children of the devil.

VIII.

Do Loyal Leagues believe in the Sermon on the Mount?

They do.

IX.

Repeat the Sermon on the Mount?

Blessed are the proud and the contractors, for theirs is the kingdom of greenbacks.

Blessed are they that do not mourn for them that are murdered in the abolition war, for they shall be comforted with office.

Blessed are the haughty, for they shall inherit shinplasters.

Blessed are they that do hunger and thirst after the blood of slaveholders, for they shall be filled.

Blessed are the unmerciful, for they shall obtain command.

Blessed are the vile in heart, for they shall be appointed judges.

Whosoever does not smite thee on one cheek, smite him on both.

And if he turn away from thee, turn and hit him again.

If thou findest a chance to steal a slaveholder's coat, steal his cloak also. Give to a negro that asketh not, but from the poor white man turn thou away.

Be ye therefore unkind, spiteful, and revengeful, even as your father the devil is the same.

Take heed that ye give alms in public to the negroes, otherwise ye have no reward of your father Abraham, who is in Washington.

Therefore when thou givest thine alms to a negro, do thou sound a trumpet before thee, as the ministers and hypocrites do in the churches and in the streets, that they may have glory of the contrabands.

And when thou doest alms, let each hand know what the other hand doeth.

That thine alms may not be secret: and thy father the devil, who established the leagues, shall reward thee openly.

And when thou prayest, go to the Academy of Music, or to Cooper's Institute, that thou mayest be seen of men, after the manner of Cora Hatch and Henry Ward Beecher.

Do not forgive men their trespasses, for if you do God will not forgive your trespasses.

Moreover, when you pretend to fast, fast not at all, but eat turkies, ducks, and especially roosters, that ye may crow over the Copperheads, and stuff yourselves with whatsoever a shinplaster buyeth.

Lay up for yourselves treasures in green backs and five-twenties, and whatever else ye may steal from the Custom House and the Treasury.

Every man can serve two masters, the devil and the Abolitionists.

Take no thought to get raiment by honest toil, but go down South and steal it. Consider the vultures and the hawks, how they toil not neither do they sow, and yet no creature was ever stuffed out with so much fatness, except a contraband that feedeth at the public crib.

Judge another without judge or jury, but destroy the laws, so that your own measure shall not be measured unto you again.

If thou hast a beam in thine own eye, shut thine eye so that it cannot be seen, and go to picking out the mote that is in the Copperhead's eye.

If a poor white man ask bread, give him a stone, if he ask a fish, give him an alligator.

Therefore, whatsoever ye would that the slaveholder should not do unto you, do it even unto him: for this is the law of the loyal leagues.

X.

Have the loyal leagues a prayer?
They have.

XI.

Repeat it.

Father Abram, who art in Washington, of glorious memory—since the date of thy proclamation to free negroes.

The kingdom come, and overthrow the republic; they will be done, and the laws perish.

Give us this day our daily supply of greenbacks.

Forgive us our plunders, but destroy the Copperheads.

Lead us into fat pastures; but deliver us from the eye of detectives; and make us the equal of the negro; for such shall be our kingdom, and the glory of thy administration.

Lesson the Fourth

I.

What is the motto of loyal leagues?
"Liberty to the slave, or death to the Union."

II.

Does this place the negro above the Union?
It does.

III.

What do loyal leagues call the masses of the people?
"A herd of cattle"—*vide* Secretary Stanton.

IV.

How many of this "Herd of cattle" have the abolitionists caused to be maimed or slain in this war?
One million.

V.

How many widows have they made?
Five hundred thousand.

VI.

How many orphans?
Ten hundred thousand.

VII.

What will Lincoln's administration cost the country?
Four thousand millions of dollars.

VIII.

What is the annual interest on this debt?
Two hundred and eighty millions of dollars.

IX.

How much will this interest amount to in ten years?
Two thousand and eight hundred million of dollars.

X.

How much will that be in twenty years?

Five thousand and six hundred million of dollars.

XI.

Would the entire surplus export production of the North pay the interest on its debt?

It would not.

XII.

How will this affect the people?

It will humble their pride, and make them feel that they have a government.

XIII.

What effect will this debt have on the farmer?

It will mortgage his farm to the Government for nearly the amount of the interest on its cash value.

XIV.

What effect will it have on the workingman?

It will mortgage his muscle and the sweat of his brow to the Government for as long as he lives.

XV.

Is there any way for the people to get rid of this debt?

None whatever, but by repudiation.

XVI.

In case of repudiation, will "five twenties" go with the rest?

Yes—all government paper will sink together.

XVII.

How do the Republicans propose to prevent repudiation?

By a standing army of *negroes,* to force the people to pay at the point of the bayonet.

XVIII.

Who must pay the expense of the standing army?

The people, which will add three hundred millions annually to their debt.

XIX.

What will be the great advantage of this debt?

It will enslave the people, and bring them into the same wholesome subjection that they are in the Old World.

XX.

Is there any other benefit?

Yes—It will enable the children of the rich to live, without industry, upon the earnings of the poor from generation to generation.

XXI.

Should Mr. Lincoln be re-elected, what debt will he leave upon the country at the end of his second term?

Eight billions, or *eight thousand millions* of dollars!

XXII.

What will be the interest annually on this debt?

Five hundred and sixty millions of dollars.

XXIII.

What will be the annual expense for interest, and the standing army?

Eight hundred and sixty millions of dollars!

XXIV.

Will it be possible for the people to stand such a pressure of taxes?

They will have to stand it, or stand the prick of the bayonet.

XXV.

Suppose the people should take it into their heads to abandon their property and quit the country?

They will not be allowed—but will be compelled to remain and work for the support of the Government.

XXVI.

Will this be just?
Yes—"the government must be supported."

Lesson the Fifth

I.

What was Abraham Lincoln by trade?
A rail-splitter.

II.

What is he now?
Union-splitter.

III.

Who is Sumner?
A free American of African descent, who would swear to support the Constitution "only as he understood it."

IV.

Who is Phillips?
One of the founders of the Republican party who "labored nineteen years to take fifteen states out of the union."

V.

Who is Garrison?
A friend of the President, who went to hell, and found the original copy of the Constitution of the United States there.

VI.

Who is Seward?
A Prophet in the Temple of black dragons, and a taster in the government whiskey distillery.

VII.

Who is Chase?
The foreman of a green paper printing office.

VIII.

Who is Banks?
A dancing master, who wanted to slide down hill with the Union.

IX.

Who is Wade?
An amiable Christian gentleman who wanted to "*wade* up to his knees in the blood of slaveholders."

X.

Who is Francis S. Spinner?
A *spinner* of black yarn, who swore he would "abolish slavery, dissolve the Union, or have civil war," now Register of the Treasury.

XI.

Who is James S. Pike?
A stale fish which Mr. Lincoln presented as a Minister to the Netherlands, because, he said, "The Union is not worth supporting in connection with the South."

XII.

Who is Judge Spaulding?
A bad pot of *glue,* which would not hold the Union together, but declared in the Fremont Convention, "I am for dissolution, and I care not how soon it comes."

XIII.

Who is Jack Hale?
A hail fellow-well-met with the negroes, who introduced a petition to dissolve the Union in 1850.

XIV.

Who is Thomas F. Meagher?
An absconding prisoner from Botany Bay, who came to New York to "squelch the Copperheads."

XV.

Who is Simeon Draper?
A political *draper* by trade, who tried to *dress out* poor *Barney* of the Custom

House, that he might make a *nice suit* for himself.

XVI.

Who is Horace Greeley?

A celebrated poet, who wrote a poem on the American Flag, beginning thus:

Tear down the flaunting lie!
Half-mast the starry flag!
Insult no sunny sky
With hate's polluted rag.

XVII.

Who is Owen Lovejoy?

A fat and spongy Albino from Illinois. When it was supposed that his soul had floated off to Tartarus on the waves of his own fat, a brother member of congress kindly wrote his epitaph:

Beneath this stone good Owen Lovejoy lies,
Little in everything except in size;
What though his burly body fills this hole,
Still through hell's key-hole crept his little soul.

And when good Owen returned to this mundane sphere, his arrival was celebrated by the following complimentary additional verse:

The Devil finding Owen there,
Began to flout and rave—and sware
That hell should ne'er endure the stain,
And kicked him back to earth again.

XVIII.

Who is Andrew Curtin?

A highly colored *screen,* to cover the whiskey in the Executive Chamber of Pennsylvania.

XIX.

Who is John A. Dix?

A brave and invincible General, who never having had a chance to show prowess in battle, seized the Park Barricks containing seventy-five sick and wronged soldiers, and twenty-seven bushels of vermin.

XX.

Who is Park Godwin?

A celebrated Lexicographer, in the pay of Mr. Lincoln, who defines theft— "annoyance" and "botheration."

XXI.

Who is Henry J. Raymond?

A giant from the blood-stained plains of Solferino, enjoying a pension as Liar Extraordinary to the Administration.

XXII.

Who is the Rev. Henry Bellows?

A *windy instrument* of the abolitionists, who is trying very hard to make himself the equal of a negro.

XXIII.

Who is General Schenck?

A creature of very mixed *black and white* principles, which made an awful stink in Maryland.

XXIV.

Who is Thad Stephens?

An amalgamationist from Pennsylvania who honestly practices what he preaches.

XXV.

Who is General Burnside?

A *firey* commander who has wonderful success in seizing peaceable and unarmed civilians, when they were asleep in their own beds at midnight; and who was once caught in a trap by a famous old trapper of the name of Lee.

XXVI.

Who is James T. Brady?

A gentleman of great political versatility, now affiliated with the amalgamationists, who believes that "A rose by any other name would smell as sweet."

XXVII.

Who is Anna Dickinson?
Ask Ben. Butler and William D. Kelly.

XXVIII.

Who is Ben. Butler?
A Satyr, who has the face of a devil and the heart of a beast, who laughed when Banks supplanted him in New Orleans, saying, "he will find it a squeezed lemon."

XXIX.

Who is William D. Kelly?
A member of Congress, and a wagon contractor, who plays a bass viol in the orchestra of the female loyal leagues.

XXX.

Who is Henry P. Stanton?
A white man, whose negro principles, are undergoing a bleaching process, in consequence of his having been made a scape-goat for all of Chase's forty thieves in the Custom House.

Lesson the Sixth

I.

What is the chief end of the loyal leagues?
The end of the Union.

II.

What are States?
Colonies of the Federal Government.

III.

What is a Judge?
A provost marshal.

IV.

What is a court of law?
A body of soldiers, appointed by a General, to try civilians without law.

V.

What is a Bastile?
A Republican meeting-house, for the involuntary assembling of men who believe in the Union as it was, and the Constitution as it is.

VI.

What is the meaning of the word "demagogue?"
Ask those members of Congress, who believe the war is for the negro, and for the destruction of the Union, and yet vote it supplies of men and money.

VII.

What is a Governor?
A general agent for the President.

VIII.

What is a negro?
A white man with a black skin.

IX.

What is a white man?
A negro with a white skin.

X.

What will be the effect of amalgamation?
It is the doctrine of the Leagues that a superior race will spring from amalgamation.

XI.

Is this according to science?
No,—science teaches that the progeny of amalgamation would run out, and become extinct after the fourth or fifth generation.

XII.

Is science true?
No—it must be a lie; or the Leaguers are the greatest fools or knaves that ever lived.

XIII.

Is amalgamation now practiced to a greater extent than formerly?
It is, to a much greater extent.

XIV.

Where?
Everywhere the Leagues prevail.

XV.

Is it prosperous in Washington?
It is—so much so that more than five thousand of the fruits of amalgamation have been born in that city since the election of Mr. Lincoln.

XVI.

Is it spreading elsewhere?
Yes—wherever the officers of our army go in the South, it is doing well.

XVII.

How is it in New Orleans?
Well;—but there are a great many squint-eyed yellow babies there, supposed to have been occasioned by fright at the presence of Ben. Butler.

XVIII.

Did the same thing occur at Fortress Monroe, after Ben. Butler was in command there?
It did.

XIX.

The effects of fright are very wonderful in such cases, are they not?
They are wonderful indeed.

XX.

Do such remarkable imitations ever spring from any other cause than fright?
Yes—as in cases which such imitations follow good looking men, like Senators Wilson and Sumner.

XXI.

Is the science of amalgamation now in its infancy?
Comparatively—but, under the patronage of the loyal leagues, a great number of practical and experimental works will soon be *issued.*

XXII.

Who are engaged on these works?
The learned abolition clergy, Members of Congress, and all *competent* loyal leaguers.

XXIII.

Are the loyal leagues intended to be *"nurseries"* of the new science of amalgamation?
They are.

XXIV.

Is amalgamation considered the true doctrine of *negro equality* as taught by Mr. Lincoln in his debates with Mr. Douglas?
It is.

XXV.

Is this what Anna Dickinson really means by "the lesson of the hour?"
It is.

XXVI.

Is this what the President means by "Rising with the occasion?"
It is.

Lesson the Seventh

I.

Were the framers of the Constitution shortsighted and foolish men?
They were.

II.

Are their pernicious sentiments condemnatory of our most righteous abolition war?
They are.

III.

What did Jefferson, the father of the Declaration of Independence, teach?
That, "the several states which framed the Constitution have the unquestionable right to judge of in-

fractions."

IV.

What did James Madison, the father of the Constitution, say?

That, "in case of a deliberate, palpable and dangerous exercise of powers not granted in the Compact, the States have a right to interfere, for maintaining within their respective limits the authorities, rights and liberties appertaining to them."

V.

What did John Quincy Adams say?

That, "if the day shall come—may Heaven avert it!—when the affections of the people of these States shall be alienated from each other, when this fraternal spirit shall give way to cold indifference, or collisions of interest shall fester into hatred—then the bands of political association will not hold together parties no longer attracted by the magnetism of conciliated interests and kindly sympathies, and far better will it be for the people of the disunited States to part in friendship from each other than to be held together by restraint."

VI.

Have still later statesmen and politicians been affected with the same damnable idea?

They have.

VII.

What did Daniel Webster say?

"A bargain broken on one side is a bargain broken on all sides."

VIII.

What did Andrew Jackson say in his farewell address?

That, "If such a struggle is once begun, and the citizens of one section of the country are arrayed in arms against those of the other, in doubtful conflict, let the battle result as it may, there will be an end of the Union, and with it an end of the hope of freedom. The victory of the injured would not secure to them the blessings of liberty; it would avenge their wrongs, but they would themselves share in the common ruin. The Constitution cannot be maintained nor the Union preserved, in opposition to public feeling, by the mere exertion of the coercive powers confided to the government."

IX.

What did Abraham Lincoln say in Congress in 1848?

That, "Any people anywhere, being inclined, and having the power, have the right to rise up and shake off the existing government, and form a new one that suits them better. This is a most valuable, a most sacred right—a right which we hope and believe, is to liberate the world. Nor is the right confined to the cause in which the whole people of an existing government may choose to exercise it. ANY PORTION of such people that can, may revolutionize and make their own of so much of the Territory as they inhabit."

X.

What did Henry Clay say?

That, "When my State is right— when it has cause for resistance—when tyranny and wrong and oppression insufferable arise, I will share her fortunes."

XI.

What did U.S. Senator Levi Woodbury of New Hampshire say?

That, "If the bonds of a common language, a common government and all the common glories of the last century, cannot make us conciliatory and kind— cannot make all sides forgive and forget something,—cannot persuade to some sacrifice even, if necessary, to hold us together, force is as unprofitable to accomplish it as fratricide is to perpetuate peace in a common family."

XII.

What did Horace Greeley say in the *Tribune,* Nov. 26, 1860?

That, "If the Cotton States unitedly and earnestly wish to withdraw peacefully from the Union, we think they should be allowed to do so. Any attempt to compel them by force to remain, would be contrary to the principles enunciated in the immortal Declaration of Independence."

XIII.

What did Mr. Greeley say in the *Tribune,* Dec. 17, 1860?

That, "We have repeatedly asked those who dissent from our view of this matter, to tell us frankly whether they do or do not assent to Mr. Jefferson's statement in the Declaration of Independence, that governments 'derive their just powers from the consent of the governed; and that, whenever any form of government becomes destructive of these ends, *it is the right of the people to alter or abolish it,* and to institute a new government, &c, &c.' We do heartily accept this doctrine, believing it intrinsically sound, beneficient, and one that, universally accepted, is calculated to *prevent the shedding of seas of human blood.* And if it justified the secession from the British Empire of three millions of colonists in 1776, we do not see why it would not justify the secession of five millions of Southerners from the Federal Union in 1861. If we are mistaken on this point why does not some one attempt to show wherein and why? For our own part, while we deny the right of slaveholders to hold slaves against the will of the latter, we cannot see how Twenty Millions of people can rightfully hold Ten or even Five Millions in a detested Union with them by Military force.

"If even 'seven or eight States' send agents to Washington to say, 'We want to get out of the Union,' we shall feel constrained by our devotion to Human Liberty to say, *Let them go!* And we do not see how we could take the other side without coming in direct contact with those rights of man which we hold paramount to all political arrangements, however convenient and advantageous.'

XIV.

What did Chancellor Walworth say March 1st, 1961?

That, "It would be as brutal to send men to butcher their brothers of the Southern States, as it would be to massacre them in Northern States."

XV.

What did David S. Dickenson say in 1860?

That, "The union is not to be maintained by force."

XVI.

What did Judge Amasa J. Parker say?

That, "our people shrink back aghast at the idea of repeating, in this enlightened age, that first great crime of man, the staining of their hands with a brother's blood."

XVII.

What did Senator Stephen A. Douglas say:

That, "I don't understand how a man can claim to be a friend of the Union, and yet be in favor of war upon ten millions of people in the Union. You cannot cover this up much longer under the pretext of love for the Union."

XVIII.

What did the address of the Democratic State Convention of New York say in 1861?

That "the worst and most ineffective argument that can be addressed by the Federal Government, or its adhering members, to the seceding States, is civil war. Civil war will not restore the Union, but will defeat forever its reconstruction."

XIX.

What did the Tammany Hall resolutions of March 1st, 1861, say?

That, "No State shall be coerced into remaining in this Union, when, in the judgment of her people, her safety requires that she should secede in order to protect the lives and property of her citizens.

"We will oppose any attempt on the part of the Republicans in power to make any armed aggression under the plea of 'enforcing the laws,' or 'preserving the Union,' upon the Southern States."

XX.

Are not the sentiments expressed by all the above named statesmen and politicians, the same as now held by such infamous traitors as Clement Vallandigham and C. Chauncey Burr?

They are.

XXI.

What ought to be done with such men as Vallandigham and Burr, who "cling to these dogmas of the dead past?"

They ought to be hanged.

XXII.

Were Gen. Jackson and John Quincy Adams to come on earth again and teach the same as they once did, would they deserve to be hanged?

They would.

XXIII.

What should be done to Tammany Hall if it held the same doctrine now that it did three years ago?

It should be hanged, individually and collectively.

XXIV.

What should be done to Abraham Lincoln if he believed now as he did in 1848?

The king can do no wrong.

XXV.

Are all who believe as our fathers taught, "traitors" and "sympathizers?"

They are.

XXVI.

What will become of all who believe in the Union as it was, and the Constitution as it is?

They shall be damned.

XXVII.

What shall be the reward of all such as believe the Union was a covenant with death, and the Constitution a compact with hell?

They shall be received into a negro Paradise.

Lesson the Ninth

I.

Is the United States a consolidated government?

It is.

II.

Who consolidated it?

Abraham Lincoln.

III.

Does consolidation mean to annihilate the States?

Yes—to a great extent.

IV.

Had he a right to do this?

Yes—under the war power.

V.

Who invented the war power?

Abraham Lincoln.

VI.

For what purpose did he invent the war power?

That he might not have to return to the business of splitting rails.

VII.

Was Mr. Lincoln ever distinguished as a military officer?
He was—In the Black Hawk war.

VIII.

What high military position did he hold in that war?
He was a cook.

IX.

Was he distinguished for anything except for his genius as a cook?
Yes—he often pretended to see Indians in the woods, where it was afterwards proved that none existed.

X.

Was he ever in any battle?
No—he prudently skedaddled, and went home at the approach of the first engagement.

XI.

It there proof of this?
Yes—there are several men still living in Sangamon County, Illinois, who were present in the brigade at the time.

XII.

Does the Republican Party intend to change the name of the United States?
It does.

XIII.

What do they intend to call it?
New Africa.

XIV.

How will New Africa be bordered?
On the North by the North Start, on the East by Boston, on the West by Sunset, and on the South by Salt-river.

XV.

Are the people of the United States happy?
They are, very.

XVI.

What do they live upon?
Chiefly on blood.

XVII.

What do the Republicans understand by the word people?
Abolitionists, mesmerisers, spiritual mediums, free-lovers and negroes.

XVIII.

What is to be the established religion of New Africa?
Infidelity.

XIX.

How are the people to be divided?
Into the rich, the poor, the wise and the foolish.

XX.

Who are the rich?
The Generals, the office-holders, and the thieves.

XXI.

Who are the poor?
The soldiers, and all the people who are neither office-holders or thieves.

XXII.

Who are the wise?
The Copperheads, because they are "serpents."

XXIII.

Who are the foolish?
The black-snakes, because they are fast wriggling into a spot where they will run against the fangs of the Copperheads.

XXIV.

Is the black-snake afraid of the Copperheads?
Yes—as he is of the devil.

XXV.

What is the uniform of a chaplain of the leagues?
A shirt, a revolver, and a dirk.

XXVI.

How was this found out?

By the discovery of a Reverend loyal leaguer in full uniform in a lady's chamber, in Massachusetts.

XXVII.

When caught did he confess that every loyal leaguer is pledged to be always armed with these implements.

He did.

XXVIII.

Did he make a clean breast of the secrets of the order?

Yes, he made a good deal cleaner *breast* than *shirt*.

XXIX.

What did the lady leaguer say when this loyal chaplain was found in her room?

She said her husband was a brute to come home when he wasn't wanted.

XXX.

Are all husbands brutes who go home when the loyal league brethren are visiting their wives?

They are, great brutes.

Lesson the Tenth

I.

Are the loyal leaguers taught to hate any man?

They are.

II.

Who is he?

George B. McClellan.

III.

Why are they taught to hate McClellan?

Because he wished to restore the Union as it was, and preserve the Constitution as our fathers made it.

IV.

Why do the loyal leagues wish the Union as it was, and the Constitution as it is, destroyed?

Because in no other way can they destroy the property of the South, and make the negro the equal of the white man.

V.

Is this the object of the war?

It is.

VI.

For what other reason are the leagues taught to hate McClellan?

Because he refused to let the army under his command steal or destroy the private property of the Southern people.

VII.

Are these the reasons why he was removed from command?

They are—because his great popularity with the soldiers might render him a stumbling-block in the Presidential campaign for 1864.

VIII.

Has Mr. Lincoln any other stumbling-blocks?

He has.

IX.

Can you name them?

General Fremont is one, and Lincoln fears, a very dangerous one.

X.

Is this the reason Mr. Lincoln has not given him a command?

It is.

XI.

Did Mr. Lincoln approve of the principles of Fremont's campaign in the West?

He did approve of every thing except his aspirations for the presidency, and his popularity among the Germans.

XII.

What other stumbling-block has Mr. Lincoln?

Chase, who is trying to buy his own nomination, by putting extra steam on his high-pressure greenback printing machines.

XIII.

What is Mr. Seward in this contest? A broken bubble.

XIV.

When does Seward think the war will end?

In sixty days.

XV.

When does Lincoln expect it will end?

When Africa's woods are moved to Washington.

XVI.

Who is Mrs. Lincoln? The wife of the government.

XVII.

Who is Mr. Lincoln? A successful contractor to supply the government with mules.

XVIII.

Who is Master Bob Lincoln?

A lucky boy, yet in his teens, who has been so happy as to obtain shares in Government Contracts by which he has realized $300,000.

Lesson the Eleventh

I.

What is the meaning of the word swamp?

It is a place in Florida where Mr. Lincoln proposes to hide a small number of Yankees, to act as presidential electors for him next fall.

II.

What is a lagoon?

A place in Louisiana to be used for the same purpose.

III.

What is the meaning of the phrase to count chickens before they are hatched?

Mr. Lincoln's reckoning upon the quiet submission of all the states to his scheme of electoral frauds.

IV.

What does he fear?

That, when the pinch comes at last, the people will fly to arms and make an end of his rotten borough system and of himself together.

V.

What is a bank-director?

A silly coon, caught in one of Chase's traps.

VI.

What is a government bank?

A new engine turned loose on the track to run over all the State banks.

VII.

What will be the result?

That all banks, State and National, will be smashed up together.

VIII.

What are Five-Twenties?

Lincoln *I.O.U's.*—made redeemable in government slips of paper, in five or twenty years.

IX.

What else are they?

Baits to catch *flat* fish.

X.

Are loyal leaguers allowed to refer to the Constitution?

Only in terms of reproach.

XI.

Is it a disloyal practice to refer to the exploded right of trial by jury?

It is very disloyal.

XII.

Is it disloyal to refer to the size of Old Abe's feet?

It is.

XIII.

Is it disloyal to speak of white men as a superior race?

It is, very.

XIV.

Is it disloyal for a husband to object to his house being visited by strange men whose acquaintance his wife forms at the meetings of the loyal leagues?

It is, shockingly disloyal.

XV.

Is it disloyal to believe in the Union as it was?

It is.

XVI.

Is it a disloyal practice to say that the abolitionists ought to do the fighting in their war for the negroes?

It is, dangerously disloyal.

XVII.

Is it disloyal to allude to the rate at which the Republicans are plundering the Treasury and the people?

It is.

XVIII.

Is it disloyal to allude to the difference between an old fashioned Democratic gold dollar and the Republican green paper dollars?

It is.

XIX.

Is it disloyal to allude to the opinions and practices of our fathers on civil liberty or the rights of the States?

It is.

Electoral Commission Act (1877)

Confederate general Robert E. Lee's surrender to Gen. Ulysses S. Grant at the courthouse in Appomattox, Virginia, on April 9, 1865, brought to a close one national trauma, the Civil War. But the end of the war marked the beginning of another painful process, the "Reconstruction" of the South. The politics of Reconstruction dominated presidential elections until 1877.

Even before the Civil War ended, President Abraham Lincoln and the Republican Congress had been seriously at odds about how to restore the defeated South to the Union. Lincoln's approach was conciliatory, Congress's punitive. The lines of disagreement between the executive and the legislature hardened after Lincoln was assassinated on April 14, 1865, and the vice president, Andrew Johnson of Tennessee, succeeded to the presidency. The political warfare between Johnson, an erstwhile Democrat, and Congress became so fierce that the House of Representatives voted to impeach the president on March 2-3, 1868.

Johnson narrowly escaped conviction and removal by the Senate (the vote against him was 35-19, one short of the constitutionally required two-thirds majority), but his power to resist Congress in matters relating to Reconstruction was destroyed. By legislative act, ten southern states were tem-porarily reorganized into five military districts, each of them ruled by an army commander. The states could be readmitted to the Union only after they had met certain conditions, such as granting the right to vote to former slaves and denying the right to former Confederates. Not surprisingly, newly enfranchised southern blacks voted overwhelmingly for Republican candidates in state and national elections.

In the presidential elections of 1868 and 1872, the Republican party nominated its most popular war hero, General Grant. By adding the support of the reconstructed and readmitted southern states to the Republicans' strong northern and western base, Grant swept the electoral college in both elections: 214 to 80 against former governor Horatio Seymour of New York in 1868, and 286 to 63 against Horace Greeley, the celebrated editor of the New York Tribune, in 1872. (Greeley was the nominee of the anti-Grant "Liberal Republicans"; the enfeebled Democratic party simply endorsed his candidacy.) Grant's popular vote majorities also were impressive: 52.7 percent to 47.3 percent in 1868, and 55.6 percent to 43.8 percent in 1872.

Grant was personally popular but, at least in civilian garb, a weak leader. During his second term, the president was overwhelmed by governmental corruption and economic depression. His and the Republican party's prestige plummeted among the voters. In 1874 the Democrats regained control of the House for the first time since the elections of 1856.

Two years later, in 1876, the major parties each nominated a large-state governor for president: Rutherford B. Hayes of Ohio was the Republican candidate, and Samuel J. Tilden of New York represented the Democrats. On election day, the results of the voting seemed to indicate a Tilden victory: he outpaced Hayes by a quarter million popular votes and won 184 electoral votes (one shy of the required 185) to Hayes's 165. Twenty electoral votes were in dispute: one from Oregon and nineteen from the three southern states of Florida, Louisiana, and South Carolina. Tilden seemed to have carried all three states, but only, the Republicans charged, because the Democrats had used fraud and intimidation to exclude black voters from participating in the election. Forced to act without clear constitutional guidance, Congress passed the Electoral Commission Act on January 29, 1877. The act referred the disputed results of the 1876 election to a special, fifteen-member, bipartisan electoral commission that consisted of Supreme Court justices, senators, and members of the House. When the commission voted eight to seven in Hayes's favor, Democrats in the Senate began a filibuster to prevent its recommendations from being approved.

On March 2, 1877, two days before the scheduled beginning of the new president's term, a compromise was forged that resolved the electoral impasse in Hayes's favor. Southern Democrats agreed to end their filibuster and allow Congress to accept the commission's report in return for Hayes's promise virtually to end Reconstruction—that is, to withdraw the remaining federal troops from the South, appoint a white southerner to the cabinet, support internal improvements in the southern states, and allow the region to return to white rule. ~

An act to provide for and regulate the counting of votes for President and Vice-President, and the decision of questions arising thereon, for the term commencing March 4, A.D. 1877.

Be it enacted by the Senate and House of Representatives of the United States of America in Congress assembled. That the Senate and House of Representatives shall meet in the Hall of the House of Representatives at the hour of one o'clock p.m. on the first Thursday in February, A.D. 1877; and the President of the Senate shall be their presiding officer. Two tellers shall be previously appointed on the part of the Senate and two on the part of the House of Representatives, to whom shall be handed, as they are opened by the President of the Senate, all the certificates and papers purporting to be certificates of the electoral votes, which certificates and papers shall be opened, presented, and acted upon in the alphabetical order of the States, beginning with the letter A; and said tellers, having then read the same in the presence and hearing of the two Houses, shall make a list of the votes as they shall appear from the said certificates; and the votes having been ascertained and counted as in this act provided, the result of the same shall be delivered to the President of the Senate, who shall thereupon announce the state of the vote, and the names of the persons, if any, elected, which announcement shall be deemed a sufficient declaration of the persons elected President and Vice-President of the United States, and, together with a list of the votes, be entered on the Journals of the two Houses. Upon such reading of any such certificate or paper when there shall be only one return from a State, the President of the Senate shall call for objections, if any. Every objection shall be made in writing, and shall state clearly and concisely, and without argument, the ground thereof, and shall be signed by at least one Senator and one member of the House of Representatives before the same shall be received. When all objections so made to any vote or paper from a State shall have been received and read, the Senate shall thereupon withdraw, and such objections shall be submitted to the Senate for its decision; and the Speaker of the House of Representatives shall in like manner submit such objections to the House of Representatives for its decision; and no electoral vote or votes from any State from which but one return has been received shall be rejected except by the affirmative vote of the two Houses. When the two Houses have voted, they shall immediately again meet, and the presiding officer shall then announce the decision of the question submitted.

Sec. 2.   That if more than one return or paper purporting to be a return from a State shall have been received by the President of the Senate, purporting to be the certificates of electoral votes given at the last preceding election for President and Vice-President in such State, (unless they shall be duplicates of the same return,) all such returns and papers shall be opened by him in the presence of the two Houses when met as aforesaid and read by the tellers, and all such returns and papers shall thereupon be submitted to the judgment and decision, as to which is the true and lawful electoral vote of such State, of a commission constituted as follows, namely:

During the session of each House on the Tuesday next preceding the first Thursday in February, 1877, each House shall, by *viva voce* vote, appoint five of its members, who, with the five associate justices of the Supreme Court of the United States, to be ascertained as hereinafter provided, shall constitute a commission for the decision of all

questions upon or in respect of such double returns named in this section.

On the Tuesday next preceding the first Thursday in February, A.D. 1877, or as soon thereafter as may be, the associate justices of the Supreme Court of the United States now assigned to the first, third, eighth, and ninth circuits shall select, in such manner as a majority of them shall deem fit, another of the associate justices of said court, which five persons shall be members of said commission; and the person longest in commission of said five justices shall be the president of said commission. The members of said commission shall respectively take and subscribe the following oath:

"I, ____ ____, do solemnly swear (or affirm, as the case may be) that I will impartially examine and consider all questions submitted to the commission of which I am a member, and a true judgment give thereon, agreeably to the Constitution and the laws: so help me God;" which oath shall be filed with the Secretary of the Senate.

When the commission shall have been thus organized, it shall not be in the power of either House to dissolve the same or to withdraw any of its members; but if any such Senator or member shall die or become physically unable to perform the duties required by this act, the fact of such death or physical inability shall be by said commission, before it shall proceed further, communicated to the Senate or House of Representatives, as the case may be, which body shall immediately and without debate proceed by *viva voce* vote to fill the place so vacated, and the person so appointed shall take and subscribe the oath herein before prescribed, and become a member of said commission; and in like manner, if any of said justices of the Supreme Court shall die or become physically incapable of performing the duties required by this act, the other of said justices, members of the said commission, shall immediately appoint another justice of said court a member of said commission; and, in such appointments, regard shall be had to the impartiality and freedom from bias sought by the original appointments to said commission, who shall thereupon immediately take and subscribe the oath herein before prescribed, and become a member of said commission to fill the vacancy so occasioned.

All the certificates and papers purporting to be certificates of the electoral votes of each State shall be opened, in the alphabetical order of the States, as provided in section 1 of this act; and when there shall be more than one such certificate or paper, as the certificates and papers from such State shall so be opened, (excepting duplicates of the same return,) they shall be read by the tellers, and thereupon the President of the Senate shall call for objections, if any. Every objection shall be made in writing, and shall state clearly and concisely, and without argument, the ground thereof, and shall be signed by at least one Senator and one member of the House of Representatives before the same shall be received. When all such objections so made to any certificate, vote, or paper from a State shall have been received and read, all such certificates, votes, and papers so objected to, and all papers accompanying the same, together with such objections, shall be forthwith submitted to said commission, which shall proceed to consider the same, with the same powers, if any, now possessed for that proceed to consider the same, with the same powers, if any, now possessed for that purpose by the two Houses acting separately or together, and, by a majority of votes, decide whether any and what votes from such State are the votes provided for by the Constitution of the United States, and how many and what persons were duly appointed electors in such State, and may therein take into view such petitions, depositions, and other

papers, if any, as shall, by the Constitution and now existing law, be competent and pertinent in such consideration; which decision shall be made in writing, stating briefly the ground thereof, and signed by the members of said commission agreeing therein; whereupon the two Houses shall again meet, and such decision shall be read and entered in the Journal of each House, and the counting of the votes shall proceed in conformity therewith, unless, upon objection made thereto in writing by at least five Senators and five members of the House of Representatives, the two Houses shall separately concur in ordering otherwise; in which case such concurrent order shall govern. No votes or papers from any other State shall be acted upon until the objections previously made to the votes or papers from any State shall have been finally disposed of.

Sec. 3. That while the two Houses shall be in meeting, as provided in this act, no debate shall be allowed and no question shall be put by the presiding officer, except to either House on a motion to withdraw; and he shall have power to preserve order.

Sec. 4. That when the two Houses separate to decide upon an objection that may have been made to the counting of any electoral vote or votes from any State, or upon objection to a report of said commission, or other question arising under this act, each Senator and Representative may speak to such objection or question ten minutes, and not oftener than once; but after such debate shall have lasted two hours, it shall be the duty of each House to put the main question without further debate.

Sec. 5. That at such joint meetings of the two Houses seats shall be provided as follows: For the President of the Senate, the Speaker's chair; for the Speaker immediately upon his left; the Senators in the body of the Hall upon the right of the presiding officer; for the

Representatives, in the body of the Hall not provided for the Senators; for the tellers, Secretary of the Senate, and Clerk of the House of Representatives, at the Clerk's desk; for the other officers of the two Houses, in front of the Clerk's desk and upon each side of the Speaker's platform. Such joint meeting shall not be dissolved until the count of electoral votes shall be completed and the result declared; and no recess shall be taken unless a question shall have arisen in regard to counting any such votes or otherwise under this act; in which case it shall be competent for either House, acting separately, in the manner herein-before provided, to direct a recess of such House not beyond the next day, Sunday excepted, at the hour of ten o'clock in the forenoon. And while any question is being considered by said commission, either House may proceed with its legislative or other business.

Sec. 6. That nothing in this act shall be held to impair or affect any right now existing under the Constitution and laws to question, by proceeding in the judicial courts of the United States, the right or title of the person who shall be declared elected or who shall claim to be President or Vice-President of the United States, if any such right exists.

Sec. 7. The said commission shall make its own rules, keep a record of its proceedings, and shall have power to employ such persons as may be necessary for the transaction of its business and the execution of its powers.

"Rum, Romanism, and Rebellion": Report of the New York World (1884)

The end of Reconstruction, which followed the disputed election of 1876, inaugurated a nearly two-decade-long era of political parity between the Republican and Democratic parties in national elections. (See "Electoral Commission Act," p. 234.)

From 1880 to 1892, partisan control of the presidency alternated between the parties in lockstep succession.

~ In 1880 Rep. James A. Garfield, the Republican nominee for president, defeated the Democratic candidate, Gen. Winfield S. Hancock, by 214 to 155 in the electoral college and by a margin of 0.02 percentage points in the popular vote.

~ In 1884 Grover Cleveland, the Democratic governor of New York, won by 0.25 percentage points in the popular vote and by 219 electoral votes to 182 electoral votes against his Republican opponent, former speaker of the House of Representatives James G. Blaine of Maine.

~ In 1888 President Cleveland, despite winning a plurality of 90,595 in the popular vote, lost by 233 to 188 in the electoral college to former Indiana senator Benjamin A. Harrison, a Republican. Not since Harrison's victory has the popular vote loser won a presidential election. (See "The Twelfth Amendment: Senate Debate," p. 89.)

~ In 1892, former president Cleveland won a rematch against President Harrison, 46.1 percent to 43.0 percent in the popular vote and 277 to 145 in the electoral college. In doing so, Cleveland became the only president in history to win nonconsecutive elections.

Partisan control of Congress also was closely fought and variable during the post-Reconstruction era. Neither party ever attained as much as a ten-seat edge in the eighty-eight member Senate. (The forty-fourth state, Wyoming, was admitted to the Union in 1892.) Majorities in the House tended to represent the president's party.

Close electoral competition did not mean clear choices for the voters during the late nineteenth century. Both political parties were dominated by conservative economic interests—the Republicans by eastern business leaders, the Democrats by the large agricultural producers of the now "solid (Democratic) South." As a consequence, presidential election campaigns often turned on emotional issues—Republicans waved the "bloody shirt" to revive memories of the Civil War, and Democrats fanned the flames of ethnic and cultural resentments.

The election of 1884 was in many ways the prototypical post-Reconstruction election. The Republican party nominated Blaine, who was known to his admirers as the "Plumed Knight." Blaine had earned his honor-

ific (and his national reputation) in 1876, when he fought against a congressional resolution to forgive those who had served the South in the Civil War. Describing the effort, Col. Robert G. Ingersoll wrote: "Like an armed warrior, like a plumed knight, James G. Blaine marched down the halls of the American Congress and threw his shining lance full and fair against the brazen forehead of every traitor to his country." It was also in 1884 that the Republicans were first referred to as the "GOP," short for "Grand Old Party."

Cleveland, the Democratic nominee, tried to run a campaign of "educational politics," distributing pamphlets on the issues by mail and at meetings. But his effort was in vain. Both parties' platforms had fudged the major issue of the day, tariffs; besides, Blaine was unwilling to make a serious appeal to the voters. Republicans waved the bloody shirt unceasingly and tried to make an issue of Cleveland's having fathered a child out of wedlock many years earlier.

In the end, Blaine's inflammatory campaign backfired. On Wednesday, October 29, 1884, he attended a meeting of Republican Protestant clergy in New York City. In the welcoming address, Rev. Samuel D. Burchard made a remark that was sure to offend Roman Catholics, who were numerous in New York: "We are Republicans, and don't propose to leave our party and identify ourselves with the party whose antecedents have been Rum, Romanism, and Rebellion." Blaine did not disavow the statement, which was widely reported in the newspapers. The New York World *headlined its story in the next day's edition, "His Black Wednesday."*

On election day, Blaine lost New York's thirty-six electors by 1,149 votes out of more than a million cast. The loss cost him the election and the presidency.   ~

His Black Wednesday

James G. Blaine rose about 9 o'clock yesterday morning. He breakfasted in company with Mrs. Blaine, Miss Margaret and Messrs. Emmons and Walker Blaine. Shortly after 10 o'clock a delegation of pastors, representing churches in New York, Brooklyn and other cities in the vicinity, gathered in Parlor F. Word was sent to Mr. Blaine that his presence was desired in the grand salon, and before Mr. Blaine made his appearance several hundred pastors of churches and divinity students were assembled. Mr. Blaine was greeted with cheers, as was his wife. Mr. Blaine was attired in a plain black Prince Albert suit. Upon his left hand he wore a glove of brown kid. The mate was carried in his hand. He appeared exceedingly haggard, giving unmistakable evidence that the recent forty days of hippodroming had told severely upon his health. He was introduced to the clergy by the Rev. Dr. King, and the Rev. Dr. Burchard, the chairman of the delegation, delivered an address of welcome. He said:

"We are very happy to welcome you to this circle. You see here a representation of all the denominations of this city. You see the large number that are represented. We are your friends, Mr. Blaine. Notwithstanding all the calumnies that have been waged in the papers against you, we stand by your side. We expect to vote for you next Tuesday. We have a higher expectation, which is that you will be the President of the United States, and that you will do honor to your name, to the United States and to the high office you will occupy. We are Republicans, and don't propose to leave our party and identify ourselves with the party whose antecedents have been RUM, ROMANISM and REBELLION. We are loyal to our flag, we are loyal to you."

The Rev. Drs. Spier, MacArthur and Roberts, and Mr. Halliday also delivered short addresses.

Mr. Blaine seemed affected by the reception and the sentiments illustrated by the addresses. When these were ended he replied as follows:

"This is altogether a very remarkable assemblage—remarkable beyond any which I have known in the history of political contests in the United States, and it does not need any personal assurance that you should know I am very deeply impressed by it. I do not feel that I am speaking to these hundreds of men merely. I am speaking to the great congregations and the great religious opinion which is behind them, and as they represent the great Christian bodies, I know and realize that full weight of that which you say to me, and of the influence which you tender to me. Were it to me personally, I confess that I should be overcome by the compliment and the weight of confidence which it carries, but I know it is extended to me as the representative of the party whose creed and whose practice are in harmony with the churches. The Republican party from its very outset stood upon the impregnable platform of opposition to the extension of human slavery, and it stood on that platform till it was dragged by the hostility it provoked into a larger assertion of national sovereignty and thence into a bloody conflict to maintain it. From that onward I defy any man to point to a single measure of the Republican party which could not challenge the approbation of Christian ministers and the approval of God; and when, as one of the reverend speakers has said, that I narrowed the issue when I spoke of its coming down to a question of the tariff, I did not mean to exclude therefrom—I could not mean it—that great history of the party which is its wealth and its creed, and which gives to you and to all that stand behind you, assurance that whatever issue it attempts to enforce it will do it in good faith. You can no more separate a party from its history than you can separate a man from his character, and when the great make-up of public opinion is ready it takes into account the origin, the process, the measures, the character of the party and the character of its public men.

What I meant by saying that the tariff was the conclusive issue was that it steps to the forefront, not in exclusion of a thousand other important issues, but for this critical occasion and at the close of this great campaign, it stands forth as that issue which represents bread to the hungry and clothing to the naked and prosperity to an entire people, and the tariff is not therefore to be presented merely as a material issue, distinct and separate from the great moral issues, because, as I have said before Western audiences, I say here, you cannot impress a man if he is hungry with any other thought than that he shall be fed; you cannot impress a man if he is naked with any other thought than that he shall be clothed, and therefore that public policy and statesmanship is highest and best that attends to the primal needs of human nature first, and says here is bread for the hungry, here is clothing for the naked, and the tariff which protects the American laborer in his wages, the American capitalist in his investment, the inventive indent of the country in its enterprises is the issue which lies at the very foundation of the prosperity of the American people, at the very foundation of the success of the Christian religion. When you send out your missions to destitute places you clothe the little naked children and get them food at the first step. Therefore I repeat that the great conflict of 1884 closes with the people of the United States standing face to face in two parties saying whether they will adhere to that policy of protection which has trebled the wealth of the United States in twenty years, or whether they will abandon it and return once more to the failing theory of free trade. It involves other issues too. No nation can grow so powerful as the United States has grown, and is growing, without continually enlarging its relations with other nations. As these relations become enlarged they become complicated, and therefore the foreign policy of the United States goes right along with its domestic policy, supplement and complement, and you cannot, in any affair of our destiny and our policy, separate the one from the other. Now, gentlemen of the Church, I address an earnest word to you.

"The policy of the United States in the past and in the future must be one of broad, liberal, Christian principles, and in that policy it must be one, in my judgment, which draws nearer within the circle of the sympathies of the United States those other struggling Republics of North and South America, which bring them first into trade relations and then into closer personal and moral relations: and I believe that I shall not only have that great gain that comes from intercourse, but we shall enlarge the civilization of the Anglo-Saxon until its limits shall include the utmost southern point of the lower continent. I did not intend in accepting and acknowledging the great sense of obligation I feel for this honor, to go into a prolonged political speech. I have but indicated two leading points which I think are involved in the pending election. It only remains for me to say to you that I recognize at its full worth— and its full worth is very great—the meaning of this assemblage. We have no union of Church and State, but we have proved that the Church is stronger without the State and we have proved that no State can be strong without the Church. Let us go forward as we have gone, the State growing and strengthening by the example of the Church and the Church growing and strengthening by liberal co-operation with all the great reforms which it is the immediate province of the Government to forward and improve. Gentlemen, I thank you

again and bid you a very cordial good morning."

At noon Mr. Blaine lunched *en famille* and then held a short conference with Chairman B. F. Jones, of the National Committee: Chairman Warren, of the State Committee: Levi P. Morton and Steve Elkinus, his boodle managers. It is said that Mr. Morton assured Mr. Blaine that his begging in Wall Street had proved successful and that the money would be ready to buy up New Jersey, Connecticut, Indiana, North Carolina and Florida on the 4th of November. Mr. Blaine then received a large number of callers among them being ex-Gov. Cornell, Senator Al Daggett, A. S. Draper, Galusha A. Grow, Collector Robertson. Senator Warner Miller, Johnny O'Brien, Mike Cregan, John Roach, Secor Robeson, Mike Dady, Barney Biglin, William H. Williams, of the Brooklyn Young Republican Club; President Knight of the Brooklyn Young Men's Republican Club; S. V. White, John Jacob Astor and Cyrus W. Field. About 1 o'clock Mr. Blaine, accompanied by his wife, daughter and ex-Senator Thomas C. Platt, went for a drive in Central Park. The party returned about 3.30 o'clock, when Mr. Blaine, with Judge Noah Davis and Capt. Williams, hastened to the platform in Madison Square to witness the business men's parade.

In spite of the steady drizzle yesterday afternoon the Republicans say they are well satisfied with the result of their long-looked-for parade. It was the first "business men's" procession in honor of James G. Blaine and his cause, and the most strenuous efforts had been made to do proper honor to the magnetic candidate. And taken altogether the procession relected credit on the hard workers that had brought so many men into line. But the term "business men's" parade was misnomer, for one-half of those who marched up Broadway yesterday were not representatives of any commercial interest. Not that there were no business men in line, for there were, and that too from some of the best and most solid houses in the city.

Still the procession was far from presenting that spontaneous outpouring of old merchants and manufacturers that was so conspicuous in the Cleveland demonstration last Saturday. Sandwiched in between the legitimate business men were scores of people imported from Maryland, Philadelphia, New Jersey and Long Island. As a fair sample of out-of-town proportion of paraders—not a single member of the jewellers committee was a citizen of New York City. All the large Republican factories gave their clerks and operatives a half holiday and free fare to join the parade, and the New York Central Railroad also gave their employees a half holiday.

Promptly at 3.30 a platoon of police charged up Broadway, just as it began to rain, and the 1,100 men from the Produce Exchange fell into line and led the procession in files sixteen deep, taking up the entire breadth of the street. All wore blue badges, carried canes and were led by Col. Charles D. Sabin, Col. Benjamin Pair, Major W. S. Haynes and Jesse Hoyt, Cappa's full Seventh Regiment Band fell in leading the contingent from the Stock Exchange. They marched with steady step and in utter silence, as though the entire affair was a too serious matter of business, and very bad business at that.

In the very front rank of the Stock Exchange paraders, just under the shadow of the silk banner from which the crafty features of Mr. Blaine looked down—there marched with stealthy step a slender little man with sandy side whiskers. It was Wash Connor, the partner of Jay Gould. Mr. Gould himself intended to march, but the nasty dampness dissuaded him and his business partner went instead. All along the line Mr. Connor's well-known features were pointed out and he was yelled at a hundred times with: "Hello,

Wash, where's the Monopoly King?" Next to Mr. Connor stepped John McCann, the confidential clerk of Russell Sage, the Western railroad manipulator, and a little further down the line that cheerful monopolist and railway magnate, Mr. C. P. Huntington, had sent his private secretary to represent him.

At 4 o'clock, when both sides of Fifth avenue from Twenty-third Street north were packed with—to all outward appearances—the same crowd which gathered thereabouts on Tuesday to see Gov. Cleveland and the National Guard, a commotion in the mob, just south of the Worth monument, announced the approach of Mr. Blaine. There was a general and sudden scattering to right and left of the citizens who blocked the roadway fronting the main entrance to the Fifth Avenue Hotel; over the heads of the people were brandished the clubs of the police; small men were gathered up and thrust with unexpected celerity into the stomachs of their larger brethren. There was a chorus of "Down there!" "Stand back, there!" and then, glorious in his new uniform; magnificent in his physical proportions, there issued from the throng the redoubtable Capt. Williams, his club raised high in the air and his handsome face wreathed in smiles. Hanging upon the left arm of the captain was Mr. Blaine. Capt. Williams wore the low-crowned regulation cap of the Police Department. Mr. Blaine wore a tall silk hat. The top of Mr. Blaine's tall silk hat reached exactly to the lobe of the gallant captain's left ear. The street was muddy, and the crowd was noisy. Mr. Blaine clung to the arm of his plucky escort with a sort of take-me-round-to-the-back-door cling, but there was nothing of the rear-door aspect about Capt. Williams. He seemed to realize that he had hooked the biggest fish in his sea, and his march to the grand-stand was triumphant in the extreme.

Mr. Blaine, who wore white gaiter tops over a pair of English shoes, minced his way along, taking five steps to every three of the captain's. His eyes were cast upon the ground, and his appearance was that of a man who had been suddenly awakened from sleep for the purpose of keeping an appointment with a dentist. Standing in front of the grand stand were Thomas C. Action, John H. Starin, Lloyd Aspinwall, John I. Davenport and Gens. A. M. Palmer and Eli Parker. Mr. Acton grasped the hand of Mr. Blaine as he approached the steps leading to the platform and hoisted him up. Mr. Davenport stood on tip-toe and shouted "Hooray!" It was raining at the time, and Mr. Blaine looked moist and unhappy.

From a casual estimate, made by impartial persons, it was asserted that fully one-third of the marchers were imported from outside posts, and had no connection with organizations behind whose signs they marched.

Many of the organizations, after they had marched up Broadway some distance, turned out of the line and marched downtown again through the side streets, where they again joined the procession. This was done in order to give the procession the appearance of being much larger than it really was.

William Jennings Bryan's "Cross of Gold" Speech to Democratic National Convention (1896)

The late nineteenth century was a period of extraordinary economic expansion and nationalization in the United States. From 1863 to 1899, the country's index of manufacturing production rose by 700 percent. With the spread of railroads, small industry and local commerce gave way to large factories and mammoth corporations as the basis of national economic activity.

In the midst of widespread economic growth, many family farmers suffered. Monopolies and cartels in the farm equipment industry, the shipping industry, even the warehouse storage industry raised production costs for farmers. Because the availability of currency in the economy was tied to the supply of gold, money was scarce and expensive to borrow. Meanwhile, the prices paid for agricultural commodities were dropping. From 1865 to 1895, the purchasing power that a farmer derived from growing and selling a bushel of grain dropped by two-thirds.

The major political parties were generally inattentive to the farmers' plight. As the party of eastern business and finance, the Republicans were unabashedly in favor of the gold standard and of high tariffs on imported goods. After 1856 the only nineteenth century Democrat to win a presidential election was Grover Cleveland, an ardent conservative who characterized one proposal to modify the gold standard as "a dangerous and reckless experiment" that was "unpatriotic."

Confused by the complex origins of their economic woes, many small farmers fixed their hopes on the currency. As the historian Richard Hofstadter has written, "If money was scarce, the farmers reasoned, then the logical thing was to increase the money supply." In 1876 western farmers formed the Greenback party, which urged the government to print paper money. Although the Greenbacks fared poorly in the presidential election, their candidates won fourteen seats in the House of Representatives in 1878 and received 3.3 percent of the popular vote for president in 1880.

By 1892 the farmers' financial panacea had become "free silver." Vowing to expand the money supply by basing it on silver as well as on gold, the newly formed People's party (commonly called "Populist") nominated former representative James B. Weaver of Iowa for president. (Weaver had been the Greenback candidate in 1880.) The Populists, who represented both western and southern small farmers, won 8.5 percent of the popular vote and twenty-two electoral votes.

After the 1892 election, fueled by the economic Panic of 1893, free-silver fervor spread rapidly through the agricultural South and Midwest and the silver-producing states of the West. In

1896 the Republican national convention stood firmly by the gold standard and nominated Gov. William L. McKinley of Ohio for president. In contrast, the "silverbug"-dominated Democratic convention adopted a free-silver platform, then rejected a resolution that praised Cleveland for his eight years of service as president.

The climactic event of the 1896 Democratic convention came near the end of the platform debate, when former representative William Jennings Bryan of Nebraska made one of the most electrifying speeches in American political history. Reaching out not just to farmers but also to industrial workers in the cities, Bryan concluded his oration with these words: "You shall not press down upon the brow of labor this crown of thorns, you shall not crucify mankind upon a cross of gold!" Bryan captivated the convention, which nominated him for president on the fifth ballot. Only thirty-six years old, he was the youngest presidential candidate in history.   ∼

I would be presumptuous, indeed, to present myself against the distinguished gentlemen to whom you have listened if this were a mere measuring of abilities; but this is not a contest between persons. The humblest citizen in all the land, when clad in the armor of a righteous cause, is stronger than all the hosts of error. I come to speak to you in defense of a cause as holy as the cause of liberty—the cause of humanity.

When this debate is concluded, a motion will be made to lay upon the table the resolution offered in commendation of the administration, and also the resolution offered in condemnation of the administration. We object to bringing this question down to the level of persons. The individual is but an atom; he is born, he acts, he dies; but principles are eternal; and this has been a contest over a principle.

Never before in the history of this country has there been witnessed such a contest as that through which we have just passed. Never before in the history of American politics has a great issue been fought out as this issue has been, by the voters of a great party. On the fourth of March, 1895, a few Democrats, most of them members of Congress, issued an address to the Democrats of the nation, asserting that the money question was the paramount issue of the hour; declaring that a majority of the Democratic party had the right to control the action of the party on this paramount issue; and concluding with the request that the believers in the free coinage of silver in the Democratic party should organize, take charge of, and control the policy of the Democratic party. Three months later, at Memphis, an organization was perfected, and Silver Democrats went forth openly and courageously proclaiming their belief, and declaring that, if successful, they would crystallize into a platform the declaration which they had made. Then began the conflict. With a zeal approaching the zeal which inspired the crusaders who followed Peter the Hermit, our silver Democrats went forth from victory unto victory until they are now assembled, not to discuss, not to debate, but to enter up the judgment already rendered by the plain people of this country. In this contest brother has been arrayed against brother, father against son. The warmest ties of love, acquaintance and association have been disregarded; old leaders have been cast aside when they have refused to give expression to the sentiments of those whom they would lead, and new leaders have sprung up to give direction to this cause of truth. Thus has the contest been waged, and we have assembled here under as binding and solemn instructions as were ever imposed upon representatives of the people.

We do not come as individuals. As individuals we might have been glad to compliment the gentleman from New York, Senator Hill, but we know that the people for whom we speak would never be willing to put him in a position where he could thwart the will of the Democratic party. I say it was not a question of persons; it was a question of principle, and it is not with gladness, my friends, that we find ourselves brought into conflict with those who are now arrayed on the other side.

The gentleman who preceded me, ex-Governor Russell, spoke of the State of Massachusetts; let me assure him that not one present in all this convention entertains the least hostility to the people of the State of Massachusetts, but we stand here representing people who are the equals, before the law, of the greatest citizens in the State of Massachusetts. When you come before us and tell us that we are about to disturb your business interests, we reply that you have disturbed our business interests by your course.

We say to you that you have made the definition of a business man too limited in its application. The man who is employed for wages is as much a business man as his employer, the attorney in a country town is as much a business man as the corporation counsel in a great metropolis; the merchant at the crossroads store is as much a business man as the merchant of New York; the farmer who goes forth in the morning and toils all day—who begins in the spring and toils all summer—and who by the application of brain and muscle to the natural resources of the country creates wealth, is as much a business man as the man who goes upon the board of trade and bets upon the price of grain; the miners who go down a thousand feet into the earth, or climb two thousand feet upon the cliffs, and bring forth from their hiding places precious metals to be poured into the channels of trade are as much business

men as the few financial magnates who, in a back room, corner the money of the world. We come to speak for this broader class of business men.

Ah, my friends, we say not one word against those who live upon the Atlantic coast, but the hardy pioneers who have braved all the dangers of the wilderness, who have made the desert to blossom as the rose—the pioneers away out there, who rear their children near to Nature's heart, where they can mingle their voices with the voices of the birds—out there where they have erected schoolhouses for the education of their young, churches where they praise their Creator, and cemeteries where rest the ashes of their dead—these people, we say, are as deserving of the consideration of our party as any people in this country. It is for these that we speak. We do not come as aggressors. Our war is not a war of conquest; we are fighting in the defense of our homes, our families, and posterity. We have petitioned, and our petitions have been scorned; we have entreated, and our entreaties have been disregarded; we have begged, and they have mocked when our calamity came. We beg no longer; we entreat no more; we petition no more. We defy them.

The gentleman from Wisconsin has said that he fears a Robespierre. My friends, in this land of the free you need not fear that a tyrant will spring up from among the people. What we need is an Andrew Jackson to stand, as Jackson stood, against the encroachment of organized wealth.

They tell us that this platform was made to catch votes. We reply to them that changing conditions make new issues; that the principles upon which Democracy rests are as everlasting as the hills, but that they must be applied to new conditions as they arise. Conditions have arisen, and we are here to meet these conditions. They tell us that the income tax ought not to be brought in here; that it is a new idea. They criticize us for our criticism of the Supreme Court of the United States. My friends, we have not criticized; we have simply called attention to what you already know. If you want criticisms, read the dissenting opinions of the court. There you will find criticisms. They say that we passed an unconstitutional law; we deny it. The income tax law was not unconstitutional when it went before the Supreme Court for the first time; it did not become unconstitutional until one of the judges changed his mind, and we cannot be expected to know when a judge will change his mind. The income tax is just. It simply intends to put the burdens of government justly upon the backs of the people. I am in favor of an income tax. When I find a man who is not willing to bear his share of the burdens of the government which protects him, I find a man who is unworthy to enjoy the blessings of a government like ours.

They say that we are opposing national bank currency; it is true. If you will read what Thomas Benton said, you will find he said that, in searching history, he could find but one parallel to Andrew Jackson; that was Cicero, who destroyed the conspiracy of Cataline and saved Rome. Benton said that Cicero only did for Rome what Jackson did for us when he destroyed the bank conspiracy and saved America. We say in our platform that we believe that the right to coin and issue money is a function of government. We believe it. We believe that it is a part of sovereignty, and can no more with safety be delegated to private individuals than we could afford to delegate to private individuals the power to make penal statutes or levy taxes. Mr. Jefferson, who was once regarded as good Democratic authority, seems to have differed in opinion from the gentleman who has addrest us on the part of the minority. Those who are opposed to this proposition tell us that the issue of paper money is a function of the bank, and

that the Government ought to go out of the banking business. I stand with Jefferson rather than with them, and tell them, as he did, that the issue of money is a function of government, and that the banks ought to go out of the governing business.

They complain about the plank which declares against life tenure in office. They have tried to strain it to mean that which it does not mean. What we oppose by that plank is the life tenure which is being built up in Washington, and which excludes from participation in official benefits the humbler members of society.

Let me call your attention to two or three important things. The gentleman from New York says that he will propose an amendment to the platform providing that the proposed change in our monetary system shall not affect contacts already made. Let me remind you that there is no intention of affecting those contracts which according to present laws are made payable in gold; but if he means to say that we cannot change our monetary system without protecting those who have loaned money before the change was made, I desire to ask him where, in law or in morals, he can find justification for not protecting the debtors when the act of 1873 was passed, if he now insists that we must protect the creditors.

He says he will also propose an amendment which will provide for the suspension of free coinage if we fail to maintain the parity within a year. We reply that when we advocate a policy which we believe will be successful, we are not compelled to raise a doubt as to our own sincerity by suggesting what we shall do if we fail. I ask him, if he would apply his logic to us, why he does not apply it to himself. He says he wants this country to try to secure an international agreement. Why does he not tell us what he is going to do if he fails to secure an international agreement? There is more reason for him to do that than there is for us to provide against the failure to maintain the parity. Our opponents have tried for twenty years to secure an international agreement, and those are waiting for it most patiently who do not want it at all.

And now, my friends, let me come to the paramount issue. If they ask us why it is that we say more on the money question than we say upon the tariff question, I reply that, if protection has slain its thousands, the gold standard has slain its tens of thousands. If they ask us why we do not embody in our platform all the things that we believe in, we reply that when we have restored the money of the Constitution all other necessary reforms will be possible; but that until this is done there is no other reform that can be accomplished.

Why is it that within three months such a change has come over the country? Three months ago, when it was confidently asserted that those who believe in the gold standard would frame our platform and nominate our candidates, even the advocates of the gold standard did not think that we could elect a President. And they had good reason for their doubt, because there is scarcely a State here to-day asking for the gold standard which is not in the absolute control of the Republican party. But note the change. Mr. McKinley was nominated at St. Louis upon a platform which declared for the maintenance of the gold standard until it can be changed into bimetallism by international agreement. Mr. McKinley was the most popular man among the Republicans, and three months ago everybody in the Republican party prophesied his election. How is it to-day? Why, the man who was once pleased to think that he looked like Napoleon—that man shudders to-day when he remembers that he was nominated on the anniversary of the battle of Waterloo. Not only that, but as he listens he can hear with ever-increasing distinctness the sound of the waves as they beat upon the lonely shores of St. Helena.

Why this change? Ah, my friends, is not the reason for the change evident to any one who will look at the matter? No private character, however pure, no personal popularity, however great, can protect from the avenging wrath of an indignant people a man who will declare that he is in favor of fastening the gold standard upon this country, or who is willing to surrender the right of self-government and place the legislative control of our affairs in the hands of foreign potentates and powers.

We go forth confident that we shall win. Why? Because upon the paramount issue of this campaign there is not a spot of ground upon which the enemy will dare to challenge battle. If they tell us that the gold standard is a good thing, we shall point to their platform and tell them that their platform pledges the party to get rid of the gold standard and substitute bimetallism. If the gold standard is a good thing, why try to get rid of it? I call your attention to the fact that some of the very people who are in this convention to-day and who tell us that we ought to declare in favor of international bimetallism— thereby declaring that the gold standard is wrong and that the principle of bimetallism is better—these very people four months ago were open and avowed advocates of the gold standard, and were then telling us that we could not legislate two metals together, even with the aid of all the world. If the gold standard is a good thing, we ought to declare in favor of its retention and not in favor of abandoning it; and if the gold standard is a bad thing why should we wait until other nations are willing to help us to let go? Here is the line of battle and we care not upon which issue they force the fight; we are prepared to meet them on either issue or on both. If they tell us that the gold standard is the standard of civilization, we reply to them that this, the most enlightened of all the nations of the earth, has never declared for a gold standard and that both the great parties this year are declaring against it. If the gold standard is the standard of civilization, why, my friends, should we not have it? If they come to meet us on that issue we can present the history of our nation. More than that; we can tell them that they will search the pages of history in vain to find a single instance where the common people of any land have ever declared themselves in favor of the gold standard. They can find where the holders of fixt investments have declared for a gold standard, but not where the masses have.

Mr. Carlisle said in 1878 that this was a struggle between "the idle holders of idle capital" and "the struggling masses, who produce the wealth and pay the taxes of the country"; and, my friends, the question we are to decide is: Upon which side will the Democratic party fight; upon the side of "the idle holders of idle capital" or upon the side of "the struggling masses?" That is the question which the party must answer first, and then it must be answered by each individual hereafter. The sympathies of the Democratic party, as shown by the platform, are on the side of the struggling masses who have ever been the foundation of the Democratic party. There are two ideas of government. There are those who believe that, if you will only legislate to make the well-to-do prosperous, their prosperity will leak through on those below. The Democratic idea, however, has been that if you legislate to make the masses prosperous, their prosperity will find its way up through every class which rests upon them.

You come to us and tell us that the great cities are in favor of the gold standard; we reply that the great cities rest upon our broad and fertile prairies.

Burn down your cities and leave our farms, and your cities will spring up again as if by magic; but destroy our farms and the grass will grow in the streets of every city in the country.

My friends, we declare that this nation is able to legislate for its own people on every question, without waiting for the aid or consent of any other nation on earth; and upon that issue we expect to carry every State in the Union. I shall not slander the inhabitants of the fair State of Massachusetts nor the inhabitants of the State of New York by saying that, when they are confronted with the proposition, they will declare that this nation is not able to attend to its own business. It is the issue of 1776 over again. Our ancestors, when but three millions in number, had the courage to declare their political independence of every other nation; shall we, their descendants, when we have grown to seventy millions, declare that we are less independent than our forefathers? No, my friends, that will never be the verdict of our people. Therefore, we care not upon what lines the battle is fought. If they say bimetallism is good, but that we cannot have it until other nations help us, we reply that, instead of having a gold standard because England has, we will restore bimetallism, and then let England have bimetallism because the Untied States has it. If they dare to come out in the open field and defend the gold standard as a good thing, we will fight them to the uttermost. Having behind us the producing masses of this nation and the world, supported by the commercial interests, the laboring interests, and the toilers everywhere, we will answer their demand for a gold standard by saying to them: You shall not press down upon the brow of labor this crown of thorns, you shall not crucify mankind upon a cross of gold.

Republican Party Platform (1896)

The election of 1896 fit precisely the political scientist V. O. Key's definition of a "critical election"—namely, "a type of election in which there occurs a sharp and durable electoral realignment between parties." Although both parties had differed little on the issues during the post-Reconstruction era, they were competitively balanced to an extent not seen before or since. (See " 'Rum, Romanism, and Rebellion': Report of the New York World," p. 239.) The Democrats' nomination of William Jennings Bryan for president in 1896 widened the ideological divide between the parties; it also inaugurated an era of Republican dominance in national politics that lasted until 1932.

The Democrats' consignment to minority party status—the "moon" to the Republican "sun" in the political analyst Samuel Lubell's metaphor—was the consequence of their own failed political gamble. In 1896 the heretofore conservative Democratic party embraced populism and, in particular, "free silver." (See "William Jennings Bryan's 'Cross of Gold' Speech to the Democratic National Convention," p. 245.) In an effort to forge a class-based coalition that united small farmers in the South and the West with industrial workers in the growing cities of the East and the factory towns of the Midwest, Bryan waged an unprecedentedly active political campaign, traveling eighteen thousand miles and delivering six hundred speeches to perhaps five million people.

Bryan's strategy failed. On election day, he swept the solid Democratic South and did well in the West. But his appeal to labor fell upon deaf ears. Workers did not believe that the small town Nebraskan really understood their urban, industrial concerns; instead, they cast their lot with the eastern business interests upon whom they depended for their livelihoods. Bryan lost every state in the East and the industrial Midwest.

The Republican party played it safe in 1896. Its nominee, Gov. William L. McKinley of Ohio, squarely fit the mold of recent Republican candidates for president, who typically were midwestern governors (Rutherford B. Hayes in 1876) or midwestern senators (James A. Garfield of Ohio in 1880 and Benjamin A. Harrison of Indiana in 1888 and 1892). The party's 1896 platform was standard Republican fare: it endorsed the gold standard, high tariffs, and an aggressive foreign policy in the Western Hemisphere. According to the political scientist Benjamin Ginsberg, the contrast between the Republican and Democratic platforms in 1896 was the third greatest in history. Finally, the Republican campaign relied on strong party organization and abundant financing.

McKinley defeated Bryan by 51.0 percent to 46.7 percent in the popular vote and by 271 to 176 in the electoral college. In their rematch in 1900, McKinley increased his margins slightly: 51.7 percent to 45.5 percent in the popular vote, 292 to 155 in the electoral college. Republicans solidified their new national majority by winning both houses of Congress in 1894, then maintaining control for the next eighteen years.

In one important sense, the new political era that was ushered in by the election of 1896 was highly competitive: it matched two different partisan approaches to government. In another sense, however, the new era was a step backward for democratic competition, because the strong national Republican majority made the outcome of elections more predictable. Voters responded more to the latter development than to the former: the turnout rate in presidential elections, which was around 80 percent in 1896, declined steadily during the next three decades to less than 50 percent.   ~

The Republicans of the United States, assembled by the representatives in National Convention, appealing for the popular and historical justification of their claims to the matchless achievements of thirty years of Republican rule, earnestly and confidently address themselves to the awakened intelligence, experience and conscience of their countrymen in the following declaration of facts and principles:

For the first time since the civil war the American people have witnessed the calamitous consequence of full and unrestricted Democratic control of the government. It has been a record of unparalleled incapacity, dishonor and disaster. In administrative management it has ruthlessly sacrificed indispensable revenue, entailed an unceasing def-

icit, eked out ordinary current expenses with borrowed money, piled up the public debt by $262,000,000 in time of peace, forced an adverse balance of trade, kept a perpetual menace hanging over the redemption fund, pawned American credit to alien syndicates and reversed all the measures and results of successful Republican rule. In the broad effect of its policy it has precipitated panic, blighted industry and trade with prolonged depression, closed factories, reduced work and wages, halted enterprise and crippled American production, while stimulating foreign production for the American market. Every consideration of public safety and individual interest demands that the government shall be wrested from the hands of those who have shown themselves incapable of conducting it without disaster at home and dishonor abroad and shall be restored to the party which for thirty years administered it with unequaled success and prosperity. And in this connection, we heartily endorse the wisdom, patriotism and success of the administration of Benjamin Harrison. We renew and emphasize our allegiance to the policy of protection, as the bulwark of American industrial independence, and the foundation of American development and prosperity. This true American policy taxes foreign products and encourages home industry. It puts the burden or revenue on foreign goods; it secures the American market for the American producer. It upholds the American standard of wages for the American workingman; it puts the factory by the side of the farm and makes the American farmer less dependent on foreign demand and price; it diffuses general thrift, and founds the strength of all on the strength of each. In its reasonable application it is just, fair and impartial, equally opposed to foreign control and domestic monopoly to sectional discrimination and individual favoritism.

We denounce the present tariff as sectional, injurious to the public credit and destructive to business enterprise. We demand such an equitable tariff on foreign imports which come into competition with the American products as will not only furnish adequate revenue for the necessary expenses of the Government, but will protect American labor from degradation and the wage level of other lands. We are not pledged to any particular schedules. The question of rates is a practical question, to be governed by the conditions of time and of production. The ruling and uncompromising principle is the protection and development of American labor and industries. The country demands a right settlement, and then it wants rest.

We believe the repeal of the reciprocity arrangements negotiated by the last Republican Administration was a National calamity, and demand their renewal and extension on such terms as will equalize our trade with other nations, remove the restrictions which now obstruct the sale of American products in the ports of other countries, and secure enlarged markets for the products of our farms, forests, and factories.

Protection and Reciprocity are twin measures of American policy and go hand in hand. Democratic rule has recklessly struck down both, and both must be re-established. Protection for what we produce; free admission for the necessaries of life which we do not produce; reciprocal agreement of mutual interests, which gain open markets for us in return for our open markets for others. Protection builds up domestic industry and trade and secures our own market for ourselves; reciprocity builds up foreign trade and finds an outlet for our surplus. We condemn the present administration for not keeping pace [faith] with the sugar producers of this country. The Republican party favors such protection as will lead to the production on American soil of all the sugar which the American people use, and for which they pay other countries more than one hundred million dollars annually. To all our products; to those of the mine and the fields, as well as to those of the shop and the factory, to hemp and wool, the product of the great industry sheep husbandry; as well as to the foundry, as to the mills, we promise the most ample protection. We favor the early American policy of discriminating duties for the upbuilding of our merchant marine. To the protection of our shipping in the foreign-carrying trade, so that American ships, the product of American labor, employed in American ship-yards, sailing under the stars and stripes, and manned, officered and owned by Americans, may regain the carrying of our foreign commerce.

The Republican party is unreservedly for sound money. It caused the enactment of a law providing for the redemption [resumption] of specie payments in 1879. Since then every dollar has been as good as gold. We are unalterably opposed to every measure calculated to debase our currency or impair the credit of our country. We are therefore opposed to the free coinage of silver, except by international agreement with the leading commercial nations of the earth, which agreement we pledge ourselves to promote, and until such agreement can be obtained the existing gold standard must be maintained. All of our silver and paper currency must be maintained at parity with gold, and we favor all measures designated to maintain inviolable the obligations of the United States, of all our money, whether coin or paper, at the present standard, the standard of most enlightened nations of the earth.

The veterans of the Union Armies deserve and should receive fair treatment and generous recognition. Whenever practicable they should be given the preference in the matter of employment. And they are entitled to the enactment of such laws as are best calculated to secure the fulfillment of the pledges made to them in the dark days of the country's peril.

We denounce the practice in the pension bureau so recklessly and unjustly carried on by the present Administration of reducing pensions and arbitrarily dropping names from the rolls, as deserving the severest condemnation of the American people.

Our foreign policy should be at all times firm, vigorous and dignified, and all our interests in the western hemisphere should be carefully watched and guarded.

The Hawaiian Islands should be controlled by the United States, and no foreign power should be permitted to interfere with them. The Nicaragua Canal should be built, owned and operated by the United States. And, by the purchase of the Danish Islands we should secure a much needed Naval station in the West Indies.

The massacres in Armenia have aroused the deep sympathy and just indignation of the American people, and we believe that the United States should exercise all the influence it can properly exert to bring these atrocities to an end. In Turkey, American residents have been exposed to gravest [grievous] dangers and American property destroyed. There, and everywhere, American citizens and American property must be absolutely protected at all hazards and at any cost.

We reassert the Monroe Doctrine in its full extent, and we reaffirm the rights of the United States to give the Doctrine effect by responding to the appeal of any American State for friendly intervention in case of European encroachment.

We have not interfered and shall not interfere, with the existing possession of any European power in this hemisphere, and to the ultimate union of all the English speaking parts of the continent by the free consent of its inhabitants; from the hour of achieving their own independence the people of the United States have regarded with sympathy the struggles of other American peoples to free themselves from European domination. We watch with deep and abiding interest the heroic battles of the Cuban patriots against cruelty and oppression, and best hopes go out for the full success of their determined contest for liberty. The government of Spain, having lost control of Cuba, and being unable to protect the property or lives of resident American citizens, or to comply with its Treaty obligations, we believe that the government of the United States should actively use its influence and good offices to restore peace and give independence to the Island.

The peace and security of the Republic and the maintenance of its rightful influence among the nations of the earth demand a naval power commensurate with its position and responsibilities. We, therefore, favor the continued enlargement of the navy, and a complete system of harbor and seacoast defenses.

For the protection of the equality of our American citizenship and of the wages of our workingmen, against the fatal competition of low priced labor, we demand that the immigration laws be thoroughly enforced, and so extended as to exclude from entrance to the United States those who can neither read nor write.

The civil service law was placed on the statute book by the Republican party which has always sustained it, and we renew our repeated declarations that it shall be thoroughly and heartily, and honestly enforced, and extended wherever practicable.

We demand that every citizen of the United States shall be allowed to cast one free and unrestricted ballot, and that such ballot shall be counted and returned as cast.

We proclaim our unqualified condemnation of the uncivilized and preposterous [barbarous] practice well known as lynching, and the killing of human beings suspected or charged with crime without process of law.

We favor the creation of a National Board of Arbitration to settle and adjust differences which may arise between employers and employed engaged in inter-State commerce.

We believe in an immediate return to the free homestead policy of the Republican party, and urge the passage by Congress of a satisfactory free homestead measure which has already passed the House, and is now pending in the senate.

We favor the admission of the remaining Territories at the earliest practicable date having due regard to the interests of the people of the Territories and of the United States. And the Federal officers appointed for the Territories should be selected from the *bona-fide* residents thereof, and the right of self-government should be accorded them as far as practicable.

We believe that the citizens of Alaska should have representation in the Congress of the United States, to the end that needful legislation may be intelligently enacted.

We sympathize fully with all legitimate efforts to lessen and prevent the evils of intemperance and promote morality. The Republican party is mindful of the rights and interests of women, and believes that they should be accorded equal opportunities, equal pay for equal work, and protection to the home. We favor the admission of women to wider spheres of usefulness and welcome their co-operation in rescuing the country from Democratic and Populist mismanagement and misrule.

Such are the principles and policies of the Republican party. By these principles we will apply it to those policies and put them into execution. We rely on the faithful and considerate judgment of the American people, confident alike of the history of our great party and in the justice of our cause, and we present our platform and our candidates in the full assurance that their selection will bring victory to the Republican party, and prosperity to the people of the United States.

"Bull Moose" Party Platform (1912)

Theodore Roosevelt attained his first national political office in 1900 when, after two years as the reformist Republican governor of New York, he was successfully promoted for the vice-presidential nomination by party regulars in his state who wanted to get him out of their affairs. Hearing of the New Yorkers' effort, but unable to thwart it, the national chair of the Republican party, Mark Hanna, fumed, "Don't you realize that there's only one life between that madman and the White House?" Hanna's remark was as prescient as it was unfair: President William L. McKinley died on September 14, 1901 (he had been shot eight days earlier), and Vice President Roosevelt succeeded to the presidency.

Roosevelt's term was marked by a succession of historical "firsts"—the first president ever to be known by his initials (TR), the first "rhetorical president" (that is, the first to try to rouse public opinion with speeches in support of his legislative policies), the youngest person ever to serve as president (forty-two years old), and the first successor president to be nominated by his party for a term in his own right. In 1904 TR won easily against Alton B. Parker, a conservative New York judge whom, curiously, the Democratic national convention nominated after enacting a liberal platform. Roosevelt's margin of victory was 336-140 in the electoral college and 56.4 percent to 37.6 percent in the popular vote.

Roosevelt was an avowed leader of the Progressive movement: he favored federal regulation of the large corporations (or "trusts"), conservation of natural resources, and reform of the corrupt practices that infused the partisan politics of the era. Publicly committed to step down as president in 1908 (he counted his three-and-one-half year succession as his first term), Roosevelt groomed Secretary of War William Howard Taft of Ohio to carry the progressive Republican flag in the election of 1908. (See "Thomas Jefferson's 'No Third Term' Letter," p. 101, and "The Twenty-second Amendment: House Debate," p. 370.)

Taft easily defeated William Jennings Bryan, who was making his third run for the presidency in the last four elections, by 321 electoral votes to 162 electoral votes and by a popular vote majority of 51.6 percent to 43.1 percent. As president, however, Taft proved to be less ardent in his pursuit of progressivism than Roosevelt had expected. Furious with his former friend and political ally, TR announced in February 1912 that he intended to challenge Taft for the Republican presidential nomination. "My hat is in the ring!" he proclaimed with characteristic enthusiasm. "The fight is on and I am stripped to the buff!"

Presidential primaries took place for the first time in 1912. Thirteen states, all of them in the North and West, allowed the voters to choose delegates to the Republican national convention. Roosevelt entered twelve primaries and won ten, including Pennsylvania, Illinois, and Taft's home state of Ohio. But Taft had enough support from the party leaders who controlled the selection of delegates in the other thirty-five states to prevail at the convention in June 1912. Vice President James S. Sherman of New York also was renominated, the first vice president ever chosen to run for a second term by a party convention.

Angered by Taft's nomination, Roosevelt's supporters stormed out of the Republican convention; TR himself announced that he planned to continue the fight. On August 5, 1912, an assortment of progressives gathered in Chicago to nominate Roosevelt for president and to adopt a platform (or "Covenant with the People") that endorsed conservation, business regulation, better working conditions for labor, the direct election of senators, women's suffrage, and a host of other reformist causes. The new party was officially called Progressive but it soon borrowed a name from a remark that Roosevelt made to reporters who asked how he felt about running for president again: "I'm feeling like a bull moose!"

The year 1912 was the highwater mark for third-party politics in presidential elections. Roosevelt finished second, with eighty-eight electoral votes and 27.4 percent of the popular vote. In addition the Socialist party ticket, which was headed by labor leader Eugene V. Debs, won 6.0 percent of the popular vote, the largest share in history for an ideological party. (See "Henry A. Wallace Announces for President," p. 453.) ~

Progressive Platform of 1912

The conscience of the people, in a time of grave national problems, has called into being a new party, born of the nation's sense of justice. We of the Progressive party here dedicate ourselves to the fulfillment of the duty laid upon us by our fathers to maintain the government of the people, by the people and for the people whose foundations they laid.

We hold with Thomas Jefferson and Abraham Lincoln that the people are the masters of their Constitution, to fulfill its purposes and to safeguard it from those who, by perversion of its intent, would convert it into an instrument of injustice. In accordance with the needs of each generation the people must use their sovereign powers to establish and maintain equal opportunity and industrial justice, to secure which this Government was founded and without which no republic can endure.

This country belongs to the people who inhabit it. Its resources, its business, its institutions and its laws should be utilized, maintained or altered in whatever manner will best promote the general interest.

It is time to set the public welfare in the first place.

The Old Parties

Political parties exist to secure responsible government and to execute the will of the people.

From these great tasks both of the old parties have turned aside. Instead of instruments to promote the general welfare, they have become the tools of corrupt interests which use them impartially to serve their selfish purposes. Behind the ostensible government sits enthroned an invisible government owing no allegiance and acknowledging no responsibility to the people.

To destroy this invisible government, to dissolve the unholy alliance between corrupt business and corrupt politics is the first task to the statesmanship of the day.

The deliberate betrayal of its trust by the Republican party, the fatal incapacity of the Democratic party to deal with the new issues of the new time, have compelled the people to forge a new instrument of government through which to give effect to their will in laws and institutions.

Unhampered by tradition, uncorrupted by power, undismayed by the magnitude of the task, the new party offers itself as the instrument of the people to sweep away old abuses, to build a new and nobler commonwealth.

A Covenant with the People

This declaration is our covenant with the people and we hereby bind the party and its candidates in State and Nation to the pledges made herein.

The Rule of the People

The National Progressive party, committed to the principles of government by a self-controlled democracy expressing its will through representatives of the people, pledges itself to secure such alterations in the fundamental law of the several States and of the United States as shall insure the representative character of the government.

In particular, the party declares for direct primaries for the nomination of State and National officers, for nation-wide preferential primaries for candidates for the presidency; for the direct election of United States Senators by the people; and we urge on the States the policy of the short ballot, with responsibility to the people secured by the initiative, referendum and recall.

Amendment of Constitution

The Progressive party, believing that a free people should have the power from time to time to amend their fundamental law so as to adapt it progressively to the changing needs of the people, pledges itself to provide a more easy and expeditious method of amending the Federal Constitution.

Nation and State

Up to the limit of the Constitution, and later by amendment of the Constitution, if found necessary, we advocate bringing under effective national jurisdiction those problems which have expanded beyond reach of the individual States.

It is as grotesque as it is intolerable that the several States should by unequal laws in matter of common concern become competing commercial agencies, barter the lives of their children, the health of their women, and the safety and well being of their working people for the benefit of their financial interests.

The extreme insistence on States' rights by the Democratic party in the Baltimore platform demonstrates anew its inability to understand the world into which it has survived or to administer the affairs of a union of States which have in all essential respects become one people.

Equal Suffrage

The Progressive party, believing that no people can justly claim to be a true democracy which denies political rights on account of sex, pledges itself to the task of securing equal suffrage to men and women alike.

Corrupt Practices

We pledge our party to legislation that will compel strict limitation of all campaign contributions and expenditures, and detailed publicity of both before as well as after primaries and elections.

Publicity and Public Service

We pledge our party to legislation compelling the registration of lobbyists; publicity of committee hearings except on foreign affairs, and recording of all votes in committee; and forbidding federal appointees from holding office in State or National political organizations, or taking part as officers or delegates in political conventions for the nomination of elective State or National officials.

The Progressive party demands such restriction of the power of the courts as shall leave to the people the ultimate authority to determine fundamental questions of social welfare and public policy. To secure this end, it pledges itself to provide:

1. That when an Act, passed under the police power of the State, is held unconstitutional under the State Constitution, by the courts, the people, after an ample interval for deliberation, shall have an opportunity to vote on the question whether they desire the Act to become law, notwithstanding such decision.

2. That every decision of the highest appellate court of a State declaring an Act of the Legislature unconstitutional on the ground of its violation of the Federal Constitution shall be subject to the same review by the Supreme Court of the United States as is now accorded to decisions sustaining such legislation.

Administration of Justice

The Progressive party, in order to secure to the people a better administration of justice and by that means to bring about a more general respect for the law and the courts, pledges itself to work unceasingly for the reform of legal procedure and judicial methods.

We believe that the issuance of injunctions in cases arising out of labor disputes should be prohibited when such injunctions would not apply when no labor disputes existed.

We also believe that a person cited for contempt in labor disputes, except when such contempt was committed in the actual presence of the court or so near thereto as to interfere with the proper administration of justice, should have a right to trial by jury.

Social and Industrial Justice

The supreme duty of the Nation is the conservation of human resources through an enlightened measure of social and industrial justice. We pledge ourselves to work unceasingly in State and Nation for:

Effective legislation looking to the prevention of industrial accidents, occupational diseases, overwork, involuntary unemployment, and other injurious effects incident to modern industry;

The fixing of minimum safety and health standards for the various occupations, and the exercise of the public authority of State and Nation, including the Federal Control over interstate commerce, and the taxing power, to maintain such standards;

The prohibition of child labor;

Minimum wage standards for working women, to provide a "living wage" in all industrial occupations;

The general prohibition of night work for women and the establishment of an eight hour day for women and young persons;

One day's rest in seven for all wage workers;

The eight hour day in continuous twenty-four-hour industries;

The abolition of the convict contract labor system; substituting a system of prison production for governmental consumption only; and the application of prisoners' earnings to the support of their dependent families;

Publicity as to wages, hours and conditions of labor; full reports upon industrial accidents and diseases, and the opening to public inspection of all tallies, weights, measures and check systems on labor products;

Standards of compensation for death by industrial accident and injury and trade disease which will transfer the burden of lost earnings from the families of working people to the industry, and thus to the community;

The protection of home life against the hazards of sickness, irregular employment and old age through the adoption of a system of social insurance adapted to American use;

The development of the creative labor power of America by lifting the last load of illiteracy from American youth and establishing continuation schools for industrial education under public control and encouraging agricultural education and demonstration in rural schools;

The establishment of industrial research laboratories to put the methods and discoveries of science at the service of American producers;

We favor the organization of the workers, men and women, as a means of protecting their interests and of promoting their progress.

Department of Labor

We pledge our party to establish a department of labor with a seat in the cabinet, and with wide jurisdiction over matters affecting the conditions of labor and living.

Country Life

The development and prosperity of country life are as important to the people who live in the cities as they are to the farmers. Increase of prosperity on the farm will favorably affect the cost of living, and promote the interests of all who dwell in the country, and all who depend upon its products for clothing, shelter and food.

We pledge our party to foster the development of agricultural credit and co-operation, the teaching of agriculture in schools, agricultural college extension, the use of mechanical power on the farm, and to re-establish the Country Life Commission, thus directly promoting the welfare of the farmers, and bringing the benefits of better farming, better business and better living within their reach.

High Cost of Living

The high cost of living is due partly to worldwide and partly to local causes; partly to natural and partly to artificial causes. The measures proposed in this platform on various subjects such as the tariff, the trusts and conservation, will of themselves remove the artificial causes.

There will remain other elements such as the tendency to leave the country for the city, waste, extravagance, bad system of taxation, poor methods of raising crops and bad business methods in marketing crops.

To remedy these conditions requires the fullest information and based on this information, effective government supervision and control to remove all the artificial causes. We pledge ourselves to such full and immediate inquiry and to immediate action to deal with every need such inquiry discloses.

Health

We favor the union of all the existing agencies of the Federal Government dealing with the public health into a single national health service without discrimination against or for any one set of therapeutic methods, school of medicine, or school of healing with such additional powers as may be necessary to enable it to perform efficiently such duties in the protection of the public from preventable diseases as may be properly undertaken by the Federal authorities, including the executing of existing laws regarding pure food, quarantine and cognate subjects, the promotion of vital statistics and the extension of the registration area of such statistics, and co-operation with the health activities of the various States and cities of the Nation.

Business

We believe that true popular government, justice and prosperity go hand in hand, and, so believing, it is our purpose to secure that large measure of general prosperity which is the fruit of legitimate and honest business, fostered by equal justice and by sound progressive laws.

We demand that the test of true prosperity shall be the benefits conferred thereby on all the citizens, not confined to individuals or classes, and that the test of corporate efficiency shall be the ability better to serve the public; that those who profit by control of business affairs shall justify that profit and that control by sharing with the public the fruits thereof.

We therefore demand a strong National regulation of inter-State corporations. The corporation is an essential part of modern business. The concentration of modern business, in some degree, is both inevitable and necessary for national and international business efficiency. But the existing concentration of vast wealth under a corporate system, unguarded and uncontrolled by the Nation, has placed in the hands of a few men enormous, secret, irresponsible power over the daily life of the citizen— a power insufferable in a free Government and certain of abuse.

This power has been abused, in monopoly of National resources, in stock watering, in unfair competition and unfair privileges, and finally in sinister influences on the public agencies of State and Nation. We do not fear commercial power, but we insist that it shall be exercised openly, under publicity, supervision and regulation of the most efficient sort, which will preserve its good while eradicating and preventing its ill.

To that end we urge the establishment of a strong Federal administrative commission of high standing, which shall maintain permanent active supervision over industrial corporations engaged in inter-State commerce, or such of them as are of public importance, doing for them what the Government now does for the National banks, and what is now done for the railroads by the Inter-State Commerce Commission.

Such a commission must enforce the complete publicity of those corporation transaction actions which are of public interest; must attack unfair competition, false capitalization and special privilege, and by continuous trained watchfulness guard and keep open equally all the highways of American commerce.

Thus the business man will have certain knowledge of the law, and will be able to conduct his business easily in conformity therewith; the investor will find security for his capital; dividends will be rendered more certain, and the savings of the people will be drawn naturally and safely into the channels of trade.

Under such a system of constructive regulation, legitimate business, freed from confusion, uncertainty and fruitless litigation, will develop normally in response to the energy and enterprise of the American business man.

We favor strengthening the Sherman Law by prohibiting agreement to divide territory or limit output; refusing to sell to customers who buy from business rivals; to sell below cost in certain areas while maintaining higher prices in other places; using the power of transportation to aid or injure special business concerns; and other unfair trade practices.

Patents

We pledge ourselves to the enactment of a patent law which will make it impossible for patents to be suppressed or used against the public welfare in the interests of injurious monopolies.

Inter-State Commerce Commission

We pledge our party to secure to the Inter-State Commerce Commission the power to value the physical property of railroads. In order that the power of the commission to protect the people may not be impaired or destroyed, we demand the abolition of the Commerce Court.

Currency

We believe there exists imperative need for prompt legislation for the improvement of our National currency system. We believe the present method of issuing notes through private agencies is harmful and unscientific.

The issue of currency is fundamentally a Government function and the system should have as basic principles soundness and elasticity. The control should be lodged with the Government and should be protected from domination or manipulation by Wall Street or any special interests.

We are opposed to the so-called Aldrich currency bill, because its provisions would place our currency and credit system in private hands, not subject to effective public control.

Commercial Development

The time has come when the Federal Government should co-operate with manufacturers and producers in ex-

tending our foreign commerce. To this end we demand adequate appropriations by congress, and the appointment of diplomatic and consular officers solely with a view to their special fitness and worth, and not in consideration of political expediency.

It is imperative to the welfare of our people that we enlarge and extend our foreign commerce.

In every way possible our Federal Government should cooperate in this important matter. Germany's policy of co-operation between government and business has, in comparatively few years, made that nation a leading competitor for the commerce of the world.

Conservation

The natural resources of the Nation must be promptly developed and generously used to supply the people's needs, but we cannot safely allow them to be wasted, exploited, monopolized or controlled against the general good. We heartily favor the policy of conservation, and we pledge our party to protect the National forests without hindering their legitimate use for the benefit of all the people.

Agricultural lands in the National forests are, and should remain, open to the genuine settler. Conservation will not retard legitimate development. The honest settler must receive his patent promptly, without hindrance, rules or delays.

We believe that the remaining forests, coal and oil lands, water powers and other natural resources still in State or National control (except agricultural lands) are more likely to be wisely conserved and utilized for the general welfare if held in the public hands.

In order that consumers and producers, managers and workmen, now and hereafter, need not pay toll to private monopolies of power and raw material, we demand that such resources shall be retained by the State or Nation, and opened to immediate use under laws which will encourage development and make to the people a moderate return for benefits conferred.

In particular we pledge our party to require reasonable compensation to the public for water power rights hereafter granted by the public.

We pledge legislation to lease the public grazing lands under equitable provisions now pending which will increase the production of food for the people and thoroughly safeguard the rights of the actual homemaker. Natural resources, whose conservation is necessary for the National welfare, should be owned or controlled by the Nation.

Good Roads

We recognize the vital importance of good roads and we pledge our party to foster their expansion in every proper way, and we favor the early construction of National highways. We also favor the extension of the rural free delivery service.

Alaska

The coal and other natural resources of Alaska should be opened to development at once. They are owned by the people of the United States, and are safe from monopoly, waste or destruction only while so owned.

We demand that they shall neither be sold nor given away, except under the Homestead Law, but while held in Government ownership shall be opened to use promptly upon liberal terms requiring immediate development.

Thus the benefit of cheap fuel will accrue to the Government of the United States and to the people of Alaska and the Pacific Coast; the settlement of extensive agricultural lands will be hastened; the extermination of the salmon will be prevented and the just and wise development of Alaskan resources will

take the place of private extortion or monopoly.

We demand also that extortion or monopoly in transportation shall be prevented by the prompt acquisition, construction or improvement by the Government of such railroads, harbor and other facilities for transportation as the welfare of the people may demand.

We promise the people of the Territory of Alaska the same measure of legal self-government that was given to other American territories, and that Federal officials appointed there shall be qualified by previous *bona-fide* residence in the Territory.

Waterways

The rivers of the United States are the natural arteries of this continent. We demand that they shall be opened to traffic as indispensable parts of a great Nation-wide system of transportation, in which the Panama Canal will be the central link, thus enabling the whole interior of the United States to share with the Atlantic and Pacific seaboards in the benefit derived from the canal.

It is a National obligation to develop our rivers, and especially the Mississippi and its tributaries, without delay, under a comprehensive general plan covering each river system from its source to its mouth, designed to secure its highest usefulness for navigation, irrigation, domestic supply, water power and the prevention of floods.

We pledge our party to the immediate preparation of such a plan, which should be made and carried out in close and friendly co-operation between the Nation, the States and the cities affected.

Under such a plan, the destructive floods of the Mississippi and other streams, which represent a vast and needless loss to the Nation, would be controlled by forest conservation and water storage at the headwaters, and by levees below; land sufficient to support millions of people would be reclaimed from the deserts and the swamps, water power enough to transform the industrial standings of whole States would be developed, adequate water terminals would be provided, transportation by river would revive, and the railroads would be compelled to co-operate as freely with the boat lines as with each other.

The equipment, organization and experience acquired in constructing the Panama Canal soon will be available for the Lakes-to-the-Gulf deep waterway and other portions of this great work, and should be utilized by the Nation in co-operation with the various States, at the lowest net cost to the people.

Panama Canal

The Panama Canal, built and paid for by the American people, must be used primarily for their benefit.

We demand that the canal shall be so operated as to break the transportation monopoly now held and misused by the transcontinental railroads by maintaining sea competition with them; that ships directly or indirectly owned or controlled by American railroad corporations shall not be permitted to use the canal, and that American ships engaged in coastwise trade shall pay no tolls.

The Progressive party will favor legislation having for its aim the development of friendship and commerce between the United States and Latin-American nations.

Tariff

We believe in a protective tariff which shall equalize conditions of competition between the United States and foreign countries, both for the farmer and the manufacturer, and which shall maintain for labor an adequate standard of living.

Primarily the benefit of any tariff should be disclosed in the pay envelope of the laborer. We declare that no industry deserves protection which is unfair to labor or which is operating in violation of Federal law. We believe that the presumption is always in favor of the consuming public.

We demand tariff revision because the present tariff is unjust to the people of the United States. Fair dealing toward the people requires an immediate downward revision of those schedules wherein duties are shown to be unjust or excessive.

We pledge ourselves to the establishment of a non-partisan scientific tariff commission, reporting both to the President and to either branch of Congress, which shall report, first, as to the costs of production, efficiency of labor, capitalization, industrial organization and efficiency and the general competitive position in this country and abroad of industries seeking protection from Congress; second, as to the revenue producing power of the tariff and its relation to the resources of Government; and, third, as to the effect of the tariff on prices, operations of middlemen, and on the purchasing power of the consumer.

We believe that this commission should have plenary power to elicit information, and for this purpose to prescribe a uniform system of accounting for the great protected industries. The work of the commission should not prevent the immediate adoption of acts reducing these schedules generally recognized as excessive.

We condemn the Payne-Aldrich bill as unjust to the people. The Republican organization is in the hands of those who have broken, and cannot again be trusted to keep, the promise of necessary downward revision.

The Democratic party is committed to the destruction of the protective system through a tariff for revenue only—a policy which would inevitably produce widespread industrial and commercial disaster.

We demand the immediate repeal of the Canadian Reciprocity Act.

Inheritance and Income Tax

We believe in a graduated inheritance tax as a National means of equalizing the obligations of holders of property to Government, and we hereby pledge our party to enact such a Federal law as will tax large inheritances, returning to the States an equitable percentage of all amounts collected.

We favor the ratification of the pending amendment to the Constitution giving the Government power to levy an income tax.

Peace and National Defense

The Progressive party deplores the survival in our civilization of the barbaric system of warfare among nations with its enormous waste of resources even in time of peace, and the consequent impoverishment of the life of the toiling masses. We pledge the party to use its best endeavors to substitute judicial and other peaceful means of settling international differences.

We favor an international agreement for the limitation of naval forces. Pending such an agreement, and as the best means of preserving peace, we pledge ourselves to maintain for the present the policy of building two battleships a year.

Treaty Rights

We pledge our party to protect the rights of American citizenship at home and abroad. No treaty should receive the sanction of our government which discriminates between American citizens because of birthplace, race, or religion, or that does not recognize the absolute right of expatriation.

The Immigrant

Through the establishment of industrial standards we propose to secure to the able-bodied immigrant and to his native fellow workers a larger share of American opportunity.

We denounce the fatal policy of indifference and neglect which has left our enormous immigrant population to become the prey of chance and cupidity.

We favor Governmental action to encourage the distribution of immigrants away from the congested cities, to rigidly supervise all private agencies dealing with them and to promote their assimilation, education, and advancement.

Pensions

We pledge ourselves to a wise and just policy of pensioning American soldiers and sailors and their widows and children by the Federal Government. And we approve the policy of the southern States in granting pensions to the ex-confederate soldiers and sailors and their widows and children.

Parcel Post

We pledge our party to the immediate creation of a parcel post, with rates proportionate to distance and service.

Civil Service

We condemn the violation of the Civil Service Law under the present administration, including the coercion and assessment of subordinate employés and the President's refusal to punish such violation after a finding of guilty by his own commission; his distribution of patronage among subservient congressmen, while withholding it from those who refuse support of administration measures; his withdrawal of nominations from the Senate until political support for himself was secured, and his open use of the offices to reward those who voted for his renomination.

To eradicate these abuses, we demand not only the enforcement of the civil service act in letter and spirit, but also legislation which will bring under the competitive system postmasters, collectors, marshals, and all other non-political officers, as well as the enactment of an equitable retirement law, and we also insist upon continuous service during good behavior and efficiency.

Government Business Organization

We pledge our party to readjustment of the business methods of the National Government and a proper co-ordination of the Federal bureaus, which will increase the economy and efficiency of the Government service, prevent duplications, and secure better results to the taxpayers for every dollar expended.

Government Supervision Over Investments

The people of the United States are swindled out of many millions of dollars every year, through worthless investments. The plain people, the wage earner and the men and women with small savings, have no way of knowing the merit of concerns sending out highly colored prospectuses offering stock for sale, prospectuses that make big returns seem certain and fortunes easily within grasp.

We hold it to be the duty of the Government to protect its people from this kind of piracy. We, therefore, demand wise, carefully thought out legislation that will give us such Governmental supervision over this matter as will furnish to the people of the United States this much-needed protection, and we pledge ourselves thereto.

Conclusion

On these principles and on the recognized desirability of uniting the Progressive forces of the Nation into an organization which shall unequivocally represent the Progressive spirit and policy we appeal for the support of all American citizens, without regard to previous political affiliations.

Woodrow Wilson's "The Old Order Changeth" Speech (1912)

On June 25, 1912, the Democrats gathered in Baltimore, Maryland, for their national convention in a mood of eager anticipation. Victory seemed all but certain in the November presidential election. Just three days earlier, the Republican national convention had split down the middle between the supporters of President William Howard Taft, the party's nominee for reelection, and loyalists of former president Theodore Roosevelt, who had announced that he would run as a third-party candidate. (See " 'Bull Moose' Party Platform," p. 256.)

Speaker of the House of Representatives James Beauchamp (Champ) Clark of Missouri, the favored candidate of most party regulars, was the front-runner for the Democratic nomination. His main rival was Woodrow Wilson, a political scientist trained at Johns Hopkins University and the former president of Princeton University. Wilson had been elected as governor of New Jersey in 1910. New Jersey's Democratic party bosses originally thought that the politically inexperienced academician would provide their corrupt state government with an honest veneer while they pulled the strings from offstage. But Wilson surprised them. He gained national fame by rousing public opinion in support of a host of Progressive causes, including an anticorruption act and public utilities regulation.

At the 1912 covention, Clark led in the early balloting; indeed, he won a majority of votes on the tenth call of the roll. But the Democratic party required a two-thirds vote for the presidential nomination, and Clark never came close. (See "Abolition of the Two-Thirds Rule: Proceedings of the Democratic National Convention," p. 344.) Wilson was nominated on the forty-sixth ballot, after William Jennings Bryan, the Democrats' standard-bearer in 1896, 1900, and 1908, transferred his support to the New Jersey governor. Gov. Thomas Marshall of Indiana was chosen as Wilson's vice-presidential running mate.

Roosevelt and Wilson were both avowed progressives, but they represented different strains in the Progressive movement. Roosevelt favored a "New Nationalism" that acknowledged the inevitability of big business and summoned the powers of the national government to punish improper corporate activities. Wilson believed that to try to regulate big business was futile; the regulator would inevitably become the servant of the regulated. "Our government has been for the past few years under the control of heads of great allied corporations with special interests," Wilson charged in a speech entitled "The Old Order Changeth." "It has not controlled these interests and assigned them a proper place in the whole system of business; it has *submitted itself to their control." Wilson, with the guidance of a brilliant young Boston lawyer, Louis Brandeis, proposed to break up the large corporations and, by so doing, to create a "New Freedom" for small businesses and consumers.*

Wilson won easily on election day: 41.8 percent to Roosevelt's 27.4 percent and Taft's 23.2 percent in the popular vote, and 435 electoral votes to 88 for Roosevelt and 8 for Taft. The Democrats gained sixty-three seats in the House of Representatives and took control of the Senate for the first time in twenty years by adding ten seats.

The combination of Wilson's reform-oriented campaign, his landslide election, and unprecedentedly long presidential coattails in the congressional elections set the stage for substantial domestic policy achievement. During his first term as president, Wilson persuaded Congress to reduce tariffs; to establish a graduated income tax; to regulate banking and unfair business competition by creating the Federal Reserve System and the Federal Trade Commission, respectively; to crack down on the trusts by passing the Clayton Antitrust Act; and to aid agriculture with the Smith-Lever Act and the Federal Farm Loan Act. ~

There is one great basic fact which underlies all the questions that are discussed on the political platform at the present moment. That singular fact is that nothing is done in this country as it was done twenty years ago.

We are in the presence of a new organization of society. Our life has broken away from the past. The life of America is not the life that it was twenty years ago; it is not the life that it was ten years ago. We have changed our economic conditions, absolutely, from top to bottom; and, with our economic society, the organization of our life. The old political formulas do not fit the present problems; they read now like documents taken out of a forgotten age. The older cries sound as if they belonged to a past age which men have almost forgotten. Things which used to be put into the party platforms of ten years ago would sound antiquated if put into a platform now. We are facing the necessity of fitting a new social organization, as we did once fit the old organization, to the happiness and prosperity of the great body of citizens; for we are conscious that the new order of society has not been made to fit and provide the convenience or prosperity of the average man. The life of the nation has grown infinitely varied. It does not centre now upon questions of governmental structure or of the distribution of governmental powers. It centres upon questions of the very structure and operation of society itself, of which government is only the instrument. Our development has run so fast and so far along the lines sketched in the earlier day of constitutional definition, has so crossed and interlaced those lines, has piled upon them such novel structures of trust and combination, has elaborated within them a life so manifold, so full of forces which transcend the boundaries of the country itself and fill the eyes of the world, that a new nation seems to have been created which the old formulas do not fit or afford a vital interpretation of.

We have come upon a very different age from any that preceded us. We have come upon an age when we do not do business in the way in which we used to do business,—when we do not carry on any of the operations of manufactures, sale, transportation, or communication as men used to carry them on. There is a sense in which in our day the individual has been submerged. In most parts of our country men work, not for themselves, not as partners in the old way in which they used to work, but generally as employees,—in a higher or lower grade,—of great corporations. There was a time when corporations played a very minor part in our business affairs, but now they play the chief part, and most men are the servants of corporations.

You know what happens when you are the servant of a corporation. You have in no instance access to the men who are really determining the policy of the corporation. If the corporation is doing the things that it ought not to do, you really have no voice in the matter and must obey the orders, and you have oftentimes with deep mortification to co-operate in the doing of things which you know are against the public interest. Your individuality is swallowed up in the individuality and purpose of a great organization.

It is true that, while most men are thus submerged in the corporation, a few, a very few, are exalted to a power which as individuals they could never have wielded. Through the great organizations of which they are the heads, a few are enabled to play a part unprecedented by anything in history in the control of the business operations of the country and in the determination of the happiness of great numbers of people.

Yesterday, and ever since history began, men were related to one another as individuals. To be sure there were the family, the Church, and the State, institutions which associated men in certain wide circles of relationship. But in the ordinary concerns of life, in the ordinary work, in the daily round, men dealt freely and directly with one another. To-day, the everyday relationships of men are largely with great impersonal concerns, with organizations, not with other individual men.

Now this is nothing short of a new social age, a new era of human relationships, a new stage-setting for the drama of life.

In this new age we find, for instance, that our laws with regard to the relations of employer and employee are in many respects wholly antiquated and impossible. They were framed for another age, which nobody now living remembers, which is, indeed, so remote from our life that it would be difficult for many of us to understand it if it were described to us. The employer is now generally a corporation or a huge company of some kind; the employee is one of hundreds or of thousands brought together, not by individual masters whom they know and with whom they have personal relations, but by agents of one sort or another. Workingmen are marshaled in great numbers for the performance of a multitude of particular tasks under a common discipline. They generally use dangerous and powerful machinery, over whose repair and renewal they have no control. New rules must be devised with regard to their obligations and their rights, their obligations to their employers and their responsibilities to one another. Rules must be devised for their protection, for their compensation when injured, for their support when disabled.

There is something very new and very big and very complex about these new relations of capital and labor. A new economic society has sprung up, and we must effect a new set of adjustments. We must not pit power against weakness. The employer is generally, in our day, as I have said, not an individual, but a powerful group; and yet the workingman when dealing with his employer is still, under our existing law, an individual.

Why is it that we have a labor question at all? It is for the simple and very sufficient reason that the laboring man and the employer are not intimate associates now as they used to be in the time past. Most of our laws were formed in the age when employer and employees knew each other, knew each other's characters, were associates with each other, dealt with each other as man with man. That is no longer the case. You not only do not come into personal contact with the men who have the supreme command in those corporations, but it would be out of the question for you to do it. Our modern corporations employ thousands, and in some instances hundreds of thousands, of men. The only persons whom you see or deal with are local superintendents or local representatives of a vast organization, which is not like anything that the workingmen of the time in which our laws were framed knew anything about. A little group of workingmen, seeing their employer every day, dealing with him in a personal way, is one thing, and the modern body of labor engaged as employees of the huge enterprises that spread all over the country, dealing with men of whom they can form no personal conception, is another thing. A very different thing. You never saw a corporation, any more than you ever saw a government. Many a workingman to-day never saw the body of men who are conducting the industry in which he is employed. And they never saw him. What they know about him is written in ledgers and books and letters, in the correspondence of the office, in the reports of the superintendents. He is a long way off from them.

So what we have to discuss is, not wrongs which individuals intentionally do,—I do not believe there are a great many of those,—but the wrongs of a system. I want to record my protest against any discussion of this matter which would seem to indicate that there are bodies of our fellow-citizens who are trying to grind us down and do us injustice. There are some men of that sort. I don't know how they sleep o' nights, but there are men of that kind. Thank God, they are not numerous. The truth is, we are all caught in a great economic system which is heartless. The modern corporation is not engaged in business as an individual. When we deal with it, we deal with an impersonal element, an immaterial piece of society. A modern corporation is a means of co-operation in the conduct of an enterprise which is so big that no one man can conduct it, and which the resources of no one man are sufficient to finance. A company is formed; that company puts out a prospectus; the promoters expect to raise a certain fund as capital stock. Well, how are they going to raise it? They are going to raise it from the public in general, some of whom will buy their stock. The moment that begins, there is formed—what? A joint stock corporation. Men begin to pool their earnings, little piles, big piles. A certain number of men are elected by the stockholders to be directors, and these directors elect a president. This president is the head of the undertaking, and the directors are its managers.

Now, do the workingmen employed by that stock corporation deal with that president and those directors? Not at all. Does the public deal with that president and that board of directors? It does not. Can anybody bring them to account? It is next to impossible to do so. If you undertake it you will find it a game of hide and seek, with the objects of your search taking refuge now behind the tree of their individual personality, now behind that of their corporate irresponsibility.

And do our laws take note of this curious state of things? Do they even attempt to distinguish between a man's act as a corporation director and as an individual? They do not. Our laws still deal with us on the basis of the old system. The law is still living in the dead past which we have left behind. This is evident, for instance, with regard to the matter of employers' liability for workingmen's injuries. Suppose that a superintendent wants a workman to use a certain piece of machinery which it is not safe for him to use, and that the workman is injured by that piece of machinery. Some of our courts have held that the superintendent is a fellow-servant, or, as the law states it, a fellow-employee, and that, therefore, the man cannot recover damages for his injury. The superintendent who probably engaged the man is not his employer. Who is his employer? And whose negligence could conceivably come in there? The board of directors did not tell the employee to use that piece of machinery; and the president of the corporation did not tell him to use that piece of machinery. And so forth. Don't you see by that theory that a man never can get redress for negligence on the part of the employer? When I hear judges reason upon the analogy of the relationships that used to exist between workmen and their employers a generation ago, I wonder if they have not opened their eyes to the modern world. You know, we have a right to expect that judges will have their eyes open, even though the law which they administer hasn't awakened.

Yet that is but a single small detail illustrative of the difficulties we are in because we have not adjusted the law to the facts of the new order.

Since I entered politics, I have chiefly had men's views confided to me privately. Some of the biggest men in the United States, in the field of commerce and manufacture, are afraid of somebody, are afraid of something. They know that there is a power somewhere so organized, so subtle, so watchful, so interlocked, so complete, so pervasive, that they had better not speak above their breath when they speak in condemnation of it.

They know that America is not a place of which it can be said, as it used to be, that a man may choose his own calling and pursue it just as far as his abilities enable him to pursue it; because to-day, if he enters certain fields, there are organizations which will use means against him that will prevent his building up a business which they do not want to have built up; organizations that will see to it that the ground is cut from under him and the markets shut against him. For if he begins to sell to certain retail dealers, to any retail deal-

ers, the monopoly will refuse to sell to those dealers, and those dealers, afraid, will not buy the new man's wares.

And this is the country which has lifted to the admiration of the world its ideals of absolutely free opportunity, where no man is supposed to be under any limitation except the limitations of his character and of his mind; where there is supposed to be no distinction of class, no distinction of blood, no distinction of social status, but where men win or lose on their merits.

I lay it very close to my own conscience as a public man whether we can any longer stand at our doors and welcome all newcomers upon those terms. American industry is not free, as once it was free; American enterprise is not free; the man with only a little capital is finding it harder to get into the field, more and more impossible to compete with the big fellow. Why? Because the laws of this country do not prevent the strong from crushing the weak. That is the reason, and because the strong have crushed the weak and strong dominate the industry and the economic life of this country. No man can deny that the lines of endeavor have more and more narrowed and stiffened; no man who knows anything about the development of industry in this country can have failed to observe that the larger kinds of credit are more and more difficult to obtain, unless you obtain them upon the terms of uniting your efforts with those who already control the industries of the country; and nobody can fail to observe that any man who tries to set himself up in competition with any process of manufacture which has been taken under the control of large combinations of capital will presently find himself either squeezed out or obliged to sell and allow himself to be absorbed.

There is a great deal that needs reconstruction in the United States. I should like to take a census of the business men,—I mean the rank and file of the business men,—as to whether they think that business conditions in this country, or rather whether the organization of business in this country, is satisfactory or not. I know what they would say if they dared. If they could vote secretly they would vote overwhelmingly that the present organization of business was meant for the big fellows and was not meant for the little fellows; that it was meant for those who are at the top and was meant to exclude those who are at the bottom; that it was meant to shut out beginners, to prevent new entries in the race, to prevent the building up of competitive enterprises that would interfere with the monopolies which the great trusts have built up.

What this country needs above everything else is a body of laws which will look after the men who are on the make rather than the men who are already made. Because the men who are already made are not going to live indefinitely, and they are not always kind enough to leave sons as able and honest as they are.

The originative part of America, the part of America that makes new enterprises, the part into which the ambitious and gifted workingman makes his way up, the class that saves, that plans, that organizes, that presently spreads its enterprises until they have a national scope and character,—that middle class is being more and more squeezed out by the processes which we have been taught to call process of prosperity. Its members are sharing prosperity, no doubt; but what alarms me is that they are not *originating* prosperity. No country can afford to have its prosperity originated by a small controlling class. The treasury of America does not lie in the brains of the small body of men now in control of the great enterprises that have been concentrated under the direction of a very small number of persons. The treasury of America lies in those ambitions, those energies, that cannot be restricted to a special favored class. It depends upon the inventions of unknown men, upon the originations of unknown men, upon the ambitions of unknown men. Every country is renewed out of the ranks of the unknown, not out of the ranks of those already famous and powerful and in control.

There has come over the land that un-American set of conditions which enables a small number of men who control the government to get favors from the government; by those favors to exclude their fellows from equal business opportunity; by those favors to extend a network of control that will presently dominate every industry in the country, and so make men forget the ancient time when America lay in every hamlet, when America was to be seen in every fair valley, when America displayed her great forces on the broad prairies, ran her fine fires of enterprise up over the mountainsides and down into the bowels of the earth, and eager men were everywhere captains of industry, not employees; not looking to a distant city to find out what they might do, but looking about among their neighbors, finding credit according to their character, not according to their connections, finding credit in proportion to what was known to be in them and behind them, not in proportion to the securities they held that were approved where they were not known. In order to start an enterprise now, you have to be authenticated, in a perfectly impersonal way, not according to yourself, but according to what you own that somebody else approves of your owning. You cannot begin such an enterprise as those that have made America until you are so authenticated, until you have succeeded in obtaining the good-will of large allied capitalists. Is that freedom? That is dependence, not freedom.

We used to think in the old-fashioned days when life was very simple that all the government had to do was to put on a policeman's uniform, and say, "Now don't anybody hurt anybody else." We used to say that the ideal of government was for every man to be left alone and not interfered with, except when he interfered with somebody else; and that the best government was the government that did as little governing as possible. That was the idea that obtained in Jefferson's time. But we are coming now to realize that life is so complicated that we are not dealing with the old conditions, and that the law has to step in and create new conditions under which we may live, the conditions which will make it tolerable for us to live.

Let me illustrate what I mean: It used to be true in our cities that every family occupied a separate house of its own, that every family had its own little premises, that every family was separated in its life from every other family. That is no longer the case in our great cities. Families live in tenements, they live in flats, they live on floors; they are piled layer upon layer in the great tenement houses of our crowded districts, and not only are they piled layer upon layer, but they are associated room by room, so that there is in every room, sometimes, in our congested districts, a separate family. In some foreign countries they have made much more progress than we in handling these things. In the city of Glasgow, for example (Glasgow is one of the model cities of the world), they have made up their minds that the entries and the hallways of great tenements are public streets. Therefore, the policeman goes up the stairway, and patrols the corridors; the lighting department of the city sees to it that the halls are abundantly lighted. The city does not deceive itself into supposing that that great building is a unit from which the police are to keep out and the civic authority to be excluded, but it says: "These are public highways, and light is needed in them, and control by the authority of the city."

I liken that to our great modern industrial enterprises. A corporation is very like a large tenement house; it isn't the premises of a single commercial family; it is just as much a public affair as a tenement house is a network of public highways.

When you offer the securities of a great corporation to anybody who wishes to purchase them, you must open that corporation to the inspection of everybody who wants to purchase. There must, to follow out the figure of the tenement house, be lights along the corridors, there must be police patrolling the openings, there must be inspection wherever it is known that men may be deceived with regard to the contents of the premises. If we believe that fraud lies in wait for us, we must have the means of determining whether our suspicions are well founded or not. Similarly, the treatment of labor by the great corporations is not what it was in Jefferson's time. Whenever bodies of men employ bodies of men, it ceases to be a private relationship. So that when courts hold that workingmen cannot peaceably dissuade other workingmen from taking employment, as was held in a notable case in New Jersey, they simply show that their minds and understandings are lingering in an age which has passed away. This dealing of great bodies of men with other bodies of men is a matter of public scrutiny, and should be a matter of public regulation.

Similarly, it was no business of the law in the time of Jefferson to come into my house and see how I kept house. But when my house, when my so-called private property, became a great mine, and men went along dark corridors amidst every kind of danger in order to dig out of the bowels of the earth things necessary for the industries of a whole nation, and when it came about that no individual owned these mines, that they were owned by great stock companies, then all the old analogies absolutely collapsed and it became the right of the government to go down into these mines to see whether human beings were properly treated in them or not; to see whether accidents were properly safeguarded against; to see whether modern economical methods of using these inestimable riches of the earth were followed or were not followed. If somebody puts a derrick improperly secured on top of a building or overtopping the street, then the government of the city has the right to see that that derrick is so secured that you and I can walk under it and not be afraid that the heavens are going to fall on us. Likewise, in these great beehives where in every corridor swarm men of flesh and blood, it is the privilege of the government, whether of the State or of the United States, as the case may be, to see that human life is protected, that human lungs have something to breathe.

These, again, are merely illustrations of conditions. We are in a new world, struggling under old laws. As we go inspecting our lives to-day, surveying this new scene of centralized and complex society, we shall find many more things out of joint.

One of the most alarming phenomena of the time,—or rather it would be alarming if the nation had not awakened to it and shown its determination to control it,—one of the most significant signs of the new social era is the degree to which government has become associated with business. I speak, for the moment, of the control over the government exercised by Big Business. Behind the whole subject, of course, is the truth that, in the new order, government and business must be associated closely. But that association is at present of a nature absolutely intolerable; the precedence is wrong, the association is upside down. Our government has been for the past few years under the control of heads of great allied corporations with special interests. It has not controlled these interests and assigned them a proper place in the whole system of business; it has submitted itself to their control. As a result, there

have grown up vicious systems and schemes of governmental favoritism (the most obvious being the extravagant tariff), far-reaching in effect upon the whole fabric of life, touching to his injury every inhabitant of the land, laying unfair and impossible handicaps upon competitors, imposing taxes in every direction, stifling everywhere the free spirit of American enterprise.

Now this has come about naturally; as we go on we shall see how very naturally. It is no use denouncing anybody, or anything, except human nature. Nevertheless, it is an intolerable thing that the government of the republic should have got so far out of the hands of the people; should have been captured by interests which are special and not general. In the train of this capture follow the troops of scandals, wrongs, indecencies, with which our politics swarm.

There are cities in America of whose government we are ashamed. There are cities everywhere, in every part of the land, in which we feel that, not the interests of the public, but the interests of special privileges, of selfish men, are served; where contracts take precedence over public interest. Not only in big cities is this the case. Have you not noticed the growth of socialistic sentiment in the smaller towns? Not many months ago I stopped at a little town in Nebraska, and while my train lingered I met on the platform a very engaging young fellow dressed in overalls who introduced himself to me as the mayor of the town, and added that he was a Socialist. I said, "What does that mean? Does that mean that this town is socialistic?" "No, sir," he said; "I have not deceived myself; the vote by which I was elected was about 20 per cent. socialist and 80 per cent. protest." It was protest against the treachery to the people of those who led both the other parties of that town.

All over the Union people are coming to feel that they have no control over the course of affairs. I live in one of the greatest States in the Union, which was at one time in slavery. Until two years ago we had witnessed with increasing concern the growth in New Jersey of a spirit of almost cynical despair. Men said: "We vote; we are offered the platform we want; we elect the men who stand on the platform, and we get absolutely nothing." So they began to ask: "What is the use of voting? We know that the machines of both parties are subsidized by the same persons, and therefore it is useless to turn in either direction."

This is not confined to some of the state governments and those of some of the towns and cities. We know that something intervenes between the people of the United States and the control of their own affairs at Washington. It is not the people who have been ruling there of late.

Why are we in the presence, why are we at the threshold, of a revolution? Because we are profoundly disturbed by the influences which we see reigning in the determination of our public life and our public policy. There was a time when America was blithe with self-confidence. She boasted that she, and she alone, knew the processes of popular government; but now she sees her sky overcast; she sees that there are at work forces which she did not dream of in her hopeful youth.

Don't you know that some man with eloquent tongue, without conscience, who did not care for the nation, could put this whole country into a flame? Don't you know that this country from one end to the other believes that something is wrong? What an opportunity it would be for some man without conscience to spring up and say: "This is the way. Follow me!"—and lead in paths of destruction!

The old order changeth—changeth under our very eyes, not quietly and equably, but swiftly and with the noise and heat and tumult of reconstruction.

I suppose that all struggle for law has been conscious, that very little of it has been blind or merely instinctive. It is the fashion to say, as if with superior knowledge of affairs and of human weakness, that every age has been an age of transition, and that no age is more full of change than another; yet in very few ages of the world can the struggle for change have been so widespread, so deliberate, or upon so great a scale as in this in which we are taking part.

The transition we are witnessing is no equable transition of growth and normal alteration; no silent, unconscious unfolding of one age into another, its natural heir and successor. Society is looking itself over, in our day, from top to bottom; is making fresh and critical analysis of its very elements; is questioning its oldest practices as freely as its newest, scrutinizing every arrangement and motive of its life; and it stands ready to attempt nothing less than a radical reconstruction, which only frank and honest counsels and the forces of generous co-operation can hold back from becoming a revolution. We are in a temper to reconstruct economic society, as we were once in a temper to reconstruct political society, and political society may itself undergo a radical modification in the process. I doubt if any age was ever more conscious of its task or more unanimously desirous of radical and extended changes in its economic and political practice.

We stand in the presence of a revolution,—not a bloody revolution; America is not given to the spilling of blood,—but a silent revolution, whereby America will insist upon recovering in practice those ideals which she has always professed, upon securing a government devoted to the general interest and not to special interests.

We are upon the eve of a great reconstruction. It calls for creative statesmanship as no age has done since that great age in which we set up the government under which we live, that government which was the admiration of the world until it suffered wrongs to grow up under it which have made many of our own compatriots question the freedom of our institutions and preach revolution against them. I do not fear revolution. I have unshaken faith in the power of America to keep its self-possession. Revolution will come in peaceful guise, as it came when we put aside the crude government of the Confederation and created the great Federal Union which governs individuals, not States, and which has been these hundred and thirty years our vehicle of progress. Some radical changes we must make in our law and practice. Some reconstructions we must push forward, for which a new age and new circumstances impose upon us. But we can do it all in calm and sober fashion, like statesmen and patriots.

I do not speak of these things in apprehension, because all is open and above-board. This is not a day in which great forces rally in secret. The whole stupendous program must be publicly planned and canvassed. Good temper, the wisdom that comes of sober counsel, the energy of thoughtful an unselfish men, the habit of co-operation and of compromise which has been bred in us by long years of free government, in which reason rather than passion has been made to prevail by the sheer virtue of candid and universal debate, will enable us to win through to still another great age without violence.

Woodrow Wilson's "Shadow Lawn" Speech on Foreign Policy (1916)

The election of 1916 was closely fought. Woodrow Wilson had served a successful first term as president, but his political base was narrow: he won just 41.8 percent of the popular vote in 1912. The Republicans, who lost to Wilson mainly because their two most prestigious leaders, President William Howard Taft and former president Theodore Roosevelt, split the convention and ran separate campaigns for president, were still the nation's majority party. (See "Woodrow Wilson's 'The Old Order Changeth' Speech," p. 267, and "Republican Party Platform [1896]," p. 251.)

In 1916, the Republicans coalesced around the candidacy of Charles Evans Hughes. From 1907 to 1910, Hughes had been a Progressive hero as the Republican governor of New York. But party regulars liked him, too. Taft appointed Hughes to the Supreme Court in 1910 and later commented, "I think he learned a great deal since he was governor." During the spring of 1916, while political efforts were undertaken in his behalf, Hughes's discreet judicial silence on the issues of the day made it even easier for Republicans of all stripes to see in him whatever they wanted to see.

At the Republican national convention in early June, Hughes was nominated for president on the third ballot. (He promptly submitted his resigna-

tion from the Court to President Wilson.) Former vice president Charles W. Fairbanks of Indiana was chosen as Hughes's running-mate.

Later in June, Wilson and Vice President Thomas R. Marshall were renominated without opposition at the Democratic national convention. The party platform praised "the splendid diplomatic victories of our great president, who has preserved the vital interests of our government and its citizens, and kept us out of war."

"He kept us out of war" became the Democrats' rallying cry in the fall campaign. In August 1914 war had broken out in Europe between the Central Powers, including Germany and Austria-Hungary, and the Allied powers, led by Great Britain, France, Russia, and Italy. Americans were divided in their hopes about the outcome of the war; more important, they were anxious not to become involved in the fighting.

Wilson's most effective speech of the campaign was delivered on September 30, 1916, to a crowd of young Democrats who assembled at Shadow Lawn, his summer home in Long Branch, New Jersey. Responding more to some bellicose remarks by Theodore Roosevelt (who had endorsed the Republican ticket) than to anything Hughes had said, Wilson warned, "[T]he certain prospect of the success of the Republi-

can party is that we shall be drawn in one form or another into the embroilments of the European war ... And the one thing I want to lay emphasis upon in this connection is—that a great, fundamental, final choice with regard to our foreign relationships is to be made on the 7th of November. Some young men ought to be interested in that."

Wilson won a narrow victory—so narrow, in fact, that both he and Hughes went to bed on election night thinking that the Republican would be the next president. In truth, Hughes's support was confined almost entirely to the early-reporting states of the Northeast and the upper Midwest. Wilson held the solid South and swept the West, eking out a 277-254 majority in the electoral college. His popular vote plurality was 49.2 percent to 46.1 percent. ～

I am very much obliged to you for giving me an opportunity to say some very plain things about the present campaign and about the future policy of this country, because young men are very much more interested in the future than they are in the present. While some of us who are older look back upon long experience and are able to take certain measurements which may not have occurred to you, nevertheless your feeling is that the world lies in front of you and not behind you. You want to know what sort of world it is going to be and what sort of guidance you are going to have in that world, and what sort of cooperation among you will be effective for the service of the world into which the years ahead will bring you.

I do not know where, from Republican quarters, you have got any suggestions as to what is going to happen in the years to come. This is a most singular campaign. I will not say an unprecedented campaign, because I happen to

remember that other parties have tried to get into power by saying nothing whatever; and I also remember with interest that they never succeeded, because the people of the United States are an inquisitive people and if you ask them to intrust you with the great power of their Government they really want to know what you are going to do with that Government if they intrust you with it. They may not insist upon your telling them what you have done in circumstances now past and gone, but they will insist upon your telling them what you intend to do in the future.

For a little while I myself expected that this campaign would be an interesting, intellectual contest; that upon both sides men would draw upon some of the essential questions of politics in order to determine the predominance of parties, but I am sorry to say I have found nothing to interest me: and I am a little bit ashamed of myself that I should have expected it, for I should have known better.

There is a fact running through all our political history of which I ought to have reminded myself. The Democratic Party, my fellow citizens, is the only party whose life has persisted and whose vigor has continued throughout all the history of this nation, and that has not happened by accident.

It has happened because it is the only party, I venture to say, all of whose life has been governed, or at any rate inspired, by a definite principle—an absolute belief in the control of the people, their right to control, their capacity to control their own affairs and shape them in the common interest.

The Democratic Party has committed many errors, the Democratic Party has made some fatal mistakes of action, but the reason it has lived, the reason it is the only party that has apparent immortality in our politics, is that it is the only party that has consistently based its beliefs upon the things and the convictions that underlie all American history—the belief in the government of the people by themselves and their own representatives.

It has witnessed the life and death of two great parties, and unless I am very much mistaken it will witness the early disappearance of another. It witnessed the life, decadence and disappearance of the Federalist Party. It witnessed the life, the increase, the demoralization, the decline and the disappearance of the Whig Party.

And then there appeared upon the scene the Republican Party, first of all organized for a great and definite purpose, to prevent the spread of the institution of slavery into the free portions of the United States. That object they greatly accomplished. And then there seemed to descend upon them the spirit of the Federalist and the Whig Parties, and ever since then the increasing demoralization of that party has been evident.

What was the spirit of those parties? The spirit of those parties was one of limited control of the affairs of the Nation by those who had the biggest material stake in the prosperity of the country. Some of them professed this very openly and some of them practiced it without professing it.

The theory of Alexander Hamilton, who founded the Federalist Party, was that the best kind of government is government by guardians and trustees, and that only those who represent the great material enterprises of the country are capable of acting as trustees and guardians. So that throughout the period when the Federalist Party was in control the whole idea was that a small group of carefully planning men should govern opinion and control administrative action in the United States.

The Whig Party, when it arose, had a somewhat more liberal conception, but before it had lasted very long it acted upon exactly the same principle—that the great body of the people is not capable of doing its own thinking and

that a small group of persons must be allowed to do its thinking for it. And the Republican party has inherited that idea—not the idea of government by the people, but of government for the people and control of the people by those who govern it.

It was a foregone conclusion that parties that held such principles could not live in America. The only reason they existed for a short time was that they did rally to their support some of the fine, planning, enterprising minds of the country and that so long as those men had the conscience of public service, great things were conceived and great things were done; but just as soon as they put in possession of the Government men who were attorneys of special interests, the decadence of the party inevitably ensued.

The Republican Party as now constituted and led believes in government by the attorneys of special interests. They are perfectly willing that the attorneys of the people should appear before them and plead for the rights of the people, but they are not willing that the counsels which determine action shall be participated in by the attorneys of the people.

One of the things that they are most constantly talking about is the protective tariff and there was a time when a very wide taking of counsel entered into the formation of our tariffs, but not toward the end. Then a small group of selected counsellors always determined what the items of the tariff should be. The only persons heard were the attorneys for the special interests, and the attorneys of the people could batter at the door as they pleased and never get a hearing.

The end of such a party was foredoomed, and now the party that believes in the people and tries to do things for the people has been in power for four years. And what has happened? It has redeemed some of the promises falsely made by the attorneys for the special interests. And it has some something more interesting than that.

You remember that four years ago there was a great body of spirited Republicans who said: "This thing is becoming a fraud and a sham. We have been taking care of some people, but we have not been taking care of the great body of the people. We have not thought about their morals; we have not thought about their health; we have not thought about their rights as human beings and we insist that you put the policy of this party in our hands or we will go off and form a party of our own."

And thereupon the great Progressive Party sprung up—great not because it turned out to be more numerous than the party from which it had seceded though it did that, but because it had the real red blood of human sympathy in its veins and was ready to work for mankind and forget the interests of a narrow party.

I want to pay my tribute of respect to the purposes and intentions of the men who formed that group in our politics. But the interesting thing is that, inasmuch as they did not get the opportunity, we took advantage of our opportunity to do the things that they wanted to do. And I want you young fellows to understand the reason for that.

There are standpatters in the Democratic Party. There are men sitting down hard on the breeching strap. There are men who are trying to hold back and to serve what they believe to be conservatism, though it is really reaction. But the interesting thing about the Democratic Party is that those men are in a small minority in its ranks, whereas in the party of the opposition they are in a majority and are in control.

The interesting thing for all politicians to remember is that the progressive voters of this country all put together outnumber either party. I venture to say they outnumber both parties put together. This country is

progressive, and if you youngsters are going to be in the running you will throw in your fortunes with the party of which the progressives have the control.

I am a progressive. I do not spell it with a capital P, but I think my pace is just as fast as those who do. It does not interfere with the running and I am very much astonished to see the company that some gentlemen who spell their name with a capital are keeping.

They are engaged in the interesting enterprise of trying to capture a party which is fortified against them and refusing to enter a party which is already captured by those who believe in their principles. The intellectual processes by which they arrive at their conclusions are entirely obscured to my intelligence.

But, you will notice that parties that merely want control do not have any principles. That is the reason why surprise that a programme has not been announced is unreasonable. Look over the ranks of the supporters of the Republican Party. Did you ever see a more motley company in your life? Did you ever see elements so absolutely contradictory of each other as the elements of that party? If they moved in any direction they would have to move in many directions; and if I am trying to get into power by the support of the people that do not agree with one another, it is very dangerous for me to profess my own opinion. Back of that party are those who want to inject into our politics the politics of Europe. But not all who have that purpose in mind are on the same side. Some want to inject those politics in order to move in one direction, and others want to inject them in order to move in exactly the opposite direction.

In these circumstances it is not wise to announce your direction. Some of them are Progressives or were and profess themselves dissatisfied with the present leadership and guidance of the party, and the others are so well satisfied with it that they are afraid that the entrance of this new element will disturb some of their favorite plans and so, looking at each other with suspicion, they have only one enthusiasm and that is the enthusiasm to get in. I see in my mind's eye this great motley company enthusiastically united in a great drive for possession.

Unfortunately, however, one thing has become reasonably clear, my fellow citizens, and it is a very serious thing indeed. One thing has become evident, not because it was explicitly stated, for nothing has been explicitly stated, but because it is unmistakably implicit in almost everything that has been said. Am I not right that we must draw the conclusion that, if the Republican Party is put into power at the next election, our foreign policy will be radically changed? I cannot draw any other inference.

All our present foreign policy is wrong, they say, and if it is wrong and they are men of conscience, they must change it; and if they are going to change it in what direction are they going to change it?

There is only one choice as against peace, and that is war. Some of the supporters of that party, a very great body of the supporters of that party, outspokenly declare that they want war; so that the certain prospect of the success of the Republican Party is that we shall be drawn in one form or other into the embroilments of the European war, and that to the south of us the force of the United States will be used to produce in Mexico the kind of law and order which some American investors in Mexico consider most to their advantage.

I do not find that anybody else's counsel is taken in respect of the policy that this country should pursue with regard to Mexico except those who have hitherto acted as the counsellors for the denied interests in Mexico. The whole country is acquainted with the gentlemen who have been consulted. There is no concealment, even by themselves, whose attorneys they are. They have talked to me. I know exactly what they want. I have declined to give it to them, and now they are going where they think that they can get it. And there is every indication, on the surface at any rate, that their calculation is well founded.

There is a more serious aspect even than that. There is an immediate result of this thing, my fellow citizens. From this time until the 7th of November it is going to be practically impossible for the present Administration to handle any critical matter concerning our foreign relations, because all foreign statesmen are waiting to see which way the election goes; and in the mean time they know that settlements will be inconclusive.

The conference which is being held with regard to Mexican affairs is embarrassed every day by the apparent evidence which is being produced that hostility to Mexico is being traded upon by one of the great political parties. These gentlemen may reconcile these influences with patriotic purpose, but it is difficult for all of us to do so. And the one thing I want to lay emphasis upon in this connection is this—that a great, fundamental, final choice with regard to our foreign relationships is to be made on the 7th of November. Some young men ought to be interested in that.

Singular, isn't it, that that should have been the only thing disclosed by the opposition. But I suspect that they are well enough content with many of the things that have been done in domestic legislation, provided they can get in and control them.

Let me illustrate it. Take the Federal Reserve System, the great banking system by which the credits of this country hitherto locked up, the credits of the average man, have been released and put into action; the great system which has made it possible for us to absorb two thousand millions' worth of American securities held on the other side of the water which have been offered for sale, nearly, if not quite 50 per cent, of the whole body of the American securities held abroad, a thing that would have been impossible otherwise.

You know that one of the many things that the Republicans promised and never did was to reform the currency system. They did what they have always done in such circumstances. They had a thorough inquiry and report made without any purpose of following it up.

The report was made after long and expensive inquiry and much interesting travel by a committee presided over by the late Senator Aldrich; and that report is a very valuable document. It is full of a great deal of useful information, along with a great deal of useless information. I dare say that in any report the useless predominate over the useful, but if you know what you are looking for, you can find it in that report.

And when we came to do this thing that ought to have been done long ago but which, because of a kind paralysis which cannot be called infantile, it was impossible for the Republican Party to do—I should call it a paralysis of the will—we found that we could take the skeleton of what we wanted to do from the Aldrich report, but that we could not take the heart out of it. We so absolutely altered the heart that Senator Aldrich himself denounced the thing that we produced.

Now the heart of the Aldrich plan was a single central bank which was susceptible of being controlled by the very men who have always dictated the financial policy of the Republican Party, whereas the heart of our system is not a great central bank, but a body appointed by and responsible to the Government and, by the same token responsible to the people of the United States.

The hand is the hand of Esau, but the heart is the heart of Jacob, and that heart is the heart of the Democratic Party, the control by representatives of the people of the things that concern the whole people.

There was universal hostility among the bankers of this country—not unanimous, but universal—to the adoption of the present system, and all of that opposition had its impulse from that central group which knew that that was going to happen which did happen—that they were going to lose their grip on the Treasury of the United States.

They are perfectly content, my fellow citizens, to take over the Federal Trade Commission, providing they can select the Commissioners and suggest whom they shall consult. They are perfectly willing to have a tariff board. At least they were willing to have before we created it, provided they can determine beforehand what its conclusions are going to be by determining the quality and antecedents of the men who compose it. You can very easily determine beforehand what is going to happen.

For example, if you want certain things to happen, select the most eminent—it may be the most honest—corporation lawyer in the country and put him on the Supreme Court. His character is not going to fail you. He may have as good a character as any man who ever lived, but his training is going to determine everything that he sees. You do not have to do these things corruptly; you only have to do them astutely.

Similarly they would be perfectly content to control the board which is to govern the rural credit system. They would be perfectly willing to appoint the board that is to control the development of the merchant marine and the regulation of marine charges in the carriage of freight on the high seas—perfectly willing. The only thing that makes them uneasy is that Democrats should be running these things.

I am not saying this in jest. I am not saying it to make a point. I am saying it out of my personal experience. Until the present Administration, Wall Street controlled the actions of the Treasury of the United States. I do not like those words, "Wall Street," because there are some men in Wall Street who have visions. There are some men who see things large and see them true; there are some men with fine statesmanlike gifts, and I do not like to include them; but the main impulse in Wall Street is not given to it by them.

Many of these gentlemen honestly believe that only they understand the interests of the country, and they were genuinely uneasy to see the Treasury conducted without their consent. Again and again I have received intimations from these quarters during the last three and a half years that they would very much like to be consulted, and I have invariably returned the same answer. I have said if these gentlemen have any advice to give I shall be most pleased to receive it. All they have to do is to ask to see me and tell me in the frankest way, like any other American citizen, what they think ought to be done. But they would not accept that kind of an invitation. They wanted to be sent for and they wanted to be reasonably certain before they went that their advice would be taken. They did not want to come in on the same terms with other citizens of the United States offering their advice as to what ought to be done.

It has been interesting and it has been very amusing that any set of men should think they knew what the interests of the country demanded and nobody else did. So that since they would not volunteer to come, we have made shift to conduct the Treasury of the United States without their assistance. And it must surprise them in their private thoughts to have to admit that it has been better conducted than ever before in our generation; more successfully as a business Administration, and infinitely more helpfully to the general body of the American people.

Such assistance as the Treasury of the United States can legitimately extend in times of financial stress used always to be extended to Wall Street. Now it is extended to the country.

It was no doubt shocking to see the money deposited in country banks and not in Wall Street, but the country banks knew how to use it and they were very much nearer the great masses of the people who need it than were the great depositaries of financial resources in New York.

I would not have you consider me prejudiced against New York City. Why gentlemen, the great City of New York is one of the most vital parts of the United States, but the city of New York does not consist of the gentlemen in Wall Street. And I would have you understand that I am very much prejudiced against them as they are against me. No not prejudice, but aware.

They have suffered another inconvenience. They used to be able to do a great deal in the way of legislation by means of a lobby the people knew very little about and the lobby, thank God, has disappeared.

I do not mean the legitimate lobby, the lobby that will go to the hearings of committees and argue their case in public with the reporters present, but I mean the buttonhole lobby. I mean the lobby that uses influence and not argument, that uses inducement and not fact, that understands some special interests and does not give a cent for the general interest, that is the lobby I mean, and the little cowards scuttled the minute they were mentioned. I had only to say in a casual interview with the representatives of the press that there was such a lobby, when all at once the rats began to scuttle.

So the instrumentalities of control have been destroyed, and the object of the present campaign on one side is to rehabilitate them.

Why do I say that? Because I see? Not more than you do. You see who are controlling the present campaign on the Republican side. There is no concealment about that. Two years ago the Republicans fancied that there was a reaction against the Democratic Party, because it had been going some, I admit. And so in the campaign for the Congressional elections two years ago some of their most distinguished leaders spoke very indiscreetly. They said that what this country needed was a business administration, which from one point of view we might have concurred in if they had not added to this definition that what the country wanted was to return to the "good old days of Mark Hanna."

Further definition was unnecessary. The good old days of Mark Hanna. No thoughtful man in this country would propose that we should return to the methods of police control practised by Senator Hanna. It happened that at that time a very lovely, trustworthy gentleman was President of the United States. I mean Mr. William McKinley. He had no part discreditable to himself, so far as I know, in the political arrangements and the expenditures of unlimited money in campaigns for which Senator Hanna was responsible.

But now, you will notice, we have returned to the good old days of Mark Hanna in the Republican Party. Some of the very gentlemen who were prominent in that odious regime are now at the head of affairs in the management of the Republican Campaign. The lieutenants of Mark Hanna have returned to authority, and the lieutenants of Mark Hanna represent the choices, the determinations and, so much as we can conjecture, the policy of the Republican Party.

What they want to do is to get control and then determine the policy in private conference. We are not going to be taken into their confidence. They want to control, possess. These are the magic words for them. They do not think we have sense enough. They do not think

we have coherence enough. They do not think a great body of free people know how to hang together in its own cause and that a little body of men that always hangs together can in the long run manage the people, and it is up to us to show them that that is impossible.

Henceforth, understand that, so far as I am concerned, I will excuse these gentlemen from answering questions, because I know they cannot answer them; that if they answered them they would lose half of their following on any particular subject and the confidence of the people of the United States altogether, therefore I, for my part, do not intend to ask them any questions. I have other uses for my mind, because I am on to the game already.

What it is our imperative duty to do, my fellow citizens, is to make everybody we know understand what the Democratic Party stands for and what it intends to do. It has begun a great process of liberalization for the business of the country and it intends to strengthen that system at every point, extend it wherever it needs extension, strengthen and fortify it against all attacks, and once for all make good the domination of the American people in their own affairs.

On that programme we are challengers to all comers. We have shown our hand. It cannot be doubted. All you have got to do, if you want to know the lines of the future policy of the Democratic Party is to extend the lines of the best policies of the Democratic Party, and you have an absolute standard. You know which way we are going. The question is, do you want to head us off? And it is for the young men of the country in particular to answer.

I do not know, for my part, how the spirit of a nation gets into one generation after another, but I do know by long contact with young men that the spirit of a nation is perhaps more intense in the generations coming on than in the more sophisticated generations that have become deeply immersed in particular lines of business.

The point of view of the young man is of the horizons. He looks abroad upon a wide world, because he is choosing his path. He looks curiously upon many of the aspects of human affairs, because he hopes and intends to play a part of importance in some of them.

And so the young men have the impulse, the momentum, the whole vision of the people more intensely in them than the older men who have grown a little tired, some of them grown a little pessimistic, some of them grown a little discouraged, some of them having had many hard knocks and suffered many disappointments, but who yet, nevertheless, with stubborn courage and steadfast strength are themselves struggling toward the light.

And they are calling to the young men, "come, recruit our ranks. Some of us are falling by the way. We need your force. We need your hope. We need your confidence. We need your capacity to get together and stay together and follow and lead. Come, strengthen the great army of men who have their eyes lifted to those horizons where shines the light of hope for men of every nation and of every generation, where rests the reassurance of the world's peace and of the world's happiness."

Warren G. Harding's "Normalcy" Speech (1920)

The presidential election of 1920 was unwinnable for the Democratic party. Despite President Woodrow Wilson's victories in 1912 and 1916, the Democrats remained the nation's minority party. Events were running squarely against them. On April 2, 1917, Wilson had asked Congress to declare war on Germany. Although the United States had been provoked to fight, its entry into World War I belied the theme of Wilson's reelection campaign—"He kept us out of war." (See "Woodrow Wilson's 'Shadow Lawn' Speech on Foreign Policy," p. 277.) In November 1918, the president's unprecedented appeal to the voters to give him a Democratic Congress on patriotic grounds backfired, and the Republicans won control of both the House of Representatives and the Senate. From 1919 until the end of his term, a series of strokes and other attacks effectively disabled Wilson. On November 11, 1919, the Senate rejected the postwar peace treaty that he had negotiated in Versailles, France. The rejection was an especially cruel blow because the treaty contained Wilson's plan for the League of Nations, an international organization he had designed to maintain world peace.

The 1920 Democratic national convention was unwilling to renominate Wilson, whose hope that the election would affirm both his leadership and the League was wildly unrealistic. But the party did write a pro-League platform and nominate a pro-League ticket: Gov. James Cox of Ohio for president and Assistant Secretary of the Navy Franklin D. Roosevelt of New York for vice president. Cox was nominated on the forty-fourth ballot, defeating former secretary of the treasury William Gibbs McAdoo and Attorney General A. Mitchell Palmer.

As expected, the Republican national convention deadlocked between Gen. Leonard Wood, the political heir to the recently deceased Theodore Roosevelt, and Illinois governor Frank Lowden, who was the favorite of party regulars. Before the convention, Harry M. Daugherty of Ohio had predicted to a reporter that Republican leaders eventually would break the deadlock by gathering during the small hours of the morning in a "smoke-filled room in some hotel" and deciding to choose his candidate, Sen. Warren G. Harding, as the party's compromise nominee. Daugherty's prediction was borne out (Harding was nominated on the tenth ballot), and the term "smoke-filled room" entered the political lexicon. The convention chose Gov. Calvin Coolidge of Massachusetts to be Harding's running mate.

The general election campaign between Cox and Harding was unexciting. Like Dwight D. Eisenhower in

1952, Richard Nixon in 1968, and George Bush in 1988, Harding perfectly captured the public's desire for consolidation after a period of domestic policy achievement and foreign entanglement. "America's present need is not heroics but healing," Harding told a Boston audience in a remarkable display of assonance and alliteration; "not nostrums but normalcy; not revolution but restoration; not agitation, but adjustment; not surgery, but serenity; not the dramatic, but the dispassionate; not experiment, but equipoise; not submergence in internationality, but sustainment in triumphant nationality." On election day, Harding handily defeated Cox by 404-127 in the electoral college and by 60.3 percent to 34.2 percent in the popular vote.

Harding died, probably of a heart attack, on August 2, 1923. Not long afterward, the "Teapot Dome" scandal broke, revealing a pattern of corruption in the leasing of federally owned oil fields that forced a number of public officials (including Attorney General Daugherty) to resign. Although not personally corrupt, Harding, through inattention, had presided over one of the most corrupt administrations in history. ～

There isn't anything the matter with the world civilization, except that humanity is viewing it through a vision impaired in a cataclysmal war. Poise has been disturbed and nerves have been racked, and fever has rendered men irrational; sometimes there have been draughts upon the dangerous cup of barbarity and men have wandered far from safe paths, but the human procession still marches in the right direction.

Here, in the United States, we feel the reflex, rather than the hurting wound, but we still think straight, and we mean to act straight, and mean to hold firmly to all that was ours when war involved us, and seek the higher attainments which are the only compensations that so supreme a tragedy may give mankind.

Normal Conditions Great Need

America's present need is not heroics, but healing; not nostrums but normalcy; not revolution, but restoration; not agitation, but adjustment; not surgery, but serenity; not the dramatic, but the dispassionate; not experiment, but equipoise; not submergence in internationality, but sustainment in triumphant nationality.

It is one thing to battle successfully against world domination by military autocracy, because the infinite God never intended such a program, but it is quite another thing to revise human nature and suspend the fundamental laws of life and all of life's acquirements.

Formal Peace Sought

The world called for peace, and has its precarious variety. America demands peace, formal as well as actual, and means to have it, regardless of political exigencies and campaign issues. If it must be a campaign issue, we shall have peace and discuss it afterward, because the actuality is imperative, and the theory is only illusive. Then we may set our own house in order. We challenged the proposal that an armed autocrat should dominate the world; it ill becomes us to assume that a rhetorical autocrat shall direct all humanity.

This republic has its ample tasks. If we put an end to false economics which lure humanity to utter chaos, ours will be the commanding example of world leadership to-day. If we can prove a representative popular government under which a citizenship seeks what it may do for the government rather than what the government may do for individuals, we shall do more to make democracy safe for the world than all armed conflict ever recorded. The world needs to be reminded that all human ills are not curable by legislation, and that quantity of statutory enactment and excess of government offer no substitute for quality of citizenship.

Should Seek Understanding

The problems of maintained civilization are not to be solved by a transfer of responsibility from citizenship to government, and no eminent page in history was ever drafted by the standards of mediocrity. More, no government is worthy of the name which is directed by influence on the one hand, or moved by intimidation on the other.

Nothing is more vital to this republic to-day than clear and intelligent understanding. Men must understand one another, and government and men must understand each other. For emergence from the wreckage of war, for the clarification of fevered minds, we must all give and take, we must both sympathize and inspire, but must learn griefs and aspirations, we must seek the common grounds of mutuality.

Work Is Solution

There can be no disguising everlasting truths. Speak it plainly, no people ever recovered from the distressing waste of war except through work and denial. There is no other way. We shall make no recovery in seeking how little men can do, our restoration lies in doing

the most which is reasonably possible for individuals to do. Under production and hateful profiteering are both morally criminal, and must be combated. America can not be content with minimums of production to-day, the crying need is maximums. If we may have maximums of production we shall have minimums of cost, and profiteering will be speeded to its deserved punishment. Money values are not destroyed, they are temporarily distorted. War wasted hundreds of billions, and depleted world storehouses, and cultivated new demands, and it hardened selfishness and gave awakening touch to elemental greed. Humanity needs renewed consecrations to what we call fellow citizenship.

Out of the supreme tragedy must come a new order and a higher order, and I gladly acclaim it. But war has not abolished work, has not established the processes of seizure or the rule of physical might. Nor has it provided a governmental panacea for human ills, or the magic touch that makes failure a success. Indeed, it has revealed no new reward for idleness, no substitute for the sweat of a man's face in the contest for subsistence and acquirement.

Supremacy of Law

There is no new appraisal for the supremacy of law. That is a thing surpassing and eternal. A contempt for international law wrought the supreme tragedy, contempt for our national and state laws will rend the glory of the republic, and failure to abide the proven laws of to-day's civilization will lead to temporary chaos.

No one need doubt the ultimate result, because immutable laws have challenged the madness of all experiment. But we are living to-day, and it is ours to save ourselves from colossal blunder and its excessive penalty.

Production Is Great Need

My best judgment of America's needs is to steady down, to get squarely on our feet, to make sure of the right path. Let's get out of the fevered delirium of war, with the hallucination that all the money in the world is to be made in the madness of war and the wildness of its aftermath. Let us stop to consider that tranquillity at home is more precious than peace abroad, and that both our good fortune and our eminence are dependent on the normal forward stride of all the American people.

Nothing is so imperative to-day as efficient production and efficient transportation, to adjust the balances in our own transactions and to hold our place in the activities of the world. The relation of real values is little altered by the varying coins of exchange, and that American is blind to actualities who thinks we can add to cost of production without impairing our hold in world markets. Our part is more than to hold, we must add to what we have.

It is utter folly to talk about reducing the cost of living without restored and increased efficiency or production on the one hand and more prudent consumption on the other. No law will work the miracle. Only the American people themselves can solve the situation. There must be the conscience of capital in omitting profiteering, there must be the conscience of labor in efficiently producing, there must be a public conscience in restricting outlay and promoting thrift.

Sober capital must make appeal to intoxicated wealth, and thoughtful labor must appeal to the radical who has no thought of the morrow, to effect the needed understanding. Exacted profits, because the golden stream is flooding, and pyramided wages to meet a mounting cost that must be halted, will speed us to disaster just as sure as the morrow comes, and we ought to think soberly and avoid it. We ought to dwell in the heights of good fortune for a generation to come, and I pray that we will, be we need a benediction of wholesome common sense to give us that assurance.

Sober Thinking Urged

I pray for sober thinking in behalf of the future of America. No worthwhile republic ever went the tragic way to destruction, which did not begin the downward course through luxury of life and extravagance of living. More, the simple living and thrifty people will be the first to recover from a war's waste and all its burdens, and our people ought to be the first recovered. Herein is greater opportunity than lies in alliance, compact or supergovernment. It is America's chance to lead in example and prove to the world the reign of reason in representative popular government where people think who assume to rule.

No overall fad will quicken our thoughtfulness. We might try repairs on the old clothes and simplicity for the new. I know the tendency to wish the thing denied, I know the human hunger for a new thrill, but denial enhances the ultimate satisfaction, and stabilizes our indulgence. A blasé people is the unhappiest in all the world.

It seems to me singularly appropriate to address this membership an additional word about production. I believe most cordially in the home market first for the American product. There is no other way to assure our prosperity. I rejoice in our normal capacity to consume our rational, healthful consumption.

Save America First

We have protected our home market with war's barrage. But the barrage has lifted with the passing of the war. The American people will not heed to-day, because world competition is not yet restored, but the morrow will soon come when the world will seek our markets and our trade balances, and we must think of America first or surrender our eminence.

The thought is not selfish. We want to share with the world in seeking becoming restoration. But peoples will trade and seek wealth in their exchanges, and every conflict in the adjustment of peace was founded on the hope of promoting trade conditions. I heard expressed, before the Foreign Relations Committee of the Senate, the aspirations of nationality and the hope of commerce to develop and expand aspiring peoples. Knowing that those two thoughts are inspiring all humanity, as they have since civilization began, I can only marvel at the American who consents to surrender either. There may be conscience, humanity and justice in both, and without them the glory of the republic is done. I want to go on, secure and unafraid, holding fast to the American inheritance and confident of the supreme American fulfillment.

The 103d Ballot (1924)

No national party convention has lasted longer or accomplished less than the 1924 Democratic national convention. The convention assembled at the sweltering Madison Square Garden in New York City on June 24 and was unable to complete its business until July 9, sixteen days and one hundred three ballots later. The party's eventual nominees for president and vice president—former ambassador to Great Britain John W. Davis of West Virginia, a corporate lawyer, and William Jennings Bryan's brother, Gov. Charles W. Bryan of Nebraska—lost the November election by an almost two-to-one popular vote majority to the Republican president, Calvin Coolidge, and his vice-presidential running mate, former budget bureau director Charles G. Dawes of Illinois.

The Democrats began their convention with little prospect for victory against Coolidge. To be sure, the Republican administration of President Warren G. Harding had been riddled with kickbacks, favoritism, and other forms of corruption. (See "Warren G. Harding's 'Normalcy' Speech," p. 286.) But when Harding died on August 2, 1923, he apparently carried the political blame for the corruption with him to the grave. Coolidge, who succeeded to the presidency, impressed the voters as being honest and upright, the soul of Yankee Puritanism. Without contro-

versy, the Republican party nominated Coolidge for a full term as president at its three-day national convention in Cleveland, Ohio.

The Democratic convention, far from being unified, was deeply divided by overlapping fault lines of region, candidate, and policy. The mainly rural, southern and western wing of the party favored former secretary of the treasury William Gibbs McAdoo of California for president and opposed platform proposals to condemn the Ku Klux Klan (KKK) and to end the prohibition of alcoholic beverages. (The KKK was a violent secret society that preached hatred of African Americans, Catholics, and Jews; Prohibition had been imposed by the Eighteenth Amendment to the Constitution in 1919.) The party's northern and eastern, mostly urban wing supported Gov. Al Smith of New York for president. It wanted to condemn the KKK and repeal Prohibition. The presence of more than a dozen "favorite-son" and other minor candidates for president complicated the convention's business even further.

Under the Democratic party's two-thirds rule, 729 votes were required for nomination. (See "Abolition of the Two-Thirds Rule: Proceedings of the Democratic National Convention," p. 344.) On the first ballot, McAdoo received 431.5 votes, Smith 241 votes, and favorite sons and other candidates 425.5 votes.

(Some delegates shared votes.) On the sixty-ninth ballot, McAdoo peaked at 530 votes, nearly 200 votes short of the nomination. Smith never rose higher than the 368 votes he received on the seventy-sixth ballot. By the ninety-fourth ballot, the convention was more fragmented than ever: McAdoo 395 votes, Smith 364.5 votes, and Davis, the third place candidate, 81 votes. Despairing of success, their supporters exhausted, Smith and McAdoo both withdrew from the race. The Democratic convention nominated Davis by acclamation on the 103d ballot.

Progressives were distressed by the candidates that the two major parties offered in 1924—the choice between Coolidge and Davis was a choice between two conservatives. A Progressive party convention met in July to nominate the bipartisan ticket of Sen. Robert M. La Follette, a Wisconsin Republican, for president and Sen. Burton K. Wheeler, a Montana Democrat, for vice president.

Coolidge prevailed easily on election day, although the voter turnout rate was the lowest (thus far) in history: only 48.9 percent of the voting age population participated. Coolidge won 54.1 percent of the popular vote to 28.9 percent for Davis and 16.6 percent for La Follette. In the electoral college, the vote was Coolidge 382, Davis 136, and La Follette 13. ～

The Acting Permanent Chairman (Mr. Barkley): The Secretary will call the roll for the next ballot. Will the aisle please be cleared here in front?

(The Acting Reading Secretary, Mr. Charles V. Truax, of Ohio, then proceeded with the roll-call of the States upon the One Hundred and Third Ballot, and received responses as follows:)

One Hundred and Third Ballot.

Alabama, 24 votes: Underwood, 24.

Arizona, 6 votes: McAdoo, 2½; Underwood, 3.

Arkansas, 18 votes: Robinson, 18.

California, 26 votes: Underwood, 2; Davis, 2; Robinson, 1; Meredith, 2; Glass, 1; Walsh, 18.

Colorado, 12 votes: Meredith, ½; John W. Davis, 3; Underwood, 5; Walsh, 1. (Two and one-half not voting.)

Connecticut, 14 votes: Walsh, 3; Underwood, 11.

Delaware, 6 votes: Underwood, 6.

Florida, 12 votes: Davis, 6; Meredith, 3; McAdoo, 3.

Georgia, 28 votes: John W. Davis, 27; Meredith, 1.

Idaho, 8 votes: John W. Davis, 8.

Illinois, 58 votes: Davis, 19; Underwood, 19; Glass, 20.

Indiana, 30 votes: Underwood, 5; John W. Davis, 25.

Iowa, 26 votes: Meredith, 26.

Kansas, 20 votes: John W. Davis, 20.

Kentucky, 26 votes: Walsh, 2½; Underwood, 1; John W. Davis, 22½.

Louisiana, 20 votes: John W. Davis, 20.

Maine, 12 votes: Davis, 2; Underwood, 10.

Maryland, 16 votes: John W. Davis, 16.

Massachusetts, 36 votes: (Passed.)

Michigan, 30 votes: John W. Davis, 29½; Walsh, ½.

Minnesota, 24 votes: Davis, 3; Walsh, 1; McAdoo, 2; Underwood, 16.

Mississippi, 20 votes: John W. Davis, 20.

Missouri, 36 votes: Davis, 36.

Montana, 8 votes: Walsh, 8.

Nebraska, 16 votes: Davis, 1; Cordell Hull, 1; Smith, 1; Meredith, 6; Underwood, 2; Senator Walsh, 5.

Nevada, 6 votes: John W. Davis, 6.

New Hampshire, 8 votes: John W. Davis, 3½; Walsh, 4½.

New Jersey, 28 votes: Underwood, 16; Glass, 11; J. W. Davis, 1.

New Mexico, 6 votes: Robinson, 2; Meredith, 2; Davis, 2.

New York, 90 votes: Daniels, 1; Gerard, 1; John W. Davis, 4; Walsh, 20; Glass, 20; Underwood, 44.

North Carolina, 24 votes: Underwood, 5½; John W. Davis, 18½.

North Dakota, 10 votes: Glass, 5; Walsh, 5.

Ohio, 48 votes: Glass, 2; Underwood, 4; Meredith, 1; Davis, 41.

Oklahoma, 20 votes: John W. Davis, 20.

Oregon, 10 votes: McAdoo, 3; Davis, 5; Underwood, 1.

Pennsylvania, 76 votes: Walsh, 1; Houston Thompson, 1; Smith, 2; McAdoo, 3; Underwood, 31½; Davis, 37½.

Rhode Island, 10 votes: Davis, 10.

South Carolina, 18 votes: Davis, 18.

South Dakota, 10 votes: Gerard, 7; Underwood, 2; McAdoo, 1.
Tennessee, 24 votes: Meredith, 1; Glass, 4; J. W. Davis, 19.
Texas, 40 votes: Davis, 40.
Utah, 8 votes: Davis, 8.
Vermont, 8 votes: Davis, 8.
Virginia, 24 votes: Glass, 12; Davis, 12.
Washington, 14 votes: Davis, 14.

Mr. H. D. Merritt (of Washington): I challenge the vote of Washington and demand a poll.

The Acting Permanent Chairman (Mr. Barkley): Washington will be passed.

The Acting Reading Secretary (continuing):

West Virginia, 16 votes: Davis, 16.
Wisconsin, 26 votes: Davis, 1; Smith, 1; Glass, 3; Underwood, 8; Walsh, 12.
Wyoming, 6 votes: John W. Davis, 6.
Alaska, 6 votes: Davis, 4; Underwood, 2.

Mr. George E. Brennan (of Illinois): Mr. Chairman, has the roll-call been concluded?

The Acting Permanent Chairman (Mr. Barkley): It has not.

Mr. George E. Brennan (of Illinois): I desire to be recognized upon the conclusion of the roll.

(Cries of: "No.")

Mr. George E. Brennan (of Illinois): Mr. Chairman.

The Acting Permanent Chairman (Mr. Barkley): For what purpose does the gentleman from Illinois arise?

Mr. George E. Brennan (of Illinois): I rise to change the vote of Illinois.

The Acting Permanent Chairman (Mr. Barkley): That will have to be done at the close of the roll-call.

Mr. George E. Brennan (of Illinois): I desire to ask leave at that time to make a change.

The Acting Reading Secretary (continuing):

District of Columbia, 6 votes: Underwood, 6.
Hawaii, 6 votes: Smith, 1; Underwood, 1; John W. Davis, 4.

Philippines, 6 votes: Walsh, 1; Underwood, 1; John W. Davis, 4.
Porto Rico, 6 votes: Underwood, 1; John W. Davis, 5.
Canal Zone, 6 votes: John W. Davis, 6.
Massachusetts, 36 votes: Underwood, 23½; Smith, 5½; Walsh, 2; Glass, 1; John W. Davis, 2.
Washington, 14 votes: John W. Davis, 14.

The Permanent Chairman: The Chair recognizes the delegate from Iowa, Mr. J. R. Files.

Mr. J. R. Files (of Iowa): Iowa changes the name of Edwin T. Meredith, and desires to have her vote cast 26 for John W. Davis.

(From this point on to the close of the balloting upon the One Hundred and Third Ballot, when John W. Davis was, by suspension of the rules, nominated by acclamation for President of the United States, the Convention was in continuous uproar, all delegates standing, many on chairs. Many delegates wildly clamoring and gesticulating for recognition. Frantic, persistent and continuous cries of "Mr. Chairman," "Mr. Chairman," "Mr. Chairman," from many delegations.)

The Permanent Chairman: The Chair recognizes the delegate from California.

Mr. William Kettner (of California): Mr. Chairman, the California delegation desires to change its vote. Meredith, 1; Walsh, 4; Davis, 21.

The Permanent Chairman: The Chair understands the accuracy of the report from the State of Washington is challenged. Is that persisted in?

Mr. R. P. Oldham (of Washington): Mr. Chairman, at the time the challenge was made, we voted seven and a half, with one absent, but since that time the delegation have all changed, except myself, and I therefore withdraw the challenge.

The Acting Reading Secretary (continuing):

Washington, 14 votes: John W. Davis, 14.

Mr. J. R. Files (of Iowa): Mr. Chairman.

The Permanent Chairman (Mr. Walsh): The Chair recognizes the delegate from Iowa.

Mr. J. R. Files (of Iowa): Iowa withdraws the name of Edwin T. Meredith, and desires to have her 26 votes cast for John W. Davis. (Applause.)

Mr. George E. Brennan (of Illinois): Mr. Chairman.

Mr. William Kettner (of California): Mr. Chairman.

The Permanent Chairman: The Chair recognizes the delegate from California.

Mr. William Kettner (of California): Mr. Chairman, the California delegation desires to change its vote from Meredith, 1; Walsh, 4; Davis, 21, to 26 votes for John W. Davis, of West Virginia.

A Delegate from Oregon: Mr. Chairman.

The Permanent Chairman: The Chair understands the accuracy of the report of the vote from the State of Washington is challenged.

Mr. H. D. Merritt (of Washington): Yes, sir, Mr. Chairman.

The Permanent Chairman: Is the challenge persisted in?

Mr. H. D. Merritt (of Washington): Mr. Chairman, the delegation at the time that the challenge was made voted seven and one-half votes with one vote absent, but since that time the delegation have all changed to Davis except myself, and therefore I withdraw the challenge, and the vote of the entire delegation stands 14 for John W. Davis, of West Virginia.

Mr. George E. Brennan (of Illinois): Mr. Chairman.

The Permanent Chairman: The delegate from Illinois is recognized.

Mr. George E. Brennan (of Illinois): Illinois desires to change its vote to 58 votes for John W. Davis.

Mr. Franklin D. Roosevelt (of New York): Mr. Chairman.

The Permanent Chairman: The Chair recognizes the delegate from New York, Mr. Roosevelt.

Mr. Franklin D. Roosevelt (of New York): Mr. Chairman, New York desires to change its vote as follows: Glass, 2; Walsh, of Montana, 28; John W. Davis, 60. (Applause.)

Mr. W. J. Fields (of Kentucky): Mr. Chairman.

The Permanent Chairman: The Chair recognizes the delegate from Kentucky, Mr. Fields.

Mr. W. J Fields (of Kentucky): Mr. Chairman, Kentucky desires to change her poll, and casts her entire 26 votes for John W. Davis.

Mr. J. Henry Goeke (of Ohio): Mr. Chairman.

The Permanent Chairman: The Chair recognizes the delegate from Ohio, Mr. J. Henry Goeke.

Mr. Josephus Daniels (of North Carolina): Mr. Chairman, Mr. Chairman.

Mr. J. Henry Goeke (of Ohio): Mr. Chairman, Ohio desires to change its vote from Glass, 2; Underwood, 4; Meredith, 1, and Davis, 41, to Meredith, 1; Underwood, 1, and John W. Davis, 46.

Senator Claude A. Swanson (of Virginia): Mr. Chairman, Mr. Chairman.

The Permanent Chairman: The Chair recognizes the delegate from Virginia, Senator Claude A. Swanson.

Mr. Claude A. Swanson (of Virginia): Mr. Chairman, Virginia desires to change its vote to 24 votes for John W. Davis. (Applause.)

The Permanent Chairman: The Chair recognizes——

Mr. Josephus Daniels (of North Carolina): Mr. Chairman.

The Permanent Chairman: The Chair recognizes the delegate from North Carolina, Mr. Josephus Daniels.

Mr. Josephus Daniels (of North Carolina): Mr. Chairman, North Carolina desires to change its vote, and solidly votes for John W. Davis. (Applause.)

Mr. W. W. Brandon (of Alabama): Mr. Chairman, Mr. Chairman.

The Permanent Chairman: The Chair recognizes the delegate from Alabama, Governor Brandon.

Mr. W. W. Brandon (of Alabama): Mr. Chairman, Alabama desires to change its entire vote from Oscar W. Underwood to John W. Davis. (Applause.)

Mr. John M. Callahan (of Wisconsin): Mr. Chairman, Mr. Chairman.

The Permanent Chairman: The Chair recognizes the delegate from Wisconsin.

Mr. John M. Callahan (of Wisconsin): Mr. Chairman, Wisconsin desires to change its vote to 1 for Meredith, 1 for Underwood, 2 for Senator Walsh, of Montana, and 22 for John W. Davis.

Mr. Thomas Taggart (of Indiana): Mr. Chairman, Indiana desires to change its vote.

A Delegate from Connecticut: Mr. Chairman.

The Permanent Chairman: The Chair recognizes the delegate from Connecticut.

Mr. David E. Fitzgerald (of Connecticut): Mr. Chairman, Connecticut desires to change its entire vote to John W. Davis.

Mr. Thomas Taggart (of Indiana): Mr. Chairman, Indiana desires to change its vote.

Mrs. Anna V. S. Wilson (of Pennsylvania): Pennsylvania, Pennsylvania—

Mr. Thomas Taggart: Indiana, Indiana.

Mrs. Anna V. S. Wilson (of Pennsylvania): Pennsylvania, Pennsylvania.

The Permanent Chairman: The Chair recognizes the delegate from Pennsylvania.

Mrs. Anna S. V. Wilson (of Pennsylvania): Mr. Chairman, Pennsylvania casts its 76 votes for John W. Davis. (Applause.)

The Permanent Chairman: The Chair begs the Convention to be in order until the vote is recorded.

The Chair recognizes the delegate from Indiana.

Mr. Thomas Taggart (of Indiana): Mr. Chairman, if it is not out of order, I move that the nomination of John W. Davis be made by acclamation. (Loud applause.)

The Permanent Chairman: The delegate from Indiana, Senator Taggart, moves that the rules be suspended and that John W. Davis be made the nominee of this Convention for the Presidency of the United States by acclamation.

(Cries of: "I second the motion," "I second the motion"; loud applause.)

Those in favor of the motion will please say aye. (Ayes.) Those opposed will please say no. (There were no noes.) The ayes have it, and it is so ordered.

The Permanent Chairman: Pursuant to the vote just had, the Chair declares the Honorable John W. Davis, of West Virginia, the nominee of this Convention for President of the United States. (Great applause and demonstration.)

H. L. Mencken's "Onward, Christian Soldiers!" Article (1928)

The presidential election of 1928, like the elections of 1920 and 1924, was all but unwinnable for the Democratic party. Prosperity seemed high, the Republicans were the majority party, and their nominee for president, Herbert Hoover, was the ideal candidate. In 1928, however, unlike 1920 and 1924, the Democrats lost the election in a way that helped to lay the groundwork for future victories.

Neither party had much trouble deciding whom to nominate in 1928. Secretary of Commerce Hoover, a self-made man from California, appeared to embody all the ideal qualities of both the mind (he was a brilliant mining engineer, a successful business leader, and an efficient government administrator) and the heart (he had directed massive efforts to feed the people of Europe during and after World War I). Hoover's conservatism appealed to Republican party regulars; his humanitarianism and his belief in nonpolitical expertise attracted support from Progressives. Hoover won a first-ballot nomination at the Republican national convention, which also chose Gov. Charles Curtis of Kansas as its nominee for vice president.

Forswearing a reenactment of the 1924 Democratic national convention (especially since the prize seemed of so little value), William Gibbs McAdoo allowed Gov. Al Smith of New York to win an uncontested, first-ballot nomination in 1928. (See "The 103d Ballot," p. 291.) In an egregious display of ticket-balancing, the convention chose Sen. Joseph T. Robinson of Arkansas— a rural, southern, Protestant, conservative "dry" (that is, prohibitionist)—as the running mate for the urban, northern, Catholic, liberal "wet" that it had just nominated for president. Franklin D. Roosevelt, the Democrats' vice-presidential candidate in 1920, provided the convention with one of its few exhilarating moments when he celebrated Smith as the "Happy Warrior" in his nominating speech.

Smith never had a chance against Hoover. As if the economy, the Republican majority, and Hoover's popularity were not enough, technology worked against the Democratic nominee. The 1928 campaign was the first in which radio played an important part, and Hoover turned out to be, if not skillful, much less awkward on the airwaves than Smith.

Anti-Catholicism undermined the Smith campaign in the traditionally strongest Democratic regions of the country, the South and the West. Smith was the first Roman Catholic ever nominated for president. Ugly rumors were spread, many of them, as reported by the famous Baltimore journalist, H. L. Mencken, absurd: the Pope would run the U.S. government, *public schools would be abolished, Protestant marriages would be annulled, and the children of Protestants would be declared illegitimate. Smith, it even was whispered, secretly planned to extend New York City's new underwater Holland Tunnel all the way to the basement of the Vatican in Rome. (See "John F. Kennedy's Speech to the Greater Houston Ministerial Association," p. 489.)*

The magnitude of Hoover's victory in November—58.2 percent to 40.8 percent in the popular vote and, with the anti-Catholic defection of five southern states to Hoover, 444 to 87 in the electoral college—concealed some important gains for the Democrats. Voter turnout rose by almost 8 million from the last election; Smith nearly doubled the popular vote of the 1924 Democratic nominee, John W. Davis. Many of the new voters were recently immigrated, urban, working-class Catholics and Jews, whom Smith's candidacy attracted into the Democratic party. In the 1930s, these voters would become core supporters of a new Democratic majority. (See "The Literary Digest Poll," p. 348.) ~

August 24, 1928

The holy war against Al in the late Confederate States seems to be breaking into two halves. On the one hand, some of the Methodist and Baptist papers begin to be extremely polite to him, and warn their customers that it is unChristian (and what is worse, unwise) to have at opponents too holy. On the other hand, there are journals which pile indignation upon indignation, and devote practically all of their space to philippics against Al, Raskob, Tammany, the Beer Trust and the Pope.

A good specimen of the former class is the *Southern Christian Advocate*, of Columbia, S.C.—like all the multitudi-nous *Christian Advocates*, a Methodist organ. In the current issue I can find but two references to Al, and both of them are quite inoffensive. Nor does Pastor E. O. Watson, the editor, print anything against the Pope. So with the *Biblical Record* (Baptist), of Raleigh, edited by Pastor Livingston Johnson. Dr. Johnson, indeed, is so moderate that he feels moved to explain his lack of ferocity. Some of his subscribers have protested against it. Says he:

> Because we have not used more vitrolic language some have thought that the editor was weakening in his position. The writer has simply endeavored to keep a cool head, as he has two or three times advised others to do.

Dr. Johnson prints several articles defending political activity by the evangelical clergy, but he publishes no assaults upon Al, nor does he denounce the Catholic Church. The *Baptist Banner*, of Parkersburg, W. Va., swings even further to the Right. It prints long articles on "State Missions," "The Book of Romans" and "Are We Going to Let Country Churches Die?", but not a word about the great Christian uprising against Rome. The *Baptist Messenger*, of Oklahoma City, goes the same way. There is no denunciation of the Pope, and Al is barely mentioned. The editor, Pastor E. C. Routh, believes that "when great moral issues arise that affect the eternal destinies of a multitude" every consecrated Christian, lay or clerical, should speak out, but he apparently believes that this speaking out should be very circumspect.

The *Baptist Record*, of Jackson, Miss., one of the holy towns of the Chigger Belt, publishes a number of arguments against Al, but they are devoid of vituperation. One of its contributors warns the Mississippi Baptists that Rome "believes in ruling the world with an iron heel," and another sends in some quotations from a Catholic "Manual of Discipline," published in Philadelphia in 1926, showing that the Pope has "a right to annul those laws or acts of government that would injure the salvation of souls or attack the natural rights of citizens," and that Rome holds that "the state should aid, protect and defend the church." but there is nothing about the villainies of the Jesuits or the plots of the Knights of Columbus.

The *Southwestern Christian Advocate,* of Cincinnati, which has a considerable circulation in the South, defends the political parsons, but does not mention the Pope. The *North Carolina Christian Advocate,* Greensboro, reprints an editorial from the Hon. Josephus Daniels' paper, the Raleigh *News and Observer,* denouncing those Tarheel Democrats who have threatened to cut off the revenues of pastors advocating Hoover, but it is silent about the crimes of Rome, and its principal articles bear such titles as "The Place of the Beautiful" and "A Good Man Gone." The *Alabama Baptist,* of Birmingham, prints a few digs at Al and Raskob, but there is no violence in them, and the Catholic Church is not mentioned.

The Richmond *Christian Advocate* prints bishop E. D. Mouzon's denunciation of the Pope and his janizaries, but not much of its own. It apologizes for discussing politics at all, on the ground that the newspapers show "a biased attitude," and promises not to be "inflammatory or bitter." The *Baptist Standard,* of Dallas, Texas, after saying that it "has not chosen to jump into partisan politics," complains that it is "being misunderstood," and that two other Baptist papers have "concluded that it is indifferent to the present crisis in our nation's life." The editor says that this is not so, but he indulges in no invective against Al. The *American Baptist,* of Lexington, Ky., takes much the same line. The editor is against Al, but he has nothing to say about the Pope and he is "opposed to mentioning the names of parties and candidates in resolutions passed by religious bodies."

The Primitive Baptist organs are too busy hunting down heresy to bother with politics. In the *Primitive Baptist,* of Thornton, Ark., the campaign is not so much as mentioned.

The *Baptist Courier,* of Greenville, S.C., belongs to the other wing. It announces Raskob as "a private chaplain *(sic)* of the papal household," and says that "without doubt he has been on his knees before the Pope." Further, it prints an article entitled "The Romish Peril," by the learned Dr. A. T. Robertson, of the Southern Baptist Theological Seminary, in which he sounds a warning that "the Pope undoubtedly longs for the wealth and power of the United States to be in his hands." He goes on:

> He will never give up that hope. He will leave no stone unturned to gain that end.... Rome means to get control of the United States sooner or later. Protestants may well understand that purpose.

Dr. Robertson does not mention Al, but his meaning is plain enough. Dr. C. M. Bishop, writing in the *Texas Christian Advocate,* of Dallas, Texas, goes further. He identifies Tammany and the Pope with the horrendous beasts mentioned in the Book of Revelation, and heads his article "Unclean Spirits Like Frogs." In the same journal Dr. Bob Shuler, the chief rival of Dr. Aimée Semple McPherson in Los Angeles, pursues the melancholy subject in his well-known trenchant style.

In the *Baptist Advance,* of Little Rock, Ark., there are many waspish items about Al, Raskob, Tammany, the Pope and the Hon. Joe Robinson. One of them says that the Catholics in Hungary have protested officially against the erection of statues there to Luther and Calvin, and cites the fact as a foretaste of what will happen in the United States if Al is elected. Dr. Robinson's speeches against intolerance are denounced as "the ravings of a demagogue and the vaporings of an ignoramus." But the editor then grows a bit cautious, and says that "we have no desire or intention to lambast anyone who cannot adopt our views with reference to the present campaign."

The *Baptist Message,* of Shreveport, La., and the *Baptist and Commoner,* of Benton, Ark., are full of hot stuff against the Pope. The latter gives three and a half pages to a diatribe under the heading of "Is the Catholic Church a Christian Church." The answer is no. The Pope, it appears, is an impostor, for "Christ said He would send the Holy Ghost into the world to direct His work." So are all priests, for Christ "called His ministers preachers and shepherds, never priests." The papal title of pontiff is pagan. The Catholic Church is "a brutal, hell-born power," and its clergy are scoundrels.

> They are always to be found at the bedside of the dying to extort money for the pretense of making prayers, and on hand to extort from the widow every penny possible for the same pretense. To meet them in the street or in the church, they seem to be devout; but when you come to know them you find that they are hypocrites and filled with iniquity.

All of them, it appears, are actively in politics. "Practically all the public offices in our large cities are held by Catholics.... The higher the percentage of Catholics, the higher the crime rate." The *Baptist Message* pursues the subject. "Every Catholic legislator, officeholder and jobholder," it says, "is expected always to remember that he is to hold office or job in the light of the fact that he is a Catholic." As for Al:

> During the Catholic Ecumenical Council, held in Chicago some time ago, while the Pope's official representative, Cardinal Bonzano, was passing through New York City, it is said that the Mayor of New York, who is also a Roman Catholic, and Governor Smith met this foreign churchman at the ship landing, and conducted him, with brass bands and military escort, to the New York City Hall, and there, placing him upon a *throne* erected for him IN THE CITY HALL—he, Governor Alfred Emanuel Smith, Governor of the Sovereign State of New York, in the United States of America, DID PROSTRATE HIMSELF BEFORE and BOWED THE KNEE to this foreign representative of a foreign potentiate, and DID KISS THE RING on the hand of this foreigner, in token of his ABJECT SUBMISSION TO THE AUTHORITY OF THE POPE OF ROME.

The *Baptist Trumpet,* of Killeen, Texas, warns its readers that if Al is elected "the Romish system will institute persecutions again, and put the cruel, blood-stained heel upon all who refuse her authority," and points for proof to Revelation 11, 21, wherein "Rome is called by the name of Jezebel, because Jezebel was a heathenish woman, married to an Israelitish king." The *Christian Index,* of Atlanta, prints a long attack upon the Knights of Columbus by Pastor T. F. Calloway, of Thomasville, Ga., wherein he quotes Priest D. S. Phelan, editor of the *Western Watchman,* as saying on June 27, 1912, that "if the Government of the United States were at war with the church, we would say tomorrow, ' "To hell with the Government of the United States!' "

The *Baptist Progress,* of Dallas, Texas, speaks of Al politely, but is hot against the Knights of Columbus. It says that "they claim that America justly belongs to the Catholic Church because a wise Jew, Columbus, who joined Catholics, discovered America in 1492." It argues that "the devil is behind both Romanism and the liquor traffic." In the *Baptist and Commoner,* previously quoted, Pastor J. A. Scarboro says the same thing, and points to texts in Daniel and Revelation to support him. He goes on furiously:

> The devil's crowd—Catholics, political demagogues, brewers, bootleggers, prostitutes—the whole motley bellygang are for Smith!

In the same paper Elder W. C. Benson rehearses his reasons for voting for Lord Hoover. I quote a few of them:

> To vote for Al Smith would be granting the Pope the right to dictate to this Government what it should do.
> A vote for Al Smith would be the sacrificing of our public schools. Rome says to hell with our public schools.
> To vote for Al Smith would be to say that all Protestants are now living in adultery because they were not married by a priest.
> To vote for Al Smith is to say our offspring are bastards. Are you ready to accept this?

And so on, and so on. I quote only a few specimens. Acres of such stuff are being printed. In some of the papers the Pope gets so much attention that he almost crowds out Prohibition. But most of them still have space to bawl out the wets. The *Wesleyan Christian Advocate,* of Atlanta, for example, denounces Governor Ritchie as one "who is not only wet, but blasphemously so." This may seem exaggerated—until one remembers that Prohibition is now an integral part of the neo-Confederate theology. To be wet down there is to be an infidel, and doomed to hell. Nothing that a wet says is honest, and nothing that a dry does is evil. The *Richmond Christian Advocate,* replying to a charge that Prohibition agents have committed more murders in the South than in the North, says complacently:

> It is a credit to these Southern States that the records show that they are trying to enforce the law, *even at the cost of human life.*

In other words, murder is a lesser crime than bootlegging! I doubt that many Southern pastors would dissent from that.

The Twentieth Amendment: Senate Debate (1932)

The Twentieth Amendment, also known as the "lame duck" amendment, was written mainly to shorten the time that separates the election of a new president and new members of Congress from their inauguration. Until the amendment was enacted, the hiatus for freshman representatives and senators (unless the president called them into special session) was thirteen months—from election day in November until the first Monday in December of the following year, the date originally established by Article I, Section 4, paragraph 2, of the Constitution as the initial meeting day for Congress. The delay for presidents had been approximately four months, from election day until the following March 4. (See "Official Call for the First Presidential Election," p. 60.)

Sen. George W. Norris, a Nebraska Republican and a leader of the Progressive movement, sought to remedy two main flaws in the traditional arrangement, which he regarded as an artifact of the age when travel was difficult and the business of the federal government was relatively minor. The first flaw was the biennial "lame duck" session of Congress, which lasted from the election until the following March and which included many members of the defeated party. Second, four months seemed too long a time for the nation to have, in effect, two presidents—an outgoing incumbent and an incoming president-elect.

To remedy the lame duck and the two-presidents problems, Section 1 of the Twentieth Amendment set noon on January 20 as the beginning of the president's and vice president's four year term and noon on January 3 as the start of the term for representatives and senators. The wisdom of moving up the president's inauguration seemed vindicated when, in the last transition to take place under the old system, a nation gripped by the Great Depression had to endure four months of governmental stalemate after Franklin D. Roosevelt defeated President Herbert Hoover in the 1932 election. (See "Franklin D. Roosevelt's Acceptance Speech to the Democratic National Convention," p. 336.)

Norris also used the Twentieth Amendment as a vehicle to address some other potential problems in the presidential and vice presidential selection process. Section 3 provided that if the president-elect were to die before the start of the term, the vice-president-elect would be inaugurated as president. If, by inauguration day, no presidential candidate had received either the electoral vote majority or the majority of state delegations in the House of Representatives that it takes to be elected, the vice-president-elect would become the acting president un-

til a president was chosen. The same would be true if a president-elect were found to be unqualified under Article II, Section 1, paragraph 5, by virtue of age (less than thirty-five years old), citizenship (not a "natural born Citizen"), or residency (less than "fourteen Years a Resident within the United States").

Section 3 of the Twentieth Amendment also authorized Congress to legislate for the possibility that a vice-president-elect might not be chosen, whether through failure to secure an electoral vote majority or inability to win a Senate election. Congress passed such a law in 1947. (See "Presidential Succession Act: House Debate," p. 420.) The law stipulates that the Speaker of the House is to serve as acting president until either a president or vice president is elected.

The possibility that a winning presidential or vice-presidential candidate might die before officially receiving "elect" status when Congress counts the electoral votes in early January underlay the writing of Section 4 of the Twentieth Amendment. It simply calls upon Congress to legislate for such a contingency. Congress never has done so, however, which means that if such a death were to occur, the legislators would have to improvise.

The Twentieth Amendment passed easily through Congress in early 1932. It was ratified quickly and without controversy by the states and became part of the Constitution on February 6, 1933. ~

The Twentieth Amendment Senate Debate (1932)

The Vice President: The question is upon the motion of the Senator from Tennessee [Mr. McKellar] that the Senate proceed to the consideration of Senate Joint Resolution 14.

Fixing Terms of President, Vice President, and Congress

The motion was agreed to; and the Senate proceeded to consider the joint resolution (S.J. Res. 14) proposing an amendment to the Constitution of the United States fixing the commencement of the terms of President and Vice President and Members of Congress and fixing the time of the assembling of Congress.

Mr. Norris: Mr. President, this joint resolution is in exactly the same form of language in which a similar measure passed the Senate in the last Congress. A like measure has passed the Senate prior to this time five times. On only two occasions was a vote reached in the House of Representatives. Once the vote, while a large majority, was not a two-thirds majority, and the joint resolution failed. In the last Congress it passed the House in a modified form and was sent to conference near the close of the short session of Congress. It died in conference, no agreement having been reached.

I do not care to take up the time of the Senate in explaining the joint resolution further, because I think all of us are perfectly familiar with the provisions. I ask unanimous consent, however, to include at this point, as a part of my remarks, the report of the committee.

The Vice President: Is there objection?

There being no objection, the report was ordered to be printed in the Record, as follows:

[Senate Report No. 26, Seventy-second Congress, first session]
Fixing the Commencement of the Terms of the President and Vice President and Members of Congress

Mr. Norris, from the Committee on the Judiciary, submitted the following report (to accompany S.J. Res. 14):

The Committee on the Judiciary, having had under consideration the joint resolution (S.J. Res. 14) proposing an amendment to the Constitution of the United States fixing the commencement of the terms of President and Vice President and Members of Congress and fixing the time of the assembling of Congress, report the same to the Senate with the recommendation that the same do pass.

This resolution is in exactly the same form as it passed the Senate in the Seventy-first Congress and in practically the same form as it passed the Senate in five preceding Congresses. There is practically unanimous sentiment in the country in favor of this amendment. No logical objection has ever been made to the constitutional changes suggested, and its passage again by the Senate will be only a response to a patriotic sentiment, country wide, for the proposed amendment.

In practically the same form as here reported this resolution passed the Senate the first time on February 13, 1923 (S.J. Res. 253, 67th Cong.). On the 22d day of February, 1923, it received a favorable report from the House committee and was placed on the House Calendar. No action was taken by the House, and it died on the 4th day of March, 1923, because of the adjournment of Congress. It passed the Senate the second time on the 18th day of March, 1924 (S.J. Res. 22, 68th Cong.), and on the 15th day of April, 1924, it was favorably reported by the House committee. It remained on the calendar of the House, without any action being taken thereon, from the 15th day of April, 1924, until the expiration of the Sixty-eighth Congress on the 4th day of March, 1925. It again passed the Senate in the Sixty-ninth Congress (S.J. Res. 9) on February 15, 1926. It was again favorably reported by the House committee on the 24th day of February, 1926, and remained on the House Calendar, without any action thereon, from said date until the expiration of the Sixty-ninth Congress on the 4th day of March, 1927. In the Seventieth Congress the resolution (S.J. Res. 47) passed the Senate on January 4, 1928, and was referred to the House committee, from which it received a favorable report. On March 9, 1928, the House acted on it, and, while it received a large majority of those voting, it failed to receive the two-thirds majority required by the Constitution.

In the Seventy-first Congress, on June 7, 1929, the resolution (S.J. Res.

3), in exactly the same form as it is here reported, passed the Senate. On the next day, June 8, 1929, it was sent to the House of Representatives. However, it was not referred to a committee but remained on the Speaker's table until the 17th day of April, 1930. On that date the Speaker referred the joint resolution to the committee having jurisdiction of the subject matter (Committee on the Election of President, Vice President, and Representatives in Congress). In the meantime, other resolutions similar to this one were introduced by Members of the House of Representatives and referred to this committee for action, and on the 8th day of April, 1930, the committee reported one of these House resolutions (H.J. Res. 292) to the House of Representatives. After this had been done, the Senate resolution was taken from the Speaker's table and referred to the committee. No action was ever taken by the committee on the Senate resolution; but, on the 24th day of February, 1931, the House of Representatives took up the House resolution (H.J. Res. 292) and, by unanimous consent, the Senate resolution (S.J. Res. 3) was taken from the committee and laid before the House, when it was amended by striking out all after the enacting clause and inserting the House resolution, which, in many respects, was practically the same as the Senate resolution. In this form it passed the House of Representatives on the same day, February 24, 1931. Conference committees were at once appointed by the Senate and the House of Representatives, but no agreement was reached and the resolution failed when the Seventy-first Congress ended on the 4th day of March, 1931.

The resolution proposes to amend the Constitution of the United States by fixing the beginning of the terms of President and Vice President at noon on the 15th day of January, and the terms of Senators and Representatives at noon on the 2d day of January following their election in the preceding November. Under existing conditions a new Congress does not actually convene in regular session until a year and one month after its Members have been elected. When our Constitution was adopted there was some reason for such a long intervention of time between the election and the actual commencement of work by the new Congress. We had neither railroads nor telegraphic communication connecting the various States and communities of the country. Under present conditions, however, the result of elections is known all over the country within a few hours after the polls close, and the Capital City is within a few days' travel of the remotest portions of the country.

Originally, Senators were elected by the legislatures, and as a rule the legislatures of the various States did not convene until after the beginning of the new year, and it was difficult and sometimes impossible for Senators to be elected until February or March. Since the adoption of the seventeenth amendment to the Constitution, however, Senators have been elected by the people at the same election at which Members of the House are elected. There is no reason, therefore, why the Congress elected in November should not be sworn in and actually enter upon the duties of office at least as soon as the beginning of the new year following their election.

The only direct opportunity that the citizens of the country have to express their ideas and their wishes in regard to national legislation is the expression of their will through the election of their representatives at the general election in November. During the campaign that precedes this election the great questions demanding attention at the hands of the new Congress are discussed at length before the people and throughout the country, and it is only fair to presume that the Members of Congress chosen at that election fairly represent the ideas of a majority of the people of the country as to what legislation is desirable. In a government "by the people" the wishes of a majority should be crystallized into legislation as soon as possible after these wishes have been made known. These mandates should be obeyed within a reasonable time.

Under existing conditions, however, more than a year elapses before the will of the people expressed at the election can be put into statutory law. This condition of affairs is not only unfair to the citizenship at large, who have expressed their will as to what legislation they desire, but it is likewise unfair to their servants whom they have elected to carry out this will. It is true that it is within the power of the President to call an extraordinary session of Congress at an earlier date than the one provided by

law, but the new Congress can not be called into extraordinary session until after the 4th of March, which would not give the new Congress very much time for the consideration of important national questions before the summer heat in the Capital City makes even existence difficult and good work almost impossible. It is conceded by all that the best time for legislatures to do good work is during the winter months. Practically all the States of the Union recognize this fact and provide for the meeting of their legislatures near the 1st of January. Moreover, the wishes of the country having been expressed at an election should not be dependent for their carrying out upon the will of the President alone. Provision should be made by law so that the new Congress could begin the performance of its important duties as soon after election as possible and under conditions that are most favorable for good work. Under existing conditions a Member of the House of Representatives does not get started in his work until the time has arrived for renominations in his district. He has accomplished nothing and has not had an opportunity to accomplish anything because Congress had not been in session. He has made no record upon which to go before his people for election. It is unfair both to him and to the people of his district. In case of a contest over a seat in the House of Representatives, history has shown that the term of office has practically expired before the House is able to settle the question as to who is entitled to the contested seat. During all this time the occupant of the seat has been drawing the salary, and if it is decided in the end that the occupant was wrongfully seated, then the entire salary must again be paid to the person who has been unjustly deprived of his seat. Double pay is therefore drawn from the Treasury of the United States and the people of the district have not been represented by the Member whom they selected for that purpose. No reason has been given why a new Congress elected at a general election to translate into law the wishes of the people should not be installed into office practically as soon as the results of the election can be determined.

Another effect of the amendment would be to abolish the so-called short session of Congress. If the terms of

Members of Congress begin and end in January instead of on the 4th of March, as heretofore, and Congress convenes in January, there would be no such thing as a short session of Congress. Every other year, under our Constitution, the terms of Members of the House and one-third of the Members of the Senate expire on the 4th day of March. The session begins on the first Monday in December and because of the expiration of such terms it necessarily follows that the session must end not later than the 4th of March. Experience has shown that this brings about a very undesirable legislative condition. It is a physical impossibility during such a short session for Congress to give attention to much general legislation for the reason that it requires practically all of the time to dispose of the regular appropriation bills. The result is a congested calendar both in the House and the Senate. It is known in advance that Congress can give attention to but a very small portion of the bills reported from the committees. The result is a congested condition that brings about either no legislation or illy considered legislation. In the closing days of such a session bad laws get through and good laws are defeated on account of this condition and the want of time to give proper consideration to anything, and the result is dissatisfaction, not only on the part of Members of Congress but on the part of the people generally. Jokers sometimes get on the statutes because Members do not have an opportunity, for the want of time, to give them proper consideration. Mistakes of a serious nature creep into all kinds of statutes which often nullify the real intent of the lawmakers, and the result is disappointment throughout the country. Such a congested condition in the National Legislature can not bring about good results. However diligent and industrious Members of Congress may be, it is a physical impossibility for them to do good work. Moreover, it enables a few Members of Congress to arbitrarily prevent the passage of laws simply by the consumption of time. In every way it brings about an undesirable legislative condition, and it is not surprising that results are so often disappointing.

There is another very important reason why this change should be made. Under the Constitution as it now stands, if it should happen that in the general election in November in presidential years no candidate for President had received a majority of all the electoral votes, the election of a President would then be thrown into the House of Representatives and the membership of that House of Representatives called upon to elect a President would be the old Congress and not the new one just elected by the people. It might easily happen that the Members of the House of Representatives, upon whom devolved the solemn duty of electing a Chief Magistrate for four years, had themselves been repudiated at the election that had just occurred, and the country would be confronted with the fact that a repudiated House, defeated by the people themselves at the general election, would still have the power to elect a President who would be in control of the country for the next four years. It is quite apparent that such a power ought not to exist, and that the people having expressed themselves at the ballot box should through the Representatives then selected, be able to select the President for the ensuing term. If the amendment we have proposed is adopted and becomes a part of the Constitution, such a condition could not happen, and in such a case the new House of Representatives fresh from the people would be the one upon which would devolve the power to select the new President.

Section 3 of the proposed amendment gives Congress the power to provide by law who shall act as President in a case where the election of a President has been thrown into the House of Representatives and the House has failed to elect a President and the Senate has likewise failed to elect a Vice President. The importance of this can be understood when we realize that under the present Constitution if the election of President and Vice President should be thrown into Congress on account of a failure of the Electoral College to elect, and that the House should fail within the time specified in the Constitution to elect a President, and the Senate should likewise fail during such time to elect a Vice President, the country would be left entirely without a Chief Magistrate and without any means of selecting one. This condition has, it is true, never happened in the history of the country, and while it may never happen, it does seem very important that some constitutional provision be enacted by which this most dangerous emergency may be avoided. The present Constitution gives power to Congress to provide who shall act as President when there is a vacancy both in the President's office and the Vice President's office caused by death, removal, or resignation, but there is no provision in the present Constitution that gives to Congress or any other authority the power to select an acting President in cases where the election has been thrown into the House of Representatives and where the House of Representatives has failed to elect a President, and the Senate has likewise failed to elect a Vice President. If such a contingency should occur, and it is liable to occur after any presidential election, the country would find itself in a condition where it would be impossible for a Chief Magistrate to be selected. The committee has corrected this defect by giving to Congress in section 3 of the proposed amendment the authority to select the acting President in such an emergency.

The question is sometimes asked. Why is an amendment to the Constitution necessary to bring about this desirable change? The Constitution does not provide the date when the terms of Senators and Representatives shall begin. It does fix the term of Senators at six years and of Members of the House of Representatives at two years. The commencement of the terms of the first President and Vice President and of Senators and Representatives composing the First Congress was fixed by an act of Congress adopted September 13, 1788, and that act provided "that the first Wednesday in March next be the time for commencing proceedings under the Constitution." It happened that the first Wednesday in March was the 4th day of March, and hence the terms of the President and Vice President and Members of Congress begin on the 4th day of March. Since the Constitution provides that the term of Senators shall be six years and the term of Members of the House of Representatives two years, it follows that this change can not be made without changing the terms of office of Senators and Representatives, which would in effect be a change of the Constitution. By another act (the act of March 1, 1792) Congress provided that the terms of President and Vice Presi-

dent should commence on the 4th day of March after their election. It seems clear, therefore, that an amendment to the Constitution is necessary to give relief from existing conditions.

Mr. Walsh of Montana: Mr. President, I want to call the attention of the Senator to two verbal matters. In line 6, section 2, occurs the word "begin." It reads:

> The Congress shall assemble at least once a year, and such meeting shall begin at noon.

I observe that in the original Constitution the word is "be" and not "begin"; that "such meeting shall be," and so forth.

Mr. Norris: Mr. President, in the original Constitution there is no hour fixed. It merely fixes the day of the month. This fixes the hour, and it seems to me the word "begin" is proper. That is the form in which we have always passed the joint resolution.

Mr. Walsh of Montana: I could not see any reason at all for the change, because it does not make any difference whether we fix a definite hour or a definite day.

Mr. Norris: My own idea is that the word "begin" is more appropriate than "be." If it was to be a meeting which would exist for a moment and pass away, "be" would probably be the most appropriate word, but the session is to run possibly for some time, and this fixes the time of its beginning.

Mr. Walsh of Montana: Let me call the attention of the Senator to the fact that the sentence begins "The Congress shall assemble at least once in every year, and such meeting"—that is, the assembling, the coming together—"shall be at noon on the 2d day of January." That is the sense of the sentence, and it occurs to me the language in the original Constitution is more appropriate.

Mr. Norris: Mr. President, in my opinion it does not change the meaning at all, but it seems to me the meeting referred to is the session. It is going to be a session. First, they shall assemble, and the word "begin," it seems to me, when we are to fix a definite time, is more appropriate than to say, "The session shall be."

Mr. Walsh of Montana: The suggestion is not of such importance as to be debated. The sense is sufficiently apparent. I merely thought the Senator would like to follow the language of the original Constitution.

Let me pass on to another matter: Should not the word "they," the second word in line 11, be "it"?

Mr. Norris: That is another instance where we are just reversed. There we follow the Constitution, and the Senator's suggestion would not follow the Constitution.

Mr. Walsh of Montana: The Senator is quite wrong about that. The Constitution uses the word "they" always when it refers to the United States, but the word "they" is not used in this connection.

Mr. Norris: Mr. President, I am satisfied that this is a direct quotation from the Constitution of the United States. But let me say to the Senator that the senior Senator from Connecticut [Mr. Bingham] is to make some remarks on the joint resolution, and if it is agreeable to the Senator from Montana, we will look this matter up while that Senator is proceeding.

Mr. Bingham: Mr. President, I hope the constitutional lawyers will have opportunity to settle this matter before we have to vote on it. I propose to offer an amendment, which I think everyone will remember was offered in the House of Representatives by the late Speaker, Mr. Longworth, who was a friend of all of us, revered by the House on both sides of the aisle.

At the time when this matter was considered by the House of Representatives, Speaker Longworth offered an amendment to it, and he broke his

almost universal practice by coming down on the floor and making a speech in favor of that amendment. The amendment is one which appeals very strongly to me and appeals to some of those who have generally supported the amendment to the Constitution which was offered by the Senator from Nebraska in repeated Congresses.

In order that those who are doing me the honor of listening to me may understand just what the amendment is, I will offer it and read it from the Congressional Record. It was offered on February 24, 1931. The gentleman from Ohio [Mr. Longworth] offered the amendment, to strike out all of section 2. If Senators will turn to their copy of the pending joint resolution, they will find that section 2 relates to the fact that Congress shall assemble at least once in every year and that such meeting shall be on the 4th day of January unless they by law appoint a different day. In other words it permits a permanent session of the Congress. It would meet every year on the 4th of January and apparently continue until the Members get tired or the next session begins.

Speaker Longworth offered this amendment, to strike out all of section 2 and insert in lieu thereof the following:

> Sec. 2. The Congress shall assemble at least once in every year. In each odd-numbered year—

In other words, the year following the presidential election—

> such meeting shall be on the 4th day of January unless they shall by law appoint a different day. In each even-numbered year—

In other words, the year in which the election is held—

> such meeting shall be on the 4th day of January, and the session shall not continue after noon on the 4th day of May.

In other words, instead of adjourning on the 4th of March, the Congress would continue for two months longer, until the 4th of May, when, as I think we will all appreciate, many Members of the House of Representatives and some Members of the Senate would like to go home and start work on their primaries, or on the election to follow a few months later.

With the indulgence of the Senate I should like to read what the distinguished Speaker said on that occasion. His remarks are not very long, being only one column of the Congressional Record. His speech is so much better than anything I could say on this matter, I am sure, that as one of the few speeches Mr. Longworth made after he became Speaker, and the last important speech he made, it will be interesting to many Senators. I read:

Mr. Longworth: Mr. Chairman, as you all know, I infrequently take the floor during the consideration of a bill or offer an amendment to a bill, but this is such an extremely important and vital matter that I think it is not only a privilege but a duty to offer this amendment.

I do not intend to debate the merits or demerits of this resolution. I desire, however, to call your attention to what, to my mind, is the fundamental objection to it in its present form. Under this resolution, as is obvious, it will be entirely possible for Congress to be in session perpetually from the time it convenes. There is no provision in the resolution for a termination either of the first session, or particularly of the second session. It seems to me obvious that great and serious danger might follow a perpetual two years' session of the Congress.

I am not one of those who says the country is better off when Congress goes home. I do not think no, but I do think that the Congress and the Country ought to have a breathing space at least once every two years.

The effect of this amendment is simply to provide that the second session of the Congress shall terminate upon the 4th day of May in the even-numbered years. That is a fair proposition. It will give at least one month more for the consideration of legislation in the sec-

ond session than is given now. There will be a clear four months' period between the assembling of the Congress in the second session and its adjournment. Can there be any real reason for opposition to a proposal which will give the Congress four months during the second session and then having May, June, July, August, September, and October clear? Those are the years when we all come up for election. Those are the years—every four years—in which national conventions are held. It is not wise that Congress should be in session during the holding of national conventions. It is wise that men should have time in which to canvass their districts and prepare for election.

The history of this matter, in so far as I have been concerned with it, is this: Something over three years ago, just before this resolution came up in the House, I was invited by perhaps the strongest organized body of intellectuals in the country, the American Bar Association, to give my views on this matter. I gave my views and stated, as I state now, that with the adoption of this amendment, providing for the termination of the second session, all my objections to this resolution would be withdrawn. The committee of the Bar Association with which I conferred adopted my views. Having indorsed the resolution previously, they withdrew that indorsement and unanimously indorsed the resolution with the inclusion of a provision such as I am now offering.

It seems to me that from every point of view this amendment ought to be adopted. I will do anything I can to help the passage of this resolution provided this amendment is adopted. This afternoon I propose to even go farther than that. In the interest of the speedy passage of this resolution, with this amendment, I will recognize a request that the Senate resolution, as amended by the House resolution, be considered in lieu of the House resolution. That will offer an opportunity to immediately send the bill to conference, and, under all the circumstances, is, I think, a proper courtesy to the Senate.

In reply to a question from Mr. Montague as to whether the amendment would interfere with the President calling an extra session, Mr. Longworth replied:

Not at all. This is precisely the provision that was in the original resolution three years ago. In case of any emergency the President may call the Congress to meet on the 4th day of May and continue the session long enough to satisfy the emergency. The amendment would have no effect in that direction.

Gentlemen, I sincerely hope this amendment may be adopted.

It was a matter of record that when the amendment was put to a vote in the House a division was taken and there were 193 ayes and 125 noes.

Mr. President, in the report made by the Judiciary Committee I find the record of the number of times the joint resolution has passed and a statement that by unanimous consent the Senate joint resolution in the last Congress was laid before the House, when it was amended by striking out all after the enacting clause and inserting the House resolution, which, in many respects, was practically the same as the Senate resolution. In this form it passed the House of Representatives.

In view of the fact that it was in so many respects the same as the Senate joint resolution I hope that the distinguished chairman of the Judiciary Committee and the author of the amendment will be willing to adopt the amendment originally proposed by former Speaker Longworth and which I now offer as an amendment to the pending joint resolution.

Mr. Dill: Mr. President—

The Presiding Officer (Mr. La Follette in the chair): Does the Senator from Connecticut yield to the Senator from Washington?

Mr. Bingham: I yield.

Mr. Dill: I am in much sympathy with the purpose of the amendment of the Senator, but I want to ask the Senator whether he does not think a later date than that in the main resolution would be better? Does he not think it would be better to make the date June 15?

Mr. Bingham: Of course the Senator from Washington would not ask that if he were a member of the Republican Party, because the Republican Party meets in national convention on June 14 and not the 15th.

Mr. Dill: That happens to be so this year.

Mr. Bingham: If the Senator will support the amendment, I shall be glad to change it to June 2.

Mr. Dill: I shall do so. I may say to the Senator that it was my understanding that the House conferees that year were willing to advance the date to a later date. I think there is much to be said for the amendment if the date is made a later one.

Mr. Bingham: Would the Senator be willing to vote for it if the date is made June 2?

Mr. Dill: I certainly will.

Mr. Bingham: Then I ask permission to change the date and make it June 2.

Mr. Barkley: Mr. President, how many changes in the date will the Senator offer in order to get votes for his amendment?

Mr. Bingham: I have stated that the Republican national convention is to be held on the 14th of June, and it is not possible to postpone it. The Democrats, as the Senator well knows, meet at a later date.

Mr. Barkley: If this is merely a matter of barter and trade and the Senator is willing to put off for a month the final adjournment date in return for a vote, I wonder how much longer he would be willing to put it off for another vote?

Mr. Bingham: June 14 is a date which concerns quite a number of us.

Mr. Barkley: I think, so far as the country is concerned, that is going to be a very ineffective date, anyway; but be that as it may, does not that still leave with us the same proposition that always faces us in the short session of Congress, whose termination is fixed by

the Constitution, when we are required
to adjourn whether we have finished the
business of Congress or not? Does it not
quite emphasize the conviction that one
session of Congress is less important
than another? That is one of the vicious
things, it seems to me, which has surrounded our whole legislative situation.
We have had three months in which we
were required to perform the duties of a
whole session, and if we could not perform them by the 4th of March, we had
to adjourn anyway.

In his amendment the Senator makes
it the 4th day of May, and he makes the
assembling of Congress one month later
so as to add only one month to the short
session. I do not think there is any more
wisdom in limiting one session of Congress than in limiting both sessions.
Congress ought to be amenable to the
people and responsive to their needs
and will. I am not one of those who
believe that the so-called short session
is of any less importance than the so-
called long session. One of them may be
as important as the other. It may frequently happen, as it has in the past,
that the short session is more important
than the long session, depending on the
questions which confront the people
and the Congress.

Mr. Smith: Mr. President, the Senator from Kentucky [Mr. Barkley] says
this is only one month longer for the
proposed short session than at present.
It is two months longer.

Mr. Barkley: Oh, no.

Mr. Smith: If we meet on the 4th of
January, then we will have January,
February, March, and April, which is
four months; whereas under the present
order of things we can practically discard December because the holidays
intervene, and so we really have only
two months of the short session. We
would have practically four months of
unbroken session under the proposal of
the Senator from Connecticut.

Mr. Barkley: That is true, in a
sense; but I think in an important mat-

ter like amending the Constitution of
the United States we ought not to take
into account holidays or political conventions or primary elections. We ought
to take into consideration the wisdom of
an amendment to our fundamental law
without regard to political conventions.

Mr. Smith: Does not the Senator
consider certain elections sometimes are
more important than a session of
Congress?

Mr. Barkley: In the minds of some
people, especially candidates for office,
that is no doubt true.

Mr. Smith: I am talking about parties. I am not talking about candidates
for office.

Mr. Barkley: In the minds of the
American people I doubt very much
whether they consider the election of
any particular person to any particular
office more important than a full session of Congress.

Mr. Smith: I am sorry the Senator
did not get the significance of the very
brilliant remark I made.

Mr. Barkley: That is due to my
own dullness and not to the Senator.

Mr. Smith: The point I was making
was that there comes a time when a
change of parties is more important
than a session of Congress. The Senator
from Connecticut [Mr. Bingham], I
think, made a very appealing and sensible suggestion.

Mr. Barkley: I am glad to hear the
Senator say that. It is such a rare thing
that it ought to be acknowleged.

Mr. Smith: Does the Senator mean
it is rare in this body that anyone
should have these accomplishments?

Mr. Barkley: Yes.

Mr. Smith: Be that as it may, I
think that the Senator from Connecticut has just about the right idea about
the situation. Four months of unbroken
consideration of legislative matters,
coupled with an interminable session
preceding it, seems to me to be the
proper thing to have. I appreciate that
under our present conditions. I never

have been able to understand how our forefathers fixed a session just antedating the holidays.

Mr. Barkley: It was purely accidental. They did not fix it.

Mr. Smith: No matter how it came about, it was so fixed, and it means that all of December and practically the first week in January are lost. We can eliminate that period of time. But under the proposition of the late Speaker of the House to give us each two years four months of unbroken consideration of legislation seems to me to be a very proper thing to do.

Mr. Barkley: Mr. President, will the Senator yield for a question?

The Presiding Officer: Does the Senator from South Carolina yield further to the Senator from Kentucky?

Mr. Smith: I yield.

Mr. Barkley: Does the Senator think that this particular Congress is better qualified to fix an arbitrary date for the adjournment of every other session of Congress for 100 years than the Members of a future Congress will be at the time it is in session, confronted as it will be by the problems which will then be before it for consideration?

Mr. Smith: I think even under the cumbersome system we have now we have done fairly well. I do not know of any great harm that has befallen the country by virtue of any of our delays. I think we ought to have one year during a given term of Members of Congress with a statutory limitation for the final adjournment of Congress. I think we are just as competent to fix it as any subsequent Congress may be to determine adventitiously whether to adjourn or to keep on working. The Senator knows that it means, if we do not put a limitation somewhere within a given Congress, that we would never adjourn. He knows that to be true.

Mr. Barkley: No; I do not know that. On the contrary, the history of our whole legislative program for 100 years, and especially since the war and at any

other time except when there is a great emergency on, shows that Congress is just as anxious to adjourn one year as it is another. We have adjourned here in May when we could have remained in session until December. We have adjourned in June when we could have remained in session until December. Congress can be depended upon, I think, each year to adjourn whenever it has concluded its business; but I do not believe there ought to be a stop watch placed upon a session of Congress, not only because we may not finish the business before us but because at an arbitrary date, when we are compelled to adjourn regardless of the state of the business, any Member of this body, as we all know, can use that fact for the purpose of filibustering against legislation that ought to be enacted. We have to go no further back than last March when it was impossible for us to enact legislation needed in the country, because it was possible for one man to hold the floor until noon on the 4th day of March and that we could not transact any business as long as that situation existed. That would be true in April or in May or in June or July, or in any other month, if an arbitrary date were fixed in the amendment for the final adjournment of a session of Congress.

Mr. Smith: But the Senator has had too much experience in life to know that we can legislate for exceptions. That was an exception.

Mr. Barkley: No; it was not an exception. It has been the rule, at least in the last two years.

Mr. Smith: I have been here a long time—

Mr. Barkley: I hope the Senator will remain much longer.

Mr. Smith: I do not recall any occasion except that, and I do not know that any very great harm was done even by the incident to which the Senator refers. However, I do not believe that it is wise for us, especially in years when there is a national political campaign, to have any Member of Congress who is up for reelection handicapped by his duty here or perhaps handicapped by his duty at home.

Mr. Barkley: Some of us could be reelected more readily by staying here than we could by leaving here and mixing with the people frequently.

Mr. Smith: That is only another exception that proves the rule.

Mr. Barkley: Of course, I had no application to the Senator from South Carolina.

Mr. Smith: Perhaps the Senator is thinking of his own case.

Mr. Barkley: I agree with the Senator from South Carolina that "charity begins at home."

Mr. George: Mr. President—

The Presiding Officer: Does the Senator from South Carolina yield to the Senator from Georgia?

Mr. Smith: I yield.

Mr. George: I merely want to make this suggestion: It is not, of course, a reason why the Constitution should be amended, but it is a practical matter that ought to be taken into consideration.

From time to time the question has arisen whether we would adopt a more stringent cloture rule of procedure in this body; from time to time we have had the threat of cloture; from time to time we have resisted it; and it seemed to be wise, in the judgment of the Senate, not to put a limitation upon debate in this body, especially upon those great questions as to which it seemed wise to the Senate to deliberate. Whenever any date is fixed by the Constitution for the adjournment of the Congress, it necessarily makes possible a filibuster; it invites it. Necessarily, therefore, it makes possible the continued agitation for stringent rules against filibustering, such rules as would restrict the freedom of speech and the freedom of debate in this body.

While the question I am now bringing to the Senator's attention is not funda-

mental, when we consider the responsible duty of amending the Federal Constitution, nevertheless it is pertinent. It would be very much wiser, it seems to me, if we should place no limitation upon any session of Congress, and should leave the matter within the discretion of the sitting Congress. I think we are justified in reposing confidence in future Congresses, and I am quite sure that the Senator from South Carolina [Mr. Smith] would not be willing to limit or restrict debate in this body; but if we have the recurrence of filibustering here that he has observed during his term in the Senate, I am quite sure that ultimately we will have what we, now at least, agree are improper and undesirable restrictions upon debate.

There is no occasion for restriction upon debate if the definite date for the termination of the Congress shall not be fixed; but if that shall be done, the question of the restriction of debate will arise from time to time and ultimately we shall have limitation upon debate that ought not to be placed upon it.

Mr. Smith: Mr. President, the Senator from Georgia is thoroughly aware of the fact that as to any proposal which is so distasteful to a group that they will enter into a determined filibuster, the probability of such a filibuster is scarcely enhanced by virtue of the imminence of the day of adjournment. Talking about putting restriction on debate, I desire to suggest that some of the most determined filibusters we have had in this body were not undertaken when the date of adjournment was imminent. We have modified the rules so that, while not arbitrarily cutting off debate, that object could be accomplished by the petition of a certain number of Senators.

Mr. George and Mr. Barkley addressed the Chair.

The President pro tempore: Does the Senator from South Carolina yield; and if so, to whom?

Mr. Smith: I yield to the Senator from Georgia.

Mr. George: The Senator from South Carolina is quite right about that; but the point is that when a definite date is fixed for adjournment a filibuster against relatively unimportant and trivial matters, over measures, let us say, that arise out of prejudice, more or less, may block all other legislation between the time when the filibuster begins and the absolute fixed date for adjournment. That sort of abuse would ultimately persuade the Senate to modify its rules under which freedom of debate is now indulged.

Mr. Smith: Mr. President, every Member of this body knows that we have postponed important legislation for one reason or another until the very last hours of the short session of Congress, and in those last hours we have had once or twice a filibuster that jeopardized proper legislation.

I maintain that under the amendment proposed by the Senator form Connecticut [Mr. Bingham], with anything like diligence, we could in the untrammeled four months enact the necessary legislation; and I do not see why as to one session of a Congress there might not be a limitation placed on its duration.

Mr. Bingham and Mr. Barkley addressed the Chair.

The President pro tempore: Does the Senator from South Carolina yield; and if so, to whom?

Mr. Smith: I yield first to the Senator from Kentucky.

Mr. Barkley: I desire merely to make this further suggestion emphasizing what the Senator from Georgia [Mr. George] has said: While, as the Senator from South Carolina has stated, it is possible at any stage of any session for one Member or a small group to organize a filibuster, the chance of its success or of effective damage being done by it is not nearly so great in the beginning or the middle of a long ses-

sion as at the end of a short session, when Congress has got to quit on a certain day at a certain hour, regardless of the circumstances. The success of obstructive methods in the Senate, by and large, depends upon whether we are compelled to adjourn on a day certain, so that Senators may hold the floor and prevent action on other measures, regardless of the situation.

Mr. Smith: The Senator from Kentucky knows that we have certain supply bills, certain appropriation bills, that are of vast importance; and we are compelled, under the present order of things, to dispose of them between January and March 4. We have merely that short time in which to act upon them. Under the proposition of the late Speaker of the House of Representatives, as presented now by the Senator from Connecticut, by continuing in session from the 4th of January to the 4th of May we should have four months—and a month longer even if we should use December, which we do not now use—in which to pass the important bills and discharge our duty.

Mr. Bingham: May I say to the Senator that in accordance with the suggestion of the Senator from Washington [Mr. Dill] I have indicated a willingness to add one month more, making it five months in all, and extending the time to the 4th of June?

Mr. Borah and Mr. Dill addressed the Chair.

The Presiding Officer (Mr. La Follette in the chair): Does the Senator from South Carolina yield; and if so, to whom?

Mr. Smith: I have stated my position. I am through, unless the Senator desires to ask me a question.

Mr. Borah: Mr. President, this is the proposition which was submitted to the conferees when the joint resolution was before them at the last session. The conferees upon the part of the Senate were unable to agree to this amendment. It seemed to those representing the Senate that it did not obviate one of the great evils which flows from fixing a day certain upon which adjournment must be taken. Against that day all the forces which want to defeat legislation can play. Notwithstanding the length of time a session may last, important—in fact, the most important—legislation may come up, as we know it often does, right at the close or before the close of a session, and any Senators or any combination of Senators desiring to prevent legislation have that day certain against which to play for time. The fixing of a day certain for adjournment is the father of filibusters in the Senate, and as we know, the occasion for a filibuster may arise upon the first day of June just as much as it may arise on the first day of March. So by fixing a date in June we would not be obviating the great evil of a fixed day for adjournment.

Mr. Dill: Mr. President—

The Presiding Officer: Does the Senator from Idaho yield to the Senator from Washington?

Mr. Borah: I yield.

Mr. Dill: Does not the fact the Senator just mentioned, namely, that it is the day certain against which everything runs, involve a consideration that Senators have not thought about, namely, that if we do not fix a day certain on which to adjourn final adjournment will be almost indefinite, because there will always be many Senators and Members of the House of Representatives who want bills passed, and they will vote against final adjournment? At present, when there is no day fixed for adjournment of the long session every other year, another session of the same Congress convenes the following December, and Senators and Members of the House have an opportunity to procure consideration of their bills during that session; but if we should provide no fixed date for the adjournment of the second session Senators

and Members of the House will be disposed to keep the Congress here.

Mr. Borah: The Senator from Washington, an experienced legislator, knows that there is never any difficulty in securing final adjournment of Congress.

Mr. Dill: I do not want to be understood as agreeing to that, because there has never been an occasion in the history of Congress when we did not have another session at which we could bring up our bills.

Mr. Fess: Mr. President—

The Vice President: Does the Senator from Idaho yield to the Senator from Ohio?

Mr. Borah: I yield.

Mr. Fess: I think there is a great deal of force in what the Senator says about fixing a time in the Constitution. It does make possible filibusters. There is the possibility of filibustering, though, without it, because we always decide by resolution at what time we will adjourn, and, of course, we can hold such a resolution off until the very last.

Mr. Borah: We decide, but we very rarely decide until the business of the session has practically been completed or it is certain that it will be completed. We do not adopt resolutions providing for a final adjournment when there is any business still pending and undisposed of; and resolutions fixing a time certain for the two Houses to adjourn almost inevitably, so far as I know, follow the disposition of important business, because otherwise there would be serious objection to considering such a resolution. The more the Senator thinks about this matter the more readily will he see that the desire to get rid of the filibuster is entirely made futile if we fix a date certain for adjournment.

Mr. Fess: I admit that; that is obvious.

Mr. Borah: But if the time for adjournment is within the discretion of the Congress, Congress can always exercise its judgment as to when it shall adjourn and, therefore, can always control the question of whether or not a particular time shall be fixed.

Mr. Robinson of Arkansas: Mr. President, will the Senator yield for a question?

Mr. Borah: I yield.

Mr. Robinson of Arkansas: If the Senate desires to rid itself of the possibility of filibuster, it can easily accomplish that end by changing its rules. The fact that the filibuster has persisted in spite of prolonged and repeated efforts to modify the rules so as to enable a Senator to force the previous question or pursue some similar method of closing debate argues conclusively that the Senate is not ready to abandon the filibuster in extreme cases. In other words, we have preserved the filibuster and we will not eliminate the filibuster by adopting the constitutional amendment proposed by the Senator from Nebraska; we will still preserve it. If we want to get rid of the filibuster, we can do it by simply providing for changes in our rules that will make impossible the carrying on of such process.

Mr. Borah: It is practically impossible to adopt a rule which operates speedily enough to shut off a filibuster which may be organized in the last 48 hours of the session if there is a time fixed for final adjournment. The Senator has seen it happen here, and so have I, that a filibuster begins the night before the time fixed for adjournment. We have seen that happen three or four times, and it is practically impossible to get a rule to operate sufficiently speedily to prevent that kind of filibuster if there is a time certain fixed for adjournment.

Mr. Robinson of Arkansas: I do not agree to that. If the Senate adopted the rule of the House of Representatives, or of other legislative bodies, it could easily conclude debate at any time; it could limit debate; it could provide for such

limitation on debate as to enable a Senator to take the floor at any time within a few hours of adjournment and move the previous question. Its rules could provide for a vote without further debate and thus conclude a question even during the very expiring hours of a session.

I took the floor merely to point out the fact that there is something strange about an effort to justify an amendment to the Constitution to end filibusters when the filibuster exists only by virtue of the rules that we ourselves have established and perpetuated.

Mr. Borah: I do not desire to see any such rule as the Senator indicates adopted by this body; I would rather suffer the evils of the present provision of the Constitution. If the amendment to the Constitution fixing a day certain would superimpose upon us that kind of a rule I would much prefer to see the matter stand as it is. Only by the most rigid exacting rules, such as moving the previous question and other rules which would destroy the Senate as a deliberative body, could we preclude the possibility of a filibuster. I would not for one moment adopt any such rules if my vote were necessary to do so.

Mr. Fess: Mr. President, will the Senator yield?

Mr. Borah: Yes.

Mr. Fess: Would the Senator resist a rule that, say, during the last six days of the session no Senator shall speak more than once nor more than 30 minutes upon any question?

Mr. Borah: I should want to reserve my discretion on a question of that kind.

Mr. Fess: That would end filibusters.

Mr. Barkley: Mr. President—

Mr. Borah: I yield to the Senator from Kentucky.

Mr. Barkley: I should like to ask for the Senator's comment on this suggestion: If there is any virtue in limiting, by statute or by constitutional provision, the length of the second session of any Congress in order to protect the country against unwise legislation, why deny them the boon of the same sort of protection at the first session? If the Congress can not be trusted to act with discretion and judgment and wisdom in the second session, by what sort of a miracle can we impute to them patriotism and wisdom as that they can do it in the first session without inflicting irreparable damage upon the country?

Mr. Borah: I agree with the Senator.

Mr. Norris: Mr. President, the Senator from Connecticut [Mr. Bingham] offers the amendment that was offered by the late Speaker of the House of Representatives. I do not care to comment on the Speaker's speech, which has been read here, because, under existing circumstances, I think it probably would not be right to get the ideas or the opinions of a man who is no longer living mixed up in this debate.

In a general way let me say that this proposition comes from the enemies of the joint resolution, the enemies of the amendment, men who have opposed it during most of the time it has been pending before the people of the United States. It is offered here by the Senator from Connecticut [Mr. Bingham], a man who has always opposed this joint resolution, who has always fought it.

I doubt whether I would be justified in telling the Senate what the impression made upon the conferees on the part of the Senate was at the time this matter was in conference; but the Senator from Montana [Mr. Walsh] is here, and the Senator from Idaho [Mr. Borah] sits here at my right. They know the controversy that went on there; and this proposal did not come to us until the very closing hours of the session, just a few days before we were compelled to adjourn on the 4th day of March. We met regularly every day in that conference committee; and I think we were all impressed with the real

thing that was behind this amendment—no compromise; nothing was possible, and we adjourned hopelessly divided.

Now, what is the proposition? It is for us to provide in the Constitution that no future Congress will be wise enough to know when to adjourn its second session. We are going to say here that a Congress that meets 40 years from now must adjourn on a particular day. Do we know enough to know when to quit? Maybe we ought to quit sometimes when we do not, but sometimes we have to quit when we ought not to be compelled to quit.

What is the objection to letting Congress determine when it shall adjourn? Then, too, as the Senator from Kentucky [Mr. Barkley] well said, you who are advocating this motion permit Congress in the first session to adjourn when it sees fit. Why not stop them then when they get up to a certain date in the calendar?

If you are going to limit a session, Senators, then you ought to limit the first session and not the last one. The last one is the more important of the two. If you want to limit a session, let me repeat, limit the first one and not the last one, because when the first one is limited you know that in that Congress there is still another session; but if you limit the second one, as far as that Congress is concerned, the last hope disappears and is gone.

I concede what the Senator from Arkansas [Mr. Robinson] says, that we could change the rules and stop all debate. By rule we could say that we could pass a bill before it is printed, as we have been asked to do to-day. We have an illustration of it right before us now in the proposal to take up Senate bill No. 1, when even the committee that was considering the amendments did not have them printed before it. The committee print is brought in here before the bill is printed for the use of the Senate, and one Senator after another is told that with the terrible condition just ahead of us, with everything going to the bowwows, we ought to pass the bill to-day.

Suppose you adopt this amendment and fix the 4th day of June as the day when you have to adjourn, and you have a President in the White House like we have now who sends a message up here on the 3d day of June, saying, "The country is going to be disrupted 12 hours from now unless you pass this legislation that I send up here," and we all tumble over each other to pass it, and we wake up the next day to find that we have all been "gypped" and fooled and nobody understood what they were doing, and you give it no consideration. If that happens in the first session, if that is limited, you can remedy it at the next session; but you can not remedy it if it happens in the second session. The Congress is ended, and unless the President should call you in session you have no way to reassemble.

We do not have any trouble about adjourning in the long session, where it is not limited. We always have some controversy over it, it is true. Some Members want to adjourn and some do not; but the majority determine the matter, and as a rule we adjourn early in June, sometimes in May. Sometimes, in case we have a tariff bill or some other very important legislation, we run through the summer months, or we take a recess sand convene again. If you put this limitation on the second session, you can not do that, and you may want to do it. It may be that the very life of the country will be at stake at a time when you want to do it, but unless you have a President who will call you back you can not do it. We may be in the midst of a war, and the Congress may be in controversy with the White House; but when the gavel falls, even if you adopt this amendment, out you go, and there is no way for you to reassemble.

Why put that burden upon Congresses whose Members have not yet been born? Why not give them credit for having some sense? Let them decide when they will adjourn, as we decide in the long session now.

I want to tell you, Mr. President, that no filibuster ever made much headway unless it was in a session of Congress where the date of adjournment was definitely fixed by law; and it does not have to occur right before the 4th of March, either. It may happen in January or December, because every Senator and every Member of the House knows that every hour of the short session that is taken up, whether it is in December, January, February, or March means that there is so much less time before the 4th of March; and if you start a filibuster in December its effect may be felt next March, when you come to the time to adjourn.

There is not any way to prevent things of that kind unless you let that Congress determine for itself when it shall adjourn, and that is a simple matter. Practically, with the exception of the short session, of course, we have always had that right. There may be a time in the history of the country, that may come next year or the year after that or 40 years from now, when to save its life Congress would not dare to adjourn when the exigencies of the occasion would demand that they be in session. Let us not cripple those Congresses now by putting manacles upon their hands and upon their feet.

We can not foresee what is in the future; and therefore it seems to me we ought to let future Congresses have the right that we have had, to fix their own date of adjournment.

Mr. Fess: Mr. President, will the Senator yield?

Mr. Norris: Yes.

Mr. Fess: The Senator knows that I have always supported this joint resolution whenever it came up.

Mr. Norris: Yes, sir.

Mr. Fess: But I have some sympathy with the suggestion of making a limit to one of the sessions, if it is not too short. I thought five months probably would be better than to make it unlimited. Has the Senator made any investigation as to why the States have limited the tenure of their legislatures? Our State does, and a great number of States do.

Mr. Norris: Yes; a great many States do, and I will say to my friend from Ohio that I would not have any particular objection to it in a State. The Congress of the United States, however, may have in its hands the very salvation and life of the country, as it has had in the past many times; and to say that at such a time we shall be compelled by the Constitution of the United States to adjourn, it seems to me, might turn out to be almost national suicide.

Mr. Fess: Mr. President, will the Senator yield to a question?

Mr. Norris: Yes.

Mr. Fess: I assume that the object in fixing the second day of January rather than the first Monday in January was to avoid the possibility of meeting on New Year's Day.

Mr. Norris: Let me say to the Senator that in the various forms which this joint resolution has gone through since it was introduced, a great many years ago, there have been some changes in the dates. As I introduced the joint resolution originally, I think it provided for the first Monday, or the first Tuesday after the first Monday, something of that kind, to avoid Congress meeting on the Sabbath day, as it will occasionally. The House committee at various times took it up, and while the joint resolution never got through the House in that form I had a great many informal discussions with Members of the House about this matter, and they were objecting to fixing a day of the week, and wanted to have a particular date named. Afterward we changed it here, and the last two or three times we

passed it, I think, we have had a definite date.

It is true that there would come times when we would have to convene on Sunday; but it is true now that we are in session on Sunday every time the 4th of March comes on Sunday. That is a common thing; and, as far as I know, it has not interfered particularly with the Congress, nor has it affected anyone's conscientious convictions, so far as I know. Personally I would a little rather it would not be on the Sabbath day, but I think it is better to have a definite day.

For instance, the Constitution says the term of a Senator shall be six years. You would have to have Congress convene on a different date from the time he actually took office in order to have him serve exactly six years. You avoid all that by fixing a definite date.

I will say to the Senator, however, that the exact date, and whether it shall be a week day or a day of the month, are, of course, matters that do not go to the fundamental principles involved in the legislation; but this amendment does, in my judgment. So I am surprised that Senators of long experience should want, by a definite constitutional arrangement, to fix a positive date when Congress must cease work.

I say to Senators that they do not realize what that might mean. In my judgment, there is no occasion for it. I think we are competent to fix a definite date for final adjournment, as well as to fix a date to adjourn over the holidays.

Mr. Dill: Mr. President, all the Congresses which have ever assembled have been under the compulsion referred to. They have been compelled to terminate their short sessions on the 4th of March, and the country has not suffered greatly by that, as I see it.

Mr. Norris: The country has suffered a good many times, in my judgment. I have seen legislation defeated by a filibuster which nearly everybody wanted to see passed. I have seen much other legislation passed without due consideration, because everybody had something else he wanted to get through, and little time could be taken in analyzing a bill, in going through it, in debating it and discussing it, and asking questions about it; every moment was precious, and Senators would let an elephant go through in order to have enacted before the gavel fell at noon on the 4th day of March something they felt to be vital. It has meant injury to the country.

There are other changes in the Constitution of which I might speak, in answering the Senator's question as to whether we have not lived so long and nothing has hurt us. That may be true, but we do not know what is going to happen in the future. We can not tell.

I implore Senators to think of this deeply before they vote in favor of a proposition which, in my judgment, has no merit, and, secondly, has been an instrumentality of the enemies of this kind of legislation from the beginning.

Mr. Barkley: Mr. President, will the Senator yield?

Mr. Norris: I yield.

Mr. Barkley: How can anyone tell with any degree of certainty that the country has not been damaged or injured because we have been living a century and a half under a system which we are now trying to change? How can anybody say how much better off the country would have been if the conditions had been different, if we had not been required to adjourn every other year on the 4th of March?

Mr. Norris: Of course.

Mr. Barkley: How can anybody be dogmatic about it?

Mr. Norris: I do not think anybody can be, I will say to the Senator. But in addition to that, in the early history of this country the importance of this kind of an amendment would not have been observed. There was a very small House of Representatives, a small Senate, and a small country, and the legislators had all the time they needed. But the country has been growing by leaps and bounds. Everybody knows now that it is impossible for us to complete the business of a session before the 4th of March. Even if the time should be extended a few months, there would probably come a time when we could not transact all the business of a session within the limits then in force, and there would have to be another change. Let Senators answer the question if they can. Why fix a date? Why not have faith enough in the Congresses which shall follow to believe that they will be able to fix their own date and fix it correctly?

Mr. McKellar: Mr. President, I will detain the Senate but a moment. I am very heartily in favor of the pending joint resolution as it is drawn.

There is one matter in connection with it to which I want to call the attention of Senators. Under the present provision we really do not have time to consider appropriation bills in the short sessions of the Congress.

Last year we appropriated $5,252,000,000 in about two months' time. I am a member of the Committee on Appropriations of the Senate, and I say to Senators that I believe every man on that committee did conscientious work, rendered faithful service in passing on those vast appropriations; but the bills passed on by the committee could not be properly considered by that committee, or by any committee, or by the Congress, or by either branch of it, for the reason that we did not have time. We were under terrific pressure every moment of the time after Congress convened.

When appropriations bills are brought over to the Senate from the House, the usual rule is that amendments only are really considered. We do not have time to go through the various provisions of the bills, either in subcommittee or in the full committee, or in the Senate or in the House.

The bill making appropriations for a particular department will be sent to Congress. If the House wants to add amendments, they are printed in italics. If the Senate wants to add amendments, they are printed in italics; and we consider only the amendments. In the Senate the bills are read for amendment. Bills carrying millions and sometimes hundreds of millions of dollars are passed by the two bodies without any consideration to the various items.

The junior Senator from Utah [Mr. King], who does not happen to be in the Chamber at the moment, has constantly inveighed against that method of legislation. It is an imperfect method; but as long as we have a 3-month session or a 4-month session, or even if we shall have a 5-month session, we are going to have the same trouble.

Therefore I say to the Senate that, in my judgment, if we consider no other reason, this joint resolution should be agreed to. I think the other reasons advanced are splendid. It is urged, first, that if his amendment were put into the Constitution there would be no further filibusters. That furnishes a perfectly valid reason for adopting the amendment. The right of every Congress to say when it wants to adjourn is another valid reason. But one of the most important reasons to the people of this country is that Congress should have time to pass upon the great appropriation bills, appropriating billions of dollars of the people's money every year.

I believe that at the last short session, if the Senate Committee on Appropriations, composed of perfectly splendid men, patriotic men, men who are seeking to do their duty by their Government and by their country, had had ample time, we would have saved hundreds of millions of dollars in the appropriation of the people's money. There were many items in those bills passed over without a word, which, if they had ever been debated, either in committee or in the Senate, would not have passed.

So, if we want to have an economical Government, if we want to cut appropriations to such figures as they ought to be cut to, we should have more time.

The Senator from Nebraska said just a moment ago that we have a very different Government now from what we had when it was founded. Our forefathers, as farseeing as they were—and they were the most farseeing set of men who ever lived—did not realize that the time might come when the Congress would have to appropriate as much as $5,000,000,000 in one year.

Mr. President, it seems to me that this joint resolution ought to be passed, not only for the reasons which have already been advanced but for this additional reason, that the Congress should have time each session properly to pass upon the appropriations which are made. We have not that time now. If the amendment of the Senator from Connecticut should be adopted, we would not have time properly to do the work.

Five billion dollars is an immense amount of money. It ought not to be treated lightly. We frequently pass appropriation bills as a matter of course. I have known of appropriation bills carrying $100,000,000 being passed in an afternoon session. That should not be. It would not be done if we had the time in the short session to discuss the measures as they ought to be discussed.

Mr. President, I am heartily in favor of this joint resolution. The Senate has shown time and again that it is in favor of this amendment to the Constitution, and I believe that it ought to be passed, and that it ought to be passed at the earliest possible moment.

Mr. Bingham: Mr. President, I have a great deal of sympathy with what the Senator from Tennessee has said. Like him, I am a member of the Committee on Appropriations, and I have often been filled with regret at the haste with which we had to consider bills.

I would like to call his attention to the fact that, notwithstanding the fact that we have no constitutional necessity for adjourning early in June at the present time, we practically always do adjourn early in June, except in time of war. It is always possible, in time of great emergency, for the President to call an extra session. It is possible under the Constitution for the Congress itself to fix an earlier day of meeting. It would have been possible for Congress last March, before it adjourned, to decide to meet on the 1st of September, had it so chosen. But it did not so choose.

Under the amendment which I have proposed, which is slightly at variance with that proposed by Speaker Longworth, because it gives an additional month, instead of there being only two active months—namely, January and February—in the short sessions, for the consideration of appropriation bills, we would get five active months, January, February, March, April, and May, until the 4th day of June.

From my observation in the last few years, I am convinced that that would provide abundant time for the consideration of appropriation bills. Therefore, it seems to me, that that argument does not hold.

Mr. McKellar: Mr. President, will the Senator yield?

Mr. Bingham: I yield.

Mr. McKellar: The Senator makes the statement that Congress usually adjourns by June. I have been a Member of the Congress, counting my service in both Houses, for a little more than 20 years. There may have been another, but I do not recall more than one session of the long Congress in that long period of time when we adjourned by June, and never, so far as I can now recall, have we adjourned prior to that in the long session of Congress. The truth of the matter is that the sessions have extended to the latter part of July, sometimes until August, and, as Champ

Clark used to say, until usually about the time the snow begins to fly.

Mr. Bingham: Mr. President, of course that Senator from Tennessee has taken advantage of the fact that I have been here for only 7 years while he has been here 20 or more, and his memory goes back much further than mine. I do not remember any Congress, except in war times, when we sat until the snow began to fly. We seldom have snow in Washington in July or August. I remember that three years ago we adjourned early in June. We have adjourned, in my recollection, about the 3d of July. But, after all, it would seem as though five months were a sufficient length of time to handle appropriation bills.

As the Senator from Nebraska has said, and in his report has mentioned, this proposed amendment to the Constitution has aroused great interest in the country. A great many newspaper editorials have appeared in favor of the so-called Norris "lame-duck" amendment. I have read a great many of those editorials. So far as I can recollect all of them refer to the fact that a Congressman elected in November of one year does not take his seat until December of the following year, and they are in favor of a Congressman taking his seat sooner after election. That is the point in which the country has been interested. But nothing has been said about that here to-day. In the amendment which I have proposed no change is made in that. There is merely a provision to prevent the continuous sitting of Congress for one reason or another.

It was pointed out in the debate in the House last year by Mr. Glover, of Arkansas, who spoke in favor of the Longworth amendment, that not only should Congress have a breathing spell, and the Members of Congress have a breathing spell, but "if we have a given task to be performed in a given time we will devote ourselves to that." He goes on to say:

Another argument made by the Senator, I think, is worth being emphasized, and that is the fact that in presidential election years, regardless of whatever party is in power, politics would enter; if we were in power, of course, we would make it hard for you, and if you were in power you would do the same thing to us. In other words, politics would be played in Congress that ought not to be played. I believe we can finish our business in the presidential year by the time specified in this resolution, and that we can accomplish our purpose, and that we can go out and have a little rest ourselves and give the people one.

Mr. President, it has been pointed out by no less a distinguished person that Prof. Everett S. Brown, of the University of Michigan, in the *American Political Science Review* that—

In public discussions of the proposed Norris "lame-duck" amendment, and in demands by Members of Congress for special sessions to meet temporary emergencies, the fact is often overlooked that Congress itself has the power to regulate the time of its meeting.

Then he goes on to point out the fact that these statements are not the result of theoretical speculation, but that prior to 1821 no fewer than 18 acts were passed by Congress appointing a different day for its meeting from that stipulated in the Constitution. I ask unanimous consent that his complete statement may be printed in the Record at the close of my remarks.

The Vice President: Without objection, it is so ordered.

(See Exhibit A.)

Mr. Bingham: Mr. President, I regret the argument used by the Senator from Nebraska [Mr. Norris] that Members of the Senate should vote against my amendment because forsooth I introduced it, who was opposed and one of the very few persons opposed to the joint resolution as introduced by the Senator from Nebraska. That argumentum ad hominem, if I may be permitted to refer to something out of the old logic book which I once studied, is one which I think should not apply to an amendment to the Constitution. Either it should stand on its own merits or not. The fact that I introduced it ought not to count against it or in its favor.

It was adopted at length in the House and adopted by a very considerable majority. I think it is a reasonable amendment. It provides a five months' short session instead of what is at the present time practically a two months' short session. It in no way affects the "lame-duck" amendment. It in no way affects the curious situation whereby a Congressman elected in November does not take his seat until a year from the following December. I hope very much that it may stand on its merits and that something may be done to prevent the things pointed out by former Speaker Longworth and by Mr. Glover.

As a matter of fact, if my recollection serves me—it has been called in question by the Senator from Tennessee [Mr. McKellar] and therefore I am a little bit afraid to refer to it—there was a filibuster conducted by the distinguished Senators from Arizona [Mr. Ashurst and Mr. Hayden] on behalf of their State during a long session of Congress in which we had many daily sessions devoted to the consideration of the Boulder Dam question. There are times when there is no way in which a small State or a small group of States can protect what they believe to be their rights in connection with undesirable legislation other than by an effort to talk it to death, by taking up a lot of time and, in other words, conducting a filibuster. Once the Senate decides that that is an undesirable proceeding, it can be changed by rule. Under Rule XXII, once two-thirds of the Senate believe any legislation should be passed without further talk, it can be done and no great harm done.

Mr. President, I very much hope the amendment may be adopted.

Exhibit A

The time of meetings of Congress: In public discussions of the proposed Norris "Lame-duck" amendment and in demands by Members of Congress for special sessions to meet temporary emergencies, the fact is often overlooked that Congress itself has the power to regulate the time of its meeting. The fourth section of Article IV of the Constitution provides: "The Congress shall assemble at least once in every year, and such meeting shall be on the first Monday in December, unless they shall by law appoint a different day." Under this provision the much-criticized rush of bills in the short session could easily be averted by an act convening Congress at an earlier date than the first Monday in December. So, too, a Congress whose final session was coming to a close could provide that its successor should meet immediately, instead of waiting until the following December. A Congress desirous of a special session on a problem like unemployment could call such a session irrespective of lack of action by the President, provided it could command a majority sufficient to override a possible presidential veto. Of course such action could be taken only while Congress was in session, because, under the provisions of the Constitution, the President is the only person who, between sessions, is empowered to call special sessions.

These statements are not the result of theoretical speculation, but rest firmly on the facts of our legislative history. Prior to 1821 no fewer than 18 acts were passed by Congress appointing a different day for its meetings from that stipulated in the Constitution. Before referring to these acts more in detail, it would perhaps clarify matters somewhat to recall to mind how March 4 was decided upon as a limit of presidential and congressional terms. Article VII of the Constitution provided that the instrument should go into effect when ratified by nine States. This was accomplished on June 21, 1788. In a resolution of September 13, 1788, the Congress of the Confederation, after providing dates for the choice of electors and the election of a President, set the first Wednesday in the following March as the time "for commencing the proceedings under said Constitution." The first Wednesday in March, 1789, fell on March 4. Lack of a quorum until April 6 prevented the counting of the electoral vote, and it was not until April 30 that Washington was inaugurated President. However, Congress decided that both congressional and presidential terms had begun on March 4, 1789, and by act of March 1, 1792, set March 4, 1793, as the date for the beginning of the next presidential term.

The First Congress adjourned its first session on September 29, 1789, but before doing so passed an act setting January 4, 1790, as the date of the beginning of its next session. This session ended on August 12, and, no further action being taken, the third session commenced on December 6, 1790, in accordance with the constitutional provision. A number of bills were introduced in the session with respect to the next meeting of Congress, and eventually by act of March 2, 1791, the date was set for the fourth Monday in October, 1791, more than a month before the date provided for in the Constitution. The precedent here established was followed with considerable frequency. The favorite date was the first Monday in November, no less than 10 of the 18 laws passed prior to 1821 selecting that day. The second, third, the fourth Mondays in November were also chosen, as were the fourth and last Mondays in October. Twice during this period—in 1809 and in 1813—the beginning of the short session was set by law for the fourth Monday in May. It is also worthy of note that nearly half of acts passed by Congress related to the long session, emphasizing the fact that Congress was concerned not merely with the brevity of the short session. The calling of the first session of a Congress at an earlier date than that set by the Constitution shortened the period between the election of members and their active participation in legislation, thus meeting much of the criticism made against that situation.

Several questions of constitutional interpretation arose in connection with these laws. For example, the act of March 3, 1797, had fixed as the date of the meeting of the Fifth Congress the first Monday in November, 1797. But President John Adams called a special session for May 15. When this Congress met the question was raised whether the act passed at the last session fixing the date of the next meeting of Congress as the first Monday in November had not been superseded by the calling of the special session. Opponents of this interpretation held that although the President had power to call extra sessions, it was the business of Congress to fix the dates of annual meetings, and, therefore, the two powers could not be allowed to infringe upon each other. However, in order to avoid any misunderstanding on the subject a new law was passed fixing the meeting of Congress on the second Monday in November, with a clause repealing the former act. Many Members of Congress did not believe the new act was necessary and opposed it on the ground that to take such action would give the President the power to repeal a law to do away with the provisions of the Constitution of this subject.

The special session called by President Adams met on May 15 and adjourned on July 10, 1797, and the regular session met on November 13, in accordance with the act passed by Congress. But what would happen if a special session called by the President had not completed its business prior to the date set for the next annual session? It was not long before this contingency arose. By the act of March 3, 1803, Congress provided that the next meeting should be on the first Monday of the following November. President Jefferson, however, called the Eighth Congress into special session on October 17, and Congress remained in session until March 27, 1804, thus continuing without a break through November 7, the date set by Congress, and through Monday, December 5, the day appointed by the Constitution for the regular annual session.

Nor was this a solitary instance. The first meeting of the Tenth Congress was convened by proclamation of President Jefferson on October 26, 1807, and remained in session until April 2, 1808, without any interruption on Monday, December 7, the constitutional day of meeting. The same was true of the Twelfth Congress, which was convened by proclamation of President Madison on November 4, 1811, and continued in session until July 6, 1812. Again, at the second session of the Thirteenth Congress a law was passed and approved April 18, 1814, setting the last Monday in November of that year for the next meeting of Congress. But a special ses-

sion was called by President Madison for September 19, 1814, and it, too, continued through the day appointed by law and by the Constitution for the beginning of the session. The reports of proceedings in Congress fail to disclose any discussions of constitutional problems here involved. If there were any questions in the minds of Members concerning distinctions between regular sessions of Congress and special ones called by presidential proclamation, presumably they were not raised.

This practice, however, was not allowed to continue, and it was later established that a special session, whether convened by law or by proclamation, ends with the day set by the Constitution for the annual meeting. During the quarrel between Congress and President Johnson Congress passed an act, approved by the President on January 22, 1867, because he realized his veto would be futile, providing that "in addition to the present regular times of meeting of Congress there shall be a meeting of the Fortieth Congress of the United States and of each succeeding Congress thereafter at 12 o'clock meridian on the 4th day of March, the day on which the term begins for which the Congress is elected. The Fortieth Congress, convened under this law, was still in session when the day approached for the regular annual meeting. A resolution was passed by both Houses that the President of the Senate and the Speaker of the House should adjourn their respective Houses without day on Monday, December 2, at 12 o'clock. In accordance with this concurrent resolution, on Monday, December 2, the presiding officers of the two Houses declared the Houses adjourned sine die. Immediately thereafter the Houses were called to order in the second session. The act of January 22, 1867, applied to three Congresses—the Fortieth, Forty-first, and Forty-second—was repealed April 20, 1871.

On October 15, 1877, the Forty-fifth Congress met in special session on the call of President Hayes, and it remained in session until December 3, the day appointed by the Constitution for the regular meeting of Congress. During the morning session on December 3, by concurrent resolution it was resolved to be the judgment of the two Houses that the current session of Congress expired by operation of law at 12 o'clock meridian on that day. The two Houses then agreed to the usual resolution authorizing the appointment of a joint committee to wait on the President and inform him of the adjournment. At 12 o'clock the new session was called.

The precedent here established was followed in later sessions. In the Fifty-eighth Congress President Roosevelt called a special session for November 9, 1903. The House adjourned on Saturday, December 6, but the Senate was still in session on Monday, December 7. At 12 o'clock on that day the President pro tempore of the Senate announced that the hour provided by law for the meeting of the first regular session of the Fifty-eighth Congress had arrived and declared the extraordinary session adjourned sine die. Immediately the Senate was called to order in regular session, as was also the House, and the second session of the Fifty-eighth Congress commenced. Almost identical action was taken by the Sixty-third Congress, when called into special session by President Wilson on April 7, the session continuing to Monday, December 1, when it was adjourned in order that the regular session might commence.

The stand here taken by Congress is an important one in the maintenance of the theory of the separation of powers in our National Government. If no distinction were made between special sessions called by the President and regular sessions provided by the Constitution, and if special sessions were to extend over the date set for regular meetings, the President would be able to exert undue pressure on the legislative branch of the Government. On the other hand, the action of Congress in its conflict with President Johnson illustrates the extent of its power to meet practically continuously, provided it has sufficient strength to override the presidential veto.

An attempt of the Twenty-fourth Congress, in 1836, to fix the date of the annual meeting of Congress on the first Monday in November in every year was vetoed by President Jackson because the same act contained a provision fixing the second Monday of May as the day of adjournment of the first session of all succeeding Congresses. Jackson admitted without question the power of Congress to fix, by law, a day for its regular annual session. But the attempt to set a definite date for the adjournment of all succeeding Congresses he regarded as unconstitutional.

It is interesting to note that, in contrast with the frequent acts of Congress prior to 1821 changing the dates of its meetings, only one law for that purpose has been passed since 1821. This was the act of January 22, 1867, which, as already noted, grew out of Congress' distrust of President Johnson. In recent years Congress has seemed content to let the President call special sessions rather than exercise its power to change the date of its meetings. Undoubtedly the development of the party system and of the party leadership of the President has had much to do with the present situation. But the fact remains that Congress has the power to change its times of meeting, just as it did so often in its earlier history. A constitutional amendment is not necessary to enable a newly elected Congress to meet for its first session on, or immediately after, March 4 following its election or to enable Congress to fix the dates of annual sessions. A change in the date of the inauguration of the President or of the beginning of the terms of Congressmen would require a constitutional amendment, and it is, perhaps, the combination of these provisions with the sessions of Congress in the Norris proposals which has obscured somewhat the real power of Congress over the time of its own meetings.

Everett S. Brown.
University of Michigan.

Mr. Barkley: Mr. President, I have no desire to detain the Senate more than a few moments. In the first place, I doubt very seriously whether the framers of our Constitution ever contemplated what we know as the short session of Congress. While in the original document they provided that Congress should meet on the first Monday in December every year, they likewise provided that the Government of the United States which was to be formed under that Constitution should not begin operation until certain preliminary things had occurred that enabled it to be represented not only in its legislative branches but in its executive department likewise.

The Constitution which had been framed by the Philadelphia convention had to be submitted to all the States, and there was no way to know how long it would require to secure its adoption: It provided that 9 of the 13 States should adopt it or ratify it before it could become effective: There was no way to foresee when the ratification by the ninth State would transpire: Then it provided for a series of events that should occur after the final ratification, including the election of Members of Congress and including the selection of members of the Electoral College who were to elect a President, all of whom had to be elected before the Government could begin operation. It so happened that the last date fell on the 4th day of March. There is nothing in the Constitution about the 4th day of March. There is nothing in the Constitution about a short session: After reading the proceedings of the Constitutional Convention and the amendments and motions offered by members of it, it is my conclusion, and the conclusion, I think, also of many able writers on the Constitution, that the convention really meant that the first session which should be held after the adoption of the Constitution and inauguration of the Government should be in the December following the November election, instead of the December, 13 months later.

But in view of the fact that a series of accidental occurrences brought the date for the beginning of the Government over the 4th day of March, which was nowhere mentioned in the Constitution, and therefore, by long practice and finally by consummation of statute, the 4th day of March was fixed as the date when new terms should begin, not only for the President of the United States but for Members of Congress, it transpired that Members elected in November did not take their seats until the following March, and, therefore, the first session of Congress which could be held after that date necessarily had to be the following December, which was 13 months after they were elected. I do not believe it was ever the intention of the framers of the Constitution that there should be any legal distinction between the first and second sessions of the Congress of the United States. So much for that.

Mr. President, in view of the fact that it was not, in my judgment, the intention of the framers of the Constitution to limit any session of Congress by fixing an arbitrary date of adjournment it seems to me that it would be presumption on our part that we possess more wisdom than any future Congress can possibly possess with reference to the date when it ought to adjourn. I do not believe we possess any greater wisdom than Congresses that may meet hereafter will possess. I do not believe it is within our province, nor is it within our duty or our wisdom or our ability, to foresee the future events of our country and say to any future Congress that they shall stay in session three months or four months or five months or any other limited time. We ought to leave it to them. I think the chances are they will have as much vision as we have. I think the chances are fair that they will be as intelligent as we are.

I certainly think, in view of the changing exigencies of our country, the multiplication of the duties of Congress, the vast ramifications of all the activities with which we are compelled to deal, that it is certainly unwise to say to any Congress that may meet 100 years from now: "Whether you have finished your business or not you must adjourn on the 4th day of some March," because forsooth we desire to get out early in the year of election in order that we may devote ourselves to our campaign for reelection. It is not a matter of any importance, in my judgment, compared to the fundamental law of our country with reference to the fixing of dates for sessions of Congress to begin or terms of office to begin. Therefore I hope the amendment will be defeated and that we will at least leave it to the discretion and judgment and wisdom of Congresses which are to meet in the years to come to determine when they shall finish their duties, and allow them to leave it to their constituents as to whether they have acted wisely or unwisely.

Mr. Dill: Mr. President, I notice that the Senator from Nebraska [Mr. Norris], in speaking against the amendment, suggested that it was an amendment presented by enemies of the measure. I want to say that if there is anyone in the Senate who is anxious to see this joint resolution become a part of the Constitution it is myself. But that does not preclude me, I hope, as a friend of constitutional government, from supporting an amendment that is wise, even though it may come from those who may have opposed the resolution in the past. If my memory serves me correctly, the resolution as reported to the Senate some years ago contained a limitation as to the time when the second session should adjourn. I may be wrong in that, but that is my recollection of the matter. The friends of the measure then, as I recall, did not feel that it was so terribly dangerous.

I believe Senators do not consider what it will mean to bring a Congress to a close when there is no opportunity to pass upon bills in which they are interested after they have voted for final adjournment. In every instance in the past when Congress adjourned voluntarily there has always been the next session of Congress at which the bills may be considered. It is only because the Constitution itself compels adjournment on the 4th of March that we have had to adjourn on that date.

I recognize the objections to filibusters. I recognize, it is possible that there will be filibusters even if the sessions run for five months. But I believe that an orderly government should not have the legislative body in session continu-

ously. I believe there ought to be a time when the work of the legislative body would come to a close in the year in which politics is uppermost in the minds of both the executive and the legislative branches of the Government. I think when we allow an unlimited time for the first session and allow approximately five months for the second session we are not endangering the country, as the Senator from Nebraska suggests.

Let me say also that I believe the adoption of the amendment of the Senator from Connecticut will hasten the submission of the constitutional amendment to the States by the House of Representatives. I recall that in the last session, when the House voted for the resolution and the matter went to conference. I stated then that I hoped the Senate would reach a compromise. I believe in the proposal as a matter of principle, and I believe the custom forced upon us by the present system of Congressmen and Senators not taking their seats and beginning their duties for 13 months after election is so hurtful to the working of popular government that this is a matter of not such great importance in comparison.

I believe, therefore, that if the amendment limiting the time to June 4 shall be adopted, the joint resolution will go through the House without any amendment whatsoever; that it will be submitted to the States and ratified probably more quickly than any amendment that has ever been submitted. On the other hand, if we do not adopt it, the House of Representatives will probably do what it did before and we shall find ourselves tied up in another conference jam, with no resolution submitted to the States, and the present objectionable situation continued.

Personally I am not worried about filibusters. I have seen a number of filibusters and I have read of a good many others. It has been my observation that very little legislation that the country really wanted and especially that the country really needed has been prevented of passage by filibuster. Any important legislation that has been prevented by the closing of the Congress on the 4th of March or by a filibuster has been very properly and quickly passed by the Congress that met in the following December. The fact of the matter is the country has been saved much legislation from which, in my judgment, it should have been saved by the fact that the Congress was compelled to adjourn on the 4th day of March.

It sounds very well for Senators to say that Congress has so much judgment that it may be depended upon always to adjourn when the best interests of the country demand, but our history does not seem to justify that statement.

Furthermore, when we allow five months from the meeting of the second session during which Congress may legislate we have not hampered it in the matter of time. For that reason, I intend to support the amendment proposed by the Senator from Connecticut [Mr. Bingham], and, of course, if it shall be defeated, I shall support the joint resolution, and I hope that it will be passed by the House of Representatives at an early date.

The Vice President: The question is on agreeing to the amendment proposed by the Senator from Connecticut [Mr. Bingham].

Mr. Bingham: I suggest the absence of a quorum.

Mr. McNary: Let us have the yeas and nays.

Mr. Bingham: Very well, I withdraw the suggestion.

The Vice President: The suggestion of the absence of a quorum is withdrawn, and the yeas and nays are demanded. Is the demand seconded?

The yeas and nays were ordered, and the legislative clerk proceeded to call the roll.

Mr. Bingham (when his name was called). I have a general pair with the junior Senator from Virginia [Mr. Glass]. I understand, however, that on this vote I am released from the pair. Therefore I am permitted to vote, and vote "yea."

Mr. Kendrick (when Mr. Carey's name was called). On this vote my colleague [Mr. Carey], who is unavoidably absent, is paired with the Senator from Ohio [Mr. Bulkley].

Mr. Hastings (when his name was called). I have a pair with the junior Senator from Alabama [Mr. Bankhead]. Not knowing how he would vote, I withhold my vote.

Mr. Jones (when his name was called). As previously announced, I am paired for the day with the senior Senator from Virginia [Mr. Swanson]. I do not know how he would vote on this question. If I were at liberty to vote, I should vote, "nay."

Mr. Moses (when his name was called). I have a general pair with the Senator from Louisiana [Mr. Broussard]. He being absent, and not knowing how he would vote, and being unable to secure a transfer, I withhold my vote.

Mr. Robinson of Indiana (when his name was called). I have a pair with the junior Senator from Mississippi [Mr. Stephens]. In his absence, and not knowing how he would vote on this question, I withhold my vote.

Mr. Smith (when his name was called). On this question I have a pair with the Senator from Indiana [Mr. Watson] and therefore withhold my vote. If permitted to vote, I should vote "yea."

The roll call was concluded.

Mr. Jones: I find that on this question I can transfer my pair with the Senator from Virginia [Mr. Swanson] to the Junior Senator from Nebraska [Mr. Howell]. I do so and will vote. I vote "nay."

Mr. King: On this vote I am paired with the Senator from Minnesota [Mr. Schall]. Not knowing how he would vote, I withhold my vote.

Mr. Barkley: I have a pair with the senior Senator from Colorado [Mr. Waterman], which I transfer to the senior Senator from Massachusetts [Mr. Walsh], and vote "nay."

Mr. Byrnes: I have a general pair with the junior Senator from Nevada [Mr. Oddie]. Not knowing how he would vote, I withhold my vote. If permitted to vote, I should vote "nay."

Mr. McKellar (after having voted in the negative). I have a pair with the junior Senator from Delaware [Mr. Townsend], who, it seems, is not present. I transfer that pair to the junior Senator from North Carolina [Mr. Bailey] and allow my vote to stand.

While I am on my feet, I desire to announce that the senior Senator from Arkansas [Mr. Robinson] is unavoidably absent and is paired with the Senator from Pennsylvania [Mr. Reed].

Mr. Moses: I find that I may transfer my pair with the senior Senator from Louisiana [Mr. Broussard] to the junior Senator from Connecticut [Mr. Walcott]. I make that transfer and vote "yea."

The result was announced—yeas 18, nays 47, as follows:

YEAS—18

Austin	Hebert
Barbour	Kean
Bingham	Keyes
Dickinson	Lewis
Dill	Metcalf
Fess	Moses
Glenn	Patterson
Goldsborough	Tydings
Hale	White

NAYS—47

Barkley	Couzens
Blaine	Cutting
Borah	Dale
Bratton	Davis
Brookhart	Fletcher
Bulow	Frazier
Capper	George
Caraway	Gore
Connally	Harris
Coolidge	Hatfield
Copeland	Hawes
Costigan	Hayden

Hull	Norris
Johnson	Nye
Jones	Sheppard
Kendrick	Shipstead
La Follette	Shortridge
Logan	Steiwer
McGill	Thomas, Idaho
McKellar	Thomas, Okla.
McNary	Wagner
Morrison	Walsh, Mont.
Neely	Wheeler
Norbeck	

NOT VOTING—30

Ashurst	Reed
Bailey	Robinson, Ark.
Bankhead	Robinson, Ind.
Black	Schall
Broussard	Smith
Bulkley	Smoot
Byrnes	Stephens
Carey	Swanson
Glass	Townsend
Harrison	Trammell
Hastings	Vandenberg
Howell	Walcott
King	Walsh, Mass.
Oddie	Waterman
Pittman	Watson

So Mr. Bingham's amendment was rejected.

The Vice President: The joint resolution is before the Senate and open to amendment. If there be no further amendment, the joint resolution will be ordered to be engrossed for a third reading and read the third time.

The joint resolution was ordered to be engrossed for a third reading and read the third time.

The Vice President: The joint resolution having been read the third time, the question is. Shall it pass?

Mr. Norris and Mr. McKellar called for the yeas and nays, and they were ordered.

The Vice President: The clerk will call the roll.

The Chief Clerk proceeded to call the roll.

Mr. Bingham (when his name was called). I have a general pair with the junior Senator from Virginia [Mr. Glass]. In his absence, and being unable to obtain a transfer, I withhold my vote.

If permitted to vote, I should vote "nay."

Mr. Byrnes (when his name was called). I have a pair with the junior Senator from Nevada [Mr. Oddie]. I understand that if present he would vote "yea." As I intend to vote the same way, I feel at liberty to vote and vote "yea."

Mr. Kendrick (when Mr. Carey's name was called). Once more I desire to announce the unavoidable absence of my colleague [Mr. Carey] and to say that he is paired with the Senator from Ohio [Mr. Bulkley].

Mr. Hastings (when his name was called). I am paired with the junior Senator from Alabama [Mr. Bankhead]. Not knowing how he would vote, I withhold my vote.

Mr. Jones (when his name was called). I understand that the Senator from Virginia [Mr. Swanson], with whom I am paired for the day, would vote as I shall vote. Therefore I am at liberty to vote. I vote "yea."

Mr. King (when his name was called). I have a pair with the Senator from Minnesota [Mr. Schall]. Not knowing how he would vote, I withhold my vote. If I were at liberty to vote, I should vote "nay."

Mr. McKellar (when his name was called). I have a general pair with the junior Senator from Delaware [Mr. Townsend], which I transfer to the junior Senator from North Carolina [Mr. Bailey], and will vote. I vote "yea."

Mr. Moses (when his name was called). I have a general pair with the senior Senator from Louisiana [Mr. Broussard]. As he is absent, I withhold my vote.

Mr. Robinson of Indiana (when his name was called). I have a general pair with the junior Senator from Mississippi [Mr. Stephens], who is detained at his home by illness. I understand that if he were present he would vote as I expect to vote. Therefore I am free to vote. I vote "yea."

The roll call was concluded.

Mr. Robinson of Arkansas (after having voted in the affirmative). I have a general pair with the Senator from Pennsylvania [Mr. Reed]. I understand that if present he would vote as I have voted, and I therefore allow my vote to stand.

Mr. Norris: I desire to announce the unavoidable absence of my colleague [Mr. Howell]. If he were present, he would vote "yea" on this question.

Mr. Bingham: The junior Senator from Virginia [Mr. Glass], with whom I have a general pair, is detained on business of the Senate and is unable to be present. If he were present, he would vote "yea."

Mr. Barkley: I transfer the pair which I have heretofore announced with the senior Senator from Colorado [Mr. Waterman] to the senior Senator from Mississippi [Mr. Harrison] and will vote. I vote "yea."

Mr. Sheppard: I desire to announce that the Senator from Alabama [Mr. Black], the Senator from Virginia [Mr. Swanson], the Senator from Mississippi [Mr. Harrison], the Senator from Virginia [Mr. Glass], the Senator from Ohio [Mr. Bulkley], and the Senator from North Carolina [Mr. Bailey] are necessarily detained on official business.

The result was announced—yeas 63, nays 7, as follows:

YEAS—63

Ashurst	Couzens
Austin	Cutting
Barbour	Davis
Barkley	Dickinson
Blaine	Dill
Borah	Fess
Bratton	Fletcher
Brookhart	Frazier
Bulow	George
Byrnes	Glenn
Capper	Gore
Caraway	Hale
Connally	Harris
Coolidge	Hatfield
Copeland	Hawes
Costigan	Hayden

Hull
Johnson
Jones
Kean
Kendrick
Keyes
La Follette
Lewis
Logan
McGill
McKellar
McNary
Morrison
Neeley
Norbeck
Norris

Nye
Robinson, Ark.
Robinson, Ind.
Sheppard
Shipstead
Steiwer
Thomas, Idaho
Thomas, Okla.
Tydings
Vandenberg
Wagner
Walsh, Mass.
Walsh, Mont.
Wheeler
White

NAYS—7

Dale
Goldsborough
Hebert
Metcalf

Patterson
Smith
Watson

NOT VOTING—25

Bailey
Bankhead
Bingham
Black
Broussard
Bulkley
Carey
Glass
Harrison
Hastings
Howell
King
Moses

Oddie
Pittman
Reed
Schall
Shortridge
Smoot
Stephens
Swanson
Townsend
Trammell
Walcott
Waterman

The Vice President: On this question the yeas are 63, the nays are 7. More than two-thirds of the Senators present having voted in the affirmative, the joint resolution is passed.

The joint resolution as passed is as follows:

Resolved, etc., That the following amendment of the Constitution be, and hereby is, proposed to the States, to become valid as a part of said Constitution when ratified by the legislatures of the several States as provided by the Constitution:

ARTICLE—

"Section 1. The terms of the President and Vice President shall end at noon on the 15th day of January, and the terms of Senators and Representatives at noon on the 2d day of January, of the years in which such terms would have ended if this article had not been ratified; and the terms of their successors shall then begin.

"Sec. 2. The Congress shall assemble at least once in every year, and such meeting shall begin at noon on the 2d day of January, unless they shall by law appoint a different day.

"Sec. 3. If the House of Representatives has not chosen a President, whenever the right of choice devolves upon them, before the time fixed for the beginning of his term, then the Vice President shall act as President, as in the case of the death or other constitutional disability of the President. The Congress shall by law provide for the case of the failure to choose the Vice President before the time fixed for the beginning of his term, declaring what officer shall then act as President, and such officer shall act accordingly until the House of Representatives chooses a President or until the Senate chooses a Vice President.

"Sec. 4. This amendment shall take effect on the 15th day of October after its ratification."

Democratic Party Platform (1932)

The elections of 1932 marked the beginning of a long period of Democratic dominance in national politics. In the thirty-six years before 1932, the Democratic party occupied the White House for only eight years and had majorities in both houses of Congress for only six years. In the thirty-six years after 1932, Democrats controlled the presidency for twenty-eight years and Congress for thirty-two years.

The Great Depression, which began with the stock market crash on October 29, 1929, was essential to the Democratic party's political success. During the seemingly prosperous, Republican-dominated 1920s, the Democrats had been riven by a host of intraparty differences: city against country dwellers in the election of 1924, Protestants against Catholics, "wets" (anti-prohibitionists) against "drys" (prohibitionists), conservatives against liberals, and northerners and easterners against southerners and westerners. In the election of 1924, John W. Davis, a conservative, Protestant, dry West Virginian, had led the party to an overwhelming defeat. The 1928 nomination of Gov. Al Smith of New York, a wet, Catholic, urbanite, also was unsuccessful. (See "The 103d Ballot," p. 291, and "H. L. Mencken's 'Onward, Christian Soldiers!' Article," p. 296.)

By raising economic concerns to the top of the national political agenda, the depression allowed the Democrats to emphasize matters on which they agreed more than they disagreed. Gov. Franklin D. Roosevelt of New York—known, like his distant cousin Theodore, by his initials, FDR—was the perfect candidate to express the party's commonalities and to mute its differences. In his 1930 reelection campaign for governor, Roosevelt had discussed depression relief, not prohibition—"Bread not Booze" was his watchword. After a landslide victory, Roosevelt prodded the state legislature to create the nation's first comprehensive system of unemployment relief and sponsored an extensive program of industrial welfare.

As the front-runner for the Democratic presidential nomination in 1932, FDR oversaw the writing of the party's platform. Like the 1932 Republican platform, which defended President Herbert Hoover's depression policies and called for a protective tariff, the Democratic platform emphasized economic issues. Unlike the Republicans, however, the Democrats were highly critical of the administration. Indeed, the political scientist Benjamin Ginsberg has found that the contrast between the two parties' 1932 platforms was the fourth sharpest in history. According to Ginsberg, almost all of the differences concerned issues of "capitalism," namely, "the aggregation of *wealth and control over the distribution of wealth by business, financial, and mercantile elites."*

As in previous eras of partisan realignment, sharply contrasting platforms helped to set the stage for major changes in public policy once the new party came to power. (See, for example, "Republican Party Platform [1980]," p. 677.) *In 1933, a Democratic-controlled Congress, led by a Democratic president, inaugurated dramatic and innovative programs to address not just the problems of capitalism but also the related concerns of workers and farmers.* ～

In this time of unprecedented economic and social distress the Democratic Party declares its conviction that the chief causes of this condition were the disastrous policies pursued by our government since the World War, of economic isolation, fostering the merger of competitive businesses into monopolies and encouraging the indefensible expansion and contraction of credit for private profit at the expense of the public.

Those who were responsible for these policies have abandoned the ideals on which the war was won and thrown away the fruits of victory, thus rejecting the greatest opportunity in history to bring peace, prosperity, and happiness to our people and to the world.

They have ruined our foreign trade; destroyed the values of our commodities and products, crippled our banking system, robbed millions of our people of their life savings, and thrown millions more out of work, produced widespread poverty and brought the government to a state of financial distress unprecedented in time of peace.

The only hope for improving present conditions, restoring employment, affording permanent relief to the people, and bringing the nation back to the proud position of domestic happiness and of financial, industrial, agricultural

and commercial leadership in the world lies in a drastic change in economic governmental policies.

We believe that a party platform is a covenant with the people to have [sic] faithfully kept by the party when entrusted with power, and that the people are entitled to know in plain words the terms of the contract to which they are asked to subscribe. We hereby declare this to be the platform of the Democratic Party:

The Democratic Party solemnly promises by appropriate action to put into effect the principles, policies, and reforms herein advocated, and to eradicate the policies, methods, and practices herein condemned. We advocate an immediate and drastic reduction of governmental expenditures by abolishing useless commissions and offices, consolidating departments and bureaus, and eliminating extravagance to accomplish a saving of not less than twenty-five per cent in the cost of the Federal Government. And we call upon the Democratic Party in the states to make a zealous effort to achieve a proportionate result.

We favor maintenance of the national credit by a federal budget annually balanced on the basis of accurate executive estimates within revenues, raised by a system of taxation levied on the principle of ability to pay.

We advocate a sound currency to be preserved at all hazards and an international monetary conference called on the invitation of our government to consider the rehabilitation of silver and related questions.

We advocate a competitive tariff for revenue with a fact-finding tariff commission free from executive interference, reciprocal tariff agreements with other nations, and an international economic conference designed to restore international trade and facilitate exchange.

We advocate the extension of federal credit to the states to provide unemployment relief wherever the diminishing resources of the states makes it impossible for them to provide for the needy; expansion of the federal program of necessary and useful construction effected [sic] with a public interest, such as adequate flood control and waterways.

We advocate the spread of employment by a substantial reduction in the hours of labor, the encouragement of the shorter week by applying that principle in government service; we advocate advance planning of public works.

We advocate unemployment and old-age insurance under state laws.

We favor the restoration of agriculture, the nation's basic industry; better financing of farm mortgages through recognized farm bank agencies at low rates of interest on an amortization plan, giving preference to credits for the redemption of farms and homes sold under foreclosure.

Extension and development of the Farm Cooperative movement and effective control of crop surpluses so that our farmers may have the full benefit of the domestic market.

The enactment of every constitutional measure that will aid the farmers to receive for their basic farm commodities prices in excess of cost.

We advocate a Navy and an Army adequate for national defense, based on a survey of all facts affecting the existing establishments, that the people in time of peace may not be burdened by an expenditure fast approaching a billion dollars annually.

We advocate strengthening and impartial enforcement of the anti-trust laws, to prevent monopoly and unfair trade practices, and revision thereof for the better protection of labor and the small producer and distributor.

The conservation, development, and use of the nation's water power in the public interest.

The removal of government from all fields of private enterprise except where necessary to develop public works and natural resources in the common interest.

We advocate protection of the investing public by requiring to be filed with the government and carried in advertisements of all offerings of foreign and domestic stocks and bonds true information as to bonuses, commissions, principal invested, and interests of the sellers.

Regulation to the full extent of federal power of

(a) Holding companies which sell securities in interstate commerce;

(b) Rates of utilities companies operating across State lines;

(c) Exchanges in securities and commodities.

We advocate quicker methods of realizing on assets for the relief of depositors of suspended banks, and a more rigid supervision of national banks for the protection of depositors and the prevention of the use of their moneys in speculation to the detriment of local credits.

The severance of affiliated security companies from, and the divorce of the investment banking business from, commercial banks, and further restriction of federal reserve banks in permitting the use of federal reserve facilities for speculative purposes.

We advocate the full measure of justice and generosity for all war veterans who have suffered disability or disease caused by or resulting from actual service in time of war and for their dependents.

We advocate a firm foreign policy, including peace with all the world and the settlement of international disputes by arbitration; no interference in the internal affairs of other nations; and sanctity of treaties and the maintenance of good faith and of good will in financial obligations; adherence to the World Court with appending reservations; the Pact of Paris abolishing war as an instrument of national policy, to be made effective by provisions for consultation and conference in case of threatened violations of treaties.

International agreements for reduction of armaments and cooperation with nations of the Western Hemisphere to maintain the spirit of the Monroe doctrine.

We oppose cancelation of the debts owing to the United States by foreign nations.

Independence for the Philippines; ultimate statehood for Porto Rico.

The employment of American citizens in the operation of the Panama Canal.

Simplification of legal procedure and reorganization of the judicial system to make the attainment of justice speedy, certain, and at less cost.

Continuous publicity of political contributions and expenditures; strengthening of the Corrupt Practices Act and severe penalties for misappropriation of campaign funds.

We advocate the repeal of the Eighteenth Amendment. To effect such repeal we demand that the Congress immediately propose a Constitutional Amendment to truly represent [sic] the conventions in the states called to act solely on that proposal; we urge the enactment of such measures by the several states as will actually promote temperance, effectively prevent the return of the saloon, and bring the liquor traffic into the open under complete supervision and control by the states.

We demand that the Federal Government effectively exercise its power to enable the states to protect themselves against importation of intoxicating liquors in violation of their laws.

Pending repeal, we favor immediate modification of the Volstead Act; to legalize the manufacture and sale of beer and other beverages of such alcoholic content as is permissible under the Constitution and to provide therefrom a proper and needed revenue.

We condemn the improper and excessive use of money in political activities.

We condemn paid lobbies of special interests to influence members of Congress and other public servants by personal contact.

We condemn action and utterances of high public officials designed to influence stock exchange prices.

We condemn the open and covert resistance of administrative officials to every effort made by Congressional Committees to curtail the extravagant expenditures of the Government and to revoke improvident subsidies granted to favorite interests.

We condemn the extravagance of the Farm Board, its disastrous action which made the Government a speculator in farm products, and the unsound policy of restricting agricultural products to the demands of domestic markets.

We condemn the usurpation of power by the State Department in assuming to pass upon foreign securities offered by international bankers as a result of which billions of dollars in questionable bonds have been sold to the public upon the implied approval of the Federal Government.[1]

And in conclusion, to accomplish these purposes and to recover economic liberty, we pledge the nominees of this convention the best efforts of a great Party whose founder announced the doctrine which guides us now in the hour of our country's need: equal rights to all; special privilege to none.

Notes

1. Inadvertently omitted from the reading of the platform, and later inlcuded, was the following statement:
   "We condemn the Hawley-Smoot Tariff Law, the prohibitive rates of which have resulted in retaliatory action by more than forty countries, created international economic hostilities, destroyed international trade, driven our factories into foreign countries, robbed the American farmer of his foreign markets, and increased the cost of production."

Franklin D. Roosevelt's Acceptance Speech to the Democratic National Convention (1932)

Franklin D. Roosevelt's victory in the 1932 election resembled in several important ways Woodrow Wilson's victory in 1912. (See "Woodrow Wilson's 'The Old Order Changeth' Speech," p. 267.) Like Wilson, Roosevelt was swept into office in an electoral landslide. His margin of victory over the Republican Herbert Hoover—57.4 percent to 40.0 percent in the popular vote and 472-59 in the electoral college—was, until 1980, the largest in history against an incumbent president. Roosevelt's party gained ninety seats in the House of Representatives (breaking Wilson's 1912 record for the longest presidential coattails) and thirteen seats in the Senate, which turned a one-seat Democratic minority into a twenty-five seat majority. Finally, FDR, like Wilson, campaigned on a theme of dramatic policy change.

Roosevelt expressed his desire for change physically, by appearing at the Democratic national convention on the night after his nomination to make an acceptance speech to the delegates. No major-party nominee ever had done so; the custom was to wait at home for a visit from a delegation of party leaders bearing official word of the convention's decision. On July 2, 1932, however, Roosevelt flew from Albany, New York, to Chicago to proclaim, "You have nominated me and I know it, and I am here to thank you for the honor.

Let it . . . be symbolic that in so doing I broke tradition. Let it be from now on the task of our Party to break foolish traditions." Nearing the end of the stirring, confidently delivered address, in which he emphasized his belief that the federal government has a "continuing responsibility for the broader public welfare," Roosevelt uttered the words that (much to his and his speechwriters' surprise) quickly became the catch phrase for his campaign and, later, for his presidency: "I pledge you, I pledge myself, to a new deal for the American people."

Roosevelt carried the theme of change into the fall campaign against President Hoover. He was seldom specific about what he intended to do as president. To be sure, FDR spoke at various times in support of farm relief, unemployment insurance, public power, tariff reduction, and other liberal causes. But more significant than any list of promises that could be extracted from his speeches was the sense of commitment Roosevelt conveyed that he would do whatever he could to remedy the awful plight of "the forgotten man at the bottom of the economic pyramid." Again and again, Roosevelt harked back to the approach to governing that he had described in an April 1932 speech at Oglethorpe University: "The country needs and, unless I mistake its temper, the country demands bold, persistent experimentation. . . . Above all, try something."

As it had for Wilson in 1913 (and as it would for Lyndon B. Johnson in 1965 and Ronald Reagan in 1981), the combination of Roosevelt's personal landslide victory, substantial gains for his party in Congress, and his change-oriented campaign created the conditions for dramatic policy innovation in 1933. (See "Lyndon B. Johnson's 'Let Us Continue' Speech to Congress," p. 511, and "The Second Reagan-Mondale Debate," p. 790.) During Roosevelt's fabled "one hundred days," Congress passed more than a dozen pieces of major administration-sponsored legislation to address the national crises in agriculture, banking, unemployment, and industrial recovery.   ~

Chairman Walsh, my friends of the Democratic National Convention of 1932:

I appreciate your willingness after these six arduous days to remain here, for I know well the sleepless hours which you and I have had. I regret that I am late, but I have no control over the winds of Heaven and could only be thankful for my Navy training.

The appearance before a National Convention of its nominee for President, to be formally notified of his selection, is unprecedented and unusual, but these are unprecedented and unusual times. I have started out on the tasks that lie ahead by breaking the absurd traditions that the candidate should remain in professed ignorance of what has happened for weeks until he is formally notified of that event many weeks later.

My friends, may this be the symbol of my intention to be honest and to avoid all hypocrisy or sham, to avoid all silly shutting of the eyes to the truth in this campaign. You have nominated me and I know it, and I am here to thank you for the honor.

Let it also be symbolic that in so doing I broke traditions. Let it be from now on the task of our Party to break foolish traditions. We will break foolish traditions and leave it to the Republican leadership, far more skilled in that art, to break promises.

Let us now and here highly resolve to resume the country's interrupted march along the path of real progress, of real justice, of real equality for all of our citizens, great and small. Our indomitable leader in that interrupted march is no longer with us, but there still survives today his spirit. Many of his captains, thank God, are still with us, to give us wise counsel. Let us feel that in everything we do there still lives with us, if not the body, the great indomitable, unquenchable, progressive soul of our commander-in-Chief, Woodrow Wilson.

I have many things on which I want to make my position clear at the earliest possible moment in this campaign. That admirable document, the platform which you have adopted, is clear. I accept it 100 percent.

And you can accept my pledge that I will leave no doubt or ambiguity on where I stand on any question of moment in this campaign.

As we enter this new battle, let us keep always present with us some of the ideals of the Party: The fact that the Democratic Party by tradition and by the continuing logic of history, past and present, is the bearer of liberalism and of progress and at the same time of safety to our institutions. And if this appeal fails, remember well, my friends, that a resentment against the failure of Republican leadership—and note well that in this campaign I shall not use the words, "Republican Party," but I shall use, day in and day out, the words, "Republican leadership"—the failure of Republican leaders to solve our troubles may degenerate into unreasoning radicalism.

The great social phenomenon of this depression, unlike others before it, is that it has produced but a few of the disorderly manifestations that too often attend upon such times.

Wild radicalism has made few converts, and the greatest tribute that I can pay to my countrymen is that in these days of crushing want there persists an orderly and hopeful spirit on the part of the millions of our people who have suffered so much. To fail to offer them a new chance is not only to betray their hopes but to misunderstand their patience.

To meet by reaction that danger of radicalism is to invite disaster. Reaction is no barrier to the radical. It is a challenge, a provocation. The way to meet that danger is to offer a workable program of reconstruction, and the party to offer it is the party with clean hands.

This, and this only, is a proper protection against blind reaction on the one hand and an improvised, hit-or-miss, irresponsible opportunism on the other.

There are two ways of viewing the Government's duty in matters affecting economic and social life. The first sees to it that a favored few are helped and hopes that some of their prosperity will leak through, sift through, to labor, to the farmer, to the small business man. That theory belongs to the party of Toryism, and I had hoped that most of the Tories left this country in 1776.

But it is not and never will be the theory of the Democratic Party. This is no time for fear, for reaction or for timidity. Here and now I invite those nominal Republicans who find that their conscience cannot be squared with the groping and the failure of their party leaders to join hands with us; here and now, in equal measure, I warn those nominal Democrats who squint at the future with their faces turned toward the past, and who feel no responsibility to the demands of the new time, that they are out of step with their Party.

Yes, the people of this country want a genuine choice this year, not a choice between two names for the same reactionary doctrine. Ours must be a party of liberal thought, of planned action, of enlightened international outlook, and of the greatest good to the greatest number of our citizens.

Now it is inevitable—and the choice is that of the times—it is inevitable that the main issue of this campaign should revolve about the clear fact of our economic condition, a depression so deep that it is without precedent in modern history. It will not do merely to state, as do Republican leaders to explain their broken promises of continued inaction, that the depression is worldwide. That was not their explanation of the apparent prosperity of 1928. The people will not forget the claim made by them then that prosperity was only a domestic product manufactured by a Republican President and a Republican Congress. If they claim paternity for the one they cannot deny paternity for the other.

I cannot take up all the problems today. I want to touch on a few that are vital. Let us look a little at the recent history and the simple economics, the kind of economics that you and I and the average man and woman talk.

In the years before 1929 we know that this country had completed a vast cycle of building and inflation; for ten years we expanded on the theory of repairing the wastes of the War, but actually expanding far beyond that, and also beyond our natural and normal growth. Now it is worth remembering, and the cold figures of finance prove it, that during that time there was little or no drop in the prices that the consumer had to pay, although those same figures proved that the cost of production fell very greatly; corporate profit resulting from this period was enormous; at the same time little of that profit was devoted to the reduction of prices. The consumer was forgotten. Very little of it went into increased wages; the worker was forgotten, and by no means an adequate proportion was even paid out in dividends—the stockholder was forgotten.

And, incidentally, very little of it was taken by taxation to the beneficent Government of those years.

What was the result? Enormous corporate surpluses piled up—the most stupendous in history. Where, under the spell of delirious speculation, did those surpluses go? Let us talk economics that the figures prove and that we can understand. Why, they went chiefly in two directions: first, into new and unnecessary plants which now stand stark and idle; and second, into the call-money market of Wall Street, either directly by the corporations, or indirectly through the banks. Those are the facts. Why blink at them?

Then came the crash. You know the story. Surpluses invested in unnecessary plants became idle. Men lost their jobs; purchasing power dried up; banks became frightened and started calling loans. Those who had money were afraid to part with it. Credit contracted. Industry stopped. Commerce declined, and unemployment mounted.

And there we are today.

Translate that into human terms. See how the events of the past three years have come home to specific groups of people: first, the group dependent on industry; second, the group dependent on agriculture; third, and made up in large part of members of the first two groups, the people who are called "small investors and depositors." In fact, the strongest possible tie between the first two groups, agriculture and industry, is the fact that the savings and to a degree the security of both are tied together in that third group—the credit structure of the Nation.

Never in history have the interests of all the people been so united in a single economic problem. Picture to yourself, for instance, the great groups of property owned by millions of our citizens,

represented by credits issued in the form of bonds and mortgages—Government bonds of all kinds. Federal, State, county, municipal; bonds of industrial companies, of utility companies; mortgages on real estate in farms and cities, and finally the vast investments of the Nation in the railroads. What is the measure of the security of each of those groups? We know well that in our complicated, interrelated credit structure if any one of these credit groups collapses they may all collapse. Danger to one is danger to all.

How, I ask, has the present Administration in Washington treated the interrelationship of these credit groups? The answer is clear: It has not recognized that interrelationship existed at all. Why, the Nation asks, has Washington failed to understand that all of these groups, each and everyone, the top of the pyramid and the bottom of the pyramid, must be considered together, that each and every one of them is dependent on every other; each and every one of them affecting the whole financial fabric?

Statesmanship and vision, my friends, require relief to all at the same time.

Just one word or two on taxes, the taxes that all of us pay toward the cost of Government of all kinds.

I know something of taxes. For three long years I have been going up and down this country preaching that Government—Federal and State and local—costs too much. I shall not stop that preaching. As an immediate program of action we must abolish useless offices. We must eliminate unnecessary functions of Government—functions, in fact, that are not definitely essential to the continuance of Government. We must merge, we must consolidate subdivisions of Government, and, like the private citizen, give up luxuries which we can no longer afford.

By our example at Washington itself, we shall have the opportunity of pointing the way of economy to local government, for let us remember well that out of every tax dollar in the average State in this Nation, 40 cents enter the treasury in Washington, D.C., 10 or 12 cents only go to the State capitals, and 48 cents are consumed by the costs of local government in counties and cities and towns.

I propose to you, my friends, and through you, that Government of all kinds, big and little, be made solvent and that the example be set by the President of the United States and his Cabinet.

And talking about setting a definite example, I congratulate this convention for having had the courage fearlessly to write into its declaration of principles what an overwhelming majority here assembled really thinks about the 18th Amendment. This convention wants repeal. Your candidate wants repeal. And I am confident that the United States of America wants repeal.

Two years ago the platform on which I ran for Governor the second time contained substantially the same provision. The overwhelming sentiment of the people of my State, as shown by the vote of that year, extends, I know, to the people of many of the other States. I say to you now that from this date on the 18th Amendment is doomed. When that happens, we as Democrats must and will, rightly and morally, enable the States to protect themselves against the importation of intoxicating liquor where such importation may violate their State laws. We must rightly and morally prevent the return of the saloon.

To go back to this dry subject of finance, because it all ties in together—the 18th Amendment has something to do with finance, too—in a comprehensive planning for the reconstruction of the great credit groups, including Government credit, I list an important place for that prize statement of principle in the platform here adopted calling

for the letting in of the light of day on issues of securities, foreign and domestic, which are offered for sale to the investing public.

My friends, you and I as common-sense citizens know that it would help to protect the savings of the country from the dishonesty of crooks and from the lack of honor of some men in high financial places. Publicity is the enemy of crookedness.

And now one word about unemployment, and incidentally about agriculture. I have favored the use of certain types of public works as a further emergency means of stimulating employment and the issuance of bonds to pay for such public works, but I have pointed out that no economic end is served if we merely build without building for a necessary purpose. Such works, of course, should insofar as possible be self-sustaining if they are to be financed by the issuing of bonds. So as to spread the points of all kinds as widely as possible, we must take definite steps to shorten the working day and the working week.

Let us use common sense and business sense. Just as one example, we know that a very hopeful and immediate means of relief, both for the unemployed and for agriculture, will come from a wide plan of the converting of many millions of acres of marginal and unused land into timberland through reforestation. There are tens of millions of acres east of the Mississippi River alone in abandoned farms, in cut-over land, now growing up in worthless brush. Why, every European Nation has a definite land policy, and has had one for generations. We have none. Having none, we face a future of soil erosion and timber famine. It is clear that economic foresight and immediate employment march hand in hand in the call for the reforestation of these vast areas.

In so doing, employment can be given to a million men. That is the kind of public work that is self-sustaining, and therefore capable of being financed by the issuance of bonds which are made secure by the fact that the growth of tremendous crops will provide adequate security for the investment.

Yes, I have a very definite program for providing employment by that means. I have done it, and I am doing it today in the State of New York. I know that the Democratic Party can do it successfully in the Nation. That will put men to work, and that is an example of the action that we are going to have.

Now as a further aid to agriculture, we know perfectly well—but have we come out and said so clearly and distinctly?—we should repeal immediately those provisions of law that compel the Federal Government to go into the market to purchase, to sell, to speculate in farm products in a futile attempt to reduce farm surpluses. And they are the people who are talking of keeping Government out of business. The practical way to help the farmer is by an arrangement that will, in addition to lightening some of the impoverishing burdens from his back, do something toward the reduction of the surpluses of staple commodities that hang on the market. It should be our aim to add to the world prices of staples products the amount of a reasonable tariff protection, to give agriculture the same protection that industry has today.

And in exchange for this immediately increased return I am sure that the farmers of this Nation would agree ultimately to such planning of their production as would reduce the surpluses and make it unnecessary in later years to depend on dumping those surpluses abroad in order to support domestic prices. That result has been accomplished in other Nations; why not in America, too?

Farm leaders and farm economists, generally, agree that a plan based on that principle is a desirable first step in the reconstruction of agriculture. It does not in itself furnish a complete program, but it will serve in great measure in the long run to remove the pall of a surplus without the continued perpetual threat of world dumping. Final voluntary reduction of surplus is a part of our objective, but the long continuance and the present burden of existing surpluses make it necessary to repair great damage of the present by immediate emergency measures.

Such a plan as that, my friends, does not cost the Government any money, nor does it keep the Government in business or in speculation.

As to the actual working of a bill, I believe that the Democratic Party stands ready to be guided by whatever the responsible farm groups themselves agree on. That is a principle that is sound; and again I ask for action.

One more word about the farmer, and I know that every delegate in this hall who lives in the city knows why I lay emphasis on the farmer. It is because one-half of our population, over 50,000,000 people, are dependent on agriculture; and, my friends, if those 50,000,000 people have no money, no cash, to buy what is produced in the city, the city suffers to an equal or greater extent.

That is why we are going to make the voters understand this year that this Nation is not merely a Nation of independence, but it is, if we are to survive, bound to be a Nation of interdependence—town and city, and North and South, East and West. That is our goal, and that goal will be understood by the people of this country no matter where they live.

Yes, the purchasing power of that half of our population dependent on agriculture is gone. Farm mortgages reach nearly ten billions of dollars today and interest charges on that alone are $560,000,000 a year. But that is not all. The tax burden caused by extravagant and inefficient local government is an additional factor. Our most immediate concern should be to reduce the interest burden on these mortgages.

Rediscounting of farm mortgages under salutary restrictions must be expanded and should, in the future, be conditioned on the reduction of interest rates. Amortization payments, maturities should likewise in this crisis be extended before rediscount is permitted where the mortgagor is sorely pressed. That, my friends, is another example of practical, immediate relief: Action.

I aim to do the same thing, and it can be done, for the small home-owner in our cities and villages. We can lighten his burden and develop his purchasing power. Take away, my friends, that spectre of too high an interest rate. Take away that spectre of the due date just a short time away. Save homes; save homes for thousands of self-respecting families, and drive out that spectre of insecurity from our midst.

Out of all the tons of printed paper, out of all the hours of oratory, the recriminations, the defenses, the happy-thought plans in Washington and in every State, there emerges one great, simple, crystal-pure fact that during the past ten years a Nation of 120,000,000 people has been led by the Republican leaders to erect an impregnable barbed wire entanglement around its borders through the instrumentality of tariffs which have isolated us from all the other human beings in all the rest of the round world. I accept that admirable tariff statement in the platform of this convention. It would protect American business and American labor. By our acts of the past we have invited and received the retaliation of other Nations. I propose an invitation to them to forget the past, to sit at the table with us, as friends, and to plan with us for the restoration of the trade of the world.

Go into the home of the business man. He knows what the tariff has done for him. Go into the home of the factory worker. He knows why goods do not move. Go into the home of the farmer.

He knows how the tariff has helped to ruin him.

At last our eyes are open. At last the American people are ready to acknowledge that Republican leadership was wrong and that the Democracy is right.

My program, of which I can only touch on these points, is based upon this simple moral principle: the welfare and the soundness of a Nation depend first upon what the great mass of the people wish and need and second, whether or not they are getting it.

What do the people of America want more than anything else? To my mind, they want two things: work, with all the moral and spiritual values that go with it; and with work, a reasonable measure of security—security for themselves and for their wives and children. Work and security—these are more than words. They are more than facts. They are the spiritual values, the true goal toward which our efforts of reconstruction should lead. These are the values that this program is intended to gain; these are the values we have failed to achieve by the leadership we now have.

Our Republican leaders tell us economic laws—sacred, inviolable, unchangeable—cause panics which no one could prevent. But while they prate of economic laws, men and women are starving. We must lay hold of the fact that economic laws are not made by nature. They are made by human beings.

Yes, when—not if when—we get the chance, the Federal Government will assume bold leadership in distress relief. For years Washington has alternated between putting its head in the sand and saying there is no large number of destitute people in our midst who need food and clothing, and then saying the States should take care of them, if they are. Instead of planning two and a half years ago to do what they are now trying to do, they kept putting it off from day to day, week to week, and month to month, until the conscience of America demanded action.

I say that while primary responsibility for relief rests with localities now, as ever, yet the Federal Government has always had and still has a continuing responsibility for the broader public welfare. It will soon fulfill that responsibility.

And now, just a few words about our plans for the next four months. By coming here instead of waiting for a formal notification, I have made it clear that I believe we should eliminate expensive ceremonies and that we should set in motion at once, tonight, my friends, the necessary machinery for an adequate presentation of the issues to the electorate of the Nation.

I myself have important duties as Governor of a great State, duties which in these times are more arduous and more grave than at any previous period. Yet I feel confident that I shall be able to make a number of short visits to several parts of the Nation. My trips will have as their first objective the study at first hand, from the lips of men and women of all parties and all occupations, of the actual conditions and needs of every part of an interdependent country.

One word more: Out of every crisis, every tribulation, every disaster, mankind rises with some share of greater knowledge, or higher decency, of purer purpose. Today we shall have come through a period of loose thinking, descending morals, an era of selfishness, among individual men and women and among Nations. Blame not Governments alone for this. Blame ourselves in equal share. Let us be frank in acknowledgment of the truth that many amongst us have made obeisance to Mammon, that the profits of speculation, the easy road without toil, have lured us from the old barricades. To return to higher standards we must abandon the false prophets and seek new leaders of our own choosing.

Never before in modern history have the essential differences between the two major American parties stood out in such striking contrast as they do today. Republican leaders not only have failed in material things, they have failed in national vision, because in disaster they have held out no hope, they have pointed out no path for the people below to climb back to places of security and of safety in our American life.

Throughout the Nation, men and women, forgotten in the political philosophy of the Government of the last years look to us here for guidance and for more equitable opportunity to share in the distribution of national wealth.

On the farms, in the large metropolitan areas, in the smaller cities and in the villages, millions of our citizens cherish the hope that their old standards of living and of thought have not gone forever. Those millions cannot and shall not hope in vain.

I pledge you, I pledge myself, to a new deal for the American people. Let us all here assembled constitute ourselves prophets of a new order of competence and of courage. This is more than a political campaign: it is a call to arms. Give me your help, not to win votes alone, but to win in this crusade to restore America to its own people.

Abolition of the Two-Thirds Rule: Proceedings of the Democratic National Convention (1936)

In 1832, the first national convention of the Democratic party decided that its candidates for president and vice president would require the votes of two-thirds of the convention's delegates to be nominated. In the rising abolitionist climate of the day, the two-thirds rule was adopted at the insistence of the party's southern wing, which wanted a virtual veto over any possible antislavery nominee. The northern- and western-based Republican party, meeting in 1856 at its first national convention, adopted instead a simple majority rule for presidential and vice presidential nominations.

In 1932, southern Democrats still insisted on the veto power that the two-thirds rule afforded them. Others in the party were losing patience. Except in 1916, when President Woodrow Wilson was renominated without opposition, every Democratic convention since 1912 had gone more than forty ballots, including the 1912 convention, which denied the nomination to its favorite candidate, Speaker of the House of Representatives James Beauchamp (Champ) Clark, and the 1924 convention, which took 103 ballots to reach a decision. Franklin D. Roosevelt considered challenging the two-thirds rule in 1932 but backed off for fear of alienating his southern supporters. Because of the rule, Roosevelt's nomination for president took four bal-

lots, even though he won the support of around three-fifths of the delegates on each of the convention's first three ballots.

Firmly in control of the 1936 Democratic national convention, Roosevelt urged the chair of the rules committee to recommend that the two-thirds rule be abolished in favor of a simple majority. The former House Speaker's son, Sen. Joel Bennett (Champ) Clark of Missouri, was happy to comply with the president's request.

Southern members of the rules committee complained that to abolish the two-thirds rule would punish the very states that had always given the Democratic party its most steadfast support. Proponents of the change argued that if the Democrats ever were to become a national majority, they could not be limited by the need to pacify one region. As a sop to southerners, the party voted to reward loyal Democratic states when apportioning delegates to future conventions. The motion to abolish the two-thirds rule passed the convention overwhelmingly.

The effects of the rule change on the Democratic party soon became apparent. In 1940, Roosevelt was able to replace Vice President John Nance Garner, a Texas conservative, on the ticket with the northern liberal secretary of agriculture, Henry A. Wallace. Since then, vice presidential nominations *have been regarded as matters more of presidential than of party prerogative, which has helped to foster a better working relationship between modern presidents and their vice presidents.*

The simple majority rule for nominations also has streamlined Democratic conventions—since 1936, only one convention has taken more than a single ballot to choose its nominee for president. The rule made it easier for the national Democratic party to reach out to black voters, who have become its most loyal supporters. Finally, by reducing the need for presidential candidates to make deals at the convention in order to attain a two-thirds majority, the new rule has given them more latitude for leadership in the White House. ～

The Permanent Chairman: The delegates in the aisles will take their seats. The convention will come to order.

The next order of business is the report of the Committee on Rules and Order of Business. The gentlemen will be seated. Those who are not entitled to the privilege of the floor will please retire as promptly as possible. The Chair takes pleasure in presenting Senator Bennett Champ Clark, chairman of the Committee on Rules. (Applause.)

Report of Committee on Rules and Order of Business, Offered by Hon. Bennett Champ Clark, of Missouri

Hon. Bennett Champ Clark: Mr. Chairman, ladies and gentlemen of the convention: By the unanimous direction of your Committee on Rules and Order of Business, I desire to submit the following report of that committee to the convention:

"Your Committee on Rules and Order of Business unanimously submits to the convention the following report, and recommends its adoption:

"*Resolved,* That the rules of the last Democratic National Convention including the rules of the House of Representatives of the Seventy-fourth Congress as far as applicable, shall be the rules of this convention, with the following exception, to-wit:

"That all questions, including the question of nominations of candidates for President of the United States and Vice President of the United States, shall be determined by a majority vote of the delegates to the convention, and the rule heretofore existing in Democratic conventions requiring a two-thirds vote in such cases is hereby specifically abrogated. (Applause.)

"*Be it Resolved,* That all nominating speeches presenting candidates for the nomination of President and Vice President shall not exceed 20 minutes, and the seconding speeches shall not exceed five minutes.

"*Be it Resolved,* That no delegate shall occupy the floor in debate for more than 30 minutes except with the unanimous consent of the convention.

"The order of business which your committee recommends is as follows:

"1. Report of Committee on Credentials.

"2. Report of Committee on Permanent Organization.

"3. Report of Committee on Rules.

"4. Report of Committee on Resolutions.

"5. Nomination and selection of a candidate for President of the United States.

"6. Nomination and selection of a candidate for Vice President of the United States.

"7. Confirmation of the selection of the members of the Democratic National Committee.

"8. Such miscellaneous business as may be in order.

"9. Adjournment of the convention.

"In addition, your committee unanimously recommends the adoption of the following resolution:

"*Be it Resolved,* That the Democratic National Committee is hereby instructed to formulate and to recommend to the next National Convention a plan for improving the system by which delegates and alternates to Democratic National Conventions are apportioned.

"*And be it Further Resolved* That in formulating this plan, the National Committee shall take into account the Democratic strength within each State, District of Columbia, and Territory, etc., in making said apportionment.

(Signed)

"Bennett Champ Clark,
"*Chairman.*
"Wesley E. McDonald,
"*Secretary.*"

Mr. Chairman, at the last National Convention in Chicago four years ago, the proposition of the abrogation of the two-thirds rule for the nomination of candidates for President and Vice President was very seriously discussed. However, the argument was strongly advanced against the abrogation at that time that to change the two-thirds rule and apply the majority rule while the strenuous contest was on for the nomination for the Presidency at that time would be to change the rule while the game was in progress. Therefore, Mr. Chairman, by unanimous vote the Chicago convention adopted a resolution specifically submitting to this convention the question of the abrogation of the two-thirds rule, and directing the Democratic National Committee to include that question for submission in its call for this convention. That submission was included in the call of the Democratic National Committee for the holding of this convention.

Mr. Chairman, your committee has been unanimously of the opinion that such a convention as this, with so much of harmony and unanimity, was the ideal and proper place for making a change for the nomination of President and Vice President, which has long been overdue in the Democratic Party, because this year, Mr. Chairman, everyone knows that it does not make the slightest difference so far as the nominees to be selected in this convention are concerned, whether we have a majority rule or a two-thirds rule, or a 99 percent rule or a 100 percent rule. (Applause.) Everyone knows, Mr. Chairman, that the present President and Vice President of the United States combine in their own prominent persons the President and Vice President of the United States, the nominee of this convention for President and the nominee for Vice President, and the next President and Vice President of the United States.

Mr. Chairman, I am happy to say that in the deliberations of the Committee on Rules and Order of Business on this important question, there has been an absolute absence of sectional feeling, of personality, or of rancor of any sort. There have been no suggestions of personalities, Mr. Chairman, either present or past. None of the great men who in past years have been candidates for the Democratic nomination of President, or who in past years have been the nominees for President of the United States by the action of Democratic conventions, could in any way be reflected upon by the action of this convention in subjecting Democratic procedure to the Jeffersonian principle of the rule of the majority.

Mr. Chairman, there could be no sectional issue, because no section of the United States could be injured or affronted by being subjected to the will of the majority of the Democratic National Convention. And, thank God, Mr. President, the Democratic Party is no longer a sectional party; it has become a great national party! (Applause and cheers.) And tonight there is not one State in the Union, North or South, or

East or West, in which it is not only possible but probable that the ticket of Roosevelt and Garner is going to carry.

Now, Mr. Chairman, what we propose is simply to subject procedure in the Democratic Convention to the rule laid down by the greatest Democrat that ever lived in the United States, the father and founder of the Democratic Party, Thomas Jefferson. In his first inaugural address, which has become a classic and which every school child in the United States should be compelled to learn by heart and recite at least once a year, in reciting the absolute necessity of success for the experiment of the young Republic upon which we were then embarking and of the rules which would guide the administration, he said in these immortal words: "Absolute acquiescence in the decisions of the majority, the vital principle of republics from which is no appeal but to force, the vital principle and immediate parent of despotism."

Mr. Chairman, I shall not detain the convention by going into the reasons which originally may have actuated the Democratic Party in adopting the two-thirds rule. I say only that whatever reason there may have been for the two-thirds rule, in my judgment passed with the Civil War, and the two-thirds rule should have been abolished with the abolition of slavery.

On behalf of the Rules and Order of Business Committee, Mr. Chairman, I move the adoption of the report, and on that the previous question.

Adoption of Report of Committee on Rules and Order of Business

The Permanent Chairman: The chairman of the committee moves the previous question on the report. As many as favor the previous question will vote "Aye"; as many as are opposed will vote "No". The "Ayes" seem to have it; the previous question is ordered.

The vote recurs on the report. As many as favor agreeing to the report will vote "Aye"; those opposed will vote "No". The "Ayes" seem to have it. The "Ayes" have it and the report is agreed to.

The Literary Digest *Poll (1936)*

Modern public opinion polling was born when Archibald Crossley, Elmo Roper, and George Gallup founded the Gallup poll in 1935. Yet the infant industry was nearly smothered in its crib when the long-established and much-celebrated Literary Digest *straw poll predicted that Gov. Alfred M. Landon of Kansas, the Republican nominee for president, would easily defeat President Franklin D. Roosevelt in the election of 1936.*

The Gallup poll endured; indeed, its reputation for accuracy was enhanced when it correctly predicted the outcome of the 1936 election. Gallup had written a doctoral dissertation on statistical sampling techniques and designed his poll accordingly. The poll was not foolproof (see "Harry S Truman's Acceptance Speech to the Democratic National Convention," p. 462), but from 1936 until 1988, it almost always came within a few percentage points of the winning candidate's share of the popular vote.

Unlike the Gallup poll, the Literary Digest poll derived its national sample in a nonrandom manner. The sample was large—10 million "ballots" were sent out through the mail, of which 2.4 million were returned. But, because the sample was drawn largely from telephone books and lists of automobile owners in an era when telephone and automobile ownership was not broadly based, poor and working class voters were underrepresented.

The outcome of the election of 1936 was in sharp contrast to the Literary Digest's October 31, 1936, prediction. In the poll, 1.3 million ballots, or 55 percent, were cast for Landon, representing 370 electoral votes, and 1.0 million ballots, or 41 percent, were cast for Roosevelt, representing 161 electoral votes. In the election, FDR won a 60.8 percent to 36.6 percent majority in the popular vote and a 523-8 majority in the electoral college.

Interestingly, the Literary Digest's class-biased sampling techniques had not prevented it from predicting the outcome of the 1920, 1924, 1928, and 1932 elections with reasonable accuracy. The poll had registered 56 percent for Roosevelt in 1932, for example, just three percentage points fewer than his actual tally.

The explanation for why the Literary Digest poll was accurate from 1920 to 1932 and inaccurate in 1936 is politically revealing. Until 1936 voting was not based primarily on economic class; hence, class-bias was not likely to render a sample inaccurate. By 1936, however, the liberal New Deal policies of Roosevelt's first term had divided the electorate along class lines, alienating the wealthy from the Democratic party but attracting support from the more numerous poor and working classes.

Indeed, the 1936 election was evidence that Roosevelt had built on the foundation of his 1932 victory a lasting New Deal coalition of workers, farmers, blacks, Catholics, Jews, and southerners, completing the realignment that transformed the Democrats into the nation's majority party on the basis of economic issues. (See "H. L. Mencken's 'Onward, Christian Soldiers!' Article," p. 296.)

As an electoral majority, the New Deal coalition endured well into the 1960s. As a governing coalition, however, it actually lost much of its potency in the aftermath of the 1936 election. In contrast to 1932, Roosevelt ran a safe, backward-looking campaign in 1936. His coattails in the congressional elections were short. Yet in 1937, falsely claiming a mandate, FDR tried to "pack" the conservative Supreme Court with additional justices who would be sympathetic to his policies. The reaction in Congress was not just defeat for the president's plan but the formation of a conservative coalition of southern Democratic and Republican legislators that, like the New Deal Democratic majority of voters, also was to last into the 1960s, thwarting presidential efforts to effect liberal policy change. ~

Landon, 1,293,669; Roosevelt, 972,897 Final Returns in *The Digest's* Poll of Ten Million Voters

October 31, 1936

Well, the great battle of the ballots in the Poll of ten million voters, scattered throughout the forty-eight States of the Union, is now finished, and in the table below we record the figures received up to the hour of going to press.

These figures are exactly as received from more than one in every five voters polled in our country—they are neither weighted, adjusted nor interpreted.

Never before in an experience covering more than a quarter of a century in taking polls have we received so many different varieties of criticism—praise from many; condemnation from many others—and yet it has been just of the same type that has come to us every time a Poll has been taken in all these years.

A telegram from a newspaper in California asks: "Is it true that Mr. Hearst has purchased *The Literary Digest?*" A telephone message only the day before these lines were written: "Has the Republican National Committee purchased *The Literary Digest?*" And all types and varieties, including "Have the Jews purchased *The Literary Digest?*" "Is the Pope of Rome a stockholder of *The Literary Digest?*" And so it goes— all equally absurd and amusing. We could add more to this list, and yet all of these questions in recent days are but repetitions of what we have been experiencing all down the years from the very first Poll.

Problem — Now, are the figures in this Poll correct? In answer to this question we will simply refer to a telegram we sent to a young man in Massachusetts the other day in answer to his challenge to us to wager $100,000 on the accuracy of our Poll. We wired him as follows:

"For nearly a quarter century, we have been taking Polls of the voters in the forty-eight States, and especially in Presidential years, and we have always merely mailed the ballots, counted and recorded those returned and let the people of the Nation draw their conclusions as to our accuracy. So far, we have been right in every Poll. Will we be right in the current Poll? That, as Mrs. Roosevelt said concerning the President's re-election, is in the 'lap of the gods.'

"We never make any claims before election but we respectfully refer you to the opinion of one of the most quoted citizens to-day, the Hon. James A. Farley, Chairman of the Democratic National Committee. This is what Mr. Farley said October 14, 1932:

" 'Any sane person can not escape the implication of such a gigantic sampling of popular opinion as is embraced in *The Literary Digest* straw vote. I consider this conclusive evidence as to the desire of the people of this country for a change in the National Government. *The Literary Digest* poll is an achievement of no little magnitude. It is a Poll fairly and correctly conducted.' "

In studying the table of the voters from all of the States printed below, please remember that we make no claims at this time for their absolute accuracy. On a similar occasion we felt it important to say:

> "In a wild year like this, however, many sagacious observers will refuse to bank upon appearances, however convincing. As for *The Digest,* it draws no conclusions from the results of its vast distribution of twenty million ballots. True to its historic non-partizan policy—or 'omni-partizan,' as some editor described it in 1928—we supply our readers with the facts to the best of our ability, and leave them to draw their own conclusions.
>
> "We make no claim to infallibility. We did not coin the phrase "uncanny accuracy" which has been so freely applied to our Polls. We know only too well the limitations of every straw vote, however enormous the sample gathered, however scientific the method. It would be a miracle if every State of the forty-eight behaved on Election day exactly as forecast by the Poll".

We say now about Rhode Island and Massachusetts that our figures indicate in our own judgment too large a percentage for Mr. Landon and too small a percentage for Mr. Roosevelt, and altho in 1932 the figures in these two States indicated Mr. Hoover's carrying both, we announced:

"A study of the returns convinces us that in those States our ballots have somehow failed to come back in adequate quantity from large bodies of Democratic voters."

Our own opinion was that they would be found in the Roosevelt column, and they were. We will not do the same this year; we feel that both States will be found in the Landon column, and we are reaching this conclusion by the same process that lead to the reverse conclusion in 1932.

Pennsylvania is another State which requires special mention. Four years ago, our figures gave the State to Mr. Roosevelt, and Mr. Hoover carried it on Election day. In comparing our ballot this year with that of 1932, we find that in many cities in Pennsylvania our figures showed a much higher trend toward Mr. Roosevelt than was justified by the election figures on Election day in 1932. In examining the very same cities now we discover the reverse trend, and in cities that in 1932 indicated an approximately 60-40 per cent. relationship between Roosevelt and Hoover, we now find 60 per cent for Landon and 40 per cent. for Roosevelt.

That's the plain language of it. Many people wonder at these great changes in a State like Pennsylvania, and we confess to wonderment ourselves.

On the Pacific Coast, we find California, Oregon and Washington all vote for Mr. Landon in our Poll, and yet we are told that the Pacific Coast is "aflame" for Mr. Roosevelt.

A State like California is always a difficult State to get an accurate opinion from by the polling method, and we may be far astray, yet every one should remember that in the Gubernatorial campaign a few years ago, we took a Poll of California when it was believed by most of California citizens that Mr. Upton Sinclair would be elected Governor, and the result of our poll showed that Mr. Sinclair would *not* be elected Governor and the Poll was correct.

The State of Washington seems to be more favorable to Mr. Landon than either Oregon or California. We can not in our Poll detect anything that would indicate a reason for this difference.

Seattle – Right here we wish to say that in 1932 our Poll in Seattle gave Mr. Roosevelt 65.43 per cent. of the vote, and he carried that city by 61.58 per cent of the vote. In one current Poll, 1936, Seattle gives Mr. Landon 58.52 per cent. and Mr. Roosevelt 40.46 per cent. Our readers will notice we overestimated Mr. Roosevelt in 1932—are we overestimating Mr. Landon now? We see no reason for supposing so. And the three Pacific Coast States which now show for Mr. Landon and which millions believe will vote for Mr. Roosevelt (they may be right) in 1924, 1928 and 1932 were correctly forecast in *The Literary Digest* Polls.

In the great Empire State, New York, the figures for so large a State are what might be called very close. After looking at the figures for New York in the column at the left, remember that in 1932 we gave Mr. Roosevelt 46.1 per cent. and Mr. Hoover 43.9 per cent., even closer than it is to-day. And yet we correctly forecast that Mr. Roosevelt would carry the State.

And so we might go on with many States that are very close, and some not so close, but in which local conditions have much to do with results, not in polls such as our Poll, but on Election day.

The Poll represents the most extensive straw ballot in the field—the most experienced in view of its twenty-five years of perfecting—the most unbiased in view of its prestige—a Poll that has always previously been correct.

Even its critics admit its value as an index of popular sentiment. As one of these critics, *The Nation,* observes:

"Because it indicates both the 1932 and 1936 vote, it offers the raw material for as careful a prognostication as it is possible to make at this time."

What Went Wrong With the Polls?

None of Straw Votes Got Exactly the Right Answer – Why?

November 14, 1936

In 1920, 1924, 1928 and 1932, *The Literary Digest* Polls were right. Not only right in the sense that they showed the winner; they forecast the *actual popular vote* with such a small percentage of error (less than 1 per cent. in 1932) that newspapers and individuals everywhere heaped such phrases as "uncannily accurate" and "amazingly right" upon us.

Four years ago, when the Poll was running his way, our very good friend Jim Farley was saying that "no sane person could escape the implication" of a sampling "so fairly and correctly conducted."

Well, this year we used precisely the same method that had scored four bull's-eyes in four previous tries. And we were far from correct. Why? We ask that question in all sincerity, because *we want to know.*

"Reasons"—Oh, we've been flooded with "reasons." Hosts of people who feel they have learned more about polling in a few months than we have learned in more than a score of years have told us just where we were off. Hundreds of astute "second-guessers" have assured us, by telephone, by letter, in the newspapers, that the reasons for our error were "obvious." Were they?

Suppose we review a few of these "obvious reasons."

The one most often heard runs something like this: "This election was different. Party lines were obliterated. For the first time in more than a century, *all* the 'have-nots' were on one side. *The Digest,* polling names from telephone books and lists of automobile owners,

Final Report: *Literary Digest ...*

	Elec-toral Vote	Landon 1936 Total Vote for State	How the Same Voters Voted in the 1932 Election						Roose-velt 1936 Total Vote for State
			Repub-licans	Demo-crats	Social-ists	Others	Did Not Vote	Vote Not Indi-cated	
Alabama	11	3,060	1,218	1,298	3	3	412	126	10,082
Arizona	3	2,337	1,431	647	18	—	129	112	1,975
Arkansas	9	2,724	1,338	953	7	9	274	—	—
California	22	89,516	65,360	16,200	315	53	3,519	4,069	77,245
Colorado	6	15,949	11,872	2,714	131	12	637	583	10,025
Connecticut	8	28,809	22,939	3,376	111	7	1,230	1,146	13,413
Delaware	3	2,918	2,242	328	9	—	134	104	2,048
Florida	7	6,087	3,121	2,051	13	5	594	303	8,620
Georgia	12	3,948	1,239	1,817	5	11	708	168	12,915
Idaho	4	3,653	2,672	698	9	8	103	163	2,611
Illinois	29	123,297	85,112	25,885	573	69	6,506	5,152	79,035
Indiana	14	42,805	31,913	7,644	134	49	1,290	1,775	26,663
Iowa	11	31,871	22,823	6,164	135	26	1,272	1,451	18,614
Kansas	9	35,408	25,315	6,489	147	15	1,466	1,976	20,254
Kentucky	11	13,365	8,957	2,939	35	14	793	627	16,592
Louisiana	10	3,686	1,366	1,742	9	3	384	182	7,902
Maine	5	11,742	8,619	1,567	25	35	713	783	5,227
Maryland	8	17,463	9,754	4,685	110	2	1,479	1,433	18,341
Massachusetts	17	87,449	70,567	10,105	330	31	3,213	3,203	25,965
Michigan	19	51,478	38,526	8,665	287	22	2,113	1,865	25,686
Minnesota	11	30,762	22,386	5,958	109	3	972	1,334	20,733
Mississippi	9	848	269	394	1	—	137	47	6,080
Missouri	15	50,022	33,551	11,149	244	45	2,975	2,058	38,267
Montana	4	4,490	3,336	828	23	—	139	164	3,562
Nebraska	7	18,280	12,436	4,241	100	7	685	811	11,770
Nevada	3	1,003	658	272	—	—	36	37	955
New Hampshire	4	9,207	7,504	1,072	21	—	253	357	2,737
New Jersey	16	58,677	45,361	8,625	251	17	2,383	2,040	27,631
New Mexico	3	1,625	1,003	444	7	1	80	90	1,662
New York	47	162,260	114,574	33,052	805	45	7,125	6,659	139,277
North Carolina	13	6,113	3,532	1,656	33	5	580	307	16,324
North Dakota	4	4,250	2,787	1,157	15	—	108	182	3,666
Ohio	26	77,896	58,232	13,391	420	66	2,747	3,040	50,778
Oklahoma	11	14,442	8,393	4,260	29	3	1,050	707	15,975
Oregon	5	11,747	8,593	2,014	72	6	521	541	10,951
Pennsylvania	36	119,086	86,433	20,097	543	115	6,461	5,437	81,114
Rhode Island	4	10,401	8,165	1,269	32	5	511	419	3,489
South Carolina	8	1,247	216	658	2	—	300	71	7,105
South Dakota	4	8,483	5,712	2,096	42	14	248	371	4,597
Tennessee	11	9,883	5,785	2,354	29	31	1,178	506	19,829
Texas	23	15,341	6,302	6,774	43	3	1,559	660	37,501
Utah	4	4,067	2,906	851	21	1	155	133	5,318
Vermont	3	7,241	5,829	822	20	2	239	329	2,458
Virginia	11	10,223	5,696	2,848	57	18	1,194	410	16,783
Washington	8	21,370	14,841	4,800	67	30	806	826	15,300
West Virginia	8	13,660	10,060	2,589	30	14	424	542	10,235
Wisconsin	12	33,796	22,587	8,495	157	12	1,142	1,403	20,781
Wyoming	3	2,526	1,830	510	15	1	83	87	1,533
State Unknown	—	7,156	4,763	1,416	35	5	263	676	6,545
Total	531	1,293,669	920,225	250,059	5,629	825	61,323	55,608	972,897

...1936 Presidential Poll

How the Same Voters Voted In the 1932 Election						Lemke 1936 Total Vote for State	How the Same Voters Voted in the 1932 Election					
Republicans	Democrats	Socialists	Others	Did Not Vote	Vote Not Indicated		Republicans	Democrats	Socialists	Others	Did Not Vote	Vote Not Indicated
371	8,530	50	1	736	394	68	5	49	4	—	4	6
248	1,555	33	—	70	69	104	22	52	8	—	10	12
228	6,655	16	8	373	328	138	14	98	4	3	9	10
15,165	53,520	1,816	63	3,578	3,103	4,977	1,620	2,560	117	25	163	492
1,747	7,256	284	13	439	286	579	136	333	29	2	26	53
2,584	9,113	408	6	788	514	1,489	245	1,006	53	3	70	112
503	1,345	34	—	96	70	35	6	19	3	—	2	5
635	6,924	41	—	614	406	195	37	116	6	2	12	22
379	10,377	42	9	1,569	539	35	3	23	1	—	6	2
398	1,989	30	8	89	97	224	69	109	8	11	9	18
14,793	54,612	1,542	57	4,790	3,241	6,415	1,172	4,219	169	17	304	534
4,513	20,247	302	22	719	860	2,166	476	1,352	64	11	73	190
3,190	13,611	258	14	829	712	2,829	560	1,831	86	11	88	253
4,182	14,121	257	11	846	837	902	226	482	52	1	43	98
1,586	13,594	95	6	703	608	732	69	554	24	—	31	54
445	6,401	39	—	697	320	841	35	667	23	2	55	59
635	3,820	41	1	289	551	418	64	277	3	2	42	30
1,891	13,540	328	5	1,366	1,211	614	56	422	22	1	34	79
5,141	17,499	744	16	1,635	930	5,415	1,002	3,670	133	3	236	371
5,114	17,402	748	26	1,472	924	3,376	680	2,145	128	4	130	289
3,699	14,855	511	22	861	785	5,426	804	3,893	115	14	157	443
88	5,396	8	1	298	289	43	5	32	1	—	2	3
4,463	30,608	455	15	1,485	1,241	2,368	322	1,680	73	4	122	167
660	2,517	94	1	151	139	212	57	108	12	1	6	28
1,677	9,045	177	2	418	451	862	157	594	31	2	18	60
163	716	2	—	42	32	36	9	22	—	—	4	1
479	1,984	51	1	114	108	372	84	238	8	—	18	24
5,495	18,642	1,032	14	1,548	900	2,444	442	1,633	89	1	104	175
212	1,290	24	—	70	66	54	13	33	1	2	2	3
18,241	99,938	4,101	141	10,604	6,252	14,656	2,106	10,414	303	20	670	1,143
820	13,778	119	6	946	655	35	5	20	3	—	4	3
694	2,679	30	2	97	164	1,111	192	743	32	5	29	110
9,465	35,864	1,315	38	2,454	1,642	8,156	1,580	5,389	249	14	375	549
1,289	12,389	53	2	687	655	217	36	143	10	—	9	19
1,966	7,666	298	7	567	447	655	196	313	46	7	30	63
14,502	56,082	1,340	55	5,733	3,402	7,507	1,121	5,089	187	11	467	632
600	2,470	90	—	208	121	794	148	545	12	3	31	55
101	5,943	6	6	701	348	20	2	11	1	—	2	4
859	3,314	46	5	125	158	770	122	539	20	10	20	59
1,419	15,510	128	33	1,938	801	100	14	63	2	—	12	9
1,860	31,262	149	5	2,668	1,557	558	58	417	13	1	28	41
954	3,935	69	8	189	163	119	30	65	8	—	5	11
489	1,756	37	—	84	83	174	48	90	2	—	18	16
1,121	13,346	141	14	1,517	644	74	17	37	4	—	8	8
2,281	11,423	278	53	709	556	683	170	374	28	27	31	53
1,278	8,229	52	11	305	360	199	51	119	4	1	11	13
3,144	15,578	582	4	799	674	3,642	412	2,727	118	—	110	285
242	1,144	27	1	63	56	78	22	46	1	1	4	4
924	4,724	97	9	231	560	693	125	406	23	1	35	103
142,942	714,194	18,420	722	57,310	39,309	83,610	14,845	55,757	2,333	233	3,679	6,773

simply did not reach the lower strata."
And so on. . . .

"Have-nots" — Well, in the first place, the "have-nots" did not reelect Mr. Roosevelt. That they contributed to his astonishing plurality, no one can doubt. But the fact remains that a majority of farmers, doctors, grocers and candlestick-makers *also* voted for the President. As Dorothy Thompson remarked in the New York *Herald Tribune,* you could eliminate the straight labor vote, the relief vote and the Negro vote, and *still* Mr. Roosevelt would have a majority.

So that "reason" does not appear to hold much water. Besides—

We *did* reach these so-called "have-not" strata. In the city of Chicago, for example, we polled *every third registered voter.* In the city of Scranton, Pennsylvania, we polled every *other* registered voter. And in Allentown, Pennsylvania, likewise other cities, we polled *every* registered voter.

Is that so? chorus the critics, a little abashed, no doubt. Well, they come back, you must have got the right answer in *those* towns, anyway.

Well, we didn't. The fact is that we were as badly off there as we were on the national total.

Cities — In Allentown, for example, 10,753 out of the 30,811 who voted returned ballots to us showing a division of 53.32 per cent. to 44.67 per cent. for Mr. Roosevelt, 41.17 per cent. for the Kansan.

In Chicago, the 100,929 voters who returned ballots to us showed a division of 48.63 per cent. to 47.56 per cent. in favor of Mr. Landon. The 1,672,175 who voted in the actual election gave the President 65.24 per cent., to 32.26 per cent. for the Republican candidate.

What happened? Why did only one in five voters in Chicago to whom *The Digest* sent ballots take the trouble to reply? And why was there a preponderance of Republicans in the one-fifth that did reply? Your guess is as good as ours. We'll go into it a little more later. The important thing in all the above is that all this conjecture about our "not reaching certain strata" simply will not hold water.

Hoover Voters — Now for another "explanation" dinned into our ears: "You got too many Hoover voters in your sample."

Well, the fact is that we've *always* got too big a sampling of Republican voters. That was true in 1920, in 1924, in 1928, and even in 1932, when we *overesti*mated the Roosevelt popular vote by three-quarters of 1 per cent.

In 1928 in Chicago, we underestimated the Democratic vote by a little more than 5 per cent., overestimated the Republican vote by the same margin.

We wondered then, as we had wondered before and have wondered since, why we were getting better cooperation in what we have always regarded as a public service from Republicans than we were getting from Democrats. Do Republicans live nearer mail-boxes? Do Democrats generally disapprove of straw polls?

We don't know that answer. All we know is that in 1932, when the tide seemed to be running away from Hoover, we were perturbed about the disproportion of Republican voters in our sampling. Republican and Democratic chieftains from all points in the country were at the telephones day after day for reports of what the Democrats called our "correctly conducted" system. And then the result came along, and it was so right, we were inclined to agree that we had been concerned without reason, and this year, when it seemed logical to suppose that the president's vote would be lighter, even if he won (hadn't that been the rule on reelections for more than a hundred years?) we decided not to worry.

Figures — So the statisticians did our worrying for us on that score, applying what they called the "compensating-ratio" in some cases, and the "switch-factor" in others. Either way, for some of the figure experts, it didn't matter; interpret our figures for 2,376,523 voters as they would, the answer was still Landon. Then other statisticians took our figures and so weighted, compensated, balanced, adjusted and interpreted them that they showed Roosevelt.

We did not attempt to interpret the figures, because we had no stake in the result other than the wish to preserve our well-earned reputation for scrupulous bookkeeping. So we sent out more than ten million ballots, exactly as we had sent them out before. We don't know what proportion went to persons who had voted for Roosevelt in 1932 or what proportion went to persons who had voted for Hoover, because our polls are secret always, and the ballots come back with no signatures, no identifying characteristics of any sort except the post-marks.

Basis – However, since the basis of the 1936 mailing-list was the 1932 mailing-list, and since the overwhelming majority of those who responded to our Poll in 1932 voted for Mr. Roosevelt, it seems altogether reasonable to assume that the majority of our ballots this year went to people who had voted for Mr. Roosevelt in 1932. There simply was no way by which *The Digest* could assure itself or the public that the marked ballots would come back in the same proportion. We couldn't very well send duplicate ballots to indifferent Democrats, or personal letters prodding them into action, because we didn't know which were Democrats and which were Republicans, let alone which would vote for Roosevelt and which for Landon.

If any of the hundreds who have so kindly offered their suggestions and criticism can tell us how we could get voters to respond proportionately, and still keep the poll secret, as we believe it ought always to be, then we wish these critics would step up and do so. And with arguments more convincing than

the familiar ones about our not reaching the "lower strata" and "sampling too many Republicans." Because those two theories explain nothing; they only add to the multiplicity and confusion of words—words—words.

Too Many – And there's another "explanation" that doesn't seem to hold much water, when you examine it closely. That's the one that argues that we polled too many voters, that cites the experience of another poll that sent out less than a fourth as many ballots and came closer to being right. The answer here is that the Baltimore *Sunpapers* polled more persons per square mile in Maryland than we did anywhere except in the cities—and the *Sunpapers* were a lot nearer right than this "model poll" for Maryland. Also, the man who came nearer the right answer than all the polls put together was Jim Farley, and Jim based his prediction on reports from tens of thousands of precinct leaders in every city, town and hamlet in the country.

So—what?

So we were wrong, altho we did everything we knew to assure ourselves of being right.

We conducted our Poll as we had always done, reported what we found, and have no alibis. We drew no special satisfaction from our figures, and we drew no conclusions from them. The result was disappointing only in the sense that it threw our figures out the window; and left us without even the satisfaction of knowing why.

Future – As for the immediate future, *The Digest* feels that in truth "the Nation has spoken." *The Digest* hails a magnificent President against whom it never uttered one word of partizan criticism. *The Digest* can not support him in the sense that newspapers support a President editorially, because *The Digest* does not editorialize. But it can obtain genuine satisfaction from the knowledge that its several Editors, as

Minor Candidates

States	Thomas 1936 Votes	Browder 1936 Votes	Colvin 1936 Votes	Aiken 1936 Votes	Others 1936 Votes	Totals	Grand Total Votes By States
Alabama	33	3	27	—	—	63	13,273
Arizona	22	24	14	—	—	60	4,476
Arkansas	37	5	21	2	5	70	10,540
California	728	967	398	44	60	2,197	173,935
Colorado	122	49	41	10	11	233	26,786
Connecticut	258	101	39	31	11	440	44,151
Delaware	16	2	8	—	1	27	5,028
Florida	58	22	31	6	2	119	15,021
Georgia	45	12	27	—	17	101	16,999
Idaho	34	3	17	1	3	58	6,546
Illinois	807	891	199	52	38	1,987	210,734
Indiana	215	69	158	13	12	467	72,101
Iowa	177	47	107	13	5	349	53,663
Kansas	156	38	107	4	3	308	56,872
Kentucky	77	23	61	4	7	172	30,861
Louisiana	85	28	37	—	6	156	12,585
Maine	53	11	8	2	5	79	17,576
Maryland	132	80	30	11	5	258	36,676
Massachusetts	544	310	72	42	32	1,000	119,829
Michigan	527	151	118	20	4	820	81,360
Minnesota	375	163	185	29	12	764	57,685
Mississippi	18	6	16	—	1	41	7,012
Missouri	468	97	103	16	13	697	91,354
Montana	58	10	18	—	2	88	8,352
Nebraska	79	34	42	1	4	160	31,072
Nevada	9	5	3	1	1	19	2,013
New Hampshire	56	17	13	—	—	86	12,402
New Jersey	601	367	87	23	24	1,102	89,854
New Mexico	12	3	7	—	—	22	3,363
New York	2,404	4,372	364	138	164	7,442	323,635
North Carolina	56	11	48	2	4	121	22,593
North Dakota	41	13	32	—	1	87	9,114
Ohio	590	325	247	65	24	1,251	138,081
Oklahoma	134	24	65	11	3	237	29,971
Oregon	164	48	74	13	12	311	23,664
Pennsylvania	1,051	608	367	63	32	2,121	209,828
Rhode Island	68	43	15	7	1	134	14,818
South Carolina	12	13	22	—	7	54	8,426
South Dakota	43	26	24	2	3	98	13,858
Tennessee	81	19	64	2	—	166	29,978
Texas	187	49	87	9	14	346	53,746
Utah	43	14	12	—	5	74	9,578
Vermont	41	6	13	1	2	63	9,936
Virginia	88	33	60	3	4	188	27,268
Washington	190	136	91	23	14	454	37,807
West Virginia	63	7	41	1	4	116	24,210
Wisconsin	686	160	97	10	6	959	59,178
Wyoming	11	2	2	—	—	15	4,152
State Unknown	67	38	52	8	2	167	14,563
Total	11,822	9,485	3,771	683	586	26,347	2,376,523

American citizens, and its millions of readers, as American citizens, will stand behind the First Citizen.

Speaking of the President, there is a spot of comfort for us in the knowledge that he himself was pretty badly off on his Electoral total, and that he "laughed it off" in his genial way. His last guess was 360 votes to Mr. Landon's 171. (On June 5 he had estimated his margin at 315 to 216.)

As for the more distant future, the questions have been asked: Will *The Digest* conduct another Poll? Will it change its methods?

The answer to the first question we phrase in others: Should the Democratic Party have quit in 1924, when it reached a modern low-ebb in power and confidence, instead of going on to the greatest triumph in its history? Should the Republican Party have quit in 1912, when it carried only two States? Should the University of Minnesota, with the greatest record in modern football, give up the sport because it finally lost one game, after a string of twenty-one victories?

The answer to the second question is: We'll cross that bridge when we come to it.

Alben W. Barkley's "Third Term" Speech to the Democratic National Convention (1940)

The two-term tradition that Thomas Jefferson deliberately created in 1807 was not overtly challenged until Franklin D. Roosevelt ran for a third term in 1940. (See "Thomas Jefferson's 'No Third Term' Letter," p. 101.) Ulysses S. Grant (in 1876) and Woodrow Wilson (in 1920) probably would have liked to serve an additional four years but were too unpopular at the end of their second terms even to be renominated by their parties. Theodore Roosevelt's situation was more complicated. He was elected president only once, in 1904, but, as the vice president who succeeded to the presidency when William L. McKinley was assassinated in 1901, he had served all but six months of McKinley's four-year term. In 1908, Roosevelt declined a certain renomination by his party, calling the two-term tradition a "wise custom." Four years later, however, he ran for president again, first as a Republican, then as a third-party candidate. (See " 'Bull Moose' Party Platform," p. 256.) That he had declined a "third cup of coffee" in 1908, Roosevelt said, did not mean that he never intended to drink coffee again.

In 1940, FDR, both publicly and in private, kept his intentions unclear until almost the last minute. Roosevelt's most pertinent statement concerning his plans for the presidential election had been made in 1937, when he de-

clared that his "great ambition on January 20, 1941," was to "turn over this desk and chair in the White House" to someone else. Emboldened by Roosevelt's silence and, in some cases, by his encouragement, other candidates launched campaigns for the 1940 Democratic presidential nomination, including Vice President John Nance Garner and Postmaster-General James A. Farley.

As the second term wore on, however, Roosevelt became increasingly concerned about the international situation. Germany, led by Adolf Hitler, began to annex territory from neighboring countries in 1938, then invaded Poland on September 1, 1939. By June 1940, Hitler had overrun most of continental Europe and seemed poised to conquer Great Britain. Meanwhile, in Asia and the Pacific, Japan was pursuing equally imperialistic ambitions of its own.

Roosevelt did not trust either the mostly isolationist Republicans or any of his less experienced fellow Democrats to lead the country into a period of likely war. On July 16, 1940, the second night of the Democratic national convention in Chicago and the eve of the balloting for the presidential nomination, Roosevelt asked Sen. Alben W. Barkley of Kentucky, the convention chair, to tell the anxious delegates that although he had no "de-

sire or purpose to continue in the office of President, . . . the delegates are free to vote for any candidate," including, by implication, the president himself.

Jubilantly, the Democrats renominated Roosevelt on July 17. FDR then announced that he would refuse the nomination if the convention did not accept his controversial choice for a vice-presidential running mate, Secretary of Agriculture Henry A. Wallace. Reluctantly, the delegates acceded to his demands. (See "Abolition of the Two-Thirds Rule: Proceedings of the Democratic National Convention," p. 344.)

Public opinion polls showed that the voters were deeply divided over the propriety of Roosevelt's candidacy. Republicans took up the cry of "No third term!" on behalf of their nominee, business leader Wendell L. Willkie. Democrats rejoined that, in perilous times, the country would be foolish to "change horses in midstream." Roosevelt was reelected but by a narrower margin than in 1936—five million popular votes, compared with eleven million popular votes in the previous election.

~

The Permanent Chairman (Honorable Alben W. Barkley, of Kentucky): Fellow Democrats, To the national committee, which recommended and to this convention which has chosen me as permanent chairman, I express my profound appreciation.

I shall endeavor to preside over your deliberations with promptness and fairness to the end that you may consummate your task in dignity and good order.

We assemble here in circumstances so uncommon, in the midst of world disorders so unprecedented and surrounded by domestic obligations so compulsive as to charge us with the duty of preparing our Nation to meet consequences which will project themselves indefinitely into the unpredictable future.

The Democratic Party has faced one crisis after another during its long and glorious history.

It has been tested in the crucible of faith and achievement. It has never faltered in its devotion to the higher interests of the people of America. It will not falter now. (Applause.)

We do not come together in any vainglorious spirit prompted by the mere desire for a partisan or personal victory. Unless by our record in the past and our concept of duty for the future, we are equipped for the tasks of statesmanship, we have no claim on the American people for further preferment.

The record we have made is written in the history of the Republic. While we lay no claim to perfection and fulminate no pretentions that this record contains no errors, nevertheless we contemplate with pride the great tasks we have undertaken and accomplished in behalf of democracy in America and those who believe in it and strive to advance it. (Applause.)

Let us be equally unequivocal in the program we shall here announce, so that the American people and the world will know what we think and what we propose to do.

The chief, if not the only reason, for the existence of political parties is to afford a vehicle for the molding and expression of public opinion and for the fixation of responsibility in the conduct of public business.

There have been occasions when political organizations were afraid to speak plainly or intelligently on problems of transcendent importance to this Nation when language was employed not to convey but to conceal thoughts; when each pronouncement made a frontal attack on all others, and the whole appeared to have been written in mud by the migratory feet of a weasel. Such is the platform adopted by the Republican Party at Philadelphia three weeks ago. (Applause.) It is the perfect example of the uncertainties and ambiguities of men who do not know where they are going or what they will do if they ever arrive. The day on which it was written was described by Walter Lippmann as "black Tuesday in Philadelphia." (Applause.)

Having assembled this political ragout and found it void and without form, its fabricators concluded that what it lacked and needed was color. They wanted not only color, but they wanted a variety of colors. But while they wanted color, they did not desire a fast color. (Laughter and applause.) They desired a color whose changing shades and shadows would be determined by the degree of regulation which a fearless Government saw fit to impose upon a vast empire of power hitherto uncontrolled in its exercise of dominion over the social, industrial, and economic life of millions of Americans. They seemed unwilling or afraid to nominate any man who had been a Republican for more than two years. (Laughter, applause, and cheers.) Hence they chose a political chameleon. (Laughter.)

The Philadelphia convention constituted the Second Charge of the Light Brigade (laughter) in the heroic Battle of Kilowatt. (Laughter, applause, and cheers.)

It is not my province or my purpose on this occasion to attempt any detailed review of the history of the world or of our own country during the past eight years. Much of that history has been spread before our eyes with such kaleidoscopic rapidity as to render the succession of events a little vague to all but the meticulous historian. It is no exaggeration to assert that no similar period in our history has been so crowded with engrossing spectacularity or fraught with such consequences to our institutions or our methods of life.

Our efforts here at home have not been inspired by the punitive desire to set group against group or to array section against section. We inherited chaos eight years ago. We inherited fear, which was almost universal. We inherited lack of confidence, not only in private enterprise, but in our public institutions. The American people had been led to the brink of a precipice by the fallacies of a smug and blind regime, which found itself impotent to draw back or to avert the disaster which it had contrived.

This impotence had wrought its devastation, not only in the field of business and industry, but had set a blight on all financial activities.

Banks and confidence in them collapsed. Wheels of industry were motionless. The market places for both money and commodities were bereft of constructive or profitable activities. Agriculture dropped and died from a dry rot inflicted by legislative and administrative incompetence, while the feet of 15,000,000 American laborers wandered in vagrant anxiety over the question of tomorrow's food and shelter and tomorrow's clothing.

Homes and firesides, millions of them, which must be the sanctuary of the true spirit of America, were on the verge of permanent loss through the cry of the auctioneer.

Abuses of the financial, economic, and social realms of our existence had grown so chronic that the Nation despaired of any constructive or effective remedy against them. The status quo became the law of our being, and the Government imitated that backward-flying bird which never knows where it is going but can only see where it has been.

American commerce with the world, which in every great industrial nation has been and must be a substantial portion of the yardstick of its prosperity, had fled from the seas and the marts of trade.

Encouraged by our own example of folly, insurmountable barriers had been erected by nation against nation through the effort of provincial minds to set metes and bounds to the genius and initiative of man. In our own hemisphere, peopled by the children of those who had fought for the creation of a new ideal of democratic thought and conduct, suspicion and fear, political and economic, retarded the efforts to consummate a solidarity essential to the preservation and protection of the common interests of all the Americas.

The effort of the past seven years on the part of our Government has been devoted to the task of remolding the faith of our people in their own brand of democracy under the leadership of one of the world's outstanding Democrats, Franklin D. Roosevelt.

We have heard much in recent days from complacent throats regarding free enterprise. The spokesmen of the Philadelphia assemblage invoked the spirits of the departed in behalf of free enterprise, and ex-President Hoover began his diatribe (boos) by proclaiming it the duty of his party to save America for free men.

He, of all men, ought to cry for the return of freedom, because he and his regime fastened more shackles on the physical, economic, and spiritual aspirations of the American people than any other group who ever mismanaged the affairs of this Republic.

What freedom is it that we have destroyed, and, by the same token, what freedom is it that the platform and nominees of the Philadelphia convention will restore?

Is it the freedom to juggle and manipulate and determine the value of the securities of American corporations in which millions of our people have invested their savings?

Do they propose to destroy the freedom we have guaranteed to labor in the United States to sit across a table from its employer on terms of equality and bargain collectively over wages, hours, and working conditions?

Do they propose to restore the uncontrolled freedom of some employers to exploit employees by long hours and low wages?

Do they propose to remove from agriculture the freedom to cooperate within itself and with the Government of the United States in securing a larger portion of the national income for the service they render to society?

Do they propose to return the American farmer to the income of 1932 instead of twice that income which he has received under the New Deal?

Mr. Hoover, who constitutes the remaining living symbol of Republican wisdom, in his speech at the convention, said that the Republican Party was the first to bring relief to the American farmer. What he no doubt meant to say was that Republican leadership was the first to bring the need for relief to the American farmer. (Applause.)

Will they restore the freedom of vast holding companies, drawing their substance from local utilities and the consumers to continue their depredations upon the public, to prevent which the Utility Holding Company Act was passed over the vehement protest of the present Republican candidate for President?

In truth, the reason for the shifting of his political roles was the enactment of this legislation, plus the completion and development of a great natural resource of nature in the Tennessee Valley, begun during the first World War in the administration of Woodrow Wilson. (Applause.)

Will they destroy or undermine the laws we have enacted for the aged and unemployed?

Will they restore the freedom as well as the compulsion of old age to descend to the grave in penury and want?

Will they restore the freedom as well as the compulsion of unemployed men to walk the streets in search of work or take their places in bread lines where they stood in 1932?

We have made but a beginning in this great field of social security. It is my opinion that we must strengthen and simplify the law, not only to provide greater assistance, but also to provide greater uniformity in the benefits accruing to those entitled to them under the Social Security Law. There ought to be greater uniformity throughout the Nation in the provisions for old-age pensions. (Applause.) And I am convinced that this uniformity can be secured only when the Federal Government assumes greater responsibility for the administration of the benefits which the law accords. (Applause.)

What is this freedom which we have driven out and which they will entice back to this land of the free?

Do the Philadelphia guarantors of a return of freedom propose to abolish the Civilian Conservation Corps or the National Youth Administration, which has prepared more than 3,000,000 young men and women for responsibilities of life and given them a new conception of the relationship between them and their government?

Mr. Hoover, in his exegesis, announced that the New Deal had stabilized unemployment. Having himself multiplied unemployment beyond all previous calculations, even he ought to welcome some stabilization.

During this pretended eclipse of free enterprise in America the national income had increased from 38 billion to 71 billion per annum. The last Republican administration had reduced it from 80 billion to 38 billion, and had inaugurated that succession of annual deficits which which they now proclaim as the peculiar patent of the Roosevelt Administration.

The fundamental difference between the two situations is that Roosevelt deficits have been reflected in vast improvements and additions to the values of property and life in every community in the United States, while there cannot be found in any part of the Nation any evidence of value or increased enjoyment of life that previous deficit spending had accomplished.

In this same period during which they believe freedom has fled from our shores and the credit of our Government has been jeopardized, the price of Government bonds on the markets of the Nation and the world rose from 80 cents on the dollar to nearly $1.20, notwithstanding a substantial decrease in the rate of interest which these obligations bare.

During the same period the total indebtedness of the American people had decreased by more than 10 billion dollars, which does not indicate that they are headed toward predicted bankruptcy.

These improvements, these aids to industry and to labor, and the general restoration of the morale of our people have cost money. We do not deny that. They have made it necessary for us to borrow money and levy taxes which under normal conditions would have been unnecessary and undesirable.

But the American people are not and will not be frightened into panic when they realize that during the past seven years, while the debt of the National Government has increased by 22 billion dollars, their total public and private indebtedness has decreased by more than 30 billion dollars and that during this same seven years their aggregate income has increased four times as much as has the indebtedness of the Federal Government.

All this has been done in order to restore the faith of the American people in their government, and to emphasize the fact that our government is not an austere, unapproachable, inanimate thing off yonder in Washington, taking no account of or interest in the affairs of those who support it. All this has been done to demonstrate that the processes of democracy can be made to respond to the needs of men and women.

It has been done in order to prove that under our constitution and without changing or undermining our form of government, it can be made an instrument of service under the stress of a great crisis. And it cannot be denied that democracy was in sore need of this proof of its efficacy and power, for never before in our history has democracy been under attack on a wider front than during the last decade.

For a century and more prior to the World War, the races of men were moving toward the goal of freedom and self-government. Beginning with our own Revolution and a little later with the French Revolution, the theory of democratic institutions found acceptance in all parts of the world. During this century most of South America established its freedom from Spain and other foreign dominations under republican forms of government, patterned largely after our own. France drove the last Bonaparte from the throne and established the French Republic.

China proclaimed a republic throughout her vast territory, and among the far-flung elements of the British Empire, a commonwealth of nations emerged, in which the people strengthened their local institutions and extended their privileges of independent action.

In the smaller nations of Europe, even those which clung to the traditions of monarchy, the people increased their power over and participation in their governments.

In Russia the Czar and all that he represented were unhorsed in what was supposed to be a revolution for the people. In Germany the Kaiser abdicated and fled his country following the establishment of a republic.

In England the House of Lords was shorn of some of its ancient prerogatives. In Italy the King became a puppet, and in South Africa the principles of self-government became an established fact following the Boer War.

Everywhere it seemed that the doctrine, proclaimed by Thomas Jefferson that all governments derived their just powers from the consent of the governed, was on the march and would at length cover the earth like the waters cover the sea.

But in the past decade or two this process seems to have gone in reverse. Whether as the result of some evil spirit loosed by the agonies of the World War, or in consequence of the impotence of existing regimes to understand or respond to the needs of the people, we need not here undertake to determine.

But we do know that autocracy rears its ugly face in larger portions of the world today than at any time since the formation of the American republic, and we do know that we are confronted with the alternative of defending and preserving our democratic institutions, as we have built them and enjoyed them, or seeing them confounded by the convergence of antagonistic ideologies in a world dedicated not to the proposition that all men are created equal but that all men are created to feed the maw of greedy, grasping totalitarian states.

In the midst of these alternatives there is but one choice that the American people can make with honor to themselves and fidelity to traditions and principles for which the Nation was created and to which it is dedicated.

That choice is to fight against those who would assault our territory, our independence, our ideals, or our vital interests, or anything which we are committed and pledged to defend and preserve, whether that assault is launched from a foreign source or is instigated by disloyal or subversive influence within our own borders.

We are charged with the responsibility of determining for ourselves whether this democracy which we have instituted and developed is, first, worth preserving; and, second, whether we have the courage, the fortitude, and the intelligence to exert the effort and make the sacrifice essential to its preservation.

We must determine whether the restoration of confidence in the American system for which we have labored the last eight years, after all, was worth the effort, and whether we are ready to announce to all the world that not only the United States but the entire Western Hemisphere has been dedicated as a sanctuary for free men, and that any effort from any outside source to encroach upon it territorially, politically, or by any other form of insidious penetration will be met by the total impact of all our resources of men, money, and material, until the encroachment and those who undertake it shall have been broken and driven back.

This does not mean that we desire war. It does not mean that we do not cherish peace and goodwill among all nations and all races. It does not mean that we propose to become involved in the military conflicts among foreign nations. It does not mean that we propose or intend to send the armed forces of this nation to the battlefields of Europe or Asia for the purpose of determining military superiority among the nations involved.

But it does mean that we propose to see that at least one continent on this earth shall be kept free for the account of the individual and collective rights and privileges of free men.

It means that we propose to hold fast to the doctrine that the State is created for the service of the people and not that the people are created for the exploitation of the State.

For this task we must be prepared, morally, spiritually, physically, mechanically, economically.

In the inept conglomeration, called the Republican platform, adopted at Philadelphia, we find the following brilliant piece of fiction:

> The Republican Party stands for Americanism, preparedness, and peace. We accordingly fasten upon the New Deal full responsibility for our unpreparedness and for the consequent danger of involvement in war.

No responsible political party ever promulgated a more deceitful alibi in all the history of political parties in the United States.

I do not relish the necessity to indulge in partisan dispute over the question of preparedness. It ought not to be a partisan question. But, in view of the fact that the Republican platform seeks to make it a partisan question, I am not afraid to discuss it on that basis.

Following the World War the nations sincerely sought peace and disarmament.

The United States, in the early days of the Harding administration, called the Washington Disarmament Conference. This conference was hailed as a great step toward lifting the burden of armaments from the people of the nations involved. War vessels were sunk. Blueprints were torn to pieces; and ships under construction were ordered scrapped.

But following this conference it turned out that under the administrations of Republican presidents, our naval building program did not approximate the ratio allowed by the agreement entered into.

Then came the so-called nine-power pact, entered into by nine nations during the control of our Government by the Republican Party under which the construction and maintenance of an adequate Army and Navy were still further retarded.

Then came the so-called Briand-Kellogg Pact, by which nearly all of the nations of the world agreed to renounce war as an instrument of national policy. This hope for world peace was made the excuse for further reductions in appropriations and in construction for our national defense.

I do not decry these efforts for world peace. The American people in common with most of the peoples of the world sincerely hoped and prayed that war would not again drench the earth in human blood.

But it cannot be claimed by those who were then in power in this Nation that anything substantial was done to build up or even maintain the minimum requirements of our national-defense equipment.

Instead of having only 75,000 we have 241,000 equipped soldiers in the United States Army, and the present Congress, on the recommendation and under the leadership of the President has authorized an increase to 375,000 men and will authorize further increases as fully and as rapidly as may be required.

In view of the aborted effort of the Republican convention to fasten on the New Deal the responsibility for any lack of preparedness that may now exist and to elude any portion of that responsibility, let us make some comparisons.

During the seven years since 1933 our Government has expended $1,300,000,000 more on the Army than was expended during the previous seven years.

In these same seven years, the United States has expended $1,500,000,000 more on the Navy than was expended during the previous seven years.

These expenditures were recommended and appropriated under President Roosevelt and they were made necessary largely because Republican administrations had sorely neglected both arms of our national defense.

During those 12 years of Harding, Coolidge and Hoover not a single battleship was laid down for construction in any navy yard in the United States.

During the last year of Woodrow Wilson's administration, when Franklin Roosevelt was Assistant Secretary of the Navy, appropriations for the Navy amounted to $960,000,000. In the first year of the Harding administration they were reduced to $485,000,000. During the twelve years of Harding, Coolidge, and Hoover, they continued to decline until the fiscal year of 1934 when they reached the insignificant sum of $266,000,000, which was the last naval appropriation enacted as Mr. Hoover was about to retire from office.

During those 12 years not a single battleship was laid down for construction and only 20 other types of combattant vessels, such as cruisers, submarines, and gunboats were constructed.

During the past 4 years we have completed 115 combattant naval vessels. We have under construction now 138 additional vessels, consisting of 10 battleships, 5 aircraft carriers, 4 heavy cruisers, 17 light cruisers, 61 destroyers, and 41 submarines.

In addition to these vessels now under construction we have provided for the construction of enough naval warcraft to give us the largest navy in the world, sufficiently strong to protect our interests in both the Atlantic and Pacific Oceans against any aggressor from any source in any part of this world.

What else does the record reveal?

When the Naval Appropriations Bill for the fiscal year 1939 was passed in the Senate a majority of Republican Senators, including the Republican candidate for Vice President, Senator McNary, voted against it.

When in the spring of 1939 there came before the Senate the bill increasing the number of Army airplanes from 5,500 to 6,000, a majority of Republican Senators, including their present candidate for Vice President, voted against it.

When in the Senate the Naval Appropriations Bill for the fiscal year 1940 was adopted, nearly half the Republican Members voted against it.

When, in May 1939, the Naval Appropriations Bill carrying a billion dollars for the Navy was before the House of Representatives, of the 58 votes cast against it, 54 were Republicans.

When the House of Representatives was considering the Army appropriations bill for 1940, 4 amendments were offered by Republicans to reduce the sums for signal service, ordinance, and airplanes. Of the 150 Members voting for these reductions 145 were Republicans.

Only eight Republicans voted against the reductions. In the United States Senate one of the Republican candidates for President, Mr. Taft, urged an amendment reducing appropriations for the Army and Navy by 25 percent; and, so far as I have been able to learn, the man who nosed him out for the Republican nomination, Mr. Wendell L. Willkie, uttered no warning or advice to his newly made Republican brethren on the subject of national defense.

He was probably too busy talking about balancing the Budget and trying to prevent the efforts of the Securities and Exchange Commission to unscramble his billion-dollar utility holding company omelet, and endeavoring to thwart the objectives of the great Tennessee Valley project which was begun 22 years ago as a part of our national-defense program.

And as late as last Thursday in the House of Representatives, when, at the urgent request and recommendation of William R. Knudsen and Edward Stettinius, members of the Advisory Committee on National Defense, and also at the urgent solicitation of Mr. Dunn, a member of the engineering firm which Mr. Willkie consulted in his fight against the Tennessee Valley Authority, an effort was made to provide for the construction of an additional dam for the purpose of inaugurating the speedy manufacture of necessary aluminum for the construction of airplanes, the effort was blocked by Republican Members of the House of Representatives.

But what of our involvement in war?

No man who ever occupied the Presidency of the United States ever strove more valiantly to avert the present war in Europe before its outbreak than did Mr. Roosevelt. No man ever condemned in more unmeasured terms the wicked determination to resort to the brutal force of arms in conquering peaceful and friendly nations, or in setting any legitimate controversies among the nations of Europe.

No political party or administration in the history of this or any Nation ever made greater sacrifices to avoid involvement in war than have been made by the Democratic Party and its present administration.

For more than a century we, as a Nation, have insisted on the freedom of the seas. We have insisted that our flag and every flag had the right to sail the seas in time of war, subject to certain rights of search and seizure. We have inisisted on the right of Americans to trade and travel under an international law that had been recognized for centuries.

It was our insistence on the observance of these rights that finally drew us into the World War in 1917.

But in order to avoid the possibility or likelihood of our involvement in this war through incidents incapable of being foreseen, we have, in the neutrality law, recommended by the President and enacted by a Democratic Congress over the protest of the Republicans, prohibited American ships to sail in belligerent or dangerous waters or American citizens to travel there; and we have prohibited even the granting of credit to belligerent nations and required them to pay cash for what they buy and to transport it in their own or other foreign vessels.

If the Republicans in Congress had been successful in defeating this legislation, we might already be involved in the war which they pretend so much to fear.

In these days of peril and uncertainty, we invoke the spirit of a united America.

We shall expect to make sacrifices. We shall expect to forego some luxuries and conveniences. Already the impact of world conditions has colored our thoughts and remolded some of our conceptions and methods of life.

But it has not lessened our resolution. It has not made us afraid. It has not cowed the spirit which discovered, populated, developed, and civilized this America of ours. It has but served to strengthen our determination and fortify our resistance.

In the midst of these threats we call on our people for unity. The relationship between a people and their government is not a one-way thoroughfare. The obligations are reciprocal. They call for that concert of soul and purpose which knows no distinction of race, origin, color, or religion.

We know that Jew and gentile, Catholic and Protestant, white and colored, rich and poor, native born and foreign born will rise in all their might and holy zeal to guard these portals against the fate which has wrecked other peoples and other civilizations.

To this high commitment we pledge ourselves and all that we shall here undertake.

In its consummation we invoke the guidance of God, who, we believe, still sits upon His throne, still rules in earth and heaven, and still holds in the hollow of His hand the destiny of nations and of men.

Presentation of a Mammoth Twist of Tobacco to the Permanent Chairman

... A mammoth twist of tobacco was presented to the Permanent Chairman. ...

The Permanent Chairman: Some of my friends from Kentucky have presented me with this huge twist of tobacco. While I desire to preserve it as a memento of this convention, I feel inclined to send it to Willkie in order to stop him from chewing the rag. (Laughter.)

Message of President Roosevelt, Delivered by Permanent Chairman

Now, my friends, I have an additional statement to make on behalf of the President of the United States. (Applause and cheers.)

I and other close friends of the President have long known that he has no wish to be a candidate again. We know, too, that in no way whatsoever has he exerted any influence in the selection of delegates, or upon the opinion of delegates to this convention.

Tonight, at the specific request and authorization of the President, I am making this simple fact clear to this convention.

The President has never had, and has not today, any desire or purpose to continue in the office of President, to be a candidate for that office, or to be nominated by the convention for that office.

He wishes in all earnestness and sincerity to make it clear that all of the delegates to this convention are free to vote for any candidate.

This is the message I bear to you tonight from the President of the United States, by authority of his word.

... A demonstration ensued, with parades of banners and cries of "We want Roosevelt!"

... A picture of President Roosevelt was handed up to Senator Barkley who held it above the rostrum with evoked louder cheering. ...

The Permanent Chairman: May I present to this great audience of Democrats my wife, Mrs. Barkley. (Applause and cheers.)

... There was a demonstration from 11:10 o'clock for fifty-three minutes. ...

Franklin D. Roosevelt's
Vice Presidential Letters (1944)

"No selection of a vice-presidential candidate," wrote the legal historian Leon Friedman, "ever contained more intrigue, suspense, confusion, and political maneuvering than the nomination of Harry S Truman." At various times during a ten-day period in July 1944, Franklin D. Roosevelt encouraged each of four different men to believe that he was the president's choice for a running mate in his fourth term reelection campaign: Vice President Henry A. Wallace, former senator and Supreme Court justice James F. Byrnes, Senator Truman of Missouri, and Supreme Court Justice William O. Douglas. In letters to Sen. Samuel D. Jackson of Indiana and to Democratic National Committee chair Robert E. Hannegan, which were released to the public on July 14 and July 19, respectively, the president expressed a preference first for Wallace, then for Truman or Douglas. The Democratic national convention, confused and irritated, acquiesced on July 21 when Roosevelt finally made clear his preference for Truman—but only after giving Wallace a plurality on the first vice presidential ballot.

Ironically, Roosevelt had been hoping to avoid controversy at the 1944 convention. Ill and preoccupied with World War II, which the United States had entered in December 1941, the president succumbed early to pressure from conservatives and party professionals to replace the liberal, unorthodox Wallace, whom Roosevelt himself liked and respected. After leaning for a time toward Byrnes, a South Carolina conservative and a convert from Roman Catholicism, Roosevelt abandoned him when he learned that liberals, Catholics, and organized labor would be appalled by a Byrnes vice presidency. ("Clear it with Sidney," the president reportedly had said of Byrnes's proposed nomination, and when Sidney Hillman, the head of the powerful Congress of Industrial Organizations Political Action Committee, objected, the trial balloon for Byrnes was deflated.) Douglas seems to have never really been in the running.

In the minds of the party professionals whose judgment Roosevelt respected, Truman was the obvious choice—a hard-working, prolabor party stalwart from a border state who recently had won plaudits for effectively chairing a Senate investigation of waste and inefficiency in the wartime defense program. "Truman was the man who would hurt him least," advised Ed Flynn, a Democratic boss from the Bronx, New York. Roosevelt, who barely knew Truman, accepted his advisers' recommendation.

The Roosevelt-Truman ticket defeated Gov. Thomas E. Dewey of New York, the Republican nominee for pres-

ident, and his running mate, Ohio governor John W. Bricker, by more than three million popular votes and by a 432-99 margin in the electoral college. On April 12, 1945, less than three months after his fourth inauguration as president, Roosevelt died of natural causes. Truman became president. ~

July 14, 1944

My dear Senator Jackson: In the light of the probability that you will be chosen as Permanent Chairman of the Convention, and because I know that many rumors accompany all Conventions, I am wholly willing to give you my own personal thought in regard to the selection of a candidate for Vice President. I do this at this time because I expect to be away from Washington for the next few days.

The easiest way of putting it is this: I have been associated with Henry Wallace during his past four years as Vice President, for eight years earlier while he was Secretary of Agriculture, and well before that. I like him and I respect him, and he is my personal friend. For these reasons, I personally would vote for his renomination if I were a delegate to the Convention.

At the same time, I do not wish to appear in any way as dictating to the Convention. Obviously the Convention must do the deciding. And it should— and I am sure it will—give great consideration to the pros and cons of its choice.

July 19, 1944

Dear Bob: You have written me about Harry Truman and Bill Douglas. I should, of course, be very glad to run with either of them and believe that either one of them would bring real strength to the ticket.

The Twenty-Second Amendment: House Debate (1947)

The Twenty-second Amendment prohibits any person from being elected president more than two times. It also limits vice-presidents who succeed to the presidency to only one election as president if they have served more than two years of a departed president's four-year term. The amendment exempted the incumbent president at the time it was enacted, Harry S. Truman, from its coverage.

For more than a century and a half after the Constitutional Convention of 1787, Americans had been dissatisfied with the original Constitution's provision for unrestricted presidential reeligibility. In 1807, President Thomas Jefferson inaugurated a two-term tradition that no president challenged until Franklin D. Roosevelt was elected to a third and fourth term in 1940 and 1944, respectively. (See "Thomas Jefferson's 'No Third Term' Letter," p. 101, and "Alben W. Barkley's 'Third Term' Speech to the Democratic National Convention," p. 358.) From 1789 to 1947, 270 resolutions to limit the president's tenure were introduced in Congress, sixty of them—an average of three per year—since 1928.

The Roosevelt years added a partisan and ideological dimension to the long-standing concern about presidential reeligibility. Republicans, who with rare exception had formed the nation's majority party from 1860 to 1928, had been driven from power by the president's New Deal Democratic coalition. Conservative Democrats, mostly southern, had lost control of their party to liberals and northerners. (See "The *Literary Digest* Poll," p. 348, and "Abolition of the Two-Thirds Rule: Proceedings of the Democratic National Convention," p. 344.)

In the midterm congressional elections of 1946, the Republicans regained control of Congress for the first time since 1930. On February 6, 1947, less than five weeks after the opening of the new Eightieth Congress, the House of Representatives passed the two-term limit amendment by a vote of 285-121. Five weeks later, on March 12, the Senate passed a slightly different version by a 59-23 vote. Every Republican member of Congress voted for the proposed amendment. The differences between the two houses were ironed out quickly; final passage took place on March 24.

Congressional debate on the Twenty-second Amendment was framed in democratic terms. Republicans contended that a two-term limit would protect the American people against the threat of an overly personalized presidency; besides, argued Rep. Leo Allen of Illinois, "the people should be given the opportunity to set limits on the time an individual can serve as Chief Executive." Democrats such as Tennessee representative Estes Kefauver rejoined that the people, "by a mere majority vote, have the opportunity of deciding every four years whether they want to terminate the services of the President if he stands for reelection."

Congress gave little, if any, consideration to the framers' original decision to place no restrictions on presidential reeligibility. (See "The Constitutional Convention: Debates on Presidential Selection," p. 1.) *Nor did Congress foresee the beneficial political effect that the amendment would have on the vice presidency. With second-term presidents barred from reelection, vice presidents are able to campaign openly for the presidency without jeopardizing their standing within the administration, as Richard Nixon did in 1960 and George Bush did in 1988.*

The proposed Twenty-second Amendment received a mixed reception in the states. No amendment to the Constitution has taken longer to ratify than the two-term limit: three years, eleven months. Eighteen state legislatures—exactly half the required number—ratified the amendment in 1947, all of them in primarily Republican states. Afterward, ratification proceeded slowly, with most victories coming in the South. Approval from the required three-fourths of the states was attained on February 27, 1951. Had the amendment not exempted Truman from its coverage, it might have foundered on charges of overt (instead of merely implicit) partisanship.

*Ironically, the constraints of the two-term limit have been felt by only two presidents, both of them Republicans. Dwight D. Eisenhower wanted to run for a third term in 1960, according to John Eisenhower, his son and deputy chief of staff. In 1988, Ronald Reagan became the second president to be denied the opportunity to run for reelection by the Twenty-second Amendment. During his second term, Reagan campaigned unsuccessfully for a constitutional amendment that would re-*peal the two-term limit, although not in such a way as to affect him.* ~

Amendment to the Constitution Relating to the Terms of Office of The President:

Feb. 6, 1947

Mr. Allen of Illinois. Mr. Speaker, I call up House Resolution 91 and ask for its immediate consideration.

The Clerk read as follows:

Resolved. That immediately upon the adoption of this resolution it shall be in order to move that the House resolve itself into the Committee of the Whole House on the State of the Union for the consideration of the joint resolution (H. J. Res. 27) proposing an amendment to the Constitution of the United States relating to the terms of office of the President. That after general debate, which shall be confined to the joint resolution and shall continue not to exceed 2 hours, to be equally divided and controlled by the chairman and ranking minority member of the Committee on the Judiciary, the joint resolution shall be read for amendment under the 5-minute rule. At the conclusion of the reading of the joint resolution for amendment, the Committee shall rise and report the same to the House with such amendments as may have been adopted, and the previous question shall be considered as ordered on the joint resolution and amendments thereto to final passage without intervening motion except one motion to recommit.

Mr. Allen of Illinois. Mr. Speaker, immediately upon the adoption of this resolution it shall be in order to move that the House resolve itself into the Committee of the Whole House on the State of the Union for the consideration of the joint resolution (H. J. Res. 27) proposing an amendment to the Constitution of the United States relating to the terms of office of the President. That after general debate, which shall be confined to the joint resolution and shall continue not to exceed 2 hours, to be equally divided and controlled by the chairman and ranking minority member of the Committee on the Judiciary, the joint resolution shall be read for amendment under the 5-minute rule. At the conclusion of the reading of the joint resolution for amendment, the committee shall rise and report the same to the House with such amendments as may have been adopted, and the previous question shall be considered as ordered on the joint resolution and amendments thereto to final passage without intervening motion except one motion to recommit.

This resolution has but one purpose. That purpose is to submit to the people, by and through their State legislatures, this very important problem of the Presidential tenure of office, and to let the people decide whether or not this limitation should be written into the Constitution.

Heretofore many resolutions have been introduced upon this very question, but for some reason or another they have fallen by the wayside, and no legislation has been passed upon this question, and our Constitution remains without amendment to this date respecting the tenure of the office of President.

Section 1, article II, of the Constitution provides:

> The executive power shall be vested in a President of the United States of America. He shall hold his office during the term of 4 years.

Again, under amendment 20, section 1, of our Constitution, we find, in that amendment, the following language.

> The terms of the President and Vice President shall end at noon on the 20th day of January, and the terms of Senators and Representatives at noon on the 3d day of January, of the years in which such terms would have ended if this article had not been ratified; and the terms of their successors shall then begin.

By reason of the lack of a positive expression upon the subject of tenure of the office of President, and by reason of a well-defined custom which has arisen in the past that no President should have more than two terms in that office, much public discussion has resulted upon this subject. Hence it is the purpose of this legislation, if passed, to submit this question to the people so they, by and through the recognized processes, may express their views upon this question, and, if they shall so elect, they may amend our Constitution and thereby set at rest this problem.

This is not a political question. The importance of the problem to the people transcends all political implications and considerations. This proposed amendment to our Constitution, if adopted, will continue throughout the future years, unless and until a further amendment may be adopted upon this subject. Therefore, in the face of general public discussions, in the face of the custom which has developed throughout the years, we are here presenting a resolution to submit this basic problem to the people.

When considering House Joint Resolution 27, amending the Constitution to limit tenure of the President to two terms, Congress must decide whether or not the people of the United States should still be permitted to choose the type of government under which they will live. This resolution merely enables our citizens through their State legislatures to express their opinion on this important question. I believe the people should make the decision, and I recommend adoption of this resolution as our expression of faith in their judgment.

When he refused nomination for a third term, George Washington warned the people that they might again be subjected to the tyranny of monarchy if they permitted any individual to become too firmly entrenched as the Chief Executive. This precedent established by our first President made unnecessary constitutional limitation of tenure of Presidency. As the precedent no longer stands to protect them, the people should be given the opportunity to set a limit on the time an individual can serve as Chief Executive. As a President can be elected by the electoral college, even without the popular vote, our citizens now have really little protection against totalitarianism. The question of Presidential tenure has never before been submitted to the people. To protect them from the oppression of dictatorships that have arisen in other countries, I recommend this resolution be adopted, allowing their expression of sovereignty.

This Undemocratic and Unwanted Constitutional Amendment is Being Rushed through with Unseemly Haste

Mr. Sabath: Mr. Speaker, I yield myself such time as I may desire.

Mr. Speaker, the rule has been correctly stated by my colleague, the new chairman of the Committee on Rules, with whom I have had the pleasure of serving for many years. I have always found him to be fair, and consequently I was rather surprised that he should have yielded to the demands for depriving the House of a reasonable time for general debate on this important legislation.

No Other Constitutional Amendment So Restricted in Debate

If I am not mistaken, this is the first time that any resolution amending the Constitution that has served us so well for 170 years has been brought before the House under a rule which permits only two short hours for general debate. I recollect in days and years gone by

that on many occasions the Republicans demanded not 2 but 6 and 8 hours, sometimes even 3 and 4 days, on minor and inconsequential proposals; but on this resolution weighted with such grave importance, proposing to change the Constitution of the United States and to limit the right of the people to choose their own President, they are liberal enough to allow only two measly hours for general debate.

Republicans in Hurry to Be Free to Attend Banquet

Of course, I understand that the gentlemen of the majority are anxious to get through with the sad business of passing this resolution in order to be free to attend a Republican feast this evening. Doubtless this pitiful victory over a great man now sleeping on the banks of the Hudson will sharpen their appetites and give zest to their banquet. I know it will be a splendid feast, and I wish that I could be with them to taste the delicious food, which I am sure I should find palatable and digestible enough; but I fear that I could not digest the words which would follow after the feasting.

Yet, still I ask, Why should the Members of this House and the people of America be deprived of the right to know the facts attending the passage of this resolution and of being informed by extended debate? Why should not the people know what this proposed constitutional amendment means? Is a banquet sufficient excuse to cancel out the democratic processes? Such haste seems indecent.

Vast Majority Favored Roosevelt

I recall that my colleague, the majority leader, the genial gentleman from Indiana (Mr. Halleck), stated yesterday that a vast majority of the American people favor this legislation. Frequently the gentleman from Indiana is right; but this time, I am sorry to say, he is entirely wrong; and I think that he knows in his heart that this unseemly haste is due to the fact that the overwhelming majority of the American people are opposed to this amendment, and the Republican leadership is hurrying to pass it through the Congress before the public clamor grows too loud to be ignored. I know, and the Republican leadership knows, that a vast majority of the American people voted for Franklin D. Roosevelt not just once, or twice, nor even three times, but for four consecutive terms. That shows how the American people stand, and how they loved this great leader.

Republicans Have No Candidate for Even a Single Term

Of course, I realize that my Republican friends have no man that they could possibly elect President for a fourth term, nor even for a third term. In fact, I do not believe they have anyone at this time, or will have in the foreseeable future, who can even be elected for a first term, notwithstanding the fact that they succeeded in misleading sufficient of the American people to gain, in the last election, a temporary majority in and control of this House.

I do not know whether or not all of you know it; but, though I am and have been always a progressive Democrat, I am ready and willing to cooperate with the Republicans whenever they are right. Unfortunately, they are not right very often. In view of the tremendous responsibility which is now theirs, I hope that they will henceforth be right; but they will not be if they follow the tactics they have followed in this case, for certainly the Republican leadership has not indicated by this procedure that it is their aim and intent to deal fairly and justly either with the minority or with the American people.

Reported by Judiciary Committee only Yesterday

Mr. Speaker, this joint resolution was reported by the Committee on the Judiciary only day before yesterday. They did not give that committee even time to introduce the amended resolution, nor to print the hearings for the benefit of the House membership. They were obliged to come in with a resolution which will have to be amended in accordance with the majority vote of the Judiciary Committee. I hope that in the future the Republican majority will not act so hastily and so harshly, bringing in legislation of major importance without giving this House and the country an opportunity to become familiar with the bills on which we are acting, and, in this instance, without any effort to explain why they believe the Constitution should be amended.

For 170 years this country has prospered and grown strong under the Constitution, without any amendment deviating from our true course toward more and more democracy, nor from the true principles of representative government laid down by the founding fathers. Today we are enjoying greater prosperity and greater liberty and greater equality than ever before in our history. I hope the Republicans will not be able to do anything to destroy that prosperity, which was brought about by the Democratic Party under the inspired leadership of our greatest President, Franklin Delano Roosevelt, during the third and even the first part of the fourth term, until his untimely death, and despite the incalculable burdens of carrying a world-wide war to final victory.

Cannot Franklin Roosevelt Be Permitted to Rest in Peace?

What hurts most, and what I strongly resent, are statements made by several Republican Members that they "must vote for this anti-Roosevelt resolution."

Perhaps, had I not overheard those remarks, I should not have said anything at all here today.

Can we not be fair enough to let rest in peace a man who has done so much for our country and for humanity? I think it is manifestly unfair for anyone to make such remarks. It was a Godsend to the world that we had Franklin D. Roosevelt, whom the people freely chose four times to direct our Government and our destinies, and who served the Nation and all mankind as no other man has ever done before.

Though Franklin Roosevelt now rests in eternal sleep, I trust and I hope that his views and his policies, for which he fought and for which he gave his life, will continue for years to come to shape our national destiny, and that this country will continue in the great material prosperity which he brought about. Most of all, Mr. Speaker, I hope that the people of the world can reach his greatest objective—a just and lasting peace—not only for America, but for all people everywhere. That is his dream, and my dream, and the dream of the common people Roosevelt so loved.

States Will Not Ratify this Amendment

In thus assailing President Roosevelt, and in attempting to besmirch his memory, Mr. Speaker, my Republican friends are overlooking the fact that just as Roosevelt loved the common people, they loved him. I do not believe that three-fourths of the States will ever ratify this amendment, which is by its nature insulting to the memory of our greatest President. I have no doubt that many of the legislatures even in solidly Republican States will refuse to approve it. Not only do the people remember Roosevelt's magnificent leadership through war to victory; they remember his stirring words in the depths of depression, "We have nothing to fear but fear itself." They remember that

our living standards, our wage levels, not only in America but the world over, rose steadily under his influence and democratic leadership. They know that he gave his life to his country as truly as did any soldier hero fallen in the battle.

This Amendment Restricts the Democratic Right of the People to Freely Choose their Own President

But, Mr. Speaker, there are other reasons why the people will rise up in anger against this proposed constitutional amendment once the facts are known.

Anyone familiar with the history of the formation of the Union and the writing of the Constitution, and with the debates in the Constitutional Convention and the commentaries of the founding fathers after the convention, knows that it was not the purpose of the delegates to that convention, nor of any of those who agreed to the language of the Constitution, to restrict the right of the people to choose their President freely, nor to limit the terms which a President could serve. No such limitation was written into the Constitution, and it would have been placed there had there been a majority sentiment for it. Our Constitution is a noble instrument of human rights, forged by the hammer of human necessity on the anvil of compromise.

We have frequently amended our Constitution, as the need arose, to extend and strengthen the democratic processes on which our Government is solidly built. This amendment goes backward, and limits the right of the majority to choose the President.

But on that score I know that the former majority leader, the great scholar and gentleman from Massachusetts [Mr. McCormack] will in his speech bring home the views of George Washington and Thomas Jefferson, and of others who helped to frame our Constitution; therefore I will not dwell upon it.

Republicans Are Inconsistent in Attack on Constitution

Mr. Speaker, how well I remember how often my Republican friends have clamored to "stand by the Constitution"—the many statements they have made, the tears they have shed, in its name. I remember how often they have charged that we, the Democrats, were trying to change or ignore the Constitution. And now, lo and behold, today and for the last 2 days, drunk with their temporary power—and by temporary I mean short-lived—they are boldly trying to change that Constitution, and the principles of our democratic form of government, by restricting the right of the American people to decide for themselves who will be their President. This denies the long-standing principle of majority rule; it restricts and dilutes rights reserved to the people under the the Constitution. I cannot and will not concur in such a backward step, and I have confidence that the American people will make their opposition known before the Senate can ever act on this resolution.

Mr. Speaker, I yield 15 minutes to the gentleman from Massachusetts [Mr. McCormack].

Mr. McCormack. Mr. Speaker, this is one of the most important questions that any Member of this body will have to pass upon and I hope each Member will determine the question in accordance with his conscience. It is not my purpose to discuss politics in connection with the proposed amendment to the Constitution, an amendment which will not have any effect upon you and me of this generation but which might have a very important effect upon generations to come after you and I are dead and gone. If this amendment is incorporated in the Constitution, it will make the Constitution rigid. It ties the hands of future generations of Americans and deprives them of the opportunity to meet any problem that might confront them.

Of course, we have lived through the experience ourselves, but I can picture two generations from now, or one or three generations from now, when Americans may be enveloped in a war with their back to the wall. We will not be here. We will have passed on. But we will have imposed this prohibition upon them. They may be with their back to the wall with a President approaching the end of his second term. Let us assume the people of that future generation have complete confidence in their President. I do not know what his party may be. I do not care. That future President will be compelled to terminate his service as President of the United States when he may be the best man qualified to lead the people of our country at that time in meeting the crisis that confronts them. I beg of you as we sit here today to realize just what we are doing. I believe in custom. A custom is one thing, but a rigid prohibition is another thing. If this amendment becomes a part of the Constitution—and you cannot say, "We are sending it to the several State legislatures"; that is not the question; that is not the answer—if this amendment becomes a part of the Constitution, it imposes upon Americans for all time until and unless the Constitution is reamended the rigid hand of a rigid prohibition that no matter what crisis may confront America in the future when a President's second term is drawing to a close they cannot reelect him so that he may continue his service to the Nation which might be vitally necessary at that particular time.

I think it is too great a risk to take. For myself, I do not want to take it. Let us see what some of the eminent men of the past have said on this question. George Washington did not want a first term even. He accepted it reluctantly as a patriotic duty. He expected to serve about 2 years. He reluctantly served a second term because of the conditions abroad. He withdrew voluntarily at the end of his second term. But what did Washington say? This is what he said in a letter to Marquis de Lafayette on April 28, 1788, in relation to the second term. This is probably the only quotation of George Washington in relation to this question which I think can be found. He said in discussing or writing about the limitation of the terms of a President:

> Under an extended view of this part of the subject, I can see no propriety in precluding ourselves from the service of any man who on some great emergency shall be deemed universally most capable of serving the public.

What about Thomas Jefferson? Thomas Jefferson, historically, is the father of the two-term custom. There is no question about that. Thomas Jefferson, however, only wanted one term. He served a second term because of the calumnies hurled upon him by the Federalist Party and the effect they were having abroad at the time. He served patriotically. He could have had a third term. As we look back in history, I think we would all agree as to that. Jefferson retired at the end of his second term, but back in the days of the Constitutional Convention he believed in rotation in office. That was the big issue then. But what did Jefferson say about this? Jefferson himself said:

> There is, however, but one circumstance that could engage my acquiescence in another election; to wit, such a division about a successor as might bring in a monarchist. But this circumstance is impossible.

In other words, Jefferson himself recognized an emergency might exist where he would run for a third term, and in those days the emergency was the danger of a division existing that might establish a monarchy in our country. So Jefferson himself definitely saw that there was a distinction between custom and rigid prohibition. He recognized that in case of an emergency he might have been compelled, patriotically, to run for a third term, but he said this circumstance was impossible, because the danger of a monarchy did not exist at that time. But he said if there was such a danger he would have run for a third time.

John Quincy Adams said it should not be incorporated in the Constitution as a rigid prohibition.

Theodore Roosevelt said:

> If, for instance, a tremendous crisis occurred at the end of the second term of a man like Lincoln, as such a crisis occurred at the end of his first term, it would be a veritable calamity if the American people were forbidden to continue to use the services of the one man whom they knew, and did not merely guess, could carry them through the crisis.

He further said:

> While it is well to keep it as a custom, it would be a mark both of weakness and unwisdom for the American people to embody it into a constitutional provision which could not do them good and on some given occasion might work real harm.

> James Buchanan, in this very House, when he was a Member of this House, said:

> Shall we pass a decree, as fixed as fate, to bind the American people, and prevent them from ever reelecting such a man? I am not afraid to trust them with this power.

Woodrow Wilson, when he was asked about a 4-year term or one 6-year term with no reelection, made this remark:

> Put the customary limitation of two terms into the Constitution, if you do not trust the people to take care of themselves, but make it two terms (not one, because 4 years is often too long), and give the President a chance to win the full service by proving himself fit for it.

"If you do not trust the people to take care of themselves," you will note he said.

Senator William E. Borah:

One of the fundamental reasons for opposing the joint resolution is that the people who could be trusted to determine whether or not they desire a President for a second term may also be trusted to determine whether or not they desire a President for a third term.

Henry Cabot Lodge, Sr.:

I have no fear that they—

The American people—

can be fully trusted with the power to say whether a man shall serve a second time or a third time.

General Grant also took the same position. Ulysses S. Grant took the position that we should not impose upon the American people a rigid prohibition that would preclude them for all time of meeting any grave emergency that might arise.

Mr. Speaker, this is not a question of the Republican Party or the Democratic Party; this is a question where as we are sitting here we are acting for tomorrow, a tomorrow when you and I in all probability will no longer be alive. What we do today, however, will be operative and binding upon Americans who come after us. Now, we are going to impose the dead hand of the past upon them on some occasion when a grave emergency confronts them, when, as I said, they might be engaged in war, with a President coming to the end of his second term but possessing the confidence of the American people of that day—not the indispensable man, but the best man; there is such a thing as the best man under certain conditions to lead a people—when the best man was the President of the United States approaching the end of his second term, what are they going to do? What can they do? The "law of the jungle" confronts them. Just as people respond to emergency situations that confront them, especially that of self-preservation, so likewise do nations.

They might be compelled to demand that such a President act extra-constitutionally, the very fear some men have in mind now might be the vehicle under certain conditions when grave danger confronts our country for the people to demand of a President: "You should continue; it is your duty to continue until the danger is over." But outside of that, when that situation exists, and it may occur again, our country is likely to be faced with that danger again in the future; it might be even worse than it was in the last war; fighting with our backs to the wall, a President, as I say, nearing the end of his second term, the people wanting him, he being the best man in the country to lead them under those circumstances, and he being a good man, the people cannot follow that which custom dictates they should do because they are met with a rigid prohibition that says that under no conditions can they reelect such a man who is President and whom the country needs, the end of whose second term is drawing near, to continue in office no matter how grave the danger that confronts the country.

Mr. Speaker, to me it is too great a risk. I am talking not as a Democrat but as an American. I served in World War I. Other Members here served in World War I, and many Members served in World War II. We are all interested in our country no matter which side of the aisle we sit on; we all believe in its fundamentals. We have got to view this from the angle of tomorrow. This amendment will operate upon future generations of Americans. This amendment at a particular time of grave crisis confronting our country in the future might place our country in a straitjacket and it might be a contributing factor to harmful results.

In no part of the Constitution will you find any limitation, any prohibition except against Congress itself: Congress shall pass no law abridging the right of free speech, freedom of the press, freedom of assemblage. You will find limitations in the Constitution, but they are limitations upon Congress; and those limitations were imposed to protect the rights of individuals to assure that the legislative body would not take away the fundamental rights that our people believe in and for which the framers of the Constitution fought. This amendment is a limitation upon the people. This is not a limitation upon the Congress. It is a limitation upon the action of the people of the future, no matter what the danger may be, no matter how urgent it may be that the second-term President continue, he cannot if this amendment becomes a part of the Constitution. Mr. Speaker, it is too grave a danger to take this step, too grave a danger for us who will be dead at that time in all probability, to impose such a limitation upon future generations of Americans. Let their hands remain unshackled. Let us not put them into a strait-jacket, a strait-jacket that might be the factor resulting in the destruction of our country at some time in the future. Leadership is important. Leadership is the big thing and a President in his second term in the future might be the leader who will bring our people to victory. His going out at such a time might be the difference between victory and defeat. We are tying the hands of Americans in the future from exercising in a grave emergency the judgment which they may deem is for the best interests of our country.

The Speaker: The time of the gentleman from Massachusetts is expired.

Mr. Allen of Illinois. Mr. Speaker, I yield 10 minutes to the gentleman from Indiana [Mr. Halleck].

Mr. Halleck: Mr. Speaker, while I do not agree with the burden of the argument just made by the gentleman from Massachusetts, I have listened with interest to what he had to say. I commend him for his approach, which is clearly one devoid of partisanship. I join with him in the statement that the matter we are discussing today is not one of partisanship but rather of what best to do, be we Democrats or Republicans, looking to the future of this great land of ours. He has pointed out certain things which he says might be dangerous in their effects. Without undertaking to say that there is no force at all to his argument, speaking for myself I think that the dangers that the gentleman envisages, if they may be said to be dangers, are certainly outweighed by the real danger that obtains from the absence of the constitutional amendment as now proposed.

We are discussing here a proposal to perfect our American system of constitutional government. In such a discussion there can be no division on mere lines of partisanship, for in this House, Democrats, no less than Republicans, are devoted to our Constitution. We all want to see our system work for the benefit of the entire Nation, and for posterity.

Throughout our entire national history, we have amended the Constitution from time to time as experience appeared to dictate.

The Constitution has served us well. It was once described by the great Gladstone as the most wonderful work ever struck off at a given time by the brain and purpose of man.

Yet the Constitution itself clearly provides the methods of amendment, demonstrating that it was never the intention of the founding fathers to regard their work as finished for all time.

These are the reasons why I am happy today to call as our witness for this proposal one of the founders of the Democratic Party, a man who was himself one of the principal architects of the Bill of Rights, so vital a part of our Constitution today—Thomas Jefferson.

Toward the end of Jefferson's second administration, in 1808, there arose an insistent demand among many of his supporters that he stand for reelection.

When the legislatures of 7 of the then 17 States had adopted petitions urging a third term, Jefferson responded:

> That I should lay down my charge at the proper period is as much a duty as to have borne it faithfully.
>
> If some termination to the services of the Chief Magistrate be not fixed by the Constitution, or supplied by practice, his office, nominally for 4 years, will, in fact, become for life; and history shows how easily that degenerates into an inheritance.
>
> Believing that a representative government, responsible at short periods by election, is that which produces the greatest sum of happiness to mankind, I feel it a duty to do no act which shall essentially impair that principle; and I should unwillingly be the person, who, disregarding sound precedent set by an illustrious predecessor, should furnish the first example of prolongation beyond the second term of office.

Now, we do not need a Philadelphia lawyer to interpret what Thomas Jefferson thought about the principle embodied in the proposal before us today.

If he were here today, in my opinion he would be supporting it.

As history demonstrates, the only reason this matter was not pressed to formal amendment many years ago was the deeply rooted belief of the American people that the principle had been firmly established by usage and broad general acceptance, to such a degree that no legal or constitutional limitation of Presidential tenure was required.

It is, of course, a common thing in American life to omit from the body of the law those things which are accepted as commonplace in the habits, customs, and traditions of the people. Indeed, our whole system of law and government is reared on certain basic assumptions of morality and attitude which are not specifically enumerated in the corpus juris. So it was with the matter of Presidential tenure.

By way of illustrating how deeply the two-term tradition had become imbedded in our legal and political assumptions, let me read to you a plank from the Democratic national platform for 1896. The plank is headed, "Third term." It reads:

> We declare it to be the unwritten law of this Republic, established by custom and usage of 100 years, and sanctioned by the examples of the greatest and wisest of those who founded and have maintained our Government, that no man should be eligible for a third term of the Presidential office.

With Thomas Jefferson as his mentor, and with the Democratic national platform of 1896 as his guide, no Democrat in this Congress need experience the slightest qualms of partisan conscience in giving unequivocal patriotic support to the amendment before us.

General Washington, the president of the Constitutional Convention, himself entertained some doubts concerning the failure of the Constitution, in its draft stage, to place a firm limitation upon Presidential tenure. In a letter to the Marquis de Lafayette under date of April 28, 1788, while the Constitution yet was in process of ratification by the States, George Washington said:

> There cannot, in my judgment, be the least danger that the President will by any practicable intrigue ever be able to continue himself one moment in office, much less perpetuate himself in it—but in the last stage of corrupted morals and political depravity.

It was this view, supported by the tremendous influence and prestige of General Washington, which at length prevailed, and led to the ratification of the Constitution without a specific limitation on Presidential tenure, as had been proposed before the convention by Edmund Randolph, of Virginia, and Charles Pinckney, of South Carolina.

But having so greatly influenced the adoption of the Constitution without that limitation, General Washington was the great author of the two-term tradition, which prevailed as almost the unwritten law of the land for 140 years.

In his historic Farewell Address of September 17, 1796, General Washington sharply warned his fellow countrymen against "that love of power, and proneness to abuse it, which predominates in the human heart."

His experience in the Presidency had confirmed him in "the necessity of reciprocal checks in the exercise of political power."

He warned against excessive partisanship, on the ground that such activities often defeated measures of sound progress and enlightened administration. And then he traced the dangers which are the very inspiration of this amendment:

> The disorders and miseries which result gradually incline the minds of men to seek security and repose in the absolute power of an individual; and sooner or later the chief of some prevailing faction, more able or more fortunate than his competitors, turns this disposition to the purposes of his own elevation, on the ruins of public liberty.

When Washington and Jefferson had, by deed and precept, firmly placed the foundations of the two-term tradition, the matter was at rest for many years, for Thomas Jefferson wrote in his biographical notes, shortly before his death in 1826:

> Though this amendment has not been made in form, yet practice seems to have established it. The example of four Presidents voluntarily retiring at the end of their eighth year, and the progress of public opinion that the principle is salutary, have given it in practice the form of precedent and usage— insomuch that should a President consent to be a candidate for a third election, I trust he would be rejected on this demonstration of ambitious views.

The House of Representatives supported and confirmed the Washington-Jefferson tradition in a resolution passed on December 15, 1875, in which it was declared to be the judgment of the House that any departure from the two-term tradition would be "unwise, unpatriotic, and fraught with peril to our free institutions."

At that time the House of the Forty-fourth Congress was composed of 181 Democrats and 107 Republicans. The resolution I have quoted was adopted by a vote of 234 to 18.

That resolution quieted all third-term discussion for a quarter century.

Immediately after his second inauguration in 1901, William McKinley became the focus of much third-term chatter, which he promptly squelched with the declaration:

> I will say now, once for all, expressing a long-settled conviction, that I not only am not and will not be a candidate for a third term but would not accept a nomination for it if it were tendered me.

I will not burden the House with a detailed review of the many minor incidents in our political history which reflect the same national sentiment—the same abiding faith of the people—that custom usage, and tradition adequately protected their constitutional system against the occasional ambitions of extended Presidential tenure.

Suffice it to say that at no point in our history has the matter ever been one of partisan decision.

On the contrary, great men of all parties have subscribed to and sustained this unwritten law of America.

Our only task today is to place the matter firmly in the Constitution.

Mr. Sabath: Mr. Speaker, I yield the remainder of my time to the gentleman from Texas [Mr. Rayburn].

Mr. Rayburn: Mr. Speaker, I think one of the greatest expressions I have ever heard is "just a minute"; wait a little while and cool off a bit.

The gentleman from Indiana said our Constitution has been amended many times. That is true. But since the first 10 amendments were adopted—and they were practically agreed upon before the Constitution was ratified—it was said by men in high office that they would be adopted—I cannot find anywhere in any of the amendments to the Constitution that a fundamental change has been made in the Constitution. This Government of yours and mine was founded upon the theory that it was to be a representative democracy. It was, it has been, and it is just that. None of the changes made in the fundamental law have ever countenanced a change from that fundamental.

Without putting any partisanship into this thing, and I do not intend to, for it is too big for that, when I say "just a minute" I think it might be well for us to take a little more time, look the situation over, and heed some of the remarks of my distinguished colleague from Massachusetts [Mr. McCormack] when we are away from the third and the fourth terms just a little. This is a representative democracy. For the people to have the privilege of choosing whom they please to be their leader is democracy, real democracy, in action.

Let us not lightly change a document that has served us well and which has been a beacon to people throughout the earth who longed to be free and who wanted to get away from the heavy hand of the few that the people themselves in a free election might choose whom they would to be their leader. I do not know—I do not know, and neither do you know, whether a time may come when one man may be the individual to carry on in an hour of great strain and stress—and danger. I believe it would be well for us to take just a minute more to consider this fundamental change in our fundamental law.

The Speaker: The time of the gentleman from Texas has expired.

Mr. Allen of Illinois. Mr. Speaker, I move the previous question on the resolution.

The previous question was ordered.

The Speaker: The question is on the resolution.

The resolution was agreed to.

Extension of Remarks

Mr. Michener: Mr. Speaker, I ask unanimous consent to include in any remarks I may make today a study of what was said about the third term by previous Presidents of the United States, a study prepared by the Legislative Reference Service in the Library of Congress.

The Speaker: Is there objection to the request of the gentleman from Michigan?

There was no objection.

Amendment to the Constitution Relating to Terms of Office of the President

Mr. Michener: Mr. Speaker, I move that the House resolve itself into the Committee of the Whole House on the State of the Union for the consideration of the resolution (H. J. Res. 27) proposing an amendment to the Constitution of the United States relating to the terms of office of the President.

The Speaker: The question is on the motion offered by the gentleman from Michigan.

The motion was agreed to.

Accordingly the House resolved itself into the Committee of the Whole House on the State of the Union for the consideration of House Joint Resolution 27, with Mr. Wolcott in the chair.

The Clerk read the title of the resolution.

By unanimous consent the first reading of the resolution was dispensed with.

The Chairman: Under the rule, the gentleman from Michigan [Mr. Michener] is recognized for 1 hour, and the gentleman from New York [Mr. Celler] is recognized for 1 hour.

Mr. Michener: Mr. Chairman, I yield 10 minutes to the gentleman from Indiana [Mr. Springer], the chairman of the subcommittee of the Committee on the Judiciary, which gave consideration to this resolution.

Mr. Springer: Mr. Chairman, the matter which is now before the House comes under House Joint Resolution 27, has been reported by the Committee on the Judiciary of the House of Representatives.

This resolution, which is rather brief, provides for submission to the people of a constitutional amendment fixing the tenure of office of the President of the United States.

At this particular point and at the very outset of what I have to say on this question, my good friend and colleague, the gentleman from Massachusetts [Mr. McCormack], indicated we were placing shackles upon the people. I cannot subscribe to that statement, because we are merely passing upon the question as to whether or not we will submit to the people a constitutional amendment, and let the people pass upon it and decide that question themselves. I do not believe there is any Member on the floor of this House who opposes submitting to the people this constitutional question, and permitting the people to decide that question themselves and return to us what their decision is.

Let us see what the provisions of this resolution are. While I say it is brief, let us read it together.

Section 1, which follows the preamble of the resolution, contains the language:

> Any person who has served as President of the United States during all, or portions of any two terms, shall thereafter be ineligible to hold the office of President; but this article shall not prevent any person who may hold the office of President during the term

within which this article is ratified from holding such office for the remainder of such term.

Section 2 provides for ratification. That is the sole and only question which we are deciding today, as to whether or not we will submit it to your people, to the people of every district in our Nation, and to the people of this Nation, and let them pass upon this question as to whether or not they believe there should be a limitation upon the terms of office of the President of the United States; and this question is not, as my good friend has said, that we are shackling the people. We are simply passing down to the people the right to determine this very highly important and basic question.

Mr. Walter: Mr. Chairman, will the gentleman yield?

Mr. Springer: Yes; I yield to the gentleman from Pennsylvania.

Mr. Walter: I know that my distinguished friend from Indiana does not mean to make a misstatement, but I am afraid he has, because, after all, this question will never be submitted to the people. It is submitted to the legislatures.

Mr. Springer: Yes, this question goes to the legislatures, and the legislatures are the representatives of the people in the various legislative districts. That has always been construed, and is today construed, as submitting the question to the people themselves.

At the very outset of what I have to say on this question I want to make clear that this question is not a political question in any sense of the word. I hope that it will not be treated as such by the membership of this great law-making body. The importance of this question, it being the submission of a constitutional amendment, far transcends all political implications and considerations. This proposed amendment to the Constitution, should it be finally adopted, would continue as a basic law of the land for years to come, and until some future amendment is adopted on this same subject. I therefore plead with the Members of the House to approach this problem in the spirit of the sacredness with which this question is enshrouded. We are meeting and facing a problem which will mean the writing of the scroll of our fundamental law, which will endure throughout time and until our words have been erased in the future by other generations.

This resolution has but one purpose. That purpose is to submit to the people of the country by and through their State legislatures the important problem of Presidential tenure, and permit the people through their legislatures to decide whether or not they desire that limitation fixed or to leave the question of Presidential tenure just as it is now set forth in the Constitution of the United States of America.

Mr. McCormack: Mr. Chairman, will the gentleman yield?

Mr. Springer: I yield to my colleague from Massachusetts.

Mr. McCormack: Does my friend agree with my contention that if in the future our country should be involved in war and the then President were in his second term, that no matter what the emergency, no matter what situation might confront the people at that time, that President must retire if this resolution becomes part of the Constitution?

Mr. Springer: I understand the gentleman's question, and thanks for submitting it. May I say that if our country were involved in any grave emergency in the future, such as war, the President does not fight the war. Our chiefs of staff, our generals, our admirals are the ones who fight our wars. Our President takes advice, of course, and acts in conjunction with them. But where is the President, of whatever political party he may be a member, who would not take that same counsel, that same advice, for the safety and for the protection of our Nation and the people in it?

Mr. McCormack: Mr. Chairman, will the gentleman yield further?

Mr. Springer: May I proceed further? I have but a short time. I appreciate the gentleman's interest.

Mr. Chairman, during the past many resolutions of this kind have been submitted but none have ever been enacted by both Houses of the Congress, and this question has not been submitted to the people. Throughout the years the Constitution has stood as originally written, and may I read just for our own consideration, as we deal with this vitally important problem, section 1 of article II of the Constitution which contains this provision. I know all of you are familiar with it, but let us review it once more:

> The executive power shall be vested in a President of the United States of America, who shall hold his office during the term of 4 years.

The Chairman: The time of the gentleman from Indiana has expired.

Mr. Michener: Mr. Chairman, I yield the gentleman three additional minutes.

Mr. Springer: May I say, Mr. Chairman, that until the lame-duck amendment to this article, amendment No. 20, there had been no amendment adopted on this question. That amendment provided—

> That the terms of President and Vice President shall end at noon on the 20th day of January and the terms of Senators and Representatives at noon on the 3d day of January of the year in which such terms should have ended if this article had not been ratified and the terms of their successors shall then begin.

Mr. Rankin: Mr. Chairman; will the gentleman yield?

Mr. Springer: I yield to the gentleman from Mississippi.

Mr. Rankin: Let me call attention to the fact that in 1861 when everyone knew we were on the verge of a war, the Confederate constitutional convention met, at a time when we had one of the greatest soldiers of all time as President of the Confederacy, and they adopted a constitutional provision limiting the Presidency of the Confederacy to 6 years and providing that he could not succeed himself.

Mr. Springer: In other words, they wanted to protect to some extent against any man perpetuating himself in public office.

Mr. Chairman, I want to recur to the words of Woodrow Wilson. Let us think for a minute what he said on this question. I obtained this interesting statement from his own remarks, now on file in the Congressional Library. This is what Woodrow Wilson said on this subject:

> To change the term to 6 years would be to increase the likelihood of its being too long, without any assurance that it would, in happy cases, be long enough. A fixed constitutional limitation to a single term of office is highly arbitrary and unsatisfactory from every point of view.

He was thinking about the one-term proposal.

> Put the present customary limitation of two terms into the Constitution, if you do not trust the people to take care of themselves, but make it two terms (not one, because 4 years is often too long), and give the President a chance to win the full service by proving himself fit for it.

Before closing I want to quote the words of Abraham Lincoln when he left Springfield, Ill., to come to Washington to assume the Presidency. He came to Indianapolis. He was worried and distressed. He stopped there. A great group of people had assembled. They asked him to speak. He spoke, and in the course of his remarks he said this to the American people:

> Remember, it is not with the President nor the officeholder, nor with the politician, but with the people alone rests the power of determining our policies of government.

Mr. Chairman, we are today proposing to submit this highly important question to the people, just as Lincoln proposed.

Mr. Celler: Mr. Chairman, I yield myself 10 minutes.

Mr. Chairman, a number of the members of the minority of the Committee on the Judiciary realize that the Constitution sets no limitation on the number of terms a President may serve. The Members also realize that a tradition was established by Washington, followed by Jefferson, Madison, Jackson, Cleveland, McKinley, and Wilson. Now attempts are being made to change the Constitution as to number of terms a President may serve.

These Members feel a change is unnecessary, but if there is to be any change these Members feel it would be preferable to change the Constitution so that a President could serve only 6 years and not be eligible for reelection.

It has always been natural for the incumbent President to have his eyes fixed on reelection, and all the acts of the first term, directly or indirectly, in some measure, are affected by the ambition for a second term. It is only natural for the incumbent President to make appointments even to his Cabinet with due consideration for political repercussions. Even appointments to important judicial positions have been at times tinctured with politics. I make no specific charge against any specific President. I speak generally. The President is one to ask himself and his intimates, "Will the appointment enhance or diminish my prospects for reelection?" You know and I know that even Ambassadors and Ministers have been appointed because of political campaign aid and assistance and in the hope of renewal of that aid at reelection time. If there is no possibility, we feel, for reelection, there is no need for the President and his Cabinet and those associated with him to canvass for delegates at the national convention; no need for the President to placate certain sections of the country that may be hostile; no need to suggest legislation that might mean the garnering of additional votes that might be useful at the national convention.

During the first term the ambition for reelection to a second term and to serve four additional years casts an ominous shadow, in my humble estimation, over all the acts and all the works of the incoming President. I could, but shall not, quote you at length the arguments advanced by numerous Presidents, notably Jackson and Hayes and Taft, in favor of a 6-year term, with no reeligibility, but I will give you the statement made by Grover Cleveland when he accepted the nomination for President. He argued for a 6-year term, with no right to reelection. He said:

> Then an election to office shall be the selection by the voters of one of their number to assume for a time a public trust, instead of his dedication to the profession of politics; when the holders of the ballot, quickened by a sense of duty, shall avenge truth betrayed and pledges broken, and when the suffrage shall be altogether free and uncorrupted, the full realization of a government by the people will be at hand. And of the means to this end not one would, in my judgment, be more effective than an amendment to the Constitution disqualifying the President from reelection. When we consider the patronage of this great office, the allurements of power, the temptations to retain public place once gained, and, more than all, the availability a party finds in an incumbent when a horde of officeholders, with a zeal born of benefits received and fostered by the hope of favors yet to come, stand ready to aid with money and trained political service, we recognize in the eligibility of the President for reelection a most serious danger to that calm, deliberate, and intelligent political action which must characterize a government by the people.

I could not and you could not put in better language, or express more succinctly or more wisely, the argument for a 6-year term, with no right to reelec-

tion. I feel that the desire to be reelected tends to build up, beyond peradventure of a doubt, for the incumbent a dangerous political machine. The attendant political strains and stresses are inconsistent with good government. Too often the President, having his eye on the reelection possibilities, wants to be all things to all people at one time. Too often in our history Presidents in their first term have actually—and I can give you chapter and verse—appeased the bosses and appeased the machines. His efficiency thereby becomes greatly impaired. Not infrequently he has the overweening desire, in order that he may get the renomination, to punish his enemies unduly and to reward his friends too lavishly.

Elections every 4 years are too often, and a great burden of taxation thereby is saddled upon the people. We know that the approach of any election sets the demagogues at work hunting issues and inventing party slogans to stir up the country, and thus the blight of discontent and uncertainty as well as fear descends upon all of us. Business is greatly retarded, and industry is hurt and hampered. That evil should not come upon us too often. It is too often, indeed, to have it come before us twice in 8 years and four times in 16 years.

For that reason, among others, I do believe it would be well for this Committee to vote for an amendment which will be offered, a substitute amendment for the amendment offered by the majority of the House Committee on the Judiciary, which substitute amendment would set up a tenure of 6 years, with no right to reelection.

I also believe this: The President's health, with a 6-year limitation, would be better protected. I believe that if President Roosevelt had not run a third and fourth time—I do not say he should or should not, I am addressing myself now to his physical condition—he might have been spared to us and we could use now and use well his prescience, his prophetic wisdom, and his statesmanship.

Mr. Michener: Mr. Chairman, I yield 10 minutes to the gentleman from Pennsylvania [Mr. Graham].

Mr. Graham: Mr. Chairman, at the outset of my remarks, in order that we may become properly oriented, let us remember how many efforts and attempts have been made to amend the Constitution of the United States. Inquiry today of the Congressional Reference Service, available to the Members of this House, reveals that 4,500 attempts have been made to amend the Constitution, of which number 1,300 were made in the first 100 years of the Constitution.

It has been argued here today that we are doing something new, dangerous, and untried.

In those first 100 years of the 1,300 attempts, 125 went to the tenure of office of the President of the United States and in a period of 39 years, from 1899 to 1928, 85 additional attempts were made to affect the tenure of office of the President of the United States. Therefore, all told, in a period of 139 years 210 attempts have been made to fix the tenure of office of the President of the United States. So we are not doing anything new, unusual, or out of the way at this time. We are simply trying to carry out the mandate of the people in order that they may have an expression and voice in the amendment of the Constitution. We must remember that our guide in this question is the Constitutional Convention. When Edmund Randolph appeared in Philadelphia on the 25th day of May 1787, and the Convention finally got down to work on the 29th the seventh ordinance that he had in his propositions was as follows, which I desire to read into the Record:

> 7. *Resolved,* That a National Executive be instituted; to be chosen by the National Legislature for the term of— ——years, to receive punctually at stated times a fixed compensation for the services rendered, in which no increase or diminution shall be made so as to affect the Magistracy, existing at the time of increase or diminution, and to be ineligible a second time.

It is true that no time was fixed to limit the debates of that Convention and in the 91 days in which they were engaged, from the 29th day of May until the 12th day of September, you will find that nearly 14 days of the time of the Convention was consumed in fixing the mode of election of the President, the time that he would serve, and the length of his term. After these propositions had been referred to the Committee of the Whole and was first debated on the 1st and 2d and 8th days of June, finally on the 26th day of July the committee made a report and in that report they fixed the term at 7 years and proposed that the incumbent would be ineligible to serve a second term. This carried through until finally the great report came through on the 4th of September under the direction of Judge Brearley, of New Jersey, chairman of the Committee on Postponed Matters. Their report was to this effect: that the term should be 4 years and the ineligibility clause stricken out. Now that is our polestar by which we must be guided today. What did the framers of the Constitution intend and what did they want done? It was known that George Washington would become the first President. Everyone knew that. The great doubt at that time was whether the country would endure for, on the 8th day of August, Nathaniel Gorman, in the Committee of the Whole, addressed George Washington, who was then presiding, and said, "Can it be supposed that 150 years hence this great country, including the western territory, will remain one nation?" Well, 160 years have gone by and Nathaniel Gorman's question has been answered. Incidentally, he was a gentleman from Massachusetts. On that score, when Washington came to the end of his second term, his Farewell Message went out to the people and thereby the precedent was established which grew into tradition which endured down through the years. What was the result of that? A few years ago that tradition was broken. What may be the other effects, if you please? Our founding fathers intended that this should be a great system of checks and balances, that the judiciary should be independent, that the legislative branch should be independent, and that the executive branch should be independent to the extent that the Executive could go ahead and administer laws enacted by the legislative bodies. I read from a statement issued by the Attorney General of the United States that in the period from 1932 down to the present there have been appointed to the United States judiciary 192 Federal judges, both district and circuit court judges, 25 in the Territories, and 14 in the lower courts, a total of 231 judges. Of that number 17 have been Republicans—9 in the United States, 6 in the Territories, and 2 in the District of Columbia. This has not reached the point where the chairman of the Committee on the Judiciary of the United States Senate has taken this matter up and publicly declared through the press and through the medium of the Congressional Record that there must be a different division in the appointment of men to fill these great and high offices of our judiciary.

That is just one illustration of the case of a President having more than two terms and entrusting too much power to one man.

I now yield to the gentleman from Massachusetts.

Mr. McCormack: In order to have the record clear, I just want to ask the gentleman if he does not agree that this was the procedure: that the 7-year term, without further eligibility, which was changed to eligibility and then changed

back again, was then sent to the Committee of Eleven, after the Committee on Detail had reported it to the Committee of the Whole? Was not that election by the National Legislature?

Mr. Graham: Up to that point the Senate was to have elected the President. At that point the electoral college was brought in.

Mr. McCormack: But the 7-year term was election by the National Legislature?

Mr. Graham: That was the first matter presented, but afterward it came down to the writing of the Constitution and the formation of the electoral college.

Mr. McCormack: And the electoral college came out of the Committee of Eleven?

Mr. Graham: Yes.

Mr. McCormack: But prior to that it was a 7-year term, to be elected by the National Legislature?

Mr. Graham: Yes.

There has been a great lack of emphasis here on the mode of election. That is what those men were principally driving toward at that time, because at the time and in that period the relative number of voters was considerably less than it is today.

In conclusion this is one point I wish to make: Our fathers realized, of course, that the day would come when it would be necessary to amend this Constitution. The great bulk of the American people have been hesitant to touch this charter of Government. The very number of amendments I have cited, nearly 4,500 attempts with only 21 successful, is proof in itself of the strong hold that this great charter of human rights has upon the minds and hearts and consciences of the American people. But by the same token, inasmuch as it has been amended, I quote you in substance the words of James Madison when he submitted the original amendments in the First Congress. This is approximately what he said:

We never need to fear an executive in this country because he will always be weak. The legislative branch will always be the stronger.

Had Mr. Madison lived within the last two decades he would have reversed that statement. Now we have come face to face with the situation where we have seen the evil of perpetuation of centralization of government, of control through great bureaucracies, appointment of courts and control of our foreign relations, all due to the built-up, accumulated potency and power of one man remaining too long in public office.

The Chairman: The time of the gentleman from Pennsylvania [Mr. Graham] has expired.

Mr. Celler: Mr. Chairman, I yield 8 minutes to the gentleman from Pennsylvania [Mr. Walter].

Mr. Walter: Mr. Chairman, I think it is extremely important, when an attempt is made to amend the Constitution, to have as the objective something more than what I believe is being attempted here today. It is very important for us to remember in connection with the present resolution that perhaps as much time was devoted in the discussions of the tenure in office of the President as was devoted in the discussions of the tenure in office of the President as was devoted to any other section of the Constitution. For 18 days the founding fathers labored with the question of whether or not the tenure should be limited, and, significantly enough, the only proposal made toward limiting the time during which the Chief Executive could serve was in connection with one term of either 6 or 7 years. It was not until after this complete debate when, in my judgment at least, the entire committee was worn out and tired, that they did nothing about it. But bear this in mind, that a great deal of thought was given to this particular section of the Constitution. I believe that if we are going to do anything at all we ought to do what the

founding fathers almost did, namely, provide for one term of 6 years.

The gentleman from Pennsylvania [Mr. Graham] has touched to some extent on the abuses that could follow when there is no limitation on the number of terms. He overlooked, however, the extremely important question of selection of personnel by the Chief Executive. Under present conditions too much attention is given to geography and politics. I could well understand there being two or three very capable men in the State of my distinguished friend the gentleman from Iowa, who could not possibly be considered because of the population of that state compared with States in which there was a much larger number of voters. No man ever occupied the seat in the White House who did not during his first term think of his reelection. It is only human nature. So I repeat, if we are going to take the first step incident to doing something as important as amending the Constitution is, we should advocate a real improvement and only after greater consideration than has been given the proposal now before us.

The Chairman: The time of the gentleman from Pennsylvania has expired.

Mr. Celler: Mr. Chairman, I yield 5 minutes to the gentleman from South Carolina [Mr. Bryson].

Mr. Bryson: Mr. Chairman, the age-old question of the third term for President is before us again. The question arose in the early days of the Republic. In 1787 when our Constitution was first adopted our founding fathers debated the question of tenure of office for the President. First, it was proposed that the President should have one 7-year term. That proposal was adopted and later thrown out. Then a 6-year term was proposed but rejected. Finally, in its great wisdom, the Convention settled on a 4-year term, with no limit to the number of terms. During the 170 years since the establishment of tenure of office for all our elective Federal officials many proposals have been made to change or limit the length of their service, but no change has ever been made. For many years, some Americans, particularly Republicans, believed that the precedents set by Washington and Jefferson, when they refused to serve three terms had established an unwritten law that no President should ever serve his country more than 8 years.

In 1940 opponents of Franklin D. Roosevelt called on that unwritten law to help them prevent his election for a third term. But this so-called precedent or tradition proved a poor substitute for the will of the people, who swept the President back into office for a third and a fourth term. To have had a constitutional limitation on the Presidential tenure of office in 1940 and again in 1944 would have been disastrous. Mr. Speaker, I submit that the gross fallacy of such a proposal as we have before us today was proved beyond the shadow of a doubt when in the face of a grave national crisis in 1940 the people of the United States believed it inadvisable to change their Chief Executive; and the utter stupidity of such a proposal was proved in 1944 when the people believed that such a change would have thrown our Nation into chaos and jeopardized our security in the face of the gravest military crisis in our Nation's history.

The proposal before us utterly ignores the possibility of future crises and exigencies which could well make it mandatory that we continue a Chief Magistrate in office beyond an 8-year period.

Before 1940 the precedent for the President's tenure of office had been established by the Presidents themselves, notably Washington and Jefferson. But in 1940 the precedent was established by the people, and that is as it should be. The President is the servant of the people, and each 4 years the

people themselves should have the privilege of deciding whether their chief servant is to continue in office or be replaced. President Wilson said, "We singularly belie our own principles by seeking to determine by fixed constitutional provision what the people shall determine for themselves."

If the people believe it unwise to continue a President in office after he has served 8 years, or 4 years, let them make that choice at the ballot box when and if the incumbent President seeks reelection and in the light of the issues involved and in consideration of the relative merits of the parties and their candidates. But in the name of democracy their exercise of free choice of a President should not be limited for all time to come by a constitutional amendment passed with only present partisan political considerations involved. It has been suggested that a constitutional amendment may at any time be repealed in the event the people should at some future time change their minds about the third term. The fallacy of that is obvious, since the President is elected by a mere majority, whereas the passage or repeal of a constitutional amendment requires a two-thirds vote of both Houses of Congress and ratification by three-fourths of the States.

Much has been said about the danger to democracy in allowing a President to remain in office beyond 8 years. There can be no danger to democracy so long as the people themselves may freely exercise the franchise. Parliamentary governments have preserved their democracy with indefinite tenure for their prime ministers.

Manifestly, if the people of the United States can be trusted to elect a President for one term, or two terms, they also can be trusted to determine whether he should be continued in office for a third one.

Mr. Springer: Mr. Chairman, I yield such time as he may desire to the gentleman from Ohio [Mr. Jenkins].

Mr. Jenkins of Ohio. Mr. Chairman, I shall favor this resolution. The two-term rule for the position of President is an American tradition which was established by Washington, ratified by Jefferson in forceful and unambiguous language and likewise ratified expressly or impliedly by every other President until the day of Franklin D. Roosevelt. The tenure of Franklin D. Roosevelt proved that Washington and Jefferson were wise.

I introduced a resolution to the same import as the resolution that we are now considering. I would have voted for my resolution and I shall vote for the one before us today.

My resolution was introduced by me several years ago and has been reintroduced in this session of Congress as House Joint Resolution 36. A copy of that resolution is as follows:

House Joint Resolution 36
Joint resolution proposing an amendment to the Constitution of the United States relating to the terms of office of the President

Resolved by the Senate and House of Representatives of the United States of America in Congress assembled (two-thirds of each House concurring therein), That the following article is hereby proposed as an amendment to the Constitution of the United States, which shall be valid to all intents and purposes as part of the Constitution when ratified by the legislatures of three-fourths of the several States:
"ARTICLE———
"Section 1. No person shall be chosen or serve as President of the United States for any term, or be eligible to hold the office of President during any term, if such person shall have theretofore served as President during the whole or any part of each of any two separate terms; but this article shall not prevent any person who may hold the office of President during the term within which this article is ratified from holding such office for the remainder of such term.
"Sec. 2. This article shall be inoperative unless it shall have been ratified as an amendment to the Constitution by the legislatures of three-fourths of the several States within 7 years from the date of its submission to the States by the Congress."

Mr. Chairman, I ask unanimous consent to revise and extend my remarks and include a resolution that I introduced on this same subject.

The Chairman: Is there objection to the request of the gentleman from Ohio?

There was no objection.

Mr. Springer: Mr. Chairman, I yield 5 minutes to the distinguished gentleman from Kentucky [Mr. Robsion].

Mr. Robsion: Mr. Chairman, I rise in support of House Joint Resolution 27. The gentleman from Michigan [Mr. Michener], one or two others, and myself introduced identical resolutions, proposing an amendment to the Constitution of the United States to limit the tenure of office of the President to the whole or any part of each of two separate terms; in other words, making ineligible any person who has served as President for a whole or part of two separate terms, and thereby placing a maximum limit of 8 years. No man could serve more than 8 years if this proposed amendment is submitted to the States and ratified by 36 of the 48 States.

I am expressing the view that I have entertained over a long period of years. My experience and observations have strengthened my position on this matter. There has been so much discussion of this subject that I feel that we should at least give the American people, through their respective legislatures, the right to determine whether or not they desire such a limitation.

President George Washington, the Father of Our Country, in his wide experience and great wisdom, declined to be considered for a third term even though there was a universal demand that he do so and at a time when our country was having serious problems with France and other nations. Thomas Jefferson, another one of our very great Americans, the author of the Declaration of Independence, and who had served our country in the highest offices in this country and in foreign countries, certainly believed in representative democracy and in protecting the liberties and freedom of the American people. He had seen at first hand in Europe how free people had lost their freedom, not through parliaments and congresses, but through ambitious heads of the executive branch of the government. Therefore, 2 years before his second term expired, he made the following statement:

> The general solicitations I have received to continue another term give me great consolation, but considerations for public as well as personal determine me inflexibly on that measure. That I should lay down my charge at a proper season is as much a duty as to have borne it faithfully. * * * These changes are necessary, too, for the security of republican government. If some period be not fixed, either by the Constitution or by practice, to the services of the First Magistrate, his office, though nominally elective, will in fact be for life; and that will soon degenerate into an inheritance. I have therefore requested my fellow citizens to think of a successor for me, to whom I shall deliver the public concern with greater joy than I received them.

In this wonderful statement Jefferson reemphasizes the principles laid down in the Declaration of Independence and our Constitution. He truly believed that the hope of this Nation and the security of our people could only be achieved through our republican form of government. He, too, realized the danger to our freedom in too long a tenure of the powerful office of the President. At the time he made this declaration and 2 years before his term expired we had very serious foreign problems with both Great Britain and France, and it might be said at that time our Nation was weak in numbers, naval and military

forces, as well as wealth. We had not yet become thoroughly established. Jefferson might well have said that by reason of the perils that confronted this new Republic there was an emergency and listened to the general solicitation not only of his own political party but many of the opposition party to consider a third term.

James Madison, James Monroe, and Andrew Jackson, all great Americans and popular heroes, declined to be considered for a third term. The first to attempt to override the wise example and admonition of Washington and Jefferson was President Ulysses S. Grant. He was a very popular war hero. Many Americans felt that he had contributed greatly in saving the Union and freeing millions of slaves. Many of his comrades in arms and many and perhaps more influential of his appointees insisted that he seek a third term. His friends made a long and determined fight to secure for him the Republican nomination. Three hundred and six delegates stood out to the end but the Republican Party refused to give to the hero of Appomattox the nomination for a third term. The Republican Party thereby rendered a great service to our country.

Theodore Roosevelt was nominated as the running mate of President McKinley in 1900. They were overwhelmingly elected. President McKinley lost his life at the hands of assassins in September 1901, less than 6 .months after his second inauguration and Theodore Roosevelt entered upon his duties of President. He was nominated in 1904 and elected by an overwhelming majority. A host of admirers and friends urged him to seek another term as he had had only one full term.

The records show that 30 of our American Presidents were conscious of this threat to the freedom of the American people and they pointed out that there should be a limitation as to the tenure of the Presidential office and one of them, a great Democrat, favored 4 years, some 6 years, others not more than 8 years. Republican and Democratic National Conventions, from time to time, have declared in favor of a limitation of the tenure of this office.

Whatever may be said of the mental attainments and the winning personality of President Franklin D. Roosevelt, he must have impressed the American people that he was an ambitious man. He insisted on having control of not only the executive branch of the Government but control of Congress and control over the courts. He created hundreds and hundreds of bureaus, commissions, and agencies and at one time had more than 4,000,000 Federal civil officeholders in this country and in foreign countries and through these agencies and officials, they attempted and did, to a large degree, control agriculture, industry, labor, and many of the normal activities of the American people. Power feeds power.

When history finally records what transpired in our Nation for the last 14 years, they will likely write that the two-term tradition was broken by these controls and by the expenditure of enormous sums of money and the granting of special favors to blocs and groups.

Soon after the election of President Roosevelt to his fourth term many of his friends and admirers were declaring themselves in favor of a fifth term, and we heard that attitude substantially expressed today by at least one of the able Members of this House, confirming the prophecy of the immortal Jefferson nearly 140 years ago. Jefferson said that there should be a limitation on the tenure of this great office, and that these changes are necessary for the security of our republican form of government, and he also stated that he should lay down his charge at a proper season and that the laying down of his duties of President is as much a duty as to have performed the duties of this office faithfully.

Who can say that some other great American, Democrat or Republican, could not have handled the affairs of this Nation from 1940 to 1945 equally as well as President Roosevelt? To take any other view we must assume that we have and do produce in this country indispensable men. This idea was only sold to one other man before President Franklin D. Roosevelt and that was President Grant.

My sincere prayer is that we shall never live to see the day when this great Republic becomes so bankrupt of leadership and patriotism that we accept the principle of the indispensable man. I am against the 6-year one term. If we should happen to pick a bad President, 6 years is too long, and if we picked a good President, under this amendment, the American people can elect him for another term. Furthermore, unless we amend the Constitution as to the election of Members of the lower House, there would be great confusion.

The two-term President would be encouraged to select suitable men for high places in our Government and conduct himself in a way that would meet the approval of the American people. Eight years of honest and faithful service is enough to break down the vitality and health of any man. While President Roosevelt won a fourth term, yet the burdens of the office greatly lessened his activities during his fourth term. The Constitution, as written provides that the term of office of the President shall be 4 years. It makes no provision for his reelection. But he set his face against this proposal. He recognized at that time that the two-term principle declared by Washington, Jefferson, and other American Presidents was generally regarded as being embodied in our country's political system.

President Wilson, our great war President, so far as I know, never showed any inclination or desire to seek a third term at the height of his popularity. President Coolidge, as the running mate of President Harding, was swept into office by a landslide in 1920. He and Mr. Harding assumed office on March 4, 1921. President Harding, after less than 3 years' service, died suddenly and Mr. Coolidge assumed the Presidency. He became a very popular President, though he had been in office less than 2 years. He was nominated by almost a unanimous vote in the Republican Convention in 1924 and was triumphantly elected. His administration of the affairs of the Nation was marked by honesty and high purpose. Tremendous pressure was brought to bear to have him seek another full term, but more than a year before the national election in 1928 he made known to the American people that he would not be a candidate. He recognized that the two-term principle was fully embodied in our political system. At the end of his term he would have had less than 6 years of service. Mr. Coolidge recognized that by accepting another full term he would have had more than two terms and violate this political principle.

This is not and must not be made a partisan issue. It is a great policy in the interest of freedom and our republican form of government laid down by the Father of our Country and followed by such great Democrats as Jefferson, Madison, Monroe, Jackson, and such outstanding Republicans as Theodore Roosevelt and Calvin Coolidge, and in only two instances in all of our history has any serious attempt been made to set aside this great political principle, in the persons of President Grant and President Franklin D. Roosevelt. No doubt, in the days of President Grant, some of his stalwart admirers looked upon him as the indispensable man but that Republican Convention believing, as we strongly believe, that this country has never had an indispensable man, refused to nominate him.

Through the 50 centuries of the world's history, chief executives, emperors, kings, princes, czars, as well as some presidents of the nations of the earth, by their own thinking and by reason of the urging of their appointees, have considered themselves the indispensable man or woman. Some of these have been cruel tyrants, others have been benevolent dictators or rulers, some have sought power and more power to accomplish their own selfish aims and those of a small coterie of favorites surrounding and cooperating with them.

Then, there have been the benevolent group of executives who, with high purposes and motives, through their own thinking and the thinking of their friends and supporters have come to believe that they alone know what is best for the people or country over which they have control, and they regard themselves as indispensable men and women. They seek power and more power to continue what they regard as their benevolent rule over the nation and the people.

As we read history no free people ever lost their liberties through their parliament or congress except in some instances through the influence and power of the executives, the law-making body is whipped into subservency and they abdicate their powers. The real hope of a republic or democracy is in a strong parliament or congress, freely chosen by the people. The parliament or congress has great power, especially in this country, to protect and preserve the rights, freedom, and liberties of the people, but such bodies do not have the power of the sword or the expenditure or disbursement of enormous sums of money, or the appointment of millions of great and small public officials. We have many examples of "yes men" in parliaments and congresses who were made subservient through the tremendous power of the chief executives. Long tenure of the Chief Executive office in this Nation was considered dangerous to the liberties and freedom of the American people, even by our early

Presidents. This danger has increased many hundredfold since the days of Washington, Jefferson, Madison, Monroe, and Jackson. In those days we had a very small Army and Navy. It was numbered by thousands rather than millions. The appointees were numbered by thousands rather than millions. The expenditures at the disposal of the President were limited to millions rather than tens of billions as it is today. In those days there were few blocs and groups that were demanding special benefits, aids, and hand-outs from the Government. It was generally accepted that the people supported their Government instead of the Government, through special privileges and benefits, supporting the people.

If long tenure of office of the President was a threat to our republican form of government as stated by President Jefferson nearly 140 years ago, with his limited powers, small disbursements, small Army and Navy and a small number of appointees, how much greater must that threat be to our republican form of government and to the liberties of the American people today. The threat to the security of our country with 48 great States and approximately 135,000,000 people with untold wealth could not have been as great as they were to our security from foreign attacks as they were in the days of Washington, Jefferson, and Madison, when our country was threatened by the French on one side and the British on the other side and the French and the British had control of the seas and much of our own North American Continent which is now a part of the United States. We have observed that even so-called benevolents, chief executives, can find emergencies and other reasons that appear to them to be good and sufficient.

I cannot believe that President Roosevelt could have or would have been nominated for a third term or even a fourth term but for the use of the Executive powers of himself and supporters to bring about his nomination for a third and fourth term. During that period the number of Federal office-holders increased by leaps and bounds. The billions of dollars of money at the disposal of the President and his subordinates increased by billions from year to year, and with all these extraordinary powers were given to the President, and practically blank checks were voted by a Congress that admittedly was dominated and controlled by the President. Immense sums of money were distributed to various groups. Of course, in each case the American people were told that all of these acts were made necessary by reason of the threat of some emergency.

At one time we reached the point that there was not only control of the executive branch of the Government but a very large control of the legislative branch and, last but not least, control of an overwhelming majority of the members of the Federal courts. All of these things violated the expressed provisions of the Constitution providing for three coordinated branches of our Government. The American people now begin to realize clearly the wisdom of Washington, Jefferson, and other great American Presidents in establishing and holding to the principle that a longer period than two terms was a real threat to our republican form of government.

Mr. Celler: Mr. Chairman, I yield 8 minutes to the gentleman from Kentucky [Mr. Chelf.]

Mr. Chelf: Mr. Chairman, I am unalterably opposed to House Joint Resolution 27. I voted against it when it came before the full Committee on the Judiciary. I joined in the minority report which sets forth our reasons for our opposition to what, in my opinion, is a legislative abortion—an untimely arrest of democratic process. I shall vote against it today on final passage.

I sincerely believe that this attempt to limit the tenure of office of the

President of the United States is unwarranted, unneeded, unwise, undesirable, unthinkable, unbelievable, unconscionable, and that it actually reeks with putrefaction insofar as keeping good faith with our basic precepts of democracy is concerned.

We are considering today a proposal that strikes right at the heart of our form of government. We are considering a proposal which would limit the rights of the American citizens as free people to govern themselves according to their expressed will as guaranteed by the tenets upon which our Nation was founded.

Perhaps one might say I am going far afield in attaching too deep a significance to this proposed amendment to our Constitution, an amendment which would do nothing more than merely limit the term of the President of the United States to two 4-year terms. Indeed, it could sound innocuous enough. Why consider over carefully a proposal that apparently does no more than limit the tenure of office of our President. To my mind, there are several vitally important factors involved which call for careful, deliberate, conscientious and even prayerful consideration.

First and foremost, we are proposing to recommend an amendment to the Constitution of the United States. For 160 years that document has outlined the principles of liberty, justice, and democracy, but it has done more than that because in guaranteeing freedom, it has also indirectly espoused the cause of the teachings of Christianity. Our Constitution has been the beacon light of hope, of faith, of comfort, and of peace to freedom-loving peoples all over the world. I do not mean to say that the founders of our Nation were able to frame an infallible pattern of government for our people throughout the ages. Quite naturally, there must be changes in our methods of operation to meet our governmental needs in a changing world. But I do say that the

principles laid down in our Constitution have proved themselves to be remarkably sound, just, and practicable. These principles have proved their roots of fairness and truth in the steady growth of our Nation.

I am informed by constitutional experts that in the 160 years of our existence as a nation, there have been some 3,000 attempts to amend our Constitution. Out of this number, only 21 have proved wise or appealing. When one pauses to consider that 10 of these amendments were the original Bill of Rights which were adopted at the same time as our Constitution itself, there are really only 11 actual amendments which were sound enough to merit favorable consideration and final adoption. Imagine, only 11 changes to our American way of life and its meaning in all of our glorious 160 years of progress and development in which we have arisen from a young, obscure, sprawling country to the greatest Nation on earth today. Incidentally, each of the 11 adopted amendments, in every instance, gave more rights, responsibilities, freedom and power to our people—only 1 of the 11 was later repealed by the people.

Whenever we can amend the Constitution to further democracy and to give a large segment of our country's population broader rights of citizenship, it should be done. For instance, when slavery was abolished, such action strengthened a link in our chain of government. When that segment of our people were given the rights of suffrage irrespective of their race, color, creed, or previous condition of servitude, this, likewise, placed another strong support in our citadel of freedom. When the people were given the right of voting directly for the Members of the Senate, such action brought more securely within the grip of the people, an additional opportunity to govern themselves. When the right of franchise was given to the women of America, that, too, was a step forward in the right direction. The Norris amendment abolishing the lame-duck session of Congress was likewise a healthy contribution. These and other amendments constitute enlargements of the democratic process and with this long history of additional responsibilities being given to the people, I profoundly regret that the majority party has now seen fit to propose this amendment which, in my humble judgment, seeks to impede and curtail the freedom and democratic power of the voter.

Mr. Chairman, we have been in session now for 33 days, and this is the second piece of legislation that has come to our attention; and will you believe it, we have only 2 hours to discuss a constitutional amendment that means so much to the people of this great Nation of ours—2 hours, 1 for the opponents and 1 for the proponents of the measure.

Mr. Springer: Mr. Chairman, will the gentleman yield?

Mr. Chelf: I am sorry, I cannot yield at the moment. I will later.

It has been argued that the American people must be protected from dictatorship by statute or constitutional fiat. But the simple fact remains that nobody can protect the American people from dictatorship because it is a well-known fact, thank God, that dictators are not bred or conceived in free and open elections such as are held in the United States of America.

Yes; only once in all of this magnificent 160 years of achievement and expansion did Americans see fit to elect any one person President for the third and then the fourth term. And as every grade-school child knows, this would never have been done had our Nation not been tottering on the brink of a horrible and ghastly world conflagration. Yes; for the first time in all of our existence as a nation, Americans realized that continuity of service, experience, and leadership were in demand far over, above, and beyond our normal

and natural tendencies to restrict, through the medium of the ballot, a President to two terms.

We cannot change the past, for what is past is prologue. Mr. Chairman, future generations are involved in this great decision which we here today must make. Who are we to say that our posterity yet unborn shall not have the same rights, privileges, and responsibilities such as we ourselves have enjoyed and participated in? If we defeat this proposed amendment today, I will make the prediction that in future ages countless thousands will laud and praise our names. We have a golden opportunity today, not only a rendezvous with destiny, but, what is more, we have a rendezvous with the future, because if by our actions we vote down this unconscionable proposal, we of our time will ring down the curtain with such a spectacular performance that the applause and acclaim therefrom shall resound and echo in the ears of grateful generations yet unborn.

The people, at present, by a mere majority vote, have the opportunity of deciding every 4 years whether they want to terminate the services of the President if he stands for reelection. I do not feel that any further limitation is justified. The American people have done nothing to warrant this restriction upon their democratic process. The fact that they saw fit in their wisdom and judgment to elect Franklin Delano Roosevelt for a third and then a fourth term is no offense.

As I see it, the man selected and the number of times he is elected or reelected comes under the heading of the people's business. That is their business. They will know how many times they want to elect a President or any other man. If they want to elect him once, twice, three times, or four times, that is the present right of the people of the United States.

Let us pray that the time may never again come when the United States may be in the throes of another global war with a dangerous enemy, but should this come to pass, by adopting this amendment—I repeat—we assume to speak for the generations to come. We have no crystal ball to gaze into and we cannot anticipate their dilemma; therefore, we should not attempt to tie their hands and require them in the midst of a titanic struggle to change leadership, be he a Republican or a Democrat, and, therefore, invite defeat and destruction of Christianity, democracy, and decency.

Does Congress propose to set itself up as a guardian or curator of the American people? By this amendment we say quite frankly that the people of this great Nation have not sufficient intelligence or judgment to know their own minds, that they cannot think for themselves, and, as a result, their Representatives in Congress must appoint themselves as the peoples' committee in order to protect the people from themselves. Yes; a committee of the people, by the people, and for the people, with malice toward none but with a straitjacket for all.

Mr. Chairman, if the Congress has nothing more to do at the present time than to attempt such legislation which seeks to detract from the rights and privileges of its citizens, then I say to you, sir, that we had better adjourn and return home.

We know we have a job to do here. Much important legislation is being held up. Let us vote this constitutional amendment down and get on with the people's business.

Mr. Springer: Mr. Chairman, will the gentleman yield?

Mr. Chelf: I yield.

Mr. Springer: I understand the gentleman's own State has a limitation of one term for your own Governor; is that correct?

Mr. Chelf: Yes; and I was not alive when that limitation was adopted, I will tell you that. I still believe the people themselves can best judge whether a man should be elected for one or more terms.

Mr. Celler: Mr. Chairman, I yield 5 minutes to the gentleman from New York [Mr. Byrne].

Mr. Byrne of New York. Mr. Chairman, it seems to me this proposal today is self-answering. I do not think anyone in the country denies that ordinarily and reasonably no party should elect a President for more than two terms. I think that is fundamental. I think it is axiomatic in a democracy. I believe the reason that this particular proposition has never been enacted or placed in the Constitution is simply because the people did not know how to make an exception to it, which exception they realize is necessary at times. Six years does not answer it, nor does 8 years answer it, because the necessity will arise suddenly, and in these times will arise more suddenly than ever right out of the clear when the absolute necessity and need for a particular man is imminent, evident, and manifest, and when everybody knows that that particular man is the logical man for that particular spot. By the way, we must not overlook the ladies because there is no question at all but what some of these days, although it may be in the distant future, there is going to be an application to this rule to the women of this country. But we cannot find, and I do not believe Solomon could have found, nor do I believe that my good friend, the gentleman from Pennsylvania [Mr. Graham], in spite of his erudition, can find the exception to the rule. Unless we can find an exception to this rule, we make our Constitution so rigid that it is unworkable. If it is unworkable, then it is not in any sense a proper democratic manifesto. That is the answer to this whole problem today, as I reason it out in my own mind. I do believe that this particular proposal is absolutely invalid because for 158 or 160 years the finest minds in our country have been attempting to find a means by which we could place in the Constitution a regulation for two terms and yet have the exception to that regulation.

They never can give us the exception. There is no question about it. When Jefferson, when Washington, when McKinley, when Cleveland, when Grant, when all of the others, including Coolidge, were looking around for a method by which they could jump the barrier and do it logically and successfully, they found it just could not be done. They found it could not be done. Today we cannot find it any more than we could before, and less readily do we find it today because the exception to the rule in Roosevelt has been proven beyond peradventure. In other words, he goes down in the pages of history unquestionably as the one man up to date who was absolutely essential and necessary at the time he was nominated and at the time he was elected. The results prove the case. In other words, it now becomes an axiom that Roosevelt was correctly placed, correctly selected, correctly elected. If you find the exception to the rule I will be happy to go along with the proponents. Otherwise I go along with the opponents.

Mr. Springer: Mr. Chairman, will the gentleman yield?

Mr. Byrne of New York. I yield.

Mr. Springer: The gentleman, I know, believes in submitting questions of this kind to the people?

Mr. Byrne of New York. Highly so.

Mr. Springer: And the gentleman certainly has no objection to a matter of this kind coming before the people and letting them determine it?

Mr. Byrne of New York. Unless the people at this time can tell me I am wrong. And I am too conceited to believe they can tell me just at the minute.

The Chairman: The time of the gentleman from New York [Mr. Byrne], has expired.

Mr. Jennings: Mr. Chairman, it is not to be determined here today that hereafter no President shall serve more than two terms. We are simply giving the people of this country, through the legislatures of the various States, the right to settle that question.

The founding fathers anticipated there might be need, from time to time, to amend the Constitution. They therefore provided a method by which it might be done.

One of the anomalies of human history is that people sacrifice and fight and die for the privilege and right to set up a government to defend themselves against the aggression and oppression of foreign powers and to protect themselves against the fraud and violence of the lawless members of society. Then, having done that, they find it necessary from time to time to protect themselves against encroachments upon their rights and liberties at the hands of their own government.

The framers of our Constitution were speaking and acting for a people who had just fought and won the Revolution to free themselves from the repeated injuries and usurpations inflicted upon them by the King of Great Britain.

The men who wrote the Constitution were familiar with every experiment in government from the dawn of history to their day. They were governmental experts. They thought in terms of government. They themselves had felt the heavy hand of despotism. They resolutely intended to protect the dignity and inviolable personality of man. They set their hands to the task of making workable under government the eternal principles and truths of the Declaration of Independence. And I quote from that immortal document:

> We hold these truths to be self-evident, that all men are created equal, that they are endowed by their Creator with certain inalienable rights, that among these are life, liberty, and the pursuit of happiness. That to secure these rights, governments are instituted among men, deriving their just powers from the consent of the governed—that

when any form of government becomes destructive of these ends, it is the right of the people to alter or to abolish it.

The first 10 amendments to the Constitution were proposed to the legislatures of the several States by the First Congress on the 25th of September 1789. They were ratified by a sufficient number of States to make them a part of the Constitution within a little more than 2 years thereafter. These 10 amendments are our Bill of Rights. They cover the citizens all over with the armor of the law.

I favor this proposed amendment. Only by its adoption can the people be assured that we shall never have a dictator in this land. Without such a limit on the number of terms a man may serve in the Presidency, the time may come when a man of vaulting ambition becomes President. Such a man, clothed with the vast powers of the Presidency and backed by a subservient Congress, as Commander in Chief of our Army and Navy, could well have in his hands the two mightiest instrumentalities of governmental power, the sword and the purse. He would have the power to put the Nation into a war without Congress having voice in or control over our going to war. The President by vetoing an act passed by Congress can kill such measure unless two-thirds of the House and Senate vote to override his veto. He appoints the members of his Cabinet, all our representatives to foreign countries, and millions of other Federal officials who have control over the business and daily lives of the people. He appoints all Federal law-enforcement officers and all Federal judges. Such a President could well name to the Supreme Court of the United States men of his political faith and economic thinking, and these men in passing upon and interpreting acts of Congress, acts of the legislatures of the States, and in construing the Constitution of our country would have the power to substitute their economic philosophy

for the law of the land. They could thus sweep aside and overthrow the safeguards of the Constitution. They could overrule the settled rules of law that have been declared and recognized for a hundred years. Such a court could legislate by judicial decision. It could transform our form of government.

Such disaster cannot hereafter happen if the proposed amendment is adopted. A vast majority of the American people favor this amendment, and rightly so. Under our constitutional form of government, the American people have made the greatest progress, have enjoyed the widest measure of liberty, and have achieved the deepest intellectual and moral and spiritual growth of any people in the history of the world.

Under the proposed amendment, no President will have the power to perpetuate himself in office, to create a dynasty, and to substitute a succession for an assured rotation in the Presidential office.

The Chairman: The time of the gentleman from Tennessee [Mr. Jennings] has expired.

Mr. Celler: Mr. Chairman, I yield 4 minutes to the gentleman from Arizona [Mr. Murdock].

Mr. Murdock: Mr. Chairman, I shall vote "no" on this proposition to deny the people the right to elect whom they please President unless the people specifically vote to deny themselves that right by constitutional limitation. The first three words in the Constitution of the United States are: "We, the people," and the enacting clause is: "We, the people, do ordain and establish this Constitution." As this bill is now written it could be made a part of the Constitution without being specifically voted on by the American people.

There has been a great deal of discussion about the nature of our Government. Of course, it is not a pure democracy. Yes, it is a representative democracy with sovereign power resting in the people. I think our Government is getting more democratic with each passing year. I believe that more and more a greater degree of responsibility is being placed upon the people, exactly where it belongs, because sovereign power resides in the people.

It is true that by our vote here today, if it carries, we are not yet making this proposal a part of the Constitution, as we are merely taking the first step; but it is conceivable that it could be submitted to the States and adopted by the necessary three-quarters of the States and then become a part of the Constitution without being subjected directly to a vote of the people. This is because the members of the State legislatures now in session or in existence were not elected on this specific issue only, they were elected on many other issues. I do not, therefore, take much stock in the argument that we are by our vote today, if this carries merely submitting it to the vote of the people.

I believe the question of whether a man is to be elected to the Presidency for more than two terms should be left to the American people at those future times, and that we should not try to determine that question today for them or this year, or at any time without their instruction. Whether any President should or should not be elected for a third term should be decided by the people themselves when the necessity arises. I myself do not favor a third term in normal times and under normal conditions, but as the gentleman from Massachusetts, the whip on our side of the House, pointed out, some time in the future the country may be faced with an emergency. We cannot forecast these emergencies. We must not tie the hands of our people thus without their specific vote to do so. This proposed constitutional amendment should not be adopted except by affirmative action by conventions chosen for the purpose in three-fourths of the States. I know there are certain republics in the Western

Hemisphere who practice rotation in office, who are apparently afraid of the man on horseback, and so place limits; but I do not believe that the American people need have any such fears nor need to place any such limits to guarantee that the man on horseback shall not appear and make himself supreme.

Each passing decade we have given more power to the people by taking away from the State legislatures the power to elect members of the other body and subjecting Senators to popular election. We have given the ballot to women. I cite these only as illustrations of extending the people's power.

I come from a far-western State that prides itself on extending the principles of democracy to a greater and greater degree. To adopt this measure into the Constitution would reverse the modern trend. I feel, Mr. Chairman, that if we should adopt this amendment providing that no man shall have more than two terms of office as President that we will be denying the people of the future the fundamental right American people have always had to select the man whom they pleased even though he has already served two terms. Let our people decide at that time what is their sovereign will.

The Chairman: The time of the gentleman from Arizona has expired.

Mr. Springer: Mr. Chairman, I yield 5 minutes to the gentleman from Illinois [Mr. Reed].

Mr. Reed of Illinois. Mr. Chairman, the Presidential tenure of office is not a political question. It is a constitutional question of the highest order. In one form or another it occupied the attention of the Constitutional Convention from the introduction of Mr. Randolph's resolutions on May 29, 1787, until the adoption of the report of the Committee on Style submitted on September 12, 5 days before final adjournment.

In one form or another it has been before the people or the Congress, or both, ever since 1803—more than 140 years—when resolutions introduced after the election of 1800 came before the House of Representatives. Indeed, it has been calculated that between that date and 1889 more than 125 amendments were proposed to change the term of office of the President or to fix the period of eligibility; and it is estimated that almost as many have been introduced since.

It is hardly necessary to remind Members of Congress that when the matter of the Presidency was considered in the Convention the members of that body repeatedly expressed the importance of placing some limitation upon the tenure of the office. That was particularly so when it was contemplated that the Chief Executive was to be chosen by Congress and that long continuance in office would lead to autocracy, intrigue, or cabal. For a long time the sentiment prevailed that the President should be limited to a single term of 7 years. When it became apparent that choice by the legislature would not be adopted, the plan of the electoral college with a provision for a fixed term of 4 years was substituted.

Members of the Constitution Convention feared autocracy. They feared perpetuation in the Executive Office. They had but emerged from war against a king with unlimited tenure of office. They had seen their State legislatures dissolved by royal governors appointed by a king. And they proposed that there should be no such usurpation of power in the Chief Executive they were about to create. And while they did not expressly prohibit reeligibility, they were not without the belief that the electoral college, as they contemplated its operation, would provide an adequate check against perpetuation in office.

Regardless of the inadequacies of the electoral college, however, the principle of a limitation upon the Presidential tenure came to develop by tradition. Even though it be contended that Mr.

Washington's refusal to accept a third term was based upon circumstances other than those intended to establish a precedent, the fact remains that his action was regarded as a precedent by his immediate successors, and the tradition of only two terms of 4 years each became attached to the Presidential office.

Jefferson expressed this sentiment in a letter dated January 1805, in which he wrote:

> My opinion originally was that the President of the United States should have been elected for 7 years, and forever ineligible afterward. I have since become sensible that 7 years is too long to be irremovable, and that there should be a peaceable way of withdrawing a man in midway who is doing wrong. The service for 8 years, with a power to remove at the end of the first four, comes nearly to my principle as corrected by experience; and it is in adherence to that that I determine to withdraw at the end of my second term. The danger is that the indulgence and attachments of the people will keep a man in the chair after he becomes a dotard, that reelection through life shall become habitual, and election for life follow that. General Washington set the example of voluntary retirement after 8 years. I shall follow it. And a few more precedents will oppose the obstacle of habit to anyone after a while who shall endeavor to extend his term. Perhaps it may beget a disposition to establish it by an amendment of the Constitution.

In his first annual message, December 1829, President Jackson said:

> I would therefore recommend such an amendment of the Constitution as may remove all intermediate agency in the election of the President and Vice President. * * * In connection with such an amendment it would seem advisable to limit the service of the Chief Magistrate to a single term of either 4 or 6 years.

And he repeated the recommendation in several succeeding messages.

In his letter of August 18, 1884, accepting the nomination for the Presidency, President Cleveland wrote:

When we consider the patronage of this great office, the allurements of power, the temptations to retain public place once gained, and, more than all, the availability a party finds in an incumbent whom a horde of officeholders, with a zeal born of benefits received and fostered by the hope of favors yet to come, stand ready to aid with money and trained political service, we recognize in the eligibility of the President for reelection a most serious danger to that calm, deliberate, and intelligent political action which must characterize a government by the people.

And I would recall to my friends on the other side of the aisle that the Democratic National Convention, held in Baltimore, Md., in 1912, adopted the following resolution:

> We favor a single Presidential term and to that end urge the adoption of an amendment to the Constitution making the President of the United States ineligible for reelection, and we pledge the candidate of this convention to this principle.

This historical feeling and tradition against unlimited tenure in the Presidential office, Mr. Chairman, is not based upon idle fear. The power and prestige of the President of the United States has grown constantly and increasingly since the first inauguration of Mr. Washington. Today, the President of the United States is perhaps the most powerful individual in the world. It is within the spirit of democracy that proper constitutional restraints be placed upon his tenure of office.

Mr. Celler: Mr. Chairman, I yield 2 minutes to the gentleman from Texas [Mr. Lyle].

Mr. Lyle: Mr. Chairman, it is a paradox that we, who generally speak so glibly of the supremacy of the people and government by the people, would, through this proposal now under consideration, limit that supremacy and power.

The statements of many of our leaders of the past have been quoted today supporting arguments both for and against this resolution. President Wilson, as suggested in last night's Washington Star, more nearly summed up arguments on this matter when he said that the President's fighting power in behalf of the people would be immensely weakened by an anti-third term amendment to the Constitution. Further quoting President Wilson, he said:

> We would singularly belie our own principles by seeking to determine by fixed constitutional provision what the people should determine for themselves.

We should not discuss at this time the issue of the number of terms the President of the United States might be privileged to serve, for the question, the unfortunate question, is that of limiting the power of the people in this regard. It perhaps would be in better taste for this body to consider this resolution had the question not been previously presented to the people.

In 1940 the sovereign voters of the United States, many millions strong, expressed themselves upon this issue. Actually, it seemed to be the only issue in the campaign, for as I checked the Congressional Record covering 1 week immediately preceding the 1940 election last night I found that more than 40 Members of the House made speeches similar, yes, almost identical, to the speeches made today predicting disaster to representative government and to this great country of ours if a President should be elected to serve more than two terms. Those predictions were made again in 1944. Both times the people of the United States repudiated the doctrine of this resolution and repudiated it overwhelmingly.

A majority in 38 States in 1940 and a majority of some 36 States in 1944 voted that a man might serve more than two terms as President of the United States.

As a matter of interest, Mr. Chairman, the very county in which the splendid Speaker of this House lives, and then lived, repudiated the theory that a President should serve no more than two terms and voted overwhelmingly for Mr. Roosevelt, as in 1944, did the people of the State of Michigan, home of the able chairman of the Judiciary Committee.

Normally, I would prefer for a new man to be President of the United States after two terms but I have a great deal more confidence and more faith in the fundamental principles of this Government—that the judgment of the people should be supreme—that the judgment of this legislative body or that of any State in this Union. Actually, I think that you have, too.

It must seem strange to the people of this country that the Republican Party is so violent at this time against a third term for the President and in the same breath are asking for a third try to impose a restriction upon the sovereignty of the people. Could it be, perhaps, that they did not like the judgment of the sovereign voters in 1940 and 1944, and have more confidence in the ability of the legislatures?

Most assuredly it is not sound at this time for any man on this floor to say that we are going to give the people an opportunity to pass on this resolution, for by the express terms of the resolution, it shall be submitted to the various legislatures. The Republican majority could have, had it desired, written the resolution and presented it for discussion, with the provision that it would be submitted to constitutional conventions in each State. I am not sure why they did not do this. Perhaps it was the memory of the people voting in 1940 and 1944.

I cannot vote for this resolution unless it provides for submission to the people; for I cannot say to them, as you will do if you pass this resolution, "We did not like your judgment in 1940 and 1944, so we are going to sidestep you and submit the question to the legisla-

tures of the various States with the hope that they will have better judgment than you have." And they might add, and perhaps have in their counsels, "It will be relatively easier to put this through in the Republican dominated legislatures of the several States."

The Chairman: The time of the gentleman from Texas has expired.

Mr. Springer: Mr. Chairman, I yield 5 minutes to the gentleman from Maine [Mr. Fellows].

Mr. Fellows: Mr. Chairman, I shall heed the injunction of our former Speaker when he used the words "just a minute," to the extent that I shall speak for just a very short time.

We must not overlook the wisdom of our forefathers, nor should we forget the accumulated experiences during the historic years. Experience is a wonderful teacher. I had this forcibly impressed upon me once. I sat in an old school house in a small town in the State of Maine, and I looked into the sweet face of an old lady with gray hair, and she said this: "Sometimes I think that the school of experience is the only one in which fools can learn anything," and she looked at me when she said it.

I have listened with great interest to the arguments that have been made against this proposed amendment. We have heard our beloved former leader of this House, the gentleman from Massachusetts, whom everybody respects, speak to this subject. The burden of Mr. McCormack's argument is this: That we may find ourselves with our backs to the wall, a President serving a second term, and that we, being in a crisis, could not find the man who could meet the situation and carry us through safely.

I think I have an answer to that, and I do not think there is any answer to my answer. I think the best answer to that is to point to the living presence of such men as the gentleman himself, who, possessors of such distinguished and preeminent ability in a country of

140,000,000 people, could and would lead us safely through any crisis. What can their reply be to that?

It has been suggested that this proposal is anti-Roosevelt. That is not true. It is not true in any sense of the word. It certainly is not retroactive legislation.

There have been some excellent statements made here but there is no better one to be found than that which appears as the minority views of two distinguished gentlemen, the gentleman from Alabama [Mr. Hobbs] and the gentleman from Texas [Mr. Gossett]. I am going to read one paragraph:

> Of course, other crises may arise in the course of our history wherein we may long to retain the experienced and able guiding hand that may then be steering the ship of state, beyond the limit of tenure fixed, and regret that we surrendered our ancient heritage of such perfect freedom. But in the exercise of our best, studied judgment we certify our conviction that the advantages of limited tenure far outweigh the disadvantages urged against it, and have confidence that, the certitude of law having removed all question of repudiation, we may count with the utmost assurance upon the patriotic service as lieutenant of every captain who steps down from the bridge.

They, I believe, are in favor of the 6-year term.

I shall vote for this proposal; first, because I believe it should be accepted by the States; and second, we are simply voting to submit this question—permitting the people, through their elected representatives in their States, to vote upon it. And let me say, when the words that inaugurate our great document are referred to, "We the people," that we the people established this system which provides that it shall go to the legislatures.

Mr. Celler: Mr. Chairman, I yield such time as he may desire to the gentleman from Tennessee [Mr. Gore].

WE MUST NOT SHACKLE THE FUTURE—OPPOSED TO PROPOSED CONSTITUTIONAL AMENDMENT—LEAVE FUTURE CITIZENS FREE TO MAKE THEIR OWN DECISIONS

Mr. Gore: Mr. Chairman, what the President's term of office should be has been a much debated question throughout our history as a nation. Even in the Constitutional Convention it was one of the principal controversies. Many different proposals were then advanced, ranging from a single term with ineligibility for reelection to tenure during good behavior or for life.

After much deliberation the constitutional framers wisely fixed the term at 4 years, but refused, by repeated votes, to limit the number of terms to which the people might elect a President.

But there was not then, nor has there ever been, complete satisfaction with this constitutional provision. In fact, a resolution to change it was introduced in the very first Congress, and over the years since, there have been more than 150 proposals to amend the Constitution so as to change the President's tenure of office.

The people have not seen fit to change it. Nevertheless, after all these years of sound democratic government, we are again debating the question today. After all these prideful years of free government and progressive extension of the right of franchise, is it now necessary or expedient to say that the people shall not be trusted to exercise their judgment in electing the man they desire as President at a particular time or any particular emergency?

This proposed amendment would be an impairment of the citizenship of the future, a limited impairment, to be sure, but a definite restriction on the freedom of choice of our children and our children's children. We must not shackle the future.

Let us suppose that in the future some crisis—a crisis even more critical than we have yet experienced—should come to hand, and that the people should consider absolutely necessary the continued service as President of a particular man who had gained their confidence through a demonstration of able patriotic leadership.

Could this question not then safely be submitted to the people, or shall we place a restriction on them because we think, perchance, they may be unable to distinguish between a patriot and a tyrant.

Under certain circumstances the people might think, and rightly so, that there was less danger to their freedom in a third term for one man than in a first term for another who did not seem to them equal to the job of running a nation.

We cannot foresee now what the election issues will be, let us say, in 1980 or whether the President will be a Republican or a Democrat. Why should we prejudge? I want to defend the rights of the American people of 1980 to judge for themselves.

To say that we must now put this restriction upon the right of the people to a free choice is to cast doubt upon the whole theory of popular government. I am one who believes that the perpetuity of government by the people depends, not upon restrictions on the people, but rather in maintaining free and frequent choice and decision by the people. The fewer restrictions on the people we place in the Constitution, the better off we will be in the long run.

We, in America, have a deep-dyed habit of citing the statements and examples of our founding fathers as evidence of the rightness of our course, even though times and circumstances may be materially different. Even so, I want to cite an example and a statement from the Father of Our Nation.

The origin of the two-term tradition is generally ascribed to President George Washington because he declined to be considered as a candidate for a third term. History, however, is abundantly clear that he did so from the standpoint of his own personal choice and not upon political precedent. Washington not only voted against limiting the terms of a president in the Constitutional Convention, but in repeated writings he branded such limitation as both unwise and unnecessary.

For instance, in a letter to General Lafayette, President Washington wrote:

> I can see no propriety in precluding ourselves from the service of any man who in some great emergency shall be deemed universally most capable of serving the public.

This is not a question, though, which should be decided solely upon the beliefs and examples of former statesmen, nor do I believe it is a political weapon, which we can wisely use for temporary political expediency. It is rather a principle which goes to the very heart of democracy—of government by the people, of the people, and for the people.

If I distrusted the free and deliberate judgment of the American people, then no matter who might be President or how short we might limit his term, I would have little faith that a system of self government by freemen could long endure in this or in any other country.

Mr. Celler: Mr. Chairman, I yield 4 minutes to the gentleman from North Carolina [Mr. Folger].

Mr. Folger: Mr. Chairman, I am frightened. I feel bad, not physically but mentally and spiritually, because this question has been brought up at this time. I do not charge that there is partisanship in the consideration of this resolution; I do not think there is. I do not even charge that there is evident partisanship in the fact that this resolution originated so quickly after the death of Franklin D. Roosevelt. But, Mr. Chairman, to my mind this is perhaps the most serious subject we will be called upon to give consideration to while we are in this Congress. It is something that is contrary to all which has been obtained for 160 years. In all that time just one man, just one, was elected to a third term as President of the United States.

The election of that man was not partisan in its character, essentially. It happened that he was nominated by the Democratic Convention which met in Chicago in July of 1940. It is a fact there were some then in that convention who thought that it would not be justified in us to nominate a man for a third term, but those were in such minority that out of about a thousand convention votes the man who was in office at that time and who was nominated for a third term received over 900 votes, in the Democratic Convention, which, as far as this action was concerned, was nonpartisan. There could not be any question as between them, whether they were Republican or Democrat. The only reason that man was chosen, who happened not to be Theodore Roosevelt, but Franklin D. Roosevelt, was because it was felt by a great majority of the people of this country that it would be in the best interests of the country and in the interest of the security of the United States of America and all its people in that hour of imminent danger. The man who had been at the helm in the several years prior thereto was not perhaps best qualified inherently but was possessed of the greatest amount of information of any other man in the United States, and while he was not an indispensable man it was the best opportunity we had to fortify ourselves against the approaching war which eventually did come and which shook the foundations of the world.

Mr. Chairman, I cannot agree with the proposition that we are withholding from the people of the United States the opportunity or privilege of speaking upon this matter. But it is natural to assume that the representatives in the State legislatures may conclude that we are in favor of it. It is yet to be accepted that Congress influences some. We set in motion a dangerous proposal. In the language of the distinguished former Speaker of this House, I would beg you to wait—wait a minute and let us consider this matter further and more seriously. Franklin Roosevelt did not personally desire a third term. The people required it in what they believed was to save our country. I beg you to vote down this resolution.

The Chairman: The time of the gentleman from North Carolina has expired.

Mr. Celler: Mr. Chairman, I yield such time as he may desire to the gentleman from California [Mr. Miller].

Mr. Miller of California. Mr. Chairman, the passage of this bill is not of the greatest importance to the American people. In a democracy we have the right to change our laws to fit the exigencies of the moment. As conditions arise we meet them. Ours is a fluid type of Government, and I am certain at this time the necessity for limiting the tenure of office of the President is not one of great concern to the people.

My opposition to the measure is based on the recent experiences that we have had with this sort of thing. In time of emergency the American people may want to continue their Chief Executive beyond the two terms as set forth in this bill, as they did at the last general election and at the general election preceding that.

Emergencies were on us, one domestic and the other international. The American people in their wisdom saw fit to reelect Franklin Delano Roosevelt for a third and a fourth term as President. His dynamic type of leadership appealed to them and they demanded his retention in office.

Being human it is understandable that those who violently opposed Mr. Roosevelt are taking this opportunity to vent their spleen.

The American people should be left free to exercise the discretionary powers granted them in this democracy.

Mr. Celler: Mr. Chairman, I yield such time as he may require to the gentleman from Michigan [Mr. Dingell].

Mr. Dingell: Mr. Chairman, while I am personally opposed in principle to a third or fourth term for the Presidency of the United States, I am nevertheless opposed to this resolution because it proposes the shackling of ourselves and future generations in the exercise of free will. It restricts the right of franchise guaranteed under the Constitution and makes slaves of free men.

What the proponents ask for is the imposition of a limitation of unrestricted choice, the abolishment of a sacred right which can be and has always heretofore been exercised by the free people of these United States.

There is no such creature as the indispensable man. I have always said that there are more capable and better men who have never held office than there are in office today, or who ever held office for that matter, and it is conceded that in the past intellectually great and saintly men have rendered priceless service to the country and to the people.

Mr. Chairman, the question of limiting tenure of the President of the United States by constitutional amendment has actually been put to the test on two separate occasions—in the campaigns of 1940 and 1944. The sovereign people spoke unmistakably on the subject. As a free people, they could have voted for the opponent of the aspirant for a third term, and again on another occasion the people could have rebuked Mr. Roosevelt when he sought a fourth term, but they did not do so. They established another far-reaching fourth-term precedent. Can anyone fail to understand the temper of the people on that question? Would anybody charge the people with lack of understanding of their prerogative, or worse still, with making an error in judgment? The people, so I hold, right or wrong, are always right. They can elect a man for a third or a fourth term, or they can turn a President out at the end of his first term as was done with Herbert Hoover.

It is the inherent right of a free-born American citizen to vote for whomsoever he chooses and as often as a candidate presents his name, once or 10 times. This right must not be abridged now or in the future. The citizen can limit Presidential tenure; he is the sovereign. He exercises this right freely and wilfully. He need not be shielded by a constitutional amendment. It should be and it is a matter of conscience. No restrictions or impediments should be placed in the path of the American voter. It works well for both the Democrats and the Republicans.

The people may some day desire to elect a Republican President, may re-elect, and may in some emergency choose to give him a fourth term if they want to do so. They shall have that right insofar as I am concerned.

Mr. Chairman, I fear that this is a belated and a misguided attempt to head off a third term for the late and beloved Franklin D. Roosevelt, who has gone to his reward, or, reduced to its lowest common denominator, it may be an attempt to besmirch his good name.

In concluding, I ask, Why should we abridge an inherent right of the people by a fixed and irrevocable rule when the individual citizen can exercise that right freely at any time he chooses? I trust the resolution is defeated.

Mr. Springer: Mr. Chairman, I yield such time as he may desire to the gentleman from Ohio [Mr. McCowen].

Mr. McCowen: Mr. Chairman, in regard to House Joint Resolution 27, proposing an amendment to the Constitution of the United States to limit the terms of office of the President, I am fully in accord with the idea to limit the terms to two terms of 4 years each.

Eight years is long enough for a good President and 4 years is too long for a bad one.

Much has already been said on the floor today on this subject. The arguments pro and con have been pretty well covered. Of course, the passage of the joint resolution will do nothing more than give the people a chance to settle the question as to whether they desire such limitations.

It is a well-known fact that the tenure of the office of President was one of the most difficult and perplexing problems before the Constitutional Convention 160 years ago. The question was not settled until the closing days of the Convention.

In the light of the breaking of the custom of 160 years to elect a President to only two terms by the four-times elected President in very recent times, it seems quite appropriate to submit the question to the people so they may have a chance to pass on the question after such experience. If this amendment should eventually become a part of the Constitution, it would be a great step toward preventing a dictatorship or some totalitarian form of government from arising in the United States.

I hope the joint resolution will pass.

Mr. Springer: Mr. Chairman, I yield such time as he may desire to the gentleman from Minnesota [Mr. O'Hara].

Mr. O'Hara: Mr. Chairman, the proposed twenty-second amendment to the Constitution presents one of the fundamental issues left unsettled by the founders of the Republic and demands the most careful consideration. The issue, moreover, is one which goes to the very heart of political theory, for the question is whether or not the "indispensable man" theory is compatible with the republican form of government.

When I speak of the "indispensable man" I am not speaking necessarily of the recent Roosevelt era, although I do think that those of us who have lived during the period when Franklin Delano Roosevelt was President recognized the dangers of continuing one man in the office of presidency for more than two terms. In lieu of the divine right of kings and the prerogatives of a dictator, we find the problems and emergencies of this or that crisis as a reason or reasons given for the continuation of one man in office.

Almost without exception we have had appointive offices filled by people of the same political philosophy as the late President Roosevelt's. This is not such a problem administratively, but the effect is tremendous so far as the judiciary branch of our Government is concerned. I have heard my colleagues on the Democratic side of the aisle complain that the test for filling judicial appointments was not whether the individual was a Democrat, but whether he was a particular brand of New Dealer.

There is nothing said or intended by these remarks as derogatory to the late President Roosevelt. The same dangers would exist had President Roosevelt been a Republican instead of a Democrat and I would have felt perhaps even more out-spokenly critical of the violation of the precedent of two terms for the Presidency. As a matter of fact, it was Thomas Jefferson himself who insisted that voluntary retirement was a matter of firm principle, and stated:

> If the principle of rotation be a sound one, as I conscientiously believe it to be with respect to this office, no pretext should ever be permitted to dispense with it, because there never will be a time when real difficulties will not exist, and furnish a plausible pretext for dispensation.

It is my conviction that we should limit the Presidency to two terms. If, in a country of 140,000,000 people there arises occasions where one man, and one man only, is capable of filling the position of the Presidency of the United

States, then I say to the advocates of that theory that both democracy and a republican form of government are a failure. However, as we stand here today, I feel that our form of government has been a bulwark against every form of attack because it is a republican form of government and it is our responsibility and our duty to safeguard it. With dictatorships and monarchies crumbling, the people of the world as well as the spirit of our forefathers look to us to preserve our form of government. The proposed constitutional amendment helps to do so, in my opinion.

Mr. Springer: Mr. Chairman, I yield such time as he may desire to the gentleman from California [Mr. Phillips].

Mr. Phillips of California. Mr. Chairman, I shall vote for this resolution, and I turn to my files of the Seventy-ninth Congress for some interesting supporting data. On June 4, 1945, I mailed to each Member of the House a questionnaire on this subject of the limitation of the term of the President of the United States. I asked only three questions—whether the Member favored a 6-year limitation; or if he favored a limitation of two terms of 4 years each, and whether the Member thought it was then an opportune time to bring up the question on the floor.

I said I would not quote any Member without his or her permission, with the result that interesting comments were received. I said the Member could sign the reply or send it back unsigned. I did not "key" the questionnaires, except on one point; I could tell which came back from Republicans, and which from Democrats, but not the individual Members. Even that was unnecessary, as a large majority signed.

Ninety-one signed replies were received from Republicans and 27 unsigned replies. Fifty-one signed replies were received from Democrats, and 17 unsigned. That made a total of 186 replies, or 43 percent of the member-

ship of the House. You could ask, Mr. Chairman, why I never reported the results to this floor. During the tabulation, I discovered that a well-known magazine writer was engaged at that moment in preparing a magazine article on this subject. She asked me to withhold my report to you, until her article was ready. Unfortunately, the magazine, after accepting it, did not use it, presumably pressed for space, and it was then too late for me. I now take out the figures and review them in the light of today's vote.

Sixty-five signed Republicans and 19 unsigned, together with 16 signed Democrats and 3 unsigned, a total of 103, favored a limitation of two terms of 4 years. Only 21 signed Republicans and 6 unsigned, with 4 signed Democrats and 3 unsigned, a total of 34, wanted a limitation of 6 years. Only 4 Republicans disapproved the idea of some limitation. Of these, No. 1 was considered by his constituents to have voted too closely to New Deal principles and was not returned last November, 1 expressed the somewhat pessimistic thought that such a resolution would somehow benefit the New Deal, 1 recommended care in amending the Constitution on any subject, and 1 gave no reason.

However, 29 signed Democrats and 11 unsigned were opposed to any limitation any time, although I noted this afternoon that 1 distinguished Member of the present minority, who wrote "Never" in a firm hand last June, today voted equally firmly in favor of 2 terms of 4 years each, which indicates that time—and possibly an election—changes all things.

There were 14 Republicans who would have preferred a 6-year limitation, but with apparent resignation accepted the likelihood of two 4-year terms, hoping for any limitation as the primary objective. I included them in the 4-year count. One Republican preferred unwritten to the written law, which causes me to suggest that the position may be academically excellent, but, to quote the first sentence of the unpublished magazine article, already referred to:

When an unwritten law is once broken, should it be replaced by a written law?

Two Republicans were thoughtful enough to raise the question of the partial term. We decided that this afternoon in favor of limitation. If a Vice President serves part of a term, due to the death or removal of a President, he may, under House Joint Resolution 27, be elected only once in his own right. It would affect the present occupant of the White House, were he to run in 1948, and to be elected, and it would have affected Theodore Roosevelt who had finished the term to which McKinley was elected, and who had been elected once in his own right. It would affect a President who had risen from the Vice Presidency only a few months before the end of his President's term, but so far as I am concerned, Mr. Chairman, if we are to set a limitation, I prefer to go in that direction, rather than the other. I favor House Joint Resolution 27.

One Republican reply brought up the question of longer terms for Representatives, tying it to the limitation on the Presidential term. Of the total replies, 78 signed Republicans and 22 unsigned, together with 13 signed and 5 unsigned Democrats, a total of 118, evidently thought if an idea were good, the sooner we make it a law the better it would be for the country. They were in favor of bringing up the resolution 18 months ago. Eleven Republicans and three Democrats felt that the Congress should wait until the war was over, or until the men had returned from the services. That thought, even if it were the minority opinion at that time, prevailed and it was not until today that the necessary resolution passed the House. The vote has been 285 ayes and 121 noes, which shows a fairly good comparison with the replies to my questionnaires of June 1945.

In the history of the Congress, 160 bills have been introduced to limit the Presidential term; it took the present one, House Joint Resolution 27, to get started on its way to the States, for their approval.

Mr. Springer: Mr. Chairman, I yield such time as he may desire to the gentleman from California [Mr. McDonough].

Mr. McDonough: Mr. Chairman, I favor the passage of House Joint Resolution 27 providing for a constitutional amendment limiting the term of President to two 4-year terms.

The action we are taking here today is not final or conclusive. We are submitting to the several States an opportunity to determine for themselves whether they want this proposed amendment to become a permanent part of the Constitution.

Should we deny the States this privilege? Should we refuse the people of the Nation an opportunity to express themselves on this vital and important issue? I say "No." To deny the people this right would be undemocratic and would be unfair.

If the custom and historic practice of limiting the term of President to two terms had not been broken in 1944, this amendment would not be before us today. Because it was broken and because we found ourselves under domination of one political party and one man as President for four terms, which terminated only by death, we have this resolution before us today.

What happened under this unprecedented administration under one man is well known. Almost unlimited power grew up in the office of President. This must not happen again and the only practical and logical way to prevent it is to adopt House Joint Resolution 27 and give the people an opportunity to say definitely and finally what they want. If they do not want a limited term for President they will say so. If we do not pass this resolution they will not have the opportunity to say whether they want a limited term or not. I urge the adoption and passage of House Joint Resolution 27.

Mr. Celler: Mr. Chairman, I yield such time as he may desire to the gentleman from Virginia [Mr. Flannagan].

Mr. Flannagan: Mr. Chairman, the reason I am against this resolution can be expressed in one sentence; I am against placing in the Constitution a limitation against the people. This never has been done, and I am in hopes never will be done.

All power originally resided in the people, and they still possess all power not specifically granted under the Constitution. And in granting power under the Constitution they only granted those powers that they could not, in the functioning of Government, exercise individually. And in granting powers to others, in order to protect their own rights, the people have ever been careful to place certain prohibitions. Congress, for instance, is prohibited from passing expost facto laws, or laws that would impair the obligation of contract, or laws interfering with freedom of speech, freedom of the press, or religious freedom, and so forth. But, my colleagues, read the Constitution from beginning to end and you will not find a single prohibition against the exercise by the sovereign people of the powers not granted.

One of the powers not granted by the people in the Constitution was the power to change their chosen representatives whenever in their judgment they saw fit. In order for the Government to orderly function, there was no need to grant or restrict, in any way, this power, because in the exercise of the ballot the people can not only limit the terms of their representatives in the Senate and House as well. And this is as it should

be. Certainly the people should not be restricted, in any way, in turning out of office or keeping in office, the representatives they desire.

Amend the resolution by limiting the terms of Senators and Representatives and the resolution would receive but few, if any, favorable votes. The people should enjoy the same freedom in keeping in or turning out of office their President that they enjoy in keeping in or turning out of office their Senators and Representatives.

... **Mr. Michener:** Mr. Chairman, I move to strike out the last word of the committee amendment.

Mr. Colmer: Mr. Chairman, will the gentleman yield for a parliamentary inquiry?

Mr. Michener: I yield to the gentleman from Mississippi.

Mr. Colmer: Mr. Chairman, I have an amendment to offer on page 1, lines 6 and 7. At what time will that amendment be in order?

The Chairman: After the committee amendment has been disposed of, the gentleman may submit his amendment.

Mr. Michener: Mr. Chairman, I take this time to make reference to the committee amendment. As chairman of the committee I assume I am ethically bound not to oppose the committee amendment which was agreed to by a very narrow margin in committee, but I have a feeling that the members of the committee who voted for that amendment would not vote for it if they had the opportunity to vote again in committee. I make that statement because the language of a constitutional amendment is most important, more so than in the case of ordinary legislation. Every comma, every semicolon, every capital letter, every word means something in a constitutional amendment, and under these circumstances we should not lightly adopt language in a constitutional amendment that has not been thoroughly weighed.

This amendment, and I am divulging nothing, was offered by a member of the committee who wrote it out with a pencil during the reading of the resolution for amendment. Grammatically, I am told by the expert draftsman of this House, the language is not the language that should be embodied in a constitutional amendment. Of course, I did not vote for the amendment, but I did vote to report the bill and I think I may be pardoned for this explanation.

Mr. Walter: Mr. Chairman, I rise in support of the committee amendment.

Mr. Chairman, the amendment that was adopted by the Judiciary Committee, offered, incidentally, by a majority member of the committee, was the only language considered with any care by the committee. Why the distinguished chairman of the committee would state that in the event the members of the committee had an opportunity to vote again the vote would be other than what it was is something I cannot understand.

Mr. Jennings: Mr. Chairman, will the gentleman yield?

Mr. Walter: I yield to the gentleman from Tennessee.

Mr. Jennings: I want to agree with what the distinguished gentleman from Pennsylvania is now saying. We carefully, deliberately, thoughtfully considered the language that we adopted by a majority vote of the Committee on the Judiciary. It is crystal clear. I do not think that the criticism is well founded or that it has any merit whatever.

Mr. Cox: Mr. Chairman, will the gentleman yield?

Mr. Walter: I yield to the gentleman from Georgia.

Mr. Cox: I have had occasion to examine the amendment. It is simply a change of verbiage which improves the grammar, that is all.

Mr. Walter: There is no question about that. The gentleman who offered the amendment made a very careful analysis of the language contained in the resolution, then offered this amendment because in his judgment and in the judgment of a majority of the Committee on the Judiciary the language agreed upon improved the language originally proposed.

I do not think the chairman of our great committee ought to come to the floor of the House and state that the committee would not have done what was done in the event it had another opportunity to vote on this particular amendment.

Mr. Michener: Mr. Chairman, will the gentleman yield?

Mr. Walter: I yield to the gentleman from Michigan.

Mr. Michener: I do not want to be misunderstood. We considered the amendment for about 5 minutes, I think the gentleman will agree. It was a penciled memorandum, such as an amendment that is offered on the floor. No attention was given at all to the language, and that is what I meant. I am not saying that the intent of the amendment is not what was intended. I am saying that the language in the resolution was given very careful consideration.

Mr. Walter: By whom was it given consideration?

Mr. Michener: Why, at least, the hearings in the Senate in 1940, the hearings in the House in 1945 and the hearings in the Senate in 1945 were considered. I am not going to oppose it. I just want to be on record, because I am confident that this language as now written in the amendment will not go into the Constitution after some of the people who did support it give it further consideration.

Mr. Walter: I do not know where the gentleman gets his information from. All I know is that our committee considered this language very carefully and we, by majority vote, concluded that it was an improvement over the language as originally written.

Mr. McCormack: Mr. Chairman, will the gentleman yield?

Mr. Walter: I yield to the gentleman from Massachusetts.

Mr. McCormack: The Committee of the Whole is now in the rather interesting position, as I see it, of this resolution being reported out only yesterday. The chairman of the committee says that if a majority of the committee had another opportunity to vote for this today, they would vote entirely different than they did only yesterday, and if I construe the remarks of my friend, the gentleman from Michigan [Mr. Michener], he was in a back-handed way politely suggesting to the Committee of the Whole to defeat the committee amendment and adopt the original verbiage, and my good friend, the gentleman from Tennessee [Mr. Jennings], at least supports the position taken by the gentleman from Pennsylvania. Now, where does that leave our friend, the gentleman from Michigan [Mr. Michener]?

Mr. Rayburn: Mr. Chairman, will the gentleman yield?

Mr. Walter: I yield to the gentleman from Texas.

Mr. Rayburn: It seems to me, Mr. Chairman, that after this confusion, more or less, it might be a good time to recommit this measure to the Committee on the Judiciary.

The Chairman: The time of the gentleman from Pennsylvania has expired.

The question is on the committee amendment.

The committee amendment was agreed to.

Mr. Colmer: Mr. Chairman, I offer amendments.

The Clerk read as follows:

Amendments offered by Mr. Colmer:
Page 1, lines 6 and 7, after the word "by" strike out the words "the legislatures of" and insert in lieu thereof the following: "conventions in."
Page 2, line 11, strike out the words

"the legislatures of" and insert the words "conventions in."

Mr. Michener: Mr. Chairman, I ask unanimous consent that all debate on this amendment close in 10 minutes, including the 5 minutes to which the gentleman from Mississippi is entitled.

The Chairman: Is there objection to the request of the gentleman from Michigan?

There was no objection.

Mr. Colmer: Mr. Chairman, the amendment is very simple. It is not subject to misconstruction. It simply provides that if the resolution is adopted it will be either ratified or not ratified, as the case may be, by conventions called in the several States for that purpose, rather than by the State legislatures. Of course the objective of the amendment is to give the people of the United States an opportunity to pass upon this momentous question without any extraneous matters entering into the discussion.

Article V of the Constitution provides:

The Congress, whenever two-thirds of both Houses shall deem it necessary, shall propose amendments to this Constitution, or, on the application of the legislatures of two-thirds of the several States, shall call a convention for proposing amendments, which, in either case, shall be valid to all intents and purposes, as part of this Constitution, when ratified by the legislatures of three-fourths of the several States, or by conventions in three-fourths thereof, as the one or the other mode of ratification may be proposed by the Congress.

In other words, it is up to this body to say which method shall be adopted.

Mr. McCormack: Mr. Chairman, will the gentleman yield?

Mr. Colmer: I yield to the gentleman from Massachusetts.

Mr. McCormack: While I have taken a position in opposition to any limitation, to two terms or to one term of 6 years, this is the nearest approach to having a question of this kind submitted to the people. We have heard continuously during the debate that this is going to be submitted to the people for ratification. This is one way the people can act upon it, and the only way they can act.

Mr. Colmer: I thank the gentleman for his contribution.

This is what we are up against. We know as a matter of common knowledge that the members of the State legislatures are elected upon various issues, upon whether or not, for instance, there shall be a tax on dogs, whether there shall be a better educational system, or what have you. Under this amendment, if adopted, the people would select their delegates to the State conventions upon the one issue of whether they wanted to adopt this amendment to the Constitution.

Mr. O'Hara: Mr. Chairman, will the gentleman yield?

Mr. Colmer: I yield to the gentleman from Minnesota.

Mr. O'Hara: Is it not true that the eighteenth amendment was submitted in the same manner as is sought to be done in this resolution?

Mr. Colmer: It is my understanding that the eighteenth amendment was handled through conventions rather than the State legislatures.

If you want to give the people who have the right to decide this question the opportunity to decide it, this amendment offers you the machinery to do it. What objection can there be by either those who are for or those who are against the principle of limiting the Presidential tenure to adopting this amendment, thereby giving the people an opportunity to express themselves directly by the election of delegates to the conventions upon the one and only issue involved, namely, whether or not the amendment to the Constitution shall be adopted?

Mr. Chairman, this is indeed a very important matter. Our forefathers in framing that great document—the Con-

stitution of the United States—debated the question as to whether or not there should be a limitation upon the number of terms a man could serve as President of this great country. There were those who took the position that there might be those ambitious ones who would desire to perpetuate themselves in office, and that the office of President was too powerful to be held by one man longer than two terms. There were others who took the position that this was a matter that the people could decide upon the merits of the time and the man; that there might come a time when the country was in the midst of a life-and-death battle with a foreign foe and that it might not be wise to change at such time. The result was that no prohibition against a man holding the office for more than a specified time was written into the Constitution. Personally, I am of the opinion that the powers and duties of this important office are of such transcending importance, and the duties of the office itself are so onerous and demanding—always resulting in serious impairment of the health of the occupant—that no man should offer himself for more than two terms. But that is my opinion. There are others who feel that there should be no limitation whatever and that a President should have the right to offer himself as a candidate to the people of the country to succeed himself as often as he desired.

But, Mr. Chairman, this country is fundamentally a democracy, and because I am elected to the National Legislature does not qualify me to pass upon that question. Neither is the representative from my county in the State legislature qualified to pass upon that question. My contention is that the people as a whole are qualified to pass upon the question, and that the best way—and, in fact, in my opinion, the only way—that they can directly pass upon the question under the Constitution is to elect the several delegates from the several States to a convention where the only issue in the selection of these delegates will be whether or not the Presidency should be limited to two terms as provided in the pending resolution. I repeat that we all know as a matter of common knowledge that when a man is elected to the State legislature he is elected not upon this issue alone but upon many and varied issues, or upon his personality. This amendment offers the only vehicle through which we can get a clear-cut and unequivocal decision of the people on the question before the House.

I had been very much in hopes that this matter could be decided upon a bipartisan issue and that party politics would not enter into it. The Republican Party, being the majority party here, is fostering this legislation. If they believe that the people want this resolution passed, then why not adopt this amendment and give the people that opportunity?

Mr. Chairman, I am not laboring under any misapprehension. We might as well be candid and realistic. If the Republican leadership are willing for the people to decide this issue, they will favor this amendment and it will be adopted because those on this side of the aisle will support the amendment. On the other hand, if the Republican leadership opposes this amendment, we all know that they have the votes to defeat it. I want to give the people an opportunity to decide it, and I want to vote for this resolution with this amendment written into it as assurance that the people will have that opportunity to pass upon it. I cannot vote for it otherwise.

The Chairman: The question is on the amendment offered by the gentleman from Mississippi [Mr. Colmer].

The question was taken; and on a division (demanded by Mr. Colmer) there were—ayes 74, noes 134.

So the amendment was rejected.

Mr. McCormack: Mr. Chairman, I move to strike out the last word.

Mr. Chairman, I want to make a few observations about some of the remarks made this afternoon. The gentleman from Indiana [Mr. Springer] clearly indicated that no President made any contribution to the winning of any war and he referred to a remark made by Madison some years ago that we would always have a weak Executive.

Mr. Springer: Mr. Chairman, will the gentleman yield?

Mr. McCormack: I yield.

Mr. Springer: I think the gentleman must have misunderstood what I said. I said that no President has participated in winning a war by leading the armies. I said the Chiefs of Staff, the generals, and admirals are the ones who carry on the war. While they consult with the President, yet the President is not the one who is responsible for the winning of a war in such an emergency.

Mr. McCormack: The gentleman then admits by his statement that my interpretation of what he originally said is correct, because certainly you have admitted it now in your own language, unless my powers of interpretation are wrong. You are going in a roundabout way, but you come back to what I understood you to say originally.

Mr. Springer: No; I am not going around Robin Hood's barn. The gentleman is going around Robin Hood's barn in respect to what I said.

Mr. McCormack: You are talking about Robin Hood's barn. If you want to get personal, we will do that, too.

Mr. Springer: I can engage in personalities, too.

Mr. McCormack: I am engaging in a discussion and not in personalities. I am giving the gentleman an opportunity to explain if I have made any misunderstanding of his statement. Certainly there is nothing of a personal nature involved in that.

Mr. Springer: Mr. Chairman, will the gentleman yield further?

Mr. McCormack: I yield.

Mr. Springer: I made the statement that the President himself was not the leader of an army in an emergency, but that the generals, admirals, and Chiefs of Staff, and officers of our Army and Navy are the ones who carry out the war. I said, of course, they consulted with the President and he consults with them, but the President is not the one who is directly responsible for the winning of the war in case of an emergency. That is what I said before and that is what I say now.

Mr. McCormack: The gentleman's statement eliminates the President as a leader in war and as a contributing factor in the determination of the outcome of a war. Does the gentleman take that position?

Mr. Springer: I did not say that at all. I said he consults with the generals.

Mr. McCormack: Then the gentleman gives sole credit to the Chiefs of Staff of the Army and Navy?

Mr. Springer: I said they consulted, and they do consult, but the President does not lead the Army.

Mr. McCormack: In the history of our country we have had Presidents who have been strong factors and strong leaders in wartime.

Mr. Springer: Not when they were sitting as President of the United States.

Mr. McCormack: Of course we have.

Mr. Springer: They consulted.

Mr. Chelf: Mr. Chairman, will the gentleman yield?

Mr. McCormack: I yield to the gentleman from Kentucky.

Mr. Chelf: Who was it that stepped up Eisenhower fourteen or fifteen points in order to make him Commander in Chief and win the war? Who was responsible for Marshall being made Chief of Staff?

Mr. McCormack: Very well, let us go back to 1861 when a man by the name of Abraham Lincoln was President and a great President. Lincoln did not know whom he could trust of those around him. He did not know what generals he could trust for a number of years until Grant came across the horizon.

According to history, Abraham Lincoln did not know what members of his Cabinet he could trust. Abraham Lincoln was the personality that led our country to victory in the War Between the States. If ever a President during wartime was a leader, not only of our civil government but in time of war, it was Lincoln. It was not until 1863, or thereabouts, that Grant came across the horizon. Prior to that time and during the remainder of the War Between the States it was Lincoln who was the leader of the civil government and also the leader of the armed forces.

When the gentleman makes the statement he does, making it in good faith, I give him back the leadership of Abraham Lincoln during the War Between the States.

The Chairman: The time of the gentleman from Massachusetts [Mr. McCormack] has expired.

The Chairman: If there are no further amendments, under the rule, the Committee will rise.

Accordingly the Committee rose; and the Speaker having resumed the chair, Mr. Wolcott, Chairman of the Committee of the Whole House on the State of the Union, reported that that Committee having had under consideration the resolution (H. J. Res. 25), pursuant to House Resolution 91, he reported the same back to the House with an amendment adopted in Committee of the Whole.

The Speaker: Under the rule, the previous question is ordered.

The question is on agreeing to the amendment.

The amendment was agreed to.

The Speaker: The question is on the engrossment and third reading of the resolution.

The joint resolution was ordered to be engrossed and read a third time, and was read the third time.

The Speaker: The question is on the passage of the joint resolution.

Mr. Rayburn: Mr. Speaker, on that I demand the yeas and nays.

The yeas and nays were ordered.

The question was taken; and there were—yeas 285, nays 121, not voting 26, as follows:

[Roll No. 4]

YEAS—285

Allen, Calif.	Andrews, N.Y.	Barrett
Allen, Ill.	Angell	Beall
Allen, La.	Arends	Bell
Andersen,	Arnold	Bender
H. Carl	Auchincloss	Bennett, Mich.
Anderson, Calif.	Bakewell	Bennett, Mo.
Andresen	Banta	Bishop
August H.	Barden	Blackney
Boggs, Del.	Harness, Ind.	Pace
Bolton	Hart	Patterson
Boykin	Hartley	Philbin
Bradley, Calif.	Hedrick	Phillips, Calif.
Bradley, Mich.	Herter	Phillips, Tenn.
Brehm	Heselton	Ploeser
Brooks	Hess	Plumley
Brophy	Hill	Poage
Brown, Ohio	Hinshaw	Poulson
Buck	Hoeven	Ramey
Buffett	Hoffman	Rankin
Burke	Holmes	Redden
Busbey	Hope	Reed, Ill.
Butler	Horan	Reed, N.Y.
Byrnes, Wis.	Howell	Rees
Canfield	Hull	Reeves
Carson	Jackson, Calif.	Rich
Case, N.J.	Jarman	Richards
Case, S. Dak.	Javits	Riehlman
Chadwick	Jenison	Riley
Chapman	Jenkins, Ohio	Rivers
Chenoweth	Jenkins, Pa.	Rizley
Chiperfield	Jennings	Robertson
Church	Jensen	Robsion
Clason	Johnson, Calif.	Rockwell
Clevenger	Johnson, Ill.	Rogers, Fla.
Clippinger	Johnson, Ind.	Rogers, Mass.
Coffin	Jones, N.C.	Rohrbough
Cole, Kans.	Jones, Ohio	Ross
Cole, N.Y.	Jones, Wash.	Russell
Corbett	Jonkman	Sadlak
Cotton	Judd	St. George
Cox	Kean	Sanborn
Crawford	Kearney	Sarbacher
Crow	Kearns	Schwabe, Mo.
Cunningham	Keating	Schwabe, Okla.
Curtis	Keefe	Scoblick
Dague	Kennedy	Scott, Hardie
Davis, Ga.	Kersten, Wis.	Scott,

Dawson, Utah	Kilburn	Hugh D., Jr.
Devitt	Kilday	Scrivner
D'Ewart	Knutson	Seely-Brown
Dirksen	Kunkel	Shafer
Dolliver	Landis	Short
Domengeaux	Larcade	Simpson, Ill.
Dondero	Latham	Simpson, Pa.
Dorn	Lea	Smathers
Doughton	LeCompte	Smith, Kans.
Drewry	LeFevre	Smith, Maine
Eaton	Lemke	Smith, Ohio
Elliott	Lewis	Smith, Va.
Ellis	Lodge	Smith, Wis.
Ellsworth	Love	Snyder
Elsaesser	McConnell	Springer
Elston	McCowen	Stanley
Engel, Mich.	McDonough	Stefan
Engle, Calif.	McDowell	Stevenson
Fellows	McGarvey	Stockman
Fenton	McGregor	Stratton
Fisher	McMahon	Sundstrom
Fletcher	McMillen, Ill.	Taber
Foote	MacKinnon	Talle
Fuller	Macy	Taylor
Fulton	Maloney	Thomas, N.J.
Gallagher	Mansfield, Tex.	Tibbott
Gamble	Martin, Iowa	Tollefson
Gathings	Mason	Towe
Gavin	Mathews	Twyman
Gearhart	Meade, Ky.	Vail
Gerlach	Meade, Md.	Van Zandt
Gifford	Merrow	Vinson
Gillette	Meyer	Vorys
Gillie	Michener	Vursell
Goff	Miller, Conn.	Wadsworth
Goodwin	Miller, Md.	Wetchel
Gossett	Miller, Nebr.	Welch
Graham	Mitchell	West
Grant, Ind.	Morton	Wheeler
Griffiths	Muhlenberg	Whittington
Gross	Mundt	Wigglesworth
Gwinn, N.Y.	Murray, Tenn.	Wilson, Ind.
Gwynne, Iowa	Murray, Wis.	Wilson, Tex.
Hale	Nixon	Wolcott
Hall,	Nodar	Wolverton
Edwin Arthur	Norblad,	Wood
Hall,	Norman	Woodruff
Leonard W.	O'Hara	Worley
Halleck	O'Konski	Youngblood
Hand	Owens	

NAYS—121

Abernethy	Burleson	Delaney
Albert	Byrne, N.Y.	Dingell
Almond	Camp	Donohue
Andrews, Ala.	Cannon	Douglas
Bates, Ky.	Celler	Durham
Beckworth	Chelf	Eberharter
Bland	Colmer	Evins
Blatnik	Combs	Fallon
Bloom	Cooley	Feighan

Boggs, La.	Courtney	Fernandez
Bonner	Cravens	Flannagan
Brown, Ga.	Crosser	Fogarty
Bryson	D'Alesandro	Folger
Buchanan	Davis, Tenn.	Forand
Bulwinkle	Deane	Gary
Gordon	Lesinski	Pfeifer
Gore	Lucas	Pickett
Granger	Lusk	Powell
Grant, Ala.	Lyle	Price, Fla.
Gregory	Lynch	Price, Ill.
Harless, Ariz.	McCormack	Priest
Harris	McMillan, S.C.	Rabin
Harrison	Madden	Rains
Havenner	Mahon	Rayburn
Hays	Manasco	Rooney
Hendricks	Mansfield,	Sabath
Hobbs	Mont.	Sheppard
Holifield	Marcantonio	Sikes
Huber	Miller, Calif.	Somers
Jackson, Wash.	Mills	Spence
Johnson, Okla.	Monroney	Stigler
Johnson, Tex.	Morgan	Teague
Jones, Ala.	Morris	Thomas, Tex.
Karsten, Mo.	Murdock	Thomason
Kee	Norton	Trimble
Kefauver	O'Brien	Walter
King	O'Toole	Whitten
Kirwan	Passman	Williams
Klein	Patman	Winstead
Lane	Peden	Zimmerman
Lanham	Peterson	

NOT VOTING—26

Bates, Mass.	Coudert	Kerr
Battle	Dawson, Ill.	Morrison
Bramblett	Gorski	Norrell
Buckley	Hagen	Potts
Carroll	Hardy	Preston
Clark	Hebert	Rayfiel
Clements	Heffernan	Sadowski
Cole, Mo.	Kelley	Sasscer
Cooper	Keogh	

So (two-thirds having voted in favor thereof) the joint resolution was passed.

The Clerk announced the following pairs:

On this vote:

Mr. Hebert and Mr. Bramblett for, with Mr. Carroll against.

Mr. Cole of Missouri and Mr. Hagen for, with Mr. Kerr against.

General pairs until further notice:

Mr. Bates of Massachusetts with Mr. Gorski.

Mr. Potts with Mr. Keogh.

Mr. Coudert with Mr. Heffernan.

The result of the vote was announced as above recorded.

Presidential Succession Act: House Debate (1947)

Article II, Section 1, paragraph 6 of the original Constitution designated the vice president as the successor to the presidency in the event of the president's death, resignation, or removal, but it did not delineate a line of succession that extended past the vice president. Instead, the article charged Congress to provide by law for situations in which the vice presidency is vacant when a presidential successor is needed.

The second Congress fulfilled its constitutional charge by passing the Succession Act of 1792. The act stipulated that a double vacancy in the presidency and the vice presidency would be remedied by the special election of a new president and vice president to a full four-year term, with the president pro tempore of the Senate (or, if there were none, the Speaker of the House of Representatives) serving as acting president until the special election took place.

In 1886, dissatisfied with the 1792 law, Congress passed another succession act. The dissatisfaction stemmed from two sources: first, uneasiness at the prospect of a congressional leader of one political party succeeding a president of the other party part way through a term; and second, concern that a longer line of succession might be needed to ensure that a legal successor would always be available. In 1881,

when President James A. Garfield was assassinated, neither a Senate president nor a House speaker had yet been chosen.

The Succession Act of 1886 addressed Congress's concerns by transferring the line of succession from the legislature to the president's cabinet in the order that the departments were created, beginning with the secretary of state. The statute was unclear about whether such a succession would be permanent or, pending a special election, temporary.

In 1933, Section 3 of the Twentieth Amendment addressed three other issues of presidential succession. If the president-elect died, resigned, or was judged to be constitutionally unqualified, the vice-president-elect would become president. If a president had not been chosen in time for the inauguration, the vice president-elect would serve as acting president. Finally, the amendment called upon Congress to legislate for the possibility that neither a president nor a vice president had been chosen by inauguration day. (See "The Twentieth Amendment: Senate Debate," p. 301.)

The issue of selection by succession was reopened in 1945 by Harry S Truman, who had succeeded to the presidency when Franklin D. Roosevelt died. Objecting to the 1886 law's provision that the secretary of state should *follow the vice president in the line of succession, Truman said: "It now lies within my power to nominate the person who would be my immediate successor in the event of my own death or inability to act. I do not believe that in a democracy this power should rest with the Chief Executive."*

Congress responded to Truman's initiative by passing the Presidential Succession Act of 1947. The act reordered the line of succession to be: Speaker of the House, president pro tempore of the Senate, then secretary of state and so on through the cabinet. The act also fulfilled Section 3 of the Twentieth Amendment by invoking the same succession line in the absence of a president-elect or a vice-president-elect on inauguration day. (The House Speaker or Senate president would have to resign from Congress before becoming the acting president.) Finally, the act forbade special presidential elections for fear of producing an excessive discontinuity of leadership within a single four-year term.

Section 2 of the Twenty-fifth Amendment, which was ratified in 1967, did not repeal the Presidential Succession Act of 1947. But, by providing a mechanism to fill vacancies in the vice presidency, the amendment reduced the possibility that the need for a longer line of succession would ever arise. (See "The Twenty-Fifth Amendment: Senate Debate," p. 522.) ∼

Mr. Michener: Mr. Speaker, pursuant to the order of the House agreed to July 8, 1947, making in order S. 564, a bill to provide for the performance of the duties of the office of President in case of the removal, resignation, death, or inability both of the President and Vice President, and providing that there shall be not to exceed 2 hours of general debate, to be equally divided and controlled by the chairman and ranking minority member of the Com-

mittee on the Judiciary, I move that the House resolve itself into the Committee of the Whole House on the State of the Union for the consideration of the bill S. 564.

The motion was agreed to.

Accordingly the House resolved itself into the Committee of the Whole House on the State of the Union for the consideration of the bill S. 564, the Presidential Succession Act, with Mr. Wolverton in the chair.

The Clerk read the title of the bill.

By unanimous consent, the first reading of the bill was dispensed with.

Mr. Michener: Mr. Chairman, the Constitution places upon the Congress the duty of enacting a Presidential succession law to determine who is to execute the office of President if there be no qualified President or Vice President.

Shortly after the adoption of the Constitution, and in 1792, the Congress passed the first Presidential succession law, and this enactment remained the law of the land until 1886—almost 100 years. In that law the President pro tempore of the Senate, next the Speaker of the House of Representatives, next the Members of the Cabinet in the order in which the Departments were created, served as President if there was no qualified President or Vice President.

In 1886 this law was repealed and the law which is now on the statute books was enacted. The present law provides that in case there is no qualified President or Vice President, the Secretary of State shall become Acting President, and the other members of the Cabinet follow in the same order as provided in the law of 1792.

The law of 1792 was the result of the recommendation of a special committee appointed by the Congress to explore the matter of Presidential succession. Reading of the annals and other records of the Congress of that day indicates that there were some political considerations involved. Thomas Jefferson was Secretary of State, Alexander Hamilton was Secretary of the Treasury. After much consideration and discussion the Congress passed the law of 1792. It is noteworthy that in the line of succession the President pro tempore of the Senate came first, the Speaker of the House of Representatives came second, and the Cabinet followed in order. Be it remembered that many of the Members of the Congress in 1792 were also members of the Constitutional Convention, which framed the Constitution. They certainly had knowledge as to what they intended concerning this succession when they wrote the Constitution. In these circumstances, the fact that the Congress of 1792 considered the President pro tempore of the Senate and the Speaker of the House of Representatives as officers eligible to serve as President under the Constitution should have great weight in arriving at what limitations the Constitution has placed upon the officers who might be considered by the Congress in determining the line of succession.

Mr. Chairman, of the 32 Presidents of the United States, 7 have died in office. No elected Vice President has ever died while acting as President. Regardless of what the law has been, the occasion has never arisen when anyone excepting the elected President or the elected Vice President has served as President.

When the President and the Vice President are both living, the country never expresses any concern about the line of Presidential succession; however, whenever a President or Vice President dies while serving in the office to which he was elected, immediately there is a revival of interest in a more adequate law taking care of the succession.

This bill, S. 564, makes two substantial changes in existing law. First, it places the Speaker of the House of Representatives next to the Vice President in the line of succession, and he is followed by the President pro tempore of the Senate. Next the Cabinet officers follow in order as now provided; however, the present law was enacted in 1886, and since that time two Cabinet offices have been created; that is, the Secretary of Labor and the Secretary of Commerce. Therefore, these two additional members of the President's Cabinet are given place in the line of succession, the same as other Cabinet officers.

There are a number of clarifications that might well be made while writing a new law controlling this important matter. For instance, it is uncertain as to just what amounts to disability on the part of an incumbent President or Acting President. This is not a new question but is a very difficult question to solve. For example, President Garfield was disabled for several months before he died, and the question arose as to how disability to act as President was to be determined. The same question was again asked when President Wilson was physically stricken. This is a difficult problem and it is admitted by all that no one has a satisfactory answer at the moment; therefore, this bill does not deal with that contingency. There are a number of resolutions now pending in the House and in the Senate providing for joint committees or commissions to study all of these details and in due season recommend if possible some salutary solution. This will take time and there is no possibility of any remedial legislation in this particular within the immediate future.

The pending bill, S. 564, had its genesis in a message by President Truman submitted to the Seventy-ninth Congress on June 19, 1945. The recommendation made by the President in that message found expression in H.R. 3587, which passed the House in the Congress in which it was introduced. That bill, however, was never acted upon by the Senate.

On February 5, 1947, the President sent a message to the Eightieth Congress reaffirming his message of June

19, 1945, and insisting on immediate action by the Congress. As a result a number of bills were introduced providing changes in the Presidential succession law. No two bills were exactly alike. Numerous plans and theories were suggested. In the House these bills were all referred to Subcommittee No. 1 of the Judiciary Committee for consideration. This subcommittee held hearings on these pending bills and gave particular consideration to H.R. 2524, introduced by the gentleman from Tennessee [Mr. Kefauver], and H.R. 2749, introduced by me, as chairman. These bills were similar and each attempted to carry out the suggestions of the President as stated in his message. After some days of consideration by the subcommittee, hearings were temporarily suspended and as chairman I addressed a letter to the President of the United States asking for his views and the views of his legal advisers as to the constitutionality of the Kefauver bill and the Michener bill, which in fact are the same as S. 564.

In response to this letter of inquiry the President courteously advised that the Attorney General would give consideration to these bills and report to the Judiciary Committee. Pursuant to this correspondence, the Attorney General of the United States on June 11, 1947, addressed a letter to the chairman of the Judiciary Committee which analyzed the several bills on Presidential succession then pending before the committee.

Mr. Chairman, that letter of the Attorney General succinctly covers this whole problem. The Attorney General has the research facilities and the lawyers, and is in a position to furnish to the Congress a factual statement, plus the benefit of his legal conclusions, as to the intent and meaning of doubtful words, phrases, and expressions used in the Constitution and in the statutes.

In the Senate this bill was debated for a large part of 2 days. No such time is available in the House; therefore, I am going to read the pertinent parts of the Attorney General's opinion. In this opinion, no words are wasted. Facts and legal conclusions only are stated and the committee reporting this bill concurs in the conclusions reached by the Attorney General.

Mr. Chairman, the Attorney General's letter reads as follows:

Office of the Attorney General,
Washington, D.C., June 11, 1947.
Hon. Earl C. Michener,
*Chairman, Committee on the
Judiciary, House of Representatives,
Washington, D.C.*

My Dear Mr. Chairman: This is in response to your request for my views concerning a group of related measures (H.R. 163, H.R. 1121, H.R. 2524, H.R. 2749, and H.J. Res. 34) relative to Presidential succession and kindred subjects.

Article II, section 1, clause 6, of the Constitution provides:

"In case of the removal of the President from office, or of his death, resignation, or inability to discharge the powers and duties of the said office, the same shall devolve on the Vice President, and the Congress may by law, provide for the case of removal, death, resignation, or inability, both of the President and Vice President, declaring what officer shall then act as President, and such officer shall act accordingly, until the disability be removed, or a President shall be elected."

Pursuant to this authorization, Congress in 1792 passed the first succession law (act of Mar. 1, 1792, ch. 8, sec. 9, 1 Stat. 240). This law provided:

"In case of removal, death, resignation, or disability both of the President and Vice President of the United States, the President of the Senate pro tempore and in case there shall be no President of the Senate, then the Speaker of the House of Representatives for the time being shall act as President of the United States until the disability be removed or a President shall be elected."

There were a number of objections to this law, both of a political and constitutional nature, and Congress accordingly changed the law in 1886 to read as follows (act of Jan. 19, 1886, ch. 4, secs. 1-2, 24 Stat. 1-2; 3 U.S.C. 21-22):

"That in case of removal, death, resignation, or inability of both the President and Vice President of the United States, the Secretary of State, or if there be none, or in case of his removal, death, resignation, or inability, then the Secretary of the Treasury, or if there be none, or in the case of his removal, death, resignation, or inability, then the Secretary of War, or if there be none, or in case of his removal, death, resignation, or inability, then the Attorney General, or if there be none, or in case of his removal, death, resignation, or inability, then the Postmaster General, or if there be none, or in case of his removal, death, resignation, or inability, then the Secretary of the Navy, or if there be none, or in case of his removal, death, resignation, or inability, then the Secretary of the Interior, shall act as President until the disability of the President or Vice President is removed or a President shall be elected: *Provided,* That whenever the powers and duties of the office of President of the United States shall devolve upon any of the persons named herein, if Congress be not then in session, or if it would not meet in accordance with law within 20 days thereafter, it shall be the duty of the person upon whom said powers and duties shall devolve to issue a proclamation convening Congress in extraordinary session, giving 20 days' notice of the time of meeting.

"Sec. 2. That the preceding section shall only be held to describe and apply to such officers as shall have been appointed by the advice and consent of the Senate to the offices therein named, and such as are eligible to the office of the President under the Constitution, and not under impeachment by the House of Representatives of the United States at the time the powers and duties of office shall devolve upon them respectively."

On June 19, 1945, the President addressed a message to Congress requesting further changes in the order of Presidential succession (91 Congressional Record 6280-6281). The President recommended that the Speaker of the House of Representatives be placed first in order of succession in case of the removal, death, resignation, or inability to act, of the President and Vice President. Under the plan recommended, the person succeeding to the Presidency would serve until the next congressional election or until a special election called for the purpose of electing a new President and Vice President. The individuals elected at such a general or special election would serve only to fill the unexpired terms. The President suggested that if there were no Speaker, or if the Speaker failed to qualify, the succession pass to the President pro tempore of the Senate and then to the members of the Cabinet, until a duly qualified Speaker is elected.

The President expressed the belief that in a democracy the power to nominate a successor (a member of the Cabinet) should not rest with the Chief Executive, and pointed out that the Speaker is elected in his own district, and is elected as presiding officer of the House by votes of the representatives of all the people of the country. Hence his selection, next to that of the President and Vice President, can most accurately be said to stem from the people themselves.

The President gave the following reasons for preferring the Speaker to the President pro tempore of the Senate: A new House is elected every 2 years, and always at the same time as the President and Vice President. It is usually in agreement politically with the Chief Executive. Only one-third of the Senate, however, is elected with the President and Vice President. It might, therefore, have a majority hostile to the policies of the President and fill the Presidential office with one not in sympathy with the will of the majority of the people. The President referred, in this connection, to the impeachment of President Johnson as suggesting the possibility of a hostile Congress seeking to oust a Vice President who had become President, in order to have the President pro tempore of the Senate become the President. This, he said, was one of the considerations which caused Congress in 1886 to change the law of 1792 under which the President pro tempore of the Senate succeeded the Vice President.

On February 5, 1947, the President renewed his request for legislation changing the order of succession. In this message, he said (93 Congressional Record 786):

"On June 19, 1945, I sent a message to the Congress of the United States suggesting that the Congress should give its consideration to the question of the Presidential succession.

"In that message, it was pointed out that under the existing statute governing the succession to the office of President, members of the Cabinet successively fill the office in the event of the death of the elected President and the Vice President. It was further pointed out that, in effect, the present law gives to me the power to nominate my immediate successor in the event of my own death or inability to act.

"I said then, and I repeat now, that in a democracy this power should not rest with the Chief Executive. I believe that, insofar as possible, the office of the President should be filled by an elective officer.

"In the message of June 19, 1945, I recommended that the Congress enact legislation placing the Speaker of the House of Representatives first in order of succession, and if there were no Speaker, or if he failed to qualify, that the President pro tempore of the Senate should act until a duly qualified Speaker was elected.

"A bill (H.R. 3587) providing for this succession that existed when I sent the message to the Congress on June 19, 1945, still exists today.

"I see no reason to change or amend the suggestion which I previously made to the Congress, but if the Congress is not disposed to pass the type of bill previously passed by the House, then I recommend that some other plan of succession be devised so that the office of the President would be filled by an officer who holds his position as a result of the expression of the will of the voters of this country.

"It is my belief that the present line of succession as provided by the existing statute, which was enacted in 1886, is not in accord with our basic concept of government by elected representatives of the people.

"I again urge the Congress to give its attention to this subject."

*   *   *

(The Attorney General's analysis of all the bills mentioned in the letter is not included here because it is not pertinent to S. 564. The letter does state the preference of the Attorney General for the Kefauver bill, H.R. 2524, and the Michener bill, H.R. 2749, both of which attempt to carry out the Presi-

dent's recommendations. The Attorney General's report continues:)

*   *   *

There are several legal questions which invariably arise upon the introduction of bills changing the order of Presidential succession. I believe, however, that these questions can be resolved in favor of the validity of legislation which would carry out the President's recommendations.

Opponents of the bill introduced in the Seventy-ninth Congress (H.R. 3587) contended that the Speaker of the House and the President pro tempore were not "officers" within the meaning of article II, section 1, clause 6, of the Constitution. In so doing, they relied heavily upon the Senate's decision in 1798 in the Blount impeachment case. In a plea to the jurisdiction of the Senate, Senator Blount contended that since he held his commission from the State of Tennessee and not from the United States, he was not a "civil officer of the United States" within the meaning of the impeachment clause of the Constitution (art. II, sec. 4). The Senate sustained the plea and dismissed the articles of impeachment.

*   *   *

The proponents countered with *Lamar* v. *United States* (241 U.S. 163, 112-113 (1916)), holding that a Member of Congress is an "officer acting under the authority of the United States" within the meaning of the impersonation statute (Criminal Code, sec. 32; 18 U.S.C. 76). In its opinion, the Court noted that on another occasion the Senate, after considering the Blount case, concluded that a Member of Congress was a civil officer within the purview of the law requiring the taking of an oath of office (Congressional Globe, 38th Cong., 1st sess., pt. 1, pp. 320-331).

The question at issue, however, is not whether a Member of Congress as such, is a civil officer within the meaning of article II, section 4. The issue is whether the Speaker of the House and the President pro tempore who, though they are Members of Congress, are chosen from those offices by their respective Houses and not by vote of their constituencies, are officers within the meaning of article II, section 1. On this question, the Blount decision is of doubtful authority. The term is used in article II, section 1, without qualification and presumably includes not only officers of the executive branch of the Government but also officers of the judicial and legislative branches.

Further support for the view that the Speaker and President pro tempore are officers within the meaning of article II can be found in the fact that the law of 1792 designated the President pro tempore and the Speaker as successors to the Presidency. This law represents a construction of article II by an early Congress, whose views of the Constitution have long been regarded as authoritative, and reflects a long-continued acquiescence in such a construction (H.Rept. 829, 79th Cong., 1st sess., p. 4).

*   *   *

In conclusion, I wish to state that I am convinced of the need for a revision of the law relating to Presidential succession and, of the measures herein discussed, have a definite preference for H.R. 2524 and H.R. 2749, which are similar in all major respects and are more nearly in harmony with the recommendations of the President. Accordingly, I recommend favorable consideration of the proposal contained in the two measures last mentioned.

I am advised by the Director of the Bureau of the Budget that there is no objection to the submission of this report.

Sincerely yours,
Douglas W. McGregor,
Acting Attorney General.

Mr. Dondero: Mr. Chairman, will the gentleman yield?

Mr. Michener: I yield to the gentleman from Michigan.

Mr. Dondero: In case there is no Vice President, as now obtains, does it provide that the President pro tempore of the Senate will succeed before the Speaker of the House will become eligible for the Presidency?

Mr. Michener: Under existing law?

Mr. Dondero: Under the present law.

Mr. Michener: Under the proposal the Speaker, as stated just a moment ago, comes first in the order of succession; the President pro tempore of the Senate comes second, and then the Cabinet officers in the order in which they were created. The Committee on the Judiciary has made no changes whatever in the Senate bill. Twenty-six of the twenty-seven Members voted to pass the bill S. 564 without amendment.

Mr. Cunningham: Mr. Chairman, will the gentleman yield?

Mr. Michener: I yield.

Mr. Cunningham: I would like to be clear on the second paragraph of S. 564. As I understand it, if there is a vacancy in the office of the President, the Speaker of the House accepts the appointment; then, the House elects another Speaker; then, if the Speaker who is acting as President dies, the second Speaker takes his place if he wishes instead of the President pro tempore of the Senate. In other words, there is no chance for a President pro tempore of the Senate to become President as long as the House has a Speaker who qualifies and is willing to serve.

Mr. Michener: That is correct.

Mr. Cunningham: I thank the gentleman.

Mr. Michener: That was discussed very thoroughly in the Senate and a number of questions were asked.

I yield to the gentleman from Pennsylvania [Mr. Eberharter].

Mr. Eberharter: Has the gentleman stated what the present law provides as to the order of succession?

Mr. Michener: The present law provides that the order of succession shall be in accordance with the order in which the Cabinet offices were created. The first is Secretary of State and so forth. But the law is incomplete because we have two Cabinet offices that were created since that law was enacted.

Mr. Dondero: Mr Chairman, will the gentleman yield for a question?

Mr. Michener: I yield.

Mr. Dondero: Suppose the Speaker of the House is not a native-born American?

Mr. Michener: We do not have to spend any time on that question for the reason that the bill is very clear on that point. No one can qualify in the line of succession who does not possess the constitutional qualifications for a President of the United States. He must be 35 years of age; he must be native-born.

The Members have before them the committee report accompanying the bill. On pages 5 and 6 of the report will be found an analysis of its provisions. Time will not permit my discussing these sections in detail; however, if there are any questions about the meaning of any section, the answers can be found in this committee analysis which is, of course, printed and presented to the membership for just that purpose. Pursuant to the permission granted to me by the House, I print with these remarks a copy of that analysis, which is as follows:

The bill S. 564 provides in section (a) (1) that in the absence of a President or Vice President to discharge the powers and duties of the Office of President, the Speaker of the House of Representatives shall act as President, provided he first retires as Speaker and as a Member of Congress. Section (a) (2) of the bill relates these same requirements to the case of the death of an individual acting as President. The selection of the Speaker to be in the first line of succession is based upon the sound reasoning that of all elected representatives of the people other than the President and Vice President, he more than any other represents the composite voice of the people by virtue of his election to the position of Speaker by the votes of the representatives of the people. He holds, in effect, a mandate from the people to carry out a particular policy or program. He, more than the President pro tempore of the Senate, reflects the latest sentiment of the people, since the 2-year term enjoyed by Representatives in Congress insures that freshness of the popular will which the 6-year senatorial term could not offer nor assure.

Moreover, because of the shorter term of a Representative, there is more likelihood of political harmony between the policies of a President and Vice President and the President pro tempore of the Senate.

Section (b) provides that in the absence of a duly qualified Speaker to succeed, the President pro tempore of the Senate shall act as President, conditioned upon his resignation as President pro tempore and as Senator.

Section (c), including subsections (1) and (2) thereunder, provides that the tenure of the person acting as President under the preceding sections shall be until the expiration of the then current Presidential term, or until the qualification or removal of disability of a prior-entitled individual, whichever period is the shorter. It will be observed that here, and in other sections of the bill, the terms "disability" and "inability" are used seemingly interchangeably. The use of the terms in this fashion is predicated upon the identical use in the Constitution in article II, section I, clause 6.

Section (d) (1) provides that in the lack of a President pro tempore, qualified to act as President, then those powers and duties shall be exercised in descending order of selection by the following officers not under a preventing disability: Secretary of State, Secretary of the Treasury, Secretary of War, Attorney General, Secretary of the Navy, Secretary of the Interior, Secretary of Agriculture, Secretary of Commerce, and the Secretary of Labor. This order parallels the order provided in the existing law, with the exception of the addition of the Secretaries of Agriculture, Commerce, and Labor. The remoteness of the contingency which would occasion such nonelective officers to act as President removes the objections now made as to that point in existing law. Subsection (d) (2) qualifies the Cabinet-officer-succession provision to the extent that the removal of the disability of a Cabinet officer higher on the list shall not terminate the service of the Cabinet officer then acting as President, although the removal of disability of any other prior-entitled individual in the line of succession would operate to terminate the Presidential tenure of the Cabinet officer then acting in such capacity.

As a further qualification to the assumption of the office of President by a

Cabinet officer, it is provided in subsection (d) (3) that the taking of the Presidential oath of office would automatically constitute his resignation as a Cabinet officer. This would preclude any question as to duality of office.

Section (e) provides that the officers named elsewhere in the bill for succession must be constitutionally eligible for the Presidency. In addition, the Cabinet officers named in the potential line of succession shall not only have been appointed by and with the advice and consent of the Senate prior to the disability of the President pro tempore, but must also not have been under impeachment by the House of Representatives at the time of devolution of the powers and duties of the Presidency upon them. The section is dictated from an abundance of caution to obviate even the barest possibility of an undesirable incumbency.

Section (f) provides the payment for the then prevailing Presidential salary to the successor, and section (g) repeals sections 1 and 2 of the Presidential Succession Act of 1886.

Now, Mr. Chairman, I have used more time than I should have used in the light of the time available. In closing, in behalf of the Judiciary Committee, I ask the Congress to pass S. 564 without amendment. If this is done, then the bill will go to the President and no further action will be required in the Senate.

Mr. Celler: Mr. Chairman, I yield myself 15 minutes.

Mr. Chairman, it is well to be specific as to what the present law is with reference to Presidential succession. In the event of the death of the President and Vice President or in the event, God forbid, of the death of President Truman, the next in succession would be Mr. Marshall, Secretary of State, then Secretary of the Treasury Snyder, then Secretary of War Patterson, then Attorney General Clark, then Postmaster General Hannegan, then Secretary of Navy Forrestal, and, finally, Secretary of the Interior Krug.

The proposed bill now before you would change the line of succession to provide for the following order of Presidential succession: First would come the Speaker of the House, the distinguished gentleman from Massachusetts [Mr. Martin]; then, the President pro tempore of the Senate, Senator Vandenberg; then Secretary Marshall; then Secretary Snyder; then Secretary Patterson; Attorney General Clark; Postmaster General Hannegan; Secretary Forrestal; and so forth.

It is interesting to delve into the history of this matter a little bit. The first act, as was said by the distinguished chairman of the Committee on the Judiciary, the gentleman from Michigan [Mr. Michener], was passed way back in 1792. That was similar to the proposed bill, except that the first in succession was to be the President pro tempore of the Senate, and the Speaker would follow. Why was that? Well, we have to consider who was in control of the Congress then. The Federalist party was in control, and Hamilton was the dominant figure of that party. He had considerable hostility to Jefferson, who was Secretary of State. Frankly, President Washington was not enamored of Mr. Jefferson, so that between the two of them they figured it would be better not to make the Secretary of State first in succession, and therefore devised a plan that the President pro tempore of the Senate would be first in succession, the Speaker second in succession, and then the Cabinet officers.

That plan continued for something like 94 years, until 1886, in the administration of Grover Cleveland. But, 33 years before 1886, in 1853, we had the administration of Franklin Pierce, but his Vice President had died, and the question arose as to his successor if he died in office. Bills were offered in the Congress in that year with reference to Presidential succession, and bills were offered in every single Congress from 1853 down to 1886, when the original statute of 1792 was changed. President

Cleveland's Vice President had died and that tragic event again high lighted the very controversial question of succession.

What happened in the interim? We know that we had lame duck Congresses in those days, and before the Speaker or the President pro tempore of the Senate was elected by their colleagues a number of months elapsed. In the debates which we find in the Congressional Record there was argument to the effect that there was danger in that situation. Since it took months before the head of the House and the head of the Senate were elected, if the succession devolved upon them, there might be considerable turmoil and uncertainty because there would not be any Speaker for a number of months—not till March—and there would not be any President pro tempore. Of course, the twentieth amendment did away with lame duck sessions.

Furthermore, there came about the impeachment proceedings of President Johnson, and that gave rise to considerable bitter debate as to who would follow President Johnson. Fear was expressed that if the President pro tempore would be first in succession, and then the Speaker of the House, a hostile Congress might evolve a clique to get control of the affairs of Government. The Tilden-Hayes contest also influenced the desire for change. So, in 1886, they passed a bill which is now the present law, namely, that the first in succession shall be the Secretary of State, and so on down among the Cabinet officers.

In the past the line of succession has been, I would say in my humble estimation, practically theoretical. There was not too much chance of the line of succession going very far. The life of today, however, is different. In the old days Presidents did not take trips to Europe, did not go to Berlin to attend conferences, did not go to Mexico, and did not ride in fast-traveling automobiles. I do not mean that as a rebuke, I

only extend that as a reminder to our present President that we all have an affectionate regard for him and want him to live many, many years, but that he should be mighty careful in his travels. I offer him much applause, however, for his courageous espousal of the purposes of the bill before us.

Strange to relate, however, during our history the Vice Presidency along since the time of Washington has been vacant by death or resignation 15 times. Not once, fortunately, did a situation develop where both the President and Vice President died. Seven Vice Presidents succeeded to the Presidency through the death of their President. They are John Tyler, Millard Fillmore, Andrew Johnson, Chester A. Arthur, Theodore Roosevelt, Calvin Coolidge, and Harry S. Truman. Seven Vice Presidents died in office leaving the succession open to the third man on the succession list. These Vice Presidents were George Clinton, Elbridge Gerry, William R. King, Henry Wilson, Thomas A. Hendricks, Garret A. Hobart, and James S. Sherman. One Vice President, strange to relate, resigned to take his office as Senator. That was John C. Calhoun.

It is well to draw attention to a peculiar situation that developed way back in 1844, in President Tyler's term. It seems that a Presidential party went on a steamer called the *Princeton*. One of its new guns was fired in salute, but the gun exploded and killed two Cabinet officers, the Secretary of State, the Secretary of the Navy, and almost killed the President. So even in those days sudden death struck unexpectedly. We can peer into the future a bit and envisage an atomic war, a bacteriological war, where a number of the highest officials of the Nation might unfortunately be done away with. So it is well to focus our attention on this question of the Presidential succession.

The present statute of 1886 provides that those who are designated to succeed the President shall only be Acting Presidents until a special election shall have been called. The bill before us does not provide for special elections, and I think wisely so, because special elections will mean recurrence of considerable political turmoil, national conventions and the usual battle for delegates and fight for nomination, with the usual flaring up of passions that accompany a national convention followed by a special election and the campaign that precedes it.

Mr. Dondero: Mr. Chairman, will the gentleman yield?

Mr. Celler: I yield.

Mr. Dondero: Did the committee or the gentleman give any thought, or would the gentleman like to discuss the question of the justification of an official who has never been elected by the people to succeed to the Presidency as provided in this bill and as provided in the laws of this land since the beginning of our Government.

Mr. Celler: I believe the answer is found in the letter that the President sent to us. He cushions the blow in a way. He first says that the Speaker of the House should be the first in succession, then the President pro tempore of the Senate. He then uses this language:

> A completely new House is elected every 2 years, and always at the same time as the President and Vice President. Usually it is in agreement politically with the Chief Executive. Only one-third of the Senate, however, is elected with the President and Vice President. The Senate might, therefore, have a majority hostile to the policies of the President and might conceivably fill the Presidential office with one not in sympathy with the will of the majority of the people.

The Chairman: The time of the gentleman from New York has expired.

Mr. Cellar: Mr. Chairman, I yield myself 10 additional minutes.

Mr. Chairman, the President there made a cogent statement when he said that the Speaker of the House is elected by representatives of the people. He is closest to the people of all mentioned in the succession. I, therefore, agree with the President that the first in succession should be one closest to the people, namely, the Speaker of the House of Representatives. He is elected.

Mr. Michener: Mr. Chairman, will the gentleman yield?

Mr. Celler: I yield to the gentleman from Michigan.

Mr. Michener: The gentleman possibly missed what I believe the gentleman from Michigan had in mind. There has been a controversy ever since the adoption of the Constitution as to whether it was necessary for the House to elect a Member of the House as its Speaker or the Senate to elect as its President pro tempore a Member of the Senate. Every once in a while we hear somebody suggest that. But the weight of authority and the common sense of the situation and the possibilities are such that that never would happen.

Mr. Celler: It never has happened and in all likelihood never will happen.

Mr. Dondero: I think the gentleman from Michigan missed the point. What I had in mind was whether or not thought had been given to the question why an individual who had never been elected by the people should succeed to the Presidency. I refer to Cabinet officers. I think the gentleman from New York has answered it in this way, that they would be in sympathy with the principles and program of the Chief Executive, who is elected by a majority of the people of the United States.

Mr. Celler: The pending bill does not take care of every conceivable contingency. It does not take care of the question of what is meant by disability of a President. Some constitutional lawyers have stated that it is not within the province of the Congress to determine what is disability and that can only be brought about by a constitutional amendment. The committee considered that matter and rather than stir up controversy in that regard we did not define what is or what is not disability; but it is interesting to note that on a number of occasions the question of disability did arise. James A. Garfield was shot and lived for almost 3 months. The question arose, is he disabled? I think the only official act that was performed during that period of critical illness was the signing of a commission for an officer. He did nothing else. But the controversy was not resolved one way or the other. The next time the question rose was with reference to the illness of President Wilson. You may recall that a committee of Senators visited Wilson and remained at his bedside. They came to the conclusion that while he was greatly impaired in health he was, in the opinion of the Senators, not disabled in the constitutional sense. The question also rose with reference to the impeachment of President Johnson. While he was under impeachment— and the proceedings of his trial took a long time—was he in that interval disabled? That question also was never determined by either House.

Mr. Snyder: Mr. Chairman, will the gentleman yield?

Mr. Celler: I yield to the gentleman from West Virginia.

Mr. Snyder: This thought occurred to me and perhaps the gentleman would like to comment on it. At least I would like to get his ideas. We always have a Speaker of the House. If something were to happen to the Chief Executive and the Speaker of the House succeeded him, the House would immediately elect another Speaker.

So consequently, following the gentleman's reasoning, we will always have a representative of the people able and eligible to succeed to the Presidency rather than to go down to the President pro tempore of the Senate and the Cabinet officers. I would like to have the gentleman's comment with reference to that.

Mr. Celler: I did touch upon that subject briefly, and President Truman in his letter, which was referred to, said that he did not wish to be placed in the position where he would designate his own successor, namely, Secretary of State Marshall, and therefore he wanted the law changed so that he would not be placed in an embarrassing situation and so that the Speaker of the House would be the first in line of succession.

Mr. Michener: Mr. Chairman, will the gentleman yield?

Mr. Celler: I yield to the gentleman from Michigan.

Mr. Michener: I think the President of the United States, Mr. Truman, is to be complimented on his second message in particular. He sent the first message in 1945, when there was a Democratic occupant of the office of President pro tempore of the Senate and a Democratic Speaker. That bill passed the House overwhelmingly. In 1947, with a Republican Speaker, with whom the President was acquainted, and with a Republican President pro tempore of the Senate, he still stood by his principle and asked for the same legislation. I might say right here that Senator Vandenberg, who would be heir apparent to the throne provided the Senate officer came ahead of the House officer, took the floor in the Senate and made a splendid speech in favor of this bill and gave reasons why the Speaker is preferable and is closer to the people than a Senator might be under certain conditions. He certainly was not selfish. Like the big man that he is, it was principle first.

Mr. Celler: As I said before, the bill does not take care of every contingency. Suppose we have a situation where we have a war and the President is accused of treason. That is a very serious crime. Now, is the President disabled while he is under that cloud? We do not cover that. That may have to be taken up by other legislation. And I can conceive of other contingencies which we do not consider, and rightly so.

This bill passed the Senate, and it is well to get it passed and out of the way. It is a good bill and one that follows the wishes of the President. It has been argued that the Speaker and the President pro tempore are not officers within the purview of article II, section 1, clause 6, of the Constitution, which provides that an officer shall succeed as President, and reliance is placed upon the case of Senator Blount, who, away back in the early days, was under impeachment, and it was held that he could not be impeached because only an officer of the United States could be impeached, and the Senator was an officer of the State of Tennessee and not of the United States.

Mr. Michener: A civil officer, emphasizing the word "civil."

Mr. Celler: A civil officer, that is correct. But in any event, the Supreme Court decided in 1915 (241 U.S.), in the October term, that a Member of the House is an officer of the United States. I shall not read the decision. It is a very lengthy decision, but covers the situation completely, and is a decision of the United States Supreme Court that a Member of the House or a Member of the Senate, within the terms of article II, clause 6, is actually an officer of the United States.

Mr. Gwynne of Iowa: Is that the Lamar case?

Mr. Celler: Yes.

The Chairman: The time of the gentleman from New York has expired.

Mr. Michener: Mr. Chairman, I yield such time as he may desire to the gentleman from South Dakota [Mr. Case].

Mr. Case of South Dakota: Mr. Chairman, the action of the Congress and the President with respect to this legislation will be a credit to their part in the developing history of our Nation.

The President made his recommendation for this type of legislation without reference to his political party and without consideration for possible personal pride in the fact that he had been a Member of the Senate of the United States. He said simply that he believed the successor should be someone most closely identified with a choice of the people. The Speaker of the House of Representatives represented most closely an expressed choice by the people in a representative way, Nationwide.

The bodies of the Congress in approving this legislation are doing it to meet a defect in our constitutional provisions for succession to the Presidency. The need for such a provision is clearer in this day of fast-moving events than it could have been when the Nation was founded.

And, Mr. Chairman, though I note the present Speaker is himself not in the chair during the debate on this bill, having turned the job of presiding over to the gentleman from Indiana, I would like to say that the action of the Congress is not retarded one whit by knowledge of who would succeed to the Presidency if the law were to be employed during your speakership.

It has been my privilege to serve in the House of Representatives during the speakerships of the gentleman from Alabama [Mr. Bankhead], the gentleman from Texas [Mr. Rayburn], and the gentleman from Massachusetts [Mr. Martin]. Each one of them would make or would have made a great President.

I shall vote for this bill, Mr. Chairman, with the knowledge that the Speakers of the House, as I have known them, merit the confidence this action implies.

Mr. Michener: Mr. Chairman, I yield to the gentleman from Kentucky [Mr. Robsion], the chairman of the Subcommittee No. 1, which held hearings and made report on the bills introduced in the House dealing with this particular subject.

Mr. Robsion: Mr. Chairman, we have before us Senate bill 564, providing for the succession to the Presidency in the event of the removal, resignation, death, or inability of both the President and Vice President to act, and this bill designates the successors to the Presidency in such a contingency as follows:

First. Speaker of the House of Representatives.

Second. President pro tempore of the Senate.

Third. Secretary of State.

Fourth. Secretary of the Treasury.

Fifth. Secretary of War.

Sixth. Attorney General.

Seventh. Postmaster General.

Eighth. Secretary of the Navy.

Ninth. Secretary of the Interior.

Tenth. Secretary of Agriculture.

Eleventh. Secretary of Commerce.

Twelfth. Secretary of Labor.

This S. 564 is identical with the bill passed by the House in the Seventy-ninth Congress, and it is identical in its terms and objectives with the bill introduced in the present Congress by our distinguished chairman, Mr. Michener, and our distinguished colleagues, Mr. Kefauver, of Tennessee, and Mr. Anderson of California. Our good friend and colleague the gentleman from Arkansas [Mr. Trimble] also introduced a very interesting bill which would take care of situations arising where all of the persons named in the Senate bill and these House bills should suffer death or inability to act as President by reason of some devastating force which might be produced by the atom bomb.

These several bills were referred to our subcommittee No. 1, of which I have the honor to be chairman, to hold hearings, give consideration, and report on the several bills. Our subcommittee held hearings and heard a number of persons who were well qualified to speak on this subject. All of the members of our subcommittee came to the conclusion that this legislation was essential and urgent, and that the persons named above should in their order suc-

ceed to the Presidency in the event of the removal, resignation, death, or inability of the President and Vice President to act.

The important question developed was whether or not the Speaker of the House and the President pro tempore of the Senate are civil officers as defined by the Constitution of the United States. In a leading case of *Lamarr* v. *The United States* (241 U.S. 103), the Supreme Court held that a Member of Congress—Representative or Senator—is a civil officer within the definition and meaning of the Constitution.

These bills were referred to the President of the United States with the request that he, through the legal departments of the Government, investigate the question carefully and make a report to the Judiciary Committee of the House. After long study, the Attorney General on June 11, 1947, submitted a written opinion in which he concurred in the decision supra Lamarr against United States and was of the opinion that the legislation proposed here is not violative of the Constitution and he recommended favorable consideration of this legislation. Soon after that report was made by the Attorney General, the Senate enacted S. 564, the bill now before the House. Our subcommittee met and after further consideration of the evidence submitted and the report of the Attorney General, found that S. 564 sought to accomplish the same objectives as the House bills and except for the transposition of some of the language, is almost identical with the House bill and identical with the bill passed by the House in the last Congress, and by unanimous vote approved S. 564 and recommended favorable action to the full Judiciary Committee.

The full Judiciary Committee read the Senate bill carefully and considered each and every part of it and at the conclusion approved unanimously S. 564 with the exception of one vote and reported favorably S. 564 to the House and the real question before us today is, Will the House accept Senate bill 564?

Of course, if the bill is amended in any respect it will likely be referred to a conference of the House and Senate, and this may prevent action on the bill at this session of Congress. The President has indicated that this legislation is urgent and therefore I strongly urge that the House accept S. 564 without amendment. This, then, will fully carry out the recommendation of the President in his message in the Seventy-ninth Congress and his message to the Eightieth Congress on February 5, 1947, and it will settle a controversy that has been going on from time to time ever since 1792 when the first succession bill was passed.

Commends President and Senate

The President, on June 19, 1945, in a message to the Congress, urged that the Congress take action on this matter of succession to the Presidency and designate, first, the Speaker of the House of Representatives instead of the President pro tempore of the Senate to become and act as President in the event of removal, death, or inability to act as President and Vice President. The House, in obedience to that request of the President, passed a bill in the last Congress, but the Senate failed to act. At that time the Democrats were in control of the House and Senate. On February 5, 1947, President Truman renewed his request for legislation and again urged that the Speaker of the House be named first in order, the President pro tempore of the Senate second in order, and members of the Cabinet in the order as we have set out above to act as President in the event of removal, death, or inability of both President and Vice President to act.

The Congress, of course, now has a Republican Speaker and a Republican President pro tempore of the Senate and if President Truman should die or be unable to act, then the Republican Speaker of the House would become President. President Truman gave the following reasons for preferring the Speaker of the House to the President pro tempore of the Senate:

> A new House is elected every 2 years and always at the same time as the President and Vice President. It usually is in agreement politically with the Chief Executive. Only one-third of the Senate, however, is elected with the President and Vice President. It might, therefore, have a majority hostile to the policies of the President and fill the Presidential office with one not in sympathy with the will of the majority of the people.

The President made it clear in his own messages that it would be more nearly in accord with our Democratic institutions to have the Speaker of the House to become President in case of the removal, death, or inability of the President and Vice President to act than it would if the President pro tempore of the Senate was designated to fill this important office. He also pointed out that under the present law, members of the Cabinet, in the order of their creation, would succeed to the Presidency, and therefore the President, under present law, could name his successor by naming certain persons of his Cabinet, persons who have not been elected by the people. I cannot commend too highly this attitude on the part of President Truman. I also desire to commend the Members of the Senate that voted to pass this bill which places the Speaker No. 1 to become President in the event of the removal, death, or inability to act of the President and Vice President.

The Senate likely could have defeated this legislation. Senator Vandenberg, who is President pro tempore of the Senate, made a very able and vigorous speech in support of S. 564 which gives the Speaker of the House preference. I regard the attitude of the President pro tempore as well as President Truman's statesmanship of a high order and in keeping with our ideals of a government of the people, by the people, and for the people, and it seems to me that each and every Member of this House could join in and pass the Senate bill, S. 564, because it is in its objectives and provisions the same as the bill the House passed in the last Congress and the bill that has been favorably considered by the committee of the House in this Congress.

Years of Debate and Consideration

I doubt if I could add much to the very able and enlightening speeches made on this bill today by the gentleman from Michigan, Chairman Michener, and ranking Democrat, the gentleman from New York [Mr. Celler], of the Judiciary Committee. The authority for the Congress to act is based primarily on article II, section 1, clause 6, of the Federal Constitution, which provides:

In case of the removal of the President from office, or of his death, resignation, or inability to discharge the powers and duties of the said office, the same shall devolve on the Vice President, and the Congress may by law provide for the case of removal, death, resignation, or inability, both of the President and Vice President, declaring what officer shall then act as President, and such officer shall act accordingly, until the disability be removed, or a President shall be elected.

Under this authorization, Congress, in March 1792, passed the first succession law. This law provides:

In case of removal, death, resignation, or disability, both of the President and Vice President of the United States, the President of the Senate pro tempore, and in case there be no President of the Senate, then the Speaker of the House of Representatives for the time being shall act as President of the United States until the disability be removed or a President shall be elected.

It will be observed that the President pro tempore of the Senate, in the act of 1792, was given preference over the Speaker of the House of Representatives. Between 1792 and 1886 a number of Presidents had died—Harrison, Taylor, Lincoln, and Garfield—and quite a number of Vice Presidents had died, and there was much discussion over this question of succession, and finally, on January 19, 1886, an act of Congress was approved which provided:

That in case of removal, death, resignation, or inability of both the President and Vice President of the United States, the Secretary of State, or if there be none, or in case of his removal, death, resignation, or inability, then the Secretary of the Treasury, and on through the Secretary of War, Attorney General should act as President.

It can be seen that this act of Congress eliminated both the President pro tempore of the Senate and the Speaker of the House of Representatives. Of course, up to that time the Senators were elected by the State legislatures instead of by popular vote and the only successors to the Presidency are the appointive officers of the President, members of his Cabinet. The Vice President, after becoming President through the removal, death, or inability to act of the President, could name his successor, and that is the situation today under the act of 1886.

President Truman is urging that the Congress change the law and first give preference to the Speaker of the House of Representatives, a man elected by the people; and second, to the President pro tempore of the Senate, a man elected by the people. If both of these fail, then in their order to the 10 Cabinet officers. As President Roosevelt is dead, Mr. Truman, as Vice President become President, can and has named his successor in the event of his removal, death, or inability to act. He does not believe this is in line with our democratic ideals, and I am sure that practically every Member of this House is in full accord with President Truman on this matter.

There has been much debate and much consideration given to this question since 1886. President McKinley and President Harding died. President Wilson was a very sick man in the latter part of his administration. President Roosevelt died in 1945. Some Vice Presidents have died, and each time the succession to the Presidency has come up for consideration.

If this becomes law, there is little likelihood that anyone can become President of the United States except a person who has been chosen by the people either as a Representative or as a Senator. Under this act, should the Speaker of the House become President and should he die, there would be little chance for the President pro tempore of the Senate to become President because when the Speaker succeeds to the Presidency, the House would elect another Speaker, and that new Speaker would become the President and not the President pro tempore of the Senate, or any member of the Cabinet. This would indicate that, if this measure becomes law, in the event of the removal, death, or inability of the President or Vice President, officers elected by the people and elected representatives of the people, the Speaker of the House will become President unless the Speaker should not have the constitutional qualifications to be President, or if he did, he declined to assume the Presidential office; in such event, the President pro tempore of the Senate would become President, and, of course, if he did not possess the constitutional qualifications to be President or refused to take the office, then members of the Cabinet in their order would become President, but all of these officials who are in line for succession to the Presidency must possess all of the constitutional qualifications of President as to being a natural-born citizen, age, and so forth.

Of course, the Speaker of the House must resign as Speaker and also as Representative in assuming the office as President and this is also true as to the President pro tempore of the Senate. He must resign his office as President pro tempore of the Senate and as Senator. Whoever succeeds to the Presidency under this bill can only hold office for the balance of the term for which the President was originally elected.

The bill also provides that if the President-elect and the Vice President-elect both fail to qualify, then the acting President shall act only until the President or Vice President qualifies. The persons who do qualify are in the order as we have named, beginning with the Speaker of the House. Some have asked what will happen in the event the House fails to elect a Speaker or the Senate fails to elect a President pro tempore of the Senate. We must bear in mind that under an amendment to the Constitution, the Congress assembles and organizes on January 3 every 2 years and the President and Vice President are sworn in and inaugurated on the following January 20 every 4 years so that when the question comes up of the President and Vice President qualifying, they will find a Congress—House and Senate—already organized with a Speaker of the House and a President pro tempore of the Senate.

This bill does not cover all of the defects in the present law. For instance, some day we must provide a way to determine when the President, because of disability or inability, is unable to act as President. Some bills and resolutions are now pending before our Judiciary Committee that undertake to provide for such a contingency. These bills and resolutions in due course will be given consideration by our Judiciary Committee and perhaps there are other defects in the law that should be remedied.

The bill before us solves the major problems of succession that now confront the Nation and the Congress. I am quite sure that every Member of the Congress expresses the hope that divine providence does not intervene in creating a vacancy during President Truman's term. President Truman was elected by the American people to the office of Vice President and he is now the legal and constitutional President of the United States but we cannot overlook the fact that under modern means of travel, to carry on the very arduous duties of the Presidency, the President must take a certain amount of risks.

If some unfortunate accident should come to President Truman and Speaker of the House Joe Martin lives, he can, under this law, take over the affairs of our great Government. He is a duly elected Representative of the people in his own district and has been made Speaker of the House by a large majority of the duly elected Representatives of the American people as a whole. He knows our Government as few men in this country know it. He has come up from the grass roots. He has been trained for years in the school of government. He has had wide experience in the affairs of our Nation. He is a loyal, patriotic, American who, too, believes profoundly in a government of the people, by the people and for the people, and should he not be available, the next man in succession would be the very able, experienced Senator Vandenberg of Michigan, President pro tempore of the Senate. Few men in this Nation have had such wide training and experience in the affairs of this country and of course, no man could be more devoted and loyal to American institutions and ideals than he is.

This bill, if enacted into law, will bring a feeling of security to the American people generally and I sincerely trust that it may be adopted unanimously. There is not and could not be partisanship in this bill. . . .

. . . **Mr. Michener:** Mr. Chairman, I yield such time as he may desire to the gentleman from New Jersey [Mr. Canfield].

Mr. Canfield: Mr. Chairman, as we prepare to enact legislation making the Speaker of the House next in line for the Presidency after the Vice President, I am reminded of a tribute paid the office of Speaker on March 3, 1893, by ex-Speaker Reed. It is reported in volume 2 of Hinds' Precedents. The occasion was the closing day of the Fifty-second Congress, and Mr. Reed's vision of the Speakership was voiced in part in these words.

> No factional or party malice ought ever to strive to diminish his standing or lessen his esteem in the eyes of Members or of the world. No disappointments or defeats ought ever to be permitted to show themselves to the injury of that high place. Whoever at any time, whether for purposes of censure or rebuke or from any other motive, attempts to lower the prestige of the House itself, whose servant and exponent the Speaker is. No attack, whether open or covert, can be made upon that great office without leaving to the future a legacy of disorder and bad government. This is not because the Speaker is himself a sacred creation; it is because he is the embodiment of the House, its power and dignity.

In drafting our Federal Constitution the founding fathers spent little time in debating the office of Speaker of the House. Apparently they felt the office would be similar to that of the Speaker of the House of Commons. This conception has changed a good deal, but by comparison we have been niggardly in providing for our Speaker.

MacDonagh, in his Pageant of Parliament, published in London in 1921, points out that the Speaker of the House of Commons "receives an emolument of £500, to be paid, free of taxes, out of the Consolidated Fund direct, without having to be voted every year by the House of Commons. Besides, a sum of £1,000 equipment money is given to the Speaker on his first appointment. He could have a secretary with a salary of £500. The Speaker has a residence furnished by the state and free of rent, rates, taxes, with coal and light supplied. The Speaker also receives a pension of £4,000 a year."

I have had the privilege of serving under two of the greatest Speakers ever chosen by the people's representatives to honor the high office of the speakership, the distinguished gentleman from Texas [Mr. Rayburn], and the distinguished gentleman from Massachusetts [Mr. Martin]. These men possess all the qualifications Americans are wont to prescribe for the highest office in our Republic—the Presidency.

Mr. Michener: Mr. Chairman, I yield 5 minutes to the gentleman from Iowa [Mr. Gwynne].

Mr. Celler: Mr. Chairman, I also yield the gentleman 5 minutes.

Mr. Gwynne of Iowa: Mr. Chairman, the bill before us provides for a contingency which has never happened but entirely ignores a contingency that has happened once and maybe more than once. Suppose in the future a President should become incapacitated, either through accident or otherwise, and could not perform the duties of his office. Suppose he should become insane. What would we do? Do you know the answer? There is no answer, so far as I am able to learn.

That has actually happened. We had it when President Garfield lingered for some time between life and death and there was some question that it did not occur at a later date also.

The Constitution, however, foresaw that contingency and provided for it in article II, section 1, in these words:

> The Congress may by law provide for the ease of removal, death, resignation, or inability, both of the President and Vice President, and declare what officer shall then act as President.

Obviously the makers of the Constitution had in mind that Congress would do its full duty and adopt a law that would cover and take care of any such contingency that might happen in the future.

In other words, I esteem it to be the duty of the Congress to legislate and set up the proper machinery to determine if and when there is this inability. Now, that is one of the questions that we have to settle, and it is not touched in this bill

Here is another contingency. Suppose after an election and before the meeting of the electoral college, the President-elect should die, then what do you do? That is another great unanswered question.

I submit, Mr. Chairman, that instead of reporting out this bill without consideration, virtually—and, incidentally, this bill has been twice reported by the Committee on the Judiciary, and on neither occasion has it had any consideration worthy of the name—that instead of that sort of a thing, it would be my suggestion that the entire subject, with all its great and dangerous possibilities, should be considered by some committee, probably the Committee on the Judiciary, or if that committee does not care to undertake it, that a nonpartisan commission be appointed to make a careful study of the entire proposition.

Now, coming to this particular bill, I think it is of doubtful constitutionality; at least, there is sufficient doubt about it that the great Committee on the Judiciary of the House, which should be the guardian of the Constitution here if any committee is, ought to give it a little more consideration than about 30 minutes.

Constitutionally, it comes down to this question: Is a Member of Congress an officer within the meaning of the Constitution? That is one question. There are, of course, others. Well, in order to determine what the Constitution makers had in mind, what they meant by the word "officer," it is well to look through the Constitution to see how the word is used in other provisions, and here are some of them:

> Article II, section 2: The President may require the opinion, in writing, of the principal officer in each of the executive departments.

Now there, of course, they did not intend to include Members of Congress.

> Article II, section 2: The President shall appoint ambassadors, other public ministers and consuls, judges of the Supreme Court, and all other officers of the United States.

Obviously, they did not intend to include Members of Congress in that.

> Article II, section 3: The President shall commission all the officers of the United States.

Well, he does not commission Members of Congress. Now, the next really calls for an explanation:

> Article II, section 4: The President, Vice President, and all civil officers of the United States, shall be removed from office on impeachment.

Is a Member of Congress subject to impeachment? Of course, it was held in the Blount case that he was not, and it was put squarely on the ground that he was not an officer within the meaning of the Constitution.

Article I, section 6, contains a provision which throws considerable light on the intent of the framers of the Constitution in these words:

> And no person holding any office under the United States, shall be a Member of either House during his continuance in office.

If you take the version that is taken by all the proponents of this bill, that section absolutely means nothing. How, I submit, can a Member of Congress be an officer to qualify to be in line of succession and not be an officer under this particular section of the Constitution?

> Article II, section 1: No Senator or Representative, or person holding an office of trust or profit under the United States, shall be appointed an elector.

This makes a clear distinction between, on the one hand, Senators and Representatives, and on the other, a person holding an office of trust or profit under the United States.

In the third section of the fourteenth amendment you find substantially that same language:

> No person shall be a Senator or Representative in Congress, or elector of President and Vice-President, or hold any office, civil or military, under the United States—

And so on, again making a clear distinction between Members of Congress, on the one hand, and officers of the Government on the other.

Article I, section 2:

> The House of Representatives shall choose their Speaker and other officers—

Indicating to me clearly that the men who wrote the Constitution meant that the Speaker was an officer of the House and not an officer of the Government.

It is interesting to note that this question has had considerable consideration, and there are respectable authorities who have placed the same interpretation on this that I have here. Here are some of them: The Supreme Court of the United States in three cases, and I will give you the citations later. The court held in substance that unless a person in the service of the Government holds his office by virtue of appointment under article II, section 2, that is, an appointment by the President or an appointment by a court or an appointment by a head of a department, he is not an officer of the United States in a Constitutional sense.

James Madison, father of the Constitution, expressed himself very clearly in accord with the views I am giving you here now. Judge Story, probably the greatest writer on the Constitution we ever had, held that view. Professor Tucker, who made a very extensive research on this subject, said that, in his opinion, the word "officer" as used in the Constitution was not meant to apply to Members of Congress. Past Attorneys General of the United States have also given it that interpretation.

Proponents of this bill refer to the case of *Lamar* v. *United States* (241 U.S. 107). That is the single authority they have to rely upon, and if you read that case you will see it absolutely does not prove their contention at all.

Mr. Celler: Mr. Chairman, will the gentleman yield?

Mr. Gwynne of Iowa: I yield to the gentleman from New York.

Mr. Celler: Did not that case hold that within a state which says that anyone impersonating a Congressman shall be guilty and suffer certain pins and penalties, and this man Lamar offered himself as Mitchell Palmer, Congressman from the State of Pennsylvania? Was it not held in the Lamar case that a Member of Congress is "an officer acting under the authority of the United States"?

Mr. Gwynne of Iowa: The gentleman is right as far as he goes. The sole question there was, Was a Member of Congress an officer within the meaning of Congress in a certain penal statute? That was the question. The Court said the Congress intended to include a Member of Congress as an officer within the meaning of that particular statute.

The Chairman: The time of the gentleman from Iowa has expired.

Mr. Michener: Mr. Chairman, I yield five additional minutes to the gentleman from Iowa.

Mr. Graham: Mr. Chairman, will the gentleman yield?

Mr. Gwynne of Iowa: I yield to the gentleman from Pennsylvania.

Mr. Graham: We all know that the only way to get rid of a Member of Congress is to expel him.

Mr. Gwynne of Iowa: That is right.

Mr. Graham: If this becomes a law, and the Speaker is eligible, and we expel him, where does the impeachment proceeding come in?

Mr. Gwynne of Iowa: That is what I am wondering myself.

This is what the Supreme Court said in the Lamar case. This is an exact quotation:

> The issue here is not a constitutional one, but who is an officer acting under the authority of the United States within the provisions of the section of the Penal Code under consideration.

That is all they were deciding, and the opinion so states.

The history of this thing is not reassuring for this type of legislation. Let me just sketch it to you briefly:

In the First Congress the matter of succession was considered. It is true there were people in that Congress who had been in the Constitutional Convention. Just the same, Marbury against Madison held unconstitutional one important bill passed by that Congress. There was a substantial group who favored the succession law we now have, in that first Congress. There was a feud between Alexander Hamilton and Thomas Jefferson. Jefferson was Secretary of State and Hamilton under no circumstances wanted him to be President. Hamilton has admitted it, and in previous debates on this bill his letter has been set out in the Record of the Congress. That First Congress did adopt a law which put the succession first in the President pro tempore of the Senate. Then, we had the Andrew Johnson impeachment proceedings. There, mind you, was the President pro tempore, the heir apparent, sitting in on that trial and voting to impeach Andrew Johnson. That demonstrated to many people the necessity for changing the succession law.

In 1886, the House Committee on the Judiciary and the Senate Committee on the Judiciary spent many days considering the matter and then wrote the present law which we now intend to change to go back to the law that they discarded.

This legislation opens up many intriguing possibilities. I think the people are entitled to have their Representatives give them some consideration. Suppose in the future there should be a feud between the Congress and the President. It could happen. It has happened—notably in the Johnson administration. Might not the Congress through the process of impeachment be able to get its representatives in the White House. That is exactly what they almost did in the Andrew Johnson impeachment case. They would have done it, except for the courage of a few Senators, including one Senator from my State.

Mr. Chairman, the possibility of this law being used under the present situation is less than a thousand-to-one shot. The next inauguration of an elected President and Vice President is less than 18 months away. Do you not think the people are entitled to have us consider this entire subject and really write a bill which would cover all these contingencies which might arise to plague us later?

I yield to the gentleman from Pennsylvania.

Mr. Walter: The thing that disturbs me about this bill is the question of fact raised by the word "inability" which appears throughout the bill. Who will pass on the question of fact as to the ability of a President to serve?

Mr. Gwynne of Iowa: I find nothing here. There is nothing in the present law either. That is something that we must study. I understand that in the administration of Woodrow Wilson consideration was given in some quarters to the necessity of someone taking over the office of the President. If we should have a situation of that character, who would determine the question of inability? Obviously, the Constitution left that to be settled by the Congress and left it to the Congress to set up some machinery to determine that question.

Mr. Cellar: Mr. Chairman, will the gentleman yield?

Mr. Gwynne of Iowa: I yield.

Mr. Celler: I think the gentleman might well know if he would make a check of it that there are a number of bills now before the Judiciary Committee of the House and the Judiciary Committee of the Senate which cover that very situation which provide for a joint committee of both Houses to investigate thoroughly the very matter as to what is or is not inability or disability of the President and what shall be done under such circumstances. But we felt it would be better not to clutter up this bill with a question of that sort which is very controversial. As I said in my main statement, it is considered by some constitutional lawyers that the Congress has no authority to determine what constitutes disability of the President and that that can only be done by a constitutional amendment.

Mr. Gwynne of Iowa: This matter is full of questions, and that is the reason I suggest setting up a commission of some sort to go into it thoroughly and make a job of it.

The cases to which I previously referred are: *United States* v. *Germaine* (99 U.S. 308); *United States* v. *Monat* (124 U.S. 307); *United States* v. *Smith* (124 U.S. 525).

Mr. Celler: Mr. Chairman, I yield 5 minutes to the gentleman from Texas [Mr. Gossett].

Mr. Gossett: Mr. Chairman, I agree that this bill is not a perfect solution and does not satisfy all the questions in the minds of all the Members. It is certainly an improvement over the existing situation. Since the President has several times asked for this legislation, I think it is timely that we act upon it. Of course, I am supporting the bill.

I do agree with my distinguished colleague who just left the well of the House that there are other issues even more important—issues akin to the matter of Presidential succession. I think we ought to get around to deciding this question of when a President is unable to serve in the office of the Presidency. There ought to be some clear legal way of making such determination.

Mr. Kefauver: Mr. Chairman, will the gentleman yield?

Mr. Gossett: I yield.

Mr. Kefauver: I might call the gentleman's attention to the fact that the Rules Committee has before it House Concurrent Resolution 18, a resolution on this side which I filed some time back. There is also a similar resolution on the Senate side to appoint a special joint committee, composed of the members of the Judiciary Committees of the Senate and the House, to go into this entire problem. There are some 8 or 10 questions that should be determined as to when "inability" begins and when it ends. I think the Congress could do a great service to the Nation to have this committee consider those problems. But I cannot see why that matter should delay the passage of this present legislation. In fact, we have always had this uncertain matter of "inability," and this bill does not make it more uncertain.

Mr. Gossett: I thank the gentleman. . . .

Mr. Robsion: Mr. Chairman, will the gentleman yield?

Mr. Gossett: I yield to the distinguished gentleman from Kentucky.

Mr. Robsion: First I think there is some misapprehension. The gentleman is a very able member of our subcommittee. I feel there is some misapprehension here that we devoted only 15 minutes to this bill.

Mr. Gossett: Oh, we devoted several days to hearings on this bill.

Mr. Robsion: Yes; and then we read the Senate bill line by line and word for word in both subcommittee and the full committee, did we not?

Mr. Gossett: That is quite true.

. . . **Mr. Celler:** Mr. Chairman, I wish to direct attention to the proposition emphasized by the gentleman from Iowa [Mr. Gwynne] and call attention to the fact that for 84 years, from 1792 to 1886 the line of succession was first to the President pro tempore, then to the Speaker of the House. During all those years there were eminent constitutional lawyers in both Houses of Congress, and many of the Presidents who held tenure during that time were themselves eminent constitutional lawyers. They never inveighed against the idea that there should be a succession first to the President pro tempore and then to the Speaker. Eminent men in not only the executive branch but also the legislative branch in those years held that President pro tempore of the Senate and the Speaker of the House were civil officers of the United States under the Constitution. It is well to read briefly from the letter sent to the chairman of the Judiciary Committee by the Attorney General.

I read one paragraph:

> The question at issue, however, is not whether a Member of Congress as such, is a "civil officer" within the meaning of article II, section 4. The issue is whether the Speaker of the House and the President pro tempore who, though they are Members of Congress, are chosen for those offices by their respective Houses and not by vote of their constituencies, are "officers" within the meaning of article II, section 1. On this question, the Blount decision is of doubtful authority. The term is used in article II, section 1, without qualification and presumably includes not only officers of the executive branch of the Government, but also officers of the judicial and legislative branches."

The Chairman: The time of the gentleman from New York has expired.

Mr. Michener: Mr. Chairman, I yield myself 3 minutes.

Mr. Chairman, our very good friend and capable lawyer the gentleman from Iowa [Mr. Gwynne] severely criticized the Judiciary Committee because he said it took only 15 minutes to consider this Presidential succession matter. As just stated by the gentleman from Texas [Mr. Gossett] a member of the subcommittee, days were taken by the subcommittee in the hearings and consideration of this problem. Then the bill was reported to the full committee. There was not a lot of time taken in the full committee because the committee had the matter up in the last Congress, reported substantially the same bill favorably, and the House after debate passed it overwhelmingly. All of the members of the Judiciary Committee, excepting the gentleman from Iowa, may be wrong. Again the gentleman from Iowa may be wrong. He stands alone in the committee in his opposition to this bill.

The gentleman from Iowa also called attention to 8 days' debate in the Senate when the law of 1886 was enacted. There was a lot of debate at that time, but I wonder if he has read all that debate. I quote from the hearings— there were hearings before the subcommittee—the testimony of our colleague from Tennessee [Mr. Kefauver], who testified as follows:

I think it would be interesting to consider briefly the succession law of 1886. The original succession law stayed on the books from 1792 to 1886.

That is practically the law we are attempting to reenact here. The Speaker, however, in this bill outranks the President pro tempore. Continuing the quotation:

At that time Cleveland was President and Vice President Hendricks had just died. The President pro tempore of the Senate was a Republican, and in the event of the death of President Cleveland he would have succeeded to the Presidency.

Thank God we are not having any 8 days of political debate here. We are giving nonpolitical consideration. We have a President who is a Democrat. We have a Republican majority and a Republican Speaker in the House. In the Seventy-ninth Congress we had a Democratic majority and a Democratic Speaker. That Congress passed this bill and this Congress is going to pass this bill today. This bill is not a cure-all, but will be an improvement.

I respect the views of our friend from Iowa. I do feel, however, that his legal deductions in this case are not well founded.

Mr. Chairman, I now yield 5 minutes to the gentleman from Indiana [Mr. Springer], a member of the Judiciary Committee.

Mr. Springer: Mr. Chairman, the succession bill which is now before the committee was considered by the House a little more than 2 years ago, or approximately at that time. Most of us recall the debate that occurred on that measure. We passed the bill in the House by a tremendous majority. It then went to the other body and when it arrived in the other body the bill was never acted upon; consequently there was not legislation which resulted from that effort on our part. However, we have the bill which is presented here this morning, and we have the additional bills which have been introduced which were mentioned by the gentleman from Tennessee [Mr. Kefauver], and the gentleman from New York [Mr. Celler].

Referring to this particular bill, I desire to call to your attention the expression of the President of the United States with reference to the passage of this particular legislation. This is what the President stated upon this particular question:

In the message of June 19, 1945, I recommended that the Congress enact legislation placing the Speaker of the House of Representatives first in order of succession, and if there were no Speaker, or if he failed to qualify, that the President pro tempore of the Senate should act until a duly qualified Speaker was elected.

That is the positive and the distinct expression of the President of the United States, and that is his expression contained in the message which he delivered to the House of Representatives. He again affirmed that same position when he delivered his message before the Eightieth Congress.

In addition to that, I also desire to call to your attention statements made by the Attorney General of the United States with reference to this particular matter and with reference to the constitutionality, if you please, of this particular legislation. I wish to quote from the concluding paragraph of the letter from the Attorney General of the United States, in which he states:

> In conclusion, I wish to state that I am convinced of the need for a revision of the law relating to Presidential succession and, of the measures herein discussed, have a definite preference for H.R. 2524 and H.R. 2749, which are similar in all major respects and are more nearly in harmony with the recommendations of the President. Accordingly I recommend favorable consideration of the proposal contained in the two measures last-mentioned.

Before I conclude I desire to call to the Members' attention a statement which was made by my very warm and distinguished friend, the gentleman from Iowa [Mr. Gwynne], when he questioned the constitutionality of this particular legislation by reason of the fact that the Constitution refers to the word "officer." In the case of *Lamar* v. *United States,* reported in the Two Hundred and Forty-first United States Reports, reading from page 113, I think that question is entirely set at rest, and I want to read into the Record the language of that decision which I think is conclusive on this question. I now read from page 112, to get the proper connection:

Guided by these rules, when the relations of Members of the House of Representatives to the Government of the United States are borne in mind and the nature and character of their duties and responsibilities are considered, we are clearly of the opinion that such Members are embraced by the comprehensive terms of the statute.

In other words they are officers within the provisions of the terms of the Constitution.

The Chairman: The time of the gentleman from Indiana has expired.

Mr. Michener: Mr. Chairman, I yield the gentleman five additional minutes.

Mr. Springer: The opinion of the Court proceeds:

> If, however, considered from the face of the statute alone the question was susceptible of obscurity or doubt— which we think is not the case—all ground for doubt would be removed by the following considerations:

Listen to this language of the Supreme Court:

> Because prior to and at the time of the original enactment in question the common understanding that a Member of the House of Representatives was a legislative officer of the United States was clearly expressed in the ordinary, as well as legal, dictionaries.

Then the Court proceeds to another section:

> Because at or before the same period in the Senate of the United States after considering the ruling in the Blount case—

And may I digress for a moment and say that the Blount case has been mentioned heretofore in this debate—

> it was concluded that a Member of Congress was a civil officer of the United States within the purview of the law requiring the taking of an oath of office.

Then the Court proceeds with its decision:

> (c) Because also in various general statutes of the United States at the

time of the enactment in question a Member of Congress was assumed to be a civil officer of the United States.

Then the Court cites the Revised Statutes:

(d) Because that conclusion is the necessary result of prior decisions of this Court and harmonizes with the settled conception of the position of members of State legislative bodies as expressed in many State decisions.

Thereafter the Court cites a large number of decisions which bear directly on this question. So, under the decision in the Lamar case, excerpts from which I have just read, there is no question of doubt in my mind, as there was no question of doubt in the minds of the Justices of the Supreme Court of the United States, that the Speaker of the House and the President pro tempore of the Senate are civil officers within the meaning and the purview of the Constitution of the United States.

Since this legislation has been before this body I have given some thought to the question as to why the President concluded in his statement that the Speaker of the House of Representatives should take precedence over the President pro tempore of the Senate. In my humble opinion, he reached that conclusion knowing that the Speaker of the House of Representatives is elected from the Members of this body, who are elected by the people every 2 years. He is very close to the people. The President pro tempore of the Senate is elected every 6 years, and is consequently not as close to the people as the Speaker of the House of Representatives. Consequently, in my opinion, and I think in the opinion of every Member of this body, he concluded that the Speaker of the House of Representatives, being closer to the people and being more representative of the will and the wish of the people, is the person who should succeed first and should have priority over the President pro tempore of the Senate.

Mr. Edwin Arthur Hall: Mr. Chairman, will the gentleman yield?

Mr. Springer: I yield to the gentleman from New York.

Mr. Edwin Arthur Hall: The point was made a little earlier in the debate that in the event the Speaker of the House should be in line to succeed to the Presidency there might be a danger that a little group of power-seeking men within the House of Representatives might impeach the President and force the Speaker of the House into the Presidency as the result of that action. What does the gentleman feel about that?

Mr. Springer: I do not think there is any danger of that in the remotest degree. Such a plan would be entirely impossible of completion. It would be necessary to impeach in the legal method, and any such conspiracy would certainly be detected and fail entirely.

As the gentleman knows, under the existing law the Cabinet officers in the order in which they were selected have priority, and the President appoints every Cabinet officer. Under the present law of succession, it merely means that the President would be selecting his own successor in office as President of the United States. Also, the Secretary of State, Secretary of the Treasury, Secretary of War, Attorney General, Postmaster General, Secretary of the Navy, Secretary of the Interior, Secretary of Agriculture, Secretary of Commerce, and Secretary of Labor are appointive offices; they have not been elected by the people. We here seek to make the succession of those who might assume this high office to come close to and direct from the people of this Nation. It is my hope this proposed legislation will be passed without dissenting votes.

The Chairman: The time of the gentleman from Indiana has again expired.

Mr. Michener: Mr. Chairman, I yield five minutes to the gentleman from New York [Mr. Keating].

Mr. Keating: Mr. Chairman, this bill, which has already received favorable action in the other body, unanimous approval of the House Committee on the Judiciary, and enthusiastic endorsement by the President, deserves speedy enactment by what I hope will prove to be an overwhelming vote.

Always when the country finds itself without a Vice President this subject of Presidential succession is urgently discussed. Seven Presidents have died in office. Each time speculation and discussion have ensued regarding a successor to the Vice President, who assumes the duties of President.

Article II, section 1, paragraph 5, of the Constitution provides as follows:

> In case of the removal of the President from office, or of his death, resignation, or inability to discharge the powers and duties of the said office, the same shall devolve on the Vice President, and the Congress may by law provide for the ease of removal, death, resignation, or inability, both of the President and Vice President, declaring what officer shall then act as President, and such officer shall act accordingly, until the disability be removed, or a President shall be elected.

The act of 1792 enacted in the Second Congress provided that the President pro tempore of the Senate should follow the Vice President in line of succession and after him the Speaker of the House. There was some discussion at that time about making members of the Cabinet eligible following the Speaker, but personalities, we are told, entered into the picture to block the suggestion. Thomas Jefferson was then Secretary of State and the violent opposition of Alexander Hamilton to him and his policies thwarted action to place Cabinet members in the line of succession.

Following the death of President Taylor in 1850, extensive hearings on this subject were held, as a result of which the House Committee on the Judiciary approved a bill, adding the Chief Justice and Justices of the Supreme Court after the Speaker in the line of succession. This bill, however, was not acted upon before a new Presidential election took place, after which the acute emergency passed, and the subject again was dropped.

It was not until the death of President Garfield that the matter was again brought up in 1886 when a radical change was made, eliminating the President pro tempore of the Senate and the Speaker, and substituting the Secretary of State, Secretary of the Treasury, and other Cabinet members in the rank which then prevailed. It is interesting to read the debates of that period, which preceded this decision and which shed light on the reasons prompting the departure from the line of succession which had prevailed for nearly a century. The principal argument, and one which, under the laws that then existed, had almost unanswerable logic behind it, was that there was a substantial period of time when there would be no one eligible to succeed. After adjournment *sine die* in those days there was no Speaker of the House nor President pro tempore of the Senate until those bodies reconvened in the succeeding Congress and elected their presiding officers. If a Vice President, who had assumed the office of President, should die or become disabled during this period, there would necessarily be no Chief Executive until the convening of the next Congress—a highly undesirable hiatus.

This has, of course, been eliminated completely by the adoption of the twentieth or so-called lame-duck amendment to the Constitution, under which the presiding officers of both legislative bodies hold over after adjournment and continue in office until the 3d day of January next succeeding when successors are chosen. This motivating cause of the change made in 1886, therefore, is now entirely without force.

The second chief argument made at that time against continuance of the President pro tempore of the Senate and the Speaker as eligibles to become acting President was that it would be undignified and potentially productive of disorder in the processes of government for the Chief Executive to be required to preside over a body where the administration of the executive branch might be the subject of criticism and attack. There was nothing in the 1792 law which relieved the presiding officer of his legislative duties upon assuming the office of the President. It is to be noted that in the first sentence of the measure now before us it is expressly provided that the Speaker shall not act as President until he has resigned as Speaker and as a representative in Congress.

Both of these arguments for the change in 1886 had at that time almost unassailable cogency, which is now, however, totally lacking.

The legislation before us prescribes the following line of succession:

First. The Speaker.
Second. The President pro tempore of the Senate.
  Third. Secretary of State.
  Fourth. Secretary of Treasury.
  Fifth. Secretary of War.
  Sixth. Attorney General.
  Seventh. Postmaster General.
  Eighth. Secretary of the Navy.
  Ninth. Secretary of the Interior.
  Tenth. Secretary of Agriculture.
  Eleventh. Secretary of Commerce.
  Twelfth. Secretary of Labor.

The last three are new because those offices have been created since 1886.

The Presidency of the United States is an elective office. Obviously, it is not practicable to elect a series of Vice Presidents who may succeed to that office. It should be filled, in the event the two elected officials are not able for any reason to serve their term, by one who as closely as possible might be said to be the choice of the people. The one man who most exactly fits that description is the Speaker of the House, chosen by the ballots of the people in his congressional district to represent them and in turn selected by a majority of the chosen representatives of all the people to preside over the deliberations of the legislative chamber. Since Representatives in Congress are chosen each 2 years, the Speaker may thus be said to represent the most recent expression of the people's choice.

Due to the rules of seniority which prevail, he will always be one who has served many years in the legislative halls, has a rich background of experience, has necessarily acquired an intimate familiarity with the administration of various departments and agencies of the executive branch of Government, enjoys the utmost respect and confidence of his colleagues, knows the science of politics in the best sense of the word, has become indoctrinated with a high sense of fairness through the demands and responsibilities of his office, and is thoroughly qualified to assume the high office of President of the United States. The country will, I am sure, pardon the pride of the Members of this House in citing as an outstanding illustration of one who fits this description, our distinguished colleague who now so ably presides over this body.

Following the Speaker in line, comes the President pro tempore of the Senate, who may have been elected at any time up to 6 years previously and who is the next closest approximation we can find to that fair cross section of an individual whom we might designate the people's choice. To a lesser degree than the Speaker, it is true, but to a greater degree than any other official of the Government he would fit such description. This was recognized in the action taken by the other body.

Another reason for placing these two elected officials before the members of the President's Cabinet is that such a procedure eliminates a natural American feeling of repugnancy to the idea of permitting the head of our Government to designate his successor. While that is not likely, it is entirely possible under the present method of succession. The prevailing sentiment of the American people, entirely apart from any consideration of the personalities involved and totally without regard to political considerations, favors the preferment of elective to appointive officials in eligibility for succession to the Presidency. This measure gives expression to that preference.

Mr. Michener: Mr. Chairman, I yield the remaining time on this side to the gentleman from Missouri [Mr. Reeves].

Mr. Reeves: Mr. Chairman, the constitutionality of S. 564 has been ably debated and, in my opinion, convincingly demonstrated. My remarks will be directed at the comment made a few minutes ago by our distinguished and respected colleague the gentleman from Iowa [Mr. Gwynne] to the effect that the need for this law is only a 1,000 to 1 chance. I am not able to agree with this viewpoint.

Seven Presidents of the United States have died in office. Six of these by an interesting coincidence have been elected President at 20-year intervals beginning with 1840. For example:

Harrison, elected in 1840, died in office on April 4, 1841.

Lincoln, elected to his first term in 1860, died in office on April 15, 1865.

Garfield, elected in 1880, died in office on September 19, 1881.

McKinley, elected to his second term in 1900, died in office on September 14, 1901.

Harding, elected, in 1920, died in office on August 2, 1923.

Roosevelt, elected to his third term in 1940, died in office on April 12, 1945.

This cycle is only a coincidence, of course, but it emphasizes that periodically the uncertainties of life and the burdens of his high office result in the death of a President of the United States. Undeniably, the heavy responsibilities of the Presidency tend to impair the health and life expectancy of any occupant of the office. The first 15 Presidents were inaugurated at an average of fifty-four and a half, and they lived an average of 11 years after leaving office. The next 14 Presidents, ending with Calvin Coolidge, were inaugurated at an average age of 49 years—5 1/2 years less than the first 15—and they lived an average of only 6 years, or slightly less, after leaving the White House.

Seven Vice Presidents have died in office: George Clinton—Jefferson—in 1812; Elbridge Gerry—Madison—in 1814; William R. King—Pierce—in 1853; Henry Wilson—Grant—in 1875; Thomas A. Hendricks—Cleveland—in 1885; Garret A. Hobart—McKinley's first term—in 1899; and James S. Sherman—Taft—in 1912.

In the 40 Presidential terms which have occurred during the constitutional history of the United States, therefore, there have been 13 terms in which the office of Vice President has been vacant for part of the term. In other words, during approximately one-third of the Presidential terms the office of Vice President has at some time been vacant, with a substantial chance that a vacancy occurring in the office of President would leave the Nation without either a President or a Vice President who had been elected by the people. It is this very real contingency which the present bill has been designed to meet.

So far as the question of policy is concerned, I am altogether in accord with the view that elected representatives of the people—rather than Cabinet members who are appointed by the President—should head the list of succession to the Presidency. For all the reasons already thoroughly discussed it seems particularly appropriate that the Speaker of the House and the President pro tempore of the Senate, in that order, should follow the Vice President in line of succession. S. 564 accomplishes that purpose, and I urge its enactment by the House.

This has become an age of uncertainty, with myriad new and destructive hazards to our national and personal security. We cannot provide against every conceivable contingency to which reference has been made, but we can assure through this bill that in the event of vacancies in the office of President and the office of Vice President the chief executive officer of the United States will be an elected representative of the people.

The Chairman: The time of the gentleman from Missouri [Mr. Reeves] has expired.

The Clerk will read.

The Clerk read as follows:

Be it enacted etc., That (a) (1), if, by reason of death, resignation, removal from office, inability, or failure to qualify, there is neither a President nor Vice President to discharge the powers and duties of the office of President, then the Speaker of the House of Representatives shall, upon his resignation as Speaker and as Representative in Congress, act as President. (2) The same rule shall apply in the case of the death, resignation, removal from office, or inability of an individual acting as President under this subsection.

(b) If, at the time when under subsection (a) a Speaker is to begin the discharge of the powers and duties of the office of President, there is no Speaker, or the Speaker fails to qualify as Acting President, then the President pro tempore of the Senate shall, upon his resignation as President pro tempore and as Senator, act as President.

(c) An individual acting as President under subsection (a) or subsection (b) shall continue to act until the expiration of the then current Presidential term, except that—

(1) if his discharge of the powers and duties of the office is founded in whole or in part on the failure of both the President-elect and the Vice-President-elect to qualify, then he shall act only until a President or Vice President qualifies; and

(2) if his discharge of the powers and duties of the office is founded in whole or in part on the inability of the President or Vice President, then he shall act only until the removal of the disability of one of such individuals.

(d) (1) If, by reason of death, resignation, removal from office, inability, or failure to qualify, there is no President pro tempore to act as President under subsection (b), then the officer of the United States who is highest on the following list, and who is not under disability to discharge the powers and duties of the office of President shall act as President: Secretary of State, Secretary of the Treasury, Secretary of War, Attorney General, Postmaster General, Secretary of the Navy, Secretary of the Interior, Secretary of Agriculture, Secretary of Commerce, Secretary of Labor.

(2) An individual acting as President under this subsection shall continue so to do until the expiration of the then current Presidential term, but not after a qualified and prior-entitled individual is able to act, except that the removal of the disability of an individual higher on the list contained in paragraph (1) or the ability to qualify on the part of an individual higher on such list shall not terminate his service.

(3) The taking of the oath of office by an individual specified in the list in paragraph (1) shall be held to constitute his resignation from the office by virtue of the holding of which he qualifies to act as President.

(c) Subsections (a), (b), and (d) shall apply only to such officers as are eligible to the office of President under the Constitution. Subsection (d) shall apply only to officers appointed, by and with the advice and consent of the Senate, prior to the time of the death, resignation, removal from office, inability, or failure to qualify, of the President pro tempore, and only to officers not under impeachment by the House of Representatives at the time the powers and duties of the office of President devolve upon them.

(f) During the period that any individual acts as president under this act, his compensation shall be at the rate then provided by law in the case of the President.

(g) Sections 1 and 2 of the act entitled "An act to provide for the performance of the duties of the office of President in case of the removal, death, resignation, or inability both of the President and Vice President," approved January 19, 1886 (24 Stat. 1: U.S.C., 1940 ed., title 3, secs. 21 and 22), are repealed.

Mr. Mathews: Mr. Chairman, I move to strike out the last word.

Mr. Chairman, I simply take this time to ask the members of the committee a question. I was not here during the entire debate and so perhaps it has been answered.

I call the attention of the committee to the first section on the first page of the bill, which includes the words "or failure to qualify." And I ask, Where is the constitutional authority for Congress to provide for succession to the Presidency or the Vice Presidency where there is merely a failure to qualify?

Mr. Michener: Will the gentleman yield?

Mr. Mathews: I yield.

Mr. Michener: The twentieth amendment, I think, takes care of that.

Mr. Mathews: Does it take care of the point fully to the satisfaction of the chairman of the committee?

Mr. Michener: It does.

Mr. Kefauver: Section 3 of the twentieth amendment expressly gives the Congress the right to name someone to act as President in the event the President and Vice-President-elect fail to qualify.

Mr. Mathews: If the committee is satisfied, I am satisfied.

Mr. Michener: We are satisfied with the bill.

Mr. Celler: Will the gentleman yield?

Mr. Mathews: Certainly I yield.

Mr. Celler: I think there is an additional reason for that. It is found in article II, section 1, clause 6, which speaks of the inability of the President or Vice President to discharge his duties. If he does not qualify he is not able to discharge his duties.

Mr. Mathews: No, that would not necessarily be sufficient to justify the authority of Congress to put in this act words which were not in the Constitu-

tion. Even if the gentleman's own opinion is that "inability" means "failure to qualify," nevertheless the same words should be used in the act as used in the Constitution. Then they may or may not be so interpreted by the courts. I do not at the moment recall the exact wording of the twentieth amendment. Exactness is essential in this type of important legislation. However, the answer which the chairman of the committee has given satisfies me that it would be within the prerogative of Congress to fix the succession in case of failure to qualify.

The Chairman: The time of the gentleman from New Jersey has expired.

Mr. Gary: Mr. Chairman, on April 29, 1947, I introduced a joint resolution proposing an amendment to the Constitution of the United States which provides that in the case of a vacancy in the office of Vice President the Senate and the House of Representatives shall, meeting jointly and by a majority vote, fill the vacancy from among those persons constitutionally eligible for the office of President. If the Congress is not in session at the time the vacancy occurs, the President is required to issue a proclamation convening the Congress.

The proposed amendment is not in conflict with the bill which is now under consideration by the House, but it will do away with the necessity of following the succession statute, except when vacancies occur simultaneously in the office of President and Vice President.

Under my proposal, whenever there is a vacancy in the office of President, the Vice President would immediately be elevated to the Presidency. The Senate and the House would then hold a joint session and by a majority vote elect a Vice President. They would not be limited in their selection to a Member of the Congress, but could elect anyone eligible for the office of President. It is to be assumed that in discharging this responsibility the Members of the House and the Senate would consider not only a person's fitness for the office of Vice President, but would also consider his qualifications for the Presidency in the event of his elevation to that high office.

I shall vote for the pending measure. I trust, however, that, notwithstanding its enactment, the Committee on the Judiciary will give serious consideration to the joint resolution which I have introduced.

Mr. Michener: Mr. Chairman, I move that the Committee do now rise and report the bill back to the House with the recommendation that the bill do pass.

The motion was agreed to.

Accordingly the Committee rose; and Mr. Halleck having assumed the Chair as Speaker pro tempore, Mr. Wolverton, Chairman of the Committee of the Whole House on the State of the Union, reported that that Committee, having had under consideration the bill (S. 564) to provide for the performance of the duties of the office of the President in case of the removal, resignation, death, or inability both of the President and Vice President, had directed him to report the same back to the House with the recommendation that the bill do pass.

Mr. Michener: Mr. Speaker, I move the previous question on the bill to final passage.

The previous question was ordered.

The bill was ordered to be read a third time and was read the third time.

The Speaker pro tempore: The question is on the passage of the bill.

Mr. Arends: Mr. Speaker, on that I ask for the yeas and nays.

The yeas and nays were ordered.

The question was taken, and there were—yeas 365, nays 11, not voting 54, as follows:

[Roll No. 106]

YEAS—365

Albert	Allen, Ill.	Almond
Allen, Calif.	Allen, La.	Anderson, Calif.

Andresen, H. Carl	Cooley	Gore
Andreson, August H.	Cooper	Gossett
	Corbett	Graham
Andrews, Ala.	Cotton	Granger
Andrews, N.Y.	Cox	Grant, Ala.
Angell	Cravens	Grant, Ind.
Arends	Crawford	Gregory
Arnold	Crosser	Griffiths
Auchincloss	Crow	Gross
Bakewell	Cunningham	Gwinn, N.Y.
Banta	Curtis	Hagen
Bates, Ky.	D'Ewart	Hale
Bates, Mass.	Dague	Hall, Edwin Arthur
Battle	Davis, Ga.	Hall, Leonard W.
Beall	Davis, Wis.	
Beckworth	Dawson, Ill.	Halleck
Bell	Dawson, Utah	Hand
Bender	Deane	Harden
Bennett, Mo.	Delaney	Hardy
Bishop	Demengeaux	Harless, Ariz.
Blackney	Dendero	Harness, Ind.
Boggs, Del.	Devitt	Harris
Boggs, La.	Dingell	Hart
Bonner	Dirksen	Havenner
Bradley	Dolliver	Hays
Bramblett	Donohue	Hebert
Brehm	Doughton	Hedrick
Brooks	Douglas	Heffernan
Brophy	Drewry	Hendricks
Brown, Ga.	Durham	Herter
Brown, Ohio	Eaton	Heselton
Bryson	Eberharter	Hess
Buchanan	Elliott	Hill
Buck	Ellis	Hinshaw
Buffett	Elsaesser	Hobbs
Burke	Elston	Hoeven
Burleson	Engle, Calif.	Hoffman
Busbey	Evins	Holifield
Butler	Fallon	Holmes
Byrne, N.Y.	Feighan	Hope
Byrnes, Wis.	Fellows	Horan
Canfield	Fenton	Howell
Cannon	Fisher	Huber
Carson	Flannagan	Hull
Case, N.J.	Fletcher	Jackson, Calif.
Case, S.Dak.	Fogarty	Jackson, Wash.
Celler	Folger	Jarman
Chadwick	Foote	Javits
Chapman	Forand	Jenison
Chelf	Fulton	Jenkins, Ohio
Chenoweth	Gallagher	Jennings
Chiperfield	Gamble	Jensen
Church	Gary	Johnson, Calif.
Clason	Gathings	Johnson, Ill.
Clevenger	Gavin	Johnson, Ind.
Clippinger	Gearhart	Johnson, Tex.
Coffin	Gillette	Jones, Ala.
Cole, Kans.	Gillie	Jones, Ohio
Colmer	Goff	Jones, Wash.
Combs	Goodwin	Jonkman
	Gordon	

Judd
Kean
Kearney
Kearns
Keating
Keefe
Kefauver
Kerr
Kilburn
Kilday
King
Kirwan
Klein
Knutson
Kunkel
Landis
Lane
Lanham
Larcade
Latham
Lea
LeCompte
LeFevre
Lemke
Lesinski
Lewis
Lodge
Love
Lucas
Lusk
Lyle
Lynch
Mack
MacKinnon
Madden
Maloney
Manasco
Mansfield,
  Mont.
Marcantonio
Martin, Iowa
Mason
Mathews
McConnell
McCormack
McCowen
McDonough
McDowell
McGarvey
McGregor
McMahon
McMillen, Ill.
Meade, Ky.
Meade, Md.
Merrow
Meyer
Michener
Miller, Calif.
Miller, Conn.

Miller, Md.
Miller, Nebr.
Mills
Mitchell
Morgan
Morton
Muhlenberg
Mundt
Murdock
Murray, Tenn.
Murray, Wis.
Nixon
Nodar
Norrell
Norton
O'Brien
O'Hara
O'Konski
Owens
Pace
Passman
Patman
Patterson
Peterson
Philbin
Phillips, Tenn.
Phillips, Calif.
Pickett
Ploeser
Plumley
Poage
Potts
Poulson
Preston
Price, Fla.
Price, Ill.
Priest
Rabin
Rains
Ramey
Rayburn
Rayfeld
Redden
Reed, Ill.
Reed, N.Y.
Rees
Reeves
Richards
Riehlman
Riley
Rivers
Rizley
Robertson
Robsion
Rockwell
Rogers, Mass.
Rohrbough
Rooney
Ross

Russell
Sabath
Sadlak
Sadowski
Sanborn
Sandstrom
Sarbacher
Sasscer
Schwabe, Mo.
Schwabe, Okla.
Scoblick
Scott, Hardie
Scott,
  Hugh D., Jr.
Scrivner
Seely-Brown
Shafer
Sheppard
Short
Simpson, Pa.
Smathers
Smith, Kans.
Smith, Maine
Smith, Wis.
Snyder
Somers
Spence
Springer
St. George
Stefan
Stevenson
Stockman
Stratton
Taber
Talle
Taylor
Teague
Thomas, N.J.
Thomas, Tex.
Thomason
Tibbett
Tollefson
Towe
Trimble
Twyman
Van Zandt
Vorys
Vursell
Walter
Wardsworth
Weichel
Welch
West
Wheeler
Whittington
Wigglesworth
Williams
Wilson, Ind.
Wilson, Tex.

Wolcott
Wolverton

Woodruff
Worley

Zimmerman

NAYS—11

Abernethy
Bulwinkle
Camp
Gwynne, Iowa

Harrison
Mahon
O'Toole
Rankin

Stanley
Whitten
Winstead

NOT VOTING—54

Barrett
Bennett, Mich.
Bland
Blatnik
Bloom
Bolton
Boykin
Buckley
Carroll
Clark
Clements
Cole, Mo.
Cole, N.Y.
Coudert
Courtney
Davis, Tenn.
Dorn
Ellsworth

Engle, Mich.
Fernandez
Fuller
Gifford
Gorski
Hartley
Jenkins, Pa.
Johnson, Okla.
Jones, N.C.
Karsten, Mo.
Kee
Kelley
Kennedy
Keogh
Kersten, Wis.
Macy
Mansfield, Tex.
McMillan, S.C.

Monroney
Morris
Morrison
Norblad
Peden
Pfeifer
Powell
Rich
Rogers, Fla.
Sikes
Simpson, Ill.
Smith, Ohio
Smith, Va.
Stigler
Vail
Vinson
Wood
Youngblood

So the bill was passed.

The Clerk announced the following pairs:

General pairs until further notice:

Mr. Macy with Mr. Carroll.
Mr. Rich with Mr. Blatnik.
Mrs. Bolton with Mr. Kennedy.
Mr. Cole of N.Y. with Mr. Dorn.
Mr. Simpson of Ill. with Mr. McMillan of S.C.
Mr. Vail with Mr. Keogh.
Mr. Cole of Mo. with Mr. Morris.
Mr. Bennett of Mi. with Mr. Kelley.
Mr. Youngblood with Mr. Gorski.
Mr. Gifford with Mr. Pfeifer.
Mr. Barrett with Mr. Clements.
Mr. Hartley with Mr. Davis of Tn.
Mr. Coudert with Mr. Fernandez.
Mr. Ellsworth with Mr. Vinson.
Mr. Fuller with Mr. Wood.
Mr. Jenkins of Pa. with Mr. Sikes.
Mr. Smith of Ohio with Mr. Monroney.
Mr. Engel of Mi. with Mr. Johnson of Ok.
Mr. Norblad with Mr. Buckley.

The result of the vote was announced as above recorded.

A motion to reconsider was laid on the table.

Henry A. Wallace Announces Candidacy for President (1947)

Third parties have appeared in various forms in American politics, including ideological parties, single-issue parties, and parties of economic protest. (See "Proceedings of the Anti-Masonic Convention," p. 143, and "William Jennings Bryan's 'Cross of Gold' Speech to the Democratic National Convention," p. 245.) The most politically successful third parties of this century, however, have been factional parties.

Factional parties arise from divisions within the Republican party or the Democratic party. Such parties usually are led by an established political leader, which means that although they tend to be one-election affairs, they have a serious effect on that one election. Former president Theodore Roosevelt's "Bull Moose" party in 1912, Sen. Robert M. La Follette's Progressive party in 1924, Gov. George C. Wallace's American Independent party in 1968, and Rep. John B. Anderson's National Unity Campaign in 1980 are examples of factional parties. (See " 'Bull Moose' Party Platform," p. 256, "New York Campaign Speech by George C. Wallace," p. 566, and "John B. Anderson Announces for President," p. 672.)

The election of 1948 was marked by the formation of two factional parties, both of which represented dissident Democrats. Southern "Dixiecrats," infuriated by the growing concern of President Harry S Truman and the national Democratic party for the civil rights of blacks, nominated Gov. J. Strom Thurmond of South Carolina and Gov. Fielding L. Wright of Mississippi as the candidates for president and vice president, respectively, of the newly formed States' Rights party. (See "Hubert H. Humphrey's Civil Rights Speech to the Democratic National Convention," p. 458.)

The other "third" party in 1948, which represented the left wing of the Democratic party, was headed by Henry A. Wallace. Wallace was the secretary of agriculture during Franklin D. Roosevelt's first two terms as president, the vice president during his third term, and, after being dropped from the ticket in favor of Truman in 1944, the secretary of commerce at the start of the fourth term. Reluctantly, Truman kept Wallace in the cabinet after he succeeded to the presidency in 1945. (See "Franklin D. Roosevelt's Vice Presidential Letters," p. 368.)

In September 1946, Wallace publicly attacked the Truman administration's foreign policies, especially the Truman Doctrine of U.S. resistance to Soviet expansion and the Marshall Plan to rebuild war-ravaged Europe. Truman promptly removed Wallace from office.

Encouraged by a diverse coalition of Communists, liberal farm and labor leaders, and disgruntled New Dealers, Wallace announced his independent

candidacy for president in a radio ad-
dress on December 29, 1947. "There is
no real fight between a Truman and a
Republican," Wallace declared. "Both
stand for a policy which opens the door
to war in our lifetime and makes war
certain for our children."

Initially, public opinion polls showed
that Wallace might draw as much as 6
or 7 percent of the popular vote from
the Democratic ticket, much of it in
states that Truman needed to carry to
win the election. But Wallace's politi-
cal stature declined sharply after the
July 1948 convention of the Progressive
party, which formally nominated him
for president and Sen. Glen ("The
Singing Cowboy") Taylor of Idaho for
vice president. The convention was
dominated by Communists and Com-
munist sympathizers, whom Wallace,
although not a Communist himself, re-
fused to repudiate.

On election day, Wallace won
enough popular votes to deny Truman
victory in New York, Maryland, and
Michigan. Yet, on balance, Wallace's
left-wing campaign, combined with
Thurmond's right-wing campaign, may
have helped Truman more than hurt
him. The extreme factional parties
made the president appear to be a
reasonable moderate in substance and
a fighting underdog in style.

The Wallace and Thurmond cam-
paigns illustrate an important quality
of third party politics in presidential
elections. Wallace's 1.2 million popular
votes, which were spread around the
country, earned him no electoral votes.
Thurmond's 1.2 million popular votes,
which were concentrated in the South,
carried four states with thirty-nine
electoral votes. Clearly the electoral
college fully rewards only those third
party candidates who have a strong
regional base.   ~

For the past fifteen months I have
traveled up and down, and back and

forth across this country. I have talked
with half a million people in public
meetings and with thousands in private
gatherings. I have been working for, and
I shall continue to work for, peace and
security.

Everywhere in the United States today, among farmers, workers, small
business men and professional men and
women, I find confusion, uncertainty
and fear. The people don't ask, "Will
there be another war?"—but "When
will the war come?"

Everywhere I find that people are
spending so much for food and rent that
they cannot afford their customary services from the doctor and dentist. They
don't ask, "Will there be another depression?" but "When will the real depression start?"

Peace and abundance mean so much
to me that I have said at a dozen press
conferences and in many speeches when
asked about a third party, "If the Democratic party continues to be a party of
war and depression, I will see to it that
the people have a chance to vote for
prosperity and peace."

To those who have come to me asking the conditions of my adherence to
the present Democratic Administration, I have said, "Let the Administration repudiate universal military training and rid itself of the Wall Street-
military team that is leading us toward
war."

I have insisted that the Democratic
Administration curb the ever-growing
power and profits of monopoly and take
concrete steps to preserve the living
standards of the American people. I
have demanded that the Democratic
Administration cease its attacks on the
civil liberties of Americans. In speeches
in the North and in the South at non-
segregated meetings I have stated the
simple truth that segregation and
discrimination of any kind or character
have no place in America.

My terms to the Democratic high
command have been well known.

By their actions and finally by their words, they have said: "Henry Wallace, we welcome your support but we will not change our policies."

In answering me, the Democratic leadership also gave its answer to millions of Americans who demand the right to vote for peace and prosperity. Thus, the leadership of the Democratic party would deprive the American people of their rightful opportunity to choose between progress and reaction in 1948.

So far as the Republican party is concerned, there is no hope—as George Norris, Fiorello LaGuardia and Wendell Willkie long ago found out.

When the old parties rot, the people have a right to be heard through a new party. They asserted that right when the Democratic party was founded under Jefferson in the struggle against the Federalist party of war and privilege of his time. They won it again when the Republican party was organized in Lincoln's day. The people must again have an opportunity to speak out with their votes in 1948.

The lukewarm liberals sitting on two chairs say, "Why throw away your vote?" I say a vote for the new party in 1948 will be the most valuable vote you have ever cast or ever will cast.

The bigger the peace vote in 1948, the more definitely the world will know that the United States is not behind the bipartisan reactionary war policy which is dividing the world into two armed camps and making inevitable the day when American soldiers will be lying in their Arctic suits in the Russian snow.

There is no real fight between a Truman and a Republican. Both stand for a policy which open the door to war in our lifetime and makes war certain for our children.

Stop saying, "I don't like it but I am going to vote for the lesser of two evils."

Rather than accept either evil, come out boldly, stand upright as men and women and say so loudly all the world can hear—

"We are voting peace and security for ourselves and our children's children. We are fighting for old-fashioned Americanism at the polls in 1948. We are fighting for freedom of speech and freedom of assembly. We are fighting to end racial discrimination. We are fighting for lower prices. We are fighting for free labor unions, for jobs, and for homes in which we can decently live."

We have just passed through the holiday season when every radio and every church proclaimed the joyous tidings of peace. Every year at this time the hearts of the American people swell with genuine good will toward all mankind. We are a kindly, well-meaning people.

But the holiday season soon passes and one of the first items on the agenda of the new Congress is universal military training. I say the first political objective of progressives is the defeat of this bill which would deliver our 18-year-olds over to the Army and cost the nation two billion dollars a year.

Universal military training is the first decisive step on the road toward fascism. We shall fight it to the limit and all Congressmen who vote for it.

The American people read that they are paying fantastic appropriations for military adventures in Greece, Turkey, China—and billions for armaments here at home. Slowly it dawns on us that these newspaper headlines have stepped into our every-day lives at the grocery store when we pay $1 for butter, 95 cents for eggs, and 90 cents for meat.

We suddenly realize that you can't have all the people of the world getting ready for the next war without paying for it in their daily lives with less food, clothing and housing. War preparations create record profits for big business but only false prosperity for the people—their purchasing power shrinks as prices rise, their needs go unfilled, and they are burdened with new debts.

Yes, corporation profits are over three times what they were in 1939, but every family is paying for our war policy at the grocery store.

A new party must stand for a positive peace program of abundance and security, not scarcity and war. We can prevent depression and war if we only organize for peace in the same comprehensive way we organize for war.

I personally was for the humanitarian aspects of the Marshall plan long before it was announced. Because I saw the post-war need of helping human beings, I was accused of wanting a quart of milk for every Hottentot.

I pushed for help for Greece against the opposition of the Administration eight months before the Truman doctrine was announced. But I have fought and shall continue to fight programs which give guns to people when they want plows.

I fight the Truman doctrine and the Marshall plan as applied because they divide Europe into two warring camps. Those whom we buy politically with our food will soon desert us. They will pay us in the base coin of temporary gratitude and then turn to hate us because our policies are destroying their freedom.

We are restoring western Europe and Germany through United States agencies rather than United Nations agencies because we want to hem Russia in. We are acting the same way as France and England after the last war and the end result will be the same—confusion, depression and war.

It just doesn't need to happen. The cost of organizing for peace, prosperity and progress is infinitely less than organizing for war.

We who believe this will be called "Russian tools" and "Communists." Let the fear mongers not distort and becloud the issues by name calling. We are not for Russia and we are not

for communism, but we recognize Hitlerite methods when we see them in our own land and we denounce the men who engage in such name calling as enemies of the human race who would rather have World War III than put forth a genuine effort to bring about a peaceful settlement of differences.

One thing I want to make clear to both Russia and the United States—peace requires real understanding between our peoples. Russia has as much to gain from peace as the United States, and just as we here fight against the spreaders of hate and falsehood against Russia, the Russian leaders can make a great contribution by restraining those extremists who try to widen the gap between our two great countries.

I insist that the United States be fully secure until there is a real peace between this country and Russia and until there is an international police force stronger than the military establishment of any nation, including Russia and the United States.

I am utterly against any kind of imperialism or expansionism, whether sponsored by Britain, Russia or the United States, and I call on Russia as well as the United States to look at all our differences objectively and free from that prejudice which the hate mongers have engendered on both sides.

What the world needs.is a United Nations disarmament conference to rid humanity for all time of the threat not only of atomic bombs but also of all other methods of mass destruction.

It happens that all of my mother's and three-fourths of my father's ancestors came to this country before the American Revolution. I love the Americanism I was taught to respect in the public schools of Iowa half a century ago.

That Americanism was betrayed after World War I by forces which found their origin in monopoly capitalism, yellow journalism and racial bigotry. Today there is a greater menace than ever before. We are losing friends, destroying basic liberties and making enemies at a time when the cost of failure is complete destruction.

That failure can be met and overcome only by a new political alignment in America which requires the organization of a new political party.

To that end I announce tonight that I shall run as an independent candidate for President of the United States in 1948.

Thousands of people all over the United States have asked me to engage in this great fight. The people are on the march. I hope that you who are listening to me tonight will lead the forces of peace, progress and prosperity in your communities and throughout our country. Will you let me know that you have come out fighting against the powers of evil?

We have assembled a Gideon's army—small in number, powerful in conviction, ready for action. We have said with Gideon, "Let those who are fearful and trembling depart." For every fearful one who leaves there will be a thousand to take his place. A just cause is worth a hundred armies.

We face the future unfettered by any principle but the principle of general welfare. We owe no allegiance to any group which does not serve that welfare. By God's grace, the people's peace will usher in the century of the common man.

Hubert H. Humphrey's Civil Rights Speech to the Democratic National Convention (1948)

The 1930s and 1940s were turbulent times in American race relations. During the Great Depression and World War II, vast numbers of African Americans migrated from the farms and the small towns of the South to the cities of the North, where they hoped to find better jobs and less discrimination. Many blacks changed their political allegiance. Stalwart members of the Republican party since the Civil War, most black voters shifted their support to the Democrats in gratitude for the New Deal economic policies of President Franklin D. Roosevelt. Gratitude was tempered by determination when, after the war, hundreds of thousands of young black veterans returned from fighting fascism abroad no longer willing to tolerate racism at home.

Roosevelt had avoided racial issues during his twelve years as president, knowing them to be politically explosive in a party that counted both blacks and white segregationists as mainstays of its electoral coalition. As the first president of the postwar era, Truman did not have that luxury. On February 2, 1948, acting on the recommendations of the President's Committee on Civil Rights, which he had appointed in 1946, Truman sent to Congress a special civil rights message that called for legislative and administrative changes in the areas of voting, employment, desegregation of the armed forces, and protection against lynching.

Truman's civil rights message provoked an angry reaction from white southerners. In May 1948, a group of southern political leaders agreed to meet in Birmingham, Alabama, after the July Democratic national convention to decide whether to form a third party. An increasing number of the president's advisers recommended that he proceed cautiously on civil rights. With Truman's approval, they eased White House pressures on Congress and instructed the Democratic convention's platform committee to draft a vague plank that endorsed civil rights in general but said nothing about specific remedies.

Liberals at the convention, displaying tactical shrewdness, decided to challenge Truman's civil rights plank with one that specifically endorsed Truman's civil rights policies. "We highly commend President Harry Truman for his courageous stand on the issue of civil rights," the liberal plank declared. "We call upon Congress to support our President in guaranteeing these basic and fundamental rights...."

On July 14, 1948, the third day of the convention, Mayor Hubert H. Humphrey of Minneapolis, a candidate for U.S. senator from Minnesota, rose to speak for the liberal proposal. He de-

livered perhaps the most passionate, politically effective speech at a party convention since William Jennings Bryan's "Cross of Gold" speech in 1896. (See p. 143.) "The time has come for the Democratic party to get out of the shadow of states' rights and walk forthrightly into the bright sunshine of human rights," Humphrey proclaimed. Caught up in the excitement of the moment, enough delegates broke ranks with the platform committee to pass the liberal civil rights plank narrowly.

Southern delegates felt angry and betrayed by the platform vote. Some walked out of the convention immediately; most stayed to vote against Truman's nomination for president. On July 17, southern segregationist leaders and their supporters gathered in Birmingham to write a virulently anti-civil rights platform and to nominate South Carolina governor J. Strom Thurmond as the presidential candidate of the newly formed States' Rights party (dubbed the "Dixiecrats"). (See "Henry A. Wallace Announces for President," p. 453.)

During the fall campaign, Truman walked the political tightrope on race adroitly. African American voters, attracted by the president's civil rights proposals and the Democratic platform's commitment to support them, voted overwhelmingly for Truman on election day. So did many southern whites, who were mollified by Truman's recent downplaying of civil rights in the fall campaign. The Dixiecrats had hoped to win all 127 southern electoral votes and throw the election into the House of Representatives. Instead, Truman carried the South by a margin of 78 electoral votes to Thurmond's 39 electoral votes.   ~

Mr. Chairman, fellow Democrats, fellow Americans:

I realize that in speaking in behalf of the minority report on civil rights as presented by Congressman Biemiller of Wisconsin, that I am dealing with a charged issue, with an issue which has been confused by emotionalism on all sides of the fence.

I realize that there are here today friends and colleagues of mine, many of them who feel just as deeply and keenly as I do about this issue, and who are yet in complete disagreement with me.

My respect and admiration for these men and their views was great when I came to this Convention. It is now far greater because of the sincerity, courtesy and forthrightness with which many of them have argued in our prolonged discussions in the Platform Committee.

Because of this very great respect, and because of my profound belief that we have a challenging task to do here, because good conscience, decent morality demands it, I feel I must rise at this time to support a report, the minority report, a report that spells out our democracy.

It is a report that the people of this country can and will understand and a report that they will enthusiastically acclaim on the greatest issue of civil rights.

Let me say this at the outset: That this proposal is made for no single religion. Our proposal is made for no single class, for no single racial or religious group in mind. All of the regions of this country, all of the states, have shared in our precious heritage of American freedom. All of the states, and all of the regions of the country have seen at least some of the infringements of that freedom.

All people, and get this; all people, white and black, all racial groups, have been the victims at times in the nation of vicious discrimination. The masterly statement of our keynote speaker, the distinguished United States Senator from Kentucky, Alben Barkley, made that plank with great force.

Speaking of the founder of our Party, Thomas Jefferson, he said this, and I quote from Alben Barkley: "He did not proclaim that all of the white or the black or the red or the yellow men are equal, that all Christian or Jewish men are equal, that all Protestant and Catholic men are equal, that all rich and poor men are equal, that all good and bad men are equal, but what he declared was that all men are equal, and the equality he proclaimed was the equality in the right to enjoy the blessings of free government in which they may participate, and to which they have given their support."

Now, these words of Senator Barkley are appropriate to this Convention, the most truly progressive political party in America. From the time of Thomas Jefferson, the time when the immortal American doctrine of individual rights, under just and fairly administered laws, the Democratic Party has tried hard to secure expanding freedoms for all citizens.

Oh, yes, I know, other political parties may have talked more about civil rights, but the Democratic Party has surely done more about civil rights. We have made great progress in every part of this country. We have made great progress in the South and we have made it in the West and in the North and in the East, but we must now focus the direction of that progress towards the realization of a full program of civil rights to all.

This convention must set out more specifically the direction in which our Party efforts are to go. We can be proud that we can be guided by the courageous trail-blazing of two great Democratic Presidents, and we can be proud of the fact that our great and beloved immortal leader, Franklin Roosevelt, gave us guidance, and we can be proud of the fact that Harry Truman has had the courage to give to the people of America the new emancipation proclamation.

It seems to me that the Democratic Party needs to make definite pledges of the kind suggested in the minority report, to maintain the trust and confidence placed in it by the people of all races and all sections of this country. Sure, we are here as Democrats, but, my good friends, we are here as Americans; we are here as the believers in the principles and the ideology of democracy, and I firmly believe that as men concerned with our country's future, we must specify in our platform the guarantees which we have mentioned in the minority report.

Yes, this is far more than a party matter. Every citizen in this country has a stake in the emergence of the United States as a leader in a free world. That world is being challenged by the world of slavery. For us to play our part effectively, we must be in a morally sound position.

We cannot use a double standard. There is no room for double standards in American politics. For measuring our own and other people's policies, our demands for democratic practices in other lands will be no more effective than the guarantee of those practices in our own country.

Friends, delegates, I do not believe that there can be any compromise on the guarantees of the civil rights which we have mentioned in the minority report. In spite of my desire for unanimous agreement on the entire platform, in spite of my desire to see everybody here in unanimous agreement, there are some matters which I think must be stated clearly and without qualification. There can be no hedging. The newspaper headlines are wrong.

There will be no hedging, and there will be no watering down, if you please, of the instruments and the principles of the civil rights program.

My friends, to those who say that we are rushing this issue of civil rights, I say to them, we are 172 years late.

To those who say that this civil rights program is an infringement on States' Rights, I say this, that the time has arrived in America for leadership and they are looking to America for precepts and example.

My good friends and my fellow Democrats, I ask you for a calm consideration of our historic opportunity. Let us not forget the evil patience and the blindness of the past. In these times of the world economic, political and spiritual, above all spiritual crisis, we cannot, and we must not, turn from the paths so plainly before us.

That path has already led us through many valleys of the shadow of death, and now is the time to recall those who were left on that path of American freedom. To all of us here, for the millions who have sent us, for the whole two billion members of the human family, our land is now more than ever before the last, best hope on earth. I know that we can, and I know that we shall, begin here the fuller and richer example of that, that promise of a land for all men truly free and equal, and each man uses his freedom and equality wisely and well.

My good friends, I ask my Party, and I ask the Democratic Party, to march down the high-road of progressive democracy. I ask this Convention to say in unmistakable terms that we proudly hail and we courageously support our President and leader, Harry Truman, in his great fight for civil rights in America.

Harry S Truman's Acceptance Speech to the Democratic National Convention (1948)

In political terms, 1948 dawned darkly for President Harry S Truman. The end of World War II in 1945 had brought high taxes, rising prices, labor strife, racial tensions, and "Cold War" with an erstwhile ally, the Soviet Union. In November 1946, campaigning on the slogan "Had enough?," the Republican party regained control of Congress for the first time in sixteen years. In October 1947, Truman's Committee on Civil Rights issued bold recommendations for racial justice that, if enacted, were certain to alienate the southern wing of the Democratic party and, if neglected, would surely provoke black and liberal resentment.

To complicate matters further, three days before the election year began, former vice president Henry A. Wallace, an anti-Cold War Democrat, announced his independent candidacy for president. Truman, whose unassuming, plainspoken style of leadership made him seem smaller than life compared with his confident, visionary predecessor, Franklin D. Roosevelt, began to sink rapidly in the polls. During the summer of 1948, the Republicans nominated and united behind their strongest presidential candidate, Gov. Thomas E. Dewey of New York; southern "Dixiecrats" marched out of the Democratic national convention to nominate Gov. J. Strom Thurmond of South Carolina for president. A Demo-

cratic defeat in the November election appeared certain. (See "Henry A. Wallace Announces for President," p. 453, and "Hubert H. Humphrey's Civil Rights Speech to the Democratic National Convention," p. 458.)

Truman's political prospects seemed little improved by November 1, 1948, the eve of the presidential election. The current issue of Life magazine carried Dewey's picture with the caption, "The next President of the United States." In a Newsweek magazine poll, fifty political reporters unanimously predicted both a Dewey victory (most of them by a landslide) and a solidly Republican Congress. Public opinion pollsters, such as George Gallup, Elmo Roper, and Archibald Crossley, had found Dewey to be so far ahead in their September and early October surveys that they reduced their interviewing, made dubious assumptions about the undecided vote and voter turnout, and lapsed into sloppy reporting procedures. On election night, November 2, the Chicago Daily Tribune even published an early edition of the next morning's paper with the headline, "DEWEY DEFEATS TRUMAN."

Yet it was Truman and his running-mate, Sen. Alben W. Barkley of Kentucky, not the Republican ticket of Dewey and Gov. Earl Warren of California, who were elected in 1948. What *is more, far from strengthening their majorities in the House of Representatives and the Senate, the Republicans lost control of Congress to the Democrats. Truman's margin of victory in the presidential election was decisive—49.5 percent to 45.1 percent in the popular vote and 303-189 in the electoral college.*

How did Truman win? More than anything else, he energized the Democratic majority that Roosevelt had forged in the 1930s by convincing most of its members that a Republican victory would place in jeopardy the economic and social gains that they had made during the New Deal. (See "The *Literary Digest* Poll," p. 348.) *On July 14, 1948, Truman opened his reelection campaign at the Democratic convention with the most aggressive acceptance speech of any presidential candidate in history. Pledging to call the Republican Eightieth Congress back into session, Truman subsequently blasted it as the "do-nothing Congress" when it met for two weeks in August and failed to enact any of his programs. From Labor Day until election day, while Dewey cautiously confined himself to issuing inoffensive platitudes, the president rode the rails on a 275-speech, cross-country, "whistle-stop" campaign that took as its theme the cries of his more enthusiastic listeners: "Give 'em hell, Harry!" Roosevelt's New Deal coalition responded to the president's appeal, and Truman was elected.* ～

I am sorry that the microphones are in the way, but I must leave them the way they are because I have got to be able to see what I am doing—as I am always able to see what I am doing.

I can't tell you how very much I appreciate the honor which you have just conferred upon me. I shall continue to try to deserve it.

I accept the nomination.

And I want to thank this convention for its unanimous nomination of my good friend and colleague, Senator Barkley of Kentucky. He is a great man, and a great public servant. Senator Barkley and I will win this election and make these Republicans like it—don't you forget that!

We will do it because they are wrong and we are right, and I will prove it to you in just a few minutes.

This convention met to express the will and reaffirm the beliefs of the Democratic Party. There have been differences of opinion, and that is the democratic way. Those differences have been settled by a majority vote, as they should be.

Now it is time for us to get together and beat the common enemy. And that is up to you.

We have been working together for victory in a great cause. Victory has become a habit of our party. It has been elected four times in succession, and I am convinced it will be elected a fifth time next November.

The reason is that the people know that the Democratic Party is the people's party, and the Republican Party is the party of special interest, and it always has been and always will be.

The record of the Democratic Party is written in the accomplishments of the last 16 years. I don't need to repeat them. They have been very ably placed before this convention by the keynote speaker, the candidate for Vice President, and by the permanent chairman.

Confidence and security have been brought to the people by the Democratic Party. Farm income has increased from less than $2½ billion in 1932 to more than $18 billion in 1946. Never in the world were the farmers of any republic or any kingdom or any other country as prosperous as the farmers of the United States; and if they don't do their duty by the Democratic Party, they are the most ungrateful people in the world!

Wages and salaries in this country have increased from 29 billion in 1933 to more than $128 billion in 1947. That's labor, and labor never had but one friend in politics, and that is the Democratic Party and Franklin D. Roosevelt.

And I say to labor what I have said to the farmers: they are the most ungrateful people in the world if they pass the Democratic Party by this year.

The total national income has increased from less than $40 billion in 1933 to $203 billion in 1947, the greatest in all the history of the world. These benefits have been spread to all the people, because it is the business of the Democratic Party to see that the people get a fair share of these things.

This last, worst 80th Congress provided just the opposite for the Republicans.

The record on foreign policy of the Democratic Party is that the United States has been turned away permanently from isolationism, and we have converted the greatest and best of the Republicans to our viewpoint on that subject.

The United States has to accept its full responsibility for leadership in international affairs. We have been the backers and the people who organized and started the United Nations, first started under that great Democratic President, Woodrow Wilson, as the League of Nations. The League was sabotaged by the Republicans in 1920. And we must see that the United Nations continues a strong and growing body, so we can have everlasting peace in the world.

We removed trade barriers in the world, which is the best asset we can have for peace. Those trade barriers must not be put back into operation again.

We have started the foreign aid program, which means the recovery of Europe and China, and the Far East. We instituted the program for Greece and Turkey, and I will say to you that all these things were done in a cooperative and bipartisan manner. The Foreign Relations Committees of the Senate and House were taken into the full confidence of the President in every one of these moves, and don't let anybody tell you anything else.

As I have said time and time again, foreign policy should be the policy of the whole Nation and not the policy of one party or the other. Partisanship should stop at the water's edge; and I shall continue to preach that through this whole campaign.

I would like to say a word or two now on what I think the Republican philosophy is; and I will speak from actions and from history and from experience.

The situation in 1932 was due to the policies of the Republican Party control of the Government of the United States. The Republican Party, as I said a while ago, favors the privileged few and not the common everyday man. Ever since its inception, that party has been under the control of special privilege; and they have completely proved it in the 80th Congress. They proved it by the things they did *to* the people, and not *for* them. They proved it by the things they failed to do.

Now, let's look at some of them—just a few.

Time and time again I recommended extension of price control before it expired June 30, 1946. I asked for that extension in September 1945, in November 1945, in a Message on the State of the Union in 1946; and that price control legislation did not come to my desk until June 30, 1946, on the day on which it was supposed to expire. And it was such a rotten bill that I couldn't sign it. And 30 days after that, they sent me one just as bad. I had to sign it, because they quit and went home.

They said, when OPA died, that prices would adjust themselves for the benefit of the country. They have been adjusting themselves all right! They have gone all the way off the chart in adjusting themselves, at the expense of the consumer and for the benefit of the people that hold the goods.

I called a special session of the Congress in November 1947—November 17, 1947—and I set out a 10-point program for the welfare and benefit of this country, among other things standby controls. I got nothing. Congress has still done nothing.

Way back 4½ years ago, while I was in the Senate, we passed a housing bill in the Senate known as the Wagner-Ellender-Taft bill. It was a bill to clear the slums in the big cities and to help to erect low-rent housing. That bill, as I said, passed the Senate 4 years ago. It died in the House. That bill was re-introduced in the 80th Congress as the Taft-Ellender-Wagner bill. The name was slightly changed, but it is practically the same bill. And it passed the Senate, but it was allowed to die in the House of Representatives; and they sat on that bill, and finally forced it out of the Banking and Currency Committee, and the Rules committee took charge, and it is still in the Rules committee.

But desperate pleas from Philadelphia in that convention that met here 3 weeks ago couldn't get that housing bill passed. They passed a bill they called a housing bill, which isn't worth the paper it's written on.

In the field of labor we needed moderate legislation to promote labor-management harmony, but Congress passed instead that so-called Taft-Hartley Act, which has disrupted labor-management relations and will cause strife and bitterness for years to come if it is not repealed, as the Democratic platform says it ought to be repealed.

On the Labor Department, the Republican platform of 1944 said, if they were in power, that they would build up a strong Labor department. They have simply torn it up. Only one bureau is left that is functioning, and they cut the

appropriation of that so it can hardly function.

I recommended an increase in the minimum wage. What did I get? Nothing. Absolutely nothing.

I suggested that the schools in this country are crowded, teachers underpaid, and that there is a shortage of teachers. One of our greatest national needs is more and better schools. I urged the Congress to provide $300 million to aid the States in the present educational crisis. Congress did nothing about it. Time and again I have recommended improvements in the social security law, including extending protection to those not now covered, and increasing the amount of benefits, to reduce the eligibility age of women from 65 to 60 years. Congress studied the matter for 2 years, but couldn't find the time to extend or increase the benefits. But they did find time to take social security benefits away from 750,000 people, and they passed that over my veto.

I have repeatedly asked the Congress to pass a health program. The Nation suffers from lack of medical care. That situation can be remedied any time the congress wants to act upon it.

Everybody knows that I recommended to the Congress the civil rights program. I did that because I believed it to be my duty under the Constitution. Some of the members of my own party disagree with me violently on this matter. But they stand up and do it openly! People can tell where they stand. But the Republicans all professed to be for these measures. But Congress failed to act. They had enough men to do it, they could have had cloture, they didn't have to have a filibuster. They had enough people in that Congress that would vote for cloture.

Now everybody likes to have low taxes, but we must reduce the national debt in times of prosperity. And when tax relief can be given, it ought to go to those who need it most, and not those who need it least, as their Republican rich man's tax bill did when they passed it over my veto on the third try.

The first one of these was so rotten that they couldn't even stomach it themselves. They finally did send one that was somewhat improved, but it still helps the rich and sticks a knife into the back of the poor.

Now the Republicans came here a few weeks ago, and they wrote a platform. I hope you have all read that platform. They adopted the platform, and that platform had a lot of promises and statements of what the Republican Party is for, and what they would do if they were in power. They promised to do in that platform a lot of things I have been asking them to do that they refused to do when they had the power.

The Republican platform cries about cruelly high prices. I have been trying to get them to do something about high prices ever since they met the first time.

Now listen! This is equally as bad, and as cynical. The Republican platform comes out for slum clearance and low-rental housing. I have been trying to get them to pass that housing bill ever since they met the first time, and it is still resting in the Rules Committee, that bill.

The Republican platform favors educational opportunity and promotion of educational opportunity and promotion of education. I have been trying to get Congress to do something about that ever since they came there, and that bill is at rest in the House of Representatives.

The Republican platform is for extending and increasing social security benefits. Think of that! Increasing social security benefits! Yet when they had the opportunity, they took 750,000 off the social security rolls!

I wonder if they think they can fool the people of the United States with such poppycock as that!

There is a long list of these promises in that Republican platform. If it weren't so late, I would tell you all about them. I have discussed a number of these failures of the Republican 80th Congress. Everyone of them is important. Two of them are of major concern to nearly every American family. They failed to do anything about high prices, they failed to do anything about housing.

My duty as President requires that I use every means within my power to get the laws the people need on matters of such importance and urgency.

I am therefore calling this Congress back into session July 26th.

On the 26th day of July, which out in Missouri we call "Turnip Day," I am going to call Congress back and ask them to pass laws to halt rising prices, to meet the housing crisis—which they are saying they are for in their platform.

At the same time I shall ask them to act upon other vitally needed measures such as aid to education, which they say they are for; a national health program; civil rights legislation, which they say they are for; an increase in the minimum wage, which I doubt very much they are for; extension of the social security coverage and increased benefits, which they say they are for; funds for projects needed in our program to provide public power and cheap electricity. By indirection, this 80th Congress has tried to sabotage the power policies the United States has pursued for 14 years. That power lobby is as bad as the real estate lobby, which is sitting on the housing bill.

I shall ask for adequate and decent laws for displaced persons in place of this anti-Semetic, anti-Catholic law which this 80th Congress has passed.

Now, my friends, if there is any reality behind that Republican platform, we ought to get some action from a short session of the 80th Congress. They can do this job in 15 days, if they want to do it. They will still have time to go out and run for office.

They are going to try to dodge their responsibility. They are going to drag all the red herrings they can across this campaign, but I am here to say that Senator Barkley and I are not going to let them get away with it.

Now, what that worst 80th Congress does in this special session will be the test. The American people will not decide by listening to mere words, or by reading a mere platform. They will decide on the record, the record as it has been written. And in the record is the stark truth, that the battle lines of 1948 are the same as they were in 1932, when the Nation lay prostrate and helpless as a result of Republican misrule and inaction.

In 1932 we were attacking the citadel of special privilege and greed. We were fighting to drive the money changers from the temple. Today, in 1948, we are now the defenders of the stronghold of democracy and of equal opportunity, the haven of the ordinary people of this land and not of the favored classes or the powerful few. The battle cry is just the same now as it was in 1932, and I paraphrase the words of Franklin D. Roosevelt as he issued the challenge, in accepting the nomination in Chicago: 'This is more than a political call to arms. Give me your help, not to win votes alone, but to win in this new crusade to keep America secure and safe for its own people."

Now my friends, with the help of God and the wholehearted push which you can put behind this campaign, we can save this country from a continuation of the 80th Congress, and from misrule from now on.

I must have your help. You must get in and push, and win this election. The country can't afford another Republican Congress.

Dwight D. Eisenhower's
Korea Speech (1952)

Harry S Truman's second term as president was dominated by the Korean War, which the United States entered after troops from Communist North Korea invaded South Korea on June 25, 1950. The war was militarily frustrating (neither side ever could gain a permanent advantage) and, as a consequence, politically unpopular. Although the newly enacted Twenty-second Amendment did not apply to Truman, on March 22, 1952, he announced that he would not run for reelection. (See "The Twenty-Second Amendment: House Debate," p. 370.) Instead, at Truman's urging, the Democratic party nominated Gov. Adlai Stevenson of Illinois for president and Sen. John Sparkman of Alabama for vice president. Stevenson was the son and namesake of President Grover Cleveland's second vice president.

Many Democrats had hoped to recruit Gen. Dwight D. Eisenhower as their party's presidential candidate. "Ike," the Supreme Allied Commander in Europe during World War II and the postwar commander of the North Atlantic Treaty Organization (NATO), was the most popular man in the country. In 1948, fearing that Truman would take their party down to defeat, an unusual alliance of liberals, southern conservatives, and party professionals had implored Eisenhower to accept the Democratic nomination for president. Ike demurred, but not until January 5, 1952, did he announce that he was a Republican.

On June 2, 1952, Eisenhower resigned his NATO post to seek the Republican nomination for president. Politically, Ike was more moderate than most members and leaders of his adopted party. In contrast to his main rival for the nomination, Senate Republican leader Robert A. Taft of Ohio, Eisenhower (like most voters) wanted to consolidate, not repeal, Franklin D. Roosevelt's New Deal programs and favored an active role for the United States in world affairs. The choice for the Republican national convention, then, was between fealty to "Mr. Republican" and an all-but-certain victory on election day. On July 10, the convention voted narrowly to nominate Eisenhower. It then chose Sen. Richard Nixon of California, considerably younger and more politically orthodox than Ike, to balance the ticket as his running-mate.

The election of 1952 was a landmark in the history of political campaigning. Television ownership was growing rapidly—in 1950, 9 percent of American homes had television sets; by 1960, 87 percent did. Eisenhower was the first candidate to use television commercials in a presidential campaign. In a typical spot, the announcer began by solemnly intoning, "Eisenhower an-

swers the nation." A man in the street then said, "General, the Democrats are telling me I never had it so good." Eisenhower replied, "Can that be true when prices have doubled, when taxes break our backs, and we are still fighting in Korea? It is tragic. It is time for a change." (See "Richard Nixon's 'Checkers' Speech," p. 474.)

The 1952 election also provided a landmark of a different sort: the three-ballot Democratic national convention was the last major-party gathering to require more than one ballot to choose its nominee for president. The combination of television and, starting in the 1960s, presidential primaries, transformed most national party conventions into coronating, not nominating, events. (See "The McGovern-Fraser Commission Report," p. 574.)

The dramatic high point of the 1952 campaign came on October 24. Speaking to an audience in Detroit, Michigan, Eisenhower not only vowed to end the Korean War but proclaimed, "I shall go to Korea." Stevenson had thought of making a similar pledge but decided that for him to do so would seem like a political stunt. He may have been right: Eisenhower's singular status as a military hero lent his statement a level of credibility that no other politician's would have had.

On election day, Eisenhower won in a landslide. He defeated Stevenson in the popular vote by 33,936,137 (55.1 percent) to 27,314,549 (44.4 percent) and by 442-89 in the electoral college.

Eisenhower was the last former military commander to be elected as president. Like George Washington, Andrew Jackson, William Henry Harrison, Zachary Taylor, and Ulysses S. Grant before him, Ike had been a popular general in a widely supported war. The Korean War of the 1950s and the Vietnam War of the 1960s produced no such heroes. ～

In this anxious autumn for America, one fact looms above all others in our people's mind. One tragedy challenges all men dedicated to the work of peace. One word shouts denial to those who foolishly pretend that ours is not a nation at war.

This fact, this tragedy, this word is: Korea.

A small country, Korea has been, for more than two years, the battleground for the costliest foreign war our nation has fought, excepting the two world wars. It has been the burial ground for 20,000 American dead. It has been another historic field of honor for the valor and skill and tenacity of American soldiers.

All these things it has been—and yet one thing more. It has been a symbol—a telling symbol—of the foreign policy of our nation.

It has been a sign—a warning sign—of the way the Administration has conducted our world affairs.

It has been a measure—a damning measure—of the quality of leadership we have been given.

Tonight I am going to talk about our foreign policy and of its supreme symbol—the Korean war. I am not going to give you elaborate generalizations—but hard, tough facts. I am going to state the unvarnished truth.

What, then, are the plain facts?

The biggest fact about the Korean war is this: It was never inevitable, it was never inescapable, no fantastic fiat of history decreed that little South Korea—in the summer of 1950—would fatally tempt Communist aggressors as their easiest victim. No demonic destiny decreed that America had to be bled this way in order to keep South Korea free and to keep freedom itself self-respecting.

We are not mute prisoners of history. That is a doctrine for totalitarians, it is no creed for free men.

There is a Korean war—and we are fighting it—for the simplest of reasons:

Because free leadership failed to check and to turn back Communist ambition before it savagely attacked us. The Korean war—more perhaps than any other war in history—simply and swiftly followed the collapse of our political defenses. There is no other reason than this: We failed to read and to outwit the totalitarian mind.

I know something of this totalitarian mind. Through the years of World War II, I carried a heavy burden of decision in the free world's crusade against the tyranny then threatening us all. Month after month, year after year, I had to search out and to weigh the strengths and weaknesses of an enemy driven by the lust to rule the great globe itself.

World War II should have taught us all one lesson. The lesson is this: To vacillate, to hesitate—to appease even by merely betraying unsteady purpose—is to feed a dictator's appetite for conquest and to invite war itself.

That lesson—which should have firmly guided every great decision of our leadership through these later years—was ignored in the development of the Administration's policies for Asia since the end of World War II. Because it was ignored, the record of these policies is a record of appalling failure.

The record of failure dates back—with red-letter folly—at least to September of 1947. It was then that Gen. Albert Wedemeyer—returned from a Presidential mission to the Far East—submitted to the president this warning: "The withdrawal of American military forces from Korea would result in the occupation of South Korea by either Soviet troops or, as seems more likely, by the Korean military units trained under Soviet auspices in North Korea."

That warning and his entire report were disregarded and suppressed by the Administration.

The terrible record of these years reaches its dramatic climax in a series of unforgettable scenes on Capitol Hill in June of 1949. By then the decision to complete withdrawal of American forces from Korea—despite menacing signs from the North—had been drawn up by the Department of State. The decision included the intention to ask Congress for aid to Korea to compensate for the withdrawal of American forces.

This brought questions from Congress. The Administration parade of civilian and military witnesses before the House Foreign Affairs Committee was headed by the Secretary of State. He and his aides faced a group of Republican Congressmen both skeptical and fearful.

What followed was historic and decisive.

I beg you to listen carefully to the words that followed, for they shaped this nation's course from that date to this.

Listen, then:

First: Republican Congressman John Lodge of Connecticut asked "(do) you feel that the Korean Government is able to fill the vacuum caused by the withdrawal of the occupation forces?"

The Administration answered: "Definitely."

Second: A very different estimate of the risk involved came from Republican Congressman Walter Judd of Minnesota. He warned: "I think the thing necessary to give security to Korea at this stage of the game is the presence of a small American force and the knowledge (on the Soviet side) that attack upon it would bring trouble with us."

"I am convinced," Representative Judd continued, "that if we keep even a battalion there, they are not going to move. And if the battalion is not there"—listen now to his warning—"the chances are they will move within a year."

What a tragedy that the Administration shrugged off that accurate warning!

Third: The Secretary of State was asked if he agreed that the South Koreans alone—and I quote—"will be able to defend themselves against any attack from the northern half of the country." To this the Secretary answered briskly: "We share the same view. Yes sir."

Rarely in Congressional testimony has so much misinformation been compressed so efficiently into so few words.

Fourth: Republican Congressman Lodge had an incisive comment on all this. "That," he said, "is wishful thinking. . . . I am afraid it confesses a kind of fundamental isolationism that exists in certain branches of the Government, which I think is a very dangerous pattern. I think the presence of our troops there is a tremendous deterrent to the Russians."

Finally: This remarkable scene of the summer of 1949 ends with a memorable document. The minority report of five Republican members of the House Foreign Affairs Committee on July 26, 1949, submitted this solemn warning.

Listen to it:

"It is reliably reported that Soviet troops, attached to the North Korean puppet armies, are in position of command as well as acting as advisors. . . . This development may well presage the launching of a full-scale military drive across the Thirty-eighth Parallel.

"Our forces . . . have been withdrawn from South Korea at the very instant when logic and common sense both demanded no retreat from the realities of the situation."

The report continues: "Already alone the Thirty-eighth Parallel aggression is speaking with the too-familiar voices of howitzers and cannons. Our position is untenable and indefensible.

"The House should be aware of these facts."

These words of eloquent, reasoned warning were spoken eleven months before the Korean war broke.

Behind these words was a fervent, desperate appeal. That appeal was addressed to the Administration. It begged at least some firm statement of American intention that might deter the foreseen attack.

What was the Administration answer to that appeal?

The first answer was silence—stubborn, sullen silence for six months.

Then, suddenly, came speech—a high Government official at long last speaking out on Asia. It was now January of 1950. What did he say? He said, "The United States Government will not provide military aid or advice to Chinese forces on Formosa."

Then, one week later, the Secretary of State announced his famous "defense perimeter"—publicly advising our enemies that, so far as nations outside this perimeter were concerned, "no person can guarantee these areas against military attach." Under these circumstances, it was cold comfort to the nations outside this perimeter to be reminded that they could appeal to the United Nations.

These nations, of course, included Korea. The armies of communism, thus informed, began their big build-up. Six months later they were ready to strike across the Thirty-eighth Parallel. They struck on June 25, 1950.

On that day, the record of political and diplomatic failure of this Administration was completed and sealed.

The responsibility for this record cannot be dodged or evaded. Even if not a single Republican leader had warned so clearly against the coming disaster, the responsibility for the fateful political decisions would still rest wholly with the men charged with making those decisions—in the Department of State and in the White House. They cannot escape that responsibility now or ever.

When the enemy struck, on that June day of 1950, what did America do? It did what it always has done in all its times of peril. It appealed to the heroism of its youth.

This appeal was utterly right and utterly inescapable. It was inescapable not only because this was the only way to defend the idea of collective freedom against savage aggression. That appeal was inescapable because there was now in the plight into which we had stumbled no other way to save honor and self-respect.

The answer to that appeal has been what any American knew it would be. It has been sheer valor—valor on all the Korean mountainsides that, each day, bear fresh scars of new graves.

Now—in this anxious autumn—from these heroic men there comes back an answering appeal. It is no whine, no whimpering plea. It is a question that addresses itself to simple reason. It asks: Where do we go from here? When comes the end? Is there an end?

These questions touch all of us. They demand truthful answers. Neither glib promises nor glib excuses will serve. They would be no better than the glib prophecies that brought us to this pass.

To these questions there are two false answers—both equally false. The first would be any answer that dishonestly pledged an end to war in Korea by any imminent, exact date. Such a pledge would brand its speaker as a deceiver.

The second and equally false answer declares that nothing can be done to speed a secure peace. It dares to tell us that we, the strongest nation in the history of freedom, can only wait—and wait—and wait. Such a statement brands its speaker as a defeatist.

My answer—candid and complete—is this:

The first task of a new Administration will be to review and re-examine every course of action open to us with one goal in view: To bring the Korean war to an early and honorable end. This is my pledge to the American people.

For this task a wholly new Administration is necessary. The reason for this is simple. The old Administration cannot be expected to repair what it failed to prevent.

Where will a new Administration begin?

It will begin with its President taking a simple, firm resolution. That resolution will be: To forego the diversions of politics and to concentrate on the job of ending the Korean war—until that job is honorably done.

That job requires a personal trip to Korea.

I shall make that trip. Only in that way could I learn how best to serve the American people in the cause of peace.

I shall go to Korea.

That is my second pledge to the American people.

Carefully, then, this new Administration, unfettered by past decisions and inherited mistakes, can review every factor—military, political and psychological—to be mobilized in speeding a just peace.

Progress along at least two lines can instantly begin. We can—first—step up the program of training and arming the South Korean forces. Manifestly, under the circumstances of today, United Nations forces cannot abandon that unhappy land. But just as troops of the Republic of Korea covet and deserve the honor of defending their frontiers, so should we give them maximum assistance to insure their ability to do so.

Then, United Nations forces in reserve positions and supporting roles would be assurance that disaster would not again strike.

We can—secondly—shape our psychological warfare program into a weapon capable of cracking the Communist front.

Beyond all this we must carefully weigh all interrelated courses of action. We will, of course, constantly confer with associated free nations of Asia and with the cooperating members of the United Nations. Thus we could bring into being a practical plan for world peace.

That is my third pledge to you.

As the next Administration goes to

work for peace, we must be guided at every instant by that lesson I spoke of earlier. The vital lesson is this: To vacillate, to appease, to placate is only to invite war—vaster war—bloodier war. In the words of the late Senator [Arthur H.] Vandenberg, appeasement is not the road to peace; it is only surrender on the installment plan.

I will always reject appeasement.

And that is my fourth pledge to you.

A nation's foreign policy is a much graver matter than rustling papers and bustling conferences. It is much more than diplomatic decisions and trade treaties and military arrangements.

A foreign policy is the face and voice of a whole people. It is all that the world sees and hears and understands about a single nation. It expresses the character and the faith and the will of that nation. In this, a nation is like any individual of our personal acquaintance; the simplest gesture can betray hesitation or weakness, the merest inflection of voice can reveal doubt or fear.

It is in this deep sense that our foreign policy has faltered and failed.

For a democracy, a great election, such as this, signifies a most solemn trial. It is the time when—to the bewilderment of all tyrants—the people sit in judgment upon the leaders. It is the time when these leaders are summoned before the bar of public decision. There they must give evidence both to justify their actions and explain their intentions.

In the great trial of this election, the judges—the people—must not be deceived into believing that the choice is between isolationism and international-

ism. That is a debate of the dead past. The vast majority of Americans of both parties know that to keep their own nation free, they bear a majestic responsibility for freedom through all the world. As practical people, Americans also know the critical necessity of unimpaired access to raw materials on other continents for our own economic and military strength.

Today the choice—the real choice— lies between policies that assume that responsibility awkwardly and fearfully—and policies that accept that responsibility with sure purpose and firm will. The choice is between foresight and blindness, between doing and apologizing, between planning and improvising.

In rendering their verdict, the people must judge with courage and with wisdom. For—at this date—any faltering in America's leadership is a capital offense against freedom.

In this trial, my testimony, of a personal kind, is quite simple. A soldier all my life, I have enlisted in the greatest cause of my life—the cause of peace.

I do not believe it a presumption for me to call the effort of all who have enlisted with me—a crusade.

I use that word only to signify two facts. First: We are united and devoted to a just cause of the purest meaning to all humankind. Second: We know that—for all the might of our effort— victory can come only with the gift of God's help.

In this spirit—humble servants of a proud ideal—we do soberly say: This is a crusade.

Richard Nixon's Checkers Speech (1952)

Following the advice of party leaders, Republican presidential nominee Dwight D. Eisenhower selected Sen. Richard Nixon of California, whom he did not know, as his vice presidential running-mate in 1952. Nixon, thirty-nine years old and a staunch Republican partisan, was chosen to balance a ticket that was headed by a sixty-two-year-old former general who had not even decided which party he belonged to until shortly before running for president. (See "Dwight D. Eisenhower's Korea Speech," p. 468.) Nixon also was known as an effective, tireless political campaigner and an ardent anticommunist.

On September 18, 1952, the New York Post printed a story that accused Nixon of using a secret $18,000 fund created by sixty-six California business leaders to pay for his personal expenses. The headline—"SECRET NIXON FUND! Secret Rich Men's Trust Fund Keeps Nixon in Style Far Beyond His Salary"—was more sensational than the story, and the story was more sensational than the reality. In truth, Nixon used the fund only to pay his political expenses; he and his family lived very frugally. Nevertheless, the charge was for a time the major issue of the campaign.

Part of the reason for the prominence of the Nixon fund story was its underlying allegation of hypocrisy—Nixon's vice presidential campaign had concentrated its fire on the corruption that supposedly infested the Democratic administration of President Harry S Truman.

Just as important, however, was the rapidly growing public perception of the importance of the vice presidency and, consequently, of the need to assess the presidential caliber of the candidates who were nominated for vice president. In 1945, when President Franklin D. Roosevelt died, Vice President Truman had succeeded to the presidency unaware of both the existence of the atomic bomb and the diplomatic plans that had been laid for the post-World War II era. Soon after, the development of intercontinental ballistic missiles armed with nuclear warheads raised the specter of virtually instant total war. In such a world, many voters realized, the nation could not afford the luxury of having an uninformed or incapable vice president succeed to the presidency.

When the charges against Nixon were made public, several of Eisenhower's advisers urged him to ask his running-mate to resign from the ticket. But on September 21, 1952, Ike encouraged Nixon "to go on a nationwide television program and tell them everything there is to tell." The Republican National Committee bought thirty minutes of television time on the eve-

ning of September 23. Nixon's political fate hung in the balance.

In 1952, television was a new but rapidly spreading feature of American presidential politics. (See "Dwight D. Eisenhower's Korea Speech," p. 468.) Speaking to fifty-five million people—until then, the largest audience for a television broadcast in history—Nixon defended his fund as a way "to pay for political expenses that I did not think should be charged to the taxpayers." He described his modest lifestyle, even noting that his wife "Pat doesn't have a mink coat. But she does have a respectable Republican cloth coat." The most memorable line from Nixon's speech came in defense of a personal gift that he vowed never to return. "You know what it was? It was a little cocker spaniel dog in a crate that [a supporter] sent all the way from Texas. Black and white spotted. And our little girl—Tricia, the six-year-old—named it Checkers."

At the end of his televised speech, Nixon called upon viewers to let the Republican National Committee know whether they thought he should resign or not. The response was overwhelmingly positive. Nixon remained on the ticket. On election day, he and Eisenhower were elected in a landslide. ~

My Fellow Americans:

I come before you tonight as a candidate for the Vice Presidency and as a man whose honesty and integrity have been questioned.

The usual political thing to do when charges are made against you is to either ignore them or to deny them without giving details.

I believe we've had enough of that in the United States, particularly with the present Administration in Washington, D.C. To me the office of the Vice Presidency of the United States is a great office, and I feel that the people have got to have confidence in the integrity

of the men who run for that office and who might obtain it.

I have a theory, too, that the best and only answer to a smear or to an honest misunderstanding of the facts is to tell the truth. And that's why I'm here tonight. I want to tell you my side of the case.

I am sure that you have read the charge and you've heard that I, Senator Nixon, took $18,000 from a group of my supporters.

Now, what was wrong? And let me say that it was wrong—I'm saying, incidentally, that it was wrong and not just illegal. Because it isn't a question of whether it was legal or illegal, that isn't enough. The question is, was it morally wrong?

I say that it was morally wrong if any of that $18,000 went to Senator Nixon for my personal use. I say that it was morally wrong if it was secretly given and secretly handled. And I say that it was morally wrong if any of the contributors got special favors for the contributions that they made.

And now to answer those questions let me say this:

Not one cent of the $18,000 or any other money of that type ever went to me for my personal use. Every penny of it was used to pay for political expenses that I did not think should be charged to the taxpayers of the United States.

It was not a secret fund. As a matter of fact, when I was on "Meet the Press," some of you may have seen it last Sunday—Peter Edson came up to me after the program and he said, "Dick, what about this fund we hear about?" And I said, Well, there's no secret about it. Go out and see Dana Smith, who was the administrator of the fund. And I gave him his address, and I said that you will find that the purpose of the fund simply was to defray political expenses that I did not feel should be charged to the Government.

And third, let me point out, and I want to make this particularly clear, that no contributor to this fund, no contributor to any of my campaigns, has ever received any consideration that he would not have received as an ordinary constituent.

I just don't believe in that and I can say that never, while I have been in the Senate of the United States, as far as the people that contributed to this fund are concerned, have I made a telephone call for them to an agency, or have I gone down to an agency in their behalf. And the record will show that, the records which are in the hands of the Administration.

But then some of you will say and rightly, "Well, what did you use the fund for, Senator? Why did you have to have it?"

Let me tell you in just a word how a Senate office operates. First of all, a Senator gets $15,000 a year in salary. He gets enough money to pay for one trip a year, a round trip that is, for himself and his family between his home and Washington, D.C.

And then he gets an allowance to handle the people that work in his office, to handle his mail. And the allowance for my State of California is enough to hire thirteen people.

And let me say, incidentally, that that allowance is not paid to the Senator—it's paid directly to the individuals that the Senator puts on his payroll, that all of these people and all of these allowances are for strictly official business. Business, for example, when a constituent writes in and wants you to go down to the Veterans Administration and get some information about his GI policy. Items of that type for example.

But there are other expenses which are not covered by the Government. And I think I can best discuss those expenses by asking you some questions. Do you think that when I or any other Senator makes a political speech, has it printed, should charge the printing of that speech and the mailing of that speech to the taxpayers?

Do you think, for example, when I or any other Senator makes a trip to his home state to make a purely political speech that the cost of that trip should be charged to the taxpayers?

Do you think when a Senator makes political broadcasts or political television broadcasts, radio or television, that the expense of those broadcasts should be charged to the taxpayers?

Well, I know what your answer is. The same answer that audiences give me whenever I discuss this particular problem. The answer is, "no." The taxpayers shouldn't be required to finance items which are not official business but which are primarily political business.

But then the question arises, you say, "Well, how do you pay for these and how can you do it legally?"

And there are several ways that it can be done, incidentally, and that it is done legally in the United States Senate and in the Congress.

The first way is to be a rich man. I don't happen to be a rich man so I couldn't use that.

Another way that is used is to put your wife on the payroll. Let me say, incidentally, my opponent, my opposite number for the Vice Presidency on the Democratic ticket, does have his wife on the payroll. And has had her on his payroll for the ten years—the past ten years.

Now just let me say this. That's his business and I'm not critical of him for doing that. You will have to pass judgment on that particular point. But I have never done that for this reason. I have found that there are so many deserving stenographers and secretaries in Washington that needed the work that I just didn't feel it was right to put my wife on the payroll.

My wife's sitting over here. She's a wonderful stenographer. She used to teach stenography and she used to teach shorthand in high school. That was when I met her. And I can tell you folks that she's worked many hours at night and many hours on Saturdays and Sundays in my office and she's done a fine job. And I'm proud to say tonight that in the six years I've been in the House and the Senate of the United States, Pat Nixon has never been on the Government payroll.

There are other ways that these finances can be taken care of. Some who are lawyers, and I happen to be a lawyer, continue to practice law. But I haven't been able to do that. I'm so far away from California that I've been so busy with my Senatorial work that I have not engaged in any legal practice.

And also as far as law practice is concerned, it seemed to me that the relationship between an attorney and the client was so personal that you couldn't possibly represent a man as an attorney and then have an unbiased view when he presented his case to you in the event that he had one before the Government.

And so I felt that the best way to handle these necessary political expenses of getting my message to the American people and the speeches I made, the speeches that I had printed, for the most part, concerned this one message—of exposing this Administration, the communism in it, the corruption in it—the only way that I could do that was to accept the aid which people in my home state of California who contributed to my campaign and who continued to make these contributions after I was elected were glad to make.

And let me say I am proud of the fact that not one of them has ever asked me for a special favor. I'm proud of the fact that not one of them has ever asked me to vote on a bill other than as my own conscience would dictate. And I am proud of the fact that the taxpayers by subterfuge or otherwise have never paid one dime for expenses which I thought were political and shouldn't be charged to the taxpayers.

Let me say, incidentally, that some of you may say, "Well, that's all right, Senator; that's your explanation, but have you got any proof?"

And I'd like to tell you this evening that just about an hour ago we received an independent audit of this entire fund.

I suggested to Gov. Sherman Adams, who is the chief of staff of the Dwight Eisenhower campaign, that an independent audit and legal report be obtained. And I have that audit here in my hand.

It's an audit made by the Price, Waterhouse & Co. firm, and the legal opinion by Gibson, Dunn & Crutcher, lawyers in Los Angeles, the biggest law firm and incidentally one of the best ones in Los Angeles.

I'm proud to be able to report to you tonight that this audit and this legal opinion is being forwarded to General Eisenhower. And I'd like to read to you the opinion that was prepared by Gibson, Dunn & Crutcher and based on all the pertinent laws and statutes, together with the audit report prepared by the certified public accountants.

"It is our conclusion that Senator Nixon did not obtain any financial gain from the collection and disbursement of the fund by Dana Smith; that Senator Nixon did not violate any Federal or state law by reason of the operation of the fund, and that neither the portion of the fund paid by Dana Smith directly to reimburse him for designated office expenses constituted income to the Senator which was either reportable or taxable as income under applicable tax laws. (signed) Gibson, Dunn & Crutcher by Alma H. Conway."

Now that, my friends, is not Nixon speaking, but that's an independent audit which was requested because I want the American people to know all the facts and I'm not afraid of having independent people go in and check the facts, and that is exactly what they did.

But then I realize that there are still some who may say, and rightly so, and let me say that I recognize that some will continue to smear regardless of what the truth may be, but that there has been understandably some honest misunderstanding on this matter, and there's some that will say:

"Well, maybe you were able, Senator, to fake this thing. How can we believe what you say? After all, is there a possibility that maybe you got some sums in cash? Is there a possibility that you may have feathered your own nest?"

And so now what I am going to do—and incidentally this is unprecedented in the history of American politics—I am going at this time to give to this television and radio audience a complete financial history; everything I've earned; everything I've spent; everything I owe. And I want you to know the facts. I'll have to start early.

I was born in 1913. Our family was one of modest circumstances and most of my early life was spent in a store out in East Whittier. It was a grocery store—one of those family enterprises. The only reason we were able to make it go was because my mother and dad had five boys and we all worked in the store.

I worked my way through college and to a great extent through law school. And then, in 1940, probably the best thing that ever happened to me happened, I married Pat—sitting over here. We had a rather difficult time after we were married, like so many of the young couples who may be listening to us. I practiced law; she continued to teach school. I went into the service.

Let me say that my service record was not a particularly unusual one. I went to the South Pacific. I guess I'm entitled to a couple of battle stars. I got a couple of letters of commendation but I was just there when the bombs were falling and then I returned. I returned to the United States and in 1946 I ran for the Congress.

When we came out of the war, Pat and I—Pat during the war had worked as a stenographer and in a bank and as an economist for a Government agency—and when we came out the

total of our savings from both my law practice, her teaching and all the time that I was in the war—the total for that entire period was just a little less than $10,000. Every cent of that, incidentally, was in Government bonds.

Well, that's where we start when I go into politics. Now what have I earned since I went into politics? Well, here it is—I jotted it down, let me read the notes. First of all I've had my salary as a Congressman and as a Senator. Second, I have received a total in this past six years of $1,600 from estates which were in my law firm at the time that I severed my connection with it.

And, incidentally, as I said before, I have not engaged in any legal practice and have not accepted any fees from business that came into the firm after I went into politics. I have made an average of approximately $1,500 a year from nonpolitical speaking engagements and lectures. And then, fortunately, we've inherited a little money. Pat sold her interest in her father's estate for $3,000 and I inherited $1,500 from my grandfather.

We live rather modestly. For four years we lived in an apartment in Park Fairfax, in Alexandria, Va. The rent was $80 a month. And we saved for the time that we could buy a house.

Now, that was what we took in. What did we do with this money? What do we have today to show for it? This will surprise you, because it is so little, I suppose, as standards generally go, of people in public life. First of all, we've got a house in Washington which cost $41,000 and on which we owe $20,000.

We have a house in Whittier, Calif., which cost $13,000 and on which we owe $10,000. My folks are living there at the present time.

I have just $4,000 in life insurance, plus my G.I. policy which I've never been able to convert and which will run out in two years. I have no life insurance whatever on Pat. I have no life insurance on our two youngsters, Patricia and Julie. I own a 1950 Oldsmobile car. We have our furniture. We have no stocks and bonds of any type. We have no interest of any kind, direct or indirect, in any business.

Now, that's what we have. What do we owe? Well, in addition to the mortgage, the $20,000 mortgage on the house in Washington, the $10,000 one on the house in Whittier, I owe $4,500 to the Riggs Bank in Washington, D.C. with interest 4½ per cent.

I owe $3,000 to my parents and the interest on that loan which I pay regularly, because it's the part of the savings they made through the years they were working so hard, I pay regularly 4 per cent interest. And then I have a $500 loan which I have on my life insurance.

Well, that's about it. That's what we have and that's what we owe. It isn't very much but Pat and I have the satisfaction that every dime that we've got is honestly ours. I should say this— that Pat doesn't have a mink coat. But she does have a respectable Republican cloth coat. And I always tell her that she'd look good in anything.

One other thing I probably should tell you because if I don't they'll probably be saying this about me too, we did get something—a gift—after the election. A man down in Texas heard Pat on the radio mention the fact that our two youngsters would like to have a dog. And, believe it or not, the day before we left on this campaign trip we got a message from Union Station in Baltimore saying they had a package for us. We went down to get it. You know what it was.

It was a little cocker spaniel dog in a crate that he sent all the way from Texas. Black and white spotted. And our little girl—Trisha, the 6-year-old—named it Checkers. And you know, the kids love the dog and I just want to say this right now, that regardless of what they say about it, we're gonna keep it.

It isn't easy to come before a nationwide audience and air your life as I've done. But I want to say some things before I conclude that I think most of you will agree on. Mr. Mitchell, the chairman of the Democratic National Committee, made the statement that if a man couldn't afford to be in the United States Senate he shouldn't run for the Senate.

And I just want to make my position clear. I don't agree with Mr. Mitchell when he says that only a rich man should serve his Government in the United States Senate or in the Congress.

I don't believe that represents the thinking of the Democratic party, and I know that it doesn't represent the thinking of the Republican Party.

I believe that it's fine that a man like Governor Stevenson who inherited a fortune from his father can run for President. But I also feel that it's essential in this country of ours that a man of modest means can also run for President. Because, you know, remember Abraham Lincoln, you remember what he said: "God must have loved the common people—he made so many of them."

And now I'm going to suggest some courses of conduct.

First of all, you have read in the papers about other funds now. Mr. Stevenson, apparently, had a couple. One of them in which a group of business people paid and helped to supplement the salaries of state employees. Here is where the money went directly into their pockets.

And I think that what Mr. Stevenson should do should be to come before the American people as I have, give the names of the people that have contributed to that fund; give the names of the people who put this money into their pockets at the same time that they were receiving money from their state government, and see what favors, if any, they gave out for that.

I don't condemn Mr. Stevenson for what he did. But until the facts are in there is a doubt that will be raised.

And as far as Mr. Sparkman is concerned, I would suggest the same thing. He's had his wife on the payroll. I don't condemn him for that. But I think that he should come before the American people and indicate what outside sources of income he has had.

I would suggest that under the circumstances both Mr. Sparkman and Mr. Stevenson should come before the American people as I have and make a complete financial statement as to their financial history. And if they don't it will be an admission that they have something to hide. And I think that you will agree with me.

Because, folks, remember, a man that's to be President of the United States, a man that's to be Vice President of the United States must have the confidence of the people. And that's why I'm doing what I'm doing, and that's why I suggest that Mr. Stevenson and Mr. Sparkman since they are under attack should do what I am doing.

Now, let me say this: I know that this is not the last of the smears. In spite of my explanation tonight other smears will be made; others have been made in the past. And the purpose of the smears, I know, is this—to silence me, to make me let up.

Well, they just don't know who they're dealing with. I'm going to tell you this: I remember in the dark days of the Hiss case some of the same columnists, some of these same radio commentators who are attacking me now and misrepresenting my position were violently opposing me at the time I was after Alger Hiss.

But I continued to fight because I knew I was right. And I can say to this great television and radio audience that I have no apologies to the American people for my part in putting Alger Hiss where he is today.

And as far as this is concerned, I intend to continue to fight.

Why do I feel so deeply? Why do I feel that in spite of the smears, the misunderstandings, the necessities for a man to come up here and bare his soul as I have? Why is it necessary for me to continue this fight?

And I want to tell you why. Because, you see, I love my country. And I think my country is in danger. And I think that the only man that can save America at this time is the man that's running for President on my ticket—Dwight Eisenhower.

You say, "Why do I think it's in danger?" and I say look at the record. Seven years of the Truman-Acheson Administration and what's happened? Six hundred million people lost to the Communists, and a war in Korea in which we have lost 117,000 American casualties.

And I say to all of you that a policy that results in a loss of 600,000,000 to the Communists and a war which costs us 117,000 American casualties isn't good enough for America.

And I say that those in the State Department that made the mistakes which caused that war and which resulted in those losses should be kicked out of the State Department just as fast as we can get 'em out of there.

And let me say that I know Mr. Stevenson won't do that. Because he defends the Truman policy and I know that Dwight Eisenhower will do that, and that he will give America the leadership that it needs..

Take the problem of corruption. You've read about the mess in Washington. Mr. Stevenson can't clean it up because he was picked by the man, Truman, under whose Administration the mess was made. You wouldn't trust a man who made the mess to clean it up—that's Truman. And by the same token you can't trust the man who was picked by the man that made the mess to clean it up—and that's Stevenson.

And so I say, Eisenhower, who owes nothing to Truman, nothing to the big city bosses, he is the man that can clean up the mess in Washington.

Take Communism. I say that as far as that subject is concerned, the danger is great to America. In the Hiss case they got the secrets which enabled them to break the secret State Department code. They got secrets in the atomic bomb case which enabled 'em to get the secret of the atomic bomb, five years before they would have gotten it by their own devices.

And I say that any man who called the Alger Hiss case a "red herring" isn't fit to be President of the United States. I say that a man who like Mr. Stevenson had pooh-poohed and ridiculed the Communist threat in the United States—he said that they are phantoms among ourselves; he's accused us that have attempted to expose the Communists of looking for Communists in the Bureau of Fisheries and Wildlife—I say that a man who says that isn't qualified to be President of the United States.

And I say that the only man who can lead us in this fight to rid the Government of both those who are Communists and those who have corrupted this Government is Eisenhower, because Eisenhower, you can be sure recognizes the problem and he knows how to deal with it.

Now let me say that, finally, this evening I want to read to you just briefly excerpts from a letter which I received, a letter which, after all this is over, no one can take away from me. It reads as follows:

"Dear Senator Nixon,

"Since I'm only 19 years of age I can't vote in this Presidential election but believe me if I could you and General Eisenhower would certainly get my vote. My husband is in the Fleet Marines in Korea. He's a corpsman on the front lines and we have a two-month-old son he's never seen. And I feel confident that with great Americans like you and General Eisenhower in the White House, lonely Americans like myself will be united with their loved ones now in Korea.

"I only pray to God that you won't be too late. Enclosed is a small check to help you in your campaign. Living on $85 a month it is all I can afford at present. But let me know what else I can do."

Folks, it's a check for $10, and it's one that I will never cash.

And just let me say this. We hear a lot about prosperity these days but I say, why can't we have prosperity built on peace rather than prosperity built on war? Why can't we have prosperity and an honest government in Washington, D.C., at the same time. Believe, me, we can. And Eisenhower is the man that can lead this crusade to bring us that kind of prosperity.

And, now, finally, I know that you wonder whether or not I am going to stay on the Republican ticket or resign.

Let me say this: I don't believe that I ought to quit because I'm not a quitter. And, incidentally, Pat's not a quitter. After all, her name was Patricia Ryan and she was born on St. Patrick's Day, and you know the Irish never quit.

But the decision, my friends, is not mine. I would do nothing that would harm the possibilities of Dwight Eisenhower to become President of the United States. And for that reason I am submitting to the Republican National Committee tonight through this television broadcast the decision which is theirs to make.

Let them decide whether my position on the ticket will help or hurt. And I am going to ask you to help them decide. Wire and write the Republican National Committee whether you think I should stay on or whether I should get off. And whatever their decision is, I will abide by it.

But just let me say this last word. Regardless of what happens I'm going to continue this fight. I'm going to campaign up and down America until we drive the crooks and the Communists and those that defend them out of Washington. And remember, folks, Eisenhower is a great man. Believe me. He's a great man. And a vote for Eisenhower is a vote for what's good for America.

Campaign Speech by Adlai Stevenson (1956)

If Dwight D. Eisenhower's most politically important statement in 1952 was "I shall go to Korea," in 1956 it was, "Ladies and gentlemen, I feel fine." Eisenhower's first term, which was marked by peace, prosperity, and presidential popularity, was marred on September 24, 1955, when he suffered a massive heart attack, and on June 8, 1956, when he underwent major surgery to remove an intestinal obstruction. Health was the only real stumbling block to Ike's reelection. When he rebounded from his setbacks with full vigor, victory was all but assured.

The Democratic party renominated former Illinois governor Adlai Stevenson for president on August 17, 1956. Stevenson's 1952 campaign had been widely celebrated for its wit and intelligence. ("Let's talk sense to the American people," he proclaimed in his acceptance speech to the 1952 Democratic national convention.) No other candidate seemed less likely to lose in 1956 or more likely to generate enthusiasm within the party than did Stevenson.

Another Democratic star was born in 1956 when, on August 18, Stevenson threw open the second spot on the national ticket to nominations from the convention floor. John F. Kennedy, a thirty-nine-year-old senator from Massachusetts, made a good run at the vice presidential nomination, then impressed party leaders and the national television audience by withdrawing gracefully in favor of Sen. Estes Kefauver of Tennessee, who had mounted a strong challenge to Stevenson in the spring primaries.

Stevenson tried hard to mix foreign policy and the president's age and health into a cutting issue in the fall campaign. As the journalist Theodore H. White characterized the Democratic candidate's October 27 speech in Los Angeles, Stevenson "made the axis of his final thrust the fact that Eisenhower (then sixty-six) was too old to be a good president; that he lacked the vigor to master foreign affairs."

International events on the eve of the election undercut Stevenson's strategy. In rapid succession, Hungarian freedom fighters rose up against their Soviet oppressors, and the combined forces of Great Britain, France, and Israel won back the Suez canal from Egypt, which had seized it in July. The uncertain global situation allowed Vice President Richard Nixon to make a hyperbolic but politically persuasive argument on behalf of the Republican ticket: "This is not the moment to replace the greatest commander-in-chief America has ever had."

Eisenhower's landslide reelection in 1956 exceeded his landslide election in 1952: he won by 35,585,245 (57.4 per-

cent) to 26,030,172 (42.0 percent) in the popular vote and by 457-73 in the electoral college.

But Eisenhower's victory was, for the most part, personal; it did little for the Republican party. A man of unknown partisanship until the year that he first ran for president, Eisenhower seldom used his office's "bully pulpit" to preach the Republican gospel. The Democrats controlled both houses of Congress for all but the first two of his eight years as president. The only enduring partisan legacy of the two Eisenhower campaigns was the crack they made for the Republican party in the previously solid Democratic South. Ike carried Virginia, Florida, Tennessee, and Texas in 1952 and added a fifth southern state, Louisiana, in 1956. (See "H. L. Mencken's 'Onward, Christian Soldiers!' Article," p. 296.)

In contrast to Eisenhower, Stevenson accomplished more for his party than for himself. His thoughtful, intellectual style attracted a generation of young lawyers and other professionals into the Democratic fold. These "Amateur Democrats," as the political scientist James Q. Wilson called them, cared more about ideals and issues than about old-style political patronage. Ironically, many of them abandoned Stevenson to support the new star of the Democratic party, Senator Kennedy, in 1960. ~

I have spoken often in this campaign of the evils of indifference in the management of our public affairs, or absentee administration, of political administration, of administration without heart, and without heart in its work. The overcrowded schools, workmen in many places, the sick and the aged, and the Government employee have all had a first-hand experience with this kind of government. To them a part-time President and an indifferent Administration is more than a phrase. The lives of many have been altered in these past four years; the lives of some blighted. Ask the thousands who have been kicked around as security risks in the Republican effort to prove one of the calumnies of 1952—that our government was riddled with subversives.

Tonight I want to tell you first what this kind of leadership or lack of leadership means—both abroad and here at home.

And I want to talk about the effort made by this Administration to cover up its errors—errors that result from abdication of responsibility.

In the last week the American people have watched anxiously the heroic efforts of the Poles and Hungarians to free themselves from the hard yoke of Moscow.

And the so-called Republican truth squad last Friday in Rock Island, Ill., celebrated the event by announcing that the great revolts were "a clear-cut result of the new American foreign policy." We have said more foolish and insulting things about other peoples during the Eisenhower-Dulles period than we like to recall and at an expense in goodwill and respect we can ill afford, but this was a new low even for the Republicans.

If it was true it would be shameful stupidity to say it; but as it is false, it was a gross effort to exploit the anguish of brave people to make votes in an American election. The credit goes where it belongs—to the heroic Poles and Hungarians who faced the tanks and guns of their Russian rulers; it belongs to those who were willing to risk all—their lives, their fortunes, their families—for freedom. No credit goes to men who in recent weeks have exposed themselves to nothing more dangerous than their own campaign oratory. And, as a postscript, let me remind the Republican truth squad that truth might be an interesting experiment for them some day; that they could have announced more accurately that we were caught off guard, that when the fighting broke out in Poland the American Ambassador wasn't even at his post—he was visiting Berlin to see his dentist. And when the revolt broke out in Hungary our envoy was not even in that country.

And you may gauge President Eisenhower's interest in this whole problem by another bit of history. In June of last year, by a vote of 367-0 the House of Representatives passed a resolution expressing its sympathy with the satellite nations and condemning colonialism. When asked about this resolution on June 29, President Eisenhower said: "I did not know about that. Maybe I was fishing that day. I don't know."

But this was not an isolated example. Let me give you another example where the issue of war and peace was at stake.

The winter and spring of 1954 were a time of deep trial and anxiety. Indochina was falling to the communists. I saw that frightening war in the rice paddies and the jungles with my own eyes. The free world was divided, troubled and alarmed, hasty voices—Mr. Nixon's with characteristic volubility, was among them—were advocating armed intervention by American troops.

On Feb. 12 the *New York Times* reported that Senate leaders "alarmed by fears of possible U.S. involvement in the Indochina war" had called high members of the Administration to an urgent secret conference. On the same day the *Times* also reported that President Eisenhower had gone South for hunting with Secretary Humphrey and had bagged his limit of quail.

Two days later the alarm had deepened in Washington and the papers reported that President Eisenhower was leaving for a six-day vacation in California. On Feb. 19, Secretary Dulles returned from the critical four-power conference in Berlin. He couldn't report to the President. The New York Times said "it was golf again for President Eisenhower" at Palm Springs.

Later on April 13, Mr. Dulles and British Foreign Secretary Anthony Eden met to explore the possibilities of joint action—joint military action—in Indochina. The New York Times reported that President Eisenhower had landed in the south "to begin a golfing vacation."

Next day it was announced that we would airlift aid to Indochina; and also that the President was playing golf in Georgia.

On April 17, The New York Times said in a headline that the United States "weighs fighting in Indochina if necessary." The President, it said, was still vacationing in Georgia.

The next day the country learned from the papers that Nixon had said that the United States might have to intervene with military force. Less spectacular news that day was that President Eisenhower had played golf in Augusta with Billy Joe Patton.

On April 23 it was announced that the last outposts around Dienbienphu, the French stronghold, had fallen. That day the President arrived in Georgia for a new golfing holiday.

The free world suffered a severe defeat in Asia and lost a rich country and more than 10,000,000 people in Indochina. And after it was all over Secretary Dulles boasted in an article in Life magazine that it had been a victory.

He also boasted that he had won this victory by our bold behavior and by bringing the country to the brink of war. And when President Eisenhower was asked his opinion, he replied: "I have not read the article."

I could go on. The President was away golfing when it was announced early last year that our Air Force had gone on a full war footing as a result of the Formosa crisis. He was shooting quail when we evacuated the Tachen Islands. He was golfing in New Hampshire in June 1954, when the Soviets shot down a U.S. plane off Alaska. In the New York Times it said, "there was no visible evidence that the President had anything on his mind other than having a good time."

In February of this year the President was golfing in Georgia during the on-again, off-again, on-again mix-up over the shipment of tanks to Saudi Arabia which so alarmed the Israeli people. Mr. Dulles as usual was out of the country. Mr. Herbert Hoover Jr. was running the store.

The President was asked this year whether Russia was leading us in guided missiles. He answered, and I quote him, that he was "astonished at the amount of information that others get that I don't."

The President was asked on April 4 of this year about an urgent message on the Middle Eastern crisis that Prime Minister Eden had sent him ten days earlier. It developed that he didn't even know the letter existed.

When asked about neutralism that long ago the President said he thought it was fine; when Mr. Dulles was asked, he said it was immoral. After they got together Mr. Dulles said that while he thought neutralism immoral he didn't know any immoral neutrals.

I suppose we have to assume that the President just doesn't know, either, of his Secretary of State's incredible blunders that have shaken the Middle East and helped the Communists do in a few months what the Czars couldn't do in centuries—penetrate the Arab lands.

The President is an honorable man. So when he smilingly assures us that all is well and America's prestige has never been higher, he just must not know that in fact the American star is low on the world's horizons.

And even what happens here at home passes the President by.

In 1953 and 1954 we had a serious drop in employment and economic activity. On Feb. 17, 1954, the Department of Commerce announced that unemployment had passed the 3,000,000 mark. The New York Times said the

President would act if there was no upturn soon. It also said that he had just departed for five days vacation at Palm Springs, Calif.

A year ago last May he was asked why Secretary Hobby had difficulty in foreseeing the great demand for Salk vaccine. He said he didn't know anything about it and to ask Mrs. Hobby.

Last February, when the head of the General Services Administration was let out for using his job to help friends get Government contracts the President thought he had resigned for "personal reasons."

When the President was asked if Republican leaders had told him why they killed an important bill to bring aid to areas suffering from unemployment he said, "No, you are telling me something now that I didn't know."

When President Eisenhower's Secretary of Labor urged extending minimum wage legislation to employees of interstate retail chain stores the President was asked where he stood. He said: "I don't know that much about it."

This list could go on endlessly.

I have left out of the list every case where the President's absence from Washington or his ignorance of crucial facts could be traced to his illnesses.

And I want to make it clear that I realize fully that any President will inevitably be gone on some occasions when a crisis arises. I surely don't begrudge the President either the recreation, the repose or the exercise necessary for health. I think even a President is entitled to enjoy himself occasionally.

But a President must assume the full responsibilities of that high post. He is the chief executive. And I say bluntly that I do not agree with President Eisenhower that the United States can be run by a board of directors, with the President presiding at occasional meetings.

Nothing could be more at odds with our constitutional system. The President was elected to the responsibilities of leadership by the American people. Dulles, Wilson, Benson, Weeks and the others were not elected at all. They are the hired hands but the President runs the store.

And we know now that the Eisenhower system just doesn't work.

The price of the President's abdication has been irresponsibility in our foreign policy. This irresponsibility has brought the coalition of the free nations to a point where even its survival has been threatened. And it has brought American prestige to the lowest level in our history.

Here at home we are in the midst of a great social transition. We have come to see with new clarity the full implications of our Bill of Rights and of our democratic faith, and we are moving forward again to assure the equal rights of man to all Americans, regardless of race or color.

Through the nation many citizens of both races are working quietly, working hard, risking much, daring much to solve the stubborn problems that lie in the path of any great social transformation.

Who but the President could say for the whole nation that those participating in this great effort—sometimes even though they disagree with the decision itself—deserve the gratitude, the respect, the moral support of their countrymen? But President Eisenhower, far from rising to this challenge of leadership, has not even expressed his views on the decision and the goal itself.

Nor has he acted with decision to sustain even the most elementary right for all adult Americans—the right to vote. The assurance of this right to all citizens is written in our laws and must surely be the keystone of our democratic institutions. But here again, Mr. Eisenhower has seen no challenge of leadership.

Nothing can be more essential to our system of government than affirmative Presidential leadership. The President was elected to these responsibilities by the American people. He is the only officer of our Government who is elected by all the people.

These four years of a part-time Presidency have been bad enough. But what would another four be like?

Well, I'll tell you. But I don't really need to, because yesterday at the Commonwealth Club in San Francisco Republican Senator Malone of Nevada put it squarely and bluntly. The "greatest sin" the Republican party has committed, this Republican Senator said, has been "carrying on what the Democrats started." Then he added, "but we'll change that in 1957 and 1958 if you elect ... President Eisenhower."

Why? Why will re-electing the same man President mean a whole new and different government policy—a new policy of wrecking twenty years of Democratic building in America?

We know exactly why.

The reason is simply that if the Republicans should be returned to office again the powers of the directorate which has governed in the last four years will be shared and perhaps pre-empted by a man you know, and know well, too well. I refer to the heir apparent, hand-picked by President Eisenhower, Richard Nixon.

President Eisenhower will not be a more vigorous leader in the next four years than in the last four years. He will almost certainly be even less disposed to lead. He will have greater need to conserve his energies. The habit of total delegation once formed is not easily changed.

More important, he will not be allowed to lead. The Republican politicians, we now know, love their leader, the President, mostly at election time. They will follow him to the polls, but no further. For four years the Democrats in Congress have repeatedly had to rescue the President's program from his own party.

Beginning in 1957, if President Eisenhower should be reelected, the Republican leaders in Congress will owe him exactly nothing. He cannot help them get elected again because, under the Twenty-second Amendment, he couldn't run again even if his age and health permitted.

We know from past experience that the President will not lead. We know that if he should try his party will not follow. And into this vacuum would come Richard Nixon—beloved by the most reactionary wing of Old Guard Republicanism.

That's why Senator Malone is so confident that a new term for Mr. Eisenhower will mean an opportunity to do a wrecking job. It's because a new term for Mr. Eisenhower will mean a new destiny for Richard Nixon.

In the last few weeks a plaintive note has entered the Republican newspaper discussion of Mr. Nixon. They say in effect: "Can't people see that this man has changed."

Well, people prefer men who don't have to be changed. And even some mighty good Republicans don't think the Republican party ought to be in the laundry business.

A lot of people just don't believe that Richard Nixon is really at home in this role as the Little Lord Fauntleroy of the Republican party. They wonder if he doesn't yearn for his old tar bucket and his brush. And they suspect that if the circumstances let him he will make a fast grab for it again.

Common decency is at stake here. But more is at stake even than that. President Eisenhower does not lead because he won't. Richard Nixon cannot lead because the American people will not follow.

This is partly because Nixon has a long record against the people. He has voted against public housing to weaken Point Four, against extending social security, against middle-income housing, against increased appropriations for school lunches, against increased R.E.A. loan funds and, of course he voted repeatedly for the Taft-Hartley Act.

People mistrust a man who votes against the people. They have an additional reason to mistrust Mr. Nixon for, on several of these issues, he has taken an equally firm stand on both sides.

Mr. Nixon's advertisers call him "adaptable." Well, that's just the trouble. For what "adaptable" means here is that this man has no standard of truth but convenience and no standard of morality except what will serve his interest in an election. The plain fact is that the people of this country just can't picture Richard Nixon as the leader of the greatest of the world's nations. They can't imagine putting Richard Nixon's hand on the trigger of the H-bomb. They just can't trust him.

John F. Kennedy's Speech to the Greater Houston Ministerial Association (1960)

In early 1960, the political scientist Clinton Rossiter compiled a historical list of "oughts" and "almost certainly musts" for would-be presidential candidates that included the following characteristics: northerner or westerner, more than forty-five but less than sixty-five years old, Protestant, a lawyer, a self-made man, and "a small town boy." In the years since Rossiter's list was published, American voters have chosen as president two southerners (Lyndon B. Johnson in 1964 and Jimmy Carter in 1976) and a sixty-nine (later seventy-three) year old (Ronald Reagan in 1980 and 1984). Except for Richard Nixon in 1968 and 1972, they have elected no lawyers at all.

No president violated more of history's canons than the man who was elected in the year that Rossiter's list appeared. In 1960, John F. Kennedy was a wealthy, forty-three-year-old urbanite. Most remarkably, he was also a Roman Catholic.

Although approximately one-fourth of the electorate was Catholic in 1960 (most of them Democrats), Catholicism was regarded by Democratic party professionals (many of them Catholic) as an insurmountable political handicap for a presidential candidate. The only Catholic nominee for president in history, Gov. Al Smith of New York, had lost by a landslide in 1928, partly be- cause anti-Catholic prejudice cost him the support of nearly half of the otherwise solid Democratic South. (See "H. L. Mencken's 'Onward, Christian Soldiers!' Article," p. 296.) In 1959, 24 percent of a national sample of voters bluntly told the Gallup poll that they could not support any Catholic for president. Renowned Protestant clergy, such as Rev. Norman Vincent Peale, argued that a Catholic president could not properly sort out his conflicting loyalties to church and state. Outside the public gaze, millions of scurrilous anti-Catholic pamphlets, no less hate-filled in 1960 than in 1928, were distributed around the country.

Kennedy used the spring 1960 primaries to demonstrate to his party's leaders that he could overcome these prejudices and be elected as president. Speaking on statewide television to an overwhelmingly Protestant and fundamentalist West Virginia audience, Kennedy faced the issue of his religion head on: "When a man stands on the steps of the Capitol and takes the oath of office of President, he is swearing to support the separation of church and state; he puts one hand on the Bible and raises the other hand to God as he takes the oath. And if he breaks his oath, he is not only committing a crime against the Constitution, for which Congress can impeach him—and should impeach him—but he is com-

mitting a sin against God. A sin against God, for he has sworn on the Bible."

Kennedy won both the May 10 West Virginia primary und, in August, the Democratic nomination for president. But the religious issue threatened to rage anew during the fall campaign. On September 12, 1960, Kennedy tried once again to lay it to rest in a televised speech to the Greater Houston Ministerial Association. After vowing to keep church and state separate in the presidency, Kennedy told the ministers, "[I]f this election is decided on the basis that 40,000,000 Americans lost their chance of being President on the day they were baptized, then it is the whole nation that will be the loser." The initially skeptical clerics greeted Kennedy's remarks warmly.

On election day, most voters cast their ballots without regard for the religious affiliations of the candidates. Even so, millions of Protestants voted against Kennedy because he was Catholic, and millions of Catholics supported him for the same reason. On balance, the concentration of Catholic voters in the large industrial states of the Northeast and Midwest probably won Kennedy more electoral votes than he lost from religious voting.   ~

I am grateful for your generous invitation to state my views.

While the so-called religious issue is necessarily and properly the chief topic here tonight, I want to emphasize from the outset that I believe that we have far more critical issues in the 1960 election: the spread of Communist influence, until it now festers only ninety miles off the coast of Florida—the humiliating treatment of our President and Vice-President by those who no longer respect our power—the hungry children I saw in West Virginia, the old people who cannot pay their doctor's bills, the families forced to give up their farms—an America with too many slums, with too few schools, and too late to the moon and outer space.

These are the real issues which should decide this campaign. And they are not religious issues—for war and hunger and ignorance and despair know no religious barrier.

But because I am a Catholic, and no Catholic has ever been elected President, the real issues in this campaign have been obscured—perhaps deliberately in some quarters less responsible than this. So it is apparently necessary for me to state once again—not what kind of church I believe in, for that should be important only to me, but what kind of America I believe in.

I believe in an America where the separation of church and state is absolute—where no Catholic prelate would tell the President (should he be a Catholic) how to act and no Protestant minister would tell his parishioners for whom to vote—where no church or church school is granted any public funds or political preference—and where no man is denied public office merely because his religion differs from the President who might appoint him or the people who might elect him.

I believe in an America that is officially neither Catholic, Protestant nor Jewish—where no public official either requests or accepts instructions on public policy from the Pope, the National Council of Churches or any other ecclesiastical source—where no religious body seeks to impose its will directly or indirectly upon the general populace or the public acts of its officials—and where religious liberty is so indivisible that an act against one church is treated as an act against all.

For while this year it may be a Catholic against whom the finger of suspicion is pointed, in other years it has been, and may someday be again, a Jew—or a Quaker—or a Unitarian—or a Baptist. It was Virginia's harassment of Baptist preachers, for example, that led to Jefferson's statute of religious freedom. Today, I may be the victim—but tomorrow it may be you—until the whole fabric of our harmonious society is ripped apart at a time of great national peril.

Finally, I believe in an America where religious intolerance will someday end—where all men and all churches are treated as equal—where every man has the same right to attend or not to attend the church of his choice—where there is no Catholic vote, no antiCatholic vote, no bloc voting of any kind—and where Catholics, Protestants and Jews, both the lay and the pastoral level, will refrain from those attitudes of disdain and division which have so often marred their works in the past, and promote instead the American ideal of brotherhood.

That is the kind of America in which I believe. And it represents the kind of Presidency in which I believe—a great office that must be neither humbled by making it the instrument of any religious group, nor tarnished by arbitrarily withholding it, its occupancy, from the members of any religious group. I believe in a President whose views on religion are his own private affair, neither imposed upon him by the nation or imposed by the nation upon him as a condition to holding that office.

I would not look with favor upon a President working to subvert the First Amendment's guarantees of religious liberty (nor would our system of checks and balances permit him to do so). And neither do I look with favor upon those who would work to subvert Article VI of the Constitution by requiring a religious test—even by indirection—for if they disagree with that safeguard, they should be openly working to repeal it.

I want a Chief Executive whose public acts are responsible to all and obligated to none—who can attend any ceremony, service or dinner his office may appropriately require him to ful-fill—and whose fulfillment of his Presidential office is not limited or conditioned by any religious oath, ritual or obligation.

This is the kind of America I believe in—and this is the kind of America I fought for in the South Pacific and the kind my brother died for in Europe. No one suggested then that we might have a "divided loyalty," that we did "not believe in liberty" or that we belonged to a disloyal group that threatened "the freedoms for which our forefathers died."

And in fact this is the kind of America for which our forefathers did die when they fled here to escape religious test oaths, that denied office to members of less favored churches, when they fought for the Constitution, the Bill of Rights, the Virginia Statute of Religious Freedom—and when they fought at the shrine I visited today—the Alamo. For side by side with Bowie and Crockett died Fuentes and McCafferty and Bailey and Bedillio and Carey—but no one knows whether they were Catholics or not. For there was no religious test there.

I ask you tonight to follow in that tradition, to judge me on the basis of fourteen years in the congress—on my declared stands against an ambassador to the Vatican, against unconstitutional aid to parochial schools, and against any boycott of the public schools (which I attended myself)—instead of judging me on the basis of these pamphlets and publications we have all seen that carefully select quotations out of context from the statements of Catholic Church leaders, usually in other countries, frequently in other centuries, and rarely relevant to any situation here—and always omitting, of course, that statement of the American bishops in 1948 which strongly endorsed church-state separation.

I do not consider these other quotations binding upon by public acts—why should you? But let me say, with respect to other countries, that I am wholly opposed to the state being used by any religious group, Catholic or Protestant, to compel, prohibit or persecute the free exercise of any other religion. And that goes for any persecution at any time, by anyone, in any country.

And I hope that you and I condemn with equal fervor those nations which deny their Presidency to Protestants and those which deny it to Catholics. And rather than cite the misdeeds of those who differ, I would also cite the record of the Catholic Church in such nations as France and Ireland—and the independence of such statesmen as de Gaulle and Adenauer.

But let me stress again that these are my views—for, contrary to common newspaper usage, I am not the Catholic candidate for President. I am the Democratic Party's candidate for President, who happens also to be a Catholic.

I do not speak for my church on public matters—and the church does not speak for me.

Whatever issues may come before me as President, if I should be elected—on birth control, divorce, censorship, gambling, or any other subject— I will make my decision in accordance with these views, in accordance with what my conscience tells me to be in the national interest, and without regard to outside religious pressure or dictate. And no power or threat of punishment could cause me to decide otherwise.

But if the time should ever come— and I do not concede any conflict to be remotely possible—when my office would require me to either violate my conscience, or violate the national interest, then I would resign the office, and I hope any other conscientious public servant would do likewise.

But I do not intend to apologize for these views to my critics of either Catholic or Protestant faith, nor do I intend to disavow either my views or my church in order to win this election. If I should lose on the real issues, I shall return to my seat in the Senate, satisfied that I tried my best and was fairly judged.

But if this election is decided on the basis that 40,000,000 Americans lost their chance of being President on the day they were baptized, then it is the whole nation that will be the loser in the eyes of Catholics and non-Catholics around the world, in the eyes of history, and in the eyes of our own people.

But if, on the other hand, I should win this election, I shall devote every effort of mind and spirit to fulfilling the oath of the Presidency—practically identical, I might add, with the oath I have taken for fourteen years in the Congress. For, without reservation, I can, and I quote, "solemnly swear that I will faithfully execute the office of President of the United States and will to the best of my ability preserve, protect and defend the Constitution, so help me God."

The First Nixon-Kennedy Debate (1960)

Richard Nixon served President Dwight D. Eisenhower as vice president for eight years and gave frequent speaking tours to fertilize the Republican party's grass roots. Official status and party service equalled an easy victory at the Republican national convention in July 1960. Nixon's quest for the presidential nomination benefited not only from the growing stature of the vice presidency but also from the Twenty-second Amendment's two-term limit on presidents, which had freed him to begin his own campaign almost as soon as Eisenhower was reelected in 1956. (See "Richard Nixon's 'Checkers' Speech," p. 474, and "The Twenty-second Amendment: House Debate," p. 370.)

From 1789 to 1956, presidential candidates never debated each other. (The famous debates between Abraham Lincoln and Stephen Douglas took place during the Illinois Senate campaign of 1858.) Even with the advent of television in the 1950s, debates were effectively forestalled by a federal law that required stations to give minor and major party candidates equal air time.

In 1960, however, the Democratic-controlled Congress voted to suspend the equal-time provision in order to force Nixon to debate the lesser known Democratic candidate, Sen. John F. Kennedy of Massachusetts. Nixon, confident of both his debating ability and, after the "Checkers" speech, of his television skills, readily agreed to debate Kennedy four times during late September and October.

The first Kennedy-Nixon debate was held in a Chicago television studio on September 26, 1960. It turned out to be politically crucial. Eighty million people watched, setting a record for the largest television audience in history. The format was less that of a classic debate than of a joint press conference—after opening statements by Nixon and Kennedy, a panel of reporters asked each candidate questions.

Since they differed little on substantive issues, the political outcome of the debate turned on matters of appearance and style. JFK won handily on both counts. He was tanned, rested, and dressed in a dark blue suit that stood out well against the studio's grey set. (Television still showed only black-and-white pictures.) Nixon, who had recently been ill, eschewed professional makeup and wore a light grey suit that faded into the background. He looked pale-skinned, hollow-eyed, and dark-bearded.

As to style, Kennedy spoke directly into the television camera and, regardless of the questions, gave answers that sounded the themes he wanted to emphasize in the campaign. His opening statement in the debate, which was supposed to be about domestic policy, stressed the supposed decline of U.S. prestige in the world. In contrast,

Nixon responded directly to Kennedy's points, often disagreeing but sometimes agreeing. Nixon's first words of the evening were, "I subscribe completely to the spirit that Sen. Kennedy has expressed tonight, the spirit that the United States should move ahead."

The first debate gave the Kennedy campaign a boost in enthusiasm and public support that carried it to a narrow victory on election day. Kennedy's electoral vote majority—303-219—was convincing, but his popular vote plurality was only 114,673 votes out of 68,828,960 votes cast.

The lesson that many political leaders learned from the Kennedy-Nixon debates was that the better-known candidate in a presidential election has more to lose by participating in such events and therefore should avoid them. The next presidential debate did not take place until 1976, when President Gerald Ford, trailing badly in the polls, debated his opponent, former Georgia governor Jimmy Carter. (See "The Second Ford-Carter Debate," p. 652.) ~

Smith: Good evening. The television and radio stations of the United States and their affiliated stations are proud to provide facilities for a discussion of issues in the current political campaign by the two major candidates for the Presidency. The candidates need no introduction. The Republican candidate, Vice President Richard M. Nixon, and the Democratic candidate, Senator John F. Kennedy.

According to the rules set by the candidates themselves each man shall make an opening statement of approximately eight minutes duration and a closing statement of approximately three minutes duration. In between the candidates will answer or comment upon answers to questions put by a panel of correspondents. In this, the first discussion in the series of four joint appearances, the subject matter as has been agreed will be restricted to internal or domestic American matters. And now for the first opening statement by Senator John F. Kennedy.

Kennedy: Mr. Smith, Mr. Nixon, in the election of 1860, Abraham Lincoln said the question was whether this nation could exist half slave or half free. In the election of 1960 and with the world around us the question is whether the world will exist half slave or half free, whether it will move in the direction of freedom, in the direction of the road that we are taking or whether it will move in the direction of slavery. I think it will depend in great measure upon what we do here in the United States, on the kind of society that we build, on the kind of strength that we maintain. We discuss tonight domestic issues but I would not want there to be any implication to be given that this does not involve directly our struggle with Mr. Khrushchev for survival.

Mr. Khrushchev is in New York and he maintains the Communist offensive throughout the world because of the productive power of the Soviet Union itself. The Chinese Communists have always had a large population but they are important and dangerous now because they are mounting a major effort within their own country. The kind of country we have here, the kind of society we have, the kind of strength we build in the United States will be the defense of freedom. If we do well here, if we meet our obligations, if we are moving ahead, then I think freedom will be secure around the world. If we fail, then freedom fails.

America's Strength

Therefore I think the question before the American people is, are we doing as much as we can do. Are we as strong as we should be? Are we as strong as we must be if we are going to maintain our independence and if we are going to maintain and hold out the hand of friendship to those who look to us for assistance, to those who look to us for survival.

I should make it very clear that I do not think we are doing enough, that I am not satisfied as an American with the progress that we are making. This is a great country but I think it could be a more powerful country.

I am not satisfied to have fifty percent of our steel mill capacity unused. I am not satisfied when the United States had last year the lowest rate of economic growth of any major industrialized society in the world because economic growth means strength and vitality, it means we are able to sustain our defenses, it means we are able to meet our commitments abroad.

I am not satisfied when we have over $9 billion worth of food, some of it rotting, even though there is a hungry world and even though four million Americans wait every month for a food package from the government which averages five cents a day per individual.

I saw cases in West Virginia, here in the United States, where children took home part of their school lunch in order to feed their families. Because of this I don't think we are meeting our obligations towards these Americans. I am not satisfied when the Soviet Union is turning out twice as many scientists and engineers as we are. I am not satisfied when many of our teachers are inadequately paid or when our children go to school in part time shifts. I think we should have an educational system second to none.

I am not satisfied when I see men like Jimmy Hoffa, in charge of the largest union in the United States, still free. I am not satisfied when we are failing to develop the natural resources of the United States to the fullest.

Here is the United States which developed the Tennessee Valley and which built the Grand Coulee and the other dams in the northwest United States. At the present rate of hydro power production, and that is the hallmark of an industrialized society, the Soviet Union by 1975 will be producing more power than we are. These are all the things I think in this country that can make our society strong or can mean that it stands still. I am not satisfied until every American enjoys his full Constitutional rights.

If a Negro baby is born, and this is true also of Puerto Ricans and Mexicans in some of our cities, he has about one half as much chance to get through high school as a white baby. He has one third as much chance to get through college as a white student. He has about a third as much chance to be a professional man, about half as much chance to own a house. He has about four times as much chance that he will be out of work in his life as the white baby. I think we can do better. I don't want the talents of any American to go to waste.

Social Legislation

I know that there are those who say that we want to turn everything over to the Government. I don't at all. I want the individuals to meet their responsibilities and I want the states to meet their responsibilities but I think there is also a national responsibility. The argument has been used against every piece of social legislation in the last 25 years. The people of the United States individually could not have developed the Tennessee Valley. Collectively they could have. A cotton farmer in Georgia or a peanut farmer, or a dairy farmer in Wisconsin or Minnesota, he cannot protect himself against the forces of supply and demand in the market place but working together in effective governmental programs he can do so.

Seventeen million Americans who live over 65 on an average Social Security check of about $78.00 a month, they are not able to sustain themselves individually but they can sustain themselves through the Social Security system.

I don't believe in big government, but I believe in effective governmental action. And I think that is the only way that the United States is going to maintain its freedom. It is the only way we are going to move ahead. I think we can do a better job. I think we are going to have to do a better job if we are going to meet the responsibilities which time and events have placed upon us. We cannot turn the job over to anyone else.

If the United States fails, then the whole cause of freedom fails and I think it depends in great measure on what we do here in this country.

The reason Franklin Roosevelt was a good neighbor in Latin America was because he was a good neighbor in the United States, because they felt that American society was moving again. I want us to recapture that image. I want people in Latin America and Africa and Asia to start to look to America to see how we are doing things, to wonder what the President of the United States is doing and not to look at Khrushchev or look at the Chinese Communists. That is the obligation upon our generation.

In 1933, Franklin Roosevelt said in his inaugural that this generation of Americans has a rendezvous with destiny. I think our generation of Americans has the same rendezvous. The question now is: can freedom be maintained under the most severe attack it has ever known. I think it can be and I think in the final analysis it depends upon what we do here. I think it is time America started moving again.

Smith: And now the opening statement by Vice President Richard M. Nixon.

Nixon: Mr. Smith, Senator Kennedy. The things that Senator Kennedy has

said, many of us can agree with. There is no question but that we cannot discuss our internal affairs in the United States without recognizing that they have a tremendous bearing on our international position. There is no question but that this nation cannot stand still because we are in a deadly competition, a competition not only with the men in the Kremlin, but the men in Peking. We are ahead in this competition as Senator Kennedy I think has implied, but when you are in a race the only way to stay ahead is to move ahead. And I subscribe completely to the spirit that Senator Kennedy has expressed tonight, the spirit that the United States should move ahead.

Where then do we disagree? I think we disagree on the implication of his remarks tonight, and on the statements that he has made on many occasions during his campaign to the effect that the United States has been standing still. We heard tonight for example, the statement made that our growth in national product last year was the lowest of any industrial nation in the world. Now, last year, of course, was 1958. That happened to be a recession year, but when we look at the growth of GNP this year, a year of recovery, we find that it is six and nine tenths percent and one of the highest in the world today. More about that later.

Looking, then, to this problem of how the United States should move ahead and where the United States is moving, I think it is well that we take the advice of a very famous campaigner: Let's look at the record. Is the United States standing still? Is it true that this administration, as Senator Kennedy has charged, has been an administration of retreat, of defeat, of stagnation? Is it true that as far as this country is concerned in the field of electric power, in all of the fields that he has mentioned, we have not been moving ahead?

Eisenhower Record

Well, we have a comparison that we can make. We have the record of the Truman Administration of seven and one-half years and the seven and one-half years of the Eisenhower Administration. When we compare these two records in the areas that Senator Kennedy has discussed tonight, I think we find that America has been moving ahead.

Let's take the schools. We have built more schools in this seven and one-half years than we have in the previous seven and one-half, for that matter in the previous twenty years.

Let's take hydroelectric power. We have developed more hydroelectric power in these seven and one-half years than was developed in any previous administration in history.

Let us take hospitals. We find more have been built in this administration than in the previous administration. The same is true of highways.

Let us put it in terms that all of us can understand. We often hear gross national product discussed. And in that respect may I say that when we compare the growth in this administration with that of the previous administration that then there was a total growth of 11 percent over seven years. In this administration there has been a total growth of 19 percent over seven years. That shows that there has been more growth in this administration than in its predecessor, but let's not put it there. Let's put it in terms of the average family. What has happened to you?

We find that your wages have gone up five times as much in the Eisenhower Administration as they did in the Truman Administration. What about the prices you pay? We find that the prices you pay went up five times as much in the Truman administration as they did in the Eisenhower Administration. What is the net result of this? This means that the average family income went up fifteen percent in the Eisenhower years as against two percent in the Truman years. Now, this is not standing still, but good as this record is, may I emphasize it isn't enough. A record is never something to stand on. It is something to build on. And in building on this record I believe we have the secret for progress; we know the way to progress and I think first of all our own record proves that we know the way.

Senator Kennedy has suggested that he believes he knows the way. I respect the sincerity with which he makes that suggestion but, on the one hand, when we look at the various programs that he offers, they do not seem to be new, they seem to be simply retreads of the programs of the Truman Administration which preceded it, and I would suggest that during the course of the evening he might indicate those areas in which his programs are new, where they will mean more progress than we had then.

What kind of programs are we for? We are for programs that will expand educational opportunities, that will give to all Americans their equal chance for education, for all of the things which are necessary and dear to the hearts of our people. We are for programs in addition which will see that our medical care for the aged is much better handled than it is at the present time. Here again may I indicate that Senator Kennedy and I are not in disagreement as to the aim. We want to see that they do have adequate medical care. The question is the means. I think that the means that I advocate will reach that goal better than the means that he advocates.

I could give better examples but whatever it is, whether it is in the field of housing—of health or medical care or schools or the development of electric power, we have programs which we believe will move America, move her forward and build on the wonderful record that we have made over these past seven and a half years.

Now, when we look at these programs, might I suggest that in evaluating them, we often have a tendency to say that the test of a program is how much you are spending. I will concede that in all the areas to which I have referred, Senator Kennedy would have the Federal Government spend more than I would have it spend. I figured out the cost of the Democratic platform. It runs a minimum of $13.2 billion a year more than we are presently spending to a maximum of $18 billion a year more than we are presently spending.

Now, the Republican platform will cost more too. It will cost a minimum of $4 billion a year more, a maximum of $4.9 billion a year more than we are presently spending. Now, does this mean that his program is better than ours? Not at all, because it isn't a question of how much the Federal Government spends, it isn't a question of which Government does the most, it is a question of which administration does the right things and in our case I do believe that our programs will stimulate the creative energies of 180 million free Americans. I believe the programs that Senator Kennedy advocates will have a tendency to stifle those creative energies. I believe, in other words, that his programs would lead to the stagnation of the motive power that we need in this country to get progress.

The final point that I would like to make is this: Senator Kennedy has suggested in his speeches that we lack compassion for the poor, for the old and for others that are unfortunate. Let us understand throughout this campaign that his motives and mine are sincere. I know what it means to be poor. I know what it means to see people who are unemployed. I know Senator Kennedy feels as deeply about these problems as I do but our disagreement is not about the goals for America but only about the means to reach those goals.

Smith: Thank you, Mr. Nixon.

That completes the opening statements and now the candidates will answer questions or comment upon one another's answers to questions put by correspondents of the networks.

The correspondents.

Vanocur: I am Sander Vanocur, NBC News.

Warren: I am Charles Warren, Mutual News.

Novins: I am Stuart Novins, CBS News.

Fleming: Bob Fleming, the ABC News.

Smith: The first question, to Senator Kennedy, from Mr. Fleming.

Kennedy Experience

Fleming: Senator, the Vice President in his campaign has said that you were naive and at times immature. He has raised the question of leadership. On this issue why do you think people should vote for you rather than the Vice President?

Kennedy: The Vice President and I came to the Congress together in 1946. We both served on the Labor Committee. I have been there now for 14 years, the same time that he has, so that our experience in government is comparable.

Secondly, I think the question is: what are the programs that we advocate? What is the party record that we lead?

I come out of the Democratic Party which in this century has produced Woodrow Wilson and Franklin Roosevelt and Harry Truman and which supported and sustained these programs which I have discussed tonight.

Mr. Nixon comes out of the Republican Party. He was nominated by it. And it is a fact that through most of these last 25 years the Republican leadership has opposed federal aid for education, medical care for the aged, development of the Tennessee Valley, development of our natural resources. I think Mr. Nixon is an effective leader of his party. I hope he would grant me the same. The question before us is which point of view and which party do we want to lead the United States.

Smith: Mr. Nixon, would you like to comment on the statement?

Nixon: I have no comment.

Nixon Proposals

Smith: The next question, Mr. Novins.

Novins: Mr. Vice President, your campaign stresses the value of your 8-year experience and the question arises as to whether that experience was as an observer or as a participant or as an initiator of policy making. Would you tell us, please, specifically, what major proposals you have made in the last eight years that have been adopted by the administration?

Nixon: It would be rather difficult to cover them in eight—in two and one-half minutes. I would suggest that these proposals could be mentioned: First, after each of my foreign trips, I have made recommendations that have been adopted. For example, after my first trip abroad, I strongly recommended that we increase our exchange programs particularly as they related to exchange of persons, of leaders in the labor field and in the information field. After my trip to South America, I made recommendations that a separate inter-American lending agency be set up which the South American nations would like much better than to participate in the lending agencies which treated all the countries of the world the same.

I have made other recommendations after each of the other trips. For example, after my trip abroad to Hungary, I made some recommendations with re-gard to the Hungarian refugee situation which were adopted not only by the President but some of them were enacted into law by the Congress.

Within the Administration as Chairman of the President's Committee on Price Stability and Economic Growth, I have had the opportunity to make recommendations which have been adopted within the Administration and which I think have been reasonably effective.

I know Senator Kennedy suggested in his speech at Cleveland that the Committee had not been particularly effective. I would only suggest that while we do not take credit for it, I would not presume to, that since the Committee has been formed, the price line has been held very well within the United States.

Kennedy: Well, I would say, in the latter, that the—and that's what I found somewhat unsatisfactory about the figures Mr. Nixon that you used in your previous speech, when you talked about the Truman Administration. Mr. Truman came to office in 1944 and at the end of the war and difficulties that were facing the United States during that period of transition, 1946 when price controls were lifted. So it is rather difficult using an over-all figure, taking those seven and one-half years and comparing them to the last eight years. I prefer to take the over-all percentage record of the last twenty years of the Democrats and the eight years of the Republicans to show an over-all period of growth.

In regard to price stability, I am not aware that the Committee did produce recommendations that ever were certainly before the Congress from the point of view of legislation in regard to controlling prices.

In regard to the exchange of students of labor unions, I am chairman of the Subcommittee on Africa. I think that one of the most unfortunate phases of our policy towards that country was the very minute number of exchanges that we had.

I think it is true of Latin America also. We did come forward with a program of students for the Congo of over three hundred, which was more than the federal government had for all of Africa the previous year. So that I don't think that we have moved, at least in those two areas, with sufficient vigor.

Farm Surpluses

Smith: The next question to Senator Kennedy from Mr. Warren.

Warren: Senator Kennedy, during your brief speech a few minutes ago, you mentioned farm surpluses.

Kennedy: That is correct.

Warren: I would like to ask this. It is a fact, I think, that presidential candidates traditionally make promises to farmers. Lots of people I think don't understand why the government pays farmers for not producing certain crops or paying farmers if they overproduce, for that matter. Let me ask, sir, why can't the farmer operate like the business man who operates a factory? If an auto company overproduces a certain model of car, Uncle Sam doesn't step in and buy up the surplus. Why this constant courting of the farmer?

Kennedy: Because I think that if the federal government moved out of the program and withdrew its supports, then I think you would have complete economic chaos. The farmer plants in the spring and harvests in the fall. There are hundreds of thousands of them. They really are not able to control their market very well. They bring their crops in or their livestock in, many of them about the same time. They have only a few purchasers that buy their milk or their hogs, a few large companies in many cases, and therefore the farmer is not in a position to bargain very effectively in the market place.

I think the experience of the Twenties has shown what a free market could do to agriculture and if the agricultural economy collapses, then the economy of the rest of the United States sooner or later will collapse. The farmers are the number one market for the automobile industry of the United States. The automobile industry is the number one market for steel, so if the farmers' economy continues to decline as sharply as it has in recent years then I think you would have a recession in the rest of the country. So I think the case for the government intervention is a good one.

Secondly, my objection to present farm policy is that there are no effective controls to bring supply and demand into better balance. The dropping of the support price in order to limit production has not worked and we now have the highest surpluses, $9 billion worth. We have had a higher tax load from the Treasury for the farmer in the last few years with the lowest farm income in many years. I think that this farm policy has failed.

Benson 'Failure'

In my judgment, the only policy that will work will be for effective supply and demand to be in balance, and that can only be done through governmental action. I therefore suggest that in those basic commodities which are supported that the federal government, after endorsement by the farmers in that commodity, attempt to bring supply and demand into balance, attempt effective production controls so that we won't have five or six percent surplus which breaks the price 15 or 20 percent.

I think Mr. Benson's program has failed. And I must say after reading the Vice President's speech before the farmers, as he read mine, I don't believe it is very much different from Mr. Benson's. I don't think it provides effective government controls. I think the support prices are tied to the average market prices for the last three years, which was Mr. Benson's theory. I therefore do not believe that this is a sharp enough breach with the past to give us any hope for success in the future.

Smith: Mr. Nixon, comment?

Nixon: I of course disagree with Senator Kennedy in so far as his suggestion as to what should be done on the farm program. He has made the suggestion that what we need is to move in the direction of more government controls, a suggestion that would also mean raising prices that the consumers pay for products and imposing upon the farmers controls on acreage even far more than they have today. I think this is the wrong direction. I don't think this has worked in the past. I do not think it will work in the future. The program that I have advocated is one which departs from the present program that we have in this respect. It recognizes that the Government has a responsibility to get the farmer out of the trouble he presently is in because the Government got him into it. And that is the fundamental reason why we can't let the farmer go by himself at the present time. The farmer produced these surpluses because the Government asked him to through legislation during the war. Now that we have these surpluses, it is our responsibility to indemnify the farmer during that period that we get rid of the surpluses.

Until we get the surpluses off the farmers' back, however, we should have a program such as I announced which will see that farm income holds up. But I would propose holding that income up not through a type of program that Senator Kennedy has suggested that would raise prices but one that would indemnify the farmer, pay the farmer in kind from the products which are in surplus.

Nixon Ideas

Smith: The next question to Vice President Nixon from Mr. Vanocur.

Vanocur: Mr. Vice President, since the question of executive leadership is a very important campaign issue I would like to follow Mr. Novins' question. Now, Republican campaign slogans, you'll see them on signs around the country as you did last week, say "it is experience that counts." That's over a picture of yourself, sir, implying that you have more governmental, executive decision-making experience than your opponent.

Now in his news conference on August 24, President Eisenhower was asked to give one example of a major idea of yours that he had adopted. His reply was, and I am quoting, "If you give me a week I might think of one, I don't remember." Now that was a month ago, sir, and the President hasn't brought it up since and I am wondering, sir, if you can clarify which version is correct, the one put out by Republican campaign leaders or the one put out by President Eisenhower?

Nixon: Well I would suggest Mr. Vanocur, that if you know the President, that was probably a facetious remark. I would also suggest that insofar as his statement is concerned, that I think it would be improper for the President of the United States to disclose the instances in which members of his official family had made recommendations, as I have made them through the years to him, which he has accepted or rejected.

The President has always maintained and very properly so that he is entitled to get what advice he wants from his cabinet and from his other advisors without disclosing that to anybody, including, as a matter of fact, the Congress.

Now I can only say this: through the years I have sat in the National Security

Council. I have been in the Cabinet. I have met with the legislative leaders. I have met with the President when he made the great decisions with regards to Lebanon, Quemoy and Matsu, other matters. The President has asked for my advice. I have given it. Sometimes my advice has been taken. Sometimes it has not.

I do not say that I have made the decisions and I would say that no President should ever allow anybody else to make the major decisions. The President only makes the decisions. All that his advisors do is to give counsel when he asks for it. As far as what experience counts and whether that is experience that counts, that isn't for me to say. I can only say that my experience is there for the people to consider.

Senator Kennedy's is there for people to consider. As he pointed out, we came to the Congress in the same year. His experience has been different from mine. Mine has been in the Executive Branch. His has been in the Legislative Branch. I would say that the people now have the opportunity to evaluate his as against mine and I think both he and I are going to abide by whatever the people decide.

Smith: Senator Kennedy:

Kennedy: Well, I will just say that the question is of experience and the question also is of what our judgment is of the future, and what our goals are for the United States, and what ability we have to implement those goals.

Abraham Lincoln came to the Presidency in 1860 after a rather little known session in the House of Representatives, and after being defeated for the Senate in '58, and was a distinguished President.

There are no certain roads to the Presidency. There are no guarantees that if you take one road or another that you will be a successful President. I have been in the Congress for 14 years. I have voted in the last eight years, when the Vice President was presiding over

the Senate and meeting his other responsibilities. I have met decisions 800 times on matters which affect not only the domestic security of the United States but as a member of the Senate Foreign Relations Committee. The question really is which candidate and which party can meet the problems that the United States is going to face in the '60s.

Smith: The next question to Senator Kennedy from Mr. Novins.

Federal Debt

Novins: Senator Kennedy, in connection with these problems of the future that you speak of and the program that you enunciated earlier in your direct talk, you call for expanding some of the welfare programs for schools, for teacher salaries, medical care, and so forth, but you also call for reducing the federal debt, and I am wondering how, if you are President in January, would go about paying the bill for all this.

Kennedy: I did not advocate reducing the federal debt because I don't believe you are going to be able to reduce the federal debt very much in 1961, '2 or '3, I think we have heavy obligations which affect our security which we are going to have to meet and, therefore, I have never suggested we should be able to retire the debt substantially or even at all in 1961 or '2. No, never—

Novins: Senator, I believe in one of your speeches you suggested that reducing the interest rate would help toward reducing the federal—

Kennedy: No, not reducing the interest—reducing the interest rate. In my judgment, the hard money, tight money policy, fiscal policy of this administration has contributed to the slowdown in our economy which helped bring the recession of '54, which made the recession of '58 rather intense and which has slowed somewhat our economic activity in 1960. What I have talked, however, the kind of programs that I talk about, in my judgment, are fiscally sound. Medical care for the aged I would put under Social Security. The Vice President and I disagree on this. The program, the Javits-Nixon or the Nixon-Javits program would have cost, if fully used, $600 million by the Government per year and $600 million by the State. The program which I advocated which failed by five votes in the United States Senate would have put medical care for the aged in Social Security and would have been paid for through the Social Security system and the Social Security tax.

Secondly, I support aid to education and federal aid for teachers' salaries. I think that is a good investment. I think we are going to have to do it, and I think to heap the burden further on the property tax which is already straining many of our communities will provide, will make, insure, in my opinion, that many children will not be adequately educated and many of our teachers not adequately compensated. There is no greater return to an economy or to a society than an educational system second to none.

On the question of the development of natural resources, I would pay as you go in the sense that they would be balanced and the power revenues would bring back sufficient money to finance the projects in the same way as the Tennessee Valley. I believe in the balanced budget and the only conditions under which I would unbalance the budget would be if there was a grave national emergency or a serious recession.

Otherwise, with a steady rate of economic growth, and Mr. Nixon and Mr. Rockefeller in their meeting said a five percent economic growth would bring by 1962 $10 billion extra in tax revenues, whatever is brought in, I think

that we can finance essential programs within a balanced budget if business remains orderly.

Smith: Mr. Nixon, your comment?

Nixon: I think what Mr. Novins is referring to was not one of Senator Kennedy's speeches, but the Democratic platform which did mention cutting the national debt. I think too that it should be pointed out that of course it is not possible, particularly under the proposals that Senator Kennedy has advocated, either to cut the national debt or to reduce taxes. As a matter of fact it will be necessary to raise taxes. As Senator Kennedy points out that as far as his one proposal is concerned, the one for medical care for the aged, that that would be financed out of Social Security. That however is raising taxes for those who pay Social Security. He points out that he would make pay-as-you-go be the basis for our natural resources development which I also support incidentally. However, whenever you appropriate money for one of these projects, you have to pay now and appropriate the money, and while they eventually do pay out, it doesn't mean that the government doesn't have to put out the money this year. And so I would say that in all these proposals Senator Kennedy has made, they will result in one or two things: Either he has to raise taxes, or he has to unbalance the budget. If he unbalances the budget, that means you have inflation and that will be, of course, a very cruel blow to the very people, the older people, that we have been talking about.

As far as an aid for school construction, I favor that as Senator Kennedy did in January of this year when he said he favored that rather than aid to teacher salaries. I favor that because I believe that is the best way to aid our schools without running any risk whatever of the Federal Government telling our teachers what to teach.

School Aid

Smith: The next question to Vice President Nixon from Mr. Warren.

Warren: Mr. Vice President, you mentioned schools. It was just yesterday I think you asked for a crash program to raise educational standards and this evening you talked about advances in education.

Mr. Vice President, you said, it was back in 1957, that salaries paid to school teachers were nothing short of a national disgrace. Higher salaries for teachers, you added were important and if the situation wasn't corrected it would lead to a national disaster. Yet you refused to vote in the Senate in order to break a tie vote when that single vote if it had been "Yes" would have granted salary increases to teachers. I wonder if you could explain that, sir?

Nixon: I am awfully glad to get that question because as you know I got into it at the last of my other question and wasn't able to complete the argument.

I think that the reason that I voted against having the Federal Government pay teachers' salaries was probably the very reason that concerned Senator Kennedy when in January of this year in his kick-off press conference he said that he favored aid for school construction but at that time did not feel that there should be aid for teachers' salaries. At least that is the way I read his remarks.

Now why should there be any question about the Federal Government aiding teachers' salaries? Why did Senator Kennedy take that position then? Why do I take it now? We both took it then and I take it now for this reason: We want higher teachers' salaries. We need higher teachers' salaries but we also want our education to be free of federal control.

When the Federal Government gets the power to pay teachers, inevitably in my opinion it will acquire the power to set standards and to tell the teachers what to teach. I think this would be bad for the country. I think it would be bad for the teaching profession. There is another point that should be made. I favor higher salaries for teachers, but as Senator Kennedy said in January of this year in the same press conference, the way that you get higher salaries for teachers is to support school construction which means that all of the local school districts in the various states then have money which is freed to raise the standards for teachers' salaries.

I should also point out this: Once you put the responsibility on the Federal Government for paying a portion of teachers' salaries, your local communities and your states are not going to meet the responsibility as much as they should. I believe, in other words, that we have seen the local communities in the states assuming more of that responsibility. Teachers' salaries, very fortunately, have gone up fifty percent in the last eight years as against only a thirty-four percent rise for other salaries. This is not enough. It should be more, but I do not believe that the way to get more salaries for teachers is to have the Federal Government get in with a massive program.

My objection here is not the cost in dollars. My objection here is the potential cost in controls and eventual freedom for the American people, by giving the Federal Government power over education and that is the greatest power a government can have.

Smith: Senator Kennedy's comment?

Kennedy: When the Vice President quotes me in January '60, I did not believe the federal government should pay directly teachers' salaries, but that was not the issue before the Senate in February. The issue before the Senate was that the money would be given to the state. The state then could determine whether the money would be spent for school construction or teachers' salaries. On that question the Vice

President and I disagreed. I voted in favor of that proposal and supported it strongly because I think that that provided assistance to our teachers for their salaries without any chance of federal control, and it is on that vote that Mr. Nixon and I disagreed, and his tie vote defeated, his breaking the tie defeated the proposal.

I don't want the Federal Government paying teachers' salaries directly, but if the money will go to the states and the states can then determine whether it shall go for school construction or for teachers' salaries, in my opinion you protect the local authority over the school board and the school committee, and supported it, and therefore I think that was a sound proposal and that is why I regret that it did not pass.

Secondly, there have been statements made that the Democratic platform would cost a good deal of money and that I am in favor of unbalancing the budget. That is wholly wrong, wholly in error. And it is a fact that in the last eight years the Democratic Congress has reduced the requests for appropriations by over $10 billion. That is not my view and I think it ought to be stated very clearly on the record. My view is that you can do these programs and they should be carefully drawn within a balanced budget if our economy is moving ahead.

August Session

Smith: The next question to Senator Kennedy from Mr. Vanocur.

Vanocur: Senator, you have been promising the voters that if you are elected President you will try and push through Congress bills on medical aid to the aged, a comprehensive minimum hourly wage bill, federal aid to education. Now, in the August post-convention session of the Congress, when you at least held up the possibility you

could one day be President and when you had overwhelming majorities, especially in the Senate, you could not get action on these bills. Now, how do you feel that you will be able to get them in January if you weren't able to get them in August?

Kennedy: If I may take the bills, we did pass in the Senate a bill to provide $1.25 minimum wage. It failed because the House did not pass it and the House failed by 11 votes. I might say two-thirds of the Republicans in the House voted against $1.25 minimum wage and a majority of the Democrats sustained it. Nearly two-thirds of them voted for the $1.25. We were threatened by a veto if we passed $1.25.

It is extremely difficult, with the great power that the President has, to pass any bill when the President is opposed to it. All the President needs to sustain his veto of any bill is one third plus one in either the House or the Senate.

Secondly, we passed a federal aid to education bill in the Senate. It failed to come to the floor of the House of Representatives. It was killed in the Rules Committee and it is a fact in the August session that the four members of the Rules Committee who were Republicans joining with two Democrats voted against sending the aid to education bill to the floor of the House. Four Democrats voted for it. Every Republican on the Rules Committee voted against sending that bill to be considered by the members of the House of Representatives.

Thirdly, on medical care for the aged, this is the same fight that has been going on for 25 years in Social Security. We wanted to tie it to Social Security. We offered an amendment to do so; 44 Democrats voted for it. One Republican voted for it, and we were informed at the time it came to a vote that if it was adopted the President of the United States would veto it. In my judgment, a vigorous Democratic President, supported by a Democratic majority and the threat of a veto hangs over the Congress, in my judgment you will continue what happened in the August session, which is a clash of parties and inaction.

Smith: Mr. Nixon, comment?

Nixon: Obviously, my views are a little different. First of all, I don't see how it is possible for one-third of a body, such as the Republicans have in the House and the Senate, to stop two-thirds if the two-thirds are adequately led.

I would say, too, that when Senator Kennedy refers to the action of the House Rules Committee there are eight Democrats on that committee and four Republicans. It would seem to me again that it was very difficult to blame the four Republicans for the eight Democrats not getting something through that particular committee.

I would say further that to blame the President and his veto power for the inability of the Senator and his colleagues to get action in this special session misses the mark.

When the President exercises his veto power, he has to have the people behind him, not just a third of the Congress, because—let's consider it. If the majority of the members of the Congress felt that these particular proposals were good issues, the majority of those who were Democrats, why didn't they pass them and send them to the President and get a veto and have an issue?

The reason why these particular bills in these various fields that have been mentioned were not passed was not because the President was against them. It was because the people were against them. It was because they were too extreme and I am convinced that the alternate proposals that I have, that the Republicans have in the field of health, in the field of education, in the field of welfare, because they are not extreme, because they will accomplish the end without too great cost in dollars

or in freedom, that they could get through the next Congress.

Smith: The next question to Vice President Nixon from Mr. Fleming.

Democratic Majorities

Fleming: Mr. Vice President, do I take it then you believe that you could work better with Democratic majorities in the House and Senate than Senator Kennedy could work with Democratic majorities in the House and Senate?

Nixon: I would say this, that we of course expect to pick up some seats in both the House and Senate. We would hope to control the House, to get a majority in the House in this election; we cannot, of course, control the Senate.

I would say that a President will be able to lead, a President will be able to get his program through to the effect that he has the support of the country, the support of the people. Sometimes we get the opinion that in getting programs through the House or the Senate it is purely a question of legislative finagling and all that sort of thing. It isn't really that. Whenever a majority of the people are for a program, the House and the Senate respond to it. And whether this House and Senate in the next session is Democratic or Republican, if the country will have voted for the candidate for the Presidency and for the proposals that he has made, I believe that you will find that the President, if it were a Republican, as it would be in my case, would be able to get his program through that Congress.

Now, I also say that as far as Senator Kennedy's proposals are concerned, that again the question is not simply one of a Presidential veto stopping programs. You must always remember that a President can't stop anything unless he has the people behind him, and the reason President Eisenhower's vetoes have been sustained, the reason the Congress does not send up bills to him which they think will be vetoed, is because the people and the Congress, the majority of them, know the country is behind the President.

Smith: Senator Kennedy:

Kennedy: Well, now, let's look at these bills that the Vice President suggests were too extreme. One was a bill for $1.25 an hour for anyone who works in a store or company that has a million dollars a year business. I don't think that is extreme at all and yet nearly 2/3 to 3/4 of the Republicans in the House of Representatives voted against that proposal.

Secondly, there was the federal aid to education bill. It was—because of the defeat of teachers' salaries—it was not a bill that met in my opinion the needs. The fact of the matter was that it was a bill that was less than you recommended, Mr. Nixon, this morning in your proposal. It was not an extreme bill and yet we could not get one Republican to join. At least I think four of the eight democrats voted to send it to the Floor of the House. Not one Republican joined with those democrats who were opposed to it. I don't say that the Democrats are united in their support of the program, but I do say a majority are, and I say a majority of the Republicans are opposed to it.

The third is medical care for the aged which was tied to Social Security and is financed out of Social Security funds. It does not put a deficit on the Treasury. The proposal advanced by you and by Mr. Javits would have cost six hundred millions of dollars. Mr. Rockefeller rejected it in New York. He said he didn't agree with the financing at all. He said it ought to be on Social Security. So there are three programs which are quite moderate. I think it shows the difference between the two parties. One party is ready to move in these pro-grams. The other party gives them lip service.

Smith: Mr. Warren's question for Senator Kennedy.

Warren: Senator Kennedy, on another subject: Communism is often described as an ideology or a belief that exists somewhere other than in the United States. Let me ask you, sir. Just how serious a threat to our national security are these Communist subversive activities in the United States today?

Kennedy: I think they are serious. I think it is a matter that we should continue to give great care and attention to. We should support the laws which the United States has passed in order to protect us from those who would destroy us from within. We should sustain the Department of Justice in its efforts, and the FBI, and we should be continually alert. I think if the United States is maintaining a strong society here in the United States, I think that we can meet any internal threat. The major threat is external and will continue.

Smith: Mr. Nixon, comment?

Nixon: I agree with Senator Kennedy's appraisal generally in this respect. The question of Communism within the United States has been one that has worried us in the past. It is one that will continue to be a problem for years to come. We have to remember that the Cold War that Mr. Khrushchev is waging and his colleagues are waging is waged all over the world and it is waged right here in the United States. That is why we have to continue to be alert. It is also essential in being alert that we be fair, because by being fair we uphold the very freedoms that the Communists would destroy. We uphold the standards of conduct which they would never follow; and in this connection I think that we must look to the future, having in mind the fact that we fight Communism at home, not only by our laws to deal with

Communists, the few who do become Communists and the few who do become fellow travelers, but we also fight Communism at home by moving against those various injustices which exist in our society which the Communists feed upon. And in that connection I again would say that while Senator Kennedy says we are for the status quo, I do believe that he would agree that I am just as sincere in believing that my proposals for federal aid to education, my proposals for health care, are just as sincerely held as his.

The question again is not one of goals. We are for those goals. It is one of means.

School Issue

Smith: Mr. Vanocur's question for Vice President Nixon.

Vanocur: Mr. Vice President, in one of your earlier statements you said we've moved ahead, we've built more schools, we've built more hospitals. Now, sir, isn't it true that the building of more schools is a local matter for financing?

Were you claiming that the Eisenhower Administration was responsible for the building of these schools, or is it the local school districts that provide for them?

Nixon: Not at all. As a matter of fact, your question brings out a point that I am very glad to make. Too often in appraising whether we are moving ahead or not, we think only of what the Federal Government is doing. Now, that isn't the test of whether America moves. The test of whether America moves is whether the Federal Government, plus the state government, plus the local government, plus the biggest segment of all, individual enterprise, moves.

We have, for example, a gross national product of approximately $500 billion. Roughly $100 billion to $125 billion of that is the result of government activity. $400 billion, approximately, is the result of what individuals do. Now, the reason the Eisenhower Administration has moved, the reason that we have had the funds, for example, locally to build the schools, and the hospitals, and the highways, to make the progress that we have, is because this administration has encouraged individual enterprise and it has resulted in the greatest expansion of the private sector of the economy that has ever been witnessed in an eight year period, and this is growth. That is the growth we are looking for, it is the growth that this administration has supported, and that its policies have stimulated.

Smith: Senator Kennedy?

Kennedy: I must say I think the reason that the schools have been constructed is because the local school districts were willing to increase the property taxes to a tremendously high figure, in my opinion, almost to a point of diminishing returns in order to sustain these schools.

Secondly, I think we have a rich country, and I think we have a powerful country. I think what we have to do, however, is have the President and the leadership set before our country exactly what we must do in the next decade, if we are going to maintain our security, in education, in economic growth, in the development of natural resources.

The Soviet Union is making great gains. It isn't enough to compare what might have been done eight years ago or ten years ago or 15 years ago or 20 years ago. I want to compare what we are doing with what our adversaries are doing so that by the year 1970 the United States is ahead in education, in health, in building, in homes, in economic strength. I think that is the big assignment, the big task, the big function of the Federal Government.

Smith: Can I have the summation time, please? We have completed our questions and our comments and in just a moment we will have the summation time.

Announcer: This will allow three minutes and twenty seconds for the summation by each candidate.

Smith: Three minutes and twenty seconds for each candidate. Vice President Nixon, will you make the first summation?

Nixon Summation

Nixon: Thank you, Mr. Smith, Senator Kennedy. First of all, I think it is well to put in perspective where we really do stand with regard to the Soviet Union in this whole matter of growth. The Soviet Union has been moving faster than we have, but the reason for that is obvious. They start from a much lower base. Although they have been moving faster in growth than we have, we find, for example, today, that their total gross national product is only forty-four percent of our total gross national product. That is the same percentage that it was twenty years ago. And as far as the absolute gap is concerned we find that the United States is even further ahead than it was twenty years ago.

Is this any reason for complacency? Not at all, because these are determined men, they are fanatical men, and we have to get the very most out of our economy. I agree completely with Senator Kennedy on that score.

Where we disagree is in the means that we would use to get the most out of our economy. I respectfully submit that Senator Kennedy too often would rely too much on the Federal Government on what it would do to solve our problems, to stimulate growth. I believe that when we examine the Democratic platform, when we examine the proposals that he has discussed tonight, when we compare them with the proposals that I have made, that these proposals that he makes would not result in greater growth for this country than would be the case if we followed the programs that I have advocated.

There are many of the points that he has made that I would like to comment upon. The one in the field of health is worth mentioning. Our health program, the one that Senator Javits and other Republican senators as well as I supported, is one that provides for all people over sixty-five who want health insurance the opportunity to have it if they want it. It provides a choice of having either government insurance or private insurance, but it compels nobody to have insurance who does not want it. His program under Social Security would require everybody who had Social Security to take government health insurance whether he wanted it or not and it would not cover several million people who are not covered by Social Security at all. Here is one place where I think that our program does a better job than his.

The other point that I would make is this: This downgrading of how much things cost, I think many of our people will understand better when they look at what happened during the Truman Administration when the government was spending more than it took in. We found savings over a lifetime eaten up by inflation. We found that people who could least afford it, people on retired incomes, people on fixed incomes, we found them unable to meet their bills at the end of the month.

It is essential that a man who is President of this country certainly stand for every program that will mean for growth, and I stand for programs that will mean growth and progress, but it is also essential that he not allow a dollar spent that could be better spent by the people themselves.

Kennedy Summation

Smith: Senator Kennedy, your conclusion.

Kennedy: The point was made by Mr. Nixon that the Soviet production is only 44 percent of ours. I must say that 44 percent in that Soviet country is causing us a good deal of trouble tonight. I want to make sure that it stays in that relationship. I don't want to see the day when it is 60 percent of ours, or 70 and 75 and 80 and 90 percent of ours, with all the force and power that it could bring to bear in order to cause our destruction.

Secondly, the Vice President mentioned medical care for the aged. Our program was an amendment to the Kerr Bill. The Kerr Bill provided assistance to all those who were not on Social Security. I think it is a very clear contrast. In 1935, when the Social Security Act was written, 94 out of 95 Republicans voted against it. Mr. Landon ran in 1936 to repeal it. In August of 1960, when we tried to get it again, this time for medical care, we received the support of one Republican in the Senate on this occasion.

Thirdly, I think the question before the American people is, as they look at this country and as they look at the world around them, the goals are the same for all Americans: the means are a question. The means are at issue. If you feel that everything that is being done now is satisfactory, that the relative power and prestige and strength of the United States is increasing in relation to that of the Communists, that we are gaining more security, that we are achieving everything as a nation that we should achieve, that we are achieving a better life for our citizens and greater strength, then I agree, I think you should vote for Mr. Nixon. But if you feel that we have to move again in the 60's, that the function of the President is to set before the people the unfinished business of our society as Franklin Roosevelt did in the 30's, the agenda for our people, what we must do as a society to meet our needs in this country and protect our security and help the cause of freedom—as I said at the beginning—the question before us all, that faces all Republicans and Democrats is: can freedom in the next generation conquer, or are the Communists going to be successful.

That is the great issue; and if we meet our responsibilities I think freedom will conquer. If we fail, if we fail to move ahead, if we fail to develop sufficient military and economic and social strength here in this country, then I think that the tide could begin to run against us and I don't want historians ten years from now to say these were the years when the tide ran out for the United States. I want them to say these were the years when the tide came in. These were the years when the United States started to move again.

That is the question before the American people and only you can decide what you want, what you want this country to be, what you want to do with the future. I think we are ready to move and it is to that great task, if we are successful, that we will address ourselves.

Smith: Thank you very much, gentlemen. This hour has gone by all too quickly. Thank you very much for permitting us to present the next President of the United States on this unique program. I have been asked by the candidates to thank the American networks and the affiliated stations for providing time and facilities for this joint appearance. Other debates in this series will be announced later, and will be on different subjects. This is Howard K. Smith. Goodnight from Chicago.

Lyndon B. Johnson's "Let Us Continue" Speech to Congress (1963)

Lyndon B. Johnson of Texas, the most powerful Senate majority leader of the twentieth century, was John F. Kennedy's main rival for the Democratic presidential nomination in 1960. In circumstances that still are disputed by participants (was Kennedy's offer sincere or merely courteous?), Johnson accepted the second slot on the ticket. By most accounts, Johnson's active campaigning kept Texas and Louisiana in the Democratic column on election day, thus providing Kennedy with his narrow margin of victory against the Republican ticket of Richard Nixon for president and United Nations ambassador Henry Cabot Lodge for vice president.

Johnson was uninfluential and, as a consequence, unhappy as Kennedy's vice president. Still, he faithfully supported the president's "New Frontier" legislative agenda, including medical care for the aged, a large income tax cut, federal aid to education, and civil rights. On November 22, 1963, Kennedy was assassinated in Dallas, Texas. For Johnson and the country, the truth of the remark made by the first vice president, John Adams, once again became apparent: "I am vice president. In this I am nothing, but I may be everything." Flanked by Mrs. Kennedy and Mrs. Johnson, the new president took the oath of office on the plane that carried them back to Washington.

As president, Kennedy had been a hero to many liberal Democrats; in death he became their idol. In contrast, Johnson's reputation among most liberals was as a southern "wheeler-dealer" whose principles, if any, embodied the conservatism of his region. The new president moved quickly to lay those perceptions to rest. On November 27, 1963, Johnson appeared before Congress and a national television audience to proclaim: "On the 20th day of January, in 1961, John F. Kennedy told his countrymen that our national work would not be finished 'in the first thousand days, nor in the life of this administration, nor even perhaps in our lifetime on this planet. But, he said, 'let us begin.' Today, in this moment of new resolve, I would say to all my fellow Americans, let us continue."

Johnson worked hard to pass Kennedy's legislative programs through Congress. Joining the public's idealized memories of the fallen president to his own extraordinary political skills, Johnson enacted every major item on the New Frontier agenda, including the Civil Rights Act of 1964. He also pursued Kennedy's foreign policy of peaceful negotiations with the Soviet Union but military aid to the beleaguered anticommunist government of South Vietnam.

Liberal Democrats were dazzled by Johnson's public commitment to their *cherished political causes and by his success in attaining their goals. Although the new president showed little affection for the late president's brother, Attorney-General Robert F. Kennedy, Johnson was nominated without opposition at the Democratic national convention in August 1964. In July, Johnson had thwarted whatever hopes Robert Kennedy may have had of pushing his way onto the ticket by announcing that no cabinet member would be considered for vice president. ("I am sorry that I had to take so many nice fellows down with me," Kennedy quipped.) To redeem himself with Democratic liberals, Johnson tapped Sen. Hubert H. Humphrey of Minnesota as his running mate.*

Johnson was the fourth of the five twentieth-century successor presidents to be renominated for a term as president in his own right; the others were Theodore Roosevelt in 1904, Calvin Coolidge in 1924, Harry S Truman in 1948, and Gerald Ford in 1976. All but Ford, who lost narrowly, were elected. In contrast, none of the four nineteenth century vice presidents who succeeded to the presidency when the president died—John Tyler in 1841, Millard Fillmore in 1850, Andrew Johnson in 1865, and Chester A. Arthur in 1881—were even nominated for president. ~

Mr. Speaker, Mr. President, Members of the House, Members of the Senate, my fellow Americans:

All I have I would have given gladly not to be standing here today.

The greatest leader of our time has been struck down by the foulest deed of our time. Today John Fitzgerald Kennedy lives on in the immortal words and works that he left behind. He lives on in the mind and memories of mankind. He lives on in the hearts of his countrymen.

No words are sad enough to express our sense of loss. No words are strong enough to express our determination to continue the forward thrust of America that he began.

The dream of conquering the vastness of space—the dream of partnership across the Atlantic—and across the Pacific as well— the dream of a Peace Corps in less developed nations—the dream of education for all of our children—the dream of jobs for all who seek them and need them—the dream of care for our elderly—the dream of an all-out attack on mental illness—and above all, the dream of equal rights for all Americans, whatever their race or color—these and other American dreams have been vitalized by his drive and by his dedication.

And now the ideas and the ideals which he so nobly represented must and will be translated into effective action.

Under John Kennedy's leadership, this Nation has demonstrated that it has the courage to seek peace, and it has the fortitude to risk war. We have proved that we are a good and reliable friend to those who seek peace and freedom. We have shown that we can also be a formidable foe to those who reject the path of peace and those who seek to impose upon us or our allies the yoke of tyranny.

The Nation will keep its commitments from South Viet-Nam to West Berlin. We will be unceasing in the search for peace; resourceful in our pursuit of areas of agreement even with those with whom we differ; and generous and loyal to those who join with us in common cause.

In this age when there can be no losers in peace and no victors in war, we must recognize the obligation to match national strength with national restraint. We must be prepared at one and the same time for both the confrontation of power and the limitation of power. We must be ready to defend the national interest and to negotiate the common interest. This is the path that we shall continue to pursue. Those who test our courage will find it strong, and those who seek our friendship will find it honorable. We sill demonstrate anew that the strong can be just in the use of strength; and the just can be strong in the defense of justice.

And let all know we will extend no special privilege and impose no persecution. We will carry on the fight against poverty and misery, and disease and ignorance, in other lands and in our own.

We will serve all the Nation, not one section or one sector, or one group, but all Americans. These are the United States—a united people with a united purpose.

Our American unity does not depend upon unanimity. We have differences; but now, as in the past, we can derive from those differences strength, not weakness, wisdom, not despair. Both as a people and a government, we can unite upon a program, a program which is wise and just, enlightened and constructive.

For 32 years Capitol Hill has been my home. I have shared many moments of pride with you, pride in the ability of the Congress of the United States to act, to meet any crisis, to distill from our differences strong programs of national action.

An assassin's bullet has thrust upon me the awesome burden of the Presidency. I am here today to say I need your help; I cannot bear this burden alone. I need the help of all Americans, and all America. This Nation has experienced a profound shock, and in this critical moment, it is our duty, yours and mine, as the Government of the United States, to do away with uncertainty and doubt and delay, and to show that we are capable of decisive action; that from the brutal loss of our leader we will derive not weakness, but strength; that we can and will act and act now.

From this chamber of representative government, let all the world know and none misunderstand that I rededicate this Government to the unswerving support of the United Nations, to the honorable and determined execution of our commitments to our allies, to the maintenance of military strength second to none, to the defense of the strength and the stability of the dollar, to the expansion of our foreign trade, to the reinforcement of our programs of mutual assistance and cooperation in Asia and Africa, and to our Alliance for Progress in this hemisphere.

On the 20th day of January, in 1961, John F. Kennedy told his countrymen that our national work would not be finished "in the first thousand days, nor in the life of this administration, nor even perhaps in our lifetime on this planet. But," he said, "let us begin."

Today, in this moment of new resolve, I would say to all my fellow Americans, let us continue.

This is our challenge—not to hesitate, not to pause, not to turn about and linger over this evil moment, but to continue on our course so that we may fulfill the destiny that history has set for us. Our most immediate tasks are here on this Hill.

First, no memorial oration or eulogy could more eloquently honor President Kennedy's memory than the earliest possible passage of the civil rights bill for which he fought so long. We have talked long enough in this country about equal rights. We have talked one hundred years or more. It is time now to write the next chapter, and to write it in the books of law.

I urge you again, as I did in 1956 and again in 1960, to enact a civil rights law so that we can move forward to eliminate from this Nation every trace of discrimination and oppression that is based upon race or color. There could be no greater source of strength to this Nation both at home and abroad.

And second, no act of ours could more fittingly continue the work of President Kennedy than the early passage of the tax bill for which he fought all this long year. This is a bill designed to increase our national income and Federal revenues, and to provide insurance against recession. That bill, if passed without delay, means more security for those now working, more jobs for those now without them, and more incentive for our economy.

In short, this is no time for delay. It is a time for action—strong, forward-looking action on the pending education bills to help bring the light of learning to every home and hamlet in America—strong, forward-looking action on youth employment opportunities; strong, forward-looking action on the pending foreign aid bill, making clear that we are not forfeiting our responsibilities to this hemisphere or to the world, nor erasing Executive flexibility in the conduct of our foreign affairs—and strong-prompt, and forward-looking action on the remaining appropriation bills.

In this new spirit of action, the Congress can expect the full cooperation and support of the executive branch. And in particular, I pledge that the expenditures of your Government will be administered with the utmost thrift and frugality. I will insist that the Government get a dollar's value for a dollar spent. The Government will set an example of prudence and economy. This does not mean that we will not meet our unfilled needs or that we will not honor our commitments. We will do both.

As one who has long served in both Houses of the Congress, I firmly believe in the independence and the integrity of the legislative branch. And I promise you that I shall always respect this. It is deep in the marrow of my bones. With

equal firmness, I believe in the capacity and I believe in the ability of the Congress, despite the divisions of opinions which characterize our Nation, to act—to act wisely, to act vigorously, to act speedily when the need arises.

The need is here. The need is now. I ask your help.

We meet in grief, but let us also meet in renewed dedication and renewed vigor. Let us meet in action, in tolerance, and in mutual understanding. John Kennedy's death commands what his life conveyed—that America must move forward. The time has come for Americans of all races and creeds and political beliefs to understand and to respect one another. So let us put an end to the teaching and the preaching of hate and evil and violence. Let us turn away from the fanatics of the far left and the far right, from the apostles of bitterness and bigotry, from those defiant of law, and those who pour venom into our Nation's bloodstream.

I profoundly hope that the tragedy and the torment of these terrible days will bind us together in new fellowship, making us one people in our hour of sorrow. So let us here highly resolve that John Fitzgerald Kennedy did not live—or die—in vain. And on this Thanksgiving eve, as we gather together to ask the Lord's blessing, and give Him our thanks, let us unite in those familiar and cherished words:

America, America,
God shed His grace on thee,
And crown thy good
With brotherhood
From sea to shining sea.

Barry M. Goldwater's Acceptance Speech to the Republican National Convention (1964)

In 1963, the political scientist James MacGregor Burns argued in his celebrated book The Deadlock of Democracy that although the United States had a two-party system in form, it had a four-party system in practice: a congressional Democratic party, which was more conservative than the Democratic party that gathered quadrennially to nominate presidential candidates, and a congressional Republican party, which was more conservative than the presidential Republican party.

Republican conservatives were especially frustrated by the situation Burns described. Not only were the party's candidates for president too liberal for their taste, in most cases they lost. Soon after Richard Nixon was defeated in the election of 1960, conservatives began working to take over the presidential party in time for the 1964 Republican national convention.

One advantage that conservative Republicans had was that they knew who their candidate would be. Sen. Barry M. Goldwater of Arizona was a plainspoken, attractive political leader. In 1960, he had published a book called The Conscience of a Conservative, which instantly became a conservative political bible.

Goldwater announced his candidacy for president on January 3, 1964, vowing that, in contrast to recent Republican nominees, he would offer the voters "a choice, not an echo." His main rival for the nomination was Nelson A. Rockefeller, the liberal governor of New York. The popular, well-financed Rockefeller had been the early front-runner in the race, but he weakened himself politically by announcing that he intended to divorce his wife of thirty-one years, then remarrying soon after.

Even against enfeebled opposition, Goldwater barely survived the nominating campaign. Almost all of his political wounds were self-inflicted. At various times, usually in offhand remarks, Goldwater suggested dropping an atomic bomb on North Vietnam, making Social Security voluntary, selling the Tennessee Valley Authority, and other unpopular measures. In his televised acceptance speech to the Republican national convention, rather than try to soften his image as a political extremist, Goldwater threw down the gauntlet to his critics: "Anyone who joins us in all sincerity we welcome. Those who do not care for our cause, we don't expect to enter our ranks in any case. . . . I would remind you that extremism in the defense of liberty is no vice! And let me remind you also that moderation in the pursuit of justice is no virtue!"

On election day, Goldwater was defeated in a landslide. President Lyndon B. Johnson won by a margin of

486-52 in the electoral college and by 61.1 percent to 38.5 percent in the popular vote. Substantial Democratic gains in the congressional elections reduced the Republican contingent in both the House of Representatives and the Senate to less than one-third. In 1965, Johnson translated his change-oriented campaign, landslide election, and long congressional coattails into legislative passage of a host of liberal social programs—his "Great Society" agenda.

But Goldwater's 1964 defeat had effects similar to Gov. Al Smith's in 1928: it laid some of the groundwork for future progress by his party. (See "H. L. Mencken's 'Onward, Christian Soldiers!' Article," p. 296.) In 1964, for the first time, a Republican nominee for president carried the Deep South, completing the collapse of the previously solid Democratic South that Dwight D. Eisenhower had begun by winning the outer southern states in 1952. In addition, the Goldwater candidacy attracted a large number of talented and hard-working conservatives into active service in the Republican party, where they remained to pursue their political agenda. (See "Republican Party Platform [1980]," p. 677.) From the ashes of defeat in 1964, the Republicans would rise to win five of the next six presidential elections. ~

My good friend and great Republican, Dick Nixon and your charming wife, Pat; my running mate—that wonderful Republican who has served us so well for so long—Bill Miller and his wife, Stephanie; to Thurston Morton, who's done such a commendable job in chairmaning this convention; to Mr. Herbert Hoover who I hope is watching, and to that great American and his wife, General and Mrs. Eisenhower. To my own wife, fellow Republicans here assembled, and Americans across this great nation:

From this moment, united and determined, we will go forward together dedicated to the ultimate and undeniable greatness of the whole man.

Together we will win.

I accept your nomination with a deep sense of humility. I accept, too the responsibility that goes with it, and I seek your continued help and your continued guidance. My fellow Republicans, our cause is too great for any man to feel worthy of it. Our task would be too great for any man did he not have with him the heart and the hands of this great Republican party.

And I promise you tonight that every fibre of my being is consecrated to our cause, that nothing shall be lacking from the struggle that can be brought to it by enthusiasm by devotion and plain hard work.

In this world no person, no party can guarantee anything, but what we can do and what we shall do is to deserve victory and victory will be ours. The Good Lord raised this mighty Republican—Republic to be a home for the Brave and to flourish as the land of the free—not to stagnate in the swampland of collectivism, not to cringe before the bully of Communism.

Now my fellow Americans, the tide has been running against freedom. Our people have followed false prophets. We must, and we shall, return to proven ways—not because they are old, but because they are true.

We must, and we shall, set the tide running again in the cause of freedom. And this party, with its every action, every word, every breath and every heart beat, has but a single resolve, and that is freedom.

Freedom made orderly for this nation by our constitutional government. Freedom under a government limited by laws of nature and of nature's God. Freedom balanced so that order lacking liberty will not become the slavery of the prison cell; balanced so that liberty lacking order will not become the license of the mob and of the jungle.

Now, we Americans understand freedom, we have earned it; we have lived for it, and we have died for it. This nation and its people are freedom's models in a searching world. We can be freedom's missionaries in a doubting world.

But, ladies and gentlemen, first we must renew freedom's mission in our own hearts and in our own homes.

During four futile years the Administration which we shall replace has distorted and lost that faith. It has talked and talked and talked and talked the words of freedom but it has failed and failed and failed in the works of freedom.

Now failure cements the wall of shame in Berlin; failures blot the sands of shame at the Bay of Pigs; failures marked the slow death of freedom in Laos; failures infest the jungles of Vietnam, and failures haunt the houses of our once great alliances and undermine the greatest bulwark ever erected by free nations, the NATO community.

Failures proclaim lost leadership, obscure purpose, weakening wills and the risk of inciting our sworn enemies to new aggressions and to new excesses.

And because of this Administration we are tonight a world divided. We are a nation becalmed. We have lost the brisk pace of diversity and the genius of individual creativity. We are plodding along at a pace set by centralized planning, red tape, rules without responsibility and regimentation without recourse.

Rather than useful jobs in our country, people have been offered bureaucratic makework; rather than moral leadership, they have been given bread and circuses; they have been given spectacles, and, yes, they've even been given scandals.

Tonight there is violence in our streets, corruption in our highest offices, aimlessness among our youth, anxiety among our elderly, and there's a virtual despair among the many who look beyond material success toward the inner meaning of their lives. And where examples of morality should be set, the opposite is seen. Small men seeking great wealth or power have too often and too long turned even the highest levels of public service into mere personal opportunity.

Now, certainly simple honesty is not too much to demand of men in government. We find it in most. Republicans demand it from everyone.

They demand it from everyone no matter how exalted or protected his position might be.

The growing menace in our country tonight, to personal safety, to life, to limb and property, in homes, in churches, on the playgrounds and places of business, particularly in our great cities, is the mounting concern or should be of every thoughtful citizen in the United States. Security from domestic violence, no less than from foreign aggression, is the most elementary and fundamental purpose of any government, and a government that cannot fulfill this purpose is one that cannot long command the loyalty of its citizens.

History shows us, demonstrates that nothing, nothing prepares the way for tyranny more than the failure of public officials to keep the streets safe from bullies and mauraders.

Now we Republicans see all this as more—much more—than the result of mere political differences, or mere political mistakes. We see this as the result of a fundamentally and absolutely wrong view of man, his nature and his destiny.

Those who seek to live your lives for you, to take your liberty in return for relieving you of yours; those who elevate the state and downgrade the citizen, must see ultimately a world in which earthly power can be substituted for Divine Will. And this nation was founded upon the rejection of that notion and upon the acceptance of God as the author of freedom.

Now those who seek absolute power, even though they seek it to do what they regard as good, are simply demanding the right to enforce their own version of heaven on earth, and let me remind you they are the very ones who always create the most hellish tyranny.

Absolute power does corrupt, and those who seek it must be suspect and must be opposed. Their mistaken course stems from false notions, ladies and gentlemen, of equality. Equality, rightly understood as our founding fathers understood it, leads to liberty and to the emancipation of creative differences; wrongly understood, as it has been so tragically in our time, it leads first to conformity and then to despotism.

Fellow Republicans, it is the cause of Republicanism to resist concentrations of power, private or public, which enforce such conformity and inflict such despotism.

It is the cause of Republicanism to insure that power remains in the hands of the people—and, so help us God, that is exactly what a Republican President will do with the help of a Republican Congress.

It is further the cause of Republicanism to restore a clear understanding of the tyranny of man over man in the world at large. It is our cause to dispel the foggy thinking which avoids hard decisions in the delusion that a world of conflict will somehow resolve itself into a world of harmony, if we just don't rock the boat or irritate the forces of aggression—and this is hogwash.

It is, further, the cause of Republicanism to remind ourselves, and the world, that only the strong can remain free; that only the strong can keep the peace.

Now I needn't remind you, or my fellow Americans regardless of party, that Republicans have shouldered this hard responsibility and marched in this cause before. It was Republican leadership under Dwight Eisenhower that kept the peace, and passed along to this Administration the mightiest arsenal for defense the world has ever known.

And I needn't remind you that it was the strength and the believable will of the Eisenhower years that kept the peace by using our strength, by using it in the Formosa Strait, and in Lebanon, and by showing it courageously at all times.

It was during those Republican years that the thrust of Communist imperialism was blunted. It was during those years of Republican leadership that this world moved closer not to war but closer to peace than at any other time in the last three decades.

And I needn't remind you, but I will, that it's been during Democratic years that our strength to deter war has been stilled and even gone into a planned decline. It has been during Democratic years that we have weakly stumbled into conflicts, timidly refusing to draw our own lines against aggression, deceitfully refusing to tell even our own people of our full participation and tragically letting our finest men die on battlefields unmarked by purpose, unmarked by pride or the prospect of victory.

Yesterday it was Korea: tonight it is Vietnam. Make no bones of this.

Don't try to sweep this under the rug. We are at war in Vietnam. And yet the President, who is the Commander in Chief of our forces, refuses to say, refuses to say mind you, whether or not the objective over there is victory, and his Secretary of Defense continues to mislead and misinform the American people, and enough of it has gone by.

And I needn't remind you, but I will, it has been during Democratic years that a billion persons were cast into communist captivity and their fate cynically sealed.

Today—today in our beloved country we have an Administration which seems eager to deal with Communism in every coin known—from gold to wheat; from consulates to confidence, and even human freedom itself.

Now the Republican cause demands that we brand Communism as the principal disturber of peace in the world today. Indeed, we should brand it as the only significant disturber of the peace. And we must make clear that until its goals of conquest are absolutely renounced, and its relations with all nations tempered, Communism and the governments it now controls are enemies, of every man on earth who is or wants to be free.

Now, we here in America can keep the peace only if we remain vigilant, and only if we remain strong. Only if we keep our eyes open and keep our guard up can we prevent war.

And I want to make this abundantly clear—I don't intend to let peace or freedom be torn from our grasp because of lack of strength, or lack of will—and that I promise you Americans.

I believe that we must look beyond the defense of freedom today to its extension tomorrow. I believe that the Communism which boasts it will bury us will instead give way to the forces of freedom. And I can see in the distant and yet recognizable future the outlines of a world worthy of our dedication, our every risk, our every effort, our every sacrifice along the way. Yes, a world that will redeem the suffering of those who will be liberated from tyranny.

I can see, and I suggest that all thoughtful men must contemplate, the flowering of an Atlantic civilization, the whole world of Europe reunified and free, trading openly across its borders, communicating openly across the world.

This is a goal far, far more meaningful than a moon shot.

It's a truly inspiring goal for all free men to set for themselves during the latter half of the twentieth century. I can see and all free men must thrill to the events of this Atlantic civilization

joined by a straight ocean highway to the United States. What a destiny! What a destiny can be ours to stand as a great central pillar linking Europe, the Americans and the venerable and vital peoples and cultures of the Pacific.

I can see a day when all the Americas—North and South—will be linked in a mighty system—a system in which the errors and misunderstandings of the past will be submerged one by one in a rising tide of prosperity and interdependence.

We know that the misunderstandings of centuries are not to be wiped away in a day or wiped away in an hour. But we pledge, we pledge, that human sympathy—what our neighbors to the South call an attitude of sympatico—no less than enlightened self-interest will be our guide.

And I can see this Atlantic civilization galvanizing and guiding emergent nations everywhere. Now I know this freedom is not the fruit of every soil. I know that our own freedom was achieved through centuries of unremitting efforts by brave and wise men. And I know that the road to freedom is a long and a challenging road, and I know also that some men may walk away from it, that some men resist challenge, accepting the false security of governmental paternalism.

And I pledge that the America I envision in the years ahead will extend its hand in help in teaching and in cultivation so that all new nations will be at least encouraged to go our way; so that they will not wander down the dark alleys of tryanny or to the dead-end streets of collectivism.

My fellow Republicans, we do no man a service by hiding freedom's light under a bushel of mistaken humility.

I seek an America proud of its past, proud of its ways, proud of its dreams and determined actively to proclaim them. But our examples to the world must, like charity, begin at home.

In our vision of a good and decent future, free and peaceful, there must be room, room for the liberation of the energy and the talent of the individual, otherwise our vision is blind at the outset.

We must assure a society here which while never abandoning the needy, or forsaking the helpless, nurtures incentives and opportunity for the creative and the productive.

We must know the whole good is the product of many single contributions. And I cherish the day when our children once again will restore as heroes the sort of men and women who, unafraid and undaunted, pursue the truth, strive to cure disease, subdue and make fruitful our natural environment, and produce the inventive engines of production, science and technology.

This nation, whose creative people have enhanced this entire span of history, should again thrive upon the greatness of all those things which we— we as individual citizens—can and should do.

During Republican years, this again will be a nation of men and women, of families proud of their role, jealous of their responsibilities, unlimited in their aspirations—a nation where all who can will be self-reliant.

We Republicans see in our constitutional form of government the great framework which assures the orderly but dynamic fulfilment of the whole man, and we see the whole man as the great reason for instituting orderly government in the first place.

We see in private property and in economy based upon and fostering private property the one way to make government a durable ally of the whole man rather than his determined enemy.

We see in the sanctity of private property the only durable foundation for constitutional government in a free society.

And beyond that we see and cherish diversity of ways, diversity of thoughts, of motives, and accomplishments. We don't seek to live anyone's life for him. We only seek to secure his rights, guarantee him opportunity, guarantee him opportunity to strive with government performing only those needed and constitutionally sanctioned tasks which cannot otherwise be performed.

We, Republicans, seek a government that attends to its inherent responsibilities of maintaining a stable monetary and fiscal climate, encouraging a free and competitive economy and enforcing law and order.

Thus do we seek inventiveness, diversity and creative difference within a stable order, for we Republicans define government's role where needed at many, many levels, preferably through the one closest to the people involved: our towns and our cities, then our counties, then our states then our regional contacts and only then the national government.

That, let me remind you, is the land of liberty built by decentralized power. On it also we must have balance between the branches of government at every level.

Balance, diversity, creative difference—these are the elements of Republican equation, Republicans agree, Republicans agree heartily, to disagree on many, many of their applications. But we have never disagreed on the basic fundamental issues of why you and I are Republicans.

This is a party—this republican party is a party for free men. Not for blind followers and not for conformists.

Back in 1858 Abraham Lincoln said this of the Republican party, and I quote him because he probably could have said it during the last week or so: It was composed of strained, discordant, and even hostile elements. End of the quote, in 1958 [sic].

Yet all of these elements agreed on one paramount objective: to arrest the progress of slavery, and place it in the course of ultimate extinction.

Today, as then, but more urgently and more broadly than then, the task of preserving and enlarging freedom at home and of safeguarding it from the forces of tryanny abroad is great enough to challenge all our resources and to require all our strength.

Anyone who joins us in all sincerity we welcome. Those, those who do not care for our cause, we don't expect to enter our ranks in any case. And let our Republicanism so focused and so dedicated not be made fuzzy and futile by unthinking and stupid labels.

I would remind you that extremism in the defense of liberty is no vice!

And let me remind you also that moderation in the pursuit of justice is no virtue!

By the—the beauty of the very system we Republicans are pledged to restore and revitalize, the beauty of this Federal system of ours is in its reconciliation of diversity with unity. We must not see malice in honest differences of opinion, and no matter how great, so long as they are not inconsistent with the pledges we have given to each other in and through our Constitution.

Our Republican cause is not to level out the world or make its people conform in computer-regimented sameness. Our Republican cause is to free our people and light the way for liberty throughout the world. Ours is a very human cause for very humane goals. This party, its good people, and its unquestionable devotion to freedom will not fulfill the purposes of this campaign which we launch here now until our cause has won the day, inspired the world, and shown the way to a tomorrow worthy of all our yesteryears.

I repeat, I accept your nomination with humbleness, with pride and you and I are going to fight for the goodness of our land. Thank you.

The Twenty-Fifth Amendment: Senate Debate (1965)

Vice President Lyndon B. Johnson's accession to the presidency after President John F. Kennedy was assassinated on November 22, 1963, left the country without a vice president for the sixteenth time in thirty-six presidencies. Vice-presidential vacancies had occurred eight times because the president died (William Henry Harrison in 1841, Zachary Taylor in 1850, Abraham Lincoln in 1865, James A. Garfield in 1881, William L. McKinley in 1901, Warren G. Harding in 1923, Franklin D. Roosevelt in 1945, and Kennedy in 1963), seven times because the vice president died (George Clinton in 1812, Elbridge Gerry in 1814, William R. King in 1853, Henry Wilson in 1875, Thomas A. Hendricks in 1885, Garret A. Hobart in 1899, and James S. Sherman in 1912), and once because the vice president resigned (John C. Calhoun in 1832).

By merest chance, no president ever died, resigned, or was impeached and convicted while the vice presidency was vacant. But the absence of a vice president during the first fourteen months of the Johnson administration was especially distressing because the next two offices in the presidential line of succession were occupied by aged and ill members of Congress, Speaker of the House of Representatives John W. McCormack of Massachusetts and President Pro Tempore of the Senate Carl Hayden of Arizona. (See "Presidential Succession Act: House Debate," p. 420.)

In early 1964, shortly after Johnson became president, the Senate began considering Indiana senator Birch Bayh's proposal for a constitutional amendment that would require the president to nominate a new vice president whenever the office became vacant, pending confirmation by a majority of both houses of Congress. Other ideas for filling vice-presidential vacancies were discussed, including one from former vice president Richard Nixon, who wanted the president to submit the nomination to the previous election's presidential electors, and another to allow Congress to choose the vice president. But Bayh's proposal prevailed. On June 30, 1965, the House approved the proposed Twenty-fifth Amendment by voice vote; the Senate followed suit with a 68-5 endorsement on July 6. The amendment was easily ratified by the states and became part of the Constitution on February 23, 1967.

In 1973 and 1974, the Twenty-fifth Amendment was put to use in circumstances scarcely imagined by its authors. Vice President Spiro T. Agnew, facing prosecution in federal court on a variety of bribery-related charges, resigned from office on October 10, 1973, as part of a plea bargain. President Richard Nixon nominated House Republican leader Gerald Ford to replace

Agnew on October 12. After a two-month investigation, Congress voted to confirm Ford's nomination—the Senate on November 27 and the House on December 6, 1973.

Barely eight months later, after Nixon resigned on August 9, 1974, to avoid impeachment for his involvement in the cover-up of the Watergate scandal, Ford became president and, on August 20, nominated Gov. Nelson A. Rockefeller of New York to be vice president. (See "The Watergate Tapes," p. 585.) Congress investigated and debated the Rockefeller nomination for four months before voting its approval in December 1974.

In addition to providing for vacancies in the vice presidency, the Twenty-fifth Amendment also created procedures to deal with presidential disabilities. The amendment states that either the president alone or the vice president and a majority of the heads of the departments may declare that the president is disabled, in which case the vice president becomes acting president until the president's disability is ended. If the president challenges the judgment of the vice president and the cabinet, Congress must decide whether the president is disabled. Unless two-thirds of both the House and the Senate vote within a three-week period to sustain the vice president and the cabinet, the president is returned to power. ~

Presidential Inability and Vacancies in the Office of Vice President — Conference Report

The Presiding Officer: Under the unanimous-consent agreement, the Chair lays before the Senate the pending business, which the clerk will state.

The Legislative Clerk: Report of the committee of conference on the disagreeing votes of the two Houses on the amendment of the House to the joint resolution (S.J. Res. 1) proposing an amendment to the Constitution of the United States relating to succession to the Presidency and Vice Presidency and to cases where the President is unable to discharge the powers and duties of his office.

The Senate resumed the consideration of the report.

The Presiding Officer: Who yields time?

Mr. Bayh: Mr. President, a parliamentary inquiry.

The Presiding Officer: The Senator will state it.

Mr. Bayh: It is my understanding that under the unanimous-consent agreement adopted by the Senate earlier, the time is to be controlled, 1 hour by the distinguished Senator from Tennessee [Mr. Gore] and 1 hour by me.

The Presiding Officer: Under the agreement, there is a limitation of 2 hours, 1 hour on each side.

Who yields time?

Mr. Bayh: Mr. President, the Senator from Tennessee [Mr. Gore] has a prepared speech. I do not desire to engage in colloquy.

I will yield myself just 2 minutes to say that this has been a much discussed subject over the 187 years of our history. The record over the past 187 years is replete with studies by the Congress, the Senate, and individuals concerned.

The purpose of the constitutional amendment, the conference report on which we are now called to approve, is to provide a means which we have devised by which the Vice President will be able to perform the powers and duties of the office of the President if the President is unable to do so.

Mr. President, in my estimation, it is impossible to devise a bill or a constitutional amendment which can cover all the contingencies in this particular, complicated field, but this Congress has gone further than any of its predecessors toward meeting the problem.

On the last day of the debate I went into some detail to specify the details of the report. I do not believe it is necessary to do so again today, unless some of my colleagues wish to question me or engage in colloquy.

Mr. Javits: Mr. President, will the Senator yield?

Mr. Bayh: I am glad to yield to the Senator from New York, who has contributed so much to bringing us in the position we now find ourselves.

Mr. Javits: I am gratified by the statement of the Senator. I read the *Record* over the weekend and thought a great deal about the subject over the weekend and thought again about the relatively close questions which the Senator from Tennessee, the Senator from Indiana, I, and other Senators discussed.

I had the good fortune to read in one of the New York newspapers, the Herald Tribune, a fine editorial on the subject, which, if the Senator will permit me, I ask unanimous consent to have printed at this point in the *Record* as a part of my remarks.

The Presiding Officer: Without objection, it is so ordered.

There being no objection, the editorial was ordered to be printed in the *Record,* as follows:

Clarifying the Presidential Succession

Hopes that this session of Congress would see the beginning of the end of a very serious hiatus in the present laws governing the succession to the Presidency—what is to be done if a President still lives, but is incapacitated from serving—have been discouraged. The Senate had passed a proposed amendment covering this contingency; the House passed a somewhat different version. A conference committee reconciled the two, and its solution was accepted by the House. Then a sudden uprising by some Democratic Senators (including our own Robert Kennedy) saw flaws in the amendment and obtained a delay in the Senate vote until tomorrow.

It is to be hoped that the Senate will weigh the theoretical objections put forward by the amendment's opponents against the very real dangers that now exist. The amendment tries manfully to cover all contingencies, but it obviously cannot prevent a group, infecting both the administration and Congress, from attempting to subvert the spirit of our institutions and affronting the good sense of the American people by seeking to have a sane and healthy President declared incapable of performing his duties. If such a desperate situation should arise, the lack of the proposed amendment would not stop the conspirators. It did not arrest the attempt to oust President Andrew Johnson by impeachment, for example—which failed by only one vote.

But the amendment would foreclose the possibility of another such constitutional nightmare as occurred when President Wilson was felled by a stroke and the country—to all appearances—was governed by his wife. This portion of the amendment is, in other words, about as sound as human forethought can make it. It relies, to some extent, upon the integrity and good sense of the men elected to high office by the American people. But so does everything else in our Constitution.

In other respects, too, the amendment makes needed reforms. It provides for filling a Vice-Presidential vacancy by Presidential appointment, confirmed by Congress. This is a better arrangement than the various succession acts passed by Congress since 1792, and fleshes out the 20th amendment, which deals chiefly with the problems arising between the election of a President and his inauguration. The amendment is good and necessary. It will require months to acquire approval by the necessary two-thirds of the States and should not be further delayed by counsels of impossible perfection nor by fears of what would be, in fact, revolution.

Mr. Javits: Mr. President, this is a tremendously important measure, a historic development in the field of Presidential succession, and we have spent a great amount of time working it out in detail. Senators who have raised questions about the matter have been statesmenlike about it and have not necessarily said that they would vote against it.

The Presiding Officer: The time of the Senator has expired.

Mr. Bayh: I yield 1 minute to the Senator from New York.

Mr. Javits: We all know that in many areas of legislation, especially in the field of constitutional amendment, we cannot spell out all the details. If an attempt to do so is made, we get into more trouble than if an effort was not made and we leave it open to further implementation.

What we discussed about the exclusivity of action of a body provided for by Congress would properly be a subject of legislation. If Congress chose not to act, it would be making a choice that the machinery provided for in the amendment should operate.

The argument that not everything is "buttoned down" by the proposed amendment is not, in my judgment, persuasive. We should not "monkey around" with the amendment to provide for something which could be taken care of by legislation by Congress.

There are many occurrences which are tantamount to revolution which could take place to immobilize our Government. Suppose the Senate and the House should refuse to approve any appropriations for the carrying on of the Government. It would immobilize us—

The Presiding Officer: The time of the Senator has expired.

Mr. Bayh: I yield 1 minute to the Senator from New York.

Mr. Javits: That would immobilize us as much as would be the case if, contrary to acting in good faith, Congress chose not to legislate in the utilization of the amendment.

So, after further deep consideration of the matter, I have come to the conclusion that notwithstanding the questions I expressed which were in the

form of exploratory questions, we have come as far as Congress can go, as the saying is, and I shall vote to approve the conference report.

Mr. Bayh: I thank the Senator. I believe that the colloquy that we had, I being in charge of the conference report, was helpful in the last discussion.

The Presiding Officer: The time of the Senator has expired.

Mr. Gore: Mr. President, I ask unanimous consent that I may suggest the absence of a quorum, and that the time be equally divided.

Mr. Bayh: Mr. President. I think this is unnecessary. If the Senator wishes to take it out of his own time?

Mr. Gore: Mr. President, I withdraw the request.

Mr. President: I suggest the absence of a quorum, and ask unanimous consent that the time be not charged to either side.

The Presiding Officer: Without objection, it is so ordered, and the clerk will call the roll.

The legislative clerk called the roll, and the following Senators answered to their names:

[No. 163 Leg.]

Allott	Inouye	Muskie
Anderson	Jackson	Pearson
Bass	Javits	Pell
Bayh	Jordan, Idaho	Proxmire
Boggs	Kennedy, N.Y.	Ribicoff
Burdick	Long, La.	Robertson
Church	McCarthy	Smith
Clark	McGovern	Sparkman
Dirksen	McNamara	Stennis
Ervin	Metcalf	Symington
Gore	Monroney	Talmadge
Harris	Morton	Young,
Hill	Moss	N. Dak.
Holland	Mundt	

The Presiding Officer: A quorum is not present.

Mr. Long of Louisiana. I announce that the Senator from Nevada [Mr. Bible], the Senator from Louisiana [Mr. Ellender], the Senator from Nevada [Mr. Cannon], the Senator from Arkansas [Mr. Fulbright], the Senator from

North Carolina [Mr. Jordan], the Senator from Missouri [Mr. Long], the Senator from Washington [Mr. Magnuson], the Senator from Montana [Mr. Mansfield], the Senator from New Mexico [Mr. Montoya], the Senator from West Virginia [Mr. Randolph], and the Senator from Oregon [Mr. Morse] are absent on official business.

I also announce that the Senator from Alaska [Mr. Bartlett], the Senator from Virginia, [Mr. Byrd], the Senator from Mississippi [Mr. Eastland], and the Senator from Indiana [Mr. Hartke] are absent on official business.

Mr. Kuchel: I announce that the Senator from Vermont [Mr. Aiken], the Senator from Colorado [Mr. Dominick], the Senator from Nebraska [Mr. Hruska], and the Senator from California [Mr. Murphy] are absent on official business.

The Senator from Utah [Mr. Bennett], the Senator from Kansas [Mr. Carlson], the Senator from New Hampshire [Mr. Cotton], the Senator from Hawaii [Mr. Fong], the Senator from Massachusetts [Mr. Saltonstall], and the Senator from Wyoming [Mr. Simpson] are necessarily absent.

Mr. Bayh: Mr. President, I move that the Sergeant at Arms be directed to request the attendance of absent Senators.

The Presiding Officer: The question is on agreeing to the motion of the Senator from Indiana.

The motion was agreed to.

The Presiding Officer: The Sergeant at Arms will execute the order of the Senate.

After a little delay Mr. Brewter, Mr. Byrd of West Virginia, Mr. Case, Mr. Cooper, Mr. Curtis, Mr. Dodd, Mr. Douglas, Mr. Fannin, Mr. Gruening, Mr. Hart, Mr. Hayden, Mr. Hickenlooper, Mr. Kennedy of Massachusetts, Mr. Kuchel, Mr. Lausche, Mr. McClellan, Mr. McGee, Mr. McIntyre, Mr. Miller, Mr. Mondale, Mr. Nelson, Mr. Pastore, Mr. Prouty, Mr. Russell of

South Carolina, Mr. Russell of Georgia, Mr. Scott, Mr. Smathers, Mr. Thurmond, Mr. Tower, Mr. Tydings, Mr. Williams of New Jersey, Mr. Williams of Delaware, Mr. Yarborough, and Mr. Young of Ohio entered the Chamber and answered to their names.

The Presiding Officer (Mr. Kennedy of Massachusetts in the chair). A quorum is present.

Who yields time?

Mr. Gore: Mr. President, I yield 15 minutes to the senior Senator from Minnesota.

Mr. McCarthy: Mr. President, I believe that the Senate acted wisely in putting off action on the conference report for a few days so that we could carefully examine the language in the proposed amendment and so that all Senators, rather than the four or five who participated in the discussion last week, might be fully aware and informed as to the committee interpretation and what would then be the congressional interpretation of what the proposed amendment to the Constitution would actually mean.

I note again that we are not enacting a statute, something which we could change in this Congress or in any subsequent Congress. We are acting on a constitutional amendment which would establish the procedure of the indefinite future.

I have serious reservations about more than the language of the amendment. I have very serious reservations about the substance of the amendment itself. It was my view when the question of presidential disability and vice-presidential succession was raised that there was sufficient authority in the Constitution to permit Congress to proceed by statute.

Paragraph 6, section 1, of article II of the Constitution gives Congress power to legislate in the area of presidential disability and of succession of a Vice President. This section of the Constitution reads:

In case of the removal of the President from office, or of his death, resignation, or inability to discharge the powers and duties of the said office, the same shall devolve on the Vice President, and the Congress may by law provide for the case of removal, death, resignation, or inability, both of the President and Vice President, declaring what officer shall then act as President, and such officer shall act accordingly, until the disability be removed, or a President shall be elected.

It is my judgment that we could act by statute to meet both the problem of succession and disability. There are constitutional authorities who feel that we have power to act in case of a vacancy in the vice-presidency. However, there is some question as to our ability to act in case of disability.

I am willing to abide by the judgment of those who thought we needed a constitutional amendment. It was my opinion that the amendment should be a simple one and should make clear the right and authority of Congress to act by statute.

This was the opinion of Deputy Attorney General Katzenbach when he testified before the committee in 1963 and in his statement submitted to the committee in 1964. He asked for a simple constitutional amendment; and, following that, for action on the part of Congress to spell out the procedures by which inability might be determined and also by which the commencement and termination of any inability would be determined.

This is not the issue involved today. Congressional committees, in both the Senate and House, have considered, I am sure, the possibility of a simple amendment to leave the way open to proceed under statute but they have not approved this method.

At this time, we are preparing to take what will probably be final action or, at least, the last chance to review the proposed amendment.

It has been argued that State legislatures would give a thorough review to the matter. We were informed last week that one State legislature was holding up action until after Congress had acted on the matter so that it would be the first State legislature to ratify the measure. It may be that the State legislature studied the matter and is fully informed as to the amendment. However, I have very grave doubts that this is so. I believe that after Congress acts on the matter, ratification by the States will be almost routine.

Mr. Gore: Mr. President, will the Senator yield?

Mr. McCarthy: I yield.

Mr. Gore: Mr. President, I wonder if the able Senator believes that the members of the legislature which was awaiting the adoption of the conference report by the Senate in order to be the first State to ratify the amendment could have had an opportunity to read the conference report and determine that the conferees had added certain words to the language. Two of the words were "pro tempore." Another was "either," and the other word was "of."

The conference report did relate that minor changes in language had been made. However, I wonder if the Senator believes that the insertion of the word "either" in the Constitution of the United States, having to do with two bodies, either of which, under the terms of the pending amendment, would play a part in the declaration of presidential disability is a minor matter, and if the State legislature to which the Senator referred was aware of this fact.

Mr. McCarthy: Mr. President, I believe that it could very well be a most serious matter. Certainly, the language of the amendment as sent to conference would be preferable to this language.

I know that the Senator from Tennessee has given much study to the meaning of the words and the application of the disjunctive alternative of "either/or" in this case.

The Senator will speak on that at some length later today. I should say that we are writing new meaning into the word "either," and that if we were to approve the draft which is before us from the conferees, we would be ignoring every treatise of grammar in which it is pointed out that if we use the word "either/or," we are providing a choice. They are alternatives. One does not include the other. We ought to use words in their logical meaning when we write them into the Constitution of the United States.

I had hoped that Senators who were handling the matter would agree to return to conference. I believe that the matter could have been cleared up in a 4- or 5-minute conference with Representatives of the House. The word "either" appears to have been dropped into the amendment almost by inadvertence. It was not used as a result of carefully considered judgment. It is not a word that was weighed or was subject to any prolonged discussion in conference.

I hope that the Senate will give consideration to the possibility of what I think might create great confusion when and if this amendment is ever put to the test. If such an occasion should arise, it could be at a time when the entire constitutional structure of the United States would be subject to its most severe test in history.

The question of having two Presidents, each of whom desires to perform the duties of office, and the question of having two cabinets or of trying to determine when the functions of one Cabinet came to an end, might be impossible of solution. The President could end the term of office of the members of the Cabinet with a mere declaration. There would be no way to determine whether they could participate in the making of the judgment provided in the proposed amendment.

It is my opinion that the Vice President should have been excluded in any case. This question has been considered by the committee. The committee has decided that the Vice President should be the key man.

No one, under this amendment, can take action with reference to the inability or disability of the President unless such action has the concurrence of the Vice President. The procedure which is provided by the Constitution for impeachment provides for action by the House of Representatives and the Senate. I believe that, as elective officials of the country, Congress should be willing to assume its full responsibility.

I had hoped that the conferees might have gone back and at least cleared up the point raised by the Senator from Tennessee, although, as I have said, my preference would be for an amendment giving Congress the clear authority to act by statute. This was evidently the position concurred in by Attorney General Katzenbach in his original testimony before the committee, and also by several other members who said that the amendment is not what they would have written had they been free to write it. I had hoped that these more substantive matters would have been considered——

Mr. Bayh: Mr. President, will the Senator yield?

Mr. McCarthy: I yield.

Mr. Bayh: Mr. President, I do not want the record to be incorrect in expressing the present position of the Attorney General. Is the senior Senator from Minnesota aware of the testimony given by the Attorney General before the committee in 1965?

Mr. McCarthy: I knew the Attorney General was supporting the amendment.

Mr. Bayh: I thank the Chair.

Mr. McCarthy: I was referring to what was his preferred position when as Deputy Attorney General he testified on the constitutional amendment dealing with Presidential inability. I believe his original position was sound, although, as in the case of many other people, he is willing to support the proposed amendment because of the urgency of the situation.

Mr. Bayh: But the Attorney General did say, before the Subcommittee on Constitutional Amendments of the Committee on the Judiciary, that he believed that proposed amendment was the best alternative that has been conceived.

Mr. McCarthy: I do not know whether he said it was the best alternative that has been conceived. He said it was the only possible course of action rather than no action at all, not that it was better than any alternative that was ever conceived. He conceived one which he thought was the best he could conceive.

Mr. Bayh: It might be well to have in the *Record* at this point the Attorney General's letter which was placed in the *Record* on the date of the debate when the Senate passed this measure 72 to nothing, if the Senator from Minnesota and the Senator from Tennessee have no objection.

Mr. McCarthy: I have no objection.

I know the Attorney General is supporting the amendment. I know what his opinion as stated publicly was. I know what his private opinion was. I know what the opinion which he gave to the Judiciary Committee was.

Mr. Bayh: May I ask that the letter may be made a part of the *Record* at this point, so that subsequent scholars may have the advantage of it?

Mr. McCarthy: Yes.

Mr. Bayh: Mr. President, I ask unanimous consent that the letter to which I have referred be printed at this point in the *Record*.

There being no objection, the letter was ordered to be printed in the *Record*, as follows:

Office of the Attorney General,
Washington, D.C.,
February 18, 1965.

Hon. Birch Bayh,
U.S. Senate, Washington, D.C.

Dear Senator Bayh: I understand that recent newspaper reports have raised some question as to whether I favor the solution for the problem of Presidential inability embodied in Senate Joint Resolution 1, or whether I prefer a constitutional amendment which would empower Congress to enact appropriate legislation for determining when inability commences and when it terminates.

Obviously, more than one acceptable solution to the problem of Presidential inability is possible. As the President said in his message of January 28, 1965, Senate Joint Resolution 1 represents a carefully considered solution that would responsibly meet the urgent need for action in this area. In addition, it represents a formidable consensus of considered opinion. I have, accordingly, testified twice in recent weeks in support of the solution embodied in Senate Joint Resolution 1 and House Joint Resolution 1.

My views on the particular question here involved were stated on January 29, 1965, before the Subcommittee on Constitutional Amendments of the Senate Judiciary Committee, as follows:

"In my testimony during the hearings of 1963, I expressed the view that the specific procedures for determining the commencement and termination of the President's inability should not be written into the Constitution, but instead should be left to Congress so that the Constitution would not be encumbered by detail. There is, however, overwhelming support for Senate Joint Resolution 1, and widespread sentiment that these procedures should be written into the Constitution. The debate has already gone on much too long. Above all, we should be concerned with substance, not form. It is to the credit of Senate Joint Resolution 1 that it provides for immediate, self-implementing procedures that are not dependent on further congressional or Presidential action. In addition, it has the advantage that the States, when called upon to ratify the proposed amendment to the Constitution, will know precisely what is intended. In view of these reasons supporting the method adopted by Senate Joint Resolution 1, I see no reason to insist upon the preference I expressed in 1963 and assert no objection on that ground."

I reaffirmed these views with the same explicit language in my prepared statement delivered on February 9, 1965, before the House Judiciary Committee. In view of the above, there should be no question that I support Senate Joint Resolution 1.

Sincerely,
Nicholas DeB. Katzenbach,
Attorney General.

Mr. Gore: Mr. President——
The Presiding Officer: How much time does the Senator from Tennessee yield to himself?

Mr. Gore: Such time as I may desire.

This is the last opportunity for any group of men in any body politic to revise or clarify the language of the proposed amendment. The House has already adopted the conference report. Should the Senate adopt the conference report in its present form, the proposed amendment would then go to the States for ratification. If the amendment is ratified by three-fourths of the State legislatures, it will then become a part of the U.S. Constitution.

The States will have no choice except to ratify or reject the amendment in the form submitted. That is why I say this is an important action on the part of the Senate.

The charter of our Republic is a precious document. Amendment of it should be approached with the greatest gravity.

In the beginning of our Republic the candidate for President who received the second largest vote became Vice President. The country's experience under that provision soon led to trouble, so much so that in 1804, I believe, the Constitution was amended so that the Vice President would be elected to a separate office by separate vote. Thus, it was sought to minimize the possibil-

ity of conflict between a President and a Vice President.

In July 1965 the U.S. Senate is again undertaking to deal with the question of the President and the Vice President of the United States.

On last Wednesday, when the conference report on Senate Joint Resolution 1 was before the Senate, I was one of those who urged that the vote on the conference report be delayed to permit additional time for Senators to examine the language of the proposed constitutional amendment before taking the final congressional action on what would be one of the more important amendments ever adopted to our Constitution.

I wish to make it clear that I did not then, nor do I now, seek either to block action on or otherwise defeat an amendment which would fill an existing procedural void in the area of presidential succession and presidential disability. The tragic events of November 1963 have served to call to the attention of the American people that failure to act on this matter might, at some time in the future, pose serious consequences to our Republic. Indeed, we should regard ourselves as most fortunate that we have not already, at some time in our history, experienced a grave constitutional crisis for want of a procedure for determining with certainty the fact of presidential disability. Clarity and certainty are the essential characteristics of any constitutional provision dealing with the subject.

The basic objective of an amendment such as we now consider should be the provision of a procedure certain for the declaration of disability of a President of the United States, but I submit that the provision now before the Senate provides an uncertain procedure.

In my opinion, the language of section 4 of the proposed amendment, which deals with the determination of the fact of Presidential disability by means other than the voluntary act of the President himself, lacks the degree of clarity and certainty required if the objective of this section of the amendment is to be achieved. If the fact of Presidential disability should ever become a matter upon which a President and other authorities designated in the amendment are in disagreement, the most essential requirement is that the procedure for making the determination be clear and precise, with the identity of those charged with responsibility for making the determination beyond question. Should the procedure not be clearly and precisely defined, or if the identity of the determining authority should be subject to conflicting interpretations, this Nation could undergo the potentially disastrous spectacle of competing claims to the power of the Presidency of the United States. This is precisely the risk which this section of the amendment is designed to avoid, but which, Mr. President, may be the result if this amendment should be adopted in its present form.

In my opinion, the language of section 4, if unchanged, is subject to conflicting interpretation—to say the least—and might create a situation in which a serious question could arise as to whether Presidential disability had been constitutionally determined.

I invite attention to the report of the Senate Judiciary Committee, on page 11:

> We must not gamble with the constitutional legitimacy of our Nation's executive branch. When a President or a Vice President of the United States assumes office, the entire Nation and the world must know without doubt that he does so as a matter of right.

I submit that under the proposed amendment one might assume or claim the power of the Presidency, not without doubt but under a cloud of doubt.

Let me read the first sentence of section 4:

> Whenever the Vice President and a majority of either the principal officers of the executive departments or of such

other body as Congress may by law provide, transmit to the President pro tempore of the Senate and the Speaker of the House of Representatives their written declaration that the President is unable to discharge the powers and duties of his office, the Vice President shall immediately assume the powers and duties of the office as Acting President.

I invite attention to four words in the above sentence—all four of which were added in conference. This is not the same language as that upon which the Senate previously voted. The words added in conference are "either," "of," and "pro tempore."

These words do not appear in the section as it was approved unanimously by the Senate. The addition of the words "pro tempore" effected a change in the Senate version to conform to the language of the House version so as to provide that a declaration of presidential disability should be transmitted to the President pro tempore of the Senate rather than the "President of the Senate."

I raise no question about that.

The statement filed by the managers on the part of the House, referring to the addition of the words "either" and "of," states that "minor change in language was made for purposes of clarification." The addition of these two words was, in my opinion, more than a minor change in language. This is a change in language which is proposed to be written into the Constitution dealing with one of the most sensitive events of our Republic; namely, the possible declaration of disability of a President of the United States.

In the absence of implementing action by Congress, it is clear that a declaration of presidential disability may be transmitted to the Congress by the Vice President acting in concert with a majority of "the principal officers of the executive departments." Hereafter I shall refer to the principal officers of the executive departments as members of the Cabinet.

To me, it also seems clear, under the language of the provision, that if Congress should "by law provide" some "other body," the Vice President might then be authorized to act in concert with either the Cabinet or such other body.

How can any other meaning be read into the words "either" and "or"?

Let us reverse the sentence. The Senator from Indiana says that the Cabinet would have the primary responsibility. The amendment does not so provide. In reversing the sentence, let us see how it would read and whether it would be changed in any way.

First, I read the sentence as it now appears:

> Whenever the Vice President and a majority of either the principal officers of the executive department or of such other body as Congress may by law provide, transmit to the President pro tempore of the Senate and the Speaker of the House of Representatives their written declaration that the President is unable to discharge the powers and duties of his office, the Vice President shall immediately assume the powers and duties of the office as Acting President.

Now, Mr. President, I read the sentence in a revised form, and ask whether it would change the meaning in any respect:

> Whenever the Vice President and a majority either of such other body as Congress may by law create or a majority of the principal officers of the executive departments transmit to the President pro tempore of the Senate and the Speaker of the House of Representatives their written declaration that the President is unable to discharge the powers and duties of his office, the Vice President shall immediately assume the powers and duties of the office as Acting President.

If one changes the sequence in which the Cabinet and some other body created by Congress appear in the sentence, one still will have "either" and "or." It would be in the alternative. I do not know how "either" and "or" would give primary responsibility to one and secondary responsibility to the other.

I do not know how the words "either" and "or" can be interpreted to mean that the part has priority, or how it could be read to mean that if the other body is created, the first body has no responsibility and no power to act.

If I understand anything about the English language, if either the Senator or I is privileged to act, then either of us can act or both of us can act. Therefore, I insist that when the conferees added these words, they did more than make a minor change of language for purposes of clarification. I believe that I know why it was added—at least I have been so advised—to make it clear that the Vice President would participate in the declaration of disability with a body created by law if such were done.

But in adding the words, they established the possibility of two coequal bodies—coequal in responsibility under the Constitution—coequal in authority to act in concert with the Vice President to declare the disability of a President of the United States.

I do not believe this effect can be eliminated by a statement of legislative intent.

If my interpretation of the language is correct—and it seems to me that is what the words used clearly say—the Vice President would be free to choose to ally himself with either of the groups, depending upon which included individuals sympathetic with his view of the then current situation. And it is entirely possible that there might be differing views among members of the Cabinet appointed by the President, on the one hand, and members of a group designated by the Congress, on the other hand, on the question of whether a President suffers "disability."

Under the above interpretation—which is my interpretation—a Vice President would be in a position to "shop around" for support of his view that the President is not able to discharge the duties of his office. When the constitutional requirements have been met, it is the Vice President upon whom the duties and powers of the Presidency would devolve.

I should not like to indulge in the assumption that at any future time some diabolical person would be Vice President of the United States. However, the Constitution is the charter for our Republic. Rights must be safeguarded; so must constitutional procedure.

Let me repeat that we seek by this proposed amendment to provide a procedure certain for a declaration of disability of the President of the United States. I submit that the language of the conference report creates uncertainty, rather than certainty. This uncertainty cannot be eliminated by a statement of legislative intent, particularly so when the stated intent is not supported by the precise language of the amendment.

I should like to suggest, although it does not involve any assumption that we shall ever have a diabolical person as Vice President, that where there is a way we must guard against possibility of the will, and beware of the old adage that where there is a will there is a way.

Questions have been raised about the approach taken by this section of the amendment. In my view there is some validity to these questions. Whether the Vice President, who would become Acting President, should have any part in making a determination of presidential disability is, to say the least, debatable.

Were I privileged to reconsider the whole matter, I should want to think about this one point a long time. However I do not press this point now. I recognize that it is perhaps not possible to devise a procedure which would meet with unanimous approval. Members of the Judiciary Committee who have worked long and diligently on this matter state that this is an approach upon which it is possible to reach agreement. I accept their statement in this regard.

I know it is difficult. We have been considering this subject for months. However, is that justification for adopting an amendment on which Senators are in disagreement as to its meaning? Does not this invite a controversy that would have to be resolved by the Supreme Court of the United States at a possibly critical hour in the history of our country? If Senators cannot agree upon the meaning of the language of the amendment, how do we expect the State legislatures to have a clear and precise understanding?

I do not seek to defeat the proposed amendment, but I ask for rejection of the conference report, which changed the language of this provision, not in a minor manner, but in a major way and, I think, in a dangerous way. I ask that the conference report be rejected and that a further conference with the House be requested. Why should there not be an attempt to clarify the meaning or to refine the language of the amendment? If it is the intent that the Cabinet have the primary responsibility, the amendment should so state. If it is the legislative intent that once Congress had created another body the Cabinet would no longer have any responsibility, the amendment should so provide. If that is what we mean, let us say what we mean. Otherwise, how can the legislatures of our respective States act with a clear understanding of what an amendment to the Constitution of the United States in this delicate field means?

If the Vice President is to participate in the disability determination procedure, there should be no question whatever about the identity of the group which would jointly exercise the responsibility with him. Under my interpretation of the language used, a Vice President would be able to act in concert with either of the two groups—and I say again that the word "either" was added in conference—assuming that Congress had acted to create the second group. This would be the language of the Constitution upon ratification of the amendment as now drafted.

In the course of the debate last Wednesday, the manager of the bill, the distinguished junior Senator from Indiana [Mr. Bayh] and the distinguished senior Senator from New York [Mr. Javits] disagreed with my interpretation of the language used. It was their view that, if and when the Congress acted to provide by a law a body other than the Cabinet to share the responsibility with the Vice President, the Cabinet would thereafter be removed from the picture altogether. How? The amendment does not so provide. The amendment, once it becomes a part of the Constitution of the United States, will vest in the Vice President and a majority of the Cabinet the power to declare the disability of the President.

My friend the distinguished junior Senator from Indiana and the senior Senator from New York maintained that, after another body was created by law, only the Vice President and the body created by act of Congress could make a declaration of disability. Does the amendment so provide? I ask my colleagues in the Senate to read it. It does not. It provides that a majority of either one or the other could act in concert with the Vice President to declare the disability of the President.

The Senator from New York contended that the Congress, in the act creating "such other body," might undertake to eliminate the Cabinet, and that the courts in applying a rule of "exclusivity" would rule that since the Congress had acted, the body designated by Congress would possess the authority exclusively. The Senator from Indiana appeared to adopt this view.

The amendment does not so provide. I know of no rule of exclusivity which provides or could provide that a legislative enactment would take precedence over an express provision of the U.S. Constitution, which this amendment, if adopted, would become.

I do not subscribe to the view that Congress, even should it affirmatively undertake to do so, could by statute deny authority and responsibility conferred upon the Cabinet by what would then be an express and integral provision of the Constitution.

I should like to read again the language proposed:

> Whenever the Vice President and a majority of either the principal officers of the executive departments—

Let us leave out the words "either" and "or." I should like to read it in this way:

> Whenever the Vice President and a majority of the principal officers of the departments transmit to the President pro tempore of the Senate a statement of the declaration of disability of the President.

That is a part of the amendment. I submit that we cannot take that language out of the Constitution by statute once we write it in. A further amendment to the Constitution would be required.

But without pressing the subject of the final judicial outcome of such a question, I submit that we cannot here decide with certainty what the Supreme Court might finally rule. It is even more certain that we on the floor of the Senate cannot eliminate the possibility that the Court might someday for necessity have to rule upon the question. And it is entirely conceivable that while the courts are in the process of making a final determination there might be two individuals each claiming the power of the Presidency.

Mr. Ervin: Mr. President, will the Senator yield for a question at that point?

Mr. Gore: I yield.

Mr. Ervin: I ask the Senator from Tennessee if the proposed amendment would not make the question of whether or not the President is capable of performing the duties of his office a political question? In my view it would be a political question and for that reason the Court would not be called upon to pass upon it. In other words, the question posed by the Senator's interpretation would be the same question which would be raised by the interpretation of the Senator from Indiana; namely, Is the President incapable of performing the duties of his office?

The amendment provides that, if the President claims he is competent, the question shall be determined by the Congress. Therefore, would not the amendment make it purely a political question as distinguished from a judicial question, since under the terms of the amendment Congress would be the sole arbiter or determiner of the question?

Mr. Gore: I submit to my distinguished friend, the able senior Senator from North Carolina, that I do not find any provision in the amendment that Congress shall be the sole arbiter. I find that the amendment would vest in the Vice President, acting in concert with the majority of the Cabinet, authority to declare the disability of a President of the United States. If that language is not in the amendment, then I simply do not understand the English language.

Mr. Ervin: Does not the Senator from Tennessee agree with the Senator from North Carolina that the resolution represents an attempt to establish a constitutional method of determining whether the President is disabled to perform the duties of his office?

Mr. Gore: I agree; but it provides two ways in which the determination could be made. That is the difficulty I have with it.

Mr. Ervin: What is the harm in providing alternatives in making the determination? Would that not improve the amendment? It would make it more flexible. If the Senator from Ten-

nessee is correct in his interpretation— and he is making a very fine argument—that the Vice President, either acting with the majority of the Cabinet or acting with the majority of an alternative body established by Congress, could declare a President to be disabled, would that not be an advantage? I feel that it would, in that it provides some flexibility instead of only one inflexible procedure.

Mr. Gore: The Senator in charge of the bill has said that that is not the correct interpretation. But to answer the Senator's question, I believe the existence of an alternate procedure would be harmful, and could be the cause of much mischief. The Senator has asked me a question. I should like very much to cite an example in which the language might even prove to be disastrous.

Let us suppose that the Congress has acted to create by law some other body to act in such cases with the Vice President. Let us suppose further that the individuals making up that body, or a majority of them, felt that the President was fully capable of discharging the duties of his office. But suppose the Vice President held a different view. And suppose further that, for one reason or another, a majority of the Cabinet shared the view of the Vice President. In such a situation if the Vice President and a majority of the Cabinet transmitted the necessary declaration to the Congress, who, then, exercises Presidential power? Will there be time for the courts to make a determination of competing claims without disaster? We all hope devoutly that such a situation never arises. But, in my opinion, it could arise, under the language contained in section 4 and under the hypothesis on which the Senator has based his question.

Mr. Ervin: Does not the Senator from Tennessee contemplate the possibility that the members of the Cabinet might have such an overpowering sense of loyalty to the President that they would be unwilling to take such action? In such a case, in my view, it would be desirable to have an alternative body that could take the action rather than run the risk of having as President of the United States a person who conceivably might be a victim of insanity.

Mr. Gore: If the answer to the Senator's question is "Yes," then clearly and beyond question only one group should be empowered to act at one time.

Let me go further. I am not at all sure that it would be wise to set up an alternative procedure. Our basic objective should be to provide a procedure certain for the declaration of the disability of the President. I should like to recall to Senators that there is now one procedure under the Constitution for the removal of a President from office, namely impeachment. It is now proposed to provide a second means by which a President could be removed and separated from the power of that office, the most powerful office in the world. If we are to take this step—and I would like to take such a step—we should do so with clear understanding and with certain procedure, not procedure which could invite a court contest at a critical hour in our Republic.

Mr. Ervin: That is where the Senator from North Carolina reaches a point of disagreement with the Senator from Tennessee. I do not understand how there would be a court contest, because the amendment provides that the Vice President acting with either the Cabinet or another body established by Congress would raise the question. They would make a temporary decision, and that temporary decision would be immediately transmitted to the Congress for its decision.

Mr. Gore: Where in the proposed amendment is there a provision for a temporary decision?

Mr. Ervin: The proposed constitutional amendment provides that the Vice President could not take over the office of President unless he had given immediate notice to the President pro tempore of the Senate and the Speaker of the House. It also provides if Congress is not already in session, it must be called immediately into session and must make a decision on the issue within 21 days; Congress would decide the question before it would ever reach the courts.

Mr. Gore: Mr. President, I would like to debate further. I am advised that I have about exhausted my time. Will the Senator from North Carolina ask consent that the time used in our colloquy thus far be equally divided or charged to his side?

Mr. Ervin: Mr. President, I ask unanimous consent that I may have 2 minutes of my own time in which to thank the Senator for yielding, and to say if the interpretation of the senior Senator from Tennessee is correct, that it would improve, instead of hurt, the amendment by making it more flexible.

Mr. Gore: Mr. President, an anomalous situation has just been revealed. The distinguished senior Senator from North Carolina, formerly a justice of the Supreme Court of North Carolina, has agreed with my interpretation and has said that the language improves the amendment. The distinguished Senator from Indiana disagrees with my interpretation.

I submit that when there is a disagreement as to interpretation between two of the authors of an amendment, this is the time to restudy, to redefine, and to clarify, before we submit the constitutional amendment to the States for their ratification or rejection. We are about to write into the Constitution of the United States an amendment that could be the most important amendment ever written.

Mr. Ervin: Mr. President, I ask unanimous consent for 1 minute.

Mr. Gore: Mr. President, I do not now yield to the Senator.

Mr. Ervin: I have merely assumed the Senator's interpretation to be correct.

The Presiding Officer: The Senator from Tennessee declines to yield.

Mr. Gore: I have only 4 minutes remaining.

In a situation involving the passing of the power of the Presidency from the hands of one individual to another it is equally important that the law be certain as that it be just or wise. Admittedly, we cannot anticipate and guard against every conceivable contingency. But in this case, we now have an opportunity to eliminate uncertainty, and to provide with certainty exactly who shall make the determination—not a temporary decision, but a determination of the disability of the President of the United States; and upon such a determination the power of the Presidency would pass to the hands of the Vice President, who could then fire the Cabinet, or part of it, and then make another declaration within 4 days of a contrary declaration by the President.

If we adopt the conference report in its present form, the matter will pass from the hands of Congress, and there will be no opportunity to change the language. There can be no language changes during the ratification process.

I am also concerned about remarks made by the junior Senator from Indiana during the debate last Wednesday which left me, at least, in doubt about the time at which it is intended by the authors of the amendment that the Congress would act to create "such other body." I had rather supposed that it was intended that the Congress would, reasonably promptly after ratification of the proposed amendment, proceed to consider this matter at a time when there was no question whatever that the then President was fully able to discharge his duties. But there is no guarantee that Congress would in fact act at a time when this question could be given dispassionate consider-

ation. I think it should. If the amendment is adopted, it seems to me that Congress should proceed forthwith to write a law in this regard, creating such a body. However, some of the remarks of the Senator from Indiana seemed to reflect a view that Congress might well not act until a question had been raised about disability on the part of the President. Is it the view of the authors of the amendment that Congress should not act until a situation arose—such as described by the senior Senator from North Carolina [Mr. Ervin]—in which the prevailing view of Members of Congress was that the President was in fact disabled but a majority of the Cabinet was disinclined to so declare?

If that is the assumption, let us look at the other side of the coin. Suppose that instead of a Cabinet being reluctant, the body created by Congress is reluctant. Then there would be the possibility of one or the other acting, not as anticipated by the authors of the amendment, but in contrast therewith. Could Congress act wisely under such circumstances? It might not be able to act at all, if we waited until such time as Congress believed the President was disabled and thought the Cabinet was reluctant to act.

If a President should be resisting a determination of disability he might veto any bill passed, thus requiring a vote of two-thirds of both Houses of Congress to override the veto. Again, we all hope that there will never be an occasion for Presidential disability to be declared, either by the President himself or by anyone else. But if the need ever arises for such action other than by voluntary act of the President, it would likely have to be done in circumstances in which the President would not concur.

If the approach followed in the proposed amendment is to be followed, I would hope that any action taken by Congress would be taken at a time and under circumstances free of constitutional crisis.

Moreover, Mr. President, I feel strongly that if Congress by law provides for some "other body" to act jointly with the Vice President in making a declaration of Presidential disability, it ought to be clear beyond all doubt that only that "body" may participate with the Vice President in making such a declaration. I do not believe it improves the amendment to provide that two bodies may act. If either of two groups possess such authority the possibility of confusion and conflicting claims is much magnified.

As I have stated, it is my opinion that the language now before the Senate would authorize either of two groups to join with the Vice President in declaring Presidential disability. At the very least there is doubt about the matter. And a doubt or a question is all that it takes to require a Supreme Court decision, with the possibility of constitutional chaos during the period of judicial proceedings.

Mr. President, we need not take that risk. The proposed amendment is still before Congress.

It two-thirds of the Senate vote "yea," the amendment will no longer be before the Senate. There will no longer be any opportunity to clarify or define the language. It should not be overly difficult to devise language to clarify this one question—and it is an important one.

Unfortunately, under the existing parliamentary situation, there is no way in which language revision can be considered other than by rejection of the conference report. Once this step has been taken, a further conference with the House can be requested—that is what I propose—and the conferees would then have an opportunity to present language free of uncertainty. We should establish a procedure with certainty for the declaration of the disability of the President of the United States. I say that this uncertainty, instead of improving the amendment, condemns it to uncertainty and unwisdom.

Should the conference report, with its present language, be approved, doubt and uncertainty will, upon ratification, become embedded in the Constitution.

For the reason I have stated, I urge Senators to vote to reject the conference report and give to the conferees an opportunity to bring to us an amendment having precise, clear meaning.

Mr. President, I reserve the remainder of my time.

Mr. Bayh: Mr. President, I yield 10 minutes to the distinguished Senator from North Carolina.

Mr. Ervin: Mr. President, the able and distinguished junior Senator from Indiana [Mr. Bayh] interprets the joint resolution to provide that if Congress does not create a substitute body as authorized by the amendment, then the Vice President, acting with the consent of the majority of the Cabinet, can declare the disability of the President, subject to congressional reversal. The Senator from Indiana also interprets the proposed amendment to mean that if Congress does create a substitute body to act, such substitute body supplants the Cabinet, and the Vice President, acting with the majority of such substitute body, can initially declare the disability of the President. The able and distinguished senior Senator from Tennessee says, on the contrary, that the Vice President may elect to use either the Cabinet or the body. I do not know what ultimate decision or construction will be placed on the amendment, but I say that a good argument can be made for either interpretation. However, I shall support the joint resolution.

The Senator from Indiana, the Senator from Tennessee, and I could have drawn a better resolution if we had had uncontrolled authority to do so. I have worked on this problem. If I were allowed to draft a resolution by myself, I think I could draw a better one. As a matter of fact, I drew what I believe to be a better one.

I did not believe the Vice President should be involved in the matter. My resolution put the matter in the hands of Congress alone. However, the measure before us reflects an amalgamation of views. As such, it represents a consensus which may not satisfy any of its proponents entirely. It may not be perfect. Indeed, in my view it is not perfect but I feel that it is the best resolution that is attainable.

I had to withdraw many of my opinions in order to obtain a resolution that would be approved by the Committee on the Judiciary and the conference committee.

I am not at all disturbed by the interpretation which my good friend, the Senator from Tennessee, places on the document. If it is a correct interpretation it would make the resolution better. This is a dangerous period in which we live, a period in which the President of the United States has his finger on the button that can start an atomic holocaust.

Many provisions of law provide alternative means. For example, in virtually every State of the Union, a prosecution for a felony can be started either by an individual in the court of a justice of the peace or by the indictment of a grand jury. However, before anybody can be convicted of a felony, he must be convicted by the same type of petit jury in a trial on the merits.

It is quite possible that in the future we may have a President who would be suffering from a mental disease, and the members of the Cabinet, appointed by the President, would be so loyal to him that they would be blind, to some extent, to his weaknesses and would not be amenable to declaring him disabled.

It would be well in a case such as that to have a body set up by Congress with

the power to act. I believe that the interpretation given by the Senator from Tennessee, instead of injuring the resolution, would make it better. After all, the Vice President could not take over the office without the approval of a majority of either the Cabinet or the body established by Congress. I presume that all of the members of either the Cabinet or the body set up by Congress would be patriotic Americans. Even in that case, before the Vice President could take over, the President pro tempore of the Senate and the Speaker of the House of Representatives would have to be notified. Congress would then have to assemble. If it were not already in session, within 48 hours. Furthermore, it would have to make a decision within 21 days. If Congress did not make a decision adverse to the President by two-thirds vote in each House within 21 days, the executive powers would automatically return to the President.

Mr. Gore: Mr. President, will the Senator yield?

Mr. Ervin: I yield.

Mr. Gore: Mr. President, I apologize to the Senator for my reluctance to yield further during the colloquy in which we engaged.

Mr. Ervin: I understand. The Senator was most generous.

Mr. Gore: Mr. President, let us suppose that the Vice President and a majority of either body provided for in the proposed amendment were to transfer to the President pro tempore of the Senate and the Speaker of the House a declaration of the disability of the President of the United States. Upon whom would the power of the Presidency then devolve?

Mr. Ervin: The power would devolve upon the Vice President temporarily, until Congress could act, and then the decision would be made by Congress.

Mr. Gore: Mr. President, who would then have the power to appoint Cabinet members?

Mr. Ervin: I do not believe that this amendment deals with that question. I believe that the Vice President could do so temporarily. However, I do not believe that Congress would confirm his appointees at a time when they were considering the question of whether he should be permitted to remain in the Office of President.

Mr. Gore: If the Vice President becomes Acting President?

Mr. Ervin: That question was raised in committee. The question was also raised concerning whether the amendment should provide for succession to the Presidency in the case of the death of the President and Vice President simultaneously or in a common disaster.

Mr. Gore: The Acting President could dismiss his predecessor's Cabinet.

Mr. Ervin: The Senator is correct.

Mr. Gore: Then he could appoint members of the Cabinet of his own choosing, subject to confirmation.

Mr. Ervin: Yes. But Congress could vacate such action by decision favorable to the President.

Mr. Gore: Suppose that under the proposed amendment, the President, over his signature, were to notify the President pro tempore that he is able to assume the duties of the office of President. Then suppose that the Acting President, in concert either with the Cabinet, or with the other body which Congress would create, were to send a second declaration to the President pro tempore of the Senate declaring the disability of the President.

Mr. Ervin: That could happen under the construction placed on the amendment by the Senator from Indiana or that made by the Senator from Tennessee. There would be no difference whatever in that situation, under either construction.

Mr. Bayh: Mr. President, will the Senator yield?

Mr. Gore: Mr. President. I should like to conclude this point first.

Mr. President, will the Senator yield further?

Mr. Ervin: I yield first to the Senator from Tennessee and then to the Senator from Indiana.

Mr. Gore: If that be the case, if the answers which the distinguished and able senior Senator from North Carolina has provided be correct, then I say that it is all the more necessary to provide a procedure certain for the declaration of disability of the President. It illustrates clearly the unwisdom and the danger of creating a situation whereby there may be competing claims and groups as to the disability or ability of the President. We are dealing with a subject which might endanger the very procedures of our Republic.

The Presiding Officer: The time of the Senator has expired.

Mr. Ervin: Mr. President, will the Senator yield me an additional minute?

Mr. Bayh: I yield 1 more minute to the Senator from North Carolina.

The Presiding Officer: The Senator from North Carolina is recognized for 1 additional minute.

Mr. Ervin: I should say that every legal and constitutional situation conjured up by the Senator from Tennessee would be possible under either interpretation. There would be absolutely no difference whatever.

Mr. Bayh: Mr. President, I yield 10 minutes to the Senator from Illinois.

The Presiding Officer: The junior Senator from Illinois is recognized for 10 minutes.

Mr. Dirksen: Mr. President, first of all, I should like to pay testimony to the distinguished Senator from Indiana for the long and painstaking labor that was involved in the preparation of the proposed amendment. He has been very patient. He has heard the testimony of many witnesses. He has been very patient in the conferences with the House.

I pay testimony also to the distinguished jurist, the Senator from North

Carolina, for the great service he has rendered.

I pay testimony likewise to the Senator from Nebraska [Mr. Hruska], good lawyer that he is, who has worked diligently on this matter, knowing its importance and knowing that sooner or later Congress would have to do something in this field.

I presume that the first thing we discover is that language is not absolute. The only word I can think of that is absolute is the word "zero." However, interpretations of all kinds can be placed upon language, and all the diversities of judicial decisions that are presumed since the beginning of the Republic, if placed in a pile, would reach up to the sky. Consequently, in dealing with the language before us, we have the same problem that we had in the subcommittee and in the conference.

Fashioning language to do what we have in mind, particularly when we are subject to the requirement of compression for constitutional amendment purposes, is certainly not an easy undertaking. However, I believe that a reading of the resolution will speak for itself.

Bruce Barton, a great advertising man who served one term in the House of Representatives and wrote that fascinating book, "The Book Nobody Knows," meaning the Bible, once observed to me that there was a penchant to read all the commentaries, but not to read the book itself. I am afraid that too often we fail to read into the *Record* exactly what is present.

They have a better custom in the House of Representatives, because when a bill goes to final reading in the Committee of the Whole, it is read a paragraph of section at a time. In the case of legislative measures, they are always read by section. In the case of appropriation bills, they are read by paragraph.

Perhaps it would be rather diverting if we started with section No. 1 of the amendment, which reads:

> In case of the removal of the President from office or of his death or resignation, the Vice President shall become President.

When Lincoln died, there was a quick transition of the Presidency into the hands of Andrew Johnson, and it offered no problem. To my knowledge, there has not been a resignation from the Presidency, and there has been no removal. Only once was an effort made to impeach a President and remove him from office. So this article of the section stands by itself and speaks for itself.

Section 2 provides:

> Whenever there is a vacancy in the office of the Vice President, the President shall nominate a Vice President who shall take office upon confirmation by a majority vote of both Houses of Congress.

When Franklin Roosevelt died, Truman acceded to the Presidency, and there was no Vice President. We then set up a line of succession, and I was in the House of Representatives when it was done. I do not know that our labor was a happy one, because it was beset with some prejudice and some bias. This question should have been taken care of long ago.

The question is taken care of through amendment to the constitution. Who better to nominate the Vice President than the President himself? He is the party responsible. There is the sense of affinity, the capacity of working with somebody. The President should be able to select his working partner. That selection would be confirmed by majority votes of both Houses of Congress. That is about as good as English language can state it. I doubt if we can set it out more clearly.

Section 3 states:

> Whenever the President transmits to the President pro tempore of the Senate and the Speaker of the House of Representatives his written declaration that he is unable to discharge the powers and duties of his office, and until he

transmits to them a written declaration to the contrary, such powers and duties shall be discharged by the Vice President as Acting President.

There is the President, on his own volition and by his own motion, advising the Congress he can no longer discharge his duties. What more natural than that the Vice President should take over, not as President, but as Acting President, because there is always the chance of recovery? It took a long time in the case of Woodrow Wilson. It required only 90 days in the case of President Garfield when he passed away. But under this proposal the duties go to the Vice President as Acting President. That appears to be the logical way, in the absence of any contrary declaration made by Congress.

Then let us go to section 4:

> Whenever the Vice President and a majority of either the principal officers of the executive departments or of such other body as Congress may by law provide, transmit to the President pro tempore of the Senate and the Speaker of the House of Representatives their written declaration that the President is unable to discharge the powers and duties of his office, the Vice President shall immediately assume the powers and duties of the office as Acting President.

One can make a hundred different assumptions under that language. The President might dismiss the Cabinet. But the President did not create the Cabinet. He appointed those who filled the positions. But it is the Congress that created the Cabinet, and Congress can always create a Cabinet, if it so desires. This is still the disciplinary branch in the Federal Government. It was no wonder that President Monroe said, "The legislative branch is the core and center of our free Government." There are only a few things that we cannot do. We cannot dismiss the President. We cannot diminish the number of the Supreme Court. We cannot abolish the Supreme Court. But we can do

just about everything else. We can reduce their number if we so desire, and, of course we can abolish every Cabinet post. There is nothing to stop the Congress from doing it.

In the light of that power, I doubt whether we need to be disturbed by the ghosts that have been created in connection with the question, largely on the basis of first one assumption and then another.

So the Vice President becomes the Acting President, and as such he continues until the disability is removed.

That section goes further.

> Thereafter, when the President transmits to the President pro tempore of the Senate and the Speaker of the House of Representatives his written declaration that no inability exists, he shall resume the powers and duties of his office unless the Vice President and a majority of either the principal officers of the executive department or of such other body as Congress may by law provide, transmit within 4 days to the President pro tempore of the Senate and the Speaker of the House of Representatives their written declaration that the President is unable to discharge the powers and duties of his office.

One would have to assume a venal Vice President; he would have to assume either a venal or very timid Cabinet, that would not carry out their duties. If they failed so to act, because of an overriding fidelity to the Chief Executive who placed them where they were, that might be a circumstance to be taken into account. But I cannot imagine a member of the Cabinet so wanting in fidelity to the Republic, rather than to the man who placed him in his position, that he would not undertake to discharge his duty. But if the Congress felt, for any reason, that that was not going to be done, we have made provision in this language for some other body, and the Congress can create that body. It can consist of civilians, including people representing every walk of life, a goodly component of doctors, and those who have the capacity to pass upon the question of whether the inability still exists or whether the inability has passed.

I cannot imagine intelligent, competent, and patriotic Americans serving as the principal officers in the executive branch, or in any other body which Congress might create, that would not deal in forthright fashion with the power that is there, to determine whether the disability had been removed and whether the elected Chief Executive was capable or not capable of carrying on his duties and responsibilities.

Mr. Gore: Mr. President, will the Senator from Illinois yield?

Mr. Dirksen: I am glad to yield to the Senator from Tennessee.

Mr. Gore: I appreciate the careful and tightly reasoned statement that the able Senator from Illinois is making. Most of us, perhaps, think of the disability of the President in the light of the tragic events of November 1963. I submit that a physical impairment of the President may not be the only condition against which we must most zealously guard. Disability may be psychiatric. It may be mental. It may be a sort on which people would honestly have differing opinions. A President might be physically fit—the picture of health; but to those who work closely with him, there might be a conviction that he had lost his mental balance, that he had psychiatric problems. In such an event, the country could be rent asunder by political passions. The able Senator has referred to the fact that the Acting President would assume the powers of the office of President. I asked the Senator from North Carolina if the Acting President could not dismiss the Cabinet of the previous President and the answer was yes, that of course he could, that he could also dismiss a few, or he could dismiss a part of them, or he could retain the few who agreed with him.

The Presiding Officer: The time of the Senator from Illinois has expired.

Mr. Bayh: Mr. President, I yield 5 additional minutes to the Senator from Illinois.

The Presiding Officer: The Senator from Illinois is recognized for 5 additional minutes.

Mr. Gore: In that event, it might be crucial, and I believe necessary, that if the man who is to succeed to the office of Acting President is to initiate a declaration—and I believe the Senator will agree that neither the Cabinet nor the other body referred to in the proposed amendment could declare the disability of a President with any effect unless the Vice President concurred in it—if the Vice President, the man to succeed to the power of the office, with the power to select his own Cabinet, or to dismiss all or a part of the Cabinet of the President is to participate in the declaration, the body which must act in concert with him should be certain and beyond doubt. I believe it is most unwise and dangerous to have two groups which might be competing in such a disastrous situation.

Mr. Dirksen: I doubt the substance of my friend's premise. I should not like to be around to enjoy the furor if ever the Vice President undertook, for venal purposes, or motivations of his own, to pursue that kind of course.

Mr. Bayh: Mr. President, will the Senator from Illinois yield?

Mr. Dirksen: I cannot imagine it, because, after all, the people of this country will have something to say about that. Where would it lead? They would not exactly run him out on a rail, but his whole political future, such as it might be, would come to an end at that point.

Let us always remember that we are dealing with human beings and human motivations, and also with the sense of fidelity and affection that people bear, one for another, when they are thrown into a common labor, such as that of a

President and Vice President, and the principal executive officers under those circumstances.

Mr. Bayh: Mr. President, will the Senator from Illinois yield?

Mr. Dirksen: I yield.

Mr. Bayh: I thought it might be helpful to ask the Senator from Illinois if he recalls the discussion in committee on this point. The committee realized that this danger lurked on the horizon, but that there was an equally severe danger that we might face a long period of Presidential disability in which a Cabinet officer might resign, or die. Unless the Vice President were given this power, he would be precluded from replacing a member whom he needed to help fill the Cabinet. I believe that the Senator from Illinois has hit the nail on the head when he advances the belief that in a time of national crisis, the American people would not tolerate an act on the part of the Vice President that was not in the best interests of the country.

Mr. Dirksen: There are some fundamentals we must remember in dealing with a matter of this kind. The first is that we do not strive for the eternal. I doubt that the English language could accomplish that, because that would be absolute. Second, we know that there will always be change, but in the change, the Constitution in its interpretation itself indicates that we would take it in our stride.

There was once a professor at Johns Hopkins University who had fashioned a thesis and a postulate that he thought would stand up under every circumstance. Then he sat down with his fellow faculty members to discuss it. When the discussion was ended, his thesis and postulate were torn apart with suppositions and other arguments to the point that he gave out a frantic cry. "In God's name, is there nothing eternal?"

One of his fellow professors answered, "Yes, one thing, and that is change."

Always there will be change. We have not done an absolute job of solving this problem, but I believe that we have done a practical job. That is what we sought to do.

Mr. Gore: Mr. President, will the Senator from Illinois yield?

Mr. Dirksen: I yield.

Mr. Gore: Instead of assuming there may be a Vice President who is venal or diabolical, let us assume that there may be one who is perfectly honest and sincere concerning circumstances on which there is a sharp division of opinion both within the Cabinet and within Congress, but despite that disagreement, the disability of the President is declared. The Vice President then becomes Acting President. There is not certainty, in this amendment, as to which body he must act in concert with.

The Presiding Officer: The time of the Senator from Illinois has expired.

Mr. Bayh: Mr. President, I yield 2 more minutes to the Senator from Illinois, but I would like to say that I intend to speak specifically to the point which the Senator from Tennessee raises. In my opinion there is no doubt. I believe that we have sufficient evidence, plus the intentions as reflected in the conference committee, to remove all questions. Whether I shall be successful, so far as the Senator from Tennessee is concerned, I do not know, but I shall do my very best.

The Presiding Officer: The Senator from Illinois is recognized for 2 additional minutes.

Mr. Gore: I am sure the Senator from Indiana will present an able argument, but there is disagreement among Senators as to whether, after Congress has created another body, the Cabinet could declare, in concert with the Vice President, the disability of the President. The Senator from Indiana asserts that it could not do so.

The Senator from Indiana says that when Congress acts to create by law another body, the provision which vests power in the majority of the Cabinet, in concert with the Vice President, would then be superseded. I ask the Senator, as a lawyer, if he believes that Congress can, by statute, supersede and strip from the Cabinet the power vested by the Constitution in a majority of that Cabinet?

Mr. Dirksen: Congress, I believe, can take away any power that any Cabinet member has. There is not a line in the Constitution of the United States which provides for a Cabinet as such. Therefore, they are endowed with powers which we give to them.

Mr. Bayh: Let me suggest to the Senator from Tennessee, who has posed some perplexing questions, that I should like to have an opportunity to answer them but would appreciate it if he would ask these questions on his own time.

I merely wish to have all of the proposed amendment appear in the *Record,* so that when the 90,000 or 100,000 copies are sent to the libraries and schools and colleges, the entire text will be available, and also that the names of the managers on the part of the House and on the part of the Senate, who served on the conference committee, will be shown. That will complete the *Record.*

There being no objection, the proposed article was ordered to be printed in the *Record,* as follows:

ARTICLE—

Section 1. In case of the removal of the President from office or of his death or resignation, the Vice President shall become President.

Sec. 2. Whenever there is a vacancy in the office of the Vice President, the President shall nominate a Vice President who shall take office upon confirmation by a majority vote of both Houses of Congress.

Sec. 3. Whenever the President transmits to the President pro tempore of the Senate and the Speaker of the House of Representatives his written declaration that he is unable to discharge the powers and duties of his

office, and until he transmits to them a written declaration to the contrary, such powers and duties shall be discharged by the Vice President as Acting President.

Sec. 4. Whenever the Vice President and a majority of either the principal officers of the executive departments or of such other body as Congress may by law provide, transmit to the President pro tempore of the Senate and the Speaker of the House of Representatives their written declaration that the President is unable to discharge the powers and duties of his office, the Vice President shall immediately assume the powers and duties of the office as Acting President.

Thereafter, when the President transmits to the President pro tempore of the Senate and the Speaker of the House of Representatives his written declaration that no inability exists, he shall resume the powers and duties of his office unless the Vice President and a majority of either the principal officers of the executive department or of such other body as Congress may by law provide, transmit within four days to the President pro tempore of the Senate and the Speaker of the House of Representatives their written declaration that the President is unable to discharge the powers and duties of his office. Thereupon Congress shall decide the issue, assembling within forty-eight hours for that purpose if not in session. If the Congress, within twenty-one days after receipt of the latter written declaration, or, if Congress is not in session, within twenty-one days after Congress is required to assemble, determines by two-thirds vote of both Houses that the President is unable to discharge the powers and duties of his office, the Vice President shall continue to discharge the same as Acting President; otherwise, the President shall resume the powers and duties of his office.

And the House agree to the same.

Emanuel Celler,
Byron G. Rogers,
James C. Corman,
William M. McCulloch,
Richard H. Poff,
Managers on the Part of the House.

Birch E. Bayh, Jr.,
James O Eastland,
Sam J. Ervin, Jr.,

Everett M. Dirksen,
Roman L. Hruska,
Managers on the Part of the Senate.

Mr. Dirksen: Mr. President, I believe we have done a reasonably worthwhile job insofar as the feeble attributes of the language can accomplish it. I compliment and congratulate the distinguished Senator from Indiana, the chairman of the subcommittee, on the good job he has done.

Mr. Bayh: Mr. President, I thank the Senator from Illinois and other Senators who have labored tirelessly to help us get this far down the road.

I yield myself such time as I may require to discuss the points which have been raised by Senators. I have no prepared speech. I have made some notes on one or two points that I wish to discuss. I shall speak with as much ability as I possess and try to clarify the question of intent in the consideration of this subject. However, I emphasize that the Senator from Tennessee and I share one intention, among others, and that is that we seek to clarify any ambiguity which may exist.

Reference has been made to the position of the Attorney General of the United States which was previously inserted in the *Record* and verified his position supporting Senate Joint Resolution 1.

Mr. President, I also quote one sentence from his testimony before the subcommittee. He said:

> I want to reaffirm my prior position that the only satisfactory method of settling the problem of Presidential inability is by constitutional amendment, as Senate Joint Resolution 1 proposes.

In this position, he was joined by a rather long list of Attorneys General of the United States, going back to Biddle and Brownell. He was also joined by such constitutional experts as Paul Freund. They felt that if there was any doubt, the Congress should propose an amendment to the Constitution.

The question has been raised as to why we have put the Vice President in the position of acting in the capacity he would have under the amendment. I believe that former President Eisenhower dramatically made this point in the presentation he made before the conference of the American Bar Association called by the President last June. President Eisenhower said he felt it was the responsibility of the Vice President to assume the authority of the Presidential office in the event that the President was unable to perform his duties, and that the Vice President could not escape that authority and obligation.

Therefore, I believe that we have done the right thing in placing the Vice President in the position of participating in that determination.

There has been a great deal of discussion about the last section, the most controversial election, of the proposed amendment. I point out, based upon my judgment, that this most controversial part of the amendment rarely if ever would be brought into play.

As the Senator from Illinois [Mr. Dirksen] has pointed out, the amendment provides for the voluntary declaration of disability by the President. Let us assume, for example, that he is undergoing a serious operation, and that he does not want to take the chance of having the enemy take advantage of the situation.

The amendment also deals with the kind of crisis which President Eisenhower described, such as a President suffering from a heart attack. For example, at the time he might be in an oxygen tent the Russians might begin to move missiles into Cuba. At that moment no person in the United States would have any power to make any decision that had to be made.

The amendment would take care of these points.

Now we get to the point to which the Senator from Tennessee has correctly alluded; namely, the question of a President who, although physically able, is not the man, from a substantive point, who was previously elected to that office. Thus arises the difficult problem of mental disability.

The Senator from Tennessee bases his argument on the fact that changes were made in the conference committee. I point out that in referring to the "either/or" change, the Senator from Tennessee overlooks the fact that several other changes were made in conference. I would not want to mislead anyone into believing that that was the only change that was made. Several others were made, in connection with which we tried to compromise with our friends in the House.

I believe that we have a better amendment now, in most respects, than when it left the Senate. I would have preferred the language which the Senator from Tennessee has suggested. This was not the case. The amendment is the product of our conference. I hope we can at least shed some light on our belief as to the validity of our contention that there is no ambiguity here.

With respect to "either/or", it is clear to me—and I invite the attention of Senators to the definition of this phrase in Black's Legal Dictionary and to most legal cases on the point—that when we talk about "either/or" it is interpreted in the disjunctive. It does not refer to two, but to either one or the other.

Reference was made—not by the Senator from Tennessee, but by another Senator—to the fact that the Vice President could in effect at one time go to either one of these bodies and use them simultaneously. I do not see how it is possible to do that.

Mr. Gore: Mr. President, will the Senator yield?

Mr. Bayh: I should like to finish my argument. Then I shall be happy to yield. We have some evidence about what the courts have indicated in this respect. Certainly it is the intention of the conference committee and it is my contention, as the floor manager of the joint resolution and as the principal sponsor of it—and I believe I can also say that it is the opinion of a majority of the Judicial Committee—that Congress should have some flexibility, and that we do not wish to nail down a plan which may not work. It is our intention for the plan, as it is enacted, to have the Vice President and a majority of the Cabinet make the decision, unless Congress, in its wisdom, at some later time, determines by statute to establish some other body to act with the Vice President. It would be rather ridiculous to give that power to Congress and provide at the same time that it may not exercise it within a certain number of years, or could not exercise it at all. We give to Congress, in its wisdom, the power to make the determination as to when another body should act in concert with the Vice President. It is our intention that at that time this other body shall supersede the Cabinet.

Mr. Lausche: Mr. President, will the Senator yield for a brief question?

Mr. Bayh: I should like to yield for only a brief question.

Mr. Lausche: Yes. Was there any discussion among the conferees about putting it in the conjunctive, instead of the disjunctive, having both a majority of the members of the Cabinet and a majority of the members of the body created by Congress act?

Mr. Bayh: This was never considered.

Mr. Lausche: It was never considered?

Mr. Bayh: It was never considered.

Since the Senator from Tennessee raised the question I have tried my best to look for cases which might soothe his concern about the ambiguity which he believes exists and which I believe does not exist.

Mr. President, I have uncovered three or four cases dealing with article V of the Constitution. They are *Hawke* v. *Smith*, 253 U.S. 221; *Dillon* v. *Gloss*,

256 U.S. 368; the *National Prohibition* cases, 253 U.S. 350; and *United States* v. *Sprague,* 282 U.S. 716.

As the Senate knows, article V deals with the means to amend the Constitution itself. Congress is given the authority to use either the means of legislative ratification or State convention ratification. Either one or the other may be used. In dealing with the fifth article, the courts have held in those cases to which I have referred—which are as close to being on the point as any I have been able to find—that Congress has full and plenary power to decide which method should be used, and once the choice is made, the other method is precluded.

These cases substantiate our feeling—at least our intention—as to what we desire to accomplish in the wording which has been placed in the conference report.

I should like to go one step further. In the debate I do not wish to concede ambiguity. But out of friendship for the Senator from Tennessee [Mr. Gore], I should like to suppose, for only a moment, that there might be ambiguity in the use of the words "either/or." What then would be the result? In the event of ambiguity there is no question that the Court would then look to the legislative intent. As a result of the insight and the perseverance of the Senator from Tennessee, we have now written a record of legislative intent, as long as our arms, to the effect that we desire only one body to act on the subject. In the event that an ambiguity is construed, I suggest that there is one last safeguard. I am certain that Congress, under the enabling provision which would permit another body to act with the Vice President, would in its wisdom at that time specify that, pursuant to section 4 of the 25th amendment to the Constitution, the other body is designated to supplant and replace the Cabinet and act in concert with the Vice President. So I am not concerned that

there might be a vexatious ambiguity present.

I should like to speak on one other point which the Senator from Tennessee raised, and which I believe is a very good point.

Mr. Long of Louisiana: Mr. President, will the Senator yield at that point?

Mr. Bayh: I yield.

Mr. Long of Louisiana: It seems to this Senator that in a dangerous time when the inability of the President might be in question, particularly with respect to his mental capacity, Congress should act on the question. As I understand, no matter which body might make the declaration that the President was not able to serve, the question would then be before the Congress and it would have to be decided by a two-thirds vote; otherwise, the man who had been elected to the office of President would continue to serve as president.

Mr. Bayh: The Senator from Louisiana is correct. To remove, for any reason or on any ground, a man who has been elected to the most powerful office in the world, the office of President of the United States, is not an action to be taken lightly. As the Senator has pointed out, and as Senators will observe in other places in the amendment, we have leaned over backward in our effort to protect the President in his office. The decision would have to be made by Congress. A two-thirds vote would be required. That is a greater safeguard than is presently available under the provision for impeachment proceedings. Under that provision a vote of two-thirds of the Senate is needed; under the proposed amendment a vote of two-thirds of both Houses would be required.

There is no need to extend the debate, but I should like to speak to the question which the Senator from Tennessee raised. The Senator said that if there is any doubt, let us wait. We cannot be certain what the Supreme Court of the

United States will do. I doubt very much that there have been many pieces of proposed legislation, certainly not related to constitutional amendments, that have passed this body in which there has not been considerable and heated debate as to whether some of the proposed language was right or wrong. Today I am certain that there are some Senators who would say that we cannot tell what the Supreme Court will do tomorrow with a constitutional amendment that is already on our books. The opinions of the Court change with time. I think we have to determine one question: Is the conference report the best piece of proposed legislation we can get and is it needed? As loudly as I can, I say that we must answer the question in the affirmative.

Some Senators might say, "What is the rush? We are not ready to adjourn yet. We can send the measure back to the conference committee and have it reworked."

To those who are students of history I do not have to document again and again the fact that we have labored for 187 years as a country and we have not yet been able to get sufficient support for any type of proposed legislation in this area. In 38 of those years we had no Vice President. We have had three serious presidential disabilities. Wilson was disabled for 16 months. Garfield was disabled for 80 days, and during that period there was no Executive running the country. Can Senators imagine what would happen to the United States and the world today if the United States were without a President? For all intents and purposes, we would be involved in world chaos from which we could not recover.

For more than 18 months the Senate has studied the proposed legislation. Two sets of hearings have been held. I appreciate the support that Senators have given us in this effort.

In the last session of Congress, the Senate passed the proposed legislation by a vote of 65 to 0; in the present session of the Congress, the Senate passed the measure by a vote of 72 to 0.

This measure is not something which we have arrived at on the spur of the moment. We have had controversy and differences of opinion over individual words. I should like to remind Senators that during the past few years we have received over 100 different proposals. Since I have been chairman of the Subcommittee on Constitutional Amendments, during the past few months 26 different proposals have been submitted.

I point out that if those who had the foresight to introduce proposed legislation on the subject—the Senator from North Carolina [Mr. Ervin], the Senator from Illinois, the Senator from Kentucky [Mr. Cooper], Senator from Idaho [Mr. Church], and others—had not been willing to agree and had not been willing to try to reach a consensus, and if it had not been for the guiding hand of the American Bar Association to try to get those with differing views together, we would not be so far as we are now. I do not believe that we should let two words separate us.

Mr. Long of Louisiana: Mr. President, will the Senator yield?

Mr. Bayh: I yield.

Mr. Long of Louisiana: If I had had my way, there are two or three changes I can think of immediately that I should like to have made. I suggested some of them to both the leadership and also to the executive branch—for the measure vitally affects the executive branch—when the subject was being considered previously. The advice that I received at that time was, "Please don't muddy the water. The amendment has been needed since the establishment of our country. If we start all over again, not only will the junior Senator from Louisiana have two or three additional suggestions that he would like to urge, but other Senators will also have suggestions to make, and we shall be another 100 years getting to the point which we now have reached."

Mr. Bayh: I thank the Senator from Louisiana. He is exactly correct.

Mr. Ervin: Mr. President, will the Senator yield?

Mr. Bayh: I yield.

Mr. Ervin: When we started to consider the proposal, the Senator from Indiana and I had a discussion. We were concerned with the old adage that too many cooks would spoil the broth. We had more cooks with more zeal concerned with preparing this "broth" than any piece of proposed legislation I have ever seen in the time I have been in the Senate. If it had not been for the perseverance, the patience, and the willingness to compromise which was manifested on a multitude of occasions by the junior Senator from Indiana, we would never have gotten the resolution out of the subcommittee, much less through the full Judiciary Committee and then through the conference with the House. I am of the opinion that the conference report which the Senator from Indiana is seeking to have approved would submit to the States the very best possible resolution on the subject obtainable in the Congress of the United States as it is now constituted. The Senator from Indiana deserves the thanks of the American people for the fact that he was willing to change the ingredients of the broth in order to appease a multitude of different cooks who had different recipes for it, including myself.

Mr. Bayh: I thank the Senator from North Carolina. I have said, and I say again, that we are greatly indebted to him for his "seasoning" and his willingness to compromise. Although there were many cooks, we had a paddle large enough so that we could all get our hands on it and stir. The conference report is the composite of the efforts of many different people.

I should like to conclude with one last thought. We know that over the great Archives Building downtown there is a statement engraved in stone. I do not know whether it is Indiana limestone, but standing out in bold letters is the statement: "What is past is prolog."

I cannot help but feel that history has been trying to tell us something.

There was a time in the history of this great Nation when carrier pigeons were the fastest means of communication and the Army was rolling on horse-drawn caissons. Perhaps it did not make any difference then whether the Nation had a President who was not able at all times to fulfill all the duties and powers of his office. But today, with the awesome power at our disposal, when armies can be moved half way around the world in a matter of hours, and when it is possible actually to destroy civilization in a matter of minutes, it is high time that we listened to history and make absolutely certain that there will be a President of the United States at all times, a President who has complete control and will be able to perform all the powers and duties of his office.

Mr. Javits: Mr. President, will the Senator yield?

Mr. Bayh: I yield.

Mr. Javits: The Senator has made an excellent argument and the right argument, concerning the effect the amendment will have in a situation of preparation for the use of executive power.

Is it not true that, with the greatest respect for the opponents of what the Senator is trying to do, it is assumed that the people will do their duty by approving the amendment through their State legislatures, but that we will not implement it in such a way as to indicate that we are not the approving power? It is one thing to say that some Vice President or President may misuse power. But we are passing the amendment. Is it not logical for us to count on ourselves to implement it effectively?

We can resolve every doubt. We have complete power to resolve every doubt by legislation that will give exclusive power to the Cabinet or to the other body.

Mr. Bayh: I agree with the Senator from New York. The main authority behind the entire legislation—in fact, behind the enactment of any legislation—is the ability of men and women in Congress and in the executive branch to act with reason. If a time comes in the history of our Nation when Senators and Representatives and Presidents are despots, our entire democratic system will be in jeopardy. I, for one, am willing to place in my successors the faith that has been placed in us today. Can we doubt that future Senators and Representatives will fulfill the responsibility that inheres in the holding of high trust and office?

Mr. Javits: If Congress were to soldier on the people in any such way as some might fear, we could sit on our hands with respect to appropriations; we would not have to declare war; there would be plenty of ways in which to sabotage the United States.

The Presiding Officer: The time of the Senator from Indiana has expired.

Mr. Cooper: Mr. President, will the Senator yield?

The Presiding Officer: Who yields time?

Mr. Gore: I yield 1 minute to the Senator from Kentucky.

Mr. Cooper: I do not wish to haggle over the meaning of the amendment, but the Senator from Tennessee asked one question which I think has not been answered.

We want to establish this body, because if we did not think it necessary and did not believe that at some point the Cabinet might not declare the President disabled, when he actually was disabled, there would not be any point in wishing to establish a second body.

The Senator from Tennessee asked the question: Assuming that Congress establishes this body, and Congress says it has exclusive jurisdiction—

The Presiding Officer: The time of the Senator from Kentucky has expired. Who yields time?

Mr. Bayh: I shall be glad to yield time.

The Presiding Officer: The time of the Senator from Indiana has expired.

Mr. Gore: I have only 3 minutes remaining. I wanted to close; however, I ask unanimous consent that the Senator from Kentucky have 5 minutes to discuss this question.

Mr. Cooper: I do not need 5 minutes.

Mr. Gore: I yield 1 minute of my remaining time to the Senator from Kentucky.

Mr. Cooper: The Senator from Tennessee made the point that since this is a constitutional amendment, Congress cannot take away the power given to the Cabinet by legislative enactment. He asks: If Congress should establish this body and give it exclusivity, would that have any force against the amendment itself, which provides that the power shall lie either in the Cabinet or in the body itself?

Mr. Javits: It is my considered judgment—and I am the one who debated this point—that Congress, having the power to establish the body, can give it exclusivity which will stand up as a matter of constitutional law.

The Presiding Officer: The time yielded by the Senator from Tennessee to the Senator from Kentucky has expired. The Senator from Tennessee has 2 minutes remaining.

Mr. Bayh: We have made the record abundantly clear.

Mr. Gore: The distinguished Senator from Kentucky has just said that a question I raised has not been answered.

The distinguished Senator from Ohio asked if this question was raised in conference. The answer was that it was not. It was not raised on the floor of either House.

Mr. Bayh: That was not the question.

Mr. Gore: The Senator from Ohio asked a question, about use of the disjunctive.

I say that the proposed amendment creates grave doubt. I should like to read from the record of the debate of last Wednesday, June 30:

> **Mr. Gore.** Do I correctly understand the able Senator to say that Congress could, immediately upon adoption of this constitutional amendment, provide by law for such a body as herein specified and that, then, either a majority of this body created by law or a majority of the Cabinet could perform this function?
>
> **Mr. Bayh:** No. The Cabinet has the primary responsibility. If it is replaced by Congress with another body, the Cabinet loses the responsibility, and it rests solely in the other body.
>
> **Mr. Gore:** But the amendment does not so provide.
>
> **Mr. Bayh:** Yes, it does. It states—
>
> **Mr. Gore:** The word is "or."
>
> **Mr. Bayh:** It says "or." It does not say "both." "Or such other body as Congress may by law prescribe."

I suggest, Mr. President, that we have time to correct this doubt. Let us return the report to conference; let it be clarified.

The Presiding Officer (Mr. Harris in the chair): All time has expired. The question is on agreeing to the conference report. [Putting the question.]

Mr. Gore: The majority leader announced that there would be a yea-and-nay vote.

Mr. Bayh: I ask for the yeas and nays.

The yeas and nays were ordered.

Mr. Ervin: Mr. President, a parliamentary inquiry.

The Presiding Officer: The Senator from North Carolina will state it.

Mr. Ervin: What is the question before the Senate?

The Presiding Officer: The ques-

tion is on agreeing to the conference report on Senate Joint Resolution 1.

Mr. Dirksen: Mr. President, a parliamentary inquiry.

The Presiding Officer: The Senator from Illinois will state it.

Mr. Dirksen: Do I correctly understand that notwithstanding that the vote is on the conference report, a two-thirds majority is required for its adoption?

The Presiding Officer: The Senator from Illinois is correct. The clerk will call the roll.

The legislative clerk called the roll.

Mr. Long of Louisiana: I announce that the Senator from New Mexico [Mr. Anderson], the Senator from Nevada [Mr. Bible], the Senator from Nevada [Mr. Cannon], the Senator from Louisiana [Mr. Ellender], the Senator from Arkansas [Mr. Fulbright], the Senator from North Carolina [Mr. Jordan], the Senator from Missouri [Mr. Long], the Senator from Washington [Mr. Magnuson], the Senator from Montana [Mr. Mansfied], the Senator from New Mexico [Mr. Montoya], the Senator from Oregon [Mr. Morse], the Senator from West Virginia [Mr. Randolph], and the Senator from Oregon [Mrs. Neuberger] are absent on official business.

I also announce that the Senator from Alaska [Mr. Bartlett], the Senator from Virginia [Mr. Byrd], the Senator from Mississippi [Mr. Eastland], and the Senator from Indiana [Mr. Hartke] are necessarily absent.

I further announce that, if present and voting, the Senator from Nevada [Mr. Bible], the Senator from North Carolina [Mr. Jordan], the Senator from Oregon [Mr. Morse], and the Senator from West Virginia [Mr. Randolph] would each vote "yea."

On this vote, the Senator from Mississippi [Mr. Eastland] and the Senator from Nebraska [Mr. Hruska] are paired with the Senator from New Mexico [Mr. Anderson]. If present and voting, the Senator from Mississippi would vote "yea," the Senator from Nebraska would vote "yea," and the Senator from New Mexico would vote "nay."

On this vote, the Senator from Nevada [Mr. Cannon] and the Senator from Louisiana [Mr. Ellender] are paired with the Senator from Washington [Mr. Magnuson]. If present and voting, the Senator from Nevada would vote "yea," and the Senator from Louisiana would vote "yea," and the Senator from Washington would vote "nay."

On this vote, the Senator from Indiana [Mr. Hartke] and the Senator from Montana [Mr. Mansfield] are paired with the Senator from New Mexico [Mr. Montoya]. If present and voting, the Senator from Indiana would vote "yea," the Senator from Montana would vote "yea," and the Senator from New Mexico would vote "nay."

Mr. Kuchel: I announce that the Senator from Vermont [Mr. Aiken], the Senator from Colorado [Mr. Dominick], the Senator from Nebraska [Mr. Hruska], and the Senator from California [Mr. Murphy] are absent on official business.

The Senator from Utah [Mr. Bennett], the Senator from Kansas [Mr. Carlson], the Senator from New Hampshire [Mr. Cotton], the Senator from Hawaii [Mr. Fong], the Senator from Massachusetts [Mr. Saltonstall], and the Senator from Wyoming [Mr. Simpson] are necessarily absent.

If present and voting, the Senator from Vermont [Mr. Aiken], the Senator from Utah [Mr. Bennett], the Senator from Colorado [Mr. Dominick], the Senator from Hawaii [Mr. Fong], the Senator from California [Mr. Murphy], the Senator from Massachusetts [Mr. Saltonstall], and the Senator from Wyoming [Mr. Simpson] would each vote "yea."

On this vote, the Senator from Nebraska [Mr. Hruska] and the Senator from Mississippi [Mr. Eastland] are paired with the Senator from New Mexico [Mr. Anderson]. If present and voting, the Senator from Nebraska and the

Senator from Mississippi would each vote "yea," and the Senator from New Mexico would vote "nay."

The yeas and nays resulted—yeas 68, nays 5, as follows:

YEAS—68

Allott	Holland	Pearson
Bass	Inouye	Pell
Bayh	Jackson	Prouty
Boggs	Javits	Proxmire
Brewster	Jordan, Idaho	Ribicoff
Burdick	Kennedy, Mass.	Robertson
Byrd, W. Va.	Kennedy, N.Y.	Russell, S.C.
Case	Kuchel	Russell, Ga.
Church	Long, La.	Scott
Clark	McClellan	Smathers
Cooper	McGee	Smith
Curtis	McGovern	Sparkman
Dirksen	McIntyre	Stennis
Dodd	NcNamara	Symington
Douglas	Metcalf	Talmadge
Ervin	Miller	Thurmond
Fannin	Monroney	Tydings
Gruening	Morton	Williams, N.J.
Harris	Moss	Williams, Del.
Hart	Mundt	Yarborough
Hayden	Muskie	Young, N. Dak.
Hickenlooper	Nelson	Young, Ohio
Hill	Pastore	

NAYS—5

Gore	McCarthy	Tower
Lausche	Mondale	

NOT VOTING—27

Aiken	Dominick	Magnuson
Anderson	Eastland	Mansfield
Bartlett	Ellender	Montoya
Bennett	Fong	Morse
Bible	Fulbright	Murphy
Byrd, Va.	Hartke	Neuberger
Cannon	Hruska	Randolph
Carlson	Jordan, N.C.	Saltonstall
Cotton	Long, Mo.	Simpson

The Presiding Officer: On this vote, the yeas are 68, the nays 5. Two-thirds of the Senators present and voting having voted in the affirmative, the conference report is agreed to.

Mr. Bayh: Mr. President, I move to consider the vote by which the conference report was agreed to.

Mr. Kuchel: Mr. President, I move to lay that motion on the table.

The motion to lay on the table was agreed to.

Eugene McCarthy Announces Candidacy for President (1967)

Like President Woodrow Wilson in 1916, President Lyndon B. Johnson campaigned in 1964 as the peace candidate in the election. (See "Woodrow Wilson's 'Shadow Lawn' Speech on Foreign Policy," p. 277.) Referring to the war in Vietnam, Johnson vowed to crowds of supporters that he would not "supply American boys to do the job that Asian boys should do." Yet, just as Wilson's election was followed by the U.S. entry into World War I, Johnson's election set the stage for the rapid escalation of the U.S. involvement in Vietnam: 23,000 troops by the end of 1964, 181,000 a year later, 389,000 a year after that, and 500,000 by the end of 1967.

In contrast to World War I, the fighting did not go well for the United States in Vietnam. Public opinion polls revealed that increasing numbers of Americans disapproved of Johnson's conduct of the war. College campuses erupted in protest. In mid-1967, New York attorney Allard K. Lowenstein and other antiwar Democrats began searching for a candidate to oppose Johnson's bid for the party's nomination in 1968. Several senators, including Robert F. Kennedy of New York, George McGovern of South Dakota, and Frank Church of Idaho, rejected Lowenstein's request as quixotic.

Sen. Eugene McCarthy of Minnesota, who had hoped to be Johnson's vice-presidential running mate in 1964, decided at last to pick up the antiwar escutcheon. On November 30, 1967, McCarthy announced that he would enter several Democratic primaries in order to challenge the administration's policy of "continued escalation and intensification of the war in Vietnam."

The McCarthy campaign caught fire among college students, many of whom cut their long hair ("Come Clean for Gene") and trekked to New Hampshire, the site of the election's first primary, to campaign on his behalf. On March 12, 1968, in an astonishing upset, McCarthy won twenty of the state's twenty-four Democratic convention delegates. Even his surprisingly narrow popular vote defeat by Johnson was declared a moral victory in the press. Overnight, the polls showed that McCarthy had surged into a commanding lead in the April 2 Wisconsin primary.

Sen. Kennedy was the first political leader to react to McCarthy's triumph: he launched an antiwar campaign of his own, entering the race for the Democratic presidential nomination on March 16. McCarthy and his supporters were furious at Kennedy's announcement, which they regarded as a purely opportunistic act that could only divide the effort to end the war.

The next to respond to the rapidly changing political situation was President Johnson. On March 31, surprising *even his closest advisers, Johnson concluded a televised address on Vietnam by announcing, "I shall not seek, and I will not accept, the nomination of my party for another term as your President."*

In the aftermath of Johnson's withdrawal, McCarthy and Kennedy battled through the remaining primaries, with Kennedy taking a narrow lead. But only about one-third of the Democratic national convention delegates were chosen in primaries in 1968; the other two-thirds were handpicked by the various state party leaders. On April 27, 1968, Vice President Hubert H. Humphrey, taking aim at the two-thirds, announced his candidacy for president. Humphrey left the battle for the other delegates to McCarthy and Kennedy, entering no primaries.

On June 4, Kennedy narrowly defeated McCarthy in the California primary. That night, flushed with victory, Kennedy was assassinated at his headquarters hotel by Sirhan Sirhan, a Palestinian activist.

The bad blood that had developed between McCarthy and Kennedy left antiwar Democrats divided even after the assassination. Many of Kennedy's delegates decided to give their votes to McGovern. Meanwhile, with Johnson's support, Humphrey built a commanding lead among the Democratic party regulars.

At the August national convention in Chicago, Humphrey was easily nominated on the first ballot. In the streets outside the convention hall, however, city police fought with thousands of enraged antiwar demonstrators. Live television cameras cut back and forth between speeches at the convention and the violence in the streets. The Democrats left Chicago a thoroughly dispirited party.   ~

I intend to enter the Democratic primaries in four states, Wisconsin, Oregon, California and Nebraska. The decision with reference to Massachusetts and also New Hampshire will be made within the next two or three weeks.

As far as Massachusetts is concerned it will depend principally upon the outcome of a meeting which is being held there if they finish their work this weekend—a meeting of the Democratic State Committee.

Since I first said that I thought the issue of Vietnam and the issues related to it should be raised in the primaries of the country I have talked with Democratic leaders from about 25 to 26 states. I've talked particularly to candidates for re-election to the Senate—Democratic candidates—some House members and also to students on campus and to other people throughout the country.

My decision to challenge the President's position and the Administration position has been strengthened by recent announcements out of the Administration, the evident intention to escalate and to intensify the war in Vietnam and on the other hand the absence of any positive indication or suggestion for a compromise or for a negotiated political settlement.

I am concerned that the Administration seems to have set no limit to the price which it's willing to pay for a military victory. Let me summarize the cost of the war up to this point:

The physical destruction of much of a small and weak nation by military operations of the most powerful nation in the world.

One hundred thousand to 150,000 civilian casualties in South Vietnam alone, to say nothing of the destruction of life and property in North Vietnam.

The uprooting and the fracturing of the structure of the society of South Vietnam where one-fourth to one-third of the population are now reported to be refugees.

For the United States as of yesterday over 15,000 combat dead and nearly

95,000 wounded through November.

A monthly expenditure in pursuit of the war amounting somewhere between $2-billion and $3-billion.

I am also concerned about the bearing of the war on other areas of the United States responsibility, both at home and abroad.

The failure to appropriate adequate funds for the poverty program here, for housing, for education, and to meet other national needs and the prospect of additional cuts as a condition to the possible passage of the surtax bill.

The drastic reduction of our foreign aid program in other parts of the world.

A dangerous rise in inflation and one of the indirect and serious consequences of our involvement in Vietnam, the devaluation of the British pound, which in many respects is more important east of Suez today than the British Navy.

In addition, there is growing evidence of a deepening moral crisis in America—discontent and frustration and a disposition to take extralegal if not illegal actions to manifest protest.

I am hopeful that this challenge which I am making, which I hope will be supported by other members of the Senate and other politicians, may alleviate at least in some degree this sense of political helplessness and restore to many people a belief in the processes of American politics and of American government.

That the college campuses especially—on those campuses—and also among adult thoughtful Americans, that it may counter the growing sense of alienation from politics which I think is currently reflected in a tendency to withdraw from political action, to talk of nonparticipation, to become cynical and to make threats of support for third parties or fourth parties or other irregular political movements.

I do not see in my move any great threat to the unity and strength of the Democratic party, whatever that unity may be today and whatever strength it may be.

The issue of the war in Vietnam is not really a separate issue but one that must be dealt with in the configuration of other problems to which it is related. It is within this broader context that I intend to make the case to the people of the United States.

To say that I'm—as I'm sure I shall be charged—I am not for peace at any price, but for an honorable, rational and political solution to this war, a solution which I believe will enhance our world position, encourage the respect of our allies and our potential adversaries, which will permit us to give the necessary attention to other commitments both at home and abroad, military and non-military and leave us with resources and moral energy to deal effectively with the pressing domestic problems of the United States itself.

In this—this total effort—I believe we can restore to this nation a clearer sense of purpose and of dedication to the achievement of our traditional purposes as a great nation in the 20th century.

Thank you very much.

Richard Nixon's Acceptance Speech to the Republican National Convention (1968)

During the twenty-year period from 1952 to 1972, Richard Nixon was the vice-presidential (1952, 1956) or presidential (1960, 1968, 1972) candidate of the Republican party in five of six national elections. It is all the more curious, then, that although Nixon was on the winning ticket in four of these elections, his political obituary was written on several occasions:

~ In 1952, Dwight D. Eisenhower, the Republican nominee for president, almost dropped Nixon from the ticket in response to charges that the then-California senator had accepted personal donations from business leaders in his state. Nixon survived the crisis by effectively explaining the purpose of the donated funds in a nationally televised address. (See "Richard Nixon's 'Checkers' Speech," p. 474.)

~ In 1956, President Eisenhower responded to the pleas of some liberal Republicans by privately encouraging Nixon to leave the vice presidency and accept a position in the cabinet. Nixon declined to withdraw voluntarily, however, and Eisenhower did not press the matter.

~ In 1962, two years after his narrow loss to Sen. John F. Kennedy in the 1960 presidential election, Nixon ran for governor of California and was handily defeated. The morning after the election, Nixon announced that he was ending his career in politics. "You won't have Nixon to kick around any more," he angrily told a group of reporters, "because, gentlemen, this is my last press conference."

Shortly after his defeat in the California gubernatorial election, Nixon moved to New York City and accepted a partnership in a major law firm. But he did not abandon politics. In 1964, Nixon gracefully presented Barry M. Goldwater to the Republican national convention on the night of the Arizona senator's acceptance speech. Two years later, he campaigned actively for Republican congressional candidates in the midterm elections. When President Lyndon B. Johnson attacked Nixon as a "chronic campaigner" and, a few days later, Republicans made substantial gains in the elections, Nixon shed part of his image as a political loser. Reporters began to write stories about a "new Nixon," seasoned by defeat, mellowed by the passage of time, and receptive to innovative ideas.

In 1967, Nixon carefully laid the groundwork for a political comeback in the coming presidential election. Having thoroughly watered the party's grass roots for almost two decades with campaign and fund-raising appearances, Nixon had the affection of state and local Republican leaders. To prove to them that he still could win a national election, Nixon entered several *primaries in the winter and spring of 1968.*

Nixon was blessed with weak opponents. The early front-runner, Gov. George Romney of Michigan, became an object of derision when he claimed that American generals had "brainwashed" him during a recent visit to Vietnam. Governors Nelson A. Rockefeller of New York and Ronald Reagan of California waited too long to enter the race. Nixon won a series of easy victories in the primaries and coasted to a first-ballot nomination at the Republican national convention in August.

In contrast to the Democratic convention, the Republican gathering in Miami, Florida, was a political love feast. (See "Eugene McCarthy Announces for President," p. 554.) Nixon capped off his nomination with an optimistic, conciliatory, and at times eloquent acceptance speech.   ~

Mr. Chairman, delegates to this convention, my fellow Americans.

Sixteen years ago I stood before this convention to accept your nomination as the running mate of one of the greatest Americans of our time or of any time—Dwight D. Eisenhower.

Eight years ago I had the highest honor of accepting your nomination for President of the United States.

Tonight I again proudly accept that nomination for President of the United States.

But I have news for you. This time there's a difference—this time we're going to win.

We're going to win for a number of reasons. First a personal one.

General Eisenhower, as you know, lies critically ill in the Walter Reed Hospital tonight. I have talked, however, with Mrs. Eisenhower on the telephone.

She tells me that his heart is with us. She says that there is nothing that he lives more for, and there is nothing that would lift him more than for us to win in November.

And I say let's win this one for Ike.

We're going to win because this great convention has demonstrated to the nation that the Republican party has the leadership, the platform and the purpose that America needs.

We're going to win because you have nominated as my running mate a statesman of the first rank who will be a great campaigner, and one who is fully qualified to undertake the new responsibilities that I shall give to the next Vice President of the United States.

And he is a man who fully shares my conviction and yours that after a period of 40 years when power has gone from the cities and the states to the Government in Washington, D.C., it's time to have power go back from Washington to the states and to the cities of this country all over America.

We're going to win because at a time that America cries out for the unity that this Administration has destroyed, the Republican party, after a spirited contest for its nomination for President and Vice President, stands united before the nation tonight.

And I congratulate Governor Reagan, I congratulate Governor Rockefeller, I congratulate Governor Romney, I congratulate all those who have made the hard fight that they have for this nomination, and I know that you will all fight even harder for the great victory our party is going to win in November because we're going to be together in that election campaign.

And a party that can unite itself will unite America.

My fellow Americans, most important we're going to win because our cause is right. We make history tonight, not for ourselves but for the ages. The choice we make in 1968 will determine not only the future of America but the future of peace and freedom in the world for the last third of the 20th century, and the question that we answer tonight: can America meet this great challenge?

Let us listen to America to find the answer to that question.

As we look at America, we see cities enveloped in smoke and flame. We hear sirens in the night. We see Americans dying on distant battlefields abroad. We see Americans hating each other; fighting each other; killing each other at home.

And as we see and hear these things, millions of Americans cry out in anguish: Did we come all this way for this? Did American boys die in Normandy and Korea and in Valley Forge for this?

Listen to the answers to these questions.

It is another voice, it is a quiet voice in the tumult of the shouting. It is the voice of the great majority of Americans, the forgotten Americans, the non-shouters, the non-demonstrators. They're not racists or sick; they're not guilty of the crime that plagues the land; they are black, they are white; they're native born and foreign born; they're young and they're old.

They work in American factories, they run American business. They serve in government; they provide most of the soldiers who die to keep it free. They give drive to the spirit of America. They give lift to the American dream. They give steel to the backbone of America.

They're good people. They're decent people; they work and they save and they pay their taxes and they care.

Like Theodore Roosevelt, they know that this country will not be a good place for any of us to live in unless it's a good place for all of us to live in.

And this I say, this I say to you tonight, is the real voice of America. In this year 1968, this is the message it will broadcast to America and to the world.

Let's never forget that despite her faults, America is a great nation. And America is great because her people are great.

With Winston Churchill we say, we have not journeyed all this way, across the centuries, across the oceans, across the mountains, across the prairies, because we are made of sugar candy.

America's in trouble today not because her people have failed, but because her leaders have failed. And what America needs are leaders to match the greatness of her people.

And this great group of Americans— the forgotten Americans and others— know that the great question Americans must answer by their votes in November is this: Whether we shall continue for four more years the policies of the last five years.

And this is their answer, and this is my answer to that question: When the strongest nation in the world can be tied down for four years in a war in Vietnam, with no end in sight, when the richest nation in the world can't manage its own economy, when the nation with the greatest tradition of the rule of law is plagued by unprecedented lawlessness, when a nation has been known for a century for equality of opportunity is torn by unprecedented racial violence, and when the President of the United States cannot travel abroad or to any major city at home without fear of a hostile demonstration—then it's time for new leadership for America.

Thank you. My fellow Americans, tonight I accept the challenge and the commitment to provide that new leadership for America and I ask you to accept it with me.

And let us accept this challenge not as a grim duty but as an exciting adventure in which we are privileged to help a great nation realize its destiny and let us begin by committing ourselves to the truth, to see it like it is and tell it like it is, to find the truth, to speak the truth and to live the truth. That's what we will do.

We've had enough of big promises and little action. The time has come for an honest government in the United States of America.

And so tonight I do not promise the millenium in the morning. I don't promise that we can eradicate poverty and end discrimination and eliminate all danger or wars in the space of four, or even eight years. But I do promise action. A new policy for peace abroad, a new policy for peace and progress and justice at home.

Look at our problems abroad. Do you realize that we face the stark truth that we are worse off in every area of the world tonight than we were when President Eisenhower left office eight years ago? That's the record.

And there is only one answer to such a record of failure, and that is the complete house cleaning of those responsible for the failures and that record.

The answer is the complete reappraisal of America's policies in every section of the world. We shall begin with Vietnam.

We all hope in this room that there's a chance that current negotiations may bring an honorable end to that war. And we will say nothing during this campaign that might destroy that chance.

But if the war is not ended when the people choose in November, the choice will be clear. Here it is: For four years this Administration has had at its disposal the greatest military and economic advantage that one nation has ever had over another in a war in history. For four years America's fighting men have set a record for courage and sacrifice unsurpassed in our history. For four years this Administration has had the support of the loyal opposition for the objective of seeking an honorable end to the struggle.

Never has so much military and economic and diplomatic power been used so ineffectively. And if after all of this time, and all of this sacrifice, and all of this support, there is still no end in sight, then I say the time has come for the American people to turn to new leadership not tied to the mistakes and

policies of the past. That is what we offer to America.

And I pledge to you tonight that the first priority foreign policy objective of our next Administration will be to bring an honorable end to the war in Vietnam.

We shall not stop there. We need a policy to prevent more Vietnams. All of America's peace-keeping institutions and all of America's foreign commitments must be reappraised.

Over the past 25 years, America has provided more than $150-billion in foreign aid to nations abroad. In Korea, and now again in Vietnam, the United States furnished most of the money, most of the arms, most of the men to help the people of those countries defend themselves against aggression. Now we're a rich country, we're a strong nation, we're a populous nation but there are 200 million Americans and there are two billion people that live in the free world, and I say the time has come for other nations in the free world to bear their fair share of the burden of defending peace and freedom around this world.

What I call for is not a new isolationism. It is a new internationalism in which America enlists its allies and its friends around the world in those struggles in which their interest is as great as ours.

And now to the leaders of the Communist world we say, after an era of confrontations, the time has come for an era of negotiations.

Where the world superpowers are concerned there is no acceptable alternative to peaceful negotiation. Because this will be a period of negotiations we shall restore the strength of America so that we shall always negotiate from strength and never from weakness.

And as we seek through negotiations let our goals be made clear. We do not seek domination over any other country. We believe deeply in our ideas but we believe they should travel on their own power and not on the power of our arms. We shall never be belligerent. But we shall be as firm in defending our system as they are in expanding theirs.

We believe this should be an era of peaceful competition not only in the productivity of our factories but in the quality of our ideas. We extend the hand of friendship to all people. To the Russian people. To the Chinese people. To all people in the world. And we shall work toward the goal of an open world, open sky, open cities, open hearts, open minds. The next eight years my friends. . . .

This period in which we're entering— I think we will have the greatest opportunity for world peace, but also face the greatest danger of world war of anytime in our history.

I believe we must have peace. I believe that we can have peace. But I do not underestimate the difficulty of this task.

Because, you see, the art of preserving peace is greater than that of waging war, and much more demanding.

But I am proud to have served in an Administration which ended one war and kept the nation out of other wars for eight years afterward.

And it is that kind of experience, and it is that kind of leadership, that America needs today and that we will give to America, with your help.

And as we commit the new policies for America tonight, let me make one further pledge—For five years hardly a day has gone by when we haven't read or heard a report of the American flag being spit on, and our embassy being stoned, a library being burned, or an ambassador being insulted some place in the world, and each incident reduced respect for the United States until the ultimate insult inevitably occurred.

And I say to you tonight that when respect for the United States of America falls so low that a fourth-rate military power like Korea will seize an American naval vessel in the high seas, it's time for new leadership to restore respect for the United States of America.

Thank you very much. My friends, America is a great nation. It is time we started to act like a great nation around the world.

It's ironic to note, when we were a small nation, weak militarily and poor economically, America was respected. And the reason was that America stood for something more powerful than military strength or economic wealth.

The American Revolution was a shining example of freedom in action which caught the imagination of the world, and today, too often, America is an example to be avoided and not followed.

A nation that can't keep the peace at home won't be trusted to keep the peace abroad. A president who isn't treated with respect at home will not be treated with respect abroad. A nation that can't manage its own economy can't tell others how to manage theirs.

If we are to restore prestige and respect for America abroad, the place to begin is at home—in the United States of America.

My friends, we live in an age of revolution in America and in the world. And to find the answers to our problems, let us turn to a revolution—a revolution that will never grow old, the world's greatest continuing revolution, the American Revolution.

The American Revolution was and is dedicated to progress. But our founders recognized that the first requisite of progress is order.

Now there is no quarrel between progress and order because neither can exist without the other.

So let us have order in America, not the order that suppresses dissent and discourages change but the order which guarantees the right to dissent and provides the basis for peaceful change.

And tonight it's time for some honest talk about the problem of order in the

United States. Let us always respect, as I do, our courts and those who serve on them, but let us also recognize that some of our courts in their decisions have gone too far in weakening the peace forces as against the criminal forces in this country.

Let those who have the responsibility to enforce our laws, and our judges who have the responsibility to interpret them, be dedicated to the great principles of civil rights. But let them also recognize that the first civil right of every American is to be free from domestic violence. And that right must be guaranteed in this country.

And if we are to restore order and respect for law in this country, there's one place we're going to begin: We're going to have a new Attorney General of the United States of America.

I pledge to you that our new Attorney General will be directed by the President of the United States to launch a war against organized crime in this country.

I pledge to you that the new Attorney General of the United States will be an active belligerent against the loan sharks and the numbers racketeers that rob the urban poor in our cities.

I pledge to you that the new Attorney General will open a new front against the pill peddlers and the narcotics peddlers who are corrupting the lives of the children of this country.

Because, my friends, let this message come through clear from what I say tonight. Time is running out for the merchants of crime and corruption in American society. The wave of crime is not going to be the wave of the future in the United States of America.

We shall re-establish freedom from fear in America so that America can take the lead of re-establishing freedom from fear in the world.

And to those who say that law and order is the code word for racism, here is a reply: Our goal is justice—justice for every American. If we are to have

respect for law in America, we must have laws that deserve respect. Just as we cannot have progress without order, we cannot have order without progress.

And so as we commit to order tonight, let us commit to progress.

And this brings me to the clearest choice among the great issues of this campaign.

For the past five years we have been deluged by Government programs for the unemployed, programs for the cities, programs for the poor, and we have reaped from these programs an ugly harvest of frustrations, violence and failure across the land. And now our opponents will be offering more of the same—more billions for Government jobs, Government housing, Government welfare. I say it's time to quit pouring billions of dollars into programs that have failed in the United States of America.

To put it bluntly, we're on the wrong road and it's time to take a new road to progress.

Again we turn to the American Revolution for our answers. The war on poverty didn't begin five years ago in this country; it began when this country began. It's been the most successful war on poverty in the history of nations. There's more wealth in America today, more broadly shared than in any nation in the world.

We are a great nation. And we must never forget how we became great. America is a great nation today, not because of what government did for people, but because of what people did for themselves over 190 years in this country.

And so it is time to apply the lessons of the American Revolution to our present problems.

Let us increase the wealth of America so we can provide more generously for the aged and for the needy and for all those who cannot help themselves.

But for those who are able to help themselves, what we need are not more millions on welfare rolls but more millions on payrolls in the United States of America.

Instead of Government jobs and Government housing let Government use its tax and credit policies to enlist in this battle the greatest engine of progress ever developed in the history of man— American private enterprise.

Let us enlist in this great cause the millions of Americans in volunteer organizations who will bring a dedication to this task that no amount of money can ever buy.

And let us build bridges, my friends, build bridges to human dignity across the gulf that separates black America from white America.

Black Americans—no more than white Americans—do not want more Government programs which perpetuate dependency. They don't want to be a colony in a nation. They want the pride and the self-respect and the dignity that can only come if they have an equal chance to own their own homes, to own their own businesses, to be managers and executives as well as workers, to have a piece of the action in the exciting ventures of private enterprise.

I pledge to you tonight that we shall have new programs which will provide that equal chance. We make great history tonight. We do not fire a shot heard round the world, but we shall light the lamp of hope in millions of homes across this land in which there is no hope today.

And that great light shining out from America will again become a beacon of hope for all those in the world who seek freedom and opportunity.

My fellow Americans, I believe that historians will recall that 1968 marked the beginning of the American generation in world history. Just to be alive in America, just to be alive at this time is an experience unparalleled in history. Here's where the action is.

Think: Thirty-two years from now most of Americans living today will celebrate a New Year that comes once in a thousand years.

Eight years from now, in the second term of the next President, we will celebrate the 200th anniversary of the American Revolution.

And by our decision in this we—all of us here, all of you listening on television and radio—we will determine what kind of a world America will be on its 200th birthday. We will determine what kind of a world America will live in in the year 2000.

This is the kind of a day I see for America on that glorious Fourth eight years from now: I see a day when Americans are once again proud of their flag: when once again at home and abroad it is honored as the world's greatest symbol of liberty and justice.

I see a day when the President of the United States is respected and his office is honored because it is worthy of respect and worthy of honor. I see a day when every child in this land, regardless of his background, has a chance for the best education that our wisdom and schools can provide, and an equal chance to go just as high as his talents will take him.

I see a day when life in rural America attracts people to the country rather than driving them away.

I see a day when we can look back on massive breakthroughs in solving the problems of slums and pollution and traffic which are choking our cities to death.

I see a day when our senior citizens and millions of others can plan for the future with the assurance that their government is not going to rob them of their savings by destroying the value of their dollar.

I see a day when we will again have freedom from fear in America and freedom from fear in the world. I see a day when our nation is at peace and the world is at peace and everyone on earth—those who hope, those who aspire, those who crave liberty will look to

America as the shining example of hopes realized and dreams achieved.

My fellow Americans, this is the cause I ask you to vote for. This is the cause I ask you to work for. This is the cause I ask you to commit to not just for victory in November but beyond that to a new Administration because the time when one man or a few leaders could save America is gone. We need tonight nothing less than the total commitment and the total mobilization of the American people if we are to succeed.

Government can pass laws but respect for law can come only from people who take the law into their hearts and their minds and not into their hands.

Government can provide opportunity, but opportunity means nothing unless people are prepared to seize it.

A president can ask for reconciliation in the racial conflict that divides Americans, but reconciliation comes only from the hearts of people.

And tonight, therefore, as we make this commitment, let us look into our hearts, and let us look down into the faces of our children.

Is there anything in the world that should stand in their way? None of the old hatreds mean anything when you look down into the faces of our children. In their faces is our hope, our love and our courage.

Tonight, I see the face of a child. He lives in a great city, he's black or he's white, he's Mexican, Italian, Polish, none of that matters. What matters he's an American child.

That child in that great city is more important than any politician's promise. He is America, he is a poet, he is a scientist, he's a great teacher, he's a proud craftsman, he's everything we've ever hoped to be in everything we dare to dream about.

He sleeps the sleep of a child, and he dreams the dreams of a child. And yet when he awakens, he awakens to a living nightmare of poverty, neglect and despair.

He fails in school, he ends up on welfare. For him the American system is one that feeds his stomach and starves his soul. It breaks his heart. And in the end it may take his life on some distant battlefield.

To millions of children in this rich land this is their prospect, but this is only part of what I see in America.

I see another child tonight. He hears a train go by. At night he dreams of faraway places where he'd like to go. It seems like an impossible dream. But he is helped on his journey through life. A father who had to go to work before he finished the sixth grade sacrificed everything he had so that his sons could go to college.

A gentle Quaker mother with a passionate concern for peace, quietly wept when he went to war but she understood why he had to go.

A great teacher, a remarkable football coach, an inspirational minister encouraged him on his way. A courageous wife and loyal children stood by him in victory and also in defeat.

And in his chosen profession of politics, first there was scores, then hundreds, than thousands, and finally millions who worked for his success.

And tonight he stands before you, nominated for President of the United States of America.

You can see why I believe so deeply in the American dream.

For most of us the American revolution has been won, the American dream has come true. What I ask of you tonight is to help me make that dream come true for millions to whom it's an impossible dream today.

One hundred and eight years ago the newly elected President of the United States, Abraham Lincoln, left Springfield, Ill., never to return again.

He spoke to his friends gathered at the railroad station. Listen to his words: "Today I leave you. I go to assume a greater task than devolved on General Washington. The Great God which helped him must help me. Without that great assistance I will surely fail. With it, I cannot fail."

Abraham Lincoln lost his life but he did not fail.

The next President of the United States will face challenges which in some ways will be greater than those of Washington or Lincoln, because for the first time in our nation's history an American President will face not only the problem of restoring peace abroad, but of restoring peace at home.

Without God's help, and your help, we will surely fail.

But with God's help and your help, we shall surely succeed.

My fellow Americans, the dark long night for America is about to end.

The time has come for us to leave the valley of despair and climb the mountain so that we may see the glory of the dawn, a new day for America, a new dawn for peace and freedom to the world.

New York Campaign Speech by George C. Wallace (1968)

As in 1948, ideological polarization split the Democratic party three ways in 1968. (See "Henry A. Wallace Announces for President," p. 453.) *Vice President Hubert H. Humphrey, the Democratic nominee for president, represented the party's center. The party's left, led by Sen. Eugene McCarthy of Minnesota and, until his assassination in June 1968, Sen. Robert F. Kennedy of New York, sat out the election after it failed to win the presidential nomination for one of its own. (See* "Eugene McCarthy Announces for President," p. 554.) *The party's right followed the 1948 precedent. George C. Wallace, the former governor of Alabama (and the current de facto governor, since he had skirted his state's one-term limit by persuading the voters to elect his wife in 1966), announced his independent candidacy for president on February 8, 1968.*

Wallace had first come to national attention in June 1963, when, for a time, he personally barred the door to black students who were trying to register for classes at the University of Alabama. Outside the South, Wallace's televised display of defiance was widely ridiculed and condemned, as was his decision to enter three northern Democratic primaries in 1964. But when Wallace won 34 percent of the vote in Wisconsin, 30 percent in Indiana, and 43 percent in Maryland

against President Lyndon B. Johnson, it became apparent that the anti-civil rights sentiments that he articulated were widespread among rank-and-file Democrats.

By 1968, four years of national civil rights legislation and urban race riots had increased the audience for Wallace's crusade against "forced integration" to include working class whites in every section of the country. A master of inflammatory rhetoric, Wallace skillfully stirred nonracial resentments as well—against antiwar demonstrators ("if any demonstrator lies down in front of my car when I'm president, that'll be the last car he lays down in front of"), "federal judges playing God," "pointy-headed professors," federal bureaucrats "who don't know how to park their bicycles straight," journalists "who are going to get some of those liberal smiles knocked off their faces," and the two major political parties ("there's not a dime's worth of difference in any of them, national Democrats or national Republicans"). At a typical campaign rally, such as the one at New York City's Madison Square Garden on October 24, 1968, reporters and hecklers served as foils that Wallace skillfully used to rouse his audience's resentments.

Wallace ran a national campaign in 1968, partly to convince southerners to take his candidacy seriously. His real strategy was to win enough electoral votes in the South to deny both Humphrey and Richard Nixon, the Republican presidential nominee, a majority of electoral votes.

For a time, it seemed possible that Wallace's strategy of deadlock would succeed. In mid-September, he reached a peak of 21 percent support in the polls. But, as the election neared, some of Wallace's southern backers abandoned him for Nixon, who was less objectionable to them than Humphrey; and some of his northern supporters, convinced by union leaders that Wallace had been an antilabor governor, defected to Humphrey. Wallace ended up with 13.5 percent of the popular vote and 46 electoral votes, all of them in the Deep South.

The major surprise of the 1968 general election (again, as in 1948) was the late resurgence of the Democratic party in the face of a complacent Republican campaign. Humphrey, who had trailed Nixon in the post-convention public opinion polls by more than fifteen percentage points, did not win the election, but he came very close. The final tally was Nixon, 43.4 percent of the popular vote and 301 electoral votes; Humphrey, 42.7 percent of the popular vote and 191 electoral votes.   ～

Well, thank you very much ladies and gentlemen. Thank you very much for your gracious and kind reception here in Madison Square Garden. I'm sure that the *New York Times* took note of the reception that we've received here in the great city of New York. I'm very grateful to the people of this city and this state for the opportunity to be on the ballot on November 5, and as you know we're on the ballot in all 50 states in this union. This is not a sectional movement. It's a national movement, and I am sure that those who are in

attendance here tonight, especially of the press, know that our movement is a national movement and that we have an excellent chance to carry the great Empire State of New York.

I have a few friends from Alabama with me and we have a number of others who were with us last week, but we have with us Willie Kirk, past president of Local 52, United Association of Plumbers and Pipefitters.

Well, I want to tell you something. After November 5, you anarchists are through in this country. I can tell you that. Yes, you'd better have your say now, because you are going to be through after November 5, I can assure you that.

I have also with me W. C. Williamson, business manager of Local 52, UAPP, Montgomery, Alabama, and R. H. Low, president of the Mobile Building and Construction Trades Council and business manager of Local 653 Operating Engineers.

And, you came for trouble, you sure got it.

And we have R. H. Bob Low, president of the MBC—We—why don't you come down after I get through and I'll autograph your sandals for you, you know?

And Charlie Ryan, recording secretary of the Steam Fitters Local 818, New York City. We have been endorsed in Alabama by nearly every local in our state: textiles workers, paper workers, steel workers, rubber workers, you name it. We've been endorsed by the working people of our state.

Regardless of what they might say, your national leaders, my wife carried every labor box in 1966, when she ran for governor of Alabama in the primary and the general election. And I also was endorsed by labor when I was elected governor in 1962.

Now, if you fellows will—I can drown—listen—if you'll sit down, ladies and gentlemen, I can drown that crowd out. If you'll just sit down, I'll drown 'em out—that—all he needs is a good haircut. If he'll go to the barbershop, I think they can cure him. So all you newsmen look up this way now. Here's the main event. I've been wanting to fight the main event a long time in Madison Square Garden, so here we are. Listen, that's just a preliminary match up there. This is the main bout right here. So let me say again as I said a moment ago, that we have had the support of the working people of our state. Alabama's a large industrial state, and you could not be elected governor without the support of people in organized labor.

Let me also say this about race, since I'm here in the State of New York, and I'm always asked the question. I am very grateful for the fact that in 1966 my wife received more black votes in Alabama than did either one of her opponents. We are proud to say that they support us now in this race for the presidency, and we would like to have the support of people of all races, colors, creeds, religions, and national origins in the state of New York.

Our system is under attack: the property system, the free enterprise system, and local government. Anarchy prevails today in the streets of the large cities of our country, making it unsafe for you to even go to a political rally here in Madison Square Garden, and that is a sad commentary. Both national parties in the last number of years have kowtowed to every anarchist that has roamed the streets. I want to say before I start on this any longer, that I'm not talking about race. The overwhelming majority of all races in this country are against this breakdown of law and order and much as those who are assembled here tonight. It's a few anarchists, a few activists, a few militants, a few revolutionaries, and a few Communists. But your day, of course, is going to be over soon. The American people are not going to stand by and see the security of our nation imperiled, and they're not going to stand by and see this nation destroyed, I can assure you that.

The liberals and the left-wingers in both national parties have brought us to the domestic mess we are in now. And also this foreign mess we are in.

You need to read the book "How to Behave in a Crowd." You really don't know how to behave in a crowd, do you?

Yes, the liberals and left-wingers in both parties have brought us to the domestic mess we are in also to the foreign policy mess we find our nation involved in at the present time, personified by the no-win war in Southeast Asia.

Now what are some of the things we are going to do when we become president? We are going to turn back to you, the people of the states, the right to control our domestic institutions. Today you cannot even go to the school systems of the large cities of our country without fear. This is a sad day when in the greatest city in the world, there is fear not only in Madison Square Garden, but in every school building in the state of New York, and especially in the City of New York. Why has the leadership of both national parties kowtowed to this group of anarchists that makes it unsafe for your child and for your family? I don't understand it. But I can assure you of this—that there's not ten cents worth of difference with what the national parties say other than our party. Recently they say most of the same things we say. I remember six years ago when this anarchy movement started, Mr. Nixon said: "It's a great movement," and Mr. Humphrey said: "It's a great movement." Now when they try to speak and are heckled down, they stand up and say: "We've got to have some law and order in this country." "We've got to have some law and order in this country." They ought to give you law and order back for nothing, because they have helped to take it away from you, along with the Supreme Court of our country that's made up of Republicans and Democrats.

It's costing the taxpayers of New York and the other states in the union almost a half billion dollars to supervise the schools, hospitals, seniority and apprenticeship lists of labor unions, and businesses. Every year on the federal level we have passed a law that would jail you without a trial by jury about the sale of your own property. Mr. Nixon and Mr. Humphrey, both three or four weeks ago, called for the passage of a bill on the federal level that would require you to sell or lease your own property to whomsoever they thought you ought to lease it to. I say that when Mr. Nixon and Mr. Humphrey succumb to the blackmail of a few anarchists in the streets who said we're going to destroy this country if you do not destroy that adage that a man's home is his castle, they are not fit to lead the American people during the next four years in our country. When I become your president, I am going to ask that Congress repeal this so-called open occupancy law and we're going to, within the law, turn back to the people of every state their public school system. Not one dime of your federal money is going to be used to bus anybody any place that you don't want them to be bussed in New York or any other state.

Yes, the theoreticians and the pseudo-intellectuals have just about destroyed not only local government but the school systems of our country. That's all right. Let the police handle it. So let us talk about law and order. We don't have to talk about it much up here. You understand what I'm talking about in, of course, the City of New York, but let's talk about it.

Yes, the pseudo-intellectuals and the theoreticians and some professors and some newspaper editors and some judges and some preachers have looked down their nose long enough at the average man on the street: the pipefitter, the communications worker, the fireman, the policeman, the barber, the white collar worker, and said we must write you a guideline about when you go to bed at night and when you get up in the morning. But there are more of us than there are of them because the average citizen of New York and of Alabama and of the other states of our union are tired of guidelines being written, telling them when to go to bed at night and when to get up in the morning.

I'm talking about law and order. The Supreme Court of our country has hand-cuffed the police, and tonight if you walk out of this building and are knocked in the head, the person who knocks you in the head is out of jail before you get in the hospital, and on Monday morning, they'll try a policeman about it. I can say I'm going to give the total support of the presidency to the policemen and the firemen in this country, and I'm going to say, you enforce the law and you make it safe on the streets, and the president of the United States will stand with you. My election as president is going to put some backbone in the backs of some mayors and governors I know through the length and breadth of this country.

You had better be thankful for the police and the firemen of this country. If it were not for them, you couldn't even ride in the streets, much less walk in the streets, of our large cities. Yes, the Kerner Commission Report, recently written by Republicans and Democrats, said that you are to blame for the breakdown of law and order, and that the police are to blame. Well, you know, of course, you aren't to blame. They said we have a sick society. Well, we don't have any sick society. We have a sick Supreme Court and some sick politicians in Washington,—that's who's sick in our country. The Supreme Court of our country has ruled that you cannot even say a simple prayer in a public school, but you can send obscene literature through the mail, and recently they ruled that a Communist can work in a defense plant. But when I become your president, we're going to take every Communist out of every defense plant in the United States, I can assure you.

The Kerner Commission report also recommended that the taxes of the American people be raised to pay folks not to destroy the country, and not to work. I never thought the day would come when a Republican and Democratic report would call for the taxes on the already over-taxed people of our country to pay people not to destroy. It is the most ludicrous and asinine report ever made to a president of our country. I want to tell you folks something. I was fighting the Nazis and Fascists before you were born. I was even shot at by them. I've been shot at by the Nazis— the Nazis and the Fascists. Now the Kerner Commission report—who is it writes these reports, ladies and gentlemen? It's usually some pointed head from one of those multi-billion dollar tax-exempt foundations. When they recommend that taxes be raised on you and me, they don't have to pay taxes because they're tax-exempt. When I become the president, I'm going to ask the Congress to remove the tax exemption feature on these multi-billion dollar tax-exempt foundations and let them pay taxes like the average citizen of New York pays also. It's estimated that 25 billion dollars goes through tax loopholes that ought to be paid by those able to pay and Senator Robert Kennedy himself said the same thing. So I say that what we ought to do is to remove that tax-exemption feature. And when we do, we can raise the workingman's dependent exemption from $600 to $1200 even in wartime.

Well now, all you television folks get a good picture over there now. Go ahead. You know—now it's all over. Get this camera turned back this way. You know—everywhere we've spoken we've had this same kind of crowd, but the television puts all its footage on a few folks that don't know how to behave in a crowd and make it appear that there are no people supporting you here. And I frankly think the networks are doing that on purpose, myself. I don't think they want to show the support we have here in New York City and throughout the country. Yes sir, but I think they know tonight and have seen something they didn't expect in Madison Square Garden, and I reckon they'll try to explain it away tomorrow, the *New York Times*, and the other papers will. But you just remember that some of these newspapers can fool some of the people some of the time, but they can't fool all the people all the time. You remember that.

We have a comprehensive platform that I hope you get copies of before the election, in which we have dealt with every problem that faces the American people. But let me tell you briefly about foreign policy. The Democrats and the Republicans are always saying: "What do the folks at Madison Square Garden supporting the American Independent Party know about foreign policy?" I ask them: "What do you know about foreign policy? We've had four wars in the last 50 years. We've spent $122 billion of our money on foreign aid. We are bogged down in a no-win war in Southeast Asia, and anarchy in the streets. What do you know about foreign policy? You haven't been so successful in conducting American foreign policy in the last 50 years yourself." I can say this: we are in Vietnam. But General Lemay knows as I know and you know that the strongest deterrent to any further global conflict is superiority in offensive and defensive capabilities of our country. We can never be on a parity nor inferior because when you are superior, you can always go to the negotiating table; you can go to the peace table; you can go to the conference table. The way I would like to see every difference between any nation settled is around the conference table. But as long as there are tensions in the world, we cannot gamble upon the security of this city or this state or this nation by having anything but absolute superiority in the matter of defensive and offensive capabilities.

We are in Vietnam whether you like it or not. I sincerely hope and pray that the conflict is soon over, but we should have learned one thing about our involvement in Southeast Asia—the same thing that Mr. Humphrey now says in his speeches: we should not march alone. I said last year in California that we should never have gone to Vietnam—by ourselves. We should have looked our allies in the face in Western Europe and our non-Communist Asian allies and said to them: it is as much your interest as it is ours and you are going to go with manpower, munitions, and money, and if you don't go and help us in Southeast Asia, and if you don't stop trading with the North Vietnamese who are killing American servicemen, we are not only going to cut off every dime of foreign aid you're getting, but we're going to ask you to pay back all you owe us from World War I right on this very day.

Yes, the average taxpayer in New York doesn't understand his money going to those nations who not only won't support us, but on the other hand actively trade with the North Vietnamese. I'm not saying we must kick our allies out. We need them in Western Europe, and they need us. We need them in non-Communist Asia, and they need us. But NATO countries of Western Europe have 55 million people more than do the United States, and in the future they're going to have to carry their share of the defense burden because we cannot carry it alone. We will not carry it alone, even though we recognize that those things that happen in other parts of the world affect us in this country, they must carry their fair share of not only the manpower commitments, but also the commitments in munitions and money, and I know you agree with that.

I sincerely hope and pray that we have a successful negotiated peace. Well, I'll drown them out, come on. I sincerely hope and pray that we have an honorably negotiated peace to arise out of the Paris peace talks. I know that you pray that, and that the American servicemen can come home. But if we fail diplomatically and politically in Southeast Asia, we're not going to stay there forever, we're not going to see hundreds of American servicemen killed every week for years and months to come. If we do not win diplomatically and politically in Paris, that is, by honorable conclusion of the war, then in my judgment, we ought to end it militarily with conventional weapons and bring the American servicemen home. If we cannot settle it diplomatically and politically, and could not win it militarily with conventional weapons, then I wonder why we're there in the first place? We're going to conclude this war one way or the other either through honorable negotiations or conventional military power.

There's something else we ought to talk about and you see some of it here in the state of New York. We should stop the morale boost for the Communists in our own country. In every state in the union, this treasonable conduct on the part of a few, and their speeches, are printed in Hanoi, Peking, Moscow, and Havana. General Westmoreland said it is prolonging the war, and it is causing New Yorkers and Alabamans to be killed in Southeast Asia. When you ask the Attorney General of our nation: "Why don't you do something about this treasonable conduct" do you know what he says? "We are too busy bussing school children in New York and Los Angeles and we don't have time." We also have some college students who raise money, food, and clothes for the Communists and fly the Viet Cong flag in the name of academic freedom, and free speech. We didn't allow that in World War II; we did not allow for anybody to call for Nazi victory, or Fascist victory.

There is such a thing as legitimate dissent. Senator Robert Kennedy from this state said we should not be in Southeast Asia, and you have a right to say it yourself, if that's what you believe because you don't believe it's in the interests of our country to be there. But if you arise and make a speech the next day and say I long for Communist victory, every average citizen in New York knows that one is dissent and the other is something else. I want to tell you that when I become your president, I'm going to have my Attorney General seek an indictment against any professor calling for Communist victory and stick him in a good jail somewhere. When you drag a few of these college students who are raising money for the Communists and put them in a good jail you'll stop that too, I can assure you. That'll stop them. We're going to destroy academic freedom in this country if we continue to abuse it as it has been abused at this time. Whether you agree with the war or not, we should agree that whatever we say or do should be in the national interests of getting the American servicemen home safely, and that sort of conduct is not conducive to the return of the American servicemen to New York and Alabama.

My friends, let me say this. We can win this election because it only takes a plurality to win when there are three or more running. If we get thirty-four percent of the vote in this state, and the other two get thirty-three percent apiece, then we win the entire electoral vote of the State of New York. That's all it takes. You know this, and that's one reason Mr. Nixon doesn't want to debate. Well, I want to tell Mr. Nixon it's a good thing he doesn't debate because if he ever does, we're going to point out that he's made so many inconsistent statements about so many matters, I would be happy to debate. But he cannot get a debate started.

That's alright. That's alright honey—that's right sweety-pie—oh, that's a he. I thought you were a she. I tell you what, I got. . . .

Well, don't worry what the newspapers say about us. Everything I've said tonight is logical and reasonable and constitutional. Not a single thing have I said tonight that anybody can argue logically with, and that's the reason they call us extremists and want to say we're Fascists. They cannot argue with the logic of the position we take here in Madison Square Garden tonight. They want to say, well, they're evil folks. I want to tell these newspapers something. These large newspapers that think they know more than the average citizen on the street of New York haven't always been right. I remember the time the *New York Times* said that Mao tse-Tung was a good man, and he turned out to be a Communist. I remember when they said that Ben Bella was a good man, and he turned out to be a Communist. When old Castro was in the hills of Cuba, the *New York Times* said he was the Robin Hood of the Caribbean, and they introduced him on national television as the George Washington of Cuba. They were mistaken about Castro.

They [newspapers] are mistaken about our movement, and they are mistaken about the good people of New York State who are here tonight supporting our candidacy because the two national parties (other than our party) has paid no attention to you. But they are paying attention to those who are making the most noise here at Madison Square Garden tonight and every other place in the country. You know that some of those people who make it unsafe for you and me are going to school on your tax money and they are exempt from the draft. Well, I tell you one thing. I'm tired of my tax money going to educate somebody who wants to raise money for the Communists in our country, and that's exactly what a lot of them do on some of the college campuses in this country. I'm certainly not talking about all the college students. You know the few that I'm talking about, and there are some in every state in the union.

Four years ago our movement received thirty-four percent of the vote in Wisconsin, thirty percent in Indiana, and forty-four percent in Maryland. We have won nearly every radio and television poll in every state in the union, so don't pay any attention to the pollsters. They said we were going to get fifteen percent of the Midwest, well, Ohio's part of the Midwest, and we got eighteen percent of the voters in that one state to sign a petition to get us on the ballot, and I would say that for every one who signed a petition in the state of Ohio, there were four more who would have signed had they been given the opportunity. Yes, we got forty-four percent of the vote four years ago in the state of Maryland.

You know, I like to tell this because— if you'll listen to this, I'll tell you a good joke—you've heard it before, but it's very good. Down in the state of Maryland that night four years ago in the presidential primary, I was leading up until about 9:30 with several hundred thousand votes in, and they called the mayor of Baltimore to the television and asked him what he thought about this man from Alabama running first in the presidential primary in our free state. Well, do you know what he said, being a big-time politician? He said: "It's sad; it's sad. We'll never live this down. What has come over the people of the free state of Maryland?" Well, if he had gone out and asked a good cab driver in Baltimore, he could have told him. You vote for me and you are going to be through with all that. Let me tell you now you continue to support our movement until November 5, together we are going to change directions in this country, and we are going to return some sanity to the American government scene. I do appreciate you being here in Madison Square Garden tonight. Thank you very much, ladies and gentlemen.

The McGovern-Fraser Commission Report (1971)

One of the major complaints of the antiwar Democrats at the 1968 Democratic national convention was that they had not been given a fair chance to compete in the delegate selection process. (See "Eugene McCarthy Announces for President," p. 554.) Only about one-third of the convention's delegates were chosen in primaries; of the remaining two-thirds, most of whom were appointed by state party leaders, nearly half had obtained their seats before the election year even began.

Although the 1968 convention made no changes in its own structure, it voted to approve the minority report of the rules committee, which required that all Democratic voters receive "full, meaningful and timely opportunity to participate in the selection of delegates" to the 1972 convention.

In February 1969, in order to implement the convention's decision, the Democratic National Committee created the Commission on Party Structure and Delegate Selection, chaired by Sen. George McGovern of South Dakota and, later, by Rep. Donald Fraser of Minnesota. The McGovern-Fraser Commission, as it came to be known, issued its report, Mandate for Change, in September 1971. The report included eighteen detailed guidelines that the state parties were obliged to follow in choosing delegates to the 1972 convention.

The McGovern-Fraser Commission drastically transformed the presidential nominating process. The commission banned a number of traditional practices, including the "unit rule" that allowed each state party to award all of its votes to the candidate who had a majority of its delegation. The commission required that racial minorities, women, and young voters be represented at the national convention in proportion to their share of the population in each state. Most important, the commission demanded that all convention delegates be chosen in an open, participatory process, either a presidential primary or a caucus in which any Democrat could vote and be heard.

To the surprise and, according to the political scientist Austin Ranney, a commission member, the dismay of the McGovern-Fraser Commission, most states decided to go the simpler, primary route: by the end of the decade, the number of presidential primaries had doubled from seventeen to thirty-five. Because new primaries required changes in state laws, state Republican parties usually followed the Democrats' lead.

Not just the process but also the politics of presidential nominations was affected by the McGovern-Fraser reforms. In 1960 John F. Kennedy, a Democrat, and eight years later, Richard Nixon, a Republican, had entered *primaries, but only as a strategy to persuade party leaders to nominate them.* (See "John F. Kennedy's Speech to the Greater Houston Ministerial Association," p. 489, and "Richard Nixon's Acceptance Speech to the Republican National Convention," p. 557.) *In 1968, Hubert H. Humphrey received the Democratic nomination for president without entering one primary. After 1968, party leaders had no choice but to accept the verdict of the primaries. Nor could any candidate expect to be nominated for president without defeating the other candidates at the ballot box.*

Subsequent Democratic rules commissions—the Mikulski Commission (1976), the Winograd Commission (1980), the Hunt Commission (1984), and the Fairness Commission (1988)— have further modified the procedures for presidential nominations. But none has substantially undone the radical changes wrought by the McGovern-Fraser Commission. ~

Mandate for Reform

Official Guidelines of the Commission

On November 19 and 20, 1969, the Commission, meeting in open session in Washington, D.C., adopted the following Guidelines for delegate selection.

Part I-Introduction

The following Guidelines for delegate selection represent the Commission's interpretation of the "full, meaningful, and timely" language of its mandate. These Guidelines have been divided into three general categories.

A. Rules or practices which inhibit access to the delegate selection process—items which compromise full and meaningful participation by inhibiting or preventing a Democrat from exercising his influence in the delegate selection process.

B. Rules or practices which dilute the influence of a Democrat in the delegate selection process, after he has exercised all available resources to effect such influence.

C. Rules and practices which have some attributes of both A and B.

Rules or practices inhibiting access

1. Discrimination on the basis of race, color, creed, or national origin.
2. Discrimination on the basis of age or sex.
3. Voter registration.
4. Costs and fees.
5. Existence of Party rules.

B. Rules or practices diluting influence

1. Proxy voting.
2. Clarity of purpose.
3. Quorum provisions.
4. Selection of alternates; filling of delegate and alternate vacancies.
5. Unit rule.
6. Adequate representation of political minority views.
7. Apportionment.

C. Rules or practices combining attributes of A and B

1. Adequate public notice.
2. Automatic (ex-officio) delegates.
3. Open and closed processes.
4. Premature delegate selection (timeliness).
5. Committee selection processes.
6. Slate-making.

Part II—The Guidelines

A-1 Discrimination on the basis of race, color, creed, or national origin

The 1964 Democratic National Convention adopted a resolution which conditioned the seating of delegations at future conventions on the assurance that discrimination in any State Party affairs on the grounds of race, color, creed or national origin did not occur. The 1968 Convention adopted the 1964 Convention resolution for inclusion in the Call to the 1972 Convention. In 1966, the Special Equal Rights Committee, which had been created in 1964, adopted six anti-discrimination standards—designated as the "six basic elements"—for the State Parties to meet. These standards were adopted by the Democratic National Committee in January 1968 as its official policy statement.

These actions demonstrate the intention of the Democratic Party to ensure a full opportunity for all minority group members to participate in the delegate selection process. To supplement the requirements of the 1964 and 1968 Conventions, the Commission requires that:

1. State Parties add the six basic elements of the Special Equal Rights Committee to their Party rules and take appropriate steps to secure their implementation;

2. State Parties overcome the effects of past discrimination by affirmative steps to encourage minority group participation, including representation of minority groups on the national convention delegation in reasonable relationship to the group's presence in the population of the State.

A-2 Discrimination on the basis of age or sex

The Commission believes that discrimination on the grounds of age or sex is inconsistent with full and meaningful opportunity to participate in the delegate selection process. Therefore, the Commission requires State Parties to eliminate all vestiges of discrimination on these grounds. Furthermore, the Commission requires State Parties to overcome the effects of past discrimina-

tion by affirmative steps to encourage representation on the national convention delegation of young people—defined as people of not more than thirty nor less than eighteen years of age—and women in reasonable relationship to their presence in the population of the State. Moreover, the Commission requires State Parties to amend their Party rules to allow and encourage any Democrat of eighteen years or more to participate in all party affairs.

When State law controls, the Commission requires State Parties to make all feasible efforts to repeal, amend, or otherwise modify such laws to accomplish the stated purpose.

A-3 Voter registration

The purpose of registration is to add to the legitimacy of the electoral process, not to discourage participation. Democrats do not enjoy an opportunity to participate fully in the delegate selection process in States where restrictive voter registration laws and practices are in force, preventing their effective participation in primaries, caucuses, conventions and other Party affairs. These restrictive laws and practices include annual registration requirements, lengthy residence requirements, literacy tests, short and untimely registration periods, and infrequent enrollment sessions.

The Commission urges each State Party to assess the burdens imposed on a prospective participant in the Party's delegate selection process by State registration laws, customs and practices, as outlined in the report of the Grass Roots Subcommittee of the Commission on Party Structure and Delegate Selection, and use its good offices to remove or alleviate such barriers to participation.

A-4 Costs and fees; petition requirements

The Commission believes that costs, fees, or assessments and excessive petition requirements made by State law and Party rule or resolutions impose a financial burden on (1) national convention delegates and alternates; (2) candidates for convention delegates and alternates; and (3) in some cases, participants. Such costs, fees assessments or excessive petition requirements discourage full and meaningful opportunity to participate in the delegate selection process.

The Commission urges the State Parties to remove all costs and fees involved in the delegate selection process. The Commission requires State Parties to remove all excessive costs and fees, and to waive all nominal costs and fees when they would impose a financial strain on any Democrat. A cost or fee of more than $10 for all stages of the delegate selection process is deemed excessive. The Commission requires State Parties to remove all mandatory assessments of delegates and alternates.

The Commission requires State Parties to remove excessive petition requirements for convention delegate candidates of presidential candidates. Any petition requirement, which calls for a number of signatures in excess of 1% of the standard use for measuring Democratic strength, whether such standard be based on the number of Democratic votes cast for a specific office in a previous election or Party enrollment figures, is deemed excessive.

When State law controls any of these matters, the Commission requires State Parties to make all feasible efforts to repeal, amend or otherwise modify such laws to accomplish the stated purpose.

This provision, however, does not change the burden of expenses borne by individuals who campaign for and/or serve as delegates and alternates. Therefore, the Commission urges State Parties to explore ways of easing the financial burden on delegates and alter-

nates and candidates for delegate and alternate.

A-5 Existence of party rules

In order for rank-and-file Democrats to have a full and meaningful opportunity to participate in the delegate selection process, they must have access to the substantive and procedural rules which govern the process. In some States the process is not regulated by law or rule, but by resolution of the State Committee and by tradition. In other States, the rules exist, but generally are inaccessible. In still others, rules and laws regulate only the formal aspects of the selection process (e.g., date and place of the State convention) and leave to Party resolution or tradition the more substantive matters (e.g., intrastate apportionment of votes; rotation of alternates; nomination of delegates).

The Commission believes that any of these arrangements is inconsistent with the spirit of the Call in that they permit excessive discretion on the part of Party officials, which may be used to deny or limit full and meaningful opportunity to participate. Therefore, the Commission requires State Parties to adopt and make available readily accessible statewide Party rules and statutes which prescribe the State's delegate selection process with sufficient details and clarity. When relevant to the State's delegate selection process, explicit written Party rules and procedural rules should include clear provisions for: (1) the apportionment of delegates and votes within the State; (2) the allocation of fractional votes, if any; (3) the selection and responsibilities of convention committees; (4) the nomination of delegates and alternates; (5) the succession of alternates to delegate status and the filling of vacancies; (6) credentials challenges; (7) minority reports.

Furthermore, the Commission requires State Parties to adopt rules which will facilitate maximum participation among interested Democrats in the processes by which National Convention delegates are selected. Among other things, these rules should provide for dates, times, and public places which would be most likely to encourage interested Democrats to attend all meetings involved in the delegate selection process.

The Commission requires State Parties to adopt explicit written Party rules which provide for uniform times and dates of all meetings involved in the delegate selection process. These meetings and events include caucuses, conventions, committee meetings, primaries, filing deadlines, and Party enrollment periods. Rules regarding time and date should be uniform in two senses. First, each stage of the delegate selection process should occur at a uniform time and date throughout the State. Second, the time and date should be uniform from year to year. The Commission recognizes that in many parts of rural America it may be an undue burden to maintain complete uniformity, and therefore exempts rural areas from this provision so long as the time and date are publicized in advance of the meeting and are uniform within the geographic area.

B-1 Proxy voting

When a Democrat cannot, or chooses not to, attend a meeting related to the delegate selection process, many States allow that person to authorize another to act in his name. This practice—called proxy voting—has been a significant source of real or felt abuse of fair procedure in the delegate selection process.

The Commission believes that any situation in which one person is given the authority to act in the name of the absent Democrat, on any issue before the meeting, gives such person an unjustified advantage in affecting the outcome of the meeting. Such a situation is inconsistent with the spirit of equal participation. Therefore, the Commission requires State Parties to add to

their explicit written rules provisions which forbid the use of proxy voting in all procedures involved in the delegate selection process.

B-2 Clarity of purpose

An opportunity for full participation in the delegate selection process is not meaningful unless each Party member can clearly express his preference for candidates for delegates to the National Convention, or for those who will select such delegates. In many States, a Party member who wishes to affect the selection of the delegation must do so by voting for delegates or Party officials who will engage in many activities unrelated to the delegate selection process.

Whenever other Party business is mixed, without differentiation, with the delegate selection process, the Commission requires State Parties to make it clear to voters how they are participating in a process that will nominate their Party's candidate for President. Furthermore, in States which employ a convention or committee system, the Commission requires State Parties to clearly designate the delegate selection procedures as distinct from other Party business.

B-3 Quorum provisions

Most constituted bodies have rules or practices which set percentage or number minimums before they can commence their business. Similarly, Party committees which participate in the selection process may commence business only after it is determined that this quorum exists. In some States, however, the quorum requirement is satisfied when less than 40% of committee members are in attendance.

The Commission believes a full opportunity to participate is satisfied only when a rank-and-file Democrat's representative attends such committee meetings. Recognizing, however, that the setting of high quorum requirements may impede the selection process, the Commission requires State Parties to adopt rules setting quorums at not less than 40% for all party committees involved in the delegate selection process.

B-4 Selection of alternates; filling of delegate and alternate vacancies

The Call to the 1972 Convention requires that alternates be chosen by one of the three methods sanctioned for the selection of delegates—i.e., by primary, convention or committee. In some States, Party rules authorize the delegate himself or the State Chairman to choose his alternate. The Commission requires State Parties to prohibit these practices—and other practices not specifically authorized by the Call—for selecting alternates.

In the matter of vacancies, some States have Party rules which authorize State Chairman to fill all delegate and alternate vacancies. This practice again involves the selection of delegates or alternates by a process other than primary, convention or committee. The Commission requires States Parties to prohibit such practices and to fill all vacancies by (1) a timely and representative Party committee; or (2) a reconvening of the body which selected the delegate or alternate whose seat is vacant; or (3) the delegation itself, acting as a committee.

When State law controls, the Commission requires State Parties to make all feasible efforts to repeal, amend or otherwise modify such laws to accomplish the stated purposes.

B-5 Unit rule

In 1968, many States used the unit rule at various stages in the processes by which delegates were selected to the National Convention. The 1968 Convention defined unit rule, did not enforce the unit rule on any delegate in 1968, and added language to the 1972 Call requiring that "the unit rule not be used in any stage of the delegate selec-

tion process." In light of the Convention action, the Commission requires State Parties to add to their explicit written rules provisions which forbid the use of the unit rule or the practice of instructing delegates to vote against their stated preferences at any stage of the delegate selection process.

B-6 Adequate representation of minority views on presidential candidates at each stage in the delegate selection process

The Commission believes that a full and meaningful opportunity to participate in the delegate selection process is precluded unless the presidential preference of each Democrat is fairly represented at all levels of the process. Therefore, the Commission urges each State Party to adopt procedures which will provide fair representation of minority views on presidential candidates and recommends that the 1972 Convention adopt a rule requiring State Parties to provide for the representation of minority views to the highest level of the nominating process.

The Commission believes that there are at least two different methods by which a State Party can provide for such representation. First, in at-large elections it can divide delegate votes among presidential candidates in proportion to their demonstrated strength. Second, it can choose delegates from fairly apportioned districts no larger than congressional districts.

The Commission recognizes that there may be other methods to provide for fair representation of minority views. Therefore, the Commission will make every effort to stimulate public discussion of the issue of representation of minority views on presidential candidates between now and the 1972 Democratic National Convention.

B-7 Apportionment

The Commission believes that the manner in which votes and delegates are apportioned within each State has a direct bearing on the nature of participation. If the apportionment formula is not based on Democratic strength and/or population the opportunity for some voters to participate in the delegate selection process will not be equal to the opportunity of others. Such a situation is inconsistent with a full and meaningful opportunity to participate.

Therefore, the Commission requires State Parties which apportion their delegation to the National Convention to apportion on a basis of representation which fairly reflects the population and Democratic strength within the State. The apportionment is to be based on a formula giving equal weight to total population and to the Democratic vote in the previous presidential election.

The Commission requires State Parties with convention systems to select at least 75% of their delegations to the National Convention at congressional district or smaller unit levels.

In convention or committee systems, the Commission requires State Parties to adopt an apportionment formula for each body actually selecting delegates to State, district and county conventions which is based upon population and/or some measure of Democratic strength. Democratic strength may be measured by the Democratic vote in the preceding presidential, senatorial, congressional or gubernatorial election, and/or by party enrollment figures.

When State law controls, the Commission requires State Parties to make all feasible efforts to repeal, amend or otherwise modify such laws to accomplish the stated purpose.

C-1 Adequate public notice

The Call to the 1968 convention required State Parties to assure voters an opportunity to "participate fully" in party affairs. The Special Equal Rights Committee interpreted this opportunity to include adequate public notice. The

Committee listed several elements—including publicizing of the time, places and rules for the conduct of all public meetings of the Democratic Party and holding such meetings in easily accessible places—which comprise adequate public notice. These elements were adopted by the Democratic National Committee in January 1968 as its official policy statement and are binding on the State Parties.

Furthermore, the Commission requires State Parties to circulate a concise and public statement in advance of the election itself of the relationship between the party business being voted upon and the delegate selection process.

In addition to supplying the information indicated above, the Commission believes that adequate public notice includes information on the ballot as to the presidential preference of (1) candidates of slates for delegate or (2) in the States which select or nominate a portion of the delegates by committees, candidates or slates for such committees.

Accordingly, the Commission requires State Parties to give every candidate for delegate (and candidate for committee, where appropriate) the opportunity to state his presidential preferences on the ballot at each stage of the delegate selection process. The Commission requires the State Parties to add the word "uncommitted" or like term on the ballot next to the name of every candidate for delegate who does not wish to express a presidential preference.

When State law controls, the Commission requires the State Parties to make all feasible efforts to repeal, amend or otherwise modify such laws to accomplish the stated purposes.

C-2 Automatic (ex-officio) delegates (see also C04)

In some States, certain public or Party officeholders are delegates to county, State and National Conventions by virtue of their official position. The Commission believes that State laws, Party rules and Party resolutions which so provide are inconsistent with the Call to the 1972 Convention for three reasons:

1. The Call requires all delegates to be chosen by primary, convention or committee procedures. Achieving delegate status by virtue of public or Party office is not one of the methods sanctioned by the 1968 Convention.

2. The Call requires all delegates to be chosen by a process which begins within the calendar year of the Convention. Ex-officio delegates usually were elected (or appointed) to their positions before the calendar year of the Convention.

3. The Call requires all delegates to be chosen by a process in which all Democrats have a full and meaningful opportunity to participate. Delegate selection by a process in which certain places on the delegation are not open to competition among Democrats is inconsistent with a full and meaningful opportunity to participate.

Accordingly, the Commission requires State Parties to repeal Party rules or resolutions which provide for ex-offico delegates. When State law controls, the Commission requires State Parties to make all feasible efforts to repeal, amend or otherwise modify such laws to accomplish the stated purpose.

C-3 Open and closed processes

The Commission believes that Party membership, and hence opportunity to participate in the delegate selection process, must be open to all persons who wish to be Democrats and who are not already members of another political party; conversely, a full opportunity for all Democrats to participate is diluted if members of other political parties are allowed to participate in the selection of delegates to the Democratic National Convention.

The Commission urges State Parties to provide for party enrollment that (1) allows non-Democrats to become Party members, and (2) provides easy access and frequent opportunity for unaffiliated voters to become Democrats.

C-4 Premature delegate selection (timeliness)

The 1968 Convention adopted language adding to the Call to the 1972 Convention the requirement that the delegate selection process must begin within the calendar year of the Convention. In many States, Governors, State Chairmen, State, district and county committees who are chosen before the calendar year of the Convention, select—or choose agents to select—the delegates. These practices are inconsistent with the Call.

The Commission believes that the 1968 Convention intended to prohibit any untimely procedures which have any direct bearing on the process by which National Convention delegates are selected. The process by which delegates are nominated is such a procedure. Therefore, the Commission requires State Parties to prohibit any practices by which officials elected or appointed before the calendar year choose nominating committees or propose or endorse a slate of delegates—even when the possibility for a challenge to such slate or committee is provided.

When State law controls, the Commission requires State Parties to make all feasible efforts to repeal, amend, or modify such laws to accomplish the stated purposes.

C-5 Committee selection processes

The 1968 Convention indicated no preference between primary, convention, and committee systems for choosing delegates. The Commission believes, however, that committee systems by virtue of their indirect relationship to the delegate selection process, offer fewer guarantees for a full and meaningful opportunity to participate than other systems.

The Commission is aware that it has no authority to eliminate committee systems in their entirety. However, the Commission can and does require State Parties which elect delegates in this manner to make it clear to voters at the time the Party committee is elected or appointed that one of its functions will be the selection of National Convention delegates.

Believing, however, that such selection system is undesirable even when adequate public notice is given, the Commission requires State Parties to limit the National Convention delegation chosen by committee procedures to not more than 10 percent of the total number of delegates and alternates.

Since even this obligation will not ensure an opportunity for full and meaningful participation, the Commission recommends that State Parties repeal rules or resolutions which require or permit Party committees to select any part of the State's delegation to the National Convention. When State law controls, the Commission recommends that State Parties make all feasible efforts to repeal, amend, or otherwise modify such laws to accomplish the stated purpose.

C-6 Slate-making

In mandating a full and meaningful opportunity to participate in the delegate selection process, the 1968 Convention meant to prohibit any practice in the process of selection which made it difficult for Democrats to participate. Since the process by which individuals are nominated for delegate positions and slates of potential delegates are formed is an integral and crucial part of the process by which delegates are actually selected, the Commission requires State Parties to extend to the nominating process all guarantees of full and meaningful opportunity to participate in the delegate selection process. When

State law controls, the Commission requires State Parties to make all feasible efforts to repeal, amend or otherwise modify such laws to accomplish the stated purpose.

Furthermore, whenever slates are presented to caucuses, meetings, conventions, committees, or to voters in a primary, the Commission requires State Parties to adopt procedures which assure that:

1. the bodies making up the slates have been elected, assembled, or appointed for the slate-making task with adequate public notice that they would perform such task;

2. those persons making up each slate have adopted procedures that will facilitate widespread participation in the slate-making process, with the proviso that any slate presented in the name of a presidential candidate in a primary State be assembled with due consultation with the presidential candidate or his representative,

3. adequate procedural safeguards are provided to assure that the right to challenge the presented slate is more than perfunctory and places no undue burden on the challengers.

When State law controls, the Commission requires State Parties to make all feasible efforts to repeal, amend or otherwise modify such laws to accomplish the stated purpose.

Conclusion

The Guidelines that we have adopted are designed to open the door to all Democrats who seek a voice in their Party's most important decision: the choice of its presidential nominee. We are concerned with the opportunity to participate, rather than the actual level of participation, although the number of Democrats who vote in their caucuses, meetings and primaries is an important index of the opportunities available to them.

As members of the Commission, we are less concerned with the product of the meetings than the process, although we believe that the product will be improved in the give and take of open fairly conducted meetings.

We believe that popular participation is more than a proud heritage of our party, more even than a first principle. We believe that popular control of the Democratic Party is necessary for its survival.

We do not believe this is an idle threat. When we view our past history and present policies alongside that of the Republican Party, we are struck by one unavoidable fact: our Party is the only major vehicle for peaceful, progressive change in the United States.

If we are not an open party; if we do not represent the demands of change, then the danger is not that people will go to the Republican Party; it is that there will no longer be a way for people committed to orderly change to fulfill their needs and desires within our traditional political system. It is that they will turn to third and fourth party politics or the anti-politics of the street.

We believe that our Guidelines offer an alternative for these people. We believe that the Democratic Party can meet the demands for participation with their adoption. We trust that all Democrats will give the Guidelines their careful consideration.

We are encouraged by the response of state Parties to date. In 40 states and territories the Democratic Party has appointed reform commissions (or subcommittees of the state committee) to investigate ways of modernizing party procedures. Of these, 17 have already issued reports and recommendations. In a number of states, party rules and state laws have already been revised, newly written or amended to insure the opportunity for participation in Party matters by all Democrats.

Rhode Island and Maryland, for example, were states that in 1968 chose their delegates by a State Committee selected in an untimely manner—that is, by a process that began before the calendar year of the convention. In 1969, the legislative bodies of those States passed presidential primary bills at the urging of Democratic members of those legislatures and Democratic Party officials. This year, the Maryland legislature has improved on the bill enacted in 1969.

Legislatures in the states of Illinois and New Mexico have also passed presidential primary laws, the latter being the first state to adopt a primary providing for proportional representation. In Nevada, a bill supported by the Democrats and calling for a presidential preference primary with proportional representation was approved by the legislature, but was vetoed by Republican Governor Paul Laxalt. A presidential primary bill has passed one house of the Delaware legislature.

In March, the Idaho legislature, at the prodding of its Democratic members, passed a law that will allow for complete modernization of the delegate selection process.

In several states there has been substantial reform of party rules governing delegate selection and party structure. In Minnesota, a new party constitution has been adopted that provides for proportional representation and modified "one Democrat—one vote." In Michigan, a meeting of 2,000 Democrats convened in January and adopted the broad recommendations of the Harber Reform Commission. In North Carolina, the State Party has adopted comprehensive reforms of its party structure, including one provision for 18-year-old participation in all party affairs and another for reasonable representation on all party committees and delegations of women, minority racial groups and young people. In Colorado, the State Committee has adopted a proposal that will ensure proportional representation for all presidential candidates at the next convention. In Oklahoma, rules have been proposed which will assure that not more than 60 percent of the membership of any committee or convention will be of the same sex, and will eliminate the role of untimely committees in the delegate selection process. In Missouri, statewide public hearings have been held to discuss proposals for party rules.

In other states, the Democratic Party has adopted significant changes in the structure and selection of their state and constituent committees. In January, Alabama reapportioned its State Committee on a one-man, one-vote basis with members now elected from districts rather than at large. The Florida Democratic Advisory Committee has provided for ex-officio representation of minority groups and youth on the State Committee.

In Washington and Virginia, the State Committee has adopted party rules that require 18-year-old participation in all party affairs. In an additional 30 states, at the urging of Democratic leaders, the 18-year-old vote is before the legislature or will be on the ballot in November.

In Mississippi, South Dakota and the Canal Zone the first set of comprehensive party rules has been adopted. The Missouri State Central Committee, upon completing its extensive statewide hearings, will adopt its first party constitution.

All of these efforts lead us to the conclusion that the Democratic Party is bent on meaningful change. A great European statesman once said, "All things are possible, even the fact that an action in accord with honor and honesty ultimately appears to be a prudent political investment." We share this sentiment. We are confident that party reform, dictated by our Party's heritage and principles, will insure a strong, winning and united Party.

The Watergate Tapes (1972)

Richard Nixon's landslide reelection victory in 1972 (he defeated the Democratic nominee for president, Sen. George McGovern of South Dakota, by 60.7 percent to 37.5 percent in the popular vote and by 520-17 in the electoral college) makes it easy to forget just how controversial and, for a time, politically precarious his administration was during its first term.

In 1971, with demonstrations against the Vietnam War raging on college campuses and public opinion polls indicating that the president was trailing in "trial heats" against a number of possible Democratic opponents, a secret "plumbers unit" was formed in the White House. The initial purpose of the unit was to plug information leaks (hence, "plumbers") in the administration. In early 1972, however, the unit was expanded and transferred to the Committee to Re-elect the President (CREEP, as it came to be known), where it was charged to conduct political espionage against Nixon's Democratic rivals.

On June 17, 1972, five burglars who were secretly employed by CREEP were caught breaking into the headquarters of the Democratic National Committee in Washington's Watergate Hotel. In an effort to avoid embarrassing revelations in the midst of the president's reelection campaign, Nixon and some of his closest aides responded to news of the burglary by trying to obstruct official investigations into what had happened.

On June 23, for example, Nixon secretly approved a plan that was suggested by his chief of staff, H. R. Haldeman, to have top officials at the Central Intelligence Agency (CIA) tell L. Patrick Gray III, the acting director of the Federal Bureau of Investigation (FBI), not to conduct a serious investigation of the Watergate break-in, citing unspecified reasons of national security. Later that day, Nixon received Haldeman's report on his conversations with CIA director Richard C. Helms and deputy director Vernon A. Walters, who refused to cooperate.

On September 15, after a federal grand jury indicted the five burglars and G. Gordon Liddy and Howard Hunt, their bosses at CREEP, Nixon met with Haldeman and John W. Dean III, the White House counsel, to discuss the progress of the cover-up. All expressed pleasure that neither the plumbers nor the break-in at the Democratic National Committee had been traced to the White House.

Despite the best efforts of two Washington Post reporters, Bob Woodward and Carl Bernstein, the cover-up survived substantially intact through election day. McGovern tried to make Watergate a major issue in the campaign, but the voters took little notice of what *the president's press secretary, Ronald L. Ziegler, publicly dismissed as a "third-rate burglary."*

In 1973, however, the Watergate cover-up began to unravel. At a Senate committee hearing, Dean testified against the president, Haldeman, and other administration officials. After the existence of a secret, voice-activated White House taping system was revealed, audiotape recordings of the president's conversations were subpoenaed and, over a period of time, released to Congress and the courts. Nixon fought the subpoena for the June 23, 1972, tapes all the way to the Supreme Court, but on July 24, 1974, in the case of United States v. Nixon, *a unanimous Court decision ordered him to comply.*

The publication of the June 23 tapes made Nixon's impeachment and conviction all but certain. The tapes were the "smoking gun" that proved even to the president's staunchest defenders that he had been involved in the cover-up virtually from the beginning. On August 9, 1974, Nixon resigned as president of the United States.   ~

Meeting: The President and Haldeman

Oval Office, June 23, 1972
(10:04 – 11:39 a.m.):

H. Now, on the investigation, you know the Democratic break-in thing, we're back in the problem area because the FBI is not under control, because Gray doesn't exactly know how to control it and they have—their investigation is now leading into some productive areas—because they've been able to trace the money—not through the money itself—but through the bank sources—the banker. And, and it goes in some directions we don't want it to go. Ah, also there have been some

things—like an informant came in off the street to the FBI in Miami who was a photographer or has a friend who is a photographer who developed some films through this guy Barker and the films had pictures of Democratic National Committee letterhead documents and things. So it's things like that that are filtering in. Mitchell came up with yesterday, and John Dean analyzed very carefully last night and concludes, concurs now with Mitchell's recommendation that the only way to solve this, and we're set up beautifully to do it, ah, in that and that—the only network that paid any attention to it last night was NBC—they did a massive story on the Cuban thing.

P. That's right.

H. That's the way to handle this now is for us to have Walters call Pat Gray and just say, "Stay to hell out of this— this is ah, business here we don't want you to go any further on it." That's not an unusual development, and ah, that would take care of it.

P. What about Pat Gray—you mean Pat Gray doesn't want to?

H. Pat does want to. He doesn't know how to, and he doesn't have, he doesn't have any basis for doing it. Given this, he will then have the basis. He'll call Mark Felt in [W. Mark Felt, FBI deputy associate director in 1972], and the two of them—and Mark Felt wants to cooperate because he's ambitious—

P. Yeah.

H. He'll call him in and say, "We've got the signal from across the river to put the hold on this." And that will fit rather well because the FBI agents who are working the case, at this point, feel that's what it is.

P. This is CIA? They've traced the money? Who'd they trace it to?

H. Well they've traced it to a name, but they haven't gotten to the guy yet.

P. Would it be somebody here?

H. Ken Dahlberg.

P. Who the hell is Ken Dahlberg?

H. He gave $25,000 in Minnesota and, ah, the check went directly to this guy Barker.

P. It isn't from the Committee, though, from Stans?

H. Yeah. It is. It's directly traceable and there's some more through some Texas people that went to the Mexican bank which can also be traced to the Mexican bank—they'll get their names today.

H. —And (pause)

P. Well, I mean, there's no way—I'm just thinking if they don't cooperate, what do they say? That they were approached by the Cubans. That's what Dahlberg has to say, the Texans too, that they—

H. Well, if they will. But then we're relying on more and more people all the time. That's the problem and they'll stop if we could take this other route.

P. All right.

H. And you seem to think the thing to do is get them to stop?

P. Right, fine.

H. They say the only way to do that is from White House instructions. And it's got to be to Helms and to—ah, what's his name....? Walters.

P. Walters.

H. And the proposal would be that Ehrlichman and I call them in, and say, ah—

P. All right, fine. How do you call him in—I mean you just—well, we protected Helms from one hell of a lot of things.

H. That's what Ehrlichman says.

P. Of course, this Hunt, that will uncover a lot of things. You open that scab there's a hell of a lot of things and we just feel that it would be very detrimental to have this thing go any further. This involves these Cubans, Hunt, and a lot of hanky-panky that we have nothing to do with ourselves. Well what the hell, did Mitchell know about this?

H. I think so. I don't think he knew the details, but I think he knew.

P. He didn't know how it was going to be handled though—with Dahlberg

and the Texans and so forth? Well who was the asshole that did? Is it Liddy? Is that the fellow? He must be a little nuts!

H. He is.

P. I mean he just isn't well screwed on is he? Is that the problem?

H. No, but he was under pressure, apparently, to get more information, and as he got more pressure, he pushed the people harder to move harder—

P. Pressure from Mitchell?

H. Apparently.

P. Oh, Mitchell. Mitchell was at the point (unintelligible).

H. Yeah.

P. All right, fine, I understand it all. We won't second-guess Mitchell and the rest. Thank God it wasn't Colson.

H. The FBI interviewed Colson yesterday. They determined that would be a good thing to do. To have him take an interrogation, which he did, and that—the FBI guys working the case concluded that there were one or two possibilities—one, that this was a White House—they don't think that there is anything at the Election Committee—they think it was either a White House operation and they had some obscure reasons for it—non-political, or it was a—Cuban and the CIA. And after their interrogation of Colson yesterday, they concluded it was not the White House, but are now convinced it is a CIA thing; so the CIA turnoff would—

P. Well, not sure of their analysis, I'm not going to get that involved. I'm (unintelligible).

H. No, sir, we don't want you to.

P. You call them in.

H. Good deal.

P. Play it tough. That's the way they play it and that's the way we are going to play it.

H. O.K.

P. When I saw that news summary, I questioned whether it's a bunch of crap, but I thought, er, well it's good to have them off us awhile, because when they start bugging us, which they have, our little boys will not know how to handle it. I hope they will though.

H. You never know.

P. Good.

(Other matters are discussed. Then the conversation returns to the break-in coverup strategy).

Return to Strategy

P. When you get in—when you get in (unintellible) people, say, "Look the problem is that this will open the whole, the whole Bay of Pigs thing, and the President just feels that ah, without going into the details—don't, don't lie to them to the extent to say there is no involvement, but just say this is a comedy of errors, without getting into it, the President believes that it is going to open the whole Bay of Pigs thing up again. And, ah, because these people are plugging for (unintelligible) and that they should call the FBI in and (unintelligible) don't go any further into this case period!

P. (Inaudible) our cause—

H. Get more done for our cause by the opposition than by us.

P. Well, can you get it done?

H. I think so.

Meeting: The President and Haldeman

**Oval Office, June 23, 1972
(1:04 — 1:13 p.m.):**

P. O.K., just postpone (scratching noises) (unintelligible) Just say (unintelligible) very bad to have this fellow Hunt, ah, he knows too dammed much, if he was involved—you happen to know that? If it gets out that this is all involved, the Cuba thing it would be a fiasco. It would make the CIA look bad, it's going to make Hunt look bad, and it is likely to blow the whole Bay of Pigs thing which we think would be very

unfortunate—both for CIA, and for the country, at this time, and for American foreign policy. Just tell him to lay off. Don't you?

H. Yep. That's the basis to do it on. Just leave it at that.

P. I don't know if he'll get any ideas for doing it because our concern political (unintelligible). Helms is not one to (unintelligible)—I would just say, lookit, because of the Hunt involvement, whole cover basically this.

H. Yep. Good move.

P. Well, they've got some pretty good ideas on this Meany thing. Shultz did a good paper. I read it all (voices fade).

Meeting: The President and Haldeman

**Executive Office Building,
June 23, 1972, (2:20 — 2:45 p.m.):**

H. No problem

P. (Unintelligible)

H. Well, it was kind of interesting. Walters made the point and I didn't mention Hunt, I just said that the thing was leading into directions that were going to create potential problems because they were exploring leads that led back into areas that would be harmful to the CIA and harmful to the government (unintelligible) didn't have anything to do (unintelligible).

(Telephone)

P. Chuck? I wonder if you would give John Connally a call he's on his trip—I don't want him to read it in the paper before Monday about this quota thing and say—look, we're going to do this, but that I checked, I asked you about the situation (unintelligible) had an understanding it was only temporary and ah (unintelligible) O.K.? I just don't want him to read it in the papers. Good. Fine.

H. (unintelligible) I think Helms did to (unintelligible) said, I've had no—

P. God (unintelligible).

H. Gray called and said, yesterday, and said that he thought—

P. Who did? Gray?

H. Gray called Helms and said I think we've run right into the middle of a CIA covert operation.

P. Gray said that?

H. Yeah. And (unintelligible) said nothing we've done at this point and ah (unintelligible) says well it sure looks to me like it is (unintelligible) and ah, that was the end of that conversation (unintelligible) the problem is it tracks back to the Bay of Pigs and it tracks back to some other the leads run out to people who had no involvement in this, except by contacts and connection, but it gets to areas that are liable to be raised? The whole problem (unintelligible) Hunt. So at that point he kind of got the picture. He said, he said we'll be very happy to be helpful (unintelligible) handle anything you want. I would like to know the reason for being helpful, and I made it clear to him he wasn't going to get explicit (unintelligible) generality, and he said fine. And Walters (unintelligible). Walters is going to make a call to Gray. That's the way we put it and that's the way it was left.

Money

P. How does that work though, how, they've got to (unintelligible) somebody from the Miami bank.

H. (unintelligible). The point John makes—the Bureau is going on and on this because they don't know what they are uncovering (unintelligible) continue to pursue it. They don't need to because they already have their case as far as the charges against these men (unintelligible) and ah, as they pursue it (unintelligible) exactly, but we didn't in any way say we (unintelligible). One thing Helms did raise. He said, Gray—he asked Gray why they thought they had run into a CIA thing and Gray said

because of the characters involved and the amount of money involved, a lot of dough. (unintelligible) and ah, (unintelligible)

P. (Unintelligible)

H. Well, I think they will

P. If it runs (unintelligible) what the hell who knows (unintelligible) contributed CIA.

H. Yeah, it's money CIA gets money (unintelligible) I mean their money moves in a lot of different ways, too.

P. Yeah. How are (unintelligible)—a lot of good—

H. (Unintelligible)

P. Well you remember what the SOB did on my book? When I brought out the fact, you know—

H. Yeah.

P. That he knew all about Dulles? (Expletive Deleted) Dulles knew. Dulles told me. I know, I mean (unintelligible) had the telephone call. Remember, I had a call put in—Dulles just blandly said and knew why.

H. Yeah.

P. Now, what the hell! Who told him to do it? The President: (Unintelligible)

H. Dulles was no more Kennedy's man than (unintelligible) was your man (unintelligible)

P. (unintelligible) covert operation— do anything else (unintelligible)

Meeting: The President and Haldeman and Dean

Oval Office, September 15, 1972 (5:27 – 6:17 p.m.):

P. Hi, how are you? You had quite a day today didn't you. You got Watergate on the way didn't you?

D. We tried.

H. How did it all end up?

D. Ah, I think we can say well at this point. The press is playing it just as we expect.

H. Whitewash?

D. No, not yet—the story right now—

P. It is a big story.

H. Five indicted plus the WH former guy and all that.

D. Plus two White House fellows.

H. That is good that takes the edge off whitewash, really, that was the thing (Nixon campaign manager John N.) Mitchell kept saying, that to people in the country Liddy and Hunt (G. Gordon Liddy and E. Howard Hunt Jr., Watergate conspirators) were big men. Maybe that is good.

P. How did MacGregor (Clark MacGregor, who succeeded Mitchell as campaign manager) handle himself?

D. I think very well he had a good statement which said that the Grand Jury had met and that it was now time to realize that some apologies may be due.

H. Fat chance.

D. Get the damn (inaudible)

H. We can't do that.

P. Just remember, all the trouble we're taking, we'll have a chance to get back one day. How are you doing on your other investigations?

H. What has happened on the bug? ... *on the what?*

D. The second bug there was a bug found in the telephone of one of the men at the DNC (Democratic National Committee).

P. You don't think it was left over from the other time?

D. Absolutely not, the Bureau has checked and re-checked the whole place after that night. The man had specifically checked and rechecked the telephone and it was not there.

P. What the hell do you think was involved?

D. I think DNC was planted.

P. You think they did it?

D. Un huh

P. (Expletive deleted) do they really want to believe that we planted that?

H. Did they get anything on the finger prints?

D. No, nothing at all either on the telephone or on the bug. The FBI has unleashed a full investigation over at the DNC starting with (Democratic chairman Lawrence F.) O'Brien right now.

H. Laughter. Using the same crew—

D. The same crew—the Washington Field Office.

P. What kind of questions are they asking him?

D. Anything they can think of because O'Brien is charging them with failing to find all the bugs.

H. Good, that will make them mad.

* * *

D. So (acting FBI director L. Patrick) Gray is pissed and his people are pissed off. So maybe they will move in because their reputation is on the line. I think that is a good development.

* * *

D. *So, so, Gray is pissed now and his people are kind of pissed off. So they're moving in because their reputation's on the line. That's uh, do you think that's a good development?*

* * *

P. I think that is a good development because it makes it look so (adjective deleted) funny. Am I wrong?

D. No, no sir. It looks silly. If we can find that the DNC planted that, the whole story will reverse. . . .

Bigger Investigation Than Of JFK Slaying

D. The resources that have been put against this whole investigation to date are really incredible. It is truly a larger investigation than was conducted against the after inquiry of the JFK assassination.

P. Oh.... Yes (Expletive deleted). (Sen. Barry) Goldwater (R Ariz.) put it in context when he said "(expletive deleted) everybody bugs everybody else. You know that."

D. That was priceless.

P. It happens to be totally true. We were bugged in '68 on the plane and in '62 even running for Governor—(expletive deleted) thing you ever saw.

D. It is a shame that evidence to the fact that that happened in '68 was never around....

H. I have some stuff too—on the bombing incident and too in the bombing halt stay.

P. The difficulty with using it, of course, it is reflects on (former President Lyndon B.) Johnson. If it weren't for that, I would use it. Is there any way we could use it without using his name—saying that the DNC did it? No-the FBI did the bugging.

D. That is the problem—would it reflect on Johnson or (former Vice President Hubert H.) Humphrey?

H. Johnson, Humphrey didn't do it.

P. Oh, hell no.

H. He was bugging Humphrey, too.

P. (Expletive deleted).... [Someone asked the President if he wanted Mitchell's call—he said, "Yeah...."]

P. Well are you still alive? I was just sitting here with John Dean and he tells me you were going to be sued or something. Good. Good. Yeah. Good. Sure. Well I tell you just don't let this keep you or your colleagues from concentrating on the big game. This thing is just one of those side issues and a month later everybody looks back and wonders what all the shooting was about. OK, John. Good night. Get a good night's sleep. And don't bug anybody without asking me? OK? Yeah. Thank you.

D. Three months ago I would have had trouble predicting there would be a day when this would be forgotten, but I think I can say that 54 days from now nothing is going to come crashing down to our surprise.

P. That what?

D. Nothing is going to come crashing down to our surprise.

'Way You Have Handled All This . . . Skillful'

P. Oh well, this is a can of worms as you know a lot of this stuff that went on. And the people who worked this way are awfully embarrassed. But the way you have handled all this seems to me has been very skillful putting your fingers in the leaks that have sprung here and sprung there. The Grand Jury is dismissed now?

D. That is correct. They have completed and they have let them go so there will be no continued investigation prompted by the Grand Jury's inquiry, the GAO (General Accounting Office) report referred over to Justice is on a shelf right now because they have hundreds of violations—they have violations of (Sen. George) McGovern (D-S.D.), of (Sen.) Humphrey (D-Minn.), violations of (Sen. Henry M.) Jackson (D-Wash.), and several hundred Congressional violations. They don't want to start prosecuting one any more than they prosecute the other.

P. They definitely will not prosecute us unless they prosecute the others.

D. Well, we are talking about technical violations referred over also.

P. What about watching the McGovern contributors and all that sort of thing?

D. We have (inaudible) eye out on that. His I understand is not in full compliance.

P. He asked?

D. No....

H. He may be getting $900,000 from somebody. He may have two or three angles.

P. I don't think he is getting a hell of a lot of small money. I don't believe (expletive deleted) Have you had the P.O. checked yet?

H. That is John's area. I don't know.

P. Well, let's have it checked.

Only Problems Are Human Problems

D. Well as I see it, the only problems we may have are the human problems and I will keep a close watch on that. . . .

P. You mean on this case?

D. On this case. There is some bitterness between the Finance Committee and the Political Committee—they feel they are taking all the heat and all the people upstairs are bad people—not being recognized.

*　　*　　*

P. We are all in it together. This is a war. We take a few shots and it will be over. We will give them a few shots and it will be over. Don't worry. I wouldn't want to be on the other side right now. Would you?

*　　*　　*

P. *They're all in it together.*

D. *That's right.*

P. *They should just, uh, just behave and, and, recognize this, this is, again, this is war. We're getting a few shots. It'll be over. Don't worry. [Unintelligible] I wouldn't want to be on the other side right now. Would you? I wouldn't want to be in Edward Bennet Williams', Williams position after this election.*

D. *No. No.*

P. *None of these bastards—*

D. *He, uh, he's done some rather unethical things that have come to light already, which in—again, Richey has brought to our attention.*

P. *Yeah.*

D. *He went down.*

H. *Keep a log on all that.*

D. *Oh, we are, on these. Yeah.*

P. *Yeah.*

H. *Because afterwards that is a guy,*

P. *We're going after him.*

H. *That is a guy we've got to ruin.*

D. *He had, he had an ex parte—*

P. *You want to remember, too, he's an attorney for the* Washington Post.

D. *I'm well aware of that.*

P. *I think we are going to fix the son-of-a-bitch. Believe me. We are going to. We've got to, because he's a bad man.*

D. *Absolutely.*

P. *He misbehaved very badly in the Hoffa matter. Our—some pretty bad conduct, there, too, but go ahead.*

*　　*　　*

Nixon Orders Enemies' List

P. I want the most comprehensive notes on all those who tried to do us in. They didn't have to do it. If we had a very close election and they were playing the other side I would understand this. No—they were doing this quite deliberately and they are asking for it and they are going to get it. We have not used the power in this first four years as you know. We have never used it. We have not used the Bureau and we have not used the Justice Department but things are going to change now. And they are either going to do it right or go.

D. What an exciting prospect.

P. Thanks. It has to be done. We have been (adjective deleted) fools for us to come into this election campaign and not do anything with regard to the Democratic Senators who are running, et cetera. And who the hell are they after? They are after us. It is absolutely ridiculous. It is not going to be that way any more.

H. Really, it is ironic that we have gone to extremes. You and your damn regulations. Everybody worries about not picking up a hotel bill.

D. I think you can be proud of the White House staff. It really has had no problems of that sort. And I love this GAO audit that is going on now. I think they have some suspicion that even a cursory investigation is going to discover something here. I don't think they can find a thing. I learned today, incidentally, and have not confirmed it, that the GAO auditor who is down here is here at the Speaker of the House's request.

P. That surprises me.

H. Well, (expletive deleted) the Speaker of the House. Maybe we better put a little heat on him.

P. I think so too.

H. Because he has a lot worse problems than he is going to find down here.

D. That's right.

H. That is the kind of thing that, you know, we really ought to do is call the Speaker and say, "I regret to say your calling the GAO down here because of what it is going to cause us to do to you."

P. Why don't you see if (former presidential counselor Bryce N.) Harlow will tell him that.

H. Because he wouldn't do it—he would just be pleasant and call him Mr. Speaker....

'Trying to Cut Our Losses'

P. You really can't sit and worry about it all the time. The worst may happen but it may not. So you just try to button it up as well as you can and hope for the best, and remember basically the damn business is unfortunately trying to cut our losses.

D. Certainly that is right and certainly it has had no effect on you. That's the good thing.

H. No, it has been kept away from the White House and of course completley from the President.... The only tie to the White House is the (former presidential special counsel Charles W.) Colson effort they keep trying to pull in.

D. And, of course, the two White House people of lower level—indicted—one consultant and one member of the Domestic Staff. That is not very much of a tie.

H. That's right. Or (convicted mass murderer Charles M.) Manson. (expletive deleted). If they had been killers. Isn't that true?

H. It is certainly true.

P. These (characterization deleted) they have had no way. They ought to move the trial away from—

D. There has been extensive clipping on the part of the counsel in this case. They may never get a fair trial. They may never get a jury that will convict them. The *Post*, you know, that they have a real large team assigned to cover this case. Believe me, the Maury Stans story about his libel sit that he had so much coverage in the *Evening News* they put way back on page 8 of the *Post* and did not even cover it in total....

*   *   *

H. *The* Post *is-*

P. *The* Post *has asked—it's going to have its problems.*

H. *[Unintelligible]*

D. *The networks, the networks are good with Maury coming back three days in a row and—*

P. *That's right. Right. The main thing is the* Post *is going to have damnable, damnable problems out of this one. They have a television station*

D. *That's right, they do.*

P. *And they're going to have to get it renewed.*

H. *They've got a radio station, too.*

P. *Does that come up too? The point is, when does it come up?*

D. I don't know. But the practice of non-licensees filing on top of licensees has certainly gotten more.

P. That's right.

D. more active in the, in the area.

P. And it's going to be God damn active here.

D. [Laughs]

P. Well, the game has to be played awfully rough. I don't know—Now, you, you'll follow through with—who will over there? Who—Timmons, or with Ford, or—How's it going to operate....

The Eagleton Affair: Statements by the Candidates (1972)

In 1974, Sen. George McGovern of South Dakota put to good use the new rules for Democratic presidential nominations that he had just helped to write. (See "The McGovern-Fraser Commission Report," p. 574.) Unfortunately, McGovern also ran afoul of an old rule (or rule of thumb) of presidential politics—namely, that the purpose of a vice-presidential nomination is to balance the party's national ticket.

McGovern began the 1972 delegate selection season as a long-shot candidate. Although he had been the legatee of some of the late Sen. Robert F. Kennedy's support in 1968 (See "Eugene McCarthy Announces for President," p. 554), McGovern initially ranked far down on a long list of candidates. The list was headed by former vice president Hubert H. Humphrey, Sen. Edmund Muskie of Maine, who had been Humphrey's running mate in 1968, Gov. George C. Wallace of Alabama, and Sen. Henry M. Jackson of Washington.

McGovern staked out a position on his party's left wing. In the ideologically charged atmosphere of the time, this stance proved to be politically popular among the Democratic rank and file who, under the new rules, now determined presidential nominations. McGovern's uncompromising opposition to the Vietnam War energized a corps of dedicated political activists. The McGovernites seized control of the state parties that chose their national convention delegates in open caucuses and worked effectively to turn out voters in the primary states.

The broad but shallow support that Muskie and Jackson enjoyed within the Democratic party proved less helpful under the new rules than it would have in the past, and their candidacies faded early. Wallace, running in 1972 as a Democrat (see "New York Campaign Speech by George C. Wallace," p. 566), did well in the primaries but was forced to abandon the race in May after he was severely wounded by an assassin at an outdoor rally in Maryland. McGovern eliminated his sole remaining rival, Humphrey, in the June 6 California primary.

McGovern's prospects for victory against Richard Nixon in the general election were slim—pathbreaking visits to China and the Soviet Union had made 1972 a triumphant year for the president. The Democratic nominee's only hope was to reach out to the very party leaders whom his rules commission had dethroned and his candidacy had defeated. In choosing his vice-presidential running mate, McGovern took ticket-balancing to an extreme, naming Sen. Thomas F. Eagleton of Missouri, a politically moderate Roman Catholic with strong ties to organized labor.

McGovern chose Eagleton hastily and did not know him well. Nor had Eagleton been his first choice: Muskie, Sen. Edward M. Kennedy of Massachusetts, and several other prospective nominees turned McGovern down. On July 25, 1972, less than two weeks after the close of the Democratic national convention, newspaper stories revealed that Eagleton had been hospitalized three times for nervous exhaustion between 1960 and 1966, and that he had been treated with a combination of psychiatric and electroshock therapy.

During the week that followed these revelations, the Eagleton story dominated the headlines. McGovern gradually went from expressing "1000 percent support" for his running mate to nudging him off the ticket. On July 31, McGovern and Eagleton announced at a joint press conference in Washington that Eagleton was stepping down, the first time in history that a vice-presidential nominee had withdrawn from an election.

On August 5, 1972, McGovern announced his choice for a new running mate, former Peace Corps director and Kennedy in-law R. Sargent Shriver. Acting under the party's rules for such contingencies, the Democratic National Committee met on August 8 to nominate Shriver formally. But by now the McGovern campaign, already weak, was fatally wounded—by its careless choice of Eagleton, its vacillation after his illness was revealed, its insensitivity to his personal anguish, and by the long delay in getting its substantive message out to the voters.   ~

Excerpts from a news conference at Rapid City, S.D., July 25, at which Sen. Thomas F. Eagleton detailed his record of psychiatric treatment, and at which he and Sen. George McGovern answered questions from the press:

Eagleton: In political campaigning it is part and parcel of that campaigning that there will be rumors about candidates. Rumors have followed me during my political career, dating back when I first ran for office in 1956 . . . there have been some rumors circulating as to my health. Thus, today I wish to give you as complete a picture as I possibly can as a layman about my personal health.

I charge no one with malice as spreading these rumors, but I think it is a legitimate question the press has to ask me about whether my health is such that I can hold the high office of Vice President of the United States.

On three occasions in my life I have voluntarily gone into hospitals as a result of nervous exhaustion and fatigue. A few in this room know me well . . . and they know me to be an intense and hard-fighting person.

I sometimes push myself too far. In 1960, John F. Kennedy was running for President and I was a Democratic nominee for Attorney General [for Missouri] . . . I was in many instances my own car driver. The day of Secret Service escorts wasn't my cup of tea in 1960, and I pushed myself, terribly hard, long hours day and night.

After that campaign was over I did experience exhaustion and fatigue. I was on my own volition hospitalized in Barnes Hospital in St. Louis, Mo. . . . The period of that hospitalization, as best I can recall it, was probably four weeks. It started around Dec. 1 and culminated perhaps the first day of January or soon afterwards in 1961.

The second experience was perhaps four days in length. I went to Mayo Clinic in Rochester, Minn., between Christmas, Dec. 25, 1964, and New Year's Day, Jan. 1, 1965. During that week, the holiday week, I was in Mayo's for four days for physical examination. Part of the manifestation of my fatigue and exhaustion relates to the stomach. I am like the fellow in the Alka-Seltzer ad who says I can't believe I ate the whole thing.

But I do get, when I do overwork and tire myself, kind of a nervous stomach situation. It's one of the physical manifestations of what I have experienced.

The third and final time, ladies and gentlemen, was in perhaps middle or late September of 1966 when I once again went back to Mayo Clinic, once again for exhaustion and fatigue. The length of that stay, I think, was approximately three weeks.

One could ask and should ask well, in light of that history, have you learned anything. All of us live our lives, I guess, in the attempt to learn more about ourselves ... in many respects we are our own worst enemies and it took these experiences, these tough experiences, for me to learn a little bit about myself.

I still am an intense person, I still push very hard. But I pace myself a great deal better than I did in earlier years. The past six years, from 1966 to date, I've experienced good, solid, sound health. I make it a regular practice to be as idle as I can on Sundays ... in the winter months that's my day to lie on the couch and watch the Redskins and the St. Louis football Cardinals and the Kansas City Chiefs, the last two being my favorite teams.

So I believe and I have every confidence that at age 42, I've learned how to pace myself and learned how to measure my own energies and know the limits of my own endurance. Insofar as this campaign is concerned, I intend to give it all I have but on a measured basis, and not to repeat the experiences that I have experienced as heretofore mentioned. So as far as the initial exposition is concerned, I've about said all I can and now I'll take questions from the press on any matter that they feel pertinent to what I have just said.

Questions and Answers

Q: Was Sen. McGovern aware of these things ... before he decided on you as a candidate?

Eagleton: No, he was not. He was made aware of it on the weekend or the Monday after the convention.

Q: How did Sen. McGovern react to it?

McGovern: Well let me say, Mr. Schumacher, that when I talked to Sen. Eagleton about my decision to ask him to go as my running mate, I asked if he had any problems in his past that were significant or worth discussing with me. He said no and I agree with that.

I am fully satisfied on the basis of everything I've learned about these brief hospital visits that what is manifested in Sen. Eagleton's part was the good judgment to seek out medical care when he was exhausted. I have watched him in the U.S. Senate for the past four years. As far as I am concerned, there is no member of that Senate who is any sounder in mind, body, and spirit than Tom Eagleton. I am fully satisfied and if I had known every detail that we discussed this morning ... he still would have been my choice for Vice President.

Q: At the risk of being indelicate, did you find during these periods of exhaustion that it affected you ability to make rational judgments?

Eagleton: No. I was in a position to make rational judgments and decisions. I was depressed. My spirits were depressed. This was one of the manifestations, along with the stomach upset, of the exhaustion and fatigue I heretofore described.

Q: Was alcohol at all involved?

A: Alcohol was not involved in any iota, in any way, shape or form whatsoever, I can assure you—categorically and without hesitation, unequivocal—there's been no trace, no hint, not one iota of alcoholism as part of these rumors—as part of the actual facts.

Q: During these periods, did you receive any psychiatric help?

A: Yes, I did.

Q: What kind of treatment?

A: As I entered the hospitals, voluntarily as I have described, my physician was an internist, Dr. William Perry of St. Louis. He's still practicing in St. Louis and he's no longer my physician since I moved to Washington I use the services of the Senate, which is Dr. Pearson and his staff. Parenthetically, not to avoid your questions, I have received a Senate exam and another one at Bethesda Naval Hospital and all the doctors have found so far is that I'm two pounds overweight and have half a hemorrhoid.... I was treated by a psychiatrist, Dr. Frank Shobez.

Q: Can you tell us what type of psychiatric treatment you received?

A: Counseling from a psychiatrist, including electric shock.

Q: Any drugs?

A: Sleeping pills.

Q: Was the electric shock treatment at all three hospitals?

A: No. Barnes in 1960 and Mayo's in 1966, not at Mayo's in 1964.

Q: What were the purposes of the electric shock treatment?

A: At that time it was part of the prescribed treatment for one who is suffering from nervous exhaustion and fatigue and manifestations of depression.

Q: Do you intend to make public the documentation of this history?

A: Medical reports are matters between one doctor and another doctor. They're not written in laymen's language.... I know of no situation where any candidate for any office has made public records of any communication between doctors and other doctors pertaining to a particular patient.

Q: Would you release your doctors from the traditional doctor-patient relationship?

A: I'm sure Dr. Perry will make a statement. I haven't talked to Dr. Perry, but he'll make a summary statement of what his findings were. He is not really the most important one because I haven't seen Dr. Perry as a patient for, I guess, over four years....

Q: What doctors did you see at Rochester?

A: I don't remember the names of the physicians. If you know how the Mayo operation is, you're more or less treated by a group of physicians ... you're sort of the patient of the entire group.

Q: Why did you decide to address yourself to the problem now when you did not decide to do so in your previous career?

A: In seeking the second highest office in the land, it is only natural that one's life becomes more and more of an open book. It's quite obvious that I haven't relished being under these lights, before 30 or 40 newsmen, describing my health. It isn't a joyous undertaking and I think it is natural that, until it is necessary to respond to rumors that were circulating, the natural tendency would be to keep one's peace.

Q: If you had this to do over again, would you have consulted Sen. McGovern before you formally accepted the vice presidential choice?

A: Sen. McGovern's staff was aware, I believe, the night before my name was put in nomination, of the rumors ... that were circulating on the floor of the convention and they were satisfied as to my health as to permit me to be the vice presidential candidate.

Q: Sen. McGovern, can you give us your assessment of your running mate's health?

A: Well, I think Tom Eagleton is fully qualified in mind, body, and spirit to be the Vice President of the United States and, if necessary, to take on the presidency on a moment's notice.... I know fully the whole case history of his illness, I know what his performance has been in the Senate over the last four years and I don't have the slightest doubt about the wisdom of my judgment in selecting him as my running mate, nor would I have any hesitance at all trusting the U.S. Government to his hands. I wouldn't have hesitated one moment if I had known everything Sen. Eagleton said here today.

McGovern Statement

Transcript of statements by Sen. George McGovern and Sen. Thomas F. Eagleton at a news conference July 31 in Washington, at which they jointly announced Eagleton's withdrawal from the ticket:

Ladies and gentlemen, Sen. Eagleton and I will each open with a brief prepared statement, and then we will be glad to respond to any questions you might have.

Sen. Eagleton and I have met this evening to discuss his vice presidential candidacy. I have consistently supported Sen. Eagleton. He is a talented, able United States senator whose ability will make him a prominent figure in American politics for many many years. I am fully satisfied that his health is excellent.

I base that conclusion upon my conversations with his doctors and my close personal and political association with him.

In the joint decision that we have reached tonight health was not a factor. But the public debate over Sen. Eagleton's past medical history continues to divert attention from the great national issues that need to be discussed.

I have referred to the growing pressures to ask for Sen. Eagleton's withdrawal. We have also seen growing vocal support for his candidacy. Sen. Eagleton and I agree that the paramount needs of the Democratic Party and the nation in 1972 are unity and a full discussion of the real issues before the country.

Continued debate between those who oppose his candidacy and those who favor it will serve to further divide the party and the nation. Therefore, we have jointly agreed that the best course is for Sen. Eagleton to step aside.

I wish nothing but the best for Sen. Eagleton and his family. He is and will remain my good friend. Furthermore he has generously agreed to campaign for the Democratic ticket this fall.

I can assure you that I welcome his strong help in this campaign.

Eagleton Statement

As Sen. McGovern has stated, he and I are jointly in agreement that I should withdraw as the Democratic candidate for Vice President.

Needless to say, this was not an easy decision for Sen. McGovern or for me.

Literally thousands and thousands of people have phoned, telegrammed or written to me and Sen. McGovern urging me to press on.

But ladies and gentlemen, I will not divide the Democratic Party, which has already too many divisions.

Therefore, tomorrow morning I will write to the chairman of the Democratic Party withdrawing my candidacy.

My personal feelings are secondary to the necessity to unify the Democratic Party and to elect George McGovern as the next President of the United States.

Thank you. Wait a minute. I've got more to say. Please be patient. The best is yet to come.

My conscience is clear, and my spirits are high.

I want to make this, to use President Nixon's favorite term, "crystal clear."

This is definitely not my last press conference and Tom Eagleton is going to be around a long time.

Wait a minute, two more sentences.

I am for George McGovern and I'm going to continue working to see him elected President of the United States.

Let me add, although it's not in the prepared statement I wish to take the liberty of adding a personal sentence to what I've just read. I said sometime during the week that there used to be a TV show called "That Was the Week That Was." And this was a week that really was. No one could have been finer to me, more considerate, more generally concerned and interested in me as a person and in my welfare as a politician than the man that I am proud to call the next President of the United States, George McGovern.

Buckley v. Valeo *(1976)*

In an extended effort to regulate the use and influence of money in presidential elections, Congress passed and, somewhat reluctantly, presidents Richard Nixon and Gerald Ford signed several pieces of campaign finance legislation during the early and mid-1970s.

The Federal Election Campaign Act of 1971 was designed mainly to bring political contributions into the light of day by forcing candidates for president and Congress to file regular reports that disclosed the sources of their campaign funding.

Congress also passed the Revenue Act of 1971. The act created the Presidential Election Campaign Fund to provide federal financing for the general election campaigns of all major party candidates for president who agreed to forsake private contributions. Taxpayers were allowed to "check off," or designate, one dollar of each year's federal income taxes for the fund.

In 1974, responding to the country's Watergate-inspired mood of revulsion against politics, Congress passed a series of amendments to the Federal Election Campaign Act of 1971 that were more sweeping than the act itself. (See "The Watergate Tapes," p. 585.) The 1974 amendments limited the amounts that a person or a political action committee (PAC) could contribute during an election cycle, either to an individual campaign for federal of-

fice or to all campaigns. (The amendments also placed a ceiling on the personal funds that candidates could spend on their own campaigns.) For presidential elections, a system of "matching funds" was established that, in addition to subsidizing the campaigns of candidates who were seeking a major party nomination, limited the amount of money that they could spend. Finally, the Federal Election Commission (FEC) was created to administer the amended act, with some of its members appointed by the president and the rest by Congress.

A broad ideological coalition (the plaintiffs included Sen. James L. Buckley of New York, a conservative Republican, and the liberal former Democratic senator from Minnesota, Eugene McCarthy) challenged the campaign finance law in federal court, raising a number of constitutional objections. The plaintiffs' main argument was that to restrict contributions was to restrict the First Amendment rights of free expression and free association. They also maintained that the law discriminated against third parties.

On January 30, 1976, in the case of Buckley v. Valeo, the Supreme Court upheld some parts of the campaign finance law and struck down others. The new system of federal financing for presidential nominations and general election campaigns passed con-

stitutional muster. So did the limits on individual and PAC contributions to particular campaigns.

Citing the First Amendment, however, the Court declared unconstitutional the ceilings on the amount of money that candidates could spend on their own campaigns and on the total amount that individuals could contribute to independent campaigns on behalf of one or more candidates. The Court also insisted that because the Constitution confined the appointment power to the president, the FEC was an improperly constituted agency.

Congress responded to Buckley v. Valeo *by passing a new series of amendments to the Federal Election Campaign Act in 1976. The main purpose of the amendments was to revive the FEC by reconstituting it as a presidentially appointed body and by strengthening its powers of investigation and enforcement.* ~

Per Curiam. [Mr. Justice Stevens took no part in the consideration or decision of these cases.]

These appeals present constitutional challenges to the key provision of the Federal Election Campaign Act of 1971, as amended in 1974.

The Court of Appeals, in sustaining the Act in large part against various constitutional challenges, viewed it as "by far the most comprehensive reform legislation [ever] passed by Congress concerning the election of the President, Vice-President, and members of Congress.". . . The Act, summarized in broad terms, contains the following provisions: (a) individual political contributions are limited to $1,000 to any single candidate per election, with an overall annual limitation of $25,000 by any contributor; independent expenditures by individuals and groups "relative to a clearly identified candidate" are limited to $1,000 a year; campaign spending by candidates for various fed-

eral offices and spending for national conventions by political parties are subject to prescribed limits; (b) contributions and expenditures above certain threshold levels must be reported and publicly disclosed; (c) a system for public funding of Presidential campaign activities is established by Subtitle H of the Internal Revenue Code; and (d) a Federal Election Commission is established to administer and enforce the Act. . . .

. . . On plenary review, a majority of the Court of Appeals rejected, for the most part, appellants' constitutional attacks. The court found "a clear and compelling interest," 519 F. 2d, at 841, in preserving the integrity of the electoral process. On that basis, the court upheld, with one exception, the substantive provisions of the Act with respect to contributions, expenditures and disclosure. It also sustained the constitutionality of the newly established Federal Election Commission. The court concluded that, notwithstanding the manner of selection of its members and the breadth of its powers, which included nonlegislative functions, the Commission is a constitutionally authorized agency created to perform primarily legislative functions. The provisions for public funding of the three stages of the Presidential selection process were upheld as a valid exercise of congressional power under the General Welfare Clause of the Constitution, Art. I, § [2] 8.

In this Court, appellants argue that the Court of Appeals failed to give this legislation the critical scrutiny demanded under accepted First Amendment and equal protection principles. In appellants' view, limiting the use of money for political purposes constitutes a restriction on communication violative of the First Amendment, since virtually all meaningful political communications in the modern setting involve the expenditure of money. Further, they argue that the reporting and disclosure provisions of the Act unconstitutionally impinge on their right to freedom of association. Appellants also view the federal subsidy provisions of Subtitle H as violative of the General Welfare Clause, and as inconsistent with the First and Fifth Amendments. Finally, appellants renew their attack on the Commission's composition and powers.

At the outset we must determine whether the case before us presents a "case or controversy" within the meaning of Art. III of the Constitution. Congress may not, of course, require this Court to render opinions in matters which are not "cases and controversies.". . . We must therefore decide whether appellants have the "personal stake in the outcome of the controversy" necessary to meet the requirements of Art. III. . . . It is clear that Congress, in enacting [Federal Election Campaign Act], intended to provide judicial review to the extent permitted by Art. III. In our view, the complaint in this case demonstrates that at least some of the appellants have a sufficient "personal stake" in a determination of the constitutional validity of each of the challenged provisions to present "a real and substantial controversy admitting of specific relief through a decree of a conclusive character, as distinguished from an opinion advising what the law would be upon a hypothetical state of facts." *Aetna Life Insurance Co. v. Haworth*, [1937]. . . .

I. Contribution and Expenditure Limitations

The intricate statutory scheme adopted by Congress to regulate federal election campaigns includes restrictions on political contributions and expenditures that apply broadly to all phases of all participants in the election process. The major contribution and expenditure limitations in the Act prohibit individuals from contributing more than $25,000 in a single year or more than $1,000 to any single candidate for an election campaign and from spending more than $1,000 a year "relative to a clearly identified candidate." Other provisions restrict a candidate's use of personal and family resources in his campaigning for federal office.

The constitutional power of Congress to regulate federal elections is well established and is not questioned by any of the parties in this case. Thus, the critical constitutional questions presented here go not to the basic power of Congress to legislate in this area, but to whether the specific legislation that Congress has enacted interferes with First Amendment freedoms or invidiously discriminates against nonincumbent candidates and minor parties in contravention of the Fifth Amendment.

[A. General Principles]

The Act's contribution and expenditure limitations operate in an area of the most fundamental First Amendment activities. Discussion of public issues and debate on the qualifications of candidates are integral to the operation of the system of government established by our Constitution. The First Amendment affords the broadest protection to such political expression in order "to assure the unfettered interchange of ideas for the bringing about of political and social changes desired by the people." *Roth v. United States* . . . (1957). . . . "[T]here is practically universal agreement that a major purpose of th[e] Amendment was to protect the free discussion of governmental affairs, . . . of course includ[ing] discussions of candidates. . . ." *Mills v. Alabama* . . . (1966). . . .

The First Amendment protects political association as well as political expression. The constitutional right of association explicated in *NAACP v. Alabama* ... (1958), stemmed from the Court's recognition that "[e]ffective advocacy of both public and private points of view, particularly controversial ones, is undeniably enhanced by group association." Subsequent decisions have made clear that the First and Fourteenth Amendments guarantee "freedom to associate with others for the common advancement of political beliefs and ideas," a freedom that encompasses "[t]he right to associate with the political party of one's choice." *Kusper v. Pontikes* ... (1973). . . .

It is with these principles in mind that we consider the primary contentions of the parties with respect to the Act's limitations upon the giving and spending of money in political campaigns. Those conflicting contentions could not more sharply define the basic issues before us. Appellees contend that what the Act regulates is conduct, and that its effect on speech and association is incidental at most. Appellants respond that contributions and expenditures are at the very core of political speech, and that the Act's limitations thus constitute restraints on First Amendment liberty that are both gross and direct.

In upholding the constitutional validity of the Act's contribution and expenditure provisions on the ground that those provisions should be viewed as regulating conduct not speech, the Court of Appeals relied upon *United States v. O'Brien* ... (1968). . . .

. . . Even if the categorization of the expenditure of money as conduct were accepted, the limitations challenged here would not meet the *O'Brien* test because the governmental interests advanced in support of the Act involve "suppressing communication." The interests served by the Act include restricting the voices of people and interest groups who have money to spend and reducing the overall scope of federal election campaigns. Although the

Act does not focus on the ideas expressed by persons or groups subjected to its regulations, it is aimed in part at equalizing the relative ability of all voters to affect electoral outcomes by placing a ceiling on expenditures for political expression by citizens and groups. . . .

. . . A restriction on the amount of money a person or group can spend on political communication during a campaign necessarily reduces the quantity of expression by restricting the number of issues discussed, the depth of their exploration, and the size of the audience reached. This is because virtually every means of communicating ideas in today's mass society requires the expenditure of money. The distribution of the humblest handbill or leaflet entails printing, paper, and circulation costs. Speeches and rallies generally necessitate hiring a hall and publicizing the event. The electorate's increasing dependence on television, radio, and other mass media for news and information has made these expensive modes of communication indispensible [indispensable] instruments of effective political speech.

The expenditure limitations contained in the Act represent substantial rather than merely theoretical restraints on the quantity and diversity of political speech. The $1,000 ceiling on spending "relative to a clearly identified candidate," ... would appear to exclude all citizens and groups except candidates, political parties, and the institutional press from any significant use of the most effective modes of communication. Although the Act's limitations on expenditures by campaign organizations and political parties provide substantially greater room for discussion and debate, they would have required restrictions in the scope of a number of past congressional and Presidential campaigns and would operate to constrain campaigning by candidates who raise sums in excess of the spending ceiling.

By contrast with a limitation upon expenditures for political expression, a limitation upon the amount that any one person or group may contribute to a candidate or political committee entails only a marginal restriction upon the contributor's ability to engage in free communication. A contribution serves as a general expression of support for the candidate and his views, but does not communicate the underlying basis for the support. The quantity of communication by the contributor does not increase perceptibly with the size of his contribution, since the expression rests solely on the undifferentiated, symbolic act of contributing. At most, the size of the contribution provides a very rough index of the intensity of the contributor's support for the candidate or campaign organization thus involves little direct restraint on his political communication, for it permits the symbolic expression of support evidenced by a contribution but does not in any way infringe the contributor's freedom to discuss candidates and issues. While contributions may result in political expression if spent by a candidate or an association to present views to the voters, the transformation of contributions into political debate involves speech by someone other than the contributor.

Given the important role of contributions in financing political campaigns, contribution restrictions could have a severe impact on political dialogue if the limitations prevented candidates and political committees from amassing the resources necessary for effective advocacy. There is no indication, however, that the contribution limitations imposed by the Act would have any dramatic adverse effect on the funding of campaigns and political associations. The overall effect of the Act's contribution ceilings is merely to require candidates and political committees to raise funds from a greater number of persons and to compel people who would otherwise contribute amounts greater than the statutory limits to expend such funds on direct political expression, rather than to reduce the total amount of money potentially available to promote political expression.

The Act's contribution and expenditure limitations also impinge on protected associational freedoms. Making a contribution, like joining a political party, serves to affiliate a person with a candidate. In addition, it enables like-minded persons to pool their resources in furtherance of common political goals. The Act's contribution ceilings thus limit one important means of associating with a candidate or committee, but leave the contributor free to become a member of any political association and to assist personally in the association's efforts on behalf of candidates. And the Act's contribution limitations permit associations and candidates to aggregate large sums of money to promote effective advocacy. By contrast, the Act's $1,000 limitation on independent expenditures "relative to a clearly identified candidate" precludes most associations from effectively amplifying the voice of their adherents, the original basis for the recognition of First Amendment protection of the freedom of association. . . .

In sum, although the Act's contribution and expenditure limitations both implicate fundamental First Amendment interests, its expenditure ceilings impose significantly more severe restrictions on protected freedoms of political expression and association than do its limitations on financial contributions.

B. Contribution Limitations

1. The $1,000 Limitation on Contributions by Individuals and Groups to Candidates and Authorized Campaign Committees

Section 608(b) provides, with certain limited exceptions, that "no person shall make contributions to any candidate with respect to any election for federal office which, in the aggregate, exceeds $1,000." The statute defines person broadly to include "an individual, partnership, committee, association, corporation, or any other organization or group of persons." ... The limitation reaches a gift, subscription, loan, advance, deposit of anything of value, or promise to give a contribution, made for the purpose of influencing a primary election, a Presidential preference primary, or a general election for any federal office.... The $1,000 ceiling applies regardless of whether the contribution is given to the candidate, to a committee authorized in writing by the candidate to accept contributions on his behalf, or indirectly via earmarked gifts passed through an intermediary to the candidate.... The restriction applies to aggregate amounts contributed to the candidate for each election—with primaries, runoff elections, and general elections counted separately and all Presidential primaries held in any calendar year treated together as a single election campaign.... .

Appellants contend that the $1,000 contribution ceiling unjustifiably burdens First Amendment freedoms, employs overbroad dollar limits, and discriminates against candidates opposing incumbent officeholders and against minor-party candidates in violation of the Fifth Amendment. We address each of these claims of invalidity in turn.

(a)

... [T]he primary First Amendment problem raised by the Act's contribution limitations is their restriction of one aspect of the contributor's freedom of political association. The Court's decisions involving associational freedoms establish that the right of association is a "basic constitutional freedom" that is closely allied to freedom of speech and a right which, like free speech, lies at the foundation of a free society.... In view of the fundamental nature of the right

to associate, governmental "action which may have the effect of curtailing the freedom to associate is subject to the closest scrutiny." *NAACP v. Alabama, supra.*... Yet, it is clear that "[n]either the right to associate nor the right to participate in political activities is absolute...." *Civil Service Comm'n v. Letter Carriers* ... (1973). Even a " 'significant interference' with protected rights of political association" may be sustained if the State demonstrates a sufficiently important interest and employs means closely drawn to avoid unnecessary abridgment of associational freedoms....

Appellees argue that the Act's restrictions on large campaign contributions are justified by three governmental interests. According to the parties and *amici*, the primary interest served by the limitations and, indeed, by the Act as a whole, is the prevention of corruption and the appearance of corruption spawned by the real or imagined coercive influence of large financial contributions on candidates' positions and on their actions if elected to office. Two "ancillary" interests underlying the Act are also allegedly furthered by the $1,000 limits on contributions. First, the limits serve to mute the voices of affluent persons and groups in the election process and thereby to equalize the relative ability of all citizens to affect the outcome of elections. Second, it is argued, the ceilings may to some extent act as a brake on the skyrocketing cost of political campaigns and thereby serve to open the political system more widely to candidates without access to sources of large amounts of money.

It is unnecessary to look beyond the Act's primary purpose ... in order to find a constitutionally sufficient justification for the $1,000 contribution limitation. Under a system of private financing of elections, a candidate lacking immense personal or family wealth must depend on financial contributions from others to provide the resources necessary to conduct a successful campaign. The increasing importance of the communications media and sophisticated mass mailing and polling operations to effective campaigning make the raising of large sums of money an ever more essential ingredient of an effective candidacy. To the extent that large contributions are given to secure political *quid pro quos* from current and potential office holders, the integrity of our system of representative democracy is undermined. Although the scope of such pernicious practices can never be reliably ascertained, the deeply disturbing examples surfacing after the 1972 election demonstrate that the problem is not an illusory one.

Of almost equal concern as the danger of actual *quid pro quo* arrangements is the impact of the appearance of corruption stemming from public awareness of the opportunities for abuse inherent in a regime of large individual financial contributions. . . .

Appellants contend that the contribution limitations must be invalidated because bribery laws and narrowly-drawn disclosure requirements constitute a less restrictive means of dealing with "proven and suspected *quid pro quo* arrangements." But laws making criminal the giving and taking of bribes deal with only the most blatant and specific attempts of those with money to influence governmental action. And while disclosure requirements serve the many salutary purposes discussed elsewhere in this option, Congress was surely entitled to conclude that disclosure was only a partial measure, and that contribution ceilings were a necessary legislative concomitant to deal with the reality or appearance of corruption inherent in a system permitting unlimited financial contributions, even when the identities of the contributors and the amounts of their contributions are fully disclosed.

The Act's $1,000 contribution limitation focuses precisely on the problem of large campaign contributions—the narrow aspect of political association where the actuality and potential for corruption have been identified—while leaving persons free to engage in independent political expression, to associate actively through volunteering their services, and to assist to a limited but nonetheless substantial extent in supporting candidates and committees with financial resources. Significantly, the Act's contribution limitations in themselves do not undermine to any material degree the potential for robust and effective discussion of candidates and campaign issues by individual citizens, associations, the institutional press, candidates, and political parties.

We find that, under the rigorous standard of review established by our prior decisions, the weighty interests served by restricting the size of financial contributions to political candidates are sufficient to justify the limited effect upon First Amendment freedoms caused by the $1,000 contribution ceiling.

(b)

Appellants' first overbreadth challenge to the contribution ceilings rests on the proposition that most large contributors do not seek improper influence over a candidate's position or an officeholder's action. Although the truth of that proposition may be assumed, it does not undercut the validity of the $1,000 contribution limitation. Not only is it difficult to isolate suspect contributions but, more importantly, Congress was justified in concluding that the interest in safeguarding against the appearance of impropriety requires that the opportunity for abuse inherent in the process of raising large monetary contributions be eliminated.

A second, related overbreadth claim is that the $1,000 restriction is unrealistically low because much more than that amount would still not be enough to enable an unscrupulous contributor to exercise improper influence over a candidate or officeholder, especially in campaigns for statewide or national office. While the contribution limitation provisions might well have been structured to take account of the graduated expenditure limitations for House, Senate and Presidential campaigns, Congress' failure to engage in such fine tuning does not invalidate the legislation. . . .

(c)

Apart from these First Amendment concerns, appellants argue that the contribution limitations work such an invidious discrimination between incumbents and challengers that the statutory provisions must be declared unconstitutional on their face. In considering this contention, it is important at the onset to note that the Act applies the same limitations on contributions to all candidates regardless of their present occupations, ideological views, or party affiliations. Absent record evidence of invidious discrimination against challengers as a class, a court should generally be hesitant to invalidate legislation which on its face imposes evenhanded restrictions. . . .

There is no such evidence to support the claim that the contribution limitations in themselves discriminate against major-party challengers to incumbents. Challengers can and often do defeat incumbents in federal elections. . . .

. . . The charge of discrimination against minor-party and independent candidates is more troubling, but the record provides no basis for concluding that the Act invidiously disadvantages such candidates. As noted above, the Act on its face treats all candidates equally with regard to contribution limitations. And the restriction would appear to benefit minor-party and independent candidates relative to their major-party opponents because major-party candidates receive far more money in large contributions. . . .

In view of these considerations, we conclude that the impact of the Act's $1,000 contribution limitation on major-party challengers and on minor-party candidates does not render the provision unconstitutional on its face.

2. The $5,000 Limitation on Contributions by Political Committees

Section 608(b)(2) of Title 18 permits certain committees, designated as "political committees," to contribute up to $5,000 to any candidate with respect to any election for federal office. In order to qualify for the higher contribution ceiling, a group must have been registered with the Commission as a political committee . . . for not less than 6 months, have received contributions from more than 50 persons and, except for state political party organizations, have contributed to five or more candidates for federal office. Appellants argue that these qualifications unconstitutionally discriminate against ad hoc organizations in favor of established interest groups and impermissibly burden free association. The argument is without merit. Rather than undermining freedom of association, the basic provision enhances the opportunity of bona fide groups to participate in the election process, and the registration, contribution, and candidate conditions serve the permissible purpose of preventing individuals from evading the applicable contribution limitations by labeling ·themselves committees.

3. Limitations on Volunteers' Incidental Expenses

The Act excludes from the definition of contribution "the value of services provided without compensation by individuals who volunteer a portion or all of their time on behalf of a candidate or political committee.". . . Certain expenses incurred by persons in providing volunteer services to a candidate are exempt from the $1,000 ceiling only to the extent that they do not exceed $500. . . .

If, as we have held, the basic contribution limitations are constitutionally valid, then surely these provisions are a constitutionally acceptable accommodation of Congress' valid interest in encouraging citizen participation in political campaigns while continuing to guard against the corrupting potential of large financial contributions to candidates. The expenditure of resources at the candidate's direction for a fundraising event at a volunteer's residence or the provision of in-kind assistance in the form of food or beverages to be resold to raise funds or consumed by the participants in such an event provides material financial assistance to a candidate.... Treating these expenses as contributions when made to the candidate's campaign or at the direction of the candidate or his staff forecloses an avenue of abuse without limiting actions voluntarily undertaken by citizens independently of a candidate's campaign.

4. The $25,000 Limitation on Total Contributions During any Calendar Year

In addition to the $1,000 limitation on the nonexempt contributions that an individual may make to a particular candidate for any single election, the Act contains an overall $25,000 limitation on total contributions by an individual during any calendar year.... The overall $25,000 ceiling does impose an ultimate restriction upon the number of candidates and committees with which an individual may associate himself by means of financial support. But this quite modest restraint upon protected political activity serves to prevent evasion of the $1,000 contribution limitation by a person who might otherwise contribute massive amounts of money to a particular candidate through the use of unearmarked contributions to political committees likely to contribute to that candidate, or huge contributions to the candidate's political party. The limited, additional re-

striction on associational freedom imposed by the overall ceiling is thus no more than a corollary of the basic individual contribution limitation that we have found to be constitutionally valid.

C. Expenditure Limitations

The Act's expenditure ceilings impose direct and substantial restraints on the quantity of political speech. The most drastic of the limitations restricts individuals and groups, including political parties that fail to place a candidate on the ballot, to an expenditure of $1,000 "relative to a clearly identified candidate during a calendar year." § 608(e)(1) Other expenditure ceilings limit spending by candidates ... their campaigns ... and political parties in connection with election campaigns.... It is clear that a primary effect of these expenditure limitations is to restrict the quantity of campaign speech by individuals, groups, and candidates. The restrictions, while neutral as to the ideas expressed, limit political expression "at the core of our electoral process and of First Amendment freedoms...." *Williams v. Rhodes* ... (1968).

1. The $1,000 Limitation on Expenditures "Relative to a Clearly Identified Candidate"

... The plan effect [of this limitation] is to prohibit all individuals, who are neither candidates nor owners of institutional press facilities, and all groups, except political parties and campaign organizations, from voicing their views "relative to a clearly identified candidate" through means that entail aggregate expenditures of more than $1,000 during a calendar year. The provision, for example, would make it a federal criminal offense for a person or association to place a single one-quarter page advertisement "relative to a clearly identified candidate" in a major metropolitan newspaper.

Before examining the interests advanced in support of [this] expenditure ceiling, consideration must be given to appellants' contention that the provision is unconstitutionally vague. . . .

. . . [I]n order to preserve the provision against invalidation on vagueness grounds, [this limitation] must be construed to apply only to expenditures for communications that in express terms advocate the election or defeat of a clearly identified candidate for federal office.

. . . We turn . . . to the basic First Amendment question—whether [this limitation], even as thus narrowly and explicitly construed, impermissibly burdens the constitutional right of free expression. . . .

. . . [T]he constitutionality of [this limitation] turns on whether the governmental interests advanced in its support satisfy the exacting scrutiny applicable to limitations on core First Amendment rights of political expression.

We find that the governmental interest in preventing corruption and the appearance of corruption is inadequate to justify [the] ceiling on independent expenditures. First, assuming *arguendo* that large independent expenditures pose the same dangers of actual or apparent *quid pro quo* arrangements as do large contributions, § 608(e)(1) does not provide an answer that sufficiently relates to the elimination of those dangers. Unlike the contribution limitations' total ban on the giving of large amounts of money to candidates, § 608(e)(1) prevents only some large expenditures. So long as persons and groups eschew expenditures that in express terms advocate the election or defeat of a clearly identified candidate, they are free to spend as much as they want to promote the candidate and his views. The exacting interpretation of the statutory language necessary to avoid unconstitutional vagueness thus undermines the limitation's effectiveness as a loophole-closing provision by facilitating circumvention by those

seeking to exert improper influence upon a candidate or officeholder. It would naively underestimate the ingenuity and resourcefulness of persons and groups desiring to buy influence to believe that they would have much difficulty devising expenditures that skirted the restriction on express advocacy of election or defeat but nevertheless benefited the candidate's campaign. Yet no substantial societal interest would be served by a loophole-closing provision designed to check corruption that permitted unscrupulous persons and organizations to expend unlimited sums of money in order to obtain improper influence over candidates for elective office. . . .

Second, quite apart from the shortcomings of § 608(e)(1) in preventing any abuses generated by large independent expenditures, the independent advocacy restricted by the provision does not presently appear to pose dangers of real or apparent corruption comparable to those identified with large campaign contributions. The parties defending § 608(e)(1) contend that it is necessary to prevent would-be contributors from avoiding the contribution limitations by the simple expedient of paying directly for media advertisements or for other portions of the candidate's campaign activities. They argue that expenditures controlled by or coordinated with the candidate and his campaign might well have virtually the same value to the candidate as a contribution and would pose similar dangers of abuse. Yet such controlled or coordinated expenditures are treated as contributions rather than expenditures under the Act. . . . Unlike contributions, such independent expenditures may well provide little assistance to the candidate's campaign and indeed may prove counterproductive. The absence of prearrangement and coordination of an expenditure with the candidate or his agent not only undermines the value of the expenditure to the candidate, but also alleviates the danger that expenditures will be given as a *quid pro quo* for improper commitments from the candidate. Rather than preventing circumvention of the contribution limitations, § 608(e)(1) severely restricts all independent advocacy despite its substantially diminished potential for abuse.

While the independent expenditure ceiling thus fails to serve any substantial governmental interest in stemming the reality or appearance of corruption in the electoral process, it heavily burdens core First Amendment expression.... Advocacy of the election or defeat of candidates for federal office is no less entitled to protection under the First Amendment than the discussion of political policy generally or advocacy of the passage or defeat of legislation.

It is argued, however, that the ancillary governmental interest in equalizing the relative ability of individuals and groups to influence the outcome of elections serves to justify the limitation on express advocacy of the election or defeat of candidates imposed by [the] expenditure ceiling. But the concept that government may restrict the speech of some elements of our society in order to enhance the relative voice of others is wholly foreign to the First Amendment.... The First Amendment's protection against governmental abridgement of free expression cannot properly be made to depend on a person's financial ability to engage in public discussion....

... For the reasons stated, we conclude that [the] independent expenditure limitation is unconstitutional under the First Amendment.

2. Limitation on Expenditures by Candidates from Personal or Family Resources

The Act also sets limits on expenditures by a candidate "from his personal funds, or the personal funds of his immediate family, in connection with his campaigns during any calendar year." ... These ceilings vary from $50,000 for

Presidential or Vice Presidential candidates to $35,000 for Senate candidates, and $25,000 for most candidates for the House of Representatives.

The ceiling on personal expenditure by candidates on their own behalf, like the limitations on independent expenditures ... imposes a substantial restraint on the ability of persons to engage in protected First Amendment expression. The candidate, no less than any other person, has a First Amendment right to engage in the discussion of public issues and vigorously and tirelessly to advocate his own election and the election of other candidates. Indeed, it is of particular importance that candidates have the unfettered opportunity to make their views known so that the electorate may intelligently evaluate the candidates' personal qualities and their positions on vital public issues before choosing among them on election day.... [The] ceiling on personal expenditures by a candidate in furtherance of his own candidacy thus clearly and directly interferes with constitutionally protected freedoms.

The primary governmental interest served by the Act—the prevention of actual and apparent corruption of the political process—does not support the limitation on the candidate's expenditure of his own personal funds.... Indeed, the use of personal funds reduces the candidate's dependence on outside contributions and thereby counteracts the coercive pressures and attendant risks of abuse to which the Act's contribution limitations are directed.

The ancillary interest in equalizing the relative financial resources of candidates competing for elective office ... is clearly not sufficient to justify the provision's infringement of fundamental First Amendment rights. First, the limitation may fail to promote financial equality among candidates. A candidate who spends less of his personal resources on his campaign may nonetheless outspend his rival as a result of more successful fundraising efforts.... Second, and more fundamentally, the First Amendment simply cannot tolerate ... [a] restriction upon the freedom of a candidate to speak without legislative limit on behalf of his own candidacy. We therefore hold that ... [the] restrictions on a candidate's personal expenditures is [sic] unconstitutional.

3. Limitations on Campaign Expenditures

Section 608 (c) of the Act places limitations on overall campaign expenditures by candidates seeking nomination for election and election to federal office. Presidential candidates may spend $10,000,000 in seeking nomination for office and an additional $20,000,000 in the general election campaign.... The ceiling on Senate campaigns is pegged to the size of the voting age population of the State with minimum dollar amounts applicable to campaigns in States with small populations. In Senate primary elections, the limit is the greater of eight cents multiplied by the voting age population of $100,000, and in the general election the limit is increased to 12 cents multiplied by the voting age population or $150,000.... The Act imposes blanket $70,000 limitations on both primary campaigns and general election campaigns for the House of Representatives with the exception that the Senate ceiling applies to campaigns in States entitled to only one Representative.... These ceilings are to be adjusted upwards at the beginning of each calendar year by the average percentage rise in the consumer price index for the 12 preceding months....

No governmental interest that has been suggested is sufficient to justify the restriction on the quantity of political expression imposed by § 608(c)'s campaign expenditure limitations. The major evil associated with rapidly increasing campaign expenditures is the danger of candidate dependence on large contributions. The interest in alle-viating the corrupting influence of large contributions is served by the Act's contribution limitations and disclosure provisions.... The Court of Appeal's assertion that the expenditure restrictions are necessary to reduce the incentive to circumvent direct contribution limits is not persuasive....

The interest in equalizing the financial resources of candidates competing for federal office is no more convincing a justification for restricting the scope of federal election campaigns. Given the limitation on the size of outside contributions, the financial resources available to a candidate's campaign, like the number of volunteers recruited, will normally vary with the size and intensity of the candidate's support....

The campaign expenditure ceilings appear to be designed primarily to serve the governmental interests in reducing the allegedly skyrocketing costs of political campaigns.... [T]he mere growth in the cost of federal election campaigns in and of itself provides no basis for governmental restrictions on the quantity of campaign spending and the resulting limitation on the scope of federal campaigns. The First Amendment denies government the power to determine that spending to promote one's political views is wasteful, excessive, or unwise....

For these reasons we hold that § 608(c) is constitutionally invalid.

In sum, the provisions of the Act that impose a $1,000 limitation on contributions to a single candidate, § 608(b)(1), a $5,000 limitation on contributions by a political committee to a single candidate, § 608(b)(2), and a $25,000 limitation on total contributions by an individual during any calendar year, § 608(b)(3), are constitutionally valid. These limitations along with the disclosure provisions, constitute the Act's primary weapons against the reality or appearance of improper influence stemming from the dependence of candidates on large campaign contributions.

The contribution ceilings thus serve the basic governmental interest in safeguarding the integrity of the electoral process without directly impinging upon the rights of individual citizens and candidates to engage in political debate and discussion. By contrast, the First Amendment requires the invalidation of the Act's independent expenditure ceiling, § 608(e)(1), its limitation on a candidate's expenditures from his own personal funds, § 608(a), and its ceilings on overall campaign expenditures, § 608(c). These provisions place substantial and direct restrictions on the ability of candidates, citizens, and associations to engage in protected political expression, restrictions that the First Amendment cannot tolerate.

II. Reporting and Disclosure Requirements

Unlike the limitations on contributions and expenditures, ... the disclosure requirements of the Act ... are not challenged by appellants as *per se* unconstitutional restrictions on the exercise of First Amendment freedoms of speech and association. Indeed, appellants argue that "narrowly drawn disclosure requirements are the proper solution to virtually all of the evils Congress sought to remedy." The particular requirements embodied in the Act are attacked as overbroad—both in their application to minor-party and independent candidates and in their extension to contributions as small as $10 or $100. Appellants also challenge the provision for disclosure by those who make independent contributions and expenditures....

... The Act presently under review replaced all prior disclosure laws. Its primary disclosure provisions impose reporting obligations on "political committees" and candidates. "Political committee" is defined ... as a group of persons that receives "contributions" or makes "expenditures" of over $1,000 in a calendar year. "Contributions" and "expenditures" are defined in lengthy parallel provisions similar to those ... discussed above. Both definitions focus on the use of money or other objects of value "for the purpose of influencing" the nomination or election of any person to federal office....

Each political committee is required to register with the Commission ... and to keep detailed records of both contributions and expenditures.... These records are required to include the name and address of everyone making a contribution in excess of $10, along with the date and amount of the contribution. If a person's contributions aggregate more than $100, his occupation and principal place of business are also to be included.... These files are subject to periodic audits and field investigations by the Commission....

Each committee and each candidate also is required to file quarterly reports.... The reports are to contain detailed financial information, including the full name, mailing address, occupation, and principal place of business of each person who has contributed over $100 in a calendar year, as well as the amount and date of the contributions.... They are to be made available by the Commission "for public inspection and copying."... Every candidate for federal office is required to designate a "principal campaign committee," which is to receive reports of contributions and expenditures made on the candidate's behalf from other political committees and to compile and file these reports, together with its own statements, with the Commission....

Every individual or group, other than a political committee or candidate, who makes "contributions" or "expenditures" of over $100 in a calendar year "other than by contribution to a political committee or a candidate" is required to file a statement with the Commission.... Any violation of these record-keeping and reporting provisions is punishable by a fine of not more than $1,000 or a prison term of not more than a year, or both. ...

A. General Principles

Unlike the overall limitations on contributions and expenditures, the disclosure requirements impose no ceiling on campaign-related activities. But we have repeatedly found that compelled disclosure, in itself, can seriously infringe on privacy of association and belief guaranteed by the First Amendment....

We long have recognized that significant encroachments on First Amendment rights of the sort that compelled disclosure imposes cannot be justified by a mere showing of some legitimate governmental interest.

... [W]e have required that the subordinating interests of the State must survive exacting scrutiny. We also have insisted that there be a "relevant correlation" or "substantial relation" between the governmental interest and the information required to be disclosed....

... [C]ompelled disclosure has the potential for substantially infringing the exercise of First Amendment rights. But we have acknowledged that there are governmental interests sufficiently important to outweigh the possibility of infringement, particularly when the "free functioning of our national institutions" is involved....

The governmental interests sought to be vindicated by the disclosure requirements are of this magnitude. They fall into three categories. First, disclosure provides the electorate with information "as to where political campaign money comes from and how it is spent by the candidate" in order to aid the voters in evaluating those who seek federal office....

Second, disclosure requirements deter actual corruption and avoid the ap-

pearance of corruption by exposing large contributions and expenditures to the light of publicity. This exposure may discourage those who would use money for improper purposes either before or after the election....

Third, and not least significant, record-keeping, reporting, and disclosure requirements are an essential means of gathering the data necessary to detect violations of the contribution limitations described above.

The disclosure requirements, as a general matter, directly serve substantial governmental interests. In determining whether these interests are sufficient to justify the requirements we must look to the extent of the burden that they place on individual rights.

It is undoubtedly true that public disclosure of contributions to candidates and political parties will deter some individuals who otherwise might contribute. In some instances, disclosure may even expose contributors to harassment or retaliation. These are not insignificant burdens on individual rights, and they must be weighed carefully against the interests which Congress has sought to promote by this legislation.... [W]e ... agree with appellants' concession that disclosure requirements—certainly in most applications—appear to be the least restrictive means of curbing the evils of campaign ignorance and corruption that Congress found to exist. Appellants argue, however, that the balance tips against disclosure when it is required of contributors to certain parties and candidates. We turn now to this contention.

B. Application to Minor Parties and Independents

Appellants contend that the Act's requirements are overbroad insofar as they apply to contributions to minor parties and independent candidates because the governmental interest in this information is minimal and the danger of significant infringement on First Amendment rights is greatly increased.

1. Requisite Factual Showing

... It is true that the governmental interest in disclosure is diminished when the contribution in question is made to a minor party with little chance of winning an election. As minor parties usually represent definite and publicized viewpoints, there may be less need to inform the voters of the interests that specific candidates represent....

... But a minor party sometimes can play a significant role in an election. Even when a minor-party candidate has little or no chance of winning, he may be encouraged by major-party interests in order to divert votes from other major-party contenders.

We are not unmindful that the damage done by disclosure to the associational interests of the minor parties and their members and to supporters of independents could be significant.... In some instances fears of reprisal may deter contributions to the point where the movement cannot survive. The public interest also suffers if that result comes to pass, for there is a consequent reduction in the free circulation of ideas both within and without the political arena.

There could well be a case ... where the threat to the exercise of First Amendment rights is so serious and the state interest furthered by disclosure so insubstantial that the Act's requirements cannot be constitutionally applied. But no appellant in this case has tendered record evidence of [this] sort....

2. Blanket Exemption

Appellants agree that "the record here does not reflect the kind of focused and insistent harassment of contributors and members that existed in the NAACP cases." They argue, however, that a blanket exemption for minor parties is necessary lest irreparable injury be done before the required evidence can be gathered....

... We recognize that unduly strict requirements of proof could impose a heavy burden, but it does not follow that a blanket exemption for minor parties is necessary. Minor parties must be allowed sufficient flexibility in the proof of injury to assure a fair consideration of their claim. The evidence offered need show only a reasonable probability that the compelled disclosure of a party's contributors' names will subject them to threats, harassment or reprisals from either government officials or private parties....

C. Section 434 (e)

Section 434(e) requires "[e]very person (other than a political committee or candidate) who makes contributions or expenditures" aggregating over $100 in a calendar year "other than by contribution to a political committee or candidate" to file a statement with the Commission. Unlike the other disclosure provisions, this section does not seek the contribution list of any association. Instead, it requires direct disclosure of what an individual or group contributes or spends.

In considering this provision we must apply the same strict standard of scrutiny, for the right of associational privacy developed in *Alabama* derives from the rights of the organization's members to advocate their personal points of view in the most effective way....

Appellants attack § 434(e) as a direct intrusion on privacy of belief, in violation of *Talley v. California* ... (1960), and as imposing "very real, practical burdens ... certain to deter individuals from making expenditures for their independent political speech" analogous to those held to be impermissible in *Thomas v. Collins* ... (1945).

1. The Role of § 434(e)

... Section 434(e) is part of Congress' effort to achieve "total disclosure" by reaching "every kind of political activity" in order to insure that the voters are fully informed and to achieve through publicity the maximum deterrence to corruption and undue influence possible. The provision is responsive to the legitimate fear that efforts would be made, as they had been in the past, to avoid the disclosure requirements by routing financial support of candidates through avenues not explicitly covered by the general provisions of the Act.

2. Vagueness Problems

In its effort to be all-inclusive, however, the provision raises serious problems of vagueness, particularly treacherous where, as here, the violation of its terms carries criminal penalties and fear of incurring these sanctions may deter those who seek to exercise protected First Amendment rights.

Section 434 (e) applies to "[e]very person . . . who makes contributions or expenditures." "Contributions" and "expenditures" are defined in parallel provisions in terms of the use of money or other valuable assets "for the purpose of . . . influencing" the nomination or election of candidates for federal office. It is the ambiguity of this phrase that poses constitutional problems. . . .

. . . To insure that the reach of § 434(e) is not impermissibly broad, we construe "expenditure" for purposes of that section in the same way we construed the terms of § 608(e)—to reach only funds used for communications that expressly advocate the election or defeat of a clearly identified candidate. This reading is directed precisely to that spending that is unambiguously related to the campaign of a particular federal candidate.

In summary, § 434(e) as construed imposes independent reporting requirements on individuals and groups that are not candidates or political committees only in the following circumstances: (1) when they make contributions earmarked for political purposes or authorized or requested by a candidate or his agent, to some person other

than a candidate or political committee, and (2) when they make an expenditure for a communication that expressly advocates the election or defeat of a clearly identified candidate.

Unlike § 608(e)(1), § 434(e) as construed bears a sufficient relationship to a substantial governmental interest. . . . It goes beyond the general disclosure requirements to shed the light of publicity on spending that is unambiguously campaign-related but would not otherwise be reported because it takes the form of independent expenditures or of contributions to an individual or group not itself required to report the names of its contributors. . . .

. . . [T]he disclosure requirement is narrowly limited to those situations where the information sought has a substantial connection with the governmental interests sought to be advanced. . . . The burden imposed by § 434(e) is no prior restraint, but a reasonable and minimally restrictive method of furthering First Amendment values by opening the basic processes of our federal election system to public view.

D. Thresholds

Appellants' third contention, based on alleged overbreadth, is that the monetary thresholds in the record-keeping and reporting provisions lack a substantial nexus with the claimed governmental interests, for the amounts involved are too low even to attract the attention of the candidate, much less have a corrupting influence.

The provisions contain two thresholds. Records are to be kept by political committees of the names and addresses of those who make contributions in excess of $10 . . . and these records are subject to Commission audit. . . . If a person's contributions to a committee or candidate aggregate more than $100, his name and address, as well as his occupation and principal place of business, are to be included in reports filed by committees and candidates with the Commission . . . and made available for public inspection. . . .

. . . The $10 and $100 thresholds are indeed low. . . . These strict requirements may well discourage participation by some citizens in the political process, a result that Congress hardly could have intended. Indeed, there is little in the legislative history to indicate that Congress focused carefully on the appropriate level at which to require recording and disclosure. Rather, it seems merely to have adopted the thresholds existing in similar disclosure laws since 1910. But we cannot require Congress to establish that it has chosen the highest reasonable threshold. . . .

We are mindful that disclosure serves informational functions, as well as the prevention of corruption and the enforcement of the contribution limitations. Congress is not required to set a threshold that is tailored only to the latter goals. . . .

. . . [T]here is no warrant for assuming that public disclosure of contributions between $10 and $100 is authorized by the Act. Accordingly, we do not reach the question whether information concerning gifts of this size can be made available to the public without trespassing impermissibly on First Amendment rights. . . .

In summary, we find no constitutional infirmities in the record-keeping, reporting, and disclosure provisions of the Act.

III. Public Financing of Presidential Election Campaigns

A series of statutes for the public financing of Presidential election campaigns produced the scheme now found in 26 U.S.C. § 6096 and Subtitle H, §§ 9001-9042, of the Internal Revenue Code of 1954. Both the District Court . . . and the Court of Appeals . . . sustained Subtitle H against a constitu-

tional attack. Appellants renew their challenge here, contending that the legislation violates the First and Fifth Amendments. We find no merit in their claims and affirm.

A. Summary of Subtitle H

Section 9006 establishes a Presidential Election Campaign Fund, financed from general revenues in the aggregate amount designated by individual taxpayers, under § 6096, who on their income tax returns may authorize payment to the Fund of one dollar of their tax liability in the case of an individual return or two dollars in the case of a joint return. The Fund consists of three separate accounts to finance (1) party nominating conventions, . . . (2) general election campaigns, . . . and (3) primary campaigns. . . .

Chapter 95 of Title 26, which concerns financing of party nominating conventions and general election campaigns, distinguishes among "major," "minor," and "new" parties. A major party is defined as a party whose candidate for President in the most recent election received 25% or more of the popular vote. . . . A minor party is defined as a party whose candidate received at least 5% but less than 25% of the vote at the most recent election. . . . All other parties are new parties, . . . including both newly created parties and those receiving less than 5% of the vote in the last election.

Major parties are entitled to $2,000,000 to defray their national committee Presidential nominating convention expenses, must limit total expenditures to that amount . . . and they may not use any of this money to benefit a particular candidate or delegate. . . . A minor party receives a portion of the major-party entitlement determined by the ratio of the votes received by the party's candidate in the last election to the average of the votes received by the major-parties' candidates. . . . The amounts given to the parties and the expenditure limit are adjusted for inflation, using 1974 as the base year.... No financing is provided for new parties, nor is there any express provision for financing independent candidates or parties not holding a convention.

For expenses in the general election campaign, § 9004(a)(1) entitles each major-party candidate to $20,000,000. This amount is also adjusted for inflation.... To be eligible for funds the candidate must pledge not to incur expenses in excess of the entitlement under § 9004(a)(1) and not to accept private contributions except to the extent that the fund is insufficient to provide the full entitlement.... Minor-party candidates are also entitled to funding, again based on the ratio of the vote received by the party's candidates.... Minor-party candidates must certify that they will not incur campaign expenses in excess of the major-party entitlement and that they will accept private contributions only to the extent needed to make up the difference between that amount and the public funding grant.... New-party candidates receive no money prior to the general election, but any candidate receiving 5% or more of the popular vote in the election is entitled to postelection payments according to the formula applicable to minor-party candidates.... Similarly, minor-party candidates are entitled to post-election funds if they receive a greater percentage of the average major-party vote than their party's candidate did in the preceding election; the amount of such payments is the difference between the entitlement based on the preceding election and that based on the actual vote in the current election.... A further eligibility requirement for minor- and new-party candidates is that the candidate's name must appear on the ballot, or electors pledged to the candidate must be on the ballot, in at least 10 States....

Chapter 96 establishes a third account in the Fund, the Presidential Primary Matching Payment Account.... This funding is intended to aid campaigns by candidates seeking Presidential nomination "by a political party," ... in "primary elections" ... The threshold eligibility requirement is that the candidate raise at least $5,000 in each of 20 States, counting only the first $250 from each person contributing to the candidate.... In addition, the candidate must agree to abide by the spending limits.... Funding is provided according to a matching formula: each qualified candidate is entitled to a sum equal to the total private contributions received, disregarding contributions from any person to the extent that total contributions to the candidate by that person exceed $250.... Payments to any candidate under Chapter 96 may not exceed 50% of the overall expenditure ceiling accepted by the candidate....

B. Constitutionality of Subtitle H

Appellants argue that Subtitle H is invalid (1) as "contrary to the 'general welfare,'" Art. I, § 8, (2) because any scheme of public financing of election campaigns is inconsistent with the First Amendment, and (3) because Subtitle H invidiously discriminates against certain interests in violation of the Due Process Clause of the Fifth Amendment. We find no merit in these contentions.

Appellants' "general welfare" contention erroneously treats the General Welfare Clause as a limitation upon congressional power. It is rather a grant of power, the scope of which is quite expansive, particularly in view of the enlargement of power by the Necessary and Proper Clause.... Congress has power to regulate Presidential elections and primaries, ... and public financing of Presidential elections as a means to reform the electoral process was clearly a choice within the granted power. It is for Congress to decide which expenditures will promote the general welfare. "[T]he power of Congress to authorize expenditure of public moneys for public purposes is not limited by the direct grants of legislative power found in the Constitution." *United States v. Butler* ... (1936). ... Any limitations upon the exercise of that granted power must be found elsewhere in the Constitution. In this case, Congress was legislating for the "general welfare"—to reduce the deleterious influence of large contributions on our political process, to facilitate communication by candidates with the electorate, and to free candidates from the rigors of fundraising. ... Whether the chosen means appear "bad," "unwise," or "unworkable" to us is irrelevant; Congress has concluded that the means are "necessary and proper" to promote the general welfare, and we thus decline to find this legislation without the grant of power in Art. I, § 8.

Appellants' challenge to the dollar check-off provision (§ 6096) fails for the same reason. They maintain that Congress is required to permit taxpayers to designate particular candidates or parties as recipients of their money. But the appropriation to the Fund in § 9006 is like any other appropriation from the general revenue except that its amount is determined by reference to the aggregate of the one- and two-dollar authorization on taxpayers' income tax returns. ...

Appellants next argue that "by analogy" to the religion clauses of the First Amendment public financing of election campaigns, however meritorious, violates the First Amendment. ... But the analogy is patently inapplicable to our issue here. Although "Congress shall make no law ... abridging the freedom of speech, or of the press," Subtitle H is a congressional effort, not to abridge, restrict, or censor speech, but rather to use public money to facilitate and enlarge public discussion and participation in the electoral process, goals vital to a self-governing people. ... Appellants argue, however, that as constructed public financing invidiously discriminates in violation of the Fifth Amendment. We turn therefore to that argument. ...

... [T]he denial of public financing to some Presidential candidates is not restrictive of voters' rights and less restrictive of candidates'. Subtitle H does not prevent any candidate from getting on the ballot or any voter from casting a vote for the candidate of his choice; the inability, if any, of minority-party candidates to wage effective campaigns will derive not from lack of public funding but from their inability to raise private contributions. Any disadvantages suffered by operation of the eligibility formulae under Subtitle H is thus limited to the claimed denial of the enhancement of opportunity to communicate with the electorate that the formula affords eligible candidates. But eligible candidates suffer a countervailing denial. As we more fully develop later, acceptance of public financing entails voluntary acceptance of an expenditure ceiling. Noneligible candidates are not subject to that limitation. Accordingly, we conclude that public financing is generally less restrictive of access to the electoral process than the ballot-access regulations dealt with in prior cases. In any event, Congress enacted Subtitle H in furtherance of sufficiently important governmental interests and has not unfairly or unnecessarily burdened the political opportunity of any party or candidate.

... [P]ublic financing as a means of eliminating the improper influence of large private contributions furthers a significant governmental interest. ... In addition, ... Congress properly regarded public financing as an appropriate means of relieving major-party Presidential candidates from the rigors of soliciting private contributions. ...

Congress' interest in not funding hopeless candidacies with large sums of public money ... necessarily justified the withholding of public assistance from candidates without significant public support....

1. General Election Campaign Financing

Appellants insist that Chapter 95 falls short of the constitutional requirement in that the provisions provide larger, and equal, sums to candidates of major parties, use prior vote levels as the sole criterion for pre-election funding, limit new-party candidates to post-election funds, and deny any funds to candidates of parties receiving less than 5% of the vote. These provisions, it is argued, are fatal to the validity of the scheme, because they work invidious discrimination against minor and new parties in violation of the Fifth Amendment. We disagree....

... Since the Presidential elections of 1856 and 1860, when the Whigs were replaced as a major party by the Republicans, no third party has posed a credible threat to the two major parties in Presidential elections. Third parties have been completely incapable of matching the major parties' ability to raise money and win elections. Congress was of course aware of this fact of American life, and thus was justified in providing both major parties full funding and all other parties only a percentage of the major-party entitlement. Identical treatment of all parties, on the other hand, "would not only make it easy to raid the United States Treasury, it would also artificially foster the proliferation of splinter parties."...

Furthermore, appellants have made no showing that the election funding plan disadvantages nonmajor parties by operating to reduce their strength below that attained without any public financing.... Thus, we conclude that the general election funding system does not work an invidious discrimination against candidates of nonmajor parties.

Appellants challenge reliance on the vote in past elections as the basis for determining eligibility. That challenge is foreclosed, however, by our holding in *Jenness v. Fortson* ... (1971) that popular vote totals in the last election are a proper measure of public support....

... Any risk of harm to minority interests is speculative due to our present lack of knowledge of the practical effects of public financing and cannot overcome the force of the governmental interests against use of public money to foster frivolous candidacies, create a system of splintered parties, and encourage unrestrained factionalism....

... Plainly campaigns can be successfully carried out by means other than public financing; they have been up to this date, and this avenue is still open to all candidates. And, after all, the important achievements of minority political groups in furthering the development of American democracy were accomplished without the help of public funds. Thus, the limited participation or nonparticipation of nonmajor parties or candidates in public funding does not unconstitutionally disadvantage them....

... Finally, appellants challenge the validity of the 5% threshold requirement for general election funding. They argue that, since most state regulations governing ballot access have threshold requirements well below 5%, and because in their view the 5% requirement here is actually stricter than that upheld in *Jenness* v. *Fortson* ... the requirement is unreasonable.... [T]he choice of the percentage requirement that best accommodates the competing interests involved was for Congress to make.... Without any doubt a range of formulations would sufficiently protect the public fisc and not foster factionalism, and also recognize the public interest in the fluidity of our political affairs. We cannot say that Congress' choice falls without the permissible range.

2. Nominating Convention Financing

The foregoing analysis and reasoning sustaining general election funding apply in large part to convention funding under Chapter 95 and suffices to support our rejection of appellants' challenge to that provision. Funding of party conventions has increasingly been derived from large private contributions to individual candidates. The expenditure limitations on major parties participating in public financing enhance the ability of nonmajor parties to increase their spending relative to the major parties; further, in soliciting private contributions to finance conventions, parties are not subject to the $1,000 contribution limit pertaining to candidates. We therefore conclude that appellants' constitutional challenge to the provisions for funding nominating conventions must also be rejected.

3. Primary Election Campaign Financing

Appellants' final challenge is to the constitutionality of Chapter 96, which provides funding of primary campaigns. They contend that these provisions are constitutionally invalid (1) because they do not provide funds for candidates not running in party primaries and (2) because the eligibility formula actually increases the influence of money on the electoral process. In not providing assistance to candidates who do not enter party primaries, Congress has merely chosen to limit at this time the reach of the reforms encompassed in Chapter 96. This Congress could do without constituting the reform a constitutionally invidious discrimination. . . .

. . . We also reject as without merit appellants' argument that the matching formula favors wealthy voters and candidates. The thrust of the legislation is to reduce financial barriers and to enhance the importance of smaller contributions. . . . In addition, one eligibility requirement for matching funds is acceptance of an expenditure ceiling, and candidates with little fundraising

ability will be able to increase their spending relative to candidates capable of raising large amounts in private funds.

For the reasons stated, we reject appellants' claims that Subtitle H is facially unconstitutional.

C. Severability

The only remaining issue is whether our holdings invalidating §§ 608(a), 608(c), and 608(e)(1) require the conclusion that Subtitle H is unconstitutional. There is of course a relationship between the spending limits in 18 U.S.C. § 608(c) and the public financing provisions; the expenditure limits accepted by a candidate to be eligible for public funding are identical to the limits in § 608(c). But we have no difficulty in concluding that Subtitle H is severable. . . . Our discussion . . . leaves no doubt that the value of public financing is not dependent on the existence of a generally applicable expenditure limit. We therefore hold Subtitle H severable from those portions of the legislation today held constitutionally infirm.

IV. The Federal Election Commission

The 1974 Amendments to the Act created an eight-member Federal Election Commission, and vest in it primary and substantial responsibility for administering and enforcing the Act. The question that we address in this portion of the opinion is whether, in view of the manner in which a majority of its members are appointed, the Commission may under the Constitution exercise the powers conferred upon it. . . .

Chapter 14 of Title 2 makes the Commission the principal repository of the numerous reports and statements which are required by that Chapter to be filed by those engaging in the regulated political activities. Its duties . . . with respect to these reports and statements include filing and indexing, making them available for public inspection, preservation, and auditing and field investigations. It is directed to "serve as a national clearinghouse for information in respect to the administration of elections."...

Beyond these record-keeping, disclosure, and investigative functions, however, the Commission is given extensive rule-making and adjudicative powers....

The Commission's enforcement power is both direct and wide-ranging....

...The body in which this authority is reposed consists of eight members. The Secretary of the Senate and the Clerk of the House of Representatives are *ex officio* members of the Commission without the right to vote. Two members are appointed by the President *pro tempore* of the Senate "upon the recommendations of the majority leader of the Senate and the minority leader of the Senate." Two more are to be appointed by the Speaker of the House of Representatives, likewise upon the recommendations of its respective majority and minority leaders. The remaining two members are appointed by the President. Each of the six voting members of the Commission must be confirmed by the majority of both Houses of Congress, and each of the three appointing authorities is forbidden to choose both of their appointees from the same political party....

A. Ripeness

...[I]n order to decide the basic question whether the Act's provision for appointment of the members of the Commission violates the Constitution, we believe we are warranted in considering all of those aspects of the Commission's authority which have been presented by [the Court of Appeals' certified questions although many of the Commission's functions have not yet been exercised]....

B. The Merits

Appellants urge that since Congress has given the Commission wide-range rule-making and enforcement powers with respect to the substantive provisions of the Act, Congress is precluded under the principle of separation of powers from vesting in itself the authority to appoint those who will exercise such authority. Their argument is based on the language of Art. II, § 2, cl. 2, of the Constitution, which provides in pertinent part as follows:

> [The President] shall nominate, and by and with the Advice and Consent of the Senate, shall appoint ... all other Officers of the United States, whose Appointments are not herein otherwise provided for, and which shall be established by Law; but the Congress may by Law vest the Appointment of such inferior Officers, as they think proper, in the President alone, in the Courts of Law, or in the Heads of Departments.

Appellants' argument is that this provision is the exclusive method by which those charged with executing the laws of the United States may be chosen. Congress, they assert, cannot have it both ways. If the legislature wishes the Commission to exercise all of the conferred powers, then its members are in fact "Officers of the United States" and must be appointed under the Appointments Clause. But if Congress insists upon retaining the power to appoint, then the members of the Commission may not discharge those many functions of the Commission which can be performed only by "Officers of the United States," as that term must be construed within the doctrine of separation of powers.

Appellee Federal Election Commission and *amici* in support of the Commission urge that the Framers of the Constitution, while mindful of the need for checks and balances among the three branches of the National Government, had no intention of denying to the Legislative Branch authority to appoint its own officers. Congress, either under the Appointments Clause or under its grants of substantive legislative authority and the Necessary and Proper Clause in Art. I, is in their view empowered to provide for the appointment to the Commission in the manner which it did because the Commission is performing "appropriate legislative functions.". . .

1. Separation of Powers

. . . Our inquiry of necessity touches upon the fundamental principles of the Government established by the Framers of the Constitution, and all litigants and all of the courts which have addressed themselves to the matter start on common ground in the recognition of the intent of the Framers that the powers of the three great branches of the National Government be largely separate from one another.

James Madison, writing in the *Federalist* No. 47, defended the work of the Framers against the charge that these three governmental powers were not *entirely* separate from one another in the proposed Constitution. . . .

Yet it is also clear from the provisions of the Constitution itself, and from the Federalist Papers, that the Constitution by no means contemplates total separation of each of these three essential branches of Government. The President is a participant in the law-making process by virtue of his authority to veto bills enacted by Congress. The Senate is a participant in the appointive process by virtue of its authority to refuse to confirm persons nominated to office by the President. . . .

. . . Mr. Justice Jackson, concurring in the opinion and the judgment of the Court in *Youngstown Co.* v. *Sawyer* . . . (1952), succinctly characterized this understanding:

> While the Constitution diffuses power the better to secure liberty, it also contemplates that practice will integrate the dispersed powers into a workable government. It enjoins upon its branches separateness but interdependence, autonomy but reciprocity.

The Framers regarded the checks and balances that they had built into the tripartite Federal Government as a self-executing safeguard against the encroachment or aggrandizement of one branch at the expense of the other. . . .

2. The Appointments Clause

The principle of separation of powers was not simply an abstract generalization in the minds of the Framers: it was woven into the document that they drafted in Philadelphia in the summer of 1787. Article I declares: "All legislative Powers herein granted shall be vested in one supreme Court, and in such inferior Courts as the Congress may from time to time ordain and establish." The further concern of the Framers of the Constitution with maintenance of the separation of powers is found in the so-called "Ineligibility" and "Incompatibility" Clauses contained in § 6 of Art. I:

> No Senator or Representative shall, during the Time for which he was elected, be appointed to any civil Office under the Authority of the United States, which shall have been created, or the emoluments whereof shall have been encreased during such time; and no Person holding any Office under the United States, shall be a Member of either House during his Continuance in Office.

It is in the context of these cognate provisions of the document that we must examine the language of Art. II, § 2, cl. 2, which appellants contend provides the only authorization for appointment of those to whom substantial executive or administrative authority is given by statute. . . . [W]e again set out the provision:

> [The President] shall nominate, and by and with the Advice and Consent of the Senate, shall appoint Ambassadors, other public Ministers and Consuls,

Judges of the supreme Court, and all other Officers of the United States, whose Appointments are not herein otherwise provided for, and which shall be established by Law, but the Congress may by Law vest the Appointment of such inferior Officers, as they think proper, in the President alone, in the Courts of Law, or in the Heads of Departments....

... We think that the term "Officers of the United States" as used in Art. II ... is a term intended to have substantive meaning. We think its fair import is that any appointee exercising significant authority pursuant to the laws of the United States is an Officer of the United States, and must, therefore, be appointed in the manner prescribed by § 2, cl. 2 of that Article.

If "all persons who can be said to hold an office under the government about to be established under the Constitution were intended to be included within one or the other of these modes of appointment," *United States v. Germaine*, [1878] it is difficult to see how the members of the Commission may escape inclusion....

Although two members of the Commission are initially selected by the President, his nominations are subject to confirmation not merely by the Senate, but by the House of Representatives as well. The remaining four voting members of the Commission were appointed by the President *pro tempore* of the Senate and by the Speaker of the House. While the second part of the Clause authorizes Congress to vest the appointment of the officers described in that part in "the Courts of Law, or in the Heads of Departments," neither the Speaker of the House nor the President *pro tempore* of the Senate comes within this language.

... Thus with respect to four of the six voting members of the Commission, neither the President, the head of any department, nor the judiciary has any voice in their selection.

... Appellee Commission and *amici* contend somewhat obliquely that because the Framers had no intention of relegating Congress to a position below that of the coequal Judicial and Executive Branches of the National Government, the Appointments Clause must somehow be read to include Congress or its officers as among those in whom the appointment power may be vested. But ... the evolution of the draft version of the Constitution, seem[s] to us to lend considerable support to our reading of the language of the Appointments Clause itself.

An interim version of the draft Constitution had vested in the Senate the authority to appoint Ambassadors, public Ministers, and Judges of the Supreme Court, and the language of Art. II as finally adopted is a distinct change in this regard. We believe that it was a deliberate change made by the Framers with the intent to deny Congress any authority itself to appoint those who were "Officers of the United States.".…

... Appellee Commission and *amici* urge that because of what they conceive to be the extraordinary authority reposed in Congress to regulate elections, this case stands on a different footing than if Congress had exercised its legislative authority in another field.... We see no reason to believe that the authority of Congress over federal election practices is of such a wholly different nature from the other grants of authority to Congress that it may be employed in such a manner as to offend well established constitutional restrictions stemming from the separation of powers.

The position that because Congress has been given explicit and plenary authority to regulate a field of activity, it must therefore have the power to appoint those who are to administer the regulatory statute is both novel and contrary to the language of the Appointments Clause. Unless their selection is elsewhere provided for, *all* officers of the United States are to be appointed in accordance with the Clause.... No class or type of officer is excluded because of its special functions....

... We are also told by appellees and *amici* that Congress had good reason for not vesting in a Commission composed wholly of President appointees the authority to administer the Act, since the administration of the Act would undoubtedly have a bearing on any incumbent President's campaign for re-election. ... [I]t would seem that those who sought to challenge incumbent Congressmen might have equally good reason to fear a Commission which was unduly responsive to Members of Congress whom they were seeking to unseat. But such fears, however rational, do not by themselves warrant a distortion of the Framers' work.

Appellee Commission and *amici* finally contend ... that whatever shortcomings the provisions for the appointment of members of the Commission might have under Art. II, Congress had ample authority under the Necessary and Proper Clause of Art. I to effectuate this result. We do not agree. The proper inquiry when considering the Necessary and Proper Clause is not the authority of Congress to create an office or a commission ... but rather its authority to provide that its own officers may appoint to such office or commission.

... [Congress may not] vest in itself, or in its officers, the authority to appoint officers of the United States when the Appointments Clause by clear implication prohibits it from doing so. ...

3. The Commission's Powers

Thus, on the assumption that all of the powers granted in the statute may be exercised by an agency whose members *have been* appointed in accordance with the Appointments Clause, the ultimate question in which, if any, of those powers may be exercised by the present Commissioners, none of whom *was* appointed as provided by that Clause. ...

Insofar as the powers confided in the Commission are essentially of an inves-

tigative and informative nature, falling in the same general category as those powers which Congress might delegate to one of its own committees, there can be no question that the Commission as presently constituted may exercise them. ...

But when we go beyond this type of authority to the more substantial powers exercised by the Commission, we reach a different result. The Commission's enforcement power, exemplified by its discretionary power to seek judicial relief, is authority that cannot possibly be regarded as merely in aid of the legislative function of Congress. A law suit is the ultimate remedy for a breach of the law, and it is to the President, and not to the Congress, that the Constitution entrusts the responsibility to "take Care that the Laws be faithfully executed." Art. II, § 3.

Congress may undoubtedly under the Necessary and Proper Clause create "offices" in the generic sense and provide such method of appointment to those "offices" as it chooses. But Congress' power under that Clause is inevitably bounded by the express language of Art. II, § 2, cl. 2, and unless the method it provides comports with the latter, the holders of those offices will not be "Officers of the United States." They may, therefore, properly perform duties only in aid of those functions that Congress may carry out by itself, or in an area sufficiently removed from the administration and enforcement of the public law as to permit them being performed by persons not "Officers of the United States.". ...

... We hold that these provisions of the Act, vesting in the Commission primary responsibility for conducting civil litigation in the courts of the United States for vindicating public rights, violate Art. II, cl. 2, § 2, of the Constitution. Such functions may be discharged only by persons who are "Officers of the United States" within the language of that section.

All aspects of the Act are brought within the Commission's broad administrative powers: rule-making, advisory opinions, and determinations of eligibility for funds and even for federal elective office itself. These functions, exercised free from day-to-day supervision of either Congress or the Executive Branch, are more legislative and judicial in nature than are the Commission's enforcement powers, and are of kinds usually performed by independent regulatory agencies or by some department in the Executive Branch under the direction of an Act of Congress. Congress viewed these broad powers as essential to effective and impartial administration of the entire substantive framework of the Act. Yet each of these functions also represents the performance of a significant governmental duty exercised pursuant to a public law. . . . [N]one of them operates merely in aid of congressional authority to legislate or is sufficiently removed from the administration and enforcement of public law to allow it to be performed by the present Commission. These administrative functions may therefore be exercised only by persons who are "Officers of the United States."

It is also our view that the Commission's inability to exercise certain powers because of the method by which its members have been selected should not affect the validity of the Commission's administration actions and determinations to this date, including its administration of those provisions, upheld today, authorizing the public financing of federal elections. The past acts of the Commission are therefore accorded *de facto* validity, just as we have recognized should be the case with respect to legislative acts performed by legislators held to have been elected in accordance with an unconstitutional apportionment plan. . . . We also draw on the Court's practice in the apportionment and voting rights cases and stay, for a period not to exceed 30 days, the Court's judgment insofar as it affects the authority of the Commission to exercise the duties and powers granted it under the Act. This limited stay will afford Congress an opportunity to reconstitute the Commission by law or to adopt other valid enforcement mechanisms without interrupting enforcement of the provisions the Court sustains, allowing the present Commission in the interim to function *de facto* in accordance with the substantive provisions of the Act. . . .

Conclusion

In summary, we sustain the individual contribution limits, the disclosure and reporting provisions, and the public financing scheme. We conclude, however, that the limitations on campaign expenditures, on independent expenditures by individuals and groups, and on expenditures by a candidate from his personal funds are constitutionally infirm. Finally, we hold that most of the powers conferred by the Act upon the Federal Election Commission can be exercised only by "Officers of the United States," appointed in conformity with Art. II, § 2, cl. 2, of the Constitution, and therefore cannot be exercised by the Commission as presently constituted.

In No. 75-436, the judgment of the Court of Appeals is affirmed in part and reversed in part. The judgment of the District Court in No. 75-437 is affirmed. The mandate shall issue forthwith, except that our judgment is stayed, for a period not to exceed 30 days, insofar as it affects the authority of the Commission to exercise the duties and powers granted it under the Act.

So ordered.

Mr. Chief Justice Burger, concurring in part and dissenting in part.

For reasons set forth more fully later, I dissent from those parts of the Court's holding sustaining the Act's provisions (a) for disclosure of small contributions, (b) for limitations on contributions, and (c) for public financing of Presidential campaigns. In my view, the Act's disclosure scheme is impermissibly broad and violative of the First Amendment as it relates to reporting $10 and $100 contributions. The contribution limitations infringe on First Amendment liberties and suffer from the same infirmities that the Court correctly sees in the expenditure ceilings. The Act's system for public financing of Presidential campaigns is, in my judgment, an impermissible intrusion by the Government into the traditionally private political process. . . .

Disclosure Provisions

Disclosure is, in principle, the salutary and constitutional remedy for most of the ills Congress was seeking to alleviate. I therefore agree fully with the broad proposition that public disclosure of contributions by individuals and by entities—particularly corporations and labor unions—is an effective means of revealing the type of political support that is sometimes coupled with expectations of special favors or rewards. That disclosure impinges on First Amendment rights is conceded by the Court . . . but given the objectives to which disclosure is directed, I agree that the need for disclosure outweighs individual constitutional claims. . . .

. . . The Court's theory, however, goes beyond permissible limits. Under the Court's view, disclosure serves broad informational purposes, enabling the public to be fully informed on matters of acute public interest. Forced disclosure of one aspect of a citizen's political activity, under this analysis, serves the public right-to-know. This open-ended approach is the only plausible justification for the otherwise irrationally low ceilings of $10 and $100 for anonymous contributions. The burdens of these low ceilings seem to me obvious, and the Court does not try to question this. . . .

. . . The public right-to-know ought not be absolute when its exercise reveals private political convictions. Secrecy, like privacy, is not *per se* criminal. On the contrary, secrecy and privacy as to political preferences and convictions are fundamental in a free society. . . .

. . . With respect, I suggest the Court has failed to give the traditional standing to some of the First Amendment values at stake here. Specifically, it has failed to confine the particular exercise of governmental power within limits reasonably required. . . .

. . . [I]t seems to me that the threshold limits fixed at $10 and $100 for anonymous contributions are constitutionally impermissible on their face. . . . To argue that a 1976 contribution of $10 or $100 entails a risk of corruption or its appearance is simply too extravagant to be maintained. No public right-to-know justifies the compelled disclosure of such contributions, at the risk of discouraging them. There is, in short, no relation whatever between the means used and the legitimate goal of ventilating possible undue influence. Congress has used a shotgun to kill wrens as well as hawks. . . .

. . . Finally, no legitimate public interest has been shown in forcing the disclosure of modest contributions that are the prime support of new, unpopular or unfashionable political causes. There is no realistic possibility that such modest donations will have a corrupting influence especially on parties that enjoy only "minor" status. Major parties would not notice them, minor parties need them. . . .

I would therefore hold unconstitutional the provisions requiring reporting of contributions of $10 or more and to make a public record of the name, address, and occupation of a contributor of $100 or more.

Contribution and Expenditure Limits

I agree fully with that part of the Court's opinion that holds unconstitutional the limitations the Act puts on campaign expenditures which "place substantial and direct restrictions on the ability of candidates, citizens, and associations to engage in protected political expression, restrictions that the First Amendment cannot tolerate." . . . Yet when it approves similarly stringent limitations on contributions, the Court ignores the reasons it finds so persuasive in the context of expenditures. For me contributions and expenditures are two sides of the same First Amendment coin. . . .

. . . The Court's attempt to distinguish the communication inherent in political *contributions* from the speech aspects of political *expenditures* simply will not wash. We do little but engage in word games unless we recognize that people—candidates and contributors—spend money on political activity because they wish to communicate ideas, and their constitutional interest in doing so is precisely the same whether they or someone else utter the words.

The Court attempts to make the Act seem less restrictive by casting the problem as one that goes to freedom of association rather than freedom of speech. I have long thought freedom of association and freedom of expression were two peas from the same pod. . . .

Public Financing

I dissent from Part III sustaining the constitutionality of the public financing provisions of the Act. . . .

. . . I would . . . fault the Court for not adequately analyzing and meeting head-on the issue whether public financial assistance to the private political activity of individual citizens and parties is a legitimate expenditure of public funds. The public monies at issue here are not being employed simply to police the integrity of the electoral process or to provide a forum for the use of all participants in the political dialog, as would, for example, be the case if free broadcast time were granted. Rather, we are confronted with the Government's actual financing, out of general revenues, a segment of the political debate itself. . . .

. . . I agree with Mr. Justice Rehnquist that the scheme approved by the Court today invidiously discriminates against minor parties. . . . The fact that there have been few drastic realignments in our basic two-party structure in 200 years is no constitutional justification for freezing the status quo of the present major parties at the expense of such future political movements. . . .

I would also find unconstitutional the system of "matching grants" which makes a candidate's ability to amass private funds the sole criterion for eligibility for public funds. Such an arrangement can put at serious disadvantage a candidate with a potentially large, widely diffused—but poor—constituency. The ability of a candidate's supporters to help pay for his campaign cannot be equated with their willingness to cast a ballot for him. . . .

I cannot join in the attempt to determine which parts of the Act can survive review here. The statute as it now stands is unworkable and inequitable.

I agree with the Court's holding that the Act's restrictions on expenditures made "relative to a clearly identified candidate," independent of any candidate or his committee, are unconstitutional. . . . Paradoxically the Court upholds the limitations on individual contributions, which embrace precisely the same sort of expenditures "relative to a clearly identified candidate" if those expenditures are "authorized or requested" by the "candidate or his agents." . . . The Act as cut back by the Court thus places intolerable pressure on the distinction between "authorized" and "unauthorized" expenditures on behalf of a candidate; even those with the most sanguine hopes for the Act might well concede that the distinction cannot be maintained....

... Moreover, the Act—or so much as the Court leaves standing—creates significant inequities. A candidate with substantial personal resources is now given by the Court a clear advantage over his less affluent opponents, who are constrained by law in fundraising, because the Court holds that the "First Amendment cannot tolerate" any restrictions on spending.... Minority parties, whose situation is difficult enough under an Act that excludes them from public funding, are prevented from accepting large single-donor contributions. At the same time the Court sustains the provision aimed at broadening the base of political support by requiring candidates to seek a greater number of small contributors, it sustains the unrealistic disclosure thresholds of $10 and $100 that I believe will deter those hoped-for small contributions. Minor parties must now compete for votes against two major parties whose expenditures will be vast. Finally, the Act's distinction between contributions in money and contributions in services remains, with only the former being subject to any limits....

The Court's piecemeal approach fails to give adequate consideration to the integrated nature of this legislation. A serious question is raised, which the Court does not consider, when central segments, key operative provisions, of this Act are stricken, can what remains function in anything like the way Congress intended? ...

Finally, I agree with the Court that the members of the Federal Election Commission were unconstitutionally appointed. However, I disagree that we should give blanket *de facto* validation to all actions of the Commission undertaken until today....

... In my view Congress can no more ration political expression than it can ration religious expression; and limits on political or religious contributions and expenditures effectively curb expression in both areas. There are many prices we pay for the freedoms secured by the First Amendment; the risk of undue influence is one of them, confirming what we have long known: freedom is hazardous, but some restraints are worse.

Mr. Justice White, concurring in part and dissenting in part....

[I]

... The disclosure requirements and the limitations on contributions and expenditures are challenged as invalid abridgments of the right of free speech protected by the First Amendment. I would reject these challenges. I agree with the Court's conclusion and much of its opinion with respect to sustaining the disclosure provisions. I am also in agreement with the Court's judgment upholding the limitations on contributions. I dissent, however, from the Court's view that the expenditure limitations of 18 U.S.C. §§ 608(c) and (e) violate the First Amendment....

... Since the contribution and expenditure limitations are neutral as to the content of speech and are not motivated by fear of the consequences of the political speech of particular candidates or of political speech in general, this case depends on whether the nonspeech interests of the Federal Government in regulating the use of money in political speech in general, this case depends on whether the nonspeech interests of the Federal Government in regulating the use of money in political campaigns are sufficiently urgent to justify the incidental effects that the limitations visit upon the First Amendment interests of candidates and their supporters....

... It would make little sense to me, and apparently made none to Congress, to limit the amounts an individual may give to a candidate or spend with his approval but fail to limit the amounts that could be spent on his behalf. Yet the Court permits the former while striking down the later limitation. ...

... Proceeding from the maxim that "money talks" the Court finds that the expenditure limitations will seriously curtail political expression by candidates and interfere substantially with their chances for election. ...

... [A]s it should be unnecessary to point out, money is not always equivalent to or used for speech, even in the context of political campaigns. I accept the reality that communicating with potential voters is the heart of an election campaign and that widespread communication has become very expensive. There are, however, many expensive campaign activities that are not themselves communicative or remotely related to speech. Furthermore, campaigns differ among themselves. Some seem to spend much less money than others and yet communicate as much or more than those supported by enormous bureaucracies with unlimited financing. The record before us no more supports the conclusion that the communicative efforts of congressional and Presidential candidates will be crippled by the expenditure limitations than it supports the contrary. The judgment of Congress was that reasonably effective campaigns could be conducted within the limits established by the Act and that the communicative efforts of these campaigns would not seriously suffer. In this posture of the case, there is no sound basis for invalidating the expenditure limitations, so long as the purposes they serve are legitimate and sufficiently substantial, which in my view they are. ...

... It is also important to restore and maintain public confidence in federal elections. It is critical to obviate or dispel the impression that federal elections are purely and simply a function of money, that federal offices are bought and sold or that political races are reserved for those who have the facility—and the stomach—for doing whatever it takes to bring together those interests, groups, and individuals that can raise or contribute large fortunes in order to prevail at the polls.

The ceiling on candidate expenditures represents the considering judgment of Congress that elections are to be decided among candidates none of whom has overpowering advantage by reason of a huge campaign war chest. At least so long as the ceiling placed upon the candidates is not plainly too low, elections are not to turn on the difference in the amounts of money that candidates have to spend. This seems an acceptable purpose and the means chosen a common sense way to achieve it. The Court nevertheless holds that a candidate has a constitutional right to spend unlimited amounts of money, mostly that of other people, in order to be elected. The holding perhaps is not that federal candidates have the constitutional right to purchase their election, but many will so interpret the Court's conclusion in this case. I cannot join the Court in this respect.

I also disagree with the Court's judgment that § 608(a), which limits the amount of money that a candidate or his family may spend on his campaign, violates the Constitution. Although it is true that this provision does not promote any interest in preventing the corruption of candidates, the provision does, nevertheless, serve salutary purposes related to the integrity of federal campaigns. ...

As with the campaign expenditure limits, Congress was entitled to determine that personal wealth ought to play a less important role in political campaigns than it has in the past. Nothing in the First Amendment stands in the way of that determination. ...

[II]

I join the answers in Part IV of the Court's opinion ... to the questions certified by the District Court relating to the composition and powers of the Federal Election Commission (FEC)....

... It is apparent that none of the members of the FEC is selected in a manner Art. II specifies for the appointment of officers of the United States....

... The challenge to the FEC, therefore, is that its members are officers of the United States the mode of whose appointment was required to, but did not, conform to the Appointments Clause. That challenge is well taken....

... This position that Congress may itself appoint the members of a body that is to administer a wide-ranging statute will not withstand examination in light of either the purpose and history of the Appointments Clause or of prior cases in this Court....

... I thus find singularly unpersuasive the proposition that because the FEC is implementing statutory policies with respect to the conduct of elections, which policies Congress has the power to propound, its members may be appointed by Congress. One might as well argue that the exclusive and plenary power of Congress over interstate commerce authorizes Congress to appoint the members of the Interstate Commerce Commission and of many other regulatory commissions....

... Congress clearly has the power to create federal offices and to define the powers and duties of those offices ... but no case in this Court even remotely supports the power of Congress to appoint an officer of the United States aside from those officers each House is authorized by Art. I to appoint to assist in the legislative processes....

Mr. Justice Marshall, concurring in part and dissenting in part.

I join in all of the Court's opinion except Part I—C—2, which deals with § 608 (a) of the Act. That section limits the amount a candidate can spend from his personal funds, or family funds under his control, in connection with his campaigns during any calendar year....

... One of the points on which all Members of the Court agree is that money is essential for effective communication in a political campaign. It would appear to follow that the candidate with a substantial personal fortune at his disposal is off to a significant "head start." Of course, the less wealthy candidate can potentially overcome the disparity in resources through contributions from others. But ability to generate contributions may itself depend upon a showing of a financial base for the campaign or some demonstration of pre-existing support, which in turn is facilitated by expenditures of substantial personal sums. Thus the wealthy candidate's immediate access to a substantial personal fortune may give him an initial advantage that his less wealthy opponent can never overcome. And even if the advantage can be overcome, the perception that personal wealth wins elections may not only discourage potential candidates without significant personal wealth from entering the political arena, but also undermine public confidence in the integrity of the electoral process....

... In view of § 608 (b)'s limitations on contributions, then, § 608 (a) emerges not simply as a device to reduce the natural advantage of the wealthy candidate, but as a provision providing some symmetry to a regulatory scheme that otherwise enhances the natural advantage of the wealthy.... I therefore respectfully dissent from the Court's invalidation of 608(a).

Mr. Justice Blackmun, concurring in part and dissenting in part. I am not persuaded that the Court makes, or indeed is able to make, a principled constitutional distinction between the contribution limitations, on the one hand, and the expenditure limitations, on the other, that are involved here. I therefore do not join Part I—B of the Court's opinion or those portions of Part I—A that are consistent with Part I—B. As to those, I dissent. . . .

Mr. Justice Rehnquist, concurring in part and dissenting in part. . . .

. . . I . . . join in all of the Court's opinion except Subpart III—B—1, which sustains, against appellants' First and Fifth Amendment challenges, the disparities found in the congressional plan for financing general Presidential elections between the two major parties, on the one hand, and minor parties and candidacies on the other. . . .

. . . Congress, of course, does have an interest in not "funding hopeless candidacies with large sums of public money,". . . and may for that purpose legitimately require " 'some preliminary showing of a significant modicum of support,' *Jenness* v. *Fortson* . . . as an eligibility requirement for public funds.". . . But Congress in this legislation has done a good deal more than that. It has enshrined the Republican and Democratic Parties in a permanently preferred position, and has estab-

lished requirements for funding minor party and independent candidates to which the two major parties are not subject. Congress would undoubtedly be justified in treating the Presidential candidates of the two major parties differently from minor party or independent Presidential candidates, in view of the long demonstrated public support for the former. But because of the First Amendment overtones of the appellants' Fifth Amendment equal protection claim, something more than a merely rational basis for the difference in treatment must be shown, as the Court apparently recognizes. I find it impossible to subscribe to the Court's reasoning that because no third party has posed a credible threat to the two major parties in Presidential elections since 1860, Congress may by law attempt to assure that this pattern will endure forever.

I would hold that, as to general election financing, Congress has not merely treated the two major parties differently from minor parties and independents, but has discriminated in favor of the former in such a way as to run afoul of the Fifth and First Amendments to the United States Constitution.

Jimmy Carter's Interview with Playboy Magazine (1976)

Jimmy Carter was the little-known former governor of Georgia when he announced his candidacy for the 1976 Democratic presidential nomination on December 12, 1974, just weeks before leaving office. His national reputation, limited as it was, owed to a 1971 cover story in Time magazine in which Carter was portrayed as one of several new southern governors who had accepted the desirability of civil rights for blacks.

Carter spent 1975 campaigning relentlessly in Iowa and New Hampshire, the two relatively small states that were scheduled to hold the first caucuses and the first primary, respectively, of the 1976 nominating season. President Richard Nixon's resignation in disgrace in August 1974, President Gerald Ford's highly unpopular pardon of Nixon in September 1974, and politically disastrous losses for the Republican party in the 1974 midterm elections seemed to augur a Democratic victory in the presidential election of 1976. A crowded field of candidates formed to seek the party's nomination: Rep. Morris K. Udall of Arizona, Gov. George C. Wallace of Alabama, former vice-presidential nominee R. Sargent Shriver of Maryland, and senators Birch Bayh of Indiana, Fred R. Harris of Oklahoma, and Henry M. Jackson of Washington. But Carter won upset victories in Iowa and New Hampshire, defeated Wallace in the Florida primary, and coasted to a first ballot nomination at the Democratic national convention in July.

Carter's political appeal was based largely on his exploitation of the anti-Washington political climate that prevailed at the time. The Watergate scandal had engendered a yearning for morality in government that Carter, a Baptist Sunday school teacher who, unlike his political opponents, felt comfortable talking publicly about moral conduct, seemed to satisfy. The Vietnam War and the recent growth of the federal bureaucracy also had fostered among the voters a desire for competence in government. Carter, proclaiming proudly that he had never been part of the Washington scene, stressed his administrative experience as the chief executive of Georgia.

Both Carter's morality and his competence were called into question in mid-September 1976 when the October issue of Playboy magazine hit the newsstands, containing a long interview with the candidate. In an exasperated answer to a series of questions about the relationship between his Christian faith and his political beliefs, Carter spoke earnestly to his nonbelieving interviewers about God's forgiveness and the Christian's responsibility not to condemn. Among other things, Carter confessed: "Christ said, 'I tell you anyone who looks on a *woman with lust has in his heart already committed adultery.' I've looked on a lot of women with lust. I've committed adultery in my heart many times. This is something that God recognizes I will do—and I have done it—and God forgives me for it. But that doesn't mean that I condemn someone who not only looks on a woman with lust but leaves his wife and shacks up with somebody out of wedlock."*

Carter's Playboy *interview became a national sensation, although less for its theological content than for its unusual (at least in politics) language—"adultery in my heart," "shack up," and so on. Cartoonists and comedians had a field day with the interview. So did hecklers: some Vanderbilt University students held up a sign to the candidate at a Nashville, Tennessee, rally that read, "Smile if you're horny!" Columnists questioned Carter's judgment. His standing dropped in the polls. Finally, despairing that his thoughtful comments would ever receive a serious hearing, Carter expressed public regret about the impropriety of giving an extended interview to* Playboy. ~

Playboy: After nearly two years on the campaign trail, don't you feel a little numbed by the routine—for instance, having to give the same speech over and over?

Carter: Sometimes. Once, when I was campaigning in the Florida primary, I made 12 speeches in one day. It was the worst day I ever had. But I generally have tried to change the order of the speech and emphasize different things. Sometimes I abbreviate and sometimes I elaborate. Of 20 different parts in a speech, I might take seven or eight and change them around. It depends on the audience—black people, Jewish people, *chicanos*—and that gives me the ability to make speeches that aren't boring to myself.

Playboy: Every politician probably emphasizes different things to different audiences, but in your case, there's been a common criticism that you seem to have several faces, that you try to be all things to all people. How do you respond to that?

Carter: I can't make myself believe these are contrivances and subterfuges I've adopted to get votes. It may be, and I can't get myself to admit it, but what I want to do is to let people know how I can stand on the issues as honestly as I can.

Playboy: If you feel you've been fully honest, why has the charge persisted that you're "fuzzy" on the issues?

Carter: It started during the primaries, when most of my opponents were members of Congress. When any question on an issue came up, they would say, "I'm for the Kennedy-Corman bill on health care, period, no matter what's in it." If the question was on employment, they would say, "I'm for the Humphrey-Hawkins bill, no matter what's in it." But those bills were constantly being amended!

I'm just not able to do that. I have to understand what I'm talking about, and simplistic answers identifying my position with such-and-such a House bill are something I can't put forward. That's one reason I've been seen as fuzzy.

Another is that I'm not an ideolog and my positions are not predictable. Without any criticism of McGovern, if the question had ever come up on abortion, you could pretty well anticipate what he was going to say. If it were amnesty, you could predict what McGovern was going to say about that. But I've tried to analyze each question individually; I've taken positions that to me are fair and rational, and sometimes my answers are complicated.

The third reason is that I wasn't a very vulnerable opponent for those who ran against me. Fuzziness was the only issue Congressman Udall, Senator

Church—and others that are hard to remember now—could adopt in their campaigns against me. I think the drumming of that factor into the consciousness of the American voter obviously had some impact.

Playboy: Still, not everybody's sure whether you're a conservative in liberal clothing or vice versa. F.D.R., for instance, turned out to be something of a surprise to people who'd voted for him, because he hadn't seemed as progressive before he was elected as he turned out to be. Could you be a surprise that way?

Carter: I don't believe that's going to be the case. If you analyze the Democratic party platform, you'll see that it's a very progressive, very liberal, very socially motivated platform. What sometimes surprises people is that I carry out my promises. People ask how a peanut farmer from the South who believes in balanced budgets and tough management of Government can possibly give the country tax and welfare reform, or a national health program, or insist on equal rights for blacks and women. Well, I'm going to *do* those things. I've promised them during the campaign, so I don't think there will be many people disappointed—or surprised—when I carry out those commitments as President.

Playboy: But isn't it true that you turned out to be more liberal as governor of Georgia than people who voted for you had any reason to suspect?

Carter: I don't really think so. No, *The Atlanta Constitution,* which was the source of all information about me, categorized me during the gubernatorial campaign as an ignorant, racist, backward, ultraconservative, rednecked South Georgia peanut farmer. Its candidate, Carl Sanders, the former governor, was characterized as an enlightened, progressive, well-educated, urbane, forceful, competent public official. I never agreed with the categorization that was made of me during the

campaign. I was the same person before and after I became governor. I remember keeping a check list and every time I made a promise during the campaign, I wrote it down in a notebook. I believe I carried out every promise I made. I told several people during the campaign that one of the phrases I was going to use in my inaugural speech was that the time for racial discrimination was over. I wrote and made that speech.

The ultraconservatives in Georgia—who aren't supporting me now, by the way—voted for me because of their animosity toward Carl Sanders. I was the alternative to him. They never asked me, "Are you a racist or have you been a member of the Ku Klux Klan?" because they knew I wasn't and hadn't been. And yet, despite predictions early this year by *The Atlanta Constitution* that I couldn't get a majority of the primary vote in Georgia against Wallace, I received about 85 percent of the votes. So I don't think the Georgia people have the feeling I betrayed them.

Playboy: Considering what you've just said about *The Atlanta Constitution,* how do you feel about the media in general and about the job they do in covering the election issues?

Carter: There's still a tendency on the part of some members of the press to treat the South, you know, as a suspect nation. There are a few who think that since I am a Southern governor, I must be a secret racist or there's something in a closet somewhere that's going to be revealed to show my true colors. There's been a constant probing back ten, twelve years in my background, even as early as the first primaries. Nobody probed like that into the background of Udall or Bayh or other people. But I don't object to it particularly, I just recognize it.

(The answer was broken off and, at a later session, Carter returned to the question of the press and its coverage of issues. This time he was tired, his head sunk far back into his airplane

seat. The exchange occurred during one of the late primaries.)

Issues? The local media are interested, all right, but the national news media have absolutely no interest in issues *at all.* Sometimes we freeze out the national media so we can open up press conferences to local people. At least we get questions from them—on timber management, on health care, on education. But the traveling press have zero interest in any issue unless it's a matter of making a mistake. What they're looking for is a 47-second argument between me and another candidate or something like that. There's nobody in the back of this plane who would ask an issue question unless he thought he could trick me into some crazy statement.

Playboy: One crazy statement you were supposed to have made was reported by Robert Shrum after he quit as your speechwriter earlier this year. He said he'd been in conversations with you when you made some slighting references to Jewish voters. What's your version of what happened?

Carter: Shrum dreamed up eight or ten conversations that never took place and nobody in the press ever asked me if they had occurred. The press just assumed that they had. I never talked to Shrum in private except for maybe a couple of minutes. If he had told the truth, if I had said all the things he claimed I had said, I wouldn't vote for *myself.*

When a poll came out early in the primaries that said I had a small proportion of the Jewish vote, I said, "Well, this is really a disappointment to me— we've worked so hard with the Jewish voters. But my pro-Israel stand won't change, even if I don't get a single Jewish vote; I guess we'll have to depend on non-Jews to put me in office." But Shrum treated it as if it were some kind of racist disavowal of Jews. Well, that's a kind of sleazy twisting of a conversation.

Playboy: While we're on the subject of the press, how do you feel about an issue that concerns the press itself—the right of journalists to keep their sources secret?

Carter: I would do everything I could to protect the secrecy of sources for the news media.

Playboy: Both the press *and* the public seem to have made an issue out of your Baptist beliefs. Why do you think this has happened?

Carter: I'm not unique. There are a lot of people in this country who have the same religious faith. It's not a mysterious or mystical or magical thing. But for those who don't know the feeling of someone who believes in Christ, who is aware of the presence of God, there is, I presume, a quizzical attitude toward it. But it's always been something I've discussed very frankly throughout my adult life.

Playboy: We've heard that you pray 25 times a day. Is that true?

Carter: I've never counted. I've forgotten who asked me that, but I'd say that on an eventful day, you know, it's something like that.

Playboy: When you say an eventful day, do you mean you pray as a kind of pause, to control your blood pressure and relax?

Carter: Well, yes. If something happens to me that is a little disconcerting, if I feel a trepidation, if a thought comes into my head of animosity or hatred toward someone, then I just kind of say a brief silent prayer. I don't ask for myself but just to let me understand what another's feelings might be. Going through a crowd, quite often people bring me a problem, and I pray that their needs might be met. A lot of times, I'll be in the back seat of a car and not know what kind of audience I'm going to face. I don't mean I'm terror-stricken, just that I don't know what to expect next. I'll pray then, but it's not something that's conscious or formal. It's just a part of my life.

Playboy: One reason some people might be quizzical is that you have a sister, Ruth, who is a faith healer. The association of politics with faith healing is an idea many find disconcerting.

Carter: I don't even know what political ideas Ruth has had, and for people to suggest I'm under the hold of a sister—or any other person—is a complete distortion of fact. I don't have any idea whether Ruth has supported Democrats or not, whereas the political views of my other sister, Gloria, are remarkably harmonious with mine.

Playboy: So you're closer to Gloria, who has described herself as a McGovern Democrat and rides motorcycles as a hobby.

Carter: I like them both. But in the past 20 or 25 years, I've been much closer to Gloria, because she lives next door to me and Ruth lives in North Carolina. We hardly saw Ruth more than once a year at family get-togethers. What political attitudes Ruth has had, I have not the slightest idea. But my mother and Gloria and I have been very compatible. We supported Lyndon Johnson openly during the 1964 campaign and my mother worked at the Johnson county headquarters, which was courageous, not an easy thing to do politically. She would come out of the Johnson headquarters and find her car smeared with soap and the antenna tied in a knot and ugly messages left on the front seat. When my young boys went to school, they were beaten. So Mother and Gloria and I, along with my Rosalynn, have had the same attitudes even when we were in a minority in Plains. But Ruth lives in a different world in North Carolina.

Playboy: Granting that you're not as close to your religious sister as is assumed, we still wonder how *your* religious beliefs would translate into political action. For instance, would you appoint judges who would be harsh or lenient toward victimless crimes—offenses such as drug use, adultery, sodomy and homosexuality?

Carter: Committing adultery, according to the Bible—which I believe in—is a sin. For us to hate one another, for us to have sexual intercourse outside marriage, for us to engage in homosexual activities, for us to steal, for us to lie—all these are sins. But Jesus teaches us not to judge other people. We don't assume the role of judge and say to another human being, "You're condemned because you commit sins." All Christians, all of us, acknowledge that we are sinful and the judgment comes from God, not from another human being.

As governor of Georgia, I tried to shift the emphasis of law enforcement away from victimless crimes. We lessened the penalties on the use of marijuana. We removed alcoholism as a crime, and so forth. Victimless crimes, in my opinion, should have a very low priority in terms of enforcing the laws on the books. But as to appointing judges, that would not be the basis on which I'd appoint them. I would choose people who were competent, whose judgment and integrity were sound. I think it would be inappropriate to ask them how they were going to rule on a particular question before I appointed them.

Playboy: What *about* those laws on the books that govern personal behavior? Should they be enforced?

Carter: Almost every state in the Union has laws against adultery and many of them have laws against homosexuality and sodomy. But they're often considered by police officers as not worthy of enforcing to the extent of disturbing consenting adults or breaking into a person's private home.

Playboy: But, of course, that gives the police a lot of leeway to enforce them selectively. Do you think such laws should be on the books at all?

Carter: That's a judgment for the individual states to make. I think the laws are on the books quite often because of their relationship to the Bible. Early in the nation's development, the Judaeo-Christian moral standards were accepted as a basis for civil law. But I don't think it hurts to have this kind of standard maintained as a goal. I also think it's an area that's been interpreted by the Supreme Court as one that can rightfully be retained by the individual states.

Playboy: Do you think liberalization of the laws over the past decade by factors as diverse as the pill and *Playboy*—an effect some people would term permissiveness—has been a harmful development?

Carter: Liberalization of some of the laws has been good. You can't legislate morality. We tried to outlaw consumption of alcoholic beverages. We found that violation of the law led to bigger crimes and bred disrespect for the law.

Playboy: We're confused. You say morality can't be legislated, yet you support certain laws because they preserve old moral standards. How do you reconcile the two positions?

Carter: I believe people should honor civil laws. If there is a conflict between God's law and civil law, we should honor God's law. But we should be willing to accept civil punishment. Most of Christ's original followers were killed because of their belief in Christ; they violated the civil law in following God's law. Reinhold Niebuhr, a theologian who has dealt with this problem at length, says that the framework of law is a balancing of forces in a society; the law itself tends to alleviate tensions brought about by these forces. But the laws on the books are not a measure of this balance nearly as much as the degree to which the laws are enforced. So when a law is anachronistic and is carried over from a previous age, it's just not observed.

Playboy: What we're getting at is how much you'd tolerate behavior that your religion considers wrong. For instance, in San Francisco, you said you considered homosexuality a sin. What does that mean in political terms?

Carter: The issue of homosexuality always makes me nervous. It's obviously one of the major issues in San Francisco. I don't have any, you know, personal knowledge about homosexuality and I guess being a Baptist, that would contribute to a sense of being uneasy.

Playboy: Does it make you uneasy to discuss it simply as a political question?

Carter: No, it's more complicated than that. It's political, it's moral and it's strange territory to me. At home in Plains, we've had homosexuals in our community, our church. There's never been any sort of discrimination—some embarrassment but no animosity, no harassment. But to inject it into a public discussion on politics and how it conflicts with morality is a new experience for me. I've thought about it a lot, but I don't see how to handle it differently from the way I look on other sexual acts outside marriage.

Playboy: We'd like to ask you a blunt question: Isn't it just these views about what's "sinful" and what's "immoral" that contribute to the feeling that you might get a call from God, or get inspired and push the wrong button? More realistically, wouldn't we expect a puritanical tone to be set in the White House if you were elected?'

Carter: Harry Truman was a Baptist. Some people get very abusive about the Baptist faith. If people want to know about it, they can read the New Testament. The main thing is that we don't think we're better than anyone else. We are taught not to judge other people. But as to some of the behavior you've mentioned, I can't change the teachings of Christ. I can't change the teachings of Christ! I believe in them, and a lot of people in this country do as well. Jews believe in the Bible. They have the same commandments.

Playboy: Then you as President, in appointing Supreme Court Justices—

Carter: I think we've pursued this conversation long enough—if you have another question.... Look, I'll try to express my views. It's not a matter of condemnation, it's not a matter of persecution. I've been a governor for four years. Anybody can come and look at my record. I didn't run around breaking down people's doors to see if they were fornicating. This is something that's ridiculous.

Playboy: We know you didn't, but we're being so persistent because of this matter of self-righteousness, because of the moral certainty of so many of your statements. People wonder if Jimmy Carter ever is unsure. Has he ever been wrong, has he ever had a failure of moral nerve?

Carter: Well, there are a lot of things I could have done differently had I known during my early life what I now know. I would certainly have spoken out more clearly and loudly on the civil rights issue. I would have demanded that our nation never get involved initially in the Vietnam war. I would have told the country in 1972 that Watergate was a much more horrible crime than we thought at the time. It's easy to say in hindsight what you would have done if you had had information you now have.

Playboy: We were asking not so much about hindsight as about being fallible. Aren't there any examples of things you did that weren't absolutely right?

Carter: I don't mind repeating myself. There are a lot of those in my life. Not speaking out for the cessation of the war in Vietnam. The fact that I didn't crusade at a very early stage for civil rights in the South, for the one-man, one-vote ruling. It might be that now I should drop my campaign for President and start a crusade for black-majority rule in South Africa or Rhodesia. It might be that later on, we'll

discover there were opportunities in our lives to do wonderful things and we didn't take advantage of them.

The fact that in 1954 I sat back and required the Warren Court to make this ruling without having crusaded myself—that was obviously a mistake on my part. But these are things you have to judge under the circumstances that prevailed when the decisions were being made. Back then, the Congress, the President, the newspaper editors, the civil libertarians all said that separate-but-equal facilities were adequate. These are opportunities overlooked, or maybe they could be characterized as absence of courage.

Playboy: Since you still seem to be saying you'd have done the right thing if you'd known what you know now, is it realistic to conclude that a person running for the highest office in the land *can't* admit many mistakes or moments of self-doubt?

Carter: I think that's a human circumstance. But if there are issues I'm avoiding because of a lack of courage, either I don't recognize them or I can't make myself recognize them.

Playboy: You mentioned Vietnam. Do you feel you spoke out at an early enough stage against the war?

Carter: No, I did not. I never spoke out publicly about withdrawing completely from Vietnam until March of 1971.

Playboy: Why?

Carter: It was the first time anybody had asked me about it. I was a farmer before then and wasn't asked about the war until I took office. There was a general feeling in this country that we ought not to be in Vietnam to start with. The American people were tremendously misled about the immediate prospects for victory, about the level of our involvement, about the relative cost in American lives. If I had known in the Sixties what I knew in the early Seventies, I think I would have spoken out more strongly. I was not in public office. When I took office as governor in 1970, I began to speak out about complete withdrawal. It was late compared with what many others had done, but I think it's accurate to say that the Congress and the people—with the exception of very small numbers of people—shared the belief that we were protecting our democratic allies.

Playboy: Even without holding office, you must have had some feelings about the war. When do you recall first feeling it was wrong?

Carter: There was an accepted feeling by me and everybody else that we ought not to be there, that we should never have gotten involved, we ought to get out.

Playboy: You felt that way all though the Sixties?

Carter: Yeah, that's right, and I might hasten to say that it was the same feeling expressed by Senators Russell and Talmadge—very conservative Southern political figures. They thought it was a serious mistake to be in Vietnam.

Playboy: Your son Jack fought in that war. Did you have any qualms about it at the time?

Carter: Well, yes, I had problems about my son fighting in the war, period. But I never make my sons' decisions for them. Jack went to war feeling it was foolish, a waste of time, much more deeply than I did. He also felt it would have been grossly unfair for him not to go when other, poorer kids had to.

Playboy: You were in favor of allocating funds for the South Vietnamese in 1975 as the war was coming to a close, weren't you?

Carter: That was when we were getting ready to evacuate our troops. The purpose of the money was to get our people out and maintain harmony between us and our Vietnamese allies, who had fought with us for 25 years. And I said yes, I would do that. But it was not a permanent thing, not to continue the war but to let us get our troops out in an orderly fashion.

Playboy: How did you respond to the argument that it was the Democrats, not the Republicans, who got us into the Vietnam war?

Carter: I think it started originally, maybe, with Eisenhower, then Kennedy, Johnson and then Nixon. It's not a partisan matter. I think Eisenhower probably first got us in there thinking that since France had failed, our country might slip in there and succeed. Kennedy thought he could escalate involvement by going beyond the mere advisory role. I guess if there was one President who made the most determined effort, conceivably, to end the war by massive force, it was certainly Johnson. And Nixon went into Cambodia and bombed it, and so forth.

It's not partisan—it's just a matter that evolved as a habit over several administrations. There was a governmental consciousness to deal in secrecy, to exclude the American people, to mislead them with false statements and sometimes outright lies. Had the American people been told the facts from the beginning by Eisenhower, Kennedy, MacNamara, Johnson, Kissinger and Nixon, I think there would have been different decisions made in our Government.

Playboy: At the Democratic Convention, you praised Johnson as a President who had vastly extended human rights. Were you simply omitting any mention of Vietnam?

Carter: It was obviously the factor that destroyed his political career and damaged his whole life. But as far as what I said at the convention, there hasn't been another President in our history—with the possible exception of Abraham Lincoln—who did so much to advance the cause of human rights.

Playboy: Except for the human rights of the Vietnamese and the Americans who fought there.

Carter: Well, I really believe that Johnson's motives were good. I think he tried to end the war even while the fighting was going on, and he was speaking about massive rehabilitation efforts, financed by our Government, to help people. I don't think he ever had any desire for permanent entrenchment of our forces in Vietnam. I think he had a mistaken notion that he was defending democracy and that what he was doing was compatible with the desires of the South Vietnamese.

Playboy: Then what about the administration that *ended* the war? Don't you have to give credit to Kissinger, the Secretary of State of a Republican President, for ending a war that a Democratic President escalated?

Carter: I think the statistics show that more bombs were dropped in Vietnam and Cambodia under Nixon and Kissinger than under Johnson. Both administrations were at fault; but I don't think the end came about as a result of Kissinger's superior diplomacy. It was the result of several factors that built up in an inexorable way: the demonstrated strength of the Viet Cong, the tremendous pressure to withdraw that came from the American people and an aroused Congress. I think Nixon and Kissinger did the proper thing in starting a phased withdrawal, but I don't consider that to be a notable diplomatic achievement by Kissinger. As we've now learned, he promised the Vietnamese things that cannot be delivered—reparations, payments, economic advantages, and so forth. Getting out of Vietnam was very good, but whether Kissinger deserved substantial diplomatic credit for it is something I doubt.

Playboy: You've said you'll pardon men who refused military service because of the Vietnam war but not necessarily those who deserted while they were in the Armed Forces. Is that right?

Carter: That's right. I would not include them. Deserters ought to be handled on a separate-case basis.

There's a difference to me. I was in the Navy for a long time. Somebody who goes into the military joins a kind of mutual partnership arrangement, you know what I mean? Your life depends on other people, their lives depend on you. So I don't intend to pardon the deserters. As far as the other categories of war resisters go, to me the ones who stayed in this country and let their opposition to the war be known publicly are more heroic than those who went and hid in Sweden. But I'm not capable of judging motives, so I'm just going to declare a blanket pardon.

Playboy: When?

Carter: The first week I'm in office.

Playboy: You've avoided the word amnesty and chosen to use the word pardon, but there doesn't seem to be much difference between the two in the dictionary. Could it be because amnesty is more emotionally charged and pardon a word more people will accept?

Carter: You know I can't deny that. But my reason for distinguishing between the two is that I think that all of those poor, and often black, young men who went to Vietnam are more worthy of recognition than those who defected, and the word pardon includes those who simply avoided the war completely. But I just want to bring the defectors back to this country without punishment and, in doing so, I would like to have the support of the American people. I haven't been able to devise for private or public presentation a better way to do it.

Playboy: Earlier this year, there was a report that as governor of Georgia, you had issued a resolution that seemed to support William Calley after his trial for the My Lai massacre and that you'd referred to him as a scapegoat. Was that a misreading of your position?

Carter: Yes. There was no reason for me to mislead anybody on the Calley thing. I thought when I first read about him that Calley was a murderer.

He was tried in Georgia and found to be a murderer. I said two things: One, that Calley was not typical of our American Servicemen and, two, that he was a scapegoat because his superiors should have been tried, too. The resolution I made as governor didn't have anything to do with Calley. The purpose of it, calling for solidarity with our boys in Vietnam, was to distinguish American Servicemen fighting an unpopular war. They weren't murderers, but they were equated, unfortunately, with a murderer in people's minds.

Playboy: In preparing for this interview, we spoke with your mother, your son Chip and your sister Gloria. We asked them what single action would most disappoint them in a Carter Presidency. They all replied that it would be if you ever sent troops to intervene in a foreign war. In fact, Miss Lillian said she would picket the White House.

Carter: They share my views completely.

Playboy: What about more limited military action? Would you have handled the Mayaguez incident the same way President Ford did?

Carter: Let me assess that in retrospect. It's obvious we didn't have adequate intelligence; we attacked an island when the Mayaguez crew was no longer there. There was a desire, I think, on the part of President Ford to extract maximum publicity from our effort, so that about 23 minutes after our crew was released, we went ahead and bombed the island airport. I hope I would have been capable of getting adequate intelligence, surrounded the island more quickly and isolated the crew so we wouldn't have had to attack the airport after the crew was released. These are some of the differences in the way I would have done it.

Playboy: So it's a matter of degree; you would have intervened militarily, too.

Carter: I would have done everything necessary to keep the crew from being taken to the mainland, yes.

Playboy: Then would you summarize your position on foreign intervention?

Carter: I would never intervene for the purpose of overthrowing a government. If enough were at stake for our national interest, I would use prestige, legitimate diplomatic leverage, trade mechanisms. But it would be the sort of effort that would not be embarrassing to this nation if revealed completely. I don't ever want to do anything as President that would be a contravention of the moral and ethical standards that I would exemplify in my own life as an individual or that would violate the principles or character of the American people.

Playboy: Do you feel it's fair criticism that you seem to be going back to some familiar faces—such as Paul Warnke and Cyrus Vance—for foreign-policy advice? Isn't there a danger of history's repeating itself when you seek out those who were involved in our Vietnam decisions?

Carter: I haven't heard that criticism. If you're raising it, then I respond to the new critic. These people contribute to foreign-affairs journals, they individually explore different concepts of foreign policy. I have 15 or 20 people who work with me very closely on foreign affairs. Their views are quite divergent. The fact that they may or may not have been involved in foreign-policy decisions in the past is certainly no detriment to their ability to help me now.

Playboy: In some respects, your foreign policy seems similar to that established by Kissinger, Nixon and Ford. In fact, Kissinger stated that he didn't think your differences were substantial. How, precisely, does your view differ from theirs?

Carter: As I've said in my speeches, I feel the policy of *détente* has given up too much to the Russians and gotten too little in return. I also feel Kissinger has equated his own popularity with the so-called advantages of *détente*. As I've traveled and spoken with world leaders—Helmut Schmidt of West Germany, Yitzhak Rabin of Israel, various leaders in Japan—I've discerned a deep concern on their part that the United States has abandoned a long-standing principle: to consult mutually, to share responsibility for problems. This has been a damaging thing. In addition, I believe we should have stronger bilateral relations with developing nations.

Playboy: What do you mean when you say we've given up too much to the Russians?

Carter: One example I've mentioned often is the Helsinki agreement. I never saw any reason we should be involved in the Helsinki meetings at all. We added the stature of our presence and signature to an agreement that, in effect, ratified the take-over of eastern Europe by the Soviet Union. We got very little, if anything in return. The Russians promised they would honor democratic principles and permit the free movement of their citizens, including those who want to emigrate. The Soviet Union has not lived up to those promises and Mr. Brezhnev was able to celebrate the major achievement of his diplomatic life.

Playboy: Are you charging that Kissinger was too soft on the Russians?

Carter: Kissinger has been in the position of being almost uniquely a spokesman for our nation. I think that is a legitimate role and a proper responsibility of the President himself. Kissinger has had a kind of Lone Ranger, secret foreign-policy attitude, which almost ensures that there cannot be adequate consultation with our allies; there cannot be a long-range commitment to unchanging principles; there cannot be a coherent evolution on foreign policy; there cannot be a bipartisan approach with support and advice from Congress. This is what I would avoid as President and is one of the major defects in the Nixon-Ford foreign policy as expressed by Kissinger.

Playboy: Say, do you always do your own sewing? *(This portion of the interview also took place aboard a plane. As he answered the interviewer's questions, Carter had been sewing a rip in his jacket with a needle and thread he carried with him.)*

Carter: Uh-huh. *(He bit off the thread with his teeth.)*

Playboy: Anyway, you said earlier that your foreign policy would exemplify your moral and ethical standards. Isn't there as much danger in an overly moralistic policy as in the kind that is too pragmatic?

Carter: I've said I don't think we should intervene militarily, but I see no reason not to express our approval, at least verbally, with those nations that develop democratically. When Kissinger says, as he did recently in a speech, that Brazil is the sort of government that is most compatible with ours— well, that's the kind of thing we want to change. Brazil is not a democratic government; it's a military dictatorship. In many instances, it's highly repressive to political prisoners. Our Government should justify the character and moral principles of the American people, and our foreign policy should not short-circuit that for temporary advantage. I think in every instance we've done that it's been counterproductive. When the CIA undertakes covert activities that might be justified if they were peaceful, we always suffer when they're revealed—it always seems as if we're trying to tell other people how to act. When Kissinger and Ford warned Italy she would be excluded from NATO if the Communists assumed power, that was the best way to make sure Communists *were* elected. The Italian voters resent it. A proper posture for our country in this sort of situation is to show, through demonstration, that our own Government works properly, that democracy is advantageous, and let the Italian people make their own decisions.

Playboy: And what if the Communists in Italy had been elected in greater numbers than they were? What if they had actually become a key part of the Italian government?

Carter: I think it would be a mechanism for subversion of the strength of NATO and the cohesiveness that ought to bind European countries together. The proper posture was the one taken by Helmut Schmidt, who said that German aid to Italy would be endangered.

Playboy: Don't you think that constitutes a form of intervention in the democratic processes of another nation?

Carter: No, I don't. I think that when the democratic nations of the world express themselves frankly and forcefully and openly, that's a proper exertion of influence. We did the same thing in Portugal. Instead of going in through surreptitious means and trying to overthrow the government when it looked like the minority Communist Party was going to assume power, the NATO countries as a group made it clear to Portugal what it would lose in the way of friendship, trade opportunities, and so forth. And the Portuguese people, recognizing that possibility, decided that the Communists should not lead their government. Well, that was legitimate exertion of influence, in my opinion. It was done openly and it was a mere statement of fact.

Playboy: You used the word subversion referring to communism. Hasn't the world changed since we used to throw words like that around? Aren't the west European Communist parties more independent of Moscow and more willing to respect democracy?

Carter: Yes, the world's changed. In my speeches, I've made it clear that as far as Communist leaders in such countries as Italy, France and Portugal are concerned, I would not want to close the doors of communication, consultation and friendship to them. That would be an almost automatic forcing of the Communist leaders into the Soviet sphere of influence. I also think we should keep open our opportunities for the east European nations—even those that are completely Communist—to trade with us, understand us, have tourist exchange and give them an option from complete domination by the Soviet Union.

But again, I don't think you could expect West Germany to lend Poland two billion dollars—which was the figure in the case of Italy—when Poland is part of the Soviet government's satellite and supportive-nation group. So I think the best way to minimize totalitarian influence within the governments of Europe is to make sure the democratic forces perform properly. The major shift toward the Communists in Italy was in the local elections, when the Christian Democrats destroyed their reputation by graft and corruption. If we can make our own Government work, if we can avoid future Watergates and avoid the activities of the CIA that have been revealed, if we can minimize joblessness and inflation, this will be a good way to lessen the inclination of people in other countries to turn away from our form of government.

Playboy: What about Chile? Would you agree that that was a case of the United States', through the CIA, intervening improperly?

Carter: Yes. There's no doubt about it. Sure.

Playboy: And you would stop that sort of thing?

Carter: Absolutely. Yes, sir.

Playboy: What about economic sanctions? Do you feel we should have punished the Allende government the way we did?

Carter: That's a complicated question, because we don't know what caused the fall of the Allende government, the murder of perhaps thousands of people, the incarceration of many others. I don't have any facts as to how deeply involved we were, but my impression is that we were involved quite deeply. As I said, I wouldn't have done that if I were President. But as to whether or not we ought to have an option on the terms of our loans, repayment schedules, interest charges, the kinds of materials we sell to them— those are options I would retain depending upon the compatibility of a foreign government with our own.

Playboy: To what do you attribute all those deceptions and secret maneuverings through the years? Why were they allowed to happen?

Carter: It was a matter of people's just saying, Well, that's politics; we don't have a right to know what our Government is doing; secrecy is OK; accepting gifts is OK; excluding the American people is OK. These are the kinds of things I want to change.

Playboy: It sounds as if you're saying Americans accepted indecency and lies in their Government all too easily. Doesn't that make your constant campaign theme, invoking the decency and honesty of the American people, somewhat naïve and ingenuous?

Carter: I say that the American people are basically decent and honest and want a truthful Government. Obviously, I know there are people in this country, out of 214,000,000, who are murderers. There are people, maybe, who don't want a decent Government. Maybe there are people who prefer lies to truth. But I don't think it's simplistic to say that our Government hasn't measured up to the ethical and moral standards of the people of this country. We've had better governments in the past and I think our people, as I've said many times, are just as strong, courageous and intelligent as they were 200 years ago. I think we still have the same inner strength they had then.

Playboy: Even though a lot of people support that feeling, many others think it makes you sound like an evangelist. And that makes it all the more confusing when they read about your hanging out with people so different from you in lifestyle and beliefs. Your publicized friendship with journalist Hunter Thompson, who makes no secret of his affinity for drugs and other craziness, is a good example.

Carter: Well, in the first place, I'm a human being. I'm not a packaged article that you can put in a little box and say, "Here's a Southern Baptist, an ignorant Georgia peanut farmer who doesn't have the right to enjoy music, who has no flexibility in his mind, who can't understand the sensitivities of an interpersonal relationship. He's gotta be predictable. He's gotta be for Calley and for the war. He's gotta be a liar. He's gotta be a racist."

You know, that's the sort of stereotype people tend to assume, and I hope it doesn't apply to me. And I don't see any mystery about having a friendship with Hunter Thompson. I guess it's something that's part of my character and it becomes a curiosity for those who see some mystery about someone of my background being elected President. I'm just a human being like everybody else. I have different interests, different understandings of the world around me, different relationships with different kinds of people. I have a broad range of friends: sometimes very serious, sometimes very formal, sometimes lighthearted, sometimes intense, sometimes casual.

Playboy: So when you find yourself at a rock concert or in some other situation that seems at odds with your rural, religious background, you never feel a sense of estrangement?

Carter: None. No. I feel at home with 'em.

Playboy: How did you get to feel this way without going through culture shock?

Carter: I have three sons, who now range from 23 to 29, and the oldest of them were very influenced by Bob Dylan in their attitudes toward civil rights, criminal justice and the Vietnam war. This was about the period of time I was entering politics. I've been fairly close to my sons and their taste in music influenced my taste, and I was able to see the impact of Bob Dylan's attitudes on young people. And I was both gratified by and involved emotionally in those changes in attitudes.

Later, when I became governor, I was acquainted with some of the people at Capricorn Records in Macon—Otis Redding and others. It was they who began to meld the white and black music industries, and that was quite a sociological change for our region. So as I began to travel around Georgia, I made contact a few days every month or two with Capricorn Records, just to stay in touch with people in the state, and got to know all the Allman Brothers, Dicky Betts and others. Later on, I met Charlie Daniels and the Marshall Tucker Band.

Then I decided to run for President. I didn't have any money and didn't have any political base, so I had to depend substantially on the friends I already had. One of my potential sources for fund raising and for recruiting young volunteers was the group of recording stars I already knew. So we began to have concerts and I got to know them even better.

Of course, I've also been close to the country-music folks in Georgia, as well as the Atlanta Symphony Orchestra. The first large contribution I got— $1,000—was from Robert Shaw, the music director of the orchestra. We've been over at the Grand Ole Opry a few times and gotten to know people like Chubby Jackson and Tom T. Hall.

Playboy: There's been a lot of publicity about your relationship with Dylan, whom you quoted in your acceptance speech at the Democratic Convention. How did that come about?

Carter: A number of years ago, my second son, Chip, who was working full time in our farming business, took a week off during Christmas. He and a couple of his friends drove all the way to New York—just to see Bob Dylan. There had been a heavy snowstorm and the boys had to park several miles from Dylan's home. It was after Dylan was injured, when he was in seclusion. Apparently, Dylan came to the door with two of his kids and shook hands with Chip. By the time Chip got to the nearest phone, a couple of miles away, and called us at home, he was nearly incoherent. Rosalynn couldn't understand what Chip was talking about, so she screamed, "Jimmy, come here quick! Something's happened to Chip!"

We finally deciphered that he had shaken Dylan's hand and was just, you know, very carried away with it. So when I read that Dylan was going on tour again, I wrote him a little personal note and asked him to come visit me at the governor's mansion. I think he checked with Phil Walden of Capricorn Records and Bill Graham to find out what kind of guy *is* this, and he was assured I didn't want to use him, I was just interested in his music.

The night he came, we had a chance to talk about his music and about changing times and pent-up emotions in young people. He said he didn't have any inclination to change the world, that he wasn't crusading and that his personal feelings were apparently compatible with the yearnings of an entire generation. We also discussed Israel, which he had a strong interest in. But that's my only contact with Bob Dylan, that night.

Playboy: That brings us back to the reason so many people find it hard to get a handle on you: On the one hand, your association with youth culture, civil rights and other liberal movements; and on the other, your apparent conservatism on many issues. Would you care to put it in a nutshell for us?

Carter: I'll try. On human rights, civil rights, environmental quality, I consider myself to be very liberal. On the management of government, on openness of government, on strengthening individual liberties and local levels of government, I consider myself a conservative. And I don't see that the two attitudes are incompatible.

Playboy: Then let's explore a few more issues. Not everyone is sure, for instance, what you mean by your call for tax reform. Does it mean that the burden will shift to corporations and upper-income groups and away from the middle- and lower-income groups, or are you talking merely about a simplified tax code?

Carter: It would involve both. One change I'm calling for is simplification, and the other involves shifting the income tax burden away from the lower-income families. But what I'm really talking about is total, comprehensive tax reform for the first time since the income tax was approved back in 1913, I think it was.

It's not possible to give you a definitive statement on tax reform any time soon. It's going to take at least a year before we can come up with a new tax structure. But there are some general provisions that would be instituted that aren't there now. The income-tax code, which now comprises 40,000 pages, will be greatly simplified. Income should be taxed only once. We should have a true progressive income tax, so that the higher the income, the higher the percentage of taxation. I see no reason why capital gains should be taxed at half the rate of income from manual labor. I would be committed to a great reduction in tax incentives, loopholes or whatever you want to call them, which are used as mechanisms to solve transient economic problems; they ought to be on a basis of annual appropriation or a time limit, rather than be built into the tax structure.

In any case, these are five or six things that would be dramatic departures from what we presently have and they should tell you what side of the issue I stand on.

Playboy: Would one of those be increasing taxes for corporations, especially the overseas and domestic profits of multinational corporations?

Carter: No, I don't think so. Obviously, there have been provisions written into the law that favor certain corporations, including those that have overseas investments; I would remove those incentives. Tax laws also benefit those who have the best lobbying efforts, those who have the most influence in Washington, and the larger the corporations are, on the average, the smaller proportion they pay in taxes. Small businesses quite often pay the flat maximum rate, 48 percent, while some larger corporations pay as little as five or six percent. That ought to be changed.

But as far as increasing over-all corporate rate taxes above the 50 percent level, I wouldn't favor that. We also have the circumstance of multinational corporations' depending on bribery as a mechanism for determining the outcome of a sale. I think bribery in international affairs ought to be considered a crime and punishable by imprisonment.

Playboy: Would you sympathize with the anticorporate attitude that many voters feel?

Carter: Well, I'm not particularly anticorporate, but I'd say I'm more oriented to consumer protection. One of the things I've established throughout the campaign is the need to break up the sweetheart arrangement between regulatory agencies and the industries they regulate. Another is the need for rigid and enthusiastic enforcement of the antitrust laws.

Playboy: To take another issue, you favor a comprehensive Federal health-care system. Why don't you just support the Kennedy-Corman bill, which provides for precisely that?

Carter: As a general philosophy, wherever the private sector can perform a function as effectively and efficiently as the Government, I would prefer to keep it within the private sector. So I would like the insurance aspect of the health program to be carried out by employer/employee contribution. There would be contributions from the general fund for those who are indigent. I would also have a very heavy emphasis on preventive health care, since I believe most of the major afflictions that beset people can be prevented or minimized. And I favor the use to a greater degree of nonphysicians, such as nurses, physicians' assistants, and so forth. Some of these things are in conflict with the provisions of the Kennedy-Corman bill.

Playboy: Let us ask you about one last stand: abortion.

Carter: I think abortion is wrong and I will do everything I can as President to minimize the need for abortions—within the framework of the decision of the Supreme Court, which I can't change. Georgia had a more conservative approach to abortion, which I personally favored, but the Supreme Court ruling suits me all right. I signed a Georgia law as governor that was compatible with the Supreme Court decision.

Playboy: You think it's wrong, but the ruling suits you? What would we tell a woman who said her vote would depend on how you stood on abortion?

Carter: If a woman's major purpose in life is to have unrestricted abortions, then she ought *not* to vote for me. But she wouldn't have anyone to vote for.

Playboy: There seem to have been relatively few women in important staff positions in your campaign. Is that accurate?

Carter: Women have been in charge of our entire campaign effort in Georgia and in New York State outside New York City. Also in Nebraska, Kansas, a third of the state of Florida and other areas.

Playboy: But whenever we hear about a meeting of top staff members, they almost always seem to be white males. Is that a failing in your organization?

Carter: I don't know about a failing. The three people with whom I consult regularly—in addition to my wife—are white males: Hamilton Jordan, Jody Powell and Charles Kirbo. But we *do* have a lot of women involved in the campaign. We are now setting up a policy committee to run a nationwide effort to coordinate Democratic races and 50 percent of the members of this committee will be women. But Jody has been my press secretary since 1970, and Hamilton and Kirbo were my major advisors in 1966. It's such an extremely stable staff that there's been no turnover at all in the past five or six years. But we've made a lot of progress, I think, in including women, and I think you'll see more.

Playboy: You mention very frequently how much you count on your wife's advice. Isn't there a strain during the campaign, with the two of you separated so much of the time?

Carter: Well, when I was in the Navy, I was at sea most of the time and I'd see her maybe one or two nights a week. Now, when I'm home in Plains, I see her almost every night. And if I'm elected President, I'll see her *every* night. So there is obviously a time to be together and a time to be separated. If you're apart three or four days and then meet again, it's almost—for me, it's a very exciting reunion. I'll have been away from Rosalynn for a few days and if I see her across an airport lobby, or across a street, I get just as excited as I did when I was, you know, 30 years younger.

We have a very close, very intimate sharing of our lives and we've had a tremendous magnification of our life's purposes in politics. Before 1966, she and I were both very shy. It was almost a painful thing to approach a stranger or make a speech. It's been a mutual change we've gone through, because we both felt it was worth while; so no matter what the outcome of the election, the relationship between Rosalynn and me will be very precious.

Playboy: Did you both have the usual share of troubles adjusting to marriage?

Carter: We did at first. We've come to understand each other much better. I was by far the dominant person in the marriage at the beginning, but not anymore. She's just as strong, if not stronger than I am. She's fully equal to me in every way in our relationship, in making business decisions, and she makes most of the decisions about family affairs. And I think it was a struggle for her to achieve this degree of independence and equality in our personal relationship. So, to summarize, years ago we had a lot of quarrels—none serious, particularly—but now we don't.

Playboy: A lot of marriages are foundering these days. Why is yours so successful?

Carter: Well, I really love Rosalynn more now than I did when I married her. And I have loved no other women except her. I had gone out with all kinds of girls, sometimes fairly steadily, but I just never cared about them. Rosalynn had been a friend of my sister's and was three years younger than I, which is a tremendous chasm in the high school years. She was just one of those insignificant little girls around the house. Then, when I was 21 and home from the Navy on leave, I took her out to a movie. Nothing extraordinary happened, but the next morning I told my mother, "That's the girl I want to marry." It's the best thing that ever happened to me.

We also share a religious faith, and the two or three times in our married life when we've had a serious crisis, I think that's what sustained our marriage and helped us overcome our difficulty. Our children, too, have been a factor binding Rosalynn and me together. After the boys, Amy came along late and it's been especially delightful for me, maybe because she's a little girl.

Playboy: This is a tough question to ask, but because it's been such a factor in American political life, we wonder if you've ever discussed with Rosalynn the possibility of being assassinated. And, assuming you have, how do you deal with it in your own mind?

Carter: Well, in the first place, I'm not afraid of death. In the second place, it's the same commitment I made when I volunteered to go into the submarine force. I accepted a certain degree of danger when I made the original decision, then I didn't worry about it anymore. It wasn't something that preyed on my mind; it wasn't something I had to reassess every five minutes. There is a certain element of danger in running for President, borne out by statistics on the number of Presidents who have been attacked, but I have to say frankly that it's something I never worry about.

Playboy: Your first answer was that you don't fear death. Why not?

Carter: It's part of my religious belief. I just look at death as not a threat. It's inevitable, and I have an assurance of eternal life. There is no feeling on my part that I *have* to be President, or that I *have* to live, or that I'm immune to danger. It's just that the termination of my physical life is relatively insignificant in my concept of over-all existence. I don't say that in a mysterious way; I recognize the possibility of assassination. But I guess everybody recognizes the possibility of other forms of death— automobile accidents, airplane accidents, cancer. I just don't worry.

Playboy: There's been some evidence that Johnson and Nixon both seemed to have gone a bit crazy while they were in the White House. Do you ever wonder if the pressures of the office might make *anyone* mentally unstable?

Carter: I really don't have the feeling that being in the White House is what caused Nixon's or Johnson's problems. Other Presidents have served without developing mental problems—

Roosevelt, Truman, Eisenhower, Kennedy, for instance. As far as I've been able to discern, President Ford approaches—or avoids—the duties of the White House with equanimity and self-assurance.

I think the ability to accept oneself and to feel secure and confident, to avoid any degree of paranoia, to face reality, these factors are fairly independent of whether or not one is President. The same factors would be important if someone were chief of police, or a schoolteacher, or a magazine editor. The pressure is greater on a President, obviously, than some of the jobs I've described, but I think the ability to accommodate pressure is a personal thing.

Playboy: We noticed your crack about President Ford's avoiding the duties of the White House. Do you agree with Senator Mondale's assessment, when he said shortly after the nomination that Ford isn't intelligent enough to be a good President?

Carter: Well, if you leave Mondale out of it, I personally think that President Ford is adequately intelligent to be President.

Playboy: And what about your Presidency, if you're elected—will you have a dramatic first 1000 days?

Carter: I would hope that my Administration wouldn't be terminated at the end of 1000 days, as was the case with one administration. I'm beginning to meet with key leaders of Congress to evolve specific legislation to implement the Democratic platform commitment. If I'm elected, there will be no delay in moving aggressively on a broad front to carry out the promises I've made to the American people. I intend to stick to everything I've promised.

Playboy: Thanks for all the time you've given us. Incidentally, do you have any problems with appearing in *Playboy*? Do you think you'll be criticized?

Carter: I don't object to that at all. I don't believe I'll be criticized.

(At the final session, which took place in the living room of Carter's home in Plains, the allotted time was up. A press aide indicated that there were other appointments for which Carter was already late, and the aide opened the front door while amenities were exchanged. As the interviewer and the Playboy *editor stood at the door, recording equipment in their arms, a final, seemingly casual question was tossed off. Carter then delivered a long, softly spoken monolog that grew in intensity as he made his final points. One of the journalists signaled to Carter that they were still taping, to which Carter nodded his assent.)*

Playboy: Do you feel you've reassured people with this interview, people who are uneasy about your religious beliefs, who wonder if you're going to make a rigid, unbending President?

Carter: I don't know if you've been to Sunday school here yet; some of the press has attended. I teach there about every three or four weeks. It's getting to be a real problem because we don't have room to put everybody now when I teach. I don't know if we're going to have to issue passes or what. It almost destroys the worship aspect of it. But we had a good class last Sunday. It's a good way to learn what I believe and what the Baptists believe.

One thing the Baptists believe in is complete autonomy. I don't accept any domination of my life by the Baptist Church, none. Every Baptist church is individual and autonomous. We don't accept domination of our church from the Southern Baptist Convention. The reason the Baptist Church was formed in this country was because of our belief in absolute and total separation of church and state. These basic tenets make us almost unique. We don't believe in any hierarchy in church. We don't have bishops. Any officers chosen by the church are defined as servants, not bosses. They're supposed to do the dirty work, make sure the church is clean and painted and that sort of thing. So it's a very good, democratic structure.

When my sons were small, we went to church and they went, too. But when they got old enough to make their own decisions, they decided when to go and they varied in their devoutness. Amy really looks forward to going to church, because she gets to see all her cousins at Sunday school. I never knew anything except going to church. My wife and I were born and raised in innocent times. The normal thing to do was to go to church.

What Christ taught about most was pride, that one person should never think he was any better than anybody else. One of the most vivid stories Christ told in one of his parables was about two people who went into a church. One was an official of the church, a Pharisee, and he said, "Lord, I thank you that I'm not like all those other people. I keep all your commandments, I give a tenth of everything I own. I'm here to give thanks for making me more acceptable in your sight." The other guy was despised by the nation, and he went in, prostrated himself on the floor and said, "Lord, have mercy on me, a sinner. I'm not worthy to lift my eyes to heaven." Christ asked the disciples which of the two had justified his life. The answer was obviously the one who was humble.

The thing that's drummed into us all the time is not to be proud, not to be better than anyone else, not to look down on people but to make ourselves acceptable in God's eyes through our own actions and recognize the simple truth that we're saved by grace. It's just a free gift through faith in Christ. This gives us a mechanism by which we can relate permanently to God. I'm not speaking for other people, but it gives me a sense of peace and equanimity and assurance.

I try not to commit a deliberate sin. I recognize that I'm going to do it anyhow, because I'm human and I'm tempted. And Christ set some almost impossible standards for us. Christ said, "I tell you that anyone who looks on a woman with lust has in heart already committed adultery."

I've looked on a lot of women with lust. I've committed adultery in my heart many times. This is something that God recognizes I will do—and I have done it—and God forgives me for it. But that doesn't mean that I condemn someone who not only looks on a woman with lust but who leaves his wife and shacks up with somebody out of wedlock.

Christ says, Don't consider yourself better than someone else because one guy screws a whole bunch of women while the other guy is loyal to his wife. The guy who's loyal to his wife ought not to be condescending or proud because of the relative degree of sinfulness. One thing that Paul Tillich said was that religion is a search for the truth about man's existence and his relationship with God and his fellow man; and that once you stop searching and think you've got it made—at that point, you lose your religion. Constant reassessment, searching in one's heart—it gives me a feeling of confidence.

I don't inject these beliefs in my answers to your secular questions.

(Carter clenched his fist and gestured sharply.)

But I don't think I would *ever* take on the same frame of mind that Nixon or Johnson did—lying, cheating and distorting the truth. Not taking into consideration my hope for my strength of character, I think that my religious beliefs alone would prevent that from happening to me. I have that confidence. I hope it's justified.

The Second Ford-Carter Debate (1976)

On August 9, 1974, Gerald Ford became the first president in history not to have been elected as either the president or the vice president. (See "The Twenty-fifth Amendment: Senate Debate," p. 522.) Entering the 1976 election year, Ford faced a number of political obstacles. He had never run a national campaign—indeed, he had never run in a constituency larger than Michigan's fifth congressional district. The combination of an economic recession and Ford's pardon of Richard Nixon, the disgraced former president, had severely damaged his political standing with the voters. Finally, the new system of primaries-based presidential nominations eased the burden of his main challenger within the Republican party, the conservative former governor of California, Ronald Reagan. (See "The McGovern-Fraser Commission Report," p. 574.)

Ford and Reagan waged a neck-and-neck race for the Republican nomination that lasted right up to the party's national convention in August 1976. Ford nosed out Reagan on the first ballot by 1,187 votes to 1,070 votes, but he trailed the Democratic nominee for president, former Georgia governor Jimmy Carter, by a wide margin in the polls. In a gesture to his party's conservatives, Ford selected Sen. Robert Dole of Kansas as his vice presidential running mate. (Ford's first choice had

been Reagan, who turned him down.) Then, in a bold move, Ford crowned his acceptance speech to the convention by challenging Carter to a series of televised debates, the first time in history that an incumbent president had issued such a challenge. Carter readily accepted.

The first Ford-Carter debate, which was held in Philadelphia on September 23, 1976, is best remembered for the twenty-five minute silence that ensued after network audio facilities broke down. (Ford and Carter stood stiffly and silently throughout the entire hiatus.) But Ford, who seemed more confident and assertive than Carter, benefited substantially from the debate. Polls showed that he was starting to gain on his Democratic rival.

Unfortunately for Ford, the second debate, which took place on October 6 in San Francisco, was the occasion for a severe self-inflicted political wound. In response to a question about U.S.-Soviet relations, Ford said, "There is no Soviet domination of Eastern Europe and there never will be under a Ford administration." Pressed for clarification, the president reiterated his answer. Carter rejoined, "I would like to see Mr. Ford convince the Polish Americans and the Czech Americans and the Hungarian Americans in this country that those countries don't live under the domination and supervision *of the Soviet Union behind the Iron Curtain."*

Most voters who watched the second debate did not catch Ford's error; indeed, the first polls showed that a plurality thought Ford had bested Carter again. But during the next several days, reporters questioned the president and his aides relentlessly about the "no Soviet domination" remark. The leaders of several East European-American ethnic associations demanded a retraction. Ford eventually succumbed—"The original mistake was mine. I did not express myself clearly. I admit it," he said on October 12, 1976—but, politically, the damage was done. Longstanding public doubts about Ford's competence as president were rekindled.

On election day, Carter and his running mate, Sen. Walter F. Mondale of Minnesota, narrowly defeated Ford and Dole. Rousing regional pride to rekindle dormant southern Democratic loyalties, Carter won by 297-240 in the electoral college and by 50.1 percent to 48.0 percent in the popular vote. ~

[Republican Record]

Q: Governor, since the Democrats last ran our foreign policy, including many of the men who are advising you, the country has been relieved of the Vietnam agony and the military draft, we've started arms control negotiations with the Russians, we've opened relations with China, we've arranged the disengagement of the Middle East, we've regained influence with the Arabs without deserting Israel. Now, maybe, we've even begun a process of peaceful change in Africa. Now you've objected in this campaign to the style with which much of this is done and you've mentioned some other things that you think ought to have been done. But do you really have a quarrel with this Republican record? Would you not have done any of those things?

Carter: Well, I think the Republican administration has been almost all style and spectacular and not substance. We've got a chance tonight to talk about first of all leadership, the character of our country and a vision of the future. And in every one of these instances the Ford administration has failed. And I hope tonight that I and Mr. Ford will have a chance to discuss the reason for those failures. Our country is not strong anymore. We're not respected anymore. We can only be strong overseas if we're strong at home. And when I become President, we'll not only be strong in those areas but also in defense. A defense capability second to none.

We've lost in our foreign policy the character of the American people. We've ignored or excluded the American people and Congress from participation in shaping of our foreign policy. It has been one of secrecy or exclusion. In addition to that we've had a chance to become now, contrary to our longstanding beliefs and principles, the arms merchant of the whole world. We've tried to buy success from our enemies at the same time we've excluded from the process the normal friendship of our allies. In addition to that, we've become fearful to compete with the Soviet Union on an equal basis. We talk about detente. The Soviet Union knows what they want in detente, and they've been getting it. We have not known what we've wanted and we've been out-traded in almost every instance.

The other point I want to make is about our defense. We've got to be a nation blessed with a defense capability—efficient, tough, capable, well organized, narrowly focused fighting capability. The ability to fight, if necessary, is the best way to avoid the chance for or the requirement to fight.

And the last point I want to make is this. Mr. Ford and Mr. Kissinger have continued on with the policies of Richard Nixon. Even the Republican platform has criticized the lack of leadership in Mr. Ford and they criticized the foreign policy of his administration. This is one instance in which I agree with the Republican platform.

I might say this in closing, and that is that as far as foreign policy goes, Mr. Kissinger has been the President of this country. Mr. Ford has shown an absence of leadership, and an absence of a grasp of what this country is and what it ought to be. That's got to be changed, and that is one of the major issues of this campaign in 1976.

Ford: Governor Carter is talking in broad generalities. Let me take just one question that he raises: The military strength and capability of the United States. Governor Carter in November of 1975 indicated that he wanted to cut the defense budget by $15-billion. A few months later he said he wanted to cut the defense budget by $8-billion or $9-billion. And more recently he talks about cutting the defense budget by $5-billion to $7-billion. There is no way you can be strong militarily and have those kind of reductions in our military appropriations.

Now let me tell you a little story. About late October of 1975, I asked the then Secretary of Defense Mr. Schlesinger to tell me what had to be done if we were going to reduce the defense budget by $3-billion to $5-billion.

A few days later Mr. Schlesinger came back and said if we cut the defense budget by $3-billion to $5-billion, we will have to cut military personnel by 250,000; civilian personnel by 100,000; jobs in America by 100,000. We would have to stretch out our aircraft procurement. We would have to reduce our naval construction program. We would have to reduce our research and development for the Army, the Navy, the Air Force and Marines by 8 per cent. We would have to close 20 military bases in the United States immediately.

That's the kind of a defense program that Mr. Carter wants.

Let me tell you this straight from the shoulder: You don't negotiate with Mr. Brezhnev from weakness, and the kind of a defense program that Mr. Carter wants will mean a weaker defense and a poor negotiating position.

[Cold War]

Q: Mr. President, my question is really the other side of the coin. For a generation, the United States has had a foreign policy based on containment of Communism. Yet we have lost the first war in Vietnam. We lost a shoving match in Angola. The Communists threatened to come to power by peaceful means in Italy and relations generally have cooled with the Soviet Union in the last few months. So let me ask you first, what do you do about such cases as Italy? And secondly, does this general drift mean that we're moving back toward something of a cold war relationship with the Soviet Union?

Ford: I don't believe we should move to a cold war relationship. I think it's in the best interest of the United States, and the world as a whole, that the United States negotiate rather than go back to the cold war relationship with the Soviet Union.

I don't look at the picture as bleakly as you indicated in your question, Mr. Trewhitt. I believe that the United States has had many successes in recent years, in recent months as far as the Communist movement is concerned. We have been successful in Portugal, where a year ago it looked like there was a very great possibility that the Communists would take over in Portugal. I didn't happen. We have democracy in Portugal today.

A few months ago, I should say maybe two years ago, the Soviet Union looked like they had continued strength in the Middle East. Today, according to Prime Minister Rabin, the Soviet Union is weaker in the Middle East than they have been in many, many years. The facts are the Soviet Union relationship with Egypt is at a low level. The Soviet Union relationship with Syria is at a very low point. The United States today, according to Prime Minister Rabin of Israel, is at a peak in its influence and power in the Middle East.

But let's turn a minute to the southern African operations that are now going on. The United States of America took the initiative in southern Africa. We wanted to end the bloodshed in southern Africa. We wanted to have the right of self-determination in Africa. We wanted to have majority rule with the full protection of the rights of the minority. We wanted to preserve human dignity in southern Africa. We have taken the initiative, and in southern Africa today the United States is trusted by the other elements in southern Africa.

The United States' foreign policy under this administration has been one of progress and success. And I believe that instead of talking about Soviet progress we can talk about American successes. And may I make an observation [about] part of the question you asked, Mr. Trewhitt. I don't believe it's in the best interest of the United States and the NATO nations to have a Communist government in NATO. Mr. Carter has said he would look with sympathy to a Communist government in NATO and I am totally opposed to it.

Carter: Unfortunately, he's just made a statement that's not true. I have never advocated a Communist government for Italy. That would obviously be a ridiculous thing for anyone to do who wanted to be President of this country. I think that this is an instance of deliberate distortion, and this has occurred also in the question about defense.

As a matter of fact, I've never advocated any cut of $15-billion in our defense budget. As a matter of fact, Mr. Ford has made a political football out of the defense budget. About a year ago, he cut the Pentagon budget $6.8-billion. After he fired James Schlesinger, the political heat got so great that he added back about $3-billion. When Ronald Reagan won the Texas primary election, Mr. Ford added back another $1.5-billion. Immediately before the Kansas City convention he added back another $1.8-billion in the defense budget.

And his own Office of Management and Budget testified that he had a $3-billion cut insurance added to the defense budget under pressure from the Pentagon. Obviously this is another indication of trying to use the defense budget for political purposes, like he's trying to do tonight.

Now we went into South Africa late; after Great Britain, Rhodesia, the black nations had been trying to solve this problem for many years. We didn't go in until right before the election, similar to what had taken place in 1972 when Mr. Kissinger announced peace was at hand just before the election at that time. And we have weakened our position in NATO because the other countries in Europe supported the democratic forces in Portugal long before we did. We stuck to the Portugal dictatorships much longer than other democracies did in this war.

[Experience, Secrecy]

Q: Governor Carter, much of what the United States does abroad is done in the name of the national interest. What is your concept of the national interest? What should the role of the United States in the world be and in that connection, concerning your limited experience in foreign affairs and the fact that you take some pride in being a Washington outsider, don't you think it would be appropriate to tell the

American voters, before the election, the people you would like to have in key positions such as Secretary of State, Secretary of Defense, national security affairs adviser at the White House?

Carter: Well, I'm not going to name my Cabinet before I get elected. I've got a little ways to go before I start doing that. But I have an adequate background I believe. I am a graduate of the U.S. Naval Academy, the first military graduate since Eisenhower. I served as governor of Georgia and have traveled extensively in foreign countries and South America, Central America, Europe, the Middle East and in Japan. I've traveled the last 21 months among the people of this country. I've talked to them and I've listened. And I've seen it first hand in a very vivid way the deep hurt that's come to this country in the aftermath of Vietnam and Cambodia and Chile and Pakistan and Angola and Watergate, CIA revelations.

What we were formerly so proud of— the strength of our country, its moral integrity, the representation in foreign affairs of what our people or what our Constitution stands for has been gone in the secrecy that has surrounded our foreign policy in the last few years. The American people, the Congress have been excluded.

I believe I know what this country ought to be. I've been one who's loved my nation as many American do and I believe there's no limit placed in what we can do in the future if we can harness the tremendous resources, militarily, economically and the stature of our people, the meaning of our Constitution in the future.

Every time we've had a serious mistake in foreign affairs, it's been because the American people have been excluded from the process. If we can just tap the intelligence and ability, the sound common sense and the good judgment of the American people, we can once again have a foreign policy to make us proud instead of ashamed, and

I'm not going to exclude the American people from that process in the future as Mr. Ford and Kissinger have done.

This is what it takes to have a sound foreign policy—strong at home, strong defense, permanent commitments, not betray the principles of our country, and involve the American people and the Congress in the shaping of our foreign policy. Every time Mr. Ford speaks from a position of secrecy in negotiations and secret treaties that have been pursued and achieved, in supporting dictatorships, in ignoring human rights, we are weak and the rest of the world knows it.

So these are the ways that we can restore the strength of our country, and they don't require a long experience in foreign policy. Nobody has that except a President who's served a long time or a Secretary of State. But my background, my experience, my knowledge of the people of this country, my commitment to our principles that don't change, those are the best bases to correct the horrible mistakes of this administration and restore our own country to a position of leadership in this world.

Q: How specifically, Governor, are you going to bring the American people into the decision-making process in foreign policy? What does that mean?

Carter: First of all, I would quit conducting the decision-making process in secret, as has been the characteristic of Mr. Kissinger and Mr. Ford. In many instances we've made agreements, like in Vietnam, that have revealed later on to our embarrassment.

Recently Ian Smith, the president of Rhodesia, announced that he had unequivocal commitments from Mr. Kissinger that he could not reveal. The American people don't know what those commitments are. We've seen in the past a destruction of the elected governments like in Chile and the strong support of military dictatorship there. These kinds of things have hurt us very much.

I would restore the concept of the fireside chat, which was an integral part of the administration of Franklin Roosevelt, and I would also restore the involvement of the Congress.

When Harry Truman was President he was not afraid to have a strong Secretary of Defense. Dean Acheson, George Marshall were strong Secretaries of Defense, excuse me, State. But he also made sure that there was a bipartisan support. The members of Congress—Arthur Vandenburg, Walter George—were part of the process. And before our nation made a secret agreement, before we made a bluffing statement, we were sure that we had the backing not only of the President and the Secretary of State but also of the Congress and the people. This is the responsibility of the President, and I think it's very damaging to our country that Mr. Ford has turned over this responsibility to the Secretary of State.

Ford: Governor Carter again contradicts himself. He complains about secrecy and yet he is quoted as saying that in the attempt to find a solution in the Middle East that he would hold unpublicized meetings with the Soviet Union, I presume for the purpose of imposing a settlement on Israel and the Arab nations.

But let me talk just a minute about what we've done to avoid secrecy in the Ford administration. After the United States took the initiative in working with Israel and with Egypt in achieving the Sinai II Agreement—and I'm proud to say that not a single Egyptian or Israeli soldier has lost his life since the signing of the Sinai Agreement. But at the time that I submitted every single document that was applicable to the Sinai II Agreement. It was the most complete documentation by any President of any agreement signed by a President on behalf of the United States.

Now as far as meeting with the Congress is concerned, during the 24 months that I've been the President of

the United States, I have averaged better than one meeting a month with responsible groups or committees of the Congress, both House and Senate. The Secretary of State has appeared in the several years that he's been the Secretary before 80 different committee hearings in the House and in the Senate. The Secretary of State has made better than 50 speeches all over the United States explaining American foreign policy. I have made myself at least 10 speeches in various parts of the country where I have discussed with the American people defense and foreign policy.

[Soviets, Eastern Europe]

Q: Mr. President, I'd like to explore a little more deeply our relationship with the Russians. Now, they used to brag during Khrushchev's day that because of their greater patience and because of our greed for business deals that they would sooner or later get the better of us. Is it possible that, despite some setbacks in the Middle East, they've proved their point? Our allies in France and Italy are now flirting with Communism. We've recognized a permanent Communist regime in East Germany. We've virtually signed in Helsinki an agreement that the Russians have dominance in Eastern Europe. We've bailed out Soviet agriculture with our huge grain sales, we've given them large loans, access to our best technology, and if the Senate hadn't interfered with the Jackson amendment, maybe you would have given them even larger loans. Is that what you call a two-way street of traffic in Europe?

Ford: I believe that we've negotiated with the Soviet Union since I've been President from a position of strength. And let me cite several examples.

Shortly after I became President, in December of 1974, I met with General

Secretary Brezhnev in Vladivostok, and we agreed to a mutual cap on ballistic missile launchers at a ceiling of 2,400, which means that the Soviet Union, if that becomes a permanent agreement, will have to make a reduction in their launchers that they now have or plan to have. I've negotiated at Vladivostok with Mr. Brezhnev a limitation on the MIRVing of their ballistic missiles at a figure of 1,320, which is the first time that any President has achieved a cap, either on launchers or on MIRV's.

It seems to me that we can go from there to the grain sales. The grain sales have been a benefit to American agriculture. We have achieved a 5¾ year sale of a minimum of 6-million metric tons, which means that they have already bought about 4-million metric tons this year and are bound to buy another 2-million metric tons, to take the grain and corn and wheat that American farmers have produced in order to have full production, and these grain sales to the Soviet Union have helped us tremendously in meeting the costs of the additional oil, and the oil that we have bought from overseas.

If we turn to Helsinki, I'm glad you raised it Mr. Frankel. In the case of Helsinki, 35 nations signed an agreement, including the Secretary of State for the Vatican. I can't under any circumstances believe that his Holiness the Pope would agree by signing that agreement that the 35 nations have turned over to the Warsaw Pact nations the domination of Eastern Europe. It just isn't true, and if Mr. Carter alleges that His Holiness, by signing that has done, he is totally inaccurate.

Now, what has been accomplished by the Helsinki agreement—number one— we have an agreement where they notify us and we notify them of any military maneuvers that are to be undertaken. They have done it in both cases where they've done so. There is no Soviet domination of Eastern Europe and

there never will be under a Ford administration.

Q: I'm sorry, could I just follow? Did I understand you to say, sir, that the Russians are not using Eastern Europe as their own sphere of influence and occupying most of the countries there and making sure with their troops that it's a Communist zone, whereas on our side of the line, the Italians and the French are still flirting with communism?

Ford: I don't believe, Mr. Frankel, that the Yugoslavians consider themselves dominated by the Soviet Union. I don't believe that the Romanians consider themselves dominated by the Soviet Union. I don't believe that the Poles consider themselves dominated by the Soviet Union. Each of those countries is independent or autonomous. It has its own territorial integrity, and the United States does not concede that those countries are under the domination of the Soviet Union. As a matter of fact, I visited Poland, Yugoslavia and Romania to make certain that the people of those countries understood that the President of the United States and the people of the United States are dedicated to their independence, their autonomy and their freedom.

Carter: Well, in the first place, I'm not criticizing His Holiness the Pope. I was talking about Mr. Ford. The fact is that secrecy has surrounded the decisions made by the Ford administration.

In the case of the Helsinki agreement—it may have been a good agreement at the beginning, but we have failed to enforce the so-called basket three part, which ensures the right of people to migrate, to join their families, to be free, to speak out. The Soviet Union is still jamming Radio Free Europe. Radio Free Europe is still being jammed. We have also seen a very serious problem with the so-called Sonnenfeldt document—which apparently Mr. Ford has just endorsed—

which says there is an organic linkage between the Eastern European countries and the Soviet Union. And I would like to see Mr. Ford convince the Polish Americans and the Czech Americans and the Hungarian Americans in this country that those countries don't live under the domination and the supervision of the Soviet Union behind the Iron Curtain.

We have also seen Mr. Ford exclude himself from access to the public. He hasn't had a tough, cross examination press conference in over 30 days. One press conference he had without sound.

He's always shown a weakness in yielding to pressure. The Soviet Union, for instance, put pressure on Mr. Ford and he refused to see a symbol of human freedom recognized around the world, Alexander Solzhenitsyn. The Arabs have put pressure on Mr. Ford, and he's yielded and has permitted a boycott by the Arab countries of American businesses who trade with Israel or have American Jews owning or taking part in the management of American companies. His own Secretary of Commerce had to be subpoenaed by the Congress to reveal the names of businesses who were subject to this boycott. They didn't volunteer the information; he had to be subpoenaed.

And the last thing I'd like to say is this. This grain deal with the Soviet Union in '72 was terrible, and Mr. Ford made up for it with three embargoes, one against our own ally Japan. That's not the way to run our foreign policy, including international trade.

[Middle East Arms]

Q: Governor, I'd like to pick up on that point, actually, and on your appeal for a greater measure of American idealism in foreign affairs. Foreign affairs come home to the American public in such issues as oil embargoes and grain sales—that sort of thing. Would you be willing to risk an oil embargo in order to promote human rights in Iran, Saudi Arabia, withhold arms from Saudi Arabia for the same purpose—or I think, for a matter of fact you've perhaps answered this final part, but would you withhold grain from the Soviet Union in order to promote civil rights in the Soviet Union?

Carter: I would never single out food as a trade embargo item. If I ever decided to impose an embargo because of a crisis in international relationships, it would include all shipments of all equipment. For instance, if the Arab countries ever again declare an embargo against our nation on oil, I would consider that not a military but an economic declaration of war. And I would respond instantly and in kind. I would not ship that Arab country anything—no weapons, no spare parts for weapons, no oil drillings rigs, no oil pipe, no nothing. I wouldn't single out just food.

Another thing that I'd like to say is this: in our international trade, as I said in my opening statement, we have become the arms merchant of the world. When this Republican administration came into office we were shipping about $1-billion worth of arms overseas. Now, $10- to $12-billion worth of arms overseas to countries, which quite often use these arms to fight each other. This shift in emphasis has been very disturbing to me.

Speaking about the Middle East, under the last Democratic administration, 60 per cent of all weapons that went into the Middle East were for Israel. Nowadays—75 per cent went for Israel before—now, 60 per cent go to the Arab countries, and this does not include Iran. If you include Iran, our present shipment of weapons to the Middle East, only 20 per cent goes to Israel.

This is a deviation from idealism; it's a deviation from our commitment to our major ally in the Middle East, which is Israel; it's a yielding to economic pressure on the part of the Arabs on the oil issue and it's also a tremendous indication that under the Ford administration we have not addressed the energy policy adequately. We still have no comprehensive energy policy in this country. And it's an overall sign of weakness.

When we are weak at home economically—high unemployment, high inflation, a confused government, a wasteful defense establishment—this encourages the kind of pressure that has been put on us successfully. It would have been inconceivable 10 or 15 years ago for us to be brought to our knees with an Arab oil embargo. But it was done three years ago and they're still putting pressure on us from the Arab countries to our discredit around the world. These are the weaknesses that I see and I believe it is not just a matter of idealism, it's a matter of being consistent. Our priorities ought to first of all be to meet our own military needs, secondly to meet the needs of our allies and friends and only then should we ship military equipment to foreign countries.

As a matter of fact, Iran is going to get 80 F-14s before we even meet our own Air Force orders for F-14s, and the shipment of Spruance class destroyers to Iran are much more highly sophisticated than the Spruance class destroyers that are presently delivered to our own Navy. This is ridiculous and it ought to be changed.

Q: Governor, let me me pursue that if I may. If I understand you correctly, you would, in fact, to use my example, withhold arms from Iran and Saudi Arabia even if the risk was an oil embargo and they should be securing those arms from somewhere else and then if the embargo came, then you'd respond in kind. Do I have it correctly?

Carter: If—Iran is not an Arab country, as you know, it's a Moslem country—but if Saudi Arabia should declare an oil embargo against us, then I would consider that an economic dec-

laration of war and I would make sure that the Saudians understood this ahead of time so that there would be no doubt in their mind. I think that under those circumstances they would refrain from pushing us to our knees as they did in 1973 with their previous oil embargo.

Ford: Governor Carter apparently doesn't realize that since I've been President we have sold to the Israelis over $4-billion in military hardware, we have made available to the Israelis over 45 per cent of the total economic and military aid since the establishment of Israel 27 years ago. So the Ford administration has done a good job in helping our good ally Israel and we're dedicated to the survival and security of Israel.

I believe that Governor Carter doesn't realize the need and necessity for arms sales to Iran. He indicates he would not make those. Iran is bordered very extensively by the Soviet Union. Iran has Iraq as one of its neighbors. The Soviet Union and the communist-dominated government of Iraq are neighbors of Iran and Iran is an ally of the United States. The history of our relationship goes back to the days of President Truman when he decided it was vitally necessary for our own security as well as for that of Iran that we should help that country, and Iran has been a good ally. In 1973 when there was an oil embargo, Iran did not participate. Iran continued to sell oil to the United States. I believe that it's in our interest and in the interest of Israel and Iran and Saudi Arabia to sell arms to those countries. It's for their security as well as ours.

[China]

Q: Mr. President, the policy of your administration is to normalize relations with mainland China. That means at some time establishing full diplomatic relations, and obviously doing something about the mutual defense treaty with Taiwan. If you are elected will you move to establish full diplomatic relations with Peking and will you abrogate the mutual defense treaty with Taiwan, and as a corollary would you provide mainland China with military equipment if the Chinese were to ask for it?

Ford: Our relationship with the People's Republic of China is based upon the Shanghai Communique of 1972 and that communique calls for the normalization of relations between the United States and the People's Republic. It doesn't set a time schedule, it doesn't make a determination as to how that relationship should be achieved in relationship to our current diplomatic recognition and obligations to the Taiwanese government. The Shanghai Communique does say that the differences between the People's Republic on the one hand and Taiwan on the other shall be settled by peaceful means. The net result is that this administration, and during my time as the President for the next four years, we will continue to move for normalization of relations in the traditional sense and we will insist that the disputes between Taiwan and the People's Republic be settled peacefully, as was agreed in the Shanghai Communique of 1972.

The Ford administration will not let down, will not eliminate or forget our obligations to the people of Taiwan. We feel that there must be a continued obligation to the people, the some 19- or 20-million people in Taiwan, and as we move during the next four years, those will be the policies of this administration.

Q: And, sir, the military equipment for the mainland Chinese?

Ford: There is no policy of this government to give the People's Republic or to sell to the People's Republic of China military equipment. I do not believe that we, the United States, should sell, give or otherwise transfer military hardware to the People's Republic of China or any other Communist nation such as the Soviet Union and the like.

Q: Governor Carter?

Carter: Well, I'd like to go back just one moment to the previous question where Mr. Ford I think confused the issue by trying to say that we were shipping Israel 40 per cent of our aid. As a matter of fact, during this current year we are shipping Iran, have contracted to ship to Iran, about $7.5-billion worth of arms, and also to Saudi Arabia about $7.5-billion worth of arms.

Also, in 1975 we almost brought Israel to their knees, after the Yom Kippur war, by the so-called reassessment of our relationship to Israel. We in effect tried to make Israel the scapegoat for the problems in the Middle East and this weakened our relationship with Israel a great deal and put a cloud on the total commitment that our people feel toward the Israelis. There ought to be a clear, unequivocal commitment, without change, to Israel.

In the Far East I think we need to continue to be strong and I would certainly pursue the normalization of relationships with the People's Republic of China. We opened up a great opportunity in 1972, which pretty well has been frittered away under Mr. Ford, that ought to be a constant inclination towards friendship. But I would never let that friendship with the People's Republic of China stand in the way of the preservation of the independence and freedom of the people of Taiwan.

['Guns and Butter']

Q: Governor, we always seem in our elections, and maybe in between, too, to argue about who can be tougher in the world. Give or take a few billion dollars, give or take one weapons system, our leading politicians and I think you two gentlemen seem to settle roughly on the same strategy in the world at roughly the same Pentagon budget cost. How bad do things have to get in our own economy or how much backwardness and hunger would it take in the world to persuade you that our national security and our survival required very drastic cutbacks in arms spending and dramatic new efforts in other directions?

Carter: Well, always in the past we've had the ability to have a strong defense and also have a strong domestic economy and also to be strong in our reputation and influence within the community of nations. These characteristics of our country have been endangered under Mr. Ford. We are no longer respected. In a showdown vote in the United Nations or in any other international council, we are lucky to get 20 per cent of the other nations to vote with us. Our allies feel that we've neglected them. The so-called Nixon shock against Japan has weakened our relationships there. Under this administration, we've also had an inclination to keep separate the European countries, thinking that if they are separate then we can dominate them and proceed with our secret, Lone Ranger type diplomatic efforts.

I would also like to point out that we in this country have let our economy go down the drain. The worst inflation since the Great Depression. The highest unemployment of any developed nation in the world. We have a higher unemployment rate in this country than Great Britain, than West Germany. Our unemployment rate is twice as high as it is in Italy, it's three or four times as high as it is in Japan, and that terrible circumstance in this country is exported overseas. We comprise about 30 per cent of the world economic trade power influence. And when we're weak at home, weaker than all our allies, that weakness weakens the whole free world. So a strong economy is very important.

Another thing that we need to do is re-establish the good relationship that we ought to have between the United States and our natural allies in France. They have felt neglected. And using that base of strength, and using the idealism, the honesty, the predictability, the commitment and the integrity of our own country, that's where our strength lies. And that would permit us to deal with the developing nations in a position of strength.

Under this administration we've had a continuation of a so-called balance of power politics where everything is looked on as a struggle between us on the one side and the Soviet Union on the other. Our allies, the smaller countries, get trampled in the rush. What we need is to try to seek individualized bilateral relationships with countries regardless of their size and to establish world order politics, which means that we want to establish peace through strength. We also want to revert back to the stature and the respect that our country had in previous administrations. Now, I can't say when this can come, but I can guarantee it will not come if Gerald Ford is re-elected and his present policies continue. It will come if I'm elected.

Q: If I hear you right, sir, you're saying guns and butter both. But President Johnson also had trouble keeping up Vietnam and his domestic program. I'm really asking when do the needs of the cities and our own needs, and those of other backward and even more needy countries and societies around the world take precedence over our own military spending? Ever?

Carter: Well, let me say very quickly that under President Johnson, in spite of the massive investment in the Vietnam War, he turned over a balanced budget to Mr. Nixon. The unemployment rate was less than 4 per cent, the inflation rate under Kennedy and Johnson was about 2 per cent— one-third what we have under this administration. So we did have at that time with good management the ability to do both. I don't think anybody can say that Johnson and Kennedy neglected the poor and destitute people in this country or around the world.

But I can say this, the number one responsibility of any President, above all else, is to guarantee the security of our nation. An ability to be free of the threat of attack or blackmail and to carry out our obligations to our allies and friends and to carry out a legitimate foreign policy. They must go hand in hand, but the security of this nation has got to go first.

Ford: Let me say very categorically, you cannot maintain the security and the strength of the United States with the kind of defense budget cuts that Governor Carter has indicated. In 1975 he wanted to cut the budget $15-billion. He's now down to a figure of $5-billion to $7-billion. Reductions of that kind will not permit the United States to be strong enough to deter aggression and maintain the peace.

Governor Carter apparently doesn't know the facts. As soon as I became President, I initiated meetings with the NATO heads of state and met with them in Brussels to discuss how we could improve the defense relationship in Western Europe. In November of 1975 I met with the leaders of the five industrial nations in France for the purpose of seeing what we could do, acting together, to meet the problems of the coming recession. In Puerto Rico this year, I met with six of the leading industrial nations' heads of state to meet the problem of inflation, so we would be able to solve it before it got out of hand.

I have met with the heads of government bilaterally as well as multilaterally. Our relations with Japan have never been better. I was the first United States President to visit Japan. And we had the Emperor of Japan here this past year, and the net result is Japan and the United States are working more closely together now than at any time in the history of our relationship.

You can go around the world, and let me take Israel for example. Just recently President Rabin said that our relations were never better.

[SALT Negotiations]

Q: Mr. President, you referred earlier to your meeting with Mr. Brezhnev at Vladivostok in 1974, and you agreed on that occasion to try to achieve another Strategic Arms Limitation SALT agreement within the year. Nothing happened in 1975, or not very much publicly at least, and those talks are still dragging and things got quieter as the current season approached. Is there a bit of politics involved there perhaps on both sides or, perhaps more important, are interim weapons developments— and I'm thinking of such things as the cruise missile and the Soviet SS20, intermediate range rocket—making SALT irrelevant, bypassing the SALT negotiations?

Ford: First we have to understand that SALT I expires Oct. 3, 1977. Mr. Brezhnev and I met in Vladivostok in December of 1974 for the purpose of trying to take the initial step so we could have a SALT II agreement that would go through 1985. As I indicated earlier, we did agree on a 2,400 limitation on launchers of ballistic missiles. That would mean a cutback in the Soviet program that would not interfere with our own program. At the same time we put a limitation of 1,320 on MIRV.

Our technicians have been working since that time in Geneva trying to put into technical language an agreement that can be verified by both parties, and in the meantime there has developed the problem of the Soviet Backfire, their high-performance aircraft, which they say is not a long-range aircraft and which some of our people say is an intercontinental aircraft. In the interim, there has been the development on our part primarily the cruise missile. Cruise missiles that could be launched from land-based mobile installations. Cruise missiles that could be launched from high performance aircraft like the B-52s or the B-1s, which I hope we proceed with. Cruise missiles which could be launched from either surface or submarine naval vessels.

Those gray area weapon systems are creating some problems in that the agreement for a SALT II negotiation. But I can say that I am dedicated to proceeding and I met just last week with the foreign minister of the Soviet Union and he indicated to me that the Soviet Union was interested in narrowing the differences and making a realistic and a sound compromise.

I hope and trust, in the best interests of both countries and in the best interests of all peoples throughout this globe, that the Soviet Union and the United States can make a mutually beneficial agreement. Because if we do not and SALT I expires on Oct. 3, 1977, you will unleash an all-out nuclear arms race with the potential of nuclear holocaust of unbelievable dimension. So it is the obligation of the President to do just that, and I intend to do so.

Q: Mr. President, let me follow that up. I'll submit that the cruise missile adds a whole new dimension to the arms competition, and then cite a statement by your office to the Arms Control Association a few days ago in which you said that the cruise missile might eventually be included in a comprehensive arms limitation agreement, but that in the meantime it was an essential part of the American strategic arsenal. Now, may I assume from that you're intending to exclude the cruise missile from the next SALT agreement? Or is it still negotiable?

Ford: I believe that the cruise missiles which we are now developing in research and development across the spectrum, from the air, sea or from the land, can be included in a SALT II agreement. They are a new weapon system that has a great potential, both conventional and nuclear arms. At the same time, we have to make certain the Soviet Union's Backfire, which they claim is not an intercontinental aircraft and which some of our people contend is, must also be included if we are to get the kind of agreement which is in the best interest of both countries. And I really believe that it's far better for us, and for the Soviet Union, and more importantly for the people around the world, that these two superpowers find an answer for a SALT II agreement before Oct. 3, 1977. I think goodwill on both parts, hard bargaining by both parties and a reasonable compromise will be in the best interest of all parties.

Carter: Well, Mr. Ford acts like he's running for President for the first time. He's been in office two years, and there has been absolutely no progress made toward a new SALT agreement. He has learned the date of the expiration of SALT I apparently. We've seen in this world a development of a tremendous threat to us. As a nuclear engineer myself, I know the limitations and capabilities of atomic power. I also know that as far as the human beings on this search are concerned, that the nonproliferation of atomic weapons is number one.

Only in the last few days, with the election approaching, has Mr. Ford taken any interest in the nonproliferation movement. I advocated last May in a speech at the United Nations that we move immediately as a nation to declare a complete moratorium on the testing of all nuclear devices, both weapons and peaceful devices—that we not ship any more atomic fuel to a country which refuses to comply with strict controls over the waste, which can be reprocessed into explosives. I've also advocated that we stop the sale by Germany and France of reprocessing plants to Pakistan and Brazil, and Mr. Ford hasn't moved on them. We also need to provide an adequate supply of enriched uranium. Mr. Ford again, under pressure from the atomic energy lobby, has insisted that this reprocessing or rather reenrichment be done by private industry and not by the existing government plants.

This kind of confusing and absence of leadership has let us drift now for two years, with the constantly increasing threat of atomic weapons throughout the world. We now have five nations that have atomic bombs that we know about. If we continue under Mr. Ford's policy, by 1985 or '90 we'll have 20 nations that have the capability of exploding atomic weapons. This has got to be stopped. That is one of the major challenges and major undertakings I will assume as the next President.

[U.S. Strength]

Q: Governor Carter, earlier tonight you said America is not strong anymore; America is not respected anymore. I must ask you, do you really believe that the United States is not the strongest country in the world? Do you really believe that the United States is not the most respected country in the world? Or is that just campaign rhetoric?

Carter: No, it's not just campaign rhetoric. I think that militarily we are as strong as any nation on earth. I think we've got to stay that way and to continue to increase our capabilities to meet any potential threat. But as far as strength derived from commitment to principle; as far as strength derived from the unity within our country, as far as strength derived from the people, the Congress, the Secretary of State, the President, sharing in the evolution and carrying out of our foreign policy, as far as strength derived from the respect of our own allies and friends— so they're assured that we will be

staunch in our commitment and will not deviate and will give them adequate attention—as far as strength derived from doing what is right, caring for the poor, providing food and becoming the breadbasket of the world instead of the arms merchant of the world, in those respects we're not strong.

Also, we'll never be strong again overseas unless we're strong at home. And with our economy in such terrible disarray and getting worse by the month, we've got 500,000 more Americans unemployed today than we had three months ago. We've got 2.5-million Americans out of work now than we had when Mr. Ford took office. This kind of deterioration in our economic strength is bound to weaken us around the world.

And we not only have problems at home, but we export those problems overseas. So as far as respect of our own people toward our own government, as far as participation in shaping of concepts and commitments, as far as the trust of our country among the nations of the world, as far as dependence of our country in meeting the needs and obligations that we have expressed to our allies, as far as the respect of our country even among our particular adversaries, we are weak. Potentially, we are strong. Under this administration, that strength has not been realized.

Ford: Governor Carter brags about the unemployment during Democratic administrations, and condemns the unemployment of the present time. I must remind him that we're at peace, and during the period that he brags about unemployment being low the United States was at war.

Not let me correct one other comment that Governor Carter just made. I have recommended to the Congress that we develop the uranium enrichment plant at Portsmouth, Ohio, which is a publicly owned, U.S. government facility. I have indicated that the private program which would follow on in Alabama is one that may or may not be constructed. But I am committed to the one at Portsmouth, Ohio.

The governor also talks about morality in foreign policy. The foreign policy of the United States meets the highest standards of morality. What is more moral than peace, and the United States is at peace today. What is more moral in foreign policy than for the administration to take the lead in the World Food Conference in Rome in 1974, when the United States committed 6-million metric tons of food—over 60 per cent of the food committed for the disadvantaged and underdeveloped nations of the world. The Ford administration wants to eradicate hunger and disease in our underdeveloped countries throughout the world. What is more moral than for the United States under the Ford administration to take the lead in southern Africa, in the Middle East? Those are initiatives in foreign policy which are of the highest moral standard, and that is indicative of the foreign policy of this country.

[Morality]

Q: Mr. President, can we stick with morality? For a lot of people, it seems to cover a bunch of sins. Mr. Nixon and Mr. Kissinger used to tell us that instead of morality we had to worry in the world about living with and letting live all kinds of governments that we really didn't like—North and South Korean dictators, Chilean fascists, Chinese Communists, Iranian emperors and so on. They said the only way to get by in the wicked world is to treat others on the basis of how they treated us, and not how they treated their own people. But, more recently, we seem to have taken a different tack. We seem to have decided that it is part of our business to tell the Rhodesians, for instance, that the way they are treating their own

black people is wrong and they've got to change their own government and put pressure on them. We're rather liberal in our advice to the Italians as to how to vote. Is this a new Ford foreign policy in the making? Can we expect that you are now going to turn to South Africa, force them to change their government, intervene in similar ways to end the bloodshed as you called it, say in Chile or Chilean prisons, or to throw our weight around for the values that we hold dear in America?

Ford: I believe that our foreign policy must express the highest standards of morality and the initiatives that we took in southern Africa, there's no doubt there would have been an acceleration of bloodshed in that part of the world. If we had not taken our initiative, it's very, very possible that the government of Rhodesia would have been overrun and that the Soviet Union and the Cubans would have dominated southern Africa. So the United States, seeking to preserve the principle of self-determination, to eliminate the possibility of bloodshed, to protect the rights of the minority as we insisted upon the rights of the majority, I believe followed the good conscience of the American people in foreign policy. And I believe that we have used our skill.

Secretary of State Kissinger has done a superb job in working with the black African nations' so-called front line nations. He has done a superb job in getting the prime minister of South Africa, Mr. Vorster, to agree that the time had come for a solution to the problem of Rhodesia. Secretary Kissinger in his meeting with Prime Minister Smith of Rhodesia was able to convince him that it was in the best interests of whites as well as blacks in Rhodesia to find an answer for a transitional government and then a majority government. This is a perfect example of the kind of leadership that the United States under this administration has taken. And I can assure you that this administration will follow that high moral principle in our future efforts in foreign policy.

Including our efforts in the Middle East, where it is vitally important because the Middle East is the crossroads of the world. There have been more disputes and it's an area where there's more volatility than any other place in the world. But because the Arab nations and the Israelis trust the United States we were able to take the lead in the Sinai II Agreement. And I can assure you the United States will take the leadership role in moving toward a comprehensive settlement of the Middle Eastern problems. I hope and trust as soon as possible and we will do with the highest moral principles.

Q: Mr. President, just clarify one point. There are lots of majorities in the world that feel they're being pushed around by minority governments. Are you saying they cannot expect to look to us for, not just good cheer, but throwing our weight on their side in South Africa, or in Taiwan, or in Chile, to help change their governments as in Rhodesia?

Ford: I would hope that as we move to one area of the world from another ... and the United States must not spread itself too thinly. That was one of the problems that helped to create the circumstances in Vietnam. But as we as a nation find that we are asked by the various parties, either one nation against another or individuals within a nation, that the United States will take the leadership and try to resolve the differences.

Let me take South Korea as an example. I have personally told President Park that the United States does not condone the kind of repressive measures that he has taken in that country. But I think in all fairness and equity we have to recognize the problem that South Korea has. On the north they have North Korea with 500,000 well-trained, well-equipped troops. They are supported by the Soviet Union.

South Korea faces a very delicate situation. Now the United States in this case, this administration has recommended a year ago and we have reiterated it again this year, that the United States, South Korea, North Korea and the People's Republic of China sit down at a conference table to resolve the problems of the Korean peninsula. This is a leadership role that the United States under this administration is carrying out. And if we do it, and I think the opportunities and the possibilities are getting better, we will have solved many of the internal domestic problems that exist in South Korea at the present time.

Carter: I noticed that Mr. Ford did not comment on the prisons in Chile. This is a typical example, maybe of many others, where this administration overthrew an elected government and helped to establish a military dictatorship. This has not been an ancient history story. Last year under Mr. Ford, of all the Food for Peace that went to South America, 85 per cent went to the military dictatorship in Chile.

Another point I want to make is this. He says we have to move from one area of the world to another. That's one of the problems with this administration's so-called shuttle diplomacy. While the Secretary of State's in one country, there are almost 150 others wondering what we're going to do next; what will be the next secret agreement. We don't have a comprehensible, understandable foreign policy that deals with world problems or even regional problems.

Another thing that concerned me was what Mr. Ford said about unemployment, insinuating that under Johnson and Kennedy, that unemployment could only be held down when this country is at war. Karl Marx said that the free enterprise in a democracy can only continue to exist when they are at war or preparing for war. Karl Marx was the grandfather of communism. I don't agree with that statement. I hope Mr. Ford doesn't either.

He has put pressure on the Congress, and I don't believe Mr. Ford will even deny this, to hold up on nonproliferation legislation until the Congress agrees for an $8-billion program for private industry to start producing enriched uranium.

And the last thing I want to make is this. He talks about peace, and I'm thankful for peace. We were peaceful when Mr. Ford went into office. But he and Mr. Kissinger and others tried to start a new Vietnam in Angola and it was only the outcry of the American people and the Congress when this secret deal was discovered that prevented our renewed involvement in that conflagration which was taking place over there.

[Panama Canal]

Q: Governor Carter, before this event, the most communications I received concerned Panama. Would you, as President, be prepared to sign a treaty which at a fixed date yields the administrative and economic control of the Canal Zone, and shared defense, which as I understand, was the position the United States took in 1974?

Carter: Well, here again, the Panamanian question is one that's been confused by Mr. Ford. He had directed his diplomatic representatives to yield to the Panamanians full sovereignty over the Panama Canal Zone at the end of a certain period of time. When Mr. Reagan raised this question in Florida, Mr. Ford not only disavowed his instructions, but he also even dropped parenthetically his use of the word detente. I would never give up complete control or practical control of the Panama Canal Zone. But I would continue to negotiate with the Panamanians.

When the original treaty was signed back in the early 1900s, Theodore Roosevelt was President, Panama retained sovereignty over the Panama Canal Zone. We retained control as though we had sovereignty. Now I would be willing to go ahead with negotiations. I believe that we can share more fully responsibilities for the Panama Canal Zone with Panama. I would be willing to continue to raise the payment for shipment of goods through the Panama Canal Zone. I might even be willing to reduce to some degree our military emplacements in the Panama Canal Zone. But I would not relinquish the practical control of the Panama Canal Zone anytime in the foreseeable future.

Ford: The United States must and will maintain complete access to the Panama Canal. The United States must maintain a defense capability of the Panama Canal and the United States will maintain our national security interest in the Panama Canal.

The negotiations for the Panama Canal started under President Johnson and have continued up to the present time. I believe those negotiations should continue but there are certain guidelines that must be followed and I just defined them.

Let me take just a minute to comment on something that Governor Carter said on nonproliferation. In May of 1975, I called for a conference of nuclear suppliers. That conference has met six times. In May of this year, Governor Carter took the first initiative, approximately 12 months after I had taken my initiative a year ago.

[Mayaguez Episode]

Q: Mr. President, the Government Accounting Office has just put out a report suggesting that you shot from the hip the Mayaguez rescue mission, that you ignored diplomatic messages that a peaceful solution was in prospect. Why didn't you do more diplomatically at the time? And a related question:

Did the White House try to prevent the release of that report?

Ford: The White House did not prevent the release of that report. On July 12 of this year, we gave full permission for the release of that report. I was very disappointed in the fact that the GAO released that report because I think it interjected political partisan politics at the present time.

But let me comment on that report. Somebody who sits in Washington, D.C., 18 months after the Mayaguez incident can be a very good grandstand quarterback. And let me make another observation. This morning I got a call from the skipper of the Mayaguez. He was furious because he told me it was the action of me, President Ford, that saved the lives of the crew of the Mayaguez. And I can assure you if we had not taken the strong and the forceful action that we did, we would have been criticized very, very severely for sitting back and not moving.

Captain Miller is thankful. The crew is thankful. We did the right thing. It seems to me that those who sit in Washington 18 months after the incident are not the best judges of the decision-making process that had to be made by the National Security Council and by myself at the time the incident was developing in the Pacific. Let me assure you that we made every possible overture to the People's Republic of China and through them to the Cambodian government. We made diplomatic protest to the Cambodian government through the United Nations. Every possible diplomatic means was utilized. But at the same time, I had a responsibility—so did the National Security Council—to meet the problem at hand. And we handled it responsibly and I think Captain Miller's testimony to that effect is the best evidence.

Carter: Well, I'm reluctant to comment on the recent report. I haven't read it. I think the American people have only one promise—that the facts about the Mayaguez be given to them accurately and completely.

Mr. Ford has been there for 18 months. He had the facts that were released today immediately after the Mayaguez incident. I understand that the report today is accurate. Mr. Ford has said, I believe, that it was accurate. That the White House made no attempt to block the issuing of that report. I don't know if that is exactly accurate or not. I understand that both the Secretary of the Department of State and the Defense Department have approved the accuracy of today's report, or yesterday's report, and also the National Security Agency.

I don't know what was right or what was wrong or what was done. The only thing I believe is that whatever the knowledge was that Mr. Ford had should have been given to the American people 18 months ago, after the Mayaguez incident occurred. This is what the American people want. When something happens and it endangers our national security, or when something happens that threatens our stature in the world, or when American people are endangered by the actions of a foreign country or just 40 sailors on the Mayaguez, we have to move aggressively and quickly to rescue them. But then after the immediate action was taken, I believe the President has an obligation to tell the American people the truth and not wait 18 months later for the report to be issued.

[Boycott of Israel]

Q: Governor Carter, if the price of gaining influence among the Arabs is closing our eyes a bit to their boycott against Israel, how would you handle it?

Carter: I believe that the boycott of American business by the Arab countries because those businesses trade with Israel or because they have American Jews who are owners or directors in the company is an absolute disgrace. This is the first time that I remember in the history of our country that we've let a foreign country circumvent or change our Bill of Rights. I'll do everything I can as President to stop the boycott of American businesses by the Arab countries.

It's not a matter of diplomacy or trade. It's a matter of morality. And I don't believe the Arab countries will pursue when we have a strong President who will protect the integrity of our country, the commitment of our constitutional Bill of Rights and protect people in this country who happen to be Jews. It may later be Catholics, it may later be Baptists who are threatened by some foreign country. But we ought to stand staunch. I think it's a disgrace that so far Mr. Ford's administration has blocked the passage of legislation that would have revealed by law every instance of the boycott and it would have prevented the boycott from continuing.

Ford: Again Governor Carter is inaccurate. The Arab boycott action was first taken in 1952 and in November of 1975 I was the first President to order the executive branch to take action, affirmative action, through the Department of Commerce and other Cabinet departments, to make certain that no American businessman or business organization should discriminate against Jews because of an Arab boycott.

And I might add that my administration, and I'm very proud of it, is the first administration that has taken an antitrust action against companies in this country that have allegedly cooperated with the Arab boycott. Just on Monday of this week, I signed a tax bill that included an amendment that would prevent companies in the United States from taking a tax deduction if they have in any way whatsoever cooperated with the Arab boycott. And last week when we were trying to get the

Export Administration Act through the Congress, necessary legislation, my administration went to Capitol Hill and tried to convince the House and the Senate that we should have an amendment on that legislation which would take strong and effective action against those who participate or cooperate with the Arab boycott.

One other point. Because the Congress failed to act, I am going to announce tomorrow that the Department of Commerce will disclose those companies that have participated in the Arab boycott. This is something that we can do, the Congress failed to do it and we intend to do it.

Q: Mr. President, if you get the accounting of missing in action you want from North Vietnam or Vietnam—I'm sorry—would you then be prepared to reopen negotiations for restoration of relations with that country?

Ford: Let me restate our policy. As long as Vietnam, North Vietnam, does not give us a full accounting of our missing in action, I will never go along with the admission of Vietnam to the United Nations. If they do give us a bona fide, complete accounting of the 800 MIAs, then I believe the United States should begin negotiation for the admission of Vietnam to the United Nations. But not until they have given us the full accounting of our MIAs.

Carter: One of the most embarrassing failures of the Ford administration and one that touches specifically on human rights is his refusal to appoint a presidential commission to go to Vietnam, to go to Laos, to go to Cambodia and try to trade for release of information on those who are missing in action in those wars. This is what the families of the MIAs want. So far, Mr. Ford has not done it. We've had several fragmentary efforts by members of the Congress, and by private citizens.

Several months ago, the Vietnam government said, "We are ready to sit down and negotiate for release of information on MIAs." So far, Mr. Ford has not responded. I also would never normalize relationships with Vietnam nor permit them to join the United Nations until they've taken this action. But that's not enough. We need to have an active and aggressive action on the part of the President, the leader of this country, to seek out every possible way to get that information, which has kept the MIA families in despair and doubt, and Mr. Ford has just not done it.

[Concluding Statements]

Carter: The purpose of this debate and the outcome of this election will determine three basic things: leadership, upholding the principles of this country and proper priorities and commitments for the future. This election will also determine what kind of world we leave our children. Will it be a nightmare world, threatened with the proliferation of atomic bombs not just in five major countries but dozens of smaller countries that have been permitted to develop atomic weapons because of a failure of our top leadership to stop proliferation? Will we have a world of hunger and hatred? And will we be living in an armed camp, stripped of our friendship and allies, hiding behind a tight defense that's been drawn in around us because of fear from the outside world? Will we have a government of secrecy that excludes the American people from participation in making basic decisions and therefore covers up mistakes and makes it possible for our government, our government, to depart from the principles of our Constitution's Bill of Rights? Or will we have a world of peace, with the threat of atomic weapons eliminated, with full trade, with our people at work, inflation controlled, openness in government, our people proud once again, Congress, citizens, President, Secretary of State working in harmony, in unity toward a common future? A world where people have enough to eat, a world where we care about those who don't? Can we become a breadbasket of the world instead of the arms merchant of the world? I believe we can and we ought to. And we've been hurt in recent years in this country, in the aftermath of Vietnam, Cambodia, Chile, Pakistan, Angola, Watergate, CIA, we've been hurt. Our people feel that we've lost something precious. That's not necessary. I want to see our nation return to a posture, an image, a standard to make us proud once again. We ought to be a beacon for nations who search for peace and who search for freedom, who search for individual liberty, who search for basic human rights. We haven't been lately. We can be once again. We'll never have that world leadership until we're strong at home, and we can have that strength if we return to the basic principles. It ought not to be a strength of bombastic threats. It ought to be a quiet strength, based on the integrity of our people, the vision of the Constitution, an innate strong will and purpose that God's given us in the greatest nation on earth.

Ford: As we have seen tonight, foreign policy and defense policy are difficult and complex issues. We can debate methods, we can debate one decision or another. But there are two things which cannot be debated: experience and results. In the last two years I have made policy decisions involving long range difficulties in policy, and made day-to-day judgments, not only as President of the United States, but as leader of the free world. What is the result of that leadership? America is strong, America is free, America is respected. Not a single young American today is fighting or dying on any foreign battlefield. America is at peace with freedom. Thank you.

John B. Anderson Announces Candidacy for President (1980)

Rep. John B. Anderson of Illinois was a fish out of water in the Republican party of the 1970s and 1980s. For almost all of its history, the Republicans had counted a substantial number of liberals among their ranks. But since the conservative senator Barry M. Goldwater's takeover of the party in 1964, liberals had become a steadily decreasing minority. (See "Barry M. Goldwater's Acceptance Speech to the Republican National Convention," p. 515.) Indeed, as the elections of 1980 drew near, it seemed apparent to Anderson, who had represented Illinois's sixteenth congressional district for twenty years and whose own personal political odyssey had taken him leftward along the ideological spectrum, that he would be defeated in his bid for renomination by a conservative Republican challenger.

Anderson decided to abandon the House of Representatives and run for president. With little money, virtually no national recognition, and hardly any support, he entered the Republican nominating contest on June 8, 1979.

In a crowded field of eight Republican candidates, Anderson took positions on the issues that stood out like a beacon or a sore thumb, depending upon the point of view. Anderson told Iowa farmers that he supported President Jimmy Carter's embargo on the sale of grain to the Soviet Union. He shocked a convention of gun owners in New Hampshire by speaking out for gun control. Audiences everywhere heard him propose a fifty-cents-per-gallon increase in the federal tax on gasoline.

By early 1980, Anderson had become the political darling of Hollywood liberals, Garry Trudeau's "Doonesbury," and NBC's "Saturday Night Live." But he made little progress in the Republican primaries. The cruelest blow fell on March 18, 1980, when Anderson was handily defeated by former California governor Ronald Reagan in his home state of Illinois.

Realizing that most of his support lay outside the Republican party, Anderson announced on April 24, 1980, that he was abandoning his quest for the nomination in order to run as an independent candidate for president in the general election.

Anderson's announcement made him the first serious third party presidential candidate in history who did not represent a widely and passionately supported political cause. Instead, Anderson appealed to the electorate on the basis of personal qualities, such as frankness and competence, that he claimed to have and that, many believed, Carter and Reagan lacked. For a time, public opinion polls recorded the perverse finding that almost a plurality of voters would cast their ballots for

Anderson if only they thought he had a chance to win. As it was, Anderson hovered between 10 and 15 percent during most of September and October. Following the historical pattern of third-party candidates, his support fell off as election day neared. (See "Henry A. Wallace Announces for President," p. 453, and "New York Campaign Speech by George C. Wallace," p. 566.)

Anderson ended up with 6.6 percent of the popular vote and, absent a regional base, no electoral votes. He seems to have drawn support about equally from Carter and Reagan, although his participation in a nationally televised debate with Reagan on September 21 (Carter declined to participate) helped the Republican nominee substantially. (See "The Carter-Reagan Debate," p. 749.)   ~

I have chosen, after careful deliberation, to pursue an independent course toward the Presidency of the United States.

I will not run as a candidate of a third party. I will pursue an independent candidacy.

Therefore, I am announcing my withdrawal from the race for the Republican nomination for President.

I do so with gratitude in my heart for the countless Americans who have offered me their support, their hard work, and their hopes.

I am also grateful for those who have exercised their precious right of franchise, and chosen to cast a ballot for my candidacy on the Republican line in the six primaries I have actively contested.

But I am not leaving any of the people I have mentioned.

I am inviting their continued support of me and my independent candidacy.

I have chosen this course of action because it is now clear that I cannot attain a majority of the delegates who will be attending the Republican national convention in July.

Therefore, it is with deep appreciation that I am releasing from any further obligation those men and women who have been elected as convention delegates pledged to support my candidacy.

At the same time, I have directed my campaign committee to return matching Federal election funds which have not been expended as determined by the Federal Election Commission.

In the course of making these decisions, I have consulted first with members of my family. I have also listened carefully to the advice and suggestions of many friends and counselors.

And I have done something else. I have gone back to reconsider the reasons that led me at the very outset, some ten months ago, to declare my intention to seek the Presidency.

What I have concluded is that in the intervening time my initial motivations to seek the Presidency have been reinforced.

I was convinced then, and I remain convinced now, that our nation is adrift in what Churchill would have called a gathering storm.

Since last June the signs that America is beset by a crisis of governance, and one of truly alarming proportions, have multiplied.

It is a crisis which manifests itself in what the President himself now concedes is an economic recession of unknown depth and duration.

Individual and business bankruptcies are approaching historic levels.

Unemployment is increasing.

The spendable income of the average worker is steadily declining.

Home ownership, once a part of the dream of the good life in America, is now fast exceeding the reach of many of our citizens because of a chronic inflation abetted by high interest rates.

Our basic industries are no longer in the robust and vigorous shape that once defined the American economy and made it a model for the world.

Instead, factory gates are closing shut, and hundreds of thousands of workers are finding themselves thrown into the swelling ranks of the unemployed and discontented.

The source of the problem is plain to see: the current administration has demonstrated a total inability to chart a clear, common sense economic policy that is capable of arresting our domestic economic decline.

The Carter Administration's failures in this regard have contributed to a growing sense of unease in the international community. There is rising concern that America, unable to deal with its domestic problems, is finally destined to relinquish her role as a leader in world affairs.

But I know something that the international community does not know. I know that the heart of America is still beating strong and that there is will and determination among our people.

Our national image of self-doubt and confusion does not stem from the fact that our people have lost confidence in themselves or in the inherent strengths of our nation.

Rather, it is because our people have grown to mistrust the motives and the abilities or our national leadership. Our people have come to doubt that they are being told the real truths about their nation's condition. And they have acquired a skepticism that President Carter will do what needs to be done.

America can no longer afford those who are more interested in perpetuating their political power than in perpetuating the ideal for which everyday Americans continue to strive.

And America will not tolerate a President who puts his finger to the prevailing political winds, rather than to the pulse of an anxious nation.

If a great nation, and we are a great nation, is to repair itself, then its leaders must recognize that the old sophistries can no longer substitute for the plain unvarnished truths.

How can a proud and seemingly affluent society justify unemployment rates ranging up to 40% for many of its young people?

How can a proud and seemingly affluent society justify dampening the hopes of millions of its people for educational opportunities, and dampen their hopes for providing their children with the very advantages enjoyed by the parents?

We cannot and we must not be satisfied with anything less than a total review of all the economic policies which have produced the situation, where a great industrial society is revealed as obsolescent, it workers declining in productivity, its exports losing their competitive edge in world markets.

The major premise of my campaign has been that America must build a new ethic of sacrifice and sharing, of conservation and saving, if we are to begin the process needed to restore a sound economy and maintain a stable democratic society.

It is my profound belief that only when we accomplish that basic goal will we recover our traditional prestige and influence in world affairs.

I have offered specific blueprints.

I have suggested that we must have an energy policy geared to the immediate objective of reducing our consumption of imported oil. This gluttony robs our national treasury of $100-billion annually, and offers our foreign policy and national security as hostage to erratic foreign leaders and uncertain events abroad.

To redress this problem will require a willingness to tax ourselves, rather than to permit OPEC to levy taxes upon our economy in the form of higher and higher prices.

I have suggested an income policy to replace the present charade of government efforts to restrain wage and price increases.

I have stated that rather than simply promising everyone an across-the-board reduction in taxes—during a period of unprecedented inflation—we must search out those specific tax reductions which will achieve the savings and investment required to rebuild our economy.

The people of America are ready for a President who will inspire the hope for our revitalization, and the people of America are ready to do their part to accomplish our revitalization.

We must put to rest the notion that as a nation of individuals we are locked in mindless competition for a bigger share of our nation's prosperity—without regard for the greater goal of a healthy, more just, and equitable society.

It is my fundamental belief that such a vision can be communicated to 225 million Americans and out of that vision will emerge a strong, confident and self-reliant nation.

Against that background, I want to turn to the rationale of my independent candidacy because the nation has a right to know what it means.

Lest anybody misunderstand, I have been a member of the Republican party for 30 years.

I will continue my membership in that party.

It is obvious that this is a most serious step, and that it is a step fraught with obstacles.

But on balance, the obstacles pale when one considers that too many people in our nation are disillusioned with the prospective choices our party structures are offering.

The result is frustration, apathy and despair.

The danger is that a significant portion of the nation may choose not to participate in the political process in November of 1980.

Yet the electoral decision taken at that time will determine the course of our nation for decades to come.

There is current statistical evidence that virtually one-half of potential voters are dissatisfied with a choice between President Carter and Ronald Reagan.

That figure takes on added significance when you consider that since 1960 the number of eligible voters who cast their ballots has steadily declined to 53%.

It seems likely that voter apathy will increase unless an alternative is available in 1980.

I believe that growing disaffection with the political process poses a far greater threat to the stability of our democratic institutions than what some are sure to charge is an oblique, perhaps frontal, attack on the two-party system.

An independent candidacy, distinguished from a third party candidacy, is an effort to broaden the choice available to millions of potential voters who simply do not participate in party primaries and caucuses.

The evidence is clear that an independent candidacy would provide a choice for those three-quarters of all eligible American voters who do not participate in party primaries or caucuses.

I also believe that an independent candidacy, unfettered by party positions, would vastly increase the likelihood that a thorough, dispassionate discussion of the host of complex issues confronting the nation and the world will take place.

Rather than simply engaging in the conventional partisan jousting to score debating points, it will become possible to conduct a positive effort to articulate positions and policies capable of leading our country into a new era of growth and achievement.

This will obviously require a willingness to communicate some harsh and even unpalatable truths and pose choices that will not be simple or easy.

I strongly disagree with those who claim that my intended action to run an independent candidacy places me in the role of a so-called spoiler.

It does not "spoil" the political process when I seek to involve in that process young people and others who in the past, and even now, consider our democratic system irrelevant to their lives.

And it does not "spoil" the political process to recognize the crisis facing us, and to provide the American people with new and alternative ideas.

There is still another consideration relating to my independent candidacy.

Public opinion polls show that I would receive between 18 and 21 percent of the vote if the election were held today, with President Carter and Ronald Reagan each falling within the 30-40 percent range.

However, 50% of the public still has little information about me, about my ideas for a revitalized America.

I can reach out and touch those people.

And that is where my campaign will succeed.

In the coming weeks, I will have to ascertain that my candidacy can overcome the numerous legal obstacles that stand in the way of an independent candidacy.

However, I am confident the legal obstacles will be overcome and that, indeed, I will remain as an independent candidate, through Election Day.

It will also be necessary in the coming weeks to ascertain that my candidacy can gather the financial and political support necessary to mount a challenge that will prevail.

I have authorized an exploratory group to begin the process of placing my name on as many states' ballots as possible, and to take steps to challenge the laws in those states which restrict access to the ballot.

In summation, I intend to pursue an independent candidacy because our nation faces a crisis and because we need alternatives.

A new national unity is required to recognize the profound problems before us, and to face up to the serious new approaches required to overcome those problems.

It is a time for patriotism, not partisanship.

It is a time for vision, not nostalgia.

It is a time for honesty and boldness.

I believe that our people are tired of evasion and postponement.

I believe there is a new willingness to accept sacrifice, to accept discipline, to accept unpleasant truths.

It is a willingness that remains only to be invited.

Our nation needs a choice in November.

Not just a choice among candidates.

I mean a choice of course for the nation.

I want to offer that choice.

And I believe the American people will want to respond.

Republican Party Platform (1980)

From the outset, 1980 offered an especially good opportunity for the Republican party to win a presidential election. The economy's "misery index" (the inflation rate plus the unemployment rate) was high, as were interest rates and energy prices. Fifty Americans were being held hostage in Iran. The incumbent Democratic president, Jimmy Carter, not only was unpopular with the voters, he faced a serious challenge for renomination from Sen. Edward M. Kennedy of Massachusetts. (See "Edward M. Kennedy's Speech to the Democratic National Convention," p. 742.)

In this propitious political setting, seven Republicans toed the line at the start of the race for the party's presidential nomination. Alphabetically, they were: Rep. John B. Anderson of Illinois, Senate Republican leader Howard Baker of Tennessee, former United Nations and China ambassador George Bush of Texas, former Democratic governor John B. Connally of Texas, Rep. Philip Crane of Illinois, Sen. Robert Dole of Kansas, and former governor Ronald Reagan of California. As it turned out, only Bush and Reagan were able to mount effective campaigns.

Bush, an energetic candidate, was first off the blocks: on January 21, 1980, he surprised the complacent frontrunner Reagan with an upset victory in the Iowa caucuses. But Reagan fought back hard, winning the New Hampshire primary five weeks later and steadily widening his lead as the spring primary season wore on. With the strong encouragement of his campaign manager, James A. Baker, Bush withdrew gracefully from the race in May, hoping to receive the vice presidential nomination.

Reagan had two outstanding political qualities that stood him well in the 1980s. First, he was an ardent conservative at a time when conservatism was triumphant within the Republican party and liberalism was increasingly unpopular among the voters. Second, in an era of "media politics," Reagan was an extremely effective communicator on television.

Both of these qualities had first become apparent in October 1964 when Reagan, previously known only as a movie and television actor, delivered a dramatic, nationally televised speech on behalf of Sen. Barry M. Goldwater's candidacy for president. Impressed by both the speech and the reactions it evoked from listeners, some conservative California business leaders recruited Reagan, a former Democrat, to run for governor as a Republican. He was elected in 1966, reelected in 1970, and made a strong bid for his party's presidential nomination against President Gerald Ford in 1976. (See "The Second Ford-Carter Debate," p. 652.)

The Republican national convention in July 1980 was a triumphant event for Reagan and his fellow conservatives. The party's platform was an unalloyed right-wing document: on social issues, it endorsed constitutional amendments to ban abortions and permit school prayer and abandoned the party's previous commitment to the Equal Rights Amendment for women; on economic issues, it supported Reagan's call for a 30 percent cut in federal income taxes and a substantial reduction in federal spending on welfare and social services; and on security issues, it pledged a massive military buildup and an aggressively anti-Communist foreign policy.

The convention, confident of victory in November, nominated Reagan on the first ballot. Reagan's effort to persuade Ford to join him on the ticket foundered when Ford insisted as a condition of his acceptance that the powers of the vice presidency be enhanced. Reagan promptly asked Bush to be his running mate and Bush, putting aside his earlier criticisms of what he had called Reagan's "voodoo economics," accepted gratefully.　～

A Preamble

The Republican Party convenes, presents this platform, and selects its nominees at a time of crisis. America is adrift. Our country moves agonizingly, aimlessly, almost helplessly into one of the most dangerous and disorderly periods in history.

At home, our economy careens, whiplashed from one extreme to another. Earlier this year, inflation skyrocketed to its highest levels in more than a century; weeks later, the economy plummeted, suffering its steepest slide on record. Prices escalate at more than 10 percent a year. More than eight million people seek employment. Manufacturing plants lie idle across the country. The hopes and aspirations of our people are being smothered.

Overseas, conditions already perilous, deteriorate. The Soviet Union for the first time is acquiring the means to obliterate or cripple our land-based missile system and blackmail us into submission. Marxist tyrannies spread more rapidly through the Third World and Latin America. Our alliances are frayed in Europe and elsewhere. Our energy supplies become even more dependent on uncertain foreign suppliers. In the ultimate humiliation, militant terrorists in Iran continue to toy with the lives of Americans.

These events are not isolated, or unrelated. They are signposts. They mark a continuing downward spiral in economic vitality and international influence. Should the trend continue, the 1980s promise to be our most dangerous years since World War II. History could record, if we let the drift go on, that the American experiment, so marvelously successful for 200 years, came strangely, needlessly, tragically to a dismal end early in our third century.

By far the most galling aspect of it all is that the chief architects of our decline—Democratic politicians—are without program or ideas to reverse it. Divided, leaderless, unseeing, uncomprehending, they plod on with listless offerings of pale imitations of the same policies they have pursued so long, knowing full well their futility. The Carter Administration is the unhappy and inevitable consequence of decades of increasingly outmoded Democratic domination of our national life. Over the past four years it has repeatedly demonstrated that it has no basic goals other than the perpetuation of its own rule and no guiding principle other than the fleeting insights provided by the latest opinion poll. Policies announced one day are disavowed or ignored the next, sowing confusion among Americans at home and havoc among our friends abroad.

Republicans, Democrats, and Independents have been watching and reading these signs. They have been watching incredulously as disaster after disaster unfolds. They now have had enough. They are rising up in 1980 to say that this confusion must end; this drift must end; we must pull ourselves together as a people before we slide irretrievably into the abyss.

It doesn't have to be this way; it doesn't have to stay this way. We, the Republican Party, hold ourselves forth as the Party best able to arrest and reverse the decline. We offer new ideas and candidates, from the top of our ticket to the bottom, who can bring to local and national leadership firm, steady hands and confidence and eagerness. We have unparalleled unity within our own ranks, especially between our Presidential nominee and our Congressional membership. Most important, we go forth to the people with ideas and programs for the future that are as powerful and compelling as they are fresh. Together, we offer a new beginning for America.

[Foremost Goal]

Our foremost goal here at home is simple: economic growth and full employment without inflation. Sweeping change in economic policy in America is needed so that Mr. Carter's promise of hard times and austerity—his one promise well kept—can be replaced with Republican policies that promise economic growth and job creation. It is our belief that the stagflation of recent years not only has consigned millions of citizens to hardship but also has bottled up the enormous ingenuity and creative powers of our people. Those energies will not be released by the sterile policies of the past: we specifically reject the Carter doctrine that inflation can be reduced only by throwing people out of work. Prosperity will not be regained simply by government fiat. Rather, we must offer broad new incentives to labor and capital to stimulate a great outpouring of private goods and services and to create an abundance of jobs. From America's grassroots to the White House we will stand united as a party behind a bold program of tax rate reductions, spending restraints, and regulatory reforms that will inject new life into the economic bloodstream of this country.

Overseas, our goal is equally simple and direct: to preserve a world at peace by keeping America strong. This philosophy once occupied a hallowed place in American diplomacy, but it was casually, even cavalierly dismissed at the outset by the Carter Administration—and the results have been shattering. Never before in modern history has the United States endured as many humiliations, insults, and defeats as it has during the past four years: our ambassadors murdered, our embassies burned, our warnings ignored, our diplomacy scorned, our diplomats kidnapped. The Carter Administration has shown that it neither understands totalitarianism nor appreciates the way tyrants take advantage of weakness. The brutal invasion of Afghanistan promises to be only the forerunner of much more serious threats to the West—and to world peace—should the Carter Administration somehow cling to power.

Republicans are united in a belief that America's international humiliation and decline can be reversed only by strong Presidential leadership and a consistent, far-sighted foreign policy, supported by a major upgrading of our military forces, a strengthening of our commitments to our allies, and a resolve that our national interests be vigorously protected. Ultimately, those who practice strength and firmness truly guard the peace.

This platform addresses many concerns of our Party. We seek to restore the family, the neighborhood, the community, and the workplace as vital alternatives in our national life to ever-expanding federal power.

We affirm our deep commitment to the fulfillment of the hopes and aspirations of all Americans—blacks and whites, women and men, the young and old, rural and urban.

[Case for the Individual]

For too many years, the political debate in America has been conducted in terms set by the Democrats. They believe that every time new problems arise beyond the power of men and women as individuals to solve, it becomes the duty of government to solve them, as if there were never any alternative. Republicans disagree and have always taken the side of the individual, whose freedoms are threatened by the big government that Democratic idea has spawned. Our case for the individual is stronger than ever. A defense of the individual against government was never more needed. And we will continue to mount it.

But we will redefine and broaden the debate by transcending the narrow terms of government and the individual; those are not the only two realities in America. Our society consists of more than that; so should the political debate. We will reemphasize those vital communities like the family, the neighborhood, the workplace, and others which are found at the center of society, between government and the individual. We will restore and strenghten their ability to solve problems in the places where people spend their daily lives and can turn to each other for support and help.

We seek energy independence through economic policies that free up our energy production and encourage conservation. We seek improvements in health care, education, housing, and opportunities for youth. We seek new avenues for the needy to break out of the tragic cycle of dependency. All of these goals—and many others—we confidently expect to achieve through a rebirth of liberty and resurgence of private initiatives, for we believe that at the root of most of our troubles today is the misguided and discredited philosophy of an all-powerful government, ceaselessly striving to subsidize, manipulate, and control individuals. But it is the individual, not the government, who reigns at the center of our Republican philosophy.

To those Democrats who say Americans must be content to passively accept the gradual but inexorable decline of America, we answer: The American people have hardly begun to marshal their talents and resources or realize the accomplishments and dreams that only freedom can inspire.

To those Democrats who say we face an "age of limits," we ask: Who knows the limit to what Americans can do when their capacity for work, creativity, optimism, and faith is enhanced and supported by strong and responsive political leadership and ideas.

To those who, with Mr. Carter, say the American people suffer from a national "malaise," we respond: The only malaise in this country is found in the leadership of the Democratic Party, in the White House and in Congress. Its symptoms are an incompetence to lead, a refusal to change, and a reluctance to act. This malaise has become epidemic in Washington. Its cure is government led by Republicans who share the values of the majority of Americans.

Republicans pledge a restoration of balance in American society. But society cannot be balanced by the actions of government or of individuals alone. Balance is found at society's vital center, where we find the family and the neighborhood and the workplace.

America will not, however, achieve any of these goals on its present course nor under its present leadership. The uncharted course of Mr. Carter will lead surely to catastrophe. By reversing our economic decline, by reversing our international decline, we can and will resurrect our dreams.

And so, in this 1980 Republican Platform, we call out to the American people: With God's help, let us now, together, make America great again; let us now, together, make a new beginning.

Free Individuals in a Free Society

It has long been a fundamental conviction of the Republican Party that government should foster in our society a climate of maximum individual liberty and freedom of choice. Properly informed, our people as individuals or acting through instruments of popular consultation can make the right decisions affecting personal or general welfare, free of pervasive and heavy-handed intrusion by the central government into the decisionmaking process. This tenet is the genius of representative democracy.

Republicans also treasure the ethnic, cultural, and regional diversity of our people. This diversity fosters a dynamism in American society that is the envy of the world.

Taxes

Elsewhere in this platform we discuss the benefits, for society as a whole, of reduced taxation, particularly in terms of economic growth. But we believe it is essential to cut personal tax rates out of fairness to the individual.

Presently, the aggregate burden of taxation is so great that the average American spends a substantial part of every year, in effect, working for government.

Substantial tax rate reductions are needed to offset the massive tax increases facing the working men and women of this country. Over the next four years, federal taxes are projected to increase by over $500 billion due to the Carter Administration's policies. American families are already paying taxes at higher rates then ever in our history; as a result of these Carter policies, the rates will go even higher. The direct and indirect burden of federal taxes alone, imposed on the average family earning $20,000, has risen to $5,451—over 27 percent of the family's gross income. During the Carter term, the federal tax alone on this family will have risen $2,000.

The Republican Party believes balancing the budget is essential but opposes the Democrats' attempt to do so through higher taxes. We believe that an essential aspect of balancing the budget is spending restraint by the federal government and higher economic growth, not higher tax burdens on working men and women.

Policies of the Democratic Party are taxing work, savings, investment, productivity, and the rewards for human ingenuity. These same tax policies subsidize debt, unemployment, and consumption. The present structure of the personal income tax system is designed to broaden the gap between effort and reward.

Therefore, the Republican Party supports across-the-board reductions in personal income tax rates, phased in over three years, which will reduce tax rates from the range of 14 to 70 percent to a range from 10 to 50 percent.

For most Americans, these reduced tax rates will slow the rate at which taxes rise. This will assure workers and savers greater rewards for greater effort by lowering the rate at which added earnings would be taxed.

These reductions have been before the Congress for three years in the Roth-Kemp legislation. The proposal will not only provide relief for all American taxpayers, but also promote non-inflationary economic growth by restoring the incentive to save, invest, and produce. These restored incentives will in turn increase investment and help reinvigorate American business and industry, leading to the creation of more jobs. In fact, Governor Reagan and Congressional Republicans have already taken the first step. Working together, they have boldly offered the American people a 10 percent tax rate cut for 1981, which will stimulate growth in our economy, and a simplification and liberalization of depreciation schedules to create more jobs.

Once tax rates are reduced, Republicans will move to end tax bracket creep caused by inflation. We support tax indexing to protect taxpayers from the automatic tax increases caused when cost-of-living wage increases move them into higher tax brackets.

Tax rate reductions will generate increases in economic growth, output, and income which will ultimately generate increased revenues. The greater justification for these cuts, however, lies in the right of individuals to keep and use the money they earn.

⅄ Improving the Welfare System

The measure of a country's compassion is how it treats the least fortunate. In every society there will be some who cannot work, often through no fault of their own.

Yet current federal government efforts to help them have become counterproductive, perpetuating and aggravating the very conditions of dependence they seek to relieve. The Democratic Congress has produced a jumble of degrading, dehumanizing, wasteful, overlapping, and inefficient programs that invite waste and fraud but inadequately assist the needy poor.

Poverty is defined not by income statistics alone, but by an individual's true situation and prospects. For two generations, especially since the mid-1960s, the Democrats have deliberately perpetuated a status of federally subsidized poverty and manipulated dependency for millions of Americans. This is

especially so for blacks and Hispanics, many of whom remain pawns of the bureaucracy, trapped outside the social and economic mainstream of American life.

For those on welfare, our nation's tax policies provide a penalty for getting a job. This is especially so for those whose new income from a job is either equal to, or marginally greater than, the amount received on welfare. In these cases, due to taxes, the individual's earned income is actually less than welfare benefits. This is the "poverty trap" which will continue to hold millions of Americans as long as they continue to be punished for working.

The Carter Administration and the Democratic Party continue to foster that dependency. Our nation's welfare problems will not be solved merely by providing increased benefits. Public service jobs are not a substitute for employable skills, nor can increases in the food stamp program by themselves provide for individual dignity. By fostering dependency and discouraging self-reliance, the Democratic Party has created a welfare constituency dependent on its continual subsidies.

The Carter Administration has proposed, and its allies in the House of Representatives actually voted for, legislation to nationalize welfare, which would have cost additional billions and made millions more dependent upon public assistance. The Democrats have presided over—and must take the blame for—the most monstrous expansion and abuse of the food stamp program to date. They have been either unable or unwilling to attack the welfare fraud that diverts resources away from the truly poor. They have sacrificed the needy to the greedy, and sent the welfare bills to the taxpayers.

We categorically reject the notion of a guaranteed annual income, no matter how it may be disguised, which would destroy the fiber of our economy and doom the poor to perpetual dependence.

As a party we commit ourselves to a welfare policy that is truly reflective of our people's true sense of compassion and charity as well as an appreciation of every individual's need for dignity and self-respect. We pledge a system that will:

Provide adequate living standards for the truly needy;

End welfare fraud by removing ineligibles from the welfare rolls, tightening food stamp eligibility requirements, and ending aid to illegal aliens and the voluntarily unemployed;

Strengthen work incentives, particularly directed at the productive involvement of able-bodied persons in useful community work projects;

Provide educational and vocational incentives to allow recipients to become self-supporting; and

Better coordinate federal efforts with local and state social welfare agencies and strengthen local and state administrative functions.

We oppose federalizing the welfare system; local levels of government are most aware of the needs in their communities. We support a block grant program that will help return control of welfare programs to the states. Decisions about who gets welfare, and how much, can be better made on the local level.

Those features of the present law, particularly the food stamp program, that draw into assistance programs people who are capable of paying for their own needs should be corrected. The humanitarian purpose of such programs must not be corrupted by eligibility loopholes. Food stamp program reforms proposed by Republicans in Congress would accomplish the twin goals of directing resources to those most in need and streamlining administration.

Through long association with government programs, the word "welfare" has come to be perceived almost exclusively as tax-supported aid to the needy. But in its most inclusive sense—

and as Americans understood it from the beginning of the Republic—such aid also encompasses those charitable works performed by private citizens, families, and social, ethnic, and religious organizations. Policies of the federal government leading to high taxes, rising inflation, and bureaucratic empire-building have made it difficult and often impossible for such individuals and groups to exercise their charitable instincts. We believe that government policies that fight inflation, reduce tax rates, and end bureaucratic excesses can help make private effort by the American people once again a major force in those works of charity which are the true signs of a progressive and humane society.

Veterans

Republicans recognize the very special sacrifice of those who have served in our nation's armed forces. Individual rights and societal values are only as strong as a nation's commitment to defend them. Because of this our country must never forget its appreciation of an obligation to our veterans.

Today the veteran population numbers 30 million. This is the largest veteran population in our nation's history. We recognize the major sacrifices they have made for their fellow Americans.

We will maintain the integrity of the Veterans Administration. We will seek to keep it separate and distinct from other federal agencies as the single agency for the administration of all veterans' programs. In particular we feel it is of vital importance to continue and expand the health programs provided to veterans through the Veterans Administration hospitals. Here we see the need for increased access to care, especially for older veterans.

We further advocate continued and expanded health care for our Vietnam veterans and consider it vital for the Veterans Administration to continue its programs for the rehabilitation of the disabled as well as its job training efforts.

We are committed to providing timely and adequate adjustments in compensation for service-disabled veterans and the survivors of those who died as a result of their service. We are also committed to maintaining the pension program for those who were disabled and impoverished, and for their widows and orphans.

We will support measures to provide for every veteran at death a final resting place for his remains in a national cemetery, and for costs of transportation thereto.

Veterans preference in federal employment in all departments and agencies will be continued and strictly enforced.

Retired military benefits deserve more than the cursory attention given them by a Department of Defense otherwise interested in ongoing programs. We believe that such benefits should be administered by the Veterans Administration.

Private Property

The widespread distribution of private property ownership is the cornerstone of American liberty. Without it neither our free enterprise system nor our republican form of government could long endure.

Under Democratic rule, the federal government has become an aggressive enemy of the human right to private property ownership. It has dissipated savings through depreciation of the dollar, enforced price controls on private exchange of goods, attempted to enforce severe land use controls, and mistreated hundreds of thousands of national park and forest inholders.

The next Republican Administration will reverse this baneful trend. It will not only protect the cherished human right of property ownership, but will also work to help millions of Americans—particularly those from disadvantaged groups—to share in the ownership of the wealth of their nation.

Transportation – Personal Mobility

Americans enjoy greater personal mobility than any other people on earth, largely as a result of the availability of automobiles and our modern highway system. Republicans reject the elitist notion that Americans must be forced out of their cars. Instead, we vigorously support the right of personal mobility and freedom as exemplified by the automobile and our modern highway system. While recognizing the importance of fuel efficiency and alternate modes of transportation, we quickly acknowledge that for millions of Americans there is no substitute on the horizon for the automobile. We reaffirm our support for a healthy domestic automobile industry, complete with continued support for the highway trust fund, which is the fairest method yet devised for financing America's highway system.

Republicans recognize the need for further improvement in highway safety. Projections indicate that highway fatalities may exceed 60,000 per year in the coming decades. Republicans support accelerated cost-effective efforts to improve highway, automobile, and individual driver safety.

Privacy

The essence of freedom is the right of law-abiding individuals to life, liberty, and the pursuit of happiness without undue governmental intervention. Yet government in recent years, particularly at the federal level, has overwhelmed citizens with demands for personal information and has accumulated vast amounts of such data through the IRS, Social Security Administration, the Bureau of the Census, and other agencies. Under certain limited circumstances, such information can serve legitimate societal interests, but there must be protection against abuse.

Republicans share the concerns of our citizens as to the nature, use, and final disposition of the volume of personal information being collected. We are alarmed by Washington's growing collection and dissemination of such data. There must be protection against its misuse or disclosure.

The Republican Party commits itself to guaranteeing an individual's right of privacy. We support efforts of state governments to ensure individual privacy.

Black Americans

For millions of black Americans, the past four years have been a long trail of broken promises and broken dreams. The Carter Administration entered office with a pledge to all minorities of a brighter economic future. Today there are more black Americans unemployed than on the day Mr. Carter became President. The unemployment rate of black teenagers is once again rising sharply. And the median income of black families has declined to less than 60 percent of white family income.

Republicans will not make idle promises to blacks and other minorities; we are beyond the day when any American can live off rhetoric or political platitudes.

Our Party specifically rejects the philosophy of the Carter Administration that unemployment is the answer to inflation. We abhor the notion that our cities should become battlegrounds in the fight against inflation and that the jobs of black Americans should be sacrificed in an attempt to counterbalance the inflationary excesses of government. Nor are we prepared to accept the practice of turning the poor into permanent wards of the state, trading their politi-

cal support for continued financial assistance.

One fundamental answer to the economic problems of black Americans is the same answer we make to all Americans—full employment without inflation through economic growth. First and foremost, we are committed to a policy of economic expansion through tax-rate reductions, spending restraint, regulatory reform and other incentives.

As the Party of Lincoln, we remain equally and steadfastly committed to the equality of rights for all citizens, regardless of race. Although this nation has not yet eliminated all vestiges of racism over the years, we are heartened by the progress that has been made, we are proud of the role that our party has played, and we are dedicated to standing shoulder to shoulder with black Americans in that cause.

Elsewhere in this platform, we set forth a number of specific proposals that will also serve to improve the quality of life for blacks. During the next four years we are committed to policies that will:

Encourage local governments to designate specific enterprise zones within depressed areas that will promote new jobs, new and expanded businesses and new economic vitality;

Open new opportunities for black men and women to begin small businesses of their own by, among other steps, removing excessive regulations, disincentives for venture capital and other barriers erected by the government;

Bring strong, effective enforcement of federal civil rights statutes, especially those dealing with threats to physical safety and security which have recently been increasing; and

Ensure that the federal government follows a non-discriminatory system of appointments up and down the line, with a careful eye for qualified minority aspirants.

Hispanic Americans

Hispanics are rapidly becoming the largest minority in the country and are one of the major pillars in our cultural, social, and economic life. Diverse in character, proud in heritage, they are greatly enriching the American melting pot.

Hispanics seek only the full rights of citizenship—in education, in law enforcement, in housing—and an equal opportunity to achieve economic security. Unfortunately, those desires have not always been fulfilled; as in so many other areas, the Carter Administration has been long on rhetoric and short on action in its approach to the Hispanic community.

We pledge to pursue policies that will help to make the opportunities of American life a reality for Hispanics. The economic policies enunciated in this platform will, we believe, create new jobs for Hispanic teenagers and adults and will also open up new business opportunities for them. We also believe there should be local educational programs which enable those who grew up learning another language such as Spanish to become proficient in English while also maintaining their own language and cultural heritage. Neither Hispanics nor any other American citizen should be barred from education or employment opportunities because English is not their first language.

The Handicapped

The Republican Party strongly believes that handicapped persons must be admitted into the mainstream of American society. It endorses efforts to enable our handicapped population to enjoy a useful and productive life.

Too often in the past, barriers have been raised to their education, employment, transportation, health care, housing, recration, and insurance. We support a concerted national effort to eliminate discrimination in all these areas. Specifically we support tax incentives for the removal of architectural and transportation barriers. We pledge continued efforts to improve communications for the handicapped and to promote a healthy, constructive attitude toward them in our society.

Women's Rights

We acknowledge the legitimate efforts of those who support or oppose ratification of the Equal Rights Amendment.

We reaffirm our Party's historic commitment to equal rights and equality for women.

We support equal rights and equal opportunities for women, without taking away traditional rights of women such as exemption from the military draft. We support the enforcement of all equal opportunity laws and urge the elimination of discrimination against women. We oppose any move which would give the federal government more power over families.

Ratification of the Equal Rights Amendment is now in the hands of state legislatures, and the issues of the time extension and rescission are in the courts. The states have a constitutional right to accept or reject a constitutional amendment without federal interference or pressure. At the direction of the White House, federal departments launched pressure against states which refused to ratify ERA. Regardless of one's position on ERA, we demand that this practice cease.

At this time, women of America comprise 53 percent of the population and over 42 percent of the work force. By 1990, we anticipate that 51 percent of the population will be women, and there will be approximately 57 million in the work force. Therefore, the following urgent problems must be resolved:

Total integration of the work force (not separate but equal) is necessary to bring women equality in pay;

Girls and young women must be given improved early career counseling and job training to widen the opportunities for them in the world of work;

Women's worth in the society and in the jobs they hold, at home or in the workplace, must be reevaluated to improve the conditions of women workers concentrated in low-status, low-paying jobs;

Equal opportunity for credit and other assistance must be assured to women in small businesses; . . .

[Child Care]

One of the most critical problems in our nation today is that of inadequate child care for the working mother. As champions of the free enterprise system, of the individual, and of the idea that the best solutions to most problems rest at the community level, Republicans must find ways to meet this, the working woman's need. The scope of this problem is fully realized only when it is understood that many female heads of households are at the poverty level and that they have a very large percentage of the nation's children.

The important secret about old age in America today is that it is primarily a woman's issue, and those over 65 are the fastest growing segment of the population. With current population trends, by the year 2020, 15.5 percent of our population will be over 65; by 2035 women in this age group will outnumber men by 13 million.

In 1980, 42 percent of women between 55 and 64 are in the work force. Half of the six million elderly women who live alone have incomes of $3,700 or less, and black women in that category have a median income of $2,600. How do they survive with the present rate of inflation? The lower salaries they earned as working women are now reflected in lower retirement benefits, if they have any at all. The Social Security system is still biased against women, and non-existent pension plans combine with that to produce a bereft elderly woman. The Republican Party must not and will not let this continue.

We reaffirm our belief in the traditional role and values of the family in our society. The damage being done today to the family takes its greatest role on the women. Whether it be through divorce, widowhood, economic problems, or the suffering of children, the impact is greatest on women. The importance of support for the mother and homemaker in maintaining the values of this country cannot be overemphasized.

In other sections of this platform, we call for greater equity in the tax treatment of working spouses. We deplore this marriage tax which penalizes married two-worker families. We call for a reduction in the estate tax burden, which creates hardships for widows and minor children. We also pledge to address any remaining inequities in the treatment of women under the Social Security system.

Women know better than anyone the decline in the quality of life that is occurring in America today. The peril to the United States and especially to women must be stressed. Women understand domestic, consumer, and economic issues more deeply because they usually manage the households and have the responsibility for them. With this responsibility must also come greater opportunity for achievement and total equality toward solution of problems.

Equal Rights

The truths we hold and the values we share affirm that no individual should be victimized by unfair discrimination because of race, sex, advanced age, physical handicap, difference of national origin or religion, or economic circumstance. However, equal opportunity should not be jeopardized by bureaucratic regulations and decisions which rely on quotas, ratios, and numerical requirements to exclude some individuals in favor of others, thereby rendering such regulations and decisions inherently discriminatory.

We pledge vigorous enforcement of laws to assure equal treatment in job recruitment, hiring, promotion, pay, credit, mortgage access, and housing.

Millions of Americans who trace their heritage to the nations of Eastern, Central, and Southern Europe have for too long seen their values neglected. The time has come to go beyond the ritual election year praise given to Ethnic Americans. We must make them an integral part of government policy. The Republican Party will take positive steps to see to it that these Americans, along with others too long neglected, have the opportunity to share the power, as well as the burdens of our society. The same holds true of our Asian-American citizens from the cultures of the Orient.

As a party we also recognize our commitment to Native Americans. We pledge to continue to honor our trusted relationship with them and we reaffirm our federal policy of self-determination. We support the assumption by Indians, Aleuts, and Eskimos themselves of the decisions and planning which will affect their lives and the end of undue federal influence on those plans and decisions.

Puerto Rico has been a territory of the United States since 1898. The Republican Party vigorously supports the right of the United States citizens of Puerto Rico to be admitted into the Union as a fully sovereign state after they freely so determine. We believe that the statehood alternative is the only logical solution to the problem of inequality of the United States citizens of Puerto Rico within the framework of the federal constitution, with full recognition within the concept of a multicultural society of the citizens' right to retain their Spanish language and traditions. Therefore we pledge to support the enactment of the necessary legislation to allow the people of Puerto Rico to exercise their right to apply for admission into the Union at the earliest possible date after the presidential election of 1980.

We also pledge that such decision of the people of Puerto Rico will be implemented through the approval of an admission bill. This bill will provide for the Island's smooth transition from its territorial fiscal system to that of a member of the Union. This enactment will enable the new state of Puerto Rico to stand economically on an equal footing with the rest of the states and to assume gradually its fiscal responsibilities as a state.

We continue to favor whatever action may be necessary to permit American citizens resident in the United States territories of the Virgin Islands and Guam to vote for President and Vice President in national elections.

Abortion

There can be no doubt that the question of abortion, despite the complex nature of its various issues, is ultimately concerned with equality of rights under the law. While we recognize differing views on this question among Americans in general—and in our own Party—we affirm our support of a constitutional amendment to restore protection of the right to life for unborn children. We also support the Congressional efforts to restrict the use of taxpayers' dollars for abortion.

We protest the Supreme Court's intrusion into the family structure through its denial of the parent's obligation and right to guide their minor children.

Strong Families

The family is the foundation of our social order. It is the school of democracy. Its daily lessons—cooperation, tolerance, mutual concern, responsibility, industry—are fundamental to the order and progress of our Republic. But the Democrats have shunted the family aside. They have given its power to the bureaucracy, its jurisdiction to the courts, and its resources to government grantors. For the first time in our history, there is real concern that the family may not survive.

Government may be strong enough to destroy families, but it can never replace them.

Unlike the Democrats, we do not advocate new federal bureaucracies with ominous power to shape a national family order. Rather, we insist that all domestic policies, from child care and schooling to Social Security and the tax code, must be formulated with the family in mind.

Education

Next to religious training and the home, education is the most important means by which families hand down to each new generation their ideals and beliefs. It is a pillar of a free society. But today, parents are losing control of their children's schooling. The Democratic Congress and its counterparts in many states have launched one fad after another, building huge new bureaucracies to misspend our taxes. The result has been a shocking drop in student performance, lack of basics in the classroom, forced busing, teacher strikes, manipulative and sometimes amoral indoctrination.

The Republican Party is determined to restore common sense and quality to education for the sake of all students, especially those for whom learning is the highway to equal opportunity. Because federal assistance should help local school districts, not tie them up in red tape, we will strive to replace the crazyquilt of wasteful programs with a system of block grants that will restore decisionmaking to local officials responsible to voters and parents. We recog-

nize the need to preserve within the structure of block grants, special educational opportunities for the handicapped, the disadvantaged, and other needy students attending public and private non-profit elementary and secondary schools.

[Teachers]

We hail the teachers of America. Their dedication to our children is often taken for granted, and they are frequently underpaid for long hours and selfless service, especially in comparison with other public employees.

We understand and sympathize with the plight of America's public school teachers, who so frequently find their time and attention diverted from their teaching responsibilities to the task of complying with federal reporting requirements. America has a great stake in maintaining standards of high quality in public education. The Republican Party recognizes that the achievement of those standards is possible only to the extent that teachers are allowed the time and freedom to teach. To that end, the Republican Party supports deregulation by the federal government of public education, and encourages the elimination of the federal Department of Education.

We further sympathize with the right of qualified teachers to be employed by any school district wishing to hire them, without the necessity of their becoming enrolled with any bargaining agency or group. We oppose any federal action, including any action on the part of the Department of Education to establish "agency shops" in public schools.

We support Republican initiatives in the Congress to restore the right of individuals to participate in voluntary, non-denominational prayer in schools and other public facilities. We applaud the action of the Senate in passing such legislation.

Our goal is quality education for all of America's children, with a special commitment to those who must overcome handicap, deprivation, or discrimination. That is why we condemn the forced busing of school children to achieve arbitrary racial quotas. Busing has been a prescription for disaster, blighting whole communities across the land with its divisive impact. It has failed to improve the quality of education, while diverting funds from programs that could make the difference between success and failure for the poor, the disabled, and minority children.

We must halt forced busing and get on with the education of all our children, focusing on the real causes of their problems, especially lack of economic opportunity.

[Tax Credits]

Federal education policy must be based on the primacy of parental rights and responsibility. Toward that end, we reaffirm our support for a system of educational assistance based on tax credits that will in part compensate parents for their financial sacrifices in paying tuition at the elementary, secondary, and post-secondary level. This is a matter of fairness,. especially for low-income families, most of whom would be free for the first time to choose for their children those schools which best correspond to their own cultural and moral values. In this way, the schools will be strengthened by the families' involvement, and the families' strengths will be reinforced by supportive cultural institutions.

We are dismayed that the Carter Administration cruelly reneged on promises made during the 1976 campaign. Wielding the threat of his veto, Mr. Carter led the fight against Republican attempts to make tuition tax credits a reality.

Next year, a Republican White House will assist, not sabotage, congressional efforts to enact tuition tax relief into law.

We will halt the unconstitutional regulatory vendetta launched by Mr. Carter's IRS Commissioner against independent schools.

We will hold the federal bureaucracy accountable for its harassment of colleges and universities and will clear away the tangle of regulation that has unconscionably driven up their expenses and tuitions. We will respect the rights of state and local authorities in the management of their school systems.

The commitment of the American people to provide educational opportunities for all has resulted in a tremendous expansion of schools at all levels. And the more we reduce the federal proportion of taxation, the more resources will be left to sustain and develop state and local institutions.

Health

Our country's unequalled system of medical care, bringing greater benefits to more people than anywhere else on earth, is a splendid example of how Americans have taken care of their own needs with private institutions.

Significant as these achievements are, we must not be complacent. Health care costs continue to rise, farther and faster than they should, and threaten to spiral beyond the reach of many families. The causes are the Democratic Congress' inflationary spending and excessive and expensive regulations.

Republicans unequivocally oppose socialized medicine, in whatever guise it is presented by the Democratic Party. We reject the creation of a national health service and all proposals for compulsory national health insurance.

Our country has made spectacular gains in health care in recent decades. Most families are now covered by private insurance, Medicare, or in the case of the poor, the entirely free services under Medicaid.

Republicans recognize that many health care problems can be solved if government will work closely with the private sector to find remedies that will enhance our current system of excellent care. We applaud, as an example, the voluntary effort which has been undertaken by our nation's hospitals to control costs. The results have been encouraging. More remains to be done.

What ails American medicine is government meddling and the straitjacket of federal programs. The prescription for good health care is deregulation and an emphasis upon consumer rights and patient choice.

As consumers of health care, individual Americans and their families should be able to make their own choices about health care protection. We propose to assist them in so doing through tax and financial incentives. These could enable them to choose their own health coverage, including protection from the catastrophic costs of major long-term illness, without compulsory regimentation.

Americans should be protected against financial disaster brought on by medical expense. We recognize both the need to provide assistance in many cases and the responsibility of citizens to provide for their own needs. By using tax incentives and reforming federal medical assistance programs, government and the private sector can jointly develop compassionate and innovative means to provide financial relief when it is most needed.

We endorse alternatives to institutional care. Not only is it costly but it also separates individuals from the supportive environment of family and friends. This is especially important for the elderly and those requiring long-term care. We advocate the reform of Medicare to encourage home-based care whenever feasible. In addition, we encourage the development of innovative alternate health care delivery systems and other out-patient services at the local level.

We must maintain our commitment to the aged and to the poor by providing quality care through Medicare and Medicaid. These programs need the careful, detailed reevaluation they have never received from the Democrats, who have characteristically neglected their financial stability. We believe that the needs of those who depend upon their programs, particularly the elderly, can be better served, especially when a Republican Administration cracks down on fraud and abuse so that program monies can be directed toward those truly in need. In the case of Medicaid, we will aid the states in restoring its financial integrity and its local direction.

We welcome the long-overdue emphasis on preventive health care and physical fitness that is making Americans more aware than ever of their personal responsibility for good health. Today's enthusiasm and emphasis on staying well holds the promise of dramatically improved health and well-being in the decades ahead. Additionally, health professionals, as well as individuals have long recognized that preventing illness or injury is much less expensive than treating it. Therefore, preventive medicine combined with good personal health habits and health education, can make a major impact on the cost of health care. Employers and employees, unions and business associations, families, schools, and neighborhood groups all have important parts in what is becoming a national crusade for better living.

Youth

The Republican Party recognizes that young people want the opportunity to exercise the rights and responsibilities of adults.

The Republican agenda for making educational and employment opportunities available to our youth has been addressed in detail in other sections of this platform.

Republicans are committed to the enactment of youth differential in the minimum wage and other vitally needed incentives for the creation of jobs for our young.

In addition, we reaffirm our commitment to broaden the involvement of young people in all phases of the political process—as voters, party workers and leaders, candidates and elected officials, and participants in government at all levels.

We pledge, as we have elsewhere in this platform, efforts to create an environment which will enable our nation's youth:

To live in a society which is safe and free;

To pursue personal, educational, and vocational goals to the utmost of their abilities;

To experience the support, encouragement, and strength that comes from maintenance of the family and its values; and

To know the stimulus of challenge, renewal through encouragement, provision of opportunities, and the growth that comes from responsible participation in numerous aspects of our society.

Older Americans

Inflation is called "the cruelest tax." It strikes most cruelly at the elderly, especially those on fixed incomes. It strikes viciously at the sick and the infirm, and those who are alone in the world.

Inflation has robbed our elderly of dignity and security. An entire generation of responsible and productive citizens who toiled and saved a full working life to build up a retirement nest egg now finds that it cannot survive on its savings. Today's inflation rates dwarf yesterday's interest rates, and the pensions and annuities of our elderly citizens cannot keep up the the rising cost of living. Millions of once-proud and independent elderly Americans face a future of welfare dependency and despair.

We propose to assist families, and individuals of all ages, to meet the needs of the elderly, primarily through vigorous private initiative. Only a comprehensive reduction in tax rates will enable families to save for retirement income, and to protect that income from ravaging inflation. Only new tax exemptions and incentives can make it possible for many families to afford to care for their older members at home.

Present laws can create obstacles to older Americans' remaining in the family home. Federal programs for the elderly, such as Medicare and Supplemental Security Income, must address, humanely and generously, the special circumstances of those who choose to stay with their families rather than enter a nursing home or other institution.

Social Security is one of this nation's most vital commitments to our senior citizens. We commit the Republican Party to first save, and then strengthen, this fundamental contract between our government and its productive citizens.

Republicans consider older Americans a community asset, not a national problem. We are committed to using the sadly wasted talents of the aged throughout our society, which sorely needs their experience and wisdom. To that end, and as a matter of basic fairness, we proudly reaffirm our opposition to mandatory retirement and our long-standing Republican commitment to end the Democrats' earnings' limitation upon Social Security benefits. In addition, the Republican Party is strongly opposed to the taxation of Social Security benefits and we pledge to oppose any attempts to tax these benefits.

Republicans have resisted Democratic electioneering schemes to spend away the Social Security trust funds for political purposes. Now the bill has come due, and the workers of America are staggering under their new tax burdens. This must stop.

Precisely because Social Security is a precious lifeline for millions of elderly, orphaned, and disabled, we insist that its financing be sound and stable. We will preserve Social Security for its original purpose.

The problems of Social Security financing are only an aspect of the overriding problems of the economy which Democratic mismanagement has produced. There is but one answer, the comprehensive tax rate reduction to which Republicans are committed. To save Social Security, we have no choice but to redirect our economy toward growth. To meet this country's commitments to Social Security recipients, present and future, we need more people at work, earning more money, thereby paying more into the trust funds. That same growth can balance the federal budget with lower taxes, over time reducing inflation, which falls so cruelly on senior citizens whose income is fixed by the size of their public or private pension.

We pledge to clean up the much-abused disability system. We will also expand eligibility for Individual Retirement Accounts to enable more persons to plan for their retirement years.

The Welfare System

The Republican agenda for welfare reform has been discussed in a previous section, but we think it important to stress that central to it is the preservation of the families the system is designed to serve. The current system does not do this. Neither would guaranteed annual income schemes. By supplanting parental responsibility and by denying children parental guidance and economic support, they encourage and reward the fragmentation of families. This is unconscionable. The values and strengths of the family provide a vital element in breaking the bonds of poverty.

Ultimately, the Republican Party supports the orderly, wholesale transfer of all welfare functions to the states

along with the tax sources to finance them.

The Family Economy

It is increasingly common for both husbands and wives to work outside the home. Often, it occurs out of economic necessity, and it creates major difficulties for families with children, especially those of pre-school age. On one hand, they are striving to improve the economic well-being of their family; on the other, they are concerned about the physical and emotional well-being of their children. This dilemma is further aggravated in instances of single parenthood due to death or divorce.

Recognizing these problems, we pledge to increase the availability of non-institutional child care. We see a special role for local, private organizations in meeting this need.

We disapprove of the bias in the federal tax system against working spouses, whose combined incomes are taxed at a proportionately higher rate than if they were single. We deplore this "marriage tax" and call for equity in the tax treatment of families.

We applaud our society's increasing awareness of the role of homemakers in the economy, not apart from the work force but as a very special part of it: the part that combines the labor of a full-time job, the skills of a profession, and the commitment of the most dedicated volunteer. Recognizing that homemaking is as important as any other profession, we endorse expanded eligibility for Individual Retirement Accounts for homemakers and will explore other ways to advance their standing and security.

Family Protection

In view of the continuing efforts of the present Administration to define and influence the family through such federally funded conferences as the

White House Conference on Families, we express our support for legislation protecting and defending the traditional American family against the on-going erosion of its base in our society.

Handicapped People

Republicans will seek every effective means to enable families more easily to assist their handicapped members and to provide for their education and special medical and therapeutic needs. In the case of handicapped children particularly, flexibility must be maintained in programs of public assistance so that, whenever possible, these youngsters may remain at home rather than in institutions.

Targeted tax relief can make it possible for parents to keep such a child at home without foregoing essential professional assistance. Similarly, tax incentives can assist those outside the home, in the neighborhood and the workplace, who undertake to train, hire, or house the handicapped.

Secure and Prosperous Neighborhoods

The quality of American neighborhoods is the ultimate test of the success or failure of government policies for the cities, for housing, and for law enforcement.

Obsessed with the demands of special interest groups and preoccupied with the design of expensive "comprehensive" programs, the Democrats in Congress and the Administration have lost sight of that simple but important criterion. They have proposed more social and fiscal tinkering with our cities and towns.

Republicans will address the real problems that face Americans in their neighborhoods day by day—deterioration and urban blight, dangerous streets

and violent crime that makes millions of Americans, especially senior citizens, fearful in their own neighborhoods and prisoners in their own homes.

In the summer of 1980, Americans suffer a rising national unemployment rate, now at nearly eight percent, and double-digit inflation and interest rates. As Republicans meet in Detroit, the policies of the Carter Administration and the Democratic Congress have pushed the economy into recession and have resulted in unemployment approaching 20 percent in our host city.

The people of Detroit have worked long and hard to revitalize their city and the evidence of its rebirth is impressive. Their efforts have been severely set back by Carter Administration policies outside of this or any city's control. The grim evidence is manifested in jobs lost as a direct consequence of bankrupt economic policies which have fostered this recession. Republicans will address and resolve the real problems of today's economy, problems that destroy jobs and deny even the hope of homeownership to millions of Americans families. We are, moreover, committed to nurturing the spirit of self-help and cooperation through which so many neighborhoods have revitalized themselves and served their residents.

Neighborhood Self-Help

The American ethic of neighbor helping neighbor has been an essential factor in the building of our nation. Republicans are committed to the preservation of this great tradition.

To help non-governmental community programs aid in serving the needs of poor, disabled, or other disadvantaged, we support permitting taxpayers to deduct charitable contributions from their federal income tax whether they itemize or not.

In contrast, the Democrats' assault against Meals-on-Wheels highlights their insensitivity to the neighborly spirit that motivates so many Americans. For over 25 years, voluntary Meals-on-Wheels organizations have been feeding needy homebound citizens—usually the elderly—with funding from local private charitable sources. Promising for the first time to "help" these neighborhood volunteer efforts in 1978, the Democratic Congress and administration instead used the carrot of federal funding and the stick of federal regulation to crowd out private ventures.

Government must never elbow aside private institutions—schools, churches, volunteer groups, labor and professional associations—in meeting the social needs in our neighborhoods and communities.

Neighborhood Revitalization

The city is the focus for the lives of millions of Americans. Its neighborhoods are places of familiarity, of belonging, of tradition and continuity. They are arenas for civic action and creative self-help. The human scale of the neighborhood encourages citizens to exercise leadership, to invest their talents, energies, and resources, to work together to create a better life for their families.

Republican economic programs will create conditions for rebirth of citizen activity in neighborhoods and cities across the land. In a Republican economic climate, America's cities can once again produce, build, and grow.

A Republican Administration will focus its efforts to revitalize neighborhoods in five areas. We will:

Cut taxes, increase incentives to save, restore sound money, and stimulate capital investment to create jobs;

Create and apply new tax incentives for employees and employers alike to stimulate economic growth and reduce red-tape for business ventures. Local government will be invited to designate specific depressed areas as jobs and enterprise zones;

Encourage our cities to undertake neighborhood revitalization and preservation programs in cooperation with the three essential local interests: local government, neighborhood property owners and residents, and local financial institutions;

Replace the categorical aid programs with block grant or revenue sharing programs and, where appropriate, transfer the programs, along with the tax sources to pay for them, back to the state and local governments; and

Remain fully committed to the fair enforcement of all federal civil rights statutes and continue minority business enterprise and similar programs begun by Republican Administrations but bungled by over-regulation and duplication during the Carter Administration.

Republican programs will revitalize the inner cities. New jobs will be created. The federal government's role will be substantially reduced. The individual citizen will reclaim his or her independence.

The revitalization of American cities will proceed from the revitalization of the neighborhoods. Cities and neighborhoods are no more nor less than the people who inhabit them. Their strengths and weaknesses provide their character. If they are to grow, it is the people who must seize the initiative and lead.

Housing and Homeownership

Our citizens must have a real opportunity to live in decent, affordable housing. Due to the disastrous policies of the Carter Administration and the Democratic Congress, however, the goal of homeownership and all that aspiration entails is now in jeopardy. These irrational policies have been catastrophic to the housing industry. The highest home mortgage interest rates in the history of the United States have depressed housing starts to the lowest level since World War II. Democratic policies guarantee shortages in owner-occupied and rental housing.

As many as 1.4 million people who depend upon homebuilding for work may lose their jobs in this recession. Many already have. In addition to the toll taken on millions of American families, intolerable pressures will build on state, local, and federal budgets as tax revenues decline and expenditures increase to aid the unemployed.

We support financing and tax incentives to encourage the construction of rental housing as an essential addition to our housing inventory.

Prospective first-time home buyers simply cannot afford to buy. The affordability of housing has become a crisis. The high rates of inflation have driven mortgage payments, house prices, and down-payment requirements beyond the means of close to 80 percent of young American families. In order to assist the record number of young families who wish to become home buyers, we propose to implement a young family housing initiative, which would include several elements such as: urban homesteading, savings and tax reforms, and innovative alternate mortgage instruments to help meet monthly payment requirements without federal subsidies. To assist older homeowners, again without federal subsidy, we urge more extensive availability of the reverse annuity mortgage which allows older homeowners to withdraw the substantial equity they have built up in their homes and thus supplement their retirement income. In order to slow increases in housing costs, regulations which artificially limit housing production and raise housing costs must be eliminated.

We favor expansion of the Republican-sponsored urban homesteading program as a means of restoring abandoned housing. This innovative program is locally administered, returns property to the tax rolls, and develops new ownership and stability within our neighborhoods.

The collapse of new home production and the distress of the housing finance system are closely related. The stop and go economic policies of the past year have created extreme volatility in financial markets which have made it impossible for thrift institutions to supply housing credit at a reasonable cost.

A set of policies aimed at higher and more stable levels of housing production will simultaneously reduce housing costs and unemployment in the economy. To assure a stable and continuous flow of funds for home mortgage financing, we pledge to allow responsible use of mortgage revenue bonds. We will work to change the tax laws to encourage savings so that young families will be able to afford their dreams.

Specifically, we will support legislation to lower tax rates on savings in order to increase funds available for housing. This will help particularly to make homeownership an accessible dream for younger families, encouraging them not to despair of ever having a home of their own, but to begin working and saving for it now. We oppose any attempt to end the income tax deductability of mortgage interest and property taxes.

Republicans will also end the mismanagement and waste that has characterized the Department of Housing and Urban Development during the Carter Administration. As presently structured, HUD programs present local governments and developers with a maze of bureaucracy, complicated applications, and inflexible requirements, often unsuited to local needs. Such programs often infringe upon the right of local government to retain jurisdiction over their own zoning laws and building codes. As a result, their cost is so high that relatively few of the needy are ultimately housed or helped. Republicans will replace many of HUD's categorical programs with decentralized block grants to provide more efficient and responsive housing assistance to the elderly, the handicapped, and the poor. In remaining programs, particular emphasis should be given to rehabilitation and preservation of existing housing stock as a priority in federal housing policy.

Crime

Safety and security are vital to the health and well-being of people in their neighborhoods and communities. Republicans are committed to ensuring that neighborhoods will be safe places in which families and individuals can live, and we support and encourage community crime fighting efforts such as neighborhood crime watch and court monitoring programs.

First, we believe that Republican economic proposals, more particularly those proposals which strengthen society and smaller communities discussed elsewhere in this document, will go a long way toward stabilizing American society.

Second, we support a vigorous and effective effort on the part of law enforcement agencies. Although we recognize the vital role of federal law enforcement agencies, we realize that the most effective weapons against crime are state and local agencies.

Just as vital to efforts to stem crime is the fair but firm and speedy application of criminal penalties. The existence and application of strong penalties are effective disincentive to criminal actions. Yet these disincentives will only be as strong as our court system's willingness to use them.

We believe that the death penalty serves as an effective deterrent to capital crime and should be applied by the federal government and by states which approve it as an appropriate penalty for certain major crimes.

We believe the right of citizens to keep and bear arms must be preserved. Accordingly, we oppose federal registration of firearms. Mandatory sentences for commission of armed felonies are the most effective means to deter abuse of this right. We therefore support Congressional initiatives to remove those provisions of the Gun Control Act of 1968 that do not significantly impact on crime but serve rather to restrain the law-abiding citizen in his legitimate use of firearms.

In recent years, a murderous epidemic of drug abuse has swept our country. Mr. Carter, through his policies and his personnel, has demonstrated little interest in stopping its ravages. Republicans consider drug abuse an intolerable threat to our society, especially to the young. We pledge a government that will take seriously its responsibility to curb illegal drug traffic. We will first and most urgently restore the ability of the FBI to act effectively in this area. Republican government will work with local law enforcement agencies to apprehend and firmly punish drug pushers and drug smugglers, with mandatory sentences where appropriate. We support efforts to crack down on the sale and advertising of drug paraphernalia. Private, nonprofit drug abuse rehabilitation agencies have taken the lead in fighting drug abuse, and they deserve greater cooperation and flexibility from federal, state, and local agencies and grant programs. We pledge the enactment of legislation to ban the utilization of federal funds by grantees of the Legal Services Corporation to render their services in cases involving the pushing or smuggling of drugs as well as in cases of repeat offenders. We commend the religious leaders, community activists, parents, and local officials who are working with fervor and dedication to protect young Americans from the drug plague.

Urban Transportation

The complex problems of mobility, congestion, and energy resources demand creative solutions if we are to improve the living conditions of our urban areas. Many urban centers of our nation need dependable and affordable mass transit systems. The first line of responsibility must lie with the local governments. They must be given the latitude to design and implement the transportation system best suited to their singular circumstances. Republicans believe we should encourage effective competition among diverse modes of transportation. The role of the federal government should be one of giving financial and technical support to local authorities, through surface transportation block grants. Because of the long planning and construction times inherent in bus, rail, and other mass transit systems, a consistent and dependable source of revenue should be established.

Mass transportation offers the prospect for significant energy conservation. In addition, both management and labor agree that ease of access to the workplace is an important factor in employment decisions and industrial plant locations. Lack of adequate access is a major reason why businesses have moved out of crowded urban areas, resulting in lower tax bases for cities. To encourage existing businesses to remain in urban centers and to attract new businesses to urban areas, it is vital that adequate public and private transportation facilities be provided.

Rural Transportation

Republicans recognize the importance of transportation in the rural areas of America.

Public transit is becoming more significant to rural areas as the costs of energy rise. While public transit will not replace the importance of private vehicles in rural America, it can serve as a vital adjunct to transportation in the neighborhoods throughout rural America.

ₓJobs and the Workplace

We propose to put Americans back to work again by restoring real growth without inflation to the United States economy. Republican programs and initiatives detailed in this platform will create millions of additional new jobs in the American workplace. As a result of Mr. Carter's recession, more than eight million Americans are now out of work.

Sweeping change in America's economic policy is needed. We must replace the Carter Administration's promise of hard times and austerity— one promise which has been kept—with Republican policies that restore economic growth and create more jobs.

The Democratic Congress and the Carter Administration are espousing programs that candidate Carter in 1976 said were inhumane: using recession, unemployment, high interest rates, and high taxes to fight inflation. The Democrats are now trying to stop inflation with a recession, a bankrupt policy which is throwing millions of Americans out of work. They say Americans must tighten their belts, abandon their dreams, and accept higher taxes, less take-home pay, fewer jobs, and no growth in the national economy.

We categorically reject this approach. Inflation is too much money chasing too few goods. Shutting down our nation's factories and throwing millions of people out of work leads only to shortages and higher prices.

We believe inflation can only be controlled by monetary and spending restraint, combined with sharp reductions in the tax and regulatory barriers to savings, investments, production, and jobs.

[Growth and its Impact on Workers]

The Republican Party believes nothing is more important to our nation's defense and social well-being than economic growth.

Since 1973, the U.S. economy has grown in real terms at a rate of only 1.9 percent a year. This is barely half of the 3.7 percent annual growth rate we experienced between 1950 and 1973 and well below the 4.6 percent growth rate we enjoyed between 1961 and 1969. If our economy continues to grow at our current rate of less than two percent a year, our Gross National Product (GNP) will barely reach $3 trillion by 1990.

But if we can regain the growth we experienced during the economic boom of the 1960s, our GNP will reach nearly $4 trillion by the end of the decade, nearly one-third higher.

With this kind of economic growth, incomes would be substantially higher and jobs would be plentiful. Federal revenues would be high enough to provide for a balanced budget, adequate funding of health, education and social spending, and unquestioned military preeminence, with enough left over to reduce payroll and income taxes on American workers and retirees. Economic growth would generate price stability as the expanding economy eliminated budget deficits and avoided pressure on the Federal Reserve to create more money. And the social gains from economic growth would be enormous. Faster growth, higher incomes, and plentiful jobs are exactly what the unemployed, the underprivileged, and minorities have been seeking for many years.

All working men and women of America have much to gain from economic growth and a healthy business environment. It enhances their bargaining position by fostering competition among potential employers to provide more attractive working conditions, better retirement and health benefits, higher wages and salaries, and generally improving job security. A stagnant economy, which Democratic policies have brought about, decreases competition among business for workers, discourages improved employee benefits, reduces income levels, and dramatically increases unemployment.

Savings, Productivity, and Jobs

Savings and investment are the keys to economic growth. Only that part of national income which goes into savings and which is not consumed by government deficits is available to finance real economic growth.

Americans now save less than any other people in the Western world because inflation and the high rates of taxation imposed by the Carter Administration and the Democratic Congress have destroyed their ability and incentive to save and invest. This has strangled economic growth, choked off private initiative, pushed up prices, and retarded productivity and job creation.

The sharp drop in the growth of American productivity is the main reason why Americans' average real weekly earnings are no more than they were 19 years ago. This problem has worsened to the point that workers earn eight percent less in real purchasing power as the Carter term comes to a close than they did when it began.

The 25 years of Democratic domination of the Congress have cost us a generation of lost opportunities. The Carter Administration in particular has opposed every Republican effort to restore the health of the economy through lower taxes and work efforts, savings, and the modernization of America's productive machinery.

Republicans are committed to an economic policy based on lower tax rates and a reduced rate of government spending.

Therefore, the Republican Party pledges to:

Reduce tax rates on individuals and businesses to increase incentives for all Americans and to encourage more savings, investment, output and productivity, and more jobs for Americans;

Provide special incentives for savings by lowering the tax rates on savings and investment income;

Revitalize our productive capacities by simplifying and accelerating tax depreciation schedules for facilities, structures, equipment, and vehicles;

Limit government spending to a fixed and smaller percentage of the Gross National Product; and

Balance the budget without tax increases at these lower levels of taxation and spending.

We also oppose Carter proposals to impose withholding on dividend and interest income. They would serve as a disincentive to save and invest and create needless paperwork burdens for government, business, industry, and the private citizen. They would literally rob the saver of the benefits of interest compounding and automatic dividend reinvestment programs.

Unless taxes are reduced and federal spending is restrained, our nation's economy faces continued inflation, recession, and economic stagnation. Tax rate reductions and spending restraint will restore the savings and investment needed to create new jobs, increase living standards, and restore our competitive position in the world.

Employment Safety-Net

To those individuals who have lost their jobs because of the Carter recession we pledge to insure that they receive their rightfully earned unemployment compensation benefits.

The Republican Party recognizes the need to provide workers who have lost

their jobs because of technological obsolescence or imports the opportunity to adjust to changing economic conditions. In particular, we will seek ways to assist workers threatened by foreign competition.

The Democratic Administration's inability to ensure fairness and equity between our nation and some of our trading partners has resulted in massive unemployment in many core industries. As we meet in Detroit, this Party takes special notice that among the hardest hit have been the automotive workers whose jobs are now targeted by aggressive foreign competition. Much of this problem is a result of the present Administration's inability to negotiate foreign trade agreements which do not jeopardize American jobs. We will take steps to ensure competitiveness of our domestic industries to protect American jobs. But for workers who have already lost their jobs, we will provide assistance, incentives for job retraining and placement, and job search and relocation allowances. Toward this end, we will pursue specific tax and regulatory changes to revitalize America's troubled basic industries. We will also seek the aid of private individuals, businesses, and non-profit organizations to formulate creative new self-supporting answers to training and placement problems as well as non-governmental sources of temporary financial support.

The Republican Party believes that protectionist tariffs and quotas are detrimental to our economic well-being. Nevertheless, we insist that our trading partners offer our nation the same level of equity, access, and fairness that we have shown them. The mutual benefits of trade require that it be conducted in the spirit of reciprocity. The Republican Party will consider appropriate measures necessary to restore equal and fair competition between ourselves and our trading partners.

The international exchange of goods and services must take place under free and unfettered conditions of market entry.

⨯ Training and Skills

Unemployment is a growing problem for millions of Americans, but it is an unparalleled disaster for minority Americans. As this country's economic growth has slowed over the past decade, unemployment has become more intractable. The gravity of the crisis is so severe that as we entered the present recession, unemployment was over six percent for the entire labor force but it was 33 percent for minority youth. In addition, the black unemployment rate was 10.8 percent and youth between the ages of 16 and 24 continued to account for about one-half of the total unemployed.

Despite the almost $100 billion spent on well-intended public sector employment and training programs, the structural unemployment problem continues to fester among minorities and young people. In addition to providing a growth climate for job creation, specific and targeted programs must be developed to alleviate these problems.

Since four out of every five jobs are in the private sector, the success of federal employment efforts is dependent on private sector participation. It must be recognized as the ultimate location for unsubsidized jobs, as the provider of means to attain this end, and as an active participant in the formulation of employment and training policies on the local and national level. Throughout America, the private and independent sectors have repeatedly helped in the creation of minority business through donated counseling and consulting services. They have encouraged equal opportunity hiring practices within their own industries and have built non-profit, self-supporting training centers where the products produced during training are sold to support the programs.

A coordinated approach needs to be developed which maximizes the use of existing community resources, offers adequate incentives to the private sector, focuses on both large and small business, and minimizes red tape.

In recognizing the seriousness of the youth employment problem, Republicans also realize that a job alone will do very little to move a disadvantaged young person beyond the poverty line. Republicans support the creation of comprehensive programs for disadvantaged youth which would offer pre-employment training, educational instruction, job placement, and retention services. Second, Republicans support efforts to establish and maintain programs which seek to match the needs of the private sector and our young people as efficiently and effectively as possible. We also support expansion of proven skill training practices, such as apprenticeship, as well as private schools and trade schools. These methods can provide quality training and point toward the acquisition of specific job skills leading to specific employment goals.

We will encourage and foster the growth of new organizations operated by public-private partnerships to help forge a closer link between the schools and private employers. These institutions can afford in-school and out-of-school disadvantaged youth with the opportunity to upgrade basic skills, acquire work habits and orientation to work, and move directly from successful completion of the program to private unsubsidized jobs.

We believe that present laws create additional barriers for unemployed youth. One of the keys to resolving the youth unemployment problem is to reduce the cost to private employers for hiring young people who lack the necessary skills and experience to become immediately productive. Unfortunately, current government policy makes it too expensive for employers to hire unskilled youths. We urge a reduction of payroll tax rates, a youth differential for the minimum wage, and alleviation of other costs of employment until a young person can be a productive employee.

Small Business

Small business is the backbone of the American economy, with unique strengths and problems which must be recognized and addressed. For more than half of all American workers, the workplace is a small business. Small business is family business both in the sense that many of them are owned and operated by single families, and also because most American families rely not only on the goods and services, but on the jobs produced there for their livelihood and standard of living.

Republicans have demonstrated their sensitivity to the problems of the small business community. The Carter Administration held a conference to learn what Republicans have long known. In the Congress, we have been working to pass legislation to solve small business problems and achieve the very goals later identified by that conference. A 1978 initiative by the late Representative Bill Steiger reduced the capital gains tax rates which were destroying capital formation in America. Under the leadership of Republicans in Congress, efforts to simplify and liberalize the restrictive depreciation schedule are a top priority. Another proposal long advocated by our Party is the drive to encourage the entrepreneur by reform of the regulatory laws which stifle the very life of business through fines, threats, and harassment. Republicans realize the immediate necessity of reducing the regulatory burden to give small business a fighting chance against the federal agencies. We believe that wherever feasible, small business should be exempt from regulations and, where exemption is not feasible, small business should be subject to a less onerous tier of regulation. We have offered legislation to reimburse small businessmen who successfully challenge the federal government in court. Republicans believe the number one priority for small business in America is the achievement of lower business and personal tax rates for small businessmen and women and we intend to work to secure them.

All of these initiatives will receive immediate attention from a Republican Administration and Congress. Without such changes as these, the small entrepreneur, who takes the risks which help make the economy grow and provides over 90 percent of all new jobs annually, will be an endangered species.

By fostering small business growth, we are promoting permanent private sector solutions to the unemployment problem. We will continue to provide for small business needs by enacting a substantial increase in the surtax exemption. The heavy estate tax burden imposed on the American people is threatening the life savings of millions of our families, forcing spouses and children to sell their homes, businesses, and family farms to pay the estate taxes. To encourage continuity of family ownership, we will seek to ease this tax burden on all Americans and abolish excessive inheritance taxes to allow families to retain and pass on their small businesses and family farms.

We will reform the patent laws to facilitate innovation and we will further this goal by encouraging a greater share of federal research and development be done by small business. Finally, we will reform those tax laws which make it more profitable to break up a small business or merge it into a conglomerate, than to allow it to grow and develop as an independent business.

Fairness to the Worker

The Republican Party is committed to full employment without inflation.

We will seek to provide more jobs, increase the standard of living, and ensure equitable treatment on the job for all American workers by stimulating economic growth.

We reaffirm our commitment to the fundamental principle of fairness in labor relations, including the legal right of unions to organize workers and to represent them through collective bargaining consistent with state laws and free from unnecessary government involvement. We applaud the mutual efforts of labor and management to improve the quality of work life.

Wage demands today often represent the attempt of working men and women to catch up with government-caused inflation and high tax rates. With the blessing of the Democrats' majority in Congress, the Council on Wage and Price Stability has put a de facto ceiling of seven to eight and one-half percent on workers' wages, while the Administration devalues their paychecks at a rate of 13 to 15 percent. The government, not the worker, is the principal cause of inflation.

We recognize the need for governmental oversight of the health and safety of the workplace, without interfering in the economic well-being of employers or the job security of workers.

The Republican Party reaffirms its long-standing support for the right of states to enact "Right-to-Work" laws under section 14(b) of the Taft-Hartley Act.

The political freedom of every worker must be protected. Therefore the Republican Party strongly supports protections against the practice of using compulsory dues and fees for partisan political purposes.

Fairness to the Consumer

The Republican Party shares the concerns of consumers that there be full disclosure and fairness in the market-place. We recognize that government regulation and taxes add significantly to costs of goods and services to the consumer, reducing the standard of living for all Americans. For example, safety and environmental standards, some of which are counterproductive, increase the average price of a new car by over $700. Compliance with those regulations alone costs motorists as much as $12 billion a year.

Fairness to the consumer, like fairness to the employer and the worker, requires that government perform certain limited functions and enforce certain safeguards to ensure that equity, free competition, and safety exist in the free market economy. However, government action is not itself the solution to consumer problems; in fact, it has become in large measure a part of the problem. By consistent enforcement of law and enhancement of fair competition, government can and should help the consumer.

An informed consumer making economic choices and decisions in the marketplace is the best regulator of the free enterprise system. Consumers are also taxpayers, workers, investors, shoppers, farmers, and producers. The Republican Party recognizes the need for consumer protection but feels that such protection will not be enhanced by the creation of a new consumer protection bureaucracy. Just as there can be no single monolithic consumer viewpoint, so the Republican Party opposes the funding of special self-proclaimed advocates to represent consumer interests in federal agency proceedings.

Fairness to the Employer

The Republican Party declares war on government overregulation. We pledge to cut down on federal paperwork, cut out excessive regulation, and cut back the bloated bureaucracy.

In addressing these problems we recognize that overregulation is particux larly harmful to America's small businesses whose survival is often threatened by the excessive costs of complying with government rules and handling federal paperwork.

While we recognize the role of the federal government in establishing certain minimum standards designed to improve the quality of life in America, we reaffirm our conviction that these standards can best be attained through innovative efforts of American business without the federal government mandating the methods of attainment.

The extraordinary growth of government, particularly since the middle 1960s, has brought mounting costs to society which, in turn, have added to inflationary pressures, reduced productivity, discouraged new investment, destroyed jobs, and increased bureaucratic intrusion into everyday life.

Regulatory costs are now running in excess of $100 billion each year, or about $1,800 for every American family. Federal paperwork annually costs businesses from $25 to $32 billion. According to official figures, it takes individuals and business firms over 143 million man-hours to complete 4,400 different federal forms each year. Government regulation produces many indirect, immeasurable costs as well and has led to increase bureaucratization of industry. Regulation also restricts personal choices, tends to undermine America's democratic public institutions, and threatens to destroy the private, competitive free market economy it was originally designed to protect.

Government Reform

In the face of a crisis of overregulation, the Carter Administration and the Democrats who control Congress have failed to recognize the problems facing workers, employers, and consumers and seem unable to come to grips with the underlying causes. While belatedly supporting transportation deregulation programs initiated by previous Republican Administrations, they have embarked on ambitious new schemes to tighten Washington's hold on energy and education. They have ignored or sidetracked Republican proposals to eliminate wasteful and outmoded spending programs and regulations. They have combined to push through more legislation and create additional programs which expand the size and power of the federal bureaucracy at the expense of ordinary taxpayers, consumers and businesses. In contradiction to 1976 Carter campaign promises to cut back on regulation, the number of pages in the Federal Register devoted to new rules and regulations has increased from 57,072 in 1976 to 77,497 in 1979 and will approach 90,000 by the end of 1980.

The result of Democratic rule in both the White House and the Congress is that government power has grown unchecked. Excessive regulation remains a major component of our nation's spiraling inflation and continues to stifle private initiative, individual freedom, and state and local government autonomy.

The Republican Party pledges itself to a comprehensive program of government reform. We propose to enact a temporary moratorium on all new federal regulations that diminish the supply of goods and services and add significantly to inflation. Such a moratorium will be consistent with the goal of achieving a safe and healthy working environment. We shall work to reduce substantially the regulatory and paperwork burdens on small businesses.

We encourage management and labor to form joint safety and health committees to make the workplace a better place to produce goods and services. At the same time we believe that the arbitrary and high-handed tactics used by OSHA bureaucrats must end. OSHA should be required to consult with, advise, and assist businesses in coping with the regulatory burden before imposing any penalty for non-compliance. Small businesses and employers with good safety records should be exempt from safety inspections, and penalties should be increased for those with consistently poor performance.

Agriculture

In no American workplace is there to be found greater productivity, cooperation, neighborly concern, creative use of applied science, information and relevant research, honesty, perseverence, hard work, and independence than on the farm and ranch.

The Republican Party takes pride in the ability of American farmers to provide abundant, high quality, and nutritious food and fiber for all our citizens including those most in need and to millions throughout the world, and at the same time to supply the largest single component in our export balance of trade.

Crisis in Agriculture

Four years of the Carter Administration and 25 consecutive years of a Congress controlled by Democrats have brought farmers and ranchers to the brink of disaster and the hardest times they have known since the Great Depression. In the last four years, more than 100,000 family farms have failed as farm income has plummeted. Even the present Administration's own figures show a decrease in real net farm income of some 40 percent in the last year alone—from $33 billion in 1979 to less than $22 billion projected for 1980.

The Democratic Party and the Carter Administration have abused their authority and failed in their responsibility to provide sound agricultural policies. Republicans pledge to make life in rural America prosperous again. We will:

Increase net farm income by supporting and refining programs to bring profitable farm prices with the goal of surpassing parity levels in a market-oriented agricultural economy;

Control inflation by adopting sound fiscal and monetary policies and by eliminating excessive and unnecessary federal regulations;

Expand markets at home by effectively utilizing the advantages of the energy potential for farm, forestry, and other biomass products. We encourage the continued innovative efforts in developing alcohol and other renewable energy sources and equipment for both on-farm and commercial use;

Aggressively expand markets abroad by effectively using the Eisenhower Food for Peace program and revolving credit incentives, working to remove foreign restraints on American products and encouraging the development of dependable new markets in developing countries;

Assure a priority allocation of fuel for U.S. agriculture, including food and fiber production, transportation, and processing; and

Combine efforts to encourage the renewable resource timber production capability of privately-owned forests and woodlands with a federal program committed to multiple-use (timber, recreation, wildlife, watershed and/or range management) where federal land has not been designated as wilderness.

Rural America

Attention to the quality of life in our rural areas is a vital necessity because rural Americans impart a special strength to the national character. It is our goal to assure that all rural citizens—whether they are farmers or not—have the same consideration in matters of economic development, in energy, credit and transportation availability, and in employment opportunities which are given to those who live in towns and cities. The opportunity for non-farm jobs enhances the ability of people to live and work in rural America in the decade ahead, and our dedication to a prosperous and energetic rural America is part and parcel of our commitment to make America great again.

Expand Export Markets

Agriculture's contribution to the U.S. trade balance makes it especially fitting that an aggressive market development program to establish dependable new markets for farm exports will be a vital part of the policies to restore profitability to American agriculture. Republicans will ensure that:

International trade is conducted on the basis of fair and effective competition and that all imported agricultural products meet the same standards of quality that are required of American producers;

The General Agreement on Tariffs and Trade becomes a meaningful vehicle for handling agricultural trade problems and grievances;

An aggressive agricultural market development program and the streamlining of the export marketing system is given top national priority;

Government-to-government sales of agricultural commodities be eliminated, except as specifically provided by law;

The future of U.S. agricultural commodities is protected from the economic evils of predatory dumping by other producing nations and that the domestic production of these commodities, so important to the survival of individuals and small rural communities is preserved; and

The important and productive potential of the commercial seafood industry is given encouragement.

Farmer-Held Reserves

We support farmer-owned grain reserves, should they become necessary, and adamantly oppose government-controlled reserves.

Grain Embargo

We believe that agricultural embargoes are only symbolic and are ineffective tools of foreign policy. We oppose singling out American farmers to bear the brunt of Carter's ill-conceived, ineffective, and improperly implemented grain embargo. The Carter grain embargo should be terminated immediately.

Excessive Regulation of Agriculture

The crushing burden of excessive federal regulation such as many of those imposed on farmers, ranchers, foresters, and commercial fishermen by OSHA, EPA, the departments of Agriculture, Labor, Justice, Interior, and other government entities are unrealistic and unnecessary.

We pledge a sensible approach to reduce excessive federal regulation that is draining the profitability from farming, ranching, and commercial fishing. Especially high on the agenda for changes in policy under Republican leadership are such regulatory issues as the Interior Department's ineffective predator control policies, EPA and FDA's excessive adherence to "zero risk" policies relative to the use of pesticides, herbicides, antibiotics, food additives, preservatives, and the like.

Soil and Water Conservation

We believe the strong soil and water conservation stewardship to which farmers, ranchers, watermen, and rural Americans are devoted is exemplary, and encourage appropriate local, state, and federal programs to give conservation practices vitality. Voluntary participation with adequate incentives is essential to the effective conservation of our soil and water resources.

Water Policy

The conservation and development of the nation's water resources are vital requisites for rebuilding America's national strength. The natural abundance of water can no longer be taken for granted. The impending crisis in water could be far more serious than our energy problems unless we act now. A dynamic water policy, which addresses our national diversity in climate, geography, and patterns of land ownership, and includes all requirements across the spectrum of water use, including Reclamation policy, will be a priority of the Republican Administration working with the advice and counsel of state and local interests. We must develop a partnership between the Executive Branch and Congress in developing and implementing that policy. Lack of such partnership has resulted in four years of bitter confrontation between the states and the obstructive policies of the Democratic Administration. The Congress has been frustrated in its efforts to conserve and develop our water resources. Working together, the states and the federal government can meet the impending water crisis through innovative and alternative approaches to such problems as cleaning our lakes and rivers, reducing toxic pollution, developing multiple-use projects, and achieving a workable balance between the many competing demands on our water resources.

Agricultural Labor

Comprehensive labor legislation, which will be fair to American workers and encourage better relations with our neighbors in Mexico and Canada with whom we wish to establish a working North American Accord, is an essential endeavor. We deplore disruptive work stoppages which interrupt the supply of food to consumers.

Taxation

Federal estate and gift taxes have a particularly pernicious effect on family farms. Young farmers who inherent farm property are often forced to sell off part of the family farm to pay taxes. Once these taxes are paid, young farmers often must begin their careers deeply in debt. Our tax laws must be reformed to encourage rather than discourage family farming and ranching.

We deplore the imposition of present excessive estate and gift taxes on family farms. We support the use of lower, productivity-based valuation when farms are transferred within the family. Further, we believe that no spouse should pay estate taxes on farm property inherited from a husband or wife. We support the Republican tax cut proposal which provides accelerated depreciation and expanded investment tax credits to farm vehicles, equipment, and structures. Finally, we support legislation which would remove tax advantages foreign investors realize on the sale of U.S. forests, farmland, and other real estate.

Rural Transportation

It is essential to the well-being and security of our nation that an adequate rural transportation system be restored as a vital link between rural areas and their markets, both domestic and export. Overall, we pledge to eliminate those rules and regulations which are restrictive to the free flow of commerce and trade of agricultural products and encourage an environment that will enhance the private development and improvement of all modes of transportation to move agricultural production swiftly, safely, and economically. Recognizing the inherent advantages of each mode of transportation, the Republican Party will work to encourage and allow those advantages to be utilized on a balanced and equitable basis.

We believe the federal 55 miles per hour speed limit is counterproductive and contributes to higher costs of goods and services to all communities, particularly in rural America. The most effective, no-cost federal assistance program available would be for each state to set its own speed limit.

A Strong USDA

We pledge an Administration dedicated to restoring profitability to agriculture. A top priority will be the selection of a qualified and effective Secretary and policy staff who will speak up for American farmers—and a President who will listen.

America's preeminence in agriculture is rooted in a system of agricultural research, extension, and teaching—unique and unequalled in the world. Land Grant Universities focus on problems of national, regional, and local concern. Cooperative extension, operating in every county of the United States and its territories, brings the results of USDA and Land Grant University research to farmers and ranchers, rural women, consumers, agribusiness, and to youth through 4-H programs.

Food Safety

The Republican Party favors a legislative effort to revise and modernize our food safety laws, providing guidelines for risk assessment, benefit assessment, peer review, and regulatory flexibility which are consistent with other government health and safety policies.

Cooperatives

We believe farmer cooperatives and rural electric and telephone cooperatives provide essential benefits to farmers and the rural Americans they serve, and we support exclusive jurisdiction of USDA in the effective administration of the Capper-Volstead Act.

We Republicans pledge ourselves to work with farmers, ranchers, and our friends and neighbors to make America great again.

The Nation

Though a relatively young nation among those of western civilization we are possessed of one of the oldest institutions of government extant. Steeped in the Judeo-Christian ethic and in Anglo-Saxon theories of law and right, our legal and political institutions have evolved over many generations to form a stable system that serves free men and women well. It governs a people of multifarious heritage dispersed across a great continent of marked geographical contrasts. It presides over a diverse economy that in its collective whole is the largest, most powerful and most resilient in the world. In the two centuries of its life, though it has from time to time been sorely tested by constitutional, economic, and social crises, it has stood and not been found wanting. Its timeless strength, coupled with and reinforced by the faith and good will, the wisdom and confidence of the people from whom it derives its powers, has preserved us as a nation of enormous vitality.

The intent of the Founders, embraced and reflected by succeeding generations of Americans, was that the central government should perform only those functions which are necessary concomitants of nationality, preserve order, and do for people only those things which they cannot do for themselves. The durability of our system lies in its flexibility and its accommodation to diversity and changing circumstance. It is notable as much for what it permits as for what it proscribes. Government must ever be the servant of the nation, not its master.

Big Government

Under the guise of providing for the common good, Democratic Party domination of the body politic over the last 47 years has produced a central government of vastly expanded size, scope, and rigidity. Confidence in government, especially big government, has been the chief casualty of too many promises made and broken, too many commitments unkept. It is time for change—time to de-emphasize big bureaucracies—time to shift the focus of national politics from expanding government's power to that of restoring the strength of smaller communities such as the family, the neighborhood, and the workplace.

Government's power to take and tax, to regulate and require has already reached extravagant proportions. As government's power continues to grow, the "consent of the governed" will diminish. Republicans support an end to the growth of the federal government and pledge to return the decisionmaking process to the smaller communities of society.

The emergence of policies and programs which will revitalize the free enterprise system and reverse the trend toward regulation is essential. To sustain the implementation of such policy, it is necessary to raise the public awareness and understanding that our free enterprise system is the source of all income, government and private, and raise the individual's awareness of his or her vested interest in its growth and vitality.

The Republican Party believes that it is important to develop a growing constituency which recognizes its direct relationship to the health and success of free enterprise, and realizes the negative impact of excessive regulation. Education and involvement in the system are the best means to accomplish this. To this end, we will actively pursue new and expanding opportunities for all Americans to become more directly involved in our free enterprise system.

Government Reorganization

The Republican Party reaffirms its belief in the decentralization of the federal government and in the traditional American principle that the best government is the one closest to the people. There, it is less costly, more accountable, and more responsive to people's needs. Against the prevailing trend toward increased centralization of government under the Democrats, Republicans succeeded in the 1970s in initiating large scale revenue sharing and block grant programs to disperse the power of the federal government and share it with the states and localities.

Our states and localities have the talent, wisdom, and determination to respond to the variety of demands made upon them. Block grants and revenue sharing provide local government with the means and the flexibility to solve their own problems in ways most appropriate for each locale. Unlike categorical grants, they do not lock states and localities into priorities and needs perceived by Washington. They are also more efficient because block grants and revenue sharing relieve both local government and the federal government from the costly and complicated process of program application, implementation, and review associated with the categorical grant system.

We pledge to continue to redouble our efforts to return power to the state and local governments. The regionalization of government encouraged by federal policies diminishes the responsiveness of state and local governments and impairs the power of the people to control their destiny.

While Republican efforts have been focused on sharing revenues and the powers that go with it, the Carter Administration has been preoccupied with the reorganization and consolidation of central authority. As a result, we have the Departments of Energy and Education, for example, but no more oil and gas, or learning, to show for it.

When we mistakenly rely on government to solve all our problems we ignore the abilities of people to solve their own problems. We pledge to renew the dispersion of power from the federal government to the states and localities. But this will not be enough. We pledge to extend the process so that power can be transferred as well to non-governmental institutions.

Government Reform

We favor the establishment of a commission of distinguished citizens to recommend ways of reorganizing and reducing the size and scope of the Executive Branch. Federal departments, agencies, and bureaus should be consolidated where possible to end waste and improve the delivery of essential services. Republicans pledge to eliminate bureaucratic red tape and reduce government paperwork. Agencies should be made to justify every official form and filing requirement. Where possible, we favor deregulation, especially in the energy, transportation, and communications industries. We believe that the marketplace, rather than the bureaucrats, should regulate management decisions.

The unremitting delegation of authority to the rule-makers by successive Democratic Congresses and the abuse of that authority has led to our current crisis of overregulation. For that reason, we support use of the Congressional veto, sunset laws, and strict budgetary control of the bureaucracies as a means of eliminating unnecessary spending and regulations. Agencies should be required to review existing regulations and eliminate those that are outmoded, duplicative, or contradictory. They must conduct cost-benefit analyses of major proposed regulations to determine their impact on the economy, on public health and safety, on state and local government, and on competition. We recommend legislation which would eliminate the present presumption of validity in favor of federal regulations. We also support legislation to require the federal government to provide restitution to those who have been wrongfully injured by agency actions. We oppose the use of tax monies by any federal agency to pay the expenses of intervenors in the rulemaking process.

We recognize that there are dangers inherent in the rapid growth of the federal bureaucracy, especially the arbitrary nature of its discretionary power and the abuses of procedural safeguards. Accordingly, we pledge to work for fundamental changes in the federal Administrative Procedures Act in order to give citizens the same constitutional protections before a government agency that they have in a courtroom. Among these reforms are requirements that agencies publish in the Federal Register all rules and statements of policy before they are adopted, that a person be guaranteed written notice and the opportunity to submit facts and arguments in any adjudicatory proceeding, that an agency decision be consistent with prior decisions unless otherwise provided by law, and that a person may seek judicial review without first exhausting his or her administrative remedies. At the same time we urge the Congress to strengthen its oversight to ensure that the agencies comply with the deadlines, report filing and other requirements mandated by law.

We propose to repeal federal restrictions and rewrite federal standards which hinder minorities from finding employment, starting their own businesses, gaining valuable work experience, or enjoying the fruits of their own labors.

Because there are too many federal employees in comparison to private sector employees, there should be no further increase in the number of civilian federal employees if that would increase the ratio of federal employees to private sector employees over the present ratio.

Election Reform

The Republican Party has consistently encouraged full participation in our electoral process and is disturbed by the steady decline in voter participation in the United States in recent years. We believe that the increased voter turnout during the past year in Republican campaigns is due to dissatisfaction with Democratic officials and their failure to heed popular demands to cut taxes, restrain spending, curb inflation, and drastically reduce regulation.

Republicans support public policies that will promote electoral participation without compromising ballot-box security. We strongly oppose national postcard voter registration schemes because they are an open invitation to fraud.

Republicans support public policies that encourage political activity by individual citizens. We support the repeal of those restrictive campaign spending limitations that tend to create obstacles to local grassroots participation in federal elections. We also oppose the proposed financing of congressional campaigns with taxpayers' dollars as an effort by the Democratic Party to protect its incumbent Members of Congress with a tax subsidy. We prefer the present system of having the states and party rules determine the presidential nominating process to the concept of a uniform national primary which would only add to the already high costs of, and excessive federal intrusion into, presidential campaigns.

We support the critical roles of competitive political parties in the recruitment of candidates, the conduct of campaigns, and the development of broad-based public policy responsible to the people. We urge Congress and state legislatures to frame their regulations of campaign finance, their nominating systems, and other election laws to strengthen rather than weaken parties.

Arts and Humanities

Recent Republican Administrations led the way in bringing together private support and governmental encouragement to effect a tremendous expansion of artistic and scholarly endeavor. The Carter Administration has crudely politicized these programs, lowering their standards of excellence and increasing federal control over them.

The Republican Party will restore the sound economy which is absolutely necessary for the arts and humanities to flourish. We will restore, as well, the integrity of federal programs in this area. Most important, to ensure the continued primacy of private funding for the arts, we reiterate our support of broader tax incentives for contributions to charitable and cultural organizations.

Transportation

America's transportation system must be designed to meet the requirements of the people, not to dictate what those requirements should be. Essential to any industrialized country is a transportation system which provides efficient and reliable service for both the movement of people and freight, urban and rural, domestic and foreign. Our nation has one of the finest transportation systems in the world but there is a danger that it will be unable to meet the future needs of a growing America.

Present levels of public and private investment will not preserve the existing system. For example, highways are deteriorating twice as fast as they are being rebuilt and inadequate rehabilitation will soon cost users more in reduced service levels than the cost of adequate rehabilitation.

The demand for transportation will grow dramatically in the next two decades with people-miles travelled increasing by over 50 percent and freight ton-miles more than doubling.

Government overregulation is inhibiting the return on investment necessary to attract capital for future growth and jobs creation.

A maze of federal agencies, Congressional committees, and conflicting policies is driving up costs and retarding innovation.

A lackluster energy policy, impeding production of oil, coal, and other forms of energy is endangering transportation's ability to keep up with demand.

Consequently, the role of government in transportation must be redefined. The forces of the free market must be brought to bear to promote competition, reduce costs, and improve the return on investment to stimulate capital formation in the private sector. The role of government must change from one of overbearing regulation to one of providing incentives for technological and innovative developments, while assuring through anti-trust enforcement that neither predatory competitive pricing nor price gouging of captive customers will occur.

Increased emphasis must be placed on the importance of having a well-balanced national transportation system where highways, passenger vehicles, buses, trucks, rail, water, pipelines, and air transportation each provide those services which they do best, while offering the widest range of reasonable choices for both passenger and freight movement. A sound transportation system is a prerequisite for the vision of America that Republicans embrace—a prosperous, growing nation where dreams can still come true.

Energy

Energy is the lifeblood of our economy. Without adequate energy supplies now and in the future, the jobs of American men and women, the security of their lives, and their ability to provide for their families will be threatened and their standard of living will be lowered. Every American is painfully aware that our national energy situation has deteriorated badly over the past four years of Democratic control. Gasoline prices have more than doubled. Our oil import bill has risen 96 percent. Our energy supplies have become increasingly vulnerable because U.S. oil production outside of Alaska is now 23 percent below 1973 levels. The threat of sudden short-

ages, curtailments, and gas lines has become a recurring reality.

This steady deterioration has not only compounded our economic problems of inflation, recession, and dollar weakness, but even more importantly, it has infected our confidence as a nation. Energy shortages, spiralling costs, and increasing insecurity are beginning to darken our basic hopes and expectations for the future.

The National Association for the Advancement of Colored People has very accurately focused on the effects that a no-growth energy policy will have on the opportunities of America's black people and other minorities. The NAACP said that "a pessimistic attitude toward energy supplies for the future ... cannot satisfy the fundamental requirement of a society of expanding economic opportunity."

In commenting on the Carter energy proposals the Association said, "We cannot accept the notion that our people are best served by a policy based upon the inevitability of energy shortage and the need for government to allocate an ever diminishing supply among competing interests ... (The plan) reflects the absence of a black perspective in its development."

Three and one-half years ago, President Carter declared energy the "moral equivalent of war" and sent Congress 109 recommendations for action, including the creation of a new Department of Energy. Since then, the federal budget for government's energy bureaucracy has grown to about $10 billion per year and more than 20,000 pages of new energy regulations and guidelines have been issued. But these have not fostered the production of a single extra unit of energy.

The Democratic Congress has joined in the stampede, taking action on 304 energy bills since 1977. As a result, the federal bureaucracy is busy from coast to coast allocating gasoline, setting building temperatures, printing rationing coupons, and readying standby plans to ban weekend boating, close factories, and pass out "no drive day" stickers to American motorists—all the time saying, "we must make do with less." Never before in the history of American government has so much been done at such great expense with such dismal results.

Republicans believe this disappointing cycle of shrinking energy prospects and expanding government regulation and meddling is wholly unnecessary. We believe that the proven American values of individual enterprise can solve our energy problems. This optimism stands in stark contrast to the grim predictions of the Democrats who have controlled Congress for the last 25 years.

[Alternative Strategy]

They seem to believe not only that we are a nation without resources, but also that we have lost our resourcefulness. Republicans believe in the common sense of the American People rather than a complex web of government controls and interventions that threaten America's ability to grow. We are committed to an alternative strategy of aggressively boosting the nation's energy supplies; stimulating new energy technology and more efficient energy use; restoring maximum feasible choice and freedom in the marketplace for energy consumers and producers alike; and eliminating energy shortages and disruptions as a roadblock to renewed national economic growth, rising living standards, and a reawakening of the hopes and dreams of the American people for a better and more abundant future.

We believe the United States must proceed on a steady and orderly path toward energy self-sufficiency. But in the interim, our pressing need for insurance against supply disruption should not be made hostage to the whims of foreign governments, as is presently the case under the Carter Administration. We believe it is necessary to resume rapid filling of strategic oil reserves to planned levels of 500 million barrels in the short-term and ultimately to the one-billion barrel level, and to insure that non-contiguous areas of the United States have their fair share of emergency oil reserves stored within their respective boundaries, as authorized by the Energy Policy and Conservation Act of 1975.

In order to increase domestic production of energy, Republicans advocate the decontrol of the price at the well head of oil and gas. We believe that the so-called windfall profits tax (which is unrelated to profit) should be repealed as it applies to small volume royalty owners, new oil, stripper wells, tertiary-recovery, and heavy crude oil, and that the phase-out of the tax on old oil should be accelerated. This tax legislation should be amended to include a plowback provision. We will seek decontrol of prices on all oil products and an end to government authority to allocate petroleum supplies except in national emergency. We also believe that market restrictions on the use of natural gas should be eliminated.

[Future of Coal]

Coal, our most abundant energy resource, can bridge the gap between our other present energy sources and the renewable energy sources of the future. The coal industry has been virtually ignored by the Carter Administration and the Democratic Congress. In 1977, President Carter promised to double coal production by 1985. Instead, because of obstructionist actions of the Administration, coal production has increased by only 11 percent to date and future prospects are dim. Today, thousands of coal miners are out of work and without hope for the future.

Republicans support a comprehensive program of regulatory reform, improved incentives, and revision of cumbersome and overly stringent Clean Air Act regulations. This program will speed conversion of utility, industrial, and large commercial oil-burning boilers to coal to the greatest extent feasible, thus substantially cutting our dependence on foreign oil. This program must begin immediately on a priority basis and be completed at the earliest date possible.

To effectively utilize this vast resource, our coal transportation systems must be upgraded and the government controls on them relaxed. Government regulation regarding the mining and use of coal must be simplified. We will propose a policy which will assure that governmental restraints, other than necessary and reasonable environmental controls, do not prevent the use of coal. We also reaffirm that mined lands must be returned to beneficial use and that states, in accordance with past Congressional mandate, have the primary responsibility to implement rules concerning the mining of coal which are adapted to the states' unique characteristics.

Coal, gas, and nuclear fission offer the best intermediate solutions to America's energy needs. We support accelerated use of nuclear energy through technologies that have been proven efficient and safe. The safe operation, as well as design, of nuclear generating plants will have our highest priority to assure the continued availability of this important energy source. The design and operation of these plants can be guaranteed in less than the 10 to 12 year lead time now required to license and build them. We believe that the licensing process can and should be streamlined through consolidation of the present process and the use of standardized reactor designs.

[Nuclear Energy Development]

The Three Mile Island incident suggests the need for certain reforms, such as in the area of operator training, but illustrates that properly designed and operated nuclear plants do not endanger public health or safety. We further encourage the research, development, and demonstration of the breeder reactor with its potential for safely contributing to our nation's future energy supplies.

Nuclear power development requires sound plans for nuclear waste disposal and storage and reprocessing of spent fuel. Technical solutions to these problems exist, and decisive federal action to choose and implement solutions is essential. The Democratic-controlled Congress and Administration have failed to address the spent fuel problem. A Republican Congress and Administration will immediately begin to implement plans for regional away-from-reactor storage of spent fuel with the goal of implementation of a program no later than 1984.

Republicans are committed to the rapid development of permanent storage facilities for nuclear wastes. Since waste disposal is a national responsibility, no state should bear an unacceptable share of this responsibility.

Republicans will also move toward reprocessing of spent fuel.

Republicans will continue to support the development of new technologies to develop liquid, gaseous, and solid hydrocarbons which can be derived from coal, oil shale, and tar sands. The decontrol of oil and gas prices will eliminate any necessity for government support for a synthetic fuel industry except possibly for limited demonstration projects. Clean air, water, waste disposal, mine reclamation, and leasing rules must be made rational and final to accelerate private investment.

Gasohol is an important, immediately available source of energy that is helping to extend our petroleum reserves. We encourage development of a domestic gasohol industry.

We also believe the government must continue supporting productive research to speed the development of renewable energy technology, including solar energy, geothermal, wind, nuclear fusion, alcohol synthesis, and biomass, to provide the next generation of energy sources.

[Incentives for Conservation]

Conservation clearly plays a vital role in the consideration and formulation of national energy policy. Republicans reject, however, the position of the Democrats which is to conserve through government fiat. Republicans understand that free markets based on the collective priorities and judgments of individual consumers will efficiently allocate the energy supplies to their most highly valued uses. We also believe that the role of government is best performed by structuring creative cost-effective incentives to achieve energy efficiency and conservation.

We reject unequivocally punitive gasoline and other energy taxes designed to artificially suppress energy consumption.

Much inefficient energy use results from government subsidization of imported oil and holding the price of natural gas substantially below its market value. When the price of energy is held artificially low, there is no incentive for conservation. This kind of energy consumption stems not from the excesses of the public, but the foolish policy distortions of government. Every BTU of genuine energy "waste" in our economy would rapidly disappear if we immediately and completely dismantle all remaining energy price controls and subsidies.

[Cost of Energy]

A Republican policy of decontrol, development of our domestic energy resources, and incentives for new supply and conservation technologies will substantially reduce our dependence on imported oil. We reject the Carter Administration's incessant excuse that the high price of imported oil and OPEC are the primary cause of inflation and recession at home and a weak dollar and declining balance of payments abroad. The fastest way to bring international oil prices under control is to stop printing so recklessly the dollar in which those prices are denominated. Fully 60 percent of the world oil price increase since 1973 represents the depreciation of our dollars rather than an increase in the real price of oil.

Virtually all major environmental legislation in the past decade reflected a bipartisan concern over the need to maintain a clean and healthful environment. While the new environmental policies have resulted in improving air quality, cleaner waters, and more careful analysis of toxic chemicals, the price paid has far exceeded the direct and necessary cost of designing and installing new control technology. In the energy area, the increased complexity of regulations, together with continual changes in the standards imposed, have brought about tremendous delays in the planning and construction of new facilities ranging from electric power plants to oil refineries, pipelines, and synthetic fuel plants.

Republicans believe that an effective balance between energy and environmental goals can be achieved. We can ensure that government requirements are firmly grounded on the best scientific evidence available, that they are enforced evenhandedly and predictably, and that the process of their development and enforcement has finality.

Republicans condemn the Democrats' withdrawal of a massive amount of the most promising federal lands from prospective energy development, including the rich potential of our Outer Continental Shelf. It has been estimated that by the end of the 1980s resources from government-controlled acreage could yield over two million barrels of oil per day and four trillion cubic feet of gas per year, the equivalent of nearly all of our imports from OPEC countries. It is clear that restrictive leasing policies have driven us further to depend on OPEC by severely impairing the exploration for, and development of, domestic oil, gas, and coal resources, thereby aggravating our balance of trade deficit and making available all suitable federal lands for multiple use purposes including exploration and production of energy resources.

Republicans believe that in order to address our energy problem we must maximize our domestic energy production capability. In the short term, therefore, the nation must move forward on all fronts simultaneously, including oil and gas, coal, and nuclear. In the longer term, renewable resources must be brought significantly on line to replace conventional sources. Finally, in conjunction with this all-out production initiative, we must strive to maximize conservation and the efficient use of energy.

The return to the traditions that gave vitality and strength to this nation is urgent.

The free world—indeed western civilization—needs a strong United States. That strength requires a prospering economy. That economy will be secure with a vigorous domestic energy industry. That vigor can only be achieved in an atmosphere of freedom—one that encourages individual initiatives and personal resourcefulness.

Environment

The Republican Party reaffirms its long standing commitment to the conservation and wise management of America's renewable natural resources.

We believe that a healthy environment is essential to the present and future well-being of our people, and to sustainable national growth.

The nature of environmental pollution is such that a government role is necessary to insure its control and the proper protection of public health. Much progress has been made in achieving the goals of clean air, clean water, and control of toxic wastes. At the same time, we believe that it is imperative that environmental laws and regulations be reviewed, and where necessary, reformed to ensure that the benefits achieved justify the costs imposed. Too often, current regulations are so rigid and narrow that even individual innovations that improve the environment cannot be implemented. We believe, in particular, that regulatory procedures must be reformed to expedite decisionmaking. Endless delay harms both the environment and the economy.

We strongly affirm that environmental protection must not become a cover for a "no-growth" policy and a shrinking economy. Our economy can continue to grow in an acceptable environment.

We believe that agricultural policy should give emphasis to the stewardship of the nation's soil and water resources. The permanent loss of productive farm land is a growing problem and we encourage states and local communities to adopt policies that help maintain and protect productive agricultural land as a national asset.

Immigration and Refugee Policy

Residence in the United States is one of the most precious and valued of conditions. The traditional hospitality of the American people has been severely tested by recent events, but it remains the strongest in the world. Republicans are proud that our people have opened their arms and hearts to strangers from abroad and we favor an immigration and refugee policy which is consistent with this tradition. We believe that to the fullest extent possible those immigrants should be admitted who will make a positive contribution to America and who are willing to accept the fundamental American values and way of life. At the same time, United States immigration and refugee policy must reflect the interests of the nation's political and economic well-being. Immigration into this country must not be determined solely by foreign governments or even by the millions of people around the world who wish to come to America. The federal government has a duty to adopt immigration laws and follow enforcement procedures which will fairly and effectively implement the immigration policy desired by American people.

The immediate adoption of this policy is essential to an orderly approach to the great problem of oppressed people seeking entry, so that the deserving can be accepted in America without adding to their hardships.

The refugee problem is an international problem and every effort should be made to coordinate plans for absorbing refugee populations with regional bodies, such as the Organization of American States and the Association of South East Asian Nations, on a global basis.

The Judiciary

Under Mr. Carter, many appointments to federal judgeships have been particularly disappointing. By his partisan nominations, he has violated his explicit campaign promise of 1976 and has blatantly disregarded the public interest. We pledge to reverse that deplorable trend, through the appointment of women and men who respect and reflect the values of the American people, and whose judicial philosophy is characterized by the highest regard for protecting the rights of law-abiding citizens, and is consistent with the belief in the decentralization of the federal government and efforts to return decision-making power to state and local elected officials.

We will work for the appointment of judges at all levels of the judiciary who

respect traditional family values and the sanctity of innocent human life.

Taxes and Government Spending

Elsewhere in this platform, we have pledged for the sake of individual freedom and economic growth to cut personal income tax rates for all. Republicans believe that these tax rate reductions should be complemented by firm limitations on the growth of federal spending as provided by the Roth-Kemp Bill. The Republican Party, therefore, pledges to place limits on federal spending as a percent of the Gross National Product. It is now over 21 percent. We pledge to reduce it. If federal spending is reduced as tax cuts are phased in, there will be sufficient budget surpluses to fund the tax cuts, and allow for reasonable growth in necessary program spending.

By increasing economic growth, tax rate reduction will reduce the need for government spending on unemployment, welfare, and public jobs programs. However, the Republican Party will also halt excessive government spending by eliminating waste, fraud, and duplication.

We believe that the Congressional budget process has failed to control federal spending. Indeed, because of its big spending bias, the budget process has actually contributed to higher levels of social spending, has prevented necessary growth in defense spending, and has been used to frustrate every Republican attempt to lower tax rates to promote economic growth.

The immediate burden of reducing federal spending rests on the shoulders of the President and the Congress. We believe a Republican President and a Republican Congress can balance the budget and reduce spending through legislative actions, eliminating the necessity for a Constitutional amendment to compel it. However, if necessary, the

Republican Party will seek to adopt a Constitutional amendment to limit federal spending and balance the budget, except in time of national emergency as determined by a two-thirds vote of Congress.

Government Lending

Not only has the Democratic Congress failed to control spending, but in the last 10 years federal credit assistance programs have soared out of control.

Many federal loan guarantees and related credit programs are off-budget. As a result, no one knows the nature and extent of our obligations or the effect such practices have on our economy. The best estimate is that outstanding federal credit is now close to $600 billion.

Runaway government lending can be just as dangerous as runaway federal spending.

The Republican Party will establish a workable federal credit policy that will bring order to the reckless lending practices of the past.

Inflation

We consider inflation and its impact on jobs to be the greatest domestic threat facing our nation today. Mr. Carter must go! For what he has done to the dollar; for what he has done to the life savings of millions of Americans; for what he had done to retirees seeking a secure old age; for what he has done to young families aspiring to a home, an education for their children, and a rising living standard, Mr. Carter must not have another four years in office.

In his three and one-half years in office, Mr. Carter has presented and supported policies which carried inflation from 4.8 percent in 1976 to a peak of 18 percent during 1980.

He has fostered a 50 percent increase in federal spending, an increase of more than $200 billion, boosting spending in an era of scarce resources, and driving up prices.

He has through both inaction and deliberate policy permitted or forced tax increases of more than 70 percent, more than $250 billion, directly increasing the cost of living and the costs of hiring and producing. This has crippled living standards, productivity, and our ability to compete in the world. It has led to reduced output, scarcity, and higher prices.

He has imposed burdensome regulations and controls on production which have reduced the availability of domestic goods and energy resources, increased our dependence on imports, particularly in the energy area, driven down the value of the dollar, and driven up prices.

He has permitted continuing federal budget deficits and increased federal borrowing, forcing higher interest rates and inflationary money creation, increasing prices.

The inflation policies of the Carter Administration have been inconsistent, counterproductive, and tragically inept. Mr. Carter has blamed everyone from OPEC to the American people themselves for this crisis of inflation—everyone, that is, but his own Administration and its policies which have been the true cause of inflation.

Inflation is too much money chasing too few goods. Much can be done to increase the growth of real output. But ultimately price stability requires a non-inflationary rate of growth of the money supply in line with the real growth of the economy. If the supply of dollars rapidly outstrips the quantity of goods, year in, year out, inflation is inevitable.

Ultimately, inflation is a decline in the value of the dollar, the monetary standard, in terms of the goods it can buy. Until the decade of the 1970s, monetary policy was automatically linked to the overriding objective of maintaining a stable dollar value. The serving of the dollar's link with real commodities in the 1960s and 1970s, in order to pursue economic goals other than dollar stability, has unleashed hyper-inflationary forces at home and monetary disorder abroad, without bringing any of the desired economic benefits. One of the most urgent tasks in the period ahead will be the restoration of a dependable monetary standard—that is, an end to inflation.

Lower tax rates, less spending, and a balanced budget are the keys to maintaining real growth and full employment as we end inflation by putting our monetary policy back on track. Monetary and fiscal policy must each play its part if we are to achieve our joint goals of full employment and price stability.

Unfortunately, Mr. Carter and the Democratic Congress seek to derail our nation's money creation policies by taking away the independence of the Federal Reserve Board. The same people who have so massively expanded government spending should not be allowed politically to dominate our monetary policy. The independence of the Federal Reserve System must be preserved.

The Republican Party believes inflation can be controlled only by fiscal and monetary restraint, combined with sharp reductions in the tax and regulatory disincentives for savings, investments, and productivity. Therefore, the Republican Party opposes the imposition of wage and price controls and credit controls.

Controls will not stop inflation, as past experience has shown. Wage and price controls will only result in shortages, inequities, black markets, and ultimately higher prices. We reject this short-sighted and misguided approach.

Peace and Freedom

Prologue

At the start of the 1980s, the United States faces the most serious challenge to its survival in the two centuries of its existence. Our ability to meet this challenge demands a foreign policy firmly rooted in principle. Our economic and social welfare in the 1980s may depend as much on our foreign and defense policy as it does on domestic policy. The Republican Party reasserts that it is the solemn purpose of our foreign policy to secure the people and free institutions of our nation against every peril; to hearten and fortify the love of freedom everywhere in the world; and to achieve a secure environment in the world in which freedom, democracy, and justice may flourish.

For three and one-half years, the Carter Administration has been without a coherent strategic concept to guide foreign policy, oblivious to the scope and magnitude of the threat posed to our security, and devoid of competence to provide leadership and direction to the free world. The Administration's conduct of foreign policy has undermined our friends abroad, and led our most dangerous adversaries to miscalculate the willingness of the American people to resist aggression. Republicans support a policy of peace through strength; weakness provokes aggression.

For three and one-half years the Carter Administration has given us a foreign policy not of constancy and credibility, but of chaos, confusion, and failure. It has produced an image of our country as a vacillating and reactive nation, unable to define its place in the world, the goals it seeks, or the means to pursue them. Despite the Administration's rhetoric, the most flagrant offenders of human rights including the Soviet Union, Vietnam, and Cuba have been the beneficiaries of Administration good will, while nations friendly to the United States have suffered the loss of U.S. commercial access and economic and military assistance.

The threat to the United States and its allies is not only a military one. We face a threat from international terrorism. Our access to energy and raw material resources is challenged by civil unrest, Soviet-sponsored subversion, and economic combinations in restraint of free trade. Our first line of defense, our network of friendly nations and alliances, has been undermined by the inept conduct of foreign affairs.

American policy since World War II has rested upon the pillars of collective security, military and technological superiority, and economic strength, and upon the perception by our adversaries that the United States possesses the will to use its power where necessary to protect its freedom. These tenets have enabled a commonwealth of free and independent nations to enjoy the benefits and confidence that come from expanding economic interchange in peace and bilateral and multilateral support in time of war. The entire structure of peace was guaranteed by American and allied military power sufficient to deter conflict, or to prevail in conflict if deterrence should fail.

The Administration's neglect of America's defense posture in the face of overwhelming evidence of a threatening military buildup is without parallel since the 1930s. The scope and magnitude of the growth of Soviet military power threatens American interest at every level, from the nuclear threat to our survival, to our ability to protect the lives and property of American citizens abroad.

[Soviet Threat]

Despite clear danger signals indicating that Soviet nuclear power would overtake that of the United States by the early 1980s, threatening the survival of the United States and making possible, for the first time in post-war history, political coercion and defeat, the Administration reduced the size and capability of our nuclear forces.

Despite clear danger signals indicating that the Soviet Union was using Cuban, East German, and now Nicaraguan, as well as its own, military forces to extend its power to Africa, Asia, and the Western Hemisphere, the Administration often undermined the very governments under attack. As a result, a clear and present danger threatens the energy and raw material lifelines of the Western world.

Despite clear danger signals indicating that the Soviet Union was augmenting its military threat to the nations of Western Europe, American defense programs such as the enhanced radiation warhead and cruise missiles, which could have offset that buildup, were cancelled or delayed—to the dismay of allies who depend upon American military power for their security.

The evidence of the Soviet threat to American security has never been more stark and unambiguous, nor has any President ever been more oblivious to this threat and its potential consequences.

The entire Western world faces complex and multi-dimensional threats to its access to energy and raw material resources. The growth of Soviet military power poses a direct threat to the petroleum resources of the Persian Gulf now that its military forces deployed in Afghanistan are less than 300 miles from the Straits of Hormuz, through which half the free world's energy supplies flow.

Soviet efforts to gain bases in areas astride the major sea lanes of the world have been successful due to their use of military power, either directly or indirectly through Cuban and other Soviet bloc forces. Since the Carter Administration took office in 1977, the Soviets or their clients have taken over Afghanistan, Cambodia, Ethiopia, and

South Yemen, and have solidified their grasp on a host of other nations in the developing world. The Soviet noose is now being drawn around southern Africa, the West's most abundant single source of critical raw materials.

[American Citizens Vulnerable]

The failure of the United States to respond to direct threats to its security has left American citizens vulnerable to terrorist assaults as well. American diplomatic personnel have been subject to seizure and assault by terrorists throughout the world without drawing a meaningful Administration response.

No failure of the Administration has been so catastrophic as its failure of leadership. Mired in incompetence, bereft of strategic vision and purpose, the President's failure to shoulder the burden of leadership in the Western alliance has placed America in danger without parallel since December 7, 1941. The United States cannot abdicate that role without inducing a diplomatic and eventually a military catastrophe.

Republicans realize that if the challenges of the 1980s are not met, we will continue to lose the respect of the world, our honor, and in the end, our freedom. Republicans pledge to meet these challenges with confidence and strength. We pledge to restore to the United States and its people a government with conviction in our cause, a government that will restore to our great nation its self-respect, its self-confidence, and its national pride.

National Security

Defense Budget Trends

In the late 1960s, the Republicans returned to the White House, inheriting a war in Southeast Asia. Because of this war, they also inherited a Fiscal Year (FY) 1968 defense budget which, if calculated in constant 1981 dollars to account for inflation, had risen to over $194 billion from $148 billion in FY 1961, the last Eisenhower year. By the beginning of the second Nixon Administration, U.S. forces were totally disengaged from Southeast Asia. The FY 1974 defense budget had dropped back to $139 billion, and the country had reaped its desired "peace dividend" of an over $50 billion reduction in annual defense spending. During this period, between 1969 and 1973, the Democrats who controlled Congress, led by Senators Mondale and Muskie, cut almost $45 billion from Nixon defense requests. Until 1975, Congress continued to ignore long-range defense needs, and made severe cuts in Republican defense proposals. The Ford Administration, however, succeeded in reversing this trend. From a low point of $134 billion in FY 1975, the FY 1976 defense budget rose, in response to President Ford's request, to $139 billion; and in FY 1977 it rose again to $147 billion.

Despite the growing sentiment for a stronger defense, candidate Carter ran on a promise of massive cuts in U.S. defense spending, one promise he has kept. In his first three years in the White House, Mr. Carter reduced defense spending by over $38 billion from President Ford's last Five Year Defense Plan. Now, in his last year in office, faced with the total collapse of his foreign policy, and with his policy advisers and their assumptions disgraced, he has finally proposed an increase beyond the rate of inflation in defense spending. But this growth for 1981 will be less than one percent.

We deplore Mr. Carter's personal attempts to rewrite history on defense budgets. His tough speeches before military audiences cannot hide his continuing opposition to Congressional defense increases. The four chiefs of the armed services have each characterized the Carter defense program as "inadequate" to meet the military threat posed to the United States. We associate ourselves with the characterization by Democratic Congressional leaders of the President's behavior on defense as "hypocritical." We would go further; it is disgraceful.

Mr. Carter cut back, cancelled, or delayed every strategic initiative proposed by President Ford. He cancelled production of the Minuteman missile and the B-1 bomber. He delayed all cruise missiles, the MX missile, the Trident submarine and the Trident II missile. He did this while the Soviet Union deployed the Backfire bomber and designed two additional bombers equal in capability to the B-1, and while it deployed four new large ICBMs and developed four others.

Mr. Carter postponed production and deployment of enhanced radiation (neutron) warheads while the Soviet Union deployed the SS-20 mobile missile and the Backfire bomber against Western Europe. He cut President Ford's proposed shipbuilding plan in half. He vetoed a nuclear aircraft carrier. He did this while the Soviet Union pursued an aggressive ship-building program capable of giving them world-wide naval supremacy in the 1980s unless current trends are reversed immediately. Mr. Carter opposed efforts to correct the terribly inadequate pay rates for our military personnel and stood by as the alarming exodus of trained and skilled personnel from the services quickened. At the same time, the Soviet Union increased its military manpower to a level of 4.8 million, more than double that of the United States.

Recovery from the Carter Administration's neglect will require effort, but Americans know that effort is the unavoidable precondition to peace and economic prosperity. The Soviet Union is now devoting over $50 billion more to defense annually than the United States, achieving military superiority as a result. We have depleted our capital and must now devote the resources essential to catching up. The Secretary of Defense has stated that even if we were to maintain a constant increase in our spending of five percent in real terms, it would require 40 years for us to catch up.

Republicans commit themselves to an immediate increase in defense spending to be applied judiciously to critically needed programs. We will build toward a sustained defense expenditure sufficient to close the gap with the Soviets, and ultimately reach the position of military superiority that the American people demand.

Defense Strategy

More is required than reversing our military decline alone. We have seen in recent years how an Administration, possessed of dwindling but still substantial strength, has stood paralyzed in the face of an inexorable march of Soviet or Soviet-sponsored aggression. To be effective in preserving our interests, we must pursue a comprehensive military strategy which guides both the design and employment of our forces. Such a strategy must proceed from a sober analysis of the diverse threats before us.

Republicans approve and endorse a national strategy of peace through strength as set forth in House Concurrent Resolution 306. We urge speedy approval of this legislation by both the U.S. House of Representatives and the U.S. Senate as a means of making clear to the world that the United States has not forgotten that the price of peace is eternal vigilance against tyranny. Therefore we commend to all Americans the text of House Concurrent Resolution 306, which reads as follows:

The foreign policy of the United States should reflect a national strategy of peace through strength. The general principles and goals of this strategy should be:

To inspire, focus, and unite the national will and determination to achieve peace and freedom;

To achieve overall military and technological superiority over the Soviet Union;

To create a strategic and civil defense which would protect the American people against nuclear war at least as well as the Soviet population is protected;

To accept no arms control agreement which in any way jeopardizes the security of the United States or its allies, or which locks the United States into a position of military inferiority;

To reestablish effective security and intelligence capabilities;

To pursue positive non-military means to roll back the growth of communism;

To help our allies and other non-Communist countries defend themselves against Communist aggression; and

To maintain a strong economy and protect our overseas sources of energy and other vital raw materials.

Our strategy must encompass the levels of force required to deter each level of foreseeable attack and to prevail in conflict in the event deterrence fails. The detailed analysis that must form the intellectual basis for the elaboration of such a strategy will be the first priority of a Republican Administration. It must be based upon the following principles.

Nuclear Forces

Nuclear weapons are the ultimate military guarantor of American security and that of our allies. Yet since 1977, the United States has moved from essential equivalence to inferiority in strategic nuclear forces with the Soviet Union. This decline has resulted from Mr. Carter's cancellation or delay of strategic initiatives like the B-1 bomber, the MX missile, and the Trident II submarine missile programs and from his decisions to close the Minuteman production line and forego production of enhanced radiation weapons.

As the disparity between American and Soviet strategic nuclear forces grows over the next three years, most U.S. land-based missiles, heavy bombers, and submarines in port will become vulnerable to a Soviet first-strike. Such a situation invites diplomatic blackmail and coercion of the United States by the Soviet Union during the coming decade.

An administration that can defend its interest only by threatening the mass extermination of civilians, as Mr. Carter implied in 1979, dooms itself to strategic, and eventually geo-political, paralysis. Such a strategy is simply not credible and, therefore is ineffectual. Yet the declining survivability of the U.S. ICBM force in the early 1980s will make this condition unavoidable unless prompt measures are taken. Our objective must be to assure the survivability of U.S. forces possessing an unquestioned, prompt, hard-target counterforce capability sufficient to disarm Soviet military targets in a second-strike. We reject the mutual assured-destruction (MAD) strategy of the Carter Administration which limits the President during crises to a Hobson's choice between mass mutual suicide and surrender. We propose, instead, a credible strategy which will deter a Soviet attack by the clear capability of our forces to survive and ultimately to destroy Soviet military targets.

In order to counter the problem of ICBM vulnerability, we will propose a number of initiatives to provide the necessary survivability of the ICBM force in as timely and effective a manner as possible. In addition, we will proceed with:

The earliest possible deployment of the MX missile in a prudent survival configuration;

Accelerated development and deployment of a new manned strategic penetrating bomber that will exploit the $5.5 billion already invested in the B-1, while employing the most advanced technology available;

Deployment of an air defense system comprised of dedicated modern interceptor aircraft and early warning support systems;

Acceleration of development and deployment of strategic cruise missiles deployed on aircraft, on land, and on ships and submarines;

Modernization of the military command and control system to assure the responsiveness of U.S. strategic nuclear forces to presidential command in peace or war; and

Vigorous research and development of an effective anti-ballistic missile system, such as is already at hand in the Soviet Union, as well as more modern ABM technologies.

For more than 20 years, commencing in the mid-1950s, the United States has maintained tactical nuclear weapons in Europe for the purpose of assuring against deep penetrations into the West by the Soviet forces. Since 1977, however, the Administration has allowed our former superiority to erode to the point where we now face a more than three-to-one disadvantage.

A Republican Administration will strive for early modernization of our theater nuclear forces so that a seamless web of deterrence can be maintained against all levels of attack, and our credibility with our European allies is restored. In consultation with them we will proceed with deployments in Europe of medium-range cruise missiles, ballistic missiles, enhanced radiation warheads, and the modernization of nuclear artillery.

Conventional Forces

The greatest single result of our loss of nuclear parity has been the manifest increase in the willingness of the Soviet Union to take risks at the conventional level. Emboldened by the Carter Administration's failure to challenge their use of surrogate Cuban forces in Africa and the later Soviet presence in Angola, Ethiopia, and South Yemen, the Soviets, for the first time in post-war history, employed their own army units outside of the Soviet bloc in a brutal invasion of Afghanistan. The invasion presents chilling evidence of the mounting threat and raises fundamental questions with respect to United States strategy.

We believe it is not feasible at this time, and in the long term would be unworkable, to deploy massive U.S. ground forces to such areas as the Persian Gulf on a permanent basis as we do in Europe and elsewhere. A more effective strategy must be built on the dual pillars of maintaining a limited full-time presence in the area as a credible interdiction force, combined with the clear capability to reinforce this presence rapidly with the forces necessary to prevail in battle. In addition, the strategy must envision military action elsewhere at points of Soviet vulnerability—an expression of the classic doctrine of global maneuver.

The forces essential to the support of such a strategy must include a much-improved Navy, the force most suitable for maintaining U.S. presence in threatened areas and protecting sea lines of communication. In addition, we will require a substantial improvement in the air and sea mobility forces and improved access to regional installations. A Republican Administration will propose their substantial improvement, to include the establishment of a permanent fleet in the Indian Ocean. We will also improve contingency planning for the use and expansion of our commercial maritime fleet, and a new rational approach to emergency use of our civil aircraft fleet.

The budget cuts imposed by Mr. Carter on the Army and his restoration of the supremacy of systems analysis in the Pentagon have resulted in slow-downs, deferrals and cost increases in nine vitally needed Army procurement programs in armor, firepower, air defense, and helicopters. These critical and long-delayed modernization programs must be restored to economical production rates and must be speeded into the field. Of equal importance is the need to bring our stocks of ammunition, spare parts and supplies—now at woefully inadequate levels—to a standard that will enable us to sustain our forces in conflict.

In addition to the strategic programs needed for our Air Force, we pledge to restore tactical aircraft development and procurement to economical levels and to speed the achievement of 26 modernized wings of aircraft able to conduct missions at night, in all weather conditions, and against the most sophisticated adversary.

We pledge to increase substantially our intra- and inter-theater airlift capability and to increase our aerial tanker fleet through procurement and speedy modernization.

Of all of the services, the Navy and Marines have suffered most from Mr. Carter's cuts. Their share of the defense budget has shrunk 40 to 33 percent during the Carter Administration. Mr. Carter slashed President Ford's 157 ship, five-year construction program to 83. He has slowed the Trident submarine and requested only one attack submarine each year in spite of a Soviet three-to-one advantage. He vetoed the Fiscal Year 1979 Defense Authorization Bill because it included an aircraft carrier which a year later Congress forced him to accept. For the fourth straight year he has requested fewer than half the number of 325 aircraft needed annually to stay even with peacetime attrition and modernization requirements. He has requested fewer than one-third of the amphibious ships needed just to keep the current level of capability for the Marines, and he has opposed Marine tactical aircraft and helicopter modernization.

The current Chief of Naval Operations has testified that, "We are trying to meet a three ocean requirement with a one-and-a-half ocean Navy." Republicans pledge to reverse Mr. Carter's dismantling of U.S. Naval and Marine forces. We will restore our fleet to 600 ships at a rate equal to or exceeding that planned by President Ford. We will build more aircraft carriers, submarines and amphibious ships. We will restore Naval and Marine aircraft procurement to economical rates enabling rapid modernization of the current forces, and expansion to meet the requirements of additional aircraft carriers.

Defense Manpower and the Draft

The Republican Party is not prepared to accept a peacetime draft at this time. Under Mr. Carter, the all-volunteer force has not been given a fair chance to succeed. The unconscionable mismanagement and neglect of personnel policy by the Carter Administration has made a shambles of the all-volunteer force concept.

Perhaps the most compelling vulnerability of our forces results from the dramatic exodus of the core of highly skilled men and women who form the backbone of our military strength. This loss is the direct result of neglect by the Commander-in-Chief.

The sustained malign neglect of our military manpower is nothing short of a national scandal. This Administration's active assault on military benefits and military retirement has been accompanied by an enforced pay-cap set at half the inflation rate. The average military family has lost between 14 percent and 25 percent in purchasing power over the past seven years. Officers and skilled enlisted personnel are leaving in droves, and 250,000 of our servicemen qualify for public assistance. Many of our career people earn less than the minimum wage. The services are currently short 70,000 senior enlisted personnel. This scandal is the direct result of Mr. Carter's willful downgrading of the military and inept mismanagement of personnel policy. As a top priority, the Republican Party pledges to end this national disgrace.

We pledge to restore a national attitude of pride and gratitude for the service of our men and women in the armed forces. We will act immediately to correct the great inequities in pay and benefits of career military personnel. Specifically, we support immediate action to:

Provide for an increase in military pay targeted in particular toward the career grades now experiencing the greatest attrition;

Increase enlistment and reenlistment bonuses;

Improve continuation bonuses for aviators;

Increase per diem travel allowances;

Increase the allowance for moving mobile homes;

Provide family separation allowances for junior personnel; and

Expand benefit entitlement under the CHAMPUS program.

A Republican Administration will index military pay and allowances to protect military personnel from absorbing the burden of inflation. We pledge that the profession of arms will be restored to its rightful place as a preeminent expression of patriotism in America.

In order to attract recruits of high ability, a Republican Administration will act to reintroduce G.I. Bill benefits for those completing two years active service. We will press for enactment of legislation denying federal funds to any educational institution that impedes access of military recruiters to their students. We regard as a serious loss the decision of many of our finest institutions of higher learning to discontinue their military officer training programs. The leadership of our armed forces must include the best trained minds in our nation. Republicans call upon our colleges and universities to shoulder their responsibilities in the defense of freedom. We will investigate legislative inducements toward this end. We will not consider a peacetime draft unless a well-managed, Congressionally-funded, full-scale effort to improve the all-volunteer force does [not] meet expectations.

Reserve Forces

The armed forces of the U.S. are today critically dependent upon our nation's Reserve components for both combat arms and combat support. The Army Reserve and National Guard provide one-third of the Army's combat divisions, 80 percent of its independent combat brigades, one-half of its artillery battalions, and one-third of its special forces groups. The Navy Reserve provides 90 percent of the Navy's ocean mine sweeping and two-thirds of its mobile construction battalions. The Air Force Reserve and Air National Guard units may be mobilized for even the smallest of conflicts and many such units today are expected to deploy immediately with the active duty units they support.

Today, however, the reserves are ill-equipped, underpaid, and under-manned by several hundred thousand personnel. Proper equipment, realistic, challenging training, and greater full-time support must be made available. We must ensure that all Americans take note of the proud and vital role played by the Reserve and National Guard components of the armed forces of the United States.

Readiness and Industrial Preparedness

History records that readiness for war is the surest means of preventing it.

Lack of preparedness is the most dangerously provocative course we can take. Yet funding requests for sufficient fuel, spare parts, ammunition, and supplies for U.S. war reserves have been cut each year for the past four years from the minimum quantities the armed services have stated they need. This has left the U.S. Armed Forces at their lowest state of preparedness since 1950, seriously compromising their ability to sustain a military conflict.

Crippling shortages of spare parts, fuel, and ammunition compromise the ability of the armed forces to sustain a major military conflict. Some critical types of ammunition could not support combat operations for more than a week although we are committed to holding a 90-day inventory of major ammunition types. In addition, critical facilities such as airfields, ammunition depots, maintenance installations, and living quarters for our troops are in serious disrepair. The backlog of deferred maintenance and the underfunded purchase of vital combat consumables is so vast that years of effort will be required to rebuild U.S. forces to the required level of readiness.

The problem of maintaining the day-to-day combat readiness of U.S. armed forces is compounded by the reduced ability of American industry to respond to wartime contingencies. Reduced acquisition of equipment for the modernization of the armed forces and the Carter Administration's failure to maintain combat readiness have eroded the incentive of American industry to maintain capacity adequate to potential defense requirements.

Republicans pledge to make the combat readiness of U.S. Armed Forces and the preparedness of the industrial base to a top priority.

Research and Development

Research and Development (R&D) provides a critical means by which our nation can cope with threats to our security. In the past, the United States' qualitative and technological superiority provided a foundation for our military superiority. Yet we are now on the verge of losing this advantage to the Soviet Union because of Mr. Carter's opposition to real increases in the R&D effort. Delays imposed on the R&D process now allow seven to 10 years or more to elapse between the time when a new weapon system is proposed and when it becomes available.

The Soviet Union now invests nearly twice as much in military research and development as does the United States. This disparity in effort threatens American technological superiority in the mid-1980s and could result in Soviet breakthroughs in advanced weapon systems.

Republicans pledge to revitalize America's military research and development efforts, from basic research through the deployment of weapons and support systems, to assure that our vital security needs will be met for the balance of the century. We will seek increased funding to guarantee American superiority in this critical area and to enable us to deal with possible breakthroughs in anti-missile defense, anti-satellite killers, high-energy directed systems, and the military and civilian exploitation of space.

America's technological advantage has always depended upon its interaction with our civilian science and technology sector. The economic policy of the Carter Administration has severely encumbered private research and development efforts, thereby depriving both our civil and military sectors of the fruits of scientific innovation.

Underfunding of beneficial government-sponsored research efforts in basic and applied scientific research has disrupted the benefits of years of effective effort. In particular, America's preeminence in the exploration of space is threatened by the failure of the Carter

Administration to fund fully the Space Shuttle program (with its acknowledged benefits for both the civil and military applications) as well as advanced exploration programs. Republicans pledge to support a vigorous space research program.

Management and Organization

The Republican Party pledges to reform the defense programming and budgeting management system established by the Carter Administration. The ill-informed, capricious intrusions of the Office of Management and Budget, and the Department of Defense Office of Program Analysis and Evaluation have brought defense planning full circle to the worst faults of the McNamara years. Orderly planning by the military services has become impossible. Waste, inefficiency, and paralysis have been the hallmarks of Carter Administration defense planning and budgeting. This has resulted in huge cost overruns and in protracted delays in placing advanced systems in the field.

National Intelligence

At a time of increasing danger, the U.S. intelligence community has lost much of its ability to supply the President, senior U.S. officials, and the Congress with accurate and timely analyses concerning fundamental threats to our nation's security. Morale and public confidence have been eroded and American citizens and friendly foreign intelligence services have become increasingly reluctant to cooperate with U.S. agencies. As a result of such problems, the U.S. intelligence community has incorrectly assessed critical foreign developments, as in Iran, and has, above all, underestimated the size and purpose of the Soviet Union's military efforts.

We believe that a strong national consensus has emerged on the need to make our intelligence community a reli-

able and productive instrument of national policy once again. In pursuing its objectives, the Soviet Union and its surrogates operate by a far different set of rules than does the United States. We do not favor countering their efforts by mirroring their tactics. However, the United States requires a realistic assessment of the threats it faces, and it must have the best intelligence capability in the world. Republicans pledge this for the United States.

A Republican Administration will seek to improve U.S. intelligence capabilities for technical and clandestine collection, cogent analysis, coordinated counterintelligence and covert action.

We will reestablish the President's Foreign Intelligence Advisory Board, abolished by the Carter Administration, as a permanent non-partisan body of distinguished Americans to perform a constant audit of national intelligence research and performance. We will propose methods of providing alternative intelligence estimates in order to improve the quality of the estimates by constructive competition.

Republicans will undertake an urgent effort to rebuild the intelligence agencies, and to give full support to their knowledgeable and dedicated staffs. We will propose legislation to enable intelligence officers and their agents to operate safely and efficiently abroad.

We will support legislation to invoke criminal sanctions against anyone who discloses the identities of U.S. intelligence officers abroad or who makes unauthorized disclosures of U.S. intelligence sources and methods.

We will support amendments to the Freedom of Information Act and the Privacy Act to permit meaningful background checks on individuals being considered for sensitive positions and to reduce costly and capricious requests to the intelligence agencies.

We will provide our government with the capability to help influence international events vital to our national security interests, a capability which only the United States among the major powers has denied itself.

A Republican Administration will seek adequate safeguards to ensure that past abuses will not recur, but we will seek the repeal of ill-considered restrictions sponsored by Democrats, which have debilitated U.S. intelligence capabilities while easing the intelligence collection and subversion efforts of our adversaries.

Terrorism

In the decade of the seventies, all civilized nations were shaken by a wave of widespread, international terrorist attacks. Time and again, nations and individuals have been subjected to extortion and murder at the hands of extremists who reject the rule of law, civil order, and the sanctity of individual human rights. Terrorism has been elevated to the level of overt national policy as authorities in Iran, encouraged by the Soviet Union, have held 53 Americans captive for more than eight months. Comprehensive support of international terrorist organizations has been a central, though generally covert, element of Soviet foreign policy.

Republicans believe that this tragic history contains lessons that must serve as the basis for a determined international effort to end this era of terrorism. We believe that certain principles have emerged from incidents in which states have defeated terrorist attacks, and we believe the United States should take the lead in a multilateral drive to eliminate the terrorist threat. A first requirement is the establishment of a military capability to deal promptly and effectively with any terrorist acts. We cannot afford, as in the abortive Iranian rescue mission, to allow months to pass while we prepare responses.

The United States must provide the leadership to forge an international consensus that firmness and refusal to con-

cede are ultimately the only effective deterrents to terrorism. The United States should take the lead in combating international terrorism. We must recognize and be prepared to deal with the reality of expanded Soviet sponsorship of international terrorist movements. Development of an effective anti-terrorist military capability and establishment of a Congressional and Executive capability to oversee our internal security efforts will no longer be neglected.

[Arms Control and Defense Policy]

The Republican approach to arms control has been markedly different from that of the Democratic Party. It has been based on three fundamental premises:

First, before arms control negotiations may be undertaken, the security of the United States must be assured by the funding and deployment of strong military forces sufficient to deter conflict at any level or to prevail in battle should aggression occur;

Second, negotiations must be conducted on the basis of strict reciprocity of benefits—unilateral restraint by the U.S. has failed to bring reductions by the Soviet Union; and

Third, arms control negotiations, once entered, represent an important political and military undertaking that cannot be divorced from the broader political and military behavior of the parties.

A Republican Administration will pursue arms control solely on the principles outlined above.

During the past three and one-half years, the Carter Administration's policy has been diametrically opposed to these principles. First, by its willful cancellation or delay of essential strategic military programs such as the B-1, the MX missile, and the Trident submarine, it has seriously damaged the credibility and effectiveness of the U.S. deterrent force. Second, by not insisting upon corresponding concessions from the Soviet Union it has, in effect, practiced unilateral disarmament and removed any incentives for the Soviets to negotiate for what they could obviously achieve by waiting. The Republican Party rejects the fundamentally flawed SALT II treaty negotiated by the Carter Administration.

The Republican Party deplores the attempts of the Carter Administration to cover up Soviet non-compliance with arms control agreements including the now overwhelming evidence of blatant Soviet violation of the Biological Warfare Convention by secret production of biological agents at Sverdlovsk.

In our platform four years ago, we stated that, "The growth of civilian nuclear technology and the rising demand for nuclear power as an alternative to increasingly costly fossil fuel resources, combine to require our recognition of the potential dangers associated with such development." We called for the formation of new multilateral arrangements to control the export of sensitive nuclear technologies. Unfortunately, the Carter Administration has failed to provide the leadership and creative diplomacy essential to forging effective international safeguards and cooperation in this vital area. In particular we oppose and deplore the pending delivery to India of nuclear material which can be directed to the manufacture of weapons.

The Republican Party reaffirms its commitment to the early establishment of effective multilateral arrangements for the safe management and monitoring of all transfers and uses of nuclear materials in the international market.

Foreign Policy

U.S. — Soviet Relations

The premier challenge facing the United States, its allies, and the entire globe is to check the Soviet Union's global ambitions. This challenge must be met, for the present danger is greater than ever before in the 200-year history of the United States. The Soviet Union is still accelerating its drive for military superiority and is intensifying its military pressure and its ideological combat against the industrial democracies and the vulnerable developing nations of the world.

Republicans believe that the United States can only negotiate with the Soviet Union from a position of unquestioned principle and unquestioned strength. Unlike Mr. Carter we see nothing "inordinate" in our nation's historic judgment about the goals, tactics, and dangers of Soviet communism. Unlike the Carter Administration, we were not surprised by the brutal Soviet invasion of Afghanistan or by other Soviet violations of major international agreements regulating international behavior, human rights, and the use of military force. And, unlike the Carter Administration, we will not base our policies toward the Soviet Union on naïve expectations, unilateral concessions, futile rhetoric, and insignificant maneuvers.

As the Soviet Union continues in its expansionist course, the potential for dangerous confrontations has increased. Republicans will strive to resolve critical issues through peaceful negotiations, but we recognize that negotiations conducted from a position of military weakness can result only in further damage to American interests.

A Republican Administration will continue to seek to negotiate arms reductions in Soviet strategic weapons, in Soviet bloc force levels in Central Europe, and in other areas that may be amenable to reductions or limitations. We will pursue hard bargaining for equitable, verifiable, and enforceable agreements. We will accept no agreement for the sake of having an agreement, and will accept no agreements that do not fundamentally enhance our national security.

[High Technology]

Republicans oppose the transfer of high technology to the Soviet Union and its Eastern European satellites, such as has been done in the past, permitting development of sophisticated military hardware which threatens the United States and our allies. The Carter Administration has encouraged the most extensive raid on American technology by the Soviet bloc since World War II. The Soviet Union has gained invaluable scientific expertise in electronics, computer sciences, manufacturing techniques, mining, transportation, aviation, agriculture, and a host of other disciplines. This has contributed to the ability of the Soviet Union to divert investment and manpower from their civilian economy to their armed forces. The fruits of Soviet access to American technology will improve the performance of the Soviet military establishment for years to come. The matter is compounded by the practice of subsidized financing of much of the Soviet bloc's acquisition of American technology through U.S. financial institutions.

Republicans pledge to stop the flow of technology to the Soviet Union that could contribute, directly or indirectly, to the growth of their military power. This objective will be pursued by a Republican Administration with our allies and other friendly nations as well. We will ensure that the Soviet Union fully understands that it will be expected to fulfill all of the commercial and diplomatic obligations it has undertaken in its international agreements.

We oppose Mr. Carter's singling out of the American farmer to bear the brunt of his failed foreign policy by imposition of a partial and incompetently managed grain embargo. Because of his failure to obtain cooperation from other grain exporting countries, the embargo has been a travesty and a substitute for policy. We call for the immediate lifting of this embargo.

[Declaration on Human Rights]

We reaffirm our commitment to press the Soviet Union to implement the United Nations Declaration on Human Rights and the Helsinki Agreements which guarantee rights such as the free interchange of information and the right to emigrate. A Republican Administration will press the Soviet Union to end its harassment and imprisonment of those who speak in opposition to official policy, who seek to worship according to their religious beliefs, or who represent diverse ethnic minorities and nationalities.

Republicans deplore growing anti-Semitism in the Soviet Union and the mistreatment of "refuseniks" by Soviet authorities. The decline in exit visas to Soviet Jews and others seeking religious freedom and the promulgation of ever more rigorous conditions inhibiting their emigration is a fundamental affront to human rights and the U.N. Charter. Republicans will make the subject of emigration from the Soviet Union a central issue in Soviet-American relations. Human rights in the Soviet Union will not be ignored as it has been during the Carter Administration. As a party to the Helsinki Conference Final Act, a Republican Administration will insist on full Soviet compliance with the humanitarian provisions of the agreement.

Republicans pledge our continued support for the people of Cuba and the captive nations of Central and Eastern Europe in their hope to achieve self-determination. We stand firmly for the independence of Yugoslavia. We support self-determination and genuine independence for new captive nations of Africa and Latin America threatened by the growing domination of Soviet power.

A Republican Administration will end the sustained Carter policy of misleading the American people about Soviet policies and behavior. We will spare no efforts to publicize to the world the fundamental differences in the two systems and will strengthen such means as the International Communication Agency, the Voice of America, Radio Free Europe, and Radio Liberty actively to articulate U.S. values and policies, and to highlight the weaknesses of totalitarianism.

We pledge to end the cover-up of Soviet violations of SALT I and II, to end the Carter cover-up of Soviet violation of the Biological Warfare Convention, and to end the cover-up of Soviet use of gas and chemical weapons in Afghanistan and elsewhere.

NATO and Western Europe

Since its inception three decades ago, the North Atlantic Treaty Organization has expressed the collective will of free nations to resist totalitarian aggression. As a cornerstone of the Western Alliance, NATO has stood on the firm foundations of American strategic strength, joint Allied defense efforts, and cooperative diplomacy based on shared interest and close consultations. The Republican Party recognizes that NATO serves the vital interests of the entire Western world and over the years we have continued to give the Alliance our undiminished and bipartisan support.

Republicans deplore the current drifts toward neutralism in Western Europe. We recognize that NATO and our Western Allies today face the greatest array of threats in their history, both from within and from without. Through its inept policies, the Carter Administration has substantially contributed to the evident erosion of Alliance security and confidence in the U.S. A Republican Administration, as one of its highest priorities and in close concert with our NATO partners, will therefore ensure that the United States

leads a concerted effort to rebuild a strong, confident Alliance fully prepared to meet the threats and the challenges of the 1980s.

The chief external threat to NATO is that of developing Soviet military superiority. In a period of supposed "détente," the NATO nations have too often cut back or delayed essential defense programs and too often placed excessive hopes in arms control negotiations, while the Soviet dominated Warsaw Pact has been transformed into the world's most powerful offensive military force.

Three-and-a-half years of Carter Administration policies have resulted in an increased threat to vital Alliance security interests. Mr. Carter's unilateral cancellations, reductions, and long delays in the B-1, Trident, MX, cruise-missile, and ship-building programs have increased the vulnerability of the U.S. strategic triad and have contributed to a developing strategic imbalance which undermines the foundation of Western deterrent and defense capabilities. His fundamentally flawed SALT II treaty would have codified Western inferiority. His reversals on the development and deployment of the "enhanced radiation" or neutron weapon, his treatment of future theater nuclear force modernization negotiations, and his manner of dealing with terrorist actions directed against Americans abroad, further undermined Alliance solidarity and security.

These Carter Administration inconsistencies have caused disunity in the Alliance. We have seen confusion in the fields of trade, fiscal, and energy policies. The lack of close coordination regarding Iran, the Middle East, Afghanistan, the Olympic boycott, nuclear proliferation, East-West trade, human rights, North-South issues, and a host of other international issues affecting Alliance interests, has reinforced Allied concerns. Republicans are concerned that these Carter Administration actions have increased Allied temptation to conduct independent diplomacy and to seek accommodation in the face of pressure from the Soviet Union. In this regard, we categorically reject unilateral moratoria on the deployment by the U.S. and NATO of theater nuclear weapons. Further, Republicans will oppose arms control agreements that interfere with the transfer of military technology to our allies.

In pledging renewed United States leadership, cooperation, and consultation, Republicans assert their expectation that each of the allies will bear a fair share of the common defense effort and that they will work closely together in support of common Alliance goals. Defense budgets, weapons acquisition, force readiness, and diplomatic coordination need to be substantially increased and improved. Within Europe as well as in areas beyond Europe which affect the shared vital interests of the Alliance, we will seek to increase our cooperative efforts, including increased planning for joint actions to meet common threats.

The Republican Party recognizes the vital importance of countries defending the flanks of NATO. We will search for an early resolution of problems that currently inhibit the effective participation of all the nations of NATO's southern region and we call for the integration of Spain into the North Atlantic Alliance.

Middle East, Persian Gulf

In the past three years, the nations of the Middle East and Persian Gulf have suffered an unprecedented level of political, economic, and military turmoil. The Soviet Union has been prompt in turning these sources of instability to its advantage and is now in an excellent position to exploit the chaos in Iran and to foment similar upheavals in other countries in the region. Today, the countries of the Middle East and Per-

sian Gulf are encircled as never before by Soviet advisers and troops based in the Horn of Africa, South Yemen, and Afghanistan. Moreover, the Soviets have close political and military ties with other states in the region.

The Soviet goal is clear—to use subversion and the threat of military intervention to establish a controlling influence over the region's resource-rich states, and thereby to gain decisive political and economic leverage over Western and Third World nations vulnerable to economic coercion. The first signs of Soviet success in this undertaking are already evidenced in the recent proposal by European countries to associate the Palestinian Liberation Organization in the West Bank autonomy talks.

Republicans believe that the restoration of order and stability to the region must be premised upon an understanding of the interrelationship between Soviet and radical Palestinian goals, the fundamental requirements of stable economic development and marketing of the area's resources, and the growing ferment among Islamic radical groups. Republicans believe that a wise and credible United States policy must make clear that our foremost concern is for the long-term peaceful development of all states in the region, not purely a self-serving exploitation of its resources. Our goal is to bring a just and lasting peace to the Arab-Israeli conflict.

[Rejection of PLO]

With respect to an ultimate peace settlement, Republicans reject any call for involvement of the PLO as not in keeping with the long-term interests of either Israel or the Palestinian Arabs. The imputation of legitimacy to organizations not yet willing to acknowledge the fundamental right to existence of the State of Israel is wrong. Repeated indications, even when subsequently denied, of the Carter Administration's involvement with the PLO has done serious harm to the credibility of U.S. policy in the Middle East and has encouraged the PLO's position of intransigence. We believe the establishment of a Palestinian State on the West Bank would be destabilizing and harmful to the peace process.

Our long- and short-term policies for the area must be developed in consultation with our NATO allies, Israel, Egypt, and other friends in the area, and we will spare no effort in seeking their consultation throughout the policy process, not merely demand their acquiescence to our plans.

The sovereignty, security, and integrity of the State of Israel is a moral imperative and serves the strategic interests of the United States. Republicans reaffirm our fundamental and enduring commitment to this principle. We will continue to honor our nation's commitment through political, economic, diplomatic, and military aid. We fully recognize the strategic importance of Israel and the deterrent role of its armed forces in the Middle East and East-West military equations.

Republicans recognize that a just and durable peace for all nations of the region is the best guarantee of continued stability and is vital to deterring further Soviet inroads. Peace between Israel and its neighbors requires direct negotiations among the states involved. Accordingly, a Republican Administration will encourage the peace process now in progress between Egypt and Israel, will seek to broaden it, and will welcome those Arab nations willing to live in peace with Israel. We are encouraged by the support given to the Middle East peace process by Sudan and Oman and the progress brought about by the strong and effective leadership of their governments.

[Relationship with Egypt]

We applaud the vision and courage of Egyptian President Anwar Sadat and we pledge to build our relationship with Egypt in cultural affairs, economic development, and military cooperation.

Republicans recognize that the Carter Administration's vacillations have left friend and foe alike unsure as to United States' policies. While reemphasizing our commitment to Israel, a Republican Administration will pursue close ties and friendship with moderate Arab states. We will initiate the economic and military framework for assuring longterm stability both in the internal development of regional states and an orderly marketplace for the area's resources. We will make clear that any reimposition of an oil embargo would be viewed as a hostile act. We will oppose discriminatory practices, including boycotts, and we will discourage arms sales which contribute to regional instability.

Republicans believe that Jerusalem should remain an undivided city with continued free and unimpeded access to all holy places by people of all faiths.

The Americas

Latin America is an area of primary interest for the United States. Yet, the Carter Administration's policies have encouraged a precipitous decline in United States relations with virtually every country in the region. The nations of South and Central America have been battered by the Carter Administration's economic and diplomatic sanctions linked to its undifferentiated charges of human rights violations.

In the Caribbean and Central America, the Carter Administration stands by while Castro's totalitarian Cuba, financed, directed, and supplied by the Soviet Union, aggressively trains, arms, and supports forces of warfare and revolution throughout the Western hemisphere. Yet the Carter Administration has steadily denied these threats and in many cases has actively worked to undermine governments and parties opposed to the expansion of Soviet power. This must end.

We deplore the Marxist Sandinista takeover of Nicaragua and the Marxist attempts to destabilize El Salvador, Guatemala, and Honduras. We do not support United States assistance to any Marxist government in this hemisphere and we oppose the Carter Administration aid program for the government of Nicaragua. However, we will support the efforts of the Nicaraguan people to establish a free and independent government.

[Cuba and the Soviet Union]

Republicans deplore the dangerous and incomprehensible Carter Administration policies toward Cuba. The Administration has done nothing about the Soviet combat brigade stationed there, or about the transfer of new Soviet offensive weapons to Cuba in the form of modern MIG aircraft and submarines. It has done nothing about the Soviet pilots flying air defense missions in Cuba or about the extensive improvements to Soviet military bases, particularly the submarine facilities in Cienfuegos, and the expanded Soviet intelligence facilities near Havana.

Republicans recognize the importance of our relations within this hemisphere and pledge a strong new United States policy in the Americas. We will stand firm with countries seeking to develop their societies while combating the subdivision and violence exported by Cuba and Moscow. We will return to the fundamental principle of treating a friend as a friend and self-proclaimed enemies, without apology. We will make it clear to the Soviet Union and Cuba that their subversion and their build-up of offensive military forces is unacceptable.

Republicans recognize the special importance of Puerto Rico and the United States Virgin Islands in the defense of freedom in the Caribbean. We believe that Puerto Rico's admission to the Union would demonstrate our common purpose in the face of growing Soviet and Cuban pressure in that area.

Republicans recognize the fundamental importance of Mexico and restoration of good working relations with that country will be of highest priority. A new Republican Administration will immediately begin high-level, comprehensive negotiations, seeking solutions to common problems on the basis of mutual interest and recognizing that each country has unique contributions to make in resolving practical problems.

Republicans pledge to reestablish close and cooperative relations with the nations of Central and South America and repair the diplomatic damage done by the Carter Administration. We pledge understanding and assistance in the efforts of these nations, and their neighbors, to deal seriously with serious domestic problems.

[Panama Canal]

We pledge to ensure that the Panama Canal remains open, secure, and free of hostile control.

The reservations and understandings to the Panama Canal treaties, including those assuring the United States of primary responsibility of protecting and defending the Canal, are an integral part of those treaties and we will hold Panama to strict interpretation of the language of the treaties, clearly established by the legislative history of Senate adoption of amendments, reservations, and understandings at the time of Senate approval of the treaties.

We would remind the American taxpayers that President Carter gave repeated assurances that the Panama Canal treaties would not cost the American taxpayers "one thin dime," and we emphasize the fact that implementing the Panama Canal treaties will cost them $4.2 billion.

We will work closely with Canada as our most important trading partner in the hemisphere. We will foster the deep affinity that exists between our two nations and our policies will be based on mutual understanding and complete equality.

We will seek a North American Accord designed to foster close cooperation and mutual benefit between the United States, Canada, and Mexico.

A new Republican Administration will, in close cooperation with its neighbors, seek to work together to build prosperity and to strengthen common efforts to combat externally produced revolution and violence.

Asia and the Pacific

The United States is and must remain a Pacific power. It is in our vital interest to maintain U.S. guaranteed stability in the area. Republicans recognize the dangerous shifts in power that have accelerated under the current Democratic Administration. The balance on the Korean peninsula has shifted dangerously toward the North. Soviet naval forces in Asia and the Pacific have steadily increased and are now at the least equal to U.S. Naval forces there. Unilateral cancellation by the United States of the mutual defense pact with Taiwan and the abrupt announcement of withdrawal of U.S. ground forces from Korea, have led countries throughout the region to question the value of alliance with the United States.

A new Republican Administration will restore a strong American role in Asia and the Pacific. We will make it clear that any military action which threatens the independence of America's allies and friends will bring a response sufficient to make its cost prohibitive to potential adversaries.

[Close Ties with Japan]

Japan will continue to be a pillar of American policy in Asia. Republicans recognize the natural interests and special relationships that exist between the two countries in their commitment to democracy and in trade, defense, and cultural matters. A new Republican Administration will work closely with the Japanese government to resolve outstanding trade and energy problems on an equitable basis. We strongly support a substantially increased Japanese national defense effort and reaffirm that our long-range objectives of military presence in the region are of mutual interest.

Republicans recognize the unique danger presented to our ally, South Korea. We will encourage continued efforts to expand political participation and individual liberties within the country, but will recognize the special problems brought on by subversion and potential aggression from the North. We will maintain American ground and air forces in South Korea, and will not reduce our presence further. Our treaty commitments to South Korea will be restated in unequivocal terms and we will reestablish the process of close consultations between our governments.

We reaffirm our special and historic relationships with the Philippines, Singapore, Malaysia, Indonesia, Thailand, New Zealand, and Australia. Republicans will recognize the long friendship with these countries and will cultivate and strengthen our diplomatic and trade relationships.

We deplore the brutal acts of Communist Vietnam against the people of Cambodia and Laos. We recognize that the suffering of refugees from these ravaged countries represents a major moral challenge to the world and one of the great human tragedies of modern times. A Republican Administration will work actively to bring relief to these suffering people, especially those who have sought refuge in Thailand. We value the special contribution the people of Thailand have made to the refugees by opening their borders and saving hundred of thousands of them from death, and we pledge to provide full economic aid and military material to assist Thailand in repelling Vietnamese aggression.

We believe that no expanded relations with Communist Vietnam should be pursued while it continues its course of brutal expansionism and genocide. We pledge that a Republican Administration will press for full accounting of Americans still listed as missing in action.

[China and Taiwan]

Recognizing the growing importance of the People's Republic of China in world affairs, Republicans—who took the historic initiative in opening the lines of communication with that nation—will continue the process of building a working relation with the PRC. Growing contacts between the United States and the People's Republic of China reflect the interests of both nations, as well as some common perceptions of recent changes in the global military balance. We will not ignore the profound differences in our respective philosophies, governmental institutions, policies, and concepts of individual liberty.

We will strive for the creation of conditions that will foster the peaceful elaboration of our relationship with the People's Republic of China. We will exercise due caution and prudence with respect to our own vital interests, especially in the field of expanding trade, including the transfer of sophisticated technology with potential offensive military applications. The relationship between the two countries must be based on mutual respect and reciprocity, with due regard for the need to maintain peace and stability in Asia.

At the same time, we deplore the Carter Administration's treatment of Taiwan, our long-time ally and friend. We pledge that our concern for the safety and security of the 17 million people of Taiwan will be constant. We should regard any attempt to alter Taiwan's status by force as a threat to peace in the region. We declare that the Republican Administration, in strengthening relations with Taiwan, will create conditions leading to the expansion of trade, and will give priority consideration to Taiwan's defense requirements.

Africa

The Republican Party supports the principle and process of self-determination in Africa. We reaffirm our commitment to this principle and pledge our strong opposition to the effort of the Soviet Union and its militant allies to subvert this process. Soviet bases, tens of thousands of Cuban troops, and Soviet-bloc subversion are unacceptable.

We recognize that much is at stake in Africa and that the United States and the industrial West have vital interests there—economically, strategically, and politically. Working closely with our allies, a Republican Administration will seek to assist the countries of Africa with our presence, our markets, our know-how, and our investment. We will work to create a climate of economic and political development and confidence. We will encourage and assist business to play a major role in support of regional industrial development programs, mineral complexes, and agricultural self-sufficiency.

Republicans believe that African nations if given a choice, will reject the Marxist, totalitarian model being forcibly imposed by the Soviet Union and its surrogates including Cuban and Nicaraguan troops as well as East German secret police. We believe that they know the Communist powers have relatively little to offer them and that, for the most part, the African peoples are convinced that the West is central to the world stability and economic growth on which their own fortunes ultimately depend.

A Republican Administration will adhere to policies that reflect the complex origins of African conflicts, demonstrate that we know what U.S. interests are, and back those interests in meaningful ways. We will recognize the important role of economic and military assistance programs and will devote major resources to assisting African development and stability when such aid is given on a bilateral basis and contributes directly to American interests on the continent.

In Southern Africa, American policies must be guided by commonsense and by our own humanitarian principles. Republicans believe that our history has meaning for Africa in demonstrating that a multiracial society with guarantees of individual rights is possible and can work. We must remain open and helpful to all parties, whether in the new Zimbabwe, in Namibia, or in the Republic of South Africa. A Republican Administration will not endorse situations or constitutions, in whatever society, which are racist in purpose or in effect. It will not expect miracles, but will press for genuine progress in achieving goals consistent with American ideals.

Foreign Assistance and Regional Security

The United States has included foreign assistance and regional security as a major element of its foreign policy for four decades. Properly administered and focused, foreign assistance can be an effective means of promoting United States foreign policy objectives, and serve to enhance American security by assisting friendly nations to become stronger and more capable of defending themselves and their regions against foreign subversion and attack.

The threat posed to individual Third World nations is beyond the means of any one of them to counter alone. A Republican Administration will seek to strengthen and assist regional security arrangements among nations prepared to assume the burden of their defense.

No longer should American foreign assistance programs seek to force acceptance of American governmental forms. The principle consideration should be whether or not extending assistance to a nation or group of nations will advance America's interests and objectives. The single-minded attempt to force acceptance of U.S. values and standards of democracy has undermined several friendly nations, and has made possible the advance of Soviet interests in Asia, the Middle East, Africa, and in the Western Hemisphere in the past four years.

American foreign economic assistance is not a charitable venture; charity is most effectively carried out by private entities. Only by private economic development by the people of the nations involved has poverty ever been overcome. U.S. foreign economic assistance should have a catalytic effect on indigenous economic development, and should only be extended when it is consistent with America's foreign policy interest. America's foreign assistance programs should be a vehicle for exporting the American idea.

A Republican Administration will emphasize bilateral assistance programs whenever possible. Bilateral programs provide the best assurance that aid programs will be fully accountable to the American taxpayer, and wholly consistent with our foreign policy interests.

[Negative Effects]

The effort of the Carter Administration to diminish the role of American military assistance and foreign military sales in our foreign policy has had several negative effects:

It has resulted in the export of many thousands of American jobs as the Soviet Union, Britain, and France have taken sales prohibited to American manufacturers;

It has reduced the ability of friendly nations to defend their independence against Soviet-sponsored supervision, resulting in several cases in abject takeovers by overtly pro-Soviet regimes; and

It has weakened the fabric of the U.S. alliance structure by making the U.S. appear to be an unreliable ally, a trend which can only lead to the undesirable attempt by nations fearful of their security to seek to acquire their own nuclear weapons.

Decisions to provide military assistance should be made on the basis of U.S. foreign policy objectives. Such assistance to any nation need not imply complete approval of a regime's domestic policy. Republicans pledge to strengthen America's presence abroad by well-constructed programs of military assistance to promote national and regional security.

[Foreign Arms Sales]

The manipulation of foreign arms sales has been one of the most seriously abused policy initiatives of the Carter Administration. The establishment of arbitrary ceilings on foreign sales, and the complex procedural and policy guidelines governing such sales have impeded the support of U.S. foreign policy objectives abroad. Friendly and allied nations alike have had to turn elsewhere for arms. This has stimulated the growth of a new arms industry in developing nations. Republicans pledge to reform and rebuild U.S. military assistance and foreign arms sales policies so that they will serve American interests in promoting regional security arrangements and the individual defense needs of friendly nations.

International Economic Policy

International Trade and Economic Policy

The American economy has an abundance of human and material resources, but nevertheless, it is part of a larger global economy. Our domestic prosperity and international competitiveness depend upon our participation in the international economy. Moreover, our security interests are in part determined by international economic factors. Yet the Carter Administration has largely ignored the role of international economics in relations between the United States and friendly nations throughout the world. The Administration has conducted its international economic policy at cross-purposes with other dimensions of its foreign policy, resulting in strains within the Western alliance and a general decline in the domestic prosperity. Under a Republican Administration, our international economic policy will be harmonized with our foreign and defense policies to leave no doubt as to the strategy and purpose of American policy.

The economic policy of the Carter Administration has led to the most serious decline in the value of the dollar in history. The ability of Americans to purchase goods and services or to invest abroad has been diminished by Carter Administration policies devaluing the dollar. Republicans will conduct international economic policy in a manner that will stabilize the value of the dollar at home and abroad.

[Aggressive Export Policy]

The Republican Party believes the United States must adopt an aggressive export policy. For too long, our trade policy has been geared toward helping our foreign trading partners. Now, we have to put the United States back on the world export map. We helped pull other countries out of the post-World War II economic chaos; it is time to remedy our own crisis. Trade, especially exporting, must be high on our list of national priorities. The Republicans will put it there and will promote trade to ensure the long-term health of the U.S. economy.

Exports can play a key role in strengthening the U.S. economy, creating jobs and improving our standard of living. A $15 billion increase in exports can increase employment by 1,000,000, the Gross National Product by $37 billion per year, and private investment by $4 billion per year. Nevertheless, the Carter Administration has placed exporting at the bottom of its priority list. The present Administration's trade policies lack coordination, cohesiveness, and true commitment to improving our export performance. Rather than helping to create strong exporters in the United States and thereby create more jobs for Americans, the Carter Administration's trade policies have discouraged traders. At best, the Administration has adopted a passive approach to trade, merely reacting to changing world economies rather than actively seeking to promote a global structure that best addresses America's needs. As a result, we lag seriously behind our foreign competitors in trade performance and economic strength. Export promotion will be a central objective of international economic policy in a Republican Administration.

A Republican Administration will emphasize a policy of free trade, but will expect our trading partners to do so as well. The failure of the Carter Administration energetically to pursue negotiations designed to improve the access of American exports to foreign markets has contributed, in part, to protectionist sentiment.

Domestic problems—over-burdensome government regulations, excessive taxation, inflationary monetary policy, and an unstable economy—have contributed to the protectionist sentiments as well. We realize that protectionist legislation has engendered retaliation by America's trading partners in the past resulting in "beggar thy neighbor" policies that had such disastrous consequences in the 1930s.

[American Jobs and American Workers]

Republicans are committed to protect American jobs and American workers first and foremost. The Republican

Party believes in free trade, and we will insist that our trade policy be based on the principles of reciprocity and equity. We oppose subsidies, tariff and non-tariff barriers that unfairly restrict access of American products to foreign markets. We will not stand idly by as the jobs of millions of Americans in domestic industries, such as automobiles, textiles, steel, and electronics are jeopardized and lost. We pledge to strengthen trade agreements and to change the Carter economic policies that have undermined the capability of American agriculture and industry to compete abroad.

Republicans believe that this nation's international trade balance can be improved through the elimination of disincentives for exporters. Statutory and regulatory requirements that inhibit exports should be reviewed and, where practical, eliminated. We further recognize that government can play a role in promoting international trade by establishing incentives for exports, especially those for small and medium size business. We pledge also to work with our trading partners to eliminate subsidies to exports and dumping.

The ability of the United States to compete in foreign markets is hampered by the excessive taxation of Americans working abroad who contributed to our domestic well-being by promoting international trade. Increased exports to our trading partners result in jobs and a rising standard of living at home. Carter Administration policy has the effect of discouraging the presence of American businessmen abroad due to the unfairly high level of taxation levied against them. A Republican Administration will support legislation designed to eliminate this inequity so that American citizens can fully participate in international commerce without fear of discriminatory taxation.

Our nation must have a strong, competitive, and efficient merchant marine to meet the needs of our international commerce and our national security. We must arrest the significant decline of recent years in the ability of American-flag shipping to compete effectively for the carriage of world commerce. A Republican Administration will revitalize our merchant marine through a responsive and sustained policy. We will encourage the development and maintenance of an American-flag ocean transportation system, staffed with trained American personnel and capable of carrying a substantial portion of our international trade in a competitive and efficient manner. We will promote the development and support of a domestic shipbuilding and ship-repair mobilization base adequate to both the commercial and the national security requirements of the United States.

[Access to Energy and Raw Materials]

The security of America's foreign sources of energy and raw material supply can no longer be ignored. The United States imports 50 percent of its domestic petroleum requirements, and depends upon foreign sources for 22 of the 74 non-fuel raw materials essential to a modern industrial economy. Nine of the most critical raw materials are almost entirely (i.e., more than 90 percent) located abroad. In contrast, the Soviet Union imports only two critical minerals at a level in excess of 50 percent of domestic consumption.

Reducing reliance on uncertain foreign sources and assuring access to foreign energy and raw materials requires the harmonization of economic policy with our defense and foreign policy. Domestic economic and regulatory pol-

icy must be adjusted to remove impediments to greater development of our own energy and raw materials resources. Democratic policies for federal land management, taxation, monetary policy, and economic regulation have served to increase America's dependence on foreign sources of energy and raw materials. Republicans pledge to work to eliminate domestic disincentives to the exploitation of these resources.

Multilateral negotiations have thus far insufficiently focused attention on U.S. long-term security requirements. A pertinent example of this phenomenon is the Law of the Sea Conference, where negotiations have served to inhibit U.S. exploitation of the sea-bed for its abundant mineral resources. Too much concern has been lavished on nations unable to carry out sea-bed mining, with insufficient attention paid to gaining early American access to it. A Republican Administration will conduct multilateral negotiations in a manner that reflects America's abilities and long-term interest in access to raw material and energy resources.

Resource access will assume an important place in defense and economic planning under a Republican Administration. Since America's allies are, in most cases, more dependent than the U.S. on foreign sources of energy and raw materials, they too have a vital interest in the defense of their access to these critical resources. Republicans pledge to promote allied defense cooperation to assure protection from military threats to overseas resources.

Edward M. Kennedy's Speech to the Democratic National Convention (1980)

Sen. Edward M. Kennedy of Massachusetts has been mentioned as a possible candidate for the Democratic presidential nomination in every election since 1968. Only once, however, in 1980, did he run. Kennedy challenged President Jimmy Carter's bid for renomination and was defeated.

Kennedy was first elected to the Senate in 1962, at the minimum constitutional age of thirty. (He did not suffer as a candidate for being the younger brother of President John F. Kennedy and Attorney General Robert F. Kennedy.) A powerful orator, an ardent crusader for liberal causes, and the presumptive heir to the presidential ambitions of his assassinated brothers, Kennedy nonetheless resisted entreaties from his party to run for president in 1972 and 1976. Unlike John and Robert, Ted Kennedy enjoyed the Senate. Unlike them, too, he had been publicly embroiled in a scandal when a car that he was driving went off the bridge at Chappaquiddick Island in Cape Cod, Massachusetts, and killed Mary Jo Kopechne, his passenger, in July 1969.

The pressures on Kennedy to seek the Democratic nomination mounted in 1979. Carter was not only an unpopular president but a more conservative one than Kennedy and many other Democrats wanted. Public opinion polls showed that the party's rank and file strongly preferred Kennedy to Carter. On Labor Day 1979, Kennedy reluctantly announced his candidacy for president.

Kennedy floundered as a candidate. In November 1979, in a nationally televised interview with Roger Mudd of CBS, he dealt awkwardly with the still smoldering issue of his conduct at Chappaquiddick and seemed not to have any answer at all to the question of why he wanted to be president. Kennedy also impressed many voters as insufficiently patriotic when he obliquely criticized Carter's measured response to the November 4, 1979, seizure of fifty American hostages in Iran. In a period of rising conservatism, Kennedy seemed personally unconfident and politically uncertain, at least in public, of his own liberal beliefs.

Despite the president's unpopularity, Kennedy was soundly defeated in the January 21, 1980, Iowa caucuses and, five weeks later, in the New Hampshire primary. With occasional exceptions, the losses continued through the spring primary season. Rather than withdraw from the race or give way to despair, however, Kennedy gradually found his voice. He became an articulate champion of the party's liberal agenda and a force to be reckoned with if Carter hoped to lead a united party into the fall campaign *against the Republican nominee for president, Ronald Reagan.*

On the second night of the Democratic national convention in August, Kennedy enjoyed his finest hour in politics. His speech roused the delegates to laughter at the expense of Reagan, enthusiasm for his unabashed endorsement of the party's historic commitment to the downtrodden, and tears in memory of his slain brothers. "For all those whose cares have been our concern," Kennedy trumpeted in conclusion, "the work goes on, the cause endures, the hope still lives, and the dream shall never die!"

The next night, on the first ballot, Kennedy lost the nomination to Carter. But the president left the convention without Kennedy's strong endorsement, the enfeebled nominee of a divided party. ~

Well, things worked out a little differently from the way I had planned, but I still love New York.

My fellow Democrats and my fellow Americans: I have come here tonight not to argue for a candidacy, but to affirm a cause.

I am asking you ... I am asking you to renew the commitment of the Democratic Party to economic justice. I am asking you to renew our commitment to a fair and lasting prosperity that can put America back to work.

This is the cause that brought me into the campaign and that sustained me for nine months, across a hundred thousand miles, in 40 different states. We had our losses; but the pain of our defeats is far, far less than the pain of the people that I have met. We have learned that it is important to take issues seriously, but never to take ourselves too seriously.

The serious issue before us tonight is the cause for which the Democratic Party has stood in its finest hours—the cause that keeps our party young—and makes it, in the second century of its age, the largest political party in this Republic and the longest lasting political party on this planet.

Our cause has been, since the days of Thomas Jefferson, the cause of the common man—and the common woman. Our commitment has been, since the days of Andrew Jackson, to all those he called "the humble members of society—the farmers, mechanics, and laborers." On this foundation, we have defined our values, refined our policies, and refreshed our faith.

Now I take the unusual step of carrying the cause and the commitment of my campaign personally to our national convention. I speak out of a deep sense of urgency about the anguish and anxiety I have seen across America. I speak out of a deep belief in the ideals of the Democratic Party, and in the potential of that party and of a president to make a difference. And I speak out of a deep trust in our capacity to proceed with boldness and common vision that will feel and heal the suffering of our time—and the division of our party.

[Economic Plank]

The economic plank of this platform on its face concerns only material things; but is also a moral issue that I raise tonight. It has taken many forms over many years. In this campaign, and in this country that we seek to lead, the challenge in 1980 is to give our voice and our vote for these fundamental Democratic principles:

Let us pledge that we will never misuse unemployment, high interest rates, and human misery as false weapons against inflation.

Let us pledge that employment will be the first priority of our economic policy.

Let us pledge that there will be security for all those who are now at work.

And let us pledge that there will be jobs for all who are out of work. And we will not compromise on the issue of jobs.

These are not simplistic pledges. Simply put, they are the heart of our tradition, and they have been the soul of our party across the generations. It is the glory and the greatness of our tradition to speak for those who have no voice, to remember those who are forgotten, to respond to the frustrations and fulfill the aspirations of all Americans seeking a better life in a better land.

We dare not forsake that tradition. We cannot let the great purposes of the Democratic Party become the bygone passages of history. We must not permit the Republicans to seize and run on the slogans of prosperity.

[Reagan's Stand on Issues]

We heard the orators at their convention all trying to talk like Democrats. They proved that even Republican nominees can quote Franklin Roosevelt to their own purpose. The Grand Old Party thinks it has found a great new trick. But 40 years ago, an earlier generation of Republicans attempted the same trick. And Franklin Roosevelt himself replied "Most Republican leaders ... have bitterly fought and blocked the forward surge of average men and women in their pursuit of happiness. Let us not be deluded that overnight those leaders have suddenly become the friends of average men and women. . . . You know," he continued, "very few of us are that gullible."

And four years later, when the Republicans tried that trick again, Franklin Roosevelt asked: "Can the Old Guard pass itself off as the New Deal? I think not. We have all seen many marvelous stunts in the circus—but no performing elephant could turn a handspring without falling flat on its back."

The 1980 Republican convention was awash with crocodile tears for our economic distress but it is by their long record and not their recent words that you shall know them.

The same Republicans who are talking about the crisis of unemployment have nominated a man who once said—and I quote: "Unemployment insurance is a prepaid vacation plan for freeloaders." And that nominee is no friend of labor.

The same Republicans who are talking about the problems of the inner cities have nominated a man who said—and I quote: "I have included in my morning and evening prayers every day the prayer that the federal government not bail out New York." And that nominee is no friend of this city and our great urban centers across this nation.

The same Republicans who are talking about security for the elderly have nominated a man who said just four years ago that participation in Social Security "should be made voluntary." And that nominee is no friend of the senior citizens of this nation.

The same Republicans who are talking about preserving the environment have nominated a man who last year made the preposterous statement, and I quote: "Eighty percent of our air pollution comes from plants and trees." And that nominee is no friend of the environment.

And the same Republicans who are invoking Franklin Roosevelt have nominated a man who said in 1976—and these are his exact words: "Fascism was really the basis of the New Deal." And that nominee, whose name is Ronald Reagan, has no right to quote Franklin Delano Roosevelt.

[Democratic Values]

The great adventure which our opponents offer is a voyage into the past.

Progress is our heritage, not theirs. What is right for us as Democrats is also the right way for Democrats to win.

The commitment I seek is not to outworn views, but to old values that will never wear out. Programs may sometimes become obsolete, but the ideal of fairness always endures. Circumstances may change, but the work of compassion must continue. It is surely correct that we cannot solve problems by throwing money at them; but it is also correct that we dare not throw out our national problems into a scrap heap of inattention and indifference. The poor may be out of political fashion, but they are not without human needs. The middle-class may be angry, but they have not lost the dream that all Americans can advance together.

The demand of our people in 1980 is not for smaller government or bigger government, but for better government. Some say that government is always bad, and that spending for basic social programs is the root of our economic evils. But we reply: The present inflation and recession cost our economy $200 billion a year. We reply: Inflation and unemployment are the biggest spenders of all.

The task of leadership in 1980 is not to parade scapegoats or to seek refuge in reaction but to match our power to the possibilities of progress.

While others talked of free enterprise, it was the Democratic Party that acted—and we ended excessive regulation in the airline and trucking industries. And we restored competition to the marketplace. And I take some satisfaction that this deregulation was legislation that I sponsored and passed in the Congress of the United States.

As Democrats, we recognize that each generation of Americans has a rendezvous with a different reality. The answers of one generation become the questions of the next generation. But there is a guiding star in the American firmament. It is as old as the revolutionary belief that all people are created equal—and as clear as the contemporary condition of Liberty City and the South Bronx. Again and again, Democratic leaders have followed that star— and they have given new meaning to the old values of liberty and justice for all.

[Party of New Hope]

We are the party of New Freedom, the New Deal, and the New Frontier. We have always been the party of hope. So this year, let us offer new hope—new hope to an America uncertain about the present, but unsurpassed in its potential for the future.

To all those who are idle in the cities and industries of America, let us provide new hope for the dignity of useful work. Democrats have always believed that a basic civil right of all Americans is the right to earn their own way. The party of the people must always be the party of full employment.

To all those who doubt the future of our economy, let us provide new hope for the reindustrialization of America. And let our vision reach beyond the next election or the next year to a new generation of prosperity. If we could rebuild Germany and Japan after World War II, then surely we can reindustrialize our own nation and revive our inner cities in the 1980s.

To all those who work hard for a living wage, let us provide new hope that the price of their employment shall not be an unsafe workplace and death at an earlier age.

To all those who inhabit our land, 'from California to the New York Island, from the Redwood Forest to the Gulfstream waters,' let us provide new hope that prosperity shall not be purchased by poisoning the air, the rivers and the natural resources that are the greatest gift of this continent. We must insist that our children and grandchildren shall inherit a land which they can truly call America the beautiful.

To all those who see the worth of their work and their savings taken by inflation, let us offer new hope for a stable economy. We must meet the pressures of the present by invoking the full power of government to master increasing prices. In candor, we must say that the federal budget can be balanced only by policies that bring us to a balanced prosperity of full employment and price restraint.

[Democratic Tax Reform]

And to all those overburdened by an unfair tax structure, let us provide new hope for real tax reform. Instead of shutting down classrooms, let us shut off tax shelters.

Instead of cutting out of school lunches, let us cut off tax subsidies for expensive business lunches that are nothing more than food stamps for the rich.

The tax cut of our Republican opponents takes the name of tax reform in vain. It is a wonderfully Republican idea that would redistribute income in the wrong direction. It is good news for any of you with incomes over $200,000 a year. For the few of you, it offers a pot of gold worth $14,000. But the Republican tax cut is bad news for the middle income families. For the many of you, they plan a pittance of $200 a year. And that is not what the Democratic Party means when we say tax reform.

The vast majority of Americans cannot afford this panacea from a Republican nominee who has denounced the progressive income tax as the invention of Karl Marx. I am afraid he has confused Karl Marx with Theodore Roosevelt, that obscure Republican president who sought and fought for a tax system based on ability to pay. Theodore Roo-

sevelt was not Karl Marx—and the Republican tax scheme is not tax reform.

[National Health Insurance]

Finally, we cannot have a fair prosperity in isolation from a fair society.

So I will continue to stand for a national health insurance. We must not surrender to the relentless medical inflation that can bankrupt almost anyone—and that may soon break the budgets of government at every level.

Let us insist on real controls over what doctors and hospitals can charge. And let us resolve that the state of a family's health shall never depend on the size of a family's wealth.

The president, the vice president, and the members of Congress have a medical plan that meets their needs in full. And whenever senators and representatives catch a little cold, the Capitol physician will see them immediately, treat them promptly, and fill a prescription on the spot. We do not get a bill even if we ask for it. And when do you think was the last time a member of Congress asked for a bill from the federal government?

And I say again, as I have said before: If health insurance is good enough for the president, the vice president and the Congress of the United States, then it is good enough for all of you and for every family in America.

[Democratic-GOP Differences]

There were some who said we should be silent about our differences on issues during this convention. But the heritage of the Democratic Party has been a history of democracy. We fight hard because we care deeply about our principles and purposes. We did not flee this struggle. We welcome this contrast with the empty and expedient spectacle last month in Detroit where no nomination was contested, no question was debated and no one dared to raise any doubt or dissent.

Democrats can be proud that we chose a different course—and a different platform.

We can be proud that our party stands for investment in safe energy instead of a nuclear future that may threaten the future itself. We must not permit the neighborhoods of America to be permanently shadowed by the fear of another Three Mile Island.

We can be proud that our party stands for a fair housing law to unlock the doors of discrimination once and for all. The American house will be divided against itself so long as there is prejudice against any American buying or renting a home.

And we can be proud that our party stands plainly and publicly, and persistently for the ratification of the Equal Rights Amendment. Women hold their rightful place at our convention; and women must have their rightful place in the Constitution of the United States. On this issue, we will not yield, we will not equivocate, we will not rationalize, explain, or excuse. We will stand for E.R.A. and for the recognition at long last that our nation is made up of founding mothers as well as funding fathers.

A fair prosperity and a just society are within our vision and our grasp. And we do not have every answer. There are questions not yet asked, waiting for us in the recesses of the future.

But of this much we can be certain, because it is the lesson of all our history:

Together a president and the people can make a difference. I have found that faith still alive wherever I have traveled across the land. So let us reject the counsel of retreat and the call to reaction. Let us go forward in the knowledge that history only helps those who help themselves.

There will be setbacks and sacrifices in the years ahead. But I am convinced that we as people are ready to give something back to our country in return for all it has given to us. Let this be our commitment: Whatever sacrifices must be made will be shared—and shared fairly. And let this be our confidence: At the end of our journey and always before us shines that ideal of liberty and justice for all.

[To Those Who 'Stayed the Course']

In closing, let me say a few words to all those I have met and all those who have supported me at this convention and across the land.

There were hard hours on our journey. And often we sailed against the wind, but always we kept our rudder true. And there were so many of you who stayed the course and shared our hope. You gave your help; but even more, you gave your hearts. And because of you, this has been a happy campaign. You welcomed Joan and me and our family into your homes and neighborhoods, your churches, your campuses, your union halls. When I think back on all the miles and all the months and all the memories, I think of you. And I recall the poet's words, and I say: "What golden friends I had."

Among you, my golden friends across this land, I have listened and learned.

I have listened to Kenny Dubois, a glass blower in Charleston, W. Va., who has 10 children to support, but has lost his job after 35 years, just three years short of qualifying for his pension.

I have listened to the Trachta family, who farm in Iowa and who wonder whether they can pass the good life and the good earth on to their children.

I have listened to a grandmother in East Oakland, who no longer has a phone to call her grandchildren, because she gave it up to pay the rent on her small apartment.

I have listened to young workers out of work, to students without the tuition for college, and to families without the chance to own a home. I have seen the closed factories and the stalled assembly lines of Anderson, Ind., and South Gate, Calif. I have seen too many—far too many—idle men and women desperate to work. I have seen too many—far too many—working families desperate to protect the value of their wages from the ravages of inflation.

Yet I have also sensed a yearning for new hope among the people in every state where I have been. And I have felt it in their handshakes; I saw it in their faces. And I shall never forget the mothers who carried children to our rallies. I shall always remember the elderly who have lived in an America of high purpose and who believe that it can all happen again.

Tonight, in their name, I have come here to speak for them. And for their sake, I ask you to stand with them. On their behalf, I ask you to restate and reaffirm the timeless truth of our party.

I congratulate President Carter on his victory here. I am confident that the Democratic Party will reunite on the basis of Democratic principles—and that together we will march toward a Democratic victory in 1980.

And someday, long after this convention, long after the signs come down, and the crowds stop cheering, and the bands stop playing, may it be said of our campaign that we kept the faith. May it be said of our party in 1980 that we found our faith again.

And may it be said of us, both in dark passages and in bright days, in the words of Tennyson that my brothers quoted and loved—and that have special meaning for me now:

I am a part of all that I have met ...
Tho much is taken, much abides ...
That which we are, we are ...
One equal temper of heroic hearts ... strong in will
To strive, to seek, to find, and not to yield.

For me, a few hours ago, this campaign came to an end. For all those whose cares have been our concern, the work goes on, the cause endures, the hope still lives, and the dream shall never die.

The Carter-Reagan Debate (1980)

The election of 1980 was a three-candidate race: President Jimmy Carter, the Democratic nominee; former California governor Ronald Reagan, the candidate of the Republican party; and Rep. John B. Anderson of Illinois, an erstwhile Republican who was running independently under the banner of the National Unity Campaign.

All three candidates wanted to debate. Carter initially trailed Reagan in the polls and sought to close the gap. Reagan, like all challengers, was eager to appear before the voters in a setting that placed him on an equal footing with the president. Anderson, as the least-known and most poorly financed candidate, wanted to reach the enormous audience that a televised presidential debate would attract. Moreover, each of the candidates thought that he was the superior debater.

One complication jeopardized the 1980 debates. Carter refused to appear on the same platform with Anderson, whose presence, the president felt, would leave him outnumbered by two Republican critics. The League of Women Voters, which was sponsoring the debates, insisted on inviting any candidate who had at least 15 percent support in the public opinion polls. When Anderson met this standard in time for the September 21, 1980, debate in Baltimore, Maryland, Carter refused to appear. A debate between

Reagan and Anderson proceeded without him.

Interestingly, the post-debate polls revealed that although Anderson had bested Reagan, Reagan was the big winner. For weeks, Carter and the Democrats had been portraying Reagan as, in turn, a warmonger and a buffoon. The Reagan whom the voters saw in the debate with Anderson appeared to be not demonic, but genial, not clownish, but self-confident. Meanwhile, Anderson scored most of his points with attacks against the absent president.

During the next few weeks, Carter declined in the polls and Anderson fell below the League's 15 percent threshhold. Carter and Reagan agreed to a two-candidate debate in Cleveland, Ohio, on October 28, one week before the election. For ninety minutes, Carter attacked relentlessly and Reagan parried amiably. Reagan had the two best lines: a rueful, head-shaking "There you go again," after Carter attacked his position on Medicare, and, in his closing statement, a simple question to frame the voters' choice: "Are you better off than you were four years ago?" Carter had the worst line. Asked about arms control, he began cloyingly, "I had a discussion with my daughter, Amy, the other day before I came here to ask me [sic] what the most important issue was. She said she thought *nuclear weaponry and the control of nuclear arms."*

The election was on November 4, 1980, the first anniversary of the day on which fifty American civilians were taken hostage in Iran. The hostage crisis had helped Carter to win the Democratic nomination; as happens during the initial stages of any international crisis, the country had "rallied round the flag" in support of the president. But when the crisis dragged on, it became a potent Republican symbol of Carter's alleged ineptness in all areas: foreign affairs, economic policy, and presidential leadership.

Reagan's victory in the election was overwhelming. In the electoral college, his margin over President Carter was 489-49, larger even than Franklin D. Roosevelt's over President Herbert Hoover in 1932. In the popular vote, Reagan received 50.7 percent, Carter 41.0 percent, and Anderson 6.6 percent. Thirty-four seats were added to the Republican minority in the House of Representatives, and a twelve-seat gain for the Republicans in the Senate put them in control of that body for the first time since 1955. ～

Hinerfeld: Good evening. I'm Ruth Hinerfeld of the League of Women Voters Education Fund. Next Tuesday is Election Day. Before going to the polls, voters want to understand the issues and know the candidates' positions. Tonight, voters will have an opportunity to see and hear the major party candidates for the Presidency state their views on issues that affect us all. The League of Women Voters is proud to present this Presidential Debate. Our moderator is Howard K. Smith.

Smith: Thank you, Mrs. Hinerfeld. The League of Women Voters is pleased to welcome to the Cleveland Ohio Convention Center Music Hall President Jimmy Carter, the Democratic Party's candidate for reelection to the Presidency, and Governor Ronald Reagan of

California, the Republican Party's candidate for the Presidency. The candidates will debate questions on domestic, economic, foreign policy, and national security issues.

The questions are going to be posed by a panel of distinguished journalists who are here with me. They are: Marvin Stone, the editor of *U.S. News & World Report;* Harry Ellis, national correspondent of the *Christian Science Monitor;* William Hilliard, assistant managing editor of the *Portland Oregonian;* Barbara Walters, correspondent, ABC News.

The ground rules for this, as agreed by you gentlemen, are these: Each panelist down here will ask a question, the same question, to each of the two candidates. After the two candidates have answered, a panelist will ask follow-up questions to try to sharpen the answers. The candidates will then have an opportunity each to make a rebuttal. That will constitute the first half of the debate, and I will state the rules for the second half later on.

Some other rules: The candidates are not permitted to bring prepared notes to the podium, but are permitted to make notes during the debate. If the candidates exceed the allotted time agreed on, I will reluctantly but certainly interrupt. We ask the Convention Center audience here to abide by one ground rule. Please do not applaud or express approval or disapproval during the debate.

Now, based on the toss of the coin, Governor Reagan will respond to the first question from Marvin Stone.

[Use of Military Power]

Stone: Governor, as you're well aware, the question of war and peace has emerged as a central issue in this campaign in the give and take of recent weeks. President Carter has been criticized for responding late to aggressive Soviet impulses, for insufficient build-up of our armed forces, and a paralysis in dealing with Afghanistan and Iran. You have been criticized for being all too quick to advocate the use of lots of muscle—military action—to deal with foreign crises. Specifically, what are the differences between the two of you on the uses of American military power?

Reagan: I don't know what the differences might be, because I don't know what Mr. Carter's policies are. I do know what he has said about mine. And I'm only here to tell you what I believe with all my heart that our first priority must be world peace, and that use of force is always and only a last resort, when everything else has failed, and then only with regard to our national security.

Now, I believe, also, that this meeting ... this mission, this responsibility for preserving the peace, which I believe is a responsibility peculiar to our country, and that we cannot shirk our responsibility as a leader of the Free World because we're the only ones that can do it. Therefore, the burden of maintaining the peace falls on us. And to maintain that peace requires strength. America has never gotten in a war because we were too strong. We can get into a war by letting events get out of hand, as they have in the last three and a half years under the foreign policies of this Administration of Mr. Carter's, until we're faced each time with a crisis. And good management in preserving the peace requires that we control the events and try to intercept before they become a crisis.

I have seen four wars in my lifetime. I'm a father of sons; I have a grandson. I don't ever want to see another generation of young Americans bleed their lives into sandy beachheads in the Pacific, or rice paddies and jungles in the ... in Asia or the muddy battlefields of Europe.

Smith: Mr. Stone, do you have a follow-up question for the Governor?

Stone: Yes. Governor, we've been hearing that the defense build-up that you would associate yourself with would cost tens of billions of dollars more than is now contemplated. Assuming that the American people are ready to bear this cost, they nevertheless keep asking the following question: How do you reconcile huge increases in military outlays with your promise of substantial tax cuts and of balancing the budget, which in this fiscal year, the one that just ended, ran more than $60 billion in the red?

Reagan: Mr. Stone, I have submitted an economic plan that I have worked out in concert with a number of fine economists in this country, all of whom approve it, and believe that over a five year projection, this plan can permit the extra spending for needed refurbishing of our defensive posture, that it can provide for a balanced budget by 1983 if not earlier, and that we can afford—along with the cuts that I have proposed in Government spending—we can afford the tax cuts I have proposed and probably mainly because Mr. Carter's economic policy has built into the next five years, and on beyond that, a tax increase that will be taking $86 billion more out of the people's pockets than was taken this year. And my tax cut does not come close to eliminating that $86 billion increase. I'm only reducing the amount of the increase. In other words, what I'm talking about is not putting government back to getting less money than government's been getting, but simply cutting the increase in ... in spending.

Smith: The same question now goes to President Carter. President Carter, would you like to have the question repeated?

Stone: Yes, President Carter, the question of war and peace, a central issue in this campaign. You've been criticized for, in the give and take, for responding late to aggressive Soviet impulses, for an insufficient build-up of our armed forces, and a paralysis in dealing with Afghanistan and Iran. Governor Reagan, on the other hand, has been criticized for being all too quick to advocate the use of lots of muscle—military action—to deal with foreign crises such as I have mentioned. Specifically, what are the differences between the two of you on the uses of American military power?

Carter: Mr. Stone, I've had to make thousands of decisions since I've been President, serving in the Oval Office. And with each one of those decisions that affect the future of my country, I have learned in the process. I think I'm a much wiser and more experienced man than I was when I debated four years ago against President Ford. I've also learned that there are no simple answers to complicated questions. H. L. Mencken said that for every problem there's a simple answer. It would be neat and plausible and wrong.

The fact is that this nation, in the eight years before I became President, had its own military strength decreased. Seven out of eight years, the budget commitments for defense went down, 37% in all. Since I've been in office, we've had a steady, carefully planned, methodical but very effective increase in our commitment for defense.

But what we've done is use that enormous power and prestige and military strength of the United States to preserve the peace. We've not only kept peace for our own country, but we've been able to extend the benefits of peace to others. In the Middle East, we've worked for a peace treaty between Israel and Egypt, successfully, and have tied ourselves together with Israel and Egypt in a common defense capability. This is a very good step forward for our nation's security, and we'll continue to do as we have done in the past.

I might also add that there are decisions that are made in the Oval Office

by every President which are profound in nature. There are always trouble spots in the world, and how those troubled areas are addressed by a President alone in that Oval Office affects our nation directly, the involvement of the United States and also our American interests. That is a basic decision that has to be made so frequently, by every President who serves. That is what I have tried to do successfully by keeping our country at peace.

Smith: Mr. Stone, do you have a follow-up for. . . ?

Stone: Yes. I would like to be a little more specific on the use of military power, and let's talk about one area for a moment. Under what circumstances would you use military forces to deal with, for example, a shut-off of the Persian Oil Gulf [*sic*], if that should occur, or to counter Russian expansion beyond Afghanistan into either Iran or Pakistan? I ask this question in view of charges that we are woefully unprepared to project sustained—and I emphasize the word sustained—power in that part of the world.

Carter: Mr. Stone, in my State of the Union address earlier this year, I pointed out that any threat to the stability or security of the Persian Gulf would be a threat to the security of our own country. In the past, we have not had an adequate military presence in that region. Now we have two major carrier task forces. We have access to facilities in five different areas of that region. And we've made it clear that working with our allies and others, that we are prepared to address any forseeable eventuality which might interrupt commerce with that crucial area of the world.

But in doing this, we have made sure that we address this question peacefully, not injecting American military forces into combat, but letting the strength of our nation be felt in a beneficial way. This, I believe, has assured that our interests will be protected in the Persian Gulf region, as we have done in the Middle East and throughout the world.

Smith: Governor Reagan, you have a minute to comment or rebut.

Reagan: Well yes, I question the figure about the decline in defense spending under the two previous Administrations in the preceding eight years to this Administration. I would call to your attention that we were in a war that wound down during those eight years, which of course made a change in military spending because of turning from war to peace. I also would like to point out that Republican presidents in those years, faced with a Democratic majority in both houses of the Congress, found that their requests for defense budgets were very often cut.

Now, Gerald Ford left a five-year projected plan for a military build-up to restore our defenses, and President Carter's Administration reduced that by 38%, cut 60 ships out of the Navy building program that had been proposed, and stopped the ... the B-1, delayed the Cruise missile, stopped the production line for the Minuteman missile, stopped the Trident or delayed the Trident submarine, and now is planning a mobile military force that can be delivered to various spots in the world, which does make me question his assaults on whether I am the one who is quick to look for use of force.

Smith: President Carter, you have the last word on this question.

Carter: Well, there are various elements of defense. One is to control nuclear weapons, which I hope we'll get to later on because that is the most important single issue in this campaign. Another one is how to address troubled areas of the world. I think, habitually, Governor Reagan has advocated the injection of military forces into troubled areas, when I and my predecessors—both Democrats and Republicans—have advocated resolving those troubles in those difficult areas of the world

peacefully, diplomatically, and through negotiation. In addition to that, the build-up of military forces is good for our country because we've got to have military strength to preserve the peace. But I'll always remember that the best weapons are the ones that are never fired in combat, and the best soldier is one who never has to lay his life down on the field of battle. Strength is imperative for peace, but the two must go hand in hand.

Smith: Thank you gentlemen. The next question is from Harry Ellis to President Carter.

[Inflation and Government Spending]

Ellis: Mr. President, when you were elected in 1976, the Consumer Price Index stood at 4.8%. It now stands at more than 12%. Perhaps more significantly, the nation's broader, underlying inflation rate has gone up from 7% to 9%. Now, a part of that was due to external factors beyond U.S. control, notably the more than doubling of oil prices by OPEC last year. Because the United States remains vulnerable to such external shocks, can inflation in fact be controlled? If so, what measures would you pursue in a second term?

Carter: Again it's important to put the situation in perspective. In 1974, we had a so-called oil shock, wherein the price of OPEC oil was raised to an extraordinary degree. We had an even worse oil shock in 1979. In 1974, we had the worst recession, the deepest and most penetrating recession since the Second World War. The recession that resulted this time was the briefest since the Second World War.

In addition, we've brought down inflation. Earlier this year, in the first quarter, we did have a very severe inflation pressure brought about by the OPEC price increase. It averaged about

18% in the first quarter of this year. In the second quarter, we had dropped it down to about 13%. The most recent figures, the last three months, on the third quarter of this year, the inflation rate is 7%—still too high, but it illustrates very vividly that in addition to providing an enormous number of jobs—nine million new jobs in the last three and a half years—that the inflationary threat is still urgent on us.

I notice that Governor Reagan recently mentioned the Reagan-Kemp-Roth proposal, which his own running mate, George Bush, described as voodoo economics, and said that it would result in a 30% inflation rate. And Business Week, which is not a Democratic publication, said that this Reagan-Kemp-Roth proposal—and I quote them, I think—was completely irresponsible and would result in inflationary pressures which would destroy this nation.

So our proposals are very sound and very carefully considered to stimulate jobs, to improve the industrial complex of this country, to create tools for American workers, and at the same time would be anti-inflationary in nature. So to add nine million new jobs, to control inflation, and to plan for the future with an energy policy now intact as a foundation is our plan for the years ahead.

Smith: Mr. Ellis, do you have a follow-up question for Mr. Carter?

Ellis: Yes. Mr. President, you have mentioned the creation of nine million new jobs. At the same time, the unemployment rate still hangs high, as does the inflation rate. Now, I wonder, can you tell us what additional policies you would pursue in a second administration in order to try to bring down that inflation rate? And would it be an act of leadership to tell the American people they are going to have to sacrifice to adopt a leaner lifestyle for some time to come?

Carter: Yes. We have demanded that the American people sacrifice, and

they have done very well. As a matter of fact, we're importing today about one-third less oil from overseas than we did just a year ago. We've had a 25% reduction since the first year I was in office. At the same time, as I have said earlier, we have added about nine million net new jobs in that period of time—a record never before achieved.

Also, the new energy policy has been predicated on two factors: One is conservation, which requires sacrifice, and the other one, increase in production of American energy, which is going along very well—more coal this year than ever before in American history, more oil and gas wells drilled this year than ever before in history.

The new economic revitalization program that we have in mind, which will be implemented next year, would result in tax credits which would let business invest in new tools and new factories to create even more new jobs—about one million in the next two years. And we also have planned a youth employment program which would encompass 600,000 jobs for young people. This has already passed the House, and it has an excellent prospect to pass the Senate.

Smith: Now, the same question goes to Governor Reagan. Governor Reagan, would you like to have the question repeated?

Ellis: Governor Reagan, during the past four years, the Consumer Price Index has risen from 4.8% to currently over 12%. And perhaps more significantly, the nation's broader, underlying rate of inflation has gone up from 7% to 9%. Now, a part of that has been due to external factors beyond U.S. control, notably the more than doubling of OPEC oil prices last year, which leads me to ask you whether, since the United States remains vulnerable to such external shocks, can inflation in fact be controlled? If so, specifically what measures would you pursue?

Reagan: Mr. Ellis, I think this idea that has been spawned here in our country that inflation somehow came upon us like a plague and therefore it's uncontrollable and no one can do anything about it, is entirely spurious and it's dangerous to say this to the people. When Mr. Carter became President, inflation was 4.8%, as you said. It had been cut in two by President Gerald Ford. It is now running at 12.7%

President Carter also has spoken of the new jobs created. Well, we always, with the normal growth in our country and increase in population, increase the number of jobs. But that can't hide the fact that there are 8 million men and women out of work in America today, and 2 million of those lost their jobs in just the last few months. Mr. Carter had also promised that he would not use unemployment as a tool to fight against inflation. And yet, his 1980 economic message stated that we would reduce productivity and gross national product and increase unemployment in order to get a handle on inflation, because in January, at the beginning of the year, it was more than 18%. Since then, he has blamed the people for inflation, OPEC, he has blamed the Federal Reserve system, he has blamed the lack of productivity of the American people, he has then accused the people of living too well and that we must share in scarcity, we must sacrifice and get used to doing with less. We don't have inflation because the people are living too well. We have inflation because the Government is living too well. And the last statement, just a few days ago, was a speech to the effect that we have inflation because Government revenues have not kept pace with Government spending.

I see my time is running out here. I'll have to get this out very fast. Yes, you can lick inflation by increasing productivity and by decreasing the cost of government to the place that we have balanced budgets, and are no longer grinding out printing press money, flooding the market with it because the Government is spending more than it takes in. And my economic plan calls for that. The President's economic plan calls for increasing the taxes to the point that we finally take so much money away from the people that we can balance the budget in that way. But we will have a very poor nation and a very unsound economy if we follow that path.

Smith: A follow-up Mr. Ellis?

Ellis: Yes. You have centered on cutting Government spending in what you have just said about your own policies. You have also said that you would increase defense spending. Specifically, where would you cut Government spending if you were to increase defense spending and also cut taxes, so that, presumably, Federal revenues would shrink?

Reagan: Well, most people, when they think about cutting Government spending, they think in terms of eliminating necessary programs or wiping out something, some service that Government is supposed to perform. I believe that there is enough extravagance and fat in government. As a matter of fact, one of the secretaries of HEW under Mr. Carter testified that he thought there was $7 billion worth of fraud and waste in welfare and in the medical programs associated with it. We've had the General Accounting Office estimate that there is probably tens of billions of dollars that is lost in fraud alone, and they have added that waste adds even more to that.

We have a program for a gradual reduction of Government spending based on these theories, and I have a task force now that has been working on where those cuts could be made. I'm confident that it can be done and that it will reduce inflation because I did it in California. And inflation went down below the national average in California when we returned the money to the people and reduced Government spending.

Smith: President Carter.

Carter: Governor Reagan's proposal, the Reagan-Kemp-Roth proposal, is one of the most highly inflationary ideas that ever has been presented to the American public. He would actually have to cut Government spending by at least $130 billion in order to balance the budget under this ridiculous proposal. I notice that his task force that is working for his future plans had some of their ideas revealed in The Wall Street Journal this week. One of those ideas was to repeal the minimum wage, and several times this year, Governor Reagan has said that the major cause of unemployment is the minimum wage. This is a heartless kind of approach to the working families of our country, which is typical of many Republican leaders of the past, but, I think, has been accentuated under Governor Reagan.

In California—I'm surprised Governor Reagan brought this up—he had the three largest tax increases in the history of that state under his administration. He more than doubled state spending while he was Governor— 122% increase—and had between a 20% and 30% increase in the number of employees. . . .

Smith: Sorry to interrupt, Mr. Carter.

Carter: . . .in California. Thank you, sir.

Smith: Governor Reagan has the last word on this question.

Reagan: Yes. The figures that the President has just used about California is a distortion of the situation there, because while I was Governor of California, our spending in California increased less per capita than the spending in Georgia while Mr. Carter was Governor of Georgia in the same four years. The size of government increased only one-sixth in California of what it increased in proportion to the population in Georgia.

And the idea that my tax-cut proposal is inflationary: I would like to ask the President why is it inflationary to let the people keep more of their money and spend it the way that they like, and it isn't inflationary to let him take that money and spend it the way he wants?

Smith: I wish that question need not be rhetorical, but it must be because we've run out of time on that. Now, the third question to Governor Reagan from William Hilliard.

[Urban Decay]

Hilliard: Yes. Governor Reagan, the decline of our cities has been hastened by the continual rise in crime, strained race relations, the fall in the quality of public education, persistence of abnormal poverty in a rich nation, and a decline in the services to the public. The signs seem to point toward a deterioration that could lead to the establishment of a permanent underclass in the cities. What, specifically, would you do in the next four years to reverse this trend?

Reagan: I have been talking to a number of Congressmen who have much the same idea that I have, and that is that in the inner city areas, that in cooperation with the local government and the national Government, and using tax incentives and with cooperating with the private sector, that we have development zones. Let the local entity, the city, declare this particular area, based on the standards of the percentage of people on welfare, unemployed, and so forth, in that area. And then, through tax incentives, induce the creation of businesses providing jobs and so forth in those areas. The elements of government through these tax incentives. . . . For example, a business that would not have, for a period of time, an increase in the property tax reflecting its development of the unused property that it was making wouldn't be any loss to the city because the city isn't getting any tax from that now. And there would simply be a delay, and on the other hand, many of the people who would then be given jobs are presently wards of the Government, and it wouldn't hurt to give them a tax incentive, because they ... that wouldn't be costing Government anything either.

I think there are things to do in this regard. I stood in the South Bronx on the exact spot that President Carter stood on in 1977. You have to see it to believe it. It looks like a bombed-out city—great, gaunt skeletons of buildings, windows smashed out, painted on one of them "Unkept promises;" on another, "Despair." And this was the spot at which President Carter had promised that he was going to bring in a vast program to rebuild this department. There are whole ... or this area ... there are whole blocks of land that are left bare, just bulldozed down flat. And nothing has been done, and they are now charging to take tourists there to see this terrible desolation. I talked to a man just briefly there who asked me one simple question: "Do I have reason to hope that I can someday take care of my family again? Nothing has been done."

Smith: Follow-up, Mr. Hilliard?

[Racial Inequities]

Hilliard: Yes, Governor Reagan. Blacks and other non-whites are increasing in numbers in our cities. Many of them feel that they are facing a hostility from whites that prevents them from joining the economic mainstream of our society. There is racial confrontation in the schools, on jobs, and in housing, as non-whites seek to reap the benefits of a free society. What do you think is the nation's future as a multi-racial society?

Reagan: I believe in it. I am eternally optimistic, and I happen to be-

lieve that we've made great progress from the days when I was young and when this country didn't even know it had a racial problem. I know those things can grow out of despair in an inner city, when there's hopelessness at home, lack of work, and so forth. But I believe that all of us together, and I believe the Presidency is what Teddy Roosevelt said it was. It's a bully pulpit. And I think that something can be done from there, because a goal for all of us should be that one day, things will be done neither because of nor in spite of any of the differences between us— ethnic differences or racial differences, whatever they may be—that we will have total equal opportunity for all people. And I would do everything I could in my power to bring that about.

Smith: Mr. Hilliard, would you repeat your question for President Carter?

Hilliard: President Carter, the decline of our cities has been hastened by the continual rise in crime, strained race relations, the fall in the quality of public education, persistence of abnormal poverty in a rich nation, and a decline in services to the public. The signs seem to point toward a deterioration that could lead to the establishment of a permanent underclass in the cities. What, specifically, would you do in the next four years to reverse this trend?

Carter: Thank you, Mr. Hilliard. When I was campaigning in 1976, everywhere I went, the mayors and local officials were in despair about the rapidly deteriorating central cities of our nation. We initiated a very fine urban renewal program, working with the mayors, the governors, and other interested officials. This has been a very successful effort. That's one of the main reasons that we've had such an increase in the number of people employed. Of the nine million people put to work in new jobs since I've been in office, 1.3 million of those has been among black

Americans, and another million among those who speak Spanish.

We are now planning to continue the revitalization program with increased commitments of rapid transit, mass transit. Under the windfall profits tax, we expect to spend about $43 billion in the next 10 years to rebuild the transportation systems of our country. We also are pursuing housing programs. We've had a 73% increase in the allotment of Federal funds for improved education. These are the kinds of efforts worked on a joint basis with community leaders, particularly in the minority areas of the central cities that have been deteriorating so rapidly in the past.

It's very important to us that this be done with the full involvement of minority citizens. I have brought into the top level, top levels of government, into the White House, into administrative offices of the Executive branch, into the judicial system, highly qualified black and Spanish citizens and women who in the past had been excluded.

I noticed that Governor Reagan said that when he was a young man that there was no knowledge of a racial problem in this country. Those who suffered from discrimination because of race or sex certainly knew we had a racial problem. We have gone a long way toward correcting these problems, but we still have a long way to go.

Smith: Follow-up question?

Hilliard: Yes. President Carter, I would like to repeat the same follow-up to you. Blacks and other non-whites are increasing in numbers in our cities. Many of them feel that they are facing a hostility from whites that prevents them from joining the economic mainstream of our society. There is racial confrontation in the schools, on jobs, and in housing, as non-whites seek to reap the benefits of a free society?

Carter: Ours is a nation of refugees, a nation of immigrants. Almost all of our citizens came here from other lands

and now have hopes, which are being realized, for a better life, preserving their ethnic commitments, their family structures, their religious beliefs, preserving their relationships with their relatives in foreign countries, but still holding themselves together in a very coherent society, which gives our nation its strength.

In the past, those minority groups have often been excluded from participation in the affairs of government. Since I've been President, I've appointed, for instance, more than twice as many black Federal judges as all previous presidents in the history of this country. I've done the same thing in the appointment of women, and also Spanish-speaking Americans. To involve them in the administration of government and the feeling that they belong to the societal structure that makes decisions in the judiciary and in the executive branch is a very important commitment which I am trying to realize and will continue to do so in the future.

Smith: Governor Reagan, you have a minute for rebuttal.

Reagan: Yes. The President talks of Government programs, and they have their place. But as governor, when I was at that end of the line and receiving some of these grants for Government programs, I saw that so many of them were dead-end. They were public employment for those people who really want to get out into the private job market where there are jobs with a future.

Now, the President spoke a moment ago about ... that I was against the minimum wage. I wish he could have been with me when I sat with a group of teenagers who were black, and who were telling me about their unemployment problems, and that it was the minimum wage that had done away with the jobs that they once could get. And indeed, every time it has increased you will find there is an increase in minority unemployment among young people. And therefore, I have been in favor of a separate minimum for them.

With regard to the great progress that has been made with this Government spending, the rate of black unemployment in Detroit, Michigan is 56%.

Smith: President Carter, you have the last word on this question.

Carter: It's obvious that we still have a long way to go in fully incorporating the minority groups into the mainstream of American life. We have made good progress, and there is no doubt in my mind that the commitment to unemployment compensation, the minimum wage, welfare, national health insurance, those kinds of commitments that have typified the Democratic party since ancient history in this country's political life are a very important element of the future. In all those elements, Governor Reagan has repeatedly spoken out against them, which, to me, shows a very great insensitivity to giving deprived families a better chance in life. This, to me, is a very important difference between him and me in this election, and I believe the American people will judge accordingly.

There is no doubt in my mind that in the downtown central cities, with the, with the new commitment on an energy policy, with a chance to revitalize homes and to make them more fuel efficient, with a chance for our synthetic fuels program, solar power, this will give us an additional opportunity for jobs which will pay rich dividends.

[Terrorism Policy]

Smith: Now, a question from Barbara Walters.

Walters: Mr. President, the eyes of the country tonight are on the hostages in Iran. I realize this is a sensitive area, but the question of how we respond to acts of terrorism goes beyond this current crisis. Other countries have policies that determine how they will respond. Israel, for example, considers hostages like soldiers and will not negotiate with terrorists. For the future, Mr. President, the country has a right to know, do you have a policy for dealing with terrorism wherever it might happen, and, what have we learned from this experience in Iran that might cause us to do things differently if this, or something similar, happens again?

Carter: Barbara, one of the blights on this world is the threat and the activities of terrorists. At one of the recent economic summit conferences between myself and the other leaders of the Western world, we committed ourselves to take strong action against terrorism. Airplane hijacking was one of the elements of that commitment. There is no doubt that we have seen in recent years—in recent months—additional acts of violence against Jews in France and, of course, against those who live in Israel, by the PLO and other terrorist organizations.

Ultimately, the most serious terrorist threat is if one of those radical nations, who believe in terrorism as a policy, should have atomic weapons. Both I and all my predecessors have had a deep commitment to controlling the proliferation of nuclear weapons. In countries like Libya or Iraq, we have even alienated some of our closest trade partners because we have insisted upon the control of the spread of nuclear weapons to those potentially terrorist countries.

When Governor Reagan has been asked about that, he makes the very disturbing comment that non-proliferation, or the control of the spread of nuclear weapons, is none of our business. And recently when he was asked specifically about Iraq, he said there is nothing we can do about it.

This ultimate terrorist threat is the most fearsome of all, and it's part of a pattern where our country must stand firm to control terrorism of all kinds.

Smith: Ms. Walters, a follow up?

Walters: While we are discussing policy, had Iran not taken American hostages, I assume that, in order to preserve our neutrality, we would have stopped the flow of spare parts and vital war materials once war broke out between Iraq and Iran. Now we're offering to lift the ban on such goods if they let our people come home. Doesn't this reward terrorism, compromise our neutrality, and possibly antagonize nations now friendly to us in the Middle East?

Carter: We will maintain our position of neutrality in the Iran and Iraq war. We have no plans to sell additional materiel or goods to Iran, that might be of a warlike nature. When I made my decision to stop all trade with Iran as a result of the taking of our hostages, I announced then, and have consistently maintained since then, that if the hostages are released safely, we would make delivery on those items which Iran owns—which they have bought and paid for—also, that the frozen Iranian assets would be released. That's been a consistent policy, one I intend to carry out.

Smith: Would you repeat the question now for Governor Reagan, please, Ms. Walters?

Walters: Yes. Governor, the eyes of the country tonight remain on the hostages in Iran, but the question of how we respond to acts of terrorism goes beyond this current crisis. There are other countries that have policies that determine how they will respond. Israel, for example, considers hostages like soldiers and will not negotiate with terrorists.

For the future, the country has the right to know, do you have a policy for dealing with terrorism wherever it might happen, and what have we learned from this experience in Iran that might cause us to do things differently if this, or something similar, should happen again?

Reagan: Barbara, you've asked that question twice. I think you ought to have at least one answer to it. I have been accused lately of having a secret plan with regard to the hostages. Now, this comes from an answer that I've made at least 50 times during this campaign to the press, when I am asked have you any ideas of what you would do if you were there? And I said, well, yes. And I think that anyone that's seeking this position, as well as other people, probably, have thought to themselves, what about this, what about that? These are just ideas of what I would think of if I were in that position and had access to the information, and which I would know all the options that were open to me.

I have never answered the question, however; second, the one that says, well, tell me, what are some of those ideas? First of all, I would be fearful that I might say something that was presently under way or in negotiations, and thus expose it and endanger the hostages, and sometimes, I think some of my ideas might require quiet diplomacy where you don't say in advance, or say to anyone, what it is you're thinking of doing.

Your question is difficult to answer, because, in the situation right now, no one wants to say anything that would inadvertently delay, in any way, the return of those hostages if there ... if there is a chance that they're coming home soon, or that might cause them harm. What I do think should be done, once they are safely here with their families, and that tragedy is over— we've endured this humiliation for just lacking one week of a year now—then, I think, it is time for us to have a complete investigation as to the diplomatic efforts that were made in the beginning, why they have been there so long, and when they come home, what did we have to do in order to bring that about—what arrangements were made? And I would suggest that Congress should hold such an investigation. In the meantime, I'm going to continue praying that they'll come home.

Smith: Follow-up question.

Walters: I would like to say that neither candidate answered specifically the question of a specific policy for dealing with terrorism, but I will ask Governor Reagan a different follow-up question. You have suggested that there would be no Iranian crisis had you been President, because we would have given firmer support to the Shah. But Iran is a country of 37 million people who are resisting a government that they regarded as dictorial.

My question is not whether the Shah's regime was preferable to the Ayatollah's, but whether the United States has the power or the right to try to determine what form of government any country will have, and do we back unpopular regimes whose major merit is that they are friendly to the United States?

Reagan: The degree of unpopularity of a regime when the choice is total authoritarianism . . . totalitarianism, I should say, in the alternative government, makes one wonder whether you are being helpful to the people. And we've been guilty of that. Because someone didn't meet exactly our standards of human rights, even though they were an ally of ours, instead of trying patiently to persuade them to change their ways, we have, in a number of instances, aided a revolutionary overthrow which results in complete totalitarianism, instead, for those people. I think that this is a kind of a hypocritical policy when, at the same time, we're maintaining a détente with the one nation in the world where there are no human rights at all—the Soviet Union.

Now, there was a second phase in the Iranian affair in which we had something to do with that. And that was, we had adequate warning that there was a threat to our embassy, and we could have done what other embassies did—

either strengthen our security there, or remove our personnel before the kidnap and the takeover took place.

Smith: Governor, I'm sorry, I must interrupt. President Carter, you have a minute for rebuttal.

Carter: I didn't hear any comment from Governor Reagan about what he would do to stop or reduce terrorism in the future. What the Western allies did decide to do is to stop all air flights—commercial air flights—to any nation involved in terrorism or the hijacking of airplanes, or the harboring of hijackers. Secondly, we all committed ourselves, as have all my predecessors in the Oval Office, not to permit the spread of nuclear weapons to a terrorist nation, or to any other nation that does not presently have those weapons or capabilities for explosives. Third, not to make any sales of materiel or weapons to a nation which is involved in terrorist activities. And, lastly, not to deal with the PLO until and unless the PLO recognizes Israel's right to exist and recognizes U.N. Resolution 242 as a basis for Middle East peace.

These are a few of the things to which our nation is committed, and we will continue with these commitments.

Smith: Governor Reagan, you have the last word on that question.

Reagan: Yes. I have no quarrel whatsoever with the things that have been done, because I believe it is high time that the civilized countries of the world made it plain that there is no room worldwide for terrorism; there will be no negotiation with terrorists of any kind. And while I have a last word here, I would like to correct a misstatement of fact by the President. I have never made the statement that he suggested about nuclear proliferation and nuclear proliferation, or the trying to halt it, would be a major part of a foreign policy of mine.

Smith: Thank you gentlemen. That is the first half of the debate. Now, the rules for the second half are quite simple. They're only complicated when I explain them. In the second half, the panelists with me will have no follow-up questions. Instead, after the panelists have asked a question, and the candidates have answered, each of the candidates will have two opportunities to follow up, to question, to rebut, or just to comment on his opponent's statement.

Governor Reagan will respond, in this section, to the first question from Marvin Stone.

[Salt II Treaty]

Stone: Governor Reagan—arms control: The President said it was the single most important issue. Both of you have expressed the desire to end the nuclear arms race with Russia, but by methods that are vastly different. You suggest that we scrap the Salt II treaty already negotiated, and intensify the build-up of American power to induce the Soviets to sign a new treaty— one more favorable to us. President Carter, on the other hand, says he will again try to convince a reluctant Congress to ratify the present treaty on the grounds it's the best we can hope to get.

Now both of you cannot be right. Will you tell us why you think you are?

Reagan: Yes. I think I'm right because I believe that we must have a consistent foreign policy, a strong America, and a strong economy. And then, as we build up our national security, to restore our margin of safety, we at the same time try to restrain the Soviet build-up, which has been going forward at a rapid pace, and for quite some time.

The Salt II treaty was the result of negotiations that Mr. Carter's team entered into after he had asked the Soviet Union for a discussion of actual reduction of nuclear strategic weapons. And his emissary, I think, came home in 12 hours having heard a very definite nyet. But taking that one no from the Soviet Union, we then went back into negotiations on their terms, because Mr. Carter had cancelled the B-1 bomber, delayed the MX, delayed the Trident submarine, delayed the Cruise missile, shut down the Missile Man—the three—the Minute Man missile production line, and whatever other things that might have been done. The Soviet Union sat at the table knowing that we had gone forward with unilateral concessions without any reciprocation from them whatsoever.

Now, I have not blocked the Salt II treaty, as Mr. Carter and Mr. Mondale suggest I have. It has been blocked by a Senate in which there is a Democratic majority. Indeed, the Senate Armed Services Committee voted 10 to 0, with seven abstentions, against the Salt II treaty, and declared that it was not in the national security interests of the United States. Besides which, it is illegal, because the law of the land, passed by Congress, says that we cannot accept a treaty in which we are not equal. And we are not equal in this treaty for one reason alone—our B-52 bombers are considered to be strategic weapons; their Backfire bombers are not.

Smith: Governor, I have to interrupt you at that point. The time is up for that. But the same question now to President Carter.

Stone: Yes. President Carter, both of you have expressed the desire to end the nuclear arms race with Russia, but through vastly different methods. The Governor suggests we scrap the Salt II treaty which you negotiated in Vienna ... or signed in Vienna, intensify the build-up of American power to induce the Soviets to sign a new treaty, one more favorable to us. You, on the other hand, say you will again try to convince a reluctant Congress to ratify the present treaty on the grounds it is the best we can hope to get from the Russians.

You cannot both be right. Will you tell us why you think you are?

Carter: Yes. I'd be glad to. Inflation, unemployment, the cities are all very important issues, but they pale into insignificance in the life and duties of a President when compared with the control of nuclear weapons. Every President who has served in the Oval Office since Harry Truman has been dedicated to the proposition of controlling nuclear weapons.

To negotiate with the Soviet Union a balanced, controlled, observable, and then reducing levels of atomic weaponry, there is a disturbing pattern in the attitude of Governor Reagan. He has never supported any of those arms control agreements—the limited test ban, Salt I, nor the Antiballistic Missile Treaty, nor the Vladivostok Treaty negotiated with the Soviet Union by President Ford—and now he wants to throw into the wastebasket a treaty to control nuclear weapons on a balanced and equal basis between ourselves and the Soviet Union, negotiated over a seven-year period, by myself and my two Republican predecessors.

The Senate has not voted yet on the Strategic Arms Limitation Treaty. There have been preliminary skirmishings in the committees of the Senate, but the Treaty has never come to the floor of the Senate for either a debate or a vote. It's understandable that a Senator in the preliminary debates can make an irresponsible statement, or, maybe, an ill-advised statement. You've got 99 other senators to correct that mistake, if it is a mistake. But when a man who hopes to be President says, take this treaty, discard it, do not vote, do not debate, do not explore the issues, do not finally capitalize on this long negotiation—that is a very dangerous and disturbing thing.

Smith: Governor Reagan, you have an opportunity to rebut that.

Reagan: Yes, I'd like to respond very much. First of all, the Soviet Union

... if I have been critical of some of the previous agreements, it's because we've been out-negotiated for quite a long time. And they have managed, in spite of all of our attempts at arms limitation, to go forward with the biggest military build-up in the history of man.

Now, to suggest that because two Republican presidents tried to pass the Salt treaty—that puts them on its side—I would like to say that President Ford, who was within 90% of a treaty that we could be in agreement with when he left office, is emphatically against this Salt treaty. I would like to point out also that senators like Henry Jackson and Hollings of South Carolina—they are taking the lead in the fight against this particular treaty.

I am not talking of scrapping. I am talking of taking the treaty back, and going back into negotiations. And I would say to the Soviet Union, we will sit and negotiate with you as long as it takes, to have not only legitimate arms limitation, but to have a reduction of these nuclear weapons to the point that neither one of us represents a threat to the other. That is hardly throwing away a treaty and being opposed to arms limitation.

Smith: President Carter?

Carter: Yes. Governor Reagan is making some very misleading and disturbing statements. He not only advocates the scrapping of this treaty—and I don't know that these men that he quotes are against the treaty in its final form—but he also advocated the possibility, he said it's been a missing element, of playing a trump card against the Soviet Union of a nuclear arms race, and is insisting upon nuclear superiority by our own nation, as a predication for negotiation in the future with the Soviet Union.

If President Brezhnev said, we will scrap this treaty, negotiated under three American Presidents over a seven-year period of time, we insist upon nuclear superiority as a basis for future negotiations, and we believe that the launching of a nuclear arms race is a good basis for future negotiations, it's obvious that I, as President, and all Americans, would reject such a proposition. This would mean the resumption of a very dangerous nuclear arms race. It would be very disturbing to American people. It would change the basic tone and commitment that all our nation has experienced ever since the Second World War, with Presidents, Democratic and Republican. And it would also be very disturbing to our allies, all of whom support this nuclear arms treaty. In addition to that, the adversarial relationship between ourselves and the Soviet Union would undoubtedly deteriorate very rapidly.

This attitude is extremely dangerous and belligerent in its tone, although it's said with a quiet voice.

Smith: Governor Reagan?

Reagan: I know the President's supposed to be replying to me, but sometimes, I have a hard time in connecting what he's saying, with what I have said or what my positions are. I sometimes think he's like the witch doctor that gets mad when a good doctor comes along with a cure that'll work.

My point I have made already, Mr. President, with regard to negotiating: it does not call for nuclear superiority on the part of the United States. It calls for a mutual reduction of these weapons, as I say, that neither of us can represent a threat to the other. And to suggest that the Salt II treaty that your negotiators negotiated was just a continuation, and based on all of the preceding efforts by two previous Presidents, is just not true. It was a new negotiation because, as I say, President Ford was within about 10% of having a solution that could be acceptable. And I think our allies would be very happy to go along with a fair and verifiable Salt agreement.

Smith: President Carter, you have the last word on this question.

Carter: I think, to close out this discussion, it would be better to put into perspective what we're talking about. I had a discussion with my daughter, Amy, the other day, before I came here, to ask her what the most important issue was. She said she thought nuclear weaponry—and the control of nuclear arms.

This is a formidable force. Some of these weapons have 10 megatons of explosion. If you put 50 tons of TNT in each one of railroad cars, you would have a carload of TNT—a trainload of TNT stretching across this nation. That's one major war explosion in a warhead. We have thousands, equivalent of megaton, or million tons, of TNT warheads. The control of these weapons is the single major responsibility of a President, and to cast out this commitment of all presidents, because of some slight technicalities that can be corrected, is a very dangerous approach.

Smith: We have to go to another question now, from Harry Ellis to President Carter.

[Alternative Fuels]

Ellis: Mr. President, as you have said, Americans, through conservation, are importing much less oil today than we were even a year ago. Yet U.S. dependence on Arab oil as a percentage of total imports is today much higher than it was at the time of the 1973 Arab oil embargo, and for some time to come, the loss of substantial amounts of Arab oil could plunge the U.S. into depression.

This means that a bridge must be built out of this dependence. Can the United States develop synthetic fuels and other alternative energy sources without damage to the environment, and will this process mean steadily higher fuel bills for American families?

Carter: I don't think there's any doubt that, in the future, the cost of oil is going to go up. What I've had as a basic commitment since I've been President is to reduce our dependence on foreign oil. It can only be done in two ways: one, to conserve energy—to stop the waste of energy—and, secondly, to produce more American energy. We've been very successful in both cases. We've now reduced the importing of foreign oil in the last year alone by one-third. We imported today 2 million barrels of oil less than we did the same date just a year ago.

This commitment has been opening up a very bright vista for our nation in the future, because with the windfall profits tax as a base, we now have an opportunity to use American technology and American ability and American natural resources to expand rapidly the production of synthetic fuels, yes; to expand rapidly the production of solar energy, yes; and also to produce the traditional kinds of American energy. We will drill more oil and gas wells this year than any year in history. We'll produce more coal this year than any year in history. We are exporting more coal this year than any year in history.

And we have an opportunity now, with improved transportation systems and improved loading facilities in our ports, to see a very good opportunity on a world international market, to replace OPEC oil with American coal as a basic energy source. This exciting future will not only give us more energy security, but will also open up vast opportunities for Americans to live a better life and to have millions of new jobs associated with this new and very dynamic industry now in prospect because of the new energy policy that we've put into effect.

Smith: Would you repeat the question now for Governor Reagan?

Ellis: Governor Reagan, Americans, through conservation, are importing much less oil today than we were even a year ago. And yet, U.S. reliance on Arab oil as a percentage of total imports is much higher today than it was during the 1973 Arab oil embargo. And the substantial loss of Arab oil could plunge the United States into depression.

The question is whether the development of alternative energy sources, in order to reduce this dependence, can be done without damaging this environment, and will it mean for American families steadily higher fuel bills?

Reagan: I'm not so sure that it means steadily higher fuel costs, but I do believe that this nation has been portrayed for too long a time to the people as being energy-poor when it is energy-rich. The coal that the President mentioned—yes, we have it—and yet one-eighth of our total coal resources is not being utilized at all right now. The mines are closed down; there are 22,000 miners out of work. Most of this is due to regulations which either interfere with the mining of it or prevent the burning of it. With our modern technology, yes, we can burn our coal within the limits of the Clean Air Act. I think, as technology improves, we'll be able to do even better with that.

The other thing is that we have only leased out—begun to explore—2% of our outer continental shelf for oil, where it is believed, by everyone familiar with that fuel and that source of energy, that there are vast supplies yet to be found. Our Government has, in the last year or so, taken out of multiple use millions of acres of public lands that once were—well, they were public lands subject to multiple use—exploration for minerals and so forth. It is believed that probably 70% of the potential oil in the United States is probably hidden in those lands, and no one is allowed to even go and explore to find out if it is there. This is particularly true of the recent efforts to shut down part of Alaska.

Nuclear power: There were 36 power plants planned in this country. And let me add the word safety; it must be done with the utmost of safety. But 32 of those have given up and canceled their plans to build, and again, because Government regulations and permits, and so forth, take—made it take—more than twice as long to build a nuclear plant in the Untied States as it does to build one in Japan or in Western Europe.

We have the sources here. We are energy rich, and coal is one of the great potentials we have.

Smith: President Carter, your comment?

Carter: To repeat myself, we have this year the opportunity, which we'll realize, to produce 800 million tons of coal—an unequalled record in the history of our country. Governor Reagan says that this is not a good achievement, and he blames restraints on coal production on regulations—regulations that affect the life and the health and safety of miners, and also regulations that protect the purity of our air and the quality of our water and our land. We cannot cast aside those regulations. We have a chance in the next 15 years, insisting upon the health and safety of workers in the mines, and also preserving the same high air and water pollution standards, to triple the amount of coal we produce.

Governor Reagan's approach to our energy policy, which has already proven its effectiveness, is to repeal, or to change substantially, the windfall profits tax—to return a major portion of $227 billion back to the oil companies; to do away with the Department of Energy; to short-circuit our synthetic fuels program; to put a minimal emphasis on solar power; to emphasize strongly nuclear power plants as a major source of energy in the gesture. He wants to put all our eggs in one basket and give that basket to the major oil companies.

Smith: Governor Reagan.

Reagan: That is a misstatement, of course, of my position. I just happen to believe that free enterprise can do a better job of producing the things that people need than government can. The Department of Energy has a multi-billion-dollar budget in excess of $10 billion. It hasn't produced a quart of oil or a lump of coal, or anything else in the line of energy. And for Mr. Carter to suggest that I want to do away with the safety laws and with the laws that pertain to clean water and clean air, and so forth. As Governor of California, I took charge of passing the strictest air pollution laws in the United States—the strictest air quality law that has even been adopted in the United States. And we created on OSHA—an Occupational Safety and Health Agency—for the protection of employees before the Federal Government had one in place. And to this day, not one of its decisions or rulings has ever been challenged.

So, I think some of those charges are missing the point. I am suggesting that there are literally thousands of unnecessary regulations that invade every facet of business, and indeed, very much of our personal lives, that are unnecessary; that Government can do without; that have added $130 billion to the cost of production in this country; and that are contributing their part to inflation. And I would like to see us a little more free, as we once were.

Smith: President Carter, another crack at that?

Carter: Sure. As a matter of fact, the air pollution standard laws that were passed in California were passed over the objections of Governor Reagan, and this is a very well-known fact. Also, recently, when someone suggested that the Occupational Safety and Health Act should be abolished, Governor Reagan responded, amen.

The offshore drilling rights is a question that Governor Reagan raises often. As a matter of fact, in the proposal for the Alaska lands legislation, 100% of all the offshore lands would be open for exploration, and 95% of all the Alaska lands, where it is suspected or believed that minerals might exist. We have, with our five-year plan for the leasing of offshore lands, proposed more land to be drilled than has been opened up for drilling since this program first started in 1954. So we're not putting restraints on American exploration, we're encouraging it in every way we can.

Smith: Governor Reagan, you have the last word on this question.

Reagan: Yes. If it is a well-known fact that I opposed air pollution laws in California, the only thing I can possibly think of is that the President must be suggesting the law that the Federal Government tried to impose on the State of California—not a law, but regulations—that would have made it impossible to drive an automobile within the city limits of any California city, or to have a place to put it if you did drive it against their regulations. It would have destroyed the economy of California, and, I must say, we had the support of Congress when we pointed out how ridiculous this attempt was by the Environmental Protection Agency. We still have the strictest air control, or air pollution laws in the country.

As for offshore oiling, only 2% now is so leased and is producing oil. The rest, as to whether the lands are going to be opened in the next five years or so—we're already five years behind in what we should be doing. There is more oil now, in the wells that have been drilled, than has been taken out in 121 years that they've been drilled.

Smith: Thank you Governor. Thank you, Mr. President. The next question goes to Governor Reagan from William Hilliard.

[Social Security]

Hilliard: Governor Reagan, wage earners in this country—especially the young—are supporting a Social Secu-

rity system that continues to affect their income drastically. The system is fostering a struggle between the young and the old, and is drifting the country toward a polarization of these two groups. How much longer can the young wage earner expect to bear the ever-increasing burden of the Social Security system?

Reagan: The Social Security system was based on a false premise, with regard to how fast the number of workers would increase and how fast the number of retirees would increase. It is actuarially out of balance, and this first became evident about 16 years ago, and some of us were voicing warnings then. Now, it is trillions of dollars out of balance, and the only answer that has come so far is the biggest single tax increase in our nation's history—the payroll tax increase for Social Security—which will only put a bandaid on this and postpone the day of reckoning by a few years at most.

What is needed is a study that I have proposed by a task force of experts to look into this entire problem as to how it can be reformed and made actuarially sound, but with the premise that no one presently dependent on Social Security is going to have the rug pulled out from under them and not get their check. We cannot frighten, as we have with the threats and the campaign rhetoric that has gone on in this campaign, our senior citizens—leave them thinking that in some way, they're endangered and they would have no place to turn. They must continue to get those checks, and I believe that the system can be put on a sound actuarial basis. But it's going to take some study and some work, and not just passing a tax increase to let the load—or the roof—fall in on the next administration.

Smith: Would you repeat that question for President Carter?

Hilliard: Yes. President Carter, wage earners in this country, especially the young, are supporting a Social Security System that continues to affect their income drastically. The system is fostering a struggle between young and old and is drifting the country toward a polarization of these two groups. How much longer can the young wage earner expect to bear the ever-increasing burden of the Social Security System?

Carter: As long as there is a Democratic president in the White House, we will have a strong and viable Social Security System, free of the threat of bankruptcy. Although Governor Reagan has changed his position lately, on four different occasions, he has advocated making Social Security a voluntary system, which would, in effect, very quickly bankrupt it. I noticed also in The Wall Street Journal early this week, that a preliminary report of his task force advocates making Social Security more sound by reducing the adjustment in Social Security for the retired people to compensate for the impact of inflation.

These kinds of approaches are very dangerous to the security, the well being and the peace of mind of the retired people of this country and those approaching retirement age. But no matter what it takes in the future to keep Social Security sound, it must be kept that way. And although there was a serious threat to the Social Security System and its integrity during the 1976 campaign and when I became President, the action of the Democratic Congress working with me has been to put Social Security back on a sound financial basis. That is the way it will stay.

Smith: Governor Reagan?

Reagan: Well, that just isn't true. It has, as I said, delayed the actuarial imbalance falling on us for just a few years with that increase in taxes, and I don't believe we can go on increasing the tax, because the problem for the young people today is that they are paying in far more than they can ever expect to get out. Now, again this state-

ment that somehow, I wanted to destroy it and I just changed my tune, that I am for voluntary Social Security, which would mean the ruin of it.

Mr. President, the voluntary thing that I suggested many years ago was that with a young man orphaned and raised by an aunt who died, his aunt was ineligible for Social Security insurance because she was not his mother. And I suggested that if this is an insurance program, certainly the person who is paying in should be able to name his own beneficiary. That is the closest I have every come to anything voluntary with Social Security. I, too, am pledged to a Social Security program that will reassure these senior citizens of ours that they are going to continue to get their money.

There are some changes that I would like to make. I would like to make a change in the regulation that discriminates against a wife who works and finds that she then is faced with a choice between her father's or her husband's benefits, if he dies first, or what she has paid in; but it does not recognize that she has also been paying in herself, and she is entitled to more than she presently can get. I'd like to change that.

Smith: President Carter's rebuttal now.

Carter: These constant suggestions that the basic Social Security System should be changed does call for concern and consternation among the aged of our country. It is obvious that we should have a commitment to them, that Social Security benefits should not be taxed and that there would be no peremptory change in the standards by which Social Security payments are made to retired people. We also need to continue to index Social Security payments, so that if inflation rises, the Social Security payments would rise a commensurate degree to let the buying power of a Social Security check continue intact.

In the past, the relationship between Social Security and Medicare has been very important to providing some modicum of aid for senior citizens in the retention of health benefits. Governor Reagan, as a matter of fact, began his political career campaigning around this nation against Medicare. Now, we have an opportunity to move toward national health insurance, with an emphasis on the prevention of disease, an emphasis on out-patient care, not in-patient care; an emphasis on hospital cost containment to hold down the cost of hospital care for those who are ill, an emphasis on catastrophic health insurance, so that if a family is threatened with being wiped out economically because of a very high medical bill, then the insurance would help pay for it. These are the kinds of elements of a national health insurance, important to the American people. Governor Reagan, again, typically is against such a proposal.

Smith: Governor?

Reagan: When I opposed Medicare, there was another piece of legislation meeting the same problem before the Congress. I happened to favor the other piece of legislation and thought that it would be better for the senior citizens and provide better care than the one that was finally passed. I was to opposing the principle of providing care for them. I was opposing one piece of legislation versus another.

There is something else about Social Security. Of course, it doesn't come of of the payroll tax. It comes out of a general fund, but something should be done about it. I think it is disgraceful that the Disability Insurance Fund in Social Security finds checks going every month to tens of thousands of people who are locked up in our institutions for crime or for mental illness, and they are receiving disability checks from Social Security every month while a state institution provides for all of their needs and their care.

Smith: President Carter, you have the last word on this question.

Carter: I think this debate on Social Security, Medicare, national health insurance typifies, as vividly any other subject tonight, the basic historical differences between the Democratic Party and Republican Party. The allusions to basic changes in the minimum wage is another, and the deleterious comments that Governor Reagan has made about unemployment compensation. These commitments that the Democratic Party has historically made to the working families of this nation, have been extremely important to the growth in their stature and in a better quality of life for them.

I noticed recently that Governor Reagan frequently quotes Democratic presidents in his acceptance address. I have never heard a candidate for President, who is a Republican, quote a Republican president, but when they get in office, they try to govern like Republicans. So, it is good for the American people to remember that there is a sharp basic historical difference between Governor Reagan and me on these crucial issues—also, between the two parties that we represent.

Smith: Thank you Mr. President, Governor Reagan. We now go to another question—a question to President Carter by Barbara Walters.

[Opponent's Weaknesses]

Walters: Thank you. You have addressed some of the major issues tonight, but the biggest issue in the minds of Americans voters is yourselves—your ability to lead this country. When many voters go into that booth just a week from today, they will be voting their gut instinct about you men. You have already given us your reasons why people should vote for you, now would you please tell us for this your final question, why they should not vote for your opponent, why his Presidency could be harmful to the nation and, having examined both your opponent's record and the man himself, tell us his greatest weakness.

Carter: Barbara, reluctant as I am to say anything critical about Governor Reagan, I will try to answer your question. First of all, there is the historical perspective that I just described. This is a contest between a Democrat in the mainstream of my party, as exemplified by the actions that I have taken in the Oval Office the last four years, as contrasted with Governor Reagan, who in most cases does typify his party, but in some cases, there is a radical departure by him from the heritage of Eisenhower and others. The most important crucial difference in this election campaign, in my judgment is the approach to the control of nuclear weaponry and the inclination to control or not to control the spread of atomic weapons to other nations who don't presently have it, particularly terrorist nations.

The inclination that Governor Reagan has exemplified in many troubled times since he has been running for President—I think since 1968—to inject American military forces in places like North Korea, to put a blockade around Cuba this year, or in some instances, to project American forces into a fishing dispute against the small nation of Ecuador on the west coast of South America. This is typical of his longstanding inclination, on the use of American power, not to resolve disputes diplomatically and peacefully, but to show that the exercise of military power is best proven by the actual use of it.

Obviously, no president wants war, and I certainly do not believe that Governor Reagan, if he were President, would want war, but a President in the Oval Office has to make a judgment on almost a daily basis about how to exercise the enormous power of our country for peace, through diplomacy, or in a careless way in a belligerent attitude which has exemplified his attitudes in the past.

Smith: Barbara, would you repeat the question for Governor Reagan?

Walters: Yes, thank you. Realizing that you may be equally reluctant to speak ill of your opponent, may I ask why people should not vote for your opponent, why his Presidency could be harmful to the nation, and having examined both your opponent's record and the man himself, could you tell us his greatest weakness?

Reagan: Well, Barbara, I believe that there is a fundamental difference—and I think it has been evident in most of the answers that Mr. Carter has given tonight—that he seeks the solution to anything as another opportunity for a Federal Government program. I happen to believe that the Federal Government has usurped powers of autonomy and authority that belong back at the state and local level. It has imposed on the individual freedoms of the people, and there are more of these things that could be solved by the people themselves, if they were given a chance, or by the levels of government that were closer to them.

Now, as to why I should be and he shouldn't be, when he was a candidate in 1976, President Carter invented a thing he called the misery index. He added the rate of unemployment and the rate of inflation, and it came, at that time, to 12.5% under President Ford. He said that no man with that size misery index has a right to seek reelection to the Presidency. Today, by his own decision, the misery index is in excess of 20%, and I think this must suggest something.

But, when I had quoted a Democratic President, as the President says, I was a Democrat. I said many foolish things back in those days. But the President that I quoted had made a promise, a Democrat promise, and I quoted him because it was never kept. And today, you would find that that promise is at the very heart of what Republicanism represents in this country today. That's why I believe there are going to be millions of Democrats that are going to vote with us this time around, because they too want that promise kept. It was a promise for less government and less taxes and more freedom for the people.

Smith: President Carter?

Carter: I mentioned the radical departure of Governor Reagan from the principles or ideals of historical perspective of his own party. I don't think that can be better illustrated than in the case of guaranteeing women equal rights under the Constitution of our nation. For 40 years, the Republican Party platforms called for guaranteeing women equal rights with a constitutional amendment. Six predecessors of mine who served in the Oval Office called for this guarantee of women's rights. Governor Reagan and his new Republican Party have departed from this commitment—a very severe blow to the opportunity for women to finally correct discrimination under which they have suffered.

When a man and a woman do the same amount of work, a man gets paid $1.00, a woman only gets paid 59 cents. And the equal rights amendment only says that equality of rights shall not be abridged for women by the Federal Government or by the state governments. That is all it says—a simple guarantee of equality of opportunity which typifies the Democratic Party, and which is a very important commitment of mine, as contrasted with Governor Reagan's radical departure from the long-standing policy of his own party.

Smith: Governor Reagan?

Reagan: Yes. Mr. President, once again, I happen to be against the amendment, because I think the amendment will take this problem out of the hands of elected legislators and put it in the hands of unelected judges. I am for equal rights, and while you

have been in office for four years and not one single state—and most of them have a majority of Democratic legislators—has added to the ratification or voted to ratify the equal rights amendment. While I was Governor, more than eight years ago, I found 14 separate instances where women were discriminated against in the body of California law, and I had passed and signed into law 14 statutes that eliminated those discriminations, including the economic ones that you have just mentioned—equal pay and so forth.

I believe that if in all these years that we have spent trying to get the amendment, that we had spent as much time correcting these laws, as we did in California—and we were the first to do it. If I were President, I would also now take a look at the hundreds of Federal regulations which discriminate against women and which go right on while everyone is looking for an amendment. I would have someone ride hard on those regulations, and we would start eliminating those discriminations in the Federal Government against women.

Smith: President Carter?

Carter: Howard, I'm a Southerner, and I share the basic beliefs of my region about an excessive government intrusion into the private affairs of American citizens and also into the private affairs of the free enterprise system. One of the commitments that I made was to deregulate the major industries of this country. We've been remarkable successful, with the help of a Democratic Congress. We have deregulated the air industry, the rail industry, the trucking industry, financial institutions. We're now working on the communications industry.

In addition to that, I believe that this element of discrimination is something that the South has seen so vividly as a blight on our region of the country which has now been corrected—not only racial discrimination but discrimination against people that have to work for a living—because we have been trying to pick ourselves up by our bootstraps, since the long depression years, and lead a full and useful life in the affairs of this country. We have made remarkable success. It is part of my consciousness and of my commitment to continue this progress.

So, my heritage as a Southerner, my experience in the Oval Office, convinces me that what I have just described is a proper course for the future.

Smith: Governor Reagan, yours is the last word.

Reagan: Well, my last word is again to say this: We were talking about this very simple amendment and women's rights. And I make it plain again: I am for women's rights. But I would like to call the attention of the people to the fact that that so-called simple amendment could be used by mischievous men to destroy discriminations that properly belong, by law, to women respecting the physical differences between the two sexes, labor laws that protect them against things that would be physically harmful to them. Those would all, could all be challenged by men. And the same would be true with regard to combat service in the military and so forth.

I thought that was the subject we were supposed to be on. But, if we're talking about how much we think about the working people and so forth, I'm the only fellow who ever ran for this job who was six times president of his own union and still has a lifetime membership in that union.

Smith: Gentlemen, each of you now has three minutes for a closing statement. President Carter, you're first.

[Closing Statements]

Carter: First of all, I'd like to thank the League of Women Voters for making this debate possible. I think it's been a very constructive debate and I hope it's helped to acquaint the American people with the sharp differences between myself and Governor Reagan. Also, I want to thank the people of Cleveland and Ohio for being such hospitable hosts during these last few hours in my life.

I've been President now for almost four years. I've had to make thousands of decisions, and each one of those decisions has been a learning process. I've seen the strength of my nation, and I've seen the crises it approached in a tentative way. And I've had to deal with those crises as best I could.

As I've studied the record between myself and Governor Reagan, I've been impressed with the stark differences that exist between us. I think the result of this debate indicates that that fact is true. I consider myself in the mainstream of my party. I consider myself in the mainstream even of the bipartisan list of Presidents who served before me. The United States must be a nation strong; the United States must be a nation secure. We must have a society that's just and fair. And we must extend the benefits of our own commitment to peace, to create a peaceful world.

I believe that since I've been in office, there have been six or eight areas of combat evolved in other parts of the world. In each case, I alone have had to determine the interests of my country and the degree of involvement of my country. I've done that with moderation, with care, with thoughtfulness; sometimes consulting experts. But, I've learned in this last three and a half years that when an issue is extremely difficult, when the call is very close, the chances are the experts will be divided almost 50-50. And the final judgment about the future of the nation—war, peace, involvement, reticence, thoughtfulness, care, consideration, concern—has to be made by the man in the Oval Office. It's a lonely job, but with the involvement of the American people in the process, with an open Government, the job is very gratifying one.

The American people now are facing, next Tuesday, a lonely decision. Those listening to my voice will have to make a judgment about the future of this country. And I think they ought to remember that one vote can make a difference. If one vote per precinct had changed in 1960, John Kennedy would never have been President of this nation. And if a few more people had gone to the polls and voted in 1968, Hubert Humphrey would have been President; Richard Nixon would not.

There is a partnership involved in our nation. To stay strong, to stay at peace, to raise high the banner of human rights, to set an example for the rest of the world, to let our deep beliefs and commitments be felt by others in other nations, is my plan for the future. I ask the American people to join me in this partnership.

Smith: Governor Reagan?

Reagan: Yes, I would like to add my words of thanks, too, to the ladies of the League of Women Voters for making these debates possible. I'm sorry that we couldn't persuade the bringing in of the third candidate, so that he could have been seen also in these debates. But still, it's good that at least once, all three of us were heard by the people of this country.

Next Tuesday is Election Day. Next Tuesday all of you will go to the polls, will stand there in the polling place and make a decision. I think when you make that decision, it might be well if you would ask yourself, are you better off than you were four years ago? Is it easier for you to go and buy things in the stores than it was four years ago? Is there more or less unemployment in the country than there was four years ago? Is America as respected throughout the world as it was? Do you feel that our security is as safe, that we're as strong as we were four years ago? And if you answer all of those questions yes, why

then, I think your choice is very obvious as to whom you will vote for. If you don't agree, if you don't think that this course that we've been on for the last four years years is what you would like to see us follow for the next four, then I could suggest another choice that you have.

This country doesn't have to be in the shape that it is in. We do not have to go on sharing in scarcity with the country getting worse off, with unemployment growing. We talk about the unemployment lines. If all of the unemployed today were in a single line allowing two feet for each of them, that line would reach from New York City to Los Angeles, California. All of this can be cured and all of it can be solved.

I have not had the experience the President has had in holding that office, but I think in being Governor of California, the most populous state in the Union—if it were a nation, it would be the seventh ranking economic power in the world—I, too, had some lonely moments and decisions to make. I know that the economic program that I have proposed for this nation in the next few years can resolve many of the problems that trouble us today. I know because we did it there. We cut the cost—the increased cost of government—in half over the eight years. We returned $5.7 billion in tax rebates, credits and cuts to our people. We, as I have said earlier, fell below the national average in inflation when we did that. And I know that we did give back authority and autonomy to the people.

I would like to have a crusade today, and I would like to lead that crusade with your help. And it would be one to take Government off the backs of the great people of this country, and turn you loose again to do those things that I know you can do so well, because you did them and made this country great. Thank you.

Smith: Gentlemen, ladies and gentlemen, for 60 years the League of

Women Voters has been committed to citizen education and effective participation of Americans in governmental and political affairs. The most critical element of all in that process is an informed citizen who goes to the polls and votes. On behalf of the League of Women Voters, now, I would like to thank President Carter and Governor Reagan for being with us in Cleveland tonight. And, ladies and gentlemen, thank you and good night.

The Democrats' Atlanta Debate (1984)

The race for the Democratic presidential nomination in 1984 was important not only in its own right but also because it vividly illustrated several qualities of the open, primaries-based, federally financed nominating process that had been created during the early 1970s by the McGovern-Fraser Commission and the Federal Election Campaign Act. (See "The McGovern-Fraser Commission Report," p. 574, and "Buckley v. Valeo," p. 601.) Among these qualities are:

~ Large fields of candidates. Under the new rules for presidential nominations, easy access to the ballot and to federal campaign funds means that virtually any political leader who wants to run for president has a chance of winning, including little-known candidates and political "outsiders." The field of eight Democratic candidates in 1984, which included three senators, a governor, a former senator, a former governor, a former vice president, and a preacher, was only slightly larger than the modern average.

~ The importance of Iowa and New Hampshire. Because the Iowa caucuses and the New Hampshire primary are the first two events of the nominating season, candidacies often rise or fall there. Because they are relatively small states, victory is the result of effort as much as of fame.

In 1972 and 1976, Sen. George McGovern of South Dakota and former Georgia governor Jimmy Carter, respectively, rose from national obscurity to national celebrity and, eventually, to the Democratic party's presidential nomination on the strength of victories in Iowa or New Hampshire. (See "The Eagleton Affair: Statements by the Candidates," p. 595; and "Jimmy Carter's Interview with *Playboy* Magazine," p. 633.)

In 1984, it was Sen. Gary Hart of Colorado (McGovern's campaign manager in 1972) who surged from the back to the front of the pack after a surprise second-place finish in the February 20 Iowa caucuses and, eight days later, an upset victory in the New Hampshire primary. Hart startled the early front-runner, former vice president Walter F. Mondale, and virtually eliminated from serious consideration every other candidate except the African-American leader, Rev. Jesse Jackson.

~ Super Tuesday. In an effort to regain influence in the nominating process from Iowa and New Hampshire, ten states decided to select their delegates on March 13, 1984, two weeks after the New Hampshire primary. (In 1988, twenty states did, including the entire South.) Hart won more states than Mondale on what was instantly dubbed "Super Tuesday," but victories for Mondale in the Georgia and Ala-

*bama primaries brought his cam-
paign's free fall to a halt.*

*In April and May, Mondale's supe-
rior organization, fund raising, and
campaigning wore Hart down. By early
June, the former vice president had
enough delegates to ensure a first-ballot nomination at the Democratic national convention in July.*

~ The importance of debates. *As in
the general election, debates between
the candidates have become an established feature of the presidential nominating process. (See "The Second Reagan-Mondale Debate," p. 790.) Hart did
well in the campaign's early debates,
forcefully declaiming the Democratic
party's need for (and his own avowed
supply of) "new ideas." On March 11,
however, in a regionally televised pre-
Super Tuesday debate in Atlanta,
Georgia, Mondale used a line from a
popular hamburger commercial to rau-
cous effect by turning to Hart and
saying, "When I hear your new ideas,
I'm reminded of that ad 'Where's the
beef?'"*

~ The media as scorekeepers. *In an
open delegate selection process that is
spread out over fifty states and eight
months, the news media inevitably become the national political scorekeepers. It was journalists who decided that
Hart's second-place finish in Iowa (he
had 16.5 percent of the vote to Mondale's 48.9 percent) was a victory; that
"Where's the beef?" was the only line
worth remembering from the Atlanta
debate; and that Mondale's winning
only two states to Hart's six on Super
Tuesday was actually a victory for the
former vice president.* ~

Following are key sections of a transcript of a debate yesterday among the
five major candidates for the Democratic
Presidential nomination in the Fox Theater in Atlanta, Ga., as recorded by The
New York Times through the facilities
of the Cable News Network.

The participants were Senator John
Glenn of Ohio, Senator Gary Hart of
Colorado, the Rev. Jesse Jackson, former
Vice President Walter F. Mondale and
former Senator George McGovern of
South Dakota. The moderator was John
Chancellor of NBC News.

Panel Discussion

Military Spending

Mr. Chancellor: Aren't most of you
for an increase in defense spending?

Jesse Jackson: Well, I'm not.

George McGovern: : I'm not, I'm
for a 25 percent cut in the President's
budget and I think it can be done without touching anything that's important
to our national defense. I'm a bomber
pilot in the Second World War. I would
not advocate anything that I thought
touched the essential defense of this
country, but some of the most thoughtful people that have looked at that military budget say that it's just loaded with
waste and cost overruns and noncompet-
itive bidding.

Mr. Chancellor: I sense that Jesse
Jackson is not out of phase with that
sentiment.

Mr. Jackson: No doubt about it.
The point is that cost overruns is a
factor that requires that we at this
point have some kind of Congressional
oversight committee of some force
that allows it to become managed.
Right now it is unmanageable—the no-
bid contracts. The second dimension is
I support the need of some conventional troops in Europe or Japan, but
300,000 troops in Europe, 50,000 in
Japan—they're better able to help
share some of that burden now. That
can be cut, similar unnecessary assistance. Whether we can cut the defense
by at least 20 to 25 percent of the
budget without cutting out defense,

that is the money to implement some new ideas

Gary Hart: I am for reducing the Reagan military buildup by 140 to 150 billions of dollars in the next four to five years, and I've spelled out in great detail where those cuts must come. But I'll tell you why I disagree with both George and Jesse. One is that we have to increase even over and above Ronald Reagan what we are paying our military personnel to retain the most skilled personnel among other things to avoid going back to a very divisive Vietnam-style draft and second even after spending 650 billions of dollars in the last three years under this Administration, the Pentagon itself admits we have fewer combat-ready divisions than we had in 1980 under the Carter-Mondale Administration. And that means even Ronald Reagan is plundering the readiness accounts of our conventional forces for a procurement build-up which is going to make us weaker.

Mr. Chancellor: Maybe we can find a way to make this more understandable—isn't it true that the President has asked for a 13 percent increase this year in the allocations for defense, allowing for inflation? That's a 13 percent increase.

Mr. Hart: What about real terms, that's 17 isn't it?

Mr. Chancellor: All right, you want to say 17 then.

Mr. Hart: It is 17.

Mr. Chancellor: What would your figure be in that context—4 or 5 percent increase?

Mr. Hart: Mine is about 3½ to 4 percent. Over the base line that was established in '80.

Walter Mondale: Not to argue with Senator Hart, about a year and a half ago, he wrote a dissenting opinion in which he seemed to say he wanted as much or more military spending as Mr. Reagan. But, let me make my point. I think one of the realities of modern Presidential leadership is that as much

as we want to bring that defense budget down—and I do—as much as we want to get rid of weapons systems that don't buy us defense—and I will—as much as we need a tough new system of bidding, of testing, of warranties, as much as we need arms control to help also bring down pressure, the inescapable fact is that the Soviet Union is a powerful military nation using its power irresponsibly in Poland, and Cambodia, and Afghanistan and Syria and elsewhere. And the President of the United States has to do everything he can to manage that budget sensibly and wisely, but he cannot fail to effectively discharge the national security interests of our country. That's a tough balance but a President must do it.

Mr. Chancellor: Will you give me a percentage figure? What are you, 3, 4, 5 percent increase?

Mr. Mondale: Yes, I would be at about 4 percent.

John Glenn: I'm at about 6 percent. My two colleagues on the right here, I feel would cut our defense establishment beyond all reality as far as keeping the security of this country.

Now I have proposed cutting about $15 billion out, I've specified where that would be, it'd be on the MX, it'd be on the division air defense, the Bradley Fighting Vehicle, and the Rapid Deployment Force, certain parts of that. The build-up of the Soviets has been relentless since those Cuban missile crisis days.

The former Vice President would cut the B-1, the Nimitz carrier, the Trident, the cruise missile, the foreign troops he would cut back, he would cut the M-1 tank, funds for the volunteer army, kill the shuttle, oppose procurement of the F-14, the Harrier and AWACs.

I propose that would leave this country emasculated. The only two of those that he's pulled back from has been the Trident missile—the Trident submarine and cruise missile.

Mr. Hart opposed the F-15, the F-18, the B-1, the big—the Nimitz carrier, the Minuteman 3, the AWACs add-on, the Patriot Hellfire MLRS missiles, and has gone to a program of leadership in Washington of smaller and simpler is better rather than stressing our technology. And that's a fundamental difference between us. And I'm saying that every single thing we put out there has to work and work properly.

But we cannot go back to a smaller, simpler day or we wind up matching our numbers for numbers of troops vs. the Soviets as opposed to using what we've done in every war and that is use our technology to keep from using so many people out there; keep a distance between you and the enemy with our technology.

I fought in those wars, I know what it's like to be up there and want the best technology because my life depended on it. And so I do not agree with this smaller is simpler is better is cheaper approach that Mr. Hart has used and I don't think most people across the South do either.

Mr. Hart: What Senator Glenn doesn't address is the need for more units of all these things. We cannot afford more aircraft carriers when they, each one, cost three and a half to four billion dollars. We are behind the Soviets in submarines by a ratio of 3 to 1. We are falling behind in almost every category of weapons system in numbers because we're worshipping technology. I want to use our technological superiority to produce conventional weapons that work in combat in sufficient numbers to defend this country's interests.

Mr. Jackson: Gary's argument now is still preparing to kill and be killed by the Russians. I think the point is that we've began to use more of our energy on talking and negotiating and engaging in trade and technology and agriculture and less upon preparing to fight, we can prepare to live. The fact is we can just wipe out the Soviet Union with 300 warheads. We've got 10,000. The only reason we're alive now is they decided not to kill us last night. They're alive because we decided not to kill them. We're beyond now talking about who can overkill each other the most. That's uncivilized behavior. We need to begin to use our minds rather than our missiles and reduce this tension and go another way. We will still be wasting money killing people in the Caribbean or in Central America or in Lebanon and we should save the money we're using killing people there and save the money from cost overruns, we can cut the budget without cutting defense, begin to use our minds and go another way.

Mr. McGovern: What we've got is this same old argument "the Russians are coming, the Russians are about to jump on us." You can be very sure that the same argument's being made over there in the Kremlin "the Americans are gaining on us." Both of these superpowers are literally scaring each other to death—each side arming in the name of defense, each side piling up more and more of these weapons of destruction at a time when our societies are deteriorating.

President Eisenhower, who probably knew more about these military matters than any other President Since World War II, put it this way: if the military spends too much, it actually weakens the country by depriving us of other sources of national power—education, housing, transportation, a balanced economy. These are things that also have to do with our national strength. And I think we need a leadership that instead of trying to get the Russians to the bargaining table by a $1.5 trillion military build-up has the common sense to say, "We're ready to bargain right now."

Reagan's undertaken this totally unjustified build-up upon the theory that the Russians would then be more humble, and they've walked out on the arms negotiations.

Mr. Mondale: I agree that the idea of just building up arms to scare the Russians so then they will agree to whatever we want, as Reagan is demonstrating, will fail. I want to be understood as being totally committed to annual summit conferences, to arms control negotiations, efforts to reduce tensions. I couldn't agree with you more.

On the other hand, and I don't want to misinterpret what you've said, but the Soviets are using their power in Poland, in Cambodia, in Afghanistan, in Syria in ways that are irresponsible and dangerous.

Mr. McGovern: Fritz, how are you going to stop that with another 4 percent of military spending or another 40 percent? That's not going to change their relation to Poland or Afghanistan or these other areas.

Mr. Mondale: I think we need to have a sensible and a strong defense, and I had really intended to respond to John Glenn. It's a question of balance and of sense in arms control. But the point I wanted to respond to John Glenn is I am for a strong defense and a sensible defense.

Let me give you one example. The B-1, which I opposed. I support the Stealth because it's a modern, advanced bomber that'll take us into the next century.

I am against the MX, but I'm for the Midgetman. I think the Navy has to be scaled to proper proportions and I would be for strengthening NATO. Those are all strong and responsible positions, coupled with an arms control position, that reflect the realities of the world as I see them.

Mr. Glenn: I'm the only one here who's put forth a five-point arms control program trying to scale arms down so that we don't have to have such big defense expenditures. Limitation, reduction, in the nuclear area, enforcing the nuclear nonproliferation act so we prevent the spread of nuclear weapons

to more and more countries around this world. Involve the other nuclear weapons states in the negotiations and overall arms control.

Gary mentioned the carriers. He and I had a debate, which I'm sure he'll recall, on the Senate floor two years ago on that. He talks about the cheaper carrier as a smaller one. But it shows such a lack of fundamental understanding of how sea power works because you have to have a whole task force that goes with any carrier that gets out there.

Mr. Jackson: You know, the thing about this argument pro and con, all of us are basically for a strong defense. Obviously, the more that we talk in terms of engaging in real trade, the less we're going to have these tensions.

President Reagan is vulnerable, and we keep talking in ways I think that kind of confuse the people, that he's cut breakfast programs out from children, he's cut lunch programs out, he's cut back on food stamps, hurting the rural farmer and the urban consumer. And while he cuts away food from children, he's got us arguing about prayer, premeditated prayer. Here's a man doesn't go to church has got us arguing about prayer!

So let's talk about a strong defense but our domestic tranquility and internal stability has to do with saving our nation from the inside out.

Role of Government

Mr. Chancellor: Half a century ago when Mr. Roosevelt became President, the United States began to change, and the Federal Government took over many of the responsibilities of the states and of the cities. We've had half a century of continued Federal involvement with people's lives, and it seems to some of us that as though it's grown much in those years. The election of 1980 may have changed that, at least many Republicans think so. Now if one of you wins the election will there be less involvement, or will it be a return to the way things were before Reagan.

Mr. Mondale: I think it's essential that the President lead us with a strong Federal Government to solve those problems that are essential to our future. No. 1, to get those deficits down dramatically, because if we don't do that we can't have a healthy economy. No. 2, to have a strong new assertive American trade policy. This is the worst trade year in American history. All through Georgia and Alabama and Florida farmers, industrialists—Alabama's got 13½ percent unemployment today, there's a lot of people left behind, a lot of that is principally because of the trade disaster. We need a renaissance of learning and education and science and training.

If this next generation is going to be able to defend themselves and compete, they simply must have the support. And finally, we need a President who leads us toward justice, and I mean enforcing those civil rights acts. I mean ratifying that equal rights amendment, I mean standing up for Social Security and Medicare. This country must be fair, and the history of America is that when a President leads us toward fairness and toward our future, it can be done.

Mr. Hart: I've made quite an issue out of the need for a new generation of leadership. I mean primarily those who have come into political life and leadership in the past decade and that's because there is a strong anti-government feeling out there. Now I fundamentally disagree with Ronald Reagan when he says he loves his country and yet he hates our Government. I don't hate our Government. I think we ought to have leaders that ask people what they can do for their country using the best instruments of our Government.

But I think there is a fundamental difference, for example, between Vice President Mondale and myself. That is

I think we can meet the basic human needs and commitments of the people of this country by restoring entrepreneurship. Ninety percent of the new jobs in this society have come from small businesses, and I think the dedication of the Democratic party to minority people in the South and elsewhere shouldn't just be jobs, it should be the opportunity to own and operate businesses that create jobs.

Mr. Mondale: When I hear your new ideas, I'm reminded of that ad "Where's the beef?"

Mr. Hart: Fritz, if you'd listen just a minute I think you'd hear. One of the other differences, by the way, is if a President goes back into office—and one of us must, I think, to save this country—you cannot go back so committed to a handful of constituency groups that you cannot make this economy grow again. And that's again a major difference, I think, between myself and Walter Mondale.

Mr. Mondale: Wait a minute! Wait a minute! I told you what I was going to do, get those deficits down, educate the next generation. Those aren't special interest groups. I said I'm going to stand up for special—uh, against special interests and for—and I'm going to support Social Security and Medicare. What's wrong with that?

Mr. Hart: Nothing wrong with that.

Mr. Mondale: Isn't that right?

Mr. Jackson: Critical to your question, the role of the government is to be a balancing wheel between big labor and big management. The Government must assume basic responsibility to enforce the laws. Right now, the Voting Rights law, for example, is not being enforced. Democrats are reluctant because we want to reconcile the interests of the boll weevil and the cotton—you can't have both.

Georgia, for example, right now, 30 percent black, 18 years after the Voting Rights Act, 10 Congresspersons, 0 black; Supreme Court, 0; Appeals Court, 0; 159

sheriffs, 0. The Government must enforce the law and not equivocate in the face of local considerations.

On the other hand, we keep focusing on what the Government should do. The private economy is $3 trillion. Five of every six jobs is in the private economy. For that $700 billion tax break to corporations, they must be obligated to reinvest in this economy, retrain our work force, and not export our jobs to slave-labor markets abroad. We can no longer allow these corporations to take this money, replace people with robots, without any sense of an adequate transition.

Mr. Glenn: Back when I was a boy in New Concord, Ohio, in the Great Depression, we estimate we had about 51 percent of the people at or below poverty level. F.D.R. came in. My dad went to work on W.P.A. We had a lot of programs at that time. It helped a lot of people. We estimated just a few years ago only 9 percent of this country were at or near poverty level. That's a record of social revolution in this country. It didn't happen with Socialism or Facism or Communism. It happened with good solid Democratic programs, and we can be very proud of those programs. Now, along with that we went a little too far in some of those programs, and we have to correct those. And now you're talking about intrusion of government. And there are some areas where I think we have some very major differences. I spelled them out between myself and Mr. Hart. Just a couple of days ago. E.R.A.—He has said that he would use that, and I'm for E.R.A., proud that Ohio led the way with that. But he said that E.R.A., he would use the power of the Federal Government to withhold projects.

Mr. Hart: No, I didn't.

Mr. Glenn: Yes, you did, Gary, I'll read it to you.

Mr. Hart: No, I didn't.

Mr. Glenn: And he, yes you did. He said he'd withhold Federal projects.

Now that's an intrusion as far as I'm concerned. I think that is flat wrong. When you're going to intrude into people's lives on that basis, with Federal projects.

Mr. McGovern: I think there are two types of concentration of power we have to worry about in the United States. One is the danger of too much Federal concentration and the other is too much corporate concentration of power. On the Federal side, to my surprise, President Reagan has increased the percentage of G.N.P. now being taken up by the Federal Government. The reason for that is obviously the dramatic increase in military spending. He has cut nutrition and education, the environment and things like that, but those cuts are less than the increase in the interest rate on the Federal debt since he took office because of this escalating deficit that he's brought on. On the corporate side, we've had more huge corporate mergers in the last three years than at any previous time in American history. Enormous oil companies taking over others to the point where I think it's a real call on all of us to see what we can do to strengthen our antitrust laws.

Mr. Mondale: I think that a private healthy economy is indispensable to everybody. If you don't have growing, healthy economy with entrepreneurship and small businesses, the key here is to make certain that the prosperity and the entrepreneurship is found in minority communities as well. There's a lot we can do through the Small Business Administration, through tax incentives, through Federal licensing laws to make certain that more blacks, Hispanics, women and other minorities can participate in the fullness of profit-making. Thirdly, through training and education and the rest, make certain that people who are not being left behind are made a part of this process. All of that depends on a private healthy economy. That's why you've got to get those deficits down and get going with an environment where we can prosper.

Mr. Jackson: When I was in Operation PUSH we began to challenge corporate America. When Reagan cut down on aid, we began to move toward trade. Burger King, for example, has made the judgment to build a plant in the middle of Eutaw, Ala., as part of our agreement. Then they will hire 200 people. They will stop small farms from going out of business by guaranteeing a market of 5 million pounds of cucumbers a year. If a company does that, they ought to get a tax incentive.

Mr. Hart: In the almost 10 years in the Senate I've cast 5,000 or 6,000 votes. Vice President Mondale in his campaign has pulled out about half a dozen of those to attack me showing that I'm not for this and not for that. I'll give you one example. One of those was a vote on O.S.H.A. Now Vice President Mondale knows full well that I am absolutely as committed to a safe workplace as he is. The vote was this, and it illustrates the point and the difference. It was to exempt from certain paperwork requirements small businesses in the country who had 10 or fewer employees and farmers who employed fewer than five people. It was that burdensome bureaucracy and paperwork that drove the Democrats out of office in the 70's.

Now I think we can have a safe workplace for people on farms and in factories without driving small business people and family farmers off their land or out of their businesses.

Mr. Mondale: I saw that vote, but I've never mentioned it. The one I talked about is where, unlike Senator Nunn and Senator Chiles and others, you refused to vote a windfall profits tax, which, if you'd been successful would have given big oil $250 billion.

Mr. Hart: There you go again.

Mr. Mondale: I am going straight ahead here. Secondly, I've talked about your $10-a-barrel tax. That is the worst idea in this campaign.

Mr. Hart: It was a Carter-Mondale initiative.

Mr. Mondale: Oh no. I have nothing to do with that. That's the worst idea. Carter's not for it. Nobody except you are for it; and you're not talking about it anymore, it's so bad.

Mr. Hart: Oh yes I am.

Mr. Mondale: A half a million people . . .

Mr. Hart: Right away.

Mr. Mondale: A half a million lose their jobs. America will become the highest cost producing area in the country. Talk about intrusion and destruction of jobs and entrepreneurship and position in international trade, this is a disaster, and I don't think you thought it through.

Mr. Hart: Well, Mr. Mondale . . .

Mr. Mondale: I don't believe you really . . .

Mr. Hart: Let me respond. Let me respond.

Mr. Chancellor: You either have a choice, it seems to me, and I'm sorry but the clock is inexorable, . . . of having a chance to say what you want to say at the end or squeezing it there at the very end and so Senator could you just say it in 25 words or less than that.

Mr. Hart: Less than that. I voted for a Carter-Mondale tariff on imported oil and I was only one of about 15 Senators that had the courage to support this Administration. And the second thing is, I proposed a windfall profits tax of 100 percent on old oil owned by the big oil companies in this country and that goes beyond the Carter-Mondale . . .

Mr. Mondale: This is a complete distortion of what he did.

Mr. Hart: It is not a distortion.

Mr. Mondale: When we needed you, you were wrong.

Mr. Hart: No, that's not right.

Mr. Mondale: That is correct.

Closing Statements

Mr. Chancellor: We're going to get your reasoned closing statements now.

Mr. Hart: I have no idea how the primaries and caucuses are going to come out next Tuesday or beyond; I obviously hope that I will be successful. I hope so for several reasons. George McGovern talked about the great leaders of our past, Democratic and otherwise, and my values are as deeply rooted in those leaders and that past and those ideals as any person on this platform, indeed in this country.

But it's interesting that the leaders he mentioned represented something else than just ideals and principles; they represented change. When this country has had to change, it came to this party for those who had a policy and a set of ideas and a vision for this country's future. That is what this campaign is all about and I think that's why people are responding to it all across this country. We cannot go back. To achieve the highest ideals, values, and goals of this country we must have new leadership and a new approach and a fresh start for this country.

Mr. Jackson: If we in fact have new leadership that replaces old leadership basically going in the same direction not sharing parity with farmers, not sharing the ticket with a woman, increasing the military budget, resisting a real commitment to enforce the Voting Rights Act, that's a new face, or a new name of an old game. We need to go in another direction. Our party must be the party of conscience. The fact is that under Reagan there are five million more people who are poor, three million more children, now up to 34 million, 15 percent of our nation, it will be 41 million by the end of this year. There must be a

commitment to lift those boats that are in fact stuck at the bottom. We must reduce the military budget without reducing our military defense, use that money to in fact create a future for our children, that they might be able to lay bricks and not throw them. If we give our children a chance, they will give our nation a chance. I remain convinced that we will suffer, that suffering breeds character, character breeds faith and in the end faith will not disappoint. We must pursue those values.

Mr. McGovern: I hope that since Gary and Fritz have both objected to being called the front-runner they'll let me be the peacemaker and take that label with me back to Boston when I go tonight. Franklin Roosevelt once said that the Presidency is pre-eminently a place of moral leadership. I think that's true, and I think it means the next President is going to have to seek above all else our salvation from nuclear annihilation, but second only to that, we've got to learn in this great country to quit intervening in these third world revolutions whether it's El Salvador or Nicaragua or Lebanon or wherever it is. Unfortunately in the name of fighting Communism we've embraced virtually every scoundrel around the world who is willing to wave an anti-Communist banner, and I think the time has come for the United States once again to assert in foreign policy not so much what we hate and fear but what this great country is for, and that ought to be the goal of the next President.

Mr. Glenn: I do regret something George just brought up here, that we have not had more of an opportunity to talk a little bit more about foreign policy because I think that's so important, what happens around the world, nuclear armswise that I mentioned earlier, but I do not agree with Gary that this is a generation gap of some kind. We go ahead as a nation and always have in the past as we've had the best interests of all of our people, of the young, of the middle-aged, of the elderly and as we had concern for everyone within our society. The South has a unique opportunity to set that course next Tuesday. It's a unique opportunity for leadership in the Democratic Party and for leadership for our nation. I see myself as the moderate, the only moderate left here. I don't believe in this politics of momentum that seems to be abroad. Politics of stampede, whatever you want to call it. I hope the people of the South will slow down, think about the issues and think about the position we've taken on the economy and foreign policy and education and research and these things and then vote on what you know about what we actually have proposed. We can control the destiny of this country. We can be No. 1 in this nation of ours again. George McGovern, a few weeks ago, said he didn't want people to throw away their conscience. Don't throw away your common sense either. Give me your vote next week, and I will guarantee you I'll give you a Presidency you can be proud of once again.

Mr. Mondale: Here in the South and throughout our country, we're about to participate in Super Tues-day. The most important single question is whether the President you want is someone who will insure our national security and will work for peace. That takes someone who knows what he's doing. This may well now be a two-man race between myself and Senator Hart.

Mr. Glenn: I'd like to disagree with that.

Mr. Mondale: If you look at the records, I think something is disclosed. A few days ago, Senator Hart said that if Persian Gulf oil were interrupted, that the allies would be on their own and they couldn't look to us for help. In my opinion, that is naïve. All history teaches us that we must stand together as an alliance and work together for the security of the Western world. Some time back he was asked whether Cuba was a totalitarian state. And he said, no. That is wrong. It is a Communist dictatorship and a President must know the difference. He has had a record on arms control which is weak, and we need a President who will push forward and provide the leadership that this country needs for our national security and to achieve the peace.

Geraldine A. Ferraro's Acceptance Speech to the Democratic National Convention (1984)

Walter F. Mondale's first-ballot nomination for president at the 1984 Democratic national convention was not an unalloyed triumph for the former vice president. For one thing, Mondale trailed President Ronald Reagan by a substantial margin in public opinion polls. For another, he faced intense pressure from the National Organization for Women (NOW) and other feminist organizations to choose a woman as the party's nominee for vice president. No woman had ever been on a major-party ticket, although the Libertarian party's vice-presidential candidate in 1972, Theodora Nathan, did receive one electoral vote from a "faithless" Republican elector. (See "The Twelfth Amendment: Senate Debate," p. 89.)

Under the right circumstances, Mondale's problems would have been opportunities. Choosing a woman as his running mate was just the sort of bold stroke that Mondale needed to change the chemistry of the general election campaign and to repair his own image as a cautious, conventional political leader. Some polls indicated that more votes would be gained than lost by choosing a female vice-presidential candidate with the proper experience and background in government.

Mondale's problem was that in 1984 the Democratic party included few women who had attained high political office of any kind. Reluctantly, he set-tled on Rep. Geraldine A. Ferraro of New York as his choice for vice president. Ferraro was best known for the commendable job she had done as the chair of the party's 1984 platform committee.

Ferraro's nomination brought certain strengths to the Democratic ticket. The choice of a woman for vice president electrified the country. Many voters shared the sentiment that Ferraro expressed at the beginning of her acceptance speech to the convention: "I can stand before you to proclaim tonight: America is the land where dreams come true." The first post-convention Gallup poll indicated that Mondale and Ferraro had drawn within two percentage points of Reagan and his running mate, Vice President George Bush.

Ferraro also proved to be an effective campaigner. On October 11, 1984, in the second vice-presidential debate in history, she more than held her own with Bush. (The first such debate had been between Mondale and his Republican counterpart, Sen. Robert A. Dole of Kansas, on October 15, 1976.) Indeed, Ferraro produced the debate's most memorable moment. When Bush offered "to help you, with the difference, Mrs. Ferraro, between Iran and the embassy in Iran," Ferraro responded with quiet fury: "Let me just say, first of all, that I almost resent,

Vice President Bush, your patronizing attitude that you have to teach me about foreign policy."

But Ferraro was a drag on Mondale's candidacy in other, more important ways. In August 1984, almost immediately after the Democratic convention, reporters peppered her with embarrassing questions about her family's financial affairs, especially her husband's activities in New York's corruption-ridden real estate industry. Soon after, Archbishop John O'Connor of New York added to the Democrats' woes by publicly doubting that a Catholic voter could support in good conscience a Catholic candidate who, like Ferraro, was pro-choice on the abortion issue. Finally, as election day drew near, doubts spread in the electorate about Ferraro's qualifications, as a three-term member of the House of Representatives with no experience in foreign policy, to succeed to the presidency if the need should arise.   ~

Ladies and gentlemen of the convention: My name is Geraldine Ferraro. I stand before you to proclaim tonight: America is the land where dreams can come true for all of us.

As I stand before the American people and think of the honor this great convention has bestowed upon me, I recall the words of Dr. Martin Luther King Jr., who made America stronger by making America more free.

He said: "Occasionally in life there are moments which cannot be completely explained by words. Their meaning can only be articulated by the inaudible language of the heart."

Tonight is such a moment for me.

My heart is filled with pride.

My fellow citizens, I proudly accept your nomination for vice president of the United States.

And I am proud to run with a man who will be one of the great presidents of this century, Walter F. Mondale.

[The Future]

Tonight, the daughter of a woman whose highest goal was a future for her children talks to our nation's oldest party about a future for us all.

Tonight, the daughter of working Americans tells all Americans that the future is within our reach—if we're willing to reach for it.

Tonight, the daughter of an immigrant from Italy has been chosen to run for [vice] president in the new land my father came to love.

Our faith that we can shape a better future is what the American dream is all about. The promise of our country is that the rules are fair. If you work hard and play by the rules, you can earn your share of America's blessings.

Those are the beliefs I learned from my parents. And those are the values I taught my students as a teacher in the public schools of New York City.

At night, I went to law school. I became an assistant district attorney, and I put my share of criminals behind bars. I believe: If you obey the law, you should be protected. But if you break the law, you should pay for your crime.

When I first ran for Congress, all the political experts said a Democrat could not win in my home district of Queens. But I put my faith in the people and the values that we shared. And together, we proved the political experts wrong.

In this campaign, Fritz Mondale and I have put our faith in the people. And we are going to prove the experts wrong again.

We are going to win, because Americans across this country believe in the same basic dream.

[Elmore, Minn., and Queens]

Last week, I visited Elmore, Minn., the small town where Fritz Mondale was raised. And soon Fritz and Joan will visit our family in Queens.

Nine hundred people live in Elmore. In Queens, there are 2,000 people on one block. You would think we would be different, but we're not.

Children walk to school in Elmore past grain elevators; in Queens, they pass by subway stops. But, no matter where they live, their future depends on education—and their parents are willing to do their part to make those schools as good as they can be.

In Elmore, there are family farms; in Queens, small businesses. But the men and women who run them all take pride in supporting their families through hard work and initiative.

On the Fourth of July in Elmore, they hang flags out on Main Street; in Queens, they fly them over Grand Avenue. But all of us love our country, and stand ready to defend the freedom that it represents.

[Playing by the Rules]

Americans want to live by the same set of rules. But under this administration, the rules are rigged against too many of our people.

It isn't right that every year, the share of taxes paid by individual citizens is going up, while the share paid by large corporations is getting smaller and smaller. The rules say: Everyone in our society should contribute their fair share.

It isn't right that this year Ronald Reagan will hand the American people a bill for interest on the national debt larger than the entire cost of the federal government under John F. Kennedy.

Our parents left us a growing economy. The rules say: We must not leave our kids a mountain of debt.

It isn't right that a woman should get paid 59 cents on the dollar for the same work as a man. If you play by the rules, you deserve a fair day's pay for a fair day's work.

It isn't right that—that if trends continue—by the year 2000 nearly all of the poor people in America will be women and children. The rules of a decent society say, when you distribute sacrifice in times of austerity, you don't put women and children first.

It isn't right that young people today fear they won't get the Social Security they paid for, and that older Americans fear that they will lose what they have already earned. Social Security is a contract between the last generation and the next, and the rules say: You don't break contracts. We're going to keep faith with older Americans.

We hammered out a fair compromise in the Congress to save Social Security. Every group sacrificed to keep the system sound. It is time Ronald Reagan stopped scaring our senior citizens.

It isn't right that young couples question whether to bring children into a world of 50,000 nuclear warheads.

That isn't the vision for which Americans have struggled for more than two centuries. And our future doesn't have to be that way.

Change is in the air, just as surely as when John Kennedy beckoned America to a new frontier; when Sally Ride rocketed into space and when Rev. Jesse Jackson ran for the office of president of the United States.

By choosing a woman to run for our nation's second highest office, you sent a powerful signal to all Americans. There are no doors we cannot unlock. We will place no limits on achievement.

If we can do this, we can do anything.

Tonight, we reclaim our dream. We're going to make the rules of American life work fairly for all Americans again.

To an Administration that would have us debate all over again whether the Voting Rights Act should be renewed and whether segregated schools should be tax exempt, we say, Mr. President: Those debates are over.

On the issue of civil, voting rights and affirmative action for minorities, we must not go backwards. We must—and we will—move forward to open the doors of opportunity.

To those who understand that our country cannot prosper unless we draw on the talents of all Americans, we say: We will pass the Equal Rights Amendment. The issue is not what America can do for women, but what women can do for America.

To the Americans who will lead our country into the 21st century, we say: We will not have a Supreme Court that turns the clock back to the 19th century.

To those concerned about the strength of American family values, as I am, I say: We are going to restore those values—love, caring, partnership—by including, and not excluding, those whose beliefs differ from our own. Because our own faith is strong, we will fight to preserve the freedom of faith for others.

To those working Americans who fear that bank, utilities, and large special interests have a lock on the White House, we say: Join us; let's elect a people's president; and let's have government by and for the American people again.

To an Administration that would savage student loans and education at the dawn of a new technological age, we say: You fit the classic definition of a cynic; you know the price of everything, but the value of nothing.

To our students and their parents, we say: We will insist on the highest standards of excellence because the jobs of the future require skilled minds.

To young Americans who may be called to our country's service, we say: We know your generation of Americans will proudly answer our country's call, as each generation before you.

This past year, we remembered the bravery and sacrifice of Americans at Normandy. And we finally paid trib-

ute—as we should have done years ago—to that unknown soldier who represents all the brave young Americans who died in Vietnam.

Let no one doubt, we will defend America's security and the cause of freedom around the world. But we want a president who tells us what America is fighting for, not just what we are fighting against. We want a president who will defend human rights—not just where it is convenient—but wherever freedom is at risk—from Chile to Afghanistan, from Poland to South Africa.

To those who have watched this administration's confusion in the Middle East, as it has tilted first toward one and then another of Israel's long-time enemies and wondered. "Will America stand by her friends and sister democracy?" We say: America knows who her friends are in the Middle East and around the world.

America will stand with Israel always.

Finally, we want a President who will keep America strong, but use that strength to keep America and the world at peace. A nuclear freeze is not a slogan: It is a tool for survival in the nuclear age. If we leave our children nothing else, let us leave them this Earth as we found it—whole and green and full of life.

I know in my heart that Walter Mondale will be that president.

A wise man once said, "Every one of us is given the gift of life, and what a strange gift it is. If it is preserved jealously and selfishly, it impoverishes and saddens. But if it is spent for others, it enriches and beautifies."

My fellow Americans: We can debate policies and programs. But in the end what separates the two parties in this election campaign is whether we use the gift of life—for others or only ourselves.

Tonight, my husband, John, and our three children are in this hall with me. To my daughters, Donna and Laura, and my son, John Jr., I say: My mother did not break faith with me . . . and I will not break faith with you. To all the children of America, I say: The generation before ours kept faith with us, and like them, we will pass on to you a stronger, more just America.

Thank you.

The Second Reagan-Mondale Debate (1984)

In the manner of presidents Woodrow Wilson, Franklin D. Roosevelt, and Lyndon B. Johnson, Ronald Reagan parlayed his change-oriented campaign and landslide election in 1980 into dramatic legislative achievements during his first two years as president: a 25 percent reduction in federal income tax rates, substantial cutbacks in federal spending on welfare and social services, and a massive military build-up. After a deep recession in 1982, the economy rebounded in 1983 and 1984 with growth rates that were high and unemployment, inflation, and interest rates that were low. (See "Woodrow Wilson's 'The Old Order Changeth' Speech," p. 267; "Franklin D. Roosevelt's Acceptance Speech to the Democratic National Convention," p. 336; and "Lyndon B. Johnson's 'Let Us Continue' Speech to Congress," p. 511.)

As the election of 1984 drew near, Reagan enjoyed strong approval from the voters. In August, he was unanimously nominated for a second term by the Republican national convention, the first time since 1956 that a president was renominated without having to fend off a challenge from within his own party. In September, following the precedent of the 1976 and 1980 elections and confident of his abilities as the "Great Communicator," Reagan agreed to debate the Democratic presidential nominee, former vice president Walter F. Mondale, two times during the general election campaign.

Reagan needed to overcome only one serious doubt among the voters in his bid for reelection: his age. In 1980, at age sixty-nine, Reagan had become the oldest person ever to be elected as president. In 1989, at the end of a second term, he would be almost seventy-eight. Reagan was an extraordinarily youthful-looking and physically robust man, but, in press conferences during his first term, he had often made confusing statements and factual errors that some attributed to senescence.

The first debate with Mondale, on October 11, 1984, in Louisville, Kentucky, was a nightmare for Reagan. His answers to the panelists' questions and his closing statement to the voters were rambling and disorganized. Mondale, after making plain at the outset that he personally liked the popular president, confidently attacked the administration's policies. Reagan's best line from his 1980 debate with President Jimmy Carter became his worst line in 1984: this time when he said, "There you go again," Mondale reminded him that his use of the remark in 1980 was in response to Carter's warning that Reagan would cut the Medicare program. Yet, Mondale continued, "you went right out and tried to cut $20 billion out of Medicare." (See "The Carter-Reagan Debate," p. 749.)

Post-debate polls revealed that both the Mondale candidacy and the public's doubts about Reagan's competence were on the rise. Another poor performance by the president in the second debate, which was scheduled for October 21 in Kansas City, Missouri, promised to close the gap between the candidates even further.

Reagan was ready, relaxed in manner and vigorous in his answers. About halfway through the second debate, panelist Henry L. Trewhitt of the Baltimore Sun *asked Reagan, "You already are the oldest president in history. . . . Is there any doubt in your mind that you would be able to function in [crisis] circumstances?" The president's deadpan reply was, "Not at all, Mr. Trewhitt. And I want you to know that also, I will not make age an issue of this campaign. I am not going to exploit, for political purposes, my opponent's youth and inexperience." The studio audience, which had groaned at the question, roared with appreciative laughter at Reagan's answer.*

In the aftermath of the second debate, the Reagan campaign sailed smoothly to a landslide victory in November. The president defeated Mondale by 525 electoral votes to 13 electoral votes and by 58.8 percent to 40.6 percent in the popular vote. ~

Mrs. Dorothy S. Ridings, Chair, The League of Women Voters Education Fund: Good evening. Good evening from the Municipal Auditorium in Kansas City. I'm Dorothy Ridings, the President of the League of Women Voters, the sponsor of this final Presidential debate of the 1984 campaign between Republican Ronald Reagan and Democrat Walter Mondale. Our panelists for tonight's debate on defense and foreign policy issues are Georgie Anne Geyer, syndicated columnist for Universal Press Syndicate, Marvin Kalb, chief

diplomatic correspondent for NBC News, Morton Kondracke, executive editor of *The New Republic* magazine, and Henry Trewhitt, diplomatic correspondent for *The Baltimore Sun*. Edwin Newman, formerly of NBC News and now a syndicated columnist for King Features, is our moderator. Ed.

Mr. Edwin Newman, King Features Syndicate: Dorothy Ridings, thank you. A brief word about our procedure tonight. The first question will go to Mr. Mondale. He will have two and a half minutes to reply. Then the panel member who put the question will ask a follow-up. The answer to that will be limited to one minute. After that, the same question will be put to President Reagan. Again, there will be a follow-up, and then each man will have one minute for rebuttal. The second question will go to President Reagan first. After that, the alternating will continue. At the end there will be four-minute summations, with President Reagan going last. We have asked the questioners to be brief. Let's begin. Ms. Geyer, your question to Mr. Mondale.

[Central America]

Ms. Georgie Anne Geyer, Universal Press Syndicate: Mr. Mondale, two related questions on the crucial issue of Central America. You and the Democratic Party have said that the only policy toward the horrendous civil wars in Central America should be on the economic development and negotiations, with perhaps a quarantine of Marxist Nicaragua. Do you believe that these answers would in any way solve the bitter conflicts there? Do you really believe that there is no need to resort to force at all? Are not these solutions to Central America's gnawing problems simply, again, too weak and too late?

Former Vice President Mondale: I believe that the question oversimplifies the difficulties of what we must do in Central America. Our objectives ought to be to strengthen the democracies, to stop Communist and other extremist influences, and stabilize the community in that area.

To do that, we need a three-pronged attack. One is military assistance to our friends who are being pressured. Secondly, a strong and sophisticated economic aid program and human rights program that offers a better life and a sharper alternative to the alternative offered by the totalitarians who oppose us. And finally, a strong diplomatic effort that pursues the possibilities of peace in the area. That's one of the big disagreements that we have with the President—that they have not pursued the diplomatic opportunities, either within El Salvador or between the countries, and have lost time during which we might have been able to achieve a peace.

This brings up the whole question of what Presidential leadership is all about. I think the lesson in Central America—this recent embarrassment in Nicaragua, where we are giving instructions for hired assassins, hiring criminals, and the rest—all of this has strengthened our opponents. A President must not only assure that we're tough, but we must also be wise and smart in the exercise of that power.

We saw the same thing in Lebanon, where we spent a good deal of America's assets. But because the leadership of this Government did not pursue wise policies, we have been humiliated and our opponents are stronger. The bottom line of national strength is that the President must be in command. He must lead. And when a President doesn't know that submarine missiles are recallable, says that 70 percent of our strategic forces are conventional, discovers three years into his Administration that our arms control efforts have failed because he didn't know that most Soviet missiles were on land—

these are things a President must know to command. A President is called the Commander in Chief. He is called that because he is supposed to be in charge of the facts and run our Government and strengthen our nation.

Ms. Geyer: Mr. Mondale, if I could broaden the question just a little bit. Since World War II, every conflict that we as Americans have been involved with has been in nonconventional or traditional terms—military terms. The Central American wars are very much in the same pattern as China, as Lebanon, as Iran, as Cuba in the early days. Do you see any possibility that we are going to realize the change in warfare in our time or react to it in those terms?

Mr. Mondale: We absolutely must, which is why I responded to your first question the way I did. It's more—it's much more complex. You must understand the region, you must understand the politics of the area, you must provide a strong alternative, and you must show strength—and all at the same time. That's why I object to the covert action in Nicaragua. That's a classic example of a strategy that's embarrassed us, strengthened our opposition, and it undermined the moral authority of our people and our country in the region. Strength requires knowledge, command. We've seen, in the Nicaraguan example, a policy that has actually hurt us, strengthened our opposition, and undermined the moral authority of our country in that region.

Ms. Geyer: Mr. President, in the last few months it has seemed more and more that your policies in Central America were beginning to work. Yet, just at this moment, we are confronted with the extraordinary story of a C.I.A. guerrilla manual for the anti-Sandinista Contras whom we are backing which advocates not only assassinations of Sandinistas, but the hiring of criminals to assassinate the guerrillas we are supporting in order to create martyrs. Is this not, in effect, our own state-supported terrorism?

President Reagan: No, and I'm glad you asked that question, because I know it's on many people's minds. I have ordered an investigation. I know that the C.I.A. is already going forward with one. We have a gentleman down in Nicaragua who is on contract to the C.I.A., advising supposedly on military tactics of the Contras. And he drew up this manual. It was turned over to the Agency head in—of the C.I.A. in Nicaragua to be printed. And a number of pages were excised by that Agency head there—the man in charge—and he sent it on up here to C.I.A., where more pages were excised before it was printed. But some way or other, there were 12 of the original copies that got out down there and were not submitted for this printing process of the C.I.A. Now, those are the details as we have them. And as soon as we have an investigation and find out where any blame lies for the few that did not get excised or changed, we certainly are going to do something about that. We will take the proper action at the proper time.

I was very interested to hear about Central America and our process down there, and I thought for a moment that instead of a debate I was going to find Mr. Mondale in complete agreement with what we're doing. Because the plan that he has outlined is the one that we have been following for quite some time, including diplomatic processes throughout Central America and working closely with the Contadora Group. So I can only tell you, about the manual, that we're not in the habit of assigning guilt before there has been proper evidence produced and proof of that guilt. But if guilt is established— whoever is guilty—we will treat with that situation then, and they will be removed.

Ms. Geyer: Well, Mr. President, you are implying then, that the C.I.A. in Nicaragua is directing the Contras

there? I would also like to ask whether having the C.I.A. investigate its own manual in such a sensitive area is not sort of like sending the fox into the chicken coop a second time?

Mr. Reagan: I'm afraid I misspoke when I said "a C.I.A. head in Nicaragua." There is not someone there directing all of this activity. There are, as you know, C.I.A. men stationed in other countries in the world, and certainly in Central America. And so it was a man down there in that area that this was delivered to, and he recognized that what was in that manual was in direct contravention of my own executive order in December of 1981 that we would have nothing to do with regard to political assassinations.

Mr. Newman: Mr. Mondale, your rebuttal.

Mr. Mondale: What is a President charged with doing when he takes his oath of office? He raises his right hand and takes an oath of office to take care to faithfully execute the laws of the land. The President can't know everything, but a President has to know those things that are essential to his leadership and the enforcement of our laws.

This manual, several thousands of which were produced, was distributed, ordering political assassinations, hiring of criminals, and other forms of terrorism. Some of it was excised, but the part dealing with political terrorism was continued. How can this happen? How can something this serious occur in an Administration and have a President of the United States, in a situation like this, say he didn't know? A President must know these things. I don't know which is worse—not knowing or knowing and not stopping it. And what about the mining of the harbors in Nicaragua, which violated international law? This has hurt this country, and a President is supposed to command.

Mr. Newman: Mr. President, your rebuttal.

Mr. Reagan: Yes. I have so many things there to respond to, I'm going to pick out something you said earlier. You've been all over the country repeating something that I will admit the press has also been repeating—that I believe that nuclear missiles could be fired and then called back. I never, ever conceived of such a thing. I never said any such thing. In a discussion of our strategic arms negotiations, I said the submarines carrying missiles and airplanes carrying missiles were more conventional type weapons, not as destabilizing as the land-based missiles, and that they were also weapons that ... or carriers, that if they were sent out and there was a change, you could call them back before they had launched their missiles. But I hope that from here on you will no longer be saying that particular thing, which is absolutely false. How anyone could think that any sane person would believe you could call back a nuclear missile, I think, is as ridiculous as the whole concept has been. So, thank you for giving me a chance to straighten the record. I'm sure that you appreciate that.

Mr. Newman: Mr. Kalb ... Mr. Kalb, your question to President Reagan.

[Soviet Union]

Mr. Marvin Kalb, NBC News: Mr. President, you have often described the Soviet Union as a powerful, evil empire intent on world domination. But this year you have said, and I quote, "If they want to keep their Mickey Mouse system, that's O.K. with me." Which is it, Mr. President? Do you want to contain them within their present borders, and perhaps try to reestablish détente or what goes for détente, or do you really want to roll back their empire?

Mr. Reagan: I have said on a number of occasions exactly what I believe about the Soviet Union. I retract nothing that I have said. I believe that many of the things they have done are evil in any concept of morality that we have. But I also recognize that as the two great superpowers in the world, we have to live with each other. And I told Mr. Gromyko [Andrei Gromyko, Foreign Minister, U.S.S.R.] we don't like their system, and they sure better not try to change ours. But, between us, we can either destroy the world or we can save it. And I suggested that certainly it was to their common interest, along with ours, to avoid a conflict and to attempt to save the world and remove the nuclear weapons. And I think that, perhaps, we established a little better understanding.

I think that in dealing with the Soviet Union one has to be realistic. I know that Mr. Mondale in the past has made statements as if they were just people like ourselves, and if we were kind and good and did something nice, they would respond accordingly. And the result was unilateral disarmament. We canceled the B-1 under the previous Administration. What did we get for it? Nothing. The Soviet Union has been engaged in the biggest military buildup in the history of man at the same time that we tried the policy of unilateral disarmament—of weakness, if you will. And now we are putting up a defense of our own. And I've made it very plain to them: we seek no superiority. We simply are going to provide a deterrent so that it will be too costly for them if they are nursing any ideas of aggression against us.

Now, they claim they are not. And I made it plain to them, we're not. But this ... there's been no change in my attitude at all. I just thought, when I came into office, it was time that there was some realistic talk to and about the Soviet Union. And we did get their attention.

Mr. Kalb: Mr. President, perhaps the other side of the coin—a related question, sir. Since World War II, the vital interests of the United States have always been defined by treaty commitments and by Presidential proclamations. Aside from what is obvious—such as NATO, for example—which countries, which regions in the world do you regard as vital national interests of this country—meaning that you would send American troops to fight there if they were in danger?

Mr. Reagan: Ah, well, now you've added a hypothetical there at the end, Mr. Kalb, about that—where we would send troops in to fight. I am not going to make the decision as to what the tactics could be. But obviously, there are a number of areas in the world that are of importance to us. One is the Middle East. And that is of interest to the whole Western world and the industrialized nations, because of the great supply of energy on which so many depend there. The ... our neighbors here in America are vital to us. We're working right now and trying to be of help in southern Africa with regard to the independence of Namibia and the removal of the Cuban surrogates—the thousands of them—from Angola. So, I can say there are a great many interests. I believe that we have a great interest in the Pacific Basin. That is where I think the future of the world lies. But I am not going to pick out one and in advance hypothetically say, "Oh yes. We would send troops there." I don't want to send troops any place—

Mr. Newman: I'm sorry, Mr. President. Your time was up.

Mr. Kalb: Mr. Mondale, you have described the Soviet leaders as, and I'm quoting, "cynical, ruthless, and dangerous," suggesting an almost total lack of trust in them. In that case, what makes you think that the annual summit meetings with them that you've proposed will result in agreements that would satisfy the interests of this country?

Mr. Mondale: Because the only type of agreements to reach with the Soviet Union are the types that are specifically defined, so we know exactly what they must do, subject to full verification—which means we know every day whether they're living up to it, and follow-ups wherever we find suggestions that they're violating it, and the strongest possible terms. I have no illusions about the Soviet Union leadership or the nature of that state. They are a tough and a ruthless adversary, and we must be prepared to meet that challenge. And I would.

Where I part with the President is that, despite all of those differences, we must—as past Presidents before this one have done—meet on the common ground of survival. And that's where the president has opposed practically every arms control agreement by every President of both political parties since the bomb went off. And he now completes this term with no progress toward arms control at all, but with a very dangerous arms race under way instead. There are now over 2,000 more warheads pointed at us today than there were when he was sworn in. And that does not strengthen us. We must be very, very realistic in the nature of that leadership, but we must grind away and talk to find ways to reducing these differences, particularly where arms races are concerned and other dangerous exercises of Soviet power.

There will be no unilateral disarmament under my Administration. I will keep this nation strong. I understand exactly what the Soviets are up to. But that, too, is a part of national strength. To do that, a President must know what is essential to command and to leadership and to strength. And that's where the President's failure to master, in my opinion, the essential elements of arms control has cost us dearly. These four years.... Three years into this Administration, he said he just discovered that most Soviet missiles are on land, and that's why his proposal didn't work. I invite the American people tomorrow ... because I will issue the statement quoting President Reagan. He said exactly what I said he said. He said that these missiles were less dangerous than ballistic missiles because you could fire them and you could recall them if you decide there had been a miscalculation.

Mr. Newman: I'm sorry, Mr.—

Mr. Mondale: A President must know those things.

[Eastern Europe]

Mr. Kalb: A related question, Mr. Mondale, on Eastern Europe: Do you accept the conventional diplomatic wisdom that Eastern Europe is a Soviet sphere of influence? And, if you do, what could a Mondale Administration realistically do to help the people of Eastern Europe achieve the human rights that were guaranteed to them as a result of the Helsinki Accords?

Mr. Mondale: I think the essential strategy of the United States ought not accept any Soviet control over Eastern Europe. We ought to deal with each of these countries separately. We ought to pursue strategies with each of them, economic and the rest, that help them pull away from their dependence upon the Soviet Union. Where the Soviet Union has acted irresponsibly, as they have in many of those countries—especially, recently, in Poland—I believe we ought to insist that Western credits extended to the Soviet Union bear the market rate. Make the Soviets pay for their irresponsibility. That is a very important objective—to make certain that we continue to look forward to progress toward greater independence by these nations, and work with each of them separately.

Mr. Newman: Mr. President, your rebuttal.

Mr. Reagan: Yes. I'm not going to continue trying to respond to these repetitions of the falsehoods that have already been stated here. But with regard to whether Mr. Mondale would be strong, as he said he would be, I know that he has a commercial out where he is appearing on the deck of the [U.S.S.] *Nimitz* and watching the F-14s take off, and that's an image of strength. Except that if he had had his way when the *Nimitz* was being planned, he would have been deep in the water out there, because there wouldn't have been any *Nimitz* to stand on. He was against it. He was against the F-14 fighter; he was against the M-1 tank; he was against the B-1 bomber; he wanted to cut the salary of all of the military; he wanted to bring home half of the American forces in Europe. And he has a record of weakness with regard to our national defense that is second to none. Indeed, he was on that side virtually throughout all his years in the Senate, and he opposed even President Carter when, toward the end of his term, President Carter wanted to increase the defense budget.

Mr. Newman: Mr. Mondale, your rebuttal.

Mr. Mondale: Mr. President, I accept your commitment to peace, but I want you to accept my commitment to a strong national defense. I have proposed a budget which would increase our nation's strength by ... in real terms, by double that of the Soviet Union. I'll tell you where we disagree. It is true, over ten years ago, I voted to delay production of the F-14, and I'll tell you why. The plane wasn't flying supposed to ... the way it was supposed to be. It was a waste of money. Your definition of national strength is to throw money at the Defense Department. My definition of national strength is to make certain that a dollar spent buys us a dollar's worth of defense. There is a big difference between the two of us. A President must manage that budget. I will keep us strong, but you'll not do that unless you command that budget and make certain we get the strength that we need. When you pay out $500 for a $5 hammer, you're not buying strength.

Mr. Newman: I would ask the audience not to applaud. All it does is take up time that we would like to devote to the debate. Mr. Kondracke, your question to Mr. Mondale.

[Use of Military Force]

Mr. Morton M. Kondracke, *The New Republic:* Mr. Mondale, in an address earlier this year, you said that before this country resorts to military force, and I'm quoting, "American interests should be sharply defined, publicly supported, Congressionally sanctioned, militarily feasible, internationally defensible, open to independent scrutiny, and alert to regional history." Now, aren't you setting up such a gauntlet of tests here that adversaries could easily suspect that as President you would never use force to protect American interests?

Mr. Mondale: No. As a matter of fact, I believe every one of those standards is essential to the exercise of power by this country. And we can see that in both Lebanon and in Central America. In Lebanon, this President exercised American power all right, but the management of it was such that our Marines were killed; we had to leave in humiliation; the Soviet Union became stronger; terrorists became emboldened. And it was because they did not think through how power should be exercised, did not have the American public with them on a plan that worked, that we ended up the way we did.

Similarly, in Central America, what we're doing in Nicaragua with this covert war—which the Congress, including many Republicans, have tried to stop—is finally end up with the public

definition of American power that hurts us, where we get associated with political assassins and the rest. We have to decline, for the first time in modern history, jurisdiction of the World Court, because they will find us guilty of illegal actions.

And our enemies are strengthened from all of this. We need to be strong. We need to be prepared to use that strength. But we must understand that we are a democracy. We are a Government by the people, and when we move, it should be for very severe and extreme reasons that serve our national interest and end up with a stronger country behind us. It is only in that way that we can persevere.

Mr. Kondracke: You've been quoted as saying that you might quarantine Nicaragua. I'd like to know what that means. Would you stop Soviet ships, as President Kennedy did in 1962, and wouldn't that be more dangerous than President Reagan's covert war?

Mr. Mondale: What I'm referring to there is the mutual self-defense provisions that exist in the Inter-American treaty, the so-called Rio pact, that permits the nations that are friends in that region to combine to take steps, diplomatic and otherwise, to prevent Nicaragua when she acts irresponsibly in asserting power in other parts outside of her border . . . to take those steps, whatever they might be, to stop it.

The Nicaraguans must know that it is the policy of our government that those . . . that that leadership must stay behind the boundaries of their nation, not interfere in other nations. And by working with all of the nations in the region, unlike the policies of this Administration—and unlike the President said, they have *not* supported negotiations in that region—we will be much stronger, because we will have the moral authority that goes with those efforts.

Mr. Kondracke: President Reagan, you introduced U.S. forces into Lebanon as neutral peacekeepers, but then you made them combatants on the side of the Lebanese Government. Eventually, you were forced to withdraw them under fire, and now Syria, a Soviet ally, is dominant in the country. Doesn't Lebanon represent a major failure on the part of your Administration and raise serious questions about your capacity as a foreign policy strategist and as Commander in Chief?

Mr. Reagan: No, Morton, I don't agree to all of those things. First of all, when we and our allies—the Italians, the French, and the United Kingdom—went into Lebanon, we went in there at the request of what was left of the Lebanese Government, to be a stabilizing force while they tried to establish a government. But the first—pardon me—the first time we went in, we went in at their request, because the war was going on right in Beirut between Israel and the P.L.O. terrorists. Israel could not be blamed for that. Those terrorists had been violating their northern border consistently, and Israel chased them all the way to there. Then, we went in with a multinational force to help remove—and did remove—more than 13,000 of those terrorists from Lebanon. We departed, and then the Government of Lebanon asked us back in as a stabilizing force while they established a government and sought to get the foreign forces all the way out of Lebanon, and that they could then take care of their own borders.

And we were succeeding. We were there for the better part of a year. Our position happened to be at the airport. Oh, there were occasional snipings and sometimes some artillery fire. But we did not engage in conflict that was out of line with our mission. I will never send troops anywhere on a mission of that kind without telling them that if somebody shoots at them, they can darn well shoot back. And this is what we did. We never initiated any kind of action. We defended ourselves there.

But we were succeeding to the point that the Lebanese Government had been organized. If you will remember, there were the meetings in Geneva in which they began to meet with the hostile factional forces and try to put together some kind of a peace plan.

We were succeeding, and that was why the terrorist acts began. There are forces there—and that includes Syria, in my mind—who don't want us to succeed, who don't want that kind of a peace with a dominant Lebanon, dominant over its own territory. And so the terrorist acts began, and led to the one great tragedy when they were killed in that suicide bombing of the building. Then the multilateral force withdrew for only one reason: we withdrew because we were no longer able to carry out the mission for which we had been sent in. But we went in in the interest of peace, and to keep Israel and Syria from getting into the sixth war between them. And I have no apologies for our going on a peace mission.

[Lebanon and Terrorism]

Mr. Kondracke: Mr. President, four years ago you criticized President Carter for ignoring ample warnings that our diplomats in Iran might be taken hostage. Haven't you done exactly the same thing in Lebanon, not once, but three times, with 300 Americans not hostages but dead. And you vowed swift retaliation against terrorists, but doesn't our lack of response suggest that you're just bluffing?

Mr. Reagan: Morton, no. I think there's a great difference between the Government of Iran threatening our diplomatic personnel—and there is a Government that you can see and can put your hand on. In the terrorist situation, there are terrorist factions all over.... In a recent 30-day period, 37 terrorist acts in 20 countries have been committed. The most recent has been the one in Brighton [England]. In dealing with terrorists, yes, we want to retaliate, but only if we can put our finger on the people responsible and not endanger the lives of innocent civilians there in the various communities and in the city of Beirut where these terrorists are operating. I have just signed legislation to add to our ability to deal, along with our allies, with this terrorist problem. And it's going to take all the nations together, just as when we banded together we pretty much resolved the whole problem of skyjackings some time ago. Well, the red light went on. I could have gone on forever.

Mr. Newman: Mr. Mondale, your rebuttal.

Mr. Mondale: Groucho Marx said, "Who do you believe—me or your own eyes?" And what we have in Lebanon is something that the American people have seen. The Joint Chiefs urged the President not to put our troops in that barracks because they were undefensible. The urged . . . they went to him five days before they were killed and said, "Please take them out of there." The Secretary of State admitted that this morning. He did not do so. The report following the explosion of the barracks disclosed that we had not taken any of the steps that we should have taken. That was the second time. Then the Embassy was blown up a few weeks ago, and once again, none of the steps that should have been taken were taken. And we were warned five days before that explosives were on their way, and they weren't taken.

The terrorists have won each time. The President told the terrorists he was going to retaliate. He didn't. They called their bluff. And the bottom line is, the United States left in humiliation and our enemies are stronger.

Mr. Newman: Mr. President, your rebuttal.

Mr. Reagan: Yes. First of all, Mr. Mondale should know that the Presi-

dent of the United States did not order the Marines into that barracks. That was a command decision made by the commanders on the spot and based with what they thought was best for the men there. That is one.

On the other things that you've just said about the terrorists, I'm tempted to ask you what you would do. These are unidentified people, and, after the bomb goes off, they're blown to bits because they are suicidal individuals who think that they're going to go to paradise if they perpetrate such an act and lose their life in doing it. We are going to . . . as I say, we're busy trying to find the centers where these operations stem from, and retaliation will be taken. But we are not going to simply kill some people to say, "Oh, look—we got even." We want to know, when we retaliate, that we're retaliating with those who are responsible for the terrorist acts. And terrorist acts are such that our own United States Capitol in Washington has been bombed twice.

Mr. Newman: Mr. Trewhitt, your question to President Reagan.

[Age and Missiles]

Mr. Henry L. Trewhitt, *The Baltimore Sun:* Mr. President, I want to raise an issue that I think has been lurking out there for two or three weeks, and cast it specifically in national security terms. You already are the oldest President in history, and some of your staff say you were tired after your most recent encounter with Mister . . . Mr. Mondale. I recall, yet, that President Kennedy, who had to go for days on end with very little sleep during the Cuba missile crisis. . . . Is there any doubt in your mind that you would be able to function in such circumstances?

Mr. Reagan: Not at all, Mr. Trewhitt. And I want you to know that also, I will not make age an issue of this campaign. I am not going to exploit, for political purposes, my opponent's youth and inexperience.

If I still have time, I might add, Mr. Trewhitt, I might add that it was Seneca or it was Cicero—I don't know which—that said, "If it was not for the elders correcting the mistakes of the young, there would be no state."

Mr. Trewhitt: Mr. President, I'd like to head for the fence and try to catch that one before it goes over, but ... but I'll go on to another question.

The ... you and Mr. Mondale have already disagreed about what you had to say about recalling submarine-launched missiles. There's another ... a similar issue out there that relates to your ... it is said, at least, that you were unaware that the Soviet retaliatory power was based on land-based missiles. First, is that correct? Secondly, if it is correct, have you informed yourself in the meantime? And third, is it even necessary for the President to be so intimately involved in strategic details?

Mr. Reagan: Yes. This had to do with our disarmament talks. And the whole controversy about land missiles came up because we thought that the strategic nuclear weapons, the most destabilizing, are the land-based. You put your thumb on a button and somebody blows up twenty minutes later. So, we thought that it would be simpler to negotiate first with those, and then we made it plain, a second phase—take up the submarine-launched ... the air ... the airborne missiles. The Soviet Union —to our surprise, and not just mine— made it plain when we brought this up that they placed, they thought, a greater reliance on the land-based missiles, and therefore they wanted to take up all three. And we agreed; we said, "All right, if that's what you want to do." But it was a surprise to us because they outnumbered us 64 to 36 in submarines and 20 percent more bombers capable of carrying nuclear missiles than we had.

So, why should we believe that they had placed that much more reliance on land-based? But even after we gave in and said, "All right, let's discuss it all," they walked away from the table. We didn't.

Mr. Trewhitt: Mr. Mondale, I'm going to hang in there. Should the President's age and stamina be an issue in the political campaign?

Mr. Mondale: No, and I have not made it an issue, nor should it be. What's at issue here is the President's application of his authority to understand what a President must know to lead this nation, secure our defense, and make the decisions and the judgments that are necessary.

A minute ago, the President quoted Cicero, I believe. I want to quote somebody a little closer to home, Harry Truman. He said, "The buck stops here." We just heard the President's answer for the problems at the barracks in Lebanon, where 241 Marines were killed. What happened? First, the Joint Chiefs of Staff went to the President, said, "Don't put those troops there." They did it. And then, five days before the troops were killed, they went back to the President through the Secretary of Defense and said, "Please, Mr. President, take those troops out of there because we can't defend them." They didn't do it. And we know what's ... what happened. After that, once again our Embassy was exploded. This is the fourth time this has happened—an identical attack in the same region, despite warnings, even public warnings from the terrorists. Who's in charge? Who's handling this matter? That's my main point.

Now, on arms control, we're completing four years. This is the first Administration since the bomb went off that made no progress. We have an arms race under way instead. A President has to lead his Government or it won't be done. Different people with different views fight with each other. For three and a half years, this Administration avoided arms control, resisted tabling arms control proposals that had any ... hope of agreeing, rebuked their negotiator in 1981 when he came close to an agreement, at least in principle, on medium-range weapons. And we have this arms race under way.

And a recent book that just came out by the ... perhaps the nation's most respected author in this field, Strobe Talbott, called "The Deadly Gambits," concludes that this President has failed to master the essential details needed to command and lead us, both in terms of security and terms of arms control. That's why they call the President the Commander in Chief. Good intentions, I grant, but it takes more than that. You must be tough and smart.

Mr. Trewhitt: This question of leadership keeps arising in different forms in this discussion already. And the President, Mr. Mondale, has called you "whining and vacillating"—among the more charitable phrases, "weak," I believe. It is ... it is a question of leadership, and he has made the point that you have not repudiated some of the semidiplomatic activity of the Reverend Jackson, particularly in Central America. Do you ... did you approve of his diplomatic activity, and are you prepared to repudiate him now?

Mr. Mondale: I ... I read his statement the other day. I don't admire Fidel Castro at all, and I've said that. Che Guevara was a contemptible figure in civilization's history. I know the Cuban state as a police state, and all my life I've worked in a way that demonstrates that. But Jesse Jackson is an independent person. I don't control him. And let's talk about people we do control. In the last debate, the Vice President of the United States said that I said the Marines had died shamefully and died in shame in Lebanon. I demanded an apology from Vice President Bush because I had instead honored these young men, grieved for their fam-

ilies, and think they were wonderful Americans that honored us all. What does the President have to say about taking responsibility for a Vice President who won't apologize for something like that?

Mr. Newman: Mr. President, your rebuttal.

Mr. Reagan: Yes. I know it'll come as a surprise to Mr. Mondale, but I am in charge. And, as a matter of fact, we haven't avoided arms control talks with the Soviet Union. Very early in my Administration I proposed—and I think something that had never been proposed by any previous Administration—I proposed a total elimination of intermediate-range missiles, where the Soviets had better than a ten ... and still have better than a ten-to-one advantage over the Allies in Europe. When they protested that and suggested a smaller number, perhaps, I went along with that. The so-called negotiation that you said I walked out on was the so-called "walk in the wood" between one of our representatives and one of the Soviet Union, and it wasn't me that turned it down; the Soviet Union disavowed it.

Mr. Newman: Mr. Mondale, your rebuttal.

Mr. Mondale: Now, there are two distinguished authors in arms control in this country. There are many others, but two that I want to cite tonight. One is Strobe Talbott in his classic book, "The Deadly Gambits." The other is John Newhouse, who's one of the most distinguished arms control specialists in our country. Both said that this Administration turned down the "walk in the woods" agreement first, and that would have been a perfect agreement from the standpoint of the United States and Europe and our security. When Mr. Nitze [Paul Nitze, Chairman, Intermediate Range Nuclear Forces Negotiations], a good negotiator, returned, he was rebuked and his boss was fired.

This is the kind of leadership that we've had in this Administration in the most deadly issue of our times. Now we have a runaway arms race. All they've got to show for four years in U.S.-Soviet relations is one meeting in the last weeks of an Administration and nothing before. They're tough negotiators, but all previous Presidents have made progress. This one has not.

[Illegal Immigration]

Mr. Newman: Miss Geyer, your question to Mr. Mondale.

Ms. Geyer: Mr. Mondale, many analysts are now saying that actually our number one foreign policy problem today is one that remains almost totally unrecognized: massive illegal immigration from economically collapsing countries. They are saying that it is the only real territorial threat to the American nation-state. You yourself said in the 1970s that we had a, quote, "hemorrhage on our borders," unquote. Yet today you have backed off any immigration reform, such as the balanced and highly crafted Simpson-Mazzoli bill. Why? What would you do instead today, if anything?

Mr. Mondale: This is a very serious problem in our country, and it has to be dealt with. I object to that part of the Simpson-Mazzoli bill which I think is very unfair and would prove to be so. That is the part that requires employers to determine the citizenship of an employee before they're hired. I am convinced that the result of this would be that people who are Hispanic, people who have different languages or speak with an accent, would find it difficult to be employed. I think that's wrong. We've never had citizenship tests in our country before, and I don't think we should have a citizenship card today. That is counterproductive.

I do support the other aspects of the Simpson-Mazzoli bill that strengthen enforcement at the border, strengthen other ways of dealing with undocumented workers in this ... in this difficult area, and dealing with the problem of settling people who have lived here for many, many years and do not have an established status. I have further strongly recommended that this Administration do something it has not done, and that is to strengthen enforcement at the border, strengthen the officials in this Government that deal with undocumented workers, and to do so in a way that's responsible and within the Constitution of the United States. We need an answer to this problem, but it must be an American answer that is consistent with justice and due process. Everyone in this room practically, here tonight, is an immigrant. We came here loving this nation, serving it, and it has served all of our most bountiful dreams. And one of those dreams is justice. And if we need a measure, and I will support a measure that brings about those objectives but voids that one aspect that I think is very serious.

The second part is to maintain and improve our relations with our friends to the south. We cannot solve this problem all on our own. And that's why the failure of this Administration to deal in effective and goodfaith ways with Mexico, with Costa Rica, with the other nations, in trying to find a peaceful settlement to the dispute in Central America has undermined our capacity to effectively to deal diplomatic in this ... diplomatically in this area, as well.

Ms. Geyer: Sir, people as well-balanced and just as Father Theodore Hesburgh at Notre Dame [University of Notre Dame], who headed the Select Commission on Immigration, have pointed out repeatedly that there will be no immigration reform without employer sanctions, because it would be an unbalanced bill and there would be simply no way to reinforce it.

However, putting that aside for the moment, your critics have also said repeatedly that you have not gone along with the bill, or with any immigration reform, because of the Hispanic groups or Hispanic leadership groups, who actually do not represent what the Hispanic Americans want—because polls show that they overwhelmingly want some kind of immigration reform. Can you say, or . . . how can you justify your position on this? And how do you respond to the criticism that this is another, or that this is an example of your flip-flopping and giving in to special interest groups at the expense of the American nation?

Mr. Mondale: I think you're right that the polls show that the majority of Hispanics want that bill. So, I'm not doing it for political reasons. I'm doing it because all my life I've fought for a system of justice in this country, a system in which every American has a chance to achieve the fullness in life without discrimination. This bill imposes upon employers the responsibility of determining whether somebody who applies for a job is an American or not. And, just inevitably, they're going to be reluctant to hire Hispanics or people with a different accent.

If I were dealing with politics here, the polls show the American people want this. I am for reform in this area, for tough enforcement at the border, and for many other aspects of the Simpson-Mazzoli bill. But all my life, I've fought for a fair nation, and despite the politics of it, I stand where I stand and I think I'm right. And before this fight is over, we're going to come up with a better bill, a more effective bill that does not undermine the liberties of our people.

Ms. Geyer: Mr. President, you, too, have said that our borders are out of control. Yet, this fall, you allowed the Simpson-Mazzoli bill—which would at least have minimally protected our borders and the rights of citizenship—because of a relatively unimportant issue of reimbursement to the states for legalized aliens. Given that, may I ask what priority can we expect you to give this forgotten national security element? How sincere are you in your efforts to control, in effect, the nation-state that is the United States?

Mr. Reagan: Georgie Anne, we, believe me, supported the Simpson-Mazzoli bill strongly, and the bill that came out of the Senate. However, there were things added in the House side that we felt made it less of a good bill—as a matter of fact, made it a bad bill. And in conference, we stayed with them in conference all the way to where even Senator Simpson [Alan Kooi Simpson, Republican, Wyoming] did not want the bill in the manner in which it would come out of the conference committee. There were a number of things in there that weakened that bill. I can't go into detail about them here. But it is true, our borders are out of control. It is also true that this has been a situation on our borders back through a number of Administrations. And I supported this bill. I believe in the idea of amnesty for those who have put down roots and who have lived here, even though some time back they . . . they may have entered illegally.

With regard to the employer sanctions, this . . . we must have that, not only to ensure that we can identify the illegal aliens, but also, while some keep protesting about what it would do to employers, there is another employer that we shouldn't be so concerned about. And these are employers, down through the years, who have encouraged the illegal entry into this country because they then hire these individuals, and hire them at starvation wages, and with none of the benefits that we think are normal and natural for workers in our country. And the individuals can't complain because of their illegal status. We don't think that those people should be allowed to continue operating free. And this was why the provisions that we had in with regard to sanctions and so forth. And I'm going to do everything I can—and all of us in the Administration are—to join in again, when Congress is back at it, to get an immigration bill that will give us, once again, control of our borders.

And with regard to friendship below the border and with the countries down there—yes, no Administration that I know has established the relationship that we have with our Latin friends. But as long as they have an economy that leaves so many people in dire poverty and unemployment, they are going to seek that employment across our borders. And we work with those other countries.

[Population Explosion]

Ms. Geyer: Mr. President, the experts also say that the situation today is terribly different, quantitatively, qualitatively different from what is has been in the past because of the gigantic population growth. For instance, Mexico's population will go from about 60 million today to 120 million at the turn of the century. Many of these people will be coming into the United States not as citizens, but as illegal workers.

You have repeatedly said, recently, that you believe that Armageddon, the destruction of the world, may be imminent in our times. Do you ever feel that we are in for an Armageddon, or a . . . a situation, a time of anarchy regarding the population explosion in the world?

Mr. Reagan: No, as a matter of fact, the population explosion . . . and if you will look at the actual figures, has been vastly exaggerated . . . overexaggerated. As a matter of fact, there are some pretty scientific and solid figures about how much space there still is in the world and how many more people we can have. It's almost

like going back to the Malthusian theory, when even then they were saying that everyone would starve, with the limited population they had then. But the problem of population growth is one here with regard to our immigration, and we have been the safety valve, whether we wanted to or not, with the illegal entry here, in Mexico, where their population is increasing and they don't have an economy that can absorb them and provide the jobs. And this is what we're trying to work out, not only to protect our own borders, but have some kind of fairness and recognition of that problem.

Mr. Newman: Mr. Mondale, your rebuttal.

Mr. Mondale: One of the biggest problems today is that the countries to our south are so desperately poor that these people, who will almost lose their lives if they don't come north, come north despite all the risks. And if we're going to find a permanent, fundamental answer to this, it goes to American economic and trade policies to permit these nations to have a chance to get on their own two feet and to get prosperity so that they can have jobs for themselves and their people.

And that's why this enormous national debt, engineered by this Administration, is harming these countries and fueling this immigration. These high interest rates, real rates that have doubled under this Administration, have had the same effect on Mexico and so on. And the cost of repaying those debts is so enormous that it results in massive unemployment, hardship, and heartache. And that drives our friends to the north . . . to the south up into our region. And we need to end those deficits, as well.

Mr. Newman: Mr. President, your rebuttal.

Mr. Reagan: Well, my rebuttal is, I've heard the national debt blamed for a lot of things, but not for illegal immigration across our border, and it has nothing to do with it. But with regard to these high interest rates too, at least give us the recognition of the fact that when you left office, Mr. Mondale, they were 21.5 [percent], the prime rate. It's now 12.25 [percent], and I predict it will be coming down a little more shortly. So, we're trying to undo some of the things that your Administration did.

Mr. Newman: Mister ... no applause, please. Mr. Kalb, your question to President Reagan.

[A Nuclear Armageddon?]

Mr. Kalb: Mr. President, I'd like to pick up this Armageddon theme. You've been quoted as saying that you do believe, deep down, that we are heading for some kind of biblical Armageddon. Your Pentagon and your Secretary of Defense have plans for the United States to fight and prevail in a nuclear war. Do you feel that we are now heading, perhaps, for some kind of nuclear Armageddon, and do you feel that this country and the world could survive that kind of calamity?

Mr. Reagan: Mr. Kalb, I think what has been hailed as something I'm supposedly, as President, discussing as principle is the result of just some philosophical discussions with people who are interested in the same things, and that is the prophecies down through the years, the biblical prophecies of what would portend the coming of Armageddon and so forth, and the fact that a number of theologians, for the last decade or more, have believed that this was true, that the prophecies are coming together to portend that. But no one knows whether Armageddon ... those prophecies mean that Armageddon is a thousand years away or day after tomorrow. So, I have never seriously warned and said, "We must plan according to Armageddon."

Now, with regard to having to say whether we would try to survive in the event of a nuclear war, of course we would. But let me also point out that to several parliaments around the world, in Europe and in Asia, I have made a statement in ... to each one of them, and I'll repeat it here: A nuclear war cannot be won and must never be fought. And that is why we are maintaining a deterrent and trying to achieve a deterrent capacity to where no one would believe that they could start such a war and escape with limited damage. But the deterrent—and that's what it is for—is also what led me to propose what is now being called the "Star Wars" concept: to propose that we research to see if there isn't a defensive weapon that could defend against incoming missiles. And if such a defense could be found, wouldn't it be far more humanitarian to say that now we can defend against a nuclear war by destroying missiles instead of slaughtering millions of people?

["Star Wars" Technology]

Mr. Kalb: Mr. President, when you made that proposal, the so-called "Star Wars" proposal, you said, if I am not mistaken, that you would share this very supersophisticated technology with the Soviet Union. After all of the distrust over the years, sir, that you have expressed towards the Soviet Union, do you really expect anyone to take seriously that offer—that you would share the best of America's technology in this weapons area with our principal adversary?

Mr. Reagan: Why not? What if we did? And I hope we can. We're still researching. What if we come up with a weapon that renders those missiles obsolete? There has never been a weapon invented in the history of man that has not led to a defensive, a counterweapon.

But suppose we came up with that? Now, some people have said, "Ah, that would make a war imminent, because they would think that we could now launch a first strike, because we could defend against the enemy." But why not do what I have offered to do and ask the Soviet Union to do? Say, "Look, here's what we can do. We'll even give it to you. Now, will you sit down with us and once and for all get rid, all of us, of these nuclear weapons, and free mankind from that threat?" I think that would be the greatest use of a defensive weapon.

Mr. Kalb: Mr. Mondale, you have been very sharply critical of the President's strategic defense initiative. And yet, what is wrong with a major effort by this country to try to use its best technology to knock out as many incoming nuclear warheads as possible?

Mr. Mondale: First of all, let me sharply disagree with the President on sharing the most advanced, the most dangerous, the most important technology in America with the Soviet Union. We have had for many years, understandably, a system of restraints on high technology, because the Soviets are behind us. And any research or development along the "Star Wars" schemes would inevitably involve our most advanced computers, most advanced engineering, and the thought that we would share this with the Soviet Union is, in my opinion, a total nonstarter. I would not let the Soviet Union get their hands on it at all.

Now what's wrong with "Star Wars?" There's nothing wrong with the theory of it. If we could develop a principle that would say both sides could fire all their missiles and no one would get hurt. I suppose it's a good idea. But the fact of it is, we're so far away from research that even comes close to that, that the director of engineering research in the Defense Department said to get there, we would have to solve eight problems, each of which are more difficult than the atomic bomb and the Manhattan Project. It would cost something like a trillion dollars to test and deploy weapons.

The second thing is, this all assumes that the Soviets wouldn't respond in kind. And they always do. We don't get behind, they won't get behind, and that's been the tragic story of the arms race. We have more at stake in space satellites than they do. If we could stop right now the testing and the deployment of these space weapons—and the President's proposals go clear beyond research—if it was just research, we wouldn't have any argument, because maybe someday somebody will think of something. But to commit this nation to a build-up of antisatellite and space weapons at this time, and their crude state, would bring about an arms race that's very dangerous indeed.

One final point—the most dangerous aspect of this proposal is, for the first time, we would delegate to computers the decision as to whether to start a war. That's dead wrong. There wouldn't be time for a President to decide. It would be decided by these remote computers; it might be an oil fire, it might be a jet exhaust, the computer might decide it's a missile, and off we go. Why don't we stop this madness now and draw a line and keep the heavens free from war?

[Nuclear Freeze]

Mr. Kalb: Mr. Mondale, in this general area, sir, of arms control, President Carter's National Security Advisor, Zbig Brzezinski [Zbigniew Brzezinski] said, "A nuclear freeze is a hoax." Yet, the basis of your arms proposals, as I understand them, is a mutual and verifiable freeze on existing weapons systems. In your view, which specific weapons systems could be subject to a mutual and verifiable freeze, and which could not?

Mr. Mondale: Every system that is verifiable should be placed on the table for negotiations for an agreement. I would not agree to any negotiations or any agreement that involved conduct on the part of the Soviet Union that we couldn't verify every day. I would not agree to any agreement in which the United States' security interest was not fully recognized and supported. That's ... that's why we say "mutual and verifiable" freezes.

Now, why do I support the freeze? Because this ever-rising arms race madness makes both nations less secure. It's more difficult to defend this nation. It is putting a hair trigger on nuclear war. This Administration, by going into the "Star Wars" system, is going to add a dangerous new escalation. We have to be tough on the Soviet Union. But I think the American people—

Mr. Newman: Time is up, Mr. Mondale.

Mr. Mondale: —and the people of the Soviet Union want it to stop.

Mr. Newman: President Reagan, your rebuttal.

Mr. Reagan: Yes. My rebuttal, once again, is that this invention that has just been created here of how I would go about the rolling over for the Soviet Union ... no, Mr. Mondale. My idea would be, with that defensive weapon, that we would sit down with them and then say, "Now, are you willing to join us? Here's what we can. ..." Give them, give them a demonstration. And then say, "Here's what we can do," Now, if you're willing to join us in getting rid of all the nuclear weapons in the world, then we'll give you this one so that we would both know that no one can cheat; that we've both got something that if anyone tries to cheat. ... But when you keep "Star-Warring" it— I never suggested where the weapons should be or what kind. I'm not a scientist. I said, and the Joint Chiefs of Staff

agreed with me, that it was time for us to turn our research ability to seeing if we could not find this kind of a defensive weapon. And suddenly somebody says, "Oh, it's got to be up there, and it's 'Star Wars,'" and so forth. I don't know what it would be. But if we can come up with one, I think the world will be better off.

Mr. Newman: Mr. Mondale, your rebuttal.

Mr. Mondale: Well, that's what a President's supposed to know—where those weapons are going to be. If they're space weapons, I assume they'll be in space. If they're antisatellite weapons, I assume they're going to be an aid ... armed against antisatellites.

Now, this is the most dangerous technology that we possess. The Soviets try to spy on us, steal this stuff. And to give them technology of this kind, I disagree with. You haven't just accepted research, Mr. President. You've set up a strategic defense initiative, an agency. You're beginning to test. You're talking about deploying. You're asking for a budget of some $30 billion for this purpose. This is an arms escalation, and we will be better off—far better off—if we stop right now, because we have more to lose in space than they do. If someday somebody comes along with an answer, that's something else. But that there would be an answer in our lifetime is unimaginable. Why do we start things that we know the Soviets will match and make us all less secure? That's what the President is for.

Mr. Newman: Mr. Kondracke, your question to Mr. Mondale.

Mr. Kondracke: Mr. Mondale, you say that with respect to the Soviet Union, you want to negotiate a mutual nuclear freeze. Yet you would unilaterally give up the MX missile and the B-1 bomber before the talks have even begun. And you have announced, in advance, that reaching an agreement with the Soviets is the most important thing in the world to you. Aren't you giving away half the store before you even sit down to talk?

Mr. Mondale: No. As a matter of fact, we have a vast range of technology and weaponry right now that provides all the bargaining chips that we need. And I support the air-launched cruise missile, ground-launched cruise missile, the Pershing missile, the Trident submarine, the D-5 submarine, the Stealth technology, the Midgetman—we have a whole range of technology. Why I disagree with the MX is that it's a sitting duck. It'll draw an attack. It puts a hair trigger . . . and it is a dangerous, destabilizing weapon. And the B-1 is similarly to be opposed, because for 15 years the Soviet Union has been preparing to meet the B-1. The Secretary of Defense himself said it would be a suicide mission if it were built.

Instead, I want to build the Midgetman, which is mobile and thus less vulnerable, contributing to stability, and a weapon that will give us security and contribute to an incentive for arms control. That's why I'm for Stealth technology: to build the Stealth bomber, which I've supported for years, that can penetrate the Soviet air defense system without any hope that they can perceive where it is because their radar system is frustrated. In other words, a President has to make choices. This makes us stronger.

The final point is, that we can use this money that we save on these weapons to spend on things that we really need. Our conventional strength in Europe is under strength. We need to strengthen that in order to assure our Western allies of our presence there—a strong defense—but also to diminish and reduce the likelihood of a commencement of a war and the use of nuclear weapons. It's in this way, by making wise choices, that we are stronger; we enhance the chances of arms control. Every President till this one has been able to do it. And this nation—the world—is more dangerous as a result.

Mr. Kondracke: I want to follow up on Mr. Kalb's question. It seems to me on the question of verifiability that you do have some problems with the extent of the freeze. It seems to me, for example, that testing would be very difficult to verify because the Soviets encode their telemetry; research would be impossible to verify by satellite, except with on-site inspection; and production of any weapon would be impossible to verify. Now, in view of that, what is going to be frozen?

Mr. Mondale: I will not agree to any arms control agreement, including a freeze, that's not verifiable. Let's take your warhead principle. The warhead principle—there've been counting rules for years. Whenever a weapon is tested we count the number of warheads on it, and whenever that warhead is used, we count that number warheads, whether they have that number or less on it or not. These are standard rules. I will not agree to any production restrictions or agreements unless we have the ability to verify those agreements. I don't trust the Russians. I believe that every agreement we reach must be verifiable, and I will not agree to anything that we cannot tell every day. In other words, we've got to be tough. But in order to stop this arms madness we've got to push ahead with tough negotiations that are verifiable, so that we know the Soviets are agreeing and living up to their agreement.

[Negotiating with Friends]

Mr. Kondracke: Mr. President, I want to ask you a question about negotiating with friends. You severely criticized President Carter for helping to undermine two friendly dictators who got into trouble with their own people: the Shah of Iran and President Somoza of Nicaragua. Now there are other such leaders heading for trouble, including President Pinochet [Augusto Pinochet Ugarte] of Chile and President Marcos [Ferdinand E. Marcos] of the Philippines. What should you do, and what can you do, to prevent the Philippines from becoming another Nicaragua?

Mr. Reagan: Morton, I did criticize the President because of our undercutting of what was a stalwart ally: the Shah of Iran. But I am not at all convinced that he was that far out of line with his people, or that they wanted that to happen. The Shah had done our bidding and carried our load in the Middle East for quite some time, and I did think that it was a blot on our record that we let him down. Have things gotten better? The Shah, whatever he might have done, was building low-cost housing, had taken land away from the mullahs, and was distributing it to the peasants so they could be landowners—things of that kind. But we turned it over to a maniacal fanatic who has slaughtered thousands and thousands of people, calling it executions.

The matter of Somoza—no. I never defended Somoza. As a matter of fact, the previous Administration stood by him. So did I. Not that I could have done anything in my position at that time. But for this revolution to take place . . . and the promise of the revolution was democracy, human rights, free labor unions, free press. And then, just as Castro had done in Cuba, the Sandinistas ousted the other parties to the revolution. Many of them are now the Contras. They exiled some, they jailed some, they murdered some, and they installed a Marxist-Leninist totalitarian government. And what I have to say about this is: many times—and this has to do with the Philippines also. . . . I know there are things there in the Philippines that do not look good to us from the standpoint, right now, of democratic rights. But what is the alternative? It is a large Communist movement to take over the Philippines. They have been our friend for . . . since their inception as a nation. And I think that we've had enough of a record of letting, under the guise of revolution, someone that we thought was a little more right than we would be, letting that person go and then winding up with totalitarianism, pure and simple, as the alternative. And I think that we're better off, for example, with the Philippines, of trying to retain our friendship and help them right the wrongs we see, rather than throwing them to the wolves and then facing a Communist power in the Pacific.

[Philippines]

Mr. Kondracke: Mr. President, since the United States has two strategically important bases in the Philippines, would the overthrow of President Marcos constitute a threat to vital American interests? And, if so, what would you do about it?

Mr. Reagan: Well, I say, we have to look at what an overthrow there would mean and what the government would be that would follow. And there is every evidence, every indication, that that government would be hostile to the United States. And that would be a severe blow to the . . . to our abilities there in the Pacific.

Mr. Kondracke: And what would you do about it?

Mr. Newman: Sorry. Sorry, you've asked the follow-up question. Mr. Mondale, your rebuttal.

Mr. Mondale: Perhaps in no area do we disagree more than this Administration's policies on human rights. I went to the Philippines as Vice President, pressed for human rights, called for the release of Aquino, *and* made progress that had been stalled on both the Subic [Bay] and Clark Airfield bases.

What explains this Administration cozying up to the Argentine dictators after they took over? Fortunately, a democracy took over. But this nation was embarrassed by this current Administration's adoption of their policies. What happens in South Africa where, for example, the Nobel Prize winner two days ago said this Administration is seen as working with the oppressive government of that region ... of South Africa. That hurts this nation. We need to stand for human rights. We need to make it clear we're for human liberty. National security and human rights must go together. But this Administration, time and time again, has lost its way in this field.

Mr. Newman: President Reagan, your rebuttal.

Mr. Reagan: Well, the invasion of Afghanistan didn't take place on our watch. I have described what has happened in Iran. And we weren't here then, either. I don't think that our record of human rights can be assailed. I think that we have observed ourselves and have done our best to see that human rights are extended throughout the world. Mr. Mondale has recently announced a plan of his to get the democracies together and to work with the whole world to turn to democracy. And I was glad to hear him say that, because that's what we've been doing ever since I announced to the British Parliament that I thought we should do this.

And human rights are not advanced when, at the same time, you then stand back and say, "Whoops, we didn't know the gun was loaded." And you have another totalitarian power on your hands.

Mr. Newman: In this segment, because of the pressure of time, there will be no rebuttals and there will be no follow-up questions. Mr. Trewhitt, your question to President Reagan.

Mr. Trewhitt: One question to each candidate?

Mr. Newman: One question to each candidate.

[Nuclear Strategy]

Mr. Trewhitt: Mr. President, can I take you back to something you said earlier? And if I am misquoting you, please correct me. But I understood you to say that if the development of space military technology was successful you might give the Soviets a demonstration and say, "Here it is," which sounds to me as if you might be trying to gain the sort of advantage that would enable you to dictate terms, and which, I would then suggest to you, might mean scrapping a generation of nuclear strategy called mutual deterrence, in which we, in effect, hold each other hostage. Is that your intention?

Mr. Reagan: Well, I can't say that I have round-tabled that and sat down with the Chiefs of Staff. But I have said that it seems to me that this could be a logical step in what is my ultimate goal, my ultimate dream: and that is the elimination of nuclear weapons in the world. And it seems to me that this could be an adjunct, or certainly a great assisting agent, in getting that done. I am not going to roll over, as Mr. Mondale suggests, and give them something that could turn around and be used against us. But I think it's a very interesting proposal—to see if we can find, first of all, something that renders those weapons obsolete, incapable of their mission. But Mr. Mondale seems to approve MAD. MAD is mutual assured destruction, meaning if you use nuclear weapons on us, the only thing we have to keep you from doing it is that we'll kill as many people of yours as you'll kill of ours. I think that to do everything we can to find, as I say, something that would destroy weapons and not humans, is a great step forward in human rights.

Mr. Trewhitt: Mr. Mondale, could I ask you to address the question of nuclear strategy? Then let's.... The formal document is very arcane, but I'm going to ask you to deal with it anyway. Do you believe in MAD—mutual assured destruction, mutual deterrence—as it has been practiced for the last generation?

Mr. Mondale: I believe in a sensible arms control approach that brings down these weapons to manageable levels. I would like to see their elimination. And in the meantime, we have to be strong enough to make certain that the Soviet Union never tempts us. Now, here we have to decide between generalized objectives and reality. The President says he wants to eliminate or reduce the number of nuclear weapons. But, in fact, these last four years have seen more weapons built, a wider and more vigorous arms race than in human history. He says he wants a system that will make nuclear arms—wars—safe, so nobody's going to get hurt. Well, maybe someday somebody can dream of that. Why threaten our space satellites upon which we depend? Why pursue a strategy that would delegate to computers the question of starting a war? A President, to defend this country and to get arms control, must master what's going on. We all ... I accept his objective of ... and his dreams. We all do. But the hard reality is that we must know what we are doing and pursue those objectives that are possible in our time. He's opposed every effort of every President to do so. And the four years of his Administration he's failed to do so. And if you want a tough President who uses that strength to get arms control and draws the line in the heavens, vote for Walter Mondale.

Mr. Newman: Please—I must, I must again ask the audience not to applaud, not to cheer, not to demonstrate its feelings in any way.

We've arrived at the point in the debate now where we call for closing statements. You have the full four minutes, each of you. Mr. Mondale, will you go first?

[Mondale's Closing Statement]

Mr. Mondale: I want to thank The League of Women Voters, the good citizens of Kansas City, and President Reagan for agreeing to debate this evening. This evening we talked about national strength. I believe we need to be strong. And I will keep us strong. By strength ... I think strength must also require wisdom and smarts in its exercise. That's key to the strength of our nation. A President must know the essential facts—essential to command. But a President must also have a vision of where this nation should go. Tonight, as Americans, you have a choice. And you're entitled to know where we would take this country if you decide to elect us.

As President, I would press for long-term vigorous economic growth. That's why I want to get these debts down and these interest rates down, restore America's exports, help rural America, which is suffering so much, and bring the jobs back here for our children. I want this next generation to be the best educated in American history, to invest in the human mind and science again so we're out front. I want this nation to protect its air, its water, its land, and its public health. America is not temporary. We're forever. And as Americans, our generation should protect this wonderful land for our children. I want a nation of fairness, where no one is denied the fullness of life or discriminated against, and we deal compassionately with those in our midst who are in trouble. And, above all, I want a nation that's strong. Since we debated two weeks ago, the United States and the Soviet Union have built 100 more warheads, enough to kill millions of Americans and millions of Soviet citizens. This doesn't strengthen us. This weakens the chances of civilization to survive.

I remember the night before I became Vice President. I was given a briefing and told that any time, night or day, I might be called upon to make the most fateful decision on earth: whether to fire these atomic weapons that could destroy the human species. That lesson tells us two things. One, pick a President that you know will know—if that tragic moment ever comes—what he must know. Because there'd be no time for staffing, committees, or advisors. A President must know right then. But, above all, pick a President who will fight to avoid the day when that god-awful decision ever needs to be made. And that's why this election is so terribly important. America and Americans decide not just what's happening in this country.

We are the strongest and most powerful free society on earth. When you make a judgment, you are deciding not only the future of our nation. In a very profound respect, you're providing the future . . . deciding the future of the world. We need to move on. It's time for America to find new leadership. Please join me in this cause to move confidently and with a sense of assurance and command, to build the blessed future of our nation.

Mr. Newman: President Reagan, your summation please.

[Reagan's Closing Statement]

Mr. Reagan: Yes. My thanks to The League of Women Voters, to the panelists, the moderator, and to the people of Kansas City for their warm hospitality and greeting.

I think the American people tonight have much to be grateful for: an eco-nomic recovery that has become expansion, freedom, and most of all, that we are at peace. I am grateful for the chance to reaffirm my commitment to reduce nuclear weapons and, one day, to eliminate them entirely. The question before you comes down to this: Do you want to see America return to the policies of weakness of the last four years, or do we want to go forward, marching together, as a nation of strength, and that's going to continue to be strong?

The . . . We shouldn't be dwelling on the past, or even the present. The meaning of this election is the future, and whether we're going to grow and provide the jobs and the opportunities for all Americans, and that they need.

Several years ago, I was given an assignment to write a letter. It was to go into a time capsule and would be read in a hundred years, when that time capsule was opened. I remember driving down the California coast one day. My mind was full of what I was going to put in that letter about the problems and the issues that confront us in our time and what we did about them.

But I couldn't completely neglect the beauty around me: the Pacific out there on one side of the highway, shining in the sunlight, the mountains of the coast range rising on the other side. And I found myself wondering what it would be like for someone . . . wondering if someone, a hundred years from now, would be driving down that highway, and if they would see the same thing.

With that thought, I realized what a job I had with that letter. I would be writing a letter to people who know everything there is to know about us. We know nothing about them. They would know all about our problems. They would know how we solved them and whether our solution was beneficial to them down through the years or whether it hurt them. They would also know that we lived in a world with terrible weapons, nuclear weapons of terrible destructive power aimed at each other, capable of crossing the ocean in a matter of minutes and destroying civilization as we knew it. And then, I thought to myself, "What . . . what are they going to say about us? What are those people a hundred years from now going to think?" They will know whether we used those weapons or not.

Well, what they will say about us a hundred years from now depends on how we keep our rendezvous with destiny. Will we do the things that we know must be done, and know that one day, down in history a hundred years, or perhaps before, someone will say, "Thank God for those people back in the 1980s—for preserving our freedom, for saving for us this blessed planet called Earth with all its grandeur and its beauty."

You know, I am grateful to all of you for giving me the opportunity to serve you for these four years, and I seek reelection because I want more than anything else to try to complete the new beginning that we charted four years

ago. George Bush—who I think is one of the finest Vice Presidents this country has ever had—George Bush and I have crisscrossed the country, and we've had, in these last few months, a wonderful experience. We have met young America. We have met your sons and daughters.

Mr. Newman: Mr. President, I am obliged to cut you off there under the rules of the debate. I'm sorry.

Mr. Reagan: All right. I was just going to . . . All right.

Mr. Newman: Perhaps I . . . perhaps I should point out that the rules under which I did that were agreed upon by the two campaigns, with The League, as you know, sir.

Mr. Reagan: I know. I know. Yes.

Mr. Newman: Thank you, Mr. President. Thank you, Mr. Mondale. Our thanks also to the panel. Finally, to our audience, we thank you, and The League of Women Voters asks me to say to you: Don't forget to vote on November 6.

Jesse Jackson's Speech to the Democratic National Convention (1988)

Jesse Jackson was not the first African-American candidate to bid for the presidential nomination of a major party—Rep. Shirley Chisholm of New York had sought to be the Democratic nominee in 1972—but he was the first to have a plausible chance to win.

Jackson, a dynamic young preacher and civil rights advocate, first ran for president in 1984. He had little money, little organization, and virtually no support from black elected officials, most of whom endorsed former vice president Walter F. Mondale or one of the other, more conventional candidates. Yet Jackson's passionate oratory and flair for publicity earned him two state primary victories, 19 percent of the total Democratic primary vote, and more than 10 percent of the delegates to the party's 1984 national convention. Jackson aimed his campaign at a "Rainbow Coalition" of blacks, whites, Native Americans, and Hispanics. In the actual voting, however, he won 77 percent of the African-American vote and only 5 percent of the white vote.

Based on his experience and performance as a candidate in 1984, Jackson was able to raise more money, build a better organization, and attract near-unanimous support from black political leaders in 1988. He also benefited both from being the best-known candidate in a Democratic field that politi-cal pundits labeled "the seven dwarfs" and from the growth of "Super Tuesday" into a de facto southern primary that took place early in the delegate selection process. (See "The Democrats' Atlanta Debate," p. 775.)

Jackson's success in the South was an unintended consequence of the regional primary's creation. Conservative white southern Democratic leaders had designed the expanded Super Tuesday of the 1988 election for the purpose of nominating a candidate who could carry the South and win the presidency in the general election. What these leaders neglected in their planning was the large proportion of labor, liberal, and African-American voters in the southern Democratic primary electorate. Thus, in 1988, although one moderate white candidate, Sen. Albert Gore of Tennessee, benefited from the March 8 Super Tuesday voting, so did Jackson and a northern white liberal, Gov. Michael S. Dukakis of Massachusetts.

After Super Tuesday, in the early spring primaries of the North, Gore faltered and Jackson and Dukakis thrived. A Jackson victory in the April 5 Wisconsin primary, which for a time seemed possible, would have made it difficult for the party to deny him the nomination, but he lost to Dukakis. The unemotional Massachusetts governor, who appealed to the voters as a *competent manager, sealed his victory with a series of primary victories in late April and May and went to the Democratic national convention in July with a first-ballot nomination securely in hand.*

Jackson's performance in the 1988 nominating contest was measurably stronger than in 1984: seven primary victories, 29 percent of the national primary vote, and 29 percent of the convention delegates. But his political appeal was essentially unchanged: Jackson's candidacy had a "high floor," consisting of virtually every black voter in the country, but a "low ceiling" because of his inability to attract support from white voters. Not just racial prejudice but also disagreement with Jackson's ardent liberalism and doubts about his lack of experience in high public office placed a firm upper limit on his potential as a presidential candidate.

After his campaign for president faltered, Jackson adjusted his sights downward, onto the vice presidential nomination. Dukakis refused to recommend him to the convention, convinced that Jackson would saddle the Democratic ticket with the same political liabilities as the vice-presidential nominee that he would as the presidential nominee. But Dukakis did accord Jackson effusive and highly public respect and attention at the convention, including an opportunity to speak to the delegates and the national television audience in prime time. Jackson's eloquent, emotional speech rang all the major chords of his campaign.   ~

Tonight we pause and give praise and honor to God for being good enough to allow us to be at this place at this time. When I look out at this convention, I see the face of America, red, yellow, brown, black and white, we're all precious in God's sight—the real rainbow coalition. All of us, all of us who are

here and think that we are seated. But we're really standing on someone's shoulders. Ladies and gentlemen, Mrs. Rosa Parks.

The mother of the civil rights movement.

I want to express my deep love and appreciation for the support my family has given me over these past months.

They have endured pain, anxiety, threat and fear.

But they have been strengthened and made secure by a faith in God, in America and in you.

Your love has protected us and made us strong.

To my wife Jackie, the foundation of our family; to our five children whom you met tonight; to my mother Mrs. Helen Jackson, who is present tonight; and to my grandmother, Mrs. Matilda Burns; my brother Chuck and his family; my mother-in-law, Mrs. Gertrude Brown, who just last month at age 61 graduated from Hampton Institute, a marvelous achievement; I offer my appreciation to [Atlanta] Mayor Andrew Young who has provided such gracious hospitality to all of us this week.

And a special salute to President Jimmy Carter.

President Carter restored honor to the White House after Watergate. He gave many of us a special opportunity to grow. For his kind words, for his unwavering commitment to peace in the world and the voters that came from his family, every member of his family, led by Billy and Amy, I offer him my special thanks, special thanks to the Carter family.

My right and my privilege to stand here before you has been won—in my lifetime—by the blood and the sweat of the innocent.

Twenty-four years ago, the late Fanny Lou Hamer and Aaron Henry—who sits here tonight from Mississippi—were locked out on the streets of Atlantic City, the head of the Mississippi Freedom Democratic Party.

But tonight, a black and white delegation from Mississippi is headed by [state party Chairman] Ed Cole, a black man, from Mississippi, 24 years later.

Many were lost in the struggle for the right to vote. Jimmy Lee Jackson, a young student, gave his life. Viola Liuzzo, a white mother from Detroit, called nigger lover, and brains blown out at point blank range.

[Michael] Schwerner, [Andrew] Goodman and [James] Chaney—two Jews and a black—found in a common grave, bodies riddled with bullets in Mississippi. The four darling little girls in the church in Birmingham, Ala. They died so that we might have a right to live.

Dr. Martin Luther King Jr. lies only a few miles from us tonight.

Tonight he must feel good as he looks down upon us. We sit here together, a rainbow, a coalition—the sons and daughters of slave masters and the sons and daughters of slaves sitting together around a common table, to decide the direction of our party and our country. His heart would be full tonight.

As a testament to the struggles of those who have gone before; as a legacy for those who will come after; as a tribute to the endurance, the patience, the courage of our forefathers and mothers; as an assurance that their prayers are being answered, their work has not been in vain, and hope is eternal; tomorrow night my name will go into nomination for the presidency of the United States of America.

Common Ground at a Crossroads

We meet tonight at a crossroads, a point of decision.

Shall we expand, be inclusive, find unity and power; or suffer division and impotence?

We come to Atlanta, the cradle of the old South, the crucible of the new South.

Tonight there is a sense of celebration because we are moved, fundamentally moved, from racial battlegrounds by law, to economic common ground. Tomorrow we will challenge to move to higher ground.

Common ground!

Think of Jerusalem—the intersection where many trails met. A small village that became the birthplace for three great religions—Judaism, Christianity and Islam.

Why was this village so blessed? Because it provided a crossroads where different people met, different cultures, and different civilizations could meet and find common ground.

When people come together, flowers always flourish and the air is rich with the aroma of a new spring.

Take New York, the dynamic metropolis. What makes New York so special?

It is the invitation of the Statue of Liberty—give me your tired, your poor, your huddled masses who yearn to breathe free.

Not restricted to English only.

Many people, many cultures, many languages—with one thing in common, they yearn to breathe free.

Common ground!

Tonight in Atlanta, for the first time in this century we convene in the South.

A state where governors once stood in school house doors. Where [former Georgia state Sen.] Julian Bond was denied his seat in the state legislature because of his conscientious objection to the Vietnam War.

A city that, through its five black universities, has graduated more black students than any city in the world.

Atlanta, now a modern intersection of the new South.

Common ground!

That is the challenge to our party tonight.

Left wing. Right wing. Progress will not come through boundless liberalism nor static conservatism, but at the critical mass of mutual survival. It takes two wings to fly.

Whether you're a hawk or a dove, you're just a bird living in the same environment, in the same world.

The Bible teaches that when lions and lambs lie down together, none will be afraid and there will be peace in the valley. It sounds impossible. Lions eat lambs. Lambs sensibly flee from lions. But even lions and lambs find common ground. Why?

Because neither lions nor lambs want the forest to catch on fire. Neither lions nor lambs want acid rain to fall. Neither lions nor lambs can survive nuclear war. If lions and lambs can find common ground, surely, we can as well, as civilized people.

The only time that we win is when we come together. In 1960, John Kennedy, the late John Kennedy, beat Richard Nixon by only 112,000 votes—less than one vote per precinct. He won by the margin of our hope. He brought us together. He reached out. He had the courage to defy his advisors and inquire about Dr. King's jailing in Albany, Georgia. We won by the margin of our hope, inspired by courageous leadership.

In 1964, Lyndon Johnson brought both wings together. The thesis, the antithesis and to create a synthesis and together we won.

In 1976, Jimmy Carter unified us again and we won. When we do not come together, we never win.

In 1968, division and despair in July led to our defeat in November.

In 1980, rancor in the spring and the summer led to [President Ronald] Reagan in the fall. When we divide, we cannot win. We must find common ground as a basis for survival and development and change and growth.

Today when we debated, differed, deliberated, agreed to agree, agreed to disagree, when we had the good judgment to argue our case and then not self-destruct, George Bush was just a little further away from the White House and a little closer to private life.

Dukakis, Jackson: In the Same Boat

Tonight, I salute Governor Michael Dukakis.

He has run a well-managed and a dignified campaign. No matter how tired or how tried, he always resisted the temptation to stoop to demagoguery.

I've watched a good mind fast at work, with steel nerves, guiding his campaign out of the crowded field without appeal to the worst in us. I've watched his perspective grow as his environment has expanded. I've seen his toughness and tenacity close up. I know his commitment to public service.

Mike Dukakis' parents were a doctor and a teacher; my parents, a maid, a beautician and a janitor.

There's a great gap between Brookline, Massachusetts, and Haney Street, the Fieldcrest Village housing projects in Greenville, South Carolina.

He studied law; I studied theology. There are differences of religion, region, and race; differences in experiences and perspectives. But the genius of America is that out of the many, we become one.

Providence has enabled our paths to intersect. His foreparents came to America on immigrant ships; my foreparents came to America on slave ships. But whatever the original ships, we're in the same boat tonight.

Our ships could pass in the night if we have a false sense of independence, or they could collide and crash. We would lose our passengers. But we can seek a higher reality and a greater good apart. We can drift on the broken pieces of Reaganomics, satisfy our baser instincts, and exploit the fears of our people. At our highest, we can call upon noble instincts and navigate this vessel to safety. The greater good is the common good.

Expansion and Inclusion

As Jesus said, "Not my will, but thine be done." It was his way of saying there's higher good beyond personal comfort or position.

The good of our nation is at stake— its commitment to working men and women, to the poor and the vulnerable, to the many in the world. With so many guided missiles, and so much misguided leadership, the stakes are exceedingly high. Our choice, full participation in a Democratic government, or more abandonment and neglect. And so this night, we choose not a false sense of independence, not our capacity to survive and endure.

Tonight we choose interdependency in our capacity to act and unite for the greater good. The common good is finding commitment to new priorities, to expansion and inclusion. A commitment to expanded participation in the Democratic Party at every level. A commitment to a shared national campaign strategy and involvement at every level. A commitment to new priorities that ensure that hope will be kept alive. A common ground commitment for a legislative agenda by empowerment for the [Michigan Rep.] John Conyers bill, universal, on-site, same-day registration everywhere—and commitment to D.C. statehood and empowerment—D.C. deserves statehood. A commitment to economic set-asides, a commitment to the [California Rep. Ronald V.] Dellums bill for comprehensive sanctions against South Africa, a shared commitment to a common direction.

Common ground. Easier said than done. Where do you find common ground at the point of challenge? This campaign has shown that politics need not be marketed by politicians, packaged by pollsters and pundits. Politics can be a marvelous arena where people come together, define common ground.

We find common ground at the plant gate that closes on workers without notice. We find common ground at the farm auction where a good farmer loses his or her land to bad loans or diminishing markets. Common ground at the schoolyard where teachers cannot get adequate pay, and students cannot get a scholarship and can't make a loan. Common ground at the hospital admitting room where somebody tonight is dying because they cannot afford to go upstairs to a bed that's empty, waiting for someone with insurance to get sick. We are a better nation than that. We must do better.

Common ground. What is leadership if not present help in a time of crisis? And so I met you at the point of challenge in Jay, Maine, where paper workers were striking for fair wages; in Greenfield, Iowa, where family farmers struggle for a fair price; in Cleveland, Ohio, where working women seek comparable worth; in McFarland, Calif., where the children of Hispanic farm workers may be dying from poison land, dying in clusters with cancer; in the AIDS hospice in Houston, Texas, where the sick support one another, 12 are rejected by their own parents and friends.

Common ground.

A Quilt of Unity

America's not a blanket woven from one thread, one color, one cloth. When I was a child growing up in Greenville, S.C., and grandmother could not afford a blanket, she didn't complain and we did not freeze. Instead, she took pieces of old cloth—patches, wool, silk, gabardine, crockersack on the patches—barely good enough to wipe off your shoes with.

But they didn't stay that way very long. With sturdy hands and strong cord, she sewed them together into a quilt, a thing of beauty and power and culture.

Now, Democrats, we must build such a quilt. Farmers, you seek fair prices and you are right, but you cannot stand alone. Your patch is not big enough. Workers, you fight for fair wages. You are right. But your patch labor is not big enough. Women, you seek comparable worth and pay equity. You are right. But your patch is not big enough. Women, mothers, who seek Head Start and day care and pre-natal care on the front side of life, rather than jail care and welfare on the back side of life, you're right, but your patch is not big enough.

Students, you seek scholarships. You are right. But your patch is not big enough. Blacks and Hispanics, when we fight for civil rights, we are right, but our patch is not big enough. Gays and lesbians, when you fight against discrimination and a cure for AIDS, you are right, but your patch is not big enough. Conservatives and progressives, when you fight for what you believe, right-wing, left-wing, hawk, dove—you are right, from your point of view, but your point of view is not enough.

But don't despair. Be as wise as my grandmama. Pool the patches and the pieces together, bound by a common thread. When we form a great quilt of unity and common ground we'll have the power to bring about health care and housing and jobs and education and hope to our nation.

Reagan: 'Reverse Robin Hood'

We the people can win. We stand at the end of a long dark night of reaction.

We stand tonight united in a commitment to a new direction. For almost eight years, we've been led by those who view social good coming from private interest, who viewed public life as a means to increase private wealth. They have been prepared to sacrifice the common good of the many to satisfy the private interest and the wealth of a few. We believe in a government that's a tool of our democracy in service to the public, not an instrument of the aristocracy in search of private wealth.

We believe in government with the consent of the governed of, for, and by the people. We must emerge into a new day with a new direction. Reaganomics, based on the belief that the rich had too much money—too little money, and the poor had too much.

That's classic Reaganomics. It believes that the poor had too much money and the rich had too little money.

So, they engaged in reverse Robin Hood—took from the poor, gave to the rich, paid for by the middle class. We cannot stand four more years of Reaganomics in any version, in any disguise.

How do I document that case? Seven years later, the richest 1 percent of our society pays 20 percent less in taxes; the poorest 10 percent pay 20 percent more. Reaganomics.

Reagan gave the rich and the powerful a multibillion-dollar party. Now, the party is over. He expects the people to pay for the damage. I take this principled position—convention, let us not raise taxes on the poor and the middle class, but those who had the party, the rich and the powerful, must pay for the party!

I just want to take common sense to high places. We're spending $150 billion a year defending Europe and Japan 43 years after the war is over. We have more troops in Europe tonight than we had seven years ago, yet the threat of war is ever more remote. Germany and Japan are now creditor nations—that means they've got a surplus. We are a debtor nation—it means we are in debt.

Let them share more of the burden of their own defense—use some of that money to build decent housing!

Use some of that money to educate our children!

Use some of that money for long-term health care!

Use some of that money to wipe out these slums and put America back to work!

I just want to take common sense to high places. If we can bail out Europe and Japan, if we can bail out Continental Bank and Chrysler—and Mr. Iacocca makes $8,000 an hour—we can bail out the family farmer.

I just want to make common sense. It does not make sense to close down 650,000 family farms in this country while importing food from abroad subsidized by the U.S. government.

Let's make sense. It does not make sense to be escorting oil tankers up and down the Persian Gulf paying $2.50 for every $1.00 worth of oil we bring out while oil wells are capped in Texas, Oklahoma and Louisiana. I just want to make sense.

Leadership must meet the moral challenge of its day. What's the moral challenge of our day? We have public accommodations. We have the right to vote. We have open housing.

End Economic Violence

What's the fundamental challenge of our day? It is to end economic violence. Plant closing without notice, economic violence. Even the greedy do not profit long from greed. Economic violence. Most poor people are not lazy. They're not black. They're not brown. They're mostly white, and female and young.

But whether white, black or brown, the hungry baby's belly turned inside out is the same color. Call it pain. Call it

hurt. Call it agony. Most poor people are not on welfare.

Some of them are illiterate and can't read the want-ad sections. And when they can, they can't find a job that matches their address. They work hard every day, I know. I live amongst them. I'm one of them.

I know they work. I'm a witness. They catch the early bus. They work every day. They raise other people's children. They work every day. They clean the streets. They work every day. They drive vans with cabs. They work every day. They change the beds you slept in these hotels last night and can't get a union contract. They work every day.

No more. They're not lazy. Someone must defend them because it's right, and they cannot speak for themselves. They work in hospitals. I know they do. They wipe the bodies of those who are sick with fever and pain. They empty their bedpans. They clean out their commode. No job is beneath them, and yet when they get sick, they cannot lie in the bed they made up every day. America, that is not right. We are a better nation than that. We are a better nation than that.

War on Drugs

We need a real war on drugs. You can't just say no. It's deeper than that. You can't just get a palm reader or an astrologer; it's more profound than that. We're spending $150 billion on drugs a year. We've gone from ignoring it to focusing on the children. Children cannot buy $150 billion worth of drugs a year. A few high profile athletes—athletes are not laundering $150 billion a year—bankers are.

I met the children in Watts who are unfortunate in their despair. Their grapes of hope have become raisins of despair, and they're turning to each other and they're self-destructing—but

I stayed with them all night long. I wanted to hear their case. They said, "Jesse Jackson, as you challenge us to say no to drugs, you're right. And to not sell them, you're right. And to not use these guns, you're right."

And, by the way, the promise of CETA [Comprehensive Employment and Training Act]—they displaced CETA. They did not replace CETA. We have neither jobs nor houses nor services nor training—no way out. Some of us take drugs as anesthesia for our pain. Some take drugs as a way of pleasure—both short-term pleasure and long-term pain. Some sell drugs to make money. It's wrong, we know. But you need to know that we know. We can go and buy the drugs by the boxes at the port. If we can buy the drugs at the port, don't you believe the federal government can stop it if they want to?

They say, "We don't have Saturday night specials any more." They say, "We buy AK-47s and Uzis, the latest lethal weapons. We buy them across the counter on Long Beach Boulevard." You cannot fight a war on drugs unless and until you are going to challenge the bankers and the gun sellers and those who grow them. Don't just focus on the children, let's stop drugs at the level of supply and demand. We must end the scourge on the American culture.

Leadership in Pursuit of Peace

Leadership. What difference will we make? Leadership cannot just go along to get along. We must do more than change presidents. We must change direction. Leadership must face the moral challenge of our day. The nuclear war build-up is irrational. Strong leadership cannot desire to look tough, and let that stand in the way of the pursuit of peace. Leadership must reverse the arms race.

At least we should pledge no first use.

Why? Because first use begat first retaliation, and that's mutual annihilation. That's not a rational way out. No use at all—let's think it out, and not fight it out, because it's an unwinnable fight. Why hold a card that you can never drop? Let's give peace a chance.

Leadership—we now have this marvelous opportunity to have a breakthrough with the Soviets. Last year, 200,000 Americans visited the Soviet Union. There's a chance for joint ventures into space, not Star Wars and the war arms escalation, but a space defense initiative. Let's build in space together, and demilitarize the heavens. There's a way out.

America, let us expand. When Mr. Reagan and Mr. [Mikhail S.] Gorbachev met, there was a big meeting. They represented together one-eighth of the human race. Seven-eighths of the human race was locked out of that room. Most people in the world tonight—half are Asian, one-half of them are Chinese. There are 22 nations in the Middle East. There's Europe; 40 million Latin Americans next door to us; the Caribbean; Africa—a half-billion people. Most people in the world today are yellow or brown or black, non-Christian, poor, female, young, and don't speak English—in the real world.

This generation must offer leadership to the real world. We're losing ground in Latin America, the Middle East, South Africa, because we're not focusing on the real world, that real world. We must use basic principles, support international law. We stand the most to gain from it. Support human rights; we believe in that. Support self-determination; we'll build on that. Support economic development; you know it's right. Be consistent, and gain our moral authority in the world.

I challenge you tonight, my friends, let's be bigger and better as a nation and as a party. We have basic challenges. Freedom in South Africa—we've already agreed as Democrats to declare

South Africa to be a terrorist state. But don't just stop there. Get South Africa out of Angola. Free Namibia. Support the front-line states. We must have a new, humane human rights assistance policy in Africa.

To Hope and to Dream

I'm often asked, "Jesse, why do you take on these tough issues? They're not very political. We can't win that way."

If an issue is morally right, it will eventually be political. It may be political and never be right. Fannie Lou Hamer didn't have the most votes in Atlantic City, but her principles have outlasted every delegate who voted to lock her out. Rosa Parks did not have the most votes, but she was morally right. Dr. King didn't have the most votes about the Vietnam war, but he was morally right. If we're principled first, our politics will fall in place.

"Jesse, why did you take these big bold initiatives?" A poem by an unknown author went something like this: We mastered the air, we've conquered the sea, and annihilated distance and prolonged life, we were not wise enough to live on this earth without war and without hate.

As for Jesse Jackson, I'm tired of sailing by little boat, far inside the harbor bar. I want to go out where the big ships float, out on the deep where the great ones are. And should my frail craft prove too slight, the waves that sweep those billows o'er, I'd rather go down in a stirring fight than drown to death in the sheltered shore.

We've got to go out, my friends, where the big boats are.

And then, for our children, young America, hold your head high now. We can win. We must not lose you to drugs and violence, premature pregnancy, suicide, cynicism, pessimism and despair. We can win.

Wherever you are tonight, I challenge you to hope and to dream. Don't submerge your dreams. Exercise above all else, even on drugs, dream of the day you're drug-free. Even in the gutter, dream of the day that you'll be upon your feet again. You must never stop dreaming. Face reality, yes. But don't stop with the way things are; dream of things as they ought to be. Dream. Face pain, but love, hope, faith, and dreams will help you rise above the pain.

Use hope and imagination as weapons of survival and progress, but you keep on dreaming, young America. Dream of peace. Peace is rational and reasonable. War is irrational in this age and unwinnable.

Dream of teachers who teach for life and not for living. Dream of doctors who are concerned more about public health than private wealth. Dream of lawyers more concerned about justice than a judgeship. Dream of preachers who are concerned more about prophecy than profiteering. Dream on the high road of sound values.

"Don't Surrender"

And in America, as we go forth to September, October and November and then beyond, America must never surrender to a high moral challenge.

Do not surrender to drugs. The best drug policy is a no first use. Don't surrender with needles and cynicism. Let's have no first use on the one hand, or clinics on the other. Never surrender, young America.

Go forward. America must never surrender to malnutrition. We can feed the hungry and clothe the naked. We must never surrender. We must go forward. We must never surrender to illiteracy. Invest in our children. Never surrender; and go forward.

We must never surrender to inequality. Women cannot compromise ERA

[Equal Rights Amendment] or comparable worth. Women are making 60 cents on the dollar to what a man makes. Women cannot buy milk cheaper. Women deserve to get paid for the work that you do. It's right and it's fair.

Don't surrender, my friends. Those who have AIDS tonight, you deserve our compassion. Even with AIDS you must not surrender in your wheelchairs. I see you sitting here tonight in those wheelchairs. I've stayed with you. I've reached out to you across our nation. Don't you give up. I know it's tough sometimes. People look down on you. It took you a little more effort to get here tonight.

And no one should look down on you, but sometimes mean people do. The only justification we have for looking down on someone is that we're going to stop and pick them up. But even in your wheelchairs, don't you give up. We cannot forget 50 years ago when our backs were against the wall, [Franklin D.] Roosevelt was in a wheelchair. I would rather have Roosevelt in a wheelchair than Reagan and [George] Bush on a horse. Don't you surrender and don't you give up.

Don't surrender and don't give up. Why can I challenge you this way? "Jesse Jackson, you don't understand my situation. You be on television. You don't understand. I see you with the big people. You don't understand my situation." I understand. You're seeing me on TV but you don't know the me that makes me, me. They wonder why does Jesse run, because they see me running for the White House. They don't see the house I'm running from.

The House He's Running From

I have a story. I wasn't always on television. Writers were not always outside my door. When I was born late one afternoon, October 8th, in Greenville, S.C., no writers asked my mother her name. Nobody chose to write down her address. My mama was not supposed to make it. And I was not supposed to make it. You see, I was born to a teen-age mother who was born to a teen-age mother.

I understand. I know abandonment and people being mean to you, and saying you're nothing and nobody, and can never be anything. I understand. Jesse Jackson is my third name. I'm adopted. When I had no name, my grandmother gave me her name. My name was Jesse Burns until I was 12. So I wouldn't have a blank space, she gave me a name to hold me over. I understand when nobody knows your name. I understand when you have no name. I understand.

I wasn't born in the hospital. Mama didn't have insurance. I was born in the bed at the house. I really do understand. Born in a three-room house, bathroom in the backyard, slop jar by the bed, no hot and cold running water. I understand. Wallpaper used for decoration? No. For a windbreaker. I understand. I'm a working person's person, that's why I understand you whether you're black or white.

I understand work. I was not born with a silver spoon in my mouth. I had a shovel programmed for my hand. My mother, a working woman. So many days she went to work with runs in her stockings. She knew better, but she wore runs in her stockings so that my brother and I could have matching socks and not be laughed at at school.

I understand. At 3 o'clock on Thanksgiving Day we couldn't eat turkey because mama was preparing someone else's turkey at 3 o'clock. We had to play football to entertain ourselves and then around 6 o'clock she would get off the Alta Vista bus when we would bring up the leftovers and eat our turkey—leftovers, the carcass, the cranberries around 8 o'clock at night. I really do understand.

Every one of these funny labels they put on you, those of you who are watching this broadcast tonight in the projects, on the corners, I understand. Call you outcast, low down, you can't make it, you're nothing, you're from nobody, subclass, underclass—when you see Jesse Jackson, when my name goes in nomination, your name goes in nomination.

I was born in the slum, but the slum was not born in me. And it wasn't born in you, and you can make it. Wherever you are tonight you can make it. Hold your head high, stick your chest out.

You can make it. It gets dark sometimes, but the morning comes. Don't you surrender. Suffering breeds character. Character breeds faith. In the end faith will not disappoint.

You must not surrender. You may or may not get there, but just know that you're qualified and you hold on and hold out. We must never surrender. America will get better and better. Keep hope alive. Keep hope alive. Keep hope alive. On tomorrow night and beyond, keep hope alive.

I love you very much. I love you very much.

George Bush's Acceptance Speech to the Republican National Convention (1988)

George Bush constructed his candidacy for president in 1988 on two main pillars: his resume of experience in government and his association with President Ronald Reagan.

Bush was the son of Prescott Bush, a wealthy Wall Street banker who represented Connecticut in the U.S. Senate. After valiant service in World War II and undergraduate studies at Yale University, Bush struck out successfully on his own, building an oil business in Texas. He was elected to the House of Representatives by the voters of Houston in 1966 and 1968 and ran a strong race for the Senate in 1970, losing to the conservative Democrat Lloyd Bentsen. (Sen. Bentsen became the Democratic nominee for vice president in 1988.) A series of appointive positions followed in the administrations of presidents Richard Nixon and Gerald Ford: ambassador to the United Nations, Republican National Committee chair, emissary to China, and director of the Central Intelligence Agency. Portraying himself as a moderate conservative, Bush ran a strong campaign for the Republican presidential nomination in 1980, finishing second to Ronald Reagan. (See "Republican Party Platform [1980]," p. 677.)

Reagan tapped Bush as his vice presidential running mate in 1980. The Reagan-Bush ticket was elected and, in 1984, was reelected. Both as a candidate and as the vice president, Bush gave his full loyalty to Reagan, avoiding any hint of disagreement or criticism and even adopting wholeheartedly the president's conservative political views.

The vice presidency is a politically anomalous office. Five of Bush's seven most recent predecessors as vice president had gone on to win their party's nomination for president: Nixon (1960), Lyndon B. Johnson (1964), Hubert H. Humphrey (1968), Ford (1976), and Walter F. Mondale (1984). Yet no incumbent vice president had been elected as president since Martin Van Buren in 1836. The vice president's years of loyal service to the president seemed to underlie both of these political patterns: party regulars appreciate the loyalty and reward it by conferring the presidential nomination on the vice president, but the broader electorate sees mostly weakness and subservience and rejects the vice president in the general election.

In the summer of 1988, Bush appeared likely to inherit the full political legacy of his office. He had raced victoriously through the early caucuses and primaries against a strong field of five other candidates, locking up the Republican nomination for president in early March. Yet going into the party's national convention in mid-August, Bush trailed his Democratic rival,

Gov. Michael S. Dukakis of Massachusetts, by as much as eighteen percentage points in the polls.

The evening of August 18, 1988, offered Bush his best chance to turn the election around: the delivery of his acceptance speech for the Republican nomination guaranteed a large television audience of voters. Bush, who was not known as an effective speaker, rose to the occasion with a speech that was well-written (by speechwriter Peggy Noonan) and confidently delivered. The speech contained several phrases that resonated with the voters throughout the fall campaign and the early part of his administration: "a thousand points of light," "a kinder and gentler nation," and "Read my lips. No new taxes."   ~

Thank you ladies and gentlemen, thank you very, very much.

I have many friends to thank tonight. I thank the voters who supported me. I thank the gallant men who entered the contest for this presidency this year, and who've honored me with their support. And, for their kind and stirring words, I thank Governor Tom Kean of New Jersey, Senator Phil Gramm of Texas, President Gerald Ford—and my friend President Ronald Reagan.

I accept your nomination for president. I mean to run hard, to fight hard, to stand on the issues—and I mean to win.

There are a lot of great stories in politics about the underdog winning—and this is going to be one of them.

And we're going to win with the help of Senator Dan Quayle of Indiana—a young leader who has become a forceful voice in preparing America's workers for the labor force of the future. What a superb job he did here tonight.

Born in the middle of the century, in the middle of America, and holding the promise of the future—I'm proud to have Dan Quayle at my side.

Many of you have asked, "When will this campaign really begin?" Well, I've come to this hall to tell you, and to tell America: Tonight is the night.

For seven and a half years I've helped the president conduct the most difficult job on earth. Ronald Reagan asked for, and received, my candor. He never asked for, but he did receive, my loyalty. And those of you who saw the president's speech last week, and listened to the simple truth of his words, will understand my loyalty all these years.

And now you must see me for what I am: the Republican candidate for president of the United States. And now I turn to the American people to share my hopes and intentions, and why and where I wish to lead.

And so tonight is for big things. But I'll try to be fair to the other side. I'll try to hold my charisma in check.

I reject the temptation to engage in personal references. My approach this evening is, as Sergeant Joe Friday used to say, "Just the facts, ma'am."

And after all, the facts are on our side.

I seek the presidency for a single purpose, a purpose that has motivated millions of Americans across the years and the ocean voyages. I seek the presidency to build a better America. It's that simple—and that big.

I'm a man who sees life in terms of missions—missions defined and missions completed.

And when I was a torpedo bomber pilot they defined the mission for us. And before we took off, we all understood that no matter what, you try to reach the target. And there have been other missions for me—Congress, and China, the CIA. But I'm here tonight, and I am your candidate, because the most important work of my life is to complete the mission we started in 1980. And how do we complete it? We build on it.

The stakes are high this year and the

choice is crucial, for the differences between the two candidates are as deep and wide as they have ever been in our long history.

Not only two very different men, but two very different ideas of the future will be voted on this Election Day.

And what it all comes down to is this: My opponent's view of the world sees a long slow decline for our country, an inevitable fall mandated by impersonal historical forces.

But America is not in decline. America is a rising nation.

He sees America as another pleasant country on the U.N. [United Nations] roll call, somewhere between Albania and Zimbabwe. And I see America as the leader—a unique nation with a special role in the world.

And this has been called the American century, because in it we were the dominant force for good in the world. We saved Europe, cured polio, went to the moon, and lit the world with our culture. And now we are on the verge of a new century, and what country's name will it bear? I say it will be another American century.

Our work is not done, our force is not spent.

There are those who say there isn't much of a difference this year. But America, don't let 'em fool ya.

Two parties this year ask for your support. Both will speak of growth and peace. But only one has proved it can deliver. Two parties this year ask for your trust, but only one has earned it.

Eight years ago, I stood here with Ronald Reagan and we promised, together, to break with the past and return America to her greatness. Eight years later, look at what the American people have produced: the highest level of economic growth in our entire history—and the lowest level of world tensions in more than 50 years.

You know, some say this isn't an election about ideology, but it's an election about competence. Well, it's nice of them to want to play on our field. But this election isn't only about competence, for competence is a narrow ideal.

Competence makes the trains run on time but doesn't know where they're going. Competence is the creed of the technocrat who makes sure the gears mesh but doesn't for a second understand the magic of the machine.

The truth is, this election is about the beliefs we share, the values we honor and the principles we hold dear.

But since someone brought up competence . . .

Consider the size of our triumph: A record number of Americans at work, a record high percentage of our people with jobs, a record high of new businesses, a high rate of new businesses, a record high rate of real personal income.

These are facts.

And one way we know our opponents know the facts is that to attack our record they have to misrepresent it. They call it a Swiss cheese economy. Well, that's the way it may look to the three blind mice.

But when they were in charge it was all holes and no cheese.

Inflation—you know the litany—inflation was 13 percent when we came in. We got it down to four. Interest rates were more than 21. We cut them in half. Unemployment was up and climbing, and now it's the lowest in 14 years.

My friends, eight years ago this economy was flat on its back—intensive care. And we came in and gave it emergency treatment: Got the temperature down by lowering regulation, and got the blood pressure down when we lowered taxes. And pretty soon the patient was up, back on his feet, and stronger than ever.

And now who do we hear knocking on the door but the same doctors who made him sick. And they're telling us to put them in charge of the case again? My friends, they're lucky we don't hit 'em with a malpractice suit!

We've created 17 million new jobs [in] the past five years—more than twice as many as Europe and Japan combined. And they're good jobs. The majority of them created in the past six years paid an average—average—of more than $22,000 a year. And someone better take a message to Michael: Tell him that we have been creating good jobs at good wages. The fact is, they talk and we deliver.

They promise and we perform.

And there are millions of young Americans in their 20s who barely remember the days of gas lines and unemployment lines. And now they're marrying and starting careers. To those young people I say, "You have the opportunity you deserve, and I'm not going to let them take it away from you."

The leaders of the expansion have been the women of America who helped create the new jobs, and filled two out of every three of them. And to the women of America I say, "You know better than anyone that equality begins with economic empowerment. You're gaining economic power, and I'm not going to let them take it away from you."

There are millions of older Americans who were brutalized by inflation. We arrested it—and we're not going to let it out on furlough.

We're going to keep the Social Security trust fund sound, and out of reach of the big spenders. To America's elderly I say, "Once again you have the security that is your right, and I'm not going to let them take it away from you."

I know the liberal Democrats are worried about the economy. They're worried it's going to remain strong. And they're right, it is—with the right leadership it will remain strong.

But let's be frank. Things aren't perfect in this country. There are people who haven't tasted the fruits of the expansion. I've talked to farmers about the bills they can't pay and I've been to the factories that feel the strain of change. And I've seen the urban children who play amidst the shattered glass and the shattered lives. And, you know, there are the homeless. And you know, it doesn't do any good to debate endlessly which policy mistake of the '70s is responsible. They're there, and we have to help them.

But what we must remember if we're to be responsible and compassionate is that economic growth is the key to our endeavors.

I want growth that stays, that broadens, and that touches, finally, all Americans, from the hollows of Kentucky to the sunlit streets of Denver, from the suburbs of Chicago to the broad avenues of New York, and from the oil fields of Oklahoma to the farms of the Great Plains.

And can we do it? Of course we can. We know how. We've done it. If we continue to grow at our current rate, we will be able to produce 30 million jobs in the next eight years.

And we will do it—by maintaining our commitment to free and fair trade, by keeping government spending down, and by keeping taxes down.

Our economic life is not the only test of our success. One issue overwhelms all the others, and that is the issue of peace.

Look at the world on this bright August night. The spirit of democracy is sweeping the Pacific rim. China feels the winds of change. New democracies assert themselves in South America. And one by one the unfree places fall, not to the force of arms but to the force of an idea: freedom works.

And we have a new relationship with the Soviet Union. The INF [intermediate-range nuclear-force] treaty, the beginning of the Soviet withdrawal from Afghanistan, the beginning of the end of the Soviet proxy war in Angola, and with it the independence of Namibia. Iran and Iraq move toward peace.

It's a watershed. It is no accident.

It happened when we acted on the ancient knowledge that strength and clarity lead to peace—weakness and ambivalence lead to war. You see, weakness tempts aggressors. Strength stops them. I will not allow this country to be made weak again—never.

The tremors in the Soviet world continue. The hard earth there has not yet settled. Perhaps what is happening will change our world forever. And perhaps not. A prudent skepticism is in order. And so is hope.

But either way, we're in an unprecedented position to change the nature of our relationship. Not by preemptive concession, but by keeping our strength. Not by yielding up defense systems with nothing won in return, but by hard, cool engagement in the tug and pull of diplomacy.

My life has been lived in the shadow of war—I almost lost my life in one.

And I hate war. Love peace.

And we have peace.

And I am not going to let anyone take it away from us.

Our economy is stronger but not invulnerable, and the peace is broad but can be broken. And now we must decide. We will surely have change this year, but will it be change that moves us forward? Or change that risks retreat?

In 1940, when I was barely more than a boy, Franklin Roosevelt said we shouldn't change horses in midstream.

My friends, these days the world moves even more quickly, and now, after two great terms, a switch will be made. But when you have to change horses in midstream, doesn't it make sense to switch to one who's going the same way?

An election that is about ideas and values is also about philosophy. And I have one.

At the bright center is the individual. And radiating out from him or her is the family, the essential unit of closeness and of love. For it is the family that communicates to our children—to the 21st century—our culture, our religious faith, our traditions and history.

From the individual to the family to the community, and then on out to the town, the church and the school, and, still echoing out, to the county, the state, and the nation—each doing only what it does well, and no more. And I believe that power must always be kept close to the individual, close to the hands that raise the family and run the home.

I am guided by certain traditions. One is that there is a God and he is good, and his love, while free, has a self-imposed cost: We must be good to one another.

I believe in another tradition that is, by now, imbedded in the national soul. It is that learning is good in and of itself. You know, the mothers of the Jewish ghettoes of the east would pour honey on a book so the children would know that learning is sweet. And the parents who settled hungry Kansas would take their children in from the fields when a teacher came. That is our history.

And there is another tradition. And that is the idea of community—a beautiful word with a big meaning. Though liberal Democrats have an odd view of it. They see "community" as a limited cluster of interest groups, locked in odd conformity. And in this view, the country waits passive while Washington sets the rules.

But that's not what community means—not to me.

For we are a nation of communities, of thousands and tens of thousands of ethnic, religious, social, business, labor union, neighborhood, regional and other organizations—all of them varied, voluntary and unique.

This is America: the Knights of Columbus, the Grange, Hadassah, the Disabled American Veterans, the Order of AHEPA [American Hellenic Educational Progressive Association], the

Business and Professional Women of America, the union hall, the Bible study group, LULAC [League of United Latin American Citizens], "Holy Name"—a brilliant diversity spread like stars, like a thousand points of light in a broad and peaceful sky.

Does government have a place? Yes. Government is part of the nation of communities—not the whole, just a part.

And I don't hate government. A government that remembers that the people are its master is a good and needed thing.

I respect old-fashioned common sense, and I have no great love for the imaginings of the social planners. You see, I like what's been tested and found to be true.

For instance.

Should public school teachers be required to lead our children in the pledge of allegiance? My opponent says no—and I say yes.

Should society be allowed to impose the death penalty on those who commit crimes of extraordinary cruelty and violence? My opponent says no—but I say yes.

And should our children have the right to say a voluntary prayer, or even observe a moment of silence in the schools? My opponent says no—but I say yes.

And should free men and women have the right to own a gun to protect their home? My opponent says no—but I say yes.

And is it right to believe in the sanctity of life and protect the lives of innocent children? My opponent says no—but I say yes.

You see, we must change, we've got to change from abortion to adoption. And let me tell you this: Barbara and I have an adopted granddaughter. And the day of her christening we wept with joy. I thank God that her parents chose life.

I'm the one who believes it is a scandal to give a weekend furlough to a hardened first-degree killer who hasn't even served enough time to be eligible for parole.

I'm the one who says a drug dealer who is responsible for the death of a policeman should be subject to capital punishment.

And I'm the one who will not raise taxes. My opponent now says he'll raise them as a last resort, or a third resort. Well, when a politician talks like that, you know that's one resort he'll be checking into. And, my opponent won't rule out raising taxes. But I will.

And the Congress will push me to raise taxes, and I'll say no, and they'll push, and I'll say no, and they'll push again. And I'll say to them: Read my lips. No new taxes.

Let me tell you more about the mission.

On jobs, my mission is: 30 in 8. Thirty million jobs in the next eight years.

Every one of our children deserves a first-rate school. The liberal Democrats want power in the hands of the federal government. And I want power in the hands of the parents. And, I will encourage merit schools. I will give more kids a head start. And I'll make it easier to save for college.

I want a drug-free America—and this will not be easy to achieve. But I want to enlist the help of some people who are rarely included. Tonight I challenge the young people of our country to shut down the drug dealers around the world. Unite with us, work with us.

"Zero tolerance" isn't just a policy, it's an attitude. Tell them what you think of people who underwrite the dealers who put poison in our society. And while you're doing that, my administration will be telling the dealers: Whatever we have to do we'll do, but your day is over, you're history.

I am going to do whatever it takes to make sure the disabled are included in the mainstream. For too long they've been left out. But they're not going to be left out anymore.

And I am going to stop ocean dumping. Our beaches should not be garbage dumps and our harbors should not be cesspools.

And I am going to have the FBI trace the medical wastes and we are going to punish the people who dump those infected needles into our oceans, lakes and rivers. And we must clean the air. We must reduce the harm done by acid rain.

And I will put incentives back into the domestic energy industry, for I know from personal experience there is no security for the United States in further dependence on foreign oil.

In foreign affairs I will continue our policy of peace through strength. I will move toward further cuts in strategic and conventional arsenals of both the United States and the Soviet Union and the Eastern Bloc and NATO. I will modernize and preserve our technological edge and that includes strategic defense.

And a priority: Ban chemical and biological weapons from the face of the Earth. That will be a priority with me.

And I intend to speak for freedom, stand for freedom, be a patient friend to anyone, East or West, who will fight for freedom.

It seems to me the presidency provides an incomparable opportunity for "gentle persuasion."

And I hope to stand for a new harmony, a greater tolerance. We've come far, but I think we need a new harmony among the races in our country. And we're on a journey into a new century, and we've got to leave that tired old baggage of bigotry behind.

Some people who are enjoying our prosperity have forgotten what it's for. But they diminish our triumph when they act as if wealth is an end in itself.

And there are those who have dropped their standards along the way, as if ethics were too heavy and slowed their rise to the top. There's graft in city hall, and there's greed on Wall Street; there's influence peddling in Washington, and the small corruptions of everyday ambition.

But you see, I believe public service is honorable. And every time I hear that someone has breached the public trust it breaks my heart.

And I wonder sometimes if we have forgotten who we are. But we're the people who sundered a nation rather than allow a sin called slavery—and we're the people who rose from the ghettoes and the deserts.

And we weren't saints, but we lived by standards. We celebrated the individual, but we weren't self-centered. We were practical, but we didn't live only for material things. We believed in getting ahead, but blind ambition wasn't our way.

The fact is prosperity has a purpose. It is to allow us to pursue "the better angels," to give us time to think and grow. Prosperity with a purpose means taking your idealism and making it concrete by certain acts of goodness.

It means helping a child from an unhappy home learn how to read—and I thank my wife Barbara for all her work in helping people to read and all her work for literacy in this country.

It means teaching troubled children through your presence that there is such a thing as reliable love. Some would say it's soft and insufficiently tough to care about these things. But where is it written that we must act as if we do not care, as if we are not moved?

Well, I am moved. I want a kinder and gentler nation.

Two men this year ask for your support. And you must know us.

As for me, I have held high office and done the work of democracy day by day. Yes, my parents were prosperous; and their children sure were lucky. But there were lessons we had to learn about life.

John Kennedy discovered poverty when he campaigned in West Virginia; there were children who had no milk.

And young Teddy Roosevelt met the new America when he roamed the immigrant streets of New York. And I learned a few things about life in a place called Texas.

And when I was working on this part of the speech, Barbara came in and asked what I was doing. And I looked up, and I said I'm working hard. And she said: "Oh dear, don't worry, relax, sit back, take off your shoes and put up your silver foot."

Now, we moved to West Texas 40 years ago—40 years ago this year. The war was over, and we wanted to get out and make it on our own. Those were exciting days. We lived in a little shotgun house, one room for the three of us. Worked in the oil business, and then started my own.

And in time we had six children. Moved from the shotgun to a duplex apartment to a house. And lived the dream—high school football on Friday nights, Little League, neighborhood barbecue.

People don't see their own experience as symbolic of an era—but of course we were.

And so was everyone else who was taking a chance and pushing into unknown territory with kids and a dog and a car.

But the big thing I learned is the satisfaction of creating jobs, which meant creating opportunity, which meant happy families, who in turn could do more to help others and enhance their own lives.

I learned that the good done by a single good job can be felt in ways you can't imagine.

It's been said that I'm not the most compelling speaker, and there are actually those who claim that I don't always communicate in the clearest, most concise way. But I dare them to keep it up—go ahead: Make my 24-hour time period!

Well, I may not be the most eloquent, but I learned that, early on, that eloquence won't draw oil from the ground.

And I may sometimes be a little awkward. But there's nothing self-conscious in my love of country.

And I am a quiet man, but I hear the quiet people others don't. The ones who raise the family, pay the taxes, meet the mortgages.

And I hear them and I am moved, and their concerns are mine.

A president must be many things.

He must be a shrewd protector of America's interests; and he must be an idealist who leads those who move for a freer and more democratic planet.

And he must see to it that government intrudes as little as possible in the lives of the people; and yet remember that it is right and proper that a nation's leader take an interest in the nation's character.

And he must be able to define—and lead—a mission.

For 7½ years, I have worked with a great president—I have seen what crosses that big desk. I have seen the unexpected crisis that arrives in a cable in a young aide's hand. And I have seen problems that simmer on for decades and suddenly demand resolution. And I have seen modest decisions made with anguish, and crucial decisions made with dispatch.

And so I know that what it all comes down to, this election—what it all comes down to, after all the shouting and the cheers—is the man at the desk. And who should sit at that desk.

My friends, I am that man.

I say it without boast or bravado.

I've fought for my country, I've served, I've built—and I will go from the hills to the hollows, from the cities to the suburbs to the loneliest town on the quietest street to take our message of hope and growth for every American to every American.

I will keep America moving forward, always forward, for a better America, for an endless enduring dream and a thousand points of light.

This is my mission. And I will complete it.

Thank you.

You know, you know it is customary to end an address with a pledge or a saying that holds a special meaning. And I've chosen one that we all know by heart. One that we all learned in school.

And I ask everyone in this great hall to stand and join me in this—we all know it.

I pledge allegiance to the flag of the United States of America and to the republic for which it stands, one nation under God, indivisible, with liberty and justice for all.

Thank you.

The Bentsen-Quayle Debate (1988)

No constitutional office has undergone a more dramatic transformation in the post-World War II era than the vice presidency. An interesting dynamic has been at play: the proliferation of nuclear weapons raised the voters' concerns that the vice president be fully competent to succeed to the presidency and immediately assume the responsibility to make life-and-death decisions; presidential candidates discovered that it was politically prudent to choose running mates of presidential caliber; vice presidents were assigned significant responsibilities and substantial resources in office; more talented political leaders sought and accepted vice-presidential nominations; and the vice presidency became the leading steppingstone to a major-party nomination for president. (See, for example, "The Twenty-second Amendment: House Debate," p. 370; "Richard Nixon's 'Checkers' Speech," p. 474; "The Twenty-fifth Amendment: Senate Debate," p. 523; and "George Bush's Acceptance Speech to the Republican National Convention," p. 825.)

In 1988, both the Democratic nominee for president, Gov. Michael S. Dukakis of Massachusetts, and Vice President George Bush, the Republican candidate, followed the practice of their recent predecessors and conducted long and thorough preconvention searches for a vice presidential running mate. Governor Dukakis, like every other presidential candidate since 1952 who lacked personal experience in Washington, tapped a Washington-based political leader, Sen. Lloyd Bentsen of Texas. Bentsen had defeated Bush in a 1970 Texas senatorial election and had risen to become the widely respected chair of the Senate Finance Committee. The Bentsen nomination was hailed by press, party, and public; indeed, by the end of the 1988 campaign, public opinion polls indicated that Bentsen was the most highly regarded candidate on either party's national ticket.

Bush searched just as thoroughly as Dukakis but, in the end, made an impulsive and controversial choice: Sen. Dan Quayle of Indiana. No sooner did Bush announce his intention to present Quayle's name to the Republican national convention than the press reported stories about the Indiana senator's mediocre academic record and his apparent use of family connections to secure a comfortable place in the National Guard during the Vietnam War. Bush's political advisers, who had been surprised by their leader's decision, assigned Quayle to campaign in small cities and rural areas, outside the bright gaze of the media spotlight.

On October 5, 1988, Bentsen and Quayle met in a nationally televised debate in Omaha, Nebraska. The sixty-

six year old Bentsen, calm and courtly, excelled during the ninety-minute encounter; his forty-one-year-old opponent, stiff and nervous, floundered. Quayle's worst moment came after he claimed to have as much experience in Congress "as Jack Kennedy did when he sought the presidency." Bentsen responded, "Senator, I served with Jack Kennedy. I knew Jack Kennedy. Jack Kennedy was a friend of mine. Senator, you're no Jack Kennedy." After the debate, Dukakis tried to capitalize on Bentsen's successful performance by campaigning alongside him and airing television commercials that raised the spectre of "President Quayle."

Quayle cost Bush a substantial number of votes on election day but not enough to lose him the presidency. Persisting in the view that he had chosen wisely, Bush pledged in 1989 that Quayle again would be his running mate in 1992. No president in history had ever made an earlier commitment to his vice president.　　　　**~**

Ms. Woodruff: By prior agreement between the two candidates, the first question goes to Senator Quayle, and you have two minutes to respond.

Senator, you have been criticized, as we all know, for your decision to stay out of the Vietnam War, for your poor academic record. But more troubling to some are some of the comments that have been made by people in your own party. Just last week, former Secretary of State Haig said that your pick was the dumbest call George Bush could have made. Your leader in the Senate, your leader in the Senate, Bob Dole, said that a better qualified person could have been chosen. Other Republicans have been far more critical in private. Why do you think that you have not made a more substantial impression on some of these people who have been able to observe you up close?

Mr. Quayle: The question goes to whether I am qualified to be vice president and, in the case of a tragedy, whether I'm qualified to be president. Qualifications for the office of vice president or president are not age alone. We must look at accomplishments, and we must look at experience. I have more experience than others that have sought the office of vice president. Now let's look at qualifications, and let's look at the three biggest issues that are going to be confronting America in the next presidency. Those three issues are national security and arms control, jobs and education, and the federal budget deficit. On each one of those issues I have more experience than does the governor of Massachusetts.

In national security and arms control you have to understand the relationship between a ballistic missile, a warhead, what throw-weight, what mega-tonnage is; you better understand about telemetry and encryption; and you better understand that you have to negotiate from a position of strength. These are important issues because we want to have more arms control and arms reductions.

In the area of jobs and education, I wrote the Job Training Partnership Act, a bipartisan bill—a bill that has trained and employed over three million economically disadvantaged youth and adults in this country. On the area of federal budget deficit, I have worked eight years on the Senate Budget Committee, and I wish that the Congress would give us the line-item veto, to help deal with that. And if qualifications alone are going to be the issue in this campaign, George Bush has more qualifications than Michael Dukakis and Lloyd Bentsen combined.

Ms. Woodruff: Senator Bentsen, Senator Bentsen. I'm going to interrupt at this point and ask once again that the audience please keep your responses as quiet as possible. We know that many of you here are for one candidate or another, but you are simply taking time away from your candidate, and more likely than not, you'll be causing the partisans for the other candidate to react again on—when their candidates speaks—so please. Senator Bentsen, you have one minute to respond.

Mr. Bentsen: This debate tonight is not about the qualifications for the vice presidency. The debate is whether or not Dan Quayle and Lloyd Bentsen are qualified to be president of the United States. Because, Judy, just as you have said, that has happened too often in the past. And if that tragedy should occur, we have to step in there without any margin for error, without time for preparation, to take over the responsibility for the biggest job in the world—that of running this great country of ours. To take over the awesome responsibility for commanding the nuclear weaponry that this country has. No, the debate tonight is a debate about the presidency itself, and a presidential decision that has to be made by you. The stakes could not be higher.

[Bentsen vs. Dukakis]

Ms. Woodruff: Senator Bentsen—a question for you, and you also have two minutes to respond. What—while this is not so much your qualifications, but your split on policy with Governor Dukakis. He has said that he does not want a clone of himself, but you disagree with him on some major issues—aid to the Nicaraguan contras, the death penalty, gun control, among others. If you had to step in to the presidency, who's agenda would you pursue? Yours, or his?

Mr. Bentsen: Well, I'm delighted to respond to that question, because we agree on so many things, and the vast majority of the issues. We agree on the fact that we have to cut this deficit, and Governor Dukakis has been able to cut that deficit ten budgets in a row in the State of Massachusetts, while he lowered the tax burden on their people from one of the highest to one of the lower in the United States. That is a major sense of achievement, and I admire that. And I'm just delighted to be on the ticket with him. Governor Dukakis and I agree that we ought to have a trade policy for this country, that we've seen this administration more than double the national debt, that they've moved this country from the number one lender nation in the world to the number one debtor nation in the world under their administration, that they have not had a trade policy, that they've let trade be a handmaiden for the foreign policy objectives of the country, that this country has exported too many jobs and not enough products.

And as I worked to pass a trade bill through the United States Senate, they threw roadblocks in the way every step of the way, but we passed a trade bill that has this premise: that any country that has full access to our markets, we're entitled to full access to their markets. Now, that means that we're going to stand tough for America, and we're going to protect those jobs, and we're going to push American products, and we're going to open up markets around the world. We'll show leadership in that respect and turn this deficit in trade around. That's the sort of thing that Michael Dukakis and I will do to bring about a better America for all of our people.

Ms. Woodruff: Senator Quayle, a minute to respond.

Mr. Quayle: As you noticed, Senator Bentsen didn't tell you very much about what Governor Dukakis would do—Governor Dukakis, one of the most liberal governors in the United States of America. The one thing he tried to point out about Governor Dukakis is that he's cut taxes. The fact of the matter is, Senator Bentsen, he's raised taxes five times. He just raised taxes this year, and that's why a lot of people refer to him as "Tax Hike Mike." That's why they refer to the state of

Massachusetts as "Taxachusetts." Because every time there's a problem the liberal governor from Massachusetts raises taxes. I don't blame Senator Bentsen for not talking about Governor Michael Dukakis; he's talking more about his record. If I had to defend the liberal policies of Governor Michael Dukakis, I wouldn't talk about it either.

Ms. Woodruff: Jon Margolis, a question for Senator Bentsen.

[Social Security]

Mr. Margolis: Senator Bentsen, you have claimed that Vice President Bush and the Republicans will raid the Social Security trust fund, and you have vowed to protect it, but as chairman of the Senate Finance Committee, you must know that there is something to the argument of your fellow Democrat, Bob Strauss, that some restraint on Social Security growth may be needed, or at least some decision to tax most Social Security benefits as regular income. In fact, you once voted for, and spoke for, a six-month delay on cost-of-living adjustment increases for Social Security. Senator, aren't you and Governor Dukakis using this issue politically, rather than dealing with it responsibly?

Mr. Bentsen: Well, I must say I hate to disappoint my good friend Bob Strauss, but we have a contract with the American people on Social Security, and Social Security is an issue where Senator Quayle voted eight times to cut the benefits on Social Security.

Mr. Quayle: (interjecting) That's wrong.

Mr. Bentsen: (continuing) When this administration came in and tried to cut the benefits, the minimum benefits—$122 a month for widows, for retirees—tried to cut the benefits for 62-year-old retirees by 40 percent, tried to do an end-run on Social Security when they first came in after promising not to

cut it, to cut it by some $20 billion. And while we were working together to reform the Social Security system and to be certain that that money was going to be there for people when they retired, at that point they tried a $40 billion end-run to cut Social Security. Now, the record is clear.

And we saw Vice President Bush fly back from the West Coast to break a tie in the United States Senate. He doesn't get to vote very often in the Senate, but he made a special trip to come back and vote against a cost-of-living increase. Now, when you talk about Social Security the people that are going to protect it are the Democrats who brought forth that program. And I think it's very important that we now see these kinds of end-runs by this administration. When they talk about the fact that they're going to continue to cut this budget, I know too well what their track record is. And we should be concerned about that kind of an effort once again after the election is over.

Ms. Woodruff: Senator Quayle, your response.

Mr. Quayle: Senator Bentsen, you know that I did not vote to cut Social Security benefits eight times. What I have voted for, and what Senator Bentsen has voted for, is to delay the cost-of-living adjustments. Sen. Bentsen, two times in the United States Senate, voted to delay the cost-of-living adjustment. The governor of Massachusetts at a governors' conference supported a resolution to delay the cost-of-living adjustment.

And, Jon, you're right, they use this for political advantage. What they try to do time and time again is to scare the old people of this country. That's the politics of the past. In 1983, Republicans and Democrats dropped their political swords and, in a bipartisan effort, saved the Social Security system. Republicans and Democrats banded together because we know that this program is not a Republican program, it's not a Democrat program; it's a program for older Americans. And that program is actuarially sound to the turn of this century.

Ms. Woodruff: Jon, a question for Senator Quayle.

[Environmental Issues]

Mr. Margolis: Senator, since coming to the Senate, you have voted against environmental protection legislation about two-thirds of the time. These include votes against pesticide controls, the toxic-waste Superfund, and health and safety protection from nuclear wastes. Senator, do you consider yourself an environmentalist? And, if you do, how do you reconcile that with your voting record?

Mr. Quayle: I have a very strong record on the environment in the United States Senate. I have a record where I voted against my president on the override of the Clean Water Act. I have voted for the major pieces of environmental legislation that have come down and been voted on in the United States Senate. This administration, and I support this administration in its environmental effort, has moved in the area for the first time to deal with the ozone problem. We now have an international treaty, a treaty that is commonly referred to as the Montreal Treaty. For the first time we are talking about the impact of CO_2 to the ozone layer. That's progress for the environment. We are committed to the environment. I take my children hiking and fishing, walking in the woods, in the wilderness. Believe me, we have a commitment to preserving the environment.

If you bring up the environment, you can't help but think about the environmental policy of the governor of Massachusetts. He talks about being an environmentalist. Let me tell you about his environmental policy. The Boston Harbor, the Boston Harbor which is the

dirtiest waterway in America. Tons of raw sewage go in there each and every day. What has the governor of Massachusetts done about that? Virtually nothing. Then he has the audacity to go down to New Jersey and tell the people in New Jersey that he's against ocean dumping. This is the same governor that applied for a license to dump Massachusetts sewage, waste off the coast of New Jersey. Who has the environmental record? Who has the environment interests? George Bush and I do.

Ms. Woodruff: Senator Bentsen?

Mr. Bentsen: Well this late conversion is interesting to me. When they talk about Boston Harbor, and he says he hasn't done anything, the facts are he has a $6 billion program under way on waste treatment, and it was this administration, their administration, that cut out the money early on to be able to clean up water and made it impossible to move ahead at that time on Boston Harbor.

We're the authors, the Democratic Party, of Clean Air, of Clean Water, of the Superfund. I'm one who played a very major role in passing the Superfund legislation. And every environmental organization that I know, every major one has now endorsed the Dukakis-Bentsen ticket. And I'm one who has just received the environmental award in Texas for the work I've done to clean up the bays, to clean up the water off the coast of Texas. Now I think we know well who's going to help clean up this environment. The record is there, the history is there, and Dukakis and Bentsen will be committed to that.

Ms. Woodruff: Tom Brokaw, a question for Senator Quayle.

[Family Assistance Programs]

Mr. Brokaw: Thank you Judy. Senator Quayle, there's been a lot of talk during the course of this campaign about family; it was the principal theme as I recall it in your acceptance speech in New Orleans. Tonight I'd like to ask you about the 65 million American children who live with their families in poverty. I'd like for you to describe to the audience the last time that you may have visited with one of those families personally, and how you explain to that family your votes against the school breakfast program, the school lunch program, and the expansion of the child immunization program.

Mr. Quayle: I have met with those people, and I met with them in Fort Wayne, Indiana, at a food bank. And you may be surprised, Tom, they didn't ask me those questions on those votes because they were glad that I took time out of my schedule to go down and to talk about how we're going to get a food bank going and making sure that a food bank goes to Fort Wayne, Indiana. And I have a very good record and a commitment to the poor, to those that don't have a family, want to have a family. This administration and a George Bush administration will be committed to eradicating poverty. Poverty hasn't gone up in this administration. It hasn't gone down much either, and that means that we have a challenge ahead of us.

But let me tell you something, what we have done for the poor. What we have done for the poor is that we, in fact—the homeless bill—the McKinney Act, which is a major piece of legislation that deals with the homeless. Congress has cut the funding that the administration recommended.

The poor and poverty—the biggest thing that we have done for poverty in America is the Tax Simplification Act of 1986. Six million working poor families got off the payroll. Six million people are off the taxpaying payrolls because of that tax reform, and they're keeping the tax money there. To help the poor, we'll have a commitment to the programs, and those programs will go on. And we

are spending more in poverty programs today than we were in 1981. That is a fact. The poverty program we are going to concentrate on is creating jobs and opportunities so that everyone will have the opportunities they want.

Ms. Woodruff: Senator Bentsen, your response.

Mr. Bentsen: I find that very interesting, because he has been of no help at all when it comes to passing the most major welfare reform bill in the history of our country, one where we're working very hard to see that people can get off welfare, break that cycle, take a step up in life, doing the kinds of things that we did there to let them have Medicaid for a year. That's a positive thing that's done. What also frustrates me with the kind of report that I just heard here is the kind of votes he's cast against child nutrition programs, the fact that he has voted against money that we needed for further immunization, the denial of polio shots to kids where the parents couldn't afford to get that kind of a shot. Now I don't really believe that is identifying with the concerns of people in poverty.

Ms. Woodruff: Tom, a question for Senator Bentsen.

[Contra Aid Qualms]

Mr. Brokaw: Senator Bentsen, I'd like to take you back to the question that Judy asked you about your differences with Michael Dukakis on contra aid. After all, contra aid is one of the cutting issues of foreign policy of this country in the last eight years. You and Michael Dukakis seem to be diametrically opposed on that.

I have been told that in a closed session of the U.S. Senate, you made one of the most eloquent and statesmanlike speeches in behalf of contra aid that anyone had made in the eight years of the Reagan term; that, in fact, you alluded to the threat the Sandinista regime could pose to your own state of Texas. Governor Dukakis, on the other hand, has described the contra aid policy as "immoral and illegal." Is he wrong?

Mr. Bentsen: Governor Dukakis and I have disagreed on the contra program—no question about that. But my big difference with this administration is they look at the contra aid program as the only way to resolve that problem. They concentrate on that. And I really think we have to give peace a chance. And that's why I've been a strong supporter of the Arias plan, a plan that won the Nobel Prize for President Arias, the president of Costa Rica. I believe that you have to work with the leaders of those other Central American countries to try to bring about the democratization of Nicaragua by negotiation, by pressure, by counseling, by diplomatic pressure—that we ought to be trying that first.

But in concentrating so much just on the contras, this administration has not paid enough attention to the rest of Central America. The concern I have is that we have a country with 85 million people sharing a 2,000-mile border with us with half of those people under the age of 15, a country that has had its standard of living cut 50 percent in the last six years. Now, we ought to be concerned about that and we ought to be involved. I was born and reared on that Mexican border. I speak their language. I spent a good part of my life down there. Governor Dukakis speaks Spanish, too. He's spent a good deal of time in Central and South America.

And we believe that we ought to be working together with a new alliance for progress, bringing in other countries to help. Bring in Europeans, the Spanish, who have a real affinity for that area. Bringing in the Japanese, who have a great capital surplus now and [are] looking for places to invest it. Those are the policy things I think we could do to

bring about peace in that area, to help raise that standard of living and give them the kind of stability where democracy can proceed and can prosper and bloom.

Those are the kinds of things that we'd be committed to in a Dukakis-Bentsen administration, to try to make this world a better place in which to live.

Ms. Woodruff: Senator Quayle, your response.

Mr. Quayle: There's no doubt, in a Dukakis administration that the aid would be cut off to the democratic resistance in Nicaragua and that is unfortunate. The reason it is unfortunate—because it is beyond me why it's okay for the Soviet Union to put in billions of dollars to prop up the communist Sandinistas, but somehow it's wrong for the United States to give a few dollars to the democratic resistance.

There's a thing called the Monroe Doctrine, something that the governor of Massachusetts has said has been superseded. I doubt if many Americans agree with that. I think they believe in the Monroe Doctrine. Senator Bentsen talked about the entire Central America. There's another issue that Michael Dukakis is wrong on in Central America and that's Grenada. He criticized our rescue mission in Grenada, according to a UPI report—criticized that, yet 85 percent of the American people supported our rescue mission and we turned a communist country into a noncommunist country. The governor of Massachusetts is simply out of step with mainstream American.

[PAC Money]

Ms. Woodruff: Brit Hume, a question for Senator Bentsen.

Mr. Hume: Good evening, Senator Bentsen, Senator Quayle. I'm sort of the clean-up man in this order, and I've been asked by my colleagues to try to deal with anything that's been left on base. Senator, I have a follow-up question for you, Senator Quayle. But Senator Bentsen, I first want to ask you a question about PAC money, something I'm sure you're prepared to talk about. Governor Dukakis has tried to make ethics a major issue in the campaign. And he has you as a running mate, a man who leads the league, at last count, in the receipt of PAC money—that being the money raised by the special-interest organizations. That is the kind of campaign financing which Governor Dukakis finds so distasteful that he has refused to accept any of it. Do you find that embarrassing, Senator?

Mr. Bentsen: No, I don't find it embarrassing at all because you have to remember that PAC money is the result of the last campaign reform bill, one that talks about employees having greater participation. And what I've done in PAC money is just what my opponent in my campaign has done in his campaign. He has, he's been raising PAC money, too. So what you have to do is comply with the laws as they are, whether you're paying taxes, or you're playing a football game; whether you like those laws or not you comply with them.

Now, I have been for campaign reform and have pushed it very hard. I believe that we have to do some things in that regard. But I've noticed that the Senator from Indiana has opposed that campaign reform and voted repeatedly against it. The things we have to do, I believe, that will cut back on "soft money," for example, which I look on as, frankly, one of those things that we have had to do because the Republicans have done it for so long, but I think it's a loophole, frankly.

But campaign reform, changing the rules of the game, is something we tried repeatedly in this session of the Congress, but only to have the Republicans lead the charge against us and defeat

us. And I wish that Senator Quayle would change his mind on that particular piece of legislation and give us the kind of a campaign reform law that I think is needed in America.

Ms. Woodruff: Senator Quayle, your response.

Mr. Quayle: Senator Bentsen is the number one PAC raiser. As a matter of fact, he used to have a $10,000 Breakfast Club. A $10,000 Breakfast Club. It only cost high-paid lobbyist special interests in Washington to come down and have breakfast with the chairman of the Senate Finance Committee—the one that oversees all the tax loopholes in the tax code—$10,000. I'm sure they weren't paying to have Corn Flakes.

Well, I'll tell you the kind of campaign reform I'm supporting, Senator Bentsen. I think it's time that we get rid of PAC money. Support our legislation where we totally eliminate contributions by special interests and political action committees, and let's have the individual contribute and the political parties contribute. That's the kind of campaign reform that Republicans are for. They want to get rid of this special interest money and rely on the individuals, and also the political parties.

Ms. Woodruff: Brit, your question for Senator Quayle. Once again, let me caution the audience: please, keep your reaction as quiet as possible. Brit.

[On Becoming President]

Mr. Hume: Senator, I want to take you back, if I can, to the question Judy asked you about some of the apprehensions people may feel about your being a heartbeat away from the presidency. And let us assume, if we can, for the sake of this question, that you become vice president and the president is incapacitated for one reason or another and you have to take the reins of power. When that moment came, what would be the first steps that you'd take and why?

Mr. Quayle: First I'd say a prayer for myself and for the country that I'm about to lead. And then I would assemble his people and talk. And I think this question keeps going back to qualifications and what kind of vice president and this hypothetical situation if I had to assume the responsibilities of the president what I would be. And, as I have said, age alone—although I can tell you, after the experience of these last few weeks on the campaign, I've added 10 years to my age—age alone is not the only qualification. You've got to look at experience, and you've got to look at accomplishments. And can you make a difference?

Have I made a difference in the United States Senate where I served for eight years? Yes, I have. Have I made a difference in the Congress that I served for twelve years? Yes, I have. As I said before, looking at the issue of qualifications, and I am delighted that it comes up, because on the three most important challenges facing America—arms control and national security, jobs and education, and budget deficit—I have more experience and accomplishments than does the governor of Massachusetts.

I have been in the Congress, and I have worked on these issues. And, believe me, when you look at arms control and trying to deal with the Soviet Union, you cannot come at it from a naive position. You have to understand the Soviet Union. You have to understand how they will respond. Sitting on that Senate Armed Services Committee for eight years has given me the experience to deal with the Soviet Union and how we can move forward. That is just one of the troubling issues that's going to be facing this nation. And I am prepared.

Mr. Hume: Senator Bentsen?

Mr. Bentsen: Well, I can't leave something on the table that he's charged me with, so let's get to that one. When you talk about the "Breakfast Club," as you know, that was perfectly legal. And I formed it and I closed it down almost immediately, because I thought the perception was bad. But it's the same law. It's the same law that lets you invite high-priced lobbyists down to Williamsburg; and bring them down there and entertain them playing golf, playing tennis and bringing Republican senators down there, to have exchanged for that contributions to their campaign.

It's the same kind of law that lets you have honorariums, and you've collected over a quarter of a million dollars of honorariums now, speaking to various interest groups. And there's no control over what you do with that money. You can spend it on anything you want to. You can spend it on golf club dues, if you want to do that. Now that's what I've seen you do in this administration, and that's why we need campaign reform laws and why I support them and you, in turn, have voted against them time and time again.

Ms. Woodruff: Jon Margolis, question for Senator Quayle.

[Workers' Rights]

Mr. Margolis: Senator Quayle, in recent years the Reagan administration has scaled back the activities of the Occupational Safety and Health Administration, prompted in part by Vice President Bush's task force on regulatory relief. The budget for the agency has been cut by 20 percent, and the number of inspections at manufacturing plants have been reduced by 33 percent.

This has had a special effect in this area where many people work in the meat-packing industry, which has a far higher rate of serious injuries than almost any other injury, a rate which appears to have been rising, although we're not really sure because some of the largest companies have allegedly been falsifying their reports. Would you acknowledge to the hundreds of injured and maimed people in Nebraska, Iowa, and elsewhere in the Midwest that, in this case, deregulation may have gone too far and the government should reassert itself in protecting workers' rights?

Mr. Quayle: The premise of your question, Jon, is that somehow this administration has been lax in enforcement of the OSHA regulations and I disagree with that, and I'll tell you why. If you want to ask some business people that I've talked to periodically, they complain about the tough enforcement of this administration.

And furthermore, let me tell you this for the record, when we have found violations in this administration there has not only been tough enforcement, but there have been the most severe penalties—the largest penalties in the history of the Department of Labor—have been levied when these violations have been found.

There is a commitment, and there will always be a commitment, to the safety of our working men and women. They deserve it, and we're committed to them. Now, the broader question goes to the whole issue of deregulation, and has deregulation worked or has deregulation not worked? In my judgment, deregulation has worked. We have a deregulated economy and we have produced through low taxes, not high taxes, through deregulation, the spirit of entrepreneurship, the individual going out and starting a business, the businessman or woman willing to go out and risk their investment and start up a business and hire people—we have produced 17 million jobs in this country since 1982.

Deregulation as a form of political philosophy is a good philosophy. It's one that our opponents disagree with. They want a centralized government. But we believe in the market; we believe in the people. And yes, there's a role of government and the role of government is to make sure that the safety and health and welfare of the people is taken care of. And we'll continue to do that.

Ms. Woodruff: Senator Bentsen?

Mr. Bentsen: I think you see once again a piece of Democratic legislation that's been passed to try to protect the working men and women of America. And then you've seen an administration that came in and really didn't have its heart in that kind of an enforcement. A good example of that is the environmental protection laws that we were talking about a moment ago. This administration came in and put in a James Watt and Anne Gorsuch. Now that's the Bonnie and Clyde, really, of environmental protection. And that's why it's important that you have people that truly believe, and trying to represent the working men and women of America. Most employers do a good job of that, but some of them put their profits before people. And that's why you have to have OSHA, and that's why you have to have tough and good and fair enforcement of it. And that's what a Democratic administration would do to help make this working place a safer and a better place to be employed.

Ms. Woodruff: Jon Margolis, another question for Senator Bentsen.

[Farm Policy]

Mr. Margolis: Senator Bentsen, since you have been in the Senate, the government has spent increasing amounts of money in an effort to protect the family farmer, but most of the subsidies seem to go, do go, to the largest and richest farmers, who presumably need it least, while it's the smaller farmers who are often forced to sell out, sometimes to their large farmer neighbor who's gotten more subsidies to begin with.

Despite the fact that I believe you, sir, are rather a large farmer yourself, do you believe it's time to uncouple the subsidy formula from the amount of land a farmer has and target federal money to the small- and medium-size farmer?

Mr. Bentsen: Well, I've supported that. I voted for the 50,000 limitation to get away from the million-dollar contributions to farmers. You know, of the four that are on this ticket, I'm the only one that was born and reared on a farm, and still involved in farming. So I think I understand their concerns and their problems. Now, I feel very strongly that we ought to be doing more for the American farmer, and what we've seen under this administration is neglect of that farmer.

We've seen them drive 220,000 farmers off the farm. They seem to think the answer is, "Move 'em to town." But we ought not to be doing that. What you have seen them do is cut farm assistance for the rural areas by over 50 percent. We're seeing rural hospitals close all over the country because of this kind of an administration. We've seen an administration that has lost much of our market abroad because they have not had a trade policy. We saw our market lost by some 40 percent. And that's one of the reasons that we've seen the cost of the farm program, which was only about $2.5 billion when they took office, now go to about $25 billion. Now we can bring that kind of a cost down and get more to market prices if we'll have a good trade policy.

I was, in January, visiting with Mr. Takeshita, the new prime minister of Japan. I said, "You're paying five times as much for beef as we pay for in our country—pay for it in our country—six times as much for rice. You have a $60 billion trade surplus with us. You could improve the standard of living of your people. You're spending 27 percent of your disposable income on food. We spent 14 or 15 percent. When you have

that kind of a barrier up against us, that's not free and fair trade, and we don't believe that should continue."

We should be pushing very hard to open up those markets, and stand up for the American farmer. And see that we recapture those foreign markets, and I think we can do it with a Dukakis-Bentsen administration.

Ms. Woodruff: Senator Quayle.

Mr. Quayle: Senator Bentsen talks about recapturing the foreign markets. Well, I'll tell you one way that we're not going to recapture the foreign markets, and that is if, in fact, we have another Jimmy Carter grain embargo. Jimmy—Jimmy Carter grain embargo—Jimmy Carter grain embargo set the American farmer back. You know what the farmer is interested in? Net farm income. Every 1 percent of increase in interest rates—a billion dollars out of the farmer's pocket. Net farm income—increase inflation another billion dollars.

Another thing that a farmer's not interested in and that's supply management the Democratic platform talks about. But, the governor of Massachusetts, he had the farm program. He went to the farmers in the Midwest, and told them not to grow corn, not to grow soybeans, but to grow Belgium endive. That's what his—that's what he and his Harvard buddies think of the American farmers. Grow Belgium endive. To come in and to tell our farmers not to grow corn, not to grow soybeans, that's the kind of farm policy you'll get under a Dukakis administration, and one I think the American farmer rightfully will reject.

Ms. Woodruff: Tom Brokaw, a question for Senator Bentsen?

[Current Economic Policies]

Mr. Brokaw: Senator Bentsen, you were a businessman before you entered the U.S. Senate. Let me offer you an inventory, if I may: lower interest rates, lower unemployment, lower inflation, and an arms control deal with the Soviet Union. Now, two guys come through your door at your business, and say, "We'd like you to change," without offering a lot of specifics. Why would you accept their deal?

Mr. Bentsen: You know, if you let me write $200 billion worth of hot checks every year, I could give you an illusion of prosperity, too. This is an administration that has more than doubled the national debt, and they've done that in less than eight years. They have taken this country from the number one lender nation in the world to the number one debtor nation in the world. And the interest on that debt next year, on this Reagan-Bush debt of our nation, is going to be $640 for every man, woman and child in America, because of this kind of a credit card mentality. So, we go out and we try to sell our securities, every week, and hope that the foreigners will buy them. And they do buy them, but every time they do, we lose some of our economic independence for the future.

Now they've turned around and they've bought 10 percent of the manufacturing base of this country. They bought 20 percent of the banks. They own 46 percent of the commercial real estate in Los Angeles. They're buying America on the cheap. Now when we have other countries that can't manage their economy down in Central and South America, we send down the American ambassador. We send down the International Monetary Fund and we tell them what they can buy and what they can sell and how to run their economies. The ultimate irony would be to have that happen to us because foreigners finally quit buying our securities.

So what we need in this country is someone like Mike Dukakis who gave 10 balanced budgets in a row there and was able to do that, meet that kind of a

commitment, set those tough priorities. We need an administration that will turn this trade policy around and open up those markets, stand tough with our trading partners to help keep the jobs at home and send the products abroad.

Ms. Woodruff: Senator Quayle?

Mr. Quayle: Senator Bentsen talks about running up the debt. Well the governor of Massachusetts has run up more debt than all the governors in the history of Massachusetts combined going back to the days of the Pilgrims. I don't believe that that's the kind of policy that we want. The question went to the heart of the matter, Tom. You asked the question that why would we change? Well we have changed since 1980. We've got interest rates down. We got inflation down. People are working again. America is held in respect once again around the world. But we're going to build on that change.

And as we made those positive change of lower interest rates, lower rate of inflation, the governor of Massachusetts fought us every step of the way. We are proud of the record of accomplishment and the opportunities and the hope for millions of Americans—hope and opportunity of these Americans is because of the policies that we have had for the last eight years and we want to build on that and change it for even the better.

Ms. Woodruff: Tom, a question for Senator Quayle.

[The Military in the Drug War]

Mr. Brokaw: Senator Quayle, as you mention here tonight, you actively supported the invasion of Grenada, which was the military operation to rescue some American medical students and to rescue an island from a Marxist takeover. If military force was necessary in that endeavor, why not use the military to go after the South American drug cartels and after General Noriega for that matter on a surgical strike, since drugs in the minds of most Americans pose a far greater danger to many more people?

Mr. Quayle: You're absolutely right. You're absolutely right, the drug problem is the number one issue.

Mr. Brokaw: But would you please address the military aspect of it?

Mr. Quayle: I will address the military aspect if I may respond. The military aspect of the drug problem is being addressed. As a matter of fact, we are using the Department of Defense in a coordinated effort on reconnaissance, but I don't believe that we're going to turn the Department of Defense into a police organization. We are using our military assets in a prudent way to deal with interdiction. And we've made some success in this area. Seventy tons of cocaine have been stopped.

But, you know, when you look at the drug problem, and it is a tremendous problem and there are no easy solutions to it, it's a complicated problem. And it's heading up the effort to try to create a drug-free America, which is a challenge and a goal of all of us. Not only will we utilize national defense and the Department of Defense, but we've got to get on the demand side of the ledger. We've got to get to education, and education ought to begin at home, and it ought to be reinforced, reinforced in our schools.

And there's another thing that will be more important than the premise of this question on a hypothetical of using troops. We'll use military assets. We're not going to, we'll use military assets, but we need to focus on another part of this problem, and that problem is law enforcement. And here's where we have a major disagreement with the governor of Massachusetts. He is opposed to the death penalty for drug kingpins. We believe people convicted of that crime deserve the death penalty, as does the

legislation that's in the Congress that's supported by a bipartisan group, including many Democrats of his party. He also was opposed to mandatory drug sentencing for drug dealers in the state of Massachusetts. You cannot have a war on drugs, you cannot be tough on drugs and weak on crime.

Ms. Woodruff: Senator Bentsen.

Mr. Bentsen: It's interesting to see that the senator from Indiana, when we had a resolution on the floor of the United States Senate sponsored by Senator Dole, that this government would make no deal with Noriega, that the senator from Indiana was one of the dozen senators that voted against it. It's also interesting to see that one of his campaign managers that's trying to help him with his image, was also hired by Noriega to help him with his image in Panama.

What we have seen under this administration, we have seen them using eight Cabinet officers, 28 different agencies, all fighting over turf. And that's one thing we'd correct under the Dukakis-Bentsen administration. We'd put one person in charge in the war against drugs, and we'd commit the resources to get that job done. Now, Mike Dukakis has been able to do that type of thing in the state of Massachusetts by cutting the drug use in high schools while it's going up around the rest of the country, by putting in a drug educational program that the Drug Enforcement Agency said was a model for the country. We'd be doing that around the rest of the country. That's a positive attack against drugs.

Ms. Woodruff: Brit Hume, a question for Senator Quayle.

[Assuming the Presidency]

Mr. Hume: Senator, I want to take you back to the question that I asked you earlier about what would happen if you were to take over in an emergency and what you would do first and why. You said you'd say a prayer and you said something about a meeting. What would you do next?

Mr. Quayle: I don't believe that it's proper for me to get into the specifics of a hypothetical situation like that. The situation is that if I was called upon to serve as the president of this country, or the responsibilities of the president of this country, would I be capable and qualified to do that? And I've tried to list the qualifications of 12 years in the United States Congress. I have served in the Congress for 12 years; I have served in the Congress and served eight years on the Senate Armed Services Committee.

I have traveled a number of times; I've been to Geneva many times to meet with our negotiators as we were hammering out the INF Treaty. I've met with the Western political leaders—Margaret Thatcher, Chancellor Kohl—I know them; they know me. I know what it takes to lead this country forward. And if that situation arises, yes, I will be prepared, and I'll be prepared to lead this country if that happens.

Mr. Hume: Senator Bentsen.

Mr. Bentsen: Well, once again, I think what we're looking at here is someone that can step in at the presidency level at the moment, if that tragedy would occur. And if that's the case, again you have to look at maturity of judgment, and you have to look at breadth of experience. You have to see what kind of leadership roles that person has played in his life before that crisis struck him. And if you do that type of thing, then you'll arrive at a judgment that I think would be a wise one, and I hope that would mean that you say, "We're going to vote for Mike Dukakis and Lloyd Bentsen."

Ms. Woodruff: Brit, a question for Senator Bentsen.

[Bentsen's Breakfast Club]

Mr. Hume: Senator, I want to take you back, if I can, to the celebrated "Breakfast Club." When it was first revealed that you had a plan to have people pay $10,000 a plate to have breakfast with you, you handled it with disarming, not to say charming, candor. You said it was a mistake and you disbanded it and called the whole idea off, and you were widely praised for having handled it deftly.

The question I have is, if the *Washington Post* had not broken that story and other media picked up on it, what can you tell us tonight as to why we should not believe that you would still be having those breakfasts to this day?

Mr. Bentsen: (Laughs) Well, I must say, Brit, I don't make many mistakes, but that one was a real doozy. And I agree with that. And, as you know, I immediately disbanded it; it was perfectly legal. And you have all kinds of such clubs on the Hill, and you know that. And—but I still believe that the better way to go is to have a campaign reform law that takes care of that kind of a situation. Even though it's legal, the perception is bad. So I would push very strong to see that we reform the entire situation. I'd work for that end and that's what my friend from Indiana has opposed repeatedly, vote after vote.

Ms. Woodruff: Senator Quayle?

Mr. Quayle: He disbanded the club, but he's still got the money. He is the number one receiver of political action committee money. Now, Senator Bentsen's talked about reform. Well, let me tell you about the reform that we're pushing. Let's eliminate political action committees to special interest money. There's legislation before the Congress to do that. That way we won't have to worry about breakfast clubs or who's the number one PAC raiser. We can go back and get the contributions from the working men and women and the individuals of America. We can also strengthen our two-party system, and it needs strengthening, and rely more on the political parties than we have in the past. That's the kind of campaign reform that I'm for, and I hope the senator will join me.

Ms. Woodruff: Jon Margolis, a question for Senator Bentsen.

["Greenhouse Effect"]

Mr. Margolis: Senator, we've all just finished—most America has just finished one of the hottest summers it can remember, and apparently this year will be the fifth out of the last nine that are among the hottest on record. No one knows, but most scientists think that something we're doing, human beings are doing, are exacerbating this problem and that this could, in a couple of generations, threaten our descendants' comfort and health and perhaps even their existence.

As vice president, what would you urge our government to do to deal with this problem? And specifically, as a Texan, could you support a substantial reduction in the use of fossil fuel, which might be necessary down the road?

Mr. Bentsen: Well, I think what you can do in that one, and which would be very helpful, is to use a lot more natural gas, which burns a lot cleaner. And what Mike Dukakis has said is that he'll try to break down those regulatory roadblocks that you have in the regulatory agency that denies much of the passage of that natural gas to the Northeast, where you, in turn, can fight against acid rain, which is another threat because it's sterilizing our lakes, it's killing our fish.

And it's interesting to me to see in the resumé of Senator Quayle that he brags on the fact that he's been able to fight the acid rain legislation. I don't think that that's a proper objective in trying to clean up this environment. But the greenhouse effect is one that has to be a threat to all of us, and we have to look for alternative sources of fuel, and I've supported that very strongly.

The Department of Energy is one that has cut back substantially on the study of those alternative sources of fuel. We can use other things that'll help the farmer. We can convert corn to ethanol, and I would push for that very strong. So absolutely, I'll do these things that are necessary to put the environment of our country number one, because if we don't protect that, we'll destroy the future of our children, and we must be committed to trying to clean up the water, clean up the air, and do everything we can not only from a research standpoint, but also in the applied legislation to see that that's carried out.

Ms. Woodruff: Senator Quayle?

Mr. Quayle: Vice President George Bush has said that he will take on the environmental problem. He has said further that he will deal with the acid rain legislation and reduce millions of tons of the SO_2 content. That legislation won't get through the Congress this year, but it will get through in a George Bush administration, a George Bush administration that is committed to the environment. Now the greenhouse effect is an important environmental issue. It is important for us to get the data in, to see what alternatives we might have to the fossil fuels, to make sure that we know what we're doing. And there are some explorations and things that we can consider in this area. The drought highlighted the problem that we have. And, therefore, we need to get on with it. And in a George Bush administration, you can bet that we will.

Ms. Woodruff: A question for Senator Quayle.

[U.S. Foreign Debt]

Mr. Margolis: Senator, as vice president, your most important contribution would be the advice you gave the president. One of the most troubling facts that's going to face the new administration is the fact that the United States has now become the world's largest debtor nation. In 1987, foreigners underwrote our debts to the tune of about $138 billion.

Last week, a top official of the Japanese Economic Planning Agency bragged that Japan now is in a position to influence the value of the dollar, of our interest rates, and even our stock prices, and he warned that one day maybe they'd do just that. If you were vice president of the United States and Japan did that, what would you tell the president to do?

Mr. Quayle: When you look at dealing with this total problem—not just with the Japanese, but the underlying question on this total world debt problem—you have got to see why are we a debtor and what is attracting the foreign investment into our country today, whether it's the Japanese or others.

I would rather have people come over here and to make investments in this country rather than going elsewhere, because by coming over here and making investments in this country, we are seeing jobs. Do you realize that today we are producing Hondas and exporting Hondas to Japan? We are the envy of the world.

The United States—some of Senator Bentsen's supporters laugh at that. They laugh at that, because they don't believe that the United States of America is the envy of the world. Well, I can tell you, the American people think the United States of America is the envy of the world.

Ms. Woodruff: Senator Bentsen— oh, I'm sorry, go ahead.

Mr. Quayle: We are the greatest nation in this world and the greatest economic power. Now, there's been some talk in Congress about forgiveness of debt. Forgiveness of debt is wrong. Forgiveness of international debt would be counterproductive. And I'd like to see those that talk about forgiving debt, Senator Bentsen, to go out and talk about the farmer that's in debt that doesn't have his forgiven. That's not the kind of policy George Bush will have.

Ms. Woodruff: Senator Bentsen.

Mr. Bentsen: Well, I've told you what I'd do about trade and trying to help turn that situation around. But [what] we also should do is get them to give us more burden-sharing when it comes to national defense. We have a situation today where on a per capita basis, people in western Europe are spending about one third as much as we are in our country. And then when you go to Japan, where we're spending 6½ percent on defense of the democracies, they're spending 1 percent.

I met with some of the Japanese business leaders, talking to them about it. And I said, "You know, we have 50,000 troops here in Japan, protecting the democracies of Asia. And it costs $3.5 billion a year. You're the number two economic power in the world. You ought to measure up to that responsibility and carry some of that cost."

I said, "If we were not doing what we're doing, we'd have a big budget surplus." And I said, "You'd have chaos, because you get 55 percent of your oil from the Persian Gulf and you wouldn't have the U.S. Navy down there to take care of that." Now, the senator from Indiana, when we passed a resolution in the United States Senate to ask for burden-sharing on that cost to keep those sea lanes open from the Japanese, he voted against that. I don't understand that.

Ms. Woodruff: Tom Brokaw, a question for Senator Quayle.

[The Presidency]

Mr. Brokaw: Senator Quayle, I don't mean to beat this drum until it has no more sound left in it, but to follow up on Brit Hume's question, when you said that it was a hypothetical situation, it is sir, after all, the reason that we're here tonight, because you are running not just for vice president. And if you cite the experience that you had in Congress, surely you must have some plan in mind about what you would do if it fell to you to become president of the United States as it has to so many vice presidents just in the last 25 years or so.

Mr. Quayle: Let me try to answer the question one more time. I think this is the fourth time that I have had this question and—

Mr. Brokaw: Third time.

Mr. Quayle: Three times, that I've had this question and I'll try to answer it again for you as clearly as I can because the question you're asking is, "What kind of qualifications does Dan Quayle have to be president?" What kind of qualifications do I have and what would I do in this kind of a situation? And what would I do in this situation?

I would make sure that the people in the Cabinet and the people and advisers to the president are called. I'll talk to them and I'll work with them. And I will know them on a firsthand basis, because as vice president, I'll sit on the National Security Council and I'll know them on a firsthand basis because I'm going to be coordinating the drug effort. I'll know them on a firsthand basis because Vice President George Bush is going to recreate the Space Council and I'll be in charge of that. I will have day-to-day activities with all the people in government.

And then if that unfortunate situation happens, if that situation which would be very tragic happens, I will be prepared to carry out the responsibilities of the presidency of the United States of America. And I will be prepared to do that. I will be prepared not only because of my service in the Congress, but because of my ability to communicate and to lead. It is not just age, it's accomplishments, it's experience. I have far more experience than many others that sought the office of vice president of this country. I have as much experience in the Congress as Jack Kennedy did when he sought the presidency. I will be prepared to deal with the people in the Bush administration if that unfortunate event would ever occur.

Ms. Woodruff: Senator Bentsen?

Mr. Bentsen: Senator, I served with Jack Kennedy. I knew Jack Kennedy. Jack Kennedy was a friend of mine. Senator, you're no Jack Kennedy. What has to be done in a situation like that, in a situation like that is to call in the joint—

Ms. Woodruff: Please, please, once again you're only taking time away from your own candidates.

Mr. Quayle: That was really uncalled for, Senator.

Mr. Bentsen: You're the one that was making the comparison, Senator, and I'm one who knew him well. And frankly, I think you're so far apart in the objectives you choose for your country that I did not think the comparison was well taken.

Ms. Woodruff: Tom, a question for Senator Bentsen.

[Middle East Hostages]

Mr. Brokaw: Since you seem to be taking no hostages on the stage, let me ask you a question about the American—nine still in brutal captivity in the Middle East. Senator Bentsen, you have been critical of the Iran-contra affair. But tell me, does the Dukakis-Bentsen ticket have any realistic plan for getting the American hostages being held in the Middle East released in any due time?

Mr. Bentsen: Tom, that's one of the toughest problems that any chief executive will face because you can't help but have the sympathy for that family and for those hostages in themselves. But the one thing we ought to have, know by now is that you can't go out and make secret deals with the Ayatollah. You can't trade arms for hostages. When you try to do that there's no question but what you just encourage more taking of hostages. And that's been the result by this dumb idea that was cooked out, cooked up in the White House basement.

And I want to tell you that George Bush, attending 17 of those meetings and having no record of what he said—if Lloyd Bentsen was in those meetings, you would certainly hear from him, and no one would be asking, "Where is Lloyd?" Because I would be making, I would be saying, "That's a dumb idea and now let's put an end to it." And I would speak up on that type of thing. So all you can do on that is to continue to push, use every bit of diplomatic pressure you can, what you can do in the way of economic pressure in addition to that. And that's what you strive to do to have a successful release, finally, of those hostages. But not to encourage more taking of hostages.

Ms. Woodruff: Senator Quayle?

Mr. Quayle: There's no doubt about it that arms for hostages is wrong, and it will never be repeated. We learn by our mistakes. But there have been a number of successes in foreign policy in this administration. But the question goes to a very difficult one: How do you do it? No one has the answer. If they did we'd, we'd certainly do it. But we won't keep trying, we'll keep trying, we'll keep the doors open. And hopefully some day Iran, and others who control those hostages, will want to return to civilized international commu-

nity. And they can do that starting now by releasing those hostages that are held illegally.

Ms. Woodruff: Brit Hume, a question for Senator Bentsen.

[Bentsen's Past Presidential Bid]

Mr. Hume: Senator, much of the Dukakis and Bentsen campaign of late has been devoted to the notion that Senator Quayle isn't ready for the vice presidency and perhaps the presidency. And certainly nothing that you have said here tonight suggests that you think otherwise. I wonder if you think it's really fair for you to advance that view in light of the fact that you ran for the presidency, not the vice presidency, in 1976, having not yet completed one full term in the Senate and having previously served three terms in the House almost a quarter of a century earlier, when in fact your time in Washington was about equal to what he has now?

Mr. Bentsen: Well, I think what you have to look at is the record of a man who has served his country— served his country in war, headed up a squadron in combat, a man who built a business, knew what it was to meet a payroll, create jobs, and then serve in the United States Senate; and one who has been able to bring about some of the kinds of legislation that I've been able to bring about in my service there. I must say I didn't do a very good job of running for the presidency, and I'm well aware of that. But what we're looking at today is trying to judge, once again, the breadth of experience and the maturity of someone taking on this kind of task. That's the judgment that has to be exercised by the people of America. It's a presidential decision that you're facing, and it's a very important one, because we're talking about who's going to lead this country into its future, and you can't have a more important responsibility than that one.

Mr. Hume: Senator Quayle?

Mr. Quayle: When you look at qualifications, you look at accomplishments as well as experience. And one of the accomplishments that I'm proudest of is the authorship of the Job Training Partnership Act that has trained and educated and employed over 3 million young people and adults that are economically disadvantaged.

And we did it in a way that we got the private sector to involve itself with the public sector on Private Industry Councils throughout America that serve over the service delivery areas. We have 51 percent of that Private Industry Council that are businessmen and women; we have members of unions; we have community-based organizations; we have education leaders. And what we've been able to do is establish a program that's working, that's putting people back to work. That is an accomplishment, and that is an accomplishment that I will take with me into the White House.

Ms. Woodruff: Brit, a question for Senator Quayle.

[Cultural Influences]

Mr. Hume: Senator, I want to ask you a question, and it may be a little off the subject of politics, it's aimed to get more at the question of what sort of person you are. I hope that, Senator Bentsen, if you choose to, you might choose to answer the same question, in your rebuttal time. Senator, can you identify any work of literature or art, or even a film that you have seen or read or experienced anywhere in the last two years that has had a particularly strong effect on you, and tell us why?

Mr. Quayle: In the last six months I think there are three very important books that I read that have had an impact. The three books are: one, Richard Nixon's *Victory in 1999,* Richard Lugar's—Senator Richard Lugar's *Letters to the Next President,* Bob Massey's *Alexandra—Nicholas and Alexandra,* which deals with the fall of the Russian empire and the coming of Leninism in 1917.

Those three books, which I read over the last spring vacation and early summer, had a very definite impact because what former President Nixon and Senator Richard Lugar were talking about was a foreign policy as we move toward the 21st century. And the historical book of the downfall of the Czar and the coming of Leninism—combining those three books together gave me a better appreciation of the challenges that we have ahead of us. In Senator Lugar's book he talks about the advancement of human rights around the world. He talked about his leadership effort in the Philippines and South Africa, where we now see human rights and advancement of the Reagan agenda.

Former President Nixon talked about what we're going to do after détente and arms control, and how we're going to pursue new arms control with the Soviet Union. He talked a little bit about how we deal with the Soviet Union. And this is one of the differences between George Bush and Michael Dukakis, because George Bush understands to deal with the Soviet Union and to get progress, you must deal from a position of strength. And the governor of Massachusetts doesn't understand that. I understand it, and a George Bush administration will pursue that policy.

Mr. Hume: Senator Bentsen?

Mr. Bentsen: I think reading—pardon me—I think reading *Winds of War* and *Guns of August* back to back, I think that really shows you how we make the same mistakes too often, over and over again. And it seems to me that the senator from Indiana is beginning to do that one. As I look on the progress that's been made toward disarmament and cutting back on nuclear weapons, and see what Ronald Reagan has been able to do with the INF Treaty—and I think he deserves great credit for that one—I see a situation where the senator from Indiana has now jumped off the reservation when we talk about building on what Ronald Reagan has done, and opposes what Ronald Reagan wants to do, the Joint Chiefs of Staff and the secretary of defense, and says, "Let's go slow on doing further disarmament and trying to get to the next treaty." I think that's a mistake.

I think that you have to deal with the Russians from strength, and we have to understand that you have to have a strong modernized nuclear deterrent. But I think we can make substantial progress, and we ought to take advantage of it. I think he's arrived at a very dangerous judgment in the question of war and peace, and it concerns me very much, because I saw him also try to sabotage the INF Treaty when it was on the floor of the United States Senate, with what he was doing there. He's listening once again—

Ms. Woodruff: Senator—

Mr. Bentsen: —to the winds of the radical right. My light was still on, Judy.

Ms. Woodruff: Jon Margolis, a question for Senator Quayle.

[Character Questions]

Mr. Margolis: Senator Quayle, I want to go back to the matter of qualifications, which I think for most people is more than just—more than just your—how long you've been in the Senate—

Mr. Bentsen: Jon, we can't hear you.

Mr. Quayle: I can hear you.

Mr. Margolis: You can hear now?

I want to go back to the question of qualifications, which I think for most

people is more than just how long you've been in the Senate and how long you've been in public life. There's also a question of candor and of consistency. And several of the things you've said, both here and earlier, I think have raised some reasonable questions.

Each of them alone might seem rather trivial, but I think together they create a pattern that needs to be asked. You've talked a few times today about the Job Training Partnership Act, which you authored. In fact, I believe you co-authored it with another senator whom you almost never name. Earlier in the campaign, when you were asked why you got a very—a desk job in the National Guard, after being trained as a welder—you said, at the time, you had a very strong background in journalism, which at that time was summer jobs at your family-owned newspaper, which you have not been very forthcoming about what they were, as you have not been very forthcoming about your college record. Now, you'll have to say—you have, at least the males on this panel have earlier agreed that your record was probably comparable to ours.

But, nonetheless, these examples of sort of overstatement and exaggeration, and not being forthcoming, this is what has led a lot of people to question this part of your qualifications. Not your—not your experiences, but your character. Would you like to set some of these things straight now, as to what you did in your summer jobs in college, what your grades were like, and would you like to identify your cosponsor of the Job Training Partnership Act?

Mr. Quayle: All in two minutes?

Mr. Margolis: Sure.

Mr. Quayle: Let me—let me start with the underlying premise that somehow I haven't been straightforward, and I have, and let's go—right to the very first question: The Job Training Partnership Act. I was the author of that. The co-author in the United States

Senate was Senator Kennedy. I was the chairman of the employment and productivity subcommittee—chairmen of the committee write that legislation. Chairmen of the committee write the legislation, and then they go out and get cosponsorship. And when you are the chairman of the committee, and you sit down and you write the legislation, you are the author of that.

And I'm proud to have been the author of that, because you know what we had, we had a CETA program, that spent $50 billion—from about 1973 through 1982. And when we concluded that program—when we concluded that program, unemployment was higher than when it began. It was a program that didn't work, and the Job Training Partnership Act does work.

Now, the issue of releasing all of my grades. I am, and I stand before you tonight, as the most investigated person ever to seek public office. Thousands of journalists have asked every professor I've had, all my teachers, and they know—and I've never professed to be anything but an average student. I have never said that I was anything more than that, but it's not whether you're an average student, it's what are you going to do with your life? And what am I going to do with my life? I have committed it to public service since I was 29 years of age: Elected to the House of Representatives, elected to the United States Senate when I was 33, and now. . . .

Ms. Woodruff: Senator? Senator Bentsen?

Mr. Bentsen: I have absolutely no quarrel with Senator Quayle's military record, but I do strongly disagree with him on some of the issues. You make great patriotic speeches, and I enjoy them. But I don't understand your vote on veterans' issues. Senator Quayle has one of the worst voting records in the United States Senate on veterans' issues. And one of them that particularly bothers me, sponsoring legislation to put a tax on combat pay and disability pay for veterans, for fighting men and women of America—tax on disability pay when lying there in the hospital, people who have sacrificed for our country. I think you ought to explain that to the people of America, and you ought to explain it tonight.

Ms. Woodruff: Jon, a question for Senator Bentsen.

[Domestic Budget Cuts]

Mr. Margolis: Senator, you're chairman of the Senate Finance Committee, and you're generally considered rather an orthodox conservative on fiscal matters, meaning someone who would be very concerned about the budget deficit. With everybody in politics afraid even to mention taxes or Social Security cuts or even very much restraint in defense spending, would you now list a few specific programs which would reduce or eliminate—which you would reduce or eliminate to cut the deficit by about $50 billion, the deficit which is expected to be about $135 billion this fiscal year?

Mr. Bentsen: One of them that I'd work on, and I do this as a farmer, I'd try to turn the situation around where we have seen the subsidy payments go from two and a half billion to 10 times that under this administration. And the way I would accomplish that was with a tough trade policy—opening up those markets, getting those prices back up to market prices. We can do that if we have an aggressive trade policy for our country, if we make trade a number one priority and not trade it off for some foreign policy objective of the moment. That means we have to stand up for the American farmers, and that cuts back on the regulation on American farmers.

That's a positive way to accomplish that. In addition to that, we'd do some of the things that I think have to be done insofar as doing a better job of procurement, particularly when we're talking about some of our military things that we should buy. I know that I've fought very hard to put in an independent inspector general for the Defense Department, but the senator from Indiana opposed me on that.

But we were finally able to put that into effect, and we saved over a quarter of a billion dollars this year—almost enough to buy a squadron of 716s. Those are the kinds of things that I'd work on, and one of the things I learned in business is that you can expect what you inspect. So we'd be doing a much tougher job of auditing to try to get rid of some of these kickbacks to consultants on military contracts, to be much more aggressive on that. In addition, those types of things would bring the interest rate down. I'd try to turn this trade deficit around and that too would help us and help us very substantially.

And I'd get rid of some things like these planes that you're going to have that the administration wants that will fly from New York to Tokyo and take those investment bankers over there in four hours. I don't think we can afford a piece of technological elegance like that. I'd strike that sort of thing from the ticket. I don't know how many people have ridden the Concorde. Not many. But I voted against it [and] said it would be a financial disaster, and it's been just that. So those are the types of things that I would work on.

Ms. Woodruff: Senator Quayle.

Mr. Quayle: The way we're going to reduce this budget deficit—and it is a challenge to make sure that it is reduced—is first to stick to the Gramm-Rudman targets. The Gramm-Rudman targets have worked. We've reduced the federal budget deficit $70 billion. Senator Bentsen voted against Gramm-Rudman—the very tool that has been used to bring the federal budget deficit down.

We're going to need all the tools possible to bring this federal budget deficit down. We need the tools of a line-item veto. A line-item veto that 43 governors in this country have, but not the president of the United States. The president of the United States needs to have a line-item veto when Congress goes ahead and puts into appropriations bills unrequested and unnecessary spending. Let the president put a line through that, send it back to the Congress, and then let the Congress vote on it again. Congress has got to help out in reducing this budget deficit as much as the executive branch.

Ms. Woodruff: Tom Brokaw, a last question for Senator Bentsen.

[Democratic Differences]

Mr. Brokaw: Senator Bentsen, I'd like to ask you about your split personality during this election year. You're running on a ticket with Michael Dukakis, a man who is opposed to the death penalty, a man who is in favor of gun control and at the same time, you're running for the United States Senate in the state of Texas where your position on many of those same issues is well-known and absolutely opposed to him. How do you explain to the people of Texas how you can be a social conservative on those cutting issues and still run with Michael Dukakis on the national ticket?

Mr. Bentsen: Michael Dukakis wasn't looking for a clone. I think it's part of the strength and the character of this man that he reaches out and that he wants someone that will speak up, and that I'll do. I've seen many chief executives come into my office and say, they're going over and tell the president of the United States off, they're going to pound the desk, and go into that office and turn to jello. Now, I dealt with many a president, and I don't hesitate for a minute to speak up.

But when you're talking about something like the death penalty, where Michael Dukakis and I do disagree, what you really ought to get to is what's being done against crime and what kind of progress he's been able to make. In the state of Massachusetts, he has the homicide rate down to the lowest of any industrial state. It's substantially ahead of the national average. He's been able to do that with an educated program for the people of that state by adding some 1,500 new police officers. He's done it in turn by the leadership that I think he will bring to the ticket when he becomes president of the United States. And fighting drugs, he's taken it down some 4 percent in the high schools of that state while it's gone up around the rest of the nation.

But you would see him as president of the United States being very aggressive in this fight against crime and having that kind of a successful result. And that's one of the reasons I'm delighted and proud to be on the ticket with him. Sure we have some differences, but overall we have so many things we agree on. This situation of a trade policy, of cutting back on the deficit, those are positive, plus things and major issues facing our nation.

Ms. Woodruff: Senator Quayle?

Mr. Quayle: One of the things that they don't agree on is in the area of national defense, national defense and how we're going to preserve the freedom in this country. Michael Dukakis is the most liberal national Democrat to seek the office of presidency since George McGovern.

He is for, he is against the MX missile, the Midgetman, cutting two aircraft carriers. He is opposed to many defense programs that are necessary to defend this country. That's why former Secretary of Defense and former Energy Secretary in the Carter administration Jim Schlesinger in an open letter to *Time* magazine asked Governor Dukakis, "Are you viscerally anti-military?"

Jim Schlesinger never got an answer and the reason he didn't is because the governor of Massachusetts doesn't want to answer former Secretary Jim Schlesinger on that very important question.

Ms. Woodruff: Tom, a last question for Senator Quayle.

[Life's Experiences]

Mr. Brokaw: Senator Quayle, all of us in our lifetime encounter an experience that helps shape our adult philosophy in some form or another. Could you describe for this audience tonight what experience you may have had and how it shaped your political philosophy?

Mr. Quayle: There are a lot of experiences that I've had that have shaped my adult philosophy, but the one that I keep coming back to time and time again, and I talk about at commencement addresses, I talk about it in the high schools, I talk about it when I visit the job training centers, and it's the advice that my maternal grandmother Martha Pulliam, who's 97 years old—we are a modern-day four-generation family. The informa—, the advice that she gave me when I was growing up is advice that I've given my children and I've given to a number of children, a number of people, and it's very simple, it's very common sense. And she says, "You can do anything you want to if you just set your mind to it and go to work."

Now the Dukakis supporters sneer at that, because it's common sense. They sneer at common sense advice, Midwestern advice, Midwestern advice from a grandmother to a grandson, important advice, something that we ought to talk about, because if you want to, you can make a difference. You, America, can make a difference. You're going to have that choice come this election. Everyone can make a difference if they want to.

Ms. Woodruff: Senator Bentsen?

Mr. Bentsen: I think being born and reared on the Rio Grande, to have spent part of my life seeing some of the struggles that have taken place in one of the lowest per capita incomes in the United States, and that's one of the reasons I've worked so hard to try to assist on education. And when I found that the bankers in that area found that they could not handle the loans because of some of the detail and the expense, couldn't make a profit on it, I went down there and helped form a non-profit organization to buy up those loans from them and to manage them, and do it in a way where they'd continue to make those loans.

Now they have, and they've educated more than 20,000 of those students, loaned out over $100 million. And it hasn't cost the taxpayers of this country one cent. It's one of the reasons I've worked so hard to bring better health care to the people, because of what I've seen in the way of poverty down there in that area, and the lack of medical attention, and trying to see that that's turned around, why I worked so hard on the welfare reform bill, to give them a chance to break these cycles of poverty, the chance for a step up in life.

Ms. Woodruff: Senator.

Mr. Bentsen: Judy, something's happened, but my light's still on.

Ms. Woodruff: Your lights aren't working?

Mr. Bentsen: All right.

Ms. Woodruff: We're sorry about that, if that's the case.

Mr. Bentsen: Okay.

Ms. Woodruff: Thank you. Thank you, Senator Bentsen. Thank you, Senator Quayle. We have now come to the end of the questions. And before I ask the candidates to make their closing remarks, on behalf of the Commission on Presidential Debates, I'd like to thank all of you for joining us. Senator Quayle, yours is the first closing statement.

[Closing Statements]

Mr. Quayle: Thank you. Tonight has been a very important evening. You have been able to see Dan Quayle as I really am, and how George Bush and I want to lead this country into the future. Thank you, America, for listening, and thank you for your fairness.

Now you will have a choice to make on election day. You will have a choice of whether America is going to choose the road of Michael Dukakis or the road of George Bush as we march toward the 21st century. The road of Michael Dukakis comes down to this: bigger government, higher taxes—they've always believed in higher taxes, they always have and they always will—cuts in national defense. Back to the old economics of high interest rates, high inflation and the old politics of high unemployment.

Now, the road of George Bush is the road to the future and it comes down to this: An America second to none, with visions of greatness, economic expansion, tough laws, tough judges, strong values, respect for the flag and our institutions. George Bush will lead us to the 21st century, a century that will be of hope and peace. Ronald Reagan and George Bush saved America from decline. We changed America. Michael Dukakis fought us every step of the way. It's not that they're not sympathetic. It's simply that they will take America backwards. George Bush has the experience, and with me, the future—a future committed to our family, a future committed to the freedom. Thank you, good night and God bless you.

Ms. Woodruff: Senator Bentsen—Senator Bentsen, your closing statement.

Mr. Bentsen: In just 34 days America will elect new leadership for our country. It's a most important decision, because there's no bigger job than governing this great country of ours and leading it into its future. Mike Dukakis and Lloyd Bentsen offer you experienced, tempered, capable leadership to meet those challenges of the future. Our opposition says, "Lower your sights, rest on your laurels." Mike Dukakis and Lloyd Bentsen think America can do better. But America can't just coast into the future, clinging to the past. This race is too close. The competition is too tough. And the stakes are too high.

Michael Dukakis and Lloyd Bentsen think America must move into that future united in a commitment to make this country of ours the most powerful, the most prosperous nation in the world. As Americans we honor our past, and we should. But our children are going to live in the future. And Mike

Dukakis says the best of America is yet to come. But that won't happen—taking care of our economy—just putting it on automatic pilot. It won't happen by accident, it's going to take leadership and it's going to take courage, and the commitment and a contribution by all of us to do that.

I've worked for the betterment of our country, both in war and peace, as a bomber pilot, as one who has been a businessman and a United States senator, working to make this nation the fairest and the strongest and the most powerful in the world. Help us bring America to a new era of greatness. The debate has been ours, but the decision is yours. God bless you.

Ms. Woodruff: Thank you both. Thank you.

The Second Bush-Dukakis Debate (1988)

On Labor Day 1988, the traditional starting date for the presidential campaign, the public opinion polls indicated a close race between Gov. Michael S. Dukakis of Massachusetts, the Democratic nominee, and his Republican opponent, Vice President George Bush.

Dukakis's appeal to the voters during the fall campaign was essentially the same that he had relied upon to win his party's nomination. "This election isn't about ideology," he told the national television audience in his acceptance speech to the Democratic convention. "It's about competence." Dukakis offered himself as a rational, hard-working manager who had wrought a dramatic economic recovery in his state—the so-called "Massachusetts Miracle"—and who could run the federal government with equal skill.

The Bush campaign took a different tack. Although not ceding the competence issue to his opponent, Bush alternated between emotional and ideological appeals to the voters. The former included his attacks on Dukakis for vetoing a state law that would have required public school teachers to lead their students in the Pledge of Allegiance and for allowing a murderer named Willie Horton to take a weekend furlough from prison, during which the convict committed another murder. The latter, ideological appeal branded

Dukakis with the "L-word" (liberal), a label that had become so unpopular during the conservative presidency of Ronald Reagan that Dukakis dissociated himself from it until just a few days before the election.

In keeping with the nature of their campaigns, Dukakis sought as many debates between the candidates as possible and Bush as few. They settled on two debates, both of them well in advance of the election.

The first Bush-Dukakis debate took place in Winston-Salem, North Carolina, on September 25, 1988. By most accounts, Dukakis made the better arguments during the ninety-minute, nationally televised encounter, but Bush was the more appealing person. The voters apparently responded with their hearts, because Bush moved into a clear lead against Dukakis in the post-debate polls.

By the time of the second debate, on October 13 in Los Angeles, California, the burden was clearly on Dukakis to reveal a warmer, more passionate side of his personality than had previously been apparent. Instead, he did the opposite. Asked in the opening question of the debate whether he would favor capital punishment for a criminal who "raped and murdered" his wife Kitty, Dukakis coolly replied that there was no evidence that the death penalty is an effective deterrent to murder. David

Broder of the Washington Post observed that as Dukakis listened to the question, his face was "as impassive as if he had been asked the time." In all, Broder concluded, the debate was "close to a total mismatch in terms of the human dimension."

Bush won the election easily, by 426 electoral votes to 111 electoral votes and by 53.4 percent to 45.6 percent in the popular vote. His victory lent itself to three plausible interpretations, each of which probably explains part of what happened. One interpretation was that his campaign appealed to the voters' emotions and values much more skillfully than did the Dukakis campaign. Another was that Bush reaped the harvest of eight years of apparent peace and prosperity under the stewardship of the Republican administration in which he had served. Finally, Bush fell heir to the strong national Republican majority in presidential politics that made the election of 1988 the Republicans' fifth victory, and their fourth landslide, in the last six presidential elections.

But Republican ascendancy was not the only recent electoral trend that was confirmed in 1988. Voter turnout declined from the preceding presidential election, as it had in every election but one for the past quarter century. The turnout rate, which was 64 percent in 1960, fell to barely 50 percent in 1988. Some political analysts attributed the fall-off, at least in part, to the growing use of emotional, negative campaigning.   ~

Mr. Shaw: By agreement between the candidates, the first question goes to Governor Dukakis. You have two minutes to respond. Governor, if Kitty Dukakis were raped and murdered, would you favor an irrevocable death penalty for the killer?

Mr. Dukakis: No, I don't, Bernard, and I think you know that I've opposed

the death penalty during all of my life. I don't see any evidence that it's a deterrent, and I think there are better and more effective ways to deal with violent crime. We've done so in my own state, and it's one of the reasons why we have had the biggest drop in crime of any industrial state in America, why we have the lowest murder rate of any industrial state in America.

But we have work to do in this nation; we have work to do to fight a real war and not a phony war against drugs. And that's something that I want to lead, something we haven't had over the course of the past many years, even though the vice president has been, at least allegedly, in charge of that war. We have much to do to step up that war, to double the number of drug enforcement agents, to fight both here and abroad, to work with our neighbors in this hemisphere. And I want to call a hemispheric summit just as soon after the 20th of January as possible to fight that war.

But we also have to deal with drug education prevention here at home. And that's one of the things that I hope I can lead personally as the president of the United States. We've had great success in my own state, and we've reached out to young people and their families and been able to help them by beginning drug education and prevention in the early elementary grades.

So we can fight this war and we can win this war, and we can do so in a way that marshals our forces, that provides real support for state and local law enforcement officers who have not been getting that kind of support, do it in a way which will bring down violence in this nation, will help our youngsters to stay away from drugs, will stop this avalanche of drugs that's pouring into the country, and will make it possible for our kids and our families to grow up in safe and secure and decent neighborhoods.

Mr. Shaw: Mr. Vice President, your one-minute rebuttal.

Mr. Bush: Well, a lot of what this campaign is about, it seems to me, Bernie, is to a question of values. And here, I do have, on this particular question, a big difference with my opponent.

You see, I do believe that some crimes are so heinous, so brutal, so outrageous—and I'd say particularly those that result in the death of a police officer—those real brutal crimes, I do believe in the death penalty. And I think it is a deterrent. And I believe we need it, and I'm glad that the Congress moved on this drug bill, and it finally called for that, related to these narcotics drug kingpins. And so, we just have an honest difference of opinion. I support it, and he doesn't.

[On the Vice Presidency]

Mr. Shaw: Now, to you, Vice President Bush. I quote to you this from Article II of the 20th Amendment of the Constitution: Quote, "If, at the time fixed for the beginning of the term of the President, the President-elect shall have died, the Vice President-elect shall become President," meaning, if you are elected and die before Inauguration Day—

Mr. Bush: Bernie!

Mr. Shaw: —automatically—automatically, Dan Quayle would become the 41st president of the United States. What have you to say about that possibility?

Mr. Bush: I'd have confidence in him, and I made a good selection. And I've never seen such a pounding, an unfair pounding, on a young senator in my entire life. And I've never seen a presidential campaign where the presidential nominee runs against my vice presidential nominee—never seen one before. You know, Lloyd Bentsen jumped on Dan Quayle when Dan Quayle said he's had roughly the same amount of experience. He had two terms in the Congress; he had two terms in the Senate, serving his second term.

He founded the—authored the Job Training Partnership Act that says to American working men and women that are thrown out of work forno fault of their own, that they're going to have jobs. We're moving intoa new, competitive age, and we need that kind of thing. He, unlikemy opponent, is an expert in national defense, helped amend the INF Treaty, so we got a good, sound treaty when these people over here were talking about a freeze. If we'd listened to them, we would never have had a treaty.

And so I have great confidence in him and he's—it's turning around. You know, the American people are fair. They don't like it when there's an unfair pounding and kind of hooting about people. They want to judge it on the record itself. And so I'm proud of my choice. And, you know, I don't think age is the only criterion. But, I'll tell you something, I'm proud that people that are 30 years old and 40 years old now have someone in their generation that is going to be vice president of the United States of America. I made a good selection. The American people are seeing it and I'm proud of it. That's what I'd say. And he could do the job.

Mr. Shaw: Governor Dukakis, your one-minute rebuttal.

Mr. Dukakis: Bernard, this was the first presidential decision that we, as nominees, were called upon to make and that's why people are so concerned because it was an opportunity for us to demonstrate what we were looking for in a running mate. More than that, it was the first national security decision that we had to make.

The vice president talks about national security. Three times since World War II, the vice president has had to suddenly become the president and commander in chief. I picked Lloyd Bentsen because I thought he was the best qualified person for the job. Mr.

Bush picked Dan Quayle and, before he did it, he said, "Watch my choice for vice president. It will tell all." And it sure did. It sure did.

Mr. Shaw: Ann Compton for the vice president.

[Taxes and the Budget]

Ms. Compton: Thank you, Bernie. Mr. Vice President, yes, we read your lips: "No new taxes." But, despite that same pledge from President Reagan, after income tax rates were cut, in each of the last five years, some federal taxes have gone up—on Social Security, cigarettes, liquor, even long-distance telephone calls. Now that's money straight out of people's wallets. Isn't the phrase "no new taxes" misleading the voters?

Mr. Bush: No, because that's—that I'm pledged to that. And, yes, some taxes have gone up. And the main point is taxes have been cut and yet income is up to the federal government by 25 percent in the last three years. And so, what I want to do is keep this expansion going. I don't want to kill it off by a tax increase.

More Americans [are] at work today than at any time in the history of this country and a greater percentage of the work force. And the way you kill expansions is to raise taxes. And I don't want to do that. And I won't do that. And what I have proposed is something much better. And it's going to take discipline of the executive branch. It's going to take discipline of the congressional branch—and that is what I call a flexible freeze that allows growth—about 4 percent or the rate of inflation—but does not permit the Congress just to add on spending.

I hear this talk about a blank check—the American people are pretty smart. They know who writes out the checks. And they know who appropriates the money. It is the United States Congress and by two to one, Congress is blamed for these deficits. And the answer is to discipline both the executive branch and the congressional branch by holding the line on taxes.

So I am pledged to do that. And those pessimists who say it can't be done, I'm sorry. I just have fundamental disagreement with them.

Mr. Shaw: Governor Dukakis, your one-minute response.

Mr. Dukakis: Ann, the vice president made that pledge; he's broken it three times in the past year already, so it isn't worth the paper it's printed on. And what I'm concerned about is that if we continue with the policies that Mr. Bush is talking about here this evening—flexible freeze—somebody described it the other day as a kind of economic Slurpee.

He wants to spend billions on virtually every weapons system around. He says he's not going to raise taxes, though he has broken that pledge repeatedly. He says he wants to give the wealthiest 1 percent in this country a five-year, $40 billion tax break, and we're going to pay for it. And he's been proposing all kinds of programs for new spending costing billions.

Now, if we continue with these policies, this trillion and a half dollars' worth of new debt that's already been added on the backs of the American taxpayers is going to increase even more. If we continue with this for another four years, then I'm worried about the next generation, whether we can ever turn this situation around.

No, we need a chief executive who's prepared to lead, who won't blame the Congress, but will lead, will bring down that deficit, will make tough choices on spending, will go out and do the job that we expect of him and do it with the Congress of the United States.

Mr. Shaw: And to Governor Dukakis.

Ms. Compton: Governor, let me follow up on that by asking you, you've said it many times, that you have balanced 10 budgets in a row in Massachusetts. Are you promising the American people, here tonight, that within a four-year presidential term, you will balance the federal budget?

Mr. Dukakis: No, I'm not sure I can promise that. I don't think either one of us can, really. There's no way of anticipating what may happen. I will say this, that we'll set as our goal a steady, gradual reduction of the deficit, which will require tough choices on spending. It will require a good strong rate of economic growth. It will require a plan that the president works out with the Congress—doesn't blame them, works it out with them—which brings that deficit down. It will require us to go out and collect billions and billions of dollars in taxes owed that aren't being paid in this country. And that's grossly unfair to the average American who's paying his taxes, and paying them on time, and doesn't have any alternative—it's taken out of his paycheck.

Mr. Bush says we're going to put the IRS on every taxpayer. That's not what we're going to do. I'm for the Taxpayer Bill of Rights. Well, I think it's unconscionable, Ann, that we should be talking or thinking about imposing new taxes on average Americans, when there are billions out there—over a hundred billion dollars in taxes owed that aren't being paid.

Now, I think if we work together on it, and if you have a president that will work with the Congress and the American people, we can bring that deficit down steadily, $20, 25, 30 billion a year, build economic growth, build a good strong future for America, invest in those things which we must invest in: economic development, good jobs, good schools for our kids, college opportunity for young people, decent health care and affordable housing, and a clean and safe environment. We can do all of those things, and at the same time build

a future in which we're standing on a good strong fiscal foundation.

Senator Bentsen said, as you recall at the debate with Senator Quayle, that if you give any of us $200 billion worth of hot checks a year, we can create an illusion of prosperity. But sooner or later, that credit card mentality isn't going to work. And I want to bring to the White House a sense of strength and fiscal responsibility which will build a good strong foundation under which this country, or above which this country can move, grow, invest and build the best America for its people and for our kids and our grand-kids.

Mr. Shaw: Mr. Vice President? Your one-minute response.

Mr. Bush: The governor has to balance a budget in his state. He's required to by law. He's raised taxes several times. I wish he would join me, as a matter of fact, in appealing to the American people for the balanced-budget amendment for the federal government and for the line-item veto. I'd like to have that line-item veto for the president, because I think that would be extraordinarily helpful.

And I won't do one other thing that he's had to do—took $29 million out of his state pension fund. That's equivalent in the federal level of taking out of the Social Security Trust Fund. I'm not going to do that. I won't do that. And so I'm still a little unclear as to whether he's for or against a tax increase. I have been all for the Taxpayer's Bill of Rights all along. And this idea of unleashing a whole bunch, an army, a conventional force army of IRS agents into everybody's kitchen—I mean, he's against most defense matters, and now he wants to get an army of IRS auditors going out there. I'm against that. I oppose that.

Mr. Shaw: I'm going to say this, and I'm going to say it once to every person in this auditorium. What these candidates are about is of utmost seriousness to the American voters. They should be heard, and you should be quiet. If you are not quiet, I'm going to implore the candidates to do something about prodding—or quieting their own partisans. But we cannot get through this program with these outbursts. Margaret Warner, for Governor Dukakis.

[Candidate Qualities]

Ms. Warner: Good evening, Governor, Mr. Vice President. Governor, you won the first debate on intellect, and yet you lost it on heart.

Mr. Bush: Just a minute.

Mr. Dukakis: I don't know about the vice—

Ms. Warner: You'll get your turn. The American public—

Mr. Dukakis: I don't know whether the vice president agrees with that.

Ms. Warner: The American public admired your performance, but didn't seem to like you much. Now Ronald Reagan has found his personal warmth to be a tremendous political asset. Do you think that a president has to be likable to be an effective leader?

Mr. Dukakis: Margaret, may I go back and just say to the vice president that I didn't raid the pension fund in Massachusetts. You're dead wrong, George. We didn't do that. As a matter of fact, I'm the first governor in the history of my state to fund that pension system, and I'm very proud of that. And you just had your—

Mr. Bush: (Inaudible.)

Mr. Dukakis: —You just have your information—no, we did not. No, we did not. I've been in politics for 25 years, Margaret. I've won a lot of elections; I've lost a few, as you know, and learned from those losses. I won the Democratic nomination in 51 separate contests. I think I'm a reasonably likable guy. I'm serious, though I think I'm a little more lovable these days than I used to be back in my youth when I began in my state

legislature. But I'm also a serious guy. I think the presidency of the United States is a very serious office. And I think we have to address these issues in a very serious way.

So I hope and expect that I'll be liked by the people of this country as president of the United States. I certainly hope I'll be liked by them on the 8th of November. But I also think it's important to be somebody who's willing to make those tough choices. Now, we've just heard two or three times from the vice president that he's not going to raise taxes. I repeat, within days after you made that pledge, you broke it. You said, "Well, maybe as a last resort, we'll do it," and you supported legislation this year that's involved tax increases not once, but twice.

So that pledge isn't realistic, and I think the vice president knows it. I think the people of this country know it. The fact of the matter is that the next president of the United States is going to have to go to the White House seriously, he's going to have to work with the Congress seriously. He can't turn to the Congress and blame them for the fact that we don't have a balanced budget and that we have billions and billions of dollars in red ink.

And I'm going to be a president who is serious, I hope and expect will be liked by the American people. But more than that, will do the kind of job that I'm elected to do, will do it with as much good humor as I can, but at the same time, will do it in a way which will achieve the goals we want for ourselves and our people. And I think we know what they are—

Mr. Shaw: Governor—

Mr. Dukakis: —a good strong future, a future in which there—

Mr. Shaw: Your time has run out, sir.

Mr. Dukakis: —is opportunity for all of our citizens.

Mr. Shaw: One minute from the vice president.

Mr. Bush: I don't think it's a question of whether people like you or not to make you an effective leader. I think it's whether you share the broad dreams of the American people, whether you have confidence in the people's ability to get things done, or whether you think it all should be turned over, as many of the liberals do, to Washington, D.C. You see, I think it's a question of values, not likability or lovability.

It's a question in foreign affairs of experience, knowing world leaders, knowing how to build on a superb record of this administration in arms control because you'd know exactly how to begin. You have to learn from experience that making unilateral cuts in the defense system is not the way that you enhance the peace.

You've got to understand that it is only the United States that can stand for freedom and democracy around the world, and we can't turn it over to the United Nations or other multilateral organizations. It is, though, trying to understand the heartbeat of the country. And I know these campaigns get knocked a lot, but I think I'd be a better president now—

Mr. Shaw: Mr. Vice President—

Mr. Bush: —for having had to travel to these communities and understand the family values and the importance of neighborhood.

Mr. Shaw: Margaret Warner for the vice president.

Ms. Warner: I'd like to follow up on that, Mr. Vice President. The tenor of the campaign you've been running in terms of both the issues and your rhetoric has surprised even some of your friends. Senator Mark Hatfield has known your family a long time and who knew your father, the late Senator Prescott Bush, said, and I quote, "If his father were alive today I'm sure his father would see it as a shocking transformation."

Is Senator Hatfield right?

Mr. Bush: What was he referring to?

Ms. Warner: He was referring to your performance in the campaign.

Mr. Bush: Well I think my dad would be pretty proud of me, because I think we've come a long, long way. And I think, you know, three months ago, I remember some of the great publications in this country had written me off. And what I've had to do is to define not just my position, but to define his [Dukakis']. And I hope I've done it fairly. And the reason I've had to do that is that he ran on the left in the Democratic primary, ran firmly and ran with conviction, and ran on his record.

And then at the Democratic Convention they made a determination. And they said there ideology doesn't matter, just competence. And in the process the negatives began. It wasn't me that was there at that convention. Thank God, I was up with Jimmy Baker camping out and I didn't have to hear all of the personal attacks on me out of that Democratic convention. It was wonderful not to listen to it. And I'm not the one that compared the president of the United States of rotting like a dead fish from the head down; I didn't do that.

But I have defined the issues and I am not going to let Governor Dukakis go through this election without explaining some of these very liberal positions. He's the one that said, "I am a liberal—traditional liberal—progressive liberal Democrat." He's the one that brought up, to garner primary votes, the whole question of the ACLU. And I have enormous difference with the ACLU on their political agenda, not on their defending some minority opinion on the right or the left. I support that. But what I don't like is this left-wing political agenda, and therefore, I have to help define that. And if he's unwilling to do it, if he says ideology doesn't matter, I don't agree with him.

Mr. Shaw: One minute, from Governor Dukakis.

Mr. Dukakis: Well, Margaret, we've heard it again tonight, and I'm not surprised. The labels. I guess the vice president called me a liberal two or three times, said I was coming from the left. In 1980, President Reagan called you a liberal for voting for federal gun control. And this is something Republicans have used for a long time. They tried it with Franklin Roosevelt and Harry Truman and John Kennedy. It's not labels, it's our vision of America, and we have two fundamentally different visions of America.

The vice president is complacent, thinks we ought to stick with the status quo, doesn't think we ought to move ahead, thinks things are okay as they are. I don't. I think this is a great country because we've always wanted to do better, to make our country better, to make our lives better. We've always been a nation which was ambitious for America, and we move forward. And that's the kind of America I want; that's the kind of leadership I want to provide.

But I don't think these labels mean a thing, and I would hope that tonight, and in the course of the rest of this campaign, we can have our good, solid disagreements on issues; there's nothing the matter with that. But let's stop labeling each other and let's get to the heart of the matter, which is the future of this country.

Mr. Shaw: Andrea Mitchell, for the Vice President.

[Weapons Systems]

Ms. Mitchell: Mr. Vice President, Governor. Mr. Vice President, let me return for a moment to the issue of the budget, because so much has already been put off limits in your campaign that most people do not believe that the flexible freeze alone will solve the problem of the deficit. So, let's turn to defense for a moment.

Pentagon officials tell us that there is not enough money in the budget to handle military readiness, preparedness, as well as new weapons systems that have been proposed, as well as those already in the pipeline. You were asked at the first debate what new weapons systems you would cut. You mentioned three that had already been canceled. Can you, tonight, share with us three new weapons systems that you would cut?

Mr. Bush: If I knew of three new weapons systems that I thought were purely waste, and weren't protected by the Congress, they wouldn't be in the budget. They would not be in the budget. But you want one now? I'll give you one. That HEMAT, that heavy truck, that's cost, what is it, $850 million and the Pentagon didn't request it and yet a member of Congress, a very powerful one, put it in the budget.

I think we can save money through this whole, very sophisticated concept, Andrea, that I know you do understand, of competitive strategies. It is new. And it is very, very different than what's happened. But it's not quite ready to be totally implemented. But it's very important. I think we can save through the Packard Commission report, and I'm very proud that David Packard, the originator of that report, is strongly supporting me. So it's not a question of saying our budget is full of a lot of waste. I don't believe that.

I do think this: We're in the serious stages of negotiation with the Soviet Union now on the strategic arms control talks. And we are protecting a couple of options in terms of modernizing our strategic forces. My secretary of defense is going to have to make a very difficult decision in which system to go forward with. But, we are protecting both of them. We're moving forward with negotiations. And, you see, I just think it would be dumb negotiating policy with the Soviets, to cut out one or the other of the two options right now. The Soviets are modernizing. They continue to modernize. And we can't simply say,

"We've got enough nuclear weapons. Let's freeze." We can't do that.

We have to have modernization. Especially if we achieve the 50 percent reduction in strategic weapons that our president is taking the leadership to attain. And so that's the way I'd reply to it. And I believe we can have the strongest and best defense possible if we modernize, if we go forward with competitive strategies, and if we do follow through on the Packard Commission report.

Mr. Shaw: Governor Dukakis, one minute.

Mr. Dukakis: Well, Andrea, we've just had another example of why the Vice President's mathematics just doesn't add up. I think you know, because you've covered these issues, that there's no way that we can build all of the weapons systems that the vice president says he wants to build within the existing defense budget. Everybody knows that, including the people at the Pentagon.

Now, my defense secretary is going to have a lot to do with some of those decisions, but it's going to be the president that's going to have to ultimately decide, before that budget goes to the Congress, what weapon systems are going to go and what are going to stay. We're not going to spend the billions and trillions that Mr. Bush wants to spend on Star Wars. We're not going to spend billions on MXs on railroad cars, which is a weapon system we don't need, can't afford, and won't help our defense posture at all. We're not going to spend hundreds of millions on a space plane from Washington to Tokyo.

Those are decisions that the chief executive has to make. Yes, we're going to have a strong and credible and effective nuclear deterrent. We're going to go forward with the Stealth, the D-5 and the advanced cruise missile and good conventional forces. But the next president of the United States will have to make some tough and difficult deci-

sions. I'm prepared to make them—

Mr. Shaw: Governor.

Mr. Dukakis: —the Vice President is not.

Mr. Shaw: Andrea has a question for you.

Ms. Mitchell: Governor, continuing on that subject then, you say that we have to do something about conventional forces. You have supported the submarine-launched missile, the D-5, you just referred to. Yet, from Jerry Ford to Jimmy Carter to Ronald Reagan, there has been a bipartisan consensus in favor of modernizing the land-based missiles. Now, you have ruled out the MX and the Midgetman. More recently, some of your aides have hinted at some flexibility that you might show about some other new form of missile. Can you tell us tonight why you have rejected the collected wisdom of people as diverse as Sam Nunn, Henry Kissinger, Al Gore, people in both parties, and what type of land-based missile would you consider?

Mr. Dukakis: Well, Andrea, today we have 13,000 strategic nuclear warheads—on land, in air and the sea. That's an incredibly powerful nuclear deterrent. I don't rule out modernization and there are discussions going on now in the Congress and over at the Pentagon about a less expensive modernized land-based leg of the triad.

But there are limits to what we can spend. There are limits to this nation's ability to finance these weapons systems. And one of the things that the vice president either ignores or won't address is the fact that you can't divorce our military security from our economic security. How can we build a strong America militarily that's teeter-tottering on a mountain of debt?

And if we go forward with the kinds of policies that the vice president is suggesting tonight and have in the past, that debt is going to grow bigger and bigger and bigger. So military security and economic security go hand in hand.

And we will have a strong and effective and credible nuclear deterrent. We're going to have conventional forces that are well maintained, well equipped, well trained, well supported. And we have serious problems with our conventional forces at the present time and they'll get worse unless we have a president who's willing to make some of these decisions.

And we also have important domestic priorities in education and housing and health care, in economic development and job training, in the environment. Now, all of these things are going to have to be addressed. That's why I say again to all of you out there who have to deal with your household budgets and know how difficult it is, that the next president has to do the same.

I want the men and women of our armed forces to have the support they need to defend us, the support they need when they risk our lives to keep us free and to keep this country free. But we cannot continue to live on a credit card. We cannot continue to tell the American people that we're going to build all of these systems, and at the same time invest in important things here at home, and be serious about building a strong and good America. And that's the kind of America I want to build.

Mr. Shaw: One minute for the vice president.

Mr. Bush: I think the foremost— Can we start the clock over? I held off for the applause. Can I get—

Mr. Shaw: You can proceed, sir.

Mr. Bush: I think the foremost responsibility of a president really gets down to the national security of this country. The governor talks about limits, what we can't do, opposes these two modernization systems, talks now about, "May, well, we'll develop some new kind of a missile." It takes eight years, 10 years to do that.

He talked about a nuclear freeze back at the time when I was in Europe, trying to convince European public opinion that we ought to go forward with the deployment of the INF weapons. And thank God the freeze people were not heard. They were wrong. And the result is we deployed and the Soviets kept deploying, and then we negotiated from strength. And now we have the first arms control agreement in the nuclear age to ban weapons. You just don't make unilateral cuts in the naive hope that the Soviets are going to behave themselves. World peace is important, and we have enhanced the peace. And I'm proud to have been a part of an administration that has done exactly that. Peace through strength works.

Mr. Shaw: Ann Compton, for Governor Dukakis.

[Today's Heroes]

Ms. Compton: Governor, today they may call them "role models," but they used to be called "heroes," the kind of public figure who could inspire a whole generation, someone who is larger than life. My question is not who your heroes were. My question instead is, who are the heroes who are there in American life today? Who are the ones that you would point out to young Americans as figures who should inspire this country?

Mr. Dukakis: Well, I think—when I think of heroes, I think back, not presently, Ann, but there are many people who I admire in this country today. Some of them are in public life, in the Senate and the Congress—some of my fellow governors who are real heroes to me. I think of those young athletes who represented us at the Olympics, who were tremendously impressive. We were proud of them. We felt strongly about them and they did so well by us.

I can think of doctors and scientists— Jonas Salk who, for example, discovered a vaccine which cured one of the most dread diseases we ever had; and he's a hero. I think of classroom teachers—classroom teachers that I have had, classroom teachers that youngsters have today who are real heroes to our young people because they inspire them, they teach them, but more than that, they are role models. Members of the clergy who have done the same. Drug counselors out there in the street who are providing help to youngsters who come up to me and others and ask for help and want help and are doing the hard work, the heroic work which it takes to provide that kind of leadership, that kind of counseling, that kind of support.

I think of people in the law enforcement community who are taking their lives in their hands every day when they go up to one of those doors and kick it down and try to stop this flow of drugs into our communities and into our kids. So there are many, many heroes in this country today. These are people that give of themselves every day and every week and every month. In many cases they're people in the community who are examples and are role models.

And I would hope that one of the things that I could do as president is to recognize them, to give them the kind of recognition that they need and deserve so that more and more young people can themselves become the heroes of tomorrow, can go into public service, can go into teaching, can go into drug counseling, can go into law enforcement and be heroes themselves to generations yet to come.

Mr. Shaw: One minute for Vice President Bush.

Mr. Bush: I think of a teacher right here—largely Hispanic school—Jamie Escalante, teaching calculus to young kids, 80 percent of them going on to college. I think of a young man now in this country named Valladeres who was released from a Cuban jail; came out and told the truth in this brilliant book, *Against All Hope,* about what is actually happening in Cuba.

I think of those people that took us back into space again—Rick Hauck and that crew—as people that are worthy of this. I agree with the governor on athletics. And there's nothing corny about having sports heroes, young people that are clean and honorable and out there setting a—setting the pace. I think of Dr. Fauci—probably never heard of him—you did? Ann heard of him. He's a very fine research, top doctor at the National Institute of Health, working hard doing something about research on this disease of AIDS.

But look, I also think we ought to give a litle credit to the President of the United States. He is the one that has gotten us that first arms control agreement and the cynics abounded—

Mr. Shaw: Mr. Vice President—

Mr. Bush: — and he is leaving office with a popularity at an all-time high—

Mr. Shaw: Mr. Vice President, your time has expired—

Mr. Bush: —because American people say, he is our hero.

Mr. Shaw: Ann has a question for you, Mr. Vice President.

[Opponent Praise]

Ms. Compton: Let's change the pace a little bit, Mr. Vice President. In this campaign, some hard and very bitter things have been spoken by each side, about each side. If you'd consider for a moment Governor Dukakis in his years of public service, is there anything nice you can say about him, anything you find admirable?

Mr. Bush: Hey, listen, you're stealing my close. I had something very nice to say in that.

Ms. Compton: Somebody leaked my question to you?

Mr. Bush: No, look, I'll tell you what, no, let me tell you something about that. And Barbara and I were sitting there before that Democratic convention, and we saw the governor and his son on television the night before, and his family and his mother who was there. And I'm saying to Barbara, "You know, we've always kept family as a bit of an oasis for us." You all know me, and we've held it back a little. But we use that as a role model, the way he took understandable pride in his heritage, what his family means to him.

And we've got a strong family and we watched that and we said, "Hey, we've got to unleash the Bush kids." And so you saw 10 grandchildren there jumping all over their grandfather at the, at the convention. You see our five kids all over this country, and their spouses. And so I would say that the concept of the Dukakis family has my great respect. And I'd say, I don't know whether that's kind or not, it's just an objective statement. And I think the man, anybody that gets into this political arena and has to face you guys every day deserves a word of praise because it's gotten a little ugly out there, it's gotten a little nasty. It's not much fun sometimes.

And I would cite again Dan Quayle. I've been in politics a long time and I don't remember that kind of piling on, that kind of ugly rumor that never was true, printed. Now, come on. So some of it's unfair, but he's in the arena. Teddy Roosevelt used to talk about the "arena"—you know, daring to fail greatly or succeed. No matter, he's in there. So, I salute these things. I salute those who participate in the political process.

Sam Rayburn had a great expression on this. He said, "You know, I hear all of these intellectuals out there griping and complaining and saying it's negative coverage." Rayburn says, "Yeah, and that guy never ran for sheriff either." Michael Dukakis has run for sheriff, and so has George Bush.

Mr. Shaw: Governor, a one-minute response, sir.

Mr. Dukakis: I didn't hear the word "liberal" or "left" one time. I thank you for that.

Mr. Bush: That's not bad; that's true.

Mr. Dukakis: And doesn't that prove the point, George, which is that values like family, and education, community—

Mr. Bush: That's where you want to take the country.

Mr. Dukakis: —decent homes for young people—that family in Long Island I visited on Monday, where Lou and Betty Tulamo bought a house for some $19,000 back in 1962, have had seven children. They're all making good livings. They can't live in the community in which they grew up in. Those are basic American values. I believe in them, I think you believe in them. They're not left or right, they're decent American values.

I guess the one thing that concerns me about this, Ann, is this attempt to label things which all of us believe in. We may have different approaches, we may think that you deal with them in different ways, but they're basically American. I believe in them, George Bush believes in them, I think the vast majority of Americans believe in them, and I hope—

Mr. Shaw: Governor.

Mr. Dukakis: —the tone we've just heard might just be the tone we have for the rest of the campaign. I think the American people would appreciate that.

Mr. Shaw: Margaret Warner, for the vice president.

[Abortion]

Ms. Warner: Vice President Bush, abortion remains with us as a very troubling issue, and I'd like to explore that for a minute with you. You have said that you regard abortion as murder, yet you would make exceptions in the cases of rape and incest. My question is, why should a woman who discovers through amniocentesis that her baby will be born with Tay-Sachs disease, for instance, that the baby will live at most two years, and those two years in incredible pain, be forced to carry the fetus to term, and yet a woman who becomes pregnant through incest would be allowed to abort her fetus?

Mr. Bush: Because you left out one other exception, the health of the mother. Let me answer your question, and I hope it doesn't get too personal, or maudlin. Bar and I lost a child, you know that. We lost a daughter, Robin. And we took—we were out—I was over running records in West Texas, and I got a call from her—"Come home." Went to the doctor. The doctor said—beautiful child—"Your child has a few weeks to live." And I said, "What can we do about it?" He said, "No, she has leukemia, acute leukemia, a few weeks to live." We took the child to New York. Thanks to the miraculous sacrifices of doctors and nurses, the child stayed alive for six months, and then died. If that child were here today, and I was told this same thing—my granddaughter Noel, for example—that child could stay alive for 10 or 15 years, or maybe for the rest of her life. And so, I don't think that you make an exception based on medical knowledge at the time. I think human life is very, very precious.

And look, this hasn't been an easy decision for me to make—work—meet. I know others disagree with it. But when I was in that little church across the river from Washington and saw our grandchild christened in our faith, I was very pleased indeed that the mother had not aborted that child, and put the child up for adoption. And so I just feel this is where I'm coming from. And it is personal. And I don't assail him on that issue or others on that issue. But that's the way I, George Bush, feel about it.

Mr. Shaw: One minute for Governor Dukakis.

Mr. Dukakis: Margaret, Kitty and I had very much the same kind of experience that the Bushes had. We lost a baby—lived about 20 minutes after it was born. But, isn't the real question that we have to answer, not how many exceptions we make—because the vice president himself is prepared to make exceptions—it's who makes the decision, who makes this very difficult, very wrenching decision.

And I think it has to be the woman, in the exercise of her own conscience and religious beliefs, that makes the decision. Who are we to say, "Well, under certain circumstances it's all right, but under other circumstances it isn't?" That's a decision that only a woman can make after consulting her conscience and consulting her religious principles. And I would hope that we would give to women in this country the right to make that decision, and to make it in the exercise of their conscience and religious beliefs.

Mr. Shaw: Governor, Margaret has a question for you.

[The Defense Budget]

Ms. Warner: Governor, I'd like to return to the topic of the defense budget for a minute. You have said in this campaign, that you would maintain a stable defense budget. Yet, you are on the board—on the advisory—

Mr. Dukakis: And incidentally, may I say that—that that's the decision of the Congress, and the president has concurred.

Ms. Warner: Yet you are on the board of a group called Jobs With Peace in Boston, that advocates a 25 percent cut in the defense budget, and the transfer of that money to the domestic economy. My question is: Do you share that goal, perhaps as a long-range goal?

And if not, are you aware of, or why do you permit this group to continue to use your name on its letterhead for fundraising?

Mr. Dukakis: Well, I think I was on the advisory committee, Margaret. No, I don't happen to share that goal. It's an example of how oftentimes we may be associated with organizations, all of whose particular positions we don't support—even though we support in general the hope that over time, particularly if we can get those reductions in strategic weapons, if we can get a comprehensive test-ban treaty, if we can negotiate with the Soviet Union and bring down the level of conventional forces in Europe with deeper cuts in the Soviet side. Yes, at some point it may be possible to reduce defense outlays and use those for important things here at home, like jobs and job training and college opportunity and health and housing and the environment, and the things that all of us care about.

But I do think this: That the next president, even within a relatively stable budget—and that's what we're going to have for the foreseeable future—will have to make those tough choices that I was talking about and that Mr. Bush doesn't seem to want to make. And that really is going to be a challenge for the next president of the United States. I don't think there's any question about it.

But I also see a tremendous opportunity now to negotiate with the Soviet Union, to build on the progress that we've made with the INF Treaty—which I strongly supported, and most Democrats did—to get those reductions in strategic weapons, to get a test-ban treaty, and to really make progress on the reduction of conventional forces in Europe.

And if we can do that, and do it in a way that gets deeper cuts on the Soviet side, which is where they ought to come from—then I think we have an opportunity over the long haul to begin to move

priorities that can provide college opportunity for that young woman whose mother wrote me from Texas just the other day, from Longview, Texas— two teachers, a mother and a father who have a child that's a freshman in college who's an electrical engineering major, a very bright student—and they can't afford to keep that child in college.

So I hope that we can begin to move those resources. It's not going to happen overnight. It certainly will have to happen on a step-by-step basis as we make progress in arms negotiation and arms control and arms reduction. But it certainly ought to be—

Mr. Shaw: Governor—

Mr. Dukakis: —a long-term goal of all Americans, and I think it is.

Mr. Shaw: One minute for the vice president.

Mr. Bush: The defense budget today takes far less percentage of the gross national product than it did in President Kennedy's time. For example—moved tremendously—and you see, I think we're facing a real opportunity for world peace. This is a big question. And it's a question as to whether the United States will continue to lead for peace. See, I don't believe any other country can pick up the mantle.

I served at the U.N. I don't think we can turn over these kinds of decisions of the collective defense to the United Nations or anything else. So, what I'm saying is, we are going to have to make choices. I said I would have the secretary of defense sit down. But while the president is negotiating with the Soviet Union, I simply do not want to make these unilateral cuts.

And I think those that advocated the freeze missed the point that there was a better way and that better way has resulted in a principle—asymmetrical cuts. The Soviets take out more than we do and the principle of intrusive verification. And those two principles can now be applied to conventional forces, to strategic forces, provided—

Mr. Shaw: Mr. Vice President—

Mr. Bush: —we don't give away our hand before we sit down at the head table.

Mr. Shaw: Andrea Mitchell for Governor Dukakis.

[Taxes and Social Security]

Ms. Mitchell: Governor, you've said tonight that you set as a goal the steady reduction of the deficit. And you've talked about making tough choices, so perhaps I can get you to make one of those tough choices. No credible economist in either party accepts as realistic your plan to handle the deficit by tightening tax collection, investing in economic growth, bringing down interest rates, and cutting weapons systems . . .

Mr. Dukakis: And some domestic programs as well, Andrea.

Ms. Mitchell: And some domestic programs as well. So let's assume now, for argument purpose, that it is the spring of 1989 and you are President Dukakis, and you discover that all of those economists were right and you were wrong. You are now facing that dreaded last resort—increase taxes. Which tax do you decide is the least onerous?

Mr. Dukakis: May I disagree with the premise of your question?

Ms. Mitchell: For the sake of argument, no.

Mr. Dukakis: As a matter of reality, I'm going to have to because we have had not one but two detailed studies which indicate that there are billions and billions of dollars to be collected that are not being paid in. These are not taxes owed by average Americans. We don't have an alternative. We lose it when it's taken out of our paycheck before we even get it. But it's the Internal Revenue Service which estimates now that we aren't collecting $100 billion or more in taxes owed in this coun-

try. And that is just absolutely unfair to the vast majority of Americans who pay their taxes and pay them on time.

The Dorgan Task Force, which included two internal revenue commissioners, one a Republican—former internal revenue commissioners—one a Republican, one a Democrat. It was a bipartisan commission, a study by two respected economists, which indicated that we could collect some $40, 45, 50 billion of those funds. The point is you've got to have a president who's prepared to do this and to begin right away and, preferably, a president who as a governor of a state that's had very, very successful experience at doing this. In my own state, we did it. In other states, we've done it. Republican governors as well as Democratic governors. And we've had great success at revenue enforcement.

Now, the vice president will probably tell you that it's going to take an army of IRS collectors again. Well, his campaign manager, who used to be the secretary of the treasury, was taking great credit about a year ago and asking and receiving from the Congress substantial additional funds to hire internal revenue agents to go out and collect these funds and I'm happy to join Jim Baker in saying that we agree on this.

But, the fact of the matter is that this is something that we must begin, it's going to take at least the first year of the new administration. But the Dorgan Task Force, the bipartisan task force, estimated that we could collect about $35 billion in the fifth year, $105 billion over five years, the other study even more than that—

Mr. Shaw: Governor.

Mr. Dukakis: —and that's where you begin.

Mr. Shaw: One minute response, Mr. Vice President.

Mr. Bush: Well, Andrea, you didn't predicate that lack of economist's support for what I call a flexible freeze 'cause some good, very good economists do support that concept. And I think where I differ with the governor of Massachusetts is, I am optimistic. They jumped on me yesterday for being a little optimistic about the United States. I am optimistic and I believe we can keep this longest expansion going.

I was not out there when that stock market dropped, wringing my hands and saying this was the end of the world, as some political leaders were— 'cause it isn't the end of the world. And what we have to do is restrain the growth of spending. And we are doing a better job of it. The Congress is doing a better job of it. And the dynamics work. But they don't work if you go raise taxes and then the Congress spends it, continues to spend that. The American working man and woman are not taxed too little, the federal government continues to spend too much. Hold it.

Mr. Shaw: Mr. Vice President, Andrea has a question for you.

Ms. Mitchell: Mr. Vice President, you have flatly ruled out any change in Social Security benefits, even for the wealthy. Now, can you stand here tonight and look a whole generation of 18 to 34 year olds in the eye, the very people who are going to have to be financing that retirement, and tell them that they should be financing the retirement of people like yourself, like Governor Dukakis, or for that matter, people such as ourselves here on this panel?

Mr. Bush: More so you than me. But—

Ms. Mitchell: —We could argue about that.

Mr. Bush: —No, but, you've got to go back to what Social Security was when it was created. It wasn't created as a welfare program, it wasn't created—it was created as a whole retirement or health supplement to retirement program. It wasn't created as a welfare program. So here's what's happened. We came into office and the Social Security Trust Fund was in great jeopardy. And the President took the lead-

ership, working with the Democrats and the Republicans in Congress. Some tough calls were made and the Social Security Trust Fund was put back into sound, solvent condition.

So I don't want to fool around with it. And there's several—there's a good political reason, because it's just about this time of year that the Democrats start saying: "The Republicans are going to take away your Social Security." It always works that way. I've seen it in precinct politics in Texas, and I've seen it at the national level.

We have made the Social Security Trust Fund sound, and it is going to be operating at surpluses. And I don't want the liberal Democratic Congress to spend out of that Social Security Trust Fund or go and take the money out for some other purpose. I don't want that. And I will not go in there and suggest changes in Social Security. I learned that the hard way.

And the Governor and I both supported slipping the COLAs for one year; he supported it at the National Governors' Conference, and I supported it in breaking a tie in a major compromise package. And we got assailed by the Democrats in the election over that. And I am going to keep that Social Security Trust Fund sound and keep our commitment to the elderly. And maybe down the line, maybe when you get two decades or one into the next century, you're going to have to take another look at it, but not now. We do not have to do it. Keep the trust with the older men and women of this country.

Mr. Shaw: Governor, you have one minute, sir.

Mr. Dukakis: Andrea, I don't know which George Bush I'm listening to. George Bush, a few years ago, said that the Social Security was basically a welfare system. And in 1985 he flew back from the West Coast to cut that COLA. I voted against that at the National Governors' Association. We won a majority; we didn't win the two-thirds that was necessary in order to pass that resolution, George, but everybody knew what we were doing, and I've opposed that.

The reason that we raised concerns not just in election years, but every year, is because Republicans, once they're elected, go in there and start cutting. You did it in 1985. The administration tried to do it repeatedly, repeatedly in '81, '82, and I'm sure you'll try to do it again because there's no way that you can finance what you want to spend, there's no way you can pay for that five-year, $40 billion tax cut for the rich and still buy all those weapon systems you want to buy, unless you raid the Social Security Trust Fund.

[Supreme Court Vacancies]

Mr. Shaw: Ann Compton, for the vice president.

Ms. Compton: Mr. Vice President, there are three justices of the Supreme Court who are in their eighties, and it's very likely the next president will get a chance to put a lasting mark on the Supreme Court. For the record, would your nominees to the Supreme Court have to pass something that has been called a kind of conservative ideological litmus test, and would you give us an idea of perhaps who two or three people on your short list are for the court?

Mr. Bush: Well, one, I don't have a list yet. I feel pretty confident tonight, but not that confident. And secondly— secondly, I don't have any litmus test. But, what I would do is appoint people to the federal bench that will not legislate from the bench, who will interpret the Constitution. I do not want to see us go to again—and I'm using this word advisedly—a liberal majority that is going to legislate from the bench.

They [Dukakis supporters] don't like the use of the word, but may I remind his strong supporters that only last year in the primary to capture that Democratic nomination, he said, "I am a progressive liberal Democratic." I won't support judges like that.

There is no litmus test on any issue. But, I will go out there and find men and women to interpret. And I don't have a list, but I think the appointments that the president has made to the bench have been outstanding, outstanding appointments—

Ms. Compton: Including Bork, including Bork?

Mr. Bush: Yeah.

Mr. Shaw: Governor—

Mr. Bush: —I supported him.

Mr. Shaw: —you have a one-minute response time.

Mr. Dukakis: If the Vice President of the United States thinks that Robert Bork was an outstanding appointment, that is a very good reason for voting for Mike Dukakis and Lloyd Bentsen on the 8th of November. And I think Mr. Bush supported the Bork nomination.

You know Mr. Bush has never appointed a judge. I've appointed over 130, so I have a record—and I'm very proud of it. I don't ask people whether they're Republicans or Democrats. I've appointed prosecutors, I've appointed defenders. I don't appoint people I think are liberal, or people who I think are conservative; I appoint people of independence and integrity and intelligence, people who will be a credit to the bench. And those are the standards that I will use in nominating people to the Supreme Court of the United States.

These appointments are for life— these appointments are for life, and when the vice president talks about liberals on the bench, I wonder who he's talking about? Is he talking about a former governor of the state of California, who was a former prosecutor—

Mr. Shaw: Governor—

Mr. Dukakis: —a Republican, named Earl Warren? Because I think Chief Justice Warren was an outstanding chief justice, and I think most Americans do too.

Mr. Shaw: Anne Compton has a question for you, Governor Dukakis.

[On Entitlements]

Ms. Compton: Governor, millions of Americans are entitled to some of the protections and benefits that the federal government provides, including Social Security, pensions, Medicare for the elderly, Medicaid for the poor. But in fact, there are so many millions of Americans who are eligible that government just can't continue to pay for all of those programs as they're currently constituted. A blue ribbon panel, shortly after the election, is likely to recommend that you go where the money is when you make budget cuts, and that means entitlements. Before the election, would you commit yourself to any of those hard choices, such as which one of those entitlements ought to be redrawn?

Mr. Dukakis: Andrea, why do people who want to balance budgets, or bring the deficit down, always go to those programs which tend to benefit people of very modest means? You know, two-thirds of the people in this country who receive Social Security checks live entirely on that check, they have no other income. And yet, Mr. Bush tried to cut their cost-of-living increase in 1985.

Medicare is not getting less expensive; medical care for the elderly is getting more expensive, with greater deductibles, with fewer benefits, the kinds of things that we've had under this administration, that have cut and chopped and reduced the kinds of benefits that one gets under Medicare. Yes, we now have catastrophic health insurance, but it's going to cost. And that's going to be an additional burden on elderly citizens. It had bipartisan support; it should have had bipartisan support, but I suggest that we understand that those are going to be additional costs on senior citizens across this country.

So I'm not going to begin, and I'm not going to go to entitlements as a means for cutting that deficit, when we're spending billions on something like Star Wars, when we're spending billions on other weapon systems which apparently the vice president wants to keep in his back pocket, or someplace, but which, if we continue to spend billions on them, will force us to cut Social Security, to cut Medicare, to cut these basic entitlements to people of very, very modest means.

Now there are some things we can do to help people who currently do get entitlements to get off of public assistance. I talked in our first debate about the possibilities of helping millions and millions of welfare families to get off of welfare, and I'm proud to say that we finally have a welfare reform bill. And the Ruby Sampsons and Dawn Lawsons, hundreds of thousands of welfare mothers in this country and in my state and across the country who today are working and earning, are examples of what can happen when you provide training for those welfare mothers, some day care for their children so that those mothers can go into a training program and get a decent job.

Mr. Shaw: Governor—

Mr. Dukakis: That's the way you bring a deficit down, and help to improve the quality of life for people at the same time.

Mr. Shaw: One minute for the vice president.

Mr. Bush: I think I've addressed it, but let me simply say for the record, I did not vote to cut COLAs. And I voted the same way that he did three months before in a National Governors' conference, and he said at that time, quote, and this is a paraphrase—A freeze, that's easy. So I don't believe that we need to do what you've suggested here, and I've said that I'm going to keep the Social Security entitlement, to keep that trust fund sound.

But I do think there are flexible ways to solve some of the pressing problems, particularly that affect our children. And I have made some good, sound proposals.

But again, we've got a big difference on child care, for example. You see, I want the families to have the choice. I want, I don't want to see the federal government licensing grandmothers. I don't want to see the federal government saying to communities, "Well, you can't do this anymore. We're going to tell you how to do it all."

I want flexibility. And I do, you know, these people laugh about the thousand points of life. You ought to go out and—light—you ought to go out and see around this country what's happening in the volunteer sector, American helping American. And I want to keep it alive in child care—

Mr. Shaw: Mr. Vice President—

Mr. Bush: —and in other entitlements.

Mr. Shaw: Margaret Warner, for Governor Dukakis.

Ms. Warner: Governor, I'm going to pass on the question I originally planned to ask you to follow up on your rebuttal to a question Andrea asked, and that involves Social Security. Now it is true, as you said, that originally you sought an exemption for Social Security COLAs in this National Governors' Association vote.

Mr. Dukakis: Right.

Ms. Warner: But when you lost that vote, you then endorsed the overall freeze proposal. And what's more, you had great criticism of your fellow governors who wouldn't go along as political cowards. You said—"It takes guts, and it takes will."

Mr. Dukakis: That is absolutely not true, Margaret. No, that is absolutely—that is absolutely not true. It

had nothing to do with the debate on Social Security. It had to do with the discussion we had had the previous day on the overall question of reducing the budget.

Ms. Warner: My question is, aren't you demagoguing the Social Security issue?

Mr. Dukakis: No, and I have to—I have to—I just have to correct the record. That simply isn't true. Now, we're not a parliamentary body—the National Governors' Association. We vote on resolutions. If you don't get a two-thirds, then your resolution doesn't pass. But everybody knew that those of us who voted against the freezing of COLAs did so—we did so emphatically and I never made that statement—never would.

The point is that as we look at this nation's future, and we have two very different visions of this future—I want to move ahead. The vice president talks about a thousand points of light. I'm interested in 240 million points of light. I'm interested in 240 million citizens in this country who—who share in the American dream—all of them, in every part of this country.

But, as we look at the decisions that the next president of the United States is going to have to make, I just don't believe the place you go first is those programs, those so-called entitlements which provide a basic floor of income and a modest amount of medical care for the elderly, for the disabled, for people who can't make their way on their own, and in many cases have given a great deal to this country.

The vice president did call Social Security a few years ago basically or largely a welfare program. It isn't. It's a contract between generations. It's something that we pay into now so that we will have a secure retirement, and our parents and grandparents will have secure retirement. It's a very sacred contract, and I believe in it. So that's not where we ought to go.

There are plenty of places to cut. There's lots we can do in the Pentagon where dishonest contractors have been lining their pockets at the expense of the American taxpayer. There are we certainly ought to be able to give our farm families a decent income without spending 20 to 25 billion dollars a year in farm subsidies and I'm sure we can do that. That's where we ought to go and those are the programs that we ought to review first.

Mr. Shaw: One minute for the vice president.

Mr. Bush: Well, let me take him up on this question of farm subsidies. We have a fundamental difference approach on agriculture. He favors this supply maintenance or production controls. He said that. He's been out in the states saying that in these Midwestern states. I don't. I think the farm bill that he criticizes was good legislation, outstanding legislation. And I believe the answer to the agricultural economy is not to get the government further involved, but to do what I'm suggesting.

First place, never go back to that Democratic grain embargo, that liberal Democrat grain embargo that knocked the markets right out from under us and made Mr. Gorbachev say to me, when he was here, "How do I know you're reliable suppliers?" We never should go back to that. And we ought to expand our markets abroad. We ought to have rural enterprise zones. We ought to move forward swiftly on my ideas of ethanol, which would use more corn and therefore make, create a bigger market for our agricultural products. But let's not go back and keep assailing a farm bill that passed with overwhelming Democrat and Republican support.

Mr. Shaw: Mr. Vice President—

Mr. Bush: The farm payments are going down because the agricultural economy is coming back.

Mr. Shaw: Margaret Warner has a question for you, Mr. Vice President.

[The Environment]

Ms. Warner: Mr. Vice President, I'd like to cover a subject that wasn't covered in the first debate. You have said in this campaign, "I am an environmentalist," and described yourself as having zero tolerance for polluters. And yet your record does seem to suggest otherwise.

When you were head of the President's Task Force of Regulatory Relief, you did urge EPA to relax regulations involving the elimination of lead from gasoline. I believe you urged suspension of rules requiring industries to treat toxic wastes before discharging them in sewers. And your group also urged OSHA to weaken the regulations requiring that workers be informed of dangerous chemicals at the worksite.

Finally, I believe you did support the President's veto of the Clean Water Act. And my question is, aren't you— how do you square your campaign rhetoric with this record?

Mr. Bush: Ninety percent reductions in lead since I chaired that regulatory task force—ninety percent. It's all—do you remember that expression—"Get the lead out"—it's almost out. Almost gone. Clean water—I'm for clean water—but what I'm not for, what I'm not for is measuring it the way the Democratic Congress does.

We sent up a good bill on clean water, a sound bill on clean water, but the only way you can express your love for clean water is to double the appropriations for clean water and then rant against the deficit. I am for clean water. I've been an outdoorsman and a sportsman all my life. I've been to these national parks. I led for the Earl-Wallop bill, or what formerly Dingell-Johnson. I headed the Task Force when I was a member of the Congress way back in the late '60s on these kinds of things on the Republican side. I led for that. And so I refuse to—to measure one's commitment as to whether you're going to double the spending. That is the same old argument that'd gotten us into the trouble on the deficit side.

So I'll just keep saying: I am one. I'm not going to go down there and try to dump the sludge from Massachusetts off the beaches off of New Jersey—I'm not going to do that. That boo was excessively loud. Can you add five seconds, Bernie, out of fairness? Come on! Give me five. I mean this guy—this is too much down there.

But I'm not gonna do that. I am an environmentalist. I believe in our parks; I believe in the President's Commission on Outdoors. And I'll do a good job because I am committed.

Mr. Shaw: Governor Dukakis, you have one minute to respond.

Mr. Dukakis: Bernard, I'm not sure I can get all of this in in one minute. George, we have supply management today under the 1985 bill, it's called "set asides." Secondly, if you were so opposed to the grain embargo, why did you ask the godfather of the grain embargo to be one of your top foreign policy advisers?

I'm against the grain embargo; it was a mistake. I'm also against the pipeline embargo which you folks attempted to impose; that was a mistake as well, and cost thousands of jobs for American workers in the Midwest and all over the United States of America.

Margaret, once again, I don't know which George Bush I'm talking about here, or looking at—the George Bush who was a charter member of the environmental wrecking crew that went to Washington in the early '80s and did a job on the EPA, or the one we've been seeing and listening to the past two or three months. But let me say this, because he spent millions and millions of dollars on advertising on the subject of Boston Harbor: George, Boston Harbor was polluted for 100 years. I'm the first Governor to clean it up. No thanks to you—no thanks to you. And we've been

cleaning it up for four years—

Mr. Shaw: Governor—

Mr. Dukakis: —we passed landmark legislation in '84. No thanks to you. Did everything you could to kill the Clean Water Act and those grants—

Mr. Shaw: Governor—

Mr. Dukakis: —which make it possible for states and local communities to clean up rivers and harbors and streams.

Mr. Shaw: Andrea Mitchell has a question for you, Mr. Vice President.

[The Campaign's Final Month]

Ms. Mitchell: Mr. Vice President, Jimmy Carter has called this the worst campaign ever. Richard Nixon has called it trivial, superficial and inane. Whoever started down this road first of negative campaigning, the American people, from all reports coming to us, are completely fed up. Now, do you have any solutions to suggest? Is there time left to fix it? There are 26 days left. For instance, would you agree to another debate before it's all over so that the American people, so that the American people would have another chance before Election Day to compare you two?

Mr. Bush: No, I will not agree to another debate. The American people are up to here with debates. They had 30 of them. We had seven of them. Now we got three of them. I am going to carry this election debate all across this country in the last, whatever remains of the last three and a half weeks or whatever we have. And the answer is no. I am not going to have any more debates. We don't need any more debates. I've spelled out my position.

In terms of negative campaigning, you know, I don't want to sound like a kid in a schoolyard—"He started it." But, take a look at the Democratic convention, take a look at it. Do you remember the senator from Boston chanting out there and the ridicule factor from that lady from Texas that was on there? I mean, come on. This was just outrageous. But, I'll try harder to keep it on a high plane.

But, let me, let me—if you could accept a little criticism. I went all across central Illinois and spoke about agricultural issues in about seven stops. We had some fun—Crystal Gayle and Loretta Lynn with us and they got up and sang. We went to little towns and I talked agriculture. And not one thing did I see, with respect, on your network about my views on agriculture and not one did I read in any newspaper. Why? 'Cause you're so interested in a poll that might have been coming out. Or because somebody had said something nasty about somebody else.

And, so, I don't know what the answer is. I don't—somebody hit me and said Barry Goldwater said you ought to talk on the issues more. How can Barry Goldwater, sitting in Arizona, know whether I'm talking on the issues or not, when we put out position paper after position paper, he puts out position paper after position paper, and we see this much about it because everyone else is fascinated with polls and who's up or down today and who's going to be up or down tomorrow.

So I think we can all share, with respect, in the fact that maybe these, the message is not getting out. But it's not getting out because there are too few debates. There will be no more debates.

Mr. Shaw: Governor Dukakis, you have one minute to respond, sir.

Mr. Dukakis: Well, I can understand, after the vice presidential debate why Mr. Bush would want no more debates. That's my five seconds, George. Andrea, I think we both have a responsibility to try to address the issues.

Yes, we have fundamental differ-

ences. I think a great many of them have come out today. And I think if we get rid of the labels and—I'm not keeping count, but I think Mr. Bush has used the label "liberal" at least 10 times. If I had a dollar, George, for every time you used that label, I'd qualify for one of those tax breaks for the rich that you want to give away.

Isn't that the point? Most Americans believe in basic values, we have differences about how to achieve them. I want to move forward. I want this nation to move forward. I'm concerned about the fact that 10 percent of our manufacturing and 20 percent of our banking and nearly half of the real estate in the city of Los Angeles are in the hands of foreign investors. I'm concerned about what that does to our future. I'm concerned about the fact that so many of our securities are in the hands of foreign banks because of these massive deficits. But, those are the issues on which we ought to be debating, and—

Mr. Shaw: Governor.

Mr. Dukakis: —if we'd just put away the flag factories and the balloons and those kinds of things and get on to a real discussion of these issues, I think we'll—

Mr. Shaw: Andrea.

Mr. Dukakis: —have a good 26 days.

Mr. Shaw: Andrea Mitchell has a question for you, Governor Dukakis.

Mr. Dukakis: I beg your pardon.

Mr. Shaw: Andrea Mitchell has a question for you, sir.

[Defense and the Pentagon]

Ms. Mitchell: While we're talking about issues, so let's return to something you said earlier about the modernization of land-based missiles. You said that you didn't rule it out but that there are limits to what we can spend.

And then you went on to talk about a much more expensive part of our defense strategy, namely conventional forces. Do you somehow see conventional forces as a substitute for our strategic forces? And in not talking about the land-based missiles and not committing to modernizing, do you somehow believe that we can have a survivable nuclear force based on the air and sea legs of our triad?

Mr. Dukakis: I think we ought to be looking at modernization. I think we ought to be exploring less expensive ways to get it on land, and we ought to make sure that we have an effective and strong and credible nuclear deterrent. But we also need well-equipped and well-trained and well-supported conventional forces. And every defense expert I know, including people in the Pentagon itself, will tell you that given the level of defense spending and the level of defense appropriations which the Congress has now approved and the president has signed, there's no way that you can do all of these things and do them well. That's why tough choices will be required, choices I'm prepared to make, Mr. Bush is not prepared to make.

But Andrea, I think we can go far beyond this as well because we have opportunities now, step by step, to bring down the level of strategic weapons and get a test ban treaty, negotiate those conventional force reductions. I would challenge Mr. Gorbachev to join with us in limiting and eliminating regional conflict in the Middle East, in Central America. Let's get him working on Syria, their client state, and see if we can't get them to join Israel and other Arab nations, if at all possible, and Arab leaders, in finally bringing peace to that troubled region. And I think that's one reason why we need fresh leadership in the White House that can make progress now in bringing peace to the Middle East.

Let's go to work and end this fiasco in Central America, a failed policy which has actually increased Cuban and Soviet influence. The democratic leaders of Central and Latin America want to work with us. I've met with them. I know them. I've spent time in South America. I speak the language; so does Senator Bentsen. We want to work with them and build a new relationship, and they with us. But not a one of those key democratic leaders support our policy in Central America. And we've got to work with them if we're going to create an environment for human rights and democracy for the people of this hemisphere, and go to work on our single most important problem, and that is the avalanche of drugs that is pouring into our country and virtually destroying those countries.

Those are the kinds of priorities, for national security and for foreign policy, that I want to pursue. Mr. Bush and I have major differences on these issues—

Mr. Shaw: Governor—

Mr. Dukakis: —and I hope very much to be president and pursue them.

Mr. Shaw: Mr. Vice President, you have one minute.

Mr. Bush: In terms of regional tensions, we have now gotten the attention of the Soviet Union. And the reason we've gotten it is because they see us now as unwilling to make the very kinds of unilateral cuts that have been called for, and to go for the discredited freeze. My opponent had trouble, criticized us on our policy in Angola. It now looks, because of steady negotiation, that we may have an agreement that will remove the Cubans from Angola.

We see the Russians coming out of Afghanistan. That wouldn't have stopped if we hadn't been willing—wouldn't have even started, the Soviets coming out, if we hadn't even been willing to support the freedom fighters there. And the policy in Central America regrettably has failed because the Congress has been unwilling to support those who have been fighting for freedom. Those Sandinistas came in and betrayed the trust of the revolution. They said it was about democracy. And they have done nothing other than solidify their Marxist domination over that country.

Mr. Shaw: Ann Compton for Governor Dukakis.

Ms. Compton: Governor, nuclear weapons need nuclear material replenished on a regular basis. And just this week, yet another nuclear manufacturing plant was closed because of safety concerns. Some in the Pentagon fear that too much priority has been put on new weapons programs, not enough on current programs, and worry that the resulting shortage would be amounting to nothing less than unilateral nuclear disarmament.

Is that a priority that you feel has been ignored by this administration? Or are the Pentagon officials making too much of it?

Mr. Dukakis: Well, its a great concern of mine, and I think of all Americans, and perhaps the vice president can tell us what's been going on. This is another example of misplaced priorities.

The administration, which wants to spend billions on weapons systems that we don't need and can't afford, and now confronts us with a very serious problem in plants that are supposed to be producing tritium and plutonium and providing the necessary materials for existing weapons.

Yes, if we don't do something about it, we may find ourselves unilaterally— if I may use that term—dismantling some of these weapons. What's been going on? Who's been in charge? Who's been managing this system? Why have there been these safety violations? Why are these plants being closed down? I don't know what the latest cost estimates are, but it's going to be in the range of $25, 50, 75, 100 billion. Now, somebody has to bear the responsibility for this.

Maybe the vice president has an answer, but I'm somebody who believes very strongly in taking care of the fundamentals first, before you start new stuff. And that's something which will be a priority of ours in the new administration, because without it we cannot have the effective and strong and credible nuclear deterrent we must have.

Mr. Shaw: Mr. Vice President, you have one minute.

Mr. Bush: That is the closest I've ever heard the governor of Massachusetts come to support anything having to do with nuclear. That's about as close as I've ever heard him. Yes, this Savannah River plant needs to be made more safe. Will he join me in suggesting that we may need another plant, maybe in Idaho, to take care of the requirements—nuclear material requirements for our Defense Department? I hope he will.

This sounds like real progress here, because we've had a big difference on the safe use of nuclear power. I believe that we—the more dependent we become on foreign oil, the less our national security is enhanced. And, therefore, I've made some proposals to strengthen the domestic oil industry, by more incentive going in to look for and find and produce oil, made him some incentives in terms of secondary and tertiary production. But we're going to have to use more gas, more coal, and more safe nuclear power for our energy base. So, I am one who believes that we can and must—

Mr. Shaw: Mr. Vice President—

Mr. Bush: —do what he's talking about now.

Mr. Shaw: Ann Compton has a question for you.

[Government Ethics]

Ms. Compton: Mr. Vice President, as many as 100 officials in this administration have left the government under an ethical cloud. Some have been indicted, some convicted. Many of the cases have involved undue influence once they are outside of government. If you become president, will you lock that revolving door that has allowed some men and women in the government to come back and lobby the very departments they once managed?

Mr. Bush: Yes, and I'll apply it to Congress too. I'll do both. I'll do both, because I think, you see, I am one who—I get kidded by being a little old fashioned on these things, but I do believe in public service. I believe that public service is honorable. And I don't think anybody has a, has a call on people and their administrations going astray. His chief education adviser is in jail. He's in jail because he betrayed the public trust. The head of education.

And yet, this man, the governor, equated the president to a rotting fish. He said that a fish rots from the head down, as he was going after Ed Meese. Look, we need the highest possible ethical standards. I will have an ethical office in the White House that will be under the president's personal concern. I will see that these standards apply to the United States Congress. I hope I will do a good job as one who has had a relatively clean record with no conflicts of interest in his own public life—as has the governor—to exhort young people to get into public service.

But, there is no corner on, on this sleaze factor, believe me. And it's a disgrace, and I will do my level best to clean it up, recognizing that you can't legislate morality. But, I do believe that with my record in Congress having led the new congressmen to a Code of Ethics through major, main emphasis on it in full disclosure, that I've got a good record. And there are more, if you want to talk about percentage appointments, more members of Congress who have been under investigation, percentage wise, than people in the executive

branch. And so it isn't want—state governments have had a tough time. His. Some of his college presidents aren't exactly holier than thou. So let's not be throwing stones about it. Let's say, "This isn't Democrat or Republican, and it isn't liberal or conservative." Let's vow to work together to do something about it.

Mr. Shaw: Governor, you have one minute to respond.

Mr. Dukakis: Well, I would agree that integrity is not a Republican or a Democratic issue. It is an American issue. But, here again, I don't know which George Bush I'm listening to. Wasn't this the Mr. Bush that supported Mr. Meese? Called James Watt an excellent Secretary of Interior? Provided support for some of these people, supported the nomination of Robert Bork to the Supreme Court of the United States? We've had dozens, we've had dozens and dozens of officials in this administration, who have left under a cloud, who have left with a special prosecutor on their arm. They've been indicted, convicted.

This isn't the kind of administration we need and one of the reasons our selection of a running mate is so important and is such a test of the kinds of standards we'll set is because it tells the American people in advance of the election just what kind of people we're looking for. I picked Lloyd Bentsen. Mr. Bush picked Dan Quaid, Dan Quayle. I think that says a great deal to the American people about the standards we'll set and the quality of the people that we will pick to serve in our administration.

Mr. Shaw: To each of you candidates, regrettably, I have to inform you that we have come to the end of our questions. That's a pity. Before I ask the candidates to make their closing remarks, on behalf of the Commission on Presidential Debates, I would like to thank all of you for joining us this evening. Governor Dukakis, yours is the first closing statement, sir.

[Closing Statements]

Mr. Dukakis: Twenty-eight years ago, as a young man, just graduated from law school, I came to this city, came clear across the country to watch John Kennedy be nominated for the presidency of the United States, right here in Los Angeles.

I never dreamed that someday I would win that nomination and be my party's nominee for president. That's America. That's why I'm proud and grateful to be a citizen of this country.

Twenty-six days from today, you and millions of Americans will choose two people to lead us into the future as president and vice president of the United States. Our opponents say, "Things are okay. Don't rock the boat. Not to worry." They say we should be satisfied.

But I don't think we can be satisfied when we're spending $150 billion a year in interest alone on the national debt, much of it going to foreign bankers, or when 25 percent of our high school students are dropping out of school, or when we have two and a half million of our fellow citizens, a third of them veterans, who are homeless and living on streets and in doorways in this country, or when Mr. Bush's prescription for our economic future is another tax give-away to the rich.

We can do better than that. Not working with government alone, but all of us working together. Lloyd Bentsen and I are optimists, and so are the American people. And we ask you for our hand—for your hands and your hearts and your votes on the 8th of November so we can move forward into the future. Kitty and I are very grateful to all of you for the warmth and the hospitality that you've given to us in your homes and communities all across this country. We love you, and we're grateful to you for everything that you've given to us. And we hope that we'll be serving you in the White House in January of 1989. Thank you, and God bless you.

Mr. Shaw: Vice President Bush, your closing statement, sir.

Mr. Bush: Sometimes it does seem that a campaign generates more heat than light. And so let me repeat, I do have respect for my opponent, for his family, for the justifiable pride he takes in his heritage.

But we have enormous differences. I want to hold the line on taxes and keep this, the longest expansion in modern history, going until everybody in America benefits. I want to invest in our children, because I mean it when I say I want a kinder and gentler nation. And by that, I want to have child care where the families, the parents, have control.

I want to keep our neighborhoods much, much better in terms of anti-crime. And that's why I would appoint judges that have a little more sympathy for the victims of crime and a little less for the criminals. That's why I do feel if some police officer is gunned down that the death penalty is required. I want to help those with disabilities fit into the mainstream.

There is much to be done. This election is about big things, and perhaps the biggest is world peace. And I ask you to consider the experience I have had in working with a president who has revolutionized the situation around the world. America stands tall again and, as a result, we are credible and we have now achieved a historic arms control agreement.

I want to build on that. I'd love to be able to say to my grandchildren, four years after my first term, I'd like to say, "Your grandfather, working with the leaders of the Soviet Union, working with the leaders of Europe, was able to ban chemical and biological weapons from the face of the Earth."

Lincoln called this country the last, best hope of man on Earth. And he was right then, and we still are the last, best hope of man on Earth. And I ask for your support on November 8th, and I will be a good president. Working together we can do wonderful things for the United States and for the free world.

Thank you very, very much.

Appendix

U.S. Presidents and Vice Presidents

President and political party	Born	Died	President's term of service	Vice president	Vice president's term of service
George Washington (F)	1732	1799	April 30, 1789-March 4, 1793	John Adams	April 30, 1789-March 4, 1793
George Washington (F)			March 4, 1793-March 4, 1797	John Adams	March 4, 1793-March 4, 1797
John Adams (F)	1735	1826	March 4, 1797-March 4, 1801	Thomas Jefferson	March 4, 1797-March 4, 1801
Thomas Jefferson (DR)	1743	1826	March 4, 1801-March 4, 1805	Aaron Burr	March 4, 1801-March 4, 1805
Thomas Jefferson (DR)			March 4, 1805-March 4, 1809	George Clinton[a]	March 4, 1805-March 4, 1809
James Madison (DR)	1751	1836	March 4, 1809-March 4, 1813	George Clinton[a]	March 4, 1809-April 12, 1812
James Madison (DR)			March 4, 1813-March 4, 1817	Elbridge Gerry[a]	March 4, 1813-Nov. 23, 1814
James Monroe (DR)	1758	1831	March 4, 1817-March 4, 1821	Daniel D. Tompkins	March 4, 1817-March 4, 1821
James Monroe (DR)			March 4, 1821-March 4, 1825	Daniel D. Tompkins	March 4, 1821-March 4, 1825
John Q. Adams (DR)	1767	1848	March 4, 1825-March 4, 1829	John C. Calhoun	March 4, 1825-March 4, 1829
Andrew Jackson (DR)	1767	1845	March 4, 1829-March 4, 1833	John C. Calhoun[b]	March 4, 1829-Dec. 28, 1832
Andrew Jackson (D)			March 4, 1833-March 4, 1837	Martin Van Buren	March 4, 1833-March 4, 1837
Martin Van Buren (D)	1782	1862	March 4, 1837-March 4, 1841	Richard M. Johnson	March 4, 1837-March 4, 1841
W. H. Harrison[a] (W)	1773	1841	March 4, 1841-April 4, 1841	John Tyler[c]	March 4, 1841-April 6, 1841
John Tyler (W)	1790	1862	April 6, 1841-March 4, 1845		
James K. Polk (D)	1795	1849	March 4, 1845-March 4, 1849	George M. Dallas	March 4, 1845-March 4, 1849
Zachary Taylor[a] (W)	1784	1850	March 4, 1849-July 9, 1850	Millard Fillmore[c]	March 4, 1849-July 10, 1850
Millard Fillmore (W)	1800	1874	July 10, 1850-March 4, 1853		
Franklin Pierce (D)	1804	1869	March 4, 1853-March 4, 1857	William R. King[a]	March 24, 1853-April 18, 1853
James Buchanan (D)	1791	1868	March 4, 1857-March 4, 1861	John C. Breckinridge	March 4, 1857-March 4, 1861
Abraham Lincoln (R)	1809	1865	March 4, 1861-March 4, 1865	Hannibal Hamlin	March 4, 1861-March 4, 1865
Abraham Lincoln[a] (R)			March 4, 1865-April 15, 1865	Andrew Johnson[c]	March 4, 1865-April 15, 1865
Andrew Johnson (R)	1808	1875	April 15, 1865-March 4, 1869		
Ulysses S. Grant (R)	1822	1885	March 4, 1869-March 4, 1873	Schuyler Colfax	March 4, 1869-March 4, 1873
Ulysses S. Grant (R)			March 4, 1873-March 4, 1877	Henry Wilson[a]	March 4, 1873-Nov. 22, 1875
Rutherford B. Hayes (R)	1822	1893	March 4, 1877-March 4, 1881	William A. Wheeler	March 4, 1877-March 4, 1881
James A. Garfield[a] (R)	1831	1881	arch 4, 1881-Sept. 19, 1881	Chester A. Arthur[c]	March 4, 1881-Sept. 20, 1881
Chester A. Arthur (R)	1830	1886	Sept. 20, 1881-March 4, 1885		
Grover Cleveland (D)	1837	1908	March 4, 1885-March 4, 1889	Thomas A. Hendricks[a]	March 4, 1885-Nov. 25, 1885
Benjamin Harrison (R)	1833	1901	March 4, 1889-March 4, 1893	Levi P. Morton	March 4, 1889-March 4, 1893
Grover Cleveland (D)	1837	1908	March 4, 1893-March 4, 1897	Adlai E. Stevenson	March 4, 1893-March 4, 1897
William McKinley (R)	1843	1901	March 4, 1897-March 4, 1901	Garret A. Hobart[a]	March 4, 1897-Nov. 21, 1899
William McKinley[a] (R)			March 4, 1901-Sept. 14, 1901	Theodore Roosevelt[c]	March 4, 1901-Sept. 14, 1901

President and political party	Born	Died	President's term of service	Vice president	Vice president's term of service
Theodore Roosevelt (R)	1858	1919	Sept. 14, 1901-March 4, 1905		
Theodore Roosevelt (R)			March 4, 1905-March 4, 1909	Charles W. Fairbanks	March 4, 1905-March 4, 1909
William H. Taft (R)	1857	1930	March 4, 1909-March 4, 1913	James S. Sherman[a]	March 4, 1909-Oct. 30, 1912
Woodrow Wilson (D)	1856	1924	March 4, 1913-March 4, 1917	Thomas R. Marshall	March 4, 1913-March 4, 1917
Woodrow Wilson (D)			March 4, 1917-March 4, 1921	Thomas R. Marshall	March 4, 1917-March 4, 1921
Warren G. Harding[a] (R)	1865	1923	March 4, 1921-Aug. 2, 1923	Calvin Coolidge[c]	March 4, 1921-Aug. 3, 1923
Calvin Coolidge (R)	1872	1933	Aug. 3, 1923-March 4, 1925		
Calvin Coolidge (R)			March 4, 1925-March 4, 1929	Charles G. Dawes	March 4, 1925-March 4, 1929
Herbert Hoover (R)	1874	1964	March 4, 1929-March 4, 1933	Charles Curtis	March 4, 1929-March 4, 1933
Franklin D. Roosevelt (D)	1882	1945	March 4, 1933-Jan. 20, 1937	John N. Garner	March 4, 1933-Jan. 20, 1937
Franklin D. Roosevelt (D)			Jan. 20, 1937-Jan. 20, 1941	John N. Garner	Jan. 20, 1937-Jan. 20, 1941
Franklin D. Roosevelt (D)			Jan. 20, 1941-Jan. 20, 1945	Henry A. Wallace	Jan. 20, 1941-Jan. 20, 1945
Franklin D. Roosevelt[a] (D)			Jan. 20, 1945-April 12, 1945	Harry S Truman[c]	Jan. 20, 1945-April 12, 1945
Harry S Truman (D)	1884	1972	April 12, 1945-Jan. 20, 1949		
Harry S Truman (D)			Jan. 20, 1949-Jan. 20, 1953	Alben W. Barkley	Jan. 20, 1949-Jan. 20, 1953
Dwight D. Eisenhower (R)	1890	1969	Jan. 20, 1953-Jan. 20, 1957	Richard Nixon	Jan. 20, 1953-Jan. 20, 1957
Dwight D. Eisenhower (R)			Jan. 20, 1957-Jan. 20, 1961	Richard Nixon	Jan. 20, 1957-Jan. 20, 1961
John F. Kennedy[a] (D)	1917	1963	Jan. 20, 1961-Nov. 22, 1963	Lyndon B. Johnson[c]	Jan. 20, 1961-Nov. 22, 1963
Lyndon B. Johnson (D)	1908	1973	Nov. 22, 1963-Jan. 20, 1965		
Lyndon B. Johnson (D)			Jan. 20, 1965-Jan. 20, 1969	Hubert H. Humphrey	Jan. 20, 1965-Jan. 20, 1969
Richard Nixon (R)	1913		Jan. 20, 1969-Jan. 20, 1973	Spiro T. Agnew	Jan. 20, 1969-Jan. 20, 1973
Richard Nixon[b] (R)			Jan. 20, 1973-Aug. 9, 1974	Spiro T. Agnew[b]	Jan. 20, 1973-Oct. 10, 1973
				Gerald R. Ford[c]	Dec. 6, 1973-Aug. 9, 1974
Gerald R. Ford (R)	1913		Aug. 9, 1974-Jan. 20, 1977	Nelson A. Rockefeller	Dec. 19, 1974-Jan. 20, 1977
Jimmy Carter (D)	1924		Jan. 20, 1977-Jan. 20, 1981	Walter F. Mondale	Jan. 20, 1977-Jan. 20, 1981
Ronald Reagan (R)	1911		Jan. 20, 1981-Jan. 20, 1985	George Bush	Jan. 20, 1981-Jan. 20, 1985
Ronald Reagan (R)			Jan. 20, 1985-Jan. 20, 1989	George Bush	Jan. 20, 1985-Jan. 20, 1989
George Bush (R)	1924		Jan. 20, 1989-	Dan Quayle	Jan. 20, 1989-

Sources: Presidential Elections Since 1789, 4th ed. (Washington, D.C.: Congressional Quarterly, 1987), 4.; Daniel C. Diller, "Biographies of the Vice Presidents," in *Guide to the Presidency*, ed. Michael Nelson (Washington, D.C.: Congressional Quarterly, 1989), 1319-1346.

Note: D—Democrat; DR—Democratic-Republican; F—Federalist; R—Republican; W—Whig.

a. Died in office.
b. Resigned.
c. Succeeded to the presidency.

Summary of Presidential Elections, 1789-1988

Year	No. of states	Candidates	Electoral vote	Popular vote
1789[a]	10	*Fed.* George Washington	*Fed.* 69	—[b]
1792[a]	15	*Fed.* George Washington	*Fed.* 132	—[b]
1796[a]	16	*Dem.-Rep.* Thomas Jefferson *Fed.* John Adams	*Dem.-Rep.* 68 *Fed.* 71	—[b]
1800[a]	16	*Dem.-Rep.* Thomas Jefferson Aaron Burr *Fed.* John Adams Charles Cotesworth Pinckney	*Dem.-Rep.* 73 *Fed.* 65	—[b]
1804	17	*Dem.-Rep.* Thomas Jefferson George Clinton *Fed.* Charles Cotesworth Pinckney Rufus King	*Dem.-Rep.* 162 *Fed.* 14	—[b]
1808	17	*Dem.-Rep.* James Madison George Clinton *Fed.* Charles Cotesworth Pinckney Rufus King	*Dem.-Rep.* 122 *Fed.* 47	—[b]
1812	18	*Dem.-Rep.* James Madison Elbridge Gerry *Fed.* George Clinton Jared Ingersoll	*Dem.-Rep.* 128 *Fed.* 89	—[b]
1816	19	*Dem.-Rep.* James Monroe Daniel D. Tompkins *Fed.* Rufus King John Howard	*Dem.-Rep.* 183 *Fed.* 34	—[b]
1820	24	*Dem.-Rep.* James Monroe Daniel D. Tompkins —[c]	*Dem.-Rep.* 231 —[c]	—[b]
1824[d]	24	*Dem.-Rep.* Andrew Jackson John C. Calhoun *Dem.-Rep.* John Q. Adams Nathan Sanford	*Dem.-Rep.* 99 *Dem.-Rep.* 84	*Dem.-Rep.* 151,271 41.3% *Dem.-Rep.* 113,122 30.9%

Year	No. of states	Dem.	Candidates	Rep.	Electoral vote Dem.	Electoral vote Rep.	Popular vote Dem.	Popular vote Rep.
1828	24	*Dem.-Rep.* Andrew Jackson, John C. Calhoun		*Nat.-Rep.* John Q. Adams, Richard Rush	*Dem.-Rep.* 178	*Nat.-Rep.* 83	*Dem.-Rep.* 642,553 56.0%	*Nat.-Rep.* 500,897 43.6%
1832[e]	24	*Dem.* Andrew Jackson, Martin Van Buren		*Nat.-Rep.* Henry Clay, John Sergeant	*Dem.* 219	*Nat.-Rep.* 49	*Dem.* 701,780 54.2%	*Nat.-Rep.* 484,205 37.4%
1836[f]	26	*Dem.* Martin Van Buren, Richard M. Johnson		*Whig* William H. Harrison, Francis Granger	*Dem.* 170	*Whig* 73	*Dem.* 764,176 50.8%	*Whig* 550,816 36.6%
1840	26	*Dem.* Martin Van Buren, Richard M. Johnson		*Whig* William H. Harrison, John Tyler	*Dem.* 60	*Whig* 234	*Dem.* 1,275,390 52.9%	*Whig* 1,128,854 46.8%
1844	26	*Dem.* James Polk, George M. Dallas		*Whig* Henry Clay, Theodore Frelinghuysen	*Dem.* 170	*Whig* 105	*Dem.* 1,339,494 49.5%	*Whig* 1,300,004 48.1%
1848	30	*Dem.* Lewis Cass, William O. Butler		*Whig* Zachary Taylor, Millard Fillmore	*Dem.* 127	*Whig* 163	*Dem.* 1,361,393 47.3%	*Whig* 1,223,460 42.5%
1852	31	*Dem.* Franklin Pierce, William R. King		*Whig* Winfield Scott, William A. Graham	*Dem.* 254	*Whig* 42	*Dem.* 1,607,510 50.8%	*Whig* 1,386,942 43.9%
1856[g]	31	James Buchanan, John C. Breckinridge		John C. Fremont, William L. Dayton	174	114	1,836,072 45.3%	1,342,345 33.1%
1860[h]	33	Stephen A. Douglas, Herschel V. Johnson		Abraham Lincoln, Hannibal Hamlin	12	180	1,380,202 29.5%	1,865,908 39.8%
1864[i]	36	George B. McClellan, George H. Pendleton		Abraham Lincoln, Andrew Johnson	21	212	1,812,807 45.0%	2,218,388 55.0%
1868[j]	37	Horatio Seymour, Francis P. Blair, Jr.		Ulysses S. Grant, Schuyler Colfax	80	214	2,708,744 47.3%	3,013,650 52.7%

Year	No. of states	Candidates Dem.	Candidates Rep.	Electoral vote Dem.	Electoral vote Rep.	Popular vote Dem.	Popular vote Rep.
1872[k]	37	Horace Greeley / Benjamin Gratz Brown	Ulysses S. Grant / Henry Wilson		286	2,834,761 43.8%	3,598,235 55.6%
1876	38	Samuel J. Tilden / Thomas A. Hendricks	Rutherford B. Hayes / William A. Wheeler	184	185	4,288,546 51.0%	4,034,311 47.9%
1880	38	Winfield S. Hancock / William H. English	James A. Garfield / Chester A. Arthur	155	214	4,444,260 48.2%	4,446,158 48.3%
1884	38	Grover Cleveland / Thomas A. Hendricks	James G. Blaine / John A. Logan	219	182	4,874,621 48.5%	4,848,936 48.2%
1888	38	Grover Cleveland / Allen G. Thurman	Benjamin Harrison / Levi P. Morton	168	233	5,534,488 48.6%	5,443,892 47.8%
1892[l]	44	Grover Cleveland / Adlai E. Stevenson	Benjamin Harrison / Whitelaw Reid	277	145	5,551,883 46.1%	5,179,244 43.0%
1896	45	William J. Bryan / Arthur Sewall	William McKinley / Garret A. Hobart	176	271	6,511,495 46.7%	7,108,480 51.0%
1900	45	William J. Bryan / Adlai E. Stevenson	William McKinley / Theodore Roosevelt	155	292	6,358,345 45.5%	7,218,039 51.7%
1904	45	Alton B. Parker / Henry G. Davis	Theodore Roosevelt / Charles W. Fairbanks	140	336	5,028,898 37.6%	7,626,593 56.4%
1908	46	William J. Bryan / John W. Kern	William H. Taft / James S. Sherman	162	321	6,406,801 43.0%	7,676,258 51.6%
1912[m]	48	Woodrow Wilson / Thomas R. Marshall	William H. Taft / James S. Sherman	435	8	6,293,152 41.8%	3,436,333 23.2%
1916	48	Woodrow Wilson / Thomas R. Marshall	Charles E. Hughes / Charles W. Fairbanks	277	254	9,126,300 49.2%	8,546,789 46.1%
1920	48	James M. Cox / Franklin D. Roosevelt	Warren G. Harding / Calvin Coolidge	127	404	9,140,884 34.2%	16,133,314 60.3%

Year	States	Candidates	Electoral Vote	Popular Vote	Candidates	Electoral Vote	Popular Vote
1924[n]	48	John W. Davis Charles W. Bryant	136	8,386,169 28.8%	Calvin Coolidge Charles G. Dawes	382	15,717,553 54.1%
1928	48	Alfred E. Smith Joseph T. Robinson	87	15,000,185 40.8%	Herbert C. Hoover Charles Curtis	444	21,411,991 58.2%
1932	48	Franklin D. Roosevelt John N. Garner	472	22,825,016 57.4%	Herbert C. Hoover Charles Curtis	59	15,758,397 39.6%
1936	48	Franklin D. Roosevelt John N. Garner	523	27,747,636 60.8%	Alfred M. Landon Frank Knox	8	16,679,543 36.5%
1940	48	Franklin D. Roosevelt Henry A. Wallace	449	27,263,448 54.7%	Wendell L. Willkie Charles L. McNary	82	22,336,260 44.8%
1944	48	Franklin D. Roosevelt Harry S Truman	432	25,611,936 53.4%	Thomas E. Dewey John W. Bricker	99	22,013,372 45.9%
1948[o]	48	Harry S Truman Alben W. Barkley	303	24,105,587 49.5%	Thomas E. Dewey Earl Warren	189	21,970,017 45.1%
1952	48	Adlai E. Stevenson II John J. Sparkman	89	27,314,649 44.4%	Dwight D. Eisenhower Richard M. Nixon	442	33,936,137 55.1%
1956[p]	48	Adlai E. Stevenson II Estes Kefauver	73	26,030,172 42.0%	Dwight D. Eisenhower Richard M. Nixon	457	35,585,245 57.4%
1960[q]	50	John F. Kennedy Lyndon B. Johnson	303	34,221,344 49.7%	Richard M. Nixon Henry Cabot Lodge	219	34,106,671 49.5%
1964	50*	Lyndon B. Johnson Hubert H. Humphrey	486	43,126,584 61.1%	Barry Goldwater William E. Miller	52	27,177,838 38.5%
1968[r]	50*	Hubert H. Humphrey Edmund S. Muskie	191	31,274,503 42.7%	Richard M. Nixon Spiro T. Agnew	301	31,785,148 43.4%
1972[s]	50*	George McGovern Sargent Shriver	17	29,171,791 37.5%	Richard M. Nixon Spiro T. Agnew	520	47,170,179 60.7%
1976[t]	50*	Jimmy Carter Walter F. Mondale	297	40,830,763 50.1%	Gerald R. Ford Robert Dole	240	39,147,793 48.0%
1980	50*	Jimmy Carter Walter F. Mondale	49	35,483,883 41.0%	Ronald Reagan George Bush	489	43,904,153 50.7%

		Candidates		Electoral vote		Popular vote	
Year	No. of states	Dem.	Rep.	Dem.	Rep.	Dem.	Rep.
1984	50*	Walter F. Mondale Geraldine Ferraro	Ronald Reagan George Bush	13	525	37,577,185 40.6%	54,455,075 58.8%
1988[u]	50*	Michael S. Dukakis Lloyd Bentsen	George Bush Dan Quayle	111	426	41,809,083 45.6%	48,886,097 53.4%

Sources: Harold W. Stanley and Richard G. Niemi, *Vital Statistics on American Politics,* 2d ed. (Washington, D.C.: CQ Press, 1990), 102-106; *Guide to U.S. Elections,* 2d ed. (Washington, D.C.: Congressional Quarterly, 1985), 329-366; Federal Election Commission.

Note: Dem.-Rep.—Democratic-Republican; Fed.—Federalist; Nat.-Rep.—National-Republican; Dem.—Democratic; Rep.—Republican.

a. Elections of 1789-1800 were held under rules that did not allow separate voting for president and vice president.

b. Popular vote returns are not shown before 1824 because consistent, reliable data are not available.

c. One electoral vote was cast for John Adams and Richard Stockton, who were not candidates.

d. 1824: All four candidates represented Democratic-Republican factions. William H. Crawford received 41 electoral votes and Henry Clay received 37 votes. Because no candidate received a majority, the election was decided (in Adams's favor) by the House of Representatives.

e. 1832: Two electoral votes were not cast.

f. 1836: Other Whig candidates receiving electoral votes were Hugh L. White, who received 26 votes, and Daniel Webster, who received 14 votes.

g. 1856: Millard Fillmore, Whig-American, received 8 electoral votes.

h. 1860: John C. Breckinridge, Southern Democrat, received 72 electoral votes. John Bell, Constitutional Union, received 39 electoral votes.

i. 1864: Eighty-one electoral votes were not cast.

j. 1868: Twenty-three electoral votes were not cast.

k. 1872: Horace Greeley, Democrat, died after the election. In the electoral college, Democratic electoral votes went to Thomas Hendricks, 42 votes; Benjamin Gratz Brown, 18 votes; Charles J. Jenkins, 2 votes; and David Davis, 1 vote. Seventeen electoral votes were not cast.

l. 1892: James B. Weaver, People's party, received 22 electoral votes.

m. 1912: Theodore Roosevelt, Progressive party, received 86 electoral votes.

n. 1924: Robert M. La Follette, Progressive party, received 13 electoral votes.

o. 1948: J. Strom Thurmond, States' Rights party, received 39 electoral votes.

p. 1956: Walter B. Jones, Democrat, received 1 electoral vote.

q. 1960: Harry Flood Byrd, Democrat, received 15 electoral votes.

r. 1968: George C. Wallace, American Independent party, received 46 electoral votes.

s. 1972: John Hospers, Libertarian party, received 1 electoral vote.

t. 1976: Ronald Reagan, Republican, received 1 electoral vote.

u. 1988: Lloyd Bentsen, the Democratic vice-presidential nominee, received 1 electoral vote for president.

* Fifty states plus District of Columbia.

Index